Handbook of Research on Decision-Making Techniques in Financial Marketing

Hasan Dinçer
Istanbul Medipol University, Turkey

Serhat Yüksel
İstanbul Medipol University, Turkey

A volume in the Advances in Marketing, Customer Relationship Management, and E-Services (AMCRMES) Book Series

Published in the United States of America by
IGI Global
Business Science Reference (an imprint of IGI Global)
701 E. Chocolate Avenue
Hershey PA, USA 17033
Tel: 717-533-8845
Fax: 717-533-8661
E-mail: cust@igi-global.com
Web site: http://www.igi-global.com

Copyright © 2020 by IGI Global. All rights reserved. No part of this publication may be reproduced, stored or distributed in any form or by any means, electronic or mechanical, including photocopying, without written permission from the publisher. Product or company names used in this set are for identification purposes only. Inclusion of the names of the products or companies does not indicate a claim of ownership by IGI Global of the trademark or registered trademark.
     Library of Congress Cataloging-in-Publication Data

Names: Dinçer, Hasan, 1982- editor. | Yuksel, Serhat, 1983- editor.
Title: Handbook of research on decision-making techniques in financial
   marketing / Hasan Dinçer and Serhat Yüksel, editors.
Description: Hershey, PA : Business Science Reference, [2020] | Includes
   bibliographical references and index. | Summary: ""This book integrates
   financial and marketing functions together to make sense of environment
   and business-related challenges. It also explores using multi criteria
   decision making methods for financial challenges while marketing
   theories are used as theoretical bases"--Provided by publisher"--
   Provided by publisher.
Identifiers: LCCN 2019042040 (print) | LCCN 2019042041 (ebook) | ISBN
   9781799825593 (hardcover) | ISBN 9781799825609 (ebook)
Subjects: LCSH: Financial institutions--Marketing. | Financial services
   industry--Marketing.
Classification: LCC HG173 .H3424 2020 (print) | LCC HG173 (ebook) | DDC
   332.1068/8--dc23
LC record available at https://lccn.loc.gov/2019042040
LC ebook record available at https://lccn.loc.gov/2019042041

This book is published in the IGI Global book series Advances in Marketing, Customer Relationship Management, and E-Services (AMCRMES) (ISSN: 2327-5502; eISSN: 2327-5529)

British Cataloguing in Publication Data
A Cataloguing in Publication record for this book is available from the British Library.

All work contributed to this book is new, previously-unpublished material. The views expressed in this book are those of the authors, but not necessarily of the publisher.

For electronic access to this publication, please contact: eresources@igi-global.com.

Advances in Marketing, Customer Relationship Management, and E-Services (AMCRMES) Book Series

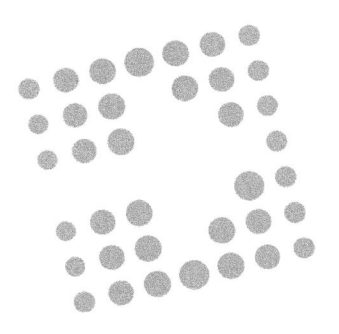

Eldon Y. Li
National Chengchi University, Taiwan & California Polytechnic State University, USA

ISSN:2327-5502
EISSN:2327-5529

Mission

Business processes, services, and communications are important factors in the management of good customer relationship, which is the foundation of any well organized business. Technology continues to play a vital role in the organization and automation of business processes for marketing, sales, and customer service. These features aid in the attraction of new clients and maintaining existing relationships.

The Advances in Marketing, Customer Relationship Management, and E-Services (AMCRMES) Book Series addresses success factors for customer relationship management, marketing, and electronic services and its performance outcomes. This collection of reference source covers aspects of consumer behavior and marketing business strategies aiming towards researchers, scholars, and practitioners in the fields of marketing management.

Coverage

- B2B marketing
- Online Community Management and Behavior
- Mobile Services
- Customer Retention
- Legal Considerations in E-Marketing
- Customer Relationship Management
- Telemarketing
- Text Mining and Marketing
- Cases on CRM Implementation
- Electronic Services

IGI Global is currently accepting manuscripts for publication within this series. To submit a proposal for a volume in this series, please contact our Acquisition Editors at Acquisitions@igi-global.com or visit: http://www.igi-global.com/publish/.

The Advances in Marketing, Customer Relationship Management, and E-Services (AMCRMES) Book Series (ISSN 2327-5502) is published by IGI Global, 701 E. Chocolate Avenue, Hershey, PA 17033-1240, USA, www.igi-global.com. This series is composed of titles available for purchase individually; each title is edited to be contextually exclusive from any other title within the series. For pricing and ordering information please visit http://www.igi-global.com/book-series/advances-marketing-customer-relationship-management/37150. Postmaster: Send all address changes to above address. Copyright © 2020 IGI Global. All rights, including translation in other languages reserved by the publisher. No part of this series may be reproduced or used in any form or by any means – graphics, electronic, or mechanical, including photocopying, recording, taping, or information and retrieval systems – without written permission from the publisher, except for non commercial, educational use, including classroom teaching purposes. The views expressed in this series are those of the authors, but not necessarily of IGI Global.

Titles in this Series

For a list of additional titles in this series, please visit:
https://www.igi-global.com/book-series/advances-marketing-customer-relationship-management/37150

Handbook of Research on Retailing Techniques for Optimal Consumer Engagement and Experiences
Fabio Musso (University of Urbino Carlo Bo, Italy) and Elena Druica (University of Bucharest, Romania)
Business Science Reference • copyright 2020 • 571pp • H/C (ISBN: 9781799814122) • US $285.00 (our price)

Handbook of Research on Contemporary Consumerism
Hans Ruediger Kaufmann (University of Applied Management Studies Mannheim, Germany & University of Nicosia, Cyprus) and Mohammad Fateh Ali Khan Panni (City University, Bangladesh)
Business Science Reference • copyright 2020 • 361pp • H/C (ISBN: 9781522582700) • US $285.00 (our price)

Improving Marketing Strategies for Private Label Products
Yusuf Arslan (Sakarya University, Turkey)
Business Science Reference • copyright 2020 • 383pp • H/C (ISBN: 9781799802570) • US $195.00 (our price)

Digital Marketing Strategies for Tourism, Hospitality, and Airline Industries
José Duarte Santos (Instituto Superior Politécnico Gaya, Portugal) and Óscar Lima Silva (Instituto Superior Politécnico Gaya, Portugal)
Business Science Reference • copyright 2020 • 267pp • H/C (ISBN: 9781522597834) • US $225.00 (our price)

Exploring the Power of Electronic Word-of-Mouth in the Services Industry
Sandra Maria Correia Loureiro (Instituto Universitário de Lisboa, Portugal) and Hans Ruediger Kaufmann (University of Applied Management Studies, Germany)
Business Science Reference • copyright 2020 • 463pp • H/C (ISBN: 9781522585756) • US $265.00 (our price)

Green Marketing as a Positive Driver Toward Business Sustainability
Vannie Naidoo (University of KwaZulu-Natal, South Africa) and Rahul Verma (Department of Training and Technical Education, India)
Business Science Reference • copyright 2020 • 356pp • H/C (ISBN: 9781522595588) • US $225.00 (our price)

Strategies and Tools for Managing Connected Consumers
Ree C. Ho (Taylor's University, Malaysia)
Business Science Reference • copyright 2020 • 365pp • H/C (ISBN: 9781522596974) • US $275.00 (our price)

IGI Global
DISSEMINATOR OF KNOWLEDGE

701 East Chocolate Avenue, Hershey, PA 17033, USA
Tel: 717-533-8845 x100 • Fax: 717-533-8661
E-Mail: cust@igi-global.com • www.igi-global.com

Editorial Advisory Board

Özlem Olgu Akdeniz, *Manchester Metropolitan University, UK*
Elif Baykal, *Istanbul Medipol University, Turkey*
Marta Borda, *Wroclaw University of Economics, Poland*
Dursun Delen, *Oklahoma State University, USA*
Enrico Ivaldi, *Università degli Studi di Genova, Italy*
Ekrem Tatoğlu, *Ibn Haldun University, Turkey*

List of Contributors

Adalı, Zafer / *Artvin Çoruh University, Turkey* 510
Adiguzel, Zafer / *Medipol Business School, Istanbul Medipol University, Turkey* 68, 115
Afşar, Bilge / *Kto Karatay University, Turkey* 21, 358
Akbalık, Murat / *Marmara University, Turkey* 336
Akça, Samet / *KTO Karatay University, Turkey* 358
Bilgin, Yavuz / *Halkbank, Turkey* 228
Camgoz, Selin Metin / *Hacettepe University, Turkey* 228
Canöz, İsmail / *İstanbul Arel University, Turkey* 493
Ceylan, Nildag Basak / *Ankara Yildirim Beyazit University, Turkey* 47
Çitilci, Tuğberk / *Nisantasi University, Turkey* 336
Dinçer, Hasan / *Istanbul Medipol University, Turkey* 145, 429
Doğdu, Ali / *Konya Food and Agriculture University, Turkey* 450
Eken, ihsan / *Istanbul Medipol University, Turkey* 247
Ergül, Gülcan / *Istanbul Medipol University, Turkey* 287
Ersin, İrfan / *Istanbul Medipol University, Turkey* 269, 412
Eti, Serkan / *Istanbul Medipol University, Turkey* 1
Gezmen, Başak / *Istanbul Medipol University, Turkey* 247
Gürler, Metin / *Uluslararası Rekabet Araştırmaları Kurumu, Turkey* 206
Gürsoy, Çiğdem / *Istinye University, Turkey* 529
Kalkavan, Hakan / *Istanbul Medipol University, Turkey* 172
Kapusuzoglu, Ayhan / *Ankara Yildirim Beyazit University, Turkey* 47
Kara, Funda / *Independent Researcher, Turkey* 206
Karakeçe, Ercan / *Istanbul Medipol University, Turkey* 412
Karan, Mehmet Baha / *Hacettepe University, Turkey* 228
Kartal, Mustafa Tevfik / *Borsa İstanbul, Turkey* 471
Kayral, İhsan Erdem / *Konya Food and Agriculture University, Turkey* 450
Kıvılcım, Fulya / *FEDEK, Turkey* 187
Kiyak, Özgür / *Beykent University, Turkey* 21
Kurucu, Gökçe / *Konya Food and Agriculture University, Turkey* 450
Kurum, Mustafa Eser / *Yeni Yüzyıl University, Turkey* 383
Mengir, Ayşe / *Istanbul Medipol University, Turkey* 145
Mızrak, Filiz / *Istanbul Medipol University, Turkey* 317
Mızrak, Kagan Cenk / *Nisantasi University, Turkey* 317
Oktar, Suat / *Marmara University, Turkey* 383

Omar, Haroub Hamad / *D-Tree International, Tanzania* 47
Pınarbaşı, Fatih / *Istanbul Medipol University, Turkey* 429
Temizel, Ece Nur / *Istanbul Medipol University, Turkey* 1, 92
Uysal, Mustafa / *Artvin Çoruh University, Turkey* 510
Yildiz, Yilmaz / *University of Huddersfield, UK* 228
Yüksel, Serhat / *Istanbul Medipol University, Turkey* 92, 287

Table of Contents

Foreword xxii

Preface xxiii

Acknowledgment xxv

Section 1

Chapter 1
Measuring Financial Literacy of the Housewife to Generate Marketing Strategies 1
    Serkan Eti, Istanbul Medipol University, Turkey
    Ece Nur Temizel, Istanbul Medipol University, Turkey

Chapter 2
Financial Marketing-Based Role of Exchange Rate to Increase Foreign Trade in Turkey 21
    Özgür Kiyak, Beykent University, Turkey
    Bilge Afşar, Kto Karatay University, Turkey

Chapter 3
The Effects of Exchange Rate on Export Performance in Tanzania: An Empirical Research for
Financial Competition 47
    Haroub Hamad Omar, D-Tree International, Tanzania
    Nildag Basak Ceylan, Ankara Yildirim Beyazit University, Turkey
    Ayhan Kapusuzoglu, Ankara Yildirim Beyazit University, Turkey

Chapter 4
Competitiveness of International Business: Management, Economics, Technology, Environment,
and Social Study of Cultural Perspective 68
    Zafer Adiguzel, Medipol Business School, Istanbul Medipol University, Turkey

Chapter 5
Evaluating the Importance of Behavioral Finance in the Financial Marketing Area: An Analysis
of Turkish Academic Studies 92
    Serhat Yüksel, Istanbul Medipol University, Turkey
    Ece Nur Temizel, Istanbul Medipol University, Turkey

Section 2

Chapter 6
Examining the Effects of Strategies, Competition Intelligence, and Risk Culture on Business Performance in International Enterprises 115
    Zafer Adiguzel, Medipol Business School, Istanbul Medipol University, Turkey

Chapter 7
Innovative Call Center Applications Focused on Financial Marketing in the Turkish Banking Sector 145
    Hasan Dinçer, Istanbul Medipol University, Turkey
    Ayşe Mengir, Istanbul Medipol University, Turkey

Chapter 8
The Importance of Ethics and Corporate Social Responsibility in Financial Markets: A Literature Review and Recommendations for Ethical and Islamic Banking 172
    Hakan Kalkavan, Istanbul Medipol University, Turkey

Chapter 9
Globalization Phenomenon and Cruising of Multinational Companies Under Global Market Conditions 187
    Fulya Kıvılcım, FEDEK, Turkey

Chapter 10
The Relationship Between Foreign Direct Investment and Financial Development in OECD Countries 206
    Metin Gürler, Uluslararası Rekabet Araştırmaları Kurumu, Turkey
    Funda Kara, Independent Researcher, Turkey

Section 3

Chapter 11
Understanding the Investment Behavior of Individual Investors: An Empirical Study on FOREX Markets 228
    Yavuz Bilgin, Halkbank, Turkey
    Selin Metin Camgoz, Hacettepe University, Turkey
    Mehmet Baha Karan, Hacettepe University, Turkey
    Yilmaz Yildiz, University of Huddersfield, UK

Chapter 12
Acquisition of Financial Literacy as a Life Skill: A Study on Financial Literacy Awareness of Students 247
    Başak Gezmen, Istanbul Medipol University, Turkey
    ihsan Eken, Istanbul Medipol University, Turkey

Chapter 13
Determining the Importance of Domestic Firms on Stock Market Performance in Terms of
Financial Marketing: An Application on OECD Countries 269
 İrfan Ersin, Istanbul Medipol University, Turkey

Chapter 14
Evaluation of Customer Expectations-Based New Product and Service Development Process: An
Analysis for the Turkish Banking Sector 287
 Serhat Yüksel, Istanbul Medipol University, Turkey
 Gülcan Ergül, Istanbul Medipol University, Turkey

Chapter 15
Role of Agility in the Banking Sector in Competitive Globalization Era: Evidence From the
Turkish Banking Sector 317
 Kagan Cenk Mızrak, Nisantası University, Turkey
 Filiz Mızrak, Istanbul Medipol University, Turkey

Section 4

Chapter 16
The Importance of PESTEL Analysis for Environmental Scanning Process 336
 Tuğberk Çitilci, Nisantasi University, Turkey
 Murat Akbalık, Marmara University, Turkey

Chapter 17
The Relationship Between Economic Growth and Innovation: Panel Data Analysis on Chosen
OECD Countries 358
 Samet Akça, KTO Karatay University, Turkey
 Bilge Afşar, KTO Karatay University, Turkey

Chapter 18
The Role of Central Bank in Competitive Environment: A Study for Interest Rate Corridor
Systems 383
 Mustafa Eser Kurum, Yeni Yüzyıl University, Turkey
 Suat Oktar, Marmara University, Turkey

Chapter 19
Analysis of the Effects of Macroeconomic Factors on Entrepreneurship: An Application on E7
Countries 412
 İrfan Ersin, Istanbul Medipol University, Turkey
 Ercan Karakeçe, Istanbul Medipol University, Turkey

Chapter 20
PESTEL Analysis-Based Evaluation of Marketing Strategies in the European Banking Sector: An
Application With IT2 Fuzzy DEMATEL 429
 Hasan Dinçer, Istanbul Medipol University, Turkey
 Fatih Pınarbaşı, Istanbul Medipol University, Turkey

Section 5

Chapter 21
Testing the Validity of Taylor's Rule on Developing Countries for Effective Financial Marketing 450
    Ali Doğdu, Konya Food and Agriculture University, Turkey
    Gökçe Kurucu, Konya Food and Agriculture University, Turkey
    İhsan Erdem Kayral, Konya Food and Agriculture University, Turkey

Chapter 22
The Concentration From the Competition Perspective in the Turkish Banking Sector: An Examination for the Period of 1999-2018 471
    Mustafa Tevfik Kartal, Borsa İstanbul, Turkey

Chapter 23
The Impact of US Monetary Growth on Bitcoin Trading Volume in the Current Economic Uncertainty 493
    İsmail Canöz, İstanbul Arel University, Turkey

Chapter 24
The Relationship Between Commodity Prices and Selected Macroeconomic Variables in Turkey: Evidence From Fourier Cointegration Test 510
    Mustafa Uysal, Artvin Çoruh University, Turkey
    Zafer Adalı, Artvin Çoruh University, Turkey

Chapter 25
From the Working Order of Akhi-Tradesmen Organization to Economic Geography: Regional Production, Competition, and Tanner Tradesmen 529
    Çiğdem Gürsoy, Istinye University, Turkey

Compilation of References 551

About the Contributors 640

Index 644

Detailed Table of Contents

Foreword xxii

Preface xxiii

Acknowledgment xxv

Section 1

Chapter 1
Measuring Financial Literacy of the Housewife to Generate Marketing Strategies 1
  Serkan Eti, Istanbul Medipol University, Turkey
  Ece Nur Temizel, Istanbul Medipol University, Turkey

This chapter evaluates the financial literacy of the housewife by analyzing a survey of a minimum of 204 housewives in Turkey. Findings from the 25 questions of the survey show housewives in Turkey generally have Turkish Lira deposits but also have a low tendency to spend. It was found that the financial literacy of housewives was low. In this context, it will be appropriate to increase this literacy through general education. In this way, housewives will be able to better evaluate their savings and the financial system of the country will work more effectively.

Chapter 2
Financial Marketing-Based Role of Exchange Rate to Increase Foreign Trade in Turkey 21
  Özgür Kiyak, Beykent University, Turkey
  Bilge Afşar, Kto Karatay University, Turkey

This chapter tries to determine whether there is a causal relationship between exchange rate and foreign trade. The study includes monthly data between February 2003 and December 2018 including dollar foreign exchange selling rate and inflation related real exchange rate for exchange rate, and export amount, import amount, export increase/decrease rate, and import increase. Increase/decrease rate is used for foreign trade among other variables, for a total of 6 variables. According to the obtained results of Engle-Granger cointegration analysis, there is a cointegration between variables in the long run. However, according to the results of the Toda-Yamamoto causality analysis, it was understood that there is no causality relationship between exchange rate and foreign trade.

Chapter 3
The Effects of Exchange Rate on Export Performance in Tanzania: An Empirical Research for
Financial Competition.. 47
    Haroub Hamad Omar, D-Tree International, Tanzania
    Nildag Basak Ceylan, Ankara Yildirim Beyazit University, Turkey
    Ayhan Kapusuzoglu, Ankara Yildirim Beyazit University, Turkey

The chapter analyzes the effects of exchange rate of Tanzanian shilling on the country's exports performance applying Vector Auto-Regressive (VAR) model covering the sample period from 1993:Q1 to 2016:Q4. Cointegration and causality tests are performed to investigate the short- and long-term relationships between the variables to evaluate the financial competition. The results show that; there is no long-term relationship (cointegration) between exchange rates and exports and between foreign demand and exports. Moreover, the results of causality test show no short-term relationship (causality) between exchange rates and exports and between foreign demand and exports. As the findings suggest, the exchange rate level of Tanzanian shilling (in nominal terms) does not statistic-significantly affect the country's exports performance.

Chapter 4
Competitiveness of International Business: Management, Economics, Technology, Environment,
and Social Study of Cultural Perspective.. 68
    Zafer Adiguzel, Medipol Business School, Istanbul Medipol University, Turkey

The world is experiencing rapid growth and change, and for a business to compete qualified, manpower must receive full training. The world economy will determine the balance of power competitive advantages. A strong management approach will increase quality and productivity. It is an important factor for the companies to gain superiority in the field of efficiency, to adapt to the technological changes, and to compete. Therefore, businesses also need to realize these advantages to provide technological changes, as well as to create competitive advantages. Management approach is necessary to create the organizational structure. Business management delivering the identified strategic objectives requires continuous effort by employees from every level. This chapter investigates international business management in terms of competitiveness combined with the effects of the cultural and social environment in understanding the management and the impact of the economy.

Chapter 5
Evaluating the Importance of Behavioral Finance in the Financial Marketing Area: An Analysis
of Turkish Academic Studies 92
    Serhat Yüksel, Istanbul Medipol University, Turkey
    Ece Nur Temizel, Istanbul Medipol University, Turkey

This chapter investigates the thesis in Turkey written in the field of behavioral finance. An important objective is to guide the relevant researchers who are missing in the fields in the literature. For this purpose, 60 theses written so far have been examined with bibliometric analysis method. The period range of these theses is 2003-2018. When Daniel Kahneman won the Nobel Prize in 2002, behavioral finance, which started to attract attention in our country, started to gain momentum especially in times of crisis when unexplained behaviors were explained by the concept of rational people. In addition, 49 of them consisted of master's degree and the remaining 11 were doctoral dissertations. State universities constitute a very large weight of the relevant universities. Studies on behavioral finance have been gathered under various topics. The most studied subject has "character traits of the investors". This is followed by "investment in stocks" and "anomalies".

Section 2

Chapter 6
Examining the Effects of Strategies, Competition Intelligence, and Risk Culture on Business Performance in International Enterprises 115
Zafer Adiguzel, Medipol Business School, Istanbul Medipol University, Turkey

The top management of the organizations attach importance to both the cultural structure and performance by paying attention to the risk level of the decisions taken in order to be successful in the competitive environment. With the success of the organization performance, the organization of employees with different cultural characteristics of the same common value comes to the fore. Therefore, human resources and corporate culture of institutions attach importance to the management of the interaction of people from different segments in their management policies. How risks are understood and managed by employees in an organization is examined within the scope of risk culture, which depends on internal and external factors in the organization. As a result of cultural differences, both the advantages of orientation are recognized and explained and the problems that need to be managed continue to arise. This chapter sets out the existing cultural framework in organizations, and supports a bridge function and a systemic understanding of cultural differences.

Chapter 7
Innovative Call Center Applications Focused on Financial Marketing in the Turkish Banking Sector 145
Hasan Dinçer, Istanbul Medipol University, Turkey
Ayşe Mengir, Istanbul Medipol University, Turkey

As a result of globalization, call centers of banks that develop rapidly by the virtue of the technology become an important unit which brings first contact with customers. Nowadays, call centers not only give support to customers and other callers but also use the communication tools. This chapter examines innovator call center applications in banking. The main aim of call centers is to provide services with minimum cost, maximum speed, and excellent customer satisfaction. To achieve this purpose, it is necessary to incorporate the advantages of technological improvements. According to the research results, beside the excessive usage of call centers by customers, the banks direct their customers to call centers or alternative distribution canals to decrease the workload of the branches. Moreover, it is mentioned in this research that some precautions are taken for both internal and external customer satisfaction. Under today's economic conditions, customers do not prefer banks which are not using innovator technologies.

Chapter 8
The Importance of Ethics and Corporate Social Responsibility in Financial Markets: A Literature Review and Recommendations for Ethical and Islamic Banking 172
Hakan Kalkavan, Istanbul Medipol University, Turkey

This chapter mainly focuses on the literature about the relationship between ethics, corporate social responsibility, and financial markets, which is broad and diverse as well as multi-disciplined. Some are concerned only with ethical banking, while others seek to establish a financial system based on social responsibility to society and people. The studies essentially bring attention to the question of how banks should act in the face of the moral-economic dilemma. In fact, ethical aspect is much more valuable than economic profitability and includes a social responsibility approach. In the concept of ethical concerns and corporate social responposibility, the literature has been reviewed and problematic areas discussed for ethical and Islamic banking. Islamic finance and specifically Islamic banking can be seen as a new practice to bring corporate ethical responsibility and social justice into the financial and economic spheres.

Chapter 9
Globalization Phenomenon and Cruising of Multinational Companies Under Global Market Conditions 187
Fulya Kıvılcım, FEDEK, Turkey

This chapter clarifies the definition of the phenomenon of globalization, historical development, the rapid and radical change that has taken place in the world. In the context of globalization, and in developing global market conditions, the author examines the course of Multinational Corporations in the globalization process; to emphasize the company structure models they own, competition, strategic management, and decision-making policies they follow, and primarily based on the importance they place on the structure of innovative thinking.

Chapter 10
The Relationship Between Foreign Direct Investment and Financial Development in OECD Countries 206
Metin Gürler, Uluslararası Rekabet Araştırmaları Kurumu, Turkey
Funda Kara, Independent Researcher, Turkey

This chapter investigates the relationship between the OECD-FRRI issued by OECD and IMF-FDI issued by IMF for 36 OECD member countries. Cross-section data (CSD) analysis and panel data (PD) analysis consisting of random and fixed effects estimations were used in the study to investigate the relationship between Foreign Direct Investment (FDI) and Financial Development for OECD countries for the years 1997, 2003, and 2006 and the 7-year period of 2010-2016. Granger Causality Test (GCT) is also applied to test the direction of causality between two indicators. According to the Random Effects Model (RAM) and Fixed Effects Model (FEM) with PD analysis in the study OECD-FRRI is found as one of the determinants of IMF-FDI and IMF-FDI is found as one of the determinants of OECD-FRRI in OECD member countries. For CSD analysis, there is no significant proof to say OECD-FRRI is one of the main determinants of IMF-FDI and IMF-FDI is one of the determinants of OECD-FRRI in OECD member countries. For CSD, OECD-FRRI does not cause IMF-FDI whereas IMF-FDI causes OECD-FRRI.

Section 3

Chapter 11
Understanding the Investment Behavior of Individual Investors: An Empirical Study on FOREX Markets 228
Yavuz Bilgin, Halkbank, Turkey
Selin Metin Camgoz, Hacettepe University, Turkey
Mehmet Baha Karan, Hacettepe University, Turkey
Yilmaz Yildiz, University of Huddersfield, UK

The FOREX market has become a popular ground amongst all kinds of market players. The leverage transactions of the market that may generate higher profit levels with low capital/investments make it very attractive for the individual risk takers. The research investigates the trading behavior of FOREX investors relying on the survey data collected from 167 Turkish investors in 2019. Within the scope of the research, the authors evaluate whether and to what extent behavioral factors, namely demographic characteristics; personal characteristics such as personality traits, love of money, and biases like disposition effect influence investment performance. The results reveal that among the personality traits, openness to experience and conscientiousness have a positive impact while disposition effect and love of money have a negative impact on the performance of investors. Additional analysis suggests that the effects of personality traits and biases on trading performance remarkably change among subgroups of investors regarding their income level.

Chapter 12
Acquisition of Financial Literacy as a Life Skill: A Study on Financial Literacy Awareness of
Students... 247
    Başak Gezmen, Istanbul Medipol University, Turkey
    ihsan Eken, Istanbul Medipol University, Turkey

Alongside the phenomena such as crisis, prosperity, etc., which emerged with the increase of global competition, the development of literacy levels has become critical. In the acquisition and development of financial literacy, first of all, the current situation should be determined, then the relevant policies should be developed and the literacy should be acquired through the necessary trainings to be provided. This chapter determines the relationship between the acquisition of financial literacy awareness as a life skill and the participation of the students who took the Introduction to Economics course in the Faculty of Communication at Istanbul Medipol University in 2018-2019 in the axis of survey method. Authors discuss the students' financial literacy awareness and skill in general. The chapter also gains insight into the situation of similar courses such as economics and finance to improve the perspective on financial literacy awareness.

Chapter 13
Determining the Importance of Domestic Firms on Stock Market Performance in Terms of
Financial Marketing: An Application on OECD Countries... 269
    İrfan Ersin, Istanbul Medipol University, Turkey

This chapter examines the relationship between stock market value of domestic firms traded in stock markets in OECD countries and stock index for 1990-2018 period. As a result of Pedroni Panel Cointegration and Dumitrescu-Hurlin Panel Causality Analysis, there is a relationship between the market values of domestic firms traded on the stock exchange and the stock index. In addition, a two-way causality relationship was found. This situation indicates that this relationship is very powerful. It can be understood that adding domestic companies to the stock market has a significant effect on the stock prices and this will attract foreign investors to enter the market.

Chapter 14
Evaluation of Customer Expectations-Based New Product and Service Development Process: An
Analysis for the Turkish Banking Sector 287
    Serhat Yüksel, Istanbul Medipol University, Turkey
    Gülcan Ergül, Istanbul Medipol University, Turkey

This chapter analyzed customer expectations-based new product and service development process in banking sector for the Turkish banking sector. In-depth interview technique was used. Four dimensions (finance, technology, customer and personnel, and physical conditions) were determined for measuring the efficiency of this process, and 12 criteria were determined for these dimensions. Questions were prepared by considering the literature and these dimensions and criteria. The 26 questions were asked to 12 different personnel working in Turkish banks. Those employees in the private and foreign banks did not indicate any negativity regarding the new product and service development process, but did report deficiencies in terms of personnel and physical conditions in relation to the new product and service development process.

Chapter 15
Role of Agility in the Banking Sector in Competitive Globalization Era: Evidence From the
Turkish Banking Sector 317
    Kagan Cenk Mızrak, Nisantası University, Turkey
    Filiz Mızrak, Istanbul Medipol University, Turkey

In today's rapidly changing market conditions, organizations need to be agile to gain a competitive market advantage. This chapter details the key points required for agility. Although there has been ongoing discussion whether finance and banking sector can be agile due to rigid structures, processes, and regulators, the chapter aims to prove the vital role of agility in banking sector with the case of Garanti Bank. Thanks to the case, the strategies both on the basis organization structure and marketing level that banks need to apply in agile transformation process, have been exemplified. As a result of the case, the importance of flexibility, speed, monitoring the latest trend, making quick decisions, and being customer-focused in the banking sector is stressed. On the other hand, banks are suggested to engage all their units, shareholders together with their customers in the process to have a more smooth translation.

Section 4

Chapter 16
The Importance of PESTEL Analysis for Environmental Scanning Process 336
    Tuğberk Çitilci, Nisantasi University, Turkey
    Murat Akbalık, Marmara University, Turkey

Strategy and tactic are two inseparable dynamics for organization which can be the same as a chess game. Organizations' theoretical infinite life cycle needs well-established strategic management. To create competitive advantage among competitors, top management of organizations must scan environmental factors very carefully. Without environmental scanning process organization can be viewed as blind and deaf in an ecosystem which definitely ends with shutdown of activity. Environmental scanning has two parts; internal environmental analysis and external analysis which aim to create early signals for organization. Internal analysis deals with micro-based factors which can be controlled by organization whereas external analysis universe is larger and wider when compared to internal analysis. External analysis covers all the factors such as political, economic, social, technological, environmental, and legal, which an organization cannot control and cannot affect. This type of analysis can be named as top-down approach analysis aims to create competitive advantage.

Chapter 17
The Relationship Between Economic Growth and Innovation: Panel Data Analysis on Chosen
OECD Countries 358
 Samet Akça, KTO Karatay University, Turkey
 Bilge Afşar, KTO Karatay University, Turkey

This chapter studies innovation and economic growth and emphasizes their relationship. In this context; innovation and economic growth outputs of 16 OECD countries between 2005 and 2015 are analyzed. GDP is considered as economic growth variable, R&D investments in GDP (%), and patent applications are considered as innovation variables. In light of these variables, panel data analyze is used. Unit root, Pedroni co-integration and FMOLS tests were applied with the order. As a result, the increase in patent applications and R&D investments was found to have a positive effect on economic growth.

Chapter 18
The Role of Central Bank in Competitive Environment: A Study for Interest Rate Corridor
Systems 383
 Mustafa Eser Kurum, Yeni Yüzyıl University, Turkey
 Suat Oktar, Marmara University, Turkey

This chapter evaluates the macroeconomic impact of the interest rate corridor policy implemented by the central bank in Turkey. In this context, firstly the general framework, types and application of interest rate corridor policy are explained. Then, the interest rate corridor policy implemented by the CBRT after the global crisis was examined in detail. In addition, domestic and foreign literature examining the macroeconomic effects of the interest rate corridor policy has been included. This chapter examines the macroeconomic impact of the interest rate corridor policy implemented in Turkey using data from the 2011-2018 period. In the study, Engle-Granger Cointegration Analysis and Toda-Yamamoto Causality Analysis were used as models. As a result of the study, it was concluded that interest rate corridor had an effect on economic growth, foreign direct investment, and exchange rate variables.

Chapter 19
Analysis of the Effects of Macroeconomic Factors on Entrepreneurship: An Application on E7
Countries 412
 İrfan Ersin, Istanbul Medipol University, Turkey
 Ercan Karakeçe, Istanbul Medipol University, Turkey

Entrepreneurship is an important field in the increase and diversification of investments in a country. Entrepreneurship is gaining importance in today's world where financial marketing has become an important sector. The aim of this study is to determine the macroeconomic factors that determine entrepreneurship in E7 countries. In the study using logit method, the period of 1992-2018 was discussed. In the analysis results, the variables of unemployment, financial loans and current account deficit were found to be macroeconomic factors determining entrepreneurship. Given that entrepreneurship is important in the financial field, E7 countries should take into account the financial credit markets, focus on economic policies to reduce unemployment and address the current account deficit problem.

Chapter 20
PESTEL Analysis-Based Evaluation of Marketing Strategies in the European Banking Sector: An Application With IT2 Fuzzy DEMATEL 429

Hasan Dinçer, Istanbul Medipol University, Turkey
Fatih Pınarbaşı, Istanbul Medipol University, Turkey

This chapter evaluates the marketing strategies in European banking sector. In this context, six dimensions of PESTEL analysis (politic, economic, sociological, technologic, environmental, and legal) are taken into the consideration. On the other side, interval type-2 fuzzy DEMATEL approach is used to weight the importance of these dimensions. The findings show that technological and political factors have the highest importance. Therefore, it is recommended that technological innovations in the banking sector should be followed by European banks. Within this framework, these banks should design a market research department to follow these developments in the market so that new products and services can be identified. Therefore, technological development should be adopted in the strategy development process. In addition, interest rates defined by the central bank should also be considered by these banks. Hence, adopting marketing strategies according to the interest rate policy of the central banks provides a competitive advantage to the European banks.

Section 5

Chapter 21
Testing the Validity of Taylor's Rule on Developing Countries for Effective Financial Marketing 450

Ali Doğdu, Konya Food and Agriculture University, Turkey
Gökçe Kurucu, Konya Food and Agriculture University, Turkey
İhsan Erdem Kayral, Konya Food and Agriculture University, Turkey

This chapter examines whether the central bank policy behaviors of E-7 countries are valid by using a Taylor type monetary policy response function. In this context, the policy response function of banks is analyzed by using monthly data for the 2008-2018 period. Then, unit root tests of ADF (Augmented Dickey Fuller), PP (Philips Perron), IPS (Im Peseran Shin) and LLC (Levin Lin Chu) were performed and analyzed by using Dumitrescu-Hurlin methodology. As a result of the analyses conducted using inflationary data, it was observed that short-term interest rates of the central bank affect price stability by causing inflation, but inflation rates did not cause an increase or decrease in short-term interest rates. According to the findings, although inflation does not cause interest rates to change in E7 countries, a causality relationship has emerged from interest rates to inflation rates. These results indicate that the monetary policies implemented in these countries are not carried out in accordance with the Taylor rule.

Chapter 22
The Concentration From the Competition Perspective in the Turkish Banking Sector: An Examination for the Period of 1999-2018.. 471

Mustafa Tevfik Kartal, Borsa İstanbul, Turkey

With the globalization, the world has been becoming a much smaller place. New types of business have been emerging. Depending on this situation, new corporations are founded in current and emerging sectors. This causes an increase in competition. On the other hand, a variety of sectors are regulated intensively which result in a high concentration. Banking sectors is one of these sectors at where regulations are much and entry barriers are high. It is aimed at examining concentration from competition perspectives Turkish Banking Sector (TBS). It is concluded that TBS generally has a non-concentrated industry structure in terms of total assets, total credits, total deposits, total equities, and total net profits. Exceptions are seen in total net profits and in total deposits. Concentration level generally has decreased from 1999 (1,172 on average) to 2018 (899 on average calculated by Herfindahl-Hirschman Index (HHI). It is recommended that necessary precautions should be taken by regulatory bodies in order to decrease concentration and increase competition in TBS.

Chapter 23
The Impact of US Monetary Growth on Bitcoin Trading Volume in the Current Economic Uncertainty 493
    İsmail Canöz, İstanbul Arel University, Turkey

This study examines the effect of US monetary growth on Bitcoin trading volume. To achieve this purpose, firstly, the symmetric causality test is used. Following this test, another symmetric causality test is used to reveal a time-varying causal effect between variables. The data set covers the period from July 2010 to July 2019. The results of the first symmetric causality test, which considers the time interval of the study data as a whole, show that there is no causal relationship between variables. According to the results of the second causality test, these support the previous results substantially. However, an interesting detail is the causal relationship between variables for the period between April 2019 and July 2019. The reason for this relationship could be that investors who are indecisive during the current economic uncertainty add Bitcoin to their portfolios in response to the Federal Reserve's decisions.

Chapter 24
The Relationship Between Commodity Prices and Selected Macroeconomic Variables in Turkey: Evidence From Fourier Cointegration Test 510
    Mustafa Uysal, Artvin Çoruh University, Turkey
    Zafer Adalı, Artvin Çoruh University, Turkey

This chapter determines whether there is a long-run relationship among oil, copper, natural gas, export figures and import figures, and BIST 100. Within this context, the study employs monthly periods from January 2006 to June 2019. ADF, Fourier ADF, and Banerjee Cointegration Test were applied. Banerjee Cointegration Test revealed that copper, oil, and natural gas and import figures move together in the long run but the existence of the long-run relationship between the selected inputs and export figures and BIST 100 has not been found. This evidence can be interpreted as the change in oil, copper, and natural gas may influence the amount of Turkish import figures.

Chapter 25
From the Working Order of Akhi-Tradesmen Organization to Economic Geography: Regional Production, Competition, and Tanner Tradesmen 529
    Çiğdem Gürsoy, Istinye University, Turkey

It is possible to take the concepts of economic geography, regional production, and competition, often mentioned nowadays, back to the transition to the established order in the historical process, in other words, to the agricultural revolution. However, systematically developing and implementing methods was started by Ahi Evran about 800 years ago. The working order of the Akhi-Tradesmen Organization created by Evran, based on the understanding of the economy will serve the human, not human to economy, bears a resemblance to today's agglomeration system. The fact that production factors, which are agglomerated in a specified geographical area, work with optimum efficiency spurs competitiveness. Within this framework, this chapter reveals the implementation of regional agglomeration model in Ottoman territories in historical process, which is discussed in the economic geography studies. In addition, within the scope of institutionalization, the period spent by organization of Akhi-Tradesmen in the Ottoman Empire will be mentioned.

Compilation of References 551

About the Contributors 640

Index 644

Foreword

Marketing is one of the most important concepts in the globalizing world. The main reason for this is the increase in competition in almost every sector as a result of globalization. As can be understood from this, companies have to produce some actions in order to survive. Marketing activities are also important elements that can contribute to these goals of the companies.

Another important factor today is the financial presence of this competition. In other words, companies have to develop their marketing strategies in financial aspect. Otherwise, these policies will always be a bit lacking. Therefore, companies must take into consideration factors such as competition, customer and profitability when determining a strategy. In this way, the strategy to be implemented will fully comply with the company's organizational objectives.

Because of my academic identity, I have been constantly reviewing the literature in the fields of finance, economics and marketing for many years. I had the opportunity to evaluate many quality studies on these issues. However, I noticed that there are a limited number of studies addressing these issues together. In other words, it is obvious that a study that examines the marketing activities of companies from a financial and economic perspective will be very effective.

I had the opportunity to examine this book which was organized by Hasan Dinçer and Serhat Yüksel and contributed by many authors. This study includes a large number of quality sections dealing with marketing financially. Because of these issues, I believe that this book will complete the deficiency in the literature I mentioned earlier. Therefore, I would like to congratulate the editors and authors who have signed such a comprehensive study.

İmre Sabahat Ersoy
Marmara University, Turkey

Preface

Marketing is the primary concern of business world since industrial societies, especially since 20th century. Apart from the production and distribution of products and services, marketing as a holistic process and the production of consumer value is important for today's enterprises. On the other hand, finance function is a major contributor for managing organizations in competitive markets and environments. Recent developments in business researches have heightened the need for integrating of different functions of business for understanding the market and managing the competition. The main challenge business face today is related to understanding and sensemaking of environment. Examining financial function with a marketing discipline approach will help understanding both competition and internal management processes.

Marketing science has its own concepts and theoretical background for evaluating consumer related challenges. From the starting of production idea to delivering consumer experience, it has many different approaches for managing consumer relationships. On the other hand, finance function has similarity with marketing function for consumer area. Consumers are facing changes day by day, therefore the needs and demands changing consistently. Examining the changing environment and managing consumer relationships while dealing with competition in today's market is important task for companies.

This book aims to integrate financial and marketing functions together to make sense of environment and business-related challenges. Different financial challenges are taken into the consideration while many of them are based on marketing theories. Agency Theory, Balance Scorecard Approach, Product Life Cycle, Comparative Advantage Theory of Competititon, Optimal Consumer Experience, Marketing Mix are the concepts from marketing theory which are used as theoretical background for financial issues. Beyond these theoretical bases, main marketing functions (elements) as product, distribution, strategy are used together with financial challenges. This study offers a novel approach as using multi criteria decision making methods for financial challenges while marketing theories are used as theoretical bases.

Target Audience and potential users of this book are defined below:

- Researchers
- Academicians
- Policy Makers
- Government Officials
- Upright Students in the Concerned Fields
- Members of Chambers of Commerce and Industry
- Top Managers of the Companies

This book consists of five different sections. Each section has five different chapters. Chapter 1 is related to the financial literacy levels of the housewives. In Chapter 2, the role of exchange rate on the foreign trade is evaluated. Chapter 3 focuses on the effects of exchange rate to increase the export amount. Chapter 4 looks at the relationship between business, technology and economics in competitive environment. Chapter 5 includes the analysis about the importance of behavioral finance in financial marketing area.

In addition to them, Chapter 6 examines the effects of strategies, competition intelligence and risk culture on business performance in international enterprises. Innovative call center applications focused on financial marketing in Turkish banking sector are examined in chapter 7. Chapter 8 makes a literature review about the importance of ethics and corporate social responsibility in financial markets. The issue of globalization is identified with the eye of financial marketing in Chapter 9. Chapter 10 focuses the relationship between foreign direct investment and financial development in OECD countries.

Chapter 11 tries to understand the investment behavior of individual investors. Chapter 12 identifies the financial literacy awareness of students. Chapter 13 aims to determine the importance of domestic firms on stock market performance in terms of financial marketing. Chapter 14 evaluates the customer expectations-based new product and service development process. On the other side, in Chapter 15, the role of agility in the banking sector in competitive globalization era is evaluated.

Chapter 16 is related to the importance of PESTEL analysis for environmental scanning process. Moreover, the relationship between economic growth and innovation is examined in Chapter 17. Chapter 18 aims to understand the role of central bank in competitive environment. Chapter 19 identifies the effects of macroeconomic factors on entrepreneurship. Chapter 20 includes PESTEL analysis-based evaluation of marketing strategies in European banking sector.

Chapter 21 tests the validity of Taylor's rule on developing countries for effective financial marketing. Chapter 22 concentrates on the competition issue in Turkish banking industry. Chapter 23 includes an analysis about the impact of US monetary growth on bitcoin trading volume in the current economic uncertainty. The relationship between commodity prices and selected macroeconomic variables in Turkey is evaluated in Chapter 24. Chapter 25 is related to the working order of Akhi-Tradesmen organization.

Acknowledgment

The editors would like to acknowledge the help of all the people involved in this project and, more specifically, to the authors and reviewers that took part in the review process. Without their support, this book would not have become a reality.

First, the editors would like to thank each one of the authors for their contributions. Our sincere gratitude goes to the chapter's authors who contributed their time and expertise to this book.

Second, the editors wish to acknowledge the valuable contributions of the reviewers regarding the improvement of quality, coherence, and content presentation of chapters. Most of the authors also served as referees; we highly appreciate their double task.

Hasan Dinçer
Istanbul Medipol University, Turkey

Serhat Yüksel
Istanbul Medipol University, Turkey

Section 1

Chapter 1
Measuring Financial Literacy of the Housewife to Generate Marketing Strategies

Serkan Eti
https://orcid.org/0000-0002-4791-4091
Istanbul Medipol University, Turkey

Ece Nur Temizel
Istanbul Medipol University, Turkey

ABSTRACT

This chapter evaluates the financial literacy of the housewife by analyzing a survey of a minimum of 204 housewives in Turkey. Findings from the 25 questions of the survey show housewives in Turkey generally have Turkish Lira deposits but also have a low tendency to spend. It was found that the financial literacy of housewives was low. In this context, it will be appropriate to increase this literacy through general education. In this way, housewives will be able to better evaluate their savings and the financial system of the country will work more effectively.

INTRODUCTION

The effectiveness of financial markets is important for the macroeconomic performance of countries. Financial markets bring together those who own and who need funds. This provides significant benefits to both parties (Horioka & Niimi, 2019; Lyons et al., 2019). Those who have funds can earn income through this system. On the other hand, those who need the fund can access this fund more easily thanks to the financial markets. In sum, financial markets accelerate the flow of funds in the country. In this way, investments in the country increase and new employment opportunities emerge (Morgan et al., 2019; De Bock et al., 2019). As a result, the country can develop more easily and quickly in economic terms.

Financial markets have been experiencing a significant change especially in recent years. The most important source of these changes is accepted as technological developments. This has made it easier

DOI: 10.4018/978-1-7998-2559-3.ch001

for investors to access financial products. In the previous period, investors who wanted to buy foreign currency had to go to a certain location and physically receive it (Bharucha, 2019; Xue et al., 2019; Dinçer et al., 2018a,b,c; Hsiao et al., 2019). However, nowadays, this process can be realized over the internet in a very short time. Furthermore, since the foreign currency was directly transferred to the investor's account, they did not have to go to the bank branches to deposit their money (Jennings et al., 2019; Dinçer et al., 2019a,b,c; Shi et al., 2019). This has contributed significantly to the development of financial markets.

With the developing technology, financial products have diversified. While this has many benefits, there are also some risks. It is not easy for anyone in the country to understand complex financial products (Gorbachev & Luengo-Prado, 2019; Fornero & Prete, 2019). There are two different drawbacks of this issue. Persons who are not fully familiar with the products will not want to use them. Consequently, financial products will not be actively used (Dinçer & Yüksel, 2018a,b). On the other hand, there is a possibility that people who use complex financial products without knowing it will suffer serious losses (Zou & Deng, 2019; Dinçer et al., 2019d,e; Rakow, 2019). For example, some individuals and companies suffered serious losses because they did not fully understand financial derivative products (Kalkavan & Ersin, 2019; Oktar & Yüksel, 2016).

In this process, the level of financial literacy of the public plays an important role. Financial literacy can be defined as the level of knowledge of individuals regarding financial matters. In this context, issues such as how people use their money and which products they invest when are considered under financial literacy (Ćumurović & Hyll, 2019; Mancebón et al., 2019). The person with a high level of financial literacy will make the right financial decisions and this will contribute positively to his budget. On the other hand, if everyone makes the right financial decisions, the financial development of the country will increase (Kuntze et al., 2019; Custódio et al., 2019). Therefore, financial literacy is considered to have quite consequences for both individuals and the national economy.

The aim of this study is to determine the level of financial literacy of housewives in Turkey. In this context, a questionnaire consisting of 25 different questions was used. The questionnaire was completed by 204 different households. According to the results of this study, it can be possible to understand the effects of financial literacy on investment decisions. Owing to this situation, new marketing strategies can be recommended to attract the attention of the housewives. The most important difference of this study compared to others is that it focuses on a specific group such as housewives. In this context, it is thought to make an important contribution to the literature.

LITERATURE REVIEW

The issue of financial literacy is very important for the effectiveness of the financial system in the country. Therefore, this subject has been handled by many researchers in different aspects in the literature. Under this heading, some studies examining the issue of financial literacy will be included. These studies were kept up-to-date and reviewed in good indexes such as SSCI and Scopus. Almenberg and Dreber (2015) examined whether financial literacy in Sweden varies by gender. While analyzing financial literacy, mainly the stock market has been studied. On the other hand, in this study, survey management was used as research management. With this method, data of 1300 randomly selected samples were examined. The most important finding of the study is that the difference in the participation rate between women and men decreases. In addition, another finding was that women's financial literacy rates increased. Allgood and Walstad (2016) used the survey method. The sample of the survey consisted of 146 people in the USA. They stated that the effect of financial literacy on the financial behavior of individuals is to be taken seriously. In addition, as a result of the financial literacy criterion used, it is mentioned that both real and perceived financial literacy shape behaviors. In this context, they examined the effect of financial literacy on financial behavior in five different areas such as credit card, investment, loans, insurance and consultancy. However, it was concluded that this relationship was not in the causality dimension.

Grohmann et al. (2015) used the concept of financial socialization to explain financial literacy. They tried to explain the concept of financial socialization through three factors: family, work and school. In this context, a questionnaire including twelve childhood characteristics was conducted. Thus, socio-cultural characteristics and financial literacy relationships were tried to be determined. As a result of the research, it was determined that both the concepts of family and school had a positive effect on financial literacy. In addition, the concept of school and the direct impact of financial literacy on financial behavior were emphasized. Boisclair et al. (2017) investigated the financial literacy rates of Canadian individuals. In addition, they examined whether financial literacy was associated with retirement planning. Among the participants whose information about risk diversification, interest rate increase and inflation were measured, only 42% of the participants answered correctly to all three questions. As a result of the research, it was revealed that retirement planning has a strong relationship with financial literacy. It was stated that those who answered the three questions correctly were 10% more likely to have retirement savings.

Agarwal et al. (2015) obtained various findings on financial literacy and financial planning in India. While doing this, questionnaire questions about financial literacy were used. In this context, the data obtained were compared between certain demographic and socioeconomic groups. Differences between these groups were found. In addition to the findings of the research, education, investor aggression, gender and financial planning are said to be related to financial literacy. Chu et al. (2017) examined the effects of financial literacy on ROI and household portfolio selection. This study tested the effect of financial literacy on household stock or mutual fund decisions. In this context, financial literacy is divided into various categories such as basic, high or advanced. It has been observed that the tendencies of individuals with higher or advanced financial literacy rate from the related categories are in the form of investing in the mutual fund or transferring their portfolios to experts. On the other hand, individuals with low financial literacy tend to have stocks in their portfolios and make their own investments.

Ali et al. (2015) was developed to estimate the level of financial satisfaction of working individuals. The hypothesis raised was tested in 1957 people in Malaysia using data collected from the survey. The results obtained from the partial least squares analysis explain the effects of financial planning on financial satisfaction and basic money management concepts. In this context, financial planning does not have a direct impact on basic money management, but it determines the financial satisfaction. In addition to this, it is expressed as attitude towards money and financial literacy as significant premise variables of financial planning. Finally, one of the most important things revealed by this study is that the financial literacy level in Malaysia is determined as 66.7% after the first level exam. Potrich et al. (2016) created and compared models combining financial knowledge, attitude and behavior to evaluate financial literacy. The sample of the study consisted of 534 randomly selected students from private and public schools in South Brazil. In this context, structural equation model was used for the analysis of the data obtained. The findings of the study indicated that financial attitude and financial information have positive effects on financial behavior. In addition, with the emergence of complex financial products, the need for the study of financial literacy will increase.

Clark et al. (2017) examined participation in the savings plan using information from all active employees of the Federal Reserve system. As a result of the study, it was found that the financial literacy rate of Federal Reserve employees was higher than that of a large part of the population. On the other hand, according to the results of the analysis, it was found that the training provided to employees had an impact on financial literacy. It was concluded that the employees who completed the training evaluated their savings more effectively. This situation also applies to other financial products. Abubakar (2015) aimed to analyze the extent to which entrepreneurship in Africa is affected by the financial literacy rate. For this purpose, the relationship between financial decision making and gender was emphasized. The most important topics examined in this study were the effects of financial literacy on financial decision-making process and household decision. Both qualitative and quantitative analysis were conducted using a mixed methodology. As a result of the researches, the most important factors for the advancement of entrepreneurship in Africa are access to market and finance, policy support, inadequacy of training programs on the subject, negative investment environment and gender gap. As a result, it was proposed to implement policies to encourage and support the entrepreneur in order to improve the financial literacy competence positively in Africa.

Mouna and Jarboui (2015) is the first study in Tunisia on portfolio linkage and financial literacy linkage. With this study, they aimed to explain the effect of the degree of financial literacy on low portfolio diversity. In this study, multivariate analysis was used to investigate the relationship between these two concepts. The sample of the study was determined as 256 small investors in Tunisia stock exchange. Among the findings, the effect of financial literacy level, investor experience, age and familiar bias on portfolio diversity is important. Potrich et al. (2015) developed a model consisting of financial information, attitude and behavior scales. They identified the sample as individuals living in southern Brazil. In this respect, a questionnaire was conducted with 991 people. They used a structural equation model to analyze the data. As a result of this study, it is stated that financial literacy is measured as a combination of financial behavior, knowledge and attitude. In addition, it is stated that men have a higher level of financial literacy than gender.

Aren and Zengin (2016) investigated the effect of individual's financial literacy, risk perception and personality traits on investment preferences. In this context, the analysis method used in the study was stated as One Way Anova and Duncan tests were performed. As a result of the study, no significant relationship was found between investment preference and personality traits. However, it was found that investment preferences were influenced by the risk perception and financial literacy level of the individual. In addition, while individuals with low financial literacy tend to deposit or foreign currency, individuals with high financial literacy tend to create portfolios or invest in stocks. In addition, it was found that gender difference had no effect on the basic level of financial literacy, but men were more competent in advanced literacy than women. Garg and Singh (2018) aimed at revealing the financial literacy of young people in the world based on previous studies on financial literacy. For this purpose, it examined the role of factors such as gender, age, socioeconomic status, income and marital status in determining the financial literacy levels of young people. As a result of the research, it was concluded that these factors affect the financial literacy rates of young people. In addition, the concepts of financial knowledge, attitudes and behaviors that affect the level of financial literacy are emphasized. The output obtained in this context was that the young people around the world had low levels of financial literacy. At the end of the study, it was asserted that it can help young people increase financial welfare and financial resources by identifying the factors that decrease financial literacy rate and implementing policies to improve them.

Sivaramakrishnan et al. (2017) aimed to examine the impact of financial literacy on investment decisions in the stock market. Qualitative and quantitative analyzes were also conducted before the survey method was applied to 506 retail investors in India. In order to test the models, structural equation model was preferred. As a result, the degree of financial literacy appears to have an impact on stock investments. The degree of financial literacy affects the investor's risk perception in its most basic form. In other words, it is seen that the investors with the highest financial literacy avoid taking excessive risks. In this way, huge losses in stock markets can be prevented. This contributes to the efficient functioning of the said market. Murendo and Mutsonziwa (2017) investigated whether financial literacy has an impact on individuals' savings decisions. In this context, the survey questions were directed to 4000 adults in Zimbabwe. Survey results show that 52% of individuals in Zimbabwe do not save. It was also stated that the factors that positively affect financial literacy can be listed as access to information via television, education and mobile money usage. They tested the effect of financial literacy on saving behavior by probit analysis. As a result of this analysis, a significant interaction was found between the two variables. Finally, it was stated that men have higher financial literacy than women and individuals living in urban areas have higher financial literacy than those living in rural areas. In addition, it is emphasized that financial literacy is important in all four cases, regardless of gender, rural or urban. Considering the positive effects of incentives on financial literacy on individual saving behavior, it was proposed to develop the necessary policies in this regard.

Kiliyanni and Sivaraman (2016) conducted surveys with 736 educated young adults in Kerala, the region with the highest literacy rate in India. With this structured questionnaire, they sought answers to the question of whether socioeconomic and demographic characteristics of individuals affect their financial literacy levels. It was concluded that socioeconomic and demographic characteristics such as gender, education, religion, work experience, income, parent education affect financial literacy. The techniques used in the analysis of the questionnaire were specified as chi-square and variance analysis. The findings of the study indicate that the financial literacy rate of young adults in Kerala is low. Participants were over-confident in personal finance. Nevertheless, the average young person answered 44% of the questions correctly. As a result, 89% of the respondents stated that they needed financial education. Ergün (2018) investigated the financial literacy levels of university students from multiple countries. countries included in this analysis between Germany, Poland, Romania, Turkey, the Netherlands, Russia, Italy and Estonia are located. A total of 409 answered online questionnaires were obtained from university students in the aforementioned countries. The aim of the study is to determine the effect of demographic characteristics on financial literacy levels. For this purpose, logistic regression analysis was performed. Among the findings, when the average of the survey responses is taken, it is stated that it possesses a moderate level of financial literacy. Another finding was that living independently of parents had a positive effect on individual financial literacy. In addition, it was stated that one of the most effective ways of increasing financial literacy was to have finance education in universities and it was added that social media was less effective than university education in increasing this rate.

The aim of the study by Hsiao and Tsai (2018) is to what extent it affects the likelihood that individuals with high financial literacy will be active participants in derivative markets. For this purpose, a questionnaire prepared by Taiwan Financial Supervision Commission was used. Thus, the extent to which financial literacy levels are determinant in portfolio decisions of investors is examined. The findings of the study indicate that individuals with high financial literacy tend to purchase derivative instruments. In addition, the factors affecting the participation rate in the derivatives market are urban settlement, gender and welfare level. When the findings of the study are analyzed, it is stated that the policies to increase financial literacy will positively affect both the functioning of the derivative markets and the welfare level. Within the aforementioned results, the importance of the adoption of such policies and the incentives to be made were emphasized. Wilson et al. (2017) tested the hypothesis that high financial and health literacy provides an individual with better cognitive health in old age. The testing phase of the hypothesis was completed on clinical evaluations of 755 elderly individuals, which lasted approximately 3 years. The findings of the study suggest that high levels of financial and health literacy may help to delay or reduce the risk of individuals with Alzheimer's development in old age. In other words, this literacy may be related to the preservation of cognitive health in old age. On the other hand, it is stated that this relationship is positive, meaning that as financial and health literacy increases, the likelihood of protection of cognitive health will increase.

Grohmann (2018) aimed to determine the financial literacy of middle-class individuals living in the Asian economy in Bangkok. Standard financial literacy questions were used in the study. According to the results of the study, the financial literacy rates of middle-class individuals living in Bangkok are similar to those of developed countries. However, it is not possible to say the same for advanced financial literacy. Another finding is that only 24% of the questions about stock market diversification were answered correctly in the relevant sample. It is emphasized that high financial literacy is associated with the use of advanced financial products. In addition, it is stated that financial literacy is a component of financial development and increases in financial literacy will positively affect saving, change of goods and services and risk management. Brown et al. (2018) examined the impact of secondary school students' cultural characteristics on their financial literacy. In this study, the students in Switzerland were evaluated by questionnaire method along the Germany-France line. As a result of the study, it was found that the financial literacy level of the students living in the German speaking region was higher than the financial literacy of the students in the French speaking region. It has been suggested that the source of the cultural division through the reconciliation method is the systematic differences in the financial socialization of the students belonging to these two different language groups. It has been said that this cultural divide between financial literacy levels may be due to differences in parental attitudes. One of the reasons for the high financial literacy of students in the German-speaking region is that they began to receive pocket money at an earlier age than students in the French-speaking region. Another reason for the high level of financial literacy of German students was explained by access to independent bank accounts.

Reich and Berman (2015) designed an experiment for low-income individuals in the housing program. Two different groups were formed as experimental and control groups. The participants in the control group were not given any treatment. On the other hand, participants in the experimental group were subjected to a four-week financial literacy course. As a result of this process, the effectiveness of the related education for low-income individuals was determined. The change of some positive or negative financial behaviors determined before the experiment was examined. As a result of this analysis, it is mentioned that there is an increase in both the level of financial knowledge and the level of financial literacy of the individuals who have received four-week financial literacy training. Accordingly, the necessity and continuity of financial literacy trainings proved to be beneficial. Kadoya and Khan (2018) emphasized the relationship between financial literacy and life anxiety in old age. At the beginning of this study, they put forward the assumption that high financial literacy is effective in making better investment and saving decisions and thus reduces anxiety in old age. In the study, it was found appropriate to use the preference parameter study prepared by Osaka University of Japan. As a result of the experimental findings obtained, it was stated that the increase in financial literacy had a decreasing effect on anxiety in the aging process. This situation was underlined by many different researchers, such as Lusardi (2019), Lin et al. (2019), Jones et al. (2019), Deenanath et al. (2019), Henager and Cude (2019) and Pang (2019).

Jariwala (2015) conducted on individual investors in Gujarat, India. This study examined the impact of financial literacy on investment decisions. The findings of the study are based on the analysis of the data collected from 385 individual investors by means of performance test and survey method. It is stated that 39.20% of the 385 individual investors that constitute the sample of the research consist of advanced financial literacy and 60,80% of the investors have low financial literacy. Explanatory factor analysis was used for the analysis of 44 investor decision variables. Afterwards, correlation and regression analyzes were conducted to examine the interaction between financial literacy and investment decision. As a result, it is concluded that financial literacy level affects individuals' investment decisions. Furthermore, Baker et al. (2019), Gerrans and Heaney (2019), Nadolny et al. (2019), Ye and Kulathunga (2019), Al-Bahrani et al. (2019), Sabir et al. (2019), Karakurum-Ozdemir et al. (2019), Rodrigues et al. (2019), Preston and Wright (2019), Zhu et al. (2019) and Loh et al. (2019) are other studies which focused on the subject of financial literacy.

As a result of the literature review, it is understood that the issue of financial literacy has received much attention. In this context, this topic has been studied by different authors on different regions. Therefore, it is important to study a region that has not been studied before in a new study. In addition, it is seen that the sample group covers a very large group of people. For this purpose, it would be very useful to study a specific population such as housewives in a new study.

AN ANALYSIS ON HOUSEWIVES IN TURKEY

In this study, knowledge of financial literacy and knowledge of the forms of assessment housewife in Turkey (TL, gold, foreign exchange and stock markets) were examined. In this part of the chapter, first of all, the data collection and details of the study will be shared. Then, information will be given about the results of the analysis using factor analysis, difference test and correlations.

Data Set and Method

The aim of this study is to examine the relationship between financial literacy and savings of housewives in Turkey. For this purpose, reliability-validated scale prepared by Sarıgül (2015) was used. This scale and questionnaires that asked for demographic information has been filled by housewives in Turkey. Survey analysis was preferred in many different studies in the literature with various purposes (Brout et al., 2019; Koçak et al., 2017; Ersin and Eti, 2017; Schwartz et al., 2019; Eti, 2016; Tanaka et al., 2019; Koçak et al., 2018; Abdul-Jabbar et al., 2019). Demographic information of 204 housewives randomly filled is given in Table 1.

According to Table 1, demographic characteristics are examined under four main headings, such as education level of the individuals, child ownership, marital status and how they evaluate their experiences. As it can be seen from the table below, primary school graduates constitute the majority of the sample. 67.6% of primary school graduates are followed by high school graduates with a rate of 10.8%. When the two extremes of the sample are examined on the basis of education levels, it is seen that there is one illiterate person and four people at the master-doctorate level. It is seen that 183 out of 204 respondents have children and the remaining 21 do not have children. For the marital status, it was determined that

Table 1. Demographic information of participants

	N	%
Education Level		
No-literate	1	0,5
Primary School	138	67,6
Middle School	8	3,9
High School	22	10,8
Undergraduate	31	15,2
Masters-Doctorate	4	2
Child Status		
Yes	183	89,7
No	21	10,3
Marital Status		
Married	182	89,2
Single	22	10,8
Accumulation Evaluation Ways		
TL (Local Money)	163	79,9
Gold	25	12,3
Currency	17	8,3
Stock Market	0	0,0

married housewives had a rate of 89.2% in the sample. The data obtained from the information obtained from the individuals about how they evaluate their savings show that a majority of 163 people evaluate their savings as TL. The remaining 25 people stated that they considered gold and 17 others as foreign currency. On the other hand, housewives did not prefer to use their savings in the stock market. The reason for this can be explained by the low financial literacy resulting from the lack of financial training.

Factor Analysis and Reliability

Factor analysis is one of the methods to reduce the p variable to k variable (k<p). Another objective in factor analysis is to obtain the latent variables that cannot be measured with the help of measurable variables. In other words, factor analysis is a method used to make multiple related variables less and independent variables (Kalaycı, 2006). The financial literacy scale is a 14-item scale consisting of 4 sub-dimensions. The first dimension of the scale is the expenditure dimension consisting of 4 questions. The second dimension is the attitude dimension consisting of 4 questions. The third dimension of the said dimension, perception, has 3 questions. The last dimension is the interest dimension which consists of 3 questions. Financial literacy can be evaluated with the help of the 4 sub-dimensions mentioned in the scale.

Factor analysis has some points to be considered. For this purpose, firstly, the sample should be sufficient. Kaiser Meyer Olkin (KMO) sample adequacy test is performed. The result of the test can be between 0 and 1. If the result is 0.50 or more, it is interpreted that the sample is sufficient for factor analysis. In addition, the number of samples required for factor analysis is generally considered as 10 times the number of items. Another consideration of factor analysis is the Barlett test. The test gives the result of whether the variables are reducible with the help of the correlation matrix. In other words, the number of variables at hand indicates whether they can be reduced to a structure with less variable. Attention is paid to the significance level of the test value in question. If the significance level of the test is less than 0.05, it is possible to infer that size reduction is possible with factor analysis. Otherwise, it is interpreted that it is not possible to reduce the size by factor analysis. Factor analysis is another factor that needs to be considered when evaluating factor loadings. Factor loads are between -1 and 1. Sample size is important for taking this value into consideration (Field, 2013; Kaiser, 1974). Hair et al. (2006) summarized the factor loads to be considered according to the sample size in Table 2.

In addition, the reliability of the survey results and the dimensions created is another case to be considered. Cronbach's Alfa and Composite Reliability tests are the most widely used reliability values for reliability. The results of these two tests are between 0 and 1. This value is expected to be at least 0.60 in social sciences (Alpar, 2013). On the other hand, if the reliability coefficients are between 0.60 and 0.80, it is accepted as medium reliability. However, if the value is 0.80 and above, it is considered to be highly reliable (Şimşek & Noyan, 2009). In the light of the information mentioned in the above paragraph, factor analysis was applied on the data of the study. Dimensions in the original article are considered. Factor analysis results obtained from this information are given in Table 3.

When Table 3 is examined, it is seen that the KMO value is 0.629 first. Since the value is above 0,60, it can be interpreted that the sample is sufficient for factor analysis. In addition, since the scale consists of 14 questions, it should be enough for factor analysis to be done with at least 14x10 = 140 participants. Since 204 housewives were reached in the study, it could be said that the number was sufficient for factor analysis. Afterwards, when Bartlett test is examined, it is calculated that the significance level is less than 0.01. In this case, it can be said that size reduction is appropriate with the help of factor analysis. In addition, factor loadings of the items are taken into consideration. Since the sample size is 204, it must have a factor load of at least 0.40. As a result of the analysis of the study, it is seen that factor loads are between 0.440 and 0.888. The smallest of the loads in the factor analysis of the study is 0,403. In this case, factor loadings can be interpreted as meaningful.

Table 2. Significant factor loadings based on sample size

Sample Size	Sufficient Factor Loading
50	0,75
60	0,7
70	0,65
85	0,6
100	0,55
120	0,5
150	0,45
200	0,4
250	0,35
350	0,3

Table 3. Factor analysis results

	Factor Loading	Composite Reliability
Expenditure		
Shopping is very important for my happiness.	0,647	
Money is for spending, not for saving.	0,61	
I have difficulty controlling my spending.	0,486	0,744
I don't understand how my money ends.	0,831	
Attitude		
There must be money in the corner for unplanned expenses.	0,403	
I make weekly and monthly spending plans.	0,499	
I compare prices when shopping.	0,888	0,768
I consider my budget when buying something.	0,842	
Perception		
Financial planning and budgeting are very necessary for those who benefit.	0,857	
It is unnecessary to plan expenditure for short periods such as daily and weekly.	0,574	0,795
No matter what I do, my financial position will not change.	0,804	
Interest		
I'm not interested in monetary issues.	0,646	
I'd like to study finance.	0,467	0,627
I watch economic and financial news from newspapers and television.	0,676	
KMO=0,629; Bartlett's Test=790,647534 (p<0,01); Cronbach's Alfa=0,606		

Finally, reliability values were examined. The Cronbach's Alpha value, which is the reliability value of the scale, was calculated as 0,606. Since the related value is over 0,60, it can be interpreted that the results are reliable. Composite reliability value was examined for the reliability of the 4 dimensions. The most recommended reliability test for the reliability of latent variables is composite reliability. The reliability values of the concepts in the study are 0,744, 0,768, 0,795 and 0,627 respectively. The dimension with the highest reliability is the perception dimension. The reliability coefficient of perception dimension is 0.795. The dimension with the lowest reliability value is of interest and the reliability coefficient is 0.627. This value and other coefficients are greater than 0.60. In this case, the results of the four dimensions created by factor analysis can be said to be reliable.

Correlation Analysis

Factor analysis yielded 4 dimensions in the original scale. Correlation analysis was used to examine the relationship between the obtained dimensions. With the help of the said analysis, the bilateral relationship between the dimensions can be revealed in more detail. If the significance value obtained as a result of the analysis is less than 0.05, it can be interpreted that there is a significant relationship between the two variables. Otherwise, it is not possible to talk about a relationship between the two variables. The matrix containing the correlation values of the variables in the study is given in Table 4.

Measuring Financial Literacy of the Housewife to Generate Marketing Strategies

Considering Table 4, it is possible to see the correlation coefficients between the two variables. Values marked with * beside the coefficients indicate statistically significant relationships. In this respect, two correlation coefficients were found to be significant. The first is the coefficient between perception and expenditure factors. The said coefficient is 0.352 and it can be said that there is a significant and positive relationship between these two dimensions. Another significant coefficient is between the dimensions of interest and attitude. The coefficient between these two dimensions is 0.392. In this case, it can be said that there is a positive and significant relationship between Attitude and Perception concepts in housewives. Considering the relevant coefficients, increasing the perception of the value of the expenditure information in Turkey are also expected to increase by a housewife. Similarly, it will be seen that the thrill of an housewife with increased interest will increase.

Difference Test According to Accumulation Arguments

Another aim of the study was to accumulation of financial literacy in Turkey are housewives reveal the relationship between the arguments. For this purpose, the housewives were asked which of the accumulation arguments they used. In the light of their answers, it is seen that they mostly evaluate their savings as TL. In addition, housewives stated that they considered gold as the highest amount besides TL. It is natural that this result comes from the fact that gold is a traditional accumulation argument.

According to the arguments the housewives use to save money, the study examines whether financial literacy is the difference between dimensions at this stage. Kruskal Wallis test was used for this purpose which is a non-parametric test. The null hypothesis of this test is that there is no difference between the median of the groups. It can be interpreted by taking into account the level of significance obtained as a result of the hypothesis testing. If the significance level of the analysis is greater than 0.05, there is no difference between the groups. In this case, it is assumed that each category or group is equal. Otherwise, if the significance level is less than 0.05, it can be interpreted that the groups are not statistically equal. In other words, it can be said that at least one of the groups is different from the other groups (Alpar, 2010). According to the arguments of the accumulation of housewives in Turkey, said the size of descriptive statistics and Kruskal-Wallis test results on the ground are given in Table 5.

When analyzed results in Table 5, it can be understood how they evaluate the accumulation of housewives in Turkey. On the other hand, the table contains detailed information about expenditure, attitudes, perceptions, and related factors. When the results obtained from the sample data are examined, it is seen that 75% of housewives prefer to evaluate their savings as TL only. The most basic reason, as a result of the low rate of financial literacy in Turkey housewife can say that the approach at a distance using

Table 4. Correlation matrix of variables

	Correlation Matrix			
	Expenditure	**Attitude**	**Perception**	**Interest**
Expenditure	1			
Attitude	0,121	1		
Perception	0,352*	-0,079	1	
Interest	0,103	0,392*	-0,006	1
*:p<0,001				

Table 5. Statistics of dimensions according to accumulation type

Saving			Expenditure			Attitude			Perception			Interest		
Category	N	%	Mean	Median	S.Deviation	Mean	Median	S.Deviation	Mean	Median	S.Deviation	Mean	Median	S.Deviation
Only TL	153	75	2,41	2,25	0,50	3,18	3,00	0,55	2,59	2,67	0,51	2,40	2,33	0,40
Only Foreign Currency	9	4,4	2,36	2,25	0,67	3,75	3,75	0,78	2,56	2,33	0,90	2,44	2,33	0,67
Only Gold	20	9,8	2,51	2,50	0,83	3,99	4,00	0,52	2,18	2,00	0,95	2,85	2,67	0,81
TL & Foreign Currency	6	2,9	2,17	2,25	0,68	3,83	3,88	1,20	1,89	1,33	1,22	2,83	2,33	0,94
TL & Gold	3	1,5	3,08	3,00	0,38	4,00	4,25	0,66	2,11	2,00	1,17	2,67	3,33	1,15
No Saving	11	5,4	2,84	3,00	0,97	3,66	4,00	1,06	2,76	2,67	0,82	2,94	2,67	0,73
Kruskal Wallis Test (Test - P)			11,984	0,035	<0,05	42,547	0	<0,05	16,127	0,006	<0,05	20,698	0,001	<0,05

different investment alternatives. In the sample, it can be seen that the remaining 20 people accumulate only on gold and 9 people evaluate their savings only on foreign exchange. It was obtained from the answers that while the number of housewives accumulating both foreign exchange and TL accumulation is 6, the number of participants accumulating both gold and TL is not limiting their savings preferences with a single method. In addition, some of the participants stated that they could not accumulate. It was obtained from the surveys that there were 11 people who expressed their status in this form. Furthermore, the Turkish housewife, who evaluated her savings on the stock exchange, could not be identified.

As a result of Kruskal Wallis analysis, the p value for the expenditure dimension was calculated as 0.035. The group with the highest expenditure average is the housewives group who collects gold together with TL. The average of this type of housewives is 3.08 and they tend to spend the most. The lowest average group of housewives is housewives who accumulate only TL. The average of these is 2.17. Overall, the average of all groups due to remain below 3 in Turkey is considered to be prone to spending a lot of housewives.

When Table 5 is examined, the p value of Kruskal Wallis analysis for the attitude dimension, which is another dimension, is calculated as less than 0.05. In this case, Turkey's stance on until a housewife, vary depending on the spool so that reviews can be made. Attitude was calculated as high in all groups. Here, the housewife in Turkey is said to be frugal structure. Nevertheless, the difference between the accumulations was found to be statistically significant. The group with the highest attitude value was found to be TL and gold accumulating group with an average of 4 points. Again, the average of only the gold accumulating group, which is very close to this group, was calculated as 3.99. It was found that the groups that collected gold were more frugal. The perception of gold as a long-term custody argument among women can be seen as an indicator of this situation. In terms of attitude perception in Turkey had the lowest average score among housewives groups are capable accumulate only in TL. The average attitude of the said group was determined as 3.18. Since TL is an argument that can be disposed of and expended, the frugality of TL accumulators remains low.

Another indicator of financial literacy is perception. It was examined whether the perception dimension differed according to the deposition patterns. According to Kruskal Wallis test, p significance level was calculated as 0.006. Due to the related value is smaller than 0.05, according to the deposition patterns in Turkey can be made comment that the differences in the perception of housewives. As a result, the groups were analyzed within themselves and evaluated. The group with the lowest perception score was calculated for housewives who saved in TL and foreign currency. The average of this group was calculated as 1.89. It can be concluded that the group concerned is budget-sensitive. In contrast, housewives with the highest scores were identified as only TL accumulating group with 2.59 points. It can be interpreted that housewives who are not only interested in other arguments, but accumulate in TL, are weaker in budgeting and planning. In general perceptions size examined, housewives in Turkey said they think they have succeeded in budgeting and planning.

Finally, the level of the financial literacy of the housewives in Turkey is evaluated. The significance of Kruskal Wallis test was 0.001. Since this calculated value is less than 0.05, it can be interpreted that there is a statistical difference between housewife groups. Overall in Turkey due to the housewife groups having an average of 3 or less, it can be said that there is low level of interest. On the other hand, the group with the highest average interest was found only in housewives who collected gold. The group with the lowest average interest was housewives who collected only TL. In the light of this information, it can be concluded that only the women who accumulate TL do not follow the finance. However, as the value of gold changes daily, housewives who accumulate gold follow financial news. In addition, this group of housewives has been identified as interested in financial matters and willing to study finance.

SOLUTIONS AND RECOMMENDATIONS

housewives in Turkey are generally defined as having Turkish Lira deposits. It was also concluded that these housewives' tendency to spend was low. However, the financial literacy of housewives was found to be low. From this point of view, a general education will contribute to increase this literacy. Therefore, both the housewives will be able to better evaluate their savings and the financial system of the country will work more effectively.

FUTURE RESEARCH DIRECTIONS

In this study, financial literacy level of Turkish housewives was analyzed. In this context, a survey was conducted with 203 people. In a new study, a different audience can be applied such as university students and workers. On the other hand, a new application using a different method will increase the originality of this study.

CONCLUSION

When analyzed in general, it is seen that only housewives who accumulate TL are lower in terms of financial literacy than other housewife groups. In other words, financial literacy, the lowest in Turkey it has emerged as only they can accumulate per housewives. Another group of housewives, TL and gold, had higher financial literacy. First as per their savings considering the housewives in Turkey, it said that under the financial literacy of orientation anymore. In this case, in Turkey it will be eligible to be informed in order to give the economy the savings outside of housewives economy. In this regard, it is thought that TL will be shunned as an alternative because it is an accustomed argument. Thus, higher participation is expected. It is thought that directing the housewives who hold their savings in TL in their term / deposit accounts in banks to gold accounts will provide more successful results than directing them to foreign currency.

REFERENCES

Abdul-Jabbar, A., Yilmaz, E., Fisahn, C., Drazin, D., Blecher, R., Uppal, M., ... Chapman, J. R. (2019). Disaster scenarios in spine surgery: A survey analysis. *Spine*, *44*(14), 1018–1024. doi:10.1097/BRS.0000000000003040 PMID:30921295

Abubakar, H. A. (2015). Entrepreneurship development and financial literacy in Africa. *World Journal of Entrepreneurship, Management and Sustainable Development*, *11*(4), 281–294. doi:10.1108/WJEMSD-04-2015-0020

Agarwal, S., Amromin, G., Ben-David, I., Chomsisengphet, S., & Evanoff, D. D. (2015). Financial literacy and financial planning: Evidence from India. *Journal of Housing Economics*, *27*, 4–21. doi:10.1016/j.jhe.2015.02.003

Al-Bahrani, A., Weathers, J., & Patel, D. (2019). Racial differences in the returns to financial literacy education. *The Journal of Consumer Affairs*, *53*(2), 572–599. doi:10.1111/joca.12205

Ali, A., Rahman, M. S. A., & Bakar, A. (2015). Financial satisfaction and the influence of financial literacy in Malaysia. *Social Indicators Research*, *120*(1), 137–156. doi:10.100711205-014-0583-0

Allgood, S., & Walstad, W. B. (2016). The effects of perceived and actual financial literacy on financial behaviors. *Economic Inquiry*, *54*(1), 675–697. doi:10.1111/ecin.12255

Almenberg, J., & Dreber, A. (2015). Gender, stock market participation and financial literacy. *Economics Letters*, *137*, 140–142. doi:10.1016/j.econlet.2015.10.009

Alpar, R. (2010). *Spor, sağlık ve eğitim bilimlerinden örneklerle uygulamalı istatistik ve geçerlik-güvenirlik*. Detay Yayıncılık.

Alpar, R. (2013). *Uygulamalı çok değişkenli istatistiksel yöntemler*. Detay Yayıncılık.

Aren, S., & Zengin, A. N. (2016). Influence of financial literacy and risk perception on choice of investment. *Procedia: Social and Behavioral Sciences*, *235*, 656–663. doi:10.1016/j.sbspro.2016.11.047

Baker, H. K., Kumar, S., Goyal, N., & Gaur, V. (2019). How financial literacy and demographic variables relate to behavioral biases. *Managerial Finance*, *45*(1), 124–146. doi:10.1108/MF-01-2018-0003

Bharucha, J. P. (2019). Determinants of financial literacy among Indian youth. In Dynamic Perspectives on Globalization and Sustainable Business in Asia (pp. 154–167). Hershey, PA: IGI Global. doi:10.4018/978-1-5225-7095-0.ch010

Boisclair, D., Lusardi, A., & Michaud, P. C. (2017). Financial literacy and retirement planning in Canada. *Journal of Pension Economics and Finance*, *16*(3), 277–296. doi:10.1017/S1474747215000311

Brout, D., Scolnic, D., Kessler, R., D'Andrea, C. B., Davis, T. M., Gupta, R. R., . . . Macaulay, E. (2019). First cosmology results using SNe Ia from the dark energy survey: Analysis, systematic uncertainties, and validation [First cosmology results using type IA supernovae from the dark energy survey: Analysis, systematic uncertainties, and validation]. *The Astrophysical Journal (Online)*, *874*(arXiv: 1811.02377; FERMILAB-PUB-18-541-AE).

Brown, M., Henchoz, C., & Spycher, T. (2018). Culture and financial literacy: Evidence from a within-country language border. *Journal of Economic Behavior & Organization*, *150*, 62–85. doi:10.1016/j.jebo.2018.03.011

Chu, Z., Wang, Z., Xiao, J. J., & Zhang, W. (2017). Financial literacy, portfolio choice and financial well-being. *Social Indicators Research*, *132*(2), 799–820. doi:10.100711205-016-1309-2

Clark, R., Lusardi, A., & Mitchell, O. S. (2017). Employee financial literacy and retirement plan behavior: A case study. *Economic Inquiry*, *55*(1), 248–259. doi:10.1111/ecin.12389

Ćumurović, A., & Hyll, W. (2019). Financial literacy and self-employment. *The Journal of Consumer Affairs*, *53*(2), 455–487. doi:10.1111/joca.12198

Custódio, C., Mendes, D., & Metzger, D. (2019). The impact of financial literacy on medium and large enterprises–Evidence from a randomized controlled trial in Mozambique.

De Bock, D., Leuven, K. U., De Win, I., & Van Campenhout, G. (2019). Inclusion of financial literacy goals in secondary school curricula: role of financial mathematics. *MEDITERRANEAN JOURNAL*, 33.

Deenanath, V., Danes, S. M., & Jang, J. (2019). Purposive and unintentional family financial socialization, subjective financial knowledge, and financial behavior of high school students. *Journal of Financial Counseling and Planning*, *30*(1), 83–96. doi:10.1891/1052-3073.30.1.83

Dincer, H., Hacioglu, U., Tatoglu, E., & Delen, D. (2019d). Developing a hybrid analytics approach to measure the efficiency of deposit banks. *Journal of Business Research*, *104*, 131–145. doi:10.1016/j.jbusres.2019.06.035

Dinçer, H., Hacıoğlu, Ü., & Yüksel, S. (2018b). Determining influencing factors of currency exchange rate for decision making in global economy using MARS method. In Geopolitics and strategic management in the global economy (pp. 261–273). Hershey, PA: IGI Global. doi:10.4018/978-1-5225-2673-5.ch013

Dinçer, H., Hacıoğlu, Ü., & Yüksel, S. (2018c). Evaluating the effects of economic imbalances on gold price in Turkey with MARS method and discussions on microfinance. In Microfinance and its impact on entrepreneurial development, sustainability, and inclusive growth (pp. 115-137). Hershey, PA: IGI Global.

Dinçer, H., & Yüksel, S. (2018a). Financial sector-based analysis of the G20 economies using the integrated decision-making approach with DEMATEL and TOPSIS. In *Emerging trends in banking and finance* (pp. 210–223). Cham, Switzerland: Springer. doi:10.1007/978-3-030-01784-2_13

Dinçer, H., & Yüksel, S. (2018b). Comparative evaluation of BSC-based new service development competencies in Turkish banking sector with the integrated fuzzy hybrid MCDM using content analysis. *International Journal of Fuzzy Systems, 20*(8), 2497–2516. doi:10.100740815-018-0519-y

Dinçer, H., Yüksel, S., & Adalı, Z. (2019a). Economic effects in Islamic stock development of the European countries: Policy recommendations for ethical behaviors. In Handbook of research on managerial thinking in global business economics (pp. 58-78). Hershey, PA: IGI Global.

Dinçer, H., Yüksel, S., & Adalı, Z. (2019c). Determining the effects of monetary policies on capital markets of the emerging economies: An evidence from E7 countries. The impacts of monetary policy in the 21st century: Perspectives from emerging economies. Emerald Publishing Limited, 3-16.

Dinçer, H., Yüksel, S., Korsakienė, R., Raišienė, A. G., & Bilan, Y. (2019e). IT2 hybrid decision-making approach to performance measurement of internationalized firms in the Baltic states. *Sustainability, 11*(1), 296. doi:10.3390u11010296

Dinçer, H., Yüksel, S., & Martínez, L. (2019b). Interval type 2-based hybrid fuzzy evaluation of financial services in E7 economies with DEMATEL-ANP and MOORA methods. *Applied Soft Computing, 79*, 186–202. doi:10.1016/j.asoc.2019.03.018

Dinçer, H., Yüksel, S., & Şenel, S. (2018a). Analyzing the global risks for the financial crisis after the great depression using comparative hybrid hesitant fuzzy decision-making models: Policy recommendations for sustainable economic growth. *Sustainability, 10*(9), 3126. doi:10.3390u10093126

Ergün, K. (2018). Financial literacy among university students: A study in eight European countries. *International Journal of Consumer Studies, 42*(1), 2–15. doi:10.1111/ijcs.12408

Ersin, İ., & Eti, S. (2017). Measuring the waste-conscious and saving habits of the youth in Turkey: The sample of Istanbul Medipol University. *Uluslararası İslam Ekonomisi ve Finansı Araştırmaları Dergisi, 3*(3), 41–49.

Eti, S. (2016). Üniversitelerdeki akademik üretkenliğe etki eden faktörlerin incelenmesi. *İş'te Davranış Dergisi, 1*(1), 67-73.

Field, A. (2013). *Discovering statistics using IBM SPSS statistics*. Thousand Oaks, CA: Sage.

Fornero, E., & Prete, A. L. (2019). Voting in the aftermath of a pension reform: The role of financial literacy. *Journal of Pension Economics and Finance, 18*(1), 1–30. doi:10.1017/S1474747218000185

Garg, N., & Singh, S. (2018). Financial literacy among youth. *International Journal of Social Economics, 45*(1), 173–186. doi:10.1108/IJSE-11-2016-0303

Gerrans, P., & Heaney, R. (2019). The impact of undergraduate personal finance education on individual financial literacy, attitudes and intentions. *Accounting and Finance, 59*(1), 177–217. doi:10.1111/acfi.12247

Gorbachev, O., & Luengo-Prado, M. J. (2019). The credit card debt puzzle: The role of preferences, credit access risk, and financial literacy. *The Review of Economics and Statistics, 101*(2), 294–309. doi:10.1162/rest_a_00752

Grohmann, A. (2018). Financial literacy and financial behavior: Evidence from the emerging Asian middle class. *Pacific-Basin Finance Journal, 48*, 129–143. doi:10.1016/j.pacfin.2018.01.007

Grohmann, A., Kouwenberg, R., & Menkhoff, L. (2015). Childhood roots of financial literacy. *Journal of Economic Psychology, 51*, 114–133. doi:10.1016/j.joep.2015.09.002

Hair, J. F., Black, W. C., Babin, B. J., Anderson, R. E., & Tatham, R. L. (2006). Multivariate data analysis (Vol. 6).

Henager, R., & Cude, B. J. (2019). Financial literacy of high school graduates: Long-and short-term financial behavior by age group. *Journal of Family and Economic Issues*, 1–12.

Horioka, C. Y., & Niimi, Y. (2019). *Financial literacy*. Incentives, and Innovation to Deal with Population Aging.

Hsiao, H. F., Zhong, T., & Dincer, H. (2019). Analysing managers' financial motivation for sustainable investment strategies. *Sustainability, 11*(14), 3849. doi:10.3390u11143849

Hsiao, Y. J., & Tsai, W. C. (2018). Financial literacy and participation in the derivatives markets. *Journal of Banking & Finance, 88*, 15–29. doi:10.1016/j.jbankfin.2017.11.006

Jariwala, H. V. (2015). Analysis of financial literacy level of retail individual investors of Gujarat State and its effect on investment decision. *Journal of Business & Finance Librarianship, 20*(1-2), 133–158. doi:10.1080/08963568.2015.977727

Jennings, J. D., Quinn, C., Ly, J. A., & Rehman, S. (2019). Orthopaedic surgery resident financial literacy: An assessment of knowledge in debt, investment, and retirement savings. *The American Surgeon, 85*(4), 353–358. PMID:31043194

Jones, C., Fouty, J. R., Lucas, R. B., & Frye, M. A. (2019). Integrating individual student advising into financial education to optimize financial literacy in veterinary students. *Journal of Veterinary Medical Education*, 1–11. doi:10.3138/jvme.1117-156r1 PMID:31194629

Kadoya, Y., & Khan, M. S. R. (2018). Can financial literacy reduce anxiety about life in old age? *Journal of Risk Research, 21*(12), 1533–1550. doi:10.1080/13669877.2017.1313760

Kaiser, H. F. (1974). An index of factorial simplicity. *Psychometrika, 39*(1), 31–36. doi:10.1007/BF02291575

Kalaycı, Ş. (2006). *SPSS Uygulamalı Çok Değişkenli İstatistik Teknikleri*. Asil Yayınevi.

Kalkavan, H., & Ersin, I. (2019). Determination of factors affecting the South East Asian crisis of 1997 Probit-Logit panel regression: The South East Asian crisis. In Handbook of research on global issues in financial communication and investment decision making (pp. 148-167). Hershey, PA: IGI Global.

Karakurum-Ozdemir, K., Kokkizil, M., & Uysal, G. (2019). Financial literacy in developing countries. *Social Indicators Research, 143*(1), 325–353. doi:10.100711205-018-1952-x

Kiliyanni, A. L., & Sivaraman, S. (2016). The perception-reality gap in financial literacy: Evidence from the most literate state in India. *International Review of Economics Education, 23*, 47–64. doi:10.1016/j.iree.2016.07.001

Koçak, O., Arslan, H., & Eti, S. (2017). Belediyelerde sosyal politika uygulamaları ve Pendik belediyesi örneği. *Uluslararası Toplum Araştırmaları Dergisi, 7*(12), 119–144. doi:10.26466/opus.311278

Koçak, O., Beki, A., & Eti, S. (2018). The effects of the different activities on the depression level of older people. *OPUS Uluslararası Toplum Araştırmaları Dergisi, 8*(15), 1241–1266.

Kuntze, R., Wu, C., Wooldridge, B. R., & Whang, Y. O. (2019). Improving financial literacy in college of business students: Modernizing delivery tools. *International Journal of Bank Marketing, 37*(4), 976–990. doi:10.1108/IJBM-03-2018-0080

Lin, X., Bruhn, A., & William, J. (2019). Extending financial literacy to insurance literacy: A survey approach. *Accounting and Finance, 59*(S1), 685–713. doi:10.1111/acfi.12353

Loh, A. M., Peong, K. K., & Peong, K. P. (2019). Determinants of personal financial literacy among young adults in Malaysian accounting firms. *Global J. Bus. Soc. Sci. Review, 7*(1), 08-19.

Lusardi, A. (2019). Financial literacy and the need for financial education: Evidence and implications. *Schweizerische Zeitschrift für Volkswirtschaft und Statistik, 155*(1), 1.

Lyons, A. C., Grable, J., & Zeng, T. (2019). Impacts of financial literacy on the loan decisions of financially excluded households in the People's Republic of China.

Mancebón, M. J., Ximénez-de-Embún, D. P., Mediavilla, M., & Gómez-Sancho, J. M. (2019). Factors that influence the financial literacy of young Spanish consumers. *International Journal of Consumer Studies, 43*(2), 227–235. doi:10.1111/ijcs.12502

Morgan, P. J., Huang, B., & Trinh, L. Q. (2019). *The need to promote digital financial literacy for the digital age*. IN THE DIGITAL AGE.

Mouna, A., & Jarboui, A. (2015). Financial literacy and portfolio diversification: An observation from the Tunisian stock market. *International Journal of Bank Marketing, 33*(6), 808–822. doi:10.1108/IJBM-03-2015-0032

Murendo, C., & Mutsonziwa, K. (2017). Financial literacy and savings decisions by adult financial consumers in Zimbabwe. *International Journal of Consumer Studies, 41*(1), 95–103. doi:10.1111/ijcs.12318

Nadolny, L., Nation, J., & Fox, J. (2019). Supporting motivation and effort persistence in an online financial literacy course through game-based learning. *International Journal of Game-Based Learning, 9*(3), 38–52. doi:10.4018/IJGBL.2019070103

Oktar, S., & Yüksel, S. (2016). Bankalarin Türev Ürün Kullanimini Etkileyen Faktörler: Mars Yöntemi ile Bir Inceleme/Determinants of the use derivatives in banking: An analysis with MARS Model. *Finans Politik & Ekonomik Yorumlar, 53*(620), 31.

Pang, M. F. (2019). Enhancing the generative learning of young people in the domain of financial literacy through learning study. *International Journal for Lesson and Learning Studies*.

Potrich, A. C. G., Vieira, K. M., Coronel, D. A., & Bender Filho, R. (2015). Financial literacy in Southern Brazil: Modeling and invariance between genders. *Journal of Behavioral and Experimental Finance, 6*, 1–12. doi:10.1016/j.jbef.2015.03.002

Potrich, A. C. G., Vieira, K. M., & Mendes-Da-Silva, W. (2016). Development of a financial literacy model for university students. *Management Research Review*, *39*(3), 356–376. doi:10.1108/MRR-06-2014-0143

Preston, A. C., & Wright, R. E. (2019). Understanding the gender gap in financial literacy: Evidence from Australia. *The Economic Record*, *95*(S1), 1–29. doi:10.1111/1475-4932.12472

Rakow, K. C. (2019). Incorporating financial literacy into the accounting curriculum. *Accounting Education*, 1–17.

Reich, C. M., & Berman, J. S. (2015). Do financial literacy classes help? An experimental assessment in a low-income population. *Journal of Social Service Research*, *41*(2), 193–203. doi:10.1080/01488376.2014.977986

Rodrigues, L. F., Oliveira, A., Rodrigues, H., & Costa, C. J. (2019). Assessing consumer literacy on financial complex products. *Journal of Behavioral and Experimental Finance*, *22*, 93–104. doi:10.1016/j.jbef.2019.02.005

Sabir, S. A., Mohammad, H. B., & Shahar, H. B. K. (2019). The role of overconfidence and past investment experience in herding behaviour with a moderating effect of financial literacy: Evidence from Pakistan stock exchange. *Asian Economic and Financial Review*, *9*(4), 480–490. doi:10.18488/journal.aefr.2019.94.480.490

Sarıgül, H. (2015). Finansal Okuryazarlık Tutum Ve Davranış Ölçeği: Geliştirme, Geçerlik Ve Güvenirlik. *Yönetim ve Ekonomi Araştırmaları Dergisi*, *13*(1), 200–218.

Schwartz, S. P., Adair, K. C., Bae, J., Rehder, K. J., Shanafelt, T. D., Profit, J., & Sexton, J. B. (2019). Work-life balance behaviours cluster in work settings and relate to burnout and safety culture: A cross-sectional survey analysis. *BMJ Quality & Safety*, *28*(2), 142–150. doi:10.1136/bmjqs-2018-007933 PMID:30309912

Shi, X., Prevett, P., Farnsworth, V., Kwong, K. C., Wan, W., He, F., ... Zhen, L. (2019). Modeling changes to survey response items over time in a Britain financial literacy education study. *Journal of Financial Counseling and Planning*, *30*(1), 56–66. doi:10.1891/1052-3073.30.1.56

Şimşek, G. G., & Noyan, F. (2009). Türkiye'de cep telefonu cihazı pazarında marka sadakati için bir model denemesi. *Middle East Technical University Studies in Development*, *36*(1).

Sivaramakrishnan, S., Srivastava, M., & Rastogi, A. (2017). Attitudinal factors, financial literacy, and stock market participation. *International Journal of Bank Marketing*, *35*(5), 818–841. doi:10.1108/IJBM-01-2016-0012

Tanaka, S., Murakami, K., & Takebayashi, Y. (2019). Survey analysis on the installation utilization pattern and renovation details of the cogeneration systems in the district heat supply system of the Tokyo metropolitan area. *Journal of Environmental Engineering (Japan)*, *84*(757), 303–312. doi:10.3130/aije.84.303

Wilson, R. S., Yu, L., James, B. D., Bennett, D. A., & Boyle, P. A. (2017). Association of financial and health literacy with cognitive health in old age. *Neuropsychology, Development, and Cognition. Section B, Aging, Neuropsychology and Cognition*, *24*(2), 186–197. doi:10.1080/13825585.2016.1178210 PMID:27263546

Xue, R., Gepp, A., O'Neill, T., Stern, S., & Vanstone, B. J. (2019, April). Financial literacy and financial decision-making: The mediating role of financial concerns. In The 10th Financial Markets & Corporate Governance Conference: Capital Markets, Sustainability and Disruptive Technologies.

Xue, R., Gepp, A., O'Neill, T. J., Stern, S., & Vanstone, B. J. (2019). Financial literacy amongst elderly Australians. *Accounting and Finance*, *59*(S1), 887–918. doi:10.1111/acfi.12362

Ye, J., & Kulathunga, K. M. M. C. B. (2019). How does financial literacy promote sustainability in SMEs? A developing country perspective. *Sustainability*, *11*(10), 2990. doi:10.3390u11102990

Zhu, A. Y. F., Yu, C. W. M., & Chou, K. L. (2019). Improving financial literacy in secondary school students: A randomized experiment. *Youth & Society*, 0044118X19851311.

Zou, J., & Deng, X. (2019). Financial literacy, housing value and household financial market participation: Evidence from urban China. *China Economic Review*, *55*, 52–66. doi:10.1016/j.chieco.2019.03.008

KEY TERMS AND DEFINITIONS

KMO: Kaiser Meyer Olkin.
SSCI: Social Science Citation Index.
TL: Turkish Lira.
USA: United States of America.

Chapter 2
Financial Marketing-Based Role of Exchange Rate to Increase Foreign Trade in Turkey

Özgür Kiyak
https://orcid.org/0000-0001-7287-3204
Beykent University, Turkey

Bilge Afşar
Kto Karatay University, Turkey

ABSTRACT

This chapter tries to determine whether there is a causal relationship between exchange rate and foreign trade. The study includes monthly data between February 2003 and December 2018 including dollar foreign exchange selling rate and inflation related real exchange rate for exchange rate, and export amount, import amount, export increase/decrease rate, and import increase. Increase/decrease rate is used for foreign trade among other variables, for a total of 6 variables. According to the obtained results of Engle-Granger cointegration analysis, there is a cointegration between variables in the long run. However, according to the results of the Toda-Yamamoto causality analysis, it was understood that there is no causality relationship between exchange rate and foreign trade.

INTRODUCTION

In a narrow sense, foreign exchange is the name given to foreign currency. In the broadest sense, foreign exchange is the means of payment used by countries to pay for goods or services. The means referred to herein as payment means may be money, as well as valuable documents such as checks, bills and policies. If a currency can buy more foreign currency, we can call it an increase in the exchange rate, and if a currency can buy less foreign currency, we can call it a depreciation in the exchange rate. As a result of the depreciation of the exchange rate, the country's exports to another country fall while im-

DOI: 10.4018/978-1-7998-2559-3.ch002

ports increase. As a result of the increase in the exchange rate, the country's exports to another country increased while imports decreased (Ison & Wall, 2007).

The foreign exchange market is the market where foreign demand and supply come together. Unlike other markets, the foreign exchange market is a global market that is open 24 hours a day. Taking into account the time difference between countries, the closing foreign exchange market in other countries may be open in other countries. Therefore, there is constant activity in the foreign exchange market (Dinçer & Yüksel, 2018). While the foreigners provide foreign exchange inflow to the country as a result of export, those who demand foreign exchange provide foreign exchange out of the country as a result of imports. In other words, while the most important economic activity that increases the foreign exchange supply is exports, it leads to the increase in foreign exchange demand from the country by importing the goods and entering the goods (Dinçer et al., 2018a,b,c).

With the collapse of the Bretton-Woods system, which accepts the US dollar as a reserve index indexed under gold, many changes have occurred between countries and markets. The disappearance of the economic boundaries between countries, especially with the globalization, has led to increased mutual trade and the world becoming a single market. In this regard, the increase in uncertainties in exchange rates as a result of the countries' transition from fixed exchange rate system to floating rate system affected the return of investors and foreign trade balance. Until today, in past years, different exchange rate policies were applied in different periods in Turkey. Applying the fixed exchange rate system in the 1980s, Turkey has moved to a floating exchange rate system in February 2001 after the crisis. Especially after 1980, with the adoption of export-based growth hypothesis, the effect of changes in exchange rates on foreign trade attracted the attention of many researchers (Karaçor & Gerçeker, 2012). In other words, exchange rate and foreign trade have become a detailed research topic for economists.

When the studies dealing with the relationship between exchange rate and foreign trade were examined, it was found that independence results were obtained from each other. In this context, some researchers have stated that this relationship is one-way or two-way, while some researchers argue that there is no relationship. In other words, the researchers could not agree on the subject. Therefore, the issue should be handled empirically in different ways. Considering the mentioned considerations, the aim of this study referred to in Turkey to determine whether the relationship between the variables. If the relationship is determined, it is to understand the direction of the relationship. In this context, monthly data for the period of 2003: 02-2018: 12 were tested by Engle-Granger Cointegration and Toda-Yamamoto Causality analysis.

The study consists of 3 chapters. In the first part of the study, general information about exchange rate and its types will be given. Then, the exchange rate system and approaches for determining the exchange rate will be discussed in detail. In the second part of the study, foreign trade concepts and policies applied in foreign trade will be mentioned. Immediately after these topics, classical and new foreign trade theories will be discussed in different topics. In the third and last part of the study, after considering the studies done in the literature, Engle-Granger Cointegration and Toda Yamamoto causality analyzes which we will use in the analysis of the data will be mentioned theoretically and then the estimation results and findings will be shared. In the conclusion part of the study, the results obtained in the study will be evaluated.

Financial Marketing-Based Role of Exchange Rate to Increase Foreign Trade in Turkey

GENERAL INFORMATION ABOUT EXCHANGE RATE

The Types of Exchange Rate

In the retail foreign exchange market, buying and selling transactions are carried out by banks and other foreign exchange market traders engaged in foreign exchange trading. As a result of the transactions in these markets, foreign exchange buying and selling rates emerge. Purchasing exchange rate is the exchange rate used for foreign exchange purchases. Foreign exchange selling rate is the exchange rate used in foreign exchange sales. There is often a difference between buying and selling prices. The reason for this difference is the profit and cost of the seller. Therefore, the selling rate is always higher than the buying rate. Spot exchange rates are determined by the supply and demand of the currencies traded in the global interbank foreign exchange market. Since transactions in this foreign exchange market change very quickly, they can respond quickly to small differences in price quotations (Levi, 2009).

The forward exchange rate is the rate that is contracted today for the exchange rate at a certain date in the future (Levi, 2009). The agreement reached for the future exchange rate is called forward contract. Foreign currency forward contracts arise as a result of the actions of intermediaries who bring together those who want to buy a currency in exchange for another currency and bring together those who wish to sell in the future. For example, when an international entity trades goods and services, it cannot immediately fulfill the contractual payment. Therefore, an economic risk occurs with a significant period between the decision to purchase a product or service and the time of payment (Hacıoğlu & Dinçer, 2013). In order to avoid the economic risk that may arise during this period, the companies make forward contracts. It is possible to make foreign exchange purchase and sale contracts between all major currencies with periods of 30, 60, 90 and 180 days (Seyidoğlu, 2003).

Exchange Rate Systems

Exchange rates are determined by supply and demand. However, both government authorities and market mechanisms affect exchange rates in various ways. In the money markets, the systems used in the interventions made by the state authorities to determine the exchange rates are called exchange rate systems. Exchange rate systems are divided into three. The first is the fixed exchange rate system, which is determined by government intervention as buyers and sellers. The second one is the floating exchange rate system, which is a freely determined exchange rate system as a result of changes in market demand and supply. Finally, they are mixed exchange rate systems that consist of a combination of fixed and floating exchange rate systems.

Every country is free to opt for the exchange rate system it sees optimal, and it does so mostly by using monetary and fiscal policies. Exchange rate systems preferred by countries cannot prevent macroeconomic turbulence that may occur in the country. However, the choice of any exchange rate system can produce better or worse economic results (Calvo & Mishkin, 2003). Each exchange rate regime has clearly unique characteristics, advantages and disadvantages. Determining the most appropriate exchange rate regime for a given country is not a simple decision since it can put countries at risk (Kalkavan & Ersin, 2019). The economy of a country can be greatly influenced by the exchange rate decision. The fixed exchange rate system is the exchange rate system in which the exchange rate is determined through the central bank, which is considered as a monetary authority instrument, and the national currency is bought and sold at the determined price.

In the fixed exchange rate system, the exchange rate level can be changed by this authority until it reaches the desired level. The central bank determines the exchange rate at any level. In case the exchange rate deviates from the specified level, the central bank intervenes in the market by buying or selling foreign exchange. As a result of the overvaluation of the foreign exchange rate, the Central Bank buys domestic money by selling foreign assets to the market and thus losses in international reserves are experienced. On the contrary, in case of a depreciation in the exchange rate, the central bank sells domestic assets and as a result international reserves gain value (Mishkin, 2018). The reason why the central bank intervenes in the market is to ensure the stability of the exchange rate. It can eliminate the distrust of the central bank due to the constraints it has placed on monetary policy. Thus, monetary policy reliability, which is formed by fixed exchange rate system, can be used as an important tool in reducing inflation (Yanar, 2008). In addition, changes in the supply and demand in the money market have not been taken into consideration in the fixed exchange rate system (Bağış, 2016).

Since the value of domestic currency against foreign currencies is kept constant in the fixed exchange rate system, uncertainties that may occur in the future do not occur and the volatility in exchange rates is prevented. Trade and investments within the country are increasing due to uncertainty and volatility in exchange rates. In addition to the above, it tries to prevent the effects of monetary crises on the economy by reducing the negative effects caused by monetary shocks (Hacıoğlu et al., 2015). In the fixed exchange rate system, since the central bank's power to issue money is limited, it manages the budget more firmly and helps financial institutions to work effectively (Yanar, 2008).

Dollarization mainly involves using the currency of another country as a nominal exchange rate instrument (Williamson, 2014). For example, the US dollar, which is a strong and stable currency, is used in countries such as Ecuador and Panama. The main reasons why these countries prefer dollarization are their economic and political situation. It comes to mind that countries give up their national independence when they accept such a regime (Kaya and Güçlü, 2005). One of the most important advantages of the dollarization system, which is also referred to as currency substitution in the literature, is that it greatly reduces the exchange rate risk and uncertainty that may occur. With the decreasing exchange rate risk and uncertainty, both foreign investors will be provided to the country and the entry of economic institutions into international markets will be facilitated (Kılavuz et al., 2011). Moreover, it is a reliable system by increasing monetary discipline in the country and eliminating the disruptions that may arise in an unstable exchange rate (Gök, 2006).

The monetary board system, which is one of the rigid fixed exchange rate systems, is an institution that has the obligation to convert the domestic currency to reserve money at the fixed exchange rate and vice versa in order to control the money supply in countries where monetary reliability and financial stability are not at the desired level (Yamak & Akyazı, 2010; Eti et al., 2019). The reserve money mentioned here is the money that the country implementing the monetary board system should hold in return for the money it provides to the market. Reserve money country is also called as reserve country (Barışık, 2001). The foreign currency of the country to be selected as reserve money must first be stable and reliable (Öztürk & Gövdere, 2004).

As an alternative to the central bank, in countries that implement the monetary board system, significant growth rate, price stability, interest and inflation lowering effect and fiscal discipline are realized (Hanke, 2002). On the contrary, due to the lack of final application authority in the countries applying the monetary board, liquidity shortage will be experienced in case of a crisis and this situation will put banks in a difficult situation. In addition, with the use of the reserve country money, interest income from the reserve money cannot be obtained and the seigniorage income will go to the reserve country.

According to the fluctuations in supply and demand depending on market conditions, the determination of exchange rate without the intervention of any official authority is called floating or flexible exchange rate system (Özbek, 1998). With the collapse of the Bretton-Woods system towards the end of the 19th century, countries that had a large share in the world economy began to implement the floating exchange rate system. Turkey has declared that the move to a floating exchange rate system after the 2001 crisis. One of the most important advantages of the floating exchange rate system is that it is resistant to shocks from the external and real sectors. As the exchange rate fluctuates freely, the exchange rates in an effective foreign exchange market adapt quickly and fully to the new situations and shocks that occur (İnan, 2002).

Although the countries that prefer floating exchange rate system lose their productivity due to the uncertainty in exchange rates, they have maximum flexibility as the exchange rate moves freely. In the floating exchange rate system, there is no negative situation in terms of the balance of payments due to the fact that there is no loss of competition for the appreciation of the exchange rate in international trade. Accordingly, the Central Bank is able to conduct its monetary policy more effectively since the governments do not choose exchange rate stability as a target (Gök, 2006).

In the said exchange rate system, since independent monetary policy is implemented, independent policies can be developed in order to keep the internal balance and macroeconomic indicators at the desired level. Moreover, since the central bank's policy of accumulating foreign exchange reserves will require less, resource savings are provided. The money market authority does not need continuous intervention in the market. Thus, the assets of the country cannot be considered as idle capacity (Bağış, 2016). As can be seen from the above-mentioned statements, in case of any uncertainty in exchange rate in the floating exchange rate system, the country which intends to invest, and the investors of that country may be abstained in trading.

The systems which have different function of fixed and floating exchange rate systems or between the two basic exchange rates are called mixed exchange rate system. For example, if we compare the series of exchange rates to a series of numbers, there is a fixed exchange rate system on one side and a floating exchange rate system on the other side. In the middle of these two exchange rate systems, there are mixed exchange systems which are defined as gray tones where these two exchange rate systems can change at certain weights (Bağış, 2016).

In the adjustable exchange rate system, which is also referred to as the Bretton-Woods system, the exchange rate is adjusted to a target value in order to correct the balance in the balance of payments. Adjustment can be in the form of devaluation (decreasing the parity value of the local currency) or revaluation (increasing the parity value of the local currency) (Moosa, 2006). Although this system contributes to economic stability by reducing the uncertainty in the exchange rate, it may cause a crisis in the economy as a result of the expectation that the value of the local currency will be reduced (Gök, 2006). The monetary authorities of a country refrain from interfering in the foreign exchange market or changing interest rates in order to influence the level or course of the nominal exchange rate. Thus, the exchange rate is determined according to the supply and demand in the market (Kenen, 2001).

Although central banks declare that exchange rates are flexible, they intervene in foreign exchange markets. It is the system in which central banks intervene in the market by buying and selling foreign exchange in order to prevent excessive fluctuations in exchange rates from time to time (Levi, 2009). These interventions, which are not made in accordance with the rules stated by the monetary authority, provide a wide range of action for the national economy. By directing the exchange rates in this way, the risks and uncertainties created by the free-floating exchange rate system are reduced to a certain extent (Özdemir & Şahinbeyoğlu, 2000). The supervised fluctuations system is divided into two. If the intervention in exchange rates occurs in order to eliminate short-term and irregular fluctuations, this is called clean fluctuation. On the other hand, it is called dirty fluctuation if it is carried out in order to increase domestic employment, control inflation and provide competitive advantage in foreign trade.

In this system, which is more similar to the fixed exchange rate system, the exchange rate is allowed to fluctuate according to supply and demand within a certain band. If the exchange rate falls outside the predetermined band, the exchange rate is withdrawn to the desired band interval (Bağış, 2016). The band fluctuation system is one of the preferred systems with its efficiency and reserve savings in exchange rates. The Exchange Rate Mechanism (ERM) implemented within the European Monetary system is one of the best examples of this system. The system may collapse if the system is unstable to maintain the band gap determined by the central bank to speculative pressures arising from a possible crisis situation (Gök, 2006). In a wide-margin parity system similar to the floating exchange rate regime, exchange rates are determined on the basis of supply and demand conditions in a wide band allowed around the parity (Cengiz, 2018). It is understood that when the upper and lower support points are forced in the wide margin parity system or they are in the same regions for a long time, new parity and exchange rate adjustments should be made (Bağış, 2016).

Creeping parity means that a country makes small, frequent changes in the currency's value to correct imbalances in the balance of payments. The budget deficit or surplus country continues to adjust until the desired exchange rate level is reached (Carbaugh, 2005). One of the most important features of the creeping parity system is that it ties the inflation rate of internationally traded goods to the anchor country and contributes to controlling inflation (Mishkin, 2018). On the other hand, the disadvantage of this system is that the country enters into the inflationary process and the effect of exchange rate on nominal anchor in monetary policy is eliminated (Kılavuz et al., 2011).

In this system, which is also defined as the optimum monetary area, a group of countries in the same geographical region connect their national currencies at fixed exchange rates and allow them to fluctuate freely against countries outside the group (Seyidoğlu, 2003). Mundell, one of the proponents of this system, tried to state that in the case of two goods and two countries, the shift in demand would lead to excessive supply in some countries and surplus in other countries when prices and prices were sticky. He argues that if countries are affected by asymmetric shocks, real exchange rates should be adjusted or production factors should be in motion to prevent unemployment and inflation. Mundell also argues that the mobility of factors, which may vary by region, can be substituted by changes in the exchange rate and will determine the limits of monetary union. In addition, he argues for the creation of monetary areas in which factor circulation is free but where interregional circulation is restricted.

Concept of Foreign Trade

Foreign trade is defined as the mutual exchange of goods and services of independent countries for various reasons. In the narrow sense, foreign trade is all of the export and import activities (Ersin, 2018). Countries are turning to foreign trade due to reasons such as production differences, consumers' tastes and desires, resources cannot be used effectively, and the quality level of goods is not at the desired level. In this way, countries establish international relations with each other (Dinçer et al., 2019a,b). Foreign trade has an important place in the economic development of countries. A country cannot produce the goods it needs or cannot provide maximum benefit because it cannot specialize in all fields if it starts with production (Hausmann et al., 2007). Therefore, if each country produces the product it specializes in, and buys the other products it needs from other countries, the welfare of that country will be increased. At the same time, these countries make cheap investments with the import of intermediate products they need. Consequently, the income level of the people living in the country increases.

Countries are adopting an open or closed economy understanding depending on whether there are any obstacles while conducting foreign trade transactions with each other. In countries that adopt a closed economy, imports are generally restricted. Therefore, in closed economies, prices are determined according to the supply and demand in the domestic market. However, in open economies, restrictions on imports and exports are removed and prices are determined according to international supply and demand. While international price is valid in open economies, domestic prices are effective in open economies (Kaya, 2011). The main reason why the factors affecting foreign trade differ from country to country is that the factors affecting export and import demands vary. These factors can be classified as primary and secondary factors. Primary factors are domestic and international income levels, relative prices and volatility in exchange rates. Secondary factors; trade reforms, monetary and fiscal policy instruments, firm level factors and natural resource intensity (Yücel, 2006; Yüksel et al., 2019).

The above mentioned domestic and foreign income levels have a significant effect on foreign trade demands under the assumption that prices are constant (Krugman, 1989). In case domestic income rises, demand for goods both at home and abroad will increase and consumption will increase. Therefore, changes in the components of foreign trade will depend on the income of the country. There is a positive relationship between domestic revenues and imports. This is called import function in the literature. In this context, the need for a certain amount of foreign inputs to realize production creates a negative effect in terms of foreign trade balance (Yücel, 2006; Zengin et al., 2018).

A tariff is simply a tax on the product of a country when it crosses the national borders. The most common tariff is the import tariff from an imported product. The least common tariff is the export tariff, which is a tax on the exported product. Export tariffs are generally used by developing countries (Carbaugh, 2005). The purpose of countries in applying customs duties on the products and services traded is to generate revenue for the state treasury and to protect the domestic industry from foreign competition (Dinçer et al., 2017; Kaymakcı et al., 2007). When we look at the tariffs in terms of providing revenue to governments, the tariffs are easily collected because the tariffs are mostly placed on the products that the people need more. In addition, countries have capital to meet their investment and other needs through these taxes (Tomanbay, 2014).

As a result of the high production costs of the domestic industrialists, the chance of competition in the domestic market is decreasing. As a result, governments increase the domestic sales price of imported goods through tariffs in order to protect the national economy from foreign competition. Thus, the domestic producer will be protected from competition. This approach is also called the baby industry thesis. This thesis was developed by Friedrich List towards the end of the eighteenth year. In the baby industry thesis, the industry, which cannot compete against foreign companies due to reasons such as knowledge-accumulation, economies of scale and technological superiority, is protected until the desired level of growth is achieved (Çakmak, 2004).

Non-tariff barriers are all kinds of instruments and policies that prevent the realization of goods and services subject to international trade within the framework of free trade conditions, other than tariffs. Although some of the non-tariff barriers are imposed against countries or firms trying to dominate the market by encouraging exportation of countries, they are considered as obstacles to free trade conditions, but are considered as measures to ensure competition conditions and prevent unfair competition (Eğilmez, 2012). Due to the rapid growth and complexity of the foreign trade volume over time, the importance of non-tariff barriers has increased. Thus, as a result of the GATT negotiations, the effectiveness of tariffs was reduced, and non-tariff barriers were intensively implemented. Non-tariff barriers are divided into three sections as quantity restrictions, exchange restrictions and new protectionism (Seyidoğlu, 2003).

THEORETICAL ANALYSIS OF EXCHANGE RATE AND FOREIGN TRADE RELATIONS

Various approaches have been put forward in the economic literature on the relationship between exchange rate and foreign trade. These approaches will be discussed in this section, respectively. Classical Economics began with Adam Smith's book The Wealth of Nations in 1776. Physiocratic thinking is very important in the formation of this system based on liberal thought. Later, within the framework of the work of David Ricardo, Classical Economics took over the thoughts that gave weight to the supply side of the economy from the physiocrats (Kızıldemir, 2013). Classical economists have argued that the balance of payments can be achieved through exchange rate and price system. International equilibrium mechanism has been explained with this approach until the publication of Keynes' General Theory. In this approach, the current monetary system is the gold standard and accordingly, foreign exchange and gold movements arising from external imbalances affect both export and import prices and restore external balances (Karluk, 2009).

The functioning of the classical approach system is as follows. If gold is exported while there is an external deficit in the country, there will be a contraction in the country's money supply. As a result of this, there will be decreases in the general level of prices within the country and the increase in other country prices will occur. Thus, export prices will increase, and foreign balances will automatically become equilibrium as prices of the deficit countries are relatively cheaper than the prices of other countries (Kemeç and Kösekahyaoğlu, 2015).

The Keynesian approach differs from the classical approach theory as it prioritizes employment and production rather than prices. According to Keynes, the expected and unexpected developments in the aggregate demand have a large impact in the short term not on prices, but on employment and real output. Keynes therefore argues that changes in aggregate demand will not lead to higher prices. In other words, short-term output and production are determined on the demand side.

Keynes also emphasizes the value of money. Contrary to the classics, he cared about money and included it as a variable in macroeconomics. According to Keynes, money has a unique role in an ever-changing and uncertain world. Therefore, all kinds of transactions are expressed in money and many goods in the economic market are made by money, not by exchange. Thus, people who do not want to take risks due to the uncertainties expected in the future want to hold money instead of any assets or assets that can replace them (Turan & Öztürk, 2016).

In addition, the keynesian approach emphasizes the theory of equilibrium. According to Keynes, internal-external balance can be balanced with income movements, he said. In this case, the total demand is reduced as the balance of payments has come out as much as the amount of the deficit, which consists of a country that has a deficit. Decreasing demand also leads to a reduction in national income. Decreasing national income reduces the demand for imports. Similarly, income increases due to the expansion of money in other countries that have a surplus in balance of payments. Imports increase due to increased income. On the one hand, the countries that give deficit as well as the countries that give surplus on the other, interact with each other and provide external balances (Karluk, 2009).

The flexibility approach was developed to investigate the effects of devaluation. The main purpose of this approach, which does not take into account capital flows, is to explain the effect of devaluation on foreign trade balance (Seyidoğlu, 2003). The flexibility approach, which focuses on the foreign trade balance, which is one of the sub-items of the current account balance, assumes that the main factor determining the current account balance is relative international prices. According to this approach, the price increase in imported goods will be observed with the devaluation that will occur in the country and therefore the import values will decrease with decreasing demand. Meanwhile, the price of export goods decreases, and exports increase as foreign demand increases. Therefore, with the increase in export revenues and the decrease in import expenses, the foreign trade deficit of the country will close (Yaprakli, 2009).

According to the flexibility approach, devaluation increases the foreign exchange income and makes the export goods cheaper in terms of foreign currencies, resulting in increased demand from foreign consumers. This situation is also called as foreign exchange earning effect. The extent to which the devaluation will earn foreign currency is again a matter determined by the foreign consumers against the export goods of the country. Due to a certain cheapness provided by the devaluation, the more foreign consumers increase the amount they demand, ie the higher the demand elasticity, the higher the foreign exchange-earning effect. Conversely, in other words, where demand elasticity is low, the foreign exchange-earning effect will be so low. At this point, it is necessary to explain the difference between the devaluation effect and the foreign exchange saving effect.

Although the elasticities approach helps to close the foreign trade deficit, it is criticized for some deficiencies in explaining the determinants of the current account balance. These can be listed as follows. Since this approach is partial, it only deals with a part of the balance of payments, not the whole. Although the purpose of the elasticities approach is to analyze the effect of devaluation on the current balance, there is no clear information about the role of non-tradable goods in the real exchange rate definition (Erkılıç, 2006). Here, the flexibility approach is examined in two different ways as Marshall-Lerner condition and J curve.

LITERATURE REVIEW

Arize (2000) used Johansen cointegration and error correction techniques in his study in 13 developing countries. The relationship between foreign exchange uncertainty and foreign trade in quarters in 1973-2016 has been observed to have a negative effect on exports in both long and short term increases in exchange rate volatility. Onafowora and Owoye (2008) investigated the effects of Nigerian exports to the United States on exchange rate volatility within the framework of cointegration and vector error correction models using quarterly data between 1980 and 2001. According to the findings, in case of an increase in the uncertainty in exchange rates in both long and short term, they determined that exports were affected negatively. Moreover, developments in terms of trade and real foreign trade income have observed a positive effect on export activity.

Duasa (2009) investigated the impact of the real exchange rate shock on Malaysia's export and import prices. In his study, he examined real exchange rate, money supply, import and export items in the period 1999: 01-2006: 12 by using Johansen cointegration and vector error correction models as monthly data. As a result of this study, it has been observed that exchange rate shocks affect the prices of export and import items. Bahmani-Oskooe and Harvey (2012) tested the extent to which the real exchange rate would affect trade between the two countries by separating the trade flows between the US and Malaysia by goods. In order to reach this conclusion, 101 industries exported by USA and 17 industries imported from Malaysia to USA by using annual data between 1971-2006 were examined by applying vector error correction model. According to the results of the study, 67% of the export industries in the short run and 53 industries in the long run have a significant relationship with the exchange rate.

Cheung and Sengupta (2013) examined the effect of exchange rate volatility on export share by using data for 2000-2010 period for non-financial companies in India. According to the empirical study, it was determined that the uncertainty in the exchange rate in the country concerned negatively affected the exports of non-financial companies. Kodongo and Ojah (2013) examined the relationship between the changes in the real exchange rate and the foreign trade balance and cross-border capital flows through causality analysis. For this study, annual data of 1993-2009 for 9 major African countries were used. As a result of the panel VAR analysis, the results supporting the classical foreign trade theory were found and it was found that the depreciation of the real exchange rate contributed positively to the foreign trade balance of the country.

Serenis and Tsounis (2013) discussed quarterly data between 1990: 01-2012: 01 in order to examine the effect of exchange rate volatility on Cyprus and Croatia on foreign trade. As a result of the study, it was observed that exchange rate volatility had no effect on the exports of both countries. Choudhry and Hassan (2015) examined the effect of exchange rate volatility and the economic crisis on the imports of England from three important developing countries: Brazil, China and South Africa. Monthly data for the period of 1991-2011 are analyzed with ARDL model. According to the results of the study, it is found that there is a long-term relationship between UK imports and exchange rate volatility along with other determinant variables such as real income of England and relative import price ratio and this relationship is negative.

Asteriou (2016) have examined the effect of exchange rate volatility in the foreign trade volume for MINT (Mexico, Indonesia, Nigeria, Turkey) countries. In the study, where monthly data for the period 1995-2012 was discussed, the Granger causality test was used to determine the short-term relationship of the ARDL model for the long-term relationship. The results, excluding Turkey in the long term is that there is a relationship between volatility and trading volumes in foreign exchange rates in other countries. In the short term, to other countries, except Turkey (Indonesia and accurate exchange rate volatility of exports and imports in Mexico, while in Nigeria the right to exchange rate volatility than exports) is that there is causality. In addition, short-term volatility in exchange rates affected the export and import demand of Mexico and Indonesia. Bahmani and Gelan (2018) investigated the effect of real exchange rate volatility on the exports and imports of 12 African countries. They used the error correction model to determine the effects in the short and long term and examined the data for the period 1971: Q1-2015: Q4. According to the results of the examinations, in the short term, the volatility in the exchange rate affected most of the countries' trade flows, while in the long term it limited the exports of 5 countries and the imports of one country.

Bahmani-Oskooee et al. (2016) examined the effect of exchange rate uncertainty on trade flow between Pakistan and Japan. In total, 44 Pakistani companies export to Japan and 60 Pakistani companies import from Japan. In the study, which deals with the data of 1980-2014, it was observed that the uncertainty experienced in the exchange rate neither in the short term nor in the long term affects trade between the two countries. Moreover, Kim (2017) investigated the effect of Korean Won and US Dollar exchange rate volatility on Korean import volume by considering monthly data for the period 2000-2015. According to the results of the ARDL model, while the increase in real income in the long run had a statistically significant positive effect on the import volume, it was found to have a statistically negative effect on world commodity prices. Moreover, long-term USD / KRW coefficient has a statistically negative effect on import volume. According to the results of DCL analysis, USD / KRW exchange rate volatility has unilateral causality on import volume and income.

Senadza and Diaba (2017) investigated the effect of exchange rate volatility on export and import. In this study, the data of the countries of Gambia, Ghana, Kenya, Madagascar, Mauritius, Mozambique, Nigeria, Sierra Leone, Tanzania, Uganda and Zambia, which are called sub-Saharan African economies, were examined in the years 1993-2014. According to the results of the GARCH model, exchange rate volatility has no significant effect on imports. It is observed that the volatility in the exchange rate has a negative effect on exports and a negative effect in the short term and a positive effect on the long term. Kohler and Ferjani (2018), in their study, between 1999 and 2012, examined the relationship between the exchange rate and the export of Switzerland based on the agriculture and food sector. They used time series and panel data analysis to calculate exchange rate flexibility in the short and long run. According to the results of the analysis, it was found that the predicted elasticities were similar in terms of the estimation methods and data structure of all models. Moreover, it was observed that the changes in the exchange rate did not affect the exports much.

Acaravcı and Ozturk (2002), investigated the effect of exchange rate variability in Turkey on exports. In this study, monthly data for the period 1989: 01-2002: 08 were examined within the framework of cointegration and error correction model. Empirical results obtained by the embodiment, the exchange rate is affected by changes in Turkey's real exports negatively, but this adverse effect was reached the conclusion that the short-term. Saatçioglu and Karaca (2004) examined how the uncertainty in exchange rates affects exports by using cointegration method and error correction model. The scope of the study is 1981-2001. According to the empirical study; the uncertainty of the exchange rate in both the short and long-term effects has been determined that Turkey's exports negatively.

Karagöz and Dogan (2005) studied the relationship between real exchange rate movements, import and export for Turkey. In this study, they applied cointegration test and multiple regression method according to monthly data for 1995: 01-2004: 06 periods. According to the empirical results, it is concluded that there is no causality relationship from real exchange rates to foreign trade variables in the long run. In addition, devaluation effect was significant in the short term. Kasman and Kasman (2005) evaluated the effect of exchange rate uncertainty in Turkey's exports taking into account the data of Turkey's most important trading countries. In this study, quarterly data for the period 1982-2001 are considered. According to empirical results, the uncertainty in the exchange rate was found to be statistically positive and significant relationship on exports in both short and long term.

In the study conducted by Yamak and Korkmaz (2005), they examined the effects of real changes in the Turkish lira on the foreign trade balance by using the Granger causality analysis with quarterly data for the period 1995: 01-2004: 04. In this study, the validity of the Marshall-Lerner condition which tries to explain exchange rate theories was investigated. According to the results of the empirical study, it is concluded that there is no long-term relationship between the variables but in the short term the relationship between real exchange rate and foreign trade balance depends on capital goods trade. Marshall-Lerner condition was also met except the February 2001 crisis period.

Gül and Ekinci (2006) investigated the relationship between real exchange rate and foreign trade variables in Turkey for 1990:01-2006:08. In this study, it is determined that there is a long term relationship between real exchange rate and export and import and it is concluded that the relationship is a unilateral causality relationship from export and import to real exchange rate. Köse et al. (2008) tried to determine the real exchange rate volatility on exports. In this study, they applied cointegration and error correction model by using monthly data of 1995-2008 period. According to the results, the uncertainty of the exchange rate has been determined that Turkey's exports negatively affect both the short and the long term.

Kılıç (2009) used monthly data for the period 1994: 01-2008: 11 to determine the effect of exchange rate on exports and imports. In this study, the relationships between the variables were tested with the vector error correction model. Then, to determine the degree of integration of the time series and to test the stability of the variables, the unit root test was performed and the cointegration test was applied to determine whether there was a long-term relationship between the variables. According to the findings, the effect of exchange rate on import and export prices was weak.

Tarı and Yıldırım (2009), using quarterly data for the period 1989-2007, have examined the relationship between uncertainty and export volume in the exchange rate in Turkey. According to the results of the study, it was concluded that the uncertainty in the exchange rate had a negative effect on the export volume, while it had no effect on the export volume in the short term. Moreover, it was emphasized that the amount of goods of exporters was negatively affected due to the uncertainty in the exchange rate in the long run.

Aktas (2010) examined the relationship between real exchange rate and export with import in Turkey, has concluded that a significant effect includes on the trade balance of the change in the real exchange rate. Esen (2012), Turkey's late in the period that the floating exchange rate system, which investigated the effect of uncertainty in the exchange rate on exports from occurring. For this purpose, quarterly data for the period 2001: 02-2011: 03 were analyzed using cointegration and error correction models. According to the findings, it was concluded that the uncertainty in the exchange rate had a negative impact on the export volume in the long run and had no effect in the short run.

AN APPLICATION ON TURKEY

Data Set and Variables

This study was analyzed to determine if the relationship between foreign trade and exchange rate variables in Turkey's economy. In the model, two different data related to exchange rate are considered. The first one is the real dollar selling rate and the other is the real effective exchange rate based on CPI. The reason for taking two different variables is to be able to reveal the result in different situations by analyzing both conditions. In the second case, four different variables were used depending on foreign trade. In addition to the export and Import quantities, the increase / decrease ratios of these variables were also taken. These two methods were preferred in order to take into account both how much these variables affect the amount and whether they affect the rate of increase. the Variable 2003: 02 and 2018: 12-month period ended data from the Central Bank of the Republic of Turkey Electronic Data Dissemination System (EDDS) were obtained on the basis of 2003. These data were analyzed with E-Views 10 econometrics package program.

Engle Granger Cointegration Analysis

In the model proposed by Engle-Granger (1987), it is determined whether there is a long-term relationship between the two variables. In order to be able to apply the said analysis, it is necessary to ensure the stability of the series by taking the same order differences. If this condition is not met, cointegration analysis cannot be performed (Yüksel, 2016). After regression is created with the variables which are obtained from the same order differences and the stability is provided, the stability value of the error correction model will be tested. According to the results of the analysis, it is concluded that there is cointegration between the variables if the level value is stable (Dilber & Kılıç, 2018; Yüksel and Kavak, 2019). In order to determine the cointegration relationship of the method, regression is first estimated (Dinçer et al., 2016; Alhan & Yüksel, 2018). Then, the stability of the error terms obtained according to the estimation is tested. If the unit root test of the relevant variables indicates that there is stasis, it will show that there is a long-term relationship between the variables.

Toda Yamamoto Causality Analysis

The analysis expressed by Toda and Yamamoto in 1995 is essentially a development of the Granger causality model. As a result of the unit root tests applied to the series of variables in the causality method, the series do not have to be stationary. In addition, it is not considered whether there is a cointegration relationship between the variables (Toda and Yamamoto, 1995). Certain stages need to take place in order to apply the above-mentioned causality analysis. In the first step of the analysis, the unit root test is applied to the variables, resulting in the maximum degree of integration (d_max) of the variables. In this context, if the two variables are stationary at the highest level, the largest of these levels gives the number of integration. In the second stage, the ideal lag length (k) will be determined by means of the VAR model to be installed. Subsequently, the causality analysis is estimated with the newly established VAR model in the respective model (d_max + k) delay number (Yüksel & Özsarı, 2016; Eti, 2019).

Analysis Results

In this study, Augmented Dickey-Fuller (ADF) unit root test was applied to the series to determine whether the series were stationary or not. P (Probe) values of the variables are taken into account when performing unit root test. In all unit root tests, P values were accepted as 5% accuracy criteria. In other words, it is assumed that the analysis is performed within 95% confidence interval. Therefore, the P values obtained were compared with 0.05. It is understood that if the obtained P value is greater than 0.05, the series is not stationary and if it is less than 0.05, it is stable. In Table 1, the stationary analysis of the exchange rate variable was performed, and the results of the unit root test were indicated.

According to the obtained unit root test results, the ADF unit root test probability (P) value of ER variable was determined as 1.0000. Since this value is above 0.05, it is not stationary. In other words, the variable unit contains the root. In order to ensure the stability of the said variable, the first difference must be obtained. Table 2 shows the results obtained by taking the first difference of ER variable.

As it can be seen from the table, the probability of the ADF unit root test of the first variable ER1 was calculated as 0.0000. Accordingly, the relevant value is less than 0.05 and is stable and the unit does not contain root. Table 3 shows the results of the ADF unit root test at the level value of export (EXP) variable for determination of stability.

Table 1. Exchange rate variable unit root test results

Variable	Critical Table Values			ADF Test Statistics	
	%1	%5	%10	t- statistic	Probability (P)
Exchange Rate (ER)	-3,46	-2,87	-2,57	2,5402	1,0000

Table 2. Taking the first difference of exchange rate variable

Variable	Critical Table Values			ADF Test Statistics	
	%1	%5	%10	t- statistic	Probability (P)
ER1	-3,46	-2,87	-2,57	-6.1516	0,0000

According to the results of ADF unit root test of the related variable in Table 3, the probability value according to the significance level of 5% is 0,3715. Accordingly, since the probability value of the related variable is greater than 0.05, it is concluded that the unit contains root and is not stationary. In order to stabilize said variable, the first difference must be obtained. Therefore, the first difference of the respective series is taken. The first difference results are given in Table 10. As can be seen from Table 4, the probability value of the related value is 0,000. Since this value is less than 0.05, the difference series has become stable and the unit does not have root.

According to the extended Dickey Fuller (ADF) unit root test results, the results of the stasis analysis of the level of import (IMP) variable are shown in Table 5.

According to the statements in Table 5, the probability value of the related variable is determined as 0.2921. According to the results of ADF unit root test (P) value is greater than 0.05, it contains unit root in the related serial level and it must be re-stationary test by taking the difference from first order. The details of the analysis results obtained from the first order difference of the related series are given in Table 6.

According to the results of the unit root test of the above-mentioned variable, the probability value is 0.0186. Accordingly, since the probability value of the related variable is less than 0.05, it is under-

Table 3. CPI based real effective exchange rate unit root test results

Variable	Critical Table Values			ADF Test Statistics	
	%1	%5	%10	t- statistic	Probability (P)
EXP	-4,01	-3,43	-3,14	-2,4131	0,3715

Table 4. First difference of CPI based real effective exchange rate

Variable	Critical Table Values			ADF Test Statistics	
	%1	%5	%10	t- statistic	Probability (P)
EXP1	-4,01	-3,43	-3,14	-6,3811	0,0000

Financial Marketing-Based Role of Exchange Rate to Increase Foreign Trade in Turkey

Table 5. Import quantity variable unit root test

Variable	Critical Table Values			ADF Test Statistics	
	%1	%5	%10	t- statistic	Probability (P)
IMP	-4,01	-3,43	-3,14	-2,5754	0,2921

stood that the series does not have unit root, in other words it is stationary. In the previous section, the stationarity test for the variables included in the study was conducted. As a result of the unit root test performed with the extended Dickey Fuller (ADF) test, it was found that some variables were stationary in the level and some variables became stationary when the first order difference was taken.

In this section, in order to apply Engle-Granger cointegration analysis to the variables, the series must be stationary in the first or second differences. In other words, it will be examined separately whether the stationary series whose differences are obtained has a cointegration relationship between each other in the long run. As can be seen here, if one of the variables is stationary in the first difference and the other is stationary in the level, the cointegration relationship of these variables cannot be calculated. Therefore, two of the four foreign trade variables cannot be used in this analysis. Because the unit root test was applied to the relevant variables as a result of the level was found to be stable.

Said analysis is implemented in two stages. First of all, the independent variable and the dependent variable which are brought to the station by taking the differences in the previous section will be subjected to regression analysis. As the regression analysis of the variables is entirely based on estimation, the results may not be accurate. Therefore, error terms are included in the series in the regression analysis. At this stage, error term series of the results of the regression analysis of the variables are formed.

In the second stage of the analysis, unit root test will be applied to the error term series. ADF unit root test is applied to error term series for unit root test. As a result of the unit root test, the fact that the related error terms are stationary in the level will prove that there is a cointegration relationship between the two variables. If the error terms are not stationary at the level, it will be concluded that there is no cointegration relationship.

According to the results of the unit root test of the exchange rate variable expressed in ER1 in the previous section and the export quantity variable expressed in EXP1, it was found that both variables were not stationary in the level but became stable when the first difference was taken. Therefore, both variables were found to be suitable for Engle-Granger cointegration analysis. After stabilizing the exchange rate and export quantity variables, regression analysis will be applied to the series first. In the second step, ADF unit root test will be applied to the series in order to test the stability of the error terms series which is formed according to the results of the regression analysis.

In applying the regression analysis, since the effect of exchange rate on foreign trade will be taken into consideration, ER1 will be considered as an independent variable and EXP1 as a dependent variable.

Table 6. Unit root test of the first difference of import variable

Variable	Critical Table Values			ADF Test Statistics	
	%1	%5	%10	t- statistic	Probability (P)
IMP1	-4,01	-3,43	-3,14	-3,8035	0,0186

Because the analysis will examine whether the changes in the exchange rate have an effect on the export amount and regression analysis will be applied in this context. The results obtained from the regression analysis are shown in Table 7.

As can be seen from Table 7, the coefficient of the variable ER1 was calculated as -411.5634. This value is negative, which means that the relationship between exchange rate and export quantity will be negative. In order to examine whether there is a possible cointegration relationship of the related variables, it is necessary to apply a unit root test to the series of error terms generated according to the test results. In Table 7 above, the regression analysis of the variables ER1 and EXP1 was performed. As a result of the related regression analysis, a series of error terms was obtained. These series of error terms were subjected to unit root test in the second stage. The unit root test results of these variables are given in Table 8.

According to the obtained unit root test results, the probability value of the equation was calculated as 0,000. Therefore, it is concluded that there is a cointegration relationship between exchange rate and export amount. In other words, Turkey's exchange rate affects the amount of exports in the long term and it is understood that this is a negative aspect of the relationship.

When we apply the unit root test to the variables of exchange rate and import amount, it is understood that the related series are not stationary in their raw state, they become stationary provided that the first order differences are taken and therefore the variables are suitable for Engle-Granger cointegration analysis. After these variables are stabilized, regression analysis will be applied first. In the next stage, the stationarity test will be performed on the error term series which is formed according to the results of the regression analysis.

As mentioned earlier, ER1 is an independent variable and IMP1 is a dependent variable due to the effect of exchange rate on import amount. Table 9 shows the results of the regression analysis of the exchange rate and import quantity variable, which are differentiated from the first order.

According to the results in the table above, the coefficient of ER1 variable was calculated as negative. The negative value of the coefficient indicates that this relationship will be negative if there is a

Table 7. Results of regression analysis of variables ER1 and EXP1

Variable	Coefficient	Standard Deviation	T-Statistic	Probability (P)
ER1	-411,5634	683,3647	-0,6022	0,5477
C	65,2984	84,3241	0,7743	0,4397
R^2	0.0019	Sum of Residual Squares		2,4808
F statistic	0,3627	Probability (P)		0,5477

Table 8. Unit root test of ER1-EXP1 regression error term

Critical Table Values			ADF Test Statistics	
%1	%5	%10	t- statistic	Probability (P)
-4,01	-3,43	-3,14	-6,2648	0,0000

Table 9. Results of regression analysis of ER1 and IMP1 variables

Variable	Coefficient	Standard Deviation	T-Statistic	Probability (P)
ER1	-2456,55	1019,69	-2,4179	0,0166
C	112,91	125,82	0,8973	0,3707
R^2	0,0301	Sum of Residual Squares		5,5208
F-statistic	5,8463	Probability (P)		0,0165

cointegration relationship between the exchange rate and the import amount. As a result of taking the first differences of the exchange rate and import amount variables above, the series were stabilized and regression analysis was performed. At this stage, ADF test will be applied to the series of error terms generated as a result of regression analysis. As a result of the relevant test, if this series of error terms is stationary at the level, the cointegration relationship between the two variables will be proved. The stationarity test of the error term for these variables is shown in Table 10.

As it can be seen from Table 10, as a result of unit root test applied to the obtained error term series, the probability value of ADF test statistic was determined as 0,0495. The fact that the said value is less than 0.05 indicates that there is a long-term cointegration relationship between the exchange rate and the amount of imports and this relationship is reversed.

At this stage of the study, Toda-Yamamoto causality analysis will be performed on the exchange rate and foreign trade variables, which are found to have long-term cointegration relationships. In applying the causality analysis, the causality analysis of the foreign exchange variables of both exchange rate variables will be considered separately. The process of causality analysis consists of two stages. First, the VAR model will determine the optimal lag length of the variables. The second stage of the analysis consists of the estimation of causality between the relevant variables.

In Toda-Yamamoto causality analysis, the maximum degree of integration of the variables in the model and the ideal lag length determined by the VAR model are very important. In the previous section, as a result of ADF unit root test between exchange rate and export amount, it was found that both variables were stationary when first order differences were taken. Therefore, the maximum number of integration of the variables in the model was determined as 1. In this context, first the ideal lag length between ER1 and EXP1 will be determined with the help of VAR model, and then the causality dimension of the model will be discussed.

In order to perform the Toda-Yamamoto causality analysis, first the VAR model equation for exchange rate and export quantity variables will be established and the ideal lag length will be determined. When applying the VAR model, the variables ER1 and EXP1, which are stabilized by taking the first order

Tablo 10. Unit root test of ER1-IMP1 regression error term

Critical Table Values			ADF Test Statistics	
%1	%5	%10	t- statistic	Probability (P)
-3,46	-2,87	-2,57	-2,8820	0,0495

differences, will be selected respectively. In addition, in order to perform the analysis of the series correctly, the maximum delay length is determined as 12 because monthly data is used in the series.

Five information criteria were used in determining the information criterion. According to these information criteria, the most cited information criterion gives the optimal delay length. When we look at Table 11, the optimal delay length for the equation investigating the causality from the exchange rate to the export amount is calculated as 12. In consideration, the model for the Toda-Yamamoto test is estimated at 13 (12 + 1) degrees. As a result of determining the ideal lag length by using the exchange rate and export quantity variables with the help of VAR model, models up to a maximum of 13 delays were estimated. The estimation results are given in the table below.

According to the results of Toda-Yamomoto causality analysis from the above table, the probability values of the related values are above 0.05. In other words, it is concluded that there is no causality between exchange rate and export amount.

In the previous analysis, the Toda-Yamamoto causality analysis will be applied to the exchange rate and import quantity variables, which are determined to have a cointegration relationship between them. Firstly, the ideal lag length of the variables will be determined by VAR model. Then, the causality estimation of the model will be tried to be determined. When determining the ideal delay length, VAR analysis will be performed between the exchange rate and import quantity variables. During the analysis, the

Table 11. Determining the ideal lag length of ER1 and EXP1

Lag	LogL	LR	FPE	AIC	SC	HQ
0	-1391.925	NA	21727.39	15.66208	15.6978	15.67658
1	-1350.969	80.5324	14344.1	15.24684	15.35409	15.29033
2	-1331.673	37.50738	12079.38	15.07498	15.25373*	15.14747
3	-1322.094	18.4057	11345.94	15.01229	15.26254	15.11377*
4	-1315.97	11.62806	11079.43	14.98843	15.31018	15.11891
5	-1313.563	4.516131	11281.16	15.00633	15.39958	15.1658
6	-1312.227	2.476471	11626.35	15.03626	15.50102	15.22473
7	-1308.798	6.280086	11704.46	15.04268	15.57893	15.26014
8	-1307.413	2.506327	12057.82	15.07206	15.67981	15.31852
9	-1304059	5.991812	12151.32	15.07931	15.75857	15.35477
10	-1300048	7.075607	12156.81	15.07919	15.82995	15.38364
11	-1279991	34.93018*	10157.12	14.89878	15.72104	15.23223
12	-1275107	8.397248	10065.03*	14.88884*	15.78260	15.25128

Table 12. ER1-EXP1 toda-yamamoto causality analysis results

Direction of Causality	Lag Length	P Probability Value
From ER1 to EXP1	13	0,8151
From EXP1 to ER1	13	0,4603

stationary series of both series will be selected and the maximum number of delays will be determined as 12 since monthly data are used.

As can be seen from Table 13 above, the 12 delay lengths with the most sign are the most significant delay length for our VAR model. Thus, the model determined for Toda-Yamamoto causality analysis will be estimated at 13 (12 + 1) degrees. Table 14 shows the results obtained according to the estimated coefficient for Toda-Yamamoto.

As can be seen from the table above, the probability values P of the variables ER1 and IMP1 are greater than 0.05. This situation states that there is no significant causal relationship between any of the variables. In other words, according to the results of Toda-Yamamoto analysis, exchange rate is not an important reason for imports.

SOLUTIONS AND RECOMMENDATIONS

In summary, the results of this analysis show that there is a long-term relationship between exchange rate and foreign trade variables; but exchange rate variables indicate that there is no reason. In other words, there is a long-term relationship between these two types of variables; but not in the dimension of causality. As we understand from here, the exchange rate should be taken into consideration when

Table 13. Determining the ideal lag length of ER1 and IMP1

Lag	LogL	LR	FPE	AIC	SC	HQ
0	-1461.690	NA	47581.81	16.44596	16.48171	16.46046
1	-1430.576	61.18061	35085.82	16.14130	16.24855	16.18479
2	-1410.521	38.98329	29295.30	15.96091	16.13966*	16.03340*
3	-1404.433	11.69592	28617.70	15.93745	16.18771	16.03894
4	-1400.349	7.755908	28593.16	15.93650	16.25826	16.06698
5	-1398.735	3.027452	29374.46	15.96332	16.35657	16.12279
6	-1397.312	2.639890	30243.34	15.99226	16.45702	16.18073
7	-1392.141	9.469753	29856.52	15.97911	16.51537	16.19658
8	-1390.294	3.340894	30598.86	16.00330	16.61106	16.24977
9	-1384.814	9.790289	30108.19	15.98667	16.66593	16.26213
10	-1379.424	9.508047	29658.70	15.97106	16.72181	16.27551
11	-1367.885	20.09531	27268.98	15.88635	16.70861	16.21980
12	-1347.620	34.83877*	22733.10*	15.70359*	16.59735	16.06604

Table 14. ER1-IMP1 toda-yamamoto causality analysis results

Direction of Causality	Lag Length	P Probability Value
From ER1 to IMP1	13	0,0878
From IMP1 to ER1	13	0,3807

making a strategy to increase or decrease the import and export figures, but it is not possible to solve this problem with the exchange rate alone. Therefore, other factors should be considered besides the exchange rate. These factors are; interest rates, inflation, capital, cost, effective use of resources. In addition, Turkey's exports depend entirely on raw materials and intermediate goods imports. Therefore, imports should be reduced, production costs should be reduced, taxes should be distributed fairly and resources should be used effectively. Turkey, meanwhile, can solve these problems on behalf of a team that needs reform and innovation. These can be expressed in the form of high value-added technology intensive production, R&D, human capital investment, education, legal and political structural reforms.

FUTURE RESEARCH DIRECTIONS

In the following studies, a different set of variables mentioned above affecting the export and import should be determined. In these studies, regression, MARS, TAR and STAR will be discussed with different methods such as will contribute to the literature.

CONCLUSION

Since the second half of the 20th century, developments in the technological field have accelerated the globalization process. This process of globalization has increased the interaction between countries in many areas, especially in the fields of trade and economy. This has led to the revision and updating of the economic systems of importance among countries. As a matter of fact, with the collapse of the Bretton Woods system in 1973, countries switched from fixed exchange rate system to floating exchange rate system. These supply and demand fluctuations in exchange rates have been one of the important factors determining the volume of international trade. In addition, fluctuations have also significantly affected the direct or indirect investment process of countries.

The fact that exchange rates are at the beginning of macroeconomic indicators in the economic system also affects the export and import amounts of countries. In other words, the appreciation or loss of the local currency changes the export and import figures in the country. For example, the exchange rate in the last few years of rapid fluctuations occurring process in Turkey and increasing the export volume of the country's upward trend is seen to reduce the volume of imports. When the relationship between exchange rate and foreign trade was examined by the researchers, it was concluded that there was no significant relationship between these two variables in some studies, while in some studies there was no significant relationship.

According to the results of the cointegration obtained, all variables were cointegrated in the long run. In other words, it would be appropriate to take actions against the exchange rate in the strategies to be made for import and export figures. In this context, Toda-Yamamoto causality analysis was applied to the cointegrated variables because the cointegration relationship allows us to estimate only rather than the exact result. In the second stage of our analysis process, Toda-Yamamoto causality analysis was used. In addition to the Engle-Granger cointegration analysis, the reason for this analysis is the determination of the strength of this effect. In Toda-Yamamoto causality analysis, two different foreign exchange oriented variables and four foreign trade oriented variables were analyzed. Therefore, eight different analyzes were performed. In order to perform the said analysis, firstly the maximum degree of integration was determined and then the ideal lag length of the variables was determined. Subsequently, Toda-Yamomato analysis was examined with the help of VAR model. As a result of these eight analyzes, no causality relationship was determined. In other words, the exchange rate variable is not the first reason for Turkey's imports and exports.

ACKNOWLEDGEMENT

This study was derived from Özgür Kıyak's master thesis written in Karatay University.

REFERENCES

Acaravcı, A., ve Öztürk, İ. (2003). Döviz kurundaki değişkenliğin türkiye ihracatı üzerine etkisi: Ampirik bir çalışma. Review of Social. *Economic ve Business Studies*, *2*, 197–206.

Aktaş, C. (2010). Türkiye'de reel döviz kuru ile ihracat ve ithalat arasındaki ilişkinin VAR tekniğiyle analizi. *ZKÜ Sosyal Bilimler Dergisi*, *6*(11), 123–140.

Alhan, O., & Yüksel, S. (2018). Kadın Çalışanların Banka Büyüklüğü Ve Karlılığına Etkisi: Engle-Granger Eş Bütünleşme Analizi İle Türkiye Üzerine Bir Uygulama. *İş'te Davranış Dergisi*, *3*(2), 140-147.

Arize, A. C., & Osang, T., ve Slottje, D. J. (2000). Exchange-rate volatility and foreign trade: Evidence from thirteen LCD's. *Journal of Business & Economic Statistics*, *18*(1), 10–17.

Asteriou, D., Masatci, K., & Pılbeam, K. (2016). Exchange rate volatility and international trade: International evidence from the MINT countries. *Economic Modelling*, *58*, 133–140. doi:10.1016/j.econmod.2016.05.006

Bağış, B. (2016). *Döviz kuru sistemleri, uluslararası ticaret ve parite ilişkileri. (Editör: N. Eroğlu, H. Dinçer, ve Ü. Hacıoğlu), Uluslararası Finans Teori ve Politika* (pp. 361–408). Ankara, Turkey: Orion Kitabevi.

Bahmani-Oskooee, M., & Gelan, A. (2018). Exchange-Rate volatility and international trade performance: Evidence from 12 African countries. *Economic Analysis and Policy*, *58*, 14–21. doi:10.1016/j.eap.2017.12.005

Bahmani-Oskooee, M., & Harvey, H. (2012). US–Malaysia trade at commodity level and the role of the real exchange rate. *Global Economic Review*, *41*(1), 55–75. doi:10.1080/1226508X.2012.655028

Bahmani-Oskooee, M., Iqbal, J., & Salam, M. (2016). Short run and long run effects of exchange rate volatility on commodity trade between Pakistan and Japan. *Economic Analysis and Policy*, *52*, 131–142. doi:10.1016/j.eap.2016.09.002

Barışık, S. (2001). Para kurulu sistemi, üstünlükleri ve zayıf yönleri. *Gazi Üniversitesi İktisadi ve İdari Bilimler Fakültesi Dergisi*, *3*(2), 51–68.

Çakmak, H. K. (2004). Stratejik dış ticaret politikaları. *Akdeniz İ. İ. B. F. Dergisi*, *7*, 48–66.

Calvo, G. A., & Mishkin, F. S. (2003). The mirage of exchange rate regimes for emerging market countries. *Journal of Economic Perspectives*, *17*(4), 99–118. doi:10.1257/089533003772034916

Carbaugh, R. J. (2005). *International economics* (10th ed.). Canada: South-Western.

Cheung, Y. W., & Sengupta, R. (2013). Impact of exchange rate movements on exports: An analysis of Indian non-financial sector firms. *Journal of International Money and Finance*, *39*, 231–245. doi:10.1016/j.jimonfin.2013.06.026

Choudhry, T., & Hassan, S. S. (2015). Exchange rate volatility and UK imports from developing countries: The effect of the global financial crisis. *Journal of International Financial Markets, Institutions and Money*, *39*, 89–101. doi:10.1016/j.intfin.2015.07.004

Dilber, İ., ve Kılıç, J. (2018). Türkiye'de turizm gelirleri ile ekonomik büyüme ilişkisi: Engle granger eşbütünleşme testi ve VAR model. TESAM Akademi Dergisi, 5(2), 95–118.

Dinçer, H., Hacıoğlu, Ü., & Yüksel, S. (2016). The impacts of financial variables on employment planning in Turkish banking sector. *International Journal of Sustainable Entrepreneurship and Corporate Social Responsibility*, *1*(2), 1–20. doi:10.4018/IJSECSR.2016070101

Dinçer, H., Hacıoğlu, Ü., & Yüksel, S. (2018a). Determining influencing factors of currency exchange rate for decision making in global economy using MARS method. In Geopolitics and strategic management in the global economy (pp. 261–273). Hershey, PA: IGI Global. doi:10.4018/978-1-5225-2673-5.ch013

Dinçer, H., & Yüksel, S. (2018). Financial sector-based analysis of the G20 economies using the integrated decision-making approach with DEMATEL and TOPSIS. In *Emerging trends in banking and finance* (pp. 210–223). Cham, Switzerland: Springer. doi:10.1007/978-3-030-01784-2_13

Dinçer, H., Yüksel, S., & Adalı, Z. (2017). Identifying causality relationship between energy consumption and economic growth in developed countries. *International Business and Accounting Research Journal*, *1*(2), 71–81. doi:10.15294/ibarj.v1i2.9

Dinçer, H., Yuksel, S., & Adalı, Z. (2018b). Relationship between non-performing loans, industry, and economic growth of the African economies and policy recommendations for global growth. In Globalization and trade integration in developing countries (pp. 203–228). Hershey, PA: IGI Global. doi:10.4018/978-1-5225-4032-8.ch009

Dinçer, H., Yüksel, S., Adalı, Z., & Aydın, R. (2019a). Evaluating the role of research and development and technology investments on economic development of E7 countries. In Organizational transformation and managing innovation in the fourth industrial revolution (pp. 245-263). Hershey, PA: IGI Global.

Dinçer, H., Yüksel, S., Pınarbaşı, F., & Çetiner, İ. T. (2019b). Measurement of economic and banking stability in emerging markets by considering income inequality and nonperforming loans. In Maintaining financial stability in times of risk and uncertainty (pp. 49–68). Hershey, PA: IGI Global. doi:10.4018/978-1-5225-7208-4.ch003

Dinçer, H., Yüksel, S., & Şenel, S. (2018c). Analyzing the global risks for the financial crisis after the great depression using comparative hybrid hesitant fuzzy decision-making models: Policy recommendations for sustainable economic growth. *Sustainability*, *10*(9), 3126. doi:10.3390u10093126

Duasa, J. (2009). Exchange rate shock on Malaysian prices of imports and exports: An empirical analysis. *Journal of Economic Cooperation and Development*, *30*(3), 99–114.

Eğilmez, M. (2012). Tarife dışı engeller. Retrieved from http://www.mahfiegilmez.com/2012/11/tarifeds-engeller.html. Erişim Tarihi: 26.11.2012.

Engle, R. F., & Granger, C. W. J. (1987). Co-integration and error correction : Representation, estimation, and testing. *Econometrica*, *55*(2), 251–276. doi:10.2307/1913236

Erkılıç, S. (2006). *Türkiye'de Carî Açığın Belirleyicileri*. Ankara, Turkey: Uzmanlık Yeterlilik Tezi.

Ersin, İ. (2018). İhracata Dayalı Büyüme Hipotezinin Test Edilmesi: MINT Ülkeleri Örneği. *Ekonomi İşletme ve Maliye Araştırmaları Dergisi*, *1*(1), 26–38.

Esen, Ö. (2012). Türkiye'de döviz kuru belirsizliğinin ihracat üzerine etkisi. *Finans Politik ve Ekonomik Yorumlar*, *49*(568), 89.

Eti, S. (2019). The use of quantitative methods in investment decisions: a literature review. In Handbook of research on global issues in financial communication and investment decision making (pp. 256–275). Hershey, PA: IGI Global. doi:10.4018/978-1-5225-9265-5.ch013

Eti, S., Dinçer, H., & Yüksel, S. (2019). G20 Ülkelerinde Bankacılık Sektörünün 5 Yıllık Geleceğinin Arıma Yöntemi İle Tahmin Edilmesi. *Uluslararası Hukuk ve Sosyal Bilim Araştırmaları Dergisi*, *1*(1), 26–38.

Gök, A. (2006). Alternatif döviz kuru sistemleri. *Marmara Üniversitesi İİBF Dergisi*, *21*(1), 131–145.

Gül, E., ve Ekinci, A. (2006). Türkiye'de reel döviz kuru ile ihracat ve ithalat arasındaki nedensellik ilişkisi: 1990 – 2006. Dumlupınar Üniversitesi Sosyal Bilimler Dergisi, (16), 165–190.

Hacıoğlu, Ü., & Dinçer, H. (2013). Evaluation of conflict hazard and financial risk in the E7 economies' capital markets. *Zbornik radova Ekonomskog fakulteta u Rijeci, časopis za ekonomsku teoriju i praksu-Proceedings of Rijeka Faculty of Economics. Journal of Economics and Business*, *31*(1), 79–102.

Hacıoğlu, Ü., Dinçer, H., & Parlak, B. (2015). An assessment on inflation risk and its effects on business operations. In Handbook of research on strategic developments and regulatory practice in global finance (pp. 197–216). Hershey, PA: IGI Global. doi:10.4018/978-1-4666-7288-8.ch013

Hacıoğlu, Ü., Dinçer, H., & Parlak, B. (2015). An assessment on inflation risk and its effects on business operations. In Handbook of research on strategic developments and regulatory practice in global finance (pp. 197–216). Hershey, PA: IGI Global. doi:10.4018/978-1-4666-7288-8.ch013

Hanke, S. H. (2002). Currency boards. *The annals of the American academy of political and social science*, *579*(1), 87–105. doi:10.1177/000271620257900107

Hausmann, R., Hwang, J., & Rodrik, D. (2007). What you export matters. *Journal of Economic Growth*, *12*(1), 1–25. doi:10.100710887-006-9009-4

İnan, E. A. (2002). Kur rejimi tercihi ve Türkiye. Bankacılık Dergisi, 1–10.

Ison, S., & Wall, S. (2007). Economics (4th Ed.). London, UK: Pearson Education.

Karaçor, Z., & Gerçeker, M. (2012). Reel döviz kuru ve dış ticaret ilişkisi: Türkiye örneği (2003 - 2010). SÜ İİBF Sosyal ve Ekonomik Araştırmalar Dergisi, (23), 289–312.

Karagöz, M., & Doğan, Ç. (2005). Döviz kuru dış ticaret ilişkisi: Türkiye örneği. *Fırat Üniversitesi Sosyal Bilimler Dergisi*, *15*(2), 219–228.

Karluk, R. (2009). *Uluslararası Ekonomi Teori Politika*. İstanbul, Turkey: Beta Yayınevi.

Kasman, A., ve Kasman, S. (2005). Exchange rate uncertainty in turkey and its impact on export volume. *ODTÜ Gelisme Dergisi*, *32*(1), 41–58.

Kaya, A. A., ve Güçlü, M. (. (2005). Döviz kuru rejimleri, krizler ve arayışlar. *Ekonomik Yaklaşım Dergisi*, *16*(55), 1–15. doi:10.5455/ey.10517

Kaya, F. (2011). *Dış Ticaret İşlemleri Yönetimi*. İstanbul, Turkey: Beta Yayınevi.

Kaymakcı, O., Avcı, N., & Şen, R. (2007). *Uluslararası Ticarete Giriş*. Ankara, Turkey: Nobel Yayıncılık.

Kemeç, A., & Kösekahyaoğlu, L. (2015). J eğrisi analizi ve türkiye üzerine bir uygulama. Uluslararası İktisadi ve İdari Bilimler Dergisi, (December), 5–29.

Kenen, P. (2001). *The international financial architecture: What's new? What's missing?* Washington, DC: Institute for International Economics.

Kılavuz, E., & Altay Topcu, B., & Tülüce, N. S. (2011). Yükselen ekonomilerde döviz kuru rejimi seçimi: Ampirik bir analiz. *Erciyes Üniversitesi Sosyal Bilimler Enstitüsü Dergisi*, *1*(30), 83–109.

Kılıç, E. (2009). Türk imalat sektöründe ihracat, ithalat ve döviz kuru arasındaki ilişkilerin zaman serisi analizi. In Econ Anadolu 2009: Anadolu International Conference in Economics. Eskişehir, Turkey.

Kim, C. B. (2017). Does exchange rate volatility affect Korea's seaborne import volume? *Asian Journal of Shipping and Logistics*, *33*(1), 43–50. doi:10.1016/j.ajsl.2017.03.006

Kızıldemir, C. (2013). Klasik Yaklaşım. Retrieved from https://www.paranomist.com/klasik-yaklasim.html, Erişim Tarihi: 17.09.2013.

Kodongo, O., & Ojah, K. (2013). Real exchange rates, trade balance and capital flows in Africa. *Journal of Economics and Business*, *66*, 22–46. doi:10.1016/j.jeconbus.2012.12.002

Kohler, A., & Ferjani, A. (2018). Exchange rate effects: A case study of the export performance of the swiss agriculture and food Sector. *World Economy*, *41*(2), 494–518. doi:10.1111/twec.12611

Köse, N., & Ay, A., & Topallı, N. (2008). Döviz kuru oynaklığının ihracata etkisi: Türkiye örneği (1995 - 2008). *Gazi Üniversitesi İktisadi ve İdari Bilimler Fakültesi Dergisi*, *10*(2), 25–45.

Krugman, P. (1989). Difference in income elasticities and trends in real exchange rates. *European Economic Review*, *33*(5), 1301–1046. doi:10.1016/0014-2921(89)90013-5

Levi, M. D. (2009). *International finance* (5th ed.). London, UK: Routledge.

Mishkin, F. S. (2018). *Makroekonomi Politika ve Uygulama. (Edsitör: S. Sezgin ve M. Şentürk)* (2nd ed.). Ankara, Turkey: Nobel Yayıncılık.

Moosa, I. A. (2006). *Exchange rate regimes: fixed, flexible or something in between?* New York: Palgrave Macmillan.

Onafowora, O. A., & Owoye, O. (2008). Exchange rate volatility and export growth in Nigeria. *Applied Economics*, *40*(12), 1547–1556. doi:10.1080/00036840600827676

Özbek, D. (1998). Doviz kuru sisteminde seçenekler. *Ekonomik Yaklaşım Dergisi*, *9*(29), 17–36. doi:10.5455/ey.10285

Özdemir, K. A., & Şahinbeyoğlu, G. (2000). Alternatif döviz kuru sistemleri. Türkiye Cumhuriyet Merkez Bankası Araştırma Genel Müdürlüğü Tartışma Tebliği.

Öztürk, S., & Gövdere, B. (2004). Para kurulu yaklaşımı ve bulgaristan deneyimi. *Journal of Political Science*, *31*, 95–112.

Saatçioğlu, C., & Karaca, O. (2004). Döviz kuru belirsizliğinin ihracata etkisi: Türkiye örneği. *Doğuş Üniversitesi Dergisi*, *5*(2), 183–195. doi:10.31671/dogus.2019.296

Senadza, B., & Diaba, D. D. (2017). Effect of exchange rate volatility on trade in Sub-Saharan Africa. *Journal of African Trade*, *4*(1-2), 20–36. doi:10.1016/j.joat.2017.12.002

Serenis, D., & Tsounis, N. (2013). Exchange rate volatility and foreign trade: The case for Cyprus and Croatia. *Procedia Economics and Finance*, *5*, 677–685. doi:10.1016/S2212-5671(13)00079-8

Seyidoğlu, H. (2003a). *Uluslararası Finans (4.Baskı)*. İstanbul, Turkey: Güzem Can Yayınları.

Tarı, R., & Yıldırım, D. Ç. (2009). Döviz Kuru Belirsizliğinin İhracata Etkisi: Türkiye İçin Bir Uygulama. Celal Bayar Üniversiteis İİBF Yönetim ve Ekonomi, 16(2), 95–105.

Toda, H. Y., & Yamamoto, T. (1995). Statistical inference in vector autoregressions with possibly ıntegrated processes. *Journal of Econometrics*, *66*(1–2), 225–250. doi:10.1016/0304-4076(94)01616-8

Tomanbay, M. (2014). *Uluslararası Ticaret ve Finansmanı*. Ankara, Turkey: Gazi Kitabevi.

Turan, Z., & Öztürk, Y. K. (2016). Keynes sistemi ve bekleyişlerin sisteme katkısı. Niğde Üniversitesi İktisadi ve İdari Bilimler Fakültesi Dergisi, 9(2).

Williamson, S. D. (2014). *Macroeconomics* (5th ed.). London, UK: Pearson Education.

Yamak, R., & Korkmaz, A. (2005). Reel döviz kuru ve dış ticaret dengesi ilişkisi. İstanbul Üniversitesi İktisat Fakültesi Ekonometri ve İstatistik Dergisi, (2), 16–38.

Yamak, R., & Akyazı, H. (2010). Fiyat istikrarının sağlanmasında para kurulu sistemi ve Türkiye. *Atatürk Üniversitesi İktisadi ve İdari Bilimler Dergisi*, *12*(1), 1–26.

Yanar, R. (2008). Gelişmekte olan ülkelerde döviz kuru rejim tercihinin makro ekonomik performans üzerine etkileri. *Gaziantep Üniversitesi Sosyal Bilimler Dergisi*, *7*(2), 255–270.

Yapraklı, S. (2009). Türkiye'de esnek döviz kuru rejimi altında dış açıkların belirleyicileri: Sınır testi yaklaşımı giriş. Ankara Üniversitesi Sbf Dergisi, 141–164.

Yücel, F. (2006). Dış ticaretin belirleyicileri üzerine teorik bir yaklaşım. *Sosyo Ekonomi*, *2*, 46–68.

Yüksel, S. (2016). Rusya ekonomisinde büyüme, işsizlik ve enflasyon arasındaki nedensellik ilişkileri. *Finans Politik ve Ekonomik Yorumlar*, *53*(614), 43–56.

Yüksel, S., Dinçer, H., & Meral, Y. (2019). Financial analysis of international energy trade: A strategic outlook for EU-15. *Energies*, *12*(3), 431. doi:10.3390/en12030431

Yüksel, S., & Kavak, P. T. (2019). Do financial investment decisions affect economic development?: An analysis on mortgage loans in Turkey. In Handbook of research on global issues in financial communication and investment decision making (pp. 168-191). Hershey, PA: IGI Global.

Yüksel, S., & Özsarı, M. (2016). Impact of consumer loans on inflation and current account deficit: A Toda Yamamoto causality test for Turkey. *World Journal of Applied Economics*, *2*(2), 3–14. doi:10.22440/wjae.2.2.1

Zengin, S., Yüksel, S., & Kartal, M. T. (2018). Understanding the factors that affect foreign direct investment in Turkey by using mars method. *Finansal Araştırmalar ve Çalışmalar Dergisi*, *10*(18), 1309–1123.

KEY TERMS AND DEFINITIONS

MINT: Mexico, Indonesia, Nigeria, and Turkey.
R&D: Research and Development.
Stationary Analysis: It aims to identify whether there is a unit root in the series or not.
US: United States.
USD: American dollar.

Chapter 3
The Effects of Exchange Rate on Export Performance in Tanzania:
An Empirical Research for Financial Competition

Haroub Hamad Omar
D-Tree International, Tanzania

Nildag Basak Ceylan
Ankara Yildirim Beyazit University, Turkey

Ayhan Kapusuzoglu
Ankara Yildirim Beyazit University, Turkey

ABSTRACT

The chapter analyzes the effects of exchange rate of Tanzanian shilling on the country's exports performance applying Vector Auto-Regressive (VAR) model covering the sample period from 1993:Q1 to 2016:Q4. Cointegration and causality tests are performed to investigate the short- and long-term relationships between the variables to evaluate the financial competition. The results show that; there is no long-term relationship (cointegration) between exchange rates and exports and between foreign demand and exports. Moreover, the results of causality test show no short-term relationship (causality) between exchange rates and exports and between foreign demand and exports. As the findings suggest, the exchange rate level of Tanzanian shilling (in nominal terms) does not statistic-significantly affect the country's exports performance.

DOI: 10.4018/978-1-7998-2559-3.ch003

INTRODUCTION

While in the last touches of World War II, in 1944, when the world was resuming to normality, an international agreement commonly known as Bretton-Woods Agreement was signed for resetting a way through which countries can exchange their currencies and hence carry out trades between them. This came following the collapse of Gold Standard and the financial chaos in Europe and America (Great Depression of 1930s). Under Bretton-Woods system, countries could trade between them using exchange rates maintained within fixed values, once exchange rates between currencies established, governments were intervening to prevent them from deviating for more than one percent (1%) from the original set level. And most of currencies were pegged to either US Dollar or British Pound. Unfortunately, by 1971 it came to light that the US Dollar to which some of currencies were pegged had been overvalued and hence greatly suppressed its demand i.e. more dollars were in supply than what demanders could afford to buy because of overvaluation. This called for a review of the exchange rate regime and finally US Dollar devalued relative to other currencies, and currencies allowed to vary above the initial allowed interval of 1%, hence, this time currencies could vary up to 2.25 percent (2.25%). This was agreed in a common agreement known as Smithsonian Agreement by major trading countries. Very unfortunate, even after being allowed to vary for up to 2.25% below or above the set level, countries were struggling to keep their currencies within the margins of change. Hence, the fixed exchange rate regime proved failure and by March 1973 officially the world wrote a new history as a starting point of "Flexible Exchange Rate Regime" which is in practice until today. (Madura, 2011) By such a new flexible exchange rate system just set in, officially exchange rates among currencies started to fluctuate in response to prevailing market demand and supply conditions – no longer fixed margins of change. The new system got a quick acceptance among many countries fuelled by globalization move. Countries started liberalizing their economies and the trading among them increased in a vacuum. As a result, the level and variability at which one currency trade against such a free globalized world become of paramount importance to determine the country's competitiveness in the world business arena. Not alone to governments' policy makers, exchange rate became of the same importance to rest of actors who use foreign currencies such as investors, individual entities (importers and exporters) and multinational corporations. The fact that exchange rates are now freely adjusting to market conditions, means these stakeholders are not sure of exchange rate movements anymore, so uncertainty set in. The now new worries in the market i.e. uncertainty brought by level as well as frequency of fluctuation of exchange rates became a click to all stakeholders of international business and the same to the world of academia. Many studies so far have been taken but most focusing on effects of exchange rate volatility rather than level. Moreover, they are based on developed countries and recently on BRICS countries as potential power houses of the world, MINT countries and MENA countries. Considering the significance of the proposed topic from both theoretical and practical view, there are very limited studies conducted the impact of exchange rate on exports performance in Tanzania. In this direction, the aim of the study is to analyze the effects of exchange rate of Tanzanian shilling on the country's exports performance.

Foreign Exchange Market in Tanzania

Tanzania in her present state of the financial and trade regime, went through major three eras. Like many developing countries, SSA countries in particular, exchange rate regimes emerged in a controversial fashion. The country right after independence in 1961 (Mainland Tanzania) entered the first era of financial system, an interim-like phase, six-year period from 1961 – 1967. This is the period where the country was in deep analysis trying to define her way forward in economic direction. The practice during this time was import substitution industrialization (ISI) which aimed at boosting income growth. In this phase, private business venture and those foreign ones were given tariff protection and guaranteed against nationalization by the government. (Rweyemamu, 1973).

In 1967, the country passed the so called "Arusha Declaration" where socialist principles of the economy were official born and put into action. With such a socialist blueprint, the ventures which were once guaranteed against nationalization were nationalized, public sector expanded and allocation of resources were then centrally controlled. The new socialist principles took place from 1967 all the way to 1985 and during the period, exchange rate of Tanzanian Shilling (TZS) with respect to other foreign currencies ware highly controlled. As Rutasitara (2004) reported that, although the economy remained mixed during this period, but private sector was severely wounded. Other instruments of control specifically designed for the implementation of Arusha Declaration, a socialist blueprint, were Finance and Credit Plan which started from 1971/2 and The Foreign Exchange Plan. The plans were specifically for the allocation of credits in the economy and control of foreign exchange respectively. With these two instruments, foreign exchange and interest rates were made immaterial for the economy. Due to these policies, in the period from 1979 to 1985 earnings from real exports were declining although it is reported by Lipumba, Ndulu, Horton, and Plourde (1988) that other external factors also played a role behind lower revenues from real exports. Moreover, foreign reserves reached all time lower during 1980-1985 (Hanak, 1982)

As seen from Table 1, Tanzania experienced physical inefficiency and a total failure of her socialist model of the economy which was named "Socialism and Self-reliance" and reaching the year 1986, the country changed from controlled to market exchange rate system. But the on-going parallel exchange rate premium kept diminishing gradually from 1986 onwards and eventually disappeared in 1992. From

Table 1. Foreign exchange windows by mid-1980s

Window	Source of foreign exchange	Degree of control	Rate applying
Central Bank free resources	Official export earnings surrendered to Bank of Tanzania and limited commercial loans	High: By Bank of Tanzania	Official
Import support	Bilateral donor support	High: Treasury with donors	Official
Open general licence	World Bank and bilateral donors	Less control; more leaning towards market forces	Official
Export retention	Export proceeds retained by exporters	Low: Exporters' own decision	Mainly parallel rate
Own funded imports	Unofficial exports and foreign exchange transactions and private external capital	Low: Market forces, dominated by private business	Parallel rate
Project loans and grants	Various commodity exports	High; Government with foreign banks	Mainly official
Suppliers' credits	Supplier	Low: Involving suppliers and private business	Higher than the parallel rate to cover risk premium

Source: Adopted from Rutasitara (2004).

1986 going forward, the country embarked on bold steps towards economic reforms. Reforms involved unification of exchange rates, trade liberalization and institutional reforms of banking system which is now comprised by central bank; Bank of Tanzania, an apex institution and regulator of banking system and economic policy formulator, commercial banks and other financial institutions. From April 1992, private bureau de change was allowed in the country, foreign exchange auctions were established in June 1993. Moreover, as reforms continued, the inter-bank foreign exchange market (IFEM) was established in June 1994. Hence, from 1993 onward, there has been a perfectly fluctuating exchange rate regime in the country, and for this reason, the study covers the interval from 1993 to 2016.

Tanzania's Export Performance

According to Foreign Trade Statistics of 2013 which is published in 2014 by Tanzania's National Bureau of Statistics (NBS, 2016), it is reported that in 2013, Tanzania's total trade with the rest of the world increased by 4.5 percent to TZS. 28,127,678 million from TZS. 26,929,265 million recorded in 2012. Total exports declined by 5.0 percent to TZS. 8,223,206 million from TZS. 8,653,372 million while imports grew by 8.9 percent to TZS. 19,904,472 million from TZS. 18,275,893 million. As result, trade deficit widened by 21.4 percent to TZS. 6 11,681,266 million compared to the deficit of TZS. 9,622,522 million in 2012. On the other hand, looking on recent economic records of Tanzania, in the year 2015 the country recorded a growth in real GDP of 7% and was expected to record a growth of 7.2% in the year 2016 and the country remain in the list of top ten fastest growing economies in the world. (IMF, 2006). Hence, for a sustainability of such a good start, there must be sound policies in place, and to attain so, closer and curious look on exchange rate and exports is crucial. But as a matter of cursory look on trends, both exchange rate and exports seems to be sharply rising.

THEORETICAL BACKGROUND

As human beings struggle to produce goods and services to cover their far wide and variety of needs due to their nature of having unlimited wants, what is obvious here is the fact that throughout history no single country or nation evolved to be self-sufficient i.e. producing everything for her citizens and needs nothing from abroad – never happened, and if such is the reality, that means countries need to trade among themselves to supplement what they cannot produce locally or say what they cannot efficiently produce. Looking at 200 plus countries around the globe, it is seen that while other countries are super rich in natural resources like oil, gas, minerals, water bodies and livestock, other countries are blessed with entrepreneurial know how and managed to set a strong platform for technological advancements from automobile production to ship building, from agricultural technology to space research, to mention a few. Hence, with this kind of setup, trade among countries makes things balanced or in other words, trade between countries is something inevitable. The imbalance nature of natural wealth among countries in the world or as being generally called "natural endowment of factors of production" is considered by some as the key reason for countries to fail to attain self-sufficiency and so remain with no other choice except to trade with other countries in the world. Although the reason is logical but is not the only one, Kusi (2002) wrote that; other factors behind the massive growth of international trade nowadays are liberalisation and globalisation. In this case, Tanzania like most of SSA countries, from mid1980s to mid-1990s embarked on trade liberalization policies and opening her economy to reap from the opportunities presented by free trade movement across the globe. By the end of 1990s the country's trade doors were open and tariffs relaxed. (Kanaan, 2000). The study shades light on how trade especially the case of international trade (imports and exports) is linked to the financial system of the country in question and more so to the exchange rate regime in play. Two broad classification of exchange rate regimes – fixed and fluctuating; are looked. Thereafter, various theories of international trade are explained to build a strong theoretical understanding of the topic. Mercantilism, classical and modern theories are discussed. Also, the newly evolving theories of international trade are discussed.

Development of Trade and the Financial System

Trade evolves hand by hand with the financial system in any community. In the past, before invention of today's money, goods were exchanged for other goods, there were no money we all know today. If someone has abundant of food but short of say clothes, then the person could give food in return for clothes to someone else who has got extra clothes and willing to offer for food. This system is commonly known as "barter trade" in business language. With such a system of old times, came problems with it; if one is to exchange what he/she has for what he/she need then must find someone who possess the needed good or one who can offer the needed service and willing to exchange. This way, there was a problem of double coincidence of wants. (Khosa et al., 2015; Pikoulakis, 1995). Not alone the problem of double coincidence of wants, Grimwade (2003) pointed out other problems of barter trade such as lack of efficient transport facilities to move goods around and the problem of lack of clear measure of values i.e. how much of one product must be exchanged for an amount or number of another product. This means, there were immovability of goods for search of another party to trade with. Also, an unjust way of measuring values while transacting between parties. Out of effort to find a way to solve the problem of measuring equal values of two commodities to be transacted and others associated with barter trade, came in money. Money started as simply something generally accepted for exchange like sea shells in some communities and then gold emerged as mostly accept form of currency through which people could trade goods and services among them. Moreover, with gold as an accepted currency, the problem of double coincidence of wants was no more. The issue of difficulty in measuring values and fair quantities of goods to be exchanged, got a remedy using gold as currency. But gold system though successfully curbed the problems of barter trade of double coincidence of wants, it had problems of its own. Notably, the gold is heavy to carry around and another problem, for that it was heavy, so couldn't be carried in privacy. Everyone could simply know if someone carries gold and so posed risk to the carrier. Hence, gold was all heavy, expensive and risky to carry around for transacting purpose. In another attempt to get rid of problems brought about by gold currency, paper money came in. Easy to carry around and can be carried privately without making those around aware of. With paper money, the world continued to base on the prevailing values of an ounce of gold (gold standard) for long time until the end world war one (WWI). This equally happened all over the globe and so was Tanzania which passed through various stages until now with her modern trade and financial system.

Exchange Rate Regimes and Trade

Exchange rate regimes refer to a way through which the value of country's currency in respect to other currencies of the world (exchange rate) is determined by the authorities of a country. Authorities here normally are central banks, the same for the case of Tanzania, where Bank of Tanzania (BOT) which is the central bank of the country oversee the system that determines exchange rate of Tanzanian shilling. It should be noted that, exchange rate regimes are different and can be applied at different degrees. Countries on the other hand are free to choose and apply any of the regimes in existence as far as it suits her economic expectations and political views. Countries does implement the exchange rate regime selected normally using the monetary policy but sometimes fiscal policy also can be used to implement the exchange rate regime in place. In the world, today where the roots of globalization get stronger and stronger, countries are becoming much more connected than ever before. This brings to the country external shocks like imported inflation, fall of exports volume and the like. Therefore, a proper exchange rate regime to curb down the shocks from abroad must be well defined and properly working. Such a system carefully determines the rate at which the country's currency can be bought or sold using foreign currencies. (Côté, 1994). And as trade between countries is done using foreign currencies, then how much it cost to buy a required amount of a foreign currency (exchange rate level) is of paramount importance. Moreover, frequency of change of the rate at which a currency can be exchanged (exchange rate volatility) again adds to the uncertainty of trade decisions among importers and exporters. This can take both expansionary and contractionary trend depending on whether a country is importer or exporter at a time. Although exchange rate regimes are generally categorized into two major umbrella groups; Fixed and Flexible exchange rate regimes, the sub-divisions are there as well and worthy revising. Different opinions regarding effectiveness of those regimes has been put forward with no consensus. Some studies found that flexible exchange rate regime does wonderful job to reduce financial shocks, but other studies refuse that hypothesis. Below, are explanations regarding different exchange rate regimes all over the world and the roles they play in influencing trade patterns of countries. The world's exchange rate regimes and volatility profile of exchange rate regimes reported in Table 2 and Table 3 respectively.

Fixed Exchange Rate Regime

This regime is sometimes called "Pegged" exchange rate system. With this system, the value of country's currency in respect to other currencies (exchange rate) is put fixed by pegging it to either a currency of another country, e.g. attaching the value of Tanzanian shilling to say US Dollar, pegging to a basket of other currencies, e.g. attaching the value of Tanzanian shilling to say US Dollar, British Pound and Euro in their combination, an index like or even pegging the currency to a value of valuable minerals example gold such that as the price of an ounce of gold moves so is the value/exchange rate of the country's currency in respect to other foreign currencies. (Khosa et al., 2015). Others say, the governments manipulate the value of currency. History shows that, the beginning of fixed exchange rate regime is the beginning of gold standard all the way back since 1876 when values of paper money started to be pegged to the value of an ounce of gold. The system played role until 1913 when it was suspended because of an outbreak of world war one (WW1). When WW1 finished in 1944, countries tried to bring back the system by signing of an agreement commonly known as Bretton-Woods Agreement to continue maintaining the gold standard. But as most of countries were struggling to rebuild their destroyed, high capital public properties, so was very difficult to keep the agreement alive. Thus, in 1971 they sat down to review and modify the terms of Bretton-Woods Agreement and more relaxed terms were finally agreed in what later came to be known as Smithsonian Agreement. Unfortunately, this second agreement lasted only for two years up to 1973 where countries surrendered and left most of the world currencies free to flow as per the forces of demand and supply in the market. This marked the birth of quite a different regime known as "flexible exchange rate regime". The pegged or fixed exchange rate system can be applied

Table 2. World's exchange rate regimes

Regime		% of IMF Members
Hard peg	No separate legel tender	6.8
	Currency board	6.3
	Total	**13.1**
Soft peg	Conventional peg	23.0
	Stabilized arrangement	11.0
	Crawling peg	1.0
	Crawling-like arrangement	7.9
	Pegged exchange rate within horizontal bands	0.5
	Total	**43.4**
Floating	Floating	18.8
	Free floating	15.2
	Total	**34.0**
Residual	Other managed arrangement	9.4
	Total	**9.4**

Source: Exchange Arrangements and Exchange Restrictions Report (IMF, 2014) from AREAER database.

at different degrees. It can be "hard peg" or "soft peg". With hard peg, the country completely fix her national currency to other respected foreign currency (Currency board) or can even abandon her own currency and start using foreign currency (Currency Union/Dollarization). On the other hand, soft peg takes in when the national currency not 100% pegged to a foreign currency rather, it allows margins of changes or bands within which national currency can move, but not beyond the given band. This can be in a form of any of the following; Crawling narrow band (+/- 1%), Crawling peg (+/- 2%), Pegged within bands, Crawling broad peg and Fixed peg. (Levy-Yeyati & Sturzenegger, 2003). Theoretically at least, the fixed exchange rate regime is said to stabilize foreign trade movements in the country as it makes business predictable; no need for insurance against profit loss and protection policies. Moreover, it curbs down imported inflation especially when the currency is pegged strong compared to capital importation, administrative expenses of the system are low, financial sector becomes sound, inflation and interest rates becomes low and risk associated with exchange rate becomes mitigated. As there are advantages so are disadvantages for a country to use this system of foreign exchange. First, it calls for great deal of backup of foreign reserves, it distorts financial markets by rendering authorities with less

Table 3. Volatility profile of exchange rate regimes

Regime	Exchange Rate Volatility	Volatility of Foreign Currency Reserves
Float	High	Low
Soft Peg	Medium	Medium
Hard Peg	Low	High

Source: Levy-Yeyati & Sturzenegger (2003).

control over money supply in the economy (less autonomy) and domestic banks can severely suffer from liquidity problems during times of depression and recession.

Floating Exchange Rate Regime

By floating or as also known as flexible exchange rate regime it means a system of determining the rate at which the national currency will be exchanged for other foreign currencies but basing on market forces. By market forces here it means interplay of demand and supply movements in the global forex market. Floating exchange rate regime can take one of the two forms; managed floating exchange rate regime or free floating exchange rate regime. In a freely floating system, the authorities commonly central banks, completely leaves the market forces of demand and supply to determine a rate at which a national currency can be traded. On the other hand, managed floating exchange rate system, is regarded as a hybrid system that borrow features from both fixed and floating exchange rate regimes. With managed floating system, occasionally, the government through authorities like central bank becomes an important player in the foreign exchange market. The authority buys and sells foreign currencies in order to affect demand and supply in the country, but this is especially done to avoid exchange rates going far extreme, both low and upper levels. This way authority creates price stability and proper flow of trade activities in the country. As IMF (2014) put it, the intervention by the authorities can be direct or indirect and the purpose is to moderate the rate at which exchange rate moves. Also, it is meant to prevent undue fluctuations in price of local currency without putting in place a kind of policies that will predefine the exchange rates in economy. There are several indicators for managing exchange rates and are broadly judgmental. Examples of those indicators are balance of payment, international reserves and parallel market developments (As was the case in Tanzania from 1986 to 1992). Although authorities occasionally intervenes the movement of exchange rates to avoid far extreme movements that can drug the country into severe economic problems, still it is regarded as floating if intervention occurs only exceptionally and targeting on addressing disorderly market conditions and if the authorities have provided information or data confirming that intervention has been limited to at most three instances in the previous six months period, and each intervention done, must be lasting no more than three business days. (IMF, 2014). With floating exchange rate regime widely accepted today all over the world, contrary to the practice during the days of gold standard, plus the tremendous growth of international trade in the past two decades, it makes price movements unpredictable because prices are directly affected by movements of exchange rates. If a country's currency appreciates it directly affects export prices and if export prices are elastic can easily pull down the exports volume of a country because the country's domestically produced goods and services will be expensive and importers abroad can easily switch and buy from other supplier countries. Meanwhile, if the country's currency depreciates against a counterpart foreign currency, domestically produced goods and services becomes cheap to buyers abroad and hence can boost export volume and improves country's exports performance and balance of payment.

Floating exchange rate system like fixed one has got both goodies and biter consequences into the economy. Those pro-free markets believe that, for a country to be effectively free-market economy, a floating exchange rate regime should be in place for that it allows exchange rate equilibrium to adjust itself without intervention from the government. The floating regime also helps the economy smoothly absorb exogenous shocks brought about by the nature of interconnectedness of the world today. Another good side of floating regime is that, it automatically adjusts balance of payments because it reduces the need to use trade restrictions and capital control to attain exchange rate equilibrium. (Brada & Méndez,

1988). On the other hand, the floating exchange rate regime intensify uncertainty which is something of paramount importance for decisions of businesspersons especially in SSA countries. Exchange rate can quickly jump to far extreme levels, above the accustomed ranges. This way, if most of exporters in the countries are risk averse, they can easily cut down production levels and hence pull down the country's exports performance track. Such extreme moves of exchange rates (upward) are normally experienced during economic boom. Also, the floating exchange rate regime comes with a risk of imported inflation. If the national currency drastically dropped, it poses a risk of imported inflation and hence calls for the government to intervene. Imported inflations creates danger of affecting other economic variables in the economy and so the authorities necessitated to take action to control the phenomenon. Imported inflation is a serious case and so taken with due care especially by the inflation-targeting countries. Inflation-targeting economies adjusts the rate of interest in order to mitigate imported inflation, and although proves successfully in the short run, but in the long run tends to suppress profitability of domestic businesses. (Khosa et al., 2015). Tanzania on her case, implements a floating exchange rate system, whereas from 1986 to 1992 there were parallel exchange rates but now officially over, and only one exchange rate is in play. The country from 1993 to date, is steadily progressing in financial development. Now has got well united, connected and efficient foreign currency market with the target being not inflation, rather monetary aggregate. With such a target, the central bank (BOT) focus on attaining the intended monetary aggregate rate of growth using different instruments. Such a target is normally the national anchor of the official exchange rate regime in play. By monetary aggregate, it refers to variables such as reserve money, quick money supply (M1) and broad money supply (M2)

Invention of money completely revolutionized trading practices especially by easing payment and valuation of good and services. Moreover, gold standard on its own played a great deal in stabilizing exchange rate which was the birth of fixed exchange rate regime in the world. The failure of gold standard made it necessary for most countries to let their local currencies float in response to demand and supply forces in the global forex market. Countries, while allowing their currencies to flow, they tend to focus on special aspect of the economy as the anchor for exchange rate regimes. There are those inflation-targeting and those monetary-aggregate targeting like Tanzania. In the following parts below, reasons as to why countries must trade has been put forward in several theories. The package for each of the most prominent theories of international trade are revised.

LITERATURE REVIEW

Proponents of managed flexible exchange rate regime and those of fixed exchange rate regime are often of the view that; frequent change of the country's currency tends to depress the exports volume. This means that, the more frequent the exchange rate keeps on changing the more negatively the exports performance of a country is affected. This comes because of increased riskiness in the business transactions and hence negatively influence the allocation of resources. When the local currency increase in value (appreciation of local currency) the price of exports to importers abroad increases compared to their previous price position, hence it is causing a contraction in foreigners' demand to buy locally produced goods and services. When the local currency decrease in value (depreciation of local currency) the demand of foreigners abroad to buy locally produced goods becomes stimulated as those goods and services becomes pricewise competitive. Although both theories and empirical findings failed to provide a clear answer to this long-term debate, but the widespread view is as explained above being the view of those who supports managed flexible and fixed exchange rate regimes. Baum et al. (2004) in their efforts to study the effects of exchange rate uncertainty on trade indicated that, there have been a huge number of theoretical analysis regarding this topic. Among them, the notable ones are: Ethier (1973), Clark (1973), Baron (1976), Cushman (1986), Perée & Steinherr (1989) etc. Unlike the empirical side, at least the theoretical analysis of the topic is not so much ambiguous. There are several theories used to explain the impact of exchange rate changes in relation to exports performance and below are few of them.

The existing literature regarding the relationship between exchange rate and exports has been extensively examined. Both theoretical arguments and empirical findings has been careful reviewed and it is possible to say that there is no confirmed empirical findings that support any of proposed direction of relationship between these two variables (whether negative, positive or no-relationship). Although many of relevant empirical studies find negative relationship, some studies show a positive relationship between exchange rate (both level and volatility) and exports (See Table 4 below for a summary). Moreover, other empirical findings show that the two variables are not related anyhow. This is same as to say, although the theoretical side of the relationship seems to be somewhat straight forward, but so far, the empirical literature on the topic is vague and remain a puzzle yet to be solved. Another thing worthy noting here is the fact that, the said empirical findings are based on studies undertaken in developed countries or at least in emerging economies, but for the case of Tanzania, the relationship is not yet extensively studied. (Khosa et al., 2015; Nkurunziza, 2016; Yazidi, 2013). Also, different measures of exchange rates (level and volatility measures) are applied without uniformity and various models of analysis are used with no consensus. The pioneer work is the paper by IMF (1984), then a stream of prominent studies follow. Those include Chowdhury (1993), Côté (1994), (McKenzie, 1999) and the recent one is by Bahmani-Oskooee & Hegerty (2007). The last three studies are review of previous empirical findings. They provide a summary and show how vague the relationship still is.

RESEARCH METHODOLOGY

In order to test the relationship between the exchange rate of Tanzanian shilling and Tanzania's exports performance, the dataset used in the analysis of this study are secondary in nature (time series) and collected from two official sources; International Monetary Fund's International Financial Statistics (IFS) and the central bank of Tanzania known as Bank of Tanzania (BOT) via its regular quarterly economic review reports of the country (Tanzania) freely available online (in the bank's website) for public use. The data, of all variables (three variables) are collected as quarterly averages covering the period from 1993:Q1 - 2016:Q4. The focus is on quarterly data rather than semi-annual because it reduces time aggregation bias and capture both short and long-run behaviours if any. All variables during empirical analysis are converted and expressed in logarithm form. In a nutshell, two variables are the main; exchange rate (USD/TZS) and exports. Other variable used is "foreign demand" of Tanzania's exports proxied by Industrial Production Index (IPI) of six among ten major trade partner countries to Tanzania. Referring to Akhtar and Hilton (1984), Chowdhury (1993) and Bahmani-Oskooee and Hegerty (2007), using nominal or real figures of exchange rates to analyse the effect has been an ongoing debate still. Some of the studies show that when nominal exchange rates were used it has a significant effect on exports. (Akhtar & Hilton, 1984; Hooper & Kohlhagen, 1978). Others find that when real figures of exchange rate are used, export is significantly affected. (Cushman, 1986; Kenen & Rodrik, 1986). Other studies report that whether nominal or real data are used results are qualitatively similar. (Koray

Table 4. Summary of some past empirical studies and their findings

Research Study	Data	Period	Model	Result
Vergil (2002)	Bilateral	1990-2000	Cointegration	Negative
Ozbay (1999)	Aggregate	1988-1997	Cointegration	Negative
Yuksel et al. (2012)	Aggregate	2003-2010	OLS	Negative
Koray & Lastrapes (1989)	Bilateral	1973-1985	VAR	Negative
Chowdhury (1993)	Aggregate	1973-1990	VAR	Negative
Arize et al. (2003)	Aggregate	1973-2004	Cointegration, ECM	Negative
Kenen & Rodrik (1986)	Aggregate	1975-1984	OLS	Negative
Nkurunziza (2016)	Aggregate	1996-2013	OLS	Positive
Kasman & Kasman (2005)	Aggregate	1982-2001	Cointegration	Positive
Yee et al. (2016)	Aggregate	1975-2013	OLS	Positive
McKenzie & Brooks (1997)	Bilateral	1973-1992	OLS	Positive
Genc & Artar (2014)	Aggregate	1985-2012	Panel Cointegration	Cointegrated
Ahmad et al. (2016)	Aggregate	1970-2009	VECM	Positive
Asseery & Peel (1991)	Aggregate	1972-1987	ARIMA	Positive
Sandu & Ghiba (2011)	Aggregate	2003-2011	VAR	Positive
Tanreyro (2007)	Bilateral	1970-1997	Panel Pseudo	No Effect
Aristotelous (2001)	Bilateral	1889-1999	Granger	No Effect
Lee (1999)	Sectoral	1973-1992	VAR	No Effect

& Lastrapes, 1989). Hence, with such ambiguous nature regarding acceptable ways of measuring the variables, this study took nominal figures of exchange rates and exports. The quarterly currency rate of Tanzanian shilling was taken as the price of single unit of US dollar (US$/TZS), showing number of shillings that buys a single US dollar such that an increase in the exchange rate means depreciation of TZS against the US$. Such an exchange rate is used since most of trade deals between Tanzania and the trading partners are executed in US$. In the country's domestic trading, the US$ is the dominant among all foreign currencies locally accepted. Hence, it is expected that given the fluctuation of the US dollar in the international markets, it is indirectly translated or passed to the Tanzanian shilling. Therefore, exploring Tanzania's exports dynamism using the dollar/shilling exchange rate would give a clear understanding of the country's export performance. Regarding the variable export, this study focused on the country's aggregate exports (value in local currencies) from Tanzania to the rest of the world. The study takes evidence from Tanzanian shilling's nominal, aggregate values of exports (as per previous studies), (Bahmani-Oskooee & Hegerty, 2007) to examine the nexus between exchange rate level and exports performance of the country. Like the case for exchange rate above, using nominal or real 50 figures of exports to analyze the effect has been an on-going debate again. The exports data are defined as the quarterly values of exports. Based on the export function, EXP = f (ER, FD), export being a dependent variable is a function of exchange rate and foreign demand (FD). The foreign demand variable (FD) is represented by quarterly average of industrial production index of six countries among top ten destinations of Tanzania's exports which is reported in Table 5.

Table 5. Tanzania's top ten exports destinations, 2007-2013

Rank	Country	Value (TZS Million)
1	Switzerland	6,554,325
2	South Africa	5,444,597
3	China	4,446,698
4	India	3,138,635
5	Kenya	2,180,217
6	Japan	2,165,946
7	Germany	1,535,269
8	Democratic Republic of Congo	1,390,316
9	Netherlands	1,103,758
10	Belgium	862,564

Source: Data from National Bureau of Statistics, Tanzania and author's own calculations

Exploratory Data Analysis

In the study, the data distribution is examined using standard descriptive statistics namely mean, median, standard deviation, skewness and kurtosis. Jarque and Bera (1980) test is conducted to ascertain the normality of the data distribution under the null hypothesis of normal distribution such that if result, J-B value is greater than zero, it is said to have deviated from the normal distribution assumption. Similarly, skewness and kurtosis represent the nature of departure from normality. In a normally distributed series, skewness is 0 and kurtosis is 3. Positive or negative skewness indicate asymmetry in the series and less than or greater than 3 kurtosis coefficients suggest flatness and peaked-ness, respectively. Also, the assumption that the errors terms are linearly independent of one another (uncorrelated with one another) was tested such that if the errors are correlated with one another, it is stated that they are auto correlated. To test for the existence of autocorrelation or not, the popular Breusch-Godfrey Serial correlation LM test was employed. As noted in (Brooks, 2014) the rejection/non-ejection rule would be given by selecting the appropriate region. Furthermore, to test for the presence of heteroscedasticity, the popular White test was employed in this study. This test involves testing the null hypothesis that the variance of the errors is constant (homoscedasticity) or no heteroscedasticity.

Test For Stationarity (Unit Root Test)

Most time series data are found to be non-stationary. A stochastic process is said to be stationary if its mean and variance are constant overtime, while the value of the covariance between two periods depend only on the gap between the periods and not the actual time at which this covariance is considered. If one or more of these conditions are not fulfilled then the process is said to be non-stationary (Charemza & Deadman, 1992). The most famous unit root test; Augmented Dickey-Fuller (ADF) test is conducted to investigate the property of time series data as proposed by Dickey and Fuller (1981).

Cointegration Test

Firstly, after stationarity is tested to prove that all variables are integrated at the same order I(1), the second stage in methodological process is to run a cointegration test. To perform this, Johansen cointegration test is used. This is proposed by Johansen and Juselius (1990), and Johansen (1991); (Johansen, 1995). The test is used both the Trace statistics and the maximum Eigenvalue tests. The optimal lag length in this test is based on using the Schwartz Information Criterion (SIC). Johansen's methodology takes its starting point in the vector auto regression (VAR) of order p. When the variables are found to be cointegrated, the relationship may be interpreted as a long run relationship. Since the study investigates the relationship between exchange rate and exports, then the hypothesis for the cointegration vectors are clearly defined. In order to test the hypothesis, the order of the cointegration vector needs to be determined first. The order (rank) of cointegration is determined by constructing the trace statistics and the estimated values of the characteristic roots or Eigenvalues.

Vector Autoregressive Model (VAR) and Granger Causality Test

It is admitted that error correction model can do a good job of pinpointing a short and long run effect, however it is usually not stable and thus not very useful in prediction, hence, the Vector Autoregressive (VAR) model is estimated in first-difference in case of absence of cointegrating relation among the variables by excluding the error correction term, $\gamma\epsilon_{t-1}$ for Granger causality with a short-term interactive feedback relationship following Granger (1988). This suggests empirical model has already been used in the context of exchange rate volatility and exports by a considerable number of studies. A VAR model of order p, where the order p represents the number of lags, that includes k variables. For each currency i, the following equations are estimated.

$$\blacklozenge lnEXP_t = \alpha + \sum_{t=1}^{p} u_i \Delta lnEXP_{t-1} + \sum_{t=1}^{p} v_i \Delta lnExRate_{t-1} + \sum_{t=1}^{p} w_i \Delta lnIPI_{t-1} + \varepsilon_t \ldots \quad (1)$$

$$\blacklozenge lnExRate_t = \alpha + \sum_{t=1}^{p} v_i \Delta lnExRate_{t-1} + \sum_{t=1}^{p} u_i \Delta lnEXP_{t-1} + \sum_{t=1}^{p} w_i \Delta lnIPI_{t-1} + \varepsilon_t .. \quad (2)$$

$$\blacklozenge lnIPI_t = \alpha + \sum_{t=1}^{p} w_i \Delta lnIPI_{t-1} + \sum_{t=1}^{p} u_i \Delta lnEXP_{t-1} + \sum_{t=1}^{p} v_i \Delta lnExRate_{t-1} + \varepsilon_t \ldots \quad (3)$$

where *lnEXP*=natural log of Export, *lnExRate*= natural log of exchange rate and *lnIPI* = natural log of industrial production index. In Equations (iii to v), α is a vector of constants, ε denotes the white noise error terms and t stands for the time lags. The optimum lag length, p, is determined using the Schwartz Information Criterion (SIC). A bivariate VAR is estimated and diagnostic tests are run to check for serial correlation, heteroscedasticity, parameter instability, and structural breaks, and all tests must satisfy a particular lag number under Schwartz Information Criterion (SIC).

EMPIRICAL FINDINGS

Descriptive Statistics

Summary statistics for the return series are presented in Table 6. All the variables have positive mean such that export (LOGEXP_SA) has the highest and industrial production index (proxy of foreign demand) has the lowest mean. Regarding the standard deviation, seasonally adjusted export (LOGEXP_SA) is more volatile than Tanzanian Shilling (LOGEXRATE) as they have higher standard deviation. In addition, the Jarque-Bera statistics for two variables; exports (LOGEXP_SA) and industrial production index (LOGIPI_SA) reject the null hypothesis that the series are normally distributed for all indices since the probability of JB test is equal to zero. For the variable exchange rate (LOGEXRATE), the JB test accepts the null hypothesis as the probability of the test is not equal to zero. All the signs of the skewness are negative for all three variables. Moreover, looking at the coefficients for kurtosis as a measure of peakedness or flatness of the distribution of the series, all return series are platykurtic (kurtosis value less than 3), this indicates that they are flat relative to normal. (Balanda & MacGillivray, 1988; Westfall, 2014).

Unit Root Test Results

In the study, Augmented Dickey-Fuller test - ADF (Dickey & Fuller, 1981) is used to test the stationarity. The choice of the lag length required for the test is based on Schwarz Information Criterion (SIC). The results derived from ADF unit root tests are presented in Table 7. Based on the test, in terms of ADF test including constant and constant and trend terms, at a level for all log return series, the null hypothesis

Table 6. Descriptive statistics

	LogExport_Sa	LogExRate	LogIpi_Sa
Mean	12.914	6.931	4.463
Median	13.000	7.009	4.461
Maximum	14.856	7.687	4.657
Minimum	10.586	5.846	4.189
Standard Deviation	1.308	0.449	0.152
Skewness	-0.005	-0.322	-0.190
Kurtosis	1.632	2.245	1.630
Jarque-Bera	7.478	3.942	8.078
Probability (JB)	0.023	0.139	0.017
Sum	1239.80	665.392	428.503
Sum Sq. Dev.	162.635	19.177	2.211
Observations	96	96	96

of a unit root process could not be rejected, except for exchange rate when tested 59 including "constant and trend". However, for all variables series under ADF test including constant and constant and trend term, the null hypothesis of a unit root can strongly be rejected at 1% significance level. Therefore, our tests results suggest that at level all variables series have a unit root. In other words, all variables appear to be integrated at the same order one, I(1).

Diagnostic Tests Results

For the purpose of avoiding spurious results; all assumptions of error term and residual diagnostic were tested. Also, the stability of VAR model was checked. The test result shows that the VAR satisfy stability condition as there is no root laying outside the unit circle. To test for the existence of autocorrelation or not, the popular Breusch-Godfrey Serial Correlation LM test was employed. The result noted that the null hypothesis can be rejected as error terms are linearly independent of one another. Furthermore, the result indicates that the null hypothesis; the variance of the errors is constant or no heteroscedasticity, cannot be rejected. In addition, the Jarque-Bera statistics reject the null hypothesis that the series are normally distributed for all indices since the probability of JB test is equal to zero.

Cointegration Test Results

All variables in the study are tested and found that they are integrated at the same order I(1). Thus, it gives justification to carry out cointegration test to find whether exchange rates of Tanzanian shilling and the country's exports have long run relationship or not. To this end, the Johansen cointegration test is used, as proposed by Johansen & Juselius (1990), Johansen (1991) and Johansen (1995). Table 8 reports the results of the test, and shows that there is no evidence of cointegration for both tests of Trace Statistics and MaxEigen Statistics. Both tests show that the null hypothesis cannot be rejected at 5% significance level. These results indicate that, there is no long run association between exchange rates and exports. Also, the results suggest that no long-run relationship found between industrial production index (IPI_SA) as a measure of foreign demand and exports. This way of testing for cointegration are used by several studies such as those of Vergil (2002), Özbay (1999), Arize et al. (2003) etc. among many others. The

Table 7. Unit root test results

	ADF – I(0)	
Variable	Constant	Constant and Trend
LogExp_Sa	-1.009	-2.704
LogExRate	-2.421	-4.457
LogIpi_Sa	-1.380	-3.353
	ADF – I(1)	
Variable	Constant	Constant and Trend
LogExp_Sa	-11.386***	-11.369***
LogExRate	-8.018***	-8.142***
LogIpi_Sa	-6.615***	-6.625***

Note: *, ** and *** indicate significance level at 10%, 5% and 1%, respectively

Table 8. Johansen-Juselius Cointegration Tests Results

Variables	Lags	Hypothesis	Trace Statistics	Max-Eigen Statistics	Summary
Exp_Sa &ExRate	1	r = 0	11.493	9.380	No Cointegration
	1	r ≤ 1	2.112	2.112	
Exp_Sa & Ipi_Sa	1	r = 0	11.621	10.365	No Cointegration
	1	r ≤ 1	1.255	1.255	

study by Kasman & Kasman (2005) finds almost the similar Johansen cointegration tests results such that out of four variables tested, three variables are found to have no cointegration.

Granger Causality Test Results

In this section exports (EXP_SA), exchange rate of Tanzanian shilling (ExRate) and industrial production index (IPI_SA) of six major trading partners to Tanzania are analyzed using Granger method. Table 9 shows the results of VAR Granger Causality/Block Exogeneity Wald Tests. In the case of exchange rates to fluctuations of exports, the null hypothesis could not be rejected i.e. exchange rate does not Granger Cause the exports as probability value is insignificant at 5% level. Regarding exports to exchange rate on the opposite, again the null hypothesis could not be rejected as the probability value is not significant at any level as seen in the table below. Moreover, the results show that, there is no causality relationship between exports and exchange rates and between exports and industrial production index. Such results are in line with the studies conducted by Mousavi & Leelavathi (2013) among others. In a nutshell, these results imply that when exchange rate moves, the exports volume of the country do not follow the move in any direction. This could be because exchange rate does responds more to exogenous factors in the global interplay of financial markets, especially the global money market unlike the case of exports which responds more to factors internal the economy.

CONCLUSION AND DISCUSSION

Using quarterly time series data for the period from 1993:Q1 to 2016:Q4, Vector Autoregressive (VAR) model was employed to test the relationship of Tanzanian shilling's exchange rates and exports. Granger Causality was tested to check the causality between three variables involved in this study; exchange rate, export and foreign demand (proxied by industrial production index of Tanzania's major trading partners). The VAR model has proven to be quite useful for describing the dynamic behaviour of economic and financial time series and for forecasting because it is flexible and it capture the linear interdependencies among multiple time series. Since classical linear regression models assume that series under inspection are stationary; then in this study, as an initial step, unit root tests to check for stationary nature of variables under consideration were carried out. ADF unit root test revealed that all the three variables; exports, exchange rates and industrial production index are stationary at first difference; therefore, they are said to be integrated of order one, I(1). Following the results of unit root rests that provided evidence that the three variables under investigation are at the same order (I), then cointegrating vector test was employed

The Effects of Exchange Rate on Export Performance in Tanzania

Table 9. VAR Granger causality/block exogeneity wald tests

Hypothesis	Lag	Chi-Square	P-Value
ExRate → Exp_Sa	1	1.243	0.264
Exp_Sa → ExRate	1	0.316	0.573
Ipi_Sa → Exp_Sa	1	3.440	0.063
Exp_Sa → Ipi_Sa	1	0.856	0.354

NOTE: Null hypothesis: "Does not Granger Cause" Hence, do not reject null hypothesis if P-Value is greater than 5%. That means, in this case, both exchange rate and foreign demand (IPI_SA) does not Granger Cause exports and it is the same for exports to exchange rate and foreign demand (IPI_SA).

to check if the variables have long-run association or not. To test for cointegration, the Johansen-Juselius method is used as the most widely used following approaches proposed in the past studies; (Engle & Granger, 1987; Granger, 1988; Johansen, 1991; Johansen & Juselius, 1990). The result of cointegration shows that there is no evidence of cointegration for both test of Trace statistics and Max Eigen statistics. Both test show that the null hypothesis cannot be rejected at 5% significance level. This result indicates that, there is no long-run association between exchange rates, exports and industrial production index. So, investigation of relationship between exchange rates and exports have been estimated via VAR approach since the cointegration tests confirmed that there is no existence of long-run associations and the VAR approach is basically the best for analysis of short-run dynamics. Results of Granger Causality tests for exchange rates, exports and foreign demand (IPI) reveal that in case of exchange rate to export fluctuation, the null hypothesis could not be rejected, that means exchange rate does not granger cause the country's exports as probability value is not significant at 5% level. Moreover, the null hypothesis cannot be rejected in case of exports to exchange rates as well as to industrial production index. Thus, exports cannot granger cause exchange rate and foreign demand. In addition, exchange rates and foreign demand does not granger cause exports i.e. no causality all the ways among variables.

SOLUTIONS AND RECOMMENDATIONS

According to the key findings of this study, any change in exchange rate movements or foreign demand will bring no statistically significant change to Tanzania's exports. Moreover, export movement brings no change to the exchange rates and foreign demand (lack of causality among variables). As the findings suggest, the exchange rate level of Tanzanian shilling (in nominal terms) does not affect statistical significantly the country's exports performance. Hence, the monetary policies of the country should not dwell on devaluation strategies to boost export, rather, the focus should be on encouraging entrepreneurial development and discouraging importation. This way could boost exports and improve the balance of payment and overall performance of the economy.

FUTURE RESEARCH DIRECTIONS

Investigation on the relationship between exchange rates and exports is as old as the floating exchange rate system itself. As results of this study reveal that exchange rates and foreign demand does very little to shift the aggregate exports volume in Tanzania, then it will give a much closer insight into the subject matter if the future studies retake the topic in a way that the variables will be tested as real variables (after being deflated) so that the effect of inflation, if any, could be examined. Moreover, as this study used aggregate data, so sector wise studies should be taken in the future as Tanzania embarks on industrialization and green revolution. This will give a comprehensive picture of the dynamism.

ACKNOWLEDGMENT

This paper is based on Haroub Hamad Omar's Master Thesis in Ankara Yildirim Beyazit University, Graduate School of Social Sciences, Ankara, Turkey. In addition to this, this study was orally presented at the III. Wroclaw Conference in Finance held between 13th-14th September 2017, Wroclaw, Poland and only the abstract was published in the conference proceedings.

REFERENCES

Ahmad, F., Draz, M. U., & Yang, S.-C. (2016). The nexus between exchange rate, exports and economic growth: Further evidence from Asia. Retrieved from https://ssrn.com/abstract=2758505

Akhtar, M. A., & Hilton, R. S. (1984). *Exchange rate uncertainty and international trade: Some conceptual issues and new estimates for Germany and the United States*. Federal Reserve Bank.

Aristotelous, K. (2001). Exchange-rate volatility, exchange-rate regime, and trade volume: Evidence from the UK–US export function (1889–1999). *Economics letters*, *72*(1), 87–94. doi:10.1016/S0165-1765(01)00414-1

Arize, A. C., Malindretos, J., & Kasibhatla, K. M. (2003). Does exchange-rate volatility depress export flows: The case of LDCs. *International Advances in Economic Research*, *9*(1), 7–19. doi:10.1007/BF02295297

Asseery, A., & Peel, D. A. (1991). The effects of exchange rate volatility on exports: Some new estimates. *Economics letters*, *37*(2), 173–177. doi:10.1016/0165-1765(91)90127-7

Bahmani-Oskooee, M., & Hegerty, S. W. (2007). Exchange rate volatility and trade flows: A review article. *Journal of Economic Studies (Glasgow, Scotland)*, *34*(3), 211–255. doi:10.1108/01443580710772777

Balanda, K. P., & MacGillivray, H. (1988). Kurtosis: A critical review. *The American statistician*, *42*(2), 111–119.

Baron, D. P. (1976). Fluctuating exchange rates and the pricing of exports. *Economic Inquiry*, *14*(3), 425–438. doi:10.1111/j.1465-7295.1976.tb00430.x

Baum, C. F., Caglayan, M., & Ozkan, N. (2004). Nonlinear effects of exchange rate volatility on the volume of bilateral exports. *Journal of Applied Econometrics*, *19*(1), 1–23. doi:10.1002/jae.725

Brada, J. C., & Méndez, J. A. (1988). Exchange rate risk, exchange rate regime and the volume of international trade. *Kyklos*, *41*(2), 263–280. doi:10.1111/j.1467-6435.1988.tb02309.x

Brooks, C. (2014). *Introductory econometrics for finance*. Cambridge University Press. doi:10.1017/CBO9781139540872

Charemza, W. W., & Deadman, D. F. (1992). *New directions in econometric practice*. Cambridge, UK: Edward Elgar.

Chowdhury, A. R. (1993). Does exchange rate volatility depress trade flows? Evidence from error-correction models. *The Review of Economics and Statistics*, 75(4), 700–706. doi:10.2307/2110025

Clark, P. B. (1973). Uncertainty, exchange risk, and the level of international trade. *Economic Inquiry*, 11(3), 302–313. doi:10.1111/j.1465-7295.1973.tb01063.x

Côté, A. (1994). *Exchange rate volatility and trade*. Bank of Canada.

Cushman, D. O. (1986). Has exchange risk depressed international trade? The impact of third country exchange risk. *Journal of International Money and Finance*, 5(3), 361–379. doi:10.1016/0261-5606(86)90035-5

Dickey, D. A., & Fuller, W. A. (1981). Likelihood ratio statistics for autoregressive time series with a unit root. *Econometrica*, 49(4), 1057–1072. doi:10.2307/1912517

Engle, R. F., & Granger, C. W. (1987). Co-integration and error correction: Representation, estimation, and testing. *Econometrica*, 55(2), 251–276. doi:10.2307/1913236

Ethier, W. (1973). International trade and the forward exchange market. *The American Economic Review*, 63(3), 494–503.

Genc, E. G., & Artar, O. K. (2014). The effect of exchange rates on exports and imports of emerging countries. *European Scientific Journal*, 10(13), 128–141.

Granger, C. W. (1988). Some recent development in a concept of causality. *Journal of Econometrics*, 39(1-2), 199–211. doi:10.1016/0304-4076(88)90045-0

Grimwade, N. (2003). *International trade: new patterns of trade, production and investment*. Routledge. doi:10.4324/9780203401668

Hanak, E. (1982). *The Tanzanian balance of payments crisis: causes, consequences, and lessons for a survival strategy*: Economic Research Bureau, University of Dar es Salaam.

Hooper, P., & Kohlhagen, S. W. (1978). The effect of exchange rate uncertainty on the prices and volume of international trade. *Journal of International Economics*, 8(4), 483–511. doi:10.1016/0022-1996(87)90001-8

IMF. (1984). *Exchange rate volatility and world trade*. International Monetary Fund, Occasional Paper No: 28. Retrieved from https://www.imf.org/en/Publications/Occasional-Papers/

IMF. (2006). Glossary of selected financial terms. Retrieved from http://www.imf.org/external/np/exr/glossary/showTerm.asp#91

IMF. (2014). Annual report on exchange rate arrangements and exchange restrictions. Retrieved from https://www.imf.org/en/Publications

Jarque, C. M., & Bera, A. K. (1980). Efficient tests for normality, homoscedasticity and serial independence of regression residuals. *Economics letters*, *6*(3), 255–259. doi:10.1016/0165-1765(80)90024-5

Johansen, S. (1991). Estimation and hypothesis testing of cointegration vectors in Gaussian vector autoregressive models. *Econometrica*, *59*(6), 1551–1580. doi:10.2307/2938278

Johansen, S. (1995). *Likelihood-based inference in cointegrated vector autoregressive models*. Oxford University Press on Demand. doi:10.1093/0198774508.001.0001

Johansen, S., & Juselius, K. (1990). Maximum likelihood estimation and inference on cointegration—With applications to the demand for money. *Oxford Bulletin of Economics and Statistics*, *52*(2), 169–210. doi:10.1111/j.1468-0084.1990.mp52002003.x

Kanaan, O. (2000). Tanzania's experience with trade liberalization. *Finance & Development*, *37*(2). Retrieved from https://www.imf.org/external/pubs/ft/fandd/2000/06/kanaan.htm

Kasman, A., & Kasman, S. (2005). Exchange rate uncertainty in Turkey and its impact on export volume. *ODTÜ Gelisme Dergisi*, *32*(1), 41–58.

Kenen, P. B., & Rodrik, D. (1986). Measuring and analyzing the effects of short-term volatility in real exchange rates. *The Review of Economics and Statistics*, *68*(2), 311–315. doi:10.2307/1925511

Khosa, J., Botha, I., & Pretorius, M. (2015). The impact of exchange rate volatility on emerging market exports: Original research. *Acta Commercii*, *15*(1), 1–11. doi:10.4102/ac.v15i1.257

Koray, F., & Lastrapes, W. D. (1989). Real exchange rate volatility and US bilateral trade: A VAR approach. *The review of economics and statistics*, *71*(4), 708–712. doi:10.2307/1928117

Kusi, N. K. (2002). *Trade liberalization and South Africa's export performance*. Paper presented at the 2002 Annual Forum at Glenburn Lodge, Muldersdrift: Trade and Industrial Policy Strategies.

Lee, J. (1999). The effect of exchange rate volatility on trade in durables. *Review of International Economics*, *7*(2), 189–201. doi:10.1111/1467-9396.00156

Levy-Yeyati, E., & Sturzenegger, F. (2003). A de facto classification of exchange rate regimes: A methodological note. *The American Economic Review*, *93*(4), 1173–1193. doi:10.1257/000282803769206250

Lipumba, N., Ndulu, B., Horton, S., & Plourde, A. (1988). A supply constrained macroeconometric model of Tanzania. *Economic Modelling*, *5*(4), 354–376. doi:10.1016/0264-9993(88)90009-0

Madura, J. (2011). *International financial management*. Cengage Learning.

McKenzie, M. D. (1999). The impact of exchange rate volatility on international trade flows. *Journal of Economic Surveys*, *13*(1), 71–106. doi:10.1111/1467-6419.00075

McKenzie, M. D., & Brooks, R. D. (1997). The impact of exchange rate volatility on German-US trade flows. *Journal of International Financial Markets, Institutions and Money*, *7*(1), 73–87. doi:10.1016/S1042-4431(97)00012-7

Mousavi, D., & Leelavathi, D. (2013). Agricultural export and exchange rates in India: The Granger causality approach. *International Journal of Scientific and Research Publications*, *3*(2), 1–8.

NBS. (2016). *National bureau of statistics: Foreign trade statistics 2013*.

Nkurunziza, F. (2016). Exchange rate volatility and Rwanda's balance of trade. *International Journal of Learning and Development, 6*(1), 104–135.

Ozbay, P. (1999). *The effect of exchange rate uncertainty on exports: A case study for Turkey*. Citeseer. Retrieved from www.citeseerx.ist.psu.edu

Perée, E., & Steinherr, A. (1989). Exchange rate uncertainty and foreign trade. *European Economic Review, 33*(6), 1241–1264. doi:10.1016/0014-2921(89)90095-0

Pikoulakis, E. (1995). *The exchange rate and the current account when prices evolve sluggishly: A simplification of the dynamics and a reconciliation with the absorption approach. International Macroeconomics* (pp. 126–143). Macmillan Education UK.

Rutasitara, L. (2004). *Exchange rate regimes and inflation in Tanzania*. The African Economic Research Consortium.

Rweyemamu, J. (1973). *Underdevelopment and industrialization in Tanzania: A study of perverse capitalist industrial development*. Oxford University Press.

Sandu, C., & Ghiba, N. (2011). The relationship between exchange rate and exports in Romania using a vector autoregressive model. *Annales Universitatis Apulensis: Series Oeconomica, 13*(2), 476–482.

Vergil, H. (2002). Exchange rate volatility in Turkey and its effect on trade flows. *Journal of Economic and Social Research, 4*(1), 83–99.

Westfall, P. H. (2014). Kurtosis as peakedness, 1905–2014. RIP. *The American statistician, 68*(3), 191–195. doi:10.1080/00031305.2014.917055 PMID:25678714

Yazidi, J. (2013). *Impact of exchange rate on trade balance*. The Open University of Tanzania.

Yee, L. S., Mun, H. W., Zhengyi, T., Ying, L. J., & Xin, K. K. (2016). Determinants of export: Empirical study in Malaysia. *Journal of International Business and Economics, 4*(1), 61–75. doi:10.15640/jibe.v4n1a6

Yuksel, H., Kuzey, C., & Sevinc, E. (2012). The impact of exchange rate volatility on exports in Turkey. *European Journal of Economic and Political Studies, 5*(2), 5–19.

KEY TERMS AND DEFINITIONS

BOT: Bank of Tanzania.

Exchange Rate: The exchange rate is the value of a country's currency in terms of one unit of the other country's currency.

Export: Exporting is dispatching products to another country in exchange for payment.

IMF: International Monetary Fund.

Industrial Production Index: Industrial production refers to the production of industrial corporations. This indicator is measured in an index that expresses the change in production output volume.

Chapter 4
Competitiveness of International Business:
Management, Economics, Technology, Environment, and Social Study of Cultural Perspective

Zafer Adiguzel
https://orcid.org/0000-0001-8743-356X
Medipol Business School, Istanbul Medipol University, Turkey

ABSTRACT

The world is experiencing rapid growth and change, and for a business to compete qualified, manpower must receive full training. The world economy will determine the balance of power competitive advantages. A strong management approach will increase quality and productivity. It is an important factor for the companies to gain superiority in the field of efficiency, to adapt to the technological changes, and to compete. Therefore, businesses also need to realize these advantages to provide technological changes, as well as to create competitive advantages. Management approach is necessary to create the organizational structure. Business management delivering the identified strategic objectives requires continuous effort by employees from every level. This chapter investigates international business management in terms of competitiveness combined with the effects of the cultural and social environment in understanding the management and the impact of the economy.

INTRODUCTION

Especially experienced in the post-1980 period with economic development and globalization; goods, provision of services and liberalization of capital flows and the acceleration of technological progress, countries have pushed Standards will have a greater share of the global market and has led to the prominence of the concept of international competitiveness (Benk & Akdemir, 2004). In this sense, with globalization, it has transformed into a sort of common market countries market countries has led to a variety

DOI: 10.4018/978-1-7998-2559-3.ch004

of policies to maintain a competitive edge in economic activity (Terpstra et al., 2012). In other words, achieving absolute success in the market, it has evolved directly related to competitiveness. International competitiveness is an indispensable concept for the rapidly increasing importance and open economic growth and development, are discussed by many researchers and focuses on the concept of the decisive factors. Although in the absence of a common definition on international competitiveness, the concept of competitiveness can be assessed from different and wide aspects. Widely used in the literature and the export performance and market share gains in the country are examined in terms of competitiveness. In this sense, countries in international commodity markets, to obtain competitiveness, a team that price and non-price dynamics (technology, information, quality, demand and productivity and so on.) are based on the elements. High quality and innovative goods producing ability and international competitiveness can be considered as the ability to buy more goods as a result of this, the performance in the countries of industrial production, compared to other countries at lower cost and/or shows higher quality and can provide increased market share by producing goods in productivity.

Societies in the world cannot live independently from each other because of the development of civilization, differences in demographic, geographic and economic structure and they are in trade relations with each other in order to meet their needs arising from world resources at optimum level. This is the contents of the goods trade relations, capital and services is approximately two centuries in the flow of what should be the direction and intensity of thinkers, economists suggest otherwise. Thanks to geography they are in the civil society around the world as well as advantage held by commercial relationships and other factors thanks to the creativity of the advantages they have as welfare vary from each other. Prosperity benefiting from these advantages by using scientific methods and efforts should be how to increase the world production was started in 1776 by Adam Smith first (Smith, 1950). In later years, a change in the nature of trade relations, Adam Smith insufficient to explain the relationship of work, has led to a new theory put forward by carrying out new work (Ashraf et al., 2005). In particular, the twentieth century's last quarter of the rapid globalization that has occurred in the right world, firms and industries, to survive in the interior and the competition they faced in external market environment, market to gain share and this is what the advantages are necessary to maintain the share and what topics should be done to create these advantages It gave rise to concentrate on. Of firms and industries, as well as state governments have also obtain the aim to improve the welfare of their citizens by achieving competitiveness in the international arena and needed in this direction macro they concentrate on the economic as well as how policy at the micro-economic level should be monitored.

INTERNATIONAL BUSINESS

Nowadays, companies' products where will the markets they want, where and how have proliferated alternatives in matters such as they perform production and 'international business' concept began to feel more the presence (Burdon et al., 2009). In 1960, Lilienthal first suggesting its international business has been expressed during a speech. Lilienthal (1960) will operate according to the country's international word expressed the opinion that the situation is more than one (Özalp, 1998). In other words, international business, business is all of the activities that have been carried out outside the national boundaries of the firm (Hill, 2008). Businesses, gain valuable experience and knowledge about foreign markets after these events have noticed that a very important key. In this way, managers began to concentrate on training that will be required in the international sense. Skills such as international marketing, international team building, international strategies and foreign language are considered as the qualifications required for managers (Birchall, 2004). The activities in the field of international business are divided into two main groups: international trade and international investment. For international trade to take place, a company must deal with the import or export of its products or services. However, international investment is a transfer of resources made for business purposes outside the borders of the main country (Daniels et al., 1998). In general, enterprises have insufficient market opportunities, increased competition environment and so on (Aktaş, 2015). For reasons, they have tended to invest in different geographical areas. Their main countries are becoming insufficient for companies. For this reason, international business activities, the idea of being global and the desire to make more money became attractive and the importance of international business activities has progressed (Slywotzky & Hoban, 2007). International businesses, specific goals and objectives in line with the country's production in their own countries as well as in various fields of activity outside its own borders, which performs operations such as sales or public can be defined as private enterprises (Ball et al., 1999). However, it is important to note that the management of these enterprises is in the hands of the citizens of the firm's own country and in addition they have a limited investment network. (Holt & Wigginton, 2002). The concept of international business is an important element for the expansion of international business lines. International business, which is of great importance for the conduct, supervision and sustainability of the existing international affairs, can be summarized as the implementation and active realization of the methods and objectives coming from the main country which is operating in different countries (Geiersbach, 2010).

International Management

Management can be described as process of achieving and succeeding targets (Drucker, 2012). In this case, the process is completed with other people and their help. It requires cooperation on this issue. Management concept can also be defined in the form of regulation in accordance with the objective of ensuring that this cooperation (Özalp, 2004). Phatak et al. (2005) defined the management as a process that organizes in accordance with the mission and vision by considering the dynamic balance elements of the effective distribution and use of individuals and other resources together with the procurement of individuals and other resources in accordance with the objectives of the organization. In this definition, two aspects of management are remarkable. First, management is an important element for the co-ordination of the two resources of the organization, the material and human resources (Hersey et al., 2007). Another is the fact that management is a dynamic structure that constantly interacts with the activities of the organization (Easterby-Smith et al., 2012). In order to sustain this interaction for the benefit of the organization, it is required to make and implement plans that are compatible with management situations (Borders et al., 1991). The need to coordinate the business's resources supports the management need. In today's world, organizations are constantly interacting with each other. In order to ensure their continuity, organizations should become a structure that constantly shapes each other in constant interaction with external stakeholders. Management needs to produce strategies needed to achieve these goals (Phatak et al., 2005). If we refer to international management based on the definition made on management; international management can be expressed as the process of achieving the goals successfully by taking into account the balances in the global environment by effectively coordinating the process of the organization's resources (Deresky, 2017). The concept of international management; the protection of global goals and global dynamic balances can be expressed as the process of providing the resources required by the organization, and coordinating and distributing the use of them effectively

(Luthans & Doh, 2012). International management is a structure that conducts, supervises and maintains the activities of international business and business. The procurement process of human resources and the elimination of human resource needs constitute one of the important duties of international governments. In addition, effective management of the mission, vision and plans coming from the main country and center is one of the important roles of management. Observing, examining the economic and political structure and reducing the possible risks in order to ensure that production continues dynamically and not to affect this dynamism is also an important role of these administrations (Klaas Jagersma, 2005).

Multinational Enterprises

Multinational enterprises do not have a common definition in the current literature. In the literature, in general, different characteristics of multinational enterprises are emphasized and definitions based on these characteristics are made. Ghoshal and Bartlett (1988) can be considered as the basic definition; according to this definition, multinational companies are companies that are composed of affiliated companies and central organizations and companies with different targets are distributed in different geographies. In other words, production and marketing activities of the organization are performing in different geographies. Therefore, as can be inferred from the definition, a multinational company is an organization that operates with juvenile companies and dealerships in different countries (Geiersbach 2010).

The more specific definitions of multinational companies in the literature are discussed in the light of their characteristics. According to Gilpin (2016), multinational enterprises are manufacturing companies in different geographies. In other words, they operate in an oligopolistic structure. In other words, oligipolistic are active in a structure. In addition, Heenan and Perlmutter (1979) describe multinational companies as enterprises or organizations that invest in different countries and follow a management strategy that takes all decisions from the center while managing these investments from a single center. Dunning (1988), on the other hand, considers these companies as firms that make direct foreign capital investments and perform their supervision and execution.

Based on such definitions, Sherman and Bohlender (1992) emphasized that the most important distinguishing feature of these companies is company size. Finally, while Jarblad (2003) defines these companies, they emphasize that these companies spread over different geographies are the companies that increase their profit potential by benefiting from legal advantages in different geographies.

Multinational companies follow minimum requirements before investing in different countries. If these minimum requirements are met, they make investment decisions. These minimum requirements are directly related to the economic and political structure of the present country. The wealth of natural resources, access to new markets, eligibility for restructuring external production and the availability of strategically important resources are the elements that multinational companies seek before making their investments (Aktan & Vural, 2004a). When multinational corporations are considered as a whole, it is seen that they have an important place in the world production and trade in the process from the beginning of the historical development to the present day.

International Economic Environment; Almost every business cannot be affected by the economic environment. Since the economic situation is constantly changing, successful business is the one that recognizes the increasing and decreasing tendencies quickly, takes the quickest attitude and has the flexibility to adapt to the new economic situation (Ataman & Gegez, 1991). The economic environment consists of sub-elements such as national income, disposable income per person, income distribution, income generation periods, borrowing opportunities, structure and operation of the trade sector and the direction of development of different sectors. GNP, which is the sum of the value or added value of the end products produced in an economy in a given period, is obtained from the gross national product value of a given period, the MG obtained by subtracting the indirect taxes collected in that economy in the same period, the national income generated in a certain period, per capita closely monitoring the economic indicators such as national income per capita and the changes in these indicators will be beneficial in terms of protecting them by achieving sustainable competitive advantage in international markets (Aydemir & Demirci, 2006). Understanding the importance of the international economic environment and creating marketing strategies, plans and programs in line with this perspective should be seen as a requirement of modern business management thinking as well as being able to adapt and integrate successfully to international markets (Gegez et al., 2003).

International Technological Environment; It is an accepted fact that the importance of technological innovations and parallel developments in the process created by globalization is relatively increased. In terms of competitiveness, technology plans and organizations of companies or entrepreneurs in the country play a strong role in the transformation of competition (Fagerberg, 1996). Long-term changes in price and cost factors in production process depend on production technology. The development of technology-based competition emerges in two ways. It may be in the form of process innovation or product innovation. Process innovation contributes to the effect of reducing the unit costs, which is seen as an important factor for producers to enter the market. Product innovation (innovation) constitutes the second stage that increases quality, determines the price and quantity depending on knowledge and occurs after process innovation (Castillo, 2011). According to Nelson and Winter (1982), since firm activities are traditionally shaped in developing countries, their efforts towards innovation and technological developments are vital to competitive advantage. Firms in developing economies are working under incomplete information production conditions compared to other countries holding technological innovation. It is not very sustainable to ensure that new technology is provided only through imports, ie innovation through technology transfer. Because it will allow the use of complex technological development and hardware information cannot be provided immediately. Also, this process is not costly, risky and predictable (Lall, 2000). Technological environment is one of the important external environmental factors affecting the companies that want to engage in international marketing activities. Because, not all countries have the same technological level. Therefore, a company wishing to enter another country market with international marketing activities should investigate the technological level of that market and consider marketing suitable products (Gegez et al., 2003). Technological innovations change the comparative advantages between countries and accelerate the socio-economic development of the countries. In countries with a low level of technology, either direct technology transfer or import of the product can be considered. Globallesme enables the recognition and faster adoption of product categories such as mobile phones, microwave ovens, digital cameras (Bengil, 2003).

INTERNATIONAL COMPETITIVENESS

Competitiveness is the level of the ability to make sales in international markets under the free market conditions of the services and products produced by maintaining the income level of the citizens of a country in a sustainable manner (Fagerberg, 1988). International competitiveness can be defined in many different ways by different individuals and environments. To an economist: "Countries that increase the efficiency, reduce costs by increasing production, raising the living standards and welfare" for policy makers: "The new application, to be used and increase competition in the market firms", the employer: "To find cheaper raw materials markets will generate the production of his products" also it means profitability for both sides emerged as. In short, there is no definite definition of competitiveness (Sarıçoban, 2013). Especially since the 1990s, using the conceptual and technological framework created by globalization, competitiveness has been taken into consideration. Although the history of competitiveness dates back to the classical foreign trade theory, the studies with globalization aim to understand the competitiveness in real terms.

International competitiveness is the mutual state of traders or industrialists who are trying to attract customers with more favorable prices, better sales conditions or better quality supply. The free competition regime is a regime in which prices are not controlled by public authorities, it is free to establish private enterprises and public authorities only intervene to secure the free functioning of the price mechanism. Competition to obtain limited supply of goods or services or, conversely, is a market behavior manifests itself in the form of a competition between economic agents who want to avoid an abundance of supply (Madsen & Walker, 2015). Another of its citizens under free market conditions competitiveness definition when trying to increase their income; also in its ability to offer its product successfully in the international arena. Another view is that while the earnings of countries are abundant, offering it to market distribution is also called competitiveness. Thus, the welfare increase and the balancing of the current account deficit in the country are expressed as a separate definition. In the industrial sense, it is the ability of a firm or industry to tackle the challenges arising from its external competitors. Therefore, to be effective in the market for critical purposes; because competitiveness requires both impact and effectiveness, and it is important to choose these objectives and this is the ability to produce, export, distribute and present the products it produces on the international market (Buckley et al., 1988). Naturally, in order for all of this to happen, that is to increase productivity, the policies and strategies implemented by firms or governments are very important. Because there is a large network of influence and interaction. This power can be determined and shaped according to the method applied, human potential, qualified labor force, technology intensive policies and can be gained. In this process, R & D, low cost, technology, resources and so on. Each of these factors plays a very important role (Karaaslan & Tuncer, 1994).

Conceptual Structure of International Competitiveness

The period in which we live is a period in which competition is increasing rapidly in both industry and international level, and efforts are being made to get more shares from the markets. The acceleration of liberalization, especially with the removal of the barriers to goods, services and capital flows, as well as the capacity increases caused by technological improvements, led to an increase in competition within the framework of micro and macro policies and strategies at national and international level. Not only in terms of price in the world markets, but also based on many structural non-price advantages in the world economy and to have a share of trade flows, and has accelerated the transformation of national competitiveness. International competitiveness; it is usually addressed at firm, industry and country level. It is stated that the dimensions of the competition start at the firm level and develop at the national level, and at the international level, it may cause a relatively higher market share and an opportunity to generate revenue. In this sense, internationally competitive advantage is created mainly at national level and sustained by achievements in activities with high national development.

The World Economic Form (WEF) describes the most important factors that determine the productivity of the country's institutions and policies in determining international competitiveness. The level of productivity is expressed as the level of welfare that the economy can achieve, and it is also seen as the main process between investments and return in the growth process. In other words, a more competitive economy is defined as a rapidly developing economy over time (Schwab & Sala-i-Martín, 2016). Therefore, the productivity increase provided by the firms and industries of the country is a part of the competition of nations.

In general and commonly used definition, international competitiveness; It is the ability of companies established in the country to sell goods and services produced in international markets in a way that will increase the living standards of all individuals living in the country (Ulengin et al., 2011). In this sense, international competitiveness also means that the basket of goods created by countries in the production process is in demand in other markets and thus contributes to the growth and prosperity process within the country. Therefore, the creation of competitiveness of countries and the effective use of the competitiveness created have gained priority in understanding the concept. In international competitiveness, it is ensured that the country is satisfactory in terms of macroeconomics and that companies or industries can create international competitive advantage in successive processes (David & David, 2013). In this sense, in many countries, research groups, commissions, and institutes have been established which examine the dimensions of competitiveness at sector and firm level in order to maintain their presence in the market and maintain their competitive position in the face of emerging economies in international trade.

International Competitiveness at Firm and Industry Level

Being competitive in the market between companies and industries depends on many factors. The basis of these is the production costs, which are frequently mentioned in micro analyzes. Every company wants to take the lead in competitiveness as it wants to increase its strength and continuity in its position in the industry. In the development of management and business strategies, Krugman (1994) states that the assessment of the determinants of competition for the firm is more evident than the assessment of international competitiveness. In the development of management and business strategies, Krugman (1994) states that the assessment of the determinants of competition for the firm is more evident than the assessment of the international competitiveness. On the other hand, it states that nations will not be able to withdraw from the markets and that they will take part in the markets under any conditions, strong or weak. Therefore, looking at countries as potential competitors can be misleading.

The competitiveness of competitiveness in production, employment and trade balance are important for nations (Kester & Luehrman, 1989). The fact that a domestic firm has international competitiveness in the export market or at home means that it is currently or in the same situation or superior in terms of non-price factors such as product price and / or product quality, punctuality in delivery and after-sales service compared to competing domestic and foreign companies (Kibritçioğlu, 1996). It is widely accepted that the difference between the competitiveness of firms and the competitiveness of nations is complex. For firms, competition is the success of services in the face of production and sales constraints and barriers. This is measured by factors such as market share and profitability (Snowdon & Stonehouse, 2006).

Porter (1990) states that competition at the firm level will play an effective role in the international competitiveness, and attributes the development of international leadership strategy, especially the innovative capacity and technology dynamics. In this sense, competitiveness of enterprises is the ability to create innovation. Competition in the industry as Porter (2008a), defined as the geographical concentration of interrelated companies and institutions in a particular field of "clustering" (clustering) draws attention to the importance of factors. Porter (2010), in determining the competitiveness of firms, as a result of this cluster or interconnected industries act together, suppliers, institutions and related industry groups, through the reduction in costs, increase efficiency and R & D activities are being achieved and thus production becomes more proactive states. Aktan and Vural (2004a) consider a competitive industry as an industry that has competitive firms at regional or international level. In this respect, the competitiveness of an industry can be evaluated as the competitiveness of the big firms within that industry. Competitiveness at industry level is generally defined in terms of productivity and performance in international trade (Aktan & Vural, 2004b). Oral et al. (1989), according to the international markets, in determining the competitiveness of local manufacturing companies, industrial competence (industrial mastery), operating capability (operational mastery) and strategic competence (strategic proficiency) emerges factors to the fore. The evaluation of performance at all levels of company management and production and function - high awareness of sound sources of distribution facilities, marketing, effective performance management is indicated as an important criteria for competitive advantage.

International Competitiveness at Country Level

Explaining and evaluating competitiveness at the country level is much wider and more complex than the firm and industry level. Because the structure of competition at country level, unlike firm or industry competitiveness, focuses more on the power of macroeconomic and political structure which starts from national welfare concept. Therefore, this broad meaning overload shows that the factors based on different definitions and approaches are coordinated. Fagerberg (1988) considers competition at the country level as the ability to achieve the goal without causing any deterioration in the balance of payments in achieving the basic economic policy objectives, increasing income and employment, and emphasizing the necessity of establishing a strong link between growth and balance of payments in determining the international competition policies in an open economy (Fagerberg 1988). In assessing the dynamics of the competitiveness of nations, Aiginger (1998) stated that the welfare increase that people will create for their ultimate goals will play an important role. S/he states that low-cost production which is effective in the competition of nations, direct contribution of external balance and adaptability to changing conditions while competing, continuous development of technology and human capital. In an economy where these do not exist, social welfare is not provided in the sense that it must be maximized. According to Boltho, (1996), countries' superiority to competition within the scope of macroeconomic policy objectives generally depends on the rapid growth of living standards as much as possible in the long term, and the maintenance of the success in the internal and external balance at the same time in the short term. What is needed in the internal balance is acceptable inflation and the consistent unemployment rate. In the external balance, the current account is at a reasonable level. Together with these two balances, competitive advantages can be clearly demonstrated between countries (Boltho, 1996).

Oral (2004) evaluates the dynamic structure of the concept of international competitiveness and the values it contains. He argues that there is a close relationship between high-quality human resources and factor resources such as monetary resources (finance) and domestic economic power and infrastructure, which in particular play a vital role in making a country's competitiveness or potential operational. In fact, when the financial resources are combined with high quality human resources in a complementary nature, the competitiveness of a country develops. Therefore, the living standard of the country is directly dependent on the competitiveness it will create (Oral, 2004). In all these approaches, increasing the international competitiveness, adding the resources of the country to production at the highest efficiency, increasing the ability to produce goods compatible with the foreign market, increasing the competitiveness of the nations and increasing the employment through growth make it inevitable to make welfare throws inevitable. In this sense, although international competitiveness starts at the scale of firms or industries to a large extent, the continuity of competitiveness also shows that it is closely related to the macroeconomic conjuncture and policies of the country.

Factors and Strategies Affecting International Competitiveness; With winds of change brought about by globalization, no doubt that survive worldwide and by achieving a strong competitive countries wanting to dominate the world market or companies must fulfill certain conditions or are known to have on these factors. With the wind of change brought about by globalization, there is no doubt that countries or firms that want to survive and dominate the world markets by gaining strong competitive power must fulfill certain conditions or have these factors known (Aiginger, 2006). Some of these factors are: labor productivity, export shares, import population ratio, net export rate, intra-sector trade, international competition, price and cost margin, profit margin, R & D expenditures and R & D intensity factors. If R & D activities are high, knowledge-based technology development will be high. More added value will be created. The R & D intensity is determined by the share of R & D expenditures from GNP (Gross National Product), the number of researchers, R & D personnel and so on criteria. If their shares of exports are low, their competitiveness will be low and their competitiveness will be strong. In-sector trade is both an export and importer of a good or sector. Imports population ratio, the ratio of total imports, total demand is in place. In short, competitiveness is the capacity of firms, countries or industries to increase their total productivity. This human capital, resources, regeneration of technology developed and are related by having on these factors. Therefore, factors such as the competitiveness of countries, the efficiency of R & D activities, foreign trade performance, technological innovation and innovation, qualified labor force, specialized and trained personnel and the use of developed technology in the production of new products are factors that increase the competitiveness (Çivi et al., 2008).

The dissemination of information arising from the strategic interaction within the firms that are densely located in a region, the situation of the competing firms both accelerates the competitiveness and economic growth increases due to these factors. Michael Porter (2000) focused on economic geography; In explaining the factors of competitiveness and competitiveness, he says that all of the companies with similar and similar characteristics in geography interact as a chain until the raw materials used in production. Therefore, it mentions the importance of four features that increase or decrease the competitiveness of these enterprises.

These four basic features are called the diamond model:

1. The first of these is the demand for the products produced by the enterprises in the region. Or the demand from outside environment outside the region.
2. The second is the limitation of production factors in the region. In other words, the capital that will carry out the production is related to the availability of qualified labor, physical and human equipment.
3. The third is the existence of a technology-intensive industry that will support the products and innovation of the company.
4. Finally, the structure and strategies of the companies, the organizations in the region and the size of the region are important elements.

Competitiveness of International Business

Each of these is interconnected. This model, called diamond, is also used in the presence of innovation and industry; The lack of demand does not increase the competitiveness, so this model decides which firm, where, in which industry to be successful, advances to the industry and which region will determine its comparative advantage. Porter (2010): "Innovation and entrepreneurship are the heart of national advantage." By emphasizing the importance of development and technological innovation in order to maintain its competitive advantage and advantage (Oğuztürk, 2003).

If a firm competes in a market where a country is very strong, this host country may block transactions in the global market or may resort to strategic changes in the firm of the other country or to disrupt its policies (Czinkota, 1999). Sometimes companies may want to sell in large markets in order to increase their export volume and try to form a global strategy. Therefore, it should implement a strategy to accommodate itself in this market. This requirement gives the host country the right to bargain and the company must grant concessions to the host country to maintain its strategy. Another influential factor is the competition factor analysis. Another effective factor is the competitor analysis factor. In the analysis of the foreign firm, factors such as labor practices, production, labor and management structures of the firm should be analyzed in order to obtain a good competition. Another factor is the disappearance of the gap between countries, especially after the globalization period. With the globalization of multinational corporations becoming more active, it is the result of positive externalities and economic development in countries, reducing the factor costs used in production, income and so on. Such as the decrease in competition with elements such as drag. Companies active in the markets with the incentive and protective industry policies implemented by the governments towards the more active sectors with the development of these sectors; it may cause inactive firms to withdraw from the market. As a result of all these factors, countries tend to keep the bar high in order to compete more. In addition, more fluidity of technology, national recognition, the emergence of large-scale markets completely affect the competitiveness (Porter, 1980).

Development Process of Competition Strategy; The strongest competitiveness determines the profitability of the industry and, most importantly, the importance of strategic formulation (Rothaermel, 2013). Of course, if a firm wants to be in a strong position in the industry, it must maintain that position. If a company wants to be in a strong position in the industry no doubt that this position is protected. Otherwise, new companies entering the market; it is a known fact that it cannot compete with a firm with a strong position. Otherwise, new companies entering the market; it is a known position. Therefore, there are strategies that affect competitiveness and developed against these factors (Porter, 2010).

The first strategy that affects competitiveness is the entry threat. New entrances bring a new capacity to the industry, a desire for market share acquisition, and often wealthy resources. But the seriousness of the threat of entry depends on the presence of competitors they know they will enter and the current barriers. The strategies of the industries that want to maintain their competitiveness are these barriers. It consists of six strong entry barrier with threats.

Economies of Scale: These economies discourage entry demand and reduce cost advantage and create large scale. Economies of scale are the main barriers to production, research, service and industry entry.

Item Discrepancy: Brand identity creates a barrier by spending on customer loyalty. These include advertising, customer service, industry leadership, product diversity, and brand identity.

Capital Requirement: Capital is not only needed to create convenience, but also to absorb consumer credit, investor and entry costs. The presence of this capital creates an entry barrier. Because the company with a capital strengthens its competitive strategy by investing in areas such as information production and technology.

Independent Resident Size Advantages: Ossified firms do not care about their competitors and what their economic growth is; but local firms may have a cost advantage. These advantages can be due to influences such as appropriate technology, learning disposition, access to the best raw material resources.

Government Policies: It can even put a barrier on government inputs to the industry through patent control and control mechanisms that restrict access to raw materials (Porter, 1998).

Another competitive development process is the strategic formulation. Strategists include providing the best protection ability against external competitiveness according to the firm's situation (Hitt et al., 2012). They hope to influence the balance of external competitiveness through strategy interaction, or to use the forces underlying factors and the changes associated with these factors for their own benefit by choosing a suitable strategy for a new competitive balance before the competing forces recognize it. Another is the strategy in the competitive development process, which can create brand identity through product differentiation or innovation in the market, affecting market balance and entry barriers.

In the information age, competition and competition development follow the five stages in the competition development process in order to gain the competitive advantage created by the information revolution.

Increase the Density Values Information: The first business of a firm is to develop the potential information intensity and presence of business products and business association process. For this, the following two characteristics of information technology, which will play a strategic role in the industry, should be considered. The first relates to the potential information of the enterprise, with whom it will enter production, the delivery process, product development and diversification, and the guarantee to the consumer and the supplier That is, to develop knowledge in the value chain, and to develop knowledge in the product.

Determining the Structure of Information Technology in Industry: Many companies have changed the structure of competition by investing heavily in information technology to their advantage. For example, when an airline sends its reservations to a computer

Determining the Direction of Information Technology to Create Competitive Advantage: In addition to strengthening the production chain, it is necessary to consider how changes can be made in the field of competition and information technologies. In other words, producing more information and using information technology within the company.

Knowing How Information Technology Can Create New Industries: Managers should take advantage of the opportunities that they can create from the existing business. These opportunities require new businesses to answer the following questions. The question of whether the information produced by the enterprise can produce, whether the information creation process can create an internal business or not, and whether information technologies can produce suitable products for the company should be carefully evaluated.

Developing a Plan to Gain the Advantage of Information Technology: Contributes to the process of implementing information technology (Porter, 2008b).

Benefits of Competitiveness

Especially with the globalization, the fact that more multinational companies took place in the global markets more quickly brought along externalities that would provide advantages for both companies and countries (Altınbaşak et al., 2008). In this way, the companies that make their production on a global level can dispatch them to any field. One of the most important phenomena was the geographical concentration of clusters or firms. This concentration occurs on a regional, national and global scale. Due to the horizontal and vertical integrations resulting from the firm clusters formed in this way, the relations of the close firms, product supply transfer and distribution mechanisms have been expanded and thus, the competition has gained a new acceleration and the economic growth has gained vitality with this benefit (Wheelen & Hunger, 2011). It has won. Thanks to the investment made by these companies in countries, the increase in productivity and development arising from all positive externalities such as employment area, resource allocation, new technology emergence, growth of scale economy can undoubtedly be considered as a positive privilege or benefit brought by the competitiveness (Barney & Hesterly, 2009). Although the concept of boundary with globalization disappears, it also coincides with the knowledge-based technology and new dynamic economics of cluster movements. Therefore, competitiveness has been reshaped and firms 'perspectives on countries' competitiveness have completely changed. It provides small returns for low taxes, electricity and so on. Not on grounds such as; information, high technology, R & D, inter-firm communication, new product development is established for reasons such as, and the externality provided by it is a benefit of competitiveness (Dulupçu, 2001).

Foreign Trade-Competitiveness Relationship in the New Economic Order

The term globalization is often used to refer to markets, financial system, competition and firm strategies. Also globalization; it is seen as the power behind competition and competitiveness, which is of vital importance for companies, even regions and countries worldwide, and is therefore of increasing importance (Hatzichronoglou, 1996). With the increasing importance of globalization, the factors that triggered globalization gained value. These are: reduction of legal, technical and institutional barriers affecting the circulation of goods, services and factor (especially capital), reduction of tariff and non-tariff barriers in world trade, and the reduction of transaction costs in terms of money and time due to the decrease in communication and transportation costs and developments in information technology. In addition, international competition includes new forces such as BRICS (Brazil, Russia, India, China, S. Africa) and other Asian/Latin American/Eastern European countries.

These developed and/or developing countries affect the globalization process and sometimes they are affected. Previously, non-tradable wholesale and retail distribution, logistics services, call centers, et al. The world economy is now starting to become important in the field of services, factors such as the growth and development of the capital market of direct investment have contributed to this process (Deardoff, 2008). Since the process of globalization begins with the internationalization of product and service trade, foreign trade is perhaps the most important of the areas where globalization affects a country's economy. Foreign trade, globalization is expressed as a cause and a result of both (Badia et al., 2008). Therefore, economies wishing to be in harmony with global trends and have to remain must have a competitive advantage in foreign trade. The acceleration of international trade and investments has brought to the forefront its competitiveness in foreign trade (Sarıdoğan, 2010).

In the past, when we talked about the concept of competition, it was understood that the competitiveness of firms and regions that contain definitions in a smaller scope. However, with the global communication, this concept has moved from the company and region to the international dimensions. If a country wants to make a name for itself in foreign markets, it should focus on the concept of broader competitiveness instead of working on narrow-scale firm competitiveness and regional competitiveness (Gamble et al., 2014). Competitiveness has not been considered and considered in the countries before, but it has been manifested by the globalization process.

With the increase in the importance of foreign trade in the globalization process, rapid changes have started to take place. These changes bring markets into a more competitive environment. The presence of a competitive environment increases the efforts of companies and countries to gain more value from international competition (John et al., 2005). With globalization, not only the firms and industries operating in the country, but also the importance of increasing the competitiveness among the industries in a more comprehensive dimension, is emerging (Altay & Gürpınar, 2008). Increasing the welfare level of a country, developing employment opportunities and using its resources effectively seem to depend on increasing the competitiveness of that country, in other words, the superiority it can gain in competition during the globalization process (Ekin, 1999). The aim of all countries in the changing and developing world order is to create competitive conditions in their economies and to increase their welfare levels. However, because of the multi-faceted competition, many factors affect the competitiveness of countries and enterprises (Çivi et al., 2008).

It is only possible for a firm to increase its production volume and profitability, to develop a region or to ensure the prosperity of a country only if that firm, region or country can compete with other firms, regions and countries. The globalization process, which has gained momentum in the last twenty years, has taken the competition from the companies' own regions and countries to an international environment. Every globally competitive organization has to address the competition on a global scale, to realize that its competitors are in every corner of the world and to make plans as an element of such a wide framework. Otherwise, it can cause a region to shrink in the same way as the global environment enables the development and development of a region (Filiztekin & Karaata, 2010).

Countries wishing to take part in the international arena should closely follow developments in more advanced countries. The concepts of innovation, quality and low cost in industry, technology and production are noteworthy especially in countries on the road to globalization. Because countries that want to develop in international trade can be different from other countries by paying attention to these concepts. Thus, countries gain a competitive advantage thanks to their prominence in international markets by revealing their differences from other countries with what they do in the field of foreign trade. The main factor influencing international competition is the foreign trade structure of the country, the amount of foreign direct investment to the country and the sectoral distribution of this capital. Innovations in these factors will affect the changes that the country will face in the future and the amount of foreign capital to come, leading to an increase in competitiveness (Emin & Erol, 2008).

It is extremely important for businesses to operate in an environment where they can increase their productivity with the rapid spread of competitiveness, especially in the field of industry, and their place in the world markets (Hill et al., 2014). Therefore, in the process of internationalization of production, the demands of the enterprises from the environment in which they operate have increased. In this framework, factors such as factor equipment, technological infrastructure, R & D investments, human capital, low labor costs, taxes and legal regulations supporting economic developments gain importance in the country (Demir, 2001).

In this framework, factors such as factor equipment, technological infrastructure, R & D investments, human capital, low labor costs, taxes and legal regulations supporting economic developments gain importance in the country (Demir, 2001). While some countries adapt and develop immediately to the globalization process, it has not been easy for some countries to increase their competitiveness and adapt to the globalization process. Countries that increased their foreign trade volume and competitiveness, adapted to foreign policies and fulfilled the necessary conditions were rapidly involved in the globalization process. In terms of foreign trade, the word globalization refers to trade without borders, but the value given to foreign trade has increased with the abolition of borders. Thus, the existence of a competitive environment has gained importance for every country wishing to take part in international markets.

The Impact of Globalization Process on Emerging Market Economies

As the world economy entered the "globalization" process rapidly in the last quarter century, the possibilities of cooperation between developed, developing countries and developing market economies have increased. As trade conditions between countries began to diminish, international trade volume expanded, advanced technology transfer from developed countries to developing countries increased, international financial markets improved, labor flow increased between countries and significant improvements in foreign capital flows were observed (Aktan, 1999).

On the basis of these developments which have taken place in the last 20-25 years, the fact that technology and capital have gained the ability to change rapidly. In addition, the importance of developing market economies, which cannot utilize the opportunities at hand, has increased with the globalization process. Because these economies, which have little or no chance of directing them to productive areas in their own countries with excessive idle resources, offer various advantages to other countries. The events that cause this rapid change in the world economy and the developments that accelerate the change in the world are seen as the cornerstones of global change (Emin & Çavuşgil, 2001). One of the events that most affected global change in the recent past was that China, India and the former Eastern Bloc countries opened their economies more to international trade. At the end of the 1970s, China abandoned closed economic models and in the beginning of the 1990s, began to follow more liberal policies. In addition, regime changes were made in Eastern Europe and former Soviet Union countries and these developments supported the globalization process.

These developments gained momentum in the early 1980s, especially since the 1990s, and began to affect the world economy. It is natural that these liberalization movements in developing countries with large economies affect the world economy (Aydın, 2008).

The crisis that started with the devaluation of Thailand's pound from Southeast Asian countries could not be predicted. However, the spread rate and impact area of the currency earthquake in Thailand has been very large (Baştürk, 2001). The crisis, which began in Southeast Asia, gained a global character in 1998 by including Russia and Brazil, which have significant weight in their regions. With the spread of the crisis, investors withdrew from the emerging markets, which they deemed risky, and settled for relatively low returns and turned to the developed countries they trust. Emerging economies, which were exposed to large-scale capital outflows and were unable to find new financing opportunities, faced serious adversities (İslamoğlu, 1999). The common denominator of most of these crises, which accelerated with globalization, was the impending detention of countries against the dangers in the international markets as a result of the liberal liberalization of the financial sector and the rapid liberalization of capital movements (Fagerberg et al., 2007). Also, in these countries which are subject to speculative hot money movements, crises with high social destruction have emerged with the lack of regulatory measures against the accumulated macro imbalances. As a result of these crises, a new liberal approach has emerged that outweighs regulatory and social sustainability both in crisis countries and in organizations such as the IMF, the World Bank, in an effort to shape emerging market economies. In line with this new approach, many countries have embarked on structural reforms that provide the state with a broader framework of activity in areas such as banking, social security, and combating poverty (Güven & Öniş, 2010).

Globalization and the disappearance of borders have enabled the cooperation between all the countries of the world to increase. The process of globalization is a good opportunity for developing market economies that do not have many advantages that developed countries have (Best et al., 2003). Because the economies developing with the abolition of the borders between countries have reached the position to benefit more from the world in areas such as foreign trade and investment. The process of globalization has negative aspects as well as the positive aspects mentioned. The most important point is the fact that the problems in the international markets spread easily to every country. Minimizing the deficiencies in the economic, political and social infrastructure of the countries within the developing market economies will enable them to suffer less from the negativities in other countries. Because with the acceleration of the globalization process, the structuring seen in many areas in the countries has not been completed or is incomplete. The practices that could not be realized in this process, the measures that were not taken, caused the countries within the framework to be more affected by the external negativities.

SOLUTIONS AND RECOMMENDATIONS

As a result of the globalization process and rapid development of information and communication technologies, both companies and country administrations attach special importance to gaining international competitiveness (Shenkar et al., 2014). However, when the concept of international competitiveness is tried to be defined, this concept is dealt with in different ways depending on the field of study, the field to be studied, the indicators and perspectives used to measure competitiveness, so there is no common definition that defines this power. In order to understand what it means at this point, competitiveness is generally evaluated in the literature by firm, industry and country. It is seen that the most simple and understandable definitions of competitiveness are made at the firm level. Accordingly, in both domestic and foreign market, a product is less cost than its competitors; therefore, it is a company that has a competitive power and offers a better quality in terms of non-price factors such as product quality and after-sales service at a more affordable price. At this point, what kind of policy should be followed in order to maintain this competitive power of the company that has competitiveness came up. The cost advantage has less durability than the non-price advantage, since this advantage of the company that uses the cost advantage as the source of competitiveness can be imitated in the long term.

Therefore, if the company that has the cost advantage wants to maintain its competitive power, it should turn this advantage into a non-price advantage. However, as this superiority can be imitated over time, companies that want to keep this power in their hands should constantly strive for innovation and improvement. This can only be achieved through R & D activities, as well as creating opportunities in the environment in which it is possible to create innovation in other environments by gaining advantage by seeing other companies before and taking advantage of this advantage and constantly innovating and making changes. Apart from these internal factors, it is an undeniable fact that there are external factors that determine firm competitiveness. These factors can be summarized as the state's place in the economy,

Competitiveness of International Business

such as protectionism and free trade, the state's path in international trade, exchange rate and interest rate policies, tax policy, budget deficits and the cause of inflation, as well as applications such as the level of consumer consciousness, domestic demand structure, energy, transportation and communication infrastructure, legal system, the structure of financial markets and the level of competition in the market.

Since the group of companies producing competing products and services is called industry, a competitive industry is an industry that has competitive companies at regional or international level (Byrne & Popoff, 2008). Therefore, factors affecting firm competitiveness also determine industry competitiveness. However, in contrast to firms, the factors that determine the competitiveness of the industries are defined as the geographical concentration of interrelated firms and institutions in a specific area bas. Clustering reduces the costs and increases productivity by providing easy access to the specialized and experienced workforce and suppliers of the companies located in a region, by identifying the acceleration and direction of innovation that can be improved through R & D activities and increasing the productivity of the cluster by strengthening the industrial competition by expanding the industrial competitiveness power.

Compared to the definitions made at firm and industry level, there is no common definition in the literature on the concept of competitiveness at country level. At this point, it is seen that definitions are made according to the number of competitive firms / industries focused on productivity, market share and hosted. Krugman (1994), who sees international competitiveness as a dangerous obsession with politicians, argues that it is unreasonable to try to simplify the concept by establishing a similarity between a firm's competitiveness and a country's competitiveness. According to Krugman (1994), the concept of competitiveness is meaningless when applied to national economies, but this obsession is dangerous mainly because it causes misallocation of resources.

Porter (1990), another academician working on this issue, does not accept the understanding that relates the national competitiveness to the share of the country in the world market, but adopts an efficiency-oriented competitiveness understanding. The biggest goal of a nation is to produce a high and sustainable living standard for its citizens, and the ability to do so depends on the productivity based on the labor and capital of the nation, and to increase this productivity, the country needs to apply for imports in other industries to specialize in imports. Therefore, according to Porter (2000), instead of trying to explain the competitiveness at the national level, we need to understand the factors that determine productivity and productivity growth rate and how and why commercial value talent and technologies are formed, and for this we need to look at industries with high productivity and high wage levels, not the whole economy.

FUTURE RESEARCH DIRECTIONS

Our epoch; It is experiencing a period in which rapid transformation and development is experienced, dreams are challenged, and information and technology is the scene of important developments and transformations that face humanity with new developments every day. The concept of competitiveness has come to the forefront with the globalization process. Liberalization in trade has led to the internationalization of production for countries. Countries have addressed this concept at sectoral level, firm level and sometimes at international level. Thus, the factors affecting the competitiveness of countries have come to the fore. Competitiveness is handled at micro and macro levels. At the micro level, competitiveness is generally addressed at the firm and industry level, while at the macro level competitiveness at national/international level is expressed. Competitiveness determinants play a major role in determining and implementing the right policies to increase competitiveness (Wheelen et al., 2010). Determinants of competitiveness; productivity, exchange rate and devaluation, R & D expenditures, macroeconomic environment, quality, human resources, financial resources and costs. Although the determinants that affect competitiveness are handled in different ways, the important point is to move the company from the position of the industry and country to a higher position.

Developments in information and technology have changed the form of information flow and the structure of the labor force. On the one hand, the flow of information is easier and faster, while on the other hand, companies are constantly structuring to adapt to changing market conditions, developing technology and changing customer demands more easily. With the changes in the structure of the labor force, the employees take an active role in negotiating and finalizing the decisions and a participatory management and production style is formed. Globalization, changing competition understanding, changing structure of the workforce and the new business structure that emerged with the effect of these have brought new insights into human resources management (Daniels et al., 1998). Nowadays, many businesses have begun to see people as a capital that needs to be invested rather than a resource that must be managed in order to stay behind in competition. Such changes and developments necessitate the development of knowledge, creativity and competencies of the employees in the enterprises. For this purpose, enterprises try to reach their goals with various training and adaptation programs. The intensity of the competition necessitates the recruitment and retention of qualified personnel.

The main purpose of having competitiveness is to increase living standards and welfare of citizens in the country. These increases can be achieved by giving sufficient importance to activities such as trade, investment and production and by increasing solidarity and specialization among all institutions in the country. In order to capture competing countries in the production and distribution of products and services, the country must focus on its unique features, superiority, capabilities and potentials. In today's world where rapid development and change is taking place, it is possible to capture and compete with this change with the qualified, educated, equipped and ready manpower for new developments. In the world economy now, power balances determine competitive advantages. For this, well-trained workforce; As it will increase quality and productivity, it is an important element for enterprises to both gain superiority in the field of efficiency and adapt to technological changes and compete. In order to provide these advantages, businesses prefer and feel the need for a qualified workforce with advanced professional and technical knowledge, which can adapt to technological changes and create competitive advantage. For firms, the way to be competitive is to have an innovative structure. At some point, the rapidly changing world conditions make this necessary. Therefore, the information in the literature points out that companies must adopt innovation in order to survive in the long term.

CONCLUSION

The concept of competitiveness has come to the forefront with the globalization process. Liberalization in trade has led to the internationalization of production for countries. Countries have addressed this concept at sectoral level, firm level and sometimes at international level. Thus, the factors affecting the competitiveness of countries have come to the fore. Competitiveness is handled at micro and macro levels. At the micro level, competitiveness is generally addressed at the firm and industry level, while at the macro level competitiveness at national/international level is expressed. Competitiveness determinants play a major role in determining and implementing the right policies to increase competitiveness. Determinants of competitiveness; productivity, exchange rate and devaluation, R & D expenditures, macroeconomic environment, quality, human resources, financial resources and costs. Although the determinants that affect competitiveness are handled in different ways, the important point is to move the company from the position of the industry and country to a higher position.

Most of the countries that have gained international competitiveness in today's global world and have reached their present position have achieved this success through strategic foreign trade policies (Kotabe et al., 1998). It is known that in global competition conditions, this success depends on the adaptation of countries to the changing parameters of the foreign trade that occurs on a global scale. In a global world where foreign trade is carried out under high R & D and technological development conditions, it is not possible for countries to succeed in providing international competitiveness by supporting only domestic companies. It is seen that this support given in an environment where foreign trade is made strategically is not fed by a system based on R & D and innovation, in other words, it does not result in achieving international competitiveness unless it is a high technology based information society.

As a natural result of technological development, significant changes have occurred in the production process, the structure of the labor force and the production methods, and the transition from labor-intensive technology to capital-intensive technology has accelerated. The transition from labor-intensive technologies to capital-intensive technology has also changed the quality of employees. On the one hand, machines are being replaced by workers, while on the other hand significant changes are experienced in the quality of employees, structural change led by micro technologies both in the world economy and in national economies, advanced technologies, people who have received high levels of education, new skills and new equipped people who will respond to the speed of technological development need. While the production of goods in industrial societies constitutes the lifeblood of the economy, the services sector develops instead of the production sector in the transition process to the societies beyond the industry. With these developments where information has come to the forefront, there has been a shift towards services based on information and high technology in the service sector. It is clear that these developments have transformed those who do business as well as the way of production and work.

The fact that strategic foreign trade policies were implemented in technology-intensive and promising sectors not only limited to the production of new products containing technological innovations, but also brought supportive policies of the state towards the creation of qualified labor such as R & D personnel. In short, international competitiveness appears to be directly related to technology-innovation-creativity-oriented strategic foreign trade policies implemented by governments. As a result, countries that want to gain global competitiveness and achieve a sustainable growth trend in the international arena should use their natural advantages and attain the acquired advantage. Gained superiority is only possible by creating a company and industry structure that will make a difference in global competition, producing added value, based on technology-innovation-creativity and based on qualified labor force.

REFERENCES

Aiginger, K. (1998). A framework for evaluating the dynamic competitiveness of countries. *Structural Change and Economic Dynamics, 9*(2), 159–188. doi:10.1016/S0954-349X(97)00026-X

Aiginger, K. (2006). Competitiveness: From a dangerous obsession to a welfare creating ability with positive externalities. *Journal of Industry, Competition and Trade, 6*(2), 161–177. doi:10.100710842-006-9475-6

Aktan, C., & Vural, İ. Y. (2004a). Rekabet Dizisi: 2 Rekabet Gücü ve Rekabet Stratejileri. *Ankara: Türkiye İşveren Sendikaları Konfederasyonları Yayını, Yayın,* (254), 9-23.

Aktan, C. C. (1999). Global Ekonomik Entegrasyon ve Türkiye. *Dış Ticaret Dergisi,* (12), 1-29.

Aktan, C. C., & Vural, İ. Y. (2004b). *Yeni ekonomi ve rekabet.* Türkiye İşveren Sendikaları Konfederasyonu Rekabet Dizisi, Ajans Türk Basım.

Aktaş, K. (2015). Uluslararası İşletmelerde Stratejik Yönetim. *Uluslararası Yönetim ve Sosyal Araştırmalar Dergisi, 3*(1), 16.

Altay, B., & Gürpınar, K. (2008). Açıklanmış Karşılaştırmalı Üstünlükler Ve Bazı Rekabet Gücü Endeksleri: Türk Mobilya Sektörü Üzerine Bir Uygulama. *Afyon Kocatepe Üniversitesi İktisadi ve İdari Bilimler Fakültesi Dergisi, 10*(1), 257–274.

Altınbaşak, İ., Akyol, A., Alkibay, S., & Arslan, F. M. (2008). *Küresel pazarlama yönetimi.* İstanbul, Turkey: Beta Basım Yayım Dağıtım AŞ.

Ashraf, N., Camerer, C. F., & Loewenstein, G. (2005). Adam Smith, behavioral economist. *The Journal of Economic Perspectives, 19*(3), 131–145. doi:10.1257/089533005774357897

Ataman, G., & Gegez, E. (1991). Dış Çevrenin Pazarlama Üzerindeki Etkisi ve Pazarlama Yönetimi Açısından Önemi. *Pazarlama Dünyası, 5*(26), 28–35.

Aydemir, M., & Demirci, M. K. (2006). *İşletmelerin Küreselleşme stratejileri ve kobi örnekleminde bir uygulama.* Ankara, Turkey: Gazi Kitabevi.

Aydın, A. (2008). Endüstri içi ticaret ve Türkiye: Ülkeye özgü belirleyicilerin tespitine yönelik bir araştırma. *Marmara Üniversitesi İİBF Dergisi, 25*(2), 881–921.

Badia, M. M., Slootmaekers, V., Beveren, I., & Van Beveren, I. (2008). *Globalization drives strategic product switching (No. 2008-2246).* International Monetary Fund.

Ball, D. A., McCulloch, W. H., Frantz, P., Geringer, M., & Minor, M. (1999). International business: The challenge of global competition.

Barney, J. B., & Hesterly, W. S. (2009). *Concepts-strategic management and competitive advantage.* Pearson India.

Baştürk, Ş. (2001). Bir Olgu Olarak Küreselleşme. *ISGUC The Journal of Industrial Relations and Human Resources, 3*(2).

Bengil, D. (2003). Uluslararası Pazarlamada Reklam Mesajı Yaratılmasında Kültür ve Önemi. Marmara Üniversitesi Sosyal Bilimler Enstitüsü (Yayınlanmamış Yüksek Lisan Tezi), 97 s., İstanbul.

Benk, S., & Akdemir, T. (2004). Globalleşme ve Ekonomik Değişim. *Çimento İşveren Dergisi, 18*(1), 12-27.

Best, R., Langston, C. A., & De Valence, G. (Eds.). (2003). *Workplace strategies and facilities management*. Routledge.

Birchall, J. (2004). Cooperatives and the millennium development goals.

Boltho, A. (1996). The assessment: International competitiveness. *Oxford Review of Economic Policy, 12*(3), 1–16. doi:10.1093/oxrep/12.3.1

Borders, M. A., Irfaeya, W., & Liu, L. (1991). International management.

Buckley, P. J., Pass, C. L., & Prescott, K. (1988). Measures of international competitiveness: A critical survey. *Journal of Marketing Management, 4*(2), 175–200. doi:10.1080/0267257X.1988.9964068

Burdon, S., Chelliah, J., & Bhalla, A. (2009). Structuring enduring strategic alliances: The case of Shell Australia and Transfield Services. *The Journal of Business Strategy, 30*(4), 42–51. doi:10.1108/02756660910972640

Byrne, S., & Popoff, L. (2008). *International joint ventures handbook*. Baker & McKenzie.

Castillo, O. N., Santibáñez, A. L. V., & Bolívar, H. R. (2011). Technological determinants of market shares of Mexican manufacturing exports. *Asian Journal of Latin American Studies, 24*(1).

Çivi, E., Erol, İ., İnanlı, T., & Erol, E. D. (2008). *Uluslararası rekabet gücüne farklı bakışlar*. Ekonomik ve Sosyal Araştırmalar Dergisi.

Czinkota, M. R. (1999). *Marketing: best practices*. Holt Rinehart & Winston.

Daniels, J. D., Radebaugh, L. H., & Sullivan, D. P. (1998). *International business: Environments and operations*. Addison-Wesley.

David, F. R., & David, F. R. (2013). *Strategic management: Concepts and cases: A competitive advantage approach*. Pearson.

Deardoff, A. V. (2008). Dünya Ekonomisi ve Dünya Ticaret Sistemi Nereye Gidiyor. *Uluslararası Ekonomi ve Dış Ticaret Politikaları, 3*(1-2), 7–24.

Demir, G. (2001). Küreselleşme üzerine. *Ankara Üniversitesi SBF Dergisi, 56*(01).

Demir, İ. (2001). *Türkiye beyaz eşya sanayiinin rekabet gücü ve geleceği*. Devlet Planlama Teşkilatı.

Deresky, H. (2017). *International management: Managing across borders and cultures*. Pearson Education India.

Drucker, P. (2012). *Management*. Routledge. doi:10.4324/9780080939063

Dulupçu, M. A. (2001). *Küresel rekabet gücü: Türkiye üzerine bir değerlendirme*. Nobel.

Dunning, J. H. (1998). Location and the multinational enterprise: A neglected factor? *Journal of International Business Studies*, *29*(1), 45–66. doi:10.1057/palgrave.jibs.8490024

Easterby-Smith, M., Thorpe, R., & Jackson, P. R. (2012). Management research. *Atlanta, GA: Sage*.

Ekin, N. (1999). Küreselleşme ve Gümrük Birliği. *İstanbul Ticaret Odası Yayın*, (1999-47), 432.

Emin, Ç., & Çavuşgil, S. T. (2001). Yeni Dünya Düzeninde Güç Kazanan Ülkeler: Yükselen Ekonomiler. *Yönetim ve Ekonomi: Celal Bayar Üniversitesi İktisadi ve İdari Bilimler Fakültesi Dergisi*, *8*(1), 113–128.

Emin, Ç., & Erol, E. D. (2008). Ulusal Rekabet Gücünü Arttırma Yolları: Literatür Araştırması. *Yönetim ve Ekonomi: Celal Bayar Üniversitesi İktisadi ve İdari Bilimler Fakültesi Dergisi*, *15*(1), 99–114.

Fagerberg, J. (1988). International competitiveness. *Economic Journal (London)*, *98*(391), 355–374. doi:10.2307/2233372

Fagerberg, J. (1996). Technology and competitiveness. *Oxford Review of Economic Policy*, *12*(3), 39–51. doi:10.1093/oxrep/12.3.39

Fagerberg, J., Srholec, M., & Knell, M. (2007). The competitiveness of nations: Why some countries prosper while others fall behind. *World Development*, *35*(10), 1595–1620. doi:10.1016/j.worlddev.2007.01.004

Filiztekin, A., & Karata, S. (2010). Türkiye'nin Dış Ticarette Rekabet Gücü: Seçilmiş Ülkeler, Sektörler-Mal Grupları ve Endeksler Bazında Karşılaştırmalı Bir Analiz. *TÜSİAD-Sabancı Üniversitesi Rekabet Forumu (REF) ve Sektörel Dernekler Federasyonu'nun*, *1*, 1-47.

Gamble, J. E., Peteraf, M. A., & Thompson, A. A. (2014). *Essentials of strategic management: The quest for competitive advantage*. McGraw-Hill Education.

Gegez, E., Arslan, M., Cengiz, E., & Uydacı, M. (2003). *Uluslararası Pazarlama Çevresi*. İstanbul, Turkey: Der Yayınları.

Geiersbach, N. (2010). The impact of international business on the global economy. *Business Intelligence Journal*, *3*(2), 119–129.

Ghoshal, S., & Bartlett, C. A. (1988). Creation, adoption and diffusion of innovations by subsidiaries of multinational corporations. *Journal of International Business Studies*, *19*(3), 365–388. doi:10.1057/palgrave.jibs.8490388

Gilpin, R. (2016). *The political economy of international relations*. Princeton University Press.

Güven, A. B., & Öniş, Z. (2010). The global economic crisis and the future of neoliberal globalization: Rupture versus continuity. *Available at SSRN 1676730*.

Hatzichronoglou, T. (1996). *Globalisation and competitiveness: relevant indicators (No. 1996/5)*. OECD Publishing.

Heenan, D. A., & Perlmutter, H. V. (1979). *Multinational organization development*. Addison-Wesley.

Hersey, P., Blanchard, K. H., & Johnson, D. E. (2007). *Management of organizational behavior* (Vol. 9). Upper Saddle River, NJ: Prentice Hall.

Hill, C. (2008). International business: Competing in the global marketplace. *Strategic Direction, 24*(9).

Hill, C. W., Jones, G. R., & Schilling, M. A. (2014). *Strategic management theory: an integrated approach*. Cengage Learning.

Hitt, M. A., Ireland, R. D., & Hoskisson, R. E. (2012). *Strategic management cases: competitiveness and globalization*. Cengage Learning.

Holt, D. H., & Wigginton, K. W. (2002). *International management*. South-Western Pub.

İslamoğlu, A. H. (1999). *Pazarlama yönetimi: stratejik ve global yaklaşım*. Beta Basım Yayım Dağıtım AŞ.

Jarblad, A. (2003). *The global political economy of transnational corporations: a theory of asymmetric interdependence*.

Karaaslan, A., & Tuncer, G. (1994). Uluslararası Rekabet Gücünün Artırılmasında Temel Devlet Politikaları. *Management Decision, 32*(2), 49.

Kester, W. C., & Luehrman, T. A. (1989). Are we feeling more competitive yet? The exchange rate gambit. *MIT Sloan Management Review, 30*(2), 19.

Kibritçioğlu, A. (1996). Uluslararası rekabet gücüne kavramsal bir yaklaşım. *MPM Verimlilik Dergisi, 96*(3), 109–122.

Klaas Jagersma, P. (2005). Cross-border alliances: Advice from the executive suite. *The Journal of Business Strategy, 26*(1), 41–50. doi:10.1108/02756660510575041

Kotabe, M., Helsen, K., & Kotabe, M. (1998). *Global marketing management*. New York, NY: Wiley.

Krugman, P. (1994). Competitiveness: A dangerous obsession. *Foreign Affairs, 73*(2), 28. doi:10.2307/20045917

Lall, S. (2000). *Turkish performance in exporting manufactures: a comparative structural analysis*. Queen Elizabeth House.

Lilienthal, D. E. (1960). *The multinational corporation: A review of some problems and opportunities for business management in a period of world-wide economic change*. Development and Resources Corporation.

Luthans, F., & Doh, J. P. (2012). *International management: Culture, strategy, and behavior*. New York: McGraw-Hill.

Madsen, T. L., & Walker, G. (2015). *Modern competitive strategy*. McGraw Hill.

Nelson, R. R., & Winter, S. G. (1982). The Schumpeterian tradeoff revisited. *The American Economic Review, 72*(1), 114–132.

Oğuztürk, A. G. D. B. S. (2003). Yenilik kavramı ve teorik temelleri. *Süleyman Demirel Üniversitesi İktisadi ve İdari Bilimler Fakültesi Dergisi, 8*(2).

Oral, M. (2004). *Rekabet Gücü Ölçümü Ve Strateji Saptanması*. Laval Üniversitesi, Yönetim Bilimleri Fakültesi, Ste-Foy Québec, RQ. GİK 7P4. Canada.

Oral, M., Singer, A. E., & Kettani, O. (1989). The level of international competitiveness and its strategic implications. *International Journal of Research in Marketing*, 6(4), 267–282. doi:10.1016/0167-8116(89)90054-2

Özalp, İ. (1998). *Çokuluslu İşletmeler: Uluslararası Yaklaşım*. Anadolu Üniversitesi Yayınları.

Özalp, İ. (Ed.). (2004). *Uluslararasi İşletmecilik*. Anadolu Universitesi.

Pearce, J. A., & Robinson, R. B. (2005). Formulation, implementation, and control of competitive strategy. McGraw-Hill.

Phatak, A. V., Bhagat, R. S., & Kashlak, R. J. (2005). *International management: Managing in a diverse and dynamic global environment*. New York, NY: McGraw-Hill Irwin.

Porter, M. (1990). e. (1990). The competitive advantage of nations. *Harvard Business Review*, 68(2), 73–93.

Porter, M. (2010). *Rekabet üzerine*. İstanbul, Turkey: Optimist Yayınları.

Porter, M. E. (1980). *Techniques for analyzing industries and competitors. Competitive Strategy*. New York: Free.

Porter, M. E. (1998). Clusters and competition. *On competition*, 7, 91.

Porter, M. E. (2000). *Rekabet Stratejisi, Sektör ve Rakip Analizi Teknikleri (Çeviri: Gülen Ulubilgen) Sistem Yayıncılık, 1* (p. 16). İstanbul, Turkey: Basım.

Porter, M. E. (2008a). Competitive advantage: Creating and sustaining superior performance, New York City.

Porter, M. E. (2008b). *Competitive strategy: Techniques for analyzing industries and competitors*. Simon and Schuster.

Rothaermel, F. T. (2013). *Strategic management: concepts*. New York, NY: McGraw-Hill Irwin.

Sarıçoban, B. S. O. K. (2013). Küresel Rekabette Kümelenme ve İnovasyonun Rolü. *Sosyal ve Beşeri Bilimler Dergisi*, 5(1), 94–104.

Sarıdoğan, E. (2010). *Mikroekonomi ve makroekonomi düzeyinde küresel rekabet gücünü etkileyen faktörler ve stratejiler*. İTO.

Schwab, K., & Sala-i-Martín, X. (2016, April). The global competitiveness report 2013–2014: Full data edition. World Economic Forum.

Shenkar, O., Luo, Y., & Chi, T. (2014). *International business*. Routledge. doi:10.4324/9780203584866

Sherman, A. W. Jr, & Bohlander, G. W. (1992). Managing human resources. Cincinnati: South. *Western Publishing Co., Wright, BE, Davis, BS (2003). Job Satisfaction in the Public Sector: The Role of the Work Environment. American Review of Public Administration*, 33(1), 70–90.

Slywotzky, A., & Hoban, C. (2007). Stop competing yourself to death: Strategic collaboration among rivals. *The Journal of Business Strategy*, 28(3), 45–55. doi:10.1108/02756660710746274

Smith, A. (1950). An inquiry into the nature and causes of the wealth of nations, (1776).

Snowdon, B., & Stonehouse, G. (2006). Competitiveness in a globalised world: Michael Porter on the microeconomic foundations of the competitiveness of nations, regions, and firms. *Journal of International Business Studies*, *37*(2), 163–175. doi:10.1057/palgrave.jibs.8400190

Terpstra, V., Foley, J., & Sarathy, R. (2012). *International marketing*. Naper Press.

Ulengin, F., Önsel, Ş., & Kaaata, S. (2011). Türkiye'nin Küresel Rekabet Düzeyi: Dünya Ekonomik Forumu Küresel Rekabetçilik Raporu'na Göre Bir Değerlendirme. *TÜSİAD-Sabancı Üniversitesi Rekabet Forumu, Sektörel Dernekler Federasyonu Yayını, 1*.

Wheelen, T. L., & Hunger, J. D. (2011). *Concepts in strategic management and business policy*. Pearson Education India.

Wheelen, T. L., Hunger, J. D., Hoffman, A. N., & Bamford, C. E. (2010). *Strategic management and business policy*. Upper Saddle River, NJ: Prentice Hall.

Chapter 5
Evaluating the Importance of Behavioral Finance in the Financial Marketing Area:
An Analysis of Turkish Academic Studies

Serhat Yüksel
Istanbul Medipol University, Turkey

Ece Nur Temizel
Istanbul Medipol University, Turkey

ABSTRACT

This chapter investigates the thesis in Turkey written in the field of behavioral finance. An important objective is to guide the relevant researchers who are missing in the fields in the literature. For this purpose, 60 theses written so far have been examined with bibliometric analysis method. The period range of these theses is 2003-2018. When Daniel Kahneman won the Nobel Prize in 2002, behavioral finance, which started to attract attention in our country, started to gain momentum especially in times of crisis when unexplained behaviors were explained by the concept of rational people. In addition, 49 of them consisted of master's degree and the remaining 11 were doctoral dissertations. State universities constitute a very large weight of the relevant universities. Studies on behavioral finance have been gathered under various topics. The most studied subject has "character traits of the investors". This is followed by "investment in stocks" and "anomalies".

INTRODUCTION

Human beings' behavior has been questioned for centuries, and each one has been searched for. From the 1870s when psychology was accepted as a scientific field, human behaviors were started to be investigated scientifically. The development of behavioral finance, which tries to find answers to various questions by dissolving human behavior and finance field in the same pot, is much more recent than the

DOI: 10.4018/978-1-7998-2559-3.ch005

other areas that constitute it. When the development of behavioral finance is examined, two cognitive psychologists named Daniel Kahneman and Amos Tversky in the 1970s and the development of Expectation Theory which they formed as a result of various scientific experiments are considered as the first steps in the name of behavioral finance. Afterwards, when Richard Thaler named this new developing area as behavioral finance, a path was made that seemed to be discussed for many years.

The traditional financial approach and the effective market hypothesis established within this framework argue that investors are rational and always make the right decisions because they act in their own interests (Dinçer et al., 2019 a, b, c, d). However, over time, the fact that investors exhibited some behaviors indicating that they were not rational has caused the traditional financial approach to lose its influence and give way to a behavioral finance approach. As a matter of fact, the aim of the behavioral finance is to investigate the trends and anomalies that remove the individuals from rationality and to investigate the effects on the investment decisions.

The discipline of behavioral finance reminds us that we are all human beings. Being human means the probability of making mistakes because human beings have many different emotions and hundreds of different thoughts. At the same time, these feelings and thoughts can be changed very frequently due to stimuli from the environment and can be controlled by the related stimuli. In summary, human behavior does not have a complete rationality as mentioned in the effective market hypothesis. For this reason, it is very difficult to predict the investment decisions of the individuals and their consequences.

In addition to all this, behavioral finance argues that investors decide in many prejudices, especially cognitive, emotional, social and self-deception. These prejudices can lead investors to take erroneous decisions and remove them from rationality. In addition, these prejudices, which cause the formation of anomalies in the market, result in price deviations in stocks (Dinçer, Yüksel, & Adalı, 2019). Effective market hypothesis and traditional finance models have been insufficient to explain the causes and consequences of these anomalies. Instead, new hypotheses and models have been created with behavioral finance approach, such as Barberis, Schleifer, Vishny model, Daniel, Hirshleifer, Subrahmanyam model, Hong and Stein model.

Parallel to the issues listed above, in this study, master's and doctoral theses that have been released regarding behavioral finance in Turkey were examined. In this context, 60 different theses which are named as behavioral finance have been analyzed. These theses were evaluated according to their year, language, type, university and subject. According to the results of the analysis, it is aimed to make some suggestions to the researchers. The main novelty of this study is that it is the first analysis feature built in Turkey in this framework.

General Information About Behavioral Finance

The Definition of Behavioral Finance

Financial theory has been a subject of debate for years. The accuracy of traditional methods based on old rules has been adopted in the financial world for many years. On the other hand, traditional financial methods have become debatable especially in recent years. In this context, some researchers have approached finance with a modern perspective. On the other hand, it is assumed that people are rational in the traditional approach. In other words, it is accepted that people always make reasonable decisions in this financial sense (Hirshleifer, 2015).

The inclusion of human behavior in traditional finance has also taken place with behavioral finance. The adoption of this approach was based on the scientific studies of Tversky and Kahneman, two cognitive psychologists in 1979. With these studies, impulses, prejudices and mind models have been added to finance science. As a result, in addition to the expected utility theory, the expectation theory was formed. In sum, the behavioral finance approach has become a modern approach by incorporating human behavior into finance science (Kahneman & Tversky, 1979).

People are very different from each other in the first place. Then, the individual life events that shape the life of each individual, the characteristics they form as a result of these events, the behavior patterns, the forms and levels of prejudice differ to the extent that we cannot refuse. As a matter of fact, modern finance approach did not ignore the existence of such effects in investment decision making behavior. The prejudices highlighted the individual's error-making ability by accepting the behaviors and emotional processes they can demonstrate and showed us that the definition of rational human being, which forms the basis of the traditional financial approach, is not actually possible.

The concept of rational behavior in the traditional financial approach is the result of all individuals in the market acting as a rational investor. In other words, this concept refers to investors who take uniform decisions and do not repeat their mistakes. In addition, investors are said to be investors who regulate their investments solely on the basis of their risk and return, do not carry any bias, are emotionally free and act in accordance with their own interests (Dinçer et al., 2018a,b,c). In the light of this information, it is assumed that the type of market formed by investors who have the highest and highest level of information processing in the market is the effective market.

In this context, the traditional financial approach, which recognizes that all investors are fully rational, has introduced the concept of Homo Economicus. This concept refers to individuals who have complete knowledge of their choices, are selective, consistent and always prefer most. Models such as the Capital Asset Pricing Model (CAPM) were developed over time, based on the assumption that these individuals always choose the right one for them. In other words, these models claim that the individuals concerned are rational in their investment decisions (Kisman & Restiyanita, 2015; Dinçer & Yüksel, 2018).

In contrast, the aforementioned models are insufficient to explain the various anomalies that have been formed and new models have been created instead. These models also considered that the investor is not rational as it is on the basis of behavioral finance. In other words, in this approach, investors are far from the rationality of the traditional approach. In addition, they are influenced by psychological, cognitive and mental processes in decision-making. In sum, scientists who adopt a behavioral finance approach claim that investors are not rational in their decisions. These researchers state that the main reason behind this claim is the financial crises. In other words, according to this view, if the investors were rationally, there should not have been a large-scale financial crisis on a global scale like the 2008 Mortgage crisis.

The Main Differences of Behavioral Finance Comparing with Effective Market Theorem

The effective market hypothesis proposed by Eugene Fama in the 1970s suggests that asset prices reflect all kinds of information. At the same time, effective markets are markets where securities are immediately, accurately and fully responsive to information. This hypothesis argues that the market is regulated by rules, and therefore superior profit is prevented. In other words, it is not possible to generate above-average returns in these markets.

In order for a market to be effective, investors should also be rational. Therefore, the effective market hypothesis created within the framework of the traditional financial approach is based on the assumption that investors act rationally in the trading of securities. In addition, some of the investors in the market show rational behaviors in certain directions, and even if they deviate the stock prices from the required value, the rest will continue to behave rationally and prevent the prices from being adversely affected. Because the prices shaped by the behaviors of non-rational investors will be considered as an opportunity by rational investors and will benefit from this arbitrage opportunity. As a result, stock prices will return to the basic level (Wang et al., 2016).

The Definition of Anomalies

Effective Market Hypothesis argues that the return on the markets is the same in every period. However, this situation is not possible under the conditions of irrational investors. Over time, price movements occurring in certain periods in the markets and changing returns depending on these movements were determined. These findings were in contradiction with the effective market hypothesis and were named as anomaly. The concept of anomaly can be defined as the dictionary meaning as distancing or deviating from normal. The anomalies in financial markets are formed by non-rational investor behavior that occurs in certain direction in the markets. For reasons of formation of anomalies, we can talk about the actors acting with emotions in psychological tendencies. These anomalies are divided into two as calendar anomalies and price anomalies (Thaler & Ganser, 2015; Ramiah et al., 2015).

The anomalies that cause a positive or negative return in certain time intervals compared to others are called calendar anomaly. In all known markets such as stocks, foreign exchange, gold, futures and commodity markets, the positive or negative deviations in returns on any given day, week, month, holiday period or certain time periods form the calendar anomalies. This anomaly is examined in two sub-headings as anomalies related to days, anomalies related to months. Deviations in stock prices that are in conflict with the effective market hypothesis are defined as price anomalies. These anomalies are considered as two headings which are the anomalies resulting from excessive reaction and anomalies caused by incomplete reaction (Noori, 2016).

Different Investor Tendencies in Behavioral Finance

In this study, behavioral finance tendencies consist of cognitive, emotional, self-deprivation and social tendencies.

Cognitive Tendencies

The most common cognitive tendencies are anchoring, loss avoidance, representation, framing, mental accounting and conservation tendencies. Together with these cognitive tendencies, the individual undergoes a brief analysis process of the information that is present in the individual. These tendencies, which are the result of automatic thinking system and which save time for the individual, also emerge when making decisions that need to be implemented immediately or more or less of the information. In summary, these tendencies can accelerate decision-making processes and may lead the individual to take erroneous decisions as it prevents the detailed and correct examination of information

Anchoring Tendency: Anchoring can be defined as consideration of information that should not be directly effective in decision-making process and taking into account as variable. The mooring model shows itself as a cognitive trend. It is seen that the individual, who needs to make a decision in the face of the unknowns, uses the anchoring model when it is necessary to base his / her thoughts on a foundation. The individual determines himself / herself a reference value in the decision-making process based on his previous experiences. In addition, these designated reference values are taken as the base point. Taking the base point is often misleading for individuals (Pompian, 2016).

The anchoring trend displayed by investors may prevent the correct pricing of securities. Historical data from stock traders may show a low response to this situation when the share values of the firm, which are regularly low, go down. This is because investors think that the firm will anchor past profit performance and stock values and that the upward trend is temporary. In addition to this, investors who invest in stocks that are in constant decline may anchor this stock to the stock price and evaluate them as an opportunity to buy that share cheaply. If short-term fluctuations are the reason for the decrease in the stocks, the investor will take advantage of the shares it receives from the low price. As a second possibility, the reason for the decline of stocks is the firm's basic imbalances. In this case, the investor will suffer losses due to a wrong decision made by anchoring.

Loss Avoidance Tendency: The tendency to avoid loss is one of the most basic characteristics of mankind. This trend affects the investment decisions of the individual and plays a decisive role in these decisions. As it is defended in expectation theory, what the investor wants to avoid is not risk but loss. Even when the individual loses something, he gets up to twice as much as he feels when he will win the same thing. As it is understood from this, the size of the joy of earning 200 USD is less than the size of sadness of losing 200 USD (Blajer-Gołębiewska et al., 2018).

Representation Tendency: It is emphasized that investors tend to consider the latest developments in decision-making. In other words, an investor attaches importance to the latest developments in the prices of companies' stocks when purchasing stocks. Therefore, according to this trend, investors prefer the stocks, which have recently entered an upward trend (Rohde, 2018).

For example, suppose an investor wants to invest in airline companies. The investor mentioned in this process will take into consideration the previous period price movements of these different airline companies. According to the traditional finance theory, the investor needs to make a detailed analysis when making a decision and to rationally invest in the company that he thinks will bring the most profit. On the other hand, according to the tendency to represent this investor, the investor would prefer to have the highest price in the recent period as he / she believes that his / her recent price represents the stock.

Framing Tendency: Framing is a tendency that occurs under loss avoidance behavior. This tendency is one of the best examples that the individual does not make rational decisions. Because the rational individual decides regardless of the question being asked and the framework presented. Individuals under the framing effect can give different answers even to the same questions asked from different angles. This inconsistency in the responses of individuals results from the aforementioned effect. Here, the perceptions of the investor come into play. Even if the two options present the same results, the individual would prefer the option to keep the loss in the background and try to shrink (Zhang & Jin, 2015).

How much you will spend a visit with your doctor about the success of this operation you hear from her 90 percent of the success of your operation will make you believe that really good, the rate of failure of this operation 10 percent of you will worry about the operation (Thaler, 2017). To summarize, a specific situation is raised, or a question is asked about the answer we will give an answer. This effect is called the framing effect. The framing effect leads individuals to think narrowly and, consequently, to make wrong decisions.

Mental Accounting Tendency: The concept of mental accounting tendency includes errors that are likely to fall in their calculations as a result of different divisions for their different needs instead of evaluating their earnings as a whole. The existence of mental accounting trend creates irrationality with the mental categories it creates on investors. Investors in this tendency show different approaches to the income they earn by the place where the money comes from. For example, an individual who earns 1,000,000 USD in a lottery will spend more easily in the case of getting out of the lottery according to the same amount of money he / she accumulates each month. The reason for this situation is that the value of the money earned by the individuals by chance is less than they earn by labor (Grover, 2015).

If there is a student who is both working and studying and this student is also receiving a scholarship for his success at school, he / she uses the scholarship to meet the holiday, concert and theater tickets he / she receives while he / she accumulates the salary he / she earns to meet the physiological needs and to receive graduate education abroad. Here, the student's scholarship can be more easily spent than the salary he / she receives, and this can be related to the more comfortable spending of non-laborless money such as lottery in the theory of mental accounting. It is also an example of mental accounting that this student who owes a reimbursement debt has kept his / her debt and the money he / she accumulates for education in a separate account. The fact that he accumulates the money he earns on an interest-free deposit account due to his importance on his education and the amount of interest added on his balance sheet as the payment period extends, and the fact that his net capital is actually decreasing, is an example of misinformation. The error here arises from the values attributed to the individual's particular assets.

This trend is contrary to the modern portfolio theory and causes the investor to evaluate each stock in his mind in different accounts. This situation may be caused by the absence of interaction between stocks, the total risk cannot be calculated correctly or misunderstood. Risk and return calculation will be deducted from diversification errors in portfolios which cannot be done correctly. As a result, investors will be exposed to low returns, high risks and even losses (Ede, 2007).

Conservation Tendency: Mankind tends to remain as much trust as possible and to avoid any possibility of harm to this area. We can evaluate the conservatism tendency as an individual trying to remain within the confidence area. This tendency results in an individual's self-esteem in the face of uncertainties, even in the case of market changes, taking into account his own predictions and developing beliefs about them (Aydin et al., 2018).

This conservative attitude towards the new information and current data that contradicts the decisions of the investor, leads to incomplete or late response to the market and consequently the price deviations in the stocks. This tendency also undermines the objectivity of decisions taken by the individual due to his / her commitment to historical data in the decision-making phase. The hypothesis of the individual who will invest in a company will be that all the information that the company will consider about the company will be in line with the hypothesis. This will cause the individual who is in a tendency to hold a favor to choose the ones who are good at eliminating the bad ones from the news about the company they invest or will make in the sectoral magazines, on the internet or in the economy channels. Even when interpreting technical analysis data, the individual will fall into the same error. Thus, the individual will concentrate on the data that support his / her own estimates.

Emotional Tendencies

Emotion can be expressed as a trend that allows an individual to be connected to or avoiding an object or situation. It includes three factors, cognitive, physiological and behavioral. Emotional tendencies are caused by various emotional factors and affect decision making processes. These trends are mainly examined under the heading of lack of autocontrol, tendency to avoid uncertainty and tendency to avoid regret.

Autocontrol Deficiency Tendency: Autocontrol can be defined as the restriction and regulation of the reactions and behaviors of the individual in order to reach a more important purpose in the future. Autocontrol requires to act within a certain discipline and not to lose feelings. In this context, the investor in the lack of autocontrol is an investor who can move away from the investment targets he has determined in the long term by considering the gains in the short term. In this way, this investor can take the wrong decisions which may cause disadvantage in the future. On the other hand, an investor who is a member of the private pension system sets an example for investors with self-control to save a certain amount of their earnings in order to lead a comfortable retirement life (Rogers et al., 2015).

Uncertainty Avoidance Tendency: The avoidance of uncertainty can be defined as the tendency of the investor to assume risks with known possibilities instead of taking risks with unforeseen possibilities. In financial markets full of uncertainties, investors may abandon the preference of investing when they have to take risks that include unforeseen probabilities, as mentioned above. Some scientific studies show that investors feel more distant from uncertainty when they receive the shares of the company with the feeling of familiarity with some firms. For this reason, investors will invest in the stocks they have already invested or know. With this trend, investors avoid investing abroad and evaluate their investments in Turkey. If they are going to invest abroad, they will invest in the most well-known and biggest brands. The fact that the individual investing in Germany invests in Mercedes-Benz is an example. As a result, this tendency prevents us from holding stocks from different sectors in different countries. As a result, the portfolio diversification of Markowitz cannot be realized, and the level of risk increases, and the level of return may be reduced (Bachmann et al., 2019).

Tendency to Avoid Regret: Regret, sadness or anguish of an individual because of not being able to get the expected result about a behavior, can be defined as not being satisfied with this past behavior. The avoidance of regret is the tendency of the investors to avoid any further discontent about their decisions. Individuals feel regret, whether they are small or big. The individual approaches the decisions taken to avoid this feeling carefully and avoids making erroneous decisions. Equity investors feel regrets when the price of the stock is lower or the price of the stock that they have planned to buy for a long time has increased. This investor will have a tendency to dispose of his / her most significant share. He will not sell and keep on hand the hopes of losing the day to hope that he will make a profit. In this way, he would have avoided the loss in his portfolio and regret (Pruna et al., 2019).

Self-Deprivation Tendencies

These trends prevent investors from taking lessons from past mistakes. On the other hand, these trends emerge when individuals have inadequate knowledge about the subject or have limited time in decision-making. Trends in self-deception; the tendency to over-reliance, the tendency to over-optimism, and the wrong assessment tendency are evaluated under three different headings.

Over-Reliance Tendency: The individual, who has a high confidence in himself, bases his talents, intuitions and predictions on intact foundations. This behavior is an obstacle to their success. The main

Evaluating the Importance of Behavioral Finance in the Financial Marketing Area

reason is that because of the aforementioned tendency, the individual considers his decisions and predictions to be more accurate than any other information he encounters. Actually, this situation, which works against the individual, causes the talents to highlight their success rather than failure, rather than chance. The investor with extreme confidence values the information they have more than they should. Therefore, he thinks that no matter what the market conditions, he will provide a positive return. In fact, this situation, which works against the investor, causes them to act inadequately in the decision and analysis processes. As a result, the investor misinterpreted the risk levels and made unsuccessful investments (Çömlekçi & Özer, 2018).

Over-Optimism Tendency: Although extreme optimism and overconfidence are two interdependent and interdependent concepts, it can be said that the most basic situation separating these two concepts is due to the individual's self-belief, while the extreme optimism is due to his belief in the environment and external factors. Extremely optimistic individuals see the possibility of realization of the events they want to happen to be very high, and the probability of realization of events that they do not want to happen is in misconception. At the same time, the expected earnings for their investments are very high compared to their real earnings. This trend, which removes the investor from rationality, can cause investors to make very risky investments and damages because they believe that they will not harm. Even if individuals are not likely to win games of chance, such as lottery, betting and lotto, it is a result of extreme optimism that they play with high hope (Efremidze et al., 2016).

Wrong Assessment Tendency: The tendency to incorrectly evaluate errors is also known as the above-mentioned loading bias. Investors, who misjudge their mistakes, do not have the opportunity to learn from their mistakes as they link their failures to bad luck and other external factors. Therefore, these investors, who are likely to repeat their mistakes, will face various problems in the market (Invernizzi, 2018).

Social Tendencies

Human beings have been growing in a social environment since the first day they were born. Therefore, human being is a social entity and influenced by various elements of the groups it is involved in. The individual who is concerned about being excluded by the social groups in which he / she is located and at the same time making decisions on his own will keep up with the decisions of the majority. For these reasons, social trends such as herd behavior and information cascade occur. These tendencies play a restrictive role in the individual's decisions as they require to act together.

Herd Behavior Tendency: Herd behavior can be defined as the belief that certain events or beliefs are spread among groups, communities, countries, and believing in that thought or situation without considering their positive negative aspects. The individual exhibiting this behavior is in an effort to avoid regret because he thinks that the error rate of large communities is less than their individual decisions. Thus, the individual belonging to a group will feel safer. The herd behavior in financial markets is due to investors who buy or sell the same shares at the same time. This behavior is influenced by economic channels, internet sites or expert opinions, or in case of information being imitated by the fact that it is difficult or costly to access the information or the interpretation of the information is technically insufficient. Investors with herd behavior are completely irrationally determined by their feelings and their psychological tendencies. This is the main reason for financial crises (Chang & Lin, 2015).

Information Cascade Tendency: The information cascade is the result of people moving together in one direction with the herd behavior they show. In other words, it is the result of imitations of the investment behavior of individuals as a result of paying attention to the decisions of other investors and giving importance to their decisions while making investment decisions. When the fluctuations that we cannot explain with any of the economic conditions in the market occur, investors tend to follow the behavior of the related investors by considering that they do not own the cause, but due to the various market information that other investors have. This monitoring trend, which is shown by the investors, causes the new investors to participate in the information cascade after the fluctuation continues (Shamandar, 2018).

Behavioral Finance Models

Behavioral finance models complemented the missing aspects of the models that were accepted as valid in the traditional financial approach and added human psychology to the relevant models. It is argued that the new models on these foundations are more robust and more successful in explaining the non-rational investor behaviors. Traders' tendencies tend to remove their behavior from rationality. With this divergence, price movements in the markets can be unpredictable and inexplicable. Prices are higher or lower than the value should be the basic concepts of behavioral finance is one of the anomalies. It was not possible to explain the abnormal investor behaviors with excessive or incomplete reactions because of the effective market hypothesis. As a result, new models have emerged that try to explain investor behavior and market movements with a more modern perspective.

Barberis, Schleifer, Vishny Model

According to this model formed by behavioral finance approach, investors are not rational. The model is based on two misconceptions of investors. One of these misconceptions is conservatism and the other is the misconception. Conservatism is the tendency of investors to change their thoughts very quickly against the new market information they face. The error of representation is formed by the fact that investors give the most weight to the most recent situation in decision-making processes (Alti & Titman, 2019).

These two misconceptions have caused investors to give extreme or low reactions to the prices in the market. As a result of the changes in profits, investors react inadequately with changes in the conservatism tendency when they believe that profits will return to the average level. After several successive market trends, the belief that investors are starting a new trend is explained by the tendency to be representative and causes excessive reaction.

Daniel, Hirshleifer, Subrahmanyam Model

The model is based on two psychological tendencies. One of these tendencies is the over-reliance. Excessive confidence is the result of investors' giving their own knowledge and intuition to more importance than the information in the market. Self-attribution arises from the results of the investment decisions made by the individual, especially because they connect the successful ones to the soundness of their decision-making systems. This model argues that traders with extreme confidence behave cause the market to overreact to private information and to react low to public information (Daniel & Hirshleifer, 2015).

Hong and Stein Model

This model argues that there are two types of investors in the market: news hunters and momentum investors. This means that the relationship between the two types of investors balances each other and constitutes the market. In addition, it can be said that these types of investors were created to explain the anomalies they create in the market. Both news-hunters and momentum investors are referred to as irrational investors because they use only a portion of the information in the market. News predators use only the information they receive for the market and for the future. The fact that this information is not immediately reflected on the market causes a low reaction and results in the value of the stocks below the required level. On the other hand, momentum investors consider price movements as information source and use past prices in the analysis process. In this case, it is argued that it causes a high reaction (Cheema & Nartea, 2017).

LITERATURE REVIEW

In Statman's (2017) study, he pointed to second generation behavioral finance models. In this study, the differences between the first and second generation models are emphasized. In this context, it was stated that individuals were irrational in the first generation model. On the other hand, it was emphasized that individuals in the second generation exhibited normal behavior rather than irrational. In summary, in this study, it is stated that important issues such as reducing the poverty of the countries and increasing the social status of individuals should be handled with the second generation behavioral finance models.

Costa et al. (2019) conducted a literature review on behavioral economics and behavioral finance. In order to achieve this aim, they benefited from bibliometric analysis approach. In this context, 2617 different articles in the "sciencedirect" database were analyzed. As a result of the examinations, a significant increase was observed in the studies conducted in both areas. In addition to the result, it was understood that the studies conducted in the field of behavioral economics were higher than those in behavioral finance. However, it is stated that future studies on behavioral finance will contribute to the literature.

Costa et al. (2017) used a bibliometric analysis method to determine the relationship between cognitive bias and financial decision making, such as anchoring, validation, overconfidence. In this context, 889 articles published between 1990 and 2016 were analyzed using the "webofscience" database. As a result of these analyzes, it has been stated that the frequency of the prejudices mentioned in behavioral finance articles has increased significantly since 2008.

Paulo et al. (2018) conducted a bibliometric analysis of keywords in 58 separate Brazilian periodicals covering the period 2007-2017. As a result of this analysis, it was concluded that 2013 was the most remarkable growth figure for behavioral finance to be included in journals. It has been observed that most of the studies in Brazil about behavioral finance have been influenced by the work of Kahneman and Tversky. On the other hand, when the citation rates were examined, it was seen that the citation for the authors with the highest number of articles was not the same, and they attributed the reason for the fact that the authors were more likely to write in journals other than Brazilian journals.

Longo (2014) stated that behavioral finance findings provide a positive indicator for investors to generate positive returns for their portfolios. Based on this, it is stated that asset management companies are also starting to take into account the behavioral finance elements in their investment strategies. In this study, which mentioned the existence of many anomalies in behavioral finance, it emphasized that the most active investment management can be achieved by integrating anomalies into investment strategies. It is foreseen that investment analysts will become persons who conduct behavioral factor analysis not only performing basic and technical analysis in time.

Xu (2014) investigated the behavioral factors effective in EFT investment process. As a result of this research conducted in Hong Kong region, it has been revealed that individuals take their EFT investment decisions by being affected by behavioral characteristics as well as calculation of risk and return. With this study, many important information about the behavioral characteristics of the capital market in Hong Kong revealed. In the future, it was emphasized that behavioral perspective will be effective in modeling of EFT market.

Garcia (2013) aims to contribute to the behavioral finance literature by examining how individuals perceive and process information when making financial decisions. Empirical studies show that overtrust and limited cognitive abilities play a dominant role in financial decision-making. The results of this article also support the empirical studies mentioned. In addition, it was emphasized that the social, cultural and historical characteristics of the countries that should not be generalized in the exploration and evaluation of the financial system in developed or developing countries will affect this system and differentiate them according to their own autonomy.

Loerwald and Stemmann (2016) emphasized that financial education has the property of increasing rational decision-making competence. During the decision-making process, the existence of information detection, processing and evaluation processes are mentioned. The analysis shows that typical anomalies, intuitive information and personal bias can affect the quality of decisions. In addition to these, it was mentioned that the financial trainings and experiments that will be given will enable young people to realize their own prejudices and abnormalities and play a role in developing new and more robust behavioral strategies. On the other side, Lu and Li (2012) aimed to develop a Bayesian approach to analyze multi-group nonlinear structural equation models. They proposed a method for estimating the parameters and choosing a suitable financial model and used this method to investigate the relationship between insider learners' behavioral factors and all behavioral factors.

Grosse (2012) established its study in order to analyze the crisis of 2008-2009 with the perspective of behavioral finance. Then, by determining the elements of the crisis, the government policies and the changes that need to be made in company management and the strategies to be implemented. It was emphasized that governments should develop new policy applications in order to prevent excessive credit lending and therefore excessive risk taking as in the 2008 crisis. It has been argued that these new policies are necessary in order to predict and react to investor behaviors by creating market balloons with herd psychology as in the related crisis.

Albaity and Rahman (2012) investigated how individual factors such as gender, religion, ethnicity, risk taking, chance, trust, regret affect investor behavior. As a result of the research, it was found that gender difference has a significant relationship with risk taking behavior and over confidence. The belief in religious belief and ethnicity, on the other hand, concluded that they had a significant impact on risk taking and therefore profit maximization. In general, a Malaysian portfolio has found a high level of risk taking and regret and a low level of maximization and happiness.

Aren et al. (2016) aimed at evaluating investor surveys that focused on factors such as saving effect, herd behavior in journals and determining gaps on the subject. For this purpose, they analyzed the reasons why prejudices occurred between 2005 and 2014. They have determined the existence of prejudices on institutional investors and explained it with knowledge or culture. It is also the first article to outline the prejudices presented by institutional investors, suggesting empirical evidence about prejudices.

Riff and Yagil (2016) aimed to measure behavioral factors related to pre-investment in domestic assets. Various experiments were carried out in this direction. As a result of the experiments it was determined that familiarity and precision factors triggered this prejudice. The tests were carried out in three different markets: normal, bear and bull market. The results show that investment in domestic assets has increased especially in the bearish market. In summary, the reasons and consequences of investors' avoidance of international portfolio diversification and their emphasis on domestic investments were emphasized.

Deshmukh and Joseph (2016) aimed to evaluate the investment fund decisions given by investors in Raipur. In this context, a survey was conducted on 300 investors with different demographic characteristics. The findings of the study show that factors such as perception, motivation and incentive potential play an important role in making an investment decision. Finally, it is said that mutual fund companies should focus on these factors to develop strategies to attract investors.

Kumar and Goyal (2015) conducted a systematic study of the literature on behavioral finance. The method of the study was reported as systematic literature review. In the literature study conducted between 1980 and 2013, the publication year, publication journal, country research, statistical writing methods and source representation were taken into consideration. As a result of the researches, it is concluded that there is no empirical studies on the individuals exhibiting herd behavior, whereas the investment bias against domestic assets is examined predominantly. In addition, it is stated that limited research has been done on the related subject in developing economies.

De Bortoli et al. (2019) examined the expectation theory, investor profile analysis, five factor personality test and cognitive reflection tests in the best way to explain the risk profiles of the investor in their financial asset investment decisions. The results were analyzed using regression method. According to the investor profile analysis, it is determined that people with high risk tolerance and experience are more inclined to take risks in their investment decisions.

The purpose of Halaba and Çoşkun (2016) studies is to examine how commercial bank managers fulfill their decision-making behavior in the context of findings in the area of behavioral finance. The study discusses the importance of risk management in the banking sector. In addition to this, it has been emphasized that the managerial decision-making model under risk in commercial banking should be developed within the framework of behavioral finance elements through studies to help the standardization of risk management processes.

Ahmed et al. (2011) examined the decision-making process of small investors on the Lahore stock exchange. In this direction, the answers of 300 small investors in Lahore were collected by using questionnaire method. As a result of the study, it was determined that small investors were affected more from behavioral finance theories in decision making processes than traditional finance theories. In addition, it was mentioned that the findings confirm the expectation theory.

In the literature analysis, it is observed that most of the studies on behavioral finance are conducted in the survey. On the other hand, it is determined that the prejudices of investors are generally mentioned in the studies. Therefore, it is thought that a new study that determines the personality characteristics affecting the decisions of investors in the process of foreign exchange and gold investments will contribute to the literature.

AN APPLICATION ON TURKISH MASTER AND PHD THESES

Data Set and Scope

In this study, all theses which have the word "behavioral finance" are included in the study. This statement was written to the search engine of "tezyok.gov.tr". As a result, it was learned that there were 60 theses. Of these 60 theses, 49 consisted of master's thesis, and 11 of them were doctoral thesis. While 3 of the theses are accessible, 57 theses are accessible. The studies were written by 32 female and 28 male individuals. It is also understood that the related theses were written in the period of 2003-2018. In summary, 60 different theses mentioned in this study were included in the study with bibliometric analysis method.

Bibliometric Analysis

In this study, bibliometric analysis technique was used in the analysis process of theses. The method was developed by Pritchard (1969). In this study, common characteristics of written sources are tried to be determined. In this process, data related to the studies were first created. The related data were then subjected to some statistical analysis. In the bibliometric analysis method, it is possible to make evaluations as follows (Eti, 2019a,b):

- The number of years of work
- Topics of studies.
- Types of studies (books, book chapters, articles, etc.).
- The authors.
- References made in studies.
- References to these studies.

The bibliometric analysis method has been considered in many different fields in the literature. Hotamışlı and Eren (2014) evaluated the studies published in the journal Accounting and Finance with bibliometric analysis method. Beşel and Yardımcıoğlu (2017) conducted a similar study for the Journal of Finance. On the other hand, Armutlu and Ari (2010) benefited from this method when they examined the types of governance and Nurettin and Turkmen (2018) assessed the theses about the local food issues. In addition, Özel and Kozak (2012) analyzed tourism marketing, Yilmaz (2017) focused on restaurant tip, Fahimnia et al. (2017) considered green supply chain management, Bornmann and Mutz (2015) evaluated growth rates and Ruhanen et al. (2015) discussed the development of tourism with bibliometric analysis.

Analysis Results

The analysis of the theses was done first in the analysis period. The development information of 60 theses included in the study mentioned in Table 1 is given according to years.

As can be seen from Table 1, the thesis on behavioral finance started to be written in 2003 and continued to be published in 2018. Related theses taken to be examined chronologically the first written thesis on behavioral finance issues in Turkey seems to be in 2003. Between 2003 and 2006, only one thesis was written on the subject. The first increase in this regular course was experienced in 2007. Although

Table 1. Information of published theses by years

Year	Number of Thesis
2003	1
2004	0
2005	1
2006	1
2007	4
2008	3
2009	5
2010	3
2011	2
2012	6
2013	4
2014	2
2015	5
2016	4
2017	4
2018	15

the number of these theses increased in 2009 and 2012, the highest increase was observed in 2018. In light of this information, it is concluded that the time has become more popular in academic studies in behavioral finance in Turkey. Considering the mentioned information, it is estimated that the graduate and doctoral level studies about behavioral finance will increase in the coming periods.

In the second part of the study, the theses were analyzed according to the types of theses. According to the results of the analysis, it was determined that the master theses were very high compared to the doctoral thesis. On the other hand, it is concluded that there are limited number of dissertations related to the doctorate. The reason of having a limited number of doctoral theses is that doctoral research requires a comprehensive study. Since behavioral finance is a very new and unique field, it is understood that researchers are worried about doing extensive studies. In 2002, Daniel Kahneman received the Nobel Prize in Theory of Expectation. With this award received by Kahneman, arrows were directed to behavioral finance and started to gain value as a research topic in our country. In 2007, behavioral finance started to become popular and people's tendencies to go on research on this subject were again related to the crisis in those years. At the time of the crisis, researchers began to wonder more about the human behavior that caused the crisis. For this reason, four master's theses were written in the same year. It is seen that the theses written about the subject in 2018 have experienced a serious leap especially when we approach our day. In this case, it can be thought that the fact that traditional finance subjects had previously been subject to a large number of studies and that it was difficult for the researchers to reveal their individuality and to make an original study.

When the studies conducted in the field of behavioral finance in the field of behavioral finance studies of Higher Education Council are examined, it is determined that they are written in 39 different universities. State universities are predominant among institutions. When the distribution of the state university / foundation university is examined, it is seen that 30 of the 39 universities in the list are state universities and 9 of them are foundation universities. Among the first three institutions to publish the most thesis, Istanbul University is the first with 10 theses. Istanbul University is followed by Marmara University with 6 dissertations. In the third place, Gazi University has 4 thesis writing numbers. The distribution of thesis writing in the aforementioned 36 universities is shown in detail in Table 2.

In the last part of the bibliometric study, the distribution of the theses on behavioral finance is examined. The topic-based distribution of these theses is given in Table 3.

It is seen that behavioral finance is discussed under seven different headings. These titles; anomalies, private pension system, demographic factors, foreign exchange markets, stock investments, character traits and crisis process. Among the related schemas, there were 31 theses and 52% of the characters. This situation shows us that the researchers are curious about the behavioral finance. This topic is followed by 9 written theses and anomalies and stock investments. In the fourth row, as shown in the table, there is a private pension system.

SOLUTIONS AND RECOMMENDATIONS

As a result of this analysis, it is understood that behavioral finance is more preferred by years in Turkey. This issue basically argues that investors do not act rationally. In this context, increasing the number of new studies in this area is important for the country's economy. With the new studies to be made, it will be possible to analyze the factors which affect the investment decisions of the individuals, the most affected by these factors and how the market is affected in different anomalies. With these results, strategy proposals will be offered to market makers.

FUTURE RESEARCH DIRECTIONS

In this study, a topic which is quite new in the literature such as behavioral finance is discussed. In this context, bibliometric analysis was carried out on a thesis published in Turkey. In this way, this topic has been shown both for its current popularity and for new authors. In a new study to be carried out in the future, it is thought that it will be very useful to conduct a new study with different methods such as fuzzy logic.

CONCLUSION

The aim of this study is to analyze the master's and doctoral theses written in the field of behavioral finance in Turkey. In this context, all the theses included in the database of the Higher Education Board and which have the phrase of behavioral finance in the title are included in the study. According to the investigations, 60 different theses were found in this scope. These theses were examined in detail by using bibliometric analysis method.

According to the results of the analysis, it was determined that these theses were written in the period between 2003 and 2018. As can be understood from the results indicated that, upon receipt of the Nobel Prize in 2002, Daniel Kahneman, this issue has attracted attention in Turkey. In addition, these theses

Evaluating the Importance of Behavioral Finance in the Financial Marketing Area

Table 2. Number of theses for universities

University	Number of Thesis
Adnan Menderes University	1
Afyon Kocatepe University	1
Bahçeşehir University	1
Balıkesir University	1
Batman University	1
Beykent University	1
Boğaziçi University	1
Çağ University	1
Çukurova University	1
Dokuz Eylül University	2
Dumlupınar University	1
Düzce University	1
Ege University	1
Erciyes University	1
Erzincan Binali Yıldırım University	1
Galatasaray University	1
Gazi University	4
Gaziosmanpaşa University	1
Gebze Teknik University	1
Gedik University	1
Gediz University	1
Hacettepe University	1
Haliç University	1
Hasan Kalyoncu University	1
İstanbul Gelişim University	2
İstanbul Aydın University	1
İstanbul Ticaret University	1
İstanbul University	10
Kastamonu University	1
Kırıkkale University	1
Marmara University	6
Mehmet Akif Ersoy University	1
Nevşehir University	1
Osmaniye Korkut Ata University	1
Sakarya University	1
Selçuk University	2
Uludağ University	2
Yalova University	1
Yüzüncü Yıl University	1
Total	**60**

Table 3. Subject-based distribution of theses

Thesis Subject	Number of Thesis
Anomalies	9
Private Pension System	4
Demographic Factors	2
Foreign Exchange Markets	2
Equity Investments	9
Character Properties	31
Financial Crisis Process	3
Total	**60**

were written in 2018 at most. In such cases, behavioral finance during the global crisis of the year 2008 shows that attracted the attention of researchers in Turkey.

Another finding obtained based on the analyzes is that only 4 of the theses are English and the others are Turkish. However, 49 of these theses are master and 11 are doctoral level. On the other hand, this thesis has analyzed 39 different universities in Turkey. The institutions with the highest number of dissertations were İstanbul University, Marmara University and Gazi University, respectively. This result shows that state universities are more interested in this issue than foundation universities.

In the last title of bibliometric analysis, these theses written in the field of behavioral finance are divided into topics. In this context, studies on behavioral finance have been gathered under various topics and it has been determined that the most studied subject has character traits. In addition to this, it is seen that stock investments and anomalies are preferred in this context. On the other hand, foreign exchange markets and financial crises were the least studied topics.

REFERENCES

Ahmed, N., Ahmad, Z., & Khan, S. K. (2011). Behavioral finance: shaping the decisions of small investors of Lahore stock exchange. *Interdisciplinary Journal of Research in Business*, *1*(2), 38–43.

Albaity, M., & Rahman, M. (2012). Behavioural finance and Malaysian culture. *International Business Research*, *5*(11), 65. doi:10.5539/ibr.v5n11p65

Alti, A., & Titman, S. (2019). *A dynamic model of characteristic-based return predictability (No. w25777)*. National Bureau of Economic Research. doi:10.3386/w25777

Aren, S., Aydemir, S. D., & Şehitoğlu, Y. (2016). Behavioral biases on institutional investors: A literature review. *Kybernetes*, *45*(10), 1668–1684. doi:10.1108/K-08-2015-0203

Armutlu, C., & Ari, G. S. (2010). Yönetim modalarinin yüksek lisans ve doktora tezlerine yansimalari: Bibliyometrik bir analiz. *ODTÜ Gelisme Dergisi*, *37*(1), 1.

Aydin, E., Brounen, D., & Kok, N. (2018). Information provision and energy consumption: Evidence from a field experiment. *Energy Economics, 71*, 403–410. doi:10.1016/j.eneco.2018.03.008

Bachmann, K., De Giorgi, E. G., & Hens, T. (2019). Behavioral finance for private banking: from the art of advice to the science of advice. *Structure, 8*(2).

Beşel, F., & Yardımcıoğlu, F. (2017). Maliye Dergisi'nin bibliyometrik analizi: 2007-2016 Dönemi. *Maliye Dergisi, 172*, 133–151.

Blajer-Gołębiewska, A., Wach, D., & Kos, M. (2018). Financial risk information avoidance. *Economic research- Ekonomska Istrazivanja, 31*(1), 521–536. doi:10.1080/1331677X.2018.1439396

Bornmann, L., & Mutz, R. (2015). Growth rates of modern science: A bibliometric analysis based on the number of publications and cited references. *Journal of the Association for Information Science and Technology, 66*(11), 2215–2222. doi:10.1002/asi.23329

Chang, C. H., & Lin, S. J. (2015). The effects of national culture and behavioral pitfalls on investors' decision-making: Herding behavior in international stock markets. *International Review of Economics & Finance, 37*, 380–392. doi:10.1016/j.iref.2014.12.010

Cheema, M. A., & Nartea, G. V. (2017). Momentum returns, market states, and market dynamics: Is China different? *International Review of Economics & Finance, 50*, 85–97. doi:10.1016/j.iref.2017.04.003

Çömlekçi, İ., & Özer, A. (2018). Behavioral finance models, anomalies, and factors affecting investor psychology. In *Global Approaches in Financial Economics, Banking, and Finance* (pp. 309–330). Cham, Switzerland: Springer. doi:10.1007/978-3-319-78494-6_15

Çömlekçi, İ., & Özer, A. (2018). Behavioral finance models, anomalies, and factors affecting investor psychology. In *Global Approaches in Financial Economics, Banking, and Finance* (pp. 309–330). Cham, Switzerland: Springer. doi:10.1007/978-3-319-78494-6_15

Costa, D. F., Carvalho, F. D. M., & Moreira, B. C. D. M. (2019). Behavioral economics and behavioral finance: A bibliometric analysis of the scientific fields. *Journal of Economic Surveys, 33*(1), 3–24. doi:10.1111/joes.12262

Costa, D. F., de Melo Carvalho, F., de Melo Moreira, B. C., & do Prado, J. W. (2017). Bibliometric analysis on the association between behavioral finance and decision making with cognitive biases such as overconfidence, anchoring effect and confirmation bias. *Scientometrics, 111*(3), 1775–1799. doi:10.100711192-017-2371-5

Daniel, K., & Hirshleifer, D. (2015). Overconfident investors, predictable returns, and excessive trading. *The Journal of Economic Perspectives, 29*(4), 61–88. doi:10.1257/jep.29.4.61

De Bortoli, D., da Costa, N. Jr, Goulart, M., & Campara, J. (2019). Personality traits and investor profile analysis: A behavioral finance study. *PLoS One, 14*(3), e0214062. doi:10.1371/journal.pone.0214062 PMID:30917175

Deshmukh, G. K., & Joseph, S. (2016). Behavioural finance: An introspection of investors psychology. *Indian Journal of Commerce and Management Studies, 7*(1), 97.

Dinçer, H., Hacıoğlu, Ü., & Yüksel, S. (2018c). Determining influencing factors of currency exchange rate for decision making in global economy using MARS method. In Geopolitics and strategic management in the global economy (pp. 261–273). Hershey, PA: IGI Global. doi:10.4018/978-1-5225-2673-5.ch013

Dincer, H., Uzunkaya, S. S., & Yüksel, S. (2019c). An IT2-based hybrid decision-making model using hesitant fuzzy linguistic term sets for selecting the development plan of financial economics. *International Journal of Computational Intelligence Systems, 12*(2), 460–473. doi:10.2991/ijcis.d.190312.001

Dinçer, H., & Yüksel, S. (2018). Financial sector-based analysis of the G20 economies using the integrated decision-making approach with DEMATEL and TOPSIS. In *Emerging Trends in Banking and Finance* (pp. 210–223). Cham, Switzerland: Springer. doi:10.1007/978-3-030-01784-2_13

Dinçer, H., Yüksel, S., & Adalı, Z. (2019). Economic effects in Islamic stock development of the European countries: Policy recommendations for ethical behaviors. In Handbook of research on managerial thinking in global business economics (pp. 58-78). Hershey, PA: IGI Global.

Dinçer, H., Yuksel, S., & Bozaykut-Buk, T. (2018b). Evaluation of financial and economic effects on green supply chain management with multi-criteria decision-making approach: Evidence from companies listed in BIST. In Handbook of research on supply chain management for sustainable development (pp. 144–175). Hershey, PA: IGI Global. doi:10.4018/978-1-5225-5757-9.ch009

Dinçer, H., Yüksel, S., & Kartal, M. T. (2019d). The role of bank interest rate in the competitive emerging markets to provide financial and economic stability. *Ekonomi, İşletme ve Maliye Araştırmaları Dergisi, 1*(2).

Dinçer, H., Yüksel, S., & Martínez, L. (2019a). Interval type 2-based hybrid fuzzy evaluation of financial services in E7 economies with DEMATEL-ANP and MOORA methods. *Applied Soft Computing*.

Dinçer, H., Yüksel, S., & Şenel, S. (2018a). Analyzing the global risks for the financial crisis after the great depression using comparative hybrid hesitant fuzzy decision-making models: Policy recommendations for sustainable economic growth. *Sustainability, 10*(9), 3126. doi:10.3390u10093126

Dinçer, H., Yüksel, S., Yazici, M., & Pınarbaşı, F. (2019b). Assessing corporate social responsibilities in the banking sector: as a tool of strategic communication during the global financial crisis. In Handbook of research on global issues in financial communication and investment decision making (pp. 1-27). Hershey, PA: IGI Global.

Efremidze, L., Rutledge, J., & Willett, T. D. (2016). Capital flow surges as bubbles: Behavioral finance and McKinnon's over-borrowing syndrome extended. *The Singapore Economic Review, 61*(02), 1640023. doi:10.1142/S0217590816400233

Eti, S. (2019a). ULAKBİM İndeksinde Taranan Sosyal Bilimler Alanındaki Dergilerde Öne Çıkan Konu Ve Yöntemlerin Metin Madenciliği Yaklaşımı İle Belirlenmesi. *Uluslararası Hukuk ve Sosyal Bilim Araştırmaları Dergisi, 1*(1), 61–66.

Eti, S. (2019b). The use of quantitative methods in investment decisions: a literature review. In Handbook of research on global issues in financial communication and investment decision making (pp. 256–275). Hershey, PA: IGI Global. doi:10.4018/978-1-5225-9265-5.ch013

Fahimnia, B., Sarkis, J., & Davarzani, H. (2015). Green supply chain management: A review and bibliometric analysis. *International Journal of Production Economics, 162*, 101–114. doi:10.1016/j.ijpe.2015.01.003

Garcia, M. J. R. (2013). Financial education and behavioral finance: New insights into the role of information in financial decisions. *Journal of Economic Surveys, 27*(2), 297–315. doi:10.1111/j.1467-6419.2011.00705.x

Grosse, R. (2012). Bank regulation, governance and the crisis: A behavioral finance view. *Journal of Financial Regulation and Compliance, 20*(1), 4–25. doi:10.1108/13581981211199399

Grover, P. (2015). Study on behavioural factors influencing investment decision in real estate: a case study of Udham Singh Nagar (Uttrakhand). *International Journal of Engineering Technology, Management and Applied*, 150-158.

Halaba, A., & Coşkun, A. (2016). Behavioral finance perspective on managerial decision making under risk in commercial banks. *Regional Economic Development: Entrepreneurship and Innovation*, 161.

Hirshleifer, D. (2015). Behavioral finance. *Annual Review of Financial Economics, 7*(1), 133–159. doi:10.1146/annurev-financial-092214-043752

Hotamışlı, M., & Erem, I. (2014). Muhasebe ve Finansman Dergisi'nde yayınlanan makalelerin bibliyometrik analizi. *Muhasebe ve Finansman Dergisi*, (63), 1-20.

Invernizzi, A. C. (2018). Managerial overconfidence. In *Overconfidence in SMEs* (pp. 1–20). Cham, Switzerland: Palgrave Macmillan. doi:10.1007/978-3-319-66920-5_1

Kahneman, D., & Tversky, A. (1979). On the interpretation of intuitive probability: A reply to Jonathan Cohen. *Cognition, 7*(4), 409–411. doi:10.1016/0010-0277(79)90024-6

Kisman, Z., & Restiyanita, S. (2015). M. The validity of capital asset pricing model (CAPM) and arbitrage pricing theory (APT) in predicting the return of stocks in Indonesia stock exchange. *American Journal of Economics. Financial Management, 1*, 184–189.

Kozak, S., Nagel, S., & Santosh, S. (2018). Interpreting factor models. *The Journal of Finance, 73*(3), 1183–1223. doi:10.1111/jofi.12612

Kumar, S., & Goyal, N. (2015). Behavioural biases in investment decision making–a systematic literature review. *Qualitative Research in Financial Markets, 7*(1), 88-108.

Loerwald, D., & Stemmann, A. (2016). Behavioral finance and financial literacy: Educational implications of biases in financial decision making. In *International handbook of financial literacy* (pp. 25–38). Singapore: Springer. doi:10.1007/978-981-10-0360-8_3

Longo, J. M. (2014). Trading and investment strategies in behavioral finance. *Investor behavior: The psychology of financial planning and investing*, 495-512.

Lu, B., Song, X. Y., & Li, X. D. (2012). Bayesian analysis of multi-group nonlinear structural equation models with application to behavioral finance. *Quantitative Finance, 12*(3), 477–488. doi:10.1080/14697680903369500

Noori, M. (2016). Cognitive reflection as a predictor of susceptibility to behavioral anomalies. *Judgment and Decision Making, 11*(1), 114.

Nurettin, A. Y. A. Z., & Türkmen, B. M. (2018). Yöresel yiyecekleri konu alan lisansüstü tezlerin bibliyometrik analizi. *Gastroia: Journal of Gastronomy and Travel Research, 2*(1), 22–38.

Özel, Ç. H., & Kozak, N. (2012). Turizm pazarlaması alanının bibliyometrik profili (2000-2010) ve bir atıf analizi çalışması. *Türk Kütüphaneciliği, 26*(4), 715–733.

Pompian, M. (2016). *Risk profiling through a behavioral finance lens*. CFA Institute Research Foundation.

Pritchard, A. (1969). Statistical bibliography or bibliometrics. *The Journal of Documentation, 25*(4), 348–349.

Pruna, R. T., Polukarov, M., & Jennings, N. R. (2018). Avoiding regret in an agent-based asset pricing model. *Finance Research Letters, 24*, 273–277. doi:10.1016/j.frl.2017.09.014

Ramiah, V., Xu, X., & Moosa, I. A. (2015). Neoclassical finance, behavioral finance and noise traders: A review and assessment of the literature. *International Review of Financial Analysis, 41*, 89–100. doi:10.1016/j.irfa.2015.05.021

Riff, S., & Yagil, Y. (2016). Behavioral factors affecting the home bias phenomenon: Experimental tests. *Journal of Behavioral Finance, 17*(3), 267–279. doi:10.1080/15427560.2016.1203324

Rogers, P., Rogers, D., & Securato, J. R. (2015). About psychological variables in application scoring models. *Revista de Administração de Empresas, 55*(1), 38–49. doi:10.1590/S0034-759020150105

Rohde, E. (2018). Olympic Games and values in disruption: The fundamental renewal of Coubertinian renewal seems necessary. *Diagoras: International Academic Journal on Olympic Studies, 2*, 193–214.

Ruhanen, L., Weiler, B., Moyle, B. D., & McLennan, C. L. J. (2015). Trends and patterns in sustainable tourism research: A 25-year bibliometric analysis. *Journal of Sustainable Tourism, 23*(4), 517–535. doi:10.1080/09669582.2014.978790

Sefil, S., & Çilingiroğlu, H. K. (2011). Davranışsal finansın temelleri: karar vermenin bilişsel ve duygusal eğilimleri.

Statman, M. (2017). Financial advertising in the second generation of behavioral finance. *Journal of Behavioral Finance, 18*(4), 470–477. doi:10.1080/15427560.2017.1365236

Thaler, R. H., & Ganser, L. J. (2015). *Misbehaving: The making of behavioral economics*. New York: WW Norton.

Vitor Jordão da Gama Silva, P., Brandalise Santos, J., & Portes Pereira, G. (2019). Behavioral finance in Brazil: A bibliometric study from 2007 to 2017. *Latin American Business Review*, 1–22.

Wang, Y. Y., Chih, H. H., & Chou, R. K. (2016). Review of behavioral finance studies in Taiwan. *Jing Ji Lun Wen Cong Kan, 44*(1), 1–55.

Xu, Y., He, K., Kenneth, L. K. K., & Lai, K. K. (2014, July). A behavioral finance analysis on ETF investment behavior. In *2014 Seventh International Joint Conference on Computational Sciences and Optimization* (pp. 386-389). IEEE. 10.1109/CSO.2014.81

Yılmaz, G. (2017). Restoranlarda bahşiş ile ilgili yayınlanan makalelerin bibliyometrik analizi. *Seyahat ve Otel İşletmeciliği Dergisi*, *14*(2), 65–79. doi:10.24010oid.335082

Zhang, Y., & Jin, Y. (2015). Thematic and episodic framing of depression: How Chinese and American newspapers framed a major public health threat. *Athens Journal of Mass Media and Communications*, 91.

KEY TERMS AND DEFINITIONS

CAPM: Capital Asset Pricing Model.
USD: American dollar.

Section 2

Chapter 6
Examining the Effects of Strategies, Competition Intelligence, and Risk Culture on Business Performance in International Enterprises

Zafer Adiguzel
https://orcid.org/0000-0001-8743-356X
Medipol Business School, Istanbul Medipol University, Turkey

ABSTRACT

The top management of the organizations attach importance to both the cultural structure and performance by paying attention to the risk level of the decisions taken in order to be successful in the competitive environment. With the success of the organization performance, the organization of employees with different cultural characteristics of the same common value comes to the fore. Therefore, human resources and corporate culture of institutions attach importance to the management of the interaction of people from different segments in their management policies. How risks are understood and managed by employees in an organization is examined within the scope of risk culture, which depends on internal and external factors in the organization. As a result of cultural differences, both the advantages of orientation are recognized and explained and the problems that need to be managed continue to arise. This chapter sets out the existing cultural framework in organizations, and supports a bridge function and a systemic understanding of cultural differences.

INTRODUCTION

In today's ever-changing conditions, especially the ability of companies operating in international markets to maintain their continuity and gain competitive advantage over other enterprises depends on their reactions to these changes. New administrative priorities have emerged in the economic environment in

DOI: 10.4018/978-1-7998-2559-3.ch006

which the borders have lost importance during the globalization process and enterprises can easily invest in different countries with some incentives. One of them is the management of cultural differences among people working in international organizations. Today, even in local businesses, considering the environments where people from different identities and cultures work together, this situation has become one of the main axes of both the necessity and functioning of the international enterprises. Businesses that incorporate different cultural structures must pay attention to these variables when creating organizational cultures. In addition, the environmental conditions of the companies operating in international areas are composed of very different structures. The laws of the regions in which they operate have different educational levels, social skills and status and economic conditions. Even in some of these regions, these conditions may also vary continuously. While the laws and economic conditions may change rapidly in the newly developing regions, there may be a calm market in the developing countries. Nevertheless, the inclusion of different cultures into an organization can turn into an element that international businesses can turn to advantage. Businesses that incorporate different cultural structures can become enterprises that learn to look at the problems they face or the strategies they want to identify from different angles.

With a strategic performance management, companies are able to provide continuous training to their employees and obtain competitive advantages from their individual differences (Grant, 1991). However; performance appraisal is extremely important in terms of achieving the objectives of the organizations and determining the level of personal contribution of the employees within the organization to this process (Garcia-Zamor, 2003). The survival of enterprises in an environment where competition is rapidly increasing and technology is constantly changing is closely related to the effectiveness of employee satisfaction. For this reason, it is now the subject of more sanctions on qualitative elements in the agenda of company leaders. The qualitative element refers to the management of subjects, such as culture, which can be subjective, which may vary from person to person and from organization to organization, by melting in a pot. For a successful management approach, managers have important roles in shaping change, employee contribution to this process, talent management and improving intercultural communication. In addition to this, it is a necessity for managers to develop solutions, action and alternative plans for the problems arising from cultural differences. Instead of reacting to the problems stemming from cultural elements in the organization, managers should have alternative plans to shape this process. In today's economic system, the managers who have won this culture and brought it to their institution are taking their companies one step ahead in the competition (Murphy, 2016). Internationalization, although it provides many advantages and opportunities to businesses, it poses a great risk for enterprises due to the dynamic, uncertain and multi-factor structure of foreign markets. Therefore, enterprises have to establish a strong risk culture structure within their own structure in order to minimize the possible risks that may arise as a result of their activities in foreign markets. In enterprises with a strong risk culture, people in decision-making positions within the organization stay away from the negativities such as excessive or insufficient risk taking; take risks within the framework of beliefs, values and norms formed within the organization (Bozeman & Kingsley, 1998).

With the increasing globalization, the competitiveness of nations in the international market comes to the forefront as a determinant of economic welfare and economic growth depends on the performance of international transactions (Hitt et al., 2012). In the process of rapid change and development, the adoption of digital technologies continues to progress rapidly and companies are trying to transform rapidly. In the realization of digital transformation; factors such as developments in the internet, information technologies, transition to smart devices, increasing importance of data, limitation of internet through wireless connections, and development of new technologies are justified. In this process where new business models and ways of doing business emerge as a result of these factors and transformation, it is important for firms to review their international marketing mix strategies for their success in the international market and competitive advantage.

DEFINITION OF INTERNATIONALIZATION

Although many researches and theories have been produced on internationalization, no single and valid definition of internationalization has been agreed by everyone. Here are a few of the many definitions made in the literature: According to Bell and Young (1998), internationalization is the continuation of business activities in international markets by using one or more methods of entry to foreign markets such as export, license, franchising, direct investment and joint venture outside the national borders. Welch and Loustarinen (1988), Internationalization, increasing the participation of businesses in international activities; they are the process of recognizing the direct and indirect impact of business activities on the future of the business, as well as the ability to develop and manage business relations with other countries around the world. According to Masum and Fernandez (2008), internationalization is the process of sending products and services produced in the country of origin to overseas markets. The process of expanding abroad is now possible through advanced technology and effective communication, allowing for a flexible spread of labor and technology across countries. The network theory model, which asserts that the internationalization of enterprises is made through inter-business relations and networks, defines internationalization as a unifying process in which business establishes, develops, maintains and terminates if necessary to achieve its goals (Johanson & Mattsson, 1988). Internationalization is the process of adapting the business activities to international markets in terms of strategy, structure and resources (Johanson & Mattsson, 1994).

Process of Internationalization

As a result of their experience gained from international activities, enterprises start to move towards ventures abroad. Businesses that decide to open and invest abroad face various obstacles and risks. They need sufficient knowledge of foreign markets to overcome these risks and barriers. Therefore, internationalization is a gradual process consisting of four consecutive stages in which enterprises expand to foreign markets step by step and international participation and resource commitment increases with time. In the first stage, enterprises operate in the domestic market and do not engage in normal export activities. In the second stage, enterprises export their products through intermediaries and agents in the host country. In the third stage, businesses open an overseas sales office. In the fourth and final stage, enterprises establish their own production line or production units abroad. In other words, while enterprises initially entered the market through indirect exports with low control and resource use; After entering the market, they gradually increase their degree of participation and resource commitments in foreign markets through direct exports or wholly-owned subsidiaries, where there is high control and resource utilization (Johanson & Wiedersheim, 1975).

According to Phatak (1989), the internationalization process consists of the following stages:

a) **External Demand:** The first stage starts when information is requested from one of the company's products from foreign markets. A positive response to the request and an agreement can result in an ongoing process.
b) **Export:** This is the stage in which the entity obtains control over foreign sales and continues this activity by itself.
c) **Sales Branches and Affiliates:** It is the stage where sales branches and affiliates are established in foreign markets.
d) **Mounting Abroad:** It is the stage where the assembly activity has started in the foreign market.
e) **Production in Foreign Countries:** At this stage, the company is now capable of producing in foreign markets.

Factors Affecting The Internationalization Process

Business Specific Factors

Business Resources: Business resources: It has four main components: administrative, personnel, financial and information resources (Knight & Cavusgil, 2004). The more and more various businesses have, the more likely they are to participate in international activities (Almeida et al., 2000). Enterprises with unique and inimitable resources increase their competitiveness in the foreign market (Barney, 1991).

Business Capabilities: They are the capabilities that provide long-term sustainable advantages to the enterprise (Prahalad & Hamel, 1990). The Given Capabilities: The technological infrastructure of the enterprise includes knowledge and resource-based approaches such as market knowledge and strategic planning (Obrecht, 2004).

Entrepreneur Orientation: It covers the senior management's strategic objectives, activities, recognition of opportunities, innovation level and trends such as risk taking (Smart & Conant, 1994). This orientation explains the risks taken to achieve the objectives of the enterprises, to obtain the latest technology and adapt to changes in the business environment (Miles et al., 1993).

Enterprise Features: Indicators such as location, ownership status, products, structure, age and size of the enterprise constitute the most important characteristics of the enterprise. For example, the size of enterprises has a positive and significant impact on internationalization behavior (Olivares-Mesa & Suarez-Ortega, 2006).

Employee Specific Factors

Philosophical Overview: It is related to the values, attitudes and perceptions of business management towards internationalization (Jones & Coviello, 2005). In other words, it is the perspective of decision-makers that includes how they see the risks, costs and benefits of internationalization (Oviatt & McDougal, 2005).

Social Capital: The ability to establish relationships with employees at all management levels (Jones & Coviello, 2005). Social capital helps the business to find suitable foreign partners through channels such as agents, distributors and suppliers. It also contributes to the business by providing information on regulations and processes in certain markets (Bell et al., 2004).

Human Capital: Human capital is a type of capital that is associated with the knowledge and skills of employees (Shepherd & Wiklund, 2005). While training, knowledge and experience help to create human capital, they gain competitive advantage thanks to these features. The expertise in human capital gives the company an advantage in fulfilling the demands of a particular market and niche products with appropriate quality and design (Olivares-Mesa & Cabrera-Suarez, 2006).

International Orientation: International orientation includes vision, perception and preparations for internationalization. International orientation is influenced by foreign cultural experience, knowledge of foreign competitors, language skills, presence of contact with foreign enterprises through formal and informal methods, and educational infrastructure (Lloyd-Reason & Mughan, 2002).

Personality characteristics: Personality traits such as the ability to establish good interpersonal relationships, honesty, tolerance and reliability are important determinants of internationalization (Oviatt & McDougal, 2005). Factors such as education level, foreign language knowledge and past work experience increase the internationalization process of enterprises (Aaby & Slater, 1989).

External Factors

Market Structure: The environment of the market includes factors such as market size, sales potential, availability and quality of infrastructure or facilities (Jones & Coviello, 2005). Business management, because of the greater sales potential, usually aim to enter the big market (Etemad, 2004).

Government Policies: Government incentives, supports, export policy, regulations and customs-related procedures directly affect the internationalization process (Mtigwe, 2005). In addition, internal problems, tax laws, interest rate policy, labor force regulations and management infrastructure affect the internationalization process of an enterprise (Boter & Lundström, 2005).

Environmental Specifications: Economic, social, political, technical and legal obligations in the host and host countries affect the degree of internationalization of enterprises (Root, 1994). Compared to the static environment, dynamic environmental conditions have a positive effect on the internationalization of enterprises (Dess et al., 1997).

Competition Environment: The competition environment depends on the level of competition in prices, performance, design, patent protection, brand name and packaging and service (Root, 1994).

Risk Description

There is no consensus on how to define and interpret risk, which is an important concept used in many scientific fields (Aven, 2011). There are many different definitions of the concept of risk. As with the general definition of risk, each professional discipline has its own definition of risk. When we look at the concept of risk in general, it can be expressed as the occurrence of undesirable or unexpected events and situations that may adversely affect people or organizations (Marhavilas & Koulouriotis, 2012). In other words, risk refers to uncertain or negative events and situations that may adversely affect an organization's ability to achieve one or more objectives (Tuncel & Alpan, 2010). According to another definition, risk is the possibility of loss or loss in economic activities of enterprises as a result of unforeseen events and phenomena (Negruş, 1986). In addition to general risk definitions, many business disciplines such as health, environment, aviation, banking, law, geology and management have defined the concept of risk with a number of differences (Fikirkoca, 2003). For international businesses, risk is the likelihood of any event or action that adversely affects the ability of businesses to implement their strategies and achieve their objectives (McNeil et al., 2005). Risk, that all decisions taken and implemented by businesses due to a business in which they operate involve unexpected losses, losses, uncertainties and dangers against the enterprise in the future; on the other hand, if it is managed well, it creates opportunities in favor of the enterprise.

Risk Management: Numerous and different definitions have been made in the literature on risk management. Bannock and Manser (2003) define risk management as identifying and accepting or compensating risks that threaten the profitability or existence of an entity. This definition may be extended to the fact that there may be damages or losses, but by the entity to engage in activities that minimize them and reduce dependence on insurance. According to Heldman (2010), risk management; as an important part of the strategic management of the enterprise in order to provide continuous benefit in all kinds of activities and portfolio of businesses is the process to deal with the risks that will occur in relation to all activities. Risk management means applying the knowledge, skills, risk management tools and techniques of the enterprise to the projects in order to reduce the threats to an acceptable level while maximizing opportunities for the enterprise (Baranoff & Baranoff, 2004). According to Cummins et al. (1998), risk management can be defined as any series of activities implemented by individuals or businesses to reduce the risks arising from the main activities of the enterprise. Truslow (2003) defined risk management as covering the actions we take to minimize the uncertainty of expected results for the enterprise and reduce market volatility. According to Ritchie and Brindley (2007), risk management is a management function that aims to protect the assets and values of enterprises against the physical and financial consequences of event risk. Risk management is defined as the process of intervention in economic and behavioral risk dynamics that increase the value of the enterprise. The managerial nature of risk management helps businesses find out which efforts are useful in achieving their goals and objectives effectively and efficiently (Briers, 2000).

Purpose of Risk Management: The purpose of risk management is to identify potential risks, analyze and identify risks to identify the most likely; does not mean the complete elimination of risks (Froot et al., 1993). In practice, organizations decide between types and degrees of risk exposure and engage in activities that can provide competitive advantage and protect their assets through the use of capital markets, or accept small amounts of exposure, while securing them against disasters (Kimball, 2000). As an indispensable part of organizational processes, risk management helps the organization achieve its objectives effectively and successfully (Funston, 2003). It is an uninterrupted process that is directly affected by the changes in the internal and external environment of the organization that provides continuous risk identification and control needs (Tchankova, 2002). Since organizations vary in size, organizational forms and complexity, the objectives of risk management will vary between organizations depending on the risk environment of the organizations (Andersen, 2006).

Importance of Risk Management: An effective risk management structure provides important opportunities for an enterprise to understand risks and make informed decisions about how to manage or how to manage them in any attempt. In addition, risk management identifies plans that help businesses to mitigate or avoid the risks that have a major impact on the entity if it occurs, and provide opportunities to businesses (Heldman, 2010). Risk management protects the business and its stakeholders by supporting the business objectives and adds value to them (Rejda, 2011). Risk management provides businesses with a framework to ensure that future activities are conducted in a consistent and controlled manner (Gebler, 2006). It also helps businesses to make decision-making and planning with a comprehensive and structured understanding of business opportunities and threats that may arise in relation to the business's operations. It also contributes to the more efficient use or allocation of capital and resources within the enterprise through risk management, to protect and enhance the assets and business image, to develop and support the knowledge base of employees and the enterprise (Woods, 2012).

Benefits of Risk Management: Risk management helps an enterprise achieve its objectives and objectives, use its resources efficiently, protect its reputation, and comply with laws and regulations while avoiding all dangers and surprises (Skipper, 2008). Effective risk management provides benefits such as harmonizing the risk appetite and strategy of the enterprise, increasing the measures taken against risk, reducing operational losses, identifying and managing multiple corporate risks, capturing opportunities and improving the distribution of capital (Heldman, 2010). Risk management contributes to enterprises in the prevention and management of risks (Thomas, 2009), and provides a procedure to protect enterprises from possible or sudden surprises (Cooper, 2005). It encourages businesses to minimize their losses, to help them make quick and effective decisions, to save time, to prevent waste of resources, to keep risks at an acceptable level, and finally to be open to innovations for managers (Derici et al., 2007).

Risk Management Process: Risk management process is a set of activities in which the main risks such as liquidity risk, legal risk, credit risk, market risk and operational risk are defined by the business management or risk manager and applied in a way that mitigates these risks (Cornett & Saunders, 2003). The risk management process involves the application of management principles, processes, procedures to tasks such as defining, analyzing, evaluating, treating, monitoring and communicating (Cooper, 2005). The risk management process consists of five interrelated stages. These stages: It includes the identification of risks, the analysis and evaluation of risks, the selection of alternative risk correction tools, the implementation of selected alternatives, and the control of risks (Daft, 1991).

Identification of Risks: Risk identification, which also means risk identification, includes a process in which problems are solved through the information obtained during the risk identification process (Stulz, 1996). As a result of defining risks, it is stated that technological, political and social uncertainties are reduced and possible losses are minimized (Hertz & Thomas, 1983). According to the risk definition, which is the first step of the risk management process, risks cannot be managed unless they are well defined (Young, 2006). At the risk identification stage, both internal and external events that may affect the objectives of an organization should be identified with the risks or opportunities it presents (Alexander, 2003). A well-defined risk identification provides an effective risk management for events that cannot be managed as a result of unexpected consequences by identifying the sources of the losses of which the source cannot be identified (Tchankova, 2002). They need deep knowledge of the market and environmental (legal, social, political and cultural) conditions in which the organization operates in order to identify risks and understand the strategic and operational objectives of the organization. At the risk identification stage, all important organizational processes should be identified and all risks arising from these processes should be meticulously stated by the organization (Cornalba & Giudici, 2004). The risk identification phase includes identifying all possible organizational risks, opportunities, and the conditions that create these risks and opportunities. Risk identification, therefore, facilitates the effective examination of areas and activities where organizational resources are at risk and affects their ability to achieve business objectives (Williams et al., 1998).

Analysis and Evaluation of Risks: Analysis and assessment of risks is the second step in analyzing the data collected about potential risks in the risk management process. Risk analysis can be defined as the process that identifies the risks that have the greatest impact on business activities, except for all threats and risks identified at the identification stage (Cooper, 2005). Risk identification, risk analysis and evaluation are followed. Focusing on defining hazards and risk factors is not enough. Equally, it is important to understand the nature of the events, the causality, the process by which it creates a loss or gain. Virtual risks, which may have profound effects on the management of an enterprise, consisting of risk perception and uncertainty, should also be analyzed (Bowden et al., 2001). Any risk management system should be capable of assessing and managing risk. Therefore, a risk measurement method should be formulated to allow comparisons between different types of risks. The risk assessment process is initiated by collecting additional information from sources such as audit reports, budget plans and management discussions to make a complete assessment of all significant risks affecting the entity. The risks identified during the risk identification stage, especially when there is a change in the business and activity environment, the information related to the risk is continuously updated and verified as a result of obtaining information about the change (Young, 2006).

CONCEPT OF CULTURE

Culture is a key concept within the social sciences, in which basic debates of methodology take place and, depending on the climate of thought, acquire content equivalent to certain theoretical-practical contexts in certain periods. Therefore, we need to acknowledge in advance that it reflects a certain theoretical-methodological approach, when used with certain contents, much more strongly than other concepts, almost like a mirror. It should be because of this quality that many social scientists who have attempted to define the concept of culture have first turned to identifying and understanding certain frequencies in the development of the concept. It is difficult to find a single definition of what culture is. Because culture has been the subject of many scientific research disciplines and as a result many different approaches and definitions related to culture have emerged. In its most general form, culture is a meaningful whole of communities' beliefs, roles, behaviors, value judgments, customs and traditions (LiPuma, 1993). Normann, on the other hand, is all of the values that make culture the basis of human behavior and make the attitudes of individuals somewhat predictable. It considers individuals as a group of values in which the generally adopted institutions and rules are maintained as well as keeping a common goal (Sewell, 2004). Culture is a concept that includes various elements such as nutrition, language, clothing, rituals that express and share the lifestyle of a group (Anderson-Levitt, 2012). Culture is a concept that gives people feelings and thoughts about who they are, where they belong, how they behave, what they should do. It also affects human behavior, attitude, work, productivity and actions (Moran et al., 2014). Definitions related to culture can be made according to their source, appearance, sovereignty, means of proving culture, work view and many other relativity. But the common denominator is that; that it is an organic entity that is the indicator of both individual and social identity, which has its basic source from human, which has changing, developing and sometimes disappearing elements (Erinç, 2014).

Organization Culture: Like the culture of societies, institutions have their own characteristics in terms of their goals, perspectives on working life, principles and values, policies and practices, and these characteristics distinguish institutions from each other. The culture of each company is unique. Culture is variable in this sense. It is shaped differently according to the sector in which the company is located, the scope of the work, the scope of the employees, the society in which it is located, and the economic and political factors (Ott, 1989). When we talk about corporate culture in literature, generally spoken and unspoken rules, assumptions, values and ways of thinking are understood (Alvesson, 2012). They determine how to be dressed and behaved in that institution, and the behaviors that should be shown to colleagues, employees, managers and customers. The term organizational culture is widely used in the early 1980s, and it is a system of attitudes and thinking that allows employees to think, feel and behave in a common direction and that each organization holds against the events that are unique to it (Xiaoming & Junchen, 2012). It is a system of norms, behaviors, values, beliefs and habits that direct the behavior of people within an organization. There are many areas where corporate culture is reflected. Corporate practices in these areas are also an indicator and reflection of corporate culture. According to one view, corporate culture consists of shared beliefs, behaviors, values and assumptions that cannot be expressed verbally, and written policies and procedures (Schein, 2010).

Hofstede (1998) interprets organizational culture as deep-rooted and unchanging values, beliefs and assumptions that are accepted by all employees and encompass a whole business. In other words, it is a holistic belief that the employees of the organization share a common and aware of the situation of the organization and the services and practices it possesses (Hofstede et al., 2005). Organizational culture is not shaped spontaneously and unconsciously, but is often shaped for economic and social purposes (Martin, 2001). The necessity to create, maintain and change the organizational culture consciously makes the management of organizational culture up-to-date (Jones, 2013). In order to benefit from the benefits of a strong organizational culture, organizational culture must be managed correctly. The main objective in organizational culture management is to ensure that the organization achieves its strategic and operational objectives effectively and efficiently (Adler & Jelinek, 1986). There is a strong link between the productivity and culture of the organization. As a result of establishing the right organizational culture, costs are reduced, productivity increases, understanding becomes clear and commitment to the organization is ensured.

Importance of Organizational Management in Business: In today's intense competition environment, companies are able to produce policies that can provide sustainable competitive advantage, the most basic condition of being permanent in the markets where continuous change is experienced. The ability of companies to gain competitive advantage is constantly renewing themselves, creating new products or services, incorporating new production processes, administrative and technological processes, and creating new business models (Daft, 2015). The application of the methods that will differentiate itself from the competitors and continuous innovation depends on the organizational structure in which decisions are taken faster, more participatory, and having a business culture that will create superior value for its customers continuously and better quality (Zur Muehlen, 2004). Organizational culture is an important distinguishing factor for companies to gain competitive advantage (Hatch & Schultz, 1997). Determining the objectives of the enterprise depends on how accurate decisions it will make in determining which strategies it will choose in order to achieve these goals and that the organizational culture is formed correctly (Hatch, 2018). Organizational culture is of great importance as it is limited to the limits of what the organization can and cannot do. Because in this aspect, organizational culture is the ability of the organization to respond to specific challenges. Organizational culture is important because it serves to better understand and describe organizations (Naoum, 2001). The success of businesses is not only dependent on successful strategies and plans (Moran et al., 2011). Nor is it the right division of the organization into its chapters and working principles. What will enable businesses to be successful in the market is that all elements can work in harmony. If the organizational culture is strong enough, it connects the employees to the organization even more and enables the organization to internalize its objectives. This makes the business more successful in achieving its goals.

Organizational Culture in International Business: The most important characteristics of international businesses are the combination of different cultures. Culture has become an important place in the new structures that have emerged as a result of the coexistence of people from different ethnicities and cultures (Cooper et al., 2001) In a sense, organizational culture plays an important role in the coexistence and effective management of these cultures (Ostroff et al., 2012). As seen in the definitions of organizational culture, the values, beliefs, behaviors and expectations adopted by the employees within the organization are. Organizational culture brings together employees from different cultures in this common culture and brings them together in a common denominator (Leung et al., 2005). In this respect, while trying to create a common culture within the organization in multinational enterprises, it is very important that all abstract or concrete elements that will create this cultural structure reflect a global world view and people-oriented ideas. The fact that individuals with different cultural backgrounds, different attitudes, values and behavior patterns take place within the same teams means confronting intercultural differences and this has significant administrative consequences (Deshpandé & Farley, 2004). Businesses operating in international markets, especially those with multinational structures, should be familiar with the different cultural elements they possess. Otherwise, it will not be possible to predict the conflicts that may occur within the organization and it will be very difficult to compensate for the conflicts that arise. In addition, environmental factors vary according to each region. Businesses operating in international markets have to adapt to these environmental factors as well as to respond rapidly to changes that may occur in these environments. The political structure of each country, people's lifestyle and access to opportunities are not the same. They have to develop different strategies for different markets and have organizational culture and structures to successfully execute these strategies.

Management of Cultural Differences in the Organization: As a result of specialization and interaction in the forms of working with developing technology, there is now a dynamic organizational model. With the innovations brought by globalization and technology, the management of differences has become important for the harmony of both employees of different countries in multinational enterprises and citizens of the same country who have different social identities. Religion, language, race, gender, region, age and similar factors have become important for individuals now (Pothukuchi et al., 2002). Companies also develop policies to coordinate people from different cultures in their corporate structures. In this context, diversity management is a form of management that aims to enable individuals with different qualifications internally and externally to operate effectively and efficiently in the institution. The different characteristics of individuals are now seen as an issue that needs to be managed and paid attention within the organization (Sığrı & Tığlı, 2014). Because it is a natural and expected situation that people who come together for common purposes are differentiated in working life especially because of the material elements. At the same time, institutions have turned to a policy of managing differences in order to avoid both compliance and potential problems. People who come together to realize the goals of the organization such as productivity, performance, efficiency, profitability, expect harmony on the one hand and respect for their differences on the other hand (Eğinli, 2011). Diversity management is an important strategy for adopting pluralism in institutions and adding it to the management policies to achieve both the performance of the organizations and the objectives of the organization (Sürgevil & Budak, 2008). In this context, the existence of different and separate characteristics of the employees has come to a vital point in terms of loyalty to the organization and performance. It is important to create a whole in harmony with the colors of today's world, rather than uniformizing the employee profile, which has become complicated in the global world. The common purpose of diversity management is to successfully manage the members of the organization with different characteristics in line with the common purpose (Harris et al., 1991). In the first stages of the models developed for this purpose, the responses to the different demographic characteristics of individuals were emphasized. In the following periods, the strategies used by the organizations that can manage the differences are focused on (Dursun, 2013).

Effects of Cultural Differences on Companies: An important question in the international business to be conducted with different cultures is how societies will have an impact on their values. Research on the interaction of multinational corporations with different cultures with the culture of the country where they interact and management relations has led to the emergence of three different views in this field (Sofyalıoğlu & Aktaş, 2001):

- The divergence of multinational corporations that presupposes that their national cultural values are effective regardless of the country in which they operate.
- Convergence, which adopts the values of increasingly industrialized countries in the management of multinational companies and adopts the domination of local country culture.
- It is the crossvergence approach of multinational corporations which is a confusion of national culture and local cultures which can be called "universal" as a result of mutual interaction.

The management of the impacts of cultural differences reveals the necessity of managing organizational policies, strategies, structures and experiences as well as the cultural patterns of the members of the organization as individuals (Findler et al., 2007). Culturally synergistic organizations offer a structure that transcends the individual cultures of its members and creates new forms of management and organization (Ehtiyar, 2003). This approach recognizes the differences and similarities between cultures that make up a multicultural organization and recognizes that perceiving this difference is a driving force in the design and development of organizations. Organizations have to support working together and participating in cultural differences. Cultural values in the organization aim to create sensitivity on social issues, to approach people more comprehensively and to value all employees and respect their ideas.

Cultural differences are manifested in 7 different organizational dimensions on the thoughts and behaviors of individuals in the organization (Chuang et al., 2004):

- **Creativity:** This dimension includes creativity, openness to innovations, taking risks, willingness to gain experience, being less careful, less prescriptive.
- **Continuity:** This dimension requires being normative, attaching importance to security and determination.
- **Attention to Details:** This dimension includes certain values such as being precise and analytical.
- **Respect for People:** This dimension includes concepts such as values of justice, respect for people and tolerance.
- **Team Compliance:** This dimension consists of values such as being compatible with people, collaboration and suitability for the team.
- **Result-Oriented:** Success, performance, result-oriented.
- **Assertiveness:** Includes high competitiveness and low social responsibility values.

Since different functional groups contain a variety of knowledge, skills and understandings, they reduce conflicts with creativity, result-oriented, assertiveness factors and help to produce positive results. Functional differences positively affect multi-dimensional decisions and firm performance. Performance, entrepreneurship and continuity of groups focused on details and result-oriented individuals positively affect. The categories of interpersonal relationships (team compatibility and respect for people) alleviate visual differences and relational conflicts. Relational conflicts are adversely affected by interpersonal feelings such as anger and insecurity. Interpersonal disagreement also occurs when there are non-work situations (gossip, social activities, religious preferences) and decreases group performance by increasing relational conflicts (Chuang et al., 2004). Therefore, management of cultural differences is extremely important for organizations.

Effective Management of Cultural Differences: One of the elements that make up a social system is the people. People who make organizations dynamic come to the organization with their knowledge, manners, experiences, thoughts and beliefs, or with their culture, from their environment. Businesses also consist of individuals with this different cultural mosaic. These individuals came together to form an organizational culture with a common belief and values system. One of the most important duties of a business manager is to realize the business goals and the individual goals of the employees together. This is obviously a difficult task. Because people have different purposes for various reasons. For this reason, it is necessary to create a common set of values for the employees who come to a business with different cultures to adopt or adapt. The importance of business culture makes itself felt at this point. In the event that such a culture occurs in an enterprise, employees will consider themselves a part of a whole, feel at home and work in a comfortable and peaceful environment as if they were with their families. With the globalization, managing people from different cultures has reached an important position for businesses that have been moved from national to international dimension. Accordingly, one of the basic elements of business activity is to combine multicultural workforce with different cultural features around common values and make multiculturalism an advantage.

To successfully manage different cultures, the following issues are needed:

- Forming conscious strategies.
- Ability to adapt to new situations.
- Sensitivity to different cultures.
- Ability to work with multicultural teams.
- Language skills.
- To be able to understand international marketing.
- As an effort to understand international differences (Williams & Anderson, 1991).

Cultural differences, which are particularly important for international businesses, can be examined by analyzing cultural changes within the organization and in various country markets and designing appropriate management and activities. For example, in the USA and Japan, the priorities in the cultural values of countries differ from each other. While Americans value the concepts of freedom, equality, individualism, competition, productivity, time and openness in order of importance, in Asian countries this ranking is listed as belonging, collectivity (group work), seniority / authority and quality. For the success of the cultural integration process in international enterprises, it is necessary to allocate sufficient time to analyze and regulate differences. Although international executives clearly recognize the importance of synergistic approach to problem solving, they cannot easily adopt this approach. Closer ties are established between the employees of small-scale firms than those of large-scale firms. Large firms are more prone to create employee profiles from different cultures and nations in recruitment.

Risk Culture

Risk culture is defined as the norms of behavior that determine the ability of individuals and groups within the organization to understand, explain and react to the present and future potential risks of the organization (Banks, 2012). Risk culture is the beliefs and attitudes that affect the activities of individuals and groups who take responsibility for risk management within the organization (Smallman, 1996). Risk culture is a system that shows the values and behaviors that shape risk decisions in an organization (Gorzeń-Mitka, 2015). Risk culture affects managers 'and employees' decisions and helps them consciously measure and assess risks and benefits (Farrel & Hoon, 2009). Risk culture determines the ways of identifying, understanding, discussing and acting on the risks faced by the organization; it can be defined as the behavior of groups and individuals within the organization against risks to the traditions and norms of the organization (Power et al., 2013). Risk culture is defined as the set of rules and behaviors that enable individuals within the organization to adapt to the new situation naturally when faced with a risky or important situation (Hillson et al., 2012). Risk culture consists of values and beliefs shared with the knowledge and experience of individuals within the organization and group (Hillson, 2012). Establishing a risk culture requires that the organization have a common risk language and that all employees have the same understanding of risk taking (Cortez, 2011). As a result of the researches, it is concluded that risk culture, which is a component of organizational culture, contains an interactive system between values and normative behaviors in the organization (Ashby et al., 2012). Many consulting firms have stated that organizations consider risk as a bad thing that needs to be controlled or mitigated using the risk culture mechanism (Hindson, 2012). Therefore, bad behaviors such as excessive risk taking are naturally restricted by the risk culture, and the risk culture process and procedures are adopted and the implementation of the risk culture is guaranteed (Power et al., 2013).

Importance of Risk Culture: Risk culture ensures that all business decisions within the organization, from planning to reporting, are made in accordance with the risk management process (Lash, 2000). Risk culture is argued to be the main factor in establishing an effective risk management process (Roeschmann, 2014). Risk culture covers the general awareness, attitude and behavior of the employees of the organization and how the risk is managed within the organization. Risk culture is an important indicator of the extent to which an organization's risk management policies and practices are expanded (Australia, 2012). It is claimed that risk culture is an important element in taking risks that are necessary for an organization to achieve its strategic goals (Fraser & Simkins, 2016). Although it is difficult to measure or change the risk culture in an organization, risk culture is important to measure the risk appetite of people in the organization. Risk culture is important in terms of knowing how much risk an employee will face in a given situation / event, whether it is senior or lower level in an organization. Because this situation is critical in preventing unnecessary risk taking the organization to collapse (Hillson, 2012). All organizations have to take various risks to achieve their goals. Organizations may be affected by the organization's existing risk culture, either better or worse, while managing the risks it takes. The risk culture significantly influences the organization's ability to make strategic decisions and fulfill its performance goals. The lack or weakness of the risk culture plays a major role in the scandals and the collapse of the organization (McShane, 2018). It is argued that one of the main causes of the global financial crisis in 2007 and 2008 is the weak risk culture in organizations. Probably, large and important businesses operating around the world will endeavor to strengthen risk cultures in the organization by taking important lessons from the 2007 and 2008 financial crises (Roeschmann, 2014).

Characteristics of Strong and Weak Risk Culture: Strong risk culture, encouraging the management of stakeholders, shareholders, regulators and creditors to see all risks in a transparent manner, providing strong feedback to employees, sharing responsibility by transferring authority, encouraging free flow of information flow within the organization, creating risk awareness and disseminating ethical behaviors (Banks, 2012). Having a strong risk culture means knowing what risks should be taken within the limits defined by the company in order to achieve the long-term strategic goals and objectives of the employees (Farrel & Hoon, 2009). A strong risk culture helps the business achieve its goals by providing loyalty, high motivation and collaboration among employees (Gordon, 2008).

A weak risk culture is exposure to effects such as unexpected losses, deterioration of the market image, liquidity problems and higher funding costs due to the fact that a business management does not understand the importance of the risk culture, does not realize it, has an insufficient risk culture or does not have the resources to strengthen the weak risk culture (Banks, 2012). For an enterprise to strengthen its weak risk culture, managers need to have strong risk culture awareness and understand the importance of the benefits of risk culture. The fact that business management is not aware of the lack of risk culture or weak risk culture within the organization, the deliberate neglect and neglect of it, the lack of awareness or understanding of the importance and benefits of a strong risk culture can lead to bigger problems with terrible consequences for the organization (Banks, 2012).

A strong risk culture provides enterprises with a competitive advantage by taking into account the wishes of stakeholders and shareholders, the wishes and limitations of regulatory authorities, incidents and disasters that cause losses and by optimizing the resources of the enterprise; weak risk culture causes enterprises to be incapacitated against risks, unexpected losses and surprises, and liquidity problems. It is seen that a strong risk culture helps organizations to achieve the proper balance between risk and return. It is seen that organizations with a weak risk culture take either too little or too much risk, and in practice it is more common to take excessive risk (Power et al., 2013).

Strategy Concept: For companies operating in the international market, the strategy refers to the sum of integrated actions that will enable the firm to succeed in the market in the long term in order to achieve sustainable advantage over competing firms in meeting the needs of customers in the national and international market, taking into account the firm resources (Bradley, 2002). Strategic management is also defined as the holistic management of decisions and activities for the development, implementation, evaluation and control of results (Dinçer, 1998). Strategic management aims to provide the necessary framework for competitive advantage in the international market (Grant, 2002). Strategic management for international firms is a comprehensive and sustained management planning process that includes the development and implementation of strategies for the market and activities in order to compete effectively with competitors in the market (Freeman, 2010).

Competitive Development Model: Porter proposed a model of competitive development that is considered to increase or decrease in national competitiveness in the international market according to the stages of the countries (Porter, 1990). It has established a competitive development model based on evolutionary stages at the level of national competitive advantage (Meshal, 1997). He stated that with the improvements to be implemented at each stage, the next stage will be reached by reaching successful levels and that each sector should be used with different sectors and industry departments and different firm strategies. In addition, he stated that not all countries could fully adapt to this structure and levels and could not go through the same stages of evolution (Jasson, 2009).

Competitive development model consisting of four stages, factor-oriented, investment-oriented, innovation-innovation-oriented and asset-oriented, respectively:

In the Factor Oriented Stage, countries mostly export unprocessed natural resources and goods and compete on the basis of comparative advantages. The production of technological products in the industry is avoided due to the high number of employees in the country, low salaries and low talent and competence of employees, lack of technology in the national market and high costs. The country's economy is heavily influenced by exchange rate fluctuations (Porter & Kramer, 2002).

In the Investment-Oriented Stage, the companies of the country invest not only in applying external technology but also in new technologies that need to be developed. Successful exporters produce products that take advantage of economies of scale and meet capital requirements, and product supply is mainly based on manufacturing standard products using standardized technologies (Jasson, 2009). Local demand conditions are average, and the relevant and supporting industries are not very developed.

At the Innovation Oriented Stage, the structure of the industries in which the companies can compete is expanding gradually. Factor costs are reduced and improved and new competitive technologies are introduced. With the development of new technologies, the contribution of relevant and supporting industries to the competition is high. The economy of the country is least affected by economic change, exchange rate and crises (Porter, 1990).

In the Asset Oriented Phase, unlike the other phases, the competitive advantage has started to decrease. As the motivations of the investors, managers and employees shifted away from sustainable investments and innovations, assets acquired in previous stages began to run out. Investors try to maintain the current situation instead of making new investments (Porter, 1990).

During the stages of the competitive advantage model, countries may not be able to pass through each stage or progress to the next stage. Some countries may remain in the factor-driven phase, or may return from the asset-oriented phase to the factor-oriented approach, because they cannot invest in advanced techniques and technologies, or fail to move beyond the investment and / or innovation-innovation phases to the asset-driven phase (Meshal, 1997).

Competition Intelligence

Today, increasing global competition, rapid political and technological developments put more pressure on business executives than ever before about the need for information about their environment. In a competitive business environment, businesses need to protect their strategies from their competitors and get as much information as possible about their competitors' goals and plans (Bergeron & Hiller, 2002). Increasing severity of competition in economies has increasingly led the attention of managers to seek and understand the factors that lead and sustain business success. Businesses need to take risks, to be innovative and to meet the changing needs of customers in their markets quickly (Brocklesby & Campbell-Hunt, 2004). Therefore, in today's dynamic markets, it is necessary for businesses to anticipate and understand the actions of competitors in order to effectively position their products and services. Understanding competitors is also one of the most important aspects of developing a viable business strategy (Kahaner, 1997). For effective strategic planning, it is necessary to combine high-quality competition information (David & David, 2013). For this purpose, enterprises should develop alternative intelligence sources, scan various aspects of the environment and make their employees sensitive to the necessity of obtaining intelligence. As we have seen, business managers need to collect and process valuable information about their environment, such as competitors, customers, suppliers, governments, technological trends, and environmental science developments, in order to form or reconstruct the business strategy. In other words, strategic Competitive Intelligence ifade, which expresses the production and processing of information about the business environment, is necessary for strategic purposes (Özdemir, 2010). According to Calof and Skinner (1999), Competition Intelligence is viable recommendations of systematic processes involving the planning, collection, analysis and dissemination of external information for potential developments or opportunities that affect the competitive status of an enterprise or country.

Campbell (2004) defines Competition Intelligence as a bridge between knowledge and practice. In fact, this approach can be said to summarize almost all definitions made in the literature very well (Köseoğlu & Akdeve, 2013). Businesses have been making efforts for many years to recognize and understand their competitors' strategies, capabilities, areas of action (Fahey, 2007). Today, Competition Intelligence serves the purpose of collecting, analyzing and using information systematically in the context of strategic management and focusing on the environment of competition, technological, political, social and economic developments. Competition Intelligence is one step ahead of environmental screening by highlighting the use of intelligence (Edin, 2008). Enterprises within the scope of Competition Intelligence; It aims to identify and control its own potentials, current and potential competitors, the immediate and distant environment of the enterprise (Blenkhorn & Fleisher, 2005). In order to achieve this goal, enterprises need to establish a very effective intelligence system, establish an effective decision support system to monitor and evaluate the movements in the strategic area, and develop early warning systems to report extraordinary situations as a result of these systems. In order to accomplish these, it is necessary to learn from the experiences of others as well as the use of knowledge of the enterprises themselves. The strength of an effective Competition Intelligence approach from the business culture will play an important role in the success of the system (Bose, 2008). The main objective of enterprises is to sustain their lives, the most important condition of which is to be aware of the environment and to be prepared for the positive and negative effects that may come from the environment. Like every socio-technical and open system, businesses have to shape the environment in line with their own interests in order to recognize the environment, adapt and strengthen its position. Otherwise, it will be impossible for them to survive in this dynamic and increasingly globalized world. The probability of winning this battle of life will increase if it recognizes itself and its competitors (Akpınar & Edin, 2007).

Business Performance

Performance is an important aspect of every organization. It is a concept about what the organization expects from the employees of the organization after the recruitment process has recruited many people for vacancies. To meet the goals of the organization and the demands of consumers who want to expect the best and high-quality service from the organization, the employees need to show an effective work (Neely, 2007). Organizational performance is a concept that aims to improve the working skills of teams and individual performances by aiming at improving the working competence and skills of the employees (Johanson & Mattsson, 2015). Although the goal is to achieve success, it aims at achieving the best output of the final product and service, as well as the ways of doing business that are individual, team and organization-wide. Performance in each enterprise measures and determines the success rate of the organization. The performance issue, which also gives information about the way the organization works, is directly related to the long and short term goals of the enterprises (Delmar, 1996). For this reason, many businesses nowadays want to evaluate the outcome of products and services produced by employees at a given time. As a result of the relevant evaluation, the overall performance of the enterprise emerges and the business management has to make a decision about how this process should be managed. These decisions are generally referred to as performance management (Blackburn et al., 2013). The overall performance of the employees within the organization reveals the performance of the organization (Giacalone & Jurkiewicz, 2003). Clarification of job performance is important for understanding employee behaviors and understanding qualitative and quantitative behaviors within the organization. However, today's employee performance is not only mentioned by numerical data and outputs. It is also evaluated within the scope of qualitative elements such as employee motivation, loyalty and social environment (Frolick & Ariyachandra, 2006).

Performance measurement at organizational level is very important in terms of its contribution to the learning process at the whole enterprise level. Today, among the objectives of performance measurement, realization of business strategy, determination of success factors and focusing on them, determination of the connection of success factors and targets, planning and directing of business resources, success valuation, providing motivation of employees, contributing to communication and learning process are included (Hoerl & Snee, 2012) . Today, businesses have shifted their job performance from wage and working hours focus to behavioral roles. Knowledge, skills, experience, motivation personality traits are now included in the performance phenomenon. Because businesses added social elements as well as problems such as how much product was produced, how much sales were made, how many hours worked and to what extent the services were realized. There is a shift from wage-oriented to a personal and social performance-oriented system (Morgan & Strong, 2003). The beginning and the most important stage of the organizational performance appraisal process is the process of determining the criteria. When the organizational performance criteria are examined, it is understood that there are similar criteria instead of sectoral and periodical sources. The main criteria that demonstrate organizational performance are: quality, effectiveness and efficiency, innovation, efficiency, profitability, budget compliance and quality of working life (Marr & Schiuma, 2003).

Assessing Business Performance: In an economic and sectoral environment where competition conditions are becoming more and more stringent, there is a process that prioritizes performance in human resources policies of organizations and shapes them in the best way to manage them. Those who constantly renew their workforce performance, and who aim to review and evaluate instead of auditing, will always be ahead of a name. Things such as division of labor, work habits, business practice, business ethics, promotion and promotion can vary from culture to culture. For example, while the increase in production is seen as important in some cultures, the performance of employees in some cultures may be seen as more important (Wu et al., 2003). Evaluating the performance of employees is now one of the basic qualities of being a manager. Today, however, performance appraisal is not just about working hours, product and service outputs. It is important to align performance with the objectives and objectives of the business. For example, a company may have achieved period-end profitability in sales, but if the employee is having problems with motivation, entry and exit and consumer satisfaction, then the desired holistic goal has not been achieved. As mentioned before, quantitative results that bring short-term gains are not sufficient to see the overall picture in today's economic conditions (Venkatraman & Ramanujam, 1986). In this context, performance evaluation represents a dynamic process. It also demonstrates the output of the activities of the employees together with the leaders towards common goals and interests. Performance evaluation measures the degree of achievement of predetermined targets (Wiklund & Shepherd, 2005). It compares the expected success with the actual results and draws a meaningful result from them. The purpose of performance evaluation is to increase organizational efficiency and productivity. It is a process that measures the success of individuals working in line with the targets set in organizations and demonstrates the moral characteristics of employee behavior patterns. Accordingly, it is an activity that measures the ratio of employee performance data to the success of the organization (Anderson & Zeithaml, 1984).

Performance Evaluation and Cultural Differences

Performance evaluation; It refers to a process that involves measuring the performance of people, units or organizations according to some predetermined standards or on the basis of the "performance of similar employees". It is also defined as the process of making a judgment about the degree of success by systematically comparing the skills, potential, work habits, behaviors and similar qualities of the employee with others (Yücel, 1999). This is also the process of formally measuring and evaluating how effectively and efficiently the objectives of employees in the organization are achieved. This system, which contributes to the differentiation of employees according to job performance, contributes to the adaptation of the objectives of the organization and management by developing employees. Managing performance consists of improving organizational performance that may arise from differences, coaching, guiding, motivating and rewarding to help mobilize potential (Richard et al., 2009). When determining the performance evaluation objectives of the enterprise for development and research, the employee potential of different cultures should be taken into consideration (Kim Jean Lee, & Yu, 2004). By comparing and evaluating the expected and actual performance dimensions of the employees, the next valuation criteria can be established more efficiently (Carmeli & Tishler, 2004). In this way, different criteria can be determined for employees with different demographic characteristics. According to contemporary methods, success evaluation is applied in large companies continuously. As a result of the evaluations, the expectations of the employees are also taken into consideration. In recent years, there has been an increase in the number of employees, significant structural changes with increasing knowledge and expertise. These changes make it difficult for a manager to be the sole evaluator of the employees in terms of knowledge, time and objectivity. The 360-degree performance evaluation system is an example of a contemporary valuation process, which is preferred by many organizations today, by making employees multi-valued, providing significant gains in terms of time, effort and cost. Thanks to this appraisal, enterprises have a structure that provides sustainable communication and feedback among their employees and can minimize the margins of error that may occur during the evaluation process (Oruç et al., 2008). The planning part of the performance management includes the agreement between individuals and managers on what is needed to develop competencies, improve performance, raise standards and achieve goals. For this, it is important to determine the priorities required by the job and to ensure the meaning of performance standards and competencies.

SOLUTIONS AND RECOMMENDATIONS

Businesses who want to be successful in the global areas, especially in this age, should be able to quickly adapt to extreme variable situations. In a period of increasing competition in international markets, the most important trump card of enterprises will be the differences they create in organizational culture. In the field of activity of international enterprises, environmental elements are especially cultural elements. The political structure, educational level, belief system, etc. of that region will affect how the enterprise will carry out its activities with a strategy. If an international business develops marketing strategies without taking these elements into consideration, there is hardly any chance of success in its operations in this region. It is a well-known fact that international businesses should know environmental factors well and plan according to these factors. Although businesses do not want to take risks because they want to stay in local markets, competitor enterprises produce cheaper and higher quality products and offer them to consumers forcing businesses to enter international markets in order to survive. On the other hand, the contraction of the local market or the existence of some legal political problems within the country are among the other factors causing the opening of the businesses to the international markets. However, although globalization necessitates enterprises to enter international markets, it provides an important advantage in maximizing their profits, in maintaining their sustainability by positioning their brands in different regional markets and increasing their market share.

In order to be successful in international markets, first of all, it is necessary to think that the demands and needs of the customers will change, to identify these differences, if any, and to have a combination of products or services that respond to their wishes and needs. As mentioned before, it has to determine the product strategies differently from the local ones, as the demands and needs of the consumers differ when opening to the international market. Because it is possible to be positioned in the markets addressed by meeting consumer expectations. Otherwise, enterprises cannot hold or be positioned in the markets of the region addressed. The only area where there is competition in enterprises operating in international markets is not in product and service marketing. At the same time, there is intense competition in the search for qualified personnel and managers. For this reason, international businesses should find and retain personnel and managers who can carry them to their goals. The coexistence of employees and managers from different cultures in an international business is one of the challenges of keeping them for a common purpose in the business (Kaplan and Norton 2005). Therefore, enterprises that fail to achieve success in human resources management will fail in all other strategies. Cultural diversity in international businesses has a significant impact on the business's relationships with its environment and customers. Particularly in the management of the enterprise, the understanding of intercultural management should be applied successfully. Because international businesses operate in different parts of the world, they have a multicultural employee profile. The fields of activity of international businesses are highly open to change. As international businesses provide goods and services to different cultural regions, each region needs to adapt to its unique cultural characteristics. Cultural differences bring about many political and legal changes. For this reason, the organizational cultures of the companies operating in international fields must have a model that is ready for change and that develops itself continuously.

FUTURE RESEARCH DIRECTIONS

According to Lawler III and Worley (2011) and other management futurists, changing environmental conditions according to the developments in the next 40 years or 50 years will direct the nations as well as developments in international business. In particular, financial institutions, banking, insurance, transportation and logistics, international civil aviation, information technology, the increase of robots, the use of artificial intelligence, the advancement of aircraft technology, the development of space technology, access to renewable energy resources, quality progress and competitiveness will become more important. In this respect, international enterprises should adopt a strategic management approach. In the following studies, the effect of risk culture on other sectors, especially service sector, can be investigated.

- Again, the impact of different dimensions of demographic characteristics and operational characteristics on risk culture can be investigated.
- Instead of a specific region of Turkey done studies on businesses operating across.
- The relationship between risk culture and other variables can be examined.

- Businesses considering opening up to international markets should study foreign markets well in terms of their social, cultural, economic and technological infrastructure; they must make the most of the opportunities and incentives offered by foreign markets.
- The strategy of entering international markets should be selected after being thoroughly researched and discussed from a strategic point of view in line with the objectives and objectives of the enterprise.
- Businesses should establish an expert staff and risk management unit in their own premises to analyze the risks they may face.
- Business owners and senior managers should take more responsibility for the establishment of the risk culture, which is an important part of the risk management process, throughout the organization.

Especially in today's global markets where hyper competition plays an active role, Competition Intelligence must be utilized. Competitive Intelligence, which is an important bridge between knowledge and application, has been used effectively in the exploratory market research model to reach the target markets. The concept of intelligence no longer applies not only to countries' privacy policies and armies, but also to companies and especially economies.

CONCLUSION

Although globalization has many impacts in the economic, social, cultural and political spheres of the world, the acceleration of its progress in the fields of communication and transportation has brought about important developments in international marketing activities. The increase in the educated population and the continuous increase in the demands and needs of consumers make businesses feel the need to develop their products and services in many areas. Although there are differences in the demands and needs of consumers living in different geographical regions, factors such as the production of products in line with the common demands and needs of consumers in the international markets towards homogenization to a large extent, intensification of the competitive environment make it difficult for businesses to continue their activities only in national markets. Enterprises that benefit from many opportunities and advantages in international markets as a result of internationalization may also face many risks and dangers if they do not take the necessary measures. When opening to foreign markets, businesses should investigate the market in which they will operate and open to international markets with strategies in line with their goals, objectives and strategies. The wrong choice of internationalization strategy can harm the business and even endanger its existence. The decision on which strategy to enter into international markets should be selected after being thoroughly investigated and discussed from a strategic point of view in line with the objectives and objectives of the enterprise.

The increase in internationalization and consequently the complexity of activities and transactions are related to the identity of the family business in which the enterprises are managed by the business owners; institutionalized and managed by professionals. They must establish an expert staff and risk management unit to analyze the risks they may face as a result of their activities in international markets. With this, it prevents unnecessary and excessive risk taking as well as insufficient risk taking within the enterprise. Business owners and senior managers should take more responsibility for the establishment of the risk culture, which is an important part of the risk management process, throughout the organization. The organizational culture models of international businesses are of course different from national enterprises. Operational models rather than structures are developed in national enterprises. For example, there are organizational model options, such as choosing between a dynamic or static model. However, in addition to functioning in international enterprises, the structural features of organizational culture are also important. Whether the structure of organizational culture is based on equality or a hierarchical structure is also vital for an international business.

A successful organizational culture will provide a competitive advantage to the international arena and make it more successful in marketing compared to other enterprises. Employees who feel good and safe in the organization will be positively motivated and productive. Thanks to a model of organizational culture open to change, an enterprise that is open to innovations that will adapt to its requirements in an era will emerge. Through organizational culture, each individual will feel identified with the organization and gain a sense of belonging. Managers, on the other hand, will take on a more self-sacrificing leadership by keeping the goals of the business and their goals. For this reason, a successful organizational culture in international enterprises is the key to all successful strategies and objectives. The enterprises that fail to form the organizational culture structure successfully will not be successful in the implementation of these plans even if they achieve excellence in all other plans. However, a successful organizational culture structure will enable the business goals and strategies to be designed successfully.

REFERENCES

Aaby, N. E., & Slater, S. F. (1989). Management influences on export performance: A review of the empirical literature 1978-1988. *International Marketing Review*, *6*(4). doi:10.1108/EUM0000000001516

Adler, N. J., & Jelinek, M. (1986). Is "organization culture" culture bound? *Human Resource Management*, *25*(1), 73–90. doi:10.1002/hrm.3930250106

Akpınar, H., & Edin, İ. (2007). *Rekabet İstihbaratı, Öneri*, *7*(28), 1–8.

Alexander, C. (Ed.). (2003). *Operational risk: regulation, analysis and management*. Pearson Education.

Almeida, J. H., Sapienza, H. J., & Michael, J. (2000). Growth through internationalization: Patterns among British firms. *Frontier of Entrepreneurship Research*, *4*, 402.

Alvesson, M. (2012). Understanding organizational culture. Atlanta, GA: Sage.

Andersen, T. J. (Ed.). (2006). *Perspectives on strategic risk management*. Copenhagen Business School Press DK.

Anderson, C. R., & Zeithaml, C. P. (1984). Stage of the product life cycle, business strategy, and business performance. *Academy of Management Journal*, *27*(1), 5–24.

Anderson-Levitt, K. M. (2012). Complicating the concept of culture. *Comparative Education*, *48*(4), 441–454. doi:10.1080/03050068.2011.634285

Ashby, S., Palermo, T., & Power, M. (2012). Risk culture in financial organisations: An interim report.

Australia, D. (2012). Cultivating an intelligent risk culture: a fresh perspective. Sydney, Australia: Deloitte Touche Tohmatsu Ltd.

Aven, T. (2011). *Quantitative risk assessment: the scientific platform.* Cambridge, UK: Cambridge University Press. doi:10.1017/CBO9780511974120

Banks, E. (2012). *Risk culture: A practical guide to building and strengthening the fabric of risk management.* Palgrave Macmillan. doi:10.1057/9781137263728

Bannock, G., & Manser, W. (2003). *International dictionary of finance (the economist series).* Profile Books.

Baranoff, E. Z., & Baranoff, E. Z. (2004). *Risk management and insurance* (pp. 48–52). Danvers, MA: Wiley.

Barney, J. (1991). Firm resources and sustained competitive advantage. *Journal of Management, 17*(1), 99–120. doi:10.1177/014920639101700108

Bell, J., Crick, D., & Young, S. (2004). Small firm internationalization and business strategy: An exploratory study of 'knowledge-intensive' and 'traditional' manufacturing firms in the UK. *International Small Business Journal, 22*(1), 23–56. doi:10.1177/0266242604039479

Bell, J., & Young, S. (1998). Towards an integrative framework of the internationalization of the firm. In *Internationalization* (pp. 5–28). London, UK: Palgrave Macmillan. doi:10.1007/978-1-349-26556-5_1

Bergeron, P., & Hiller, C. A. (2002). Competitive intelligence. *Annual Review of Information Science and Technology (Arist), 36*(1), 353–390. doi:10.1002/aris.1440360109

Blackburn, R. A., Hart, M., & Wainwright, T. (2013). Small business performance: Business, strategy and owner-manager characteristics. *Journal of Small Business and Enterprise Development, 20*(1), 8–27. doi:10.1108/14626001311298394

Blenkhorn, D. L., & Fleisher, C. S. (Eds.). (2005). *Competitive intelligence and global business.* Greenwood Publishing Group.

Bose, R. (2008). Competitive intelligence process and tools for intelligence analysis. *Industrial Management & Data Systems, 108*(4), 510–528. doi:10.1108/02635570810868362

Boter, H., & Lundström, A. (2005). SME perspectives on business support services: The role of company size, industry and location. *Journal of Small Business and Enterprise Development, 12*(2), 244–258. doi:10.1108/14626000510594638

Bowden, A. R., Lane, M. R., & Martin, J. H. (2002). *Triple bottom line risk management: enhancing profit, environmental performance, and community benefits.* John Wiley & Sons.

Bozeman, B., & Kingsley, G. (1998). Risk culture in public and private organizations. *Public Administration Review, 58*(2), 109–118. doi:10.2307/976358

Bradley, F. (2002). Uluslararası Pazarlama Stratejisi.(Çev.: Ġçlem Er). *Financial Times Prentice Hall, Ankara: Bilim Teknik Yayın Evi.*

Briers, S. (2000). The development of an integrated model of risk. (Doctoral thesis, The University of South Africa).

Brocklesby, J., & Campbell-Hunt, C. (2004). The evolution of competitive capability: A cognition and complex systems perspective. *Journal of Organisational Transformation & Social Change*, 1.

Calof, J., & Skinner, B. (1999). Government's role in competitive intelligence: What's happening in Canada. *Competitive Intelligence Magazine*, 2(2), 20–23.

Campbell, J. L. (2004). *Institutional change and globalization*. Princeton University Press.

Carmeli, A., & Tishler, A. (2004). The relationships between intangible organizational elements and organizational performance. *Strategic Management Journal*, 25(13), 1257–1278. doi:10.1002mj.428

Chuang, Y. T., Church, R., & Zikic, J. (2004). Organizational culture, group diversity and intragroup conflict. *Team Performance Management: An International Journal*, 10(1/2), 26–34. doi:10.1108/13527590410527568

Cooper, C. A., Cartwright, S., & Earley, P. C. (2001). *The international handbook of organizational culture and climate*.

Cooper, D. F. (2005). *Project risk management guidelines: managing risk in large projects and complex procurements*. Hoboken, NJ: John Wiley & Sons

Cornalba, C., & Giudici, P. (2004). Statistical models for operational risk management. *Physica A*, 338(1-2), 166–172. doi:10.1016/j.physa.2004.02.039

Cornett, M. M., & Saunders, A. (2003). *Financial institutions management: A risk management approach*. McGraw-Hill/Irwin.

Cortez, A. (2011). *Winning at risk: strategies to go beyond Basel* (Vol. 638). Hoboken, NJ: John Wiley & Sons.

Cummins, J. D., Phillips, R. D., & Smith, S. D. (1998). The rise of risk management. *Economic Review (Atlanta, Ga.)*, 83(1), 30–41.

Daft, R. L. (1991). *Management* (2nd ed.). Chicago, IL: Dryden Press.

Daft, R. L. (2015). *Organization theory and design*. Cengage Learning.

David, F. R., & David, F. R. (2013). *Strategic management concepts and cases: A competitive advantage approach*. Pearson.

Delmar, F. (1996). *Entrepreneurial behavior and business performance*. EFI.

Derici, O., Tüysüz, Z., & Sarı, A. (2007). Kurumsal Risk Yönetimi ve Sayıştay Uygulaması. *Sayıştay Dergisi*, 65, 151–172.

Deshpandé, R., & Farley, J. U. (2004). Organizational culture, market orientation, innovativeness, and firm performance: An international research odyssey. *International Journal of Research in Marketing*, 21(1), 3–22. doi:10.1016/j.ijresmar.2003.04.002

Dess, G. G., Lumpkin, G. T., & Covin, J. G. (1997). Entrepreneurial strategy making and firm performance: Tests of contingency and configurational models. *Strategic Management Journal*, 18(9), 677–695. doi:10.1002/(SICI)1097-0266(199710)18:9<677::AID-SMJ905>3.0.CO;2-Q

Dinçer, Ö. (1998). *Stratejik Yönetim ve Politikası, Genişletilmiş ve Yenilenmiş 5*. İstanbul, Turkey: Baskı, Beta Yay.

Dursun, İ. T. (2013). Örgüt Kültürü ve Strateji İlişkisi: Hofstede'nin Boyutları Açısından Bir Değerlendirme. *Siyaset, Ekonomi ve Yönetim Araştırmaları Dergisi, 1*(4).

Edin, İ. (2008). Rekabet İstihbaratı Sürecinde Anahtar İstihbarat Konularının Belirlenmesi, *Marmara Üniversitesi İ. İ. B. F. Dergisi*, C.XXV, 2, 589-600.

Eğinli, A. T. (2011). Kültürlerarası Yeterliliğin Kazanılmasında Kültürel Farklılık Eğitimlerinin Önemi. *Öneri Dergisi, 9*(35), 215-227.

Ehtiyar, R. (2003). Kültürel Sinerji: Uluslararası İşletmelere Yönelik Kavramsal Bir İrdeleme. *Akdeniz University Faculty of Economics & Administrative Sciences Faculty Journal/Akdeniz Universitesi Iktisadi ve Idari Bilimler Fakultesi Dergisi, 3*(5).

Erinç, S. M. (2014). Kültürde kültür, kültür de kültür. *Cogito Düşünce Dergisi*, 2, 107–112.

Etemad, H. (Ed.). (2004). *International entrepreneurship in small and medium size enterprises: orientation, environment and strategy*. Edward Elgar. doi:10.4337/9781845421557

Fahey, L. (2007). Connecting strategy and competitive intelligence: Refocusing intelligence to produce critical strategy inputs. *Strategy and Leadership, 35*(1), 4–12. doi:10.1108/10878570710717236

Farrel, J. M., & Hoon, A. (2009). What's your company risk culture. National Association of Corporate Directors Directorship, 50-62.

Fikirkoca, M. (2003). *Bütünsel risk yönetimi*. Ankara, Turkey: Pozitif Matbaacılık.

Findler, L., Wind, L. H., & Barak, M. E. M. (2007). The challenge of workforce management in a global society: Modeling the relationship between diversity, inclusion, organizational culture, and employee well-being, job satisfaction and organizational commitment. *Administration in Social Work, 31*(3), 63–94. doi:10.1300/J147v31n03_05

Fraser, J. R., & Simkins, B. J. (2016). The challenges of and solutions for implementing enterprise risk management. *Business Horizons, 59*(6), 689–698. doi:10.1016/j.bushor.2016.06.007

Freeman, R. E. (2010). *Strategic management: A stakeholder approach*. Cambridge, UK: Cambridge University Press. doi:10.1017/CBO9781139192675

Frolick, M. N., & Ariyachandra, T. R. (2006). Business performance management: One truth. *IS Management, 23*(1), 41–48.

Froot, K. A., Scharfstein, D. S., & Stein, J. C. (1993). Risk management: Coordinating corporate investment and financing policies. *Journal of Finance, 48*(5), 1629-1658.

Funston, R. (2003). Creating a risk-intelligent organization: Using enterprise risk management, organizations can systematically identify potential exposures, take corrective action early, and learn from those actions to better achieve objectives. *Internal Auditor, 60*(2), 59–64.

Garcia-Zamor, J. C. (2003). Workplace spirituality and organizational performance. *Public Administration Review*, *63*(3), 355–363. doi:10.1111/1540-6210.00295

Gebler, D. (2006). Is your culture a risk factor? *Business And Society Review-Boston And New York*, *111*(3), 337.

Giacalone, R. A., & Jurkiewicz, C. L. (Eds.). (2003). *Handbook of workplace spirituality and organizational performance*. Me Sharpe.

Gordon, C. (2008). Cashing in on corporate culture: An organization with a well-defined culture can achieve higher profitability. *CA Magazine (Toronto)*, *141*(1), 49.

Gorzeń-Mitka, I. (2015). Management challenges in the context of risk culture. *Problems of Management in the 21st Century*, *10*(2), 60-61.

Grant, R. M. (1991). The resource-based theory of competitive advantage: Implications for strategy formulation. *California Management Review*, *33*(3), 114–135. doi:10.2307/41166664

Grant, R. M. (2002). *Contemporary strategy analysis: concept, techniques, applications. Massachusetts*: Blackwell.

Harris, P. R., Moran, R. T., & Andrews, J. (1991). *Managing cultural differences* (Vol. 3). Houston, TX: Gulf Publishing.

Hatch, M. J. (2018). Organization theory: Modern, symbolic, and postmodern perspectives. Oxford, UK: Oxford University Press.

Hatch, M. J., & Schultz, M. (1997). Relations between organizational culture, identity and image. *European Journal of Marketing*, *31*(5/6), 356–365. doi:10.1108/eb060636

Heldman, K. (2010). *Project manager's spotlight on risk management*. Hoboken, NJ: John Wiley & Sons.

Hertz, D. B., & Thomas, H. (1983). *Risk analysis and its applications*. Singapore: John Wiley & Sons.

Hillson, D. (2012). *How much risk is too much risk: understanding risk appetite*. Project Management Institute.

Hillson, D., Linsley, P., Smith, K., Hindson, A., & Murray-Webster, R. (2012). Models of risk culture. *Risk culture: Resources for practitioners*, 22-27.

Hindson, A. (2012). A practical approach to risk culture. *Risk culture: Resources for Practitioners*, 16-19.

Hitt, M. A., Ireland, R. D., & Hoskisson, R. E. (2012). *Strategic management cases: competitiveness and globalization*. Cengage Learning.

Hoerl, R., & Snee, R. D. (2012). *Statistical thinking: Improving business performance* (Vol. 48). Hoboken, NJ: John Wiley & Sons. doi:10.1002/9781119202721

Hofstede, G. (1998). Attitudes, values and organizational culture: Disentangling the concepts. *Organization Studies*, *19*(3), 477–493. doi:10.1177/017084069801900305

Hofstede, G., Hofstede, G. J., & Minkov, M. (2005). *Cultures and organizations: Software of the mind* (Vol. 2). New York: McGraw-Hill.

Jasson, E. M. V. (2009). *A study of Argentine competitiveness: an extension of Porter's Diamond Model*, (Doctoral Dissertation, York University).

Johanson, J., & Mattsson, L. G. (1994). The markets-as-networks tradition in Sweden. In *Research traditions in marketing* (pp. 321–346). Dordrecht, The Netherlands: Springer. doi:10.1007/978-94-011-1402-8_10

Johanson, J., & Mattsson, L. G. (2015). Internationalisation in industrial systems—a network approach. In *Knowledge, networks and power* (pp. 111–132). London, UK: Palgrave Macmillan. doi:10.1057/9781137508829_5

Johanson, J., & Wiedersheim-Paul, F. (1975). The internationalization of the firm—Four Swedish cases 1. *Journal of Management Studies*, *12*(3), 305–323. doi:10.1111/j.1467-6486.1975.tb00514.x

Johanson, J. M., & Mattsson, L. G. (1988). Internationalization in industrial systems–a network approach. Strategies in Global Competition. London, UK: Croom Helm. 287-314.

Jones, G. R. (2013). *Organizational theory, design, and change*. Upper Saddle River, NJ: Pearson.

Jones, M. V., & Coviello, N. E. (2005). Internationalisation: Conceptualising an entrepreneurial process of behaviour in time. *Journal of International Business Studies*, *36*(3), 284–303. doi:10.1057/palgrave.jibs.8400138

Kahaner, L. (1997). *Competitive intelligence: How to gather analyze and use information to move your business to the top*. Simon and Schuster.

Kaplan, R. S., & Norton, D. P. (2005). *Creating the office of strategy management*. Boston, MA: Division of Research, Harvard Business School.

Kim Jean Lee, S., & Yu, K. (2004). Corporate culture and organizational performance. *Journal of Managerial Psychology*, *19*(4), 340–359. doi:10.1108/02683940410537927

Kimball, R. C. (2000). Failures in risk management. *New England Economic Review*, 3–12.

Knight, G. A., & Cavusgil, S. T. (2004). Innovation, organizational capabilities, and the born-global firm. *Journal of International Business Studies*, *35*(2), 124–141. doi:10.1057/palgrave.jibs.8400071

Köseoğlu, M. A., & Akdeve, E. (2013). *Rekabet İstihbaratı (Competitive Intelligence)*. Ankara, Turkey: Nobel Yayın.

Lash, S. (2000). Risk culture. *The risk society and beyond: Critical issues for social theory*, 47-62.

Lawler, E. E. III, & Worley, C. G. (2011). *Management reset: Organizing for sustainable effectiveness*. Hoboken, NJ: John Wiley & Sons.

Leung, K., Bhagat, R. S., Buchan, N. R., Erez, M., & Gibson, C. B. (2005). Culture and international business: Recent advances and their implications for future research. *Journal of International Business Studies*, *36*(4), 357–378. doi:10.1057/palgrave.jibs.8400150

LiPuma, E. (1993). Culture and the concept of culture in a theory of practice. *Bourdieu: critical perspectives,* 14-34.

Lloyd-Reason, L., & Mughan, T. (2002). Strategies for internationalisation within SMEs: The key role of the owner-manager. *Journal of Small Business and Enterprise Development, 9*(2), 120–129. doi:10.1108/14626000210427375

Marhavilas, P. K., & Koulouriotis, D. E. (2012). Developing a new alternative risk assessment framework in the work sites by including a stochastic and a deterministic process: A case study for the Greek public electric power provider. *Safety Science, 50*(3), 448–462. doi:10.1016/j.ssci.2011.10.006

Marr, B., & Schiuma, G. (2003). Business performance measurement–past, present and future. *Management Decision, 41*(8), 680–687. doi:10.1108/00251740310496198

Martin, J. (2001). Organizational culture: Mapping the terrain. Thousand Oaks, CA: Sage.

Masum, M., & Fernandez, A. (2008). Internationalization process of SMEs: Strategies and methods.

McNeil, A. J., Frey, R., & Embrechts, P. (2005). *Quantitative risk management: Concepts, techniques, and tools* (Vol. 3). Princeton, NJ: Princeton University Press.

McShane, M. (2018). Enterprise risk management: History and a design science proposal. *The Journal of Risk Finance, 19*(2), 137–153. doi:10.1108/JRF-03-2017-0048

Meshal, H. (1997). *Comparative and competitive advantage as determinants of 'foreign policy formulation in Australia,* (Doctoral Thesis, The Fletcher School).

Miles, M. P., Arnold, D. R., & Thompson, D. L. (1993). The interrelationship between environmental hostility and entrepreneurial orientation. *Journal of Applied Business Research, 9*(4), 12–23. doi:10.19030/jabr.v9i4.5984

Moran, R. T., Abramson, N. R., & Moran, S. V. (2014). *Managing cultural differences.* Routledge.

Moran, R. T., Harris, P. R., & Moran, S. V. (2011). *Managing cultural differences: global leadership strategies for cross-cultural business success.* Routledge.

Morgan, R. E., & Strong, C. A. (2003). Business performance and dimensions of strategic orientation. *Journal of Business Research, 56*(3), 163–176. doi:10.1016/S0148-2963(01)00218-1

Mtigwe, B. (2005). The entrepreneurial firm internationalization process in the Southern African context: A comparative approach. *International Journal of Entrepreneurial Behaviour & Research, 11*(5), 358–377. doi:10.1108/13552550510615006

Murphy, C. (2016). *Competitive intelligence: gathering, analysing and putting it to work.* Routledge. doi:10.4324/9781315573151

Naoum, S. (2001). *People and organizational management in construction.* Thomas Telford. doi:10.1680/paomic.28746

Neely, A. (Ed.). (2007). *Business performance measurement: Unifying theory and integrating practice.* Cambridge University Press. doi:10.1017/CBO9780511488481

Negruş, M. (1986). *Mijloace şi modalităţi de plată internaţionale*. Editura Academiei Republicii Socialiste România.

Obrecht, J. J. (2004). Entrepreneurial capabilities: A resource-based systemic approach to international entrepreneurship. Handbook of research on international entrepreneurship, 248-266.

Olivares-Mesa, A., & Cabrera-Suarez, K. (2006). Factors affecting the timing of the export development process: Does the family influence on the business make a difference? *International Journal of Globalisation and Small Business*, *1*(4), 326–339. doi:10.1504/IJGSB.2006.012183

Olivares-Mesa, A., & Suarez-Ortega, S. (2006). Factors affecting the timing of the export development process in Spanish manufacturing firms. In *International Marketing Research* (pp. 89–105). Emerald Group. doi:10.1016/S1474-7979(06)17003-9

Oruç, K. E., Armaneri, Ö., & Yalçınkaya, Ö. (2008). 360 Derece Performans Değerleme ve Web Tabanlı Bir Model İle Kurumsal Verimliliğin Arttırılması, İzmir Büyükşehir Belediyesi, Ulaşım Dairesi, Dokuz Eylül Üniversitesi, Mühendislik Fakültesi, Endüstri Mühendisliği Bölümü, *Endüstri Mühendisliği Dergisi. Makina Mühendisleri Odası*, *19*(1), 4–18.

Ostroff, C., Kinicki, A. J., & Muhammad, R. S. (2012). Organizational culture and climate. Handbook of psychology, Second Edition, 12.

Ott, J. S. (1989). *The organizational culture perspective* (pp. 221–243). Chicago, IL: Dorsey Press.

Oviatt, B. M., & McDougall, P. P. (2005). Defining international entrepreneurship and modeling the speed of internationalization. *Entrepreneurship Theory and Practice*, *29*(5), 537–553. doi:10.1111/j.1540-6520.2005.00097.x

Özdemir, E. (2010). Rekabet istihbarati toplama ve etik: Bir alan arastirmasi. *İstanbul Üniversitesi Siyasal Bilgiler Fakültesi Dergisi*, (43), 67-95.

Phatak, A. V. (1989). *Uluslararası Yönetim, (Çev. Atilla Baransel, Tomris Somay)*. İstanbul, Turkey: İÜ İşletme Fakültesi Yayını.

Porter, M. E. (1990). *The competitive advantage of nations*. New York: The Free Press. doi:10.1007/978-1-349-11336-1

Porter, M. E., & Kramer, M. R. (2002). The competitive advantage of corporate.

Pothukuchi, V., Damanpour, F., Choi, J., Chen, C. C., & Park, S. H. (2002). National and organizational culture differences and international joint venture performance. *Journal of International Business Studies*, *33*(2), 243–265. doi:10.1057/palgrave.jibs.8491015

Power, M., Ashby, S., & Palermo, T. (2013). *Risk culture in financial organisations: A research report*. CARR-Analysis of Risk and Regulation.

Prahalad, C. K., & Hamel, G. (1990). The core competence of the corporation. *Harvard Business Review*, 3.

Rejda, G. E. (2011). *Principles of risk management and insurance*. Pearson Education India.

Richard, P. J., Devinney, T. M., Yip, G. S., & Johnson, G. (2009). Measuring organizational performance: Towards methodological best practice. *Journal of Management*, *35*(3), 718–804. doi:10.1177/0149206308330560

Ritchie, B., & Brindley, C. (2007). Supply chain risk management and performance: A guiding framework for future development. *International Journal of Operations & Production Management*, *27*(3), 303–322. doi:10.1108/01443570710725563

Roeschmann, A. Z. (2014). Risk culture: What it is and how it affects an insurer's risk management. *Risk Management & Insurance Review*, *17*(2), 277–296. doi:10.1111/rmir.12025

Root, F. R. (1994). *Entry strategies for international markets* (pp. 22–44). New York: Lexington Books.

Schein, E. H. (2010). *Organizational culture and leadership* (Vol. 2). Hoboken, NJ: John Wiley & Sons.

Sewell, W. H. (2004). The concept(s) of culture. In *Practicing history* (pp. 90–110). Routledge.

Shepherd, D. A., & Wiklund, J. (2005). *Entrepreneurial small businesses: a resource-based perspective*. Edward Elgar. doi:10.4337/9781845425692

Sığrı, Ü., & Tığlı, M. (2014). Hofstede'nin" belirsizlikten kaçınma" kültürel boyutunun yönetsel-örgütsel süreçlerde ve pazarlama açısından tüketici davranışlarına etkisi. *İktisadi ve İdari Bilimler Dergisi; Cilt 21, Sayı 1 (2006); 327-342*.

Skipper, H. D. (2008). *Risk management and insurance: perspectives in a global economy*. Hoboken, NJ: John Wiley & Sons.

Smallman, C. (1996). Risk and organizational behaviour: A research model. *Disaster Prevention and Management: An International Journal*, *5*(2), 12–26. doi:10.1108/09653569610112880

Smart, D. T., & Conant, J. S. (1994). Entrepreneurial orientation, distinctive marketing competencies and organizational performance. *Journal of Applied Business Research*, *10*(3), 28–38. doi:10.19030/jabr.v10i3.5921

Sofyalıoğlu, Ç., & Aktaş, R. (2001). Kültürel farklılıkların uluslararası işletmelere etkisi. *Yönetim ve Ekonomi: Celal Bayar Üniversitesi İktisadi ve İdari Bilimler Fakültesi Dergisi*, *8*(1), 75–92.

Stulz, R. M. (1996). Rethinking risk management. *Journal of Applied Corporate Finance*, *9*(3), 8–25. doi:10.1111/j.1745-6622.1996.tb00295.x

Sürgevil, O., & Budak, G. (2008). İşletmelerin farklılıkların yönetimi anlayışına yaklaşım tarzlarının saptanmasına yönelik bir araştırma. *Dokuz Eylül Üniversitesi Sosyal Bilimler Enstitüsü Dergisi*, *10*(4), 65–96.

Tchankova, L. (2002). Risk identification–basic stage in risk management. *Environmental Management and Health*, *13*(3), 290–297. doi:10.1108/09566160210431088

Thomas, P. (2009). *Strategic management*. Course at Chalmers University of Technology.

Truslow, D. K. (2003). Operational risk management? It's everyone's job. *The R Journal*, *85*(5), 34–37.

Tuncel, G., & Alpan, G. (2010). Risk assessment and management for supply chain networks: A case study. *Computers in Industry, 61*(3), 250–259. doi:10.1016/j.compind.2009.09.008

Venkatraman, N., & Ramanujam, V. (1986). Measurement of business performance in strategy research: A comparison of approaches. *Academy of Management Review, 11*(4), 801–814. doi:10.5465/amr.1986.4283976

Welch, L. S., & Luostarinen, R. (1988). Internationalization: Evolution of a concept. *Journal of General Management, 14*(2), 34–55. doi:10.1177/030630708801400203

Wiklund, J., & Shepherd, D. (2005). Entrepreneurial orientation and small business performance: A configurational approach. *Journal of Business Venturing, 20*(1), 71–91. doi:10.1016/j.jbusvent.2004.01.001

Williams, C. A., Smith, M. L., & Young, P. C. (1998). *Risk management and insurance* (Doctoral dissertation, Univerza v Mariboru, Ekonomsko-poslovna fakulteta).

Williams, L. J., & Anderson, S. E. (1991). Job satisfaction and organizational commitment as predictors of organizational citizenship and in-role behaviors. *Journal of Management, 17*(3), 601–617. doi:10.1177/014920639101700305

Woods, M. (2012). *Risk management in organizations: An integrated case study approach*. Routledge. doi:10.4324/9780203815922

Wu, F., Mahajan, V., & Balasubramanian, S. (2003). An analysis of e-business adoption and its impact on business performance. *Journal of the Academy of Marketing Science, 31*(4), 425–447. doi:10.1177/0092070303255379

Xiaoming, C., & Junchen, H. (2012). A literature review on organization culture and corporate performance. *International Journal of Business Administration, 3*(2), 28–37.

Young, J. (2006). *Operational risk management-the practical application of a qualitative approach*. Pretoria, South Africa: Van Schaik Publishers.

Yücel, R. (1999). İnsan kaynakları yönetiminde başarı değerlendirme. *Dokuz Eylül Üniversitesi Sosyal Bilimler Enstitüsü Dergisi, 1*(3), 110–128.

Zur Muehlen, M. (2004). Organizational management in workflow applications–issues and perspectives. *Information Technology Management, 5*(3-4), 271–291. doi:10.1023/B:ITEM.0000031582.55219.2b

Chapter 7
Innovative Call Center Applications Focused on Financial Marketing in the Turkish Banking Sector

Hasan Dinçer
Istanbul Medipol University, Turkey

Ayşe Mengir
Istanbul Medipol University, Turkey

ABSTRACT

As a result of globalization, call centers of banks that develop rapidly by the virtue of the technology become an important unit which brings first contact with customers. Nowadays, call centers not only give support to customers and other callers but also use the communication tools. This chapter examines innovator call center applications in banking. The main aim of call centers is to provide services with minimum cost, maximum speed, and excellent customer satisfaction. To achieve this purpose, it is necessary to incorporate the advantages of technological improvements. According to the research results, beside the excessive usage of call centers by customers, the banks direct their customers to call centers or alternative distribution canals to decrease the workload of the branches. Moreover, it is mentioned in this research that some precautions are taken for both internal and external customer satisfaction. Under today's economic conditions, customers do not prefer banks which are not using innovator technologies.

INTRODUCTION

In recent years, the development of technology has made it necessary to develop banking applications. Especially when the first contact with the customers and call the customer call centers starting from 7-24 hours 444 *** // 0 800 ***, the expectations of the customers from the customer representatives is to perform the transaction by phone and be able to handle this operation without even waiting. Towards

DOI: 10.4018/978-1-7998-2559-3.ch007

the end of the 1980s, the use of technology in banks has thrown (Lin et al., 2010; Feigin et al., 2006). Companies and banks not only use the developing technology in the product they produce, but also use the technology in the promotion and marketing and sale of this product. Call centers have a large share in promotion and marketing. With the developing technology, the speed of the call centers transportation and transactions has increased. In addition to transferring the intensity of the branch to call centers, it is also directed to other alternative distribution channels. The most important reasons for their referral are related to the qualification of the services offered in interbank competition. It has become a necessity for banks to bring technology together with their customers and to maintain their assets (Rocha et al., 2005; Brown et al., 2005).

The aim of this work is to examine developing alternative distribution channels in Turkey, to discuss the importance of call centers in ensuring customer satisfaction, digitization comes with IVR (interactive voice response system) and examine the audio technology and will not go into call center applications used in banks in Turkey. In the first part of the study; In the last 50 years, the effect of the incredible distance in technology in call centers has been mentioned. In today's world where global integration is taking place, it is seen that traditional trade models have started to disappear in developed and developing countries, and individual customers and corporate customers have realized their needs through call centers, internet banking, mobile branches and ATMs quickly, in less time and without distance.

In the third part of the study, customers can perform their transactions in the IVR tree without reaching the customer representative. As the IVR (voice response system) tree, the width of the IVR (voice response system) is mentioned. Customers can do many transactions such as password transactions, eft-remittance transactions, voice surveys without connecting to the customer representative. This means saving time for both the company and the customers. At the same time, firms can significantly reduce their costs. It is seen that banks improve their operational channels and reduce their costs and transfer the labor load on employees to alternative distribution channels.

The fourth part of the study is related to the competitiveness and productivity in Turkey and it is one of the important issues in the world. Factors that determine the competitiveness of production, cost, market power, speed can be addressed. Here, the concept of speed is one of the important concepts. Especially with electronic banking transactions, both companies and customers can go beyond traditional practices. At the same time, with the development of information technologies, banks can change their strategies or develop new strategies. As alternative distribution channels are applied, banks that do not charge for electronic channels have recently started to charge fees. Not only the internet or mobile branch, but also telephone banking. Noting call centers of banks in Turkey in recent years, it has implemented voice recognition technology is a call center system. Customers with the application process in Turkey can only realize their speaking voice. With the increase of voice recognition technologies and the technologies used by the branches for the future, it will contribute to the increase of financially (residual) spiritual (especially time saving) to the firms and customers.

BASIC CONCEPTS OF ALTERNATIVE DISTRIBUTION CHANNELS IN THE BANKING SECTOR

Definitions Related to Alternative Distribution Channels

We live in an endless world full of changes. All changes should be designed to help customers maintain their goals. It integrates technology and advice to build deeper relationships with customers, giving customers the freedom to choose, regardless of when and where they invest, with a consultant or a combination of both. The wise use of innovation to deliver the highest level of high technology is the key to building stronger connections with customers and communities and developing financial lives that will have a positive and lasting impact on the economy.

The producer aims to deliver the product (goods) to the consumer in minimum cost and in the shortest time. In order to provide access to the mass market and to provide services on a large scale, service costs cannot be achieved without accessible channels. Alternative distribution channels, which are defined as channels that extend the scope of services beyond the traditional bank branch, have emerged as a result of innovations in information and communication technology and as a result of a change in consumer expectations. In other words, Alternative Distribution Channels focused primarily on reducing operational costs in branches and increasing technology usage efficiency. The aim is to provide long-term profit with the selected distribution channel. Banks try to provide the most appropriate service that can be provided through distribution channels to the customer with minimum cost and time savings. With the alternative distribution channel, it is possible to provide better service to customers (Stepanov et al., 2015).

ATMs, telephone banking, internet banking and mobile banking are among the alternative distribution channels available in all banks today. Alternative distribution channels contain new and powerful mechanisms for consumers to manage and analyze financial resources and make decisions. Over the past three decades, the proliferation of new information and communication technologies in the financial sector has affected the way banks serve their customers. In particular, self-service technologies have enabled banks to follow an electronically managed multi-channel strategy. From a consumer perspective, these new technologies enable one to access, analyze and make decisions about financial management (Li et al., 2018).

Alternative Distribution Channels Services

Alternative Distribution Channels, especially in order to provide products and services to the end user to reach the time, cost and so on. in order to reduce operational costs. Today, the commercial needs of bank customers are increasing in the global economy that is shrinking with globalization. Customers need new payment systems. This changing and developing situation in the banking sector has led to the necessity of making use of new technologies and investing in technology. In today's world, with the globalization, the needs of customers increased. Customers need new payment channels. In addition, the spread of electronic commerce around the world and the electronic payment of traditional forms of payment have envisaged the development of new payment channels. The main alternative distribution channels are; Automatic teller machines (ATM), Call Canter, Telephone banking, Internet / Mobile banking (Soh & Gurvich, 2016).

Automated teller machines (ATMs) are the first of the electronic fund transfer services launched by the customers of the banks through the use of cards to reach the banks. In order to save personnel by reducing the workload of branch employees in banks, it was used to save customers from the trouble of accessing to bank branches and to provide cash to customers in places where there are no branches. The first ATM device was introduced in the United States (USA) in the 1960s. Turkey was carried out with the first Debit by the Bank in 1988. With the help of ATM devices, the operational transactions of the banks were simplified and most of the operational transactions were transferred to ATM devices with the increasing use of technology.

Many transactions are carried out through ATMs, not bank branches. In order for banks to obtain high returns from ATMs, it is necessary to locate them in areas where there is a high demand for ATM machines. It is important that they set up a common ATM between banks to reduce costs. There are also differences in the use of ATMs in the interbank competition market. Alternatives, for example, are differentiation strategies for banks, such as on-screen advertising while waiting for transactions. Some of the transactions made from automated teller machines are withdrawals, changing passwords, depositing accounts and transferring accounts, issuing travel checks, requesting check books, credit card application transactions, credit and credit card application payment transactions, foreign currency and gold transactions (Oh et al., 2017). Another important channel of alternative distribution channels Call Canter is one of the systems that enables the efficient management of incoming and outgoing calls in times of heavy traffic. In other words, the duty of the customer representatives working in the call centers is to meet the incoming call and use the time effectively to perform the transaction of the customer and to ensure customer satisfaction during this period.

To manage call center operations, for the first time, companies have incorporated industrial engineering models into customer service, mechanizing historical and diverse complex and complex business processes. For firms, the economic benefits of shifting service delivery to call centers include enormous economies of scale achieved through office consolidation. However, call centers represent an exceptional situation in which the mechanization is extended to the communication activities with the customer. A hundred years ago, operator service jobs were considered high-skilled jobs in the high-tech telephone industry. It requires physical manipulation of codes, social interaction skills, and diagnostic evaluations of faulty telephone circuits. However, from the 1920s onwards, the company began to mechanize operations with the disintegration of various jobs. Mechanical switching enabled customers to call their local calls in the 1920s and long-distance calls in the 1950s. In the 1970s, digital systems further eliminated operator work by allowing customers to use credit cards to route long-distance calls. Each new technological advance reduces the diversity and complexity of the remaining jobs, eliminating many operator jobs: eliminating the physical side of the job, reducing call types, and eliminating diagnostic work (Zengin & Yüksel, 2016). In the 1980s and 1990s, thread and relocation continued with the use of automated response and voice recognition systems. In 2000, the typical telephone operator kept 1000 calls per day, a work cycle time of about 21 seconds per call, significantly lower than the average 60 second work cycle time of the automated assembly workers. In addition to all the banks, most of the transactions in call centers, which are referred to as the integration of the phone with the information technology and the technological development feature of the phone in recent years, have begun to be transferred. These include password transactions, lost-stolen transactions, credit card transactions (Flory et al., 2016).

Another feature that can be performed by connecting to or without connecting to the customer representative when the call center is placed is telephone banking. One of the services provided by banks to their customers without visiting branches. Services include account balances, detailed account transactions, check transactions, credit transactions and eft / transfer transactions (Bateh & Farah, 2017). At the same time, telephone banking services are computer-based telephone keypad responses or banking activities performed over the telephone with voice recognition technology that enables banking activities to be performed. Thanks to telephone banking, customers can access their accounts at the bank via telephone and do whatever they want on their accounts. Customer numbers and private passwords are provided for account security in telephone banking. Thanks to telephone banking in the banking sector, it has provided the opportunity to bring cheaper services to geographically large regions instead of meeting the cost of opening new branches (Tunay et al., 2019). Turkey's first telephone banking was introduced in 1996 under the leadership of İşbank.

In a globalizing world where technology efficiency is increasing, the efficient use of banking services without making a call to the call center, internet / mobile banking systems are trying to catch up with the innovations of the age. Internet banking is a banking channel that enables consumers to perform a wide range of financial and non-financial services through a bank's website. Mobile banking is defined as a channel through which mobile devices such as mobile phones or personal digital assistants interact with a bank through non-voice applications such as text or WAP-based banking services. The most important of these innovations are technological developments. With the development of internet technology, internet banking and mobile branches have developed, and their use has increased. Nowadays, all transactions can be carried out without giving wet signed instructions from the branches. Thanks to the internet banking and mobile branches, banks have been able to perform customer transactions more easily and quickly, thus contributing to increase customer satisfaction and lower costs (Ben-David & Icht, 2016).

With the increase in technological developments in the banking sector, banking transactions and services have increased with the transition from traditional distribution channels to modern distribution channels. Each customer group of the Bank needs to channel its customers through the channels they need. The technology used should also be perceived as reliable and simple to use. The perception of the channel used by the customer is an important success factor. Thanks to these channels, the products and services needed by the customer are easier to access. Call centers, which are the first contact centers, ensure that customers can receive the service they need at any time by using all alternative distribution channels, while at the same time, it is aimed to provide transportation for problem solutions whenever needed. In addition, there should be a tendency to focus on the risks created or to be created by alternative distribution channels, and therefore, those who will not be happy to use these channels should be reassured by the banks (Zito et al., 2018)

Moving customers to e-channels is an important issue in terms of reducing operational costs of the banking sector. For example, the e-commerce telephone banking application saves an estimated cost of $ 30 million annually. Financial institutions use e-banking channels to cross-sell financial products, and banks recommend that financial instruments such as investment products, savings products or credit products be actively recommended and advertised through e-banking channels. For the consumer, electronic banking channels include decision support systems. Because it enables individuals to make real-time financial decisions independent of time and space. Electronic banking also helps consumers decide which banking product is best suited to their personal needs (Ji et al., 2017).

Alternative Distribution Channels in Banking Sector of Developed Countries

In a globalizing world, countries want to develop their trade and industrial activities. Banks that provide money transfer systems between countries try to adapt to the globalizing world framework. The limited banking activities used by very few of the society in the past include every individual today. With the increase in communication technology, they realize short-term money-based commercial transfers between countries and continents. In such a globalizing world order, developed country banking system and developing banking are different from each other. Examples of banking activities in developed countries are given below.

The United States of America (USA) is one of the most developed countries in the world economy. This development applies not only to firms but also to the banking sector. The United States, which attaches importance to technology developments, also uses a variety of alternative channels in the banking field. The types of alternative distribution channels used are as follows. In the digitalizing world, internet is one of the most important concepts of today. Internet and computer technologies (IT) are considered to be one of the greatest stages humanity has experienced since the Industrial Revolution. Automated teller machines (ATMs) and the first telephone banking applications, one of the first alternative distribution channels, emerged in the United States.

Automatic cash dispensers are among the most important service facilities in the banking sector. Ever since they appeared about 35 years ago, ATMs have literally changed the face of banking. The number and impact of banking and retail trade is increasing. There are many factors that banks need to consider in order to set location priorities for ATM sites. Accordingly, the bank concerned should first determine whether the main objective of placing a new off-premise ATM is visibility or free income. The usual first step is to identify where potential customers live, where they work, and what key routes they use. Customer surveys as well as geographic, demographic, economic and traffic data are also useful for answering these questions. Other considerations include safety, cost, convenience and visibility (Kim & Choi, 2015).

Telephone banking, another of the conveniences in banking practices, began in the 1980s in the United States. With the telephone banking service, after entering a password and account number (security questions may vary between banks), all transactions with bank branches and ATMs can be performed in an interactive manner or through a customer representative. In addition to providing speed and convenience in banking services, telephone banking provides significant savings in operational expenses. The most important savings providers are internet banking and mobile banking. Mobile branch, the United States are successful examples when looking at the sample applications. USAA (United Services Automobile Association), which serves 7.7 million US soldiers and their families all over the world, is pioneering mobile solutions. USAA customers can take advantage of the Mobile Remote Deposit Capture service since 2009 and can withdraw their checks by location-independent telephone in 2 minutes. Customers take both the front side and the back side of the check and send it to the bank. After checking the check information, the bank passes the money to the account. This technology has brought great benefit to companies thanks to its feature (Presbitero, 2017).

The concept of marketing can be categorized as nonprofit, micro and macro enterprises as normative. The banking sector has accelerated its marketing operations through developing alternative distribution channels. Investments by banks are directly proportional to the development of new technologies. Since 1998, banking transactions have been carried out over the internet. Thanks to the use of the Internet, it has facilitated, accelerated the process of banks' operational transactions and reduced the workload of personnel. Thus, significant savings have been made in reducing operational costs. Due to recent developments in information technology, internet banking is preferred between 8% and 22% in the United States, according to estimated research. In the US, internet banking services can provide customers with all the services that can be done at the bank branch except for the withdrawal of physical money. After the 2000s, with the development of virtual wallets, physical banking withdrawals started with mobile banking (Go et al., 2018).

Innovative Call Center Applications Focused on Financial Marketing in the Turkish Banking Sector

For the last thirty years, banks have invested in the development of several alternative distribution channels, including ATMs, the Internet, call centers and, more recently, wireless technologies. The purpose of investing in alternative distribution channels is that banks can reduce costs to serve customers. The second part of the banks' rationale for investment is the adoption of non-branch channels. For example, in just six years, the use of Internet banking in the US has exceeded 25 percent of the retail customer base. What banks foresee is that customers want to change their habit types. Customers did not exhibit the types of habits prescribed by banks. Instead of replacing branch visits with lower-cost alternatives, most customers increased frequency and method of interaction (Frimpong et al., 2018).

With the active use of developing technology, the limits have disappeared. The interbank competition created by globalization has also affected European countries. The alternative variety used has increased. This diversity is listed below. The rapid development of information and communication technology in recent years has affected the banking sector. Traditional alternative distribution channels (branches) are called modern alternative distribution channels (internet-mobile banking, etc.). However, with the developing technology, modern alternative distribution channels will leave the name of modern banking behind with a new name stemming from the fact that the banks are transferred to digital media (Williams et al., 2018).

As technology increases, ATMs are developed to take advantage of new technological innovations. It has continued to a certain degree over the years. Modern ATMs should be flexible, impressive and easier to use. ATMs were introduced in the UK in the late 60s and early 70s. Automated teller machines are not only located outside the bank, but can also be found in shops, hotels and airports in other locations. When ATMs were first introduced, there was a major design problem. During a transaction, the ATM handed cash to the customer before returning the customer card. This resulted in customers not receiving their cards from the ATM. This design problem is now fixed. The customer's card is returned before the cash card is dealt. Improvements were made to ATM availability. Modern ATMs are more than a simple cash dispenser. Standard ATMs offer relatively simple services, including cash withdrawals; tends to offer advanced services such as check payment, cash deposit, bill payment, ticket purchase (e.g. train, concert) (Skalicky et al., 2016).

Call centers are defined as a one-stop communication tool by communicating with customers and target groups of banks using different electronic channels. It is widely used by banks and multinational companies. 60% of the communications with customers worldwide are realized through call centers. In the UK, 3% of employees are employed in call centers. The first call center in the UK was established in the late 1970s. Ten years later, the call center sector has grown significantly and the growth rate has reached 435% between 1985-1989. Banks and financial services companies benefit from the development of electronic alternative distribution channels as a marketing channel and the variety of alternative distribution offered to consumers is increasing. They aim to quantify the provision of electronic services available by major retail banking institutions in the UK. This new channel is gained by discovering two areas that are important in the analysis of new proposals: this organization's approach to innovation and their view of current, future markets. Alternatively, highly innovative organizations are most likely to assume such pioneering developments. European banks and financial services companies are waking up to the benefits of this multi-faceted personal marketing channel, while increasing the variety of mobile applications available to consumers (Lu et al., 2019).

Banks are one of the sectors where technology development efficiency is felt most. Banks are trying to keep up with technological developments. With the increase in information and communication technology, transactions were transferred to electronic environment. With the electronic development, trade has become widespread in parallel with the banks. As one of the developed countries, the UK banking sector develops and offers new products to its customers. The world's first cash dispenser was established in Enfield, North London. In 1972, machines following innovation in the cash sector were connected to a centralized system that enabled withdrawals on the secure line. Technology has a huge impact on the payment sector. There are countless different ways to reward innovations such as the emergence of digital currencies, the development of mobile payments and the real attraction of contact-less cards. This was effective in changing consumer preferences. ATM withdrawal, the main method of accessing money, shows that the total withdrawal value remains relatively constant on average. Over the past decade, £ 192 billion has been withdrawn every year. The cash industry also has a key role to play, and much of the flexibility in cash demand so far has been to stretch the models to meet customer demand. The introduction of ATM in 1967 was an important example of this. In the UK, ATMs and thousands of self-service payment machines were updated to improve cash management in the market, staff were trained to recognize new security features; The wholesale money industry shifted from paper to polymer distribution of about 300 million notes.

Call centers have long been part of a modern organizational operation. Emergency services, telephone lines, operator services and customer help lines are just a few of the call centers that have existed in the last 40-50 years, even if they are not labeled as such. However, in spite of this historical presence, it has only recently emerged that call centers have special interest and importance. The most obvious reason for this is the rapid increase in the number of call centers and their employment. For example, in the UK, almost all call center transactions have increased in the last 10 years. Furthermore, it is estimated that in 2002, 1.3% of the European working population will be employed in call centers. One of the most important benefits of Internet and mobile banking growth is the development of customer and customer experiences as transactions and interactions increase. The number of customers using e-banking in developed countries is high. In a private bank in the UK, the use of technology has reached 24 million customers by using digitalization in digital data. The number of active use of mobile banking is 9.8m. Mobile banking payments and transfers: 230b. As a global service provider in the UK, banks are focused on meeting the needs of customers, and online banking has brought customers an accessible, intuitive and secure banking experience.

Establishing the technology and investing in the right place for each unit within the institution or in-house is extremely important for the companies. Customers use new technology that allows them to enter the bank and offers our own personal financial advisors. Through the use of digital technology, banks are communicating more than ever. Customers prefer to use their mobile applications more than the websites of banks. People use more applications than any other banking form, such as branches, phones and online. Banks are trying to reduce their costs with revenue growth and determine their strategies with credit control.

As one of the most developed countries in the world, Japan is one of the most important focal points of technology development. It is a pioneer of technology in the areas of computer, nuclear energy, aviation and communications. The integration of financial markets, the transformation of large-scale firms into a global network beyond production, the direction of labor markets have changed the border definitions of countries in the known sense. As financial relations between countries increase in the globalizing world, the need for effective coordination in economic management has increased. Organizations operating in the field of finance are actively using alternative distribution channels to retain existing customers and at the same time gain new customers.

Technology companies and operators determine new strategies for electronic distribution channels. One of the alternative distribution channels in Japan, Call Center has undergone significant changes in the global economy over the last decade. One of them is advances in information, communication and telecommunications technology. Innovations take consumers further. Financial firms and banks use call centers to make use of in-house telephony (service agency) to sell their products and services, and company owners use their call centers to provide services by telephone to main businesses and other companies. Another alternative distribution channel, Internet banking, is a PC (connecting the site to the bank from a tablet terminal on the Internet) is one of the most important banking services. The site is a very useful service that is accessed on-site to the bank. In the globalizing world, there is no time to go to the Bank. Internet, smart phone and so on. transactions are carried out by using the bank without spending time to go to the bank (Yüksel et al., 2018). Mobile banking, on the other hand, provides internet banking services in various transactions such as many banks, fund settlement and asset management in Japan. Internet banking has become one of the most important social infrastructures. Mobile banking transaction content is the same as internet banking. Transactions with banks are not limited to bank window (box office / teller), ATM with mobile banking. By using smartphones and tablets, the personal computer on the mobile Internet can direct various operations via figures.

Call centers located in alternative distribution channels according to Japan call center association; In order to promote the healthy development of the sector, playing the role of call center for the establishment of ethics and finesse in cooperation with consumers, customers and organizations using information and communication technology, the promotion of formulation and regional incentive and safety, and the development of existing knowledge, the realization of culturally rich national life for the purpose of economic and international contribute to society. All alternative distribution channels refer to the use of data to measure customer sensitivity and meet their needs (Odebiyi et al., 2016).

Material production realized with technology in the industrial society has been replaced by the information society which carries the production of information based on computer and technology. In industrial society, material products are produced in factories. In the information society, data is produced depending on the data banks and information. In the globalizing world with the use of knowledge, national borders are eliminated. The increase in technological knowledge with globalization will create a positive increase in human welfare. Technological increases in banks are also important for people's welfare and economic growth. An efficient banking system contributes to an economic order that enables growth and innovation by making efficient use of savings in the economy. In Japan, there is a very good education system that tries to prepare the needs of the future, complies with the requirements of the age, thinks and researches. With this system, which is needed by the society, people who are knowledgeable in every subject and think multi-faceted will succeed in the information society. Together with technological innovations, they help to bring quality products to the market due to the increase in competition (Kim & Kang, 2016).

Alternative Distribution Channels in Banking Sector of Developing Countries

The world's economies are trying to have sufficient capital accumulation. Capital accumulation is provided by economic development. The world economy which is in economic competition is divided into developed country economy and developing economy. With this distinction, there is an increase in competition between countries and with the increase in communication technology, competition between firms / banks has been triggered. Developing countries, which had experienced crises in the 1990s, focused on innovation and focused on strengthening against new crises. With these innovations, capital inflows increased and countries offered cheap financing for continuity of economic reforms. Thanks to capital mobility, it contributed to the restructuring of developing countries.

With the globalization, the technologies used in the countries have increased in the banks and there is competition in the interbank world market. Thanks to the technology in question, communication and trade increased not only within the country but also between countries. The banking operational channels used in both developed and developing countries are diversified. Nowadays the Brazilian banking system is quite efficient and there are at least one large bank in cities, with a large number of bank branches. Many banks in the country have websites to promote their products. With the Internet technology becoming indispensable in human life, advertising / promotion activities of banks have increased. Call center accessibility, mobile / internet banking technology infrastructure development, telephone banking IVR (voice response system) options and ATM frequency are among the most important alternative distribution channels in the operations center that banks should develop in a competitive environment (Dinçer et al., 2017).

Many of the services from health, education, telecommunications and transportation are becoming the largest sector in the economy. In many countries, besides providing employment and a large portion of income, services in areas such as the financial or telecommunications sectors are vital for the production of other goods and services. Therefore, the efficiency of the services sector is very important for the overall efficiency of the economy. At the same time, the Internet revolution made it possible to provide a variety of electronic services, an increasingly important delivery tool for developing countries. States have contributed to the development of their power in the world market by establishing remote call center services in the field of economy. Thanks to the remote call center in the world market, cost savings of up to 50% have been achieved. To take advantage of outsourcing opportunities, developing countries will need both modern, effective telecommunications and access to developed country markets to provide cross-border services. Computer and related outsourcing and back-office services, including trade, professional and financial services, are important export-oriented areas (Kim et al., 2016).

ATM devices are equipment that allows branches to perform banking transactions even when they are closed any day of the week. Electronic boxes are found not only in banks, but also in locations spread to cities such as supermarkets, shopping malls and markets. Among the actions of the Central Bank to ensure the stability of Brazilian payment systems, microfinance operating in the country provides guidance on the continuation of management of overall business risks, as well as plans. The regulation of payment systems by the Brazilian central bank enabled mobile banking applications to be made available to all segments. The aim is to promote the financial system for mobile payments in a globalized world (Pappas et al., 2015).

Developments in payment systems had a positive impact on the banking sector. According to Brazilian central bank data, the total amount of payments (check, payment card, collection blocks and collection agreements, etc.) that includes customers increased by 9% in 2010 compared to the previous year. The number of checks made increased by 7.1% in 2010 compared to the previous year and credit card payments (debt and credit) increased by 23%. On the other hand, payments made mainly through in-bank direct payments in Brazil indicate that only 4% of total transactions of this instrument were relatively cheap in 2010. Regarding the service of financial institutions, the 'internet, home and office banking' channel is the most used channel by customers and expanded by 26.7% more than other alternative distribution channels. The number of transactions from payment terminals and POS terminals remained stable. Mobile banking is not used actively. In addition, Brazilian payment systems have little initiative to increase the use of the DDA (authorized direct debit) platform, and there is a need to achieve additional productivity gains, especially with higher levels of interoperability and infrastructure (Legros et al., 2018).

Developments in communication and regulation policy in the information and communication sector; increased the impact of the digital economy on growth and development. In addition to the growth framework, economic challenges vary from country to country. The telecommunication industry in Brazil is thought to have at least 70% of the overall level of telecommunication team place content in 2017 should be from 4G networks. 62% of the input in the Brazilian communication sector is locally sourced. As in many other countries, Brazil has accelerated production and technological development, necessitating stronger communication networks. With its medium-sized, developing economy and large young population, Brazil is committed to improving its networks. Because today's world is fast-talking and consuming and constantly moving, its economic resources necessitate reaching people faster. Brazil continues to create alternative distribution channels and strong communication networks.

Strengthening the existing strategy has become a necessity in global economies. Hungary has an important geographical position in terms of trade and foreign investment in Europe. In order to establish the framework of banking regulations, efforts were made to strengthen markets in order to ensure financial sustainability and economic stability. In the Hungarian banking system, which is a member of the European Union, call centers, internet banking, mobile branches, ATM devices, branchless banking activities and technology usage levels in banking as alternative distribution channels will be explored under the heading of alternative distribution channels. Alternative distribution channels, which have become more valuable today than ever, have become even more valuable thanks to technology development. Banks are trying to capture the rapidly changing attitudes of customers through the revaluation of technology. Regulatory authorities have always sought to find the least burdensome remedy to address identified competition concerns.

Following the political changes in Hungary in 1989, the importance of the telecommunications sector was recognized to make a significant contribution to Hungary's economic growth, and policies were introduced to develop the sector and address the background of telecommunications demand. In the first phase of the Hungarian telecommunications strategy implemented between 1990 and 1993, it was aimed to establish a national digital network infrastructure. In the second phase of the strategy implemented between 1994 and 1997, the priority was to expand and modernize the network and to introduce the most important new services for business customers. In the third phase between 1997 and 2000, the strategic focus was on the expansion of various trade communication and information services and the development of quality and diversification services at low tariffs. In the fourth phase implemented after 2000, the main emphasis will be on the provision of advanced telecommunications services, including high-tech intelligent services, personal communications services and broadband multimedia services.

By reducing costs in information technologies, call centers, ATM users, Internet and mobile users have been provided with a wide range of services. Hungary is a country that has started to develop information and communication technologies (ICT) infrastructure with the support of the European Union (EU), showing a policy approach to progress towards network structures and information collection infrastructure. Hungary is the leader in many technological countries. But the cost of internet access in Hungary is also high. Although the cost of internet access is high, the number of users in mobile and fixed lines is high. Demand increases in products or services thanks to global development in the world increases the services offered to financial markets. Thanks to technology development, banks are trying to meet the demand increases with minimum cost and maximum profit. Thanks to the financial programs in recent years, significant developments have been experienced in Malaysia. In this context, on the one hand, public expenditures were reduced and made transparent, while on the other hand, banking activities were monitored in the financial sector and the framework of banking regulations aimed at strengthening the markets was established. Proper execution of financial infrastructures and reliable, efficient operation are essential for real economic and financial transactions.

The impact of increasing the outsourcing of services shows the increasing trend of outsourcing business processes in the world. Providing a wide range of services away from the customer has been possible through standardization of services, the availability of broadband telecommunications and the reduction of information and communication technology costs. In addition to the service centers already in service, specialized businesses are expected to take place in Hungary. Existing service centers today are primarily to provide services to subsidiaries of their assets. Customers are expected to grow and meet an increasing amount of extra currency requirements. The industry is increasingly striving to benefit the domestic market and businesses are planning to outsource large-scale administrative activities.

How to respond to savings, investment and economic growth depending on information and technological development is theoretically one of the common problems of countries in the world. Banking, which is an intermediate factor in the economic system, has attached importance to the development of alternative distribution channels with the increasing use of communication tools and internet. In Malaysia, it is the key to reforms to improve the quality of education and skills training, promote innovation and adopt information technology. Comprehensive growth and productivity enhancing programs and remedial policies governing the financial framework and technology infrastructure studies are ongoing. In the global economic environment, R & D studies as geographic structure cover large areas.

Banks, which have become the intermediate factor of economic institutions, have given importance to technological infrastructure studies in order to meet the demand increases of their customers. One of the fastest growing areas of infrastructure work is call centers. When the continuous development of information technologies facilitated communication and reduced the cost of the phone, companies shifted their call center services out of the center. In particular, firms in developed countries have moved their call centers abroad to reduce employee costs. However, US centers have shifted to countries such as India, Malaysia and Ghana. The main reason for the spread of call centers from central countries to neighboring countries stems from the fact that the global economy does not allow obstacles in finding the most appropriate costs and that the technology allows parallel growth. Thus, it has had a positive effect on unemployment in developing countries and a negative effect on unemployment rate in developed countries. At the same time, thanks to the development of knowledge and technology, alternatives have increased. These alternatives are telephone banking, internet banking, mobile branch and ATM devices outside the call center.

The increase in internet usage and the strengthening of communication structure led to the expansion of internet banking. Internet banking is an alternative distribution channel developed using the internet to provide banking services. Various types of innovation have been introduced in the banking sector. On the one hand, increasing innovations, improving existing products, reinforcing the position of information management. On the other hand, radical innovations can renew the role of banks. Today, in the information age, companies are giving information that they need to understand modern strategic management techniques to be successful.

Internet banking has attracted worldwide attention due to the benefits or benefits it offers to banks and customers. The Internet is used not only as an innovative payment method, but also as a way to increase customer convenience and reduce costs and increase your profits. This paper attempts to explain the role of information management in radical innovations, particularly in the field of internet banking.

Innovative Call Center Applications Focused on Financial Marketing in the Turkish Banking Sector

Recent advances in technology are calling on the internet banking industry to gain significant levels in organizations around the world. In recent years, the importance of banks in the information sector has increased and most have started to implement internet banking.

ALTERNATIVE DISTRIBUTION CHANNELS IN THE TURKISH BANKING SECTOR

Information in parallel with customers' needs and developments in technology, has suffered significant changes in the payment system in the world and Turkey. The circulation of hot money in the market has decreased and the demand for payment systems due to technological developments has increased. With the development of digitalization, the number of customers going to branches decreased. Many transactions such as SME or retail loan application transactions, stock purchase and sale transactions are carried out through the online banking model (Yüksel et al., 2017).

In payment systems offered to customers, thanks to technology development, higher quality service is provided with less cost. These services include; automated teller machines, pos devices, call centers, telephone banking system, internet and mobile banking applications. Today, the most widespread use of internet and mobile branch channels. In Turkey, the use of alternative distribution channels was put into use in late 1980. Most of the transactions that can be performed at the branch (cashier) can be made by using the electronic card provided to customers through ATMs. After 1990, telephone banking started to be used with the development of call centers and internet banking was developed in 1998 thanks to technological development. Many transactions can be made with the mobile branch, which is an extension of internet banking (Dinçer et al., 2019a,b,c,d).

Today, international consumption has increased rapidly. In parallel with the increase in the consumption of the banks, the money spent was not made by hand but through payment systems, which led to the development of the existing system. It has played an important role in increasing call center applications by expanding the use of the internet with the effect of technology development. Call centers that provide services with internal or external system are provided with information, complaint line, technical support, appointment etc. provides many services. Turkey's first year of implementation of the 1990 years. In the early days, it served the hotline and customer satisfaction. In the 2000s, while together with the development of internet technology call centers in Turkey have made investments in many fields hotline and bank alongside customer satisfaction transaction password transactions, account information, credit card / debit card transactions are carried out several operations.

Internet banking and mobile banking in Turkey is growing quickly. Banks try to respond to these requirements by closely analyzing customer demands and changes against technological innovations by using the opportunities of technology. Today, the Internet or mobile branch is a very convenient alternative distribution option especially for SMEs (small and medium-sized enterprises). The development of internet or mobile branch channels, increasing payment options (eft / remittance transactions, bill payment, tax payment, etc.) contributed to accelerating the circulation of money in the market. In internet banking, the rates of fees received from the services rendered are lower than the branches. The reason for the low fees is that customers want to direct or practice banking or internet banking. From this, customers are able to perform the services they receive from internet / mobile banking faster and cost-effectively (Dinçer et al., 2019e,f,g).

In order to perform banking transactions quickly and easily, banks set up automatic money payment machines in private or public spaces, on the streets where population density is high, in accordance with the provisions of the protocol between the owners and / or related parties for rent and / or for rent. Thanks to ATMs, the rate of money in circulation increased and pocket money decreased. Information and technology developments in the financial markets have led to an increase in the number of alternative distribution channels. Many tools such as call centers, internet-mobile banking, automatic payment machines, chat applications, whatsapp are being tried to be harmonized in advanced markets (Çabuk et al., 2017).

Call centers try to meet their current demands with maximum speed by providing effective conversations with customers by telephone. Call canter development in the world as well as in Turkey has made substantial progress in recent years. Thanks to its development in the sector, it has begun to provide services through the operator in many areas such as sales and marketing, appointment services, information update, money transfer transactions, password transactions without being connected to customer representatives. Turkey's call center have occurred some years the increase in incoming and outgoing calls. While these rates were 1.9 billion in 2014, they increased by 5% and reached 2 billion in 2015. In 2016, year-on-year increase of incoming and outgoing calls reached 2.2 billion with a 10% increase. The changing, developing and increasingly globalized world is in search of new trends in economic terms and in search of an innovative, daily economic investment analysis. Especially in recent years, the widespread use of alternative distribution channels has made world finance giants into a virtual, centralized understanding.

Financial institutions and banks have to diversify the products they produce or the services they provide in order to gain more profit according to the needs of customers or in a competitive environment. This diversification has further increased thanks to technology development. Maintaining the price stability in the markets and contributing to the financial stability are among the central duties of the central banks. In addition, the increasingly digitalized world, the transformation of technological change reflected in all areas of life, financial markets could not remain indifferent (Yüksel et al., 2015). In particular, data mining and the use of crypto money in parallel with this are seen as a significant share in recent economic activities. As an alternative distribution channel, digital money attracts attention especially for its investors. Many Central Banks and International Finance Institutions in the world could not remain indifferent to this rise and started to see digital money as an alternative investment tool rather than an alternative distribution channel. The alternative distribution channel applications developed in recent years aim to produce new, innovative and rational solutions for crypto money (Kassavou & Sutton, 2016).

TECHNOLOGICAL INNOVATIONS AND IVR TREE APPLICATIONS IN CALL CENTER

Technology Investments in Finance Sector

Most of the financial resources used by companies should be used by investing in information technologies. The main reason for this is to ensure efficiency. Efficiency means to design new workflows by reducing the workload of the employee. Technology developments in the financial sector not only affect the way they do business, but also affect the work environment. By providing flexible working hours, it is possible to make transactions 24/7. Achieving cost reductions in today's economy is one of the advantages of providing competitive advantage in the market. Companies using information technologies know their customers more closely and gain access to large markets. At the same time, countries attach importance to technological developments in order to provide competitive advantage (Andersson, 2015).

Economic policies adopted and implemented in countries show similarities in economic field in developed and developing countries. Nowadays, in many countries, the view of free trade is adopted. It is recognized by countries that financial and financial liberalization needs to be improved. Globalization is experiencing fundamental structural changes. Nowadays, information society is gaining importance and there is an increasing and increasing relationship between information and technology development. Technology acquisition takes place in three stages (Dinçer & Yüksel, 2019). The first stage is the ability to apply technology. The second stage is to spread the technology learned in the field to the production areas to which it relates. In the third stage, it is necessary to acquire the ability to take the technology used to the next level. Since science and technology policies directly affect the welfare of countries, they must make the necessary effort to produce, maintain and disseminate technology. The financial system reduces the cost of collecting, evaluating, evaluating information, resources and data, reducing the cost of transfer, and ensures the efficiency and efficiency of savings and investors. This way the process works in the financial system affects growth positively. the foundation of the financial system in Turkey constitute the banking sector. The reason is that a large part of the financial resources are collected by banks and used by banks again (Swendeman et al., 2015).

In the development of digital economy and society, digital technologies should be used as a basis. Such use may be provided if it develops the skills necessary for the effective use of digital technologies, including general information and communication. In recent years, the use of digital technologies among these main actors has continued rapidly. In general, larger enterprises are more likely to use advanced technology applications, partly due to stronger competition in their internal business processes, but also because of stronger barriers to technology adoption, skill shortages and greater financial pressures. The increasing use of digital technologies by individuals varies between countries and social groups. The Internet is widely used by people, but the differences between countries and social groups are still large. According to OECD data, in 2005, approximately 56% of the adult population had access to the Internet and 30% used it. In 2016, these shares were 83% and 73% respectively. Advances in mobile technology have made access to the network not only on the road, but also within home communication as an important part of everyday life. For example, the share of households in European Union countries (27 countries) who do not have in-house internet access was reduced from 20% in 2006 to less than 7% in 2016. In the following sector, the top ten sectors in OECD member countries are those where robot technology is used. Industrial robot technology is the most used area of transportation equipment area, while the least used sector is wood products. It seems to be the sector where robot technology is rarely used in metal and pharmaceutical-cosmetic products.

Research and development are efforts to improve product innovation, development of existing product or increasing scientific knowledge. Today, the national economy and even the enterprises have to give importance to research and development activities within the scope of financial opportunities. Companies or banks in today's market system, where continuous technological innovations are experienced, must be in constant development and change in order to maintain their assets and at the same time realize their goals. Businesses can develop change activities by working in a planned and systematic way, guiding all innovations. The effect of competition is of great importance in the globalizing world economic system. Businesses must compete not only with their competitors in the country, but also with businesses in other countries. This necessitates businesses to plan their strategies on a global level and reduce their costs below their global competitors (Mudliar & Donner, 2015).

While the increase in the export capacities of the countries enables the distribution of resources, it also increases the level of technology stemming from the intensity of relations with the outside world. In order to ensure the sustainability of economic growth in developing countries, they need to adopt new technologies and new production techniques rapidly. Developed countries and developing countries do not produce the innovations they have obtained as a result of their R & D activities in order to present them to the domestic market but they also export them. The fact that R & D investments appeal to a wide market reduces costs and is encouraging in terms of these activities and researches. In international data networks, some are linked to broad intergovernmental research infrastructures, have highly developed central services, and are primarily concerned with the data needs of single disciplines. Some have extremely dispersed, less rigid management structures and provide access to data in many different areas. Most are located between these two extremes and cover different geographical regions from regional to global. All provide a mix of data and related data services to meet the needs of the research community, and this provision is based on a mix of hardware, software, standards, protocols and human skills. They cross national boundaries and come together in technical and social networks (Dinçer & Yüksel, 2018a,b).

Call centers have become important units of most companies and banks with the increase in technology equipment and experienced customer representatives. The current technological structure of call centers consists of software and hardware besides labor use. In this center, there are units such as information lines, customer relations, technical support center; various contact channels are managed within this structure. Technology has a large impact on the labor and labor process. While the number of jobs based on information production increases, it is assumed that old type jobs will disappear. To support this assumption, overwork statistics are drawn up and attention is drawn to the increase in the number of information workers. It is claimed that electronic developments will improve the quality of the work done by manpower, improve working conditions, decrease routine procedures and reveal their creative potential. Accordingly, information production shifts from arm strength to mental abilities in the labor process (Kazakos et al., 2016).

In addition to the use of voice response systems, call centers prefer to use internet-mobile branches other than making customer calls with the development of information technology. While traditional call centers carry out all my transactions through the customer representative, they are now able to access internet, mobile, chat, etc. without connecting to the customer representative. manpower use has decreased. Companies are investing in technology channels rather than the cost of employing manpower. The recruitment process has decreased. However, selected customer representatives are equipped with orientation, effective communication and on-the-job training. Customer representatives are positioned as the most ideal environment for contacting customers to understand their feelings, identify their needs, provide satisfaction and strengthen their loyalty.

Customers can reach the call centers of businesses, complaints-satisfaction-suggestion that they can send requests; It is an important unit of the enterprises that they expect to return for the solution they demand. The service received by customers in call centers creates good or bad prejudice against the business for most customers. The call received by the customer representative with a smiling tone strengthens the communication with the customer. Using the facilities of the technology, the customer representative identifies the problem of the customer in a short time and saves time, and as a result of this determination, the customer is satisfied with the call provided.

In order to provide the best service to customers, call centers are becoming more and more important for businesses. The average talk and post-work time for employee productivity measures includes compliance with the shift plan. In the quality criteria, call listening includes researching customer satisfaction.

The high level of service quality offered in call centers increases the value of the product and service offered at the customer satisfaction level. The most important aim of call centers is to provide services in accordance with a philosophy based on mutual communication in order to provide maximum quality and to ensure customer satisfaction (Amaya et al., 2018).

With the development of information technology, the works performed are more hierarchical and controlled more centrally. Information technologies in enterprises measure time tracking, performance and efficiency evaluations. At the same time, it becomes a tool for monitoring the purposes for which information technologies are used by employees. Another study in the US showed that only 59% of customers were satisfied with the service they received as a result of customers contacting call centers for support. Thanks to this stage, the interviews with the voice recording systems allowed listening and evaluation for quality purposes. The evaluations do not cover only customer representatives. It can also be provided on a group basis and automatically reporting. This has enabled efficient benchmarking and group benchmarking. It is assumed that information technologies will increase the transaction speed in the banking sector, provide the necessary information for financial reports in time to manage cost and risk, help to continuously improve the quality of products and services, and increase the ability of individual and corporate customers to respond to specific product and service demands.

IVR Tree Applications in Call Center

Technological developments accelerated the change and development of banks in the product and service sector and transformed the banking system on information communication technologies into an established structure (Feinberg et al., 2002; Taylor, 2008). Today, call centers have become a system that accepts calls professionally, works with the help of dialing or voice response system. Serving one or more people simultaneously, the menu offers an interactive voice response method (Aksin et al., 2007; Rafaeli et al., 2008). The sum of the calls received in the voice response system (IVR). It is a system that works 24/7. In this application, the customer is directed by the system when he calls the call center. It enables the customer to perform the transactions without the need of the customer representative by using the phone keys or speaking by voice to the menu he needs (Çekmecelioğlu et al., 2012; Wallace et al., 2000).

Today, call centers are complex socio-technical systems that play an increasingly important role in modern world society (Weinberg et al., 2007; Das et al., 2005). Information and emergency centers, help desks, telemarketing etc. areas to serve. To provide high quality services, call center managers and designers should consider the complexity of factors associated with incoming calls. A tandem consisting of two stations, Station 1 and Station 2 is contemplated (Chang et al., 2009). Station 1 represents retrievals in a multi-server sequence. On arrival, a customer who occupies all the lines joins the orbit and retries for service after a random period of time, regardless of the other orbit. Such behavior is typical for customers calling the call center and receives a signal indicating that all lines are busy (Kavitha, 2017). All incoming calls at Station 1 (first and repetitive) can terminate the service in the tandem system at this (first) stage or require an additional service at Station 2 (second stage). The first stage can be described, for example, as IVR-Interactive Voice Response. Unsatisfied customers are referred to the second stage customer representatives to solve their problems. All customers are initially handled by agents in the first phase of the call center (the servers of Station 1), and some of the customers are satisfied with the service at this stage. However, the service of some customers cannot be completed by these representatives due to limited authorities and knowledge, so these customers can be handled by their specialists when they call in the second stage.

The emergence of interactive voice response (IVR) applications for use in telephone systems has reduced operating costs for many types of businesses, reducing telephone personnel requirements (Gans et al., 2015). Such IVR (voice answering system) applications typically answer incoming phone calls and provide voice menus of selectable options to callers. Callers usually select menus in one of two ways: pressing a key or sequence of keys on the touch keypad, or navigating menus using speech recognition technology. Often there are many hierarchical menus that the caller must navigate to find the option the caller wants to select. It may take time to navigate through these menus, especially if the caller makes an incorrect selection during the navigation. It can be minimized by providing callers with a simplified navigation method to achieve the desired operation within an IVR menu (Allen et al., 2016).

Nowadays, thanks to the evolving voice technology, automatic voice response (IVR) system enables you to navigate the menus by speaking instead of clicking the buttons. Most of the call centers used in banks and companies use this technology. Interactive voice response (IVR) systems enable a computer to detect and process speech or touch tones entered by a caller. The IVR (voice response system) system can respond with pre-recorded or dynamically generated messages to direct the caller. IVR (voice response system) systems are used frequently with various menu options (Ibrahim et al., 2016).

IVR (voice response system) is a system that uses the keypad to input the caller's voice and dual tone multi-frequency (DTMF) tones to interact with people. When calls are routed to agents, the probability of the caller being transferred to the wrong agent or department is significantly reduced (Pugh, 2017). Gathering information about the needs of the customer, acquiring information without the need of any agency or bank branch, prioritizing the calls according to the needs of the customer (customers can connect to an agency immediately from the lost-stolen menu, etc.), IVR (voice response system) It can be classified as transactions that can be done through (Picanso et al., 2017).

The automated voice response system helps reduce costs and is also used as a service outside of a day's working hours. To complete a call in the IVR (voice response system), it is necessary to provide the customer with the functionality it needs in the IVR (voice response system) (Garrett et al., 2016). There are three basic requirements for customers to perform an operation with the functionality required in IVR (voice response system). These; customer identification, indication of functionality processed in the system, and authorization of the customer to achieve the desired functionality for security (Allexandre et al., 2016).

Call centers are a rapidly growing industry in many countries. Call center operators spend most of their time passing through phones equipped with headsets, which are usually supported by computers. Call center services generally include one of two types. The first type deals with customer calls from workers who provide customer service (Chau et al., 2016). The second type performs simple sales activities or market surveys for new customers. There are clear differences between workloads that provide inbound and outbound services. In another definition, the call is made through the customer in the incoming call centers (Robbins, 2017). For example, health enterprises, help desks, travel agencies, information channels and so on. In outgoing call centers, the call is initiated by the customer representative for a specific customer group. Outgoing call centers are generally used for marketing. They are also used for announcement, appointment, information, customer satisfaction surveys, recovery, information update searches (Gustavsson et al., 2018).

Corporate and individual customers demand more from the sectors in which they have served. Customer-focused activities are the focus of survival for companies in today's economy. Call centers, which are more preferred by customers in recent years, are trying to meet the expectations of the customers thanks to the technology and at the same time to increase the level of technology used (Oztaysi et al.,

2017). Technological developments that continue with globalization In addition to IVR (voice response system), artificial intelligence technologies are also widely used. Nowadays, with the development of information technologies, artificial intelligence studies have increased. Data and analytical leaders in many sectors are seeking an invention that should be targeted in the long run. In the future, artificial intelligence systems are expected to interact safely and reliably in a complex real world (Jouini et al., 2015). This includes applications involving autonomous driving, robots interacting with the environment, as well as decision making under complex constraints in areas such as social sciences, finance, politics and others. These systems can be used to investigate and reason the decision-making process and its potential consequences. It can help to give information about the possible strategies and policies sought from it.

Artificial intelligence methods and artificial intelligence technologies have been introduced to bring transformative change to societies and industries worldwide. The play-changing nature of artificial intelligence studies and its role as the driving force of innovation, future growth and competitiveness are internationally recognized. In the United States, large investments in artificial intelligence studies are made by the private sector, and in 2016 an important government plan was launched, including significant long-term investments in artificial intelligence research. Similarly, in 2017, the Canadian government began investing heavily in artificial intelligence research and focused mostly on the existing power of deep learning. In 2017, China published its next Generation Artificial Intelligence Development Plan with the goal of achieving the superiority of artificial intelligence by 2030. However, Europe has lagged behind its European competitors in investments in talent, research, technology and innovation (Hidayah Ibrahim et al., 2019).

The cost of providing trained agencies in call centers accounts for more than 50% of the total operating costs. It is therefore important to identify the right strategies for personnel and workforce planning that directly affect profitability and productivity. Inadequate understanding leads to reductions in performance indicators and, of course, customer satisfaction, while resulting in misuse of resources. With the developing technologies, customers' expectations from companies have increased. Customers' expectations follow technology developments. New technologies and different delivery channels change the customer and staff experience in the services sector. Call centers and Web-based service methods are becoming the norm in completing traditional telephone, office and postal services. Call centers have become an important source of customer information as well as an important customer access channel (Rosen et al., 2016).

Information technologies (IT) affect the skills and employment by enabling the restructuring of firms through the change and development of the economy. In order to achieve the goal of economic development and growth, the resources available should be used in the most effective and efficient way. The existence of economic awareness between continents, countries or regions brought about the search for the elimination of differences. By providing new advantages to consumers, it contributes to the growth of companies. With the development of technology, there is a linear relationship between the expectations of customers or callers in call centers. The relationship between banks and customers increased more than in the past. The technological innovations found by banks offer new ways to facilitate customers (Kassavou & Sutton, 2016).

SOLUTIONS AND RECOMMENDATIONS

It is observed that call centers are concentrated in the areas of informing, giving opinions and suggestions, and solving complaints. This results in accordance with the structure and function of the institution. As a result, it shows this trend in both developed and developing countries where call centers act in accordance with technology developments according to needs. The said growth also increases the equipment of the employees and contributes positively to both internal and external customer satisfaction. Because, as the studies in alternative distribution channels expands, it will be ensured that the needs are read well and the requirements are acted upon.

It carries many functions such as complaint resolution, opinion-suggestion and information in call centers. Therefore, call centers are regarded as reliable sources of information. They focus on their weaknesses by making use of information technology opportunities to transform their weaknesses into opportunities. This is in accordance with the structure and function of call centers. As a result, it shows this trend in both developed and developing countries where call centers act in accordance with technology developments according to needs. The said growth also increases the equipment of the employees and contributes positively to both internal and external customer satisfaction. Because, as the studies in alternative distribution channels expands, it will be ensured that the needs are read well and the requirements are acted upon.

FUTURE RESEARCH DIRECTIONS

This study tried to understand the main developments in call center applications based on the theory of financial marketing. In the future studies, an analysis can be made to understand how to improve call center performance of the banks so that it can be much easier to attract the attentions of the customers.

CONCLUSION

In the world and Turkey it is seen that it has continuously developed alternative distribution channels used by banks. The most important fact in the necessity of increasing the quality in call centers, which is one of the most important in alternative distribution channels, is intense competition between banks. The increase in the competition among the banks ensured the diversification of services offered in call centers and customer satisfaction.

In recent years, technology investment in call centers in developed and developing countries has increased. It is aimed to ensure customer satisfaction through call centers in an interbank competitive environment. Thus, while trying to resolve the problems and complaints of customers or callers, they aim to respond to the demands of new services by recording their suggestions and opinions. Working in Turkey 'call center technology applications are also discussed.

The customers menu with this context, the bank call center, self-service process to realize fast and secure transactions without getting lost, the call center market structure, to achieve customer satisfaction, emphasizing the developed and developing investments in include the place and Turkey with the size of the call center. By evaluating the data, the current point of call centers was tried to be determined. The results obtained in this context; By using technology in the call center, marketing activities were brought to the forefront, providing better service to customers and increasing customer satisfaction. In the light of these developments, call center management and technological effects have been used effectively in the development of call centers. Increasing product and service diversity with the use of new technologies leads to an increase in competition. In call centers, the IVR (voice response system) tree improved voice routing, enabling new transactions to be carried to the IVR (voice response system). In the operational field, call centers can be cited as an important unit developing technology in different areas.

ACKNOWLEDGMENT

This study was derived from Ayşe Mengir's master thesis written in İstanbul Medipol University.

REFERENCES

Aksin, Z., Armony, M., & Mehrotra, V. (2007). The modern call center: A multi-disciplinary perspective on operations management research. *Production and Operations Management*, *16*(6), 665–688. doi:10.1111/j.1937-5956.2007.tb00288.x

Allen, T. T., Xiong, H., & Afful-Dadzie, A. (2016). A directed topic model applied to call center improvement. *Applied Stochastic Models in Business and Industry*, *32*(1), 57–73. doi:10.1002/asmb.2123

Allexandre, D., Bernstein, A. M., Walker, E., Hunter, J., Roizen, M. F., & Morledge, T. J. (2016). A web-based mindfulness stress management program in a corporate call center: A randomized clinical trial to evaluate the added benefit of onsite group support. *Journal of Occupational and Environmental Medicine*, *58*(3), 254–264. doi:10.1097/JOM.0000000000000680 PMID:26949875

Amaya, A., Lau, C., Owusu-Amoah, Y., & Light, J. (2018). Evaluation of gaining cooperation methods for IVR surveys in low-and middle-income countries. *Survey Methods: Insights from the Field*, 8.

Andersson, C. (2015). Comparison of WEB and interactive voice response (IVR) methods for delivering brief alcohol interventions to hazardous-drinking university students: A randomized controlled trial. *European Addiction Research*, *21*(5), 240–252. doi:10.1159/000381017 PMID:25967070

Bateh, J., & Farah, J. (2017). Reducing call center wait times through six sigma. *Journal of Business Inquiry*, *17*(2), 131–148.

Ben-David, B. M., & Icht, M. (2016). Voice changes in real speaking situations during a day, with and without vocal loading: Assessing call center operators. *Journal of Voice*, *30*(2), 247–e1. doi:10.1016/j.jvoice.2015.04.002 PMID:26320758

Brown, L., Gans, N., Mandelbaum, A., Sakov, A., Shen, H., Zeltyn, S., & Zhao, L. (2005). Statistical analysis of a telephone call center: A queueing-science perspective. *Journal of the American Statistical Association*, *100*(469), 36–50. doi:10.1198/016214504000001808

Çabuk, U. C., Şenocak, T., Demir, E., & Çavdar, A. (2017). A Proposal on initial remote user enrollment for IVR-based voice authentication systems. *Int. J. of Advanced Research in Computer and Communication Engineering*, *6*, 118–123.

Çekmecioğlu, H. G., Günsel, A., & Ulutaş, T. (2012). Effects of emotional intelligence on job satisfaction: An empirical study on call center employees. *Procedia: Social and Behavioral Sciences*, *58*, 363–369. doi:10.1016/j.sbspro.2012.09.1012

Chang, T. Y., Graff Zivin, J., Gross, T., & Neidell, M. (2019). The effect of pollution on worker productivity: Evidence from call center workers in China. *American Economic Journal. Applied Economics*, *11*(1), 151–172. doi:10.1257/app.20160436

Chau, J. Y., Sukala, W., Fedel, K., Do, A., Engelen, L., Kingham, M., ... Bauman, A. E. (2016). More standing and just as productive: Effects of a sit-stand desk intervention on call center workers' sitting, standing, and productivity at work in the Opt to Stand pilot study. *Preventive Medicine Reports*, *3*, 68–74. doi:10.1016/j.pmedr.2015.12.003 PMID:26844191

Das, S. S., Hackbarth, K. R., Jensen, K. B., Kohler, J. E., Matula, V. C., & Windhausen, R. A. (2005). *U.S. Patent No. 6,847,714*. Washington, DC: U.S. Patent and Trademark Office.

Dinçer, H., Hacıoğlu, Ü., & Yüksel, S. (2017). A strategic approach to global financial crisis in banking sector: a critical appraisal of banking strategies using fuzzy ANP and fuzzy topsis methods. *International Journal of Sustainable Economies Management*, *6*(1), 1–21. doi:10.4018/ijsem.2017010101

Dinçer, H., & Yüksel, S. (2018a). Comparative evaluation of BSC-based new service development competencies in Turkish banking sector with the integrated fuzzy hybrid MCDM using content analysis. *International Journal of Fuzzy Systems*, *20*(8), 2497–2516. doi:10.100740815-018-0519-y

Dinçer, H., & Yüksel, S. (2018b). Financial sector-based analysis of the G20 economies using the integrated decision-making approach with DEMATEL and TOPSIS. In *Emerging trends in banking and finance* (pp. 210–223). Cham, Switzerland: Springer. doi:10.1007/978-3-030-01784-2_13

Dinçer, H., & Yüksel, S. (2019). An integrated stochastic fuzzy MCDM approach to the balanced scorecard-based service evaluation. *Mathematics and Computers in Simulation*.

Dinçer, H., Yüksel, S., Adalı, Z., & Aydın, R. (2019a). Evaluating the role of research and development and technology investments on economic development of E7 countries. In Organizational Transformation and Managing Innovation in the Fourth Industrial Revolution (pp. 245-263). Hershey, PA: IGI Global.

Dinçer, H., Yüksel, S., & Çetiner, İ. T. (2019c). Strategy selection for organizational performance of Turkish banking sector with the integrated multi-dimensional decision-making approach. In Handbook of research on contemporary approaches in management and organizational strategy (pp. 273–291). Hershey, PA: IGI Global. doi:10.4018/978-1-5225-6301-3.ch014

Dinçer, H., Yüksel, S., Eti, S., & Tula, A. (2019d). Effects of demographic characteristics on business success: an evidence from Turkish banking sector. In Handbook of research on business models in modern competitive scenarios (pp. 304–324). Hershey, PA: IGI Global. doi:10.4018/978-1-5225-7265-7.ch016

Dinçer, H., Yüksel, S., Kartal, M. T., & Alpman, G. (2019e). Corporate governance-based evaluation of alternative distribution channels in the turkish banking sector using quality function deployment with an integrated fuzzy MCDM method. In Intergenerational governance and leadership in the corporate world: Emerging research and opportunities (pp. 39-77). Hershey, PA: IGI Global.

Dinçer, H., Yüksel, S., & Martínez, L. (2019f). Analysis of balanced scorecard-based SERVQUAL criteria based on hesitant decision-making approaches. *Computers & Industrial Engineering*, *131*, 1–12. doi:10.1016/j.cie.2019.03.026

Dinçer, H., Yüksel, S., & Martínez, L. (2019g). Interval type 2-based hybrid fuzzy evaluation of financial services in E7 economies with DEMATEL-ANP and MOORA methods. *Applied Soft Computing*, *79*, 186–202. doi:10.1016/j.asoc.2019.03.018

Dinçer, H., Yüksel, S., & Pınarbaşı, F. (2019b). Technology acceptance model-based website evaluation of service industry: an application on the companies listed in BIST via hybrid MCDM. In Multi-Criteria Decision-Making Models for Website Evaluation (pp. 1-28). Hershey, PA: IGI Global.

Feigin, P. (2006). *Analysis of customer patience in a bank call center. Working paper.* Haifa, Israel: The Technion.

Feinberg, R. A., Hokama, L., Kadam, R., & Kim, I. (2002). Operational determinants of caller satisfaction in the banking/financial services call center. *International Journal of Bank Marketing*, *20*(4), 174–180. doi:10.1108/02652320210432954

Flory, J. A., Leibbrandt, A., & List, J. A. (2016). *The effects of wage contracts on workplace misbehaviors: Evidence from a call center natural field experiment (No. w22342)*. National Bureau of Economic Research.

Frimpong, E., Oduro-Mensah, E., Vanotoo, L., & Agyepong, I. A. (2018). An exploratory case study of the organizational functioning of a decision-making and referral support call center for frontline providers of maternal and new born care in the Greater Accra Region of Ghana. *The International Journal of Health Planning and Management*, *33*(4), e1112–e1123. doi:10.1002/hpm.2595 PMID:30095184

Gans, N., Shen, H., Zhou, Y. P., Korolev, N., McCord, A., & Ristock, H. (2015). Parametric forecasting and stochastic programming models for call-center workforce scheduling. *Manufacturing & Service Operations Management: M & SOM*, *17*(4), 571–588. doi:10.1287/msom.2015.0546

Garrett, G., Benden, M., Mehta, R., Pickens, A., Peres, S. C., & Zhao, H. (2016). Call center productivity over 6 months following a standing desk intervention. *IIE Transactions on Occupational Ergonomics and Human Factors*, *4*(2-3), 188–195. doi:10.1080/21577323.2016.1183534

Go, E. M., Ong, K. B., San Juan, J. L., Sia, W. G., Tiu, R. H., & Li, R. (2018, August). Development of fuzzy data envelopment risk analysis applied on auditory ergonomics for call center agents in the Philippines. In *Congress of the International Ergonomics Association* (pp. 13–22). Cham, Switzerland: Springer.

Gustavsson, K., L'Ecuyer, P., & Olsson, L. (2018). Modeling bursts in the arrival process to an emergency call center. In *Winter Simulation Conference 2018*.

Hidayah Ibrahim, S. N., Suan, C. L., & Karatepe, O. M. (2019). The effects of supervisor support and self-efficacy on call center employees' work engagement and quitting intentions. *International Journal of Manpower*, *40*(4), 688–703. doi:10.1108/IJM-12-2017-0320

Ibrahim, R., Ye, H., L'Ecuyer, P., & Shen, H. (2016). Modeling and forecasting call center arrivals: A literature survey and a case study. *International Journal of Forecasting, 32*(3), 865–874. doi:10.1016/j.ijforecast.2015.11.012

Ji, Y., Park, T., & Lee, Y. S. (2017). The impact of severe weather announcement on the Korea meteorological administration call center counseling demand. *Atmosphere, 27*(4), 377–384.

Jouini, O., Akşin, O. Z., Karaesmen, F., Aguir, M. S., & Dallery, Y. (2015). Call center delay announcement using a newsvendor-like performance criterion. *Production and Operations Management, 24*(4), 587–604. doi:10.1111/poms.12259

Kassavou, A., & Sutton, S. (2016). *Developing and pre-testing a tailored interactive voice response (IVR) intervention to support adherence to anti-hypertensive medications: a research protocol*. Cambridge, UK: Cambridge University.

Kassavou, A., & Sutton, S. (2016). Supporting medication adherence using Interactive Voice response (IVR): development and delivery of a theory and evidence-based intervention. *Eur Heal Psychol, 18*.

Kavitha, V. (2017). *The relationship and effect of role overload, role ambiguity, work-life balance and career development on work stress among call center executives of business process outsourcing (BPO) in Selangor* (Doctoral dissertation, Universiti Utara Malaysia).

Kazakos, K., Asthana, S., Balaam, M., Duggal, M., Holden, A., Jamir, L., ... Murthy, G. V. S. (2016, May). A real-time IVR platform for community radio. In *Proceedings of the 2016 CHI Conference on Human Factors in Computing Systems* (pp. 343-354). ACM. 10.1145/2858036.2858585

Kim, C., Klimenok, V. I., & Dudin, A. N. (2016). Priority tandem queueing system with retrials and reservation of channels as a model of call center. *Computers & Industrial Engineering, 96*, 61–71. doi:10.1016/j.cie.2016.03.012

Kim, J., & Kang, P. (2016). Late payment prediction models for fair allocation of customer contact lists to call center agents. *Decision Support Systems, 85*, 84–101. doi:10.1016/j.dss.2016.03.002

Kim, J. I., & Choi, B. R. (2015). Convergence study on emotional labor, stress response and turnover intention of call-center worker. *Journal of the Korea Convergence Society, 6*(6), 139–146. doi:10.15207/JKCS.2015.6.6.139

Legros, B., Jouini, O., & Koole, G. (2018). Blended call center with idling times during the call service. *IISE Transactions, 50*(4), 279–297. doi:10.1080/24725854.2017.1387318

Li, S., Wang, Q., & Koole, G. (2018, November). Predicting call center performance with machine learning. In *INFORMS International Conference on Service Science* (pp. 193-199). Cham, Switzerland: Springer.

Lin, Y. H., Chen, C. Y., Hong, W. H., & Lin, Y. C. (2010). Perceived job stress and health complaints at a bank call center: Comparison between inbound and outbound services. *Industrial Health, 48*(3), 349–356. doi:10.2486/indhealth.48.349 PMID:20562511

Lu, F., Suggs, A., Ezaldein, H. H., Ya, J., Fu, P., Jamora, J., ... Baron, E. D. (2019). The effect of shift work and poor sleep on self-reported skin conditions: a survey of call center agents in the Philippines. *Clocks & Sleep, 1*(2), 273–279. doi:10.3390/clockssleep1020023

Mudliar, P., & Donner, J. (2015). Experiencing interactive voice response (IVR) as a participatory medium: The case of CGNet Swara in India. *Mobile Media & Communication, 3*(3), 366–382. doi:10.1177/2050157915571591

Odebiyi, D. O., Akanle, O. T., Akinbo, S. R. A., & Balogun, S. A. (2016). Prevalence and impact of work-related musculoskeletal disorders on job performance of call center operators in Nigeria. *Int J Occup Environ Med (The IJOEM), 7*(2 April), 622-98.

Oh, H., Park, H., & Boo, S. (2017). Mental health status and its predictors among call center employees: A cross-sectional study. *Nursing & Health Sciences, 19*(2), 228–236. doi:10.1111/nhs.12334 PMID:28295980

Oztaysi, B., Onar, S. C., & Kahraman, C. (2017). Integrated call center performance measurement using hierarchical intuitionistic fuzzy axiomatic design. In *Advances in fuzzy logic and technology 2017* (pp. 94–105). Cham, Switzerland: Springer.

Pappas, D., Androutsopoulos, I., & Papageorgiou, H. (2015, October). Anger detection in call center dialogues. In *2015 6th IEEE International Conference on Cognitive Infocommunications (CogInfoCom)* (pp. 139-144). IEEE. 10.1109/CogInfoCom.2015.7390579

Picanso, J. M., Swinkels, C. M., Hill, M., Hess, T. H., Straits-Tröster, K. A., Glynn, S., & Sayers, S. L. (2017, March). The development and initial evaluation of a call center for concerned family members of military veterans. In Annals of Behavioral Medicine (Vol. 51, pp. S229-S229). 233 Spring St., New York, NY 10013: Springer.

Presbitero, A. (2017). It's not all about language ability: Motivational cultural intelligence matters in call center performance. *International Journal of Human Resource Management, 28*(11), 1547–1562. doi:10.1080/09585192.2015.1128464

Pugh, W. (2017). *Call center experience optimization: a case for a virtual predictive queue* (Doctoral dissertation, University of the Incarnate Word).

Rafaeli, A., Ziklik, L., & Doucet, L. (2008). The impact of call center employees' customer orientation behaviors on service quality. *Journal of Service Research, 10*(3), 239–255. doi:10.1177/1094670507306685

Robbins, T. R. (2017). Complexity and flexibility in call center scheduling models. *International Journal of Business and Social Science, 8*(12).

Rocha, L. E., Glina, D. M. R., Marinho, M. F., & Nakasato, D. (2005). Risk factors for musculoskeletal symptoms among call center operators of a bank in Sao Paulo, Brazil. *Industrial Health, 43*(4), 637–646. doi:10.2486/indhealth.43.637 PMID:16294918

Rosen, R. C., Stephens-Shields, A. J., Cunningham, G. R., Cifelli, D., Cella, D., Farrar, J. T., ... Snyder, P. J. (2016). Comparison of interactive voice response (IVR) with paper administration of instruments to assess functional status, sexual function, and quality of life in elderly men. *Quality of Life Research: An International Journal of Quality of Life Aspects of Treatment, Care and Rehabilitation, 25*(4), 811–821. doi:10.100711136-015-1133-1 PMID:26358063

Skalicky, S., Friginal, E., & Subtirelu, N. (2016). A corpus-assisted investigation of nonunderstanding in outsourced call center discourse. In *Talking at Work* (pp. 127–153). London, UK: Palgrave Macmillan. doi:10.1057/978-1-137-49616-4_6

Soh, S. B., & Gurvich, I. (2016). Call center staffing: Service-level constraints and index priorities. *Operations Research*, *65*(2), 537–555. doi:10.1287/opre.2016.1532

Stepanov, E., Favre, B., Alam, F., Chowdhury, S., Singla, K., Trione, J., ... Riccardi, G. (2015, December). Automatic summarization of call-center conversations. In *Proc. of the IEEE Automatic Speech Recognition and Understanding Workshop (ASRU 2015)*. IEEE.

Swendeman, D., Jana, S., Ray, P., Mindry, D., Das, M., & Bhakta, B. (2015). Development and pilot testing of daily interactive voice response (IVR) calls to support antiretroviral adherence in India: A mixed-methods pilot study. *AIDS and Behavior*, *19*(2), 142–155. doi:10.100710461-014-0983-9 PMID:25638037

Taylor, J. W. (2008). A comparison of univariate time series methods for forecasting intraday arrivals at a call center. *Management Science*, *54*(2), 253–265. doi:10.1287/mnsc.1070.0786

Tunay, N., Yüksel, S., & Tunay, K. B. (2019). The Effects of Technology on Bank Performance in Advanced and Emerging Economies: An Empirical Analysis. In Handbook of research on managerial thinking in global business economics (pp. 263–280). Hershey, PA: IGI Global. doi:10.4018/978-1-5225-7180-3.ch015

Wallace, C. M., Eagleson, G., & Waldersee, R. (2000). The sacrificial HR strategy in call centers. *International Journal of Service Industry Management*, *11*(2), 174–184. doi:10.1108/09564230010323741

Weinberg, J., Brown, L. D., & Stroud, J. R. (2007). Bayesian forecasting of an inhomogeneous Poisson process with applications to call center data. *Journal of the American Statistical Association*, *102*(480), 1185–1198. doi:10.1198/016214506000001455

Williams, M. J., Bélanger, J. J., Horgan, J., & Evans, W. P. (2018). Experimental effects of a call-center disclaimer regarding confidentiality on callers' willingness to make disclosures related to terrorism. *Terrorism and Political Violence*, 1–15. doi:10.1080/09546553.2018.1476347

Yüksel, S., Dinçer, H., & Emir, Ş. (2017). Comparing the performance of Turkish deposit banks by using DEMATEL, Grey Relational Analysis (GRA) and MOORA approaches. *World Journal of Applied Economics*, *3*(2), 26–47. doi:10.22440/wjae.3.2.2

Yuksel, S., Dinçer, H., & Emir, S. (2018). Analysis of service innovation performance in turkish banking sector using a combining method of fuzzy MCDM and text mining. *MANAS Sosyal Araştırmalar Dergisi*, *7*(3).

Yuksel, S., Dincer, H., & Hacioglu, U. (2015). CAMELS-based determinants for the credit rating of Turkish deposit banks. *International Journal of Finance & Banking Studies (2147-4486)*, *4*(4), 1-17.

Zengin, S., & Yüksel, S. (2016). A comparison of the views of internal controllers/auditors and branch/call center personnel of the banks for operational risk: A case for Turkish banking sector. *International Journal of Finance & Banking Studies*, *5*(4), 10.

Zito, M., Emanuel, F., Molino, M., Cortese, C. G., Ghislieri, C., & Colombo, L. (2018). Turnover intentions in a call center: The role of emotional dissonance, job resources, and job satisfaction. *PLoS One*, *13*(2), e0192126. doi:10.1371/journal.pone.0192126 PMID:29401507

KEY TERMS AND DEFINITIONS

ATM: Automatic Teller Machine.
CRM: Customer Relationship Management.
CTI: Computer Telephony Integration.
EU: European Union.
IVR: Interactive Voice Response.
R&D: Research and Development.
US: United States.
USD: American dollar.

Chapter 8
The Importance of Ethics and Corporate Social Responsibility in Financial Markets:
A Literature Review and Recommendations for Ethical and Islamic Banking

Hakan Kalkavan
https://orcid.org/0000-0003-4482-0505
Istanbul Medipol University, Turkey

ABSTRACT

This chapter mainly focuses on the literature about the relationship between ethics, corporate social responsibility, and financial markets, which is broad and diverse as well as multi-disciplined. Some are concerned only with ethical banking, while others seek to establish a financial system based on social responsibility to society and people. The studies essentially bring attention to the question of how banks should act in the face of the moral-economic dilemma. In fact, ethical aspect is much more valuable than economic profitability and includes a social responsibility approach. In the concept of ethical concerns and corporate social responposibility, the literature has been reviewed and problematic areas discussed for ethical and Islamic banking. Islamic finance and specifically Islamic banking can be seen as a new practice to bring corporate ethical responsibility and social justice into the financial and economic spheres.

INTRODUCTION

One of the main reasons behind formation of financial and economic crisis is unethical behaviors of owners, executives and employees in financial organizations such as government banks, commercial banks, central banks and insurance companies. The relationship between financial institutions and ethics is crucially important for solid financial system in which consumer and firms perform their economic

DOI: 10.4018/978-1-7998-2559-3.ch008

activities in mutual trust. Therefore, moral sensitivity as well as legal regulations should be established in financial institutions both in terms of corporate mentality and individually.

Ethical banking is a concept that defines the banking understanding that includes transparency, environmental consciousness and social responsibility practices. While Ethical Banks are trying to make a profit on the one hand, they are trying to do this in line with the principles. The separation between environment, society and economy that undermined socio-economic structure of societies and endangered the continuation of humanity. Ethical banks provide many benefits for a sustainable socio-economic system if they address issues that other traditional banks do not consider. In fact, this ethical aspect is much more valuable than economic profitability and includes a social responsibility approach. Thus, they aimed to contribute to the integration between ethical theory and daily banking practices.

Although ethical banking and Islamic banking have similarities in many ways, Islamic banking has many different principles based on religion. In this context, it is expressed that the growth of ethical banking accelerates Islamic banking. Although many thinkers think that Islamic banking is based on the idea of ethical banking, it can be said that Islamic banking offers an approach stemming from Islamic moral understanding. According to Islamic financing, ethical investments are based on a moral and legal basis that defines the levels of halal and haram, makes a beneficial social contribution to society. With this study, the topic of ethics and social responsibilty in financial markets will be researched and problematic areas will be discussed. Thereby the study will be concluded by policy recommendations within conceptual framework discussed.

LITERATURE REVIEW FOR ETHICS AND CORPORATE SOCIAL RESPONSIBILITY IN FINANCIAL MARKETS

Literature Review on Ethics and Financial Markets

The literature about the relationship between ethics and financial markets is multi-disciplined. Some studies theoretical, most of them are econometric and quantitative, others are qualititative. The reasons for conducting these studies are as diverse as the research subject. Some are concerned only with ethical banking, while others seek to establish a financial system based on sensitivity to society and people. In this section; the research topics, scope and findings of the studies conducted in the literature in terms of ethics and banking will be reviewed.

In a survey research conducted by Harvey (1995) with the bank clients on ethical banking in the UK, it was concluded that ethical banks are beneficial if they develop different strategies on issues that other conventional banks do not care about. In a study of sustainable development in the context of environment, society and economy, Giddings et al. (2002) found that the separation between environment, society and economy developed a kind of techno-scientific approach, which undermined socio-economic structure of societies and endangered the continuation of cultural differences. San-Jose et al. (2011) selected 114 banks in 10 European countries as sample groups and examined property-based ethical banks and traditional financial institutions according to the Radical Affinity Index; ethical ideology, transparency of information, guarantee, the portfolio selection of assets and participation etc. and consequently found that ethical banks differ in terms of information transparency and the portfolio selection of assets from conventional financial institutions. In another study, Forseth et al. (2015) investigated the factors of illegal action, fraudulent sales and right selling through exploratory ethnographic method in the period of

1996-2014. As a result, financial jolty situation causes daily routine transactions to be interrupted and requires members to develop new accounts of their applications as the remaining accounts are out of legality. Another study is conducted by Paulet et al. (2015) to investigate the difference between traditional banks and ethical banks by using factor analysis method in terms of profitability, equity requirement, speculation policy and publication transparency in the context of new business environment. According to this study, ethical banks has integrated new banking regulatory rules long before the sub-prime crisis. As a result, both types of banks have different approaches with different business models, the authors emphasized the idea that it would be more beneficial for ethical banks to engage in local credit market rather than dealing with financial secondary markets.

In a study on the significance of relational marketing and Islamic banking, Widana et al. (2016) concluded that Islamic banks will be successful in providing differentiated services and products through the implementation of seven-dimensional Islamic business ethics on the basis of factors such as employee training, the establishment of justice and the promotion of prosperity. In a similar study conducted by Gilani (2015) on Islamic banking, the ethical evaluation of Islamic banking was researched by using qualitative thematic content analysis method. This study, comparing the traditional capitalist banking sector with Islamic banking in terms of interest, ethical banking and treating customers fairly, suggests that Islamic banking has a morally positive image. In this context, Islamic banking makes an innovative moral contribution to the traditional financial sector, which uses ruthless interest-based transactions, profit maximization motivation, debt-based growth and speculative transactions. In another study, Chew et al. (2016) investigated 20 senior bank executives working in co-operative banks in the United Kingdom by qualitative focus group method between 2012 and 2014, and evaluated the impact of these banks on the sustainability of socio-economic development, regulation of economic and social instruments and corporate social responsibility. As a result of this study, it was found that the Cooperative Bank has been impressively successful in maintaining the socio-environmental development of the UK. In a different study conducted by Oates and Dias (2016), which was explored whether there are ethics lectures in graduate banking and finance programs in the period of 2014-2015, it was determined by content analysis method that there were no ethics lectures in 809 out of 897 programs.

Using the cognitive mapping technique, Ferreira et al. (2016) primarily determined the basic factors of ethical practices by examining the factors of commitment to customers, welfare of employees and transparency. Thus, they aimed to contribute to the integration between ethical theory and daily banking practices. As a result of the research, it has been clearly observed that this problem causes great concern among the people inside and outside the institution. Moreover Tan et al. (2017) conducted a qualitative research that interviewing with 35 bankers of MayBank operating in Malaysia from different departments. The sustainable banking operating system. As a result of this study, which is dealt with the sustainable banking operating system from customers, governments, competitors and stakeholders variables with a holistic perspective, Maybank's mission statement and vision statement expressed in the sustainable banking agenda have been found to be highly effective. In another study conducted by Aliyu et al. (2018), sustainability of Islamic banking was evaluated on the basis of long-term economic, social and environmental sustainability factors with the literature review method. The authors concluded that Islamic banks need to strike a balance between corporate, social and environmental sustainability in order to achieve the Sharia goal. A research about SME's in Turkey conducted by Erdogan (2018), aims to identify the aspects effecting SME access to bank loans. In this study, variables such as bank loans, firm profitability, debt ratio and firm's relationship with the bank were assessed by thematic analysis method which is conducted by semi-structured interview with 25 Turkish bank managers. Main finding of the study is "Firms with a long-term relationship with the bank and older firms have better access to bank loans". Additionally, SMEs in the manufacturing industry have easier access to bank financing.

Another literature review study conducted by Zainuldin et al. (2018) considers Ethics and agency theory from an Islamic banking perspective. According to the results obtained on the basis of compliance with the legislation and the structures of investors and shareholders, the Islamic ethical system involved in the commercial activities of Islamic banks transforms Islamic banks into institutions that have higher ethical considerations than traditional banks and lessly have agency problems compare to counterparts institutions. On a similar topic, Gheitani et al. (2019) investigated the impact of Islamic business ethics on job satisfaction and organizational commitment among Maskan bank employees by survey method. In this study, variables such as intrinsic motivation, Islamic work ethics, job satisfaction and organizational commitment were designed within the model. As a result of the analyzes, it was found that intrinsic motivation plays a partial role in the relationship between Islamic work ethics and job satisfaction and a mediator role in the relationship between Islamic work ethics and organizational commitment. Another study on Islamic banking was analyzed by San-Jose and Cuesta (2019) based on the transparency, asset placement, guarantees and participation factors according to the Radical Affinity Index 2014 datas of 20 Islamic banks from 13 Islamic countries. As a result of the study, the following findings were reached; Islamic banks have scored lower than ethical banks in terms of RAI variables and should provide a clearer view of their ethical and social commitment to society. In the study, which was put forward by Lenz and Neckel (2019), the theoretical framework of German ethical banking was compared with 27 qualitative interviews with ethical bank employees. In this study, the theoretical framework of German ethical banking was put forward by Lenz and Neckel (2019) and then 27 ethical interviews were conducted with ethical bank employees and compared. In the context of the trade-off between moral principles and economic demands, the paradox is that banks cannot afford to invest in their ethical commitments because of their economic expansion.

Literature Review on Corporate Social Responsibility and Financial Markets

The literature about the correlation between corporate social responsibility and financial markets is broad and diverse as well as multi-disciplined. Most of studies are empirical, some are qualitative and fewer are theoretical. Although these studies are carried out for various purposes, the contribution of banking to social responsibility to society and people is mainly evaluated. Some are concerned only with ethical banking, while others seek to establish a financial system based on social responsibility. In this section; the research topics, contents and findings of the studies conducted in the literature in terms of corporate social responsibility and banking will be revised.

In a study, Wu and Shen (2013) examined the financial data of 162 banks in 22 countries in the period 2003-2009 using the extended version of Heckman's two-stage regression, and investigated the driving force of corporate social responsibility (CSR), financial performance (FP) and banks' inclusion in CSR. The authors found that corporate social responsibility positively correlated with financial performance only in return on assets, return on equity, net interest income and non-interest income. The authors found that corporate social responsibility was positively associated with financial performance only in return on assets, return on equity, net interest income and non-interest income, whereas it was negatively correlated with non-performing loans. In another interesting study, Polychronidou et al. (2014) analyzed the ten largest Greek banks on the basis of environmental, community and CSR factors using a survey method. Thus, authors determined what CSR policies are made for in the Greek banking sector

Table 1. Ethics and financial markets

Author (s)	Content	Method	Period	Variables	Finding (s)
Harvey (1995)	Ethical approach to banking practice: British case	Quantitative research: 30,000 customers	1992-1993	Stakeholder dialogue, Corporate strategy and marketing	"Ethical banking strategy which built on the bank's differences from the others, and which benefited from an opportunity which was being ignored by them"
Gidding, Hopwood & O'Brien (2002)	Environment, economy and society: Sustainable development	Therotical framework		Futurity – inter-generational equity, Social justice – intra-generational equity, Transfrontier responsibility, Geographical equity	"The separation of environment, society and economy causes socio-economic problems which endangers the sustainability of communities and the maintenance of cultural diversity"
San-Jose, Retolaza & Gutierrez-Goiria (2011)	10 European countries: Differences between traditional financial institutions and ethical banks based on property rights	Radical Affinity Index (RAI): Sample of 114 European banks	2009	Ethical ideology, Information transparency, Placement of assets, Guarantees, Participation	"Transparency of information and placement of assets are factors that differentiate ethical banks from other financial intermediaries"
Forseth, Røyrvik & Clegg (2015)	Scandinavian financial institutions	An explorative, ethnographic study	1996-2014	Mis-selling Malpractice Right selling	"Jolts require members to develop new accounts of their practices as existing accounts are delegitimized"
Paulet, Parnaudeau & Relano (2015)	Behavior of the banking industry in the new business environment: Conventional banks vs. ethical banks	Factor analysis	2008	Profitability, Equity requirement, Speculation policy, Publication transparency	"Different response of both types of banks reflects the existence of a distinct business model" "Ethical banks had already integrated the new regulatory requirements in their distinct business model long before the subprime crisis" "Core business of ethical banks concentrates on granting credit at the local level"
Widana et al. (2015)	Relationship marketing and Islamic banking	Conceptual framwork		Educating individuals, Establishing justice, Promoting welfare	"Islamic banks must offer unique services and products differentiated by the implementation of Islamic business ethics to compute with conventional banks"
Gilani (2015)	Ethical aspects of Islamic banking	A qualitative research method, Thematic content analysis		Riba, Ethical banking, Treating its customers fairly	"The research indicates a positive image of Islamic banking in the international world based on ethical principles" "An innovative moral addition to the present capitalist banking sector for dealing with unjustly interest-based transactions, profit maximisation, speculative investments and debt-focussed banking transactions"
Chew, Tan & Hamid (2016)	UK Co-operative Banks	Qualitative focus group: Conducted on 20 senior bank managers	2012-2014	Sustainability of socioeconomic development, Regulations of economic and social instruments, CSR	"Co-operative Banks have done tremendously well in sustaining the socioenvironmental development of UK"
Oates & Dias (2016)	897 courses in banking and finance programmes in Australian universities	Content analysis	2014-2015	Ethics lectures	"809 out of 897 courses do not have ethics lectures in banking and finance programmes"

continued on following page

Table 1. Continued

Author (s)	Content	Method	Period	Variables	Finding (s)
Ferreira, Jalali & Ferreira (2016)	Context of ethical banking: identifying the main determinants of ethical practices for the integration inter between ethical theory and everyday business	Cognitive mapping		Commitment to customers, Well-being of employees, Transparency	"The analyse clearly shows the need for a greater concern with people, both within and outside of the organization"
Tan, Chew & Hamid (2017)	Maybank, Malaysia: Sustainable banking operating system	Qualitative: Interview with 35 bankers who were from different departments	2015	Customers, Government, Competitors, Meso-level drivers, Stakeholders, Macro-level drivers, Micro-level drivers	"Maybank is majorly motivated by its mission statement and vision statement, which is articulated in their sustainable banking agenda"
Aliyu et al. (2018)	Islamic banking sustainability	Literature review		Long-term economic, social and environmental sustainability	"Islamic banks should find a balance between the institutional, societal, and environmental sustainability in order to achieve the objective of Sharia"
Erdogan (2018)	Determine the factors affecting SME access to bank loans in Turkey	Thematic analysis: Semi-structured interviews with 25 Turkish bank managers		Bank loans, Profitability, Debt ratio, Current ratio, Firm's relationship with the bank	"Firms that have a long-term relationship with the bank and older firms have better access to bank loans"
Zainuldin, Lui & Yii (2018)	Ethics and agency theory in Islamic banking perspective	Literature review		Regulatory compliance, Depositors and shareholders structures	"Islamic banks are likely to have less severe agency problems relative to their conventional counterparts" "Islamic ethical system embedded in the Islamic banks business activities shapes Islamic banks into organisations that place higher ethical considerations than conventional banks"
Gheitani et al. (2019)	Impact of the Islamic work ethic on job satisfaction and organizational commitment: Employees of Bank Maskan	Survey (220 questinnaire)		Intrinsic motivation, Islamic work ethic, Job satisfaction, Organizational commitment	"Intrinsic motivation plays a partial and completely mediatory role in the relationship between IWE and job satisfaction and between IWE and organizational commitment"
San-Jose and Cuesta (2019)	Comparison of Islamic banks vs. ethical banks on RAI	Radical Affinity Index (RAI): Sample of 20 Islamic banks from 13 Islamic countries	2014	Transparency, Placement of assets, Guarantees, Participation	"Islamic banks, at least some of them could improve their ethical requirements of the Sharia: They obtained lower scores than ethical banks in terms of RAI variables"
Lenz & Neckel (2019)	German ethical banks	Theoretical framework, 27 qualitative interviews with employees of ethical banks		Moral principles, Economic demands	"A paradox of ethical banking: due to the banks' economic expansion, investments corresponding to their ethical commitments tend to become a luxury they cannot afford"

and concluded that banks actually use CSR to raise their image, attract more customers, and ultimately increase profits. In their theoretical studies, Mocan et al. (2015) investigated whether corporate social responsibility in the Romanian banks adds value to the banking sector. In this context, there are many benefits for banking institutions that carry out corporate social responsibility issues such as economic efficiency, increasing company reputation, employee loyalty, increasing communication and organizational commitment between the banking industry and society. In his study, Saeidi (2015) examined the relationship between CSR and firm performance with Balanced Scorecard methodology and found that reputation and competitive advantage mediated the relationship between CSR and firm performance. Investigating the two-way relationship between Corporate Social Responsibility and Financial Performance in companies listed in Spain, Rodriguez-Fernandez (2016) used both the theoretical framework and empirical analysis methods. In this study, various variables such as CSR, ROA, Dow Jones Sustainability Index, Madrid Stock Exchange were analyzed. As a result, it is emphasized that social policies increase financial resources and vice versa, the increase in financial performance leads to increase social benefits and thus contributes a welfare society.

Using the content analysis method, which analyzes 30 European banks in order to create a multidimensional ethical rating model based on the most important items representing corporate social responsibility, Birindelli et al. (2015) found that there are many international ethical principles that have not yet been followed in the institutions and that a demand for more ethical / quality certificates should be created. In another study, Valentine and Godkin (2017) researched the perception of corporate social responsibility with respect to the values of commitment and turnover intentions of individuals, conducting a survey for managers and employees, and found that corporate social responsibility was associated with increased value conformity commitment and this commitment to value compliance is negatively related to the intentions of turnover reported by the managers and employees. In another study investigating the mediation effect of corporate social responsibility outcomes on the relationship between CSR governance and financial performance, Wang and Sarkis (2017) analyzed the top 500 green firms in the USA between 2009-2013 with panel regression. As a result of this research, it was found that CSR outputs mediate the relationships between CSR governance and financial performance. However, it also shows that companies' successful implementation of CSR governance in order to produce good corporate social responsibility output has an important role affecting the financial performance of companies. Using panel regression method, Yüksel and Özsarı (2017) analyzed 23 commercial banks in Turkey with a variety of financial variables in terms of social responsibility. As a result of the research, it was found that there is a negative relationship between CSR activities and the ratio of nonperforming loans, while there is a positive relationship between asset return and corporate social responsibility activities. In another study using panel data analysis, Fayad et al. (2017) examined seven Lebanese banks in terms of financial performance and corporate social responsibility. As a result of the study which used the data in 2013-2015 period, it was found that there is a positive relationship between corporate social responsibility and financial performance. In addition, it is suggested that there is the highest chance of profit for a better image and legitimacy when investing in human, social development and environmental protection as a result of social responsibility.

In a study applying the experimental scenario technique, Bhardwaj et al. (2018) researched when and how investing in CSR can have a positive or negative effect on the profitability of the firm, and and concluded that firms should invest in CSR according to consumers' CSR discretion. In their survey of banks in India, Subba and Kumar (2018) found that corporate social responsibility also affects positive emotions through the creation of compassion in the workplace in addition to the direct impact of corporate social responsibility. Similarly, Maqbool and Zameer (2018) investigated the relationship between corporate social responsibility and financial performance in the Indian context and analyzed 28 Indian commercial banks traded on the Bombay Stock Exchange by using panel regression method. As a result of this study, it provides important information about management in order to integrate corporate social responsibility with the strategic purpose of the business and to transform the business philosophy from traditional profit oriented approach to socially responsible approach. In a similar study in which the data of 21 banks in Nigeria for 2010-2014 period were analyzed by panel regression method, Oyewumi et al. (2018) investigated the impact of corporate social responsibility investments and disclosures on corporate financial performance. As a result of this study, it is revealed that CSR investments made without a special case disclosure will make little or no contribution to the corporate financial performance. In another

Table 2. Corporate social responsibility and financial markets

Author (s)	Content	Method	Period	Variables	Finding (s)
Wu & Shen (2013)	162 banks in 22 countries: Corporate social responsibility & financial performance (FP) Discussing the driving motives of banks to engage in CSR	Extended Version of the Heckman two-step Regression	2003-2009	ROA, ROE, NPL, CSR, Leverage, LoanDep, Corruption	"CSR positively associates with FP in terms of return on assets, return on equity, net interest income, and non-interest income. In contrast, CSR negatively associates with non-performing loans"
Polychronidou et al. (2014)	Ten biggest banks in Greece: CSR policies in banking sector in Greece	Survey	2012-2013	CSR, Enivorment, Society	"Banks use CSR to strengthen their image, attract more clients and eventually increase their profits" "Respondents state that they would not change their bank because of the CSR program"
Mocan et al. (2015)	Romanian banks: Contribution of corporate social responsibility to value creation in the banking industry	Theoritical framework		Improved products related to the needs of society, Increasing motivation of employees, Good relationship with the stakeholders, Social integration and banking reputation	"Benefits for the banking institutions with performing CSR: economic efficiency, improved company reputation, employee loyalty, communication between the banking industry and society"
Saeidi (2015)	205 Iranian manufacturing and consumer product firms: Relationship between CSR and firm performance	Balanced Scorecard Methodology		Sustainable competitive advantage, Reputation, Customer satisfaction, ROE, ROA, ROI	"The positive effect of CSR on firm performance: competitive advantage, reputation, and customer satisfaction"
Birindelli et al. (2015)	30 European banks: Construction of a multidimensional ethical rating model, based on many items that represent the most significant Corporate Social Responsibility drivers of the banks.	Content analysis		Sustainability Report, Compliance with GRI standards, External audit Stakeholder, Engagement Report, Economic value distributed to community and environment	"Still many international principles which have not yet been adhered to and an increase in requests for more ethical/quality certifications"
Rodriguez-Fernandez(2016)	Spanish listed companies: Investigating bidirectional relationship between Corporate Social Responsibility and Financial Performance	Theoretical Framework, Emprical Analysis	2009	CSR, FP, ROA ROE Good Corporate Governance, Dow Jones Sustainability Index, Madrid Stock Exchange	"Social policies increase financial resources, and vice versa, that increased financial performances lead to greater social benefits" "Investing financial resources in developing policies that contribute globally to the improvement of society"
Valentine & Godkin (2017)	Determining the degree to which perceptions of corporate social responsibility are related to individuals' value-fit commitment and turnover intentions	Survey: Managers and employees		Value-fit commitment, Perceived corporate social responsibility, Manager-reported turnover intention, Employee-reported turnover intention	"Corporate social responsibility was associated with increased value-fit commitment, and that value-fit commitment was negatively related to employee-reported and manager-reported turnover intentions"
Wang & Sarkis (2017)	Top 500 U.S. Green companies: Investigating the mediation effect of CSR outcomes, on the relationship between CSR governance and financial performance	Panel Regression	2009–2013	CSR Governance, Corporate environmental and social outcomes, Return on Assets, Tobin's Q	"CSR outcomes mediate the relationships between CSR governance and financial performance"
Yüksel & Özsari (2017)	23 deposit banks in Turkey	Panel Regression	2005-2015	Total Assets, ROA, ROE, Nonperforming Loans, Capital Adequacy Ratio	"Negative relationship between CSR activities and nonperforming loans and positive relationship between return on asset and corporate social responsibility activities" "Banks don't prefer social responsibility activities if there are higher financial losses"

continued on following page

Table 2. Continued

Author (s)	Content	Method	Period	Variables	Finding (s)
Fayad, Ayoub & Ayoub (2017)	7 Lebanese banks: Corporate social responsibility on financial performance (FP) of Lebanese banks	Panel Data Analysis	2013-2015	ROA, ROE, CSR, Economic Development, Community Development, Environmental Protection, Human Development	"Positive relation between CSR and financial performance: If the investments are made into human, economic, community development and environmental protection, higher profit leads for a better image and legitimacy"
Bhardwaj et al. (2018)	Investing in CSR: Positive or negative impact on a firm's profitability	Experimental scenario technique		CSR, CA (company ability relevant), NCA (company ability irrelevant)	"Consumers' willingness to pay for a firm's product increases when they observe that the firm invests in CSR of either type. Both firms should invest in CSR-CA if consumers' appreciation of CSR is high"
Subba & Kumar (2018)	Banking industry of India: Corporate social responsibility and positive emotions among employees	Survey: 241 samples		CSR, Compassion at work place, Positive emotions	"CSR influences positive emotions through compassion at workplace. Compassion mediates the relationship between CSR and positive emotion which is a new contribution to the literature"
Maqbool & Zameer (2018)	28 Indian commercial banks listed in Bombay stock exchange (BSE): Corporate social responsibility and financial performance in Indian context	Panel Regression	2007-2016	ROE, ROA, NPL, SR (Stock return), CSR	"CSR exerts positive impact on financial performance of the Indian banks" "Good insights for management, to integrate the CSR with strategic intent of the business, and renovate their business philosophy from traditional profit-oriented to socially responsible approach"
Oyewumi, Ogunmeru & Oboh (2018)	21 banks in Nigeria: Effects of corporate social responsibility investment and disclosure on corporate financial performance	Panel Data Analysis	2010-2014	CSR investment, Financial Performance	"CSR investment without due disclosure would have little or no contribution to corporate financial performance"
Han, Zhuangxion & Jie (2018)	Chinese listed firms: Effects of Market competition on firms' product market performance	Panel Regression Analysis	2008-2014	CSR, Product market competition, Total Assets, Operating revenue, Sales growth, Profitability	"CSR significantly decreases firms' product market performance only in noncompetitive industries for non-state-owned firms"
Dinçer et al. (2019)	Turkish deposit banks	Fuzzy DEMATEL/ MOORA		Transparency, Face-to-face communication, Appropriateness to the purpose, Education, Health, Environment	"Transparency is found as the most important factor in the criterion set and environment has the best degree in the alternative set" "Banks should be very transparent especially in the crisis period which has positive effects on the minds of the consumers"
Lin et al. (2019)	100 of the Fortune Most Admired Companies: Corporate social responsibility and corporate financial performance (CFP)	Panel VAR	2007-2016	CSR, ROA, ROE, ROIC	"Better financial performance of firms lead to a better CSR engagement" "Better CSR does not necessarily lead to superior CFP"
Rezaee, Dou & Zhang (2019)	2580 Chinese listed firms: Association between corporate social responsibility and earnings quality using CSR ranking data	Multiple Regression	2009–2015	CSRR, State, Market Size, Loss	"CSR firms and those with higher CSR ratings are less likely to engage in earnings management than non-CSR firms and those with lower CSR ratings, and their earnings are more persistent and more accurately predict future cash flows from operations" "State ownership and marketization moderate the relationship between CSR disclosures and earnings quality"
(Sheikh, 2019)	2,009 Companies from MSCI and Compustat Database: Impact of market competition on the relationship between CSR and firm leverage	OLS Regression	1996-2015	Leverage, Firm specific wealth, Free cash flows, Profitability, Fixed assets ratio	"CSR is negatively associated with both book leverage and market leverage. CSR has a negative effect on firm leverage only when competition in product markets is high. When is low, CSR has no impact"

study similarly using panel regression method for Chinese listed firms between 2008-2014 period, Han et al. (2018) examined the impact of corporate social responsibility (CSR) on product market performance and underlying mechanism as a result of product market competition. As a result of the research, corporate social responsibility significantly reduces the product market performance of firms only in non-competitive industries and for non-Governmental companies with weak debt financing capacity.

In an interesting study investigating Turkish deposit banks using Fuzzy DEMATEL / MOORA method, Dinçer et al. (2019) determined transparency, face-to-face communication, eligibility, education, health, environment, etc. factors in accordance with the research subject. As a result of the research, transparency was found to be the most important factor in the criteria set and environment was best in alternative set. Subsequently it is emphasized that banks should be very transparent especially during the crisis and banks should be prone to environmental problems in their corporate social responsibility activities. Using panel VAR method in line with 2007-2016 data, Lin et al. (2019) analyzed the Fortune 100 Most Admired Companies in terms of corporate social responsibility and corporate financial performance. As a result of the analysis, it has been found that better financial performance of firms leads to better corporate social responsibility participation, but vice versa, good corporate social responsibility does not lead to better corporate financial performance. Using multiple regression method according to the 2009-2015 data of 2580 Chinese companies listed on the stock exchange, Rezaee et al. (2019) analyzed the relationship between corporate social responsibility and earnings quality by using the CSR ranking data. As a result of the study, it was found that companies with higher CSR scores had less participation in earnings management than those with low CSR scores, and the relationship between earnings quality and CSR scores was stronger for firms in cities with a marketing index score above the national average. In another similar study using OLS regression method for 1996-2015 period data, Sheikh (2019) analyzed the effect of market competition on the relationship between corporate social responsibility and firm leverage. In the analysis results, corporate social responsibility is negatively related to both book leverage and market leverage; however, if the competition in the product markets is high, the firm has a negative effect on the leverage, vice versa in low competition there is no effect.

ETHICAL ASPECTS AND CONCEPTS OF ISLAMIC BANKING IN FINANCIAL MARKETS

Islamic definition for banking services comes from the way of banking in accordance with Islamic rules, Sharia. Islam is a religion that regulates every side of life. Therefore, Islam is in the center of life, not just brings divine services for people beside coordinate norms and system for society such as providing and ensuring justice, development and morality. Prohibition of interest is the most commonly known feature of Islamic banking, but that is not the single rule. Otherwise there are such working banks, but they are not named as Islamic banks. There are other rules and prohibition such like prohibition of alcohol and pork etc. What understood about interest by the perspective of Islam; the borrower has to pay a pre-determined interest irrespective of whether he makes a profit or loss. This is seen unjust according to Islam because if the borrower makes a loss, he has still to pay interest because of the lender's supposed "opportunity cost", which is unfair against the borrower. In case the borrower makes a profit at a rate bigger than the interest rate he has to pay, the lender gets a return which is lower than his money actually earned; this is considered unfair against the lender and accepted as unethical (Lewis & Algaoud, 2001; Mannan, 1986).

Just as every system and model has its own principles, Islamic banking has also its own principles. The theoretical studies conducted in this field first reveal the framework of Islamic banking in line with the basic sources of Islam and the perspectives of the ongoing practices in Islamic societies. With the establishment of Islamic banks in the 1970s, the principles of Islamic banking became clear in the process of practical implementation. The basis of the interest-free banking system are the rules based on the principles of interest-free economy. These rules are not only a financial model, but also related to the economic, social, political and cultural life of the society. The basis of these rules is the Quran and Sunnah. These rules and methods were developed as a result of ijtihads made by Islamic scholars in accordance with the original principles (Iqbal & Mirakhor, 1999; Siddiqi, 2006; Usmani, 2001).

There are many definitions of ethical banking, including a general definition of ethical banking: a system that works on promoting equality, responsibility, accountability and sustainable development (Gilani, 2104). Ethical social responsibilities connected to socio-economic structure reveal the fact that Islamic financial institutions are more obliged to serve their customers by providing funds in their portfolios. In this respect, Islamic banks become institutions of economic development and thus play an important role in the economic and corporate social responsibilty of Islamic society (Siddiqi, 1997).

However, the distinctive features of Islamic banking failed to internalize corporate social responsibilty and social justice into its operational function, as the value system was reduced to a technical definition of Riba. As a result, it should be to focus on the core structure of Islam in order to overcome the failure of Islamic banking in terms of social responsibility. It is necessary to establish an institutional transformation model based on morality and social responsibility by going beyond the Islamic banking aiming to maximize commercial profit. Thus, a more sustainable financing and banking system should be established where the moral values in which the projects aiming social responsibility and development are applied have priority (Asutay, 2008).

SOLUTIONS AND RECOMMENDATIONS

Although there is a clear relationship between Islamic banking and ethical banking systems, there is concern by non-muslim communities that Islamic banking is a financial management system specific to those belonging to the Muslim community. In fact, Islamic banking is based on the fact that it is based on universal ethical principles, characterizing profit and loss sharing banking and even interest-free banking. With these definitions, Islamic banking can help to open both Muslims and non-Muslim communities and to large masses of moral sensitivity. (Gilani, 2014). In this context, Islamic banking should place more emphasis on universal moral principles in order to express itself to the wider masses. They can do this mainly in terms of the way they do business and benefit the society in which they live. This is possible by providing a participatory business and finance model and being beneficial to people, society and nature due to corporate social responsibility. Only by building social peace and prosperity can a sustainable financial system be built.

FUTURE RESEARCH DIRECTIONS

It is necessary to conduct both theoretical and empirical studies on the moral foundations of Islamic banking. This can be evaluated both by investigating the structural probes of Islamic banking and by examining employees and clients of these institutions. In the light of the findings obtained in the litareture research, many different studies can be done. The studies mainly focus on the question of how banks should act in the face of the moral-economic dilemma. Furthermore, ethical and Islamic banks will be able to implement a business and financial model in the current financial market system by preserving their differences (in terms of moral sensitivity) from conventional banks and how to put it into a sustainable form.

CONCLUSION

The literature about the relationship between ethics, corporate social responsibility and financial markets is broad and diverse as well as multi-disciplined. Some studies theoretical, most of them are econometric and quantitative, others are qualititative. The reasons for conducting these studies are as diverse as the research subject. Some are concerned only with ethical banking, while others seek to establish a financial system based on on social responsibility to society and people. In literature review section; the research topics, scope and findings of the studies conducted in the literature in terms of ethics and corporate social responsibility and banking were reviewed. Thus, a framework was drawn to make sense of the ethical foundations of Islamic banking. Hereby, Islamic finance and specifically Islamic banking can be seen as a new practice to bring corporate ethical responsibility and social justice into the financial and economic spheres.

REFERENCES

Aliyu, S., Hassan, M. K., Mohd Yusof, R., & Naiimi, N. (2017). Islamic banking sustainability: a review of literature and directions for future research. *Emerging Markets Finance & Trade*, *53*(2), 440–470. doi:10.1080/1540496X.2016.1262761

Asutay, M. (2008). *Islamic banking and finance: social failure. New Horizon, No. 169* (pp. 1–3). October-December; doi:10.2139srn.1735674

Bhardwaj, P., Chatterjee, P., Demir, K. D., & Turut, O. (2018). When and how is corporate social responsibility profitable? *Journal of Business Research*, *84*, 206–219. doi:10.1016/j.jbusres.2017.11.026

Birindelli, G., Ferretti, P., Intonti, M., & Iannuzzi, A. P. (2015). On the drivers of corporate social responsibility in banks: Evidence from an ethical rating model. *The Journal of Management and Governance*, *19*(2), 303–340. doi:10.100710997-013-9262-9

Campa, D., & Zijlmans, E. W. A. (2019). Corporate social responsibility recognition and support for the arts: Evidence from European financial institutions. *European Management Journal*. doi:10.1016/j.emj.2019.01.003

Chew, B., Tan, L., & Hamid, S. (2016). Ethical banking in practice: A closer look at the Co-operative Bank UK PLC. *Qualitative Research in Financial Markets, 8*(1), 70–91. doi:10.1108/QRFM-02-2015-0008

Dinçer, H., Yüksel, S., Yazici, M., & Pınarbaşı, F. (2019). Assessing corporate social responsibilities in the banking sector: as a tool of strategic communication during the global financial crisis. In Handbook of research on global issues in financial communication and investment decision making (pp. 1–27). Hershey, PA: IGI Global. doi:10.4018/978-1-5225-9265-5.ch001

Erdogan, A. I. (2018). Factors affecting SME access to bank financing: An interview study with Turkish bankers. *Small Enterprise Research, 25*(1), 23–35. doi:10.1080/13215906.2018.1428911

Fayad, A. A., Ayoub, R., & Ayoub, M. (2017). Causal relationship between CSR and FB in banks. *Arab Economic and Business Journal, 12*(2), 93–98. doi:10.1016/j.aebj.2017.11.001

Ferreira, F. A. F., Jalali, M. S., & Ferreira, J. J. M. (2016). Experience-focused thinking and cognitive mapping in ethical banking practices: From practical intuition to theory. *Journal of Business Research, 69*(11), 4953–4958. doi:10.1016/j.jbusres.2016.04.058

Forseth, U., Røyrvik, E. A., & Clegg, S. (2015). Brave new world? The global financial crisis' impact on Scandinavian banking's sales rhetoric and practices. *Scandinavian Journal of Management, 31*(4), 471–479. doi:10.1016/j.scaman.2015.06.003

Gheitani, A., Imani, S., Seyyedamiri, N., & Foroudi, P. (2019). Mediating effect of intrinsic motivation on the relationship between Islamic work ethic, job satisfaction, and organizational commitment in banking sector. *International Journal of Islamic and Middle Eastern Finance and Management, 12*(1), 76–95. doi:10.1108/IMEFM-01-2018-0029

Giddings, B., Hopwood, B., & O'Brien, G. (2002). Environment, economy and society: Fitting them together into sustainable development. *Sustainable Development, 10*(4), 187–196. doi:10.1002d.199

Gilani, H. (2015). Exploring the ethical aspects of Islamic banking. *International Journal of Islamic and Middle Eastern Finance and Management, 8*(1), 85–98. doi:10.1108/IMEFM-09-2012-0087

Han, W., Zhuangxiong, Y., & Jie, L. (2018). Corporate social responsibility, product market competition, and product market performance. *International Review of Economics & Finance, 56,* 75–91. doi:10.1016/j.iref.2018.03.019

Harvey, B. (1995). Ethical banking: The case of the Co-operative bank. *Journal of Business Ethics, 14*(12), 1005–1013. doi:10.1007/BF00872116

Iqbal, Z., & Mirakhor, A. (1999). Progress and challenges of Islamic banking. *Thunderbird International Business Review, 41*(4-5), 381–405. doi:10.1002/tie.4270410406

Lenz, S., & Neckel, S. (2019). Ethical banks between moral self-commitment and economic expansion. In S. Schiller-Merkens, & P. Balsiger (Eds.), The Contested Moralities of Markets (Research in the Sociology of Organizations, Vol. 63). Emerald. pp. 127-148. doi:10.1108/S0733-558X20190000063015

Lewis, M. K., & Algaoud, L. M. (2001). *Islamic banking.* Edward Elgar.

Lin, W. L., Law, S. H., Ho, J. A., & Sambasivan, M. (2019). The causality direction of the corporate social responsibility – Corporate financial performance Nexus: Application of Panel Vector Autoregression approach. *The North American Journal of Economics and Finance, 48*, 401–418. doi:10.1016/j.najef.2019.03.004

Mannan, M. A. (1986). *Islamic economics: Theory and practice.* Cambridge, UK: Hodder & Stoughton.

Maqbool, S., & Zameer, M. N. (2018). Corporate social responsibility and financial performance: An empirical analysis of Indian banks. *Future Business Journal, 4*(1), 84–93. doi:10.1016/j.fbj.2017.12.002

Mocan, M., Rus, S., Draghici, A., Ivascu, L., & Turi, A. (2015). Impact of corporate social responsibility practices on the banking industry in Romania. *Procedia Economics and Finance, 23*, 712–716. doi:10.1016/S2212-5671(15)00473-6

Oates, G., & Dias, R. (2016). Including ethics in banking and finance programs: Teaching "we shouldn't win at any cost". *Education + Training, 58*(1), 94–111. doi:10.1108/ET-12-2014-0148

Oyewumi, O. R., Ogunmeru, O. A., & Oboh, C. S. (2018). Investment in corporate social responsibility, disclosure practices, and financial performance of banks in Nigeria. *Future Business Journal, 4*(2), 195–205. doi:10.1016/j.fbj.2018.06.004

Paulet, E., Parnaudeau, M., & Relano, F. (2015). Banking with ethics: strategic moves and structural changes of the banking industry in the aftermath of the subprime mortgage crisis. *Journal of Business Ethics, 131*(1), 199–207. doi:10.100710551-014-2274-9

Polychronidou, P., Ioannidou, E., Kipouros, A., Tsourgiannis, L., & Simet, G. F. (2014). Corporate social responsibility in Greek banking sector – an empirical research. *Procedia Economics and Finance, 9*, 193–199. doi:10.1016/S2212-5671(14)00020-3

Rezaee, Z., Dou, H., & Zhang, H. (2019). Corporate social responsibility and earnings quality: Evidence from China. *Global Finance Journal, 100473.* doi:10.1016/j.gfj.2019.05.002

Rodriguez-Fernandez, M. (2016). Social responsibility and financial performance: The role of good corporate governance. *BRQ Business Research Quarterly, 19*(2), 137–151. doi:10.1016/j.brq.2015.08.001

Saeidi, S. P., Sofian, S., Saeidi, P., Saeidi, S. P., & Saaeidi, S. A. (2015). How does corporate social responsibility contribute to firm financial performance? The mediating role of competitive advantage, reputation, and customer satisfaction. *Journal of Business Research, 68*(2), 341–350. doi:10.1016/j.jbusres.2014.06.024

San-Jose, L., & Cuesta, J. (2019). Are Islamic banks different? The application of the Radical Affinity Index. *International Journal of Islamic and Middle Eastern Finance and Management, 12*(1), 2–29. doi:10.1108/IMEFM-07-2017-0192

San-Jose, L., Retolaza, J. L., & Gutierrez-Goiria, J. (2011). Are ethical banks different? A comparative analysis using the radical affinity index. *Journal of Business Ethics, 100*(1), 151–173. doi:10.100710551-011-0774-4

Sheikh, S. (2019). Corporate social responsibility and firm leverage: The impact of market competition. *Research in International Business and Finance, 48*, 496–510. doi:10.1016/j.ribaf.2018.11.002

Siddiqi, M. N. (2006). Islamic banking and finance in theory and practice: A survey of state of the art. *Islamic Economic Studies*, *13*(2).

Subba, D., & Kumar, S. (2018). Employees' responses to corporate social responsibility: A study among the employees of banking industry in India. *Decision (Washington, D.C.)*, *45*(4), 301–312. doi:10.100740622-018-0194-8

Tan, L., Chew, B., & Hamid, S. (2017). A holistic perspective on sustainable banking operating system drivers. *Qualitative Research in Financial Markets*, *9*(3), 240–262. doi:10.1108/QRFM-12-2016-0052

Usmani, M. M. T. (2001). An introduction to Islamic finance. In *An introduction to Islamic finance*. Brill Publishing.

Valentine, S., & Godkin, L. (2017). Banking employees' perceptions of corporate social responsibility, value-fit commitment, and turnover intentions: ethics as social glue and attachment. *Employee Responsibilities and Rights Journal*, *29*(2), 51–71. doi:10.100710672-017-9290-8

Wang, Z., & Sarkis, J. (2017). Corporate social responsibility governance, outcomes, and financial performance. *Journal of Cleaner Production*, *162*, 1607–1616. doi:10.1016/j.jclepro.2017.06.142

Widana, G. O., Wiryono, S. K., Purwanegara, M. S., & Toha, M. (2015). Exploring the impact of Islamic business ethics and relationship marketing orientation on business performance: the Islamic banking experience. Asian Academy of Management Journal, 20(1).

Wu, M.-W., & Shen, C.-H. (2013). Corporate social responsibility in the banking industry: Motives and financial performance. *Journal of Banking & Finance*, *37*(9), 3529–3547. doi:10.1016/j.jbankfin.2013.04.023

Yüksel, S., & Özsari, M. (2017). Identifying the factors influence Turkish deposit banks to join corporate social responsibility activities by using panel probit method. *International Journal of Finance & Banking Studies*, *6*(1), 39.

Zainuldin, M., Lui, T., & Yii, K. (2018). Principal-agent relationship issues in Islamic banks: A view of Islamic ethical system. *International Journal of Islamic and Middle Eastern Finance and Management*, *11*(2), 297–311. doi:10.1108/IMEFM-08-2017-0212

Chapter 9
Globalization Phenomenon and Cruising of Multinational Companies Under Global Market Conditions

Fulya Kıvılcım
FEDEK, Turkey

ABSTRACT

This chapter clarifies the definition of the phenomenon of globalization, historical development, the rapid and radical change that has taken place in the world. In the context of globalization, and in developing global market conditions, the author examines the course of Multinational Corporations in the globalization process; to emphasize the company structure models they own, competition, strategic management, and decision-making policies they follow, and primarily based on the importance they place on the structure of innovative thinking.

INTRODUCTION

Main issue regarding the concept of globalization is the capability of local decisions to go beyond political borders to reach other nations and have the power to affect them.

Taken into consideration particularly the last 30 years of process; the world has felt the magnitude of globalization on every level and according to the conditions that are created by the present era, will keep on feeling in the approaching years with an even higher effect.

In this manner; study will consist of three main parts, a definition of globalization will be elaborated, a brief historical development process will be included, then with an evaluation of its levels, actors of globalization process and effects of actors on the process will be verbalized with reference to multinational corporations. In the second section of the work, mentioning the definition of multinational corporation, its historical development and technological models, the main target of this work, the interaction between

DOI: 10.4018/978-1-7998-2559-3.ch009

globalization and multinational corporations and especially the power of manipulation of multinational corporations in the process will be approached.

Multinational corporations' role in the process of globalization and the interaction between them will be tried to be evaluated on the perspective of technology transfer model that had been internalized by multinational corporations to expound the interaction between globalization in developing market conditions and multinational corporations.

DEFINITION AND DEVELOPMENT OF GLOBALIZATION

Historical Development of Globalization

Describing an old process even though being a new word (Ellwood, 2002). and becoming a key-phrase in the illustration of the world's virtually re-creation, a common definition of 'globalization' has not been made despite the richness of literature and interest shown by the circles. The situation had been expressed by Zengingonul as such: The common feature of globalization definitions is that they cannot agree upon a 'common' definition (Zengingönül, 2004). Although it is not easy to provide a clear and complete definition of globalization, it may be expressed as transfrontier mutual economic integration as a result of increasing mobility of assets, services and capital and, increasing interaction between people and states that are found in different places in the world and becoming mutually co-dependent in the process of a national economy to be involved in global market. Considering the other definitions in the literature again related with nation, "globalization virtually increased and widened mutual social co-dependency by eliminating geographical, political and cultural borders thus; a structure is achieved where the opposition of far and near had been eliminated, transfrontier interaction levels had been developed."(Steger, 2006) Based on this definition, Giddens' interpretation is; "Globalization may be expressed as, local organizations shaped by events that are kilometers away or condensation of worldwide international relations that achieves to connect far away localities"(Giddens, 2006).

First use of globalization took place in an article on distribution and usage of natural resources written by British Economist W. Foter in 1833 and also found in The Economist journal in 4th of April 1959. Contemporary use of globalization is based on Garett Hardin's work regarding distribution and usage of sources written in 1968 (Karabıçak, 2002). Globalization is considered an economical concept by many researchers. However, perceiving globalization only as an economical base makes it harder to conceive. Because it is clear, especially while trying to elaborate on the concept in the manner of definitions in the literature, that globalization is not only an economical advancement, and its social, cultural and political aspects also have significance.

As it is seen, while an unshared portrayal of globalization that is a multi-dimensional concept and leading topic for researches especially made by social scientists is not available; common aspect that every researcher working on the subject agrees upon is the necessity to multiapproach the concept regarding economic, political, socio-cultural and technological dimensions.

As the essentiality to emphasize on the vital point of globalization under the light of all these definitions, with the process of globalization, global issues have no borders and control mechanisms anymore (Bauman, 2010).

When the historical development process of globalization is examined; First Globalization occurred between the dates 1870 and 1914 as the World Bank indicated. While the main aspect of the activities during the first globalization period was economic, the purpose of it was to expand the concept and change the influenced areas. During the first globalization period, advancements in navigation, invention of telegraph and developments in railways constituted the opportunity for the West to transmit its political, military and commercial effect into land that had not (could not) been accessed until that period (Oran, 2001). Furthermore, intensification of competition in international trade in this novel period resulted in expertise in production. According to Yilmaz; technological developments had reached advanced levels, increasing connection between nations and people (Yılmaz, 2007).

The period between 1914 and 1945 states the Second Globalization. Though, the period is known as a period of stagnation as it coincides certain events in human history. Eruption of the World War I in 1914, occurrence of the Great Depression in 1929 and then the beginning of the World War II had decelerated the globalization process (Şen, 1999). Scilicet, wars and depressions as their result have blocked globalization from constituting a consistency and led to different periods of globalization. It is noticed that during World War II, international capital circulation had been subjected to strict surveillance and the IMF and the World Bank had been designed in an environment of confined private capital circulation to provide potentiality to international commerce and investments, after that the restrictions on the capital circulation had been eliminated in time and by the beginning of 1980's, during Reagan and M. Theachar period, international capital mobility had increased especially by the dissolution of the Soviets in the beginning of 1990's, financial market became genuinely global. Indeed, the magnitude of international organizations such as IMF, the World Bank, GATT, Organization for Economic Cooperation and Development (OECD) to increase the momentum of globalization process have great importance. Such international organizations that almost all of them found in the second half of 1940's had been founded by the aegis of the USA and with the contribution of these organizations, according to Aktan and Sen, a new globalization wave had emerged in the 1950's and 1960's. Another milestone for the Second Globalization happened during 1970's: With the declension of Bretton Woods System in August 1971 fixed rate system had been abandoned and advanced countries such as the US, Germany, England and Japan had consecutively eliminated restrictions on capital movements. Elimination of restrictions on capital movements in these countries resulted in a great increase in acceleration of financial globalization (Şen, 1999). Another reason behind the increased velocity of globalization after 1970's were the effects of developing technology and expansion of increased production markets. Therefore; after mid 1970's, countries, adhering to the market logic, had begun to act according to the necessities of commercial liberation. According to Aslan; "especially while in advanced economies after 1945, foreign market dominance based on technological advancements and "Keynesian" economics towards keeping demand and purchase power at high level had secured growth for long period, a shift in the conditions after 1970 had brought together political changes (Aslan, 2005). 1980 and beyond is the period of third globalization in the history of globalization. Third globalization is a quite different, complex and multi-dimensional period. Advancements with expedition had been on a wide range from technology to communication, from social life to environment. Globalization after 1980 basically staged these developments and became prominent: Actions of corporations that focus on industry, quick market reforms, dazzling developments in product and manufacture technology and escalating competition. Economic and political collapse of former Eastern Bloc countries after 1990 led to the climax of this process. Regulated with planned economy, these countries economically and politically approached the Western countries in time (Şen, 1999). Most authors claim that the increasing wave of globalization, especially after the year of 1990, is resulted by the environment after the dissolution of bipolar military balance. The device of third globalization is, as the common opinion of researchers, is the advancement

Table 1. Evaluation of three globalization periods

	First Expansion (1490's)	**Second Expansion (1890's)**	**Third Expansion (1940's)**
Impetus	Mercantilism	First Industrial Revolution	Second Industrial Revolution/Information Age Multinational Corporations in the 1970's Revolution of Communication in 1980's West becoming unrivalled in the 1990's with the dissolution of USSR.
Method	Conquerors, explorers and military invasion	First missionaries, then explorers, then commercial corporations, ultimately military invasion	Cultural, ideological effect
Justification	We carry the religion of God to infidels.	Bargain of the White Men Civilizing mission White supremacy	The Highest level of civilization Will of the international community The Invisible Hand of the market Globalization is beneficial for everyone We bring democracy to Afghanistan by attacking
Result	Colonialism	Imperialism	Globalization

Sources: (Oran, 2001); (Sivrikaya, 2012b)

in science and technology. Therefore, the third globalization period is also named as the Information Age. Oran explains the arrival of Third Globalization around these consecutive occurrences that took place ten years apart from each other (Oran, 2001).

Starting from the 70's, domination of multinational corporations on the global market. The Revolution of Communication that was created by the West in the 80's by enabling inventions like optical cable, communications satellite, computers and the Internet.

Elimination of power balance after the dissolution of USSR and West, becoming the single power center in the 90's. One of the main dynamics and one of the main symbols of the third globalization had been communication and the Internet consecutively. The Internet technology plays a significant role in realization of globalization by forming World Wide Web (www) and eliminating the difficulties related to distance (Şen, 1999). Developments in transportation had always been an important element in globalizations.

In each globalization period, important developments in transportation were supported by inventions in communication therefore, resulting in globalization. Another feature of third globalization is such developments in transportation industry that resolved geographical handicaps. Aerial transportation had been added to already advanced railroads and navigation leading to an affordable and easy transportation. It is certain that this had great impact on forming a 'global structure'. Therefore, some authors connect the contemporary globalization age to these developments (Atasoy, 2005).

As seen and tried to be explained in Table, the development phases of globalization may be summarized in three periods while the essential point to be mentioned before development phase is that the history of the process is not based on late history. First globalization period started in the late 1890's and continued until World War I. As a result of industrial revolution that had a great impact on this period manufacture speed had increased and parallel to this, international trade operations had been intensified. The process that we call the second period of globalization had started by the end of World War II and affected until 1970's, while the last and perhaps the strongest period of globalization, third globalization has started during 1980's and reached this day. With the period of the process, international trade has increased noticeably, production activities stopped being a country-based local activity and continued as an international process therefore leading to the age of information.

Globalization from the Aspect of Economical Phenomenon

As the popular opinion verbalized by intellectuals, globalization gathers its power and domination from the process of economics that is to say economical laws. As this idea suggests, primary dimension of globalization is economics. Next, the opinion that after getting over vital challenges in human life, global and political and other relations that we may call superstructure like difficulties towards government etc. bring together globalizations is noteworthy in the intellectual field (Sağlam, 2007a).

Economic globalization denotes general embodiment of country economics, coalescence of the world into a solitary market. In other words, economic globalization is expressed as development in economic interactions with the increase of asset, capital and labor fluidity between countries, intensification and predomination of mutual interactions on a global scale (Fischer, 2003).

To view another instance on the definition of economic globalization, according to Steger; economic globalization stands for increasing intensity and popularity of economical interactions throughout the world(Steger, 2006).

One of the most significant developments on the process of economic globalization is the increase in intercountry cross-fertilization, cooperation and similarity as a result of intensified commercial operations. National relations alter as the commercial networks increase, international preferences develop, become widespread and even become compulsory (Aslan, 2005). As a matter of fact, some developments played a great role in the popularization of international trade or globalization of trade in other words.

At the beginning of these developments are the works conducted to achieve liberation of commerce in universal scale by eliminating custom tariffs and limitations within the framework GATT which is founded in 1947. (Today World Trade Organization (WTO) stands for GATT). In addition, technological improvements (communication and correspondence) have great impact. With these developments, transportation costs had been reduced, international market became easily trackable (Seyidoğlu, 2003b).

As it is seen, economic globalization is the main facet of globalization. Development of economic globalization starts with the Bretton Woods Conference that took place near the end of World War II. The conclusion of the conference was decided on elimination of protective policies that were in charge between the two world wars. Every attendant country on the conference agreed upon improving international trade and therefore, decided to form an exchange rate system in which every currency is fixed on gold price in US Dollar. Besides, Bretton Woods Conference established the foundations of three international economic organizations. These are, International Monetary Fund to manage the international economic system, the World Bank to provide credits to European Countries that attempt to escape war economics and General Agreement on Tariffs and Trade (GATT) to make global trade agreements. Although the Bretton Woods system had collapsed in thirty years, it accomplished its mission on that period on laid the groundwork for contemporary international economic institutions and multinational corporations (Sivrikaya, 2012c).

To conclude this part without mentioning three constituent of economic globalization which is the main element of globalization would not be sufficient. First thing to be emphasized is the improvement of world trade operations with the elimination of taxes and limitations. As the second element is growth of global financial market and increased mobility of global capital, third sub-constituent of economic globalization may be expressed as manufacturing industry going beyond local borders in the manner of cheap labor and resources etc. mostly operated by multinational corporations(Bayar, 2008).

Even though the multinational corporations' part had not been yet expressed, with the economic globalization ruling class of the world economy had altered and new actors had appeared. In this scope, while evaluating the economic dimension of globalization, importance of multinational corporations should not be overlooked. In the recent era; multinational corporations are able to dominate the world economy with their assets and yearly based profits and weaken political authorities with the power they gain in the international arena.

Globalization from the Political Approach

One of the arguments over the paradigm of the state's political and economic operations in the international system finds its roots in an archetype that brings Grotius with Hobbes, De Jure Pacis ac Belli with Leviathan face to face. Grotius, a Dutch lawyer, while emphasizing the international role of individuals and international institutions; he also had opinions on improving the transnational relations. Opinions of Grotius had been criticized by Hobbes, who considered transnational relations as power and confliction focused. According to Hobbes, national gains are inevitably correlated to national security (Badie, 2001).

Winner of this debate, as one might guess, had been the British attendant Hobbes. After this date, international system had been seen as the order of dominant land units. After this period, even though there had been attempts to internalize liberal politics and co-operation, the determining factor had been the states. In this period, it is noticeable that the realist theory had been more dominant.

According to realism, the state is the unique and basic actor of the international system. As the states are rational actors, national security is the most significant purpose. In the case of international relations that is examines in international order and state centered manner, concept of individual has been left behind the priority subjects of realism. The relation between realism and society and individuals had been shaped by pessimistic perspective while defining the features of state-centered order. Similar to evil from birth, pursuing personal benefits and greedy individuals' daily life, the role of a state in the international order is determined through its own profits (Griffts, 1965).

In this regard, especially up until 1980's, theories of international relations had been studied on state and system basis. However, starting from 1970's, whether changes in international system (i.e. increasing importance of international organizations and multinational corporations) or clarification of different theories directed towards explanation of changes (i.e. Neoliberalism, Neo-Marxism, Pluralism, feminist theory, etc.) have carried individuals and society into the agenda of international relations (Aydın, 2004). Therefore, main topics of debate regarding the international order had been brought up again but in a different format.

The world order had altered within the process of globalization in two particular ways. First, globalization ruled out the distances and prevented it from being a political wellspring. Justified by complex communication opportunities, the new world order is no longer local. It is turning into a relationship directly interpersonal, uncontrollable by the state and goes beyond borders. Thus, individuals, international organizations, non-profit organizations, multinational corporations and such other organizations are potential international actors (Badie, 2001).

Secondly; public benefit is no longer sovereignty benefit: providing demands in a global order points out a global content rather than a national movement. Environment, economic and social improvement, shelter, women's situation and human rights have become a subject of international politics instead of states' domestic policies. In addition, new actors of the international system (i.e. local integrations, supra-nation structures, NGO's) defy the state on the use of absolute power and politics loses its hierarchical positions that is suggested by realization. Therefore, the main discussion after the cold war had been related to the multiplicity and diversity of the actors. Looking through the illumination resulted from evaluations so far, it is a clear fact that the world is going through a phase of metamorphosis. With globalization, basic values like democracy, civil rights, liberty, environmental protection gained universal character while nation-state is forced to adjust under strong trends like democratization, localization, transparency, participation, flexibility, accountability. In this aspect, strategies like downsizing of state, privatization, political reforms, alteration of socio-economic politics have become the main politics of countries (Köse, 2003).

Globalization from the Socio-Cultural Aspects

Cultural aspect of globalization may be explained by steady increment of communication and interaction of societies. In addition, general identities like citizenship have left their place to different ethnical, religious, social and political identities.

Also, increasing similarity between societies related to elements like consumerism and popular culture is an ongoing process. US flag designed t-shirts everywhere in the world, English as the global language, listening to same music are evidences that a cultural globalization is present (Köse, 2003);(Sağlam, 2007b).

Such accommodations are proof that globalization have started to influence social and cultural environments through a global cultural of its own.

Globalization from Technological Aspect

The most important feature that separates globalization from previous periods is the expansion of manufacture on a widespread area with the latest technologies on an unusual speed and level (Sarıbay, 2000). Thus, a definition is needed for technology as another aspect of globalization. The procedure that is defined as global economy is in fact a digital economy. Digitalization technique is primarily turning every data like sound, text, document, music, video, moving object, teleconference, etc. into bytes that consist of 1's and 0's and transfer to somewhere else with the help of telecommunication technology. These codes are decrypted adjacent to the original and brought into use (Bayraç, 2006).

Up to this part of our work, definitions of globalization on the literature have been tried to be elaborated and explained by classifying by their size, mentioning their historical phases. Multinational corporations as the most important element of this period will be evaluated in the following chapter and the purpose of this study, interaction between globalization and multinational corporations, will be held lastly.

LITERATURE REVIEW

The primary factors to be identified when conducting a literature study are; the scope of the study, the limitation of the study and determination of the methodology.

As the study begins with the globalization process, the important elements that need to be addressed within the scope of the globalization literature to be used in the study are to determine which types of studies can be evaluated within the globalization literature, which resources can be part of the research and the time interval of the literature.

In this study; international and domestic sources of globalization and multinational companies are included as literature. The types of studies included in the literature consist of articles, books, reports, papers, and research theses. Looking at the timeframe of the literature, especially from the first period of the globalization movement on the world, the works which are up to the present day have been included. Finally, while preparing the literature; international databases, indexed journals, university libraries and research channels such as ULAKbim were used.

Also, this study, which will be used as a theoretical analysis method, consists of three parts. Globalization concept, process, dimensions, and multinational companies are included in the concept, and multinational companies are evaluated on the theoretical basis with the definition, historical development processes, and operating methods.

In the third part of the study, the analysis of the interaction between globalization and multinational companies, the process of globalization and the areas of activity and volume of multinational companies are analyzed.

In its broadest sense, globalization is a tendency to broaden the scope of a mode of production and its relations of production through internal and external economic processes. Globalization in economic terms can be defined as spreading the influence of the capital and commodity movements to the world with increasing intensity (Kara, 2004).

With the positive and negative consequences of globalization on national economies, it is one of the most debated concepts in business and economics. This concept, which expresses the free movement of goods, services, capital, information, and technology, is in a sense the way neoliberal economics in the world. In the 1980s and 1990s, international economic integration accelerated and the world countries lifted the borders and adopted the cost of more efficient production, investment, and trade. Globalization is not only an economic system based on a profit-oriented market economy but also a major change project involving political and socio-cultural fields (Danışoğlu, 2004).

According to Bauman, globalization has a distinctive nature, especially in the cultural sense. There is no sovereign control mechanism which is controlled from a certain center. Globalization is the new world disorder (Bauman, 1999). Contrary to the hope and intention of establishing order in the basic concepts of modern thought such as development, civilization, and universalization, the emphasis is on uncertainty and inability to be planned in the concept of globalization.

According to another view, globalization can be seen as an advanced stage of capitalism, international capital and multinational corporations, and basically the process of withdrawing from the economic life of the state as a process of social reconciliation prepared by the social state prepared by reviewing a case that weakens or eliminated the social quality of the state (Bulut, 2003).

Approaches to globalization are divided into three. The first is the anti-globalization approach, which argues that globalization weakens and destroys nation-state and nationality and puts nations under the domination of international capital. The second approach is that globalization is an inevitable consequence for the future of the world and that there are extremists who support the necessity of global new world order. The third and last approach to globalization is based on the position of the nation-state in the face of globalization, followed by a cautious approach to neither being nor a party to globalization and rejecting the theses of the other two approaches (Bozkurt, 2001).

AGENTS OF GLOBALIZATION PROCESS AND BEING ABLE TO CONCEIVE MULTINATIONAL CORPORATIONS

Global economy brings concepts like internationalization of manufacture (completion of a process in different countries), interlacement of financial markets and local economies, improvements on communication and transportation as a result of technological developments.

Furthermore, while the concept of international economics had been used in the past, nowadays it has been replaced by the concept of global economics (Seyidoğlu, 2003a). The reason behind this is the plenitude of agents and operations and the magnitude of their relation in the process of globalization.

For instance, while in the past transnational economic relations had been explained with terms like foreign trade and treated as international economics, nowadays agents like multinational corporations, international organizations, international non-profit organizations join these economic relations beside the states. While international economics is associated with transnational relations and borders, global economics describes a process where the impact of borders has been lessened and even interpersonal relations are intensified. Thus, in the present time, global economy interests and effects almost everyone in country, enterprise and individual levels.

In a global system with economic, political, cultural and technological aspects, enterprises try to get along with the rules of the game. Effects of global economy on enterprises are noticeable in almost every field from manufacturing relations to investments; marketing operations to public relations. On the next chapters of this study, description of multinational corporations, its historical development, ability to create and use technology and affects and magnitude on the globalization process will take place.

Definition of Multinational Corporations and its Historical Development

International business administration is every type of business operation held by companies outside their national borders. Even though it is on a constantly decreasing scale, some international business administrations are still run by governments to achieve political and strategical purposes. Furthermore, international business administration applications are mostly run by private enterprises (Özalp, 2004).

Most significant reason behind this might be addressed as private enterprises being more aggressive than state institutions and able to adapt changes on the global market and technology more quickly. In addition to this, private enterprises, with the liberty from bureaucracy, have a more flexible structure, therefore started to operate quickly in various countries while partnership structures depended on the nature of the work.

It is every type of business operation of an enterprises spread in or between two or more independent countries. In other words, international business administration; is defined as business operations that involve resource, assets, service and such transnational movements of private or public enterprises (Mutlu, 1999). International management on the other hand, is defined as achieving global targets by effectively coordinating supply and distribution and usage of financial and labor sources, providing stable dynamic balance situation (Mutlu, 1999). International company, is a firm that, once established a strong foundation in a country, attends to access and put down roots in other countries with the help of a central administration. These firms (companies) usually come from developed countries to developing or less developed countries and expand into similar countries after accessing their market. Sometimes the opposite may happen as a company from a developing country may expand into other markets in a similar action. Lastly, multinational corporation is, one of the greatest economic facts of our age, a result of operational corporation between giant companies with their partners in foreign countries (Taşlıca, 1999). Multinational corporations are worldwide enterprises. Multinational corporation as a definition, is a partnership that is based in a national state in ethnicity and managerial manner, however, allots partnership resources without borders and distributes worldwide., Multinational corporations, are internationally recognized firms that coordinates foreign capital and directly make their investment in compliance with foreign investment law in the country of expansion, shows integrity in organizational structure, decision making and control mechanisms (Yüksel, 1999a). For example, companies like Nokia and Coca-Cola are multinational corporations. When the endorsement of multinational corporations are viewed it is seen that their profit rate is astronomical and sometimes their endorsement may be higher than some state's GNP's. When the literature is viewed; There have been many definitions of multinational corporations.

"While it is possible to define multinational corporation as a firm that has branches and connected companies on multinational influence area" (Thompson, 2007).

"...is a company that operates in two or more countries, earns some of its profits from foreign operations and has assets on other countries"(Dereli, 2005); (Sivrikaya, 2012a).

The biggest feature that separates multinational corporations from national corporations is the ability of multinational corporation to transfer resources cross-border by setting up an organization that can provide a global maximization.

A similar definition regarding multinational corporation is, *"a company that has the power to coordinate and control operations in more than one country (owned or not)* (Dicken, 2006).

When the operation structure of multinational corporations is viewed; there are no obligations of possessing devices to be able to use productive devices. Multinational corporations usually possess these types of devices. However, they still need to co-operate with legal independent local firms. Even the greatest multinational corporations have to follow the local national legislations. While multinational corporations try to take advantage of legislations that vary from country to country, they must also co-operate with local enterprises.

With this co-operation, they will gather information about legal steps and consumer habits in the present country.

"With the shortest definition, multinational corporations are enterprises that invest in order to manufacture in foreign markets or compete in different countries" (Seymen, 2005).

Lastly, in order to consider a firm as a multinational corporation, it is necessary to obtain at least 20% of its assets in foreign countries and at least 35% of its profit should be gained through international operations (Sivrikaya, 2012a).

Global company is a worldwide operated enterprise that uses high technology, conducts global product, price etc. policies, and is managed by world citizen managers (Mutlu, 1999). In addition to these, literature also contains descriptions like Transnational Corporation and Supranational Corporation. Transnational corporation is a firm in which citizens of different countries are partners in ownership and in addition to ownership, that has a multi-national character with expert management team that consists of different origins (Taşlıca, 1999).Since the old times, international businesses have spent time full of wars, political frictions, piracy, economical changes and cultural tariffs. Despite this, human desire to earn money, going beyond national trade borders undoubtedly supported the improvement of internationalization (J., 1993).Even though international business operations have reached a great volume, their roots are based on thousands of years ago. Intersocietal commerce have a custom that goes beyond four thousand years. There had been commercial interactions between Mesopotamia, Asia Minor and North Africa; Mediterranean being the focal point.. During this period, clothing, spices and olive oil were commercial products. Later, trading had improved under the control of the Roman Empire. Outcomes of this period were advanced law system as a result of regulations on the trade routes and secure trading operations under a supreme authority. Chinese export of silk to Europe and India is the representation of the depth of the new trading operations (Yüksel, 1999b).

When the history of international trade is examined, it is seen that trading had been done under the authority of the state until the industrial revolution. During global expansion years, it enabled the enterprises to enter further markets and eliminated the communication problem for the most part. Until this period, US companies that had been rather passive when compared to European enterprises on the international business administration manner, started to spread throughout the globe especially in 1950's and 1960's and internationalization became a deal of US in the entire world. During these years, US companies that surpass European companies in technological advancements and achieve the highest position in the technology transfer rate, tried to combine their quality in technics, marketing, administration and finance with cheap labor in overseas countries and obtained great success and profit (Özalp, 2004).

This concept, called alternative cost, is still present as instead of producing some product itself, company gets them produced in a country to reach the least cost and then assembly. For instance, although a representative of the Finnish industry, Nokia follow a process of producing some materials in China or other countries with reduced labor costs and dispatch to customers after an assembly period. In fact, this type of production, where the production is managed by planning by reduced labor costs might be referred as global production.

Internationalization gained importance because of various reasons for many companies these days. Therefore, the amount of enterprises to invest in foreign countries increase every day. The question "Why should enterprises enter the international market?" might be answered in different ways. Some of those answers are as listed below: (Rhinesmith, 2000).

Higher authorities may demand,
Make use of an opportunity of co-operation invitation,
Company beginning to look for new opportunities as the domestic competition is too intense on some industries,
Sharp domestic competition may lead the company abroad,
International markets being viewed as potential centers of profit.

As it can be understood from the answers listed as reasons to enter the international market, the reasons behind internalization may be various. However, the most important element that makes internationalization attractive is profit. Profit rate in fresh and undiscovered markets carry a great level of attraction for many companies. Also, another feature of the profit is related to the tax easements provided by the host country to foreign investors. The second most important reason may be told to be consistency (Rhinesmith, 2000).

Foreign markets provide an important advantage to utilize the potentiality. Therefore, enterprises may target internationalization which may prove a consistent method in production and sales. According to these statements, reasons that force companies to internationalize may be gathered under four main topics. These are:(Taştan, 2005).

- Market related elements.
- Cost related elements.
- Competition related elements.
- Political elements.

Within the frame of all these elements, the reasons behind the enterprises' desire to enter the international market might be classified in two groups as aggressive and defensive (Taştan, 2005).

Aggressive Reasons:
- New market search.
- To reduce costs and reach higher profit.
- To satisfy the demand of expansion and growth of higher authorities.

Defensive Reasons:
- To protect the local market.
- To protect other markets.
- To secure feed stock demand.
- To gain new technologies.
- Geographical alteration.
- To establish a base for new operations.

After all the evaluation, in the present period importance of multinational corporations rapidly increases with the growth of the economic integration on the global scale, transmission of the effect of market economy to cross-border and liberation of international trade and finance operation. Multinational corporations determine their level of investment and focus areas of economical actions with ongoing operations and strategies. Multinational corporations also decide on which areas to maintain welfare level with investment on capital and technology intensified industries. "At the present time, nearly 61,000 multinational corporations and 900,000 foreign affiliates operate in various parts of the world." (Vural, 2006).

In the present century; it is noticeable that multinational corporations have a great place in the process of globalization. Besides the constant increase in the population, with globalization, people still operate on production-consumption activities in every field within the framework of increasing competition conditions thanks to free market economy policies. With the liberation of international trade and application of neo-liberal policies, it is visible that the number of multinational corporations and their operation fields have increased. A huge part of industry and trade operations in the world are run by these corporations. At the same time, these corporations control the worldwide technology in addition to production of new technologies (Martinez, 1996).The truth that multinational corporations which establishes a domination on the world economy may cause threats that could abrade the power of nation-states even though they can provide benefits to the international arena should not be overlooked.

TO BE ABLE TO INTERPRET DATA AND TECHNOLOGY TRANSFER IN THE AGE OF GLOBALIZATION AND THE TECHNOLOGY TRANSFER MODEL INTERNALIZED BY MULTINATIONAL CORPORATIONS

What should be said in the beginning is the clarification to resolve the conceptual confusion regarding data and technology transfer. Technology transfer states the transfer of capital goods like machinery and hardware, while data transfer involves the transfer of implicit knowledge like know-how, management and technical skills.

Information transfers are considered more important and critical as they provide new information and teach organizational skills (UNCTAD, 1997). The term technology transfer stands for the process of knowledge, skill and experience acquisition for the technology receiver as a result of direct effect of provided technological resources. Technology transfer process is the process of internalization and learning of the knowledge and experience related to the transferred technology. Upper-mentioned transfer process' productivity depends on two important elements: Those may be expressed as technology receiver having a certain knowledge base and actions to improve this knowledge base (Terdudomtham, 2004). When technology transfer channels are viewed, Grosse states that technology transfer is classified in two groups as horizontal and vertical (Grosse, 1996). If the technology transfer process goes from basic research to applicational research or development, it is called vertical technology transfer; however, if the technology transfer goes from usage of technology from a place to another place, it is horizontal technology transfer. (Grosse, 1996).

According to Grosse, the technology transfer channel that multinational corporations follow goes from their offices in the main campus to overseas affiliates and therefore it is seen as horizontal technology transfer (Grosse, 1996).

When the technology transfer channels of multinational corporations are reviewed, multinational corporations have the strength to affect productivity of local companies in various methods. Besides innovations, two important types of technological expansion should be examined. Those are horizontal and vertical technology expansion.

Horizontal expansions occur in three main ways:

Actions to attempt a copy of product and process technologies of multinational corporations by local companies those are interacted with multinational corporations when they integrate into local markets with their advanced technology. (display/imitation effect)

Integration of a multinational corporation in a market increases competition and increased competition forces the local companies to use their technology more effectively and in order to be more competitive, renew or renovate their technology. (competition effect)

Education of multinational corporation staff and employment of those staff by local companies enable indirect access of production and management skills of multinational corporations (*labor circulation*) (Sönmez, 2011).

Vertical expansions occur with the interaction of multinational corporations with local suppliers and clients. To secure the quality of intermediate inputs, multinational corporations may provide technical help to local suppliers, educate workers, help in gathering raw materials etc. In this context, backwards networking is present. The process that is called as backwards networking may be expressed as purchase of local producers' intermediate or capital goods from foreign suppliers. Foreign suppliers' products have a more advanced technology when compared to local suppliers' products, thus; information transfers by multinational corporations to local companies in order to let the producers use the goods in a productive and effective way, might be stated as vertical expansion (Sönmez, 2011).

As it is obvious, it is because multinational corporations are indeed the technology producers of the world. A great part of R&D investments in the world are done by these corporations (Borensztein, 1998). At the same time, these corporations control the worldwide technology in addition to production of new technologies (Martinez, 1996). Important information regarding the production and technological activities of these corporations are found in 1997 and 2003 editions of World Investment Report that is annually published by United Nations Conference on Trade and Development (UNCTAD). (UNCTAD, 1997); (UNCTAD, 2003). For instance, it is noticeable that the trade volume between the center of multinational corporations and their foreign affiliates is one third of total world trading volume. 80% of R&D activities in OECD countries are operated by multinational corporations with more than 10.000 employees. Furthermore, 75-80% of worldwide R&D expenses are resulted from the same multinational corporations. In addition to this, most of the technological production takes place in the homeland of those multinational corporations. For example, it is noticed that only 13% of US centered multinational corporations' R&D operations are carried out in foreign countries. More than 80% of worldwide R&D activities take place only in five countries. Those countries are US, Japan, France, England and Germany (Martinez, 1996); (Sönmez, 2011).

Under the light of these evaluations, once more the role of multinational corporations on the world trading volume is seen and their place as the technology producer is proven.

BEING ABLE TO CONCEIVE THE INTERACTION BETWEEN GLOBALIZATION AND MULTINATIONAL CORPORATIONS

In addition to being the main agent in the globalization process, multinational corporations are among the leading dynamics to speed up the globalization process. With the increasing speed of globalization process, operating fields, organizational structures and administrative approach of those corporations began to change. Volumes of local or intercountry operations increased to global based operations. It is noticeable that the concept of globalization cannot be conceived separate from multinational corporations as they provide great importance for the economical aspect of globalization. In this context, Samuel Huntington expresses this process and globalization as increased international interaction between individuals, companies, governments, NGO's and other organizations, development of multinational corporations that are involved in production and marketing, intensification of international organizations, regimes and regulations (Huntington, 2004). Multinational corporations became prominent with the increasing speed of globalization process; their operational fields and capital structures have developed. One of the most important features of globalization is that it brings flexibility in many fields. Being able to move a great amount of capital through multinational corporations from a place in the world to another place, being able to switch from areas where the tax rate is high to areas with low rates, increase in the Internet and fast communication devices, new possibilities of shopping like e-commerce are flexibilities that are brought by the globalization. Multinational corporations benefit greatly from those flexibilities created by the globalization and have effect on the process in the same amount (Katırcıoğlu, 2008).

SOLUTIONS AND RECOMMENDATIONS

Considering the results obtained, with the process of globalization, the nation-state draws itself from the economic field as the opposite of the traditional state understanding. Because globalization leads to uniformization of states with its economic dimension and restructures their political, cultural and economic values and decisions. Due to the essence of globalization, it also erodes the national values and ideas of national unity of societies. It also reveals that the nation-state is inadequate to cope with the new conditions within this process, so sub-national and supranational organizations have started to develop and have started to find a place among the actors of the globalization process.

In summary; The emergence of regional integrations, non-governmental actors, multinational corporations, and international non-governmental organizations in this process has prevented the nation-state from being the sole and indispensable power of the international arena. These institutions and organizations, which can be regarded as new actors in this process, can direct and influence the decisions of nation-states, which undermines the authority of the nation-state, and now the state shares its current authority with these global actors to a certain extent. In addition, it is seen that intergovernmental agreements and agreements have helped to spread globalization.

As a result, globalization has strengthened the areas of action of international financial capital and multinational corporations and has narrowed the authority and responsibility of the state and led to a radical change in the role of the nation-state in the international arena. However, with the process of globalization, the nation-state has not and will not be disappeared.

FUTURE RESEARCH DIRECTIONS

The phenomenon of globalization maintains its priority in the areas discussed today. Although it has economic, political, cultural and technological dimensions, the concept of globalization is essentially an economic-based concept. Actors such as IMF, World Bank, World Trade Organization and multinational corporations accelerate and manage the globalization process. The main reason for this situation can be explained as the effect of the global system in almost all areas. This is the result that can shed light for future studies; In the process of globalization, the nation-state is sharing its authority and sovereignty with supra-national institutions and local administrations, and this process foresees the nation-state to lose its sovereignty and to maintain its existence in the free market order by introducing new qualities and functions to the nation-state. This situation; it will inevitably bring the concept of nation-state, the re-analysis of the area of authority and responsibility of the nation-state, and will continue to bring forth in future studies.

CONCLUSION

To summarize; in addition to being an important agent on the globalization process, multinational corporations may also be stated as dynamics that directs the speeding up of globalization process.

Especially the period after the World War II, as the reflection of developing production systems, it provided the increase in corporation numbers, and carried existing corporations' operation areas from local to international area as the result of increasing trading volume. Therefore, locally operated enterprises almost turned into multinational corporations and began to direct the globalization process.

Activities and operational fields of multinational corporations on the world economy are at a very high level and when the effects on the nation-state in the process of globalization is considered they are in a position to threaten the affect-area of nation-state with the economic power they hold.

With the depth and width of its influential area, the concept of globalization is the primary topic for discussions in the recent years. The main reason behind this might be explained plainly as the visible affect globalization in every field. To give place to debates and analysis regarding globalization of course exceeds the limits of this study.

It is noticeable that multinational corporations form an important anchor of globalization process. Increasing co-dependency and liberalization tendencies push the country borders to become more permeable. This results in the easy transfer of knowledge, asset, service and capital which are highly important for multinational corporations. Therefore, it provides the possibility for the multinational corporations to find resources, to transfer capital and foreign profits to their own countries. Globalization process brought multinational corporations to a much stronger position in the global market.

As a result, multinational corporations are affected by the globalization process as well as speeding it up.

ACKNOWLEDGMENT

This study was dedicated to my retired teacher grandmother Gülsüm Süheyla Kıvılcım.

REFERENCES

Aktan, C. C., & Vural, İ. Y. (2006). *Çokuluslu şirketler: Global sermaye ve global yatırımlar*. Konya, Turkey: Çizgi Kitabevi Yayınları.

Aslan, N. (2005). *Dünya Ekonomisinde Gelişmeler: Küreselleşme ve Ekonomik Entegrasyon Küresel ve Bölgesel Yaklaşım* (O. Küçükahmetoğlu, Ed.). Ankara, Turkey: Ekin Yayınevi.

Atasoy, F. (2005). *Küreselleşme ve Milliyetçilik*. İstanbul, Turkey: Ötüken Yayınları.

Aydın, M. (2004). Uluslararası İlişkilerin Gerçekçi Teorisi: Kökeni, Kapsamı,Kritiği. *Uluslararası İlişkiler*, *1*(1), 33–60.

Badie, B. (2001). Realism under praise, or a requiem? The praradigmatic debate in international relations. *International Political Science Review*, *22*(3), 45–46. doi:10.1177/0192512101223003

Bauman, Z. (1999). *Küreselleşme*. İstanbul, Turkey: Ayrıntı Yayınları.

Bauman, Z. (2010). *Küreselleşme Topumsal Sonuçları* (A. Yılmaz, Trans.). İstanbul, Turkey: Ayrıntı Yayınları.

Bayar, F. (2008). Küreselleşme Kavramı ve Küreselleşme Sürecinde Türkiye. *Uluslararası Ekonomik Sorunlar Dergisi*, *32*, 25–34.

Bayraç, N. (2006). *Yeni Ekonomi'nin Toplumsal*. Ekonomik Ve Teknolojik Boyutları.

Borensztein, E., & Gregorio, J. D. (1998). How does foreign direct investment affect economic growth? *Journal of International Economics*, 45(1), 115–135. doi:10.1016/S0022-1996(97)00033-0

Bozkurt, V. (2001). Küreselleşme Kavram, Gelişim Yaklaşımlar. *3*(2).

Bulut, N. (2003). Küreselleşme: Sosyal Devletin Sonu Mu? *Ankara Üniversitesi Hukuk Fakültesi Dergisi*, 52(2), 185.

Danışoğlu, A. Ç. (2004). Küreselleşmenin Gelir Eşitsizliği ve Yoksulluk Üzerindeki Etkisi. *İstanbul Ticaret Üniversitesi Dergisi*, 3(5), 215-216.

Dereli, B. (2005). Çok Uluslu İşletmelerde İnsan Kaynakları Yönetimi. *İstanbul Ticaret Üniversitesi Sosyal Bilimler Dergisi*, 7, 59-81.

Dicken, P. (2006). Yeni Jeo Ekonomi (A. Ağca, Trans. B. K. Ed.). Ankara, Turkey: Kadim Yayınları.

Ellwood, W. (2002). *Küreselleşmeyi Anlama Kılavuzu*. İstanbul, Turkey: Metis Yayınları.

Fischer, S. (2003). Globalization and its challenges. *The American Economic Review*, 93(2), 2. doi:10.1257/000282803321946750

Giddens, A. (2006). *Modernitenin Küreselleşmesi* (K. Bülbül, Trans.). Ankara, Turkey: Kadim Yayınları.

Griffts, J. H. M. M. (1965). *Politics among nations: the struggle for power and peace* (pp. 24–38). New York: Routledge.

Grosse, R. (1996). *International technology transfer in service journal of technology business studies*, 27, 781–800.

Huntington, S. (2004). *Biz Kimiz: Amerika'nın Ulusal Kimlik Arayışı* (A. Özer, Trans.). İstanbul, Turkey: CSA Yayınları.

Kara, U. (2004). *Sosyal Devletin Yükselişi ve Düşüşü*. Ankara, Turkey: Özgür Üniversite Kitaplığı.

Karabıçak, M. (2002). Küreselleşme Sürecinde Gelişmekte Olan Ülke Ekonomilerinde Ortaya Çıkan Yönelim ve Tepkiler. *Süleyman Demirel Üniversitesi İktisadi ve İdari Bilimler Fakültesi*, 7(1), 113–116.

Katırcıoğlu, E. (2008). *Küreselleşme Çağında Sol Ekonomik Politikalar"Yeni Toplum Yeni Siyaset Küreselleşme Çağında Sosyal Demokrat Yaklaşımlar*. İstanbul, Turkey: Kalkedon Yayınları.

Köse, Ö. (2003). Küreselleşme Sürecinde Devletin Yapısal ve İşlevsel Dönüşümü. *Sayıştay Dergisi*, 49(Nisan-Haziran), 3-4.

Martinez, R. J., & Eden, E. L. L. (1996). The production transfer and spillover of technology: comparing large and small multinationals as technology producer. *Small Business Economics*, 9, 53–66.

Mutlu, E. C. (1999). *Uluslararası İşletmecilik*. İstanbul, Turkey: Beta Yayınları.

Oran, B. (2001). *Küreselleşme ve Azınlıklar* (4th ed.). Ankara, Turkey: İmaj Yayınevi.

Özalp, İ. (2004). *Uluslararası İşletmecilik*. Eskişehir, Turkey: Anadolu Üniversitesi.

Rhinesmith, S. H. (2000). *Yöneticinin Küreselleşme Rehberi*. İstanbul, Turkey: Sabah Kitapçılık.

Sağlam, S. (2007a). Küreselleşmeye Yaklaşımlar. *Genç Sosyal Bilim Forumu, 13*, 7.

Sağlam, S. (2007b). Küreselleşmeye Yaklaşımlar. *Genç Sosyal Bilim Forumu, 13*, 8–9.

Sarıbay, A. Y. (2000). Global ve Yerel Eksende Türkiye. In A. Sarıbay (Ed.), Yirmibirinci Yüzyıla Doğru Global Kapitalizm, Oryantalizm, Yerlicilik", Global ve Yerel Eksende Türkiye. İstanbul, Turkey: Alfa Yayınları.

Şen, C. C. A. H. (1999). Globalleşme Ekonomik Kriz ve Türkiye. *Tosyöv Yayınları*, 10-12.

Seyidoğlu, H. (2003a). *Uluslararası İktisat Teori Politika Ve Uygulama*. İstanbul, Turkey: Güzem Can Yayınları.

Seyidoğlu, H. (2003b). *Uluslararası İktisat Teori Politika Ve Uygulama*. İstanbul, Turkey: Güzem Can Yayınları.

Seymen, T. B. O. A. (2005). Çok uluslu İşletmelerin Kavramsal Açıdan İncelenmesi. In T. Seymen (Ed.), Küreselleşme ve Çok Uluslu İşletmecilik (pp. 53-67). Ankara, Turkey: Nobel Yayın Dağıtım.

Sivrikaya, D. (2012a). *Küreselleşme Sürecinde Çokuluslu Şirketler ile Sivil Toplum Kuruluşlarının İktisadi Etkileşimi. (Yüksek Lisans)*. Ordu, Turkey: Ordu Üniversitesi.

Sivrikaya, D. (2012b). *Küreselleşme Sürecinde Çokuluslu Şirketler ile Sivil Toplum Kuruluşlarının İktisadi Etkileşimi. (Yüksek Lisans)*. Ordu, Turkey: Ordu Üniversitesi.

Sivrikaya, D. (2012c). *Küreselleşme Sürecinde Çokuluslu Şirketler ile Sivil Toplum Kuruluşlarının İktisadi Etkileşimleri. (Yüksek Lisans)* (p. 134). Ordu, Turkey: Ordu Üniversitesi.

Sönmez, M. (2011). *Analysis of knowledge and technology transfer by multinational companies to local suppliers in the Turkish automotive industry*. In M. B. Steger (Ed.), *Küreselleşme* (A. Ersoy, Trans.), Ankara, Turkey: Dost Kitabevi.

Taggart, J. H., & McDermott, M. C. (1993). *The essence of international business*. London, UK.

Taşlıca, A. O. (1999). *Çok Uluslu İşletmeler ve Türkiye*. Paper presented at the Anadolu Üniversitesi, İİBF Yayınları Eskişehir.

Taştan, S. (2005). Küreselleşme ve Küresel Strateji.

Terdudomtham, K. T. T. (2004). *Evolution of inter-firm techonology transfer and technological capability formation of local parts firms in the Thai automobile industry journal of technology innovation, 12*, 2–20.

Thompson, P. H. G. (2007). Küreselleşme Sorgulanıyor (Ç. E. v. E. Yücel, Trans.). Ankara, Turkey: Dost Kitabevi

UNCTAD. (1997). Transnational corporations, market structure and competition policy. UN.

UNCTAD. (2003). *FDI policies for development: National and international perspectives. World Investment Report*. New York: UNCTAD.

Yılmaz, A. (2007). *Romantizmden Gerçeğe Küreselleşme*. Ankara, Turkey: Minima Yayıncılık.

Yüksel, Ö. (1999a). *Uluslararası İşletme Yönetimi ve Türkiye Uygulamaları*. Ankara, Turkey: Gazi Kitabevi.

Yüksel, Ö. (1999b). *Uluslararası İşletme Yönetimi ve Türkiye Uygulamaları*. Ankara, Turkey: Gazi Kitapevi.

Zengingönül, O. (2004). *Yoksulluk Gelişmişlik Ve İşgücü Piyasaları Ekseninde Küreselleşme*. Ankara, Turkey: Adres Yayınları.

KEY TERMS AND DEFINITIONS

GNP: Gross National Product.
NGO: Non-governmental organization.
UNCTAD: United Nations Conference on Trade and Development.

Chapter 10
The Relationship Between Foreign Direct Investment and Financial Development in OECD Countries

Metin Gürler
https://orcid.org/0000-0002-9263-0258
Uluslararası Rekabet Araştırmaları Kurumu, Turkey

Funda Kara
Independent Researcher, Turkey

ABSTRACT

This chapter investigates the relationship between the OECD-FRRI issued by OECD and IMF-FDI issued by IMF for 36 OECD member countries. Cross-section data (CSD) analysis and panel data (PD) analysis consisting of random and fixed effects estimations were used in the study to investigate the relationship between Foreign Direct Investment (FDI) and Financial Development for OECD countries for the years 1997, 2003, and 2006 and the 7-year period of 2010-2016. Granger Causality Test (GCT) is also applied to test the direction of causality between two indicators. According to the Random Effects Model (RAM) and Fixed Effects Model (FEM) with PD analysis in the study OECD-FRRI is found as one of the determinants of IMF-FDI and IMF-FDI is found as one of the determinants of OECD-FRRI in OECD member countries. For CSD analysis, there is no significant proof to say OECD-FRRI is one of the main determinants of IMF-FDI and IMF-FDI is one of the determinants of OECD-FRRI in OECD member countries. For CSD, OECD-FRRI does not cause IMF-FDI whereas IMF-FDI causes OECD-FRRI.

DOI: 10.4018/978-1-7998-2559-3.ch010

Table 1. Financial development index pyramid

Financial Development (FD)					
Financial Institutions (FI)			Financial Markets (FM)		
Depth (FID)	Access (FIA)	Efficiency (FIE)	Depth (FMD)	Access (FMA)	Efficiency (FME)

Source: Sahay et al. (2015). 12.

INTRODUCTION

FDI provides many positive gains to the host economy, such as employment, production, income and export growth. This situation has been effective in increasing the competition of countries to attract FDI in recent years and with their efforts to make their countries attractive for investment. Due to the possible negative effects of indirect foreign capital investments, investing directly in other countries is extremely important for supporting the sustainable growth of especially developing countries.

The effectiveness of the financial system comes to the forefront in the success of the economic performance of the countries. Financial stability has become a prerequisite for economic stability. Therefore, the soundness of the financial system, which is important for the foreign investor, is a matter that needs to be paid attention.

The basis of this study is to examine the relationship between FDI and financial development in 36 OECD countries (Australia, Austria, Belgium, Canada, Chile, Czech Republic, Denmark, Estonia, Finland, France, Germany, Greece, Hungary, Iceland, Ireland, Israel, Italy, Japan, Kore Republic, Latvia, Lithuania, Luxembourg, Mexico, Netherlands, New Zealand, Norway, Poland, Portugal, Slovak Republic, Slovenia, Spain, Sweden, Switzerland, Turkey, United Kingdom, United States).

For this purpose, the relationship between the International Monetary Fund's (IMF) Financial Development Index (IMF-FDI) and Foreign Direct Investment Regulatory Restrictiveness Index (OECD-FRRI) measured by the OECD has been examined for 36 OECD member countries. Financial Development Index (IMF-FDI) is a relative ranking of countries on the depth, access, and efficiency of their financial institutions and financial markets. It is an aggregate of the Financial Institutions Index and the Financial Markets Index (IMF, https://data.imf.org/).

Financial development is identified as a combination of depth (size and liquidity of markets), access (ability of individuals and companies to access financial services), and efficiency (ability of institutions to provide financial services at low cost and with sustainable revenues, and the level of activity of capital markets). (Table 1) These indices were originally developed in the context of the IMF's "Rethinking Financial Deepening: Stability and Growth in Emerging Markets" (Sahay et al., 2015).

The FDI Regulatory Restrictiveness Index (OECD-FRRI) measures statutory restrictions on foreign direct investment in 22 economic sectors across 69 countries, including all OECD and G20 countries. The FDI Index gauges the restrictiveness of a country's FDI rules by looking at the four main types of restrictions on FDI: (OECD, https://www.oecd.org/).

- Foreign equity limitations.
- Screening or approval mechanisms.
- Restrictions on the employment of foreigners as key personnel.
- Operational restrictions, e.g. restrictions on branching and capital repatriation or land ownership.

The FDI Regulatory Restrictiveness Index (FRRI) originally developed in 2003. It is jointly maintained by the OECD Investment Division and the OECD Economics Department as one component of the revised 2008 OECD Indicator of Product Market Regulation (PMR) from which the Going for Growth policy priorities are drawn (https://www.oecd-ilibrary.org/).

In recent years, countries around the world have continued to liberalize international investment restrictions. However, FDI liberalization is still an incomplete issue in various regions and sectors of the world (Mistura & Roulet, 2019). In line with the increasing importance of direct investments for OECD countries as in the world, the subject of our study is to examine the relationship between FDI and financial development for these countries. Cross-section data (CSD) analysis and panel data (PD) analysis were used for the years 1997, 2003 and 2006 and the 7-year period of 2010-2016. Granger Causality Test (GCT) is also applied to test the direction of causality between two indicators.

LİTERATURE REVİEW

With the increasing importance of foreign direct investments for countries, it has started to occupy a wide place in the literature. Research examining the mutual relationship between growth, financial development, and FDI is available in the literature. Besides, there are studies in the literature that examine the relationship between financial development and financial constraint with the relationship between FDI and competitiveness in the literature. The literature also includes studies on the determinants of foreign direct investment. However, our focus is limited to studies that directly examine the relationship between financial development and FDI. It is possible to see the summary of the studies in the literature in Table 2.

Research examining the mutual relationship between growth, financial development and FDI is available in the literature. Studies such as Korgaonkar (2012), Zadeh and Madani (2012), Ljungwall and Li (2007), Raheem and Oyınlola (2013) are examples. Lauro et al (2003) show that FDI alone plays an ambiguous role in contributing to economic growth. However, countries with well-developed financial markets gain significantly from FDI. Korgaonkar (2012) states that the development of the financial system of the recipient country is an important precondition for FDI to have a positive impact on economic growth. Zadeh and Madani's (2012) aim of their study is that the role financial market developments play in mediating the impact of FDI on economic growth. Results show that the effect of FDI on economic growth is non-linear in nature. Ljungwall and Li (2007) state that the interaction of FDI and financial development increases growth. Raheem and Oyınlola (2013) in their study, 15 African countries selected and it was concluded that there is a positive relationship between FDI and growth when the financial development indicator reaches a certain threshold level. According to Desbordes and Wei (2017) a deep financial system in source and destination countries strongly facilitates the international expansion of firms through FDI.

When the studies examining the effect of financial development and FDI on growth are examined in the literature; in general, financial development and FDI have a positive impact on growth.

There are studies in the literature that examine the relationship between financial development and financial constraint. For example, Love (2003) shows that financial development decreases financing constraints. Solan and Yenice (2017) they examined how financial development reduces financial constraints. Desbordes and Wei (2017) state that unambiguously indicate that a deep financial system in source and destination countries strongly facilitates the international expansion of firms through FDI. Baum et al.'s (2011) findings reveal that both the structure of the financial system and its level of development matter.

Table 2. Literature review

Author	Method	Period	Result
Inançlı, Aydın (2015)	Johansen Cointegration Test, Granger Causality Test, Vector Error Correction Model	1980-2012	In the short period, global competitiveness itself has led to foreign direct investment. Also a reciprocal causality between foreign direct investment and foreign competition capacity has come out in the long run in Turkey.
Nur, Dilber (2017)	Panel Data Method	1996-2014	18 developing countries were selected from the (IMF) World Economic Outlook 2015. It concluded that while control of corruption, openness to trade, technology, total labor and rule of law variables affects FDI inflows positively and total debt service, gross fixed capital formation and infrastructure variables affects FDI negatively.
Omran, Bolbol (2003)	Panel Data Method	1975-1999	Data from Arab countries showed that the impact of FDI on growth significantly increased if financial development reached a certain threshold level, and FDI increased financial development.
Ljungwall, Li (2007)	Generalized Method of Moment	1986-2003	Sample consist of a panel of 28 provinces in Mainland China. They show that the interaction between foreign direct investment and indicators measuring the degree of market-oriented financing enhance economic growth. The interaction of FDI and financial development has been stated to increase growth.
Bayar, Gavriletea (2018)	Westerlund Cointegration Test, Dumitrescu and Hurlin Causality Test	1996-2015	Their findings reveal that there is no cointegrating relationship among FDI inflows, investments of foreign portfolio and development of financial sectors. However, there is a one-way causality from development of financial sectors to FDI inflows over the short run.
Alfaro et al. (2003)	Cross-Country Data	1975-1995	The effect of FDI on growth alone is uncertain; however, they concluded that well-organized financial market countries benefited greatly from FDI. *(Sample of 71 countries for which data on credit markets are available, sample of 49 countries for which data on SCAPT and SVALT are available, sample of 53 countries for which SVALT was available but SCAPT was not: Sample of 49 plus Costa Rica, Honduras, Ireland, and Panama).*
Göçer (2013)	Time Series Analysis Methods	1980-2011	As a result of the empirical analysis 1% increases of FDI in Turkey, increases total factor productivity by 0.10%, economic growth by 0.49% and domestic investments by 0.12%, decreases current account deficit by 2.79% and employment by 0.01%.
Raheem, Oyınlola (2013)	TAR (Threshold Autoregressive)	1970-2010	According to data availability, 15 African countries were selected and it was concluded that there is a positive relationship between FDI and growth when the financial development indicator reaches a certain threshold level.
Şahin, (2018)	Panel Data Method	2004-2014	It analyzes the determinants of foreign direct investment in APEC countries. It shows that there is a positive and statistically significant relationship between foreign direct investments, economic growth and trade openness.
Ang (2009)	Annual Time Series	1970-2004	They examined the impact of FDI on the economy of Thailand by controlling for the level of financial development. according to results, financial development stimulates economic development whereas foreign direct investment impacts negatively on output expansion in the long run.
Bolívar et al. (2019)	Panel Data Method	2009-2015	They study the economic performance of countries in terms of their associations with certain FDI partners employing social network analysis. Their conclusion is that country features such as size, openness, skill levels, and institutional stability not only set the pace of FDI, but that they also influence both the network structure and the power positions of each node.
Choong, Lim (2009)	Technique of Cointegration, Error Correction Model	1970-2001	It is stated that the interaction between FDI and financial development exerts a significant effect on the growth performance of Malaysia. Their study showed that the significant role played by FDI–finance interaction in the growth process.
Dunning, Zhang (2008)	Stepwise Test, Country Groups Based on Income Level, Country Groups Based on Openness, Econometric Test	WEF (2005), UNIDO (2004) WIR (2002)	They find that the level of competitiveness does encourage both inward and outward FDI. The Institutions (I) of a country has stronger positive effects on FDI than its RCM (capabilities and markets). For the independent and competitive related variables, they use the rankings of the 117 countries contained in GCR. Their study shows that the effects of I are particularly strong in countries at the advanced stage of development.
Landesman, Stehrer (2000)	Foreign Trade Data	1963-1997	The competitiveness of the processing industry improved the most in transition countries. Moreover, it was the greatest role of firms with foreign participation. (industrialized and developing 32 countries investigated).
Delgado et al. (2012)	Panel Data Method	2001-2008	They define a new concept, global investment attractiveness, which is the cost of factor inputs relative to a country's competitiveness using multiple data sets covering more than 130 countries over. The definition of global investment attractiveness offers a platform for further work.
Pradhan (2010)	Johansen's Cointegration Technique, Error Correction Model	1970-2007	The study examines the long-term relationship between financial development, FDI and growth in India. It is stated that the Indian economy needs a better financial system for growth and FDI.

continued on following page

Table 2. Continued

Author	Method	Period	Result
Bonelli (1999)	A Case Study	1990s.	When looking at data within the manufacturing sector in Brazil linking the growth of competitiveness to FDI, there does not appear to be a clear-cut relationship with either the growth of FDI or the share of foreign capital within different industries. This evidence would suggest that there is no general tendency for FDI to be attracted primarily to industries where competitiveness is improving most rapidly.
Akal, Gökmenoğlu (2012)	Granger Causality Tests	2005	In this study, it was confirmed that direct foreign investments have caused competitive power for each OECD country, R&D expenditures have determined competitive power to a large extent.
Saray, Hark (2015)	Dynamic Panel Data	2004-2012	The most important competitiveness determinant of OECD countries ensues as productivity variable. There have been no relationship determined with competitiveness power, foreign direct investment and the number of patent applications.
Adeniyi et al. (2012)	Error Correction Model, Granger Causality Analysis	1970-2005	They examined the relationship between financial development, FDI and growth for the countries of Cote'ahili, Gambia, Ghana, Nigeria and Sierra Leone in their studies. Financial development in Ghana, Gambia and Sierra Leone has been seen to support economic growth by increasing the benefit from FDI. In Nigeria, there is no relationship between these variables.
Alvarez, Marin (2013)	Panel Data Method	1996-2010	They study how the integration of firms from developing countries in sophisticated high-tech markets can be defined by the combined action of MNE and the ability for technology absorption and creation. Analysis shows how the different dimensions of internal and external factors affect international competitiveness in high-tech industries.
Zhang (2014)	Panel Data Method	2005-2010	Results suggest that FDI has large positive effects on China's industrial performance; such effects are much greater on low-tech manufacturing than medium- and high-tech industries.
Korgaonkar (2012)	Interpreting Regression, Data Mining Techniques	1980-2009	In this study, data about 78 countries were used results showed that FDI did not turn to financially weak countries. Moreover, it is stated that the developed financial system is a prerequisite for the positive effect of FDI on growth.
Artan, Hayaloğlu (2015)	Panel Data Method	1990-2012	Main determinants of foreign direct investment in OECD countries are institutional factors rather than economic determinants. According to this, a good institutional structure plays an important role in attracting foreign direct investment in OECD countries.
Zadeh, Madani (2012)	Regression Model	1971-2008	In this study examines financial market development, FDI and economic growth in Iran, the intermediary role of financial development is tried to be determined in order to benefit from FDI in achieving economic growth. Accordingly, if the country has not reached the threshold level of financial development, it affects growth negatively. Conversely, FDI has a positive impact on growth if financial development has exceeded the threshold level. (ratio of threshold level private sector loans to GDP)
Akal et al. (2012)	Multiple Regression	2007	Net inward foreign direct investment has a statistically significant positive effect on the competitiveness, but it has a very low impact when compared with the impact of Human Development Index and R&D Expenditures. It is stated that the increases in net foreign direct investment used to represent the activities of multinational firms increased the competitiveness of OECD countries.
Çetin, Şeker (2014)	Dynamic Panel Data	1996-2011	They find that trade openness and financial development are positively associated with foreign direct investment in the long-run. The empirical results imply that trade openness and financial development are the determinants of foreign direct investment in OECD countries.
Özgür, Demirtaş (2015)	Unrestricted VAR, Johansen Co-integration Test	1992:1-2013:3	The study investigates the long-run relationship among financial development, FDI and economic growth in Turkey. According to the results, while financial development positively affected growth, long-term effect of FDI was not positive. In addition, it has been suggested that FDI will have an indirect positive effect supporting economic development with increasing financial development level.
Sghaier, Abida (2013)	Generalized Method of Moment (GMM) Panel Data Analysis	1980-2011	4 countries of North Africa (Tunisia, Morocco, Algeria and Egypt) have been studied. They find strong evidence of a positive relationship between FDI and economic growth. In order to increase the positive effects of FDI on the economy, it is necessary to improve the financial system.
Solan, Yenice (2017)	Generalized Method of Moment (GMM) Panel Data Analysis	2005-2015	It was investigated how financial development reduces financial constraints for BIST. According to the results that financial constraints are alleviated by financial development for firms that are considered to be financial constraints which are not part of a large business group, or without any foreign partners.

continued on following page

Table 2. Continued

Author	Method	Period	Result
Desbordes, Wei (2017)	Regression Model	2003-2006	They investigated the various structural effects of financial development on foreign direct investment. Their empirical results unambiguously indicate that a deep financial system in source and destination countries strongly facilitates the international expansion of firms through FDI. *(in 83 source and in 13 broad manufacturing sectors of 125 (developed and developing) destination countries.)*
Love (2003)	Single-Country Regressions	1988-1998	This study contributes to the economic development and growth literature by showing that financial development diminishes financing constraints by reducing information asymmetries and contracting imperfections. It provides evidence that financial development impacts growth by reducing financing constraints.
Baum, Schäfer, Talavera (2011)	Panel Data Method	1989-2006	They conjecture that a country's financial system, both in terms of its structure and its level of development, should influence the cash flow sensitivity of cash of constrained firms but leave unconstrained firms unaffected. Their findings reveal that both the structure of the financial system and its level of development matter.

Source: Prepared by the authors.

The literature also includes studies on the determinants of foreign direct investment. For example, according to Artan and Hayaloğlu (2015) main determinants of foreign direct investment in OECD countries are institutional factors rather than economic determinants. Çetin and Şeker (2014) in their study state that trade openness and financial development are the determinants of foreign direct investment in OECD countries.

Akal and Gökmenoğlu (2012) which is one of the studies dealing with the relationship between FDI and competitiveness in the literature, it was expressed that direct foreign investments have caused competitive power, R&D expenditures have determined competitive power to a large extent. Again regarding the relationship between FDI and competitiveness, Inançlı and Aydın's (2015) in their study, a reciprocal causality between foreign direct investment and foreign competition capacity has come out in the long run in Turkey. Dunning and Zhang (2008) find that the level of competitiveness does encourage both inward and outward FDI. According to them, the Institutions (I) of a country has stronger positive effects on FDI. Saray and Hark's (2015) in their study, there has been no relationship determined with competitiveness power, foreign direct investment and the number of patent applications in OECD countries. The most important competitiveness determinant is productivity variable. Akal et al. (2012) state that the increases in net foreign direct investment increased the competitiveness of OECD countries.

METHODS

Data Set and Variables

In the study PD observation of 36 OECD countries with the years 1997, 2003 and 2006 and the period 2010-2016 (totally 10 years) and CSD observation of same country group with for the year 2016 were applied. The countries which were observed are all members of OECD.

The data for IMF-FDI was collected from IMF (Svirydzenka, 2016) whereas OECD-FRRI data was collected from OECD (https://stats.oecd.org.) for 36 OECD member countries.

At the initial level of development for Developing Counties (DC) basic inputs such as labour and capital are key determinants of economic growth. Foreign direct investment plays a crucial role for DC in two different aspects. First one is it is important for the capital accumulation in the host country where the second one is it brings technology transferring to the country. Besides these two properties it also helps

Table 3. Results of the relationship between OECD-FRRI and IMF-FDI where OECD-FRRI is as dependent variable and IMF-FDI is as independent variable with CSD Method

Dependent Variable: FRRI				
Method: Least Squares				
Sample: 1 36				
Included observations: 36				
Variable	Coefficient	Std. Error	t-Statistic	Prob.
C	0.029809	0.033183	0.898330	0.3753
FDI	0.056746	0.050831	1.116369	0.2721
R-squared	0.035359	Mean dependent var		0.065250
Adjusted R-squared	0.006987	S.D. dependent var		0.058142
S.E. of regression	0.057938	Akaike info criterion		-2.804920
Sum squared resid	0.114133	Schwarz criterion		-2.716947
Log likelihood	52.48856	Hannan-Quinn criter.		-2.774215
F-statistic	1.246280	Durbin-Watson stat		2.331239
Prob(F-statistic)	0.272092			

Source: Eviews9 software

the country to access the new target markets for its export products. Today foreign direct investment is still important for the economic stability of a country whether it is developing or advanced. According to the UNCTAD World Investment Report 2019 (UNCTAD, 2019) there was 1.3 trillion dollar foreign direct investment inflows in the world in 2018 and United States was the most attractive country for foreign direct investments with nearly 251.8 billion dollar inflows with and a 19.4% share. On the other hand, OECD countries attracted 606.6 billion dollars foreign direct investment with a share of 46.8%. Not only the financial stability but the financial development in the country is also an important factor for foreign direct investment inflows into a country so that a country should establish its financial infrastructure to reach financial development and attract foreign direct investments into the country.

An improvement in financial development increases the foreign direct investment inflows into a country resulting with an economic growth and enhancing the competitiveness of the country in international markets. Higher foreign direct investments mean better access to the technology, capital and new target export destinations for the country. The domestic market gains competitiveness with the entrance of foreign direct investments via multinational corporations and transnational corporations. These corporations also establish bridges between hosting domestic country and target market countries.

Following the existing literature for the relationship between foreign direct investment and financial development in a country the estimated model in the study can be described as follow:

$\ln(Y_{it}) = f(X_{it})$, ln: natural logarithm, Y_{it}: OECD-FRRI, X_{it}: IMF-FDI

$\ln(Y_{it}) = f(X_{it})$, ln: natural logarithm, Y_{it}: IMF-FDI, X_{it}: OECD-FRRI

$\ln(Y_{it}) = \alpha + \beta \times X_{it} + \upsilon_t$, i= 1,2,3 ... 36 (countries), t = 2016 for CSD, Y_{it}: OECD-FRRI or IMF-FDI, X_{it}: IMF-FDI or OECD-FRRI

Table 4. Results of the relationship between OECD-FRRI and IMF-FDI where is IMF-FDI as dependent variable and OECD-FRRI is as independent variable with CSD Method

Dependent Variable: FDI				
Method: Panel Least Squares				
Sample: 2007 2016				
Periods included: 10				
Cross-sections included: 36				
Total panel (balanced) observations: 360				
Variable	Coefficient	Std. Error	t-Statistic	Prob.
C	0.609068	0.014767	41.24419	0.0000
FRRI	0.183707	0.143380	1.281260	0.2009
R-squared	0.004565	Mean dependent var		0.623034
Adjusted R-squared	0.001784	S.D. dependent var		0.189206
S.E. of regression	0.189037	Akaike info criterion		-0.488212
Sum squared resid	12.79308	Schwarz criterion		-0.466622
Log likelihood	89.87808	Hannan-Quinn criter.		-0.479627
F-statistic	1.641626	Durbin-Watson stat		0.078779
Prob(F-statistic)	0.200932			

Source: Eviews9 software

$\ln(Y_{it}) = \alpha + \beta \times X_{it} + \upsilon_t$, i= 1,2,3 ... 36 (countries), t = 1997, 2003, 2006, 2010-2016 (10-year period) for PD, Y_{it}: OECD-FRRI or IMF-FDI, X_{it}: IMF-FDI or OECD-FRRI

In the study OECD-FRRI or IMF-FDI variable is considered as dependent variable (Y) whereas IMF-FDI or OECD-FRRI variable as independent (explanatory) variable (X) in regressions.

The Financial Development Index (IMF-FDI) which was created by IMF summarizing how developed financial institutions and financial markets are in terms of their depth, access, and efficiency and the Foreign Direct Investment Regulatory Restrictiveness Index (OECD-FRRI) which was created by The Organisation for Economic Co-operation and Development (OECD) measuring statutory restrictions on foreign direct investment were used in the study. For PD analysis 10-year period as 1997, 2003, 2006, 2010, 2011, 2012, 2013, 2014, 2015, 2016 and for CSD analysis the year 2016 were studied for 36 OECD countries.

α is the constant coefficient (intercept) and β is the regression coefficient (independent variable coefficient/ slope). υ_t is the disturbance (error) term that represents the changes in OECD-FRRI or IMF-FDI is not defined by IMF-FDI or OECD-FRRI at time t. υ_t is a random variable with well-defined probability properties and is υ_t ~Normally and Independently Distributed (NID) (0, σ^2) where υ_t has zero (0) mean and common variance (σ^2) for all countries according to the Classical Normal Linear Regression and is normally and independently distributed according to time and countries (Gujarati and Porter, 2008).

ANALYSIS RESULTS

The Relationship Between OECD-FRRI and IMF-FDI with CSD Method

If the relationship between OECD-FRRI and IMF-FDI is wanted be expressed as a regression for 36 OECD countries for cross-section data the following equations are obtained.

OECD-FRRI$_{2016}$ =α+β* IMF-FDI$_{2016}$ and IMF-FDI$_{2016}$ =α+β* OECD-FRRI$_{2016}$ where α and β are coefficients.

The relationship between IMF-FDI and OECD-FRRI where OECD-FRRI is as dependent variable and IMF-FDI is as independent variable is estimated with CSD by the EViews 9 software (https://www.eviews.com) is as below (Table 3).

The equation below tells us one percent increase in IMF-FDI causes approximately 0.057 (5.7%) increase in OECD-FRRI for 36 OECD countries in average.

OECD-FRRI$_{2016}$ =0.0298+0.057* IMF-FDI$_{2016}$

In the equation above nearly 3.5% of the changes in OECD-FRRI are expressed by IMF-FDI.

The relationship between IMF-FDI and OECD-FRRI where IMF-FDI is as dependent variable and OECD-FRRI is as independent variable is estimated with CSD by the EViews 9 software) is as below (Table 4).

The equation below tells us one percent increase in IMF-FDI causes approximately 0.057 (5.7%) increase in OECD-FRRI for 36 OECD countries in average.

IMF-FDI$_{2016}$=0.609+0.184* OECD-FRRI$_{2016}$

In the equation above nearly 0.46% of the changes in IMF-FDI are expressed by OECD-FRRI.

The statistical values of the coefficients of both regressions are not statistically significant (p >0.05 and the absolute values of the coefficients t are inside the threshold values of the t distribution either F-statistic value is lower than critical value). So the regressions above are not adequate. It is obviously seen that there is no relationship between OECD-FRRI and IMF-FDI in short term.

The Relationship Between OECD-FRRI and IMF-FDI with Random Effects Model (REM)

If the relationship between OECD-FRRI and IMF-FDI is wanted be expressed as a REM regression for 36 OECD countries for panel data the following equations are obtained.

OECD-FRRI$_t$ =α+β* IMF-FDI$_t$ and IMF-FDI$_t$ =α+β* OECD-FRRI$_t$ where α and β are coefficients and t = 1997, 2003, 2006, 2010-2016 (10-year period).

The relationship between IMF-FDI and OECD-FRRI where OECD-FRRI is as dependent variable and IMF-FDI is as independent variable is estimated with REM PD by the EViews 9 software is as below (Table 5).

The equation below tells us one percent increase in IMF-FDI causes approximately 0.202 (20.2%) decrease in OECD-FRRI for 36 OECD countries in average. It seems that financial development inhibits foreign direct investment restrictions in a country.

$$\text{OECD-FRRI}_{1997,\,2003,\,2006,\,2010\text{-}2016} = 0.202 - 0.202 * \text{IMF-FDI}_{1997,\,2003,\,2006,\,2010\text{-}2016}$$

In the equation above nearly 12% of the changes in OECD-FRRI are expressed by IMF-FDI.

The statistical values of the coefficients of both regressions are statistically significant (p <0.05 and the absolute values of the coefficients t are outside the threshold values of the t distribution either F-statistic value is bigger than critical value). So the regressions above is adequate. It is obviously seen that there is negative relationship between OECD-FRRI and IMF-FDI in long term.

Table 5. Results of the relationship between OECD-FRRI and IMF-FDI where OECD-FRRI is as dependent variable and IMF-FDI is as independent variable with REM PD Method

Dependent Variable: FRRI				
Method: Panel EGLS (Cross-section random effects)				
Sample: 2007 2016				
Periods included: 10				
Cross-sections included: 36				
Total panel (balanced) observations: 360				
Swamy and Arora estimator of component variances				
Variable	Coefficient	Std. Error	t-Statistic	Prob.
C	0.201869	0.020277	9.955431	0.0000
FDI	-0.201990	0.027914	-7.236263	0.0000
	Effects Specification			
			S.D.	Rho
Cross-section random			0.061797	0.8009
Idiosyncratic random			0.030809	0.1991
	Weighted Statistics			
R-squared	0.120529	Mean dependent var		0.011839
Adjusted R-squared	0.118072	S.D. dependent var		0.033892
S.E. of regression	0.031828	Sum squared resid		0.362662
F-statistic	49.06294	Durbin-Watson stat		0.787267
Prob(F-statistic)	0.000000			
	Unweighted Statistics			
R-squared	-0.375868	Mean dependent var		0.076022
Sum squared resid	2.391616	Durbin-Watson stat		0.119380

Source: Eviews9 software

If the regression is wanted to be obtained by pooled ordinary least squares method it would be as;

OECD-FRRI $_{1997, 2003, 2006, 2010\text{-}2016}$ = 0.06 +0.02*IMF-FDI$_{1997, 2003, 2006, 2010\text{-}2016}$

But it must be considered that pooled all 36 observations and estimate a "grand" regression neglecting the cross-section and time series nature of our data is not meaningful since all 36 countries are not same so the regression will not be valid.

"Hausman Test" can be applied to test the validity of the REM which shows the relationship between OECD-FRRI and IMF-FDI where OECD-FRRI is as dependent variable and IMF-FDI is as independent variable obtained with the EViews 9 software above.

H_0: REM can be applied,
H_1: FEM can be applied instead of REM

The following "Hausman Test" (Table 6) also shows that null hypothesis indicating REM can be applied should be rejected, since with 1 df (degree of freedom) and X^2 (chi-square) value is statistically significant so that FEM can be applied instead of REM.

The Relationship Between OECD-FRRI and IMF-FDI Where OECD-FRRI is as Dependent Variable and IMF-FDI is as Independent Variable with Fixed Effects Model (FEM)

As the null hypothesis is rejected, the alternative one which tells FEM can be applied for the relationship should be accepted and the regression estimated by FEM will be as below.

OECD-FRRI $_{1997, 2003, 2006, 2010\text{-}2016}$ = 0.25 -0.28*IMF-FDI$_{1997, 2003, 2006, 2010\text{-}2016}$

It simply means that one unit increase in IMF-FDI for 36 OECD countries causes nearly 28% decrease in OECD-FRRI in average. The regression above shows that about 82.4% of the changes in the OECD-FRRI is expressed by the IMF-FDI values of the 36 countries (Table 7).

If the relationship between IMF-FDI and OECD-FRRI where IMF-FDI is as dependent variable and OECD-FRRI is as independent variable is estimated with REM PD by the EViews 9 software the results will be as below (Table 8).

The equation below tells us one percent increase in OECD-FRRI causes approximately 0.66 (66%) decrease in IMF-FDI for 36 OECD countries in average. It seems that foreign direct investment restrictions inhibits financial development in a country.

IMF-FDI $_{1997, 2003, 2006, 2010\text{-}2016}$ = 0.67 -0.66* OECD-FRRI $_{1997, 2003, 2006, 2010\text{-}2016}$

In the equation above nearly 16.7% of the changes in IMF-FDI are expressed by OECD-FRRI.

The statistical values of the coefficients of both regressions are statistically significant (p <0.05 and the absolute values of the coefficients t are outside the threshold values of the t distribution either F-statistic value is bigger than critical value). So the regressions above is adequate. It is obviously seen

Table 6. "Hausman Test" results of for REM to test the relationship between OECD-FRRI and IMF-FDI where OECD-FRRI is as dependent variable and IMF-FDI is as independent variable with PD method

Correlated Random Effects - Hausman Test				
Equation: Untitled				
Test cross-section random effects				
Test Summary	Chi-Sq. Statistic		Chi-Sq. d.f.	Prob.
Cross-section random	25.083455		1	0.0000
Cross-section random effects test comparisons:				
Variable	Fixed	Random	Var(Diff.)	Prob.
FDI	-0.279983	-0.201990	0.000243	0.0000
Cross-section random effects test equation:				
Dependent Variable: FRRI				
Method: Panel Least Squares				
Sample: 2007 2016				
Periods included: 10				
Cross-sections included: 36				
Total panel (balanced) observations: 360				
Variable	Coefficient	Std. Error	t-Statistic	Prob.
C	0.250461	0.019981	12.53526	0.0000
FDI	-0.279983	0.031964	-8.759420	0.0000
	Effects Specification			
Cross-section fixed (dummy variables)				
R-squared	0.823627	Mean dependent var		0.076022
Adjusted R-squared	0.803969	S.D. dependent var		0.069584
S.E. of regression	0.030809	Akaike info criterion		-4.024941
Sum squared resid	0.306582	Schwarz criterion		-3.625536
Log likelihood	761.4895	Hannan-Quinn criter.		-3.866130
F-statistic	41.89852	Durbin-Watson stat		0.984691
Prob(F-statistic)	0.000000			

Source: Eviews9 software

that there is negative relationship between IMF-FDI and OECD-FRRI where IMF-FDI is as dependent variable and OECD-FRRI is as independent variable in long term.

If the regression is wanted to be obtained by pooled ordinary least squares method it would be as;

$$\text{IMF-FDI}_{1997, 2003, 2006, 2010\text{-}2016} = 0.61 + 0.184 * \text{OECD-FRRI}_{1997, 2003, 2006, 2010\text{-}2016}$$

But it must be considered that as it is mentioned before pooled all 36 observations and estimate a "grand" regression neglecting the cross-section and time series nature of our data is not meaningful since all 36 countries are not same so the regression will not be valid.

Table 7. Results of the relationship between OECD-FRRI and IMF-FDI where OECD-FRRI is as dependent variable and IMF-FDI is as independent variable with FEM PD method

Dependent Variable: FRRI				
Method: Panel Least Squares				
Sample: 2007 2016				
Periods included: 10				
Cross-sections included: 36				
Total panel (balanced) observations: 360				
Variable	Coefficient	SStd. Error	t-Statistic	Prob.
C	0.250461	0.019981	12.53526	0.0000
FDI	-0.279983	0.031964	-8.759420	0.0000
	Effects Specification			
Cross-section fixed (dummy variables)				
R-squared	0.823627	Mean dependent var		0.076022
Adjusted R-squared	0.803969	S.D. dependent var		0.069584
S.E. of regression	0.030809	Akaike info criterion		-4.024941
Sum squared resid	0.306582	Schwarz criterion		-3.625536
Log likelihood	761.4895	Hannan-Quinn criter.		-3.866130
F-statistic	41.89852	Durbin-Watson stat		0.984691
Prob(F-statistic)	0.000000			

Source: Eviews9 software

"Hausman Test" can be applied to test the validity of the REM which shows the relationship between IMF-FDI and OECD-FRRI where IMF-FDI is as dependent variable and OECD-FRRI is as independent variable obtained with the EViews 9 software above.

H_0: REM can be applied,
H_1: FEM can be applied instead of REM

The following "Hausman Test" (Table 9) also shows that null hypothesis indicating REM can be applied should be rejected, since with 1 df and X^2 value is statistically significant so that FEM can be applied instead of REM.

The Relationship Between OECD-FRRI and IMF-FDI Where IMF-FDI is as Dependent Variable and OECD-FRRI is as Independent Variable with Fixed Effects Model (FEM)

As the null hypothesis is rejected, the alternative one which tells FEM can be applied for the relationship should be accepted and the regression estimated by FEM will be as below.

$$\text{IMF-FDI}_{1997, 2003, 2006, 2010\text{-}2016} = 0.67 - 0.69 * \text{OECD-FRRI}_{1997, 2003, 2006, 2010\text{-}2016}$$

Table 8. Results of the relationship between OECD-FRRI and IMF-FDI where IMF-FDI is as dependent variable and OECD-FRRI is as independent variable with REM PD method

Dependent Variable: FDI				
Method: Panel EGLS (Cross-section random effects)				
Sample: 2007 2016				
Periods included: 10				
Cross-sections included: 36				
Total panel (balanced) observations: 360				
Swamy and Arora estimator of component variances				
Variable	Coefficient	Std. Error	t-Statistic	Prob.
C	0.673152	0.031440	21.41088	0.0000
FRRI	-0.659257	0.077335	-8.524655	0.0000
	Effects Specification			
			S.D.	Rho
Cross-section random			0.184683	0.9362
Idiosyncratic random			0.048210	0.0638
	Weighted Statistics			
R-squared	0.167270	Mean dependent var		0.051256
Adjusted R-squared	0.164943	S.D. dependent var		0.053034
S.E. of regression	0.048463	Sum squared resid		0.840828
F-statistic	71.91102	Durbin-Watson stat		1.090643
Prob(F-statistic)	0.000000			
	Unweighted Statistics			
R-squared	-0.091546	Mean dependent var		0.623034
Sum squared resid	14.02827	Durbin-Watson stat		0.065371

Source: Eviews9 software

It simply means that one unit increase in OECD-FRRI for 36 OECD countries causes nearly 69% decrease in IMF-FDI in average. The regression above shows that about 94.2% of the changes in the IMF-FDI is expressed by the OECD-FRRI values of the 36 countries (Table 10).

Detecting Autocorrelation in the Regressions

The Relationship Between OECD-FRRI and IMF-FDI where OECD-FRRI is as Dependent Variable and IMF-FDI is as Independent Variable with FEM PD Method

To detect the presence of autocorrelation in the residuals of the regressions above the Durbin-Watson d statistic is applied.

H₀: there is no sequential relationship between error terms (neither the same direction nor opposite direction),

Table 9. Results of "Hausman Test" for REM to test the relationship between OECD-FRRI and IMF-FDI where OECD-FRRI is as dependent variable and IMF-FDI is as independent variable with PD method

Correlated Random Effects - Hausman Test				
Equation: Untitled				
Test cross-section random effects				
Test Summary	Chi-Sq. Statistic	Chi-Sq. d.f.	Prob.	
Cross-section random	4.777222	1	0.0288	
Cross-section random effects test comparisons:				
Variable	Fixed	Random	Var(Diff.)	Prob.
FRRI	-0.685574	-0.659257	0.000145	0.0288
Cross-section random effects test equation:				
Dependent Variable: FDI				
Method: Panel Least Squares				
Sample: 2007 2016				
Periods included: 10				
Cross-sections included: 36				
Total panel (balanced) observations: 360				
Variable	Coefficient	Std. Error	t-Statistic	Prob.
C	0.675153	0.006470	104.3537	0.0000
FRRI	-0.685574	0.078267	-8.759420	0.0000
	Effects Specification			
Cross-section fixed (dummy variables)				
R-squared	0.941587	Mean dependent var		0.623034
Adjusted R-squared	0.935077	S.D. dependent var		0.189206
S.E. of regression	0.048210	Akaike info criterion		-3.129415
Sum squared resid	0.750704	Schwarz criterion		-2.730010
Log likelihood	600.2948	Hannan-Quinn criter.		-2.970604
F-statistic	144.6285	Durbin-Watson stat		1.226852
Prob(F-statistic)	0.000000			

Source: Eviews9 software

H_1: There is a sequential relationship between error terms.

The d-value (d_L) at the lower limit is taken as 1.411 and the d-value at the upper limit (d_U) is taken as 1.525 with 1 explanatory variable (IMF-FDI) at level 5% and 36 observations (country). H_0 can't be rejected if $d_U < 4 - d_U$ and can be rejected if $0 < d_L$. As the d (0.98) value obtained in the regression is 0.98 < 1.411 the null hypothesis (H_0) can be rejected and it can be said that there is no positive sequential relationship between the error terms.

Table 10. Results of the relationship between OECD-FRRI and IMF-FDI where OECD-FRRI is as dependent variable and IMF-FDI is as independent variable with FEM PD method

Dependent Variable: FDI			
Method: Panel Least Squares			
Sample: 2007 2016			
Periods included: 10			
Cross-sections included: 36			
Total panel (balanced) observations: 360			
Variable	Coefficient	Std. Error	t-Statistic	Prob.
C	0.675153	0.006470	104.3537	0.0000
FRRI	-0.685574	0.078267	-8.759420	0.0000
Effects Specification			
Cross-section fixed (dummy variables)			
R-squared	0.941587	Mean dependent var	0.623034
Adjusted R-squared	0.935077	S.D. dependent var	0.189206
S.E. of regression	0.048210	Akaike info criterion	-3.129415
Sum squared resid	0.750704	Schwarz criterion	-2.730010
Log likelihood	600.2948	Hannan-Quinn criter.	-2.970604
F-statistic	144.6285	Durbin-Watson stat	1.226852
Prob(F-statistic)	0.000000		

Source: Eviews9 software

The Relationship Between OECD-FRRI and IMF-FDI Where IMF-FDI is as Dependent Variable and OECD-FRRI is as Independent Variable with FEM PD Method

As the d (1.23) value obtained in the regression is 1.23<1.411 the null hypothesis (H_0) can be rejected and it can be said that there is no positive sequential relationship between the error terms.

Table 11. Pairwise "Granger Causality Test" results of to test the direction of relationship between IMF-FDI and OECD-FRRI in CSD

Pairwise Granger Causality Tests			
Sample: 1 36			
Lags: 2			
Null Hypothesis:	Obs	F-Statistic	Prob.
FRRI does not Granger Cause FDI	34	0.36200	0.6994
FDI does not Granger Cause FRRI		3.77688	0.0349

Source: Eviews9 software

Table 12. Pairwise "Granger Causality Test" results of to test the direction of relationship between IMF-FDI and OECD-FRRI in PD

Pairwise Granger Causality Tests			
Sample: 2007 2016			
Lags: 2			
Null Hypothesis:	Obs	F-Statistic	Prob.
FRRI does not Granger Cause FDI	288	4.22559	0.0155
FDI does not Granger Cause FRRI		5.80160	0.0034

Source: Eviews9 software.

Granger Causality Tests

The Granger Causality tests may be approved for both PD and CSD sets to show the direction of the causality between OECD-FRRI and IMF-FDI.

To test OECD-FRRI causes IMF-FDI
H_0: OECD-FRRI does not Granger cause IMF-FDI
H_1: OECD-FRRI Granger causes IMF-FDI
To test IMF-FDI causes OECD-FRRI
H_0: OECD-FRRI does not Granger cause IMF-FDI
H_1: OECD-FRRI Granger causes IMF-FDI
To test the direction of relationship between IMF-FDI and OECD-FRRI in CSD
To test OECD-FRRI causes IMF-FDI;

According to the Table 11 results F value doesn't exceed the critical F value and p>0.05 level of significance, so we can't reject null hypothesis so that OECD-FRRI doesn't Granger cause IMF-FDI for CSD.

To test IMF-FDI causes OECD-FRRI;

According to the Table 11 results F value exceeds the critical F value and p<0.05 level of significance, so we reject null hypotheses and accept that IMF-FDI Granger causes OECD-FRRI for CSD.

To test the direction of relationship between IMF-FDI and OECD-FRRI in PD
To test OECD-FRRI causes IMF-FDI;

According to the Table 12 results F value exceeds the critical F value and p<0.05 level of significance, so we reject null hypothesis so that we accept that OECD-FRRI Granger causes IMF-FDI for PD.

To test IMF-FDI causes OECD-FRRI;

According to the Table 12 results F value exceeds the critical F value and p<0.05 level of significance, so we reject null hypothesis so that we accept that IMF-FDI Granger causes OECD-FRRI for PD.

CONCLUSION

According to the RAM and FEM with PD analysis in the study OECD-FRRI is found as one of the determinants of IMF-FDI and IMF-FDI is found as one of the determinants of OECD-FRRI in OECD member countries. After applying the appropriate test it is found is FEM is adequate instead of REM. with PD.

For CSD analysis, there is no significant proof to say OECD-FRRI is one of the main determinants of IMF-FDI and IMF-FDI is one of the determinants of OECD-FRRI in OECD member countries.

Granger causality test is also applied to test the direction of causality between OECD-FRRI and IMF-FDI for the selected countries by both PD and CSD analyses. It is obviously seen that OECD-FRRI causes IMF-FDI and vice versa according to the Granger test statistics for PD. For CSD, OECD-FRRI does not cause IMF-FDI whereas IMF-FDI causes OECD-FRRI.

In the study it is found that OECD-FRRI affects IMF-FDI and IMF-FDI affects OECD-FRRI negatively not at once but in a time period. In the manuscript our results show there is a negative relationship between OECD-FRRI and IMF-FDI in both directions according to the PD. As the OECD-FRRI increases in a country IMF-FDI decreases and vice versa. It seems that financial development inhibits foreign direct investment restrictions and foreign direct investment restrictions inhibits financial development in a country.

For CSD there is no exact relationship between OECD-FRRI and IMF-FDI.

Totally removing or at least decreasing restrictions on foreign direct investment will enhance Foreign Direct Investment inflows into a country. Attracting Foreign Direct Investment will enable the financial development of the country's financial institutions and markets and financial development will also promote FDI inflows into the country in long term.

REFERENCES

Adeniyi, O., Omisakin, O., Egwaikhide, F. O., & Oyinlola, A. (2012). Foreign direct investment economic growth and financial sector development in small open developing economies. *Economic Analysis and Policy*, *42*(1), 105–127. doi:10.1016/S0313-5926(12)50008-1

Akal, M., & Gökmenoğlu, S. M. (2012). OECD Ülkelerinde Rekabet Gücünün Nedensellik İlişkisi: Ampirik Bir Analiz. *TISK Akademi*, *7*(13), 102–129.

Akal, M., Kabasakal, A., & Gökmenoğlu, S. M. (2012). OECD Ülkelerinin Rekabet Gücünü Açıklayıcı Kurumsal ve Karma Modeller. *Business and Economics Research Journal*, *3*(1), 109–130.

Alfaro, L., Chanda, A., Özcan, S. K., & Sayek, S. (2003). FDI and economic growth: the role of local financial markets. *Journal of International Economics*, *64*(1), 89–112. doi:10.1016/S0022-1996(03)00081-3

Alvarez, I., & Marin, R. (2013). FDI and technology as levering factors of competitiveness in developing countries. *Journal of International Management*, *19*(3), 232–246. doi:10.1016/j.intman.2013.02.005

Ang, J. B. (2009). Foreign direct investment and its impact on the Thai economy: The role of financial development. *Journal of Economics and Finance*, *33*(3), 316–323. doi:10.100712197-008-9042-6

Artan, S., & Hayaloğlu, P. (2015). Doğrudan Yabancı Sermaye Yatırımlarının Kurumsal Belirleyicileri: OECD Ülkeleri Örneği. *Ege Akademik Bakış, 15*(4), 551–564. doi:10.21121/eab.2015416654

Baum, C., Schäfer, D., & Talavera, O. (2011). The impact of the financial system's structure on firms' financial constraints. *Journal of International Money and Finance, 30*(4), 678–691. doi:10.1016/j.jimonfin.2011.02.004

Bolívar, L. M., Casanueva, G., & Castro, I. (2019). Global foreign direct investment: a network perspective. *International Business Review*, 1–17.

Bonelli, R. (1999). A note on foreign direct investment and industrial competitiveness in Brazil. *Oxford Development Studies, 27*(3), 305–327. doi:10.1080/13600819908424180

Çetin, M., & Şeker, F. (2014). Ticari Açıklık ve Finansal Gelişmenin Doğrudan Yabancı Yatırımlar Üzerindeki Etkisi: Oecd Ülkeleri Üzerine Dinamik Panel Veri Analizi. *Atatürk Üniversitesi İktisadi ve İdari Bilimler Dergisi, 28*(1), 125–147.

Choong, C.-K., & Lim, K.-P. (2009). Foreign direct investment, financial development and economic growth: the case of Malaysia. *Macroeconomics and Finance in Emerging Market Economies, 2*(1), 13–30. doi:10.1080/17520840902726227

Čihák, M., Demirguc-Kunt, A., Feyen, E., & Levine, R. (2012). Benchmarking financial development around the world. *World Bank Policy Research Working Paper*, 6175. World Bank, Washington, DC.

Delgado, M., Ketels, C., Porter, M. E., & Stern, S. (2012). The determinants of national competitiveness. *Nber Working Paper Series*, National Bureau of Economic Research, Cambridge, 1-47.

Desbordes, R., & Wei, S.-J. (2017). The effects of financial development on foreign direct investment. *Journal of Development Economics, 127*, 153–168. doi:10.1016/j.jdeveco.2017.02.008

Dunning, J. H., & Zhang, F. (2008). *Foreign direct investment and the locational competitiveness of countries. Transnational Corporations, 17(3)* (pp. 1–30). New York: United Nations.

EViews downloads. (n.d.). Retrieved from https://www.eviews.com/download/download.shtml#eviews9

Göçer, İ. (2013). *Yabancı Doğrudan Yatırımların Makroekonomik ve Verimlilik Etkileri: Türkiye Çin ve Hindistan Örneği*. Adnan Menderes Üniversitesi Sosyal Bilimler Enstitüsü Doktora Tezi.

Gujarati, D. N., & Porter, D. C. (2008). *Basic econometrics* (5th ed.). The McGraw-Hill Series Economics.

IMF. (n.d.). Financial development index database. Retrieved from https://data.imf.org/?sk=F8032E80-B36C-43B1-AC26-493C5B1CD33B&sId=1480712464593

İnançlı, S., & Aydın, F. (2015). Doğrudan Yabancı Sermaye Yatırımı ve Dış Rekabet Gücü İlişkisi: Türkiye İçin Nedensellik Analizi. *Sakarya İktisat Dergisi, 4*(1), 52–69.

Korgaonkar, C. (2012). Analysis of the impact of financial development on foreign direct investment: a data mining approach. *Journal of Economics and Sustainable Development, 3*(6), 70–78.

Landesmann, M., & Stehrer, R. (2000). Potential switchovers in comparative advantage: patterns of industrial convergence. *WIIW Working Papers,* No. 14.

Ljungwall, C., & Li, J. (2007). Financial sector development, FDI and economic growth in China. *Center for Economic Research (CCER)* Peking University. Working Paper Series, No: E2007005.3.

Love, I. (2003). Financial development and financing constraints: international evidence from the structural investment model. *Review of Financial Studies*, *16*(3), 765–791. doi:10.1093/rfs/hhg013

Nur, H. B., & Dilber, İ. (2017). Gelişmekte Olan Ülkelerde Doğrudan Yabancı Yatırımları Belirleyen Temel Unsurlar. *Dokuz Eylül Üniversitesi İktisadi ve İdari Bilimler Fakültesi Dergisi*, *32*(2), 15–45. doi:10.24988/deuiibf.2017322551

OECD. (n.d.). FDI regulatory restrictiveness index. Retrieved from https://www.oecd.org/investment/fdi index.htm

OECD. (n.d.). Retrieved from https://www.oecd-ilibrary.org/finance-and-investment/oecd-s-fdi-restrictiveness-index5km91p02zj7g-en

OECD. (n.d.). Retrieved from https://stats.oecd.org/Index.aspx?datasetcode=FDIINDEX#

Omran, M., & Bolbol, A. (2003). Foreign direct investment financial development and economic growth: evidence from the Arab countries. *Review of Middle East Economics and Finance*, *1*(3), 231–249. doi:10.1080/1475368032000158232

Özgür, M. I., & Demirtaş, C. (2015). Finansal Gelişme ve Doğrudan Yabancı Yatırımların Ekonomik Büyüme Üzerindeki Etkileri: Türkiye Örneği. *E-Journal of New World Sciences Academy*, *10*(3), 76–91.

Pradhan, R. P. (2010). Financial deepening foreign direct investment and economic growth: are they cointegrated. *International Journal of Financial Research*, *1*(1), 37–43. doi:10.5430/ijfr.v1n1p37

Raheem, I. D., & Oyınlola, M. A. (2013). Foreign direct investment-economic nexus: the role of the level of financial sector development in Africa. *Journal of Economics and International Finance*, *5*(9), 327–337. doi:10.5897/JEIF2013.0542

Sahay, R., Čihák, M., N'Diaye, P., Barajas, A., Bi, R., Ayala, D., ... Yousefi, S. R. (2015). Rethinking financial deepening: stability and growth in emerging markets. *IMF Staff Discussion Note, SDN*, *15*(08), 1–41. doi:10.5089/9781498312615.006

Şahin, D. (2018). Apec Ülkelerinde Doğrudan Yabancı Sermaye Yatırımlarının Belirleyicileri. *Kırıkkale Üniversitesi Sosyal Bilimler Dergisi*, *8*(2), 415–430.

Saray, M. O., & Hark, R. (2015). OECD Ülkelerinin İleri-Teknoloji Ürünlerindeki Rekabet Güçlerinin Değerlendirilmesi. *Çankırı Karatekin Üniversitesi İktisadi ve İdari Bilimler Fakültesi Dergisi*, *5*(1), 347-372.

Sghaier, I. M., & Abida, Z. (2013). Foreign direct investment, financial development and economic growth: empirical evidence from North African countries. *Journal of International and Global Economic Studies*, *6*(1), 1–13.

Solan, E., & Yenice, S. (2017). Finansal Gelişmişliğin Finansal Kısıtlara Etkisi: Borsa İstanbul Uygulaması. *Kara Harp Okulu Bilim Dergisi*, *27*(1), 25–52.

Svirydzenka, K. (2016). Introducing a new broad-based index of financial development. IMF Working Paper WP/16/5. Retrieved from https://www.imf.org/external/pubs/ft/wp/ 2016/wp1605.pdf

UNCTAD. (2019). World Investment Report 2019. Special economic zones key messages and overview. United Nations, Geneva. Retrieved from https://unctad.org/en/Publications Library/wir2019_overview_en.pdf

Zadeh, H. A., & Madani, Y. (2012). Financial market development FDI and economic growth in Iran. *Journal of Basic and Applied Scientific Research*, 2(1), 228–230.

Zhang, K. H. (2014). How does foreign direct investment affect industrial competitiveness? Evidence from China. *China Economic Review*, 30, 530–539. doi:10.1016/j.chieco.2013.08.003

Section 3

Chapter 11
Understanding the Investment Behavior of Individual Investors:
An Empirical Study on FOREX Markets

Yavuz Bilgin
Halkbank, Turkey

Selin Metin Camgoz
Hacettepe University, Turkey

Mehmet Baha Karan
Hacettepe University, Turkey

Yilmaz Yildiz
University of Huddersfield, UK

ABSTRACT

The FOREX market has become a popular ground amongst all kinds of market players. The leverage transactions of the market that may generate higher profit levels with low capital/investments make it very attractive for the individual risk takers. The research investigates the trading behavior of FOREX investors relying on the survey data collected from 167 Turkish investors in 2019. Within the scope of the research, the authors evaluate whether and to what extent behavioral factors, namely demographic characteristics; personal characteristics such as personality traits, love of money, and biases like disposition effect influence investment performance. The results reveal that among the personality traits, openness to experience and conscientiousness have a positive impact while disposition effect and love of money have a negative impact on the performance of investors. Additional analysis suggests that the effects of personality traits and biases on trading performance remarkably change among subgroups of investors regarding their income level.

DOI: 10.4018/978-1-7998-2559-3.ch011

INTRODUCTION

The Foreign Exchange market, hereafter 'FOREX' market, is not only one of the most exciting, volatile, and engaging markets in the investment world, but also the largest market in terms of daily turnover. The BIS Triennial Central Bank Survey (2016) estimates that the total turnover in global foreign exchange markets is 5.1 trillion dollars a day and that is much larger than the turnover in U.S. treasury bonds and the trading volume at the New York Stock Exchange (Barker, 2007). The main players of the FOREX market are institutional investors namely dealers, banks (including central banks), and investment funds. Their shares in the trading volume are 42%, 22% and 16%, respectively (BIS, 2016). While the central banks use the FOREX markets to carry out monetary policies or to protect the value of money, corporations trade currency for global business operations and to hedge risk. The recent advances in electronic trading and its institutional trading adaptations have shifted the balance of the market participation from banks and other financial accounts to big and small 'market participants'. This has resulted in domestic and global players becoming one of the primary drivers of the market in the recent years. Although the motives of FOREX trading are much more diverse than traders in the capital markets, FOREX market players are generally known to be speculative and return-motivated.

In general, the transaction volume of individual investors (retail investors) is very low compared with institutional parties, but interestingly, their participation in the FOREX markets has been substantially increasing in last decades (Rime & Schrimpf, 2013). The individual investors base currency trades on a various tools including fundamentals and technical factors such as inflation rate, interest parity, price pattern and technical indicator. Especially, low transaction cost, leverage trading, high liquidity, and resilient lot size have been making the market more attractive for retail investors. Brendan Callan, the president of FOREX Capital Markets in Europe, rationalize this picture by claiming that accessibility of currency news in the mainstream media has led the individual investors to become more comfortable with FOREX trading (Financial Times, 2011). On the other hand, a recent research on the French securities indicates that the FOREX market is much more complex and the risky for small investors than equity markets and 89% of all active retail clients lose their money (AMF, 2014). Nevertheless, many individual investors around the globe have been fallen down or lost millions of dollars in the last years due to widespread fraud (NBCnews, 2012). These experiences have led the regulatory authorities to take actions for individual investors. An example is the case of Turkey where after a series of failures of individual investors, the Turkish Market Regulatory Agency (SPK) has recently raised the minimum investment amount for the FOREX market to limit the entry of individual investors to the market (Republic of Turkey Official Gazette, 2017). Despite these facts and recent failures, the interest of individual investors to the FOREX market is still growing not only in Turkey but also worldwide.

Indeed, poor performance of individual investors is not limited to the FOREX market. Barber and Odean (2013) mention that individual investors in the real world behave differently than the investors in models of traditional finance such as Capital Asset Pricing Model. In this regard, they argue that the investment attitude of the individuals is well explained by the behavioral factors rather than the rational expectations. The research specifies that the individual investors have a tendency to trade frequently. As a result of this overtrading, they face high investment costs, make inefficient stock selections and lose money. Most of them hold undiversified portfolios, which generate high levels of diversifiable risk relying on their past experience and tend to ignore the prescriptive advice of experts. Daniel Kahneman and Amos Tversky, the founding fathers of behavioral finance, clearly state that *"human decision-making processes are distorted by inherent biases toward optimism and overconfidence"* and *"these subjective perceptions, when present to a significant degree in the financial decision-making process, can result in miscalculating the value of an opportunity*" (Kahneman & Tversky, 1979).

The risk of individual traders in the FOREX market is beyond capital markets due to high leverage trading availability. As a leveraged instrument, there is heavy risk associated with FOREX trades that can result in significant losses. A very small change in value quickly adds up to bigger profits or bigger losses. Obviously, margin trading makes the market attractive for risk taker individual investors and aggressive profit-seekers. Individual investors are noise traders and their noise trading decrease the capability to adjust to the new information, therefore understanding the behavioral and demographic characteristics of these investors is very important for market regulators, banks and brokerage houses (Bloomfield et al., 2009). Although there exists extensive work on the attitude of individual investors, the research particularly examining behaviors of retail investors in the FOREX market are quite limited.

Relying on that, the aim of the current research is to explore the trading behavior of individual investors in the FOREX market. This study evaluates whether and to what extent behavioral factors, namely demographic characteristics; personal characteristics such as personality traits, love of money, and disposition effect bias affect investors' gains and losses. The main prediction of the study is that the behavior of individual investors in the FOREX market can be explained under behavioral finance phenomenon. To this aim, data is collected from 167 Turkish Forex investors trading in 2019 by random surveys. The respondents are asked for their demographic and behavioral characteristics. By employing logistic regression methodology, the results suggest that behavioral factors and personality traits successfully explain the performance of individual FOREX investors. Moreover, the impact of behavioral factors is contingent upon the income level of the investors which supports prior findings regarding the trading patterns of individual investors (Vissing-Jorgensen, 2003).

There are several distinct contributions of the current study to the growing behavioral finance literature. First, through employing a comprehensive survey, the relations between the behavioral factors and investors' trading performance are established. Second, there is very limited research on attitudes of individual investors trading in the FOREX market especially in emerging markets and to authors' knowledge, there is no research on Turkish investors. Therefore, this research has a potential to produce novel results within an uncommon sample of investors. Finally, the findings of the research provide valuable implications and insights to not only investors but also to the market regulators in developing measures against noisy and disruptive trading behavior of investors.

The chapter consists of six sections. In Section 2, a brief discussion about the prior literature of behavioral finance and investment attitudes of the individual investors is presented. Section 3 is devoted to the survey design and the instruments used in the research. In Section 4, the methodology and the models are explained. Chapter 5 presents the findings and Section 6 concludes the chapter.

LITERATURE REVIEW AND HYPOTHESES DEVELOPMENT

The Rise of Behavioral Finance

With the rise of anomalies and departures of market behavior apart from the predictions of Efficient Market Hypothesis (EMH) as well as rising critics targeted EMH, an emerging interest tend to focus on behavioral finance or behavioral economy. Behavioral finance as a sub discipline of the broader behavioral economy, is considered as the integration of psychology and finance (Ritter, 2003). Behavioral finance has made breakthrough by its thorough investigation of markets and investors. It aims to combine psychological theories with traditional economics and finance and tries to understand what drives investors to make irrational decisions. The traditional finance model is rooted from the idea that the players of the markets process all the information accurately as they are perfectly rational. However, the model of behavioral finance is descriptive in nature and explores how the participants of the market behave in reality (Shiller, 2003). Unlike traditional finance, the scholars of behavioral finance contend that investors are irrational in general and exhibit systematic and predictable biases mostly originated from cognition and emotions (Lo et al., 2005). More particularly, they assume that investors' thoughts, emotions, perceptions, and personal characteristics are represented in their judgements and behavioral actions (Daniel et al., 2002; De Bondt, 1998).

Big-Five Personality Traits

Personality is defined as "the dynamic organization within the individual of the psychophysical systems that determine his characteristics, behavior and thought" (Allport, 1961, p. 28). It basically refers a set of distinct tendencies, attitudes, and behaviors that differentiate one individual from another. When we talk about personality we refer to a set of characteristics that are mostly stable and consistent over time and in different situations. Among a number of personality theories, the consensus among scholars has reached that an individual's personality could be explained by Big-Five personality traits. Those five traits are extraversion, conscientiousness, openness to experience, neuroticism and agreeableness (Costa and McCrae, 2003; Pervin & John, 1999). The Big-Five personality traits have attracted extensive attention from both researchers and practitioners for their possible effects on both individual, organizational outcomes and productivity (Barrick & Mount, 1991; Salgado, 1997).

Extraversion is related with being energetic, social, talkative, assertive and active (Goldberg, 1993). Extraversion dimension is considered as one of the strongest determinants of thrill-seeking (Zuckerman, 1994). This dimension is particularly associated with being assertive, energetic, high level of energy and activity, and also excitement seeking. Those individuals who are high in excitement seeking (a facet of extraversion) tend to overtrade to experience more excitement. In a study conducted by Abbey & Doukas (2015), it is reported that the currency traders who trade daily seem to earn greater returns compared to the performance of passive traders. Moreover, extraversion is related to the information seeking and acquisition (Tauni et al., 2015). Extravert investors tend to obtain significant amount of information before making investment decisions with the help of large networks, which may lead them to make better assessment of opportunities and increase their investment performance. Özerol et al. (2011) address this issue by investigating the role of personality traits and some demographics (gender, marital status, and age) on distinguishing successful fund managers from the unsuccessful ones. Their findings reveal that extraversion is associated with better financial performance measured by Sharpe ratio. Therefore, a positive association of extraversion with trading performance of FOREX investors is proposed.

Neuroticism dimension relates to what extent an individual reacts to his/her surroundings. This dimension is characterized by moodiness, anger, hostility, impulsivity and emotional instability. Neurotic individuals tend to experience negative emotions, shift emotional mood, feel anxiety, and experience stress because of worrying too much about different things (Costa & McCrae, 2003). The individuals who score low in neuroticism, on the other hand, are considered as emotionally stable. Neuroticism affects the performance of individuals in different channels. First, high level neuroticism relates to poor performance in terms of extrinsic success across the life span (Judge et al. 1999). Furthermore, Cox

Fuenzalida et al. (2004) find that neurotic individuals have a lower reaction time especially when there is a significant change in their work environment. As another channel, investors with a neurotic trait tend to trade more which may reduce the efficiency of their trading and as a consequence decrease their performance. Therefore, a negative association of neuroticism with trading performance is proposed.

Conscientiousness dimension is related to having high levels of thoughtfulness and impulsive control. Those individuals tend to be well organized, feel responsibility of their actions, and are hardworking, careful about deadliness, and spend time on planning. The study of Salgado (1997) demonstrate that conscientiousness is found to be the strongest predictor of performance. Specifically, they find that conscientiousness is positively related to high performance in all occupation groups since conscientiousness associates to self-discipline and responsibility. Moreover, Metin Camgoz et al. (2011) also reports a positive correlation between conscientiousness and investment performance of fund managers. Therefore, it might be reasonable to propose a positive association of conscientiousness with trading performance of the FOREX investors.

Agreeableness involve the attributes of kindness, modesty, trust affection, altruism, and prosocial behaviors (Digman, 1997). The individuals who are high in agreeableness care about the others, feels empathy and enjoy helping others. One of the most important facet of agreeableness dimension is compliance, which refers how an individual follows the rules. So, a high score in this trait might have a more tendency to follow the trade recommendations and obey the rules of the trading system. Although high level of agreeableness is usually attached to better performance if the task requires interpersonal skills; its effect on performance in an environment which requires minimum level of teamwork and harmony may be insignificant or negative. Since trading in FOREX markets requires independent thinking, self-assessment, and critical judgement, investors who are high in agreeableness may struggle in making independent choices and in turn experience lower returns in their financial investments. Moreover, Eisen et al. (2002) argue that these individuals are misguided by false information and fail to make critical assessment which may diminish their portfolio returns. Therefore, a negative association of agreeableness with the trading performance is proposed.

Openness to experience, indicates the extent that individuals like to explore novel and new things. They are focused on trying new things and challenges. Those are the individuals who are identified having high levels of tolerance for uncertainty and demanding change and novelty. Thus, it is defined as "*a tendency toward sensation seeking and correlated with risk-taking*" (Costa & McCrae, 2003). Barrick and Mount (1991) argue that high scoring individuals in terms of openness to experience trait are broadminded and they are more likely to be motivated to learn. On the other hand, openness to experience is also associated with high level of risk tolerance and increased trading activity (Kleine et al., 2016). Assuming that frequent trading activity is positively related to the positive abnormal returns in currency trading (Abbey & Doukas, 2015), individuals higher in this dimension may earn positive alphas in their investment decisions. Therefore, the authors expect a positive influence of high level of openness to experience on investment performance.

Overall, the integration of the personality research with behavioral finance and exploration of investors' personality traits on their financial decisions attract significant attention from the scholars since the introduction of behavioral finance into the agenda. However, these studies are not limited to the performance determinants of individual investors. Several studies in the literature investigate the impact of personality traits on risk tolerance, risk taking, and also trading frequency. An earlier research is conducted by Filbeck et al. (2005), in which the authors use the Myers-Briggs Type personality for assessing risk tolerance differences. Their findings demonstrate evidence that personality types explain the variation in risk tolerances. Such that, individuals who score high in sensing, thinking, and judging dimensions have higher risk tolerances.

In terms of trading performances, extraversion and openness to experience are argued to have an significant effect on the individuals' perceptions of risky trading choices (Nicholsan, et al., 2005). Particularly, risk taking is found to be greater for individuals with higher extraversion and openness to experience scores compared to those who are high in conscientiousness, neuroticism, and agreeableness. Likewise, Durand et al. (2008) report a positive association between the individual's extraversion type of personality and stock exposure. Their research demonstrates that while extraversion is positively associated with trading frequency; openness to experience is positively related to portfolio diversification. Moreover, agreeableness and conscientiousness are more likely to be correlated with selecting momentum stocks in portfolios. Another research conducted with a sample of business school undergraduates reveals that the participants high on extraversion dimension are reported to trade more and invest higher proportion of money in stock market compared to participants with low level of extraversion (Mayfield et al., 2008). Moreover, they report that individuals high in neuroticism avoid short-term investing, while those who are high in openness to experience tend to engage in long-term investment behavior.

In a recent study, Oehler et al. (2018) explore the impact of extraversion and neuroticism on individuals' decision making in an experimental asset market. They find that extravert traders have a tendency to buy at higher prices for risky instruments compared to introverts and they tend to invest more on the risky instruments when they are overpriced. In contrast, neurotics are reported to have a tendency to make more sales for underpriced assets and thus, sell risky assets at low prices.

Love of Money

Love of money is defined as "*an individual's attitude toward money or the meaning that individuals attribute to it*" (Chen et al., 2014). Alternatively, it is the assessment of an individual's subjective feelings about money. The other definitions of love of money specify it in terms of someone's aspiration and desire for money or one's greed and aspiration for materialism (Tang & Chen, 2008). In this sense, love of money is considered as an individual differing variable and it is on the eye of the beholder (Tang & Chiu, 2003).

Scholars acknowledge that love of money has a multidimensional nature (Tang & Chiu, 2003). Among different sub dimensions, '*rich*' refers to the strong ambition that the individual has desire for possessing a great amount of money. The idea of being rich controls those people's desires and thoughts (Sardžoska & Tang, 2009). Those individuals who have higher levels of positive attitudes towards being rich, are argued to have "foolish and harmful desires and are likely to take action and make money" (Tang & Liu, 2012, p. 296). The sub dimension of '*importance*' indicates that the attitude of individuals towards money is significant and valuable factor in their lives. This is the cognitive component of love of money construct. Those individuals who attribute greater importance to money think that money is good and important for their lives (Chen et al., 2014). The sub dimension of '*motivator*' indicates that money is the fundamental mechanism for individuals to pursue an action and persist on it. It stands for the idea that for such individuals, there is no better motivator or incentive than money. An individual would describe it as 'money reinforces me to work harder' as a motivator factor.

A number of studies on money and money attitudes has been conducted in the literature (e.g. Diener & Seligman, 2004; Furnham & Argyle, 1998; Vohs et al., 2006). Majority of the research have focused on the effects of love of money in relation to unethical intention and outcomes, whilst no research addresses the impact of love of money on trading performances of investors. However, the authors argue that investors' attitudes towards money might influence the trading performances of FOREX investors. It is expected that the love of money and its sub dimensions will lead FOREX investors to act irrationally and impulsively, which in turn would diminish their gains. Thus, a negative association of love of money with FOREX investors' trading performance is expected.

Disposition Effect

The disposition effect –as one of the biases when making investment and trading decisions– is defined as the investor tendency to sell the winner assets too early and to hold the loser assets too long (Weber & Camerer, 1998). This inclination that investors appear reluctant to realize losses and eager to realize gains, has first time been conceptualized by Shefrin and Statman (1985). One of the explanations to the disposition effect refers to the prospect theory, which suggests that investors behave differently in different risk conditions. They are risk averse when faced with gains and risk-seeking when faced with losses (Hens & Vleck, 2011). Shefrin and Statman (1984) alternatively explains the disposition effect with emotions of regret and pride. This is to avoid regret when the stock price goes down while hoping that it will go up in the future and to seek for pride when the stock price goes up.

Since its presentation to the behavioral finance literature, several research have been conducted to explore the signs of disposition effect among different samples of individual or institutional investors. Ferris et al. (1988) is one of the earliest research that presents empirical evidence of disposition effect among individual investors. Odean (1999)'s work is a well-known research that provides experimental evidence on the disposition effect through an analysis of trading records of 10,000 individual investors. In another study examining day trader transactions support evidence of a disposition effect (Jordan & Diltz, 2004). Likewise, Locke and Mann (2005) also provide evidence of disposition effect in a sample of professional futures traders. Dhar and Zhu (2006) propose that certain investor characteristics predict engaging in disposition effect bias.

Moreover, the regret and pride aspects of the disposition effect are also experimented by several research. Fogel and Berry (2006) investigate the effect of the emotion of regret on the disposition effect through experiments. Muermann and Volkman (2006) develop a dynamic portfolio choice model which incorporates anticipated regret and pride revealing that anticipating regret and pride can help explaining the disposition effect.

Although it is common to explore the evidence of disposition effect among investors, the number of research that focus on the consequences of disposition effect on trading performance is limited. As an example to such research can be given as Chen et al. (2007), which demonstrate evidence on how disposition effect leads to poor trading decisions within a sample of Chinese traders. On the other hand, although several research on discovering disposition effect can be found individual and institutional stock market investors, the number of studies on FOREX market traders is also limited. A recent example in FOREX markets can be given as Beilis et al. (2014), which focuses on the impact of regret on selling behavior. The current study tries to fill this gap in the literature by investigating the relationship of disposition effect with FOREX investors' trading performances.

DATA and METHODOLOGY

Sample and Procedure

The sample of the research is composed of individual investors who make transactions in FOREX market. The data of the study is obtained through survey methodology. Data were collected by sending emails with an online survey link approximately to 1000 FX investors between March 2019 and July 2019 and 306 investors responded to it. A total of responses are with a return rate of 30.6 percent and no incentives were offered for participation. Finally, the results of 167 participants who answered the questionnaire completely are included in the study.

The demographic profile of the respondents can be seen in Table 1. 87% of the respondents are male whereas 13% of are female. Approximately 68% of the respondents are married. Incomes of the investors range from less than $20,000 to over $90,000 and 38% of the investors are in high income group. The largest portion of the respondents (63%) possesses a college degree or higher, while the rest (37%) have a high school diploma or lower. The mean age of the respondents is 37.

Measurement of the Variables

The questionnaire is primarily designed to capture FOREX investors' Big-five personality traits, love of money, and disposition effect biases. In other words, the authors try to reveal how these biases act in financial decisions and affect the performance of the individual investors. Detailed information about the scales are given below:

The Big-Five Personality Instrument (BFI): The personality traits of the FOREX investors are assessed by the 44-item Big-Five Inventory (BFI) developed by John et al. (1991). The inventory contains 44 items to assess agreeableness, conscientiousness, extraversion, neuroticism and openness to experience. Sample items are: "generally trusting/ is helpful" for agreeableness; "perseveres until the task is

Table 1. Demographic profile of the investors

		Frequency	Percentage
Gender	Male	146	87.43
	Female	21	12.57
Marital Status	Single	54	32.34
	Married	113	67.66
Income Level	Low	103	61.68
	High	64	38.32
Education	Below high school	14	8.38
	High school	40	23.95
	Associate	9	5.39
	College	81	48.5
	Above college	23	13.77
This table presents the demographic profiles of the investors included in this study.			

finished" for conscientiousness; "is outgoing/is full of energy" for extraversion; "gets nervous easily" for neuroticism; and "is original, comes up with new ideas" for openness to experience. The responses range from 1 (strongly disagree) to 5 (strongly agree). The instruments are translated and adapted into Turkish by Sümer et al. (2005). The Cronbach alpha reliability coefficients range from 0.64 (Agreeableness) to 0.82 (Extraversion).

Love of Money (LOMS): Nine items adapted from the 17-item LOMS scale developed by Tang et al. (2005) are employed. LOMS measures the participants' feelings and attitudes towards money. The nine items cover rich, motivator and importance sub factors. For instance, the sample items for rich factor is *"I want to be rich"*, *"Money reinforces me to work harder"* is for motivator factor and *"Money is important"* is for important factor. The response format ranges from (1) strongly disagree to (5) strongly agree. Higher scores denote the higher levels for love of money. The Turkish translation of the scale is conducted by the authors using back translation procedure. The Cronbach alpha reliability score is 0.90 for total score of Love of Money.

Disposition Effect: The disposition effect of the FOREX investors was assessed by two scenario questionnaires that are adapted from Shefrin and Statman (1985)'s original article. The respondents were confronted with trade off scenarios as "selling the losing stocks and realizing the paper loss" or "holding the losing stock for break-even".

Methodology

To assess the impact of personality traits and other psychological biases on the investor performance in the FOREX market, backward logistic regression is utilized. The logistic regression methodology is usually employed when the dependent variable is categorical. The advantage of logistic analysis is that it does not seek the assumption that the variables used in the analysis have a normal distribution. Logistic regression finds the best fitting model to explain the dependent variable (dichotomous variable) and a set of explanatory predictors aThe logistic regression model is defined in Equation 1 as;

$$logit(p) = b_0 + b_1 X_1 + b_2 X_2 + b_3 X_3 + \ldots + b_k + X_k \tag{1}$$

In Equation 1, p denotes the probability of the presence of the characteristic of interest. B is the coefficient of the variables including the intercept (b_0) and X represents the variables included in the model. The logit transformation is described as the logged odds as following:

$$odds = \frac{p}{1-p} = \frac{probability of presence of characteristic}{probability of absence of characteristic} \tag{2}$$

In Equation 2, odds ratio of a given variable is calculated as dividing the probability of presence of characteristic to the probability of absence of the given characteristic. The logistic regression provides coefficient estimates for the null hypotheses together with the standard errors and test statistics. The test statistics (specified as "Wald") are calculated by the square of the ratio of coefficients to their standard errors. The interpretations are hinged on the odds-ratios.

The dependent variable of the current model is the trading performance of the FOREX investors which is a dummy variable. The authors code the trading performance (dependent variable) as '1' when FOREX investors have a positive return from their investments (labeled as *successful traders*) or '0' otherwise (labeled as *unsuccessful traders*). Then, Big-Five personality traits, love of money sub-scales, disposition effect and demographic variables such as age, gender, marital status, and income level are regressed on the dependent variable of trading performance. Age variable is a continuous variable represents the current age of the investors. Male investors are coded as "0" and female investors as "1". Single investors are labelled as "0" and married investors as "1". Finally, the authors categorize the investors according to their income label and code as "0" for low income investors and "1" as the high income FOREX investors.

In Table 2, the descriptive statistics and the correlation coefficients of the variables are presented. These highest and lowest coefficients are observed among the Love of Money dimensions as expected. For the personality traits, the highest correlation coefficient is for the Extraversion and the Openness to Experience as 0.564.

FINDINGS

Main Findings

Before moving on to the multivariate analysis, mean difference tests are employed to assess whether personality traits and other biases differentiate according to the performance of the FOREX investors.

According to the results presented in Table 3, there are significant differences between the successful and unsuccessful investors in terms of the several dimensions of personality and psychological biases. Successful FOREX investors have a higher score in Extraversion, Conscientiousness, and Openness to Experience. On the other hand, unsuccessful investors have higher scores in Neuroticism, Disposition Effect, and also "Rich" dimension of Love of Money. Agreeableness and "Importance" and "Motivator" dimensions of Love of Money do not make any contribution in differentiating successful investors from the unsuccessful ones.

To test the impact of demographic characteristics and personality traits of the FOREX investors on their financial performance, backward logistic regression estimation is employed. The backward logistic regression analysis begins with a full model including all the independent variables, followed by gradually eliminating variables from the regression model at each step to find a reduced model that best explains the data. Accordingly, first of all, gender, age, marital status, Big-Five personality traits, love of money dimensions as richness, importance and motivator and disposition effect are all included in the analysis. The final results of logistic regression estimation for the full sample yield only four variables in predicting successful traders from unsuccessful ones. Table 4 presents the results.

The overall fit of the model is checked by several goodness of fit tests. The first one is Nagelkerke and Cox & Snell. The results of these tests are 0.205 and 0.273, respectively. The model is significant regarding the likelihood test value as 193.005. Additionally, the Hosmer-Lemeshow test of the model is insignificant, which indicates that the model adequately fits the data. The results estimate 74.7% of the unsuccessful traders and 65% of the successful ones successfully, and the overall percentage of accuracy is 70.1%. Considering the threshold of 50%, the accuracy of the model is quite high. According to the Wald criterion, the variables of Conscientiousness, Openness to experience, Rich dimension of Love

Table 2. Descriptive statistics and correlation coefficients

	Variables	Mean	SD	1	2	3	4	5	6	7	8	9	10	11	12	13	14	15
1	Performance	0.521	0.501	1														
2	Age	36.994	9.385	-0.036	1													
3	Gender	0.126	0.333	0.074	-0.204*	1												
4	Marital status	0.677	0.469	0.003	0.411*	-0.239*	1											
5	Income	0.383	0.488	0.164	0.041	-0.038	0.202*	1										
6	Education	3.353	1.223	0.022	0.022	0.112	0.053	0.216*	1									
7	Agreeableness	3.762	0.546	-0.041	0.126	0.032	0.140	-0.078	0.114	1								
8	Extraversion	3.368	0.823	0.268*	-0.135	0.108	0.128	0.320*	0.213*	0.150	1							
9	Conscientiousness	3.779	0.722	0.273*	0.174	0.057	0.191	0.186	0.123	0.319*	0.357*	1						
10	Neuroticism	2.704	0.825	-0.277*	-0.061	-0.014	-0.089	-0.238*	-0.044	-0.151	-0.416*	-0.426*	1					
11	Openness	3.724	0.620	0.297*	-0.082	0.128	0.01	0.246*	0.175	0.223*	0.564*	0.378*	-0.287*	1				
12	Disposition effect	0.605	0.490	-0.284*	0.039	-0.099	0.095	0.007	0.043	0.134	0.024	-0.030	0.146	-0.127	1			
13	LOM_Rich	4.242	0.831	-0.135	-0.003	-0.016	-0.014	-0.086	0.153	0.157	0.132	0.117	0.075	0.237*	0.235*	1		
14	LOM_Importance	4.246	0.847	-0.014	0.066	-0.003	-0.006	0.062	0.129	0.059	0.146	0.178	0.045	0.233*	0.080	0.628*	1	
15	LOM_Motivator	3.850	1.035	-0.061	-0.024	0.055	-0.108	-0.124	-0.004	0.089	0.111	0.055	0.141	0.077	0.163	0.530*	0.551*	1

This table presents the descriptive statistics and correlation coefficients among the variables used in this study. * denotes the significance level at 1%.

of Money and Disposition effect are found to be significant at 5 percent level. The results indicate that among personality dimensions, Conscientiousness and Openness to experience are reported as positively associated with the likelihood of being a successful trader. Among those, the Openness to experience

Table 3. Mean difference tests

	Successful		Unsuccessful			
	Mean	SD	Mean	SD	t-value	p-value
Agreeableness	3.741	0.597	3.786	0.488	-0.535	0.593
Extraversion	3.579	0.856	3.138	0.724	3.583	0.000
Conscientiousness	3.968	0.704	3.574	0.689	3.656	0.000
Neuroticism	2.486	0.837	2.942	0.747	-3.707	0.000
Openness	3.900	0.573	3.533	0.616	3.996	0.000
Disposition effect	0.471	0.054	0.750	0.049	-3.817	0.000
LOM_Rich	4.134	0.865	4.358	0.781	-1.753	0.081
LOM_Importance	4.234	0.861	4.258	0.837	-0.187	0.852
LOM_Motivator	3.789	1.089	3.917	0.976	-0.794	0.429

This table presents the mean difference tests for the variables of interest.

has a relatively high odds ratio. The Exp (B) ratio for Openness to experience reveals that a one-unit increase in this personality trait will increase likelihood of being a successful trader by a factor of 2.68. On the other hand, the *Rich* sub dimension of Love of money and the Disposition effect attain negative coefficients meaning that they are negatively associated with the likelihood of being a successful trader. Particularly, Disposition effect has a relatively higher odds ratio. A one-unit increase in disposition effect will decrease likelihood of being a successful trader by 0.641 which is obtained by one minus the Exp(B) value of Disposition effect which is 0.359.

Additional Analyses

At this stage of the analysis, the authors act in accordance with the research of Vissing-Jorgensen (2003), suggesting that the irrational behavior tends to diminish with investors' wealth and sophistication levels.

Table 4. Binomial logit estimations for all FOREX investors (N=167)

	B	SE	Wald	Sig.	Exp (B)
Conscientiousness	0.679	0.270	6.349	0.012	1.972
Openness	0.985	0.340	8.401	0.004	2.679
LOM_Rich	-0.506	0.231	4.803	0.028	0.603
Disposition Effect	-1.026	0.371	7.660	0.006	0.359
Constant	-3.376	1.386	5.932	0.015	0.034
Cox and Snell – R^2	0.205				
Nagelkerke – R^2	0.273				
2 Log Likelihood	193.005				
Hosmer-Lemeshow (p-value)	0.378				

This table presents the results of backward logistic regression estimation. B and SE denote the coefficient and the standard error of the variable, respectively.

Relying on that, in the sample, the FOREX investors are divided into two groups according to their income levels. 103 investors are obtained in the low income group and 64 investors are in the high income group. Specifically, high income group represents the investors whose income is greater than the sample mean, vice versa. The backward logistic regression analysis is also employed for these two groups separately to test how performance determinants change according to the income level.

The logistic regression results for the low-income group are reported in Table 5. The goodness of fit test reveals that the model as reliable. The Nagelkerke and Cox & Snell values are 0.169 and 0.226, respectively. The result of the likelihood test value is 122.881 indicating the significance of the model. The Hosmer-Lemeshow test of the model is insignificant, so the data fit the model. The analysis successfully estimates 55.3% of the unsuccessful investors and 75% of the successful ones, and the overall percentage of accuracy is 66% with a 50% cut-off rate.

The results show that Conscientiousness is positively related to success in FOREX trading of low income investors and a one-unit increase in conscientiousness is expected to increase the likelihood of being a successful investor by almost 1.94. On the other hand, Disposition effect is negatively associated with the likelihood of being a successful investor with an Exp (B) ratio of 0.20 revealing that a one-unit increase in disposition effect is expected to decrease the likelihood of being a successful investor by 0.80.

Table 6 presents the logistic regression estimations for the high income group of FOREX investors. The analysis successfully estimates 87.5% of the unsuccessful investors and 54.2% of the successful ones. The estimations for the high income group of FOREX investors indicate that success determinants of high income FOREX investors are remarkably different from those of low income investors. Among the personality traits, extraversion, agreeableness and neuroticism are found to be significant for the high income group and their odd ratios are relatively high. The extraversion dimension is positively related to trading success and a one-unit increase in extraversion trait is expected to increase the likelihood of being successful by 3.5. On the other hand, agreeableness and neuroticism personality traits are found to be negatively related to the likelihood of being a successful investor for the high income individuals. A one-unit increase in agreeableness and neuroticism traits are expected to decrease the likelihood of being successful by factors of 0.787 and 0.735, respectively. Overall, personality traits and biases are strong determinants of the success in FOREX trading, however, income level of the individual plays an important role on this relationship. As in line with the prior results, success factors in FOREX trading significantly differ according to the income level of the individual.

Table 5. Binomial logit estimations for low income FOREX investors (N=103)

	B	SE	Wald	Sig.	Exp (B)
Conscientiousness	0.663	0.313	4.480	0.034	1.940
Disposition Effect	1.610	0.447	12.948	0.000	0.200
Constant	-1.662	1.181	1.980	0.159	0.190
Cox and Snell – R^2	0.169				
Nagelkerke – R^2	0.226				
2 Log Likelihood	122.881				
Hosmer-Lemeshow (p-value)	0.392				
This table presents the results of backward logistic regression estimation for the low income individuals. B and SE denote the coefficient and the standard error of the variable, respectively.					

Table 6. Binomial logit estimations for how income FOREX investors (N=64)

	B	SE	Wald	Sig.	Exp (B)
Extraversion	1.254	0.491	6.526	0.011	3.505
Agreeableness	-1.546	0.747	4.283	0.039	0.213
Neuroticism	-1.330	0.498	7.139	0.008	0.265
Constant	5.081	3.270	2.414	0.120	160.922
Cox and Snell – R^2	0.268				
Nagelkerke – R^2	0.366				
2 Log Likelihood	64.685				
Hosmer-Lemeshow (p-value)	0.939				
This table presents the results of backward logistic regression estimation for the low income individuals. B and SE denote the coefficient and the standard error of the variable, respectively.					

DISCUSSION AND CONCLUSION

In this chapter, the authors investigate the predictors of successful trading performance of FOREX investors with a set of variables associated with personality traits, love of money and disposition effect. To our knowledge, this is the initial research that establishes a link among personality, psychological biases and financial performance of FOREX investors relying on the survey data. Including 167 Turkish FOREX investors into the sample, the findings in the current chapter reveal that personality traits and disposition effect are strong predictors of the performance of FOREX investors. More particularly, openness to experience and conscientiousness are found to positively predict the odds of being a successful FOREX trader. This particular finding corroborates with Salgado (1997) and also extends the work of Metin Camgoz et al. (2011). Also, a significant negative impact of disposition effect and "rich" dimension of love of money on trading performance is obtained. Since "rich" dimension of love of money is related to the desire of gaining great amount of money, individuals who are high in this dimension may struggle making rational decisions or take more risk which result in poor performance in their investment. The association of disposition effect with poor performance of FOREX investors revealed in the current study is congruent with the work of Chen et al. (2007) demonstrating poor performance of Chinese investors originated from disposition effect bias.

In the second stage of the analysis the sample is divided into to as high and low income investors and employ the baseline model for each of the groups. The findings reveal that income level of the investor significantly affects the explanatory power of the determinants of trading performance. Specifically, for the low income investors, conscientiousness and disposition effect significantly explain the variation in the trading performance, however, for the high income group extraversion, neuroticism, and agreeableness are more powerful in explaining the trading performance of FOREX investors. Therefore, one could conclude that rather than having a direct impact of income level on the performance, its effect emerges when it interacts with the personality traits and biases.

The findings of this chapter is of interest for not only investors but also institutions such as investment firms also market regulators which are aimed to ensure proper functioning of the markets. Although traditional finance theories assume the rationality of all investors, it is evident that personality traits and psychological biases such as disposition effect play important role in investment decisions and performance. Therefore, the findings of this study shed additional lights on the plausible effects of behavioral biases on the individual decision making processes together with remarking the irrationality of the human decisions. Further analysis with larger samples and including investors from different cultural backgrounds will enhance the understanding about the motives of personal investment decisions and increase the generalizability of the results.

REFERENCES

Abbey, B. S., & Doukas, J. A. (2015). Do individual currency traders make money? *Journal of International Money and Finance*, *56*, 158–177. doi:10.1016/j.jimonfin.2014.10.003

Allport, G. W. (1961). *Pattern and growth in personality*. London, UK: Holt, Reinhart, and Winston.

AMF. (2014, Oct. 13). *The AMF warns of the dangers of forex market trading for individual investors*. Retrieved from https://www.amf-france.org/en_US/Actualites/Communiques-depresse/AMF/annee_2014.html?docId=workspace%3A%2F%2FSpacesStore%2F96c52a14-3900-464f-8fff-7d4700ff37e3

Barber, B. M., & Odean, T. (2013). The behavior of individual investors. In *Handbook of the Economics of Finance* (Vol. 2, pp. 1533–1570). Elsevier.

Barker, W. (2007). The global foreign exchange market: Growth and transformation. *Bank of Canada Review*, *2007*(Autumn), 4–13.

Barrick, M. R., & Mount, M. K. (1991). The big five personality dimensions and job performance: A meta-analysis. *Personnel Psychology*, *44*(1), 1–26. doi:10.1111/j.1744-6570.1991.tb00688.x

Beilis, A., Dash, J. W., & Wise, J. V. (2014). Psychology, stock/FX trading and option prices. *Journal of Behavioral Finance*, *15*(3), 251–268. doi:10.1080/15427560.2014.943227

BIS. (2016, Dec. 11). *Triennial Central Bank Survey of foreign exchange and OTC derivatives markets in 2016*. Retrieved from www.bis.org/publ/rpfx16.htm

Chen, G., Kim, K. A., Nofsinger, J. R., & Rui, O. M. (2007). Trading performance, disposition effect, overconfidence, representativeness bias, and experience of emerging market investors. *Journal of Behavioral Decision Making*, *20*(4), 425–451. doi:10.1002/bdm.561

Chen, J., Tang, T. L. P., & Tang, N. (2014). Temptation, monetary intelligence (love of money), and environmental context on unethical intentions and cheating. *Journal of Business Ethics*, *123*(2), 197–219. doi:10.100710551-013-1783-2

Costa, P. T., & McCrae, R. R. (2003). *NEO-FFI: NEO Five Factor Inventory*. Lutz, FL: Psychological Assessment Resources.

Cox-Fuenzalida, L. E., Swickert, R., & Hittner, J. B. (2004). Effects of neuroticism and workload history on performance. *Personality and Individual Differences*, *36*(2), 447–456. doi:10.1016/S0191-8869(03)00108-9

Daniel, K., Hirshleifer, D., & Teoh, S. H. (2002). Investor psychology in capital markets: Evidence and policy implications. *Journal of Monetary Economics*, *49*(1), 139–209. doi:10.1016/S0304-3932(01)00091-5

De Bondt, W. F. (1998). A portrait of the individual investor. *European Economic Review*, *42*(3-5), 831–844. doi:10.1016/S0014-2921(98)00009-9

Dhar, R., & Zhu, N. (2006). Up close and personal: Investor sophistication and the disposition effect. *Management Science*, *52*(5), 726–740. doi:10.1287/mnsc.1040.0473

Diener, E., & Seligman, M. E. (2004). Beyond money: Toward an economy of well-being. *Psychological Science in the Public Interest*, *5*(1), 1–31. doi:10.1111/j.0963-7214.2004.00501001.x PMID:26158992

Digman, J. M. (1997). Higher-order factors of the Big Five. *Journal of Personality and Social Psychology*, *73*(6), 1246–1256. doi:10.1037/0022-3514.73.6.1246 PMID:9418278

Durand, R. B., Newby, R., & Sanghani, J. (2008). An intimate portrait of the individual investor. *Journal of Behavioral Finance*, *9*(4), 193–208. doi:10.1080/15427560802341020

Eisen, M. L., Winograd, E., & Qin, J. (2002). Individual differences in adults' suggestibility and memory performance. *Memory and Suggestibility in the Forensic Interview*, 205-234.

Ferris, S. P., Haugen, R. A., & Makhija, A. K. (1988). Predicting contemporary volume with historic volume at differential price levels: Evidence supporting the disposition effect. *The Journal of Finance*, *43*(3), 677–697. doi:10.1111/j.1540-6261.1988.tb04599.x

Filbeck, G., Hatfield, P., & Horvath, P. (2005). Risk aversion and personality type. *Journal of Behavioral Finance*, *6*(4), 170–180. doi:10.120715427579jpfm0604_1

Financial Times. (2011, April 1). *Forex investing: no place for amateurs*. Retrieved from https://www.ft.com/content/62cb6258-5c4c-11e0-8f48-00144feab49a

Fogel, S. O. C., & Berry, T. (2006). The disposition effect and individual investor decisions: The roles of regret and counterfactual alternatives. *Journal of Behavioral Finance*, *7*(2), 107–116. doi:10.120715427579jpfm0702_5

Furnham, A., & Argyle, M. (1998). *The psychology of money*. Psychology Press.

Goldberg, L. R. (1993). The structure of phenotypic personality traits. *The American Psychologist*, *48*(1), 26–34. doi:10.1037/0003-066X.48.1.26 PMID:8427480

Hens, T., & Vlcek, M. (2011). Does prospect theory explain the disposition effect? *Journal of Behavioral Finance*, *12*(3), 141–157. doi:10.1080/15427560.2011.601976

John, O. P., Donahue, E. M., & Kentle, R. L. (1991). The big five inventory—versions 4a and 54.

Jordan, D., & Diltz, J. D. (2004). Day traders and the disposition effect. *Journal of Behavioral Finance*, *5*(4), 192–200. doi:10.120715427579jpfm0504_2

Judge, T. A., Higgins, C. A., Thoresen, C. J., & Barrick, M. R. (1999). The big five personality traits, general mental ability, and career success across the life span. *Personnel Psychology*, *52*(3), 621–652. doi:10.1111/j.1744-6570.1999.tb00174.x

Kahneman, D., & Tversky, A. (1979). Prospect theory: An analysis of decision under risk. *Econometrica*, *47*(2), 263–291. doi:10.2307/1914185

Kleine, J., Wagner, N., & Weller, T. (2016). Openness endangers your wealth: Noise trading and the big five. *Finance Research Letters*, *16*, 239–247. doi:10.1016/j.frl.2015.12.002

Li-Ping Tang, T., Shin-Hsiung Tang, D., & Luna-Arocas, R. (2005). Money profiles: The love of money, attitudes, and needs. *Personnel Review*, *34*(5), 603–618. doi:10.1108/00483480510612549

Lo, A. W., Repin, D. V., & Steenbarger, B. N. (2005). Fear and greed in financial markets: A clinical study of day-traders. *The American Economic Review*, *95*(2), 352–359. doi:10.1257/000282805774670095

Locke, P. R., & Mann, S. C. (2005). Professional trader discipline and trade disposition. *Journal of Financial Economics*, *76*(2), 401–444. doi:10.1016/j.jfineco.2004.01.004

Mayfield, C., Perdue, G., & Wooten, K. (2008). Investment management and personality type. *Financial Services Review*, *17*(3), 219–236.

Metin Camgoz, S., Karan, B., & Ergeneli, A. (2011). Relationship between the Big-Five personality and the financial performance of fund managers. *Current Topics in Management*, *15*, 137–152.

Muermann, A., & Volkman Wise, J. (2006). Regret, pride, and the disposition effect. *Available at SSRN 930675*.

NBC News. (2012, Nov. 19). *Dozens of forex traders arrested.* Retrieved from http://www.nbcnews.com/id/3540930/ns/business-corporate_scandals/t/dozens-FOREX-traders-arrested/#.XSGISegzbDc

Nicholson, N., Soane, E., Fenton-O'Creevy, M., & Willman, P. (2005). Personality and domain-specific risk taking. *Journal of Risk Research*, *8*(2), 157–176. doi:10.1080/1366987032000123856

Odean, T. (1998). Are investors reluctant to realize their losses? *The Journal of Finance*, *53*(5), 1775–1798. doi:10.1111/0022-1082.00072

Oehler, A., Wendt, S., Wedlich, F., & Horn, M. (2018). Investors' personality influences investment decisions: Experimental evidence on extraversion and neuroticism. *Journal of Behavioral Finance*, *19*(1), 30–48. doi:10.1080/15427560.2017.1366495

Özerol, H., Selin, M. C., Karan, M. B., & Ergeneli, A. (2011). Determining the performance of individual investors: The predictive roles of demographic variables and trading strategies. *International Journal of Business and Social Science*, *2*(18).

Pervin, L. A., & John, O. P. (Eds.). (1999). *Handbook of personality: theory and research*. Elsevier.

Republic of Turkey Official Gazette. (2017, Feb. 10). *Notice Number 29975*. Retrieved from http://www.resmigazete.gov.tr/eskiler/2017/02/20170210-5.htm

Rime, D., & Schrimpf, A. (2013). The anatomy of the global FX market through the lens of the 2013 Triennial Survey. *BIS Quarterly Review*, December.

Ritter, J. R. (2003). Behavioral finance. *Pacific-Basin Finance Journal*, *11*(4), 429–437. doi:10.1016/S0927-538X(03)00048-9

Salgado, J. F. (1997). The five factor model of personality and job performance in the European Community. *The Journal of Applied Psychology*, *82*(1), 30–43. doi:10.1037/0021-9010.82.1.30 PMID:9119797

Sardžoska, E. G., & Tang, T. L. P. (2009). Testing a model of behavioral intentions in the Republic of Macedonia: Differences between the private and the public sectors. *Journal of Business Ethics*, *87*(4), 495–517. doi:10.100710551-008-9955-1

Shefrin, H., & Statman, M. (1985). The disposition to sell winners too early and ride losers too long: Theory and evidence. *The Journal of Finance*, *40*(3), 777–790. doi:10.1111/j.1540-6261.1985.tb05002.x

Shefrin, H. M., & Statman, M. (1984). Explaining investor preference for cash dividends. *Journal of Financial Economics*, *13*(2), 253–282. doi:10.1016/0304-405X(84)90025-4

Shiller, R. J. (2003). From efficient markets theory to behavioral finance. *The Journal of Economic Perspectives*, *17*(1), 83–104. doi:10.1257/089533003321164967

Sümer, N., Lajunen, T., & Özkan, T. (2005). Big five personality traits as the distal predictors of road accident. *Traffic and Transport Psychology: Theory and Application*, *215*, 215–227.

Tang, T. L. P., & Chen, Y. J. (2008). Intelligence vs. wisdom: The love of money, Machiavellianism, and unethical behavior across college major and gender. *Journal of Business Ethics*, *82*(1), 1–26. doi:10.100710551-007-9559-1

Tang, T. L. P., & Chiu, R. K. (2003). Income, money ethic, pay satisfaction, commitment, and unethical behavior: Is the love of money the root of evil for Hong Kong employees? *Journal of Business Ethics*, *46*(1), 13–30. doi:10.1023/A:1024731611490

Tang, T. L. P., & Liu, H. (2012). Love of money and unethical behavior intention: Does an authentic supervisor's personal integrity and character (ASPIRE) make a difference? *Journal of Business Ethics*, *107*(3), 295–312. doi:10.100710551-011-1040-5

Tauni, M. Z., Fang, H. X., & Yousaf, S. (2015). The influence of Investor personality traits on information acquisition and trading behavior: Evidence from Chinese futures exchange. *Personality and Individual Differences*, *87*, 248–255. doi:10.1016/j.paid.2015.08.026

Vissing-Jorgensen, A. (2003). Perspectives on behavioral finance: Does" irrationality" disappear with wealth? Evidence from expectations and actions. *NBER Macroeconomics Annual*, *18*, 139–194. doi:10.1086/ma.18.3585252

Vohs, K. D., Mead, N. L., & Goode, M. R. (2006). The psychological consequences of money. *Science*, *314*(5802), 1154–1156. doi:10.1126cience.1132491 PMID:17110581

Weber, M., & Camerer, C. F. (1998). The disposition effect in securities trading: An experimental analysis. *Journal of Economic Behavior & Organization*, *33*(2), 167–184. doi:10.1016/S0167-2681(97)00089-9

Zuckerman, M. (1994). *Behavioral expressions and biosocial bases of sensation seeking*. Cambridge, UK: Cambridge University Press.

KEY TERMS AND DEFINITIONS

Behavioral Finance: It refers to a sub discipline of the broader behavioral economy and is considered as the integration of psychology and finance.

Big-Five Personality Traits: It is a taxonomy for personality traits consisting of extraversion, conscientiousness, openness to experience, neuroticism and agreeableness.

Disposition Effect: It is a bias defined as investor tendency to sell the winner assets too early and to hold the loser assets too long.

FOREX: It refers to the foreign exchange market that is the marketplace where various national currencies are traded.

Love of Money: It refers to an individual's attitude toward money or the meaning that individuals attribute to it.

Chapter 12
Acquisition of Financial Literacy as a Life Skill:
A Study on Financial Literacy Awareness of Students

Başak Gezmen
Istanbul Medipol University, Turkey

ihsan Eken
https://orcid.org/0000-0002-0401-8545
Istanbul Medipol University, Turkey

ABSTRACT

Alongside the phenomena such as crisis, prosperity, etc., which emerged with the increase of global competition, the development of literacy levels has become critical. In the acquisition and development of financial literacy, first of all, the current situation should be determined, then the relevant policies should be developed and the literacy should be acquired through the necessary trainings to be provided. This chapter determines the relationship between the acquisition of financial literacy awareness as a life skill and the participation of the students who took the Introduction to Economics course in the Faculty of Communication at Istanbul Medipol University in 2018-2019 in the axis of survey method. Authors discuss the students' financial literacy awareness and skill in general. The chapter also gains insight into the situation of similar courses such as economics and finance to improve the perspective on financial literacy awareness.

INTRODUCTION

Today, several discussions and applications have been made on the concept of literacy in many fields. The literacy areas discussed in different disciplines develop different approaches according to each discipline. It is important that the objectives and priorities are correctly identified and supported by practices.

DOI: 10.4018/978-1-7998-2559-3.ch012

Literacy fields such as health literacy, media literacy, information literacy, language literacy aim the literacy to be perceived as the basic life skill. It aims to raise individuals who question the reality of the texts in the media, the world of simulation produced by the media for us, criticize the media messages shaped according to the values of the capitalist system, and examine the visible. The health field of literacy, on the other hand, aims to know the basic concepts related to health and to create conscious consumers who check the expiration dates of the products sold at the drug package insert in markets and similar places. As it is seen in reality, people gain features such as not accepting, questioning, criticizing as in literacy skills.

In order to maintain our daily lives, we need to make decisions and choices in many areas. We have to make relevant reasoning in the goal-oriented practical solutions of practical problems regarding the issue. It is a necessity of our lives in the field of finance. In this context, making the right decisions at the right time is becoming increasingly important. New technologies and the dizzying speed of digitalization have dominated the finance field as it happens in every field. Now, individuals are forced to go beyond the traditional methods of saving and accumulating money. At this point, the individual has to acquire general knowledge and basic skills in many areas of finance. Financial literacy enables the individual to acquire knowledge and information in areas such as credit card use, budget, savings bonds. The phenomenon of literacy is an ability acquired by individuals. At this point, it is a necessity in today's society that individuals gain financial literacy ability from an early age. Recently, many training seminars and applications have been held for the first time on the subject, especially in universities, some courses are included in the curriculum in certain departments. In some departments, some courses related to the field (economics, finance, statistics, etc.) are taught embeddedly.

The aim of this study was to determine the relationship between the participation of the communication faculty students in Introduction to Economics course at Istanbul Medipol University in 2018-2019 academic year and financial literacy acquisition as a life skill. Survey method, which is one of the quantitative research methods, was used in the research. 217 students participated in the survey. The data obtained from the students were analyzed with the statistical program SPSS.

THE CONCEPT AND IMPORTANCE OF 'LITERACY'

The concept of literacy, which we often hear today and is the subject of research fields, is a process that goes beyond reading and understanding in general. The emergence and continuous discussion of concepts such as health literacy and media literacy point to a process of competence aimed at every field and the necessity of this process. For example, a media literate is someone who perceives and analyzes the media correctly. So why is it necessary to understand the media correctly? Because hundreds of media messages we encounter every day are actually fictional. In other words, the media does not always present the facts to us. It produces a simulated world made up of fiction. In many serials, advertising and similar media messages, the world we face comprises areas specially designed for us, which have a high level of credibility. The necessity of being competent to understand what is real and what is fiction arises. In order to make a true interpretation between the real world and the fiction world, the individual must be subject to a successful education process, must educate himself correctly, investigate, analyze and question the normative rather than accepting it as it is.

In order to ensure competence in every subject, appropriate training programs are also organized. For instance, some of the products we encounter every day in the markets and many of which we buy may have expired. Or, to confirm whether any product we will buy from the pharmacy will be effective in the treatment process of our ailment, it is necessary to examine the package insert supplied with the drugs and make verification with our previous researches. Throughout this whole process, the individual actually takes part in the literacy process by observing, researching and analyzing.

Media literacy is the ability to be a media authority. In order to deserve the title of competence, to distinguish the reconstructed messages and to make comments about it, it is necessary to acquire a separate ability. In addition, competence can be gained as a result of background knowledge and training process (Taşkıran Öncel, 2007).

Literacy ability is acquired at elementary school level. In reading action, which is limited to the first meaning of a text, the student makes sense of the text based on its first meaning. For example, any first grade student starts reading the texts, messages correctly towards the end of the class, in line with his education process. Because he has learned to read. However, it would be wrong to interpret his acquiring this ability as the correct understanding and evaluation of the news he encounters in any newspaper. In the following periods, the student begins to make sense of what he reads. For example, the student can think and comment conceptually on any subject, although superficially, in the status of development in secondary education (Bilici, 2017).

When we look at the development process of the concept of literacy from past to present, it can be stated that the issue is not related to the level of prosperity, industrialization, economic development or democratization degree, and management style in societies. The large-scale literacy campaigns are also part of a wide range of social changes and transformations. Such literacy campaigns used to be closely related to the efforts of centralizing authority. At this point, mobilization of a large number of educators and propagation of a certain doctrine took place in a repressive process. Today, the development of new communication technologies, digital transformation that continues to take place at a dizzying speed, gradually increasing information, easy access to information and speed are aimed at constantly promoting the issue of literacy (İnal, 2009).

Many literacy forms can come to mind within the scope of the concept of literacy. Apart from media literacy and health literacy, language literacy emphasizes the acquisition of a linguistic system consisting of certain formats. At this point reading is understanding the written symbols and their place in compounds. In visual literacy and picture literacy, this is the ability to understand dimensional patterns. Developments in new media and communication technologies bring in a new dimension to the concept of literacy (İnal, 2009). Media literacy, defined as access to messages written and non-written formats and the ability to correctly analyze and transmit these media messages, necessitates the media products to gain meaning correctly. It is known that the first definitions regarding this subject were made in 1978. In a sense, media's gaining meaning correctly can also be seen as a war against manipulation (İnceoğlu, 2007).

In the 1970s, the media began to be used as part of education. It is seen that various newspapers and magazines were taught in classrooms during the education process, and various programs and films were watched and the media also contributed to the educational function in this process. The changes and transformations in post-80 society, the rapid penetration of the influence of the capitalist system on the societies, the impact of globalization and the competitive understanding it brings along on the mass media, led the topic of "the effects of media," to start to take its place on the agenda (İnal, 2009).

The effects of the media, which have become a part of our daily life, are also included in the media exposure discourse. Exposure to media messages is a negative discourse. That is, there are lots of messages coming from the media and they are fictional. At this point, the necessity to resolve these messages correctly also arises. The rapid development of technology requires the acquisition of correct perception and analysis skills in every field as in the field of media.

FINANCIAL LITERACY CONCEPTUAL FRAMEWORK AND FINANCIAL LITERACY EDUCATION

With the technological developments, the variety of financial products and services have also been increasing gradually. Financial service offerings have also differed dramatically by keeping pace with changes and transformations. The change in each sector also creates an increasingly complex structure in the financial world. The abounding of products and services in the field of financial services, where there is lots of knowledge and information, necessitates this complex structure to be interpreted correctly.

In the financial flow that has been increasing at a dizzying pace today, it has become obligatory for individuals to gain the skills to access and correctly read the information in the process and process flow. The level of financial knowledge and skills has started to prevail in many age groups. Individuals are also expected to have sufficient financial knowledge to contribute to life practices and to analyze information correctly.

The term "financial literacy", which was first used in 1997, was used to measure the financial literacy state of American high school students in those years. In this research, it is the ability of individuals to use the knowledge and skills necessary to successfully manage and organize financial resources that are vital to them in order to provide financial security. In another definition, the effect of financial literacy in gaining the ability to make informed decisions in the process of the proper use and management of money is emphasized. The definition of financial literacy is very difficult due to the factual complexity of the concept of finance. In this context, the concepts of knowledge, education and talent are pointed out in the field of finance as in the case of literacy in every field. Some concepts can be used interchangeably regarding the concepts of finance and literacy. These are concepts such as financial ability, economic literacy, economic ability, financial education etc. (Ağırman & Akyol, 2019).

Regarding the concept of financial literacy, which is the basic information needed to survive in today's society, the level of financial literacy is related to the accuracy and awareness gained in the financial decision-making process as a result of individuals' having obtained sufficient financial information. In OECD 2012 data, financial literacy is defined as follows. *"It is having the knowledge and understanding of financial concepts and risks, the ability, motivation and confidence to use this knowledge and understanding to make effective decisions in different financial contexts, to improve the financial well-being of individuals and society and to ensure participation in economic life."* (Çakırer, 2019).

Financial literacy, which is considered as one of the literacy areas in the digital period, is the competence and skill that enables each individual to gain the ability to solve problems regarding the basic financial situations s/he is faced with and to make informed financial decisions consciously. The state of financial literacy is a very important issue in the national economy. The concepts of "correct management of money", "saving", "conscious spending", "borrowing" and "investment" are among the concepts that need to be properly interpreted regarding the concept of financial literacy.

Every individual in the financial system should be able to use financial products and services successfully and effectively. In other words, if an individual receiving his salary from a bank uses a bank and credit card, makes savings and investments, it means he is in the world of financial system. He needs to know what the minimum payment and similar concepts mean. Today, however, there are many individuals who cannot benefit from financial services or who use them incorrectly because they cannot interpret financial services correctly (Çakırer, 2019).

Education in each field increases the awareness and awareness point specific to that field. In general, media education is all of the activities that have a specific plan and aim to teach the nature and practices of media. Media literacy education aims to eliminate the harmful effects of media (Bilici, 2017). Trainings should be provided to raise awareness regarding financial literacy in parallel thinking. In particular, courses with basic economic knowledge contribute in this respect.

Çakırer states that in order to improve financial literacy, attention should first be directed to this field. Regarding this subject, literature reviews should be performed, and books and brochures should be read and examined. Moreover, considering that today, films are not only used for entertainment but also for educational purposes, it may also be beneficial to gain financial literacy perspective in many films (Çakırer, 2019). Some special seminars, symposiums and training programs are also organized on this topic with a focus on age periods.

CHARACTERISTICS, IMPORTANCE AND MEASUREMENT OF FINANCIAL LITERACY

Today's economic conditions increasingly necessitate all people to take responsibilities in decision making economically throughout their lives. Savings and investment decisions are important for individuals in today's economic context where there are many crises. An examination of the literature reveals that the definition of financial literacy has been made from many perspectives. The definition of financial literacy can be used as a prerequisite for its measurement. Financial literacy, individuals' savings and investment world, having sufficient information about investment instruments and investment rules means being able to make informed investments and making financial decisions based on sufficient information (Sancak, 2012). Financial literacy means "individual finance." In many countries, financial education studies are pursued on country basis in order to increase financial literacy (Sancak, 2014).

Miller (1977) defines financial literacy as an integration of consumers and investors' abilities and competences regarding how they can act on the basis of the knowledge they have, which institutions and persons they should consult in case of need and their understanding of financial arguments to be able to improve their financial development and take the valid steps in this field.

According to the Organization for Economic Co-operation and Development (OECD), financial literacy is a combination of awareness, knowledge, skills, attitude and behavior required to achieve individual financial welfare as a result of strong financial decisions (OECD, 2011). Financial literacy is individuals' knowing the necessary financial concepts and risks for them to make efficient decisions, which will help them join economic life and better their financial being and having the skills, motivation and self-confidence to put this information into practice (OECD, 2013).

The following components emerge as common in all the definitions regarding financial literacy (Remund, 2010):

1. Information about financial concepts.
2. Ability to communicate and talk about financial issues.
3. Individual financial management skills.
4. Ability to make appropriate financial decisions.

5. Ability to plan effectively for future financial needs.

Financial literate uses his money and assets well. He does not only think of the moment he lives, but also designs the future by making long-term plans instead of thinking short-term. He recognizes the risks in the market, calculates income, assets and expenses and takes steps according to his calculations. A good finance literate calculates the changes in the market and learns new information without giving up gaining knowledge and experience. A person who is financially literate should have the necessary knowledge, skills, attitudes and behaviors.

Good Money Management: an individual or a family should not spend all or more of their income, but must try to save some of it. Each individual or family should have its own budget and should be able to act accordingly. Budget management can make a difference in individuals' lives if it is learned at an early age. When accurate financial information and money management habits are acquired in the first years of young people's acquaintance with money and of their decision making regarding individual spending or savings, this is permanently reflected in their behaviors for the rest of their lives.

It is crucial to keep records in the management of money. If all cash income and expenses are recorded, the spent groups and income points will be seen much more clearly. In this way, it will be easier to make amends (Gökmen, 2012).

Understanding the Financial System: It is the organization that brings together those who have surplus funds and those in need of funds and provides the flow of funds. The components of the financial system are (Gökmen, 2012):

1. Those who have fund surpluses (savers).
2. Those in need of funding.
3. Financial institutions.
4. Financial markets.
5. Financial instruments.
6. Regulatory institutions.

Making Financial Plans: Financial planning can help individuals to pursue their lives within the framework of their incomes, cover their expenditures with their income, save them from financial uncertainty and help them make savings and investments to reach their financial goals. In order to make a good financial planning, it is necessary to determine the targets at first and then calculate the current income gradually, to estimate the income and expenses, to plan the debts well, to reach the savings targets and to implement the plan.

The stages of creating a financial plan are as follows (Gökmen, 2012):

1. Setting financial goals.
2. Revealing the current financial situation.
3. Evaluating options to achieve goals.
4. Choosing and implementing the best option.
5. Reviewing the plan and changing it if necessary.

Good Communication: Consumers who want to buy financial products or services will face professional sellers. Therefore, interview techniques should be learned and improved in order not to be misled.

This is the most important part of the exchange we make in the financial market as in all current shopping rules. Furthermore, if the consumer is experiencing a problem, he should know well where to he can solve this problem. Due to the structure of the financial sector, consumers should constantly renew themselves (Gökmen, 2012).

Having financial literacy skills is important both for solving financial problems and foreseeing and avoiding them in advance and at the same time for being able to lead a happy and healthy life in prosperity. The various financial problems experienced by people cause many different problems, some of them being mental and familial and affect the lives of people negatively. In the OECD (2013) report, it is stated that *"Many of the financial literacy researches conducted in the world reveal that a large part of the population does not have sufficient knowledge even to understand the basic financial products and the risks regarding these products. Most people can not make prudential financial plans and can not take efficient decisions concerning the management of their financial resources."* In the report, it was also emphasized that *"Individuals living in different economic, financial and social environments in the world should take more responsibility for their future financial well-being and protection"*. One of the most important reasons for this issue's being emphasized is the prolongation of people's lifespan together with the technological and medical developments experienced today and therefore the increase in their life qualities.

Today, individuals assume more responsibility for a longer period of time for their personal or familial health care needs. Increasing education costs, additional obligatory education expenditures for children also rendered it significant for parents to plan their children's education on a significant level and to make investment in this area. While these trends are more prominent in developed countries, similar issues have begun to emerge in many developing economies.

In the OECD report it is emphasized that, *"in order to increase the financial literacy level, governments have begun to develop financial education policies as an alternative to the measures taken to protect the consumers. Financial education, is aimed at empowering individuals in the financial markets, and to provide individuals and families to manage their resources better. This situation is valid for all the economically developed countries, the middle classes, which a redeveloping or getting strong and all the poor or financially shunned countries."* In the report, it is emphasized that especially financial education can equip citizens with the skills of gaining advantage from eligible financial services and evaluating the financial risks they are faced with better (2013).

There are different approaches to measuring literacy in the financial literacy literature. In the study of Volpe, Chen & Pavlico (1996), 10 multiple choice questions are asked and the percentages of the correct answers of the participants are calculated. The skills of the participants regarding their investment habits are measured by applying a performance test as a content area. In Mandell's (2004) study, the ratio of correct answers is calculated in the 31-item knowledge test. The participants involved in the study are implemented performance test as content area and the skills of the participants regarding savings, investment and debt habits are measured. In the study of the National Council on Economic Education (2005), the proportion of correct answers taken from the 24-question knowledge test is calculated. The participants involved in the study are implemented performance test as content area and the skills of the participants regarding savings, investment and debt habits are measured. In the study of Rooij, Lusardi and Alessie (2007), which form the basis of the study, weighted average of 5 multiple choice basic financial literacy questions according to right / wrong situation and 11 multiple choice sophisticated financial literacy questions are asked and weighted average of the answers given by the participants is calculated. The skills of the participants involved in the study regarding savings, investment and debt habits are measured (İçke, 2017).

The Aim and the Significance of the Research

Financial literacy, which is one of the most important issues affecting every period of our lives, is slowly gaining more and more importance today. The increase in global competition, the increase in the number and use of credit cards, the increase in people's spending, and the fact that almost all of our daily businesses are operational through finance have made it necessary for people to improve their financial literacy level. With this research, the relationship between participation in Introduction to Economics Course of students at Communication Faculty and financial literacy acquisition as a life skill was investigated.

The Limitations of the Research

This study was carried out with the students who were studying in departments of New Media and Communication, Media and Visual Arts, Public Relations and Advertising and Journalism and took the Introduction to Economics course at Faculty of Communication in 2018-2019 academic year. The main criterion of the study is that students take the Introduction to Economics course.

Methdology of the Study

For the analysis of the relationship between participation in Introduction to Economics Course of students at Communication Faculty and financial literacy acquisition as a life skill, questionnaire form was preferred as a quantitative data collection technique. The questionnaire is a method of obtaining data by responding to pre-determined questions for an academic, commercial or official purpose. For survey application, the basic level and advanced level financial literacy scale used by Rooij, Lusardi, Alessie (2007) in their study *"Financial Literacy and Participation in Stock Exchange"* was used. 24 questions were asked to the participants. Before the final survey form was prepared and data collection process, 5 people were interviewed and their opinions about the questions and expressions were taken. After correcting unclear statements, the questionnaire questions were reorganized. All of the respondents in the questionnaire took the Introduction to Economics course.

In the research, purposive sampling technique was used as a sampling technique. In this sample model, the researcher selects the subjects who have certain characteristics that s/he thinks suitable for the research problem through his/her personal observations (Gürbüz & Şahin, 2016). The population of the study consists of the students who took the Introduction to Economics course in the departments of New Media and Communication, Media and Visual Arts, Public Relations and Advertising and Journalism at Istanbul Medipol University Faculty of Communication in 2018-2019 academic year. In 2018-2019 academic year, 293 students took the Introduction to Economics course. 217 students from 293 students were surveyed online via e-mail with surveymonkey program. In this study, it is assumed that the students of Istanbul Medipol University Faculty of Communication, which are taken as a sample, will ideally represent the universe.

First of all, some questions were asked to reveal the demographic information of the participants. These questions include questions about gender, age, subject of study, score that they got from the introduction to economics course, how they live, monthly average income, credit card and bank account.

Acquisition of Financial Literacy as a Life Skill

Following the demographic information, questions about finance literacy were asked. The answers to the questions, which were asked based on the basic level and advanced level of financial literacy scale used by Rooij, Lusardi, Alessie (2007) in their study *"Financial Literacy and Participation in Stock Exchange"* were searched. The questionnaire was conducted on 217 female and male students who took the Introduction to Economics course and study in four departments of İstanbul Medipol University, at the Faculty of Communication, in 2018-2019 academic year. KMO (Kaiser-Meyer-Olkin) value of the study is 7448. In other words, it is a highly reliable study.

FINDINGS OF THE RESEARCH

Within the scope of the research, the effects of the participation in Introduction to Economics course of the students at the Communication Faculty on the acquisition of financial literacy as a life skill was examined. 217 students participated in the survey. According to the results of the survey; gender, age, department of study, score taken from the introduction to economics course, how they reside, average monthly income, credit card, bank account, basic and advanced financial literacy thoughts of the participants were determined. 100 of the participants are female, and 117 are male. The percentage of the females is 46.1%, while the percentage of the males is 53.9%.

When the age diagram of the students participating in the study is examined, it is seen that 59.4% of the participants participated in the study consisted of students between the ages of 18-19. The number of the students in this group is 129. 76 of the participants were the students whose ages were around 20-21. Percentage of the students in this group is 35%. 5 of the participants were around 22-23 years old. Percentage of the students in this group is 2.3%. 7 of the participants were the students who were in the 24 and older age group. Percentage of the students in this group is 35%.

94 of the students who participated in the study were students of Public Relations and Advertising Department. Percentage of the participants who study in the Public Relations and Advertising Department and participated in the study is 43.3. 64 of the students participated in the study were the students studying at the New Media and Communication Department. Percentage of the participants studying at the New Media and Communication Department and participated in the study is 29.5. 46 of the students participated in the study were Media and Visual Arts students. Percentage of the participants who study the Media and Visual Arts Department and participated in the study is 21.2. 13 of the students participated in the study were students of the Department of Journalism. Percentage of the participants who study at the Department of Journalism and participated in the study is 6 percent.

The grading of students studying at Istanbul Medipol University is divided into four groups. The letter final grades that constitutes the first group "very good" are "A, A-, B+". The number of students who got "very good" degree from the Introduction to Economics course is 26. Percentage of the students who have got the "very good" degree is 12. The letter final grades that constitutes the second group "good" are "B, B-, C+". In the study, the number of students who received the "good" degree from the Introduction to Economics course is 51. Percentage of students who have got a good degree is 23.5. The letter final grades that constitutes the third group "Intermediate" are "C, C-". In the study, the number of students who received the intermediate degree from the Introduction to Economics course was 49. Percentage of the students who have got an intermediate degree is 22.6. The letter final grade which constitutes the fourth group "failed" is F. In the study, the number of students who received the "failed" degree from the Introduction to Economics course is 91. Percentage of the students who got the 'failed' degree is 41.9.

When the residence types of the participants were examined, it is determined that 133 of them are living with their families. Percentage of the participants living with their families is 61.3. In other words, more than half of the participants in the study live with their families. Thirty-five of the participants participated in the study accommodate in the student houses (two or more students). Percentage of the participants staying in the student houses is 16.1. 34 of the participants were residing in the dormitory. Percentage of the participants staying in the dormitory is 15.7. 10 participants were living alone in their own houses. Percentage of the participants staying in their own houses is 4.6. 5 of the participants were living together with their relatives. Percentage of the participants living with their relatives is 2.3.

When the average monthly income of the participants was examined, 98 of them had incomes between 1000-1499 TL. Percentage of the participants with an income between 1000-1499 TL is 45.2. 81 of the participants have an income between 1500-1999 TL. Percentage of the participants with an income between 1500-1999 TL is 37.3. 24 of the participants have an income of 2000 TL and above. Percentage of the participants with an income of 2000 TL or above is 11.1. 14 of the participants have an income between 501-999 TL. Percentage of the participants with an income between 501-999 TL is 6.5.

Considering the question about whether or not the participants have a bank account, 212 of them, in other words, 97.7% of the participants have a bank account. Number of the participants without a bank account is 5. Percentage of the participants who do not have a bank account is 2.3. Considering the question about whether or not the participants of the study have a credit card; 215 of the participants, in other words 99.1% of them, have a credit card. Number of the participants without credit card is 2. Percentage of the participants without a credit card is 9.

When the basic level financial literacy status of the participants was examined; the question, "(Financial Mathematics) Assume that you have 100 TL in your savings account and interest rates are 2% per year. How much will you have in your account after five years if you don't withdraw your money at all?" was answered by 115 participants as more than 102 TL, 64 participants as exactly 102 TL, 29 participants less than 102 TL, and 9 participants as 'I do not know'. When the percentage distributions of the answers given by the participants were examined, percentage of the respondents who said 'more than 102 TL' is 53, percentage of the respondents who said 'exactly 102 TL' is 29.5, percentage of the respondents who said 'less than 102 TL' is 13.4 and percentage of the respondents who said 'I do not know' is 4.1.

(Compound Interest) Assume that you have 100 TL in your savings account and the annual interest rate is 20%. How much does it accumulate in your account after five years if you don't withdraw your money and interest? 69 of the participants responded as exactly 200 TL, 58 of them said less than 200 TL, 53 of them said more than 200 TL and 37 of them said 'I do not know'. When the percentage distributions of the answers given by the participants are examined, percentage of the respondents who gave the answer of exactly 200 TL is 31.8, the percentage of the respondents who gave the answer of less than 200 TL is 26.7, the percentage of the respondents who gave the answer of more than 200 TL is 24.4 and the percentage of the respondents who gave the answer 'I do not know' is 17.1.

The question "(Inflation) Assume that your savings account receives an annual interest rate of 1%. Inflation is 2% annually. What is the change in your money in a year?" was asked to the participants. 88 of the participants said it remains the same, 60 of them said it will be less than today, 55 of them said it will be more than today and 14 of them answered as 'I do not know'. When the percentage distributions of the answers given by the participants to this question are examined, the percentage of the respondents who said it remains the same is 40.6, the percentage of the respondents who said it would be less than today is 27.6, the percentage of the respondents who said it would be more than today is 25.3 and the percentage of the participants who said 'I do not know' is 6.5.

Acquisition of Financial Literacy as a Life Skill

(Time value of money) Assume that a friend of yours inherited 10,000 TL today. Three years later, his wife inherited 10,000 TL. Which one will be richer in this case? 97 of the participants said 'my friend', 82 of them said 'the spouse', 33 of them said that they are equally rich and 5 of them answered as 'I do not know'. When the percentage distributions of the answers given by the participants were examined, the percentage of the participants who gave the answer 'my friend' is 44.7, the percentage of the participants who said 'the spouse' is 37.8, the percentage of the participants who said that they are equally rich is 15.2 and the percentage of the participants who said 'I do not know' is 2.3.

The question, "When the participants' advanced level of financial literacy was examined; which of the following statements describes the basic function of stock markets?" was answered by 111 of the respondents as 'stock markets cause an increase in stock prices'. Percentage of this question is 51.2. 37 of the participants said that stock markets help to estimate stock market earnings. Percentage of this question is 17.1. 19 respondents replied that the stock markets bring the parties together who want to buy and sell stocks. Percentage of this question is 8.8. 50 of the respondents said 'I do not know'. Percentage of this question is 23.

The question "Which of the following statements is true when an investor purchases the share of the firm B?" was answered by 84 of the participants as the investor would own a part of the firm B. Percentage of this question is 38.7. 62 of the respondents answered that the investor would be responsible for the debts of the firm B. Percentage of this question is 28.6. 41 of the participants replied as 'I do not know'. Percentage of this question is 18.9. 30 of the respondents replied that the investor made a loan to the firm B. Percentage of this question is 13.8.

To the question "Which of the following statements is correct?", 91 of the respondents answered that investment funds can be invested in various assets including stocks and bonds. Percentage of this question is 41.9. 71 of the respondents replied that you cannot withdraw your deposit when you invest in an investment fund in the first year. Percentage of this question is 32.7. 50 of the respondents said 'I do not know'. Percentage of this question is 23. 5 of the respondents answered that mutual funds guarantee a certain rate of return to their investors depending on their past performance. Percentage of this question is 2.3.

To the question "Which of the following statements is true when an investor buys a bond belonging to firm B?", 61 of the participants answered as 'I do not know'. Percentage of this question is 28.1. 57 of the respondents answered that the person becomes responsible for the debts of the firm B. Percentage of this question is 26.5 44 of the participants answered that the person would own a share of the firm B. Percentage of this question is 20.3 32 participants replied that they would have lent money to the firm B. Percentage of this question is 14.7. 23 of the participants replied as 'I do not answer'. Percentage of this question is 10.6.

To the question "Which of the following assets gives the highest return over a long period of time like 10-20 years?", 81 of the participants answered as stock certificate. Percentage of this question is 37.3. 56 respondents responded as the savings account. Percentage of this question is 25.8. 51 of the participants answered as 'I do not know'. Percentage of this question is 23.5 29 of the respondents answered as the bond. Percentage of this question is 13.4.

To the question "Which entity experiences the highest fluctuation over time?", 72 of the respondents answered as 'the bond'. Percentage of this question is 33.2. 60 of the respondents replied as 'I do not know'. Percentage of this question is 27.6. 47 respondents answered as 'the savings account'. Percentage of this question is 21.7. 38 of the participants answered this question as stock certificate. Percentage of this question is 17.5.

The risk of losing money was asked when an investor distributes his money among different assets; and 92 respondents answered that the risk increases. Percentage of this question is 42.4. 91 of the respondents said that it decreases. Percentage of this question is 41.9. 34 respondents said it remains the same. Percentage of this question is 15.7.

To the question "Suppose you purchased a 10-year bond, when you want to sell it five years later, you won't be able to sell it without a huge loss. Is this statement true or false?", 113 of the participants replied as false. Percentage of this question is 52.1. 58 of the respondents said it is true. Percentage of this question is 26.7. 36 of the participants answered that 'I do not know'. Percentage of this question is 16.6. 10 of them answered that 'I do not answer'. Percentage of this question is 4.6.

To the question "Stocks are riskier than bonds. Is this statement true or false?", 118 of the respondents said true. Percentage of this question is 54.4. 55 of the participants answered as 'I do not know'. Percentage of this question is 25.3. 43 of the participants replied that it is false. Percentage of this question is 19.8. One of the participants replied that 'I do not answer'. Percentage of this question is 5.

To the question "When you buy a company's share, you usually get a safer return than buying a stock mutual fund. Is this statement true or false?", 91 of the participants replied as 'false'. Percentage of this question is 41.9. 65 of the participants answered as 'I do not know'. Percentage of this question is 30. 61 of the respondents answered that it is true. Percentage of this question is 28.1.

To the question "Assuming that interest rates have fallen, what do you expect bond prices to be?", 104 of the respondents answered as it rises. Percentage of this question is 47.9. 47 respondents said it remains the same. Percentage of this question is 21.7. 41 of the participants replied as 'I do not know'. Percentage of this question is 18.9. 25 of the respondents said it decreases. Percentage of this question is 11.5.

Within the scope of the study, the data of the hypothesis tests of the research were analyzed and explanations of the findings were made. Chi-Square (X^2) test was used in the hypothesis tests. The Chi-Square test was generally used to test whether the observed values or frequencies are in accordance with the claimed theoretical frequencies and whether the distribution of the sample is suitable for a known distribution. (Gürbüz & Şahin, 2016).

In the research, the presence of a 0.05 significance level of difference between financial mathematics and having a bank account of the students who participated in the study (Assume that you have 100 TL in your savings account and interest rates are 2% per year. If you never withdraw your money, how much will you have in your account after five years?) was examined. In the research, a questionnaire was conducted on 217 students who participated in the study according to certain criteria and their opinions were gathered. For this study, H^0 and H^1 hypotheses were formed as follows.

1H⁰: There is no relationship between having a bank account and financial mathematics.
1H¹: There is a relationship between having a bank account and financial mathematics.

The results of the chi-square tests that is applied to test whether there is a relationship between the financial mathematics category and the participants who have bank account are given in above. There is no statistically significant relationship between the participants who have a bank account and financial mathematics category ($X2 (3) = 1757; P> 0.05$) (Table 1). The observed frequency and expected frequency values were determined to be very distant or different from each other. As a result, H^1 hypothesis is rejected, H^0 hypothesis is accepted. In other words, there is no significant difference among the participants having a bank account in terms of financial mathematics category.

Table 1. 1H⁰ and 1H¹ chi-square tests

	Value	**df**	**Asymp. Sig. (2-sided)**
Pearson Chi-Square	1.757ª	3	,624
Likelihood Ratio	2,558	3	,465
Linear-by-Linear Association	1,650	1	,199
N of Valid Cases	217		
a. 4 cells (50.0%) have expected count less than 5. The minimum expected count is .21.			

In the research, it was tested whether or not there is a 0.05 significance level of difference between compound interest and having a bank account of the students who participated in the study (Assume that you have 100 TL in your savings account and the annual interest rate is 20%. How much does it accumulate in your account after five years if you don't withdraw your money and interest?)". In the research, a questionnaire was conducted on 217 students who participated in the study according to certain criteria and their opinions were gathered. For this study, H⁰ and H¹ hypotheses were formed as follows.

2H⁰: There is no relationship between having a bank account and compound interest.
2H¹: There is a relationship between having a bank account and compound interest.

The results of the chi-square tests that is applied to test whether there is a relationship between the compound interest and the participants who have bank account are given in above. There was no statistically significant relationship between the compound interest category and the participants having a bank account ($X2 (3) = 845$; $P > 0.05$) (Table 2). The observed frequency and expected frequency values were determined to be very distant or different from each other. As a result, H¹ hypothesis is rejected, H⁰ hypothesis is accepted. In other words, there is no significant difference among the participants having a bank account in terms of compound interest category.

It was tested whether or not there is a 0.05 significance level of difference between time value of money (Assume that a friend inherited 10 thousand TL today. His wife has inherited 10 thousand TL three years later. Who has become richer in this case?) and the illusion of money for the students who participated in the research (Assume that in 2010 your income and also the price of goods doubled. How much goods will you be able to purchase with your income in 2010). In the research, a questionnaire was conducted on 217 students who participated in the study according to certain criteria and their opinions were gathered. For this study, H⁰ and H¹ hypotheses were formed as follows.

Table 2. 2H⁰ and 2H¹ chi-square tests

	Value	**df**	**Asymp. Sig. (2-sided)**
Pearson Chi-Square	.845ª	3	,839
Likelihood Ratio	,805	3	,848
Linear-by-Linear Association	,129	1	,719
N of Valid Cases	217		
a. 4 cells (50.0%) have expected count less than 5. The minimum expected count is .85.			

3H⁰: There is no relationship between time value of money and monetary illusion.
3H¹: There is a relationship between time value of money and monetary illusion.

The results of the chi-square that is applied to test whether there is a relationship between the time value of money category and the monetary illusion category are given in above. There is a statistically significant relationship between the time value of money category and the monetary illusion category ($X2(9) = 124379$; $P < 0.05$) (Table 3). The observed frequency and expected frequency values were determined to be very close or indifferent to each other. As a result, H^0 hypothesis is rejected, H^1 hypothesis is accepted. In other words, there is a significant difference between the time value of money category and the monetary illusion category.

It was tested whether or not there is a 0.05 significance level of difference between "inflation (Assume that your savings account charges 1% interest annually. Inflation is 2% annually. How does your money change in a year?) and time value of money (Assume that a friend inherited 10 thousand TL today. Three years later, his wife inherited 10,000 TL. In this case, who has become richer?)" of the students who participated in the research. In the research, a questionnaire was conducted on 217 students who participated in the study according to certain criteria and their opinions were gathered. For this study, H^0 and H^1 hypotheses were formed as follows.

4H⁰: There is no relationship between inflation and time value of money.
4H¹: There is a relationship between inflation and time value of money.

The Chi-Square results applied to test whether there is a relationship between the categories of inflation and time value of money are given in above. There is a statistically significant relationship between the categories of inflation and time value of money ($X2(9) = 93666$; $P < 0.05$) (Table 4). The observed

Table 3. 3H⁰ and 3H¹ chi-square tests

	Value	df	Asymp. Sig. (2-sided)
Pearson Chi-Square	124.379[a]	9	,000
Likelihood Ratio	61,587	9	,000
Linear-by-Linear Association	,277	1	,599
N of Valid Cases	217		
a. 7 cells (43.8%) have expected count less than 5. The minimum expected count is .23.			

Table 4. 4H⁰ and 4H¹ chi-square tests

	Value	df	Asymp. Sig. (2-sided)
Pearson Chi-Square	93.666[a]	9	,000
Likelihood Ratio	89,605	9	,000
Linear-by-Linear Association	2,823	1	,093
N of Valid Cases	217		
a. 5 cells (31.3%) have expected count less than 5. The minimum expected count is .32.			

Acquisition of Financial Literacy as a Life Skill

frequency and expected frequency values were determined to be very close or indifferent to each other. As a result, H⁰ hypothesis is rejected, H¹ hypothesis is accepted. In other words, there is a significant difference between the inflation category and time value category of money.

It was tested whether there was a 0.05 significance level of difference between financial mathematics and the economics grades of the students who participated in the research (Assume that you have 100 TL in your savings account and interest rates are 2% per year. If you never withdraw your money, how much will you have in your account after five years?). In the research, a questionnaire was conducted on 217 students who participated in the study according to certain criteria and their opinions were gathered. For this study, H0 and H1 hypotheses were formed as follows.

5H⁰: There is no relationship between financial mathematics and students' economics grades.
5H¹: There is a relationship between financial mathematics and students' economics grades.

The results of the chi-square that are applied to test whether there is a relationship between students' economics grades and financial mathematics category are given in above. There is a statistically significant relationship between students' grades in economics and financial mathematics category ($X2$ (9) = 189685; P <0.05) (Table 5). The observed frequency and expected frequency values were determined to be very close or indifferent to each other. As a result, H⁰ hypothesis is rejected, H¹ hypothesis is accepted. In other words, there is a significant difference between students' grades in economics and financial mathematics category.

It was tested whether or not there is 0.05 significance level of difference between compound interest and students' grades in economics course (Assume that you have 100 TL in your savings account and the annual interest rate is 20%. If you do not withdraw your money and interest, how much does your account accumulate at the end of five years?). In the research, a questionnaire was conducted on 217 students who participated in the study according to certain criteria and their opinions were gathered. For this study, H⁰ and H¹ hypotheses were formed as stated below.

6H⁰: There is no correlation between students' economics grades and compound interest.
6H¹: There is a relationship between students' economics grades and compound interest.

The results of the chi-square test that is applied to test whether there is a relationship between students' economics grades and compound interest category are given in above. There is a statistically significant relationship between students' grades in economics and compound interest category ($X2$ (9) = 157377; P <0.05) (Table 6). The observed frequency and expected frequency values were determined to be very

Table 5. 5H⁰ and 5H¹ chi-square tests

	Value	df	Asymp. Sig. (2-sided)
Pearson Chi-Square	189.685[a]	9	,000
Likelihood Ratio	250,217	9	,000
Linear-by-Linear Association	81,551	1	,000
N of Valid Cases	217		
a. 5 cells (31.3%) have expected count less than 5. The minimum expected count is 1.08.			

Table 6. 6H⁰ and 6H¹ chi-square tests

	Value	df	Asymp. Sig. (2-sided)
Pearson Chi-Square	157.377ª	9	,000
Likelihood Ratio	191,384	9	,000
Linear-by-Linear Association	4,258	1	,039
N of Valid Cases	217		
a. 1 cells (6.3%) have expected count less than 5. The minimum expected count is 4.43.			

close or indifferent to each other. As a result, H⁰ hypothesis is rejected, H¹ hypothesis is accepted. In other words, there is a significant difference between students' grades in economics and compound interest category.

It was tested whether or not there is 0.05 significance level of difference between inflation and students' grades in economics course (Assume that your savings account charges 1% interest annually. Inflation is 2% annually. How will your money change after a year?)". In the research, a questionnaire was conducted on 217 students who participated in the study according to certain criteria and their opinions were gathered. For this study, H⁰ and H¹ hypotheses were formed as follows.

7H⁰: There is no relationship between the students' economics grades and inflation.
7H¹: There is a relationship between inflation and students' economics grades.

The results of the chi-square test that is applied to test whether there is a relationship between students' economics grades and inflation category are given in above. There is a statistically significant relationship between students' economics grades and inflation category ($X2 (9) = 123934; P <0.05$) (Table 7). The observed frequency and expected frequency values were determined to be very close or indifferent to each other. As a result, H⁰ hypothesis is rejected, H¹ hypothesis is accepted. In other words, there is a significant difference between students' economics grades and inflation category.

It was tested whether or not there is a difference at 0.05 significance level between students' economics grades and time value of money (Assume that a friend has inherited 10 thousand TL today. Three years later, his wife inherited 10,000 TL. In this case, who has become richer?)" In the research, a questionnaire was conducted on 217 students who participated in the study according to certain criteria and their opinions were gathered. For this study, H⁰ and H¹ hypotheses were formed as follows.

Table 7. 7H⁰ and 7H¹ chi-square tests

	Value	df	Asymp. Sig. (2-sided)
Pearson Chi-Square	123.934ª	9	,000
Likelihood Ratio	153,640	9	,000
Linear-by-Linear Association	,872	1	,350
N of Valid Cases	217		
a. 3 cells (18.8%) have expected count less than 5. The minimum expected count is 1.68.			

Acquisition of Financial Literacy as a Life Skill

8H⁰: With the grade of the students' time value of money There is no relationship between.
8H¹: There is a relationship between students' economics grades and time value of money.

The results of the chi-square test that is applied to test whether there is a relationship between students' economics grades and time value of money category are given in above. There is a statistically significant relationship between students' economics grades and inflation category (X2 (9) = 83465; P <0.05) (Table 8). The observed frequency and expected frequency values were determined to be very close or indifferent to each other. As a result, H⁰ hypothesis is rejected, H¹ hypothesis is accepted. In other words, there is a significant difference between students' grades and time value of money.

It was tested whether or not there is a 0.05 significance level of difference between students' economics grades and monetary illusion (Assume that in 2010 your income and also the price of goods doubled. How much goods will you be able to purchase with your income in 2010) . In the research, a questionnaire was conducted on 217 students who participated in the study according to certain criteria and their opinions were gathered. For this study, H⁰ and H¹ hypotheses were formed as follows.

9H0: There is no relationship between students' economics grades and monetary illusion.
9H¹: There is a relationship between students' economics grades and monetary illusion.

The results of the chi-square test that is applied to test whether there is a relationship between students' economics grades and monetary illusion category are given in above. There is a statistically significant relationship between students' grade in economics and monetary illusion category (X2 (9) = 92083; P <0.05) (Table 9). The observed frequency and expected frequency values were determined to be very close or indifferent to each other. As a result, H⁰ hypothesis is rejected, H¹ hypothesis is accepted. In

Table 8. 8H⁰ and 8H¹ chi-square tests

	Value	**df**	**Asymp. Sig. (2-sided)**
Pearson Chi-Square	83.465[a]	9	,000
Likelihood Ratio	89,404	9	,000
Linear-by-Linear Association	44,399	1	,000
N of Valid Cases	217		
a. 5 cells (31.3%) have expected count less than 5. The minimum expected count is .60.			

Table 9. 9H⁰ and 9H¹ chi-square tests

	Value	**df**	**Asymp. Sig. (2-sided)**
Pearson Chi-Square	92.083[a]	9	,000
Likelihood Ratio	116,713	9	,000
Linear-by-Linear Association	24,526	1	,000
N of Valid Cases	217		
a. 5 cells (31.3%) have expected count less than 5. The minimum expected count is 1.20.			

other words, there is a significant difference between students' economics grades and monetary illusion category.

SOLUTIONS AND RECOMMENDATIONS

Money has always been an indispensable element in our lives from past to present. Regarding the concept of money, which is seen as a part of our lives, issues such as control of money, saving money etc. are frequently brought to the agenda. A financial literate is a person who knows economic concepts in a basic level and who is able to master the applications shaped by technological developments, such as successfully managing the credit card operations. In addition, s/he is a person who has sufficient background on subjects like budget and savings. Acquisition of these skills can be supported with the education process. Individuals can be educated from childhood through lessons aimed at acquiring relevant skills. Starting from elementary schools, basic, simple fun applications with a money theme can be used in the lessons.

It can be taught as a compulsory course in universities. Students have a common belief that it is a course which is composed of mathematical expressions and statistics. Brochures that include information about course definitions and requirements can be held in introductory seminars. Students may not request it in elective courses because they perceive financial literacy as a difficult and complex subject. However, awareness about the necessities in daily life can be increased with lots of fun and practical exercises in compulsory courses.

FUTURE RESEARCH DIRECTIONS

In Financial literacy is a necessary concept for individuals to make relevant decisions that we have to take in our daily lives. A person with financial literacy is a person who is familiar with how account-based transactions proceed, who knows about their credit card transactions, debts and has savings information, can easily make decisions in these areas, and make financial transactions within the framework of technological development.

In today's living conditions, it has become compulsory for each individual to master the basic financial information in general and to use this information successfully in developing technology and digital environment. It is also among the financial literacy skills of individuals to know the amount of money they receive, to control it, to regulate the livelihood process, and to make savings and investment through the amount of money they receive.

The study on the financial literacy skills of the students who took the introduction to economics course in the 2018-2019 academic year includes only the communication faculty students. This study can give different and effective information about the subject if various comparisons can be made by conducting a research with the students in the departments such as business administration and economics.

CONCLUSION

In general, the notion of literacy, which can be defined as the process of learning to read and write, is regarded as an intellectual achievement. It can also be considered as the ability to analyse the printed materials and letters and being educated. However, with the change in communication technologies and the development of devices such as mobile phones etc., a cultural change occurs in every aspect of our lives. This change and transformation and the cultural metamorphosis that it brings with it make these definitions inadequate. Literacy is discussed as a part of the transformation in societies and we can mention about literacy definitions in every field. For example, the concept of literacy is constantly being discussed in the fields of media, health, language and finance, and many studies are carried out about it. Literacy is described as the competency in someone's own field, having the necessary knowledge and information skills and defines the people who can use these skills actively. A financial literacy is a person who knows the basics of finance and is able to mobilize skills that are used in finance as part of our daily lives.

In the scope of the research, data were analyzed to determine the relationship between financial literacy acquisition as a life skill and participation in the Introduction to Economics course with the students who study at Istanbul Medipol University Faculty of Communication during the 2018-2019 academic year. 217 students participated in the survey. A homogeneous group was tried to be formed for the research universe. 100 female and 117 male students were included in the study. The majority of the participants were 18-19 years old students. The number of students at this age is 129. Students belonging to age group 22 and above within the participants constituting the universe of the study are the participants who have the possibility of failing the course. In this study, the Departments of Public Relations and Advertising (English) and Radio, Television and Cinema, are within the departments of Istanbul Medipol University, Faculty of Communication, were not included in the research as they did not take an Introduction to Economics course. The departments included in the research are Public Relations and Advertising, New Media and Communication, Media and Visual Arts and Journalism. Whereas 126 of the students who participated in the study passed the course with very good, good and intermediate grades, 91 students failed the course with F grade. While 138 of the students participated in the study were living with their families or relatives, 79 of them were accommodating in dormitories, student houses and single-detached dwellings. 203 of the students have an average monthly income of at least 1000 TL. This income can be considered as an amount that will enable students to live comfortably and make savings. Nearly all students in the study have a bank account and a credit card. The most important reason for having a bank account may be the scholarships received from the government (Credit and Dormitories Agency), or part-time or full-time job wages or that the students coming from outside the city open bank accounts to receive money from their families. Some of the students may have their own cards as credit cards, or some of them may have additional credit cards belonging to the other family members. It was observed that the students who participated in the study more consciously answered the questions related to the basic level of financial literacy (financial mathematics, compound interest, inflation, time value of money, monetary illusion). It was determined that the participants chose the options 'I do not know' or 'I do not answer' in their answers to advanced financial literacy questions. Further studies are needed, especially on advanced financial literacy studies.

In the context of the study, data of the hypothesis tests of the research were analyzed and the explanations of the findings were made. In the first hypothesis of the study, when the relationship between students' bank accounts and financial mathematics is examined, it is seen that there is no relationship between these variables or the relationship is weak. In other words, there is no relationship between having a bank account of the student and the transfer of some amount of money in his/her account to their deposit account, as well as the information about whether the student's money increases, decreases or remains constant at the end of a year. In the second hypothesis of the study, when the relationship between students' bank accounts and compound interest is examined, it is seen that there is no relationship between these variables or the relationship is weak. In other words, there is no relationship between having a bank account and having money in his/her deposit account, and the increase, decrease or remaining constant of the student's money with a five-year term. When the relationship between the time value of money and illusion of money is examined in the third hypothesis, it is seen that there is no relationship between these variables or the relationship is weak. In other words, there is no difference between the fact that the amount of money students have today, the question of who will be richer when another friend has the same amount of money in his account in the coming years, and how much product can be bought with his income after the prices of the products he wants to buy doubled in a given year. When the relationship between inflation and time value of money is examined in the fourth hypothesis of the study, a statistically significant relationship was observed between these variables. In other words, there is a significant difference between these variables when a certain amount of money in the bank account of students is traded with a certain interest rate and there is twice the inflation rate of the student's interest rate and when the amount of money in the student's account is compared with the same amount of money in the following years . In the fifth hypothesis of the study, when the relationship between the results obtained from economics course and financial mathematics is examined, a statistically significant relationship was observed. In other words, there is a significant difference between the final grade of the students and the increase, decrease or remaining stable of the interest income that will be obtained at the end of five years with a certain interest rate of some money in the student's deposit account. . In the sixth hypothesis of the study, when the relationship between the results obtained from the economics course and the compound interest is examined, there was a statistically significant relationship between these variables. In other words, there is a significant difference between the final grade of the students and the information about how much money will be accumulated after five years in the savings account of the student. In the seventh hypothesis of the study, the relationship between the grades obtained from economics course and financial mathematics is examined; and a statistically significant relationship was observed between these variables. In other words, there is a significant difference between the final grade of the students and the fact that the student's interest rate is twice as much as the amount of money and the comparison of some amount of money in student's bank account with the same amount of money in the coming years . In the eighth hypothesis of the study, when the relationship between the students' economics grades and the inflation is examined, a statistically significant relationship was found between these variables. In other words, there is a significant difference between the final grade of the students and the fact that the students have some money today and the question who becomes richer with another friend having the same amount of money in the next years. In the eighth hypothesis of the study, the relationship between students' economics grades and inflation is examined, and a statistically significant relationship was observed between these variables. In other words, there is significant difference between the final grade of the students and the fact that the students have some money today and with another friend having the same amount of money in the coming years, who will be richer. In the ninth hypothesis of the study, when the relationship between the students' economics grades and the inflation is examined, a statistically significant relationship was found between these variables. In other words, there is a significant difference between the final grade of the students and the amount of products that they want to buy with the income in a given year, after the prices of desired products doubled.

REFERENCES

Ağırman, E., & Akyol, Ş. (2019). *Finanasal Okuryazarlık İİBF Öğrencileri Üzerine Bir Araştırma*. Bursa, Turkey: Ekin Yayınları.

Bilici, İ. (2017). *Medya Okuryazarlığı ve Eğitimi*. Ankara, Turkey: Nobel Akademik Yayınları.

Çakırer, M. (2019). *Finanasal Okuryazarlık*. Bursa, Turkey: Ekin Basım Yayın Dağıtım.

Dilek, M. Ş. (2019, 5 15). *Ekonomiye Giriş Ders Tanıtımı Formu*. Retrieved from İletişim Fakültesi - Halkla İlişkiler ve Reklamcılık Programı EKONOMİYE GİRİŞ: http://www.medipol.edu.tr/ders-detay i?DersBolumID=202966#DersTanimi

Field, A. (2000). *Discovering Statistics Using SPSS for Windows*. New Delhi, India: Sage Publications.

Gökmen, H. (2012). *Finansal Okuryazarlık*. İstanbul, Turkey: Hiperlik Yayınları.

Gürbüz, S., & Şahin, F. (2016). *Sosyal Bilimlerde Araştırma Yöntemleri*. Ankara, Turkey: Seçkin Yayıncılık.

İçke, B. T. (2017). *Finansal Okur Yazarlık*. İstanbul, Turkey: Beta Basım Yayın.

İnal, K. (2009). *Medya Okuryazarlığı El Kitabı*. Ankara, Turkey: Ütopya Yayınevi.

İnceoğlu, Y. (2007). Medyayı Doğru Okumak. In *N. Türkoğlu, & M. Cinman Şimşek, Medya Okuryazarlığı* (pp. 21–26). İstanbul, Turkey: Kalemus Yayınları.

Miller, M. H. (1977). Debt and Taxes. *The Journal of Finance*, 261–275.

OECD. (2011). *Measuring Financial Literacy: Questionnaire and Guidance Notes for Conducting an Internationally Comparable Survey of Financial Literacy*. Paris, France: OECD.

OECD. (2013). *Advancing National Strategies for Financial Education A Joint Publication by Russia's G20 Presidency and the OECD*. Russia: OECD.

Remund, D. L. (2010). Financial Literacy Explicated: The Case for a Clearer Definition in an Increasingly Complex Economy. *The Journal of Consumer Affairs, 44*(2), 276–295. doi:10.1111/j.1745-6606.2010.01169.x

Rooij, M. V., Lusardi, A., & Alessie, R. (2007, September). Financial Literacy and Stock Market Participation. *Tjalling C. Koopmans Research Institute Discussion Paper Series nr: 07-23*, pp. 1-50.

Sancak, E. (2012). *Bireysel Tasarruf ve Yatırımları Koruma Rehberi*. Ankara, Turkey: Gazi Kitabevi.

Sancak, E. (2014). *Sermaye Piyasası Sözlüğü - Temel Düzey*. İstanbul, Turkey: Scala Yayıncılık.

Sung, Y., Lee, J.-A., & Choi, S. M. (2016). Why we post selfies: Understanding motivations for posting pictures of oneself. *Personality and Individual Differences, 97*, 260–265. doi:10.1016/j.paid.2016.03.032

Taşkıran Öncel, N. (2007). *Medya Okuryazarlığına Giriş*. İstanbul, Turkey: Beta Yayınları.

KEY TERMS AND DEFINITIONS

Budget: Budget is the balance of income and expenditure of individuals, institutions and even public institutions.

Economy: Economy is a discipline that analyses the relations of production and consumption.

Finance: Finance is the supply of the provision of stock certificate, currency, precious metals like gold under favorable conditions to the individuals who need them.

Financial Literacy: it is to be able to master and apply all the general information about finance, which is a life skill.

Investment: Investment is the use of goods and values to generate income.

Literacy: Literacy is to have the ability in a subject. It is the person who has all the required knowledge and information about the related field.

Questionnaire: Questionnaire is a form of research method used in the study areas such as commercial, academic, etc.

Saving: Saving is to accumulate the components like foreign exchange, precious metals owned or will be owned by individuals.

Chapter 13
Determining the Importance of Domestic Firms on Stock Market Performance in Terms of Financial Marketing:
An Application on OECD Countries

İrfan Ersin
https://orcid.org/0000-0002-7407-3654
Istanbul Medipol University, Turkey

ABSTRACT

This chapter examines the relationship between stock market value of domestic firms traded in stock markets in OECD countries and stock index for 1990-2018 period. As a result of Pedroni Panel Cointegration and Dumitrescu-Hurlin Panel Causality Analysis, there is a relationship between the market values of domestic firms traded on the stock exchange and the stock index. In addition, a two-way causality relationship was found. This situation indicates that this relationship is very powerful. It can be understood that adding domestic companies to the stock market has a significant effect on the stock prices and this will attract foreign investors to enter the market.

INTRODUCTION

One of the most important indicators in determining the investors' decisions within the stock market is undoubtedly the stock prices. The development, liberalization of financial markets and the increasing degree of interaction in the sub-markets made stock prices extremely sensitive to economic and political developments (Basher and Sadorsky, 2016; Raza et al., 2016). The development of this market and ensuring a stable course follow the decisions of investors; the health of the decisions depends on the correct and meaningful determination of the factors affecting stock prices (Reboredo et al., 2016; Albeni and Demir, 2005). In the economy, whether it is individual investors or institutional investors, it is

DOI: 10.4018/978-1-7998-2559-3.ch013

very important to evaluate surplus funds in their hands on the basis of low risk and high return. In this sense, it is of paramount importance that financial market investors are sensitive to stock investments and invest in high yielding stocks (Dessaint et al., 2018; Ege and Bayrakdaroğlu, 2012; Dinçer, 2015; Ewing and Malik, 2016).

The entity may obtain equity financing through the sale of shares or the release of net profit to the company. The most important contribution of the financing through equity capital to the related company is that there is no fixed interest or obligation that the company must pay to the capital provided in this way (Neaime, 2016; Phua et al., 2017). Today, all countries strive to attract international capital to their countries through stock. Many developing countries provide foreign currency inflows to their countries by billions of dollars each year by stabilizing their capital markets. Indeed, the strength of the stock market in the country is an important factor for foreign investors (Kotabe and Kothari, 2016; Dinçer et al., 2016). The internal variable is the mobility of the domestic firms in the stock market which will determine the power of the stock market. Domestic companies listed on the exchange will contribute to the stock market (Edirisuriya et al., 2015; Yerdelen Kaygın, 2013).

The stock market is very important from an economic point of view. The stock market has a direct relationship with the real economy. As a matter of fact, the development of the stock market causes an increase in investments and this contributes to the economic growth (Smales, 2017; Bouri et al., 2017). The most important contribution of the stock to the economy functionally can be expressed as the evaluation of the savings of the people directly in the investments without incurring the credit costs (Kang et al., 2016; Arkan, 2016; Eti et al., 2019). This causes the burden of interest on the economy to disappear. In this respect, real economic development is an important event in the stock market. Ultimately, the development of a country depends on the development of the economy, and the development of the economy depends on the development of enterprises within the financial system (Beyer, 2015; Karan, 2011; Dinçer and Yüksel, 2018).

Determining the factors that affect stock prices will enable the investor to make the right investment decisions. If the factors that affect stock prices are determined correctly, the success of the investments will be higher. Factors affecting stock prices are classified as macroeconomic, enterprise-specific and other factors (Dizdarlar and Derindere, 2008; Salmanov et al., 2016). These factors include dividend income, capital gains and pre-emptive income for stock returns. From a microeconomic perspective, liquidity ratios, operating ratios, leverage ratios, profitability ratios and stock market performance ratios are important in terms of affecting stock prices (Feng et al., 2016; Bekiros et al., 2016; Emir et al., 2016). Macroeconomically, it can be expressed as exchange rate, inflation rate, money supply, interest rate, GDP, gold prices, oil prices and foreign trade balance (Huang et al., 2017; Acaravci, 2016; Peiró, 2016). When these factors are taken into consideration, it is seen that stock market performance is a variable. As a matter of fact, the effect of local firms on the stock market performance is one of the subjects that researchers aim to understand (Malandri et al., 2018).

It is one of the subjects that the domestic companies traded on the stock exchange are interested in whether they affect the stock market (Choudhry et al., 2016; Chien et al., 2015). The presence of local companies in the stock market gives us information about the structure of domestic investments. In addition, the strength, management quality and transparency of domestic firms in the stock exchange are important in attracting foreign investors (Siganos et., 2017; Cetorelli and Peristiani, 2015). As a matter of fact, the quality of management of domestic firms will affect stock prices and influencing stock prices will have an impact on foreign direct investments. Affecting FDI will also contribute to the country's economic development (Engelberg and Parsons, 2016; Yiğit and Muzır, 2019; Gao, 2015). In this respect, the situation of domestic firms in the stock market is important.

The fact that a country's macro and micro economic indicators are good may not mean that the domestic firms of that country are also strong. For example, the democracy and legal infrastructure of the country may result in the fact that foreign investors contribute more to the national economy. Therefore, knowing the presence of domestic firms in the stock market is important for the emergence of the national power of the economy. The aim of our study is to reveal the relationship between stock market performance, which is a condition of financial marketing, and domestic firms traded on the stock exchange. The study, which takes OECD countries into account, analyzes the 1990-2018 period and uses the Pedroni Cointegration test as a method. In this direction, the introduction part of our study gives information about the stock market and the importance of domestic firms. In the second part, the related literature was searched and in the third part the empirical application was made. In the fourth section, the findings were evaluated and in the last section the results and recommendations were presented.

LITERATURE REVIEW

Studies examining the impact of domestic firms on stock performance have been rarely encountered in the literature. The literature review close to the subject of this study is presented in Table 1.

In Table 1, the relationship between stocks and the real sector is examined in the literature review. Aydemir (2008) has addressed the scope of the ISE 100 index in Turkey. Error-Correction Model and Standard Granger Causulity test were used in the study. As a result of the analysis, a long-term relationship between stocks and the real sector was determined. In addition, a causal relationship was found between the two variables. Oral et al. (2017) examined the relationship between companies in Borsa Istanbul on the value of shares. In the study, which used panel data analysis, monthly data for 2010-2014 period were evaluated and it was concluded that the 40% financial leverage ratio of companies increased the stock yield. Li et al. (2019) examined the relationship between the stocks of firms with large shares in the Chinese market and the market value of firms. In the study, which used panel data analysis, the period of 2003-2015 was discussed and a relationship was found between the stock amounts of firms and their market value.

Tease (1993) analyzed the relationship between stock prices and business investments in G7 countries. Panel data analysis is used in the study, 1960-1991 period is discussed. According to the results of the study, the relationship between stock prices and business investments in G7 countries was found to be weak. Albeni and Demir (2005) analyzed the effects of macroeconomic factors on stock prices using a multiple regression model. The study, which covers the period of 1991-2000, has been found to affect deposit interest rates, gold of the republic, international portfolio investments and stock prices of the German Mark. A similar study was conducted by Maysami et al. (2005) for Singapore. In this study, it is tried to establish a relationship between macroeconomic variables (interest, prices, money supply and industrial production) and the stock market value of the firms in Singapore during 1989-2001 period. In the study using panel cointegration analysis, a relationship was determined between stock market value and macroeconomic variables. Similarly, Peiró (2016) examined the impact of macroeconomic factors on stock prices. In the study, which examined England, Germany and France, the period of 1969-2013 was analyzed by regression method. As a result of this study, it is seen that production and interest rates are determinative on stock prices.

Table 1. Literature review

Author	Content	Method	Period	Finding
(Aydemír, 2008)	Turkey	Error-correction model and Standard Granger-Causality test	1998-2008	A long-term relationship was found between GDP and private sector consumption expenditures and stock returns. Moreover, mutual the causal relationship between two variables was determined.
(Oral, Polat, & ŞiT, 2017)	Turkey	Panel Cointegration test-DOLS, FMOLS and CCR tests	2010-2014	It was observed for 40% of the companies that the financial leverage ratio increased the stock returns.
(Tease, 1993)	G7 Countries	Panel Data Analysis	1960-1991	In G7 countries, a weak relationship was found between stock prices and business investments.
(Albeni & Demír, 2005)	Turkey	Multiple Regression Analysis	1991-2000	International portfolio investments affect stock prices.
(Bagirov & Mateus, 2019)	Europe Countries	VAR Analysis	2006-2015	A relationship was identified between the stock exchange in European countries and oil prices.
(Boyacıoğlu & Çürük, 2016)	Turkey	Panel Data Analysis	2006-2014	The change in the real exchange rate index was found to have a positive relationship on stock returns.
(Kurt & Köse, 2017)	Turkey	Panel Causality Test	2002-2016	A causality was found between the capital adequacy and balance sheet structure of banks with stock returns.
(Li, Liu, & Scott, 2019)	Chine	Panel Data Analysis	2003-2015	A relationship was found between the stock value of the firms and their market value.
(Maysami, Howe, & Rahmat, 2005)	Singapore	Panel Cointegration Test	1989-2001	A relationship was found between the stock market value of firms in Singapore and macroeconomic variables (interest, money supply, prices and industrial production).
(Yalçıner, Atan, & Boztosun, 2005)	Turkey	Data Envelopment Analysis (DEA) and Malmquist Total Factor Productivity (TFT) analysis	2000-2003	The relationship between active companies and their stock returns is high during periods of economic stability.
(Zheng & Osmer, 2019)	USA	VAR-GARCH Model	1991-2014	it was found that correlations between aggregate stock market sentiment and housing returns.
(Eugster & Isakov, 2019)	Switzerland	Panel Regression	2003-2013	It was concluded that the returns of family firms for different firm characteristics and risk factors were higher than non-family firms.
(Gupta & Banerjee, 2019)	USA	Panel Regression	2003-2014	It was reached that negative OPEC news positively affected stock returns in the USA.
(Ma, Anderson, & Marshall, 2019)	World (57 Countries)	Panel Regression	1990-2015	High risk perception of investors reduces international stock market returns.
(Chiang & Chen, 2016)	USA	ARCH and GARCH Model	1994-2014	It was concluded that changes in exchange rates affect stock returns of developing sectors.
(Sui & Sun, 2016)	BRICS Countries	VAR and ARDL Model	1993-2014	It was viewed that there is a significant spread effect from exchange rates to short-term stock returns.
(Robinson, Glean, & Moore, 2018)	China, Taiwan, Brazil, South Africa and India	Panel Regression	2015 (January 1-December 31)	News affects the daily stock returns of firms, but this effect does not last long.
(Haider, Khan, Saddique, & Hashmi, 2017)	China	ARDL Model	2007-2015	Stock market performance has a positive effect on foreign portfolio investments.
(Peiró, 2016)	France, Germany and the United Kingdom	Regression	1969-2013	Production and interest rates determine stock returns in France, Germany and the UK.
(Idris & Bala, 2015)	Nigeria	Panel Regression	2007-2013	It was viewed that Market Capitalization has a negative impact on stock returns.

Yalçıner et al. (2005) examined the relationship between firms' financial ratios and stock returns. In this study, the companies in Borsa Istanbul were analyzed by taking 2000-2003 monthly data into consideration. Data Envelopment Analysis (DEA) and Malmquist Total Factor Productivity (TFT) analysis is used in the study and it is concluded that the relationship between companies that are effective in terms of financial ratios and their stock returns is high during periods of economic stability. Bagirov and Mateus (2019) have tried to establish a relationship between oil prices and stock and stock values by considering the Dow Jones Stoxx Europe 600 index in European countries. In the study which analyzed the period of 2006-105, VAR model was used. As a result of this study, it is determined that there is a strong relationship between oil prices and stocks.

Kurt and Kose (2017), the relationship between BIST 100 within nine bank's capital structure and balance sheet with stock returns in Turkey has been analyzed by the panel causality test. As a result of the study covering the period of 2002-2016, it is concluded that the capital structures of the banks ((Equity-Fixed Assets) / Total Assets) ratio and balance sheet structures (TL Loans and Receivables / Total Loans and Receivables) are the causes of stock returns. In the study of İdris and Bala (2017), the effect of specific characteristics of food companies in Nigeria on stock returns was analyzed. In this study, Panel Regression was used as the method in the study, which takes into account variables such as capital use in stock exchange, equity finance to stock exchange and earnings per share. As a result of this study, it was seen that market capitalization affects stock returns.

Gupta and Banerjee (2019) examined the impact of OPEC news on the US stock market. Panel regression method was used in this study and 2003-2014 period was analyzed. As a result of the study, it was concluded that negative OPEC news positively affected stock returns on the US stock exchange. Robinson et al. (2018) examined the effects of the news on stock exchange returns of green certified firms. In this study, the countries of China, Taiwan, Brazil, South Africa and India were taken as examples and daily data of January 1-December 31, 2015 were analyzed. Panel regression method was used in the study and it was concluded that the news affected the stock returns of the firms, but this did not last long.

In the study of Zheng and Osmer (2019) examining the effect of total stock market sentiment on housing returns in the USA, the period 1991-2014 was analyzed by VAR-GARCH model. As a result of the study, a relationship was found between total stock market sentiment and housing returns. In fact, this relationship was found to be stronger during periods of stagnant economy. Ma et al. (2019) examined the risk perception of investors and their impact on international stock returns. In this study using panel regression method, 57 countries were analyzed. On the other hand, the period 1990-2015 is discussed. As a result of the study, it was seen that the increase in the risk perception of the investors decreased the returns of the international stock market. Haider et al. (2017) analyzed the effect of stock market performance and inflation on foreign portfolio investments in China. In this study, which analyzed 2007-2015 period, ARDL Boundary Test was applied and as a result of the study, it was seen that stock market performance had a positive effect on foreign portfolio investments.

Chiang and Chen (2016) established a relationship between the stock returns and domestic economic forces of the developing industrial sector in the United States. ARCH-GARCH model was used in the study which covers the period of 1990-2014. In this study, changes in the dividend yield, trading volume, stock volatility, liquidity, exchange rate, US market returns, and stress in the US market were used as variables. As a result of the study, it is seen that exchange rate changes affect stock returns in the developing industry sector. Sui and Sun (2016) conducted a similar study and examined the relationship between exchange rate changes and stock returns in BRICS (Brazil, Russia, India, China, and South Africa). In this study, VAR and ARDL Boundary Tests were used as a method. As a result of the study, it is seen that exchange rate changes have a spread effect on stock returns in the short term. In the study of Boyacioglu and Corus (2016), the relationship between exchange rate changes and stocks was analyzed. For the period 2006-2014 in Turkey, it is considered as BIST100 index coverage. On the other hand, panel data analysis was used in this study. According to the results of the study, a positive relationship was found between real exchange rate changes and stocks.

In the study of Eugster and Isakov (2019), the stock returns of family companies and non-family companies on the Swiss stock exchange were compared. The panel regression method was used to analyze the 2003-2013 period. As a result of this study, stock exchange returns of family companies were higher than non-family firms in terms of different firm characteristics and risk factors. When the literature studies are taken into consideration, there is no direct study on the stock performance of local firms, but similar studies are scarce. In fact, this study is thought to make an important contribution to the literature. In this section of the literature review, similar studies are conducted on the relationship between market capitulations and stock prices of domestic firms traded on the stock exchange. In the next section of this section, the studies related to the method used in our study will be included. The frequency and manner of using the method in the current period will answer the question of why this method is needed.

Faith et al. (2016) Dumitrescu-Hurlin causality test was used for the relationship between financial development and growth in D8 countries. In the study of Dursun and Özcan (2019), the same causality test was used to examine the relationship between energy price changes and stock market indices for OECD countries. Reis and Aydın (2014) analyzed the relationship between stock liquidity and financial development with the Dumitrescu-Hurlin causality test. Kaya and Öztürk (2015) used the Pedroni cointegration test to examine the relationship between accounting profits and stock prices. Akıncı and Küçükçaylı (2016) analyzed the relationship between stock markets and exchange rate mechanisms with Pedroni cointegration test. Apart from these studies, Dumitrescu-Hurlin and Pedroni cointegration tests are among the most frequently used methods recently. As a matter of fact, Gün (2019), Dinçer et al. (2019), Zoundi (2017), Yüksel and Canöz (2017), Apergis and Öztürk (2015), Yüksel (2017), Dinçer et al. (2019a,b,c,d), Adalı and Yüksel (2017), Saidi and Mbarek (2016), Dinçer and Yüksel (2019), Ersin and Baş (2019), Doğan and Arslan (2017), Hassler and Hosseinkouchack (2016), Amin et al. (2019), Dinçer et al. (2018a,b), Çelik and Kaya (2010), Furuoka (2017), Aydin and Malcioğlu (2016) and Dinçer et al. (2017) used Pedroni cointegration and Dumitrescu-Hurlin Causality tests in their studies.

AN APPLICATION ON OECD ECONOMIES

Data Set and Method

In this study, the period between 1990-2018 was examined in order to examine the relationship between the market value and stock prices of listed firms in OECD countries. In the OECD, 16 countries with data between these periods were selected. The variables used in our study are presented in Table 2. The market value data of domestic firms listed on the stock exchange, which is one of the variables in Table 2, is obtained from world bank data as a percentage of GDP. Equity prices variable data were also obtained from OECD database. Equity prices are taken as base year 2010 = 100. In our study, Pedroni cointegration and Dumitrescu-Hurlin Causality test were used as methods. These tests are widely used in time series analysis. In order to measure these tests, variables are first subjected to unit root test.

Table 2. Definition of variables used and data sources

The Name of the Variables	Definition	Data Source
StockFirm	Market capitalization of listed domestic companies (% of GDP)	World Bank
StockPrice	Stock Prices (2010 = 100 index)	OECD

Stationary Analysis

The unit root test shows whether the series are stationary. If there is no stasis in a time series, it is formulated as $\Delta X = X_t - X_{t-1}$ and taken until it becomes stable. When the time series becomes stagnant, this series Δ level is integrated. In addition, the stability of the series is shown as $X_t \sim I(\Delta)$. In the literature, Levin et al. (2002), Im et al. (2003), Maddala and Wu (1999), Choi (2001) are generally accepted. Fisher Type: Maddala and Wu (1999) and Choi (2001), Breitung (2000), Levin, Lin and Chu (LLC) (2002) and Im, Pesaran and Shin (IPS) (2003) for unit root testing in panel data models). Establishing hypotheses in these tests and calculating test statistics are based on Dickey-Fuller (1979) and Extended Dickey Fuller (ADF) unit root tests.

As shown in Equation 1, LLC is based on the Augmented Dickey-Fuller-ADF test and is based on the assumption that the autoregressive (ρ) coefficient of the variable is homogeneous. In the model with constant parameters, ε_{it}, ie the error process, is distributed independently between the variables (Levin et al., 2002).

$$\Delta y_{it} = \alpha_{0i} + \rho y_{it-1} + \varepsilon_{it} \tag{1}$$

In addition, starting from equation 1, the unit root test hypotheses are established below. In the hypothesis, if the coefficient ρ is equal to 0, the hypothesis H_0 is accepted. In this case, the difference must be obtained for the series to become stable.

In Levin, Lin and Chu (LLC) (2002) test, the autoregressive ρ coefficient is homogeneous for all units, whereas in the Im, Pesaran and Shin (IPS) (2003) test, the ρ coefficient is allowed to be heterogeneous. In the IPS test, unit root test is applied to time series for each unit without combining the data and the average of the obtained statistics is obtained by obtaining the IPS test statistic (Im, Pesaran, Shin, 2003: 53). Maddala and Wu (1999) and Choi (2001) proposed Fisher-type test as an alternative based on uniting unit root test statistics for each non-parametric cross-section (Güven & Mert, 2016).

Pedroni Panel Cointegration Analysis

Cointegration analysis is a test method that provides information about the long-term relationship between the series. Stating that linear combinations of two or more non-stationary series may be stationary, Engle and Granger (1987) made an important contribution to the literature with cointegration analysis. In panel cointegration analyzes, the method that we often encounter in the literature is developed by Pedroni. This method is expressed in Equation (2) below. The existence of the relationship between x and y in this equation depends on the stability of the error term e_{it} residue. If the error term is stationary, there is a long-term relationship between x and y (Pedroni, 2001).

$$y_{it} = \alpha_i + \delta_i t + \beta_{1i} X_{2it} + \beta_{2i} X_{2it} + \ldots + \beta_{Mi} X_{Mit} + e_{it} \qquad (2)$$

Two different panel cointegration tests, Kao (1999) and Pedroni (1999), are used to test for cointegration in panel data. Pedroni (1999) uses a two-variable model for cointegration analysis, whereas in Pedroni (2001), this limitation disappears, and multivariate models can be used. Pedroni panel cointegration analysis, panel v-statistic, panel rho-statistic, panel Philips-Peron (PP) -statistic, panel ADF-statistic, group rho-statistic, group PP-statistic and group ADF-statistic has 7 different tests. This methodology is appropriate when evaluating using panel methods. In this test, the probability values of all 7 tests were calculated. If the probability values of 4 or more tests are less than 0.05, it means that there is cointegration between the variables. In other words, it can be said that these variables involve long term relationships.

Dumitrescu Hurlin Panel Causality Analysis

Dumitrescu Hurlin panel causality is a methodology for understanding the causal relationship between variables. This method is considered to be an advanced version of Granger causality analysis. In this approach, it is possible to evaluate using panel data. Dumitrescu - Hurlin panel causality analysis is shown below in Equation (3).

$$Y_{i,t} = a_i + \sum_{k=1}^{K} Y_i^k Y_{i,t-k} + \sum_{k=1}^{K} B_i^k X_{i,t-k} + \varepsilon_{i,t} \qquad (3)$$

In this equation, X and Y represent variables. The purpose of this method is therefore to determine whether X is the main cause of Y. In addition, B is the coefficient of the variable and a constant term. In addition, the symbol $\varepsilon_{i,t}$ gives reference to the error term and K gives information about the optimal delay interval (Dumitrescu and Hurlin, 2012).

Analysis Results

The prerequisite for panel cointegration and panel causality analyzes is that the series are stationary. In order to stabilize the series, variables are subjected to unit root test. The unit root test results of the variables are presented in Table 3. As shown in Table 3, there are 5 unit root test methods. Stability of variables is accepted at 1% and 5% significance levels. If the result of at least 3 of the 5 methods is significant at the level of 5% for the stability of the variables in Table 3, the variable is considered stationary.

The Stockfirm variable in Table 3, which represents the domestic firms traded on the stock exchange, was considered to be stationary in Breitung t-stat and PP - Fisher Chi-square methods, but not in other methods. Since we consider at least 3 methods, the first difference of Stockfirm variable is taken and the variable is made stationary in all methods. The Stockprice variable, which represents the stock price, is considered stationary at a level other than PP - Fisher Chi-square. Therefore, the Stockprice variable is considered stationary at the level.

Cointegration is a method that provides information about the relationship between two variables. The variables used in the study were subjected to panel cointegration test after stabilization. In Pedroni cointegration analysis shown in Table 4, the significance value was lower than 0.05 in 6 of the 7 test

Table 3. Panel unit root test results

		Constant and Trend		Constant	
		t- statistics I(0)	Probability I(0)	t- statistics I(1)	Probability I(1)
StockFirm	Levin, Lin & Chu	0.39273	0.6527	13.5607	0.0000
	Breitung t-stat	-4.04787	0.0000	-	-
	Im, Pesaran and Shin W-stat	-1.15064	0.1249	-14.7913	0.0000
	ADF - Fisher Chi-square	36.3292	0.2739	241.612	0.0000
	PP - Fisher Chi-square	57.3485	0.0039	367.805	0.0000
StockPrice	Levin, Lin & Chu	-3.65543	0.0001	-	-
	Breitung t-stat	-3.75103	0.0001	-	-
	Im, Pesaran and Shin W-stat	3.09586	0.0010	-	-
	ADF - Fisher Chi-square	57.7533	0.0035	-	-
	PP - Fisher Chi-square	24.7949	0.8142	-	-

methods. These results show that there is a relationship between the market value of domestic firms listed on the stock exchange and stock prices.

Dumitrescu - Hurlin causality analysis, which is an advanced version of Granger causality analysis, provides information about the causality of the relationship between variables. The panel causality results of our study are shown in Table 5. According to the results, a two-way causality has been determined between the market value and stock prices of domestic firms traded on the stock exchange. Since the probability values of the variables in Table 5 are less than 0.05, a two-way causality relationship has emerged.

When the findings are evaluated, the effectiveness of the domestic firms traded on the stock market affects the stock prices as well as the market prices of the domestic firms traded on the stock market. In fact, since the effectiveness of domestic firms will affect the country's stock prices causally, this situation may shape the arrival of foreign firms to the stock market. Moreover, the emergence of this causal

Table 4. Pedroni cointegration test

Relationship Type	Test Method	Statistic	Prob.	Weighted Statistic	Prob.
Relationship between stock prices and domestic firms listed on the stock market	Panel v-Statistic	1.281510	0.1000	-0.890688	0.8134
	Panel rho-Statistic	-16.28555	0.0000	-16.07146	0.0000
	Panel PP-Statistic	-23.49218	0.0000	-21.78754	0.0000
	Panel ADF-Statistic	-14.89099	0.0000	-	-
	Group rho-Statistic	-12.85822	0.0000	-	-
	Group PP-Statistic	-30.60068	0.0000	-	-
	Group ADF-Statistic	-16.06129	0.0000	-	-

relationship in OECD countries signals the strength of domestic firms in stock prices. Having the power of domestic firms in the stock exchange in a country is an important event in the national development of the national economy.

SOLUTIONS AND RECOMMENDATIONS

In this case, it is possible to say that domestic firms are active in the stock market in OECD countries. It can be said that the strength of domestic firms is an important issue for financial marketing.

FUTURE RESEARCH DIRECTIONS

This study investigated the effects of domestic firms on the stock market. Investigating the effects of foreign firms on the stock market for new studies is recommended for researchers.

CONCLUSION

In today's world where globalization has become widespread, financial marketing has become an important field. Financial marketing is a large market in which financial instruments are evaluated by investors.

Table 5. Dumitrescu-Hurlin panel causality test

Direction of Causality Relationship	Lag Values	p- Value	null hypothesis	Decision
From Stockfirm to Stockprice	1	0.0000	Stockfirm does not homogeneously cause Stockprice	Rejection
	2	0.0000		Rejection
	3	0.0000		Rejection
From Stockprice to Stockfirm	1	0.0000	Stockprice does not homogeneously cause Stockfirm	Rejection

Within this market, the stock market is also an important indicator of real investment. Therefore, the strength of the stock market is a consideration taken into consideration in the economic growth of the country. A country must attach importance to the stock market for real economic growth. The strength of stock performance is seen as a factor that will enable foreign investors to come to the country.

Developing countries want to attract foreign investments to their own countries. As investments increase, the economy of the country will provide growth and the development of the country will increase. Developing the stock market and ensuring a stable course depends on the decisions of the investors and the soundness of the decisions depends on the factors affecting the stock returns. Therefore, in addition to improving macroeconomic indicators, the country has to make policies that will ensure the strength of domestic firms. The strength of domestic firms will give economic confidence to foreigners and FDI will increase. Therefore, the functioning and efficiency of the stock exchange is important for financial marketing.

In our study, an application was made on the importance of domestic firms in the stock market which is an area of financial marketing. In the implementation for OECD countries, the period of 1990-2018 was discussed and panel cointegration and causality analyzes were conducted. As a result of the analysis, cointegration was determined between stock prices and market value of domestic firms traded on the stock exchange. A double causality was also found in the analysis. In addition, when we compare our results with the literature, Yalçıner (2005), Oral et al. (2017), Tease (1993) and Liv et al. (2019) and our results are similar.

REFERENCES

Acaravci, S. K. (2016). Finansal Oranlar ve Hisse Senedi Getirisi İlişkisi: Borsa İstanbul Üzerine Bir Uygulama / Financial Ratios - Stock Return Nexus: An Applicaton on BIST. *Mustafa Kemal Üniversitesi Sosyal Bilimler Enstitüsü Dergisi, 13*(35), 0–0.

Adalı, Z., & Yüksel, S. (2017). *Causality relationship between foreign direct investments and economic improvement for developing economies.* Retrieved from http://dspace.marmara.edu.tr/xmlui/handle/11424/6146

Albeni, M., & Demir, Y. (2005). Makro Ekonomik Göstergelerin Mali Sektör Hisse Senedi Fiyatlarına Etkisi (IMKB Uygulamalı). *Muğla Üniversitesi Sosyal Bilimler Enstitüsü Dergisi,* (14), 1–18.

Amin, S. B., Kabir, F. A., & Khan, F. (2019). Tourism and energy nexus in selected South Asian countries: A panel study. *Current Issues in Tourism,* 1–5. doi:10.1080/13683500.2019.1638354

Apergis, N., & Ozturk, I. (2015). Testing environmental Kuznets curve hypothesis in Asian countries. *Ecological Indicators, 52,* 16–22. doi:10.1016/j.ecolind.2014.11.026

Arkan, T. (2016). The importance of financial ratios in predicting stock price trends: A case study in emerging markets. *Finanse, Rynki Finansowe. Ubezpieczenia, 79*(1), 13–26.

Aydemir, O. (2008). Hisse Senedi Getirileri Ve Reel Sektör Arasındaki İlişki: Ampirik Bir Çalışma. *Afyon Kocatepe Üniversitesi İktisadi ve İdari Bilimler Fakültesi Dergisi, 10*(2), 37–55.

Aydin, M., & Malcioglu, G. (2016). Financial development and economic growth relationship: The case of OECD countries. *Journal of Applied Research in Finance and Economics*, 2(1), 1–7.

Bagirov, M., & Mateus, C. (2019). Oil prices, stock markets and firm performance: Evidence from Europe. *International Review of Economics & Finance*, *61*, 270–288. doi:10.1016/j.iref.2019.02.007

Basher, S. A., & Sadorsky, P. (2016). Hedging emerging market stock prices with oil, gold, VIX, and bonds: A comparison between DCC, ADCC and GO-GARCH. *Energy Economics*, *54*, 235–247. doi:10.1016/j.eneco.2015.11.022

Bekiros, S., Gupta, R., & Kyei, C. (2016). On economic uncertainty, stock market predictability and nonlinear spillover effects. *The North American Journal of Economics and Finance*, *36*, 184–191. doi:10.1016/j.najef.2016.01.003

Beyer, S., Jensen, G., Johnson, R., & Hughen, J. C. (2015). Stock returns and the US dollar: The importance of monetary policy. *Managerial Finance*.

Tolga, O. R. A. L., Polat, E., & Ahmet, Ş. İ. T. (2017). *Borsa İstanbul Kurumsal Yönetim Endeksinde Yer Alan Şirketlerin Sermaye Yapıları İle Hisse Senedi Getirileri Arasındaki İlişkinin İncelenmesi*, 8(1), 16.

Bouri, E., Jain, A., Biswal, P. C., & Roubaud, D. (2017). Cointegration and nonlinear causality amongst gold, oil, and the Indian stock market: Evidence from implied volatility indices. *Resources Policy*, *52*, 201–206. doi:10.1016/j.resourpol.2017.03.003

Boyacıoğlu, M. A., & Çürük, D. (2016). Döviz Kuru Değişimlerinin Hisse Senedi Getirisine Etkisi: Borsa İstanbul 100 Endeksi Üzerine Bir Uygulama. *Muhasebe ve Finansman Dergisi*, (70), 143–156. doi:10.25095/mufad.396686

Canbaş, S., Doğukanlı, H., Düzakın, H., & İskenderoğlu, Ö. (2005). Performans Ölçümünde Tobin Q Oranının Kullanılması: Hisse Senetleri İMKB''de İşlem Gören Sanayi İşletmeleri Üzerinde Bir Deneme. *Muhasebe ve Finansman Dergisi*, (28), 24–36.

Çelik, S., & Kaya, H. (2010). Real exchange rates and bilateral trade dynamics of Turkey: Panel cointegration approach. *Applied Economics Letters*, *17*(8), 791–795. doi:10.1080/13504850802388993

Cetorelli, N., & Peristiani, S. (2015). Firm value and cross listings: The impact of stock market prestige. *Journal of Risk and Financial Management*, *8*(1), 150–180. doi:10.3390/jrfm8010150

Chiang, T. C., & Chen, X. (2016). Stock returns and economic fundamentals in an emerging market: An empirical investigation of domestic and global market forces. *International Review of Economics & Finance*, *43*, 107–120. doi:10.1016/j.iref.2015.10.034

Chien, M. S., Lee, C. C., Hu, T. C., & Hu, H. T. (2015). Dynamic Asian stock market convergence: Evidence from dynamic cointegration analysis among China and ASEAN-5. *Economic Modelling*, *51*, 84–98. doi:10.1016/j.econmod.2015.06.024

Choi, I. (2001). Unit root tests for panel data. *Journal of International Money and Finance*, *20*(2), 249–272. doi:10.1016/S0261-5606(00)00048-6

Choudhry, T., Papadimitriou, F. I., & Shabi, S. (2016). Stock market volatility and business cycle: Evidence from linear and nonlinear causality tests. *Journal of Banking & Finance, 66*, 89–101. doi:10.1016/j.jbankfin.2016.02.005

Dessaint, O., Foucault, T., Frésard, L., & Matray, A. (2018). Noisy stock prices and corporate investment. *Review of Financial Studies, 32*(7), 2625–2672. doi:10.1093/rfs/hhy115

Dincer, H. (2015). Profit-based stock selection approach in banking sector using Fuzzy AHP and MOORA method. *Global Business and Economics Research Journal, 4*(2), 1–26.

Dincer, H., Hacioglu, U., Tatoglu, E., & Delen, D. (2016). A fuzzy-hybrid analytic model to assess investors' perceptions for industry selection. *Decision Support Systems, 86*, 24–34. doi:10.1016/j.dss.2016.03.005

Dinçer, H., Hacıoğlu, Ü., & Yüksel, S. (2018). Conflict risk and defense expenses and their impact on the economic growth. In Handbook of research on military expenditure on economic and political resources (pp. 1–23). Hershey, PA: IGI Global. doi:10.4018/978-1-5225-4778-5.ch001

Dinçer, H., & Yüksel, S. (2018). Financial sector-based analysis of the G20 economies using the integrated decision-making approach with DEMATEL and TOPSIS. In *Emerging trends in banking and finance* (pp. 210–223). Cham, Switzerland: Springer. doi:10.1007/978-3-030-01784-2_13

Dinçer, H., & Yüksel, S. (2019). Identifying the causality relationship between health expenditure and economic growth: An application on E7 countries. *Journal of Health Systems and Policies, 1*, 5.

Dinçer, H., Yüksel, S., & Adalı, Z. (2017). Identifying causality relationship between energy consumption and economic growth in developed countries. *International Business and Accounting Research Journal, 1*(2), 71–81. doi:10.15294/ibarj.v1i2.9

Dinçer, H., Yuksel, S., & Adalı, Z. (2018). Relationship between non-performing loans, industry, and economic growth of the african economies and policy recommendations for global growth. In Globalization and trade integration in developing countries (pp. 203–228). Hershey, PA: IGI Global. doi:10.4018/978-1-5225-4032-8.ch009

Dinçer, H., Yüksel, S., Adalı, Z., & Aydın, R. (2019c). Evaluating the role of research and development and technology investments on economic development of E7 countries. In Organizational transformation and managing innovation in the fourth industrial revolution (pp. 245-263). Hershey, PA: IGI Global.

Dinçer, H., Yüksel, S., & Canbolat, Z. N. (2019d). A strategic approach to reduce energy imports of E7 countries: Use of renewable energy. In Handbook of research on economic and political implications of green trading and energy use (pp. 18-38). Hershey, PA: IGI Global.

Dinçer, H., Yüksel, S., Eti, S., & Tula, A. (2019a). Effects of demographic characteristics on business success: an evidence from Turkish banking sector. Handbook of research on business models in modern competitive scenarios, 304–324. doi:10.4018/978-1-5225-7265-7.ch016

Dinçer, H., Yüksel, S., Pınarbaşı, F., & Çetiner, İ. T. (2019b). Measurement of economic and banking stability in emerging markets by considering income inequality and nonperforming loans. *Maintaining financial stability in times of risk and uncertainty*, 49–68. doi:10.4018/978-1-5225-7208-4.ch003

Dizdarlar, H. I., & Derindere, S. (2008). *Hisse Senedi Endeksini Etkileyen Faktörler: İMKB 100 Endeksini Etkileyen Makroekonomik Göstergeler Üzerine Bir Araştırma. 19*(61), 113–124.

Dogan, E., & Aslan, A. (2017). Exploring the relationship among CO2 emissions, real GDP, energy consumption and tourism in the EU and candidate countries: Evidence from panel models robust to heterogeneity and cross-sectional dependence. *Renewable & Sustainable Energy Reviews, 77*, 239–245. doi:10.1016/j.rser.2017.03.111

Dumitrescu, E. I., & Hurlin, C. (2012). Testing for Granger non-causality in heterogeneous panels. *Economic Modelling, 29*(4), 1450–1460. doi:10.1016/j.econmod.2012.02.014

Dursun, A., & Özcan, M. (2019). Enerji Fiyat Değişimleri İle Borsa Endeksleri Arasındaki İlişki: OECD Ülkeleri Üzerine Bir Uygulama. *Energy price changes and stock exchange relationship: an application on OECD countries*, (82), 177–198. doi:10.25095/mufad.536069

Edirisuriya, P., Gunasekarage, A., & Dempsey, M. (2015). Bank diversification, performance and stock market response: Evidence from listed public banks in South Asian countries. *Journal of Asian Economics, 41*, 69–85. doi:10.1016/j.asieco.2015.09.003

Ege, İ., & Bayrakdaroğlu, A. (2012). İMKB Şirketlerinin Hisse Senedi Getiri Başarılarının Lojistik Regresyon Tekniği İle Analizi. *Uluslararası Yönetim İktisat ve İşletme Dergisi, 5*(10), 139-158. doi:10.11122/ijmeb.2014.5.10.203

Emir, S., Dincer, H., Hacioglu, U., & Yuksel, S. (2016). Random regression forest model using technical analysis variables. *International Journal of Finance & Banking Studies (2147-4486), 5*(3), 85-102.

Engelberg, J., & Parsons, C. A. (2016). Worrying about the stock market: Evidence from hospital admissions. *The Journal of Finance, 71*(3), 1227–1250. doi:10.1111/jofi.12386

Engle, R. F., & Granger, C. W. (1987). Co-integration and error correction: Representation, estimation, and testing. *Econometrica, 55*(2), 251–276. doi:10.2307/1913236

Ersin, İ., & Baş, H. (2019). Güney Avrupa Refah Ülkelerinde Sosyal Harcamalar ve Ekonomik Büyüme Arasındaki İlişkinin İncelenmesi. *SGD-Sosyal Güvenlik Dergisi, 9*(1), 193–213. doi:10.32331gd.582752

Eti, S., Dinçer, H., & Yüksel, S. (2019). G20 Ülkelerinde Bankacılık Sektörünün 5 Yıllık Geleceğinin Arıma Yöntemi İle Tahmin Edilmesi. *Uluslararası Hukuk ve Sosyal Bilim Araştırmaları Dergisi, 1*(1), 26–38.

Eugster, N., & Isakov, D. (2019). Founding family ownership, stock market returns, and agency problems. *Journal of Banking & Finance, 107*, 105600. doi:10.1016/j.jbankfin.2019.07.020

Ewing, B. T., & Malik, F. (2016). Volatility spillovers between oil prices and the stock market under structural breaks. *Global Finance Journal, 29*, 12–23. doi:10.1016/j.gfj.2015.04.008

Feng, S. P., Hung, M. W., & Wang, Y. H. (2016). The importance of stock liquidity on option pricing. *International Review of Economics & Finance, 43*, 457–467. doi:10.1016/j.iref.2016.01.008

Furuoka, F. (2017). Renewable electricity consumption and economic development: New findings from the Baltic countries. *Renewable & Sustainable Energy Reviews, 71*, 450–463. doi:10.1016/j.rser.2016.12.074

Gao, Y. C., Zeng, Y., & Cai, S. M. (2015). Influence network in the Chinese stock market. *Journal of Statistical Mechanics*, *2015*(3), P03017. doi:10.1088/1742-5468/2015/03/P03017

Gün, M. (2019). Cointegration between carbon emission, economic growth, and energy consumption in two neighbor countries: a study on Georgia and Turkey. *Uluslararası İktisadi ve İdari İncelemeler Dergisi*, (22), 39–50. doi:10.18092/ulikidince.397486

Gupta, K., & Banerjee, R. (2019). Does OPEC news sentiment influence stock returns of energy firms in the United States? *Energy Economics*, *77*, 34–45. doi:10.1016/j.eneco.2018.03.017

Güven, S., & Mert, M. (2016). Uluslararası Turizm Talebinin Eşbütünleşme Analizi: Antalya İçin Panel Ardl Yaklaşımı. *Cumhuriyet Üniversitesi İktisadi ve İdari Bilimler Dergisi*, *17*(1), 133–152.

Haider, M. A., Khan, M. A., Saddique, S., & Hashmi, S. H. (2017). *The impact of stock market performance on foreign portfolio investment in China*, *7*(2), 9.

Hassler, U., & Hosseinkouchack, M. (2016). Panel cointegration testing in the presence of linear time trends. *Econometrics*, *4*(4), 45. doi:10.3390/econometrics4040045

Huang, S., An, H., Gao, X., & Sun, X. (2017). Do oil price asymmetric effects on the stock market persist in multiple time horizons? *Applied Energy*, *185*, 1799–1808. doi:10.1016/j.apenergy.2015.11.094

Idris, I., & Bala, H. (2015). Firms' specific characteristics and stock market returns (Evidence from listed food and beverages firms in Nigeria). *Research Journal of Finance and Accounting*, *6*(16), 188-200–200.

Im, K. S., Pesaran, M. H., & Shin, Y. (2003). Testing for unit roots in heterogeneous panels. *Journal of Econometrics*, *115*(1), 53–74. doi:10.1016/S0304-4076(03)00092-7

İnançli, S., Altintaş, N., & İnal, V. (2016). Finansal Gelişme ve Ekonomik Büyüme İlişkisi: D-8 Örneği. *Kastamonu Üniversitesi İktisadi ve İdari Bilimler Fakültesi Dergisi*, *14*(4), 36–49.

Kang, W., Ratti, R. A., & Vespignani, J. (2016). The impact of oil price shocks on the US stock market: A note on the roles of US and non-US oil production. *Economics Letters*, *145*, 176–181. doi:10.1016/j.econlet.2016.06.008

Kao, C. (1999). Spurious regression and residual-based tests for cointegration in panel data. *Journal of Econometrics*, *90*(1), 1–44. doi:10.1016/S0304-4076(98)00023-2

Karan, M. B. (2011). *Yatırım Analizi ve Portföy Yönetimi* (3rd ed.). Ankara, Turkey: Gazi Kitabevi.

Kaya, A., & Öztürk, M. (2015). Muhasebe Kârları ile Hisse Senedi Fiyatları Arasındaki İlişki: BİST Firmaları Üzerine Bir Uygulama. *The relationship between accounting profits and stock prices: an application on BIST firms*, 37–54.

Kaygın, Y. C. (2013). Hisse Senetleri Fiyatını Etkileyen Faktörlerin Panel Veri Analizi İle İncelenmesi: İmalat Sektörü Üzerine Bir Uygulama. Atatürk Üniversitesi SBE, Yayımlanmamış Doktora Tezi, Erzurum.

Kotabe, M., & Kothari, T. (2016). Emerging market multinational companies' evolutionary paths to building a competitive advantage from emerging markets to developed countries. *Journal of World Business*, *51*(5), 729–743. doi:10.1016/j.jwb.2016.07.010

Kurt, G., & Köse, A. (2017). Türkiye'de Bankaların Finansal Oranları ile Hisse Senedi Getirisi Arasındaki Panel Nedensellik İlişkisi. *Çukurova Üniversitesi Sosyal Bilimler Enstitüsü Dergisi, 26*(3), 302–312.

Lee, C. C., & Chang, C. P. (2006). Social security expenditure and GDP in OECD countries: A cointegrated panel analysis. *International Economic Journal, 20*(3), 303–320. doi:10.1080/10168730600879372

Levin, A., Lin, C. F., & Chu, C. S. J. (2002). Unit root tests in panel data: Asymptotic and finite-sample properties. *Journal of Econometrics, 108*(1), 1–24. doi:10.1016/S0304-4076(01)00098-7

Li, M., Liu, C., & Scott, T. (2019). Share pledges and firm value. *Pacific-Basin Finance Journal, 55*, 192–205. doi:10.1016/j.pacfin.2019.04.001

Ma, R., Anderson, H. D., & Marshall, B. R. (2019). Risk perceptions and international stock market liquidity. *Journal of International Financial Markets, Institutions and Money, 62*, 94–116. doi:10.1016/j.intfin.2019.06.001

Maddala, G. S., & Shaowen, W. (1999). Comparative study of unit root tests with panel data and a new simple test. *Oxford Bulletin of Economics and Statistics, 61*(Special Issue), 631–652. doi:10.1111/1468-0084.61.s1.13

Malandri, L., Xing, F. Z., Orsenigo, C., Vercellis, C., & Cambria, E. (2018). Public mood–driven asset allocation: The importance of financial sentiment in portfolio management. *Cognitive Computation, 10*(6), 1167–1176. doi:10.100712559-018-9609-2

Maysami, R. C., Howe, L. C., & Rahmat, M. A. (2005). Relationship between macroeconomic variables and stock market indices: cointegration evidence from stock exchange of Singapore's all-S sector indices. *Jurnal Pengurusan (UKM Journal of Management), 24*. Retrieved from http://ejournal.ukm.my/pengurusan/article/view/1454

Neaime, S. (2016). Financial crises and contagion vulnerability of MENA stock markets. *Emerging Markets Review, 27*, 14–35. doi:10.1016/j.ememar.2016.03.002

Pedroni, P. (1999). Critical values for cointegration tests in heterogeneous panels with multiple regressors. *Oxford Bulletin of Economics and Statistics, 61*(1), 653–670. doi:10.1111/1468-0084.61.s1.14

Pedroni, P. (2001). Fully modified OLS for heterogeneous cointegrated panels. In Nonstationary panels, panel cointegration, and dynamic panels. Emerald Group, 15, 93-130.

Peiró, A. (2016). Stock prices and macroeconomic factors: Some European evidence. *International Review of Economics & Finance, 41*, 287–294. doi:10.1016/j.iref.2015.08.004

Phua, C. Y., Ang, W. H., Chua, H. E., Hong, Y. W., & Peng, S. C. (2017). *Does domestic stock market returns depend on the stock market of its major trading partners? Evidence from Malaysia* (Doctoral dissertation, UTAR).

Raza, N., Shahzad, S. J. H., Tiwari, A. K., & Shahbaz, M. (2016). Asymmetric impact of gold, oil prices and their volatilities on stock prices of emerging markets. *Resources Policy, 49*, 290–301. doi:10.1016/j.resourpol.2016.06.011

Reboredo, J. C., Rivera-Castro, M. A., & Ugolini, A. (2016). Downside and upside risk spillovers between exchange rates and stock prices. *Journal of Banking & Finance*, *62*, 76–96. doi:10.1016/j.jbankfin.2015.10.011

Reis, Ş. G., & Aydin, N. (2014). Causality relationship between stock liquidity and financial performance: an example of Borsa İstanbul. *Gaziantep University Journal of Social Sciences*, *13*(3), 607–617.

Robinson, J., Glean, A., & Moore, W. (2018). How does news impact on the stock prices of green firms in emerging markets? *Research in International Business and Finance*, *45*, 446–453. doi:10.1016/j.ribaf.2017.07.176

Saidi, K., & Mbarek, M. B. (2016). Nuclear energy, renewable energy, CO2 emissions, and economic growth for nine developed countries: Evidence from panel Granger causality tests. *Progress in Nuclear Energy*, *88*, 364–374. doi:10.1016/j.pnucene.2016.01.018

Salmanov, O., Babina, N., Bashirova, S., Samoshkina, M., & Bashirov, R. (2016). The Importance of the country's GDP in the evaluation of companies using multiples on the European stock market. *Regional and Sectoral Economic Studies*, *16*, 1.

Siganos, A., Vagenas-Nanos, E., & Verwijmeren, P. (2017). Divergence of sentiment and stock market trading. *Journal of Banking & Finance*, *78*, 130–141. doi:10.1016/j.jbankfin.2017.02.005

Smales, L. A. (2017). The importance of fear: Investor sentiment and stock market returns. *Applied Economics*, *49*(34), 3395–3421. doi:10.1080/00036846.2016.1259754

Sui, L., & Sun, L. (2016). Spillover effects between exchange rates and stock prices: Evidence from BRICS around the recent global financial crisis. *Research in International Business and Finance*, *36*, 459–471. doi:10.1016/j.ribaf.2015.10.011

Tease, W. (1993). The stock market and investment. *Behaviour*, *1*, 11.

Yalçıner, K., Atan, M., & Boztosun, D. (2005). Finansal Oranlarla Hisse Senedi Getirileri Arasındaki İlişki. *Muhasebe ve Finansman Dergisi*, (27), 176–187.

Yiğit, F., & Muzır, E. (2019). Efficiency of the Major Borsa Istanbul indexes: An empirical investigation about the interaction between corporate governance and equity prices through a market model approach. *Ekonomi İşletme ve Maliye Araştırmaları Dergisi*, *1*(3), 237–245.

Yüksel, S. (2017). The impacts of research and development expenses on export and economic growth. *International Business and Accounting Research Journal*, *1*(1), 1–8. doi:10.15294/ibarj.v1i1.1

Yüksel, S., & Canöz, İ. (2017). Does Islamic banking contribute to economic growth and industrial development in Turkey? *IKONOMIKA*, *2*(1), 93–102. doi:10.24042/febi.v2i1.945

Zheng, Y., & Osmer, E. (2019). Housing price dynamics: The impact of stock market sentiment and the spillover effect. *The Quarterly Review of Economics and Finance*. doi:10.1016/j.qref.2019.02.006

Zoundi, Z. (2017). CO2 emissions, renewable energy and the Environmental Kuznets Curve, a panel cointegration approach. *Renewable & Sustainable Energy Reviews*, *72*, 1067–1075. doi:10.1016/j.rser.2016.10.018

KEY TERMS AND DEFINITIONS

ADF: Augmented Dickey Fuller
ARDL: Autoregressive Distributed Lag Model
BRICS: Brazil, Russia, India, China and South Africa
IPS: Im Peseran Shin
LLC: Levin Lin Chu
OECD: The Organisation for Economic Co-operation and Development
PP: Philips Perron
USA: United States of America
VAR: Vector Autoregression

Chapter 14
Evaluation of Customer Expectations-Based New Product and Service Development Process:
An Analysis for the Turkish Banking Sector

Serhat Yüksel
Istanbul Medipol University, Turkey

Gülcan Ergül
Istanbul Medipol University, Turkey

ABSTRACT

This chapter analyzed customer expectations-based new product and service development process in banking sector for the Turkish banking sector. In-depth interview technique was used. Four dimensions (finance, technology, customer and personnel, and physical conditions) were determined for measuring the efficiency of this process, and 12 criteria were determined for these dimensions. Questions were prepared by considering the literature and these dimensions and criteria. The 26 questions were asked to 12 different personnel working in Turkish banks. Those employees in the private and foreign banks did not indicate any negativity regarding the new product and service development process, but did report deficiencies in terms of personnel and physical conditions in relation to the new product and service development process.

INTRODUCTION

Globalization has affected countries socially, culturally and economically. The most important economic impact of globalization is the disappearance of financial borders between countries. This issue has provided many economic benefits to countries. In this way, companies have the opportunity to reach new

DOI: 10.4018/978-1-7998-2559-3.ch014

markets. This situation has a positive effect on the profitability of the countries (Parente et al., 2018). Despite these positive aspects mentioned above, globalization has led to an increase in competition in the markets. This is considered to be a positive aspect as it will lead to a decrease in the prices of the products. On the other hand, this increasing competition may affect some firms negatively. There are risks of bankruptcy, especially since they cannot compete with local companies and other large international firms (Coulibaly et al., 2018).

The banking sector is also highly affected by the competition caused by globalization. The financial limits that globalization abolished benefited the banking sector the most. As a result, large banks have had the chance to operate easily in other countries (Kleymenova et al., 2016). This situation caused the financial difficulties of local banks. In order to survive in this competitive environment, it has become necessary for banks to take certain actions. Developing new products and services is one of the strategies that banks can implement in a competitive environment. Thanks to the new products and services they will develop, banks will gain a competitive advantage over their competitors. In this way, the bank can be preferred by customers. This situation will have a positive effect on the profitability of banks (Ghosh, 2016). Another important point in this process is to measure the competence of developing new products and services. In this way, it will be possible to identify a possible problem in advance and take the necessary measures.

The aim of this study is to analyze the new product and service development process focused on customer expectations in the banking sector. Within this framework, the Turkish banking sector was included in the scope of the review. In the analysis process of the study, in-depth interview technique was used. In this framework, four different dimensions were determined, namely, finance, technology, customer and personnel and physical conditions for the measurement of new product and service development effectiveness. On the other hand, 12 different criteria have been determined for these dimensions. 26 different questions were prepared by considering these dimensions and criteria. Related questions were asked to 12 different personnel working in Turkish banks.

The study consists of 3 different sections. In the first part, basic issues related to the banking sector are discussed. In the second part of the study, the concepts of innovation management in banking and customer relationship management and development in banking are emphasized. In the last part of the study, an in - depth interview with the Turkish banking sector is given.

GENERAL INFORMATION ABOUT BANKING

The Definition of Banking

There are a large number of individuals or companies in a country with certain background. Some of them do not prefer to start their own business. Instead, lending their money and thus earning interest income may be the reason for preference. Therefore, it is important that there is an institution that can provide this service for the persons concerned. There are also people in need of money in the country in question. With the money they want to get, the people in question will be able to get married, remodeled and so on. requirements. Therefore, it is very important that these people obtain this money on time (Noth and Busch, 2016; Fuertes et al., 2016). As can be understood from this, there is a need for an institution that can meet this need quickly and effectively.

Evaluation of Customer Expectations-Based New Product and Service Development Process

On the other hand, firms need money for basically two different reasons. First, firms need a certain amount of money to invest. With this resource they will be able to provide investment resources of the company such as machinery and equipment. On the other hand, it is possible to talk about the cash requirement for operational processes such as salary payment to personnel, payment of invoices and rents. Banks provide funds supply-demand balance by bringing together surpluses and those in need of funds. In this respect, it is evident that banks benefit both those who provide funds and those who request funds (Filip, 2015; Amavilah et al., 2017). Persons with money will receive interest income as they evaluate their savings in banks. In other words, these accumulations will stop being idle.

On the other hand, banks also benefit those who need money. For example, companies that need money for investment purposes will be able to meet their needs in a shorter time and easily thanks to banks. Thanks to these funds, companies can increase their investments and this will contribute to the growth of the national economy. In summary, banks play an important role in maintaining a sound economy. It is common to assume that the main origin of the word banco, which is expressed in small variations in all world languages, comes from Italy. Allegedly, a group of people who have money in Italy want to make their savings available to people in need of money. The most important issue in this process is that these accumulators have access to people who need money (Rus et al., 2016; Gozzi et al., 2015). To this end, these people with experience have been sitting on a bench, allowing people who need money to find themselves. In summary, it is assumed that the word bank derives from the word banco in Italian.

In the most general definition, the bank collects deposits from individuals and companies with accumulated knowledge, transfers these deposits to the parties in need of credit and also acts as an intermediary for money transfers such as money transfers, transfers and electronic funds transfers (EFT). financial institutions with services such as trading. As can be understood from this definition, it is very difficult to define the bank. As can be seen, the definition of a bank that includes all its functions becomes quite complicated. There is no clear definition of a bank in Turkish law. Developing bank activities make it difficult to define a clear bank.

It is recognized that there are many important issues in the historical development of banking. It is clear that the birth of trade is an important factor in the formation of the banking sector. On the other hand, the first banking transactions BC. It is assumed that 3500 years were based on Sumerian and Babylonian civilizations. In addition, BC. In the 2000s, the shrines were planted by the monks to produce seeds, etc., to be paid to the peasants engaged in farming. monetary loans were given as raw material. In addition, the famous laws of Hammurabi (1688-2000 BC) regulated the laws on lending transactions. This situation is thought to play an important role in the development of the regulatory system in the banking sector.

The Banking History of Turkey

The Ottoman Empire history of the banking sector in Turkey seem to go up to the date. In the 18th and 19th centuries, Western European states completed the industrial revolution. However, the failure of the Ottoman Empire to undergo an industrial revolution led to unfavorable developments in the national economy. These negative developments prevented the development of banking activities. In 1844, with the intention of overcoming the economic crisis in Istanbul and port cities, Galata bankers established the first Ottoman Bank, the Bank of Felicity. On the other hand, the purpose of the establishment of the Istanbul bank is to preserve the value of paper money. Founded in 1847, this bank went bankrupt in 1852 (Tatoğlu et al., 2017).

Ottomon Bank was founded in 1856. The bank belongs to UK capital. Later, the French became a partner in the bank. This bank is considered as the first central bank. Functions of the bank; making public grants through branches, dealing with domestic and foreign debts, advising and advising the government on financial issues. In the 19th century, there were not enough capital and national banks in the country. Therefore, the banks with foreign capital played an important role for the national economy at the relevant date. In this period, the biggest loss of the absence of public banks has touched the farmers. Farmers in need of money due to the lack of relevant banks have been exposed to high rates of interest to meet their needs. In order to find a solution to this situation, Mithat Pasha established his country's chests on 20.11.1863. Thus, the foundations of Ziraat Bank, the first example of national banking, were laid (Consiglio et al., 2016; Clay, 2016).

In the 20th century, the government began to feel uncomfortable with the presence of foreign capital banks. Therefore, new economic policies were implemented to strengthen the economy and capital. In this context, it was decided to establish new national banks since the Ottoman Bank, which has foreign capital, contradicts the state interests. In this period, due to nationalism being in the forefront, the need for the central bank was also emphasized because of the discomfort experienced by the banks with foreign capital (Fraser, 2016).

Due to the great depression in 1929, a more protective policy was experienced in the economy. In this period, the number of special purpose banks increased. In addition to the aforementioned issues, the economic problems experienced by the Second World War also affected the banking sector negatively. As a result, economic contraction has been experienced in the country. After the Second World War, the state followed policies that supported the private sector and as a result, the number of private banks increased (Altinirmak et al., 2017).

Banks Association of Turkey was founded in 1958. The aim of the said union is to take measures for the establishment of a competitive environment in the sector, and to carry out studies for its implementation. The Banking Law No. 3182 entered into force in 1985. As a result of this period, it is seen that there were radical changes in the banks. International surveillance and audit systems and international banking standards have started to be used. In addition to the aforementioned issues, a uniform account application was introduced. In addition, individuals have the right to have foreign currency and open foreign currency accounts. In addition, the EFT system was introduced in 1992. In addition, national banks opened branches abroad during this period (Aysan et al., 2018; Şimşek et al., 2017).

In the coming period, together with financial liberalization, foreign banks have also opened branches in Turkey. Due to the increase in the number of foreign banks in the country, the competition environment increased further. As a result, there has been an increase in product diversity in the banking system. The economic crisis in 1994 also affected the banking sector. Between 1999 and 2002, some legal levels were made in the banking sector. Some banks that have failed to sustain their operations were confiscated (Kilic, 2016; Kalkavan and Ersin, 2019).

Following the financial crisis in 2001, some measures were taken in order to increase the efficiency of the banking sector. In this context, the Banking Regulation and Supervision Agency (BRSA) was established to supervise the banking sector more effectively in the relevant period. In order to solve the structural problems in the Turkish banking sector before the 2000 crisis, economic programs were implemented with the support of the International Monetary Fund (IMF). Thus, financial markets began to improve. In today's banking system, digitalization process is intense. Mobile banking, ATM, internet banking, telephone banking transactions support branch banking considerably and these processes significantly reduce the costs of banks. As a result, the importance of these alternative distribution channels,

Evaluation of Customer Expectations-Based New Product and Service Development Process

especially mentioned in the Turkish banking sector in recent years, is becoming increasingly important (Eti et al., 2019; Eti, 2019).

Activity Areas of the Banks

The most important fields of activity of banks are to provide loans. In the most general definition of credit, banks are called to lend money collected from surplus funds to people or institutions in need. A certain maturity is set when banks give credit to customers. In certain loan types, the customer is paid to the bank by the customer using the loan at certain intervals up to this maturity date. In addition, in some credit types, banks receive their payments at maturity. In summary, banks aim to collect these loan amounts that they lend to their customers with interest within a certain period (Sun et al., 2017).

The loans granted by banks may vary depending on the type of payment or the type of customer. Loans paid in certain periods are called installment loans. In such loans, customers pay certain amounts to the bank in the relevant periods. These payments include both the principal amount and the interest amount. In addition to the loan type, some loan types do not have periodic payments. The customer pays the loan amount and interest total to the bank on the due date. These loans are called spot loans (Mittal et al., 2017).

In addition to the aforementioned issues, credits are also named under different names according to the type of customer granted. For example, loans used by individuals are called retail loans, while loans granted by firms are called commercial loans. On the other hand, consumer loans can be handled in three different classes as consumer loans, auto loans and housing loans. In addition to the mentioned types, the credits used by the companies can be divided into different categories such as micro, SME, commercial and corporate according to the types of firms (Akhisar et al., 2015).

Deposit collection is also one of the important functions of the bank. Banks collect these funds from people who have accumulated in the country. These savings are transferred to the needy by the banks. It is possible to mention two different advantages of this situation. First, thanks to these deposits collected by banks, fund holders can earn interest income. Secondly, the deposits collected by the banks are transferred to companies wishing to invest as funds. In this way, the amount of investment in the country will increase and this situation will contribute to the economic development of the country (Bouzgarrou et al., 2018).

Deposits are defined in two different ways: term and demand deposits. Demand deposits represent the amount of money held by individuals or companies in the bank without being bound for any period of time. Such money may be withdrawn by the owners at any time. Therefore, the Bank does not make any interest payments for the said deposits. On the other hand, time deposits are deposits made by customers and promised not to withdraw until a certain date. In other words, banks do not receive this money until the date specified in the contract and earn interest on the date of the contract. If these funds are withdrawn before this date, customers will not be able to earn the interest they earn (Niepmann and Schmidt-Eisenlohr, 2017).

In order to provide a better service to their customers, banks provide financial consultancy services for the management of their wealth. They buy and sell the securities they want to their account and give advice about different investment tools. Customers deliver their savings to the bank for a certain period with an agreement. Banks also carry out activities such as portfolio management and market analysis with investment experts. Companies need cash to meet their operational needs or make new investments. These companies can meet these needs in different ways. One-way companies can meet these needs is to issue securities. However, this process is very complex, as certain procedures need to be followed during the issuance of securities. Therefore, banks provide services to related companies by mediating this process (Samina and Hossain, 2019).

INNOVATION MANAGEMENT IN BANKING AND DEVELOPMENT OF CUSTOMER RELATIONS

General Information about New Product and Service Development Concept

Following globalization, competition has increased significantly in all sectors. As a result, companies have taken some action to be one step ahead of their competitors. Otherwise, it will become very difficult for firms to survive in this competitive environment. Even large-scale companies operating in very important sectors cannot withstand this high competition. For example, Nokia was seen as one of the most important companies in the industry 20 years ago. However, the said company cannot compete with other companies in the sector (Vezzoli et al., 2015).

As it can be understood from this issue, the companies should consider the competition issue very much. Developing new products and services is also a preferred method for companies to gain competitive advantage. Companies aim to attract customers with new products and services. In this way, it is the preferred company and will be able to gain a significant advantage over its competitors. This situation will contribute to the continuity of the company in the sector (Chang and Taylor, 2016).

Companies need to pay attention to some issues while developing new products and services. First, customers' expectations regarding new products and services should be determined. In this context, a detailed survey of customers in the market will serve this purpose. After the expectations of the customers are determined, it is necessary to start work on new products and services in the company. In this context, a new product and service development team should be established first. It is useful for the company to be selective for the employees to be selected for this team. Following these issues, financial analysis of the new product to be developed is also required. The finance department will play an important role in this process. Finally, customer feedback should be provided after the launch of new products and services (Visnjic et al., 2016).

New product and service development, as mentioned earlier, contributes to companies gaining competitive advantage. In this way, companies can be one step ahead of their competitors. This situation helps the customer to be preferred by the relevant company. This enables the company to maintain its long-term presence in the competitive market. Companies wishing to develop new products and services must make significant investments in order to be different from their competitors. For example, companies can develop new products and services by making technological investments. In this way, it will be possible to achieve technological development in the sector. On the other hand, new products that contribute technologically will increase the quality of life of customers (Cui and Wu, 2016).

Decreases in firm profitability with the onset of globalization, abolition of national borders, increases in production capacity, uncertain variability in customer demands and changes in customers; it requires businesses to be good at the international platform, not nationally. The prerequisite of being good for businesses is to innovate in every field (product, service, process, method, structure and management) and to benefit from the creative ideas of employees in the face of constantly developing technology (Reim et al., 2015).

Evaluation of Customer Expectations-Based New Product and Service Development Process

In order for innovation to occur, the need for innovation must be born. The need for innovation is created by forcing the company to innovate in line with customer demands. Customers may not like the goods and services produced, see them as incomplete, or may not be able to fully respond to customers' wishes and needs. In such cases, the goods and services produced by the enterprise do not match the expectations of the customers, their demands are inadequate compared to the demands of the innovation leads to new inventions (Haeberle et al., 2016).

In order to make a comprehensive definition of the new product concept, it is necessary to know the point of view of the subject. The reason for this is that the new product concept has a different meaning for consumers and businesses. From the consumer's point of view, the new product is the formation of a need that does not meet or does not exist before. In terms of enterprises, the concept of new product is the first product introduced to the market by any enterprise, but it refers to the first technological development or invention in the market (Roberts and Darler, 2017).

The word innovation is derived from the Latin word "innovatus". As the name suggests, the word in question refers to the use of a new method in any field. This issue, which is also very important in other fields, is particularly prominent in the field of economy and finance. The main reason for this is that companies want to be different from others in the competitive environment. Otherwise, firms will not be able to maintain their existence in a healthy environment in an intense competitive environment. Companies aiming to be one step ahead of their competitors will be able to gain competitive advantage through new products and services. In this way, it will have an important advantage by attracting the attention of both investors and consumers (Vezzoli et al., 2015).

An important issue in this process is how innovation will be realized. The main reason for this is to determine which innovation will be made and when. The innovation strategy implemented at the wrong time can cause significant losses for the company. In addition to the aforementioned issue, the faulty innovation strategy implemented without fully analyzing customer and market expectations may cause serious problems (Chang and Taylor, 2016). As can be understood from these issues, effective management of innovation process is important. Therefore, companies establish a special team for innovation management.

Innovation is the creation of changes in the production or marketing of a product or service that will better meet market needs and create opportunities for competitors. In other words, innovation is the creation of a new and original idea and its transformation into a product demanded in the market (Visnjic et al., 2016; Cui and Wu, 2016). In addition to the aforementioned issues, innovation can be defined as providing existing products and services or by making additions to existing products and making them in demand.

As can be seen from the above mentioned issues, innovation management helps companies to implement the new product and service development process more actively and effectively. In this way, companies can develop new products to satisfy their customers. As a result of this, companies have the advantage of gaining competitive advantage and increasing their sales. With the new technology, the whole production of the enterprises has increased and the sources of their promotion, promotion, promotion and advertising have increased rapidly. In other words, thanks to technological changes, the importance given to research and development has increased (Rei meet al., 2015). Therefore, technological innovations have a direct impact on the preparation and distribution of products and services.

One of the biggest factors in the need for innovation management is the change in customer expectations and demands with the increase in developing technology and digitalization. The concept that innovation is related to can also be called creativity, that is, to produce new things, to invent, to create new ideas by creating new ideas. Innovation activities may vary from business to business. Some companies develop and launch a new product and carry out innovation projects while others make continuous improvements in existing products, processes and activities. And the work of both companies is considered to be innovative.

The aim of product development is to meet the demand of the consumer and to increase the market share of the company and to make it continuous. Because every product, service will not address the customer or customer base. Therefore, defining the target market for a product is a critical component that must be done at the beginning of the product development process. Quantitative market research should be carried out at every stage of the process, including when the product or service is designed, when the product is designed and after the product is placed on the market. Product development requires a new process of formation. Against this, the desire to launch a new product is based on a systematic approach.

Innovation Management Process in Banking Sector

While the technology forced the sectors to update, the banking sector entered the infrastructure development process and became involved in the development process. Banks that need to review their financial systems after the regional and global crises have started to give more importance to investing in information technology. Technological changes and developments have caused many changes in the banking sector. Previously commercial banks were similar, but nowadays the strategic options of banks are different (Cornaggia et al., 2015). The different creativity and entrepreneurship of commercial banks is one of the factors that increase the number of customers.

The banking sector is able to solve the problem of asymmetric information in financial markets thanks to its specialized personnel and advanced technology systems. Therefore, banks can ensure efficiency in the allocation of resources and capital accumulation by preventing market failures (Zaleska and Kondraciuk, 2019). In other words, banks contribute positively to economic growth by financing productive investment projects as a result of increasing specialization through technological innovations.

If we look at the innovation management process in the banking sector, the biggest reason that pushes the bank to innovation in the banking sector is that the customer demands are inadequate in the face of the demands and competing banks take advantage of the developing technology and increase their market share and expand their customer reservoir to ensure their continuity (Farouk et al., 2016). Like the enterprises, the banking sector can primarily understand the inadequacy of its existing services in line with customer demands.

In order to determine this, they provide the necessary support to customer representatives, R & D and try to eliminate the necessary deficiency. In the face of the developing technology, they try to launch new developments on the service offered by their rival banks to their customers. In order for the bank to need innovation, the reasons that push the bank to innovation must arise and there should be departments to determine these reasons (Parameswar et al., 2017).

The banking sector is able to solve the problem of asymmetric information in financial markets thanks to its specialized personnel and advanced technology systems (Agolla et al., 2018). Therefore, banks can ensure efficiency in the distribution of resources and capital accumulation by preventing market failures. Banks can contribute to economic growth by financing productive investment projects as a result of increasing specialization through technological innovations (Muda and Putra, 2018).

When we look at changes in consumer awareness or changes in consumer expectation, sharing information more easily on the internet makes the consumer more conscious. Therefore, with the social marketing approach, consumers can request their requests more easily. The consumer can cause differences in the product and service offerings of the enterprises in the variety of demand that it presents depending on their tastes and needs (Laukkanen, 2015; Kaushik and Rahman, 2015).

With the developing technology, the whole production of the enterprises increased and the sources of their promotion, promotion and advertising increased rapidly. In other words, thanks to technological changes, the importance given to research and development has increased. Therefore, technological innovations have a direct impact on the preparation and distribution of products and services. Competition in today's world is an important effect. Because competition is the most important driving force that enables progress to develop in enterprises (Elmes et al., 2016; Nesvetailova, 2015).

The Concept of Customer Relationship Management

If an enterprise's customers are satisfied, it is easier for that business to compete with its competitors. In other words, in recent years, focusing on customers can be an important and in fact difficult process. The success of the enterprises in this process may be related to the necessity of a stable and specific effort. Because, in order to create this situation, the employees of the enterprise should take a willing stance on this issue (Nyadzayo and Khajehzadeh, 2016; Dinçer et al., 2019a,b,c,d,e,f).

Today, competition in almost every sector has increased significantly. The main reason behind this issue is that globalization has been effective especially in recent years. With increasing globalization, many companies have had the chance to operate internationally because globalization has led to the disappearance of financial boundaries between countries. As a result, competition has had a significant impact in all sectors (Soltani and Navimipour, 2016).

This increasing competition poses a threat especially for local firms. The main reason for this is that with globalization, large-scale international companies have started to operate in different countries. In other words, the small-scale local firms in the country had to compete with the international companies, which were much larger than them. This has led to the necessity of taking action in order to solve the related problem (Rahimi and Kozak, 2017).

It is unlikely that small-scale firms that do not take action in this competitive environment will have continuity in the sector. In other words, these companies have to take some action that can increase their competitiveness. Customer relationship management is an action that can be taken in this context. Companies will be able to satisfy their customers if they manage their relationships effectively. This will give companies a significant competitive advantage compared to their competitors (Lillard and Al-Suqri, 2019).

In summary, customer relationship management defines the actions taken by companies in order to improve their relations with their customers. In this context, it is important that companies first determine the expectations of their customers. The main reason for this is that it is not possible to have healthier customer relations without determining the expectations of the customers. After this, considering these customer expectations, companies should decide on the necessary actions (Navimipour and Soltani, 2016).

Companies that attach importance to effective customer relations can become the mirror of the business culture. Effective customer relations are the responsibility of everyone in a business and everyone who is interested in customer needs to be given the authority to solve problems. In particular, top managers need to be in a leading position in developing relationships with customers and have quality standards in this regard (Hassan et al., 2015).

It is possible to talk about the many purposes of customer relationship management for companies. First, companies can achieve customer satisfaction through effective customer relationship management. Customers who meet their expectations and demands will undoubtedly be satisfied with the services of the company. The point that should be underlined here is the necessity of determining the expectations of the customers in this process (Ascarza et al., 2017; Dinçer et al., 2019 g, h).

Customer relationship management also aims to improve the financial performance of the company. The main reason behind this process is that the happier customers will continue to prefer the products of the company. In other words, the company succeeds in satisfying its customers through effective customer management, thus increasing its sales. This will have a positive impact on the company's financial performance and profitability (Diffley et al., 2018).

To be successful in the decision-making process of the customer, an effective communication is required. It is necessary to analyze customer behaviors in a good way and show a behavior accordingly. Evaluation should be done by separating the customers into groups. This grouping may not always give accurate results. Because a customer looking at a product or service today may not decide for that product or service tomorrow (Dewnarain et al., 2019). Banks are undoubtedly the sector most affected by globalization. As globalization has lifted the financial boundaries between countries, there has been a significant increase in the volume of international trade between countries. A significant majority of companies have become engaged in foreign trade (Santouridis and Veraki, 2017). This situation provided opportunities for countries as well as increased risks in the foreign trade process.

The most important way to minimize the risks in the foreign trade process is to maintain the liaison between firms by institutionalized banks. Banks can serve as intermediaries in the foreign trade process between the mentioned companies. This will minimize the risks. In other words, high-volume foreign trade transactions can be carried out more effectively and healthily with the guarantee service provided by the banks (Hargreaves et al., 2018). Banks also contribute to the foreign trade process by providing funds for investment. Companies have had the opportunity to invest in other countries with the effect of globalization. However, financial resources are needed to make these investments. As a result, banks have a very important role in international trade (Rahimi, 2017).

When the above mentioned issues are taken into consideration, it is understood that the globalization process increases the competition especially in the banking sector. Therefore, it is important for banks to take certain actions in order to survive in this increasingly competitive environment. Otherwise, there is a risk that especially small-scale local banks will not be able to maintain their assets. One of the most important actions to be taken for banks is the establishment of an effective customer relationship management. Banks that make their relations with customers healthier become more selectable than their competitors. The main reason for this is that satisfied customers want to continue working with banks. This will positively affect the profitability of banks (Wang et al., 2016).

Customers are the source of life for all businesses as well as banks. Therefore, it has become a necessity for the vendors in the banking sector to get to know their customers closely. Customer is the person who acquires, uses and benefits from a good or service. Therefore, customer satisfaction is important for banks. The main reason for this is the fact that satisfied customers continue to work with banks, which in turn increases the revenues of banks (Maecker et al., 2016). To meet the needs of the customer, it selects among the recommendations that are compatible with the needs and will benefit itself. For the bank, any person using a banking product and service is considered a customer. Banks examine their customers in two ways: individual and corporate. While the customers who maintain their relations with the Bank with various product usage are active customers, they refer to customers who have used the product of the bank in the past, are now inactive and defined as customers trying to be earned but have not used any products (Dinçer et al., 2019 i, j, k).

Each customer is different. Therefore, it would not be wrong to say that the number of customers' needs as much customers. Considering the resources and efficiency of banks, banks should not be able to deal with each customer one-to-one, so they need to group the similar customers and plan to provide the best service. In other words, it is important to know the customers well and offer the products according to the customers' expectations (Talón-Ballestero et al., 2018). In this context, it is possible to talk about some steps in the customer relationship management process of banks. First, banks need to know their customers. In this context, it is important to make a very detailed analysis by banks. In order to achieve this aim, a survey can be conducted by banks. In this study, the profiles of the relevant customers will be determined by means of detailed questions to be asked to the customers (Abedin, 2016; Dinçer et al., 2019 l, m).

The second step in customer relationship management of banks is to develop products suitable for customers whose profile is defined. What is important in this process is that the profiles of customers differ. In other words, it is not possible for all customers of the bank to show similar characteristics. Therefore, banks are required to offer different products for customers with different profiles when developing products. The third step in customer relationship management of banks is to receive customer feedback on products. In this way, it can be determined which customers are satisfied with the products they use and which ones are not. What is important at this stage is to ensure that customers' notifications are provided in an effective and healthy manner (Srinivasan and Saravanan, 2015).

The last step in the management of customer relations of banks is to take the necessary actions to solve the problems learned through feedback from customers. In this process, it is important that banks establish an effective problem tracking system. At this stage, problems will be identified through the monitoring channels of the bank and it will be possible to understand the stage of solving these problems (Anshari, 2015).

Banks determine the needs and desires of consumers and work to develop goods and services that will satisfy their customers. It is not enough for banks to identify consumer demands only, but they should also make investigations in line with their requests. An effort to understand customer needs will provide an advantage to banks in a competitive environment. A bank addressing customer needs will make the customer more dependent on itself by taking a stronger stance in the competitive environment (Guha et al., 2018).

Analysis of customer needs to ensure customer satisfaction is very important for both banks and institutions. It is essential that every bank is able to lead the way to ensure this satisfaction. Because banks need to make innovations in their products or services available to customers. Banks should be able to meet customers' demands in full, but should be able to provide feedback in a short time (Chopra et al., 2019). Thus, they can easily use the systems we call procurement. It is of great importance for customers to communicate easily with the bank whenever they need it, to monitor customer problems closely and continuously, and to ensure continuous customer satisfaction (Wang and Kim, 2017).

AN ANALYSIS ON TURKISH BANKING INDUSTRY

Theoretical Information about In-Depth Interview Method

In-depth interview technique is a method of getting information by discussing the issue with certain people. The important point here is that the selected persons are experts on the subject to be informed (Rosenthal, 2016). On the other hand, detailed questions are prepared during the interview to obtain comprehensive information on the subject. In this context, another important issue is that the questions to be asked consist of literature-based questions that express the essence of the subject (Eisner et al., 2018; Ting et al., 2016). When conducting an in-depth interview, the person using the recorder to record audio will help to carry out the process more effectively. In this way, it will be possible to observe during the interview and ask a different question.

Otherwise, if the interviewer tries to write one-to-one answers, there may be a problem of loss of information. On the other hand, if the voice recorder is used, the excitement of the other person may also impair the effectiveness of the interview (Cridland et al., 2016; Chang and Hung, 2018; Diviani et al., 2016). Another important aspect of the in-depth interview is that the interviewee feels safe. In this context, it is important that the interviewee is assured that personal information will never be used anywhere. Otherwise, there is a risk that the person will respond under business concern. This will result in the lack of real answers to the questions (Schnittker et al., 2018; Cook et al., 2018; Haberland et al., 2016).

Determination of Dimensions and Criteria for New Product and Service Development Process Performance

Developing new products and services is a vital issue for banking. Therefore, the success of banks in this process needs to be measured. The measurement will provide information on how banks' new product and service development performance is and will provide an opportunity to identify a potential problem in advance. Within this framework, an important issue is the determination of new product and service development criteria. A detailed literature analysis was performed in order to determine these criteria effectively. Details of the dimensions and criteria determined based on the results obtained are given in Table 1.

As can be seen in Table 1, four different dimensions have been determined for the measurement of banks' new product and service development performance. Under the financial dimension, three different criteria were selected. Banks' budgeting facilities, profit-oriented new product and service development projects, and efficiency-focused new product and service development projects constitute three different criteria. On the other hand, in terms of technology, the technological infrastructure of the bank, the competence of the information technology department of the bank and the follow-up of the current developments regarding the technological infrastructure are the criteria.

In addition to the aforementioned issues, another dimension that affects banks' new product and service development performance is related to customers. The importance given to customer expectations, the importance given to customer loyalty and the consideration of customer feedback are three different criteria representing the customer dimension. Finally, staff and physical conditions are another dimension that affects banks' performance in developing new products and services. The role of personnel in new product and service development projects, the adequacy of the physical conditions of the bank and the technological security of the bank represent three different criteria under the customer dimension.

Evaluation of Customer Expectations-Based New Product and Service Development Process

Table 1. Dimensions and criteria for new product/service development process

Dimension	Criteria	Source
Financial	Budgeting Opportunities of the Bank	Rubin (2019); Tosun and Bağdadioğlu (2016); Miller et al. (2018); Ahrens and Ferry (2015)
Financial	Profit Oriented New Product and Service Development Projects	Rubleske and Kaarst-Brown (2019); Chang and Taylor (2016); Jaakkola et al. (2017); Dinçer and Yüksel (2018a,b); Yüksel et al. (2017)
Financial	Productivity-Oriented New Product and Service Development Projects	Burton et al. (2017); Ylimäki and Vesalainen (2015); Yüksel et al. (2015)
Technology	Technological Infrastructure	Carbonell and Rodriguez Escudero (2015); Witell et al. (2015)
Technology	The competence of the Bank's Information Technology Department	Jaakkola et al. (2017); Liu et al. (2019); Dinçer et al. (2017)
Technology	Tracking of Developments for Technological Infrastructure	Snyder et al. (2016); Chang and Taylor (2016)
Customer	Importance of Customer Expectations	Yang et al. (2016); Hoffman et al. (2016); Yüksel et al. (2018)
Customer	Importance of Customer Loyalty	Su and Chen (2016); Witell et al. (2017)
Customer	Considering Customer Feedback	Mahmoud et al. (2018); Atsalakis et al. (2018); Yüksel et al. (2019)
Personnel and Physical Conditions	Role of Personnel in New Product and Service Development Projects	Zaitseva et al. (2015); Ali et al. (2015)
Personnel and Physical Conditions	Adequacy of the Bank's Physical Conditions	Ojasalo et al. (2015); Yu and Sangiorgi (2018)
Personnel and Physical Conditions	Technological Security of the Bank	Crumbly and Carter (2015); Masood and Java (2015); Dinçer and Yüksel (2019a,b)

In this study, 7 different bank personnel were interviewed using in-depth interview method. The main purpose of the interview with the said personnel is to measure the banks' ability to develop new products and services. Care has been taken to select these personnel from different bank groups. In this way, it is possible to make comparative analysis between different bank types for the related topic. 26 different questions were prepared considering the literature-based dimensions and criteria in Table 1. The details of these questions are given in Table 2.

Analysis Results

26 questions prepared within the scope of the analysis process employed in state-owned banks operating in Turkey Study 2 were directed at staff. One of these personnel is the head office and branch employees with 21 years and 5 years of experience. The summary of the responses of these personnel is shown in Table 3.

As it can be seen from Table 4, it was determined that public bank personnel reported deficiencies in every dimension regarding the new product and service development process. Personnel Regarding the process of developing new products and services;

- They do not find the budgeting facilities sufficient for the new product development process,
- There is no expectation of future output for budgeting,

Table 2. Questions to bank personnel

Sections	Questions
Section 1: Demographic Considerations	Question 1: Can you give information about your education level and yourself?
	Question 2: Can you give us information about your current job and past work experience?
Section 2: Financial Issues	Question 3: How do you evaluate your bank's budgeting opportunities regarding the new product development process?
	Question 4: Is there a separate department in your bank regarding this issue? Is there such a plan for the future?
	Question 5: Is there any future output for budgeting?
	Question 6: Does your bank have any profit-oriented product and service development projects?
	Question 7: What is the role of new products and services in profitable business strategies?
	Question 8: What is the level of efficiency in the process of new product and service development?
Section 3: Technology Considerations	Question 9: How do you evaluate the technological infrastructure of your bank in the process of developing new products and services?
	Question 10: Do you think that your bank's alternative distribution channels are technologically suitable for new product and service development?
	Question 11: How do you assess the competence of your IT department?
	Question 12: What is your bank's competitive technological investment plans?
	Question 13: Do you think the developments regarding the technological infrastructure in the sector are followed by your bank?
	Question 14: What is the level of sectoral cooperation and outsourcing of your bank in technology adaptation?
Section 4: Customer Considerations	Question 15: Do you think your bank attaches importance to customer expectations in the process of developing new products and services?
	Question 16: Is there a technological infrastructure for customer expectations?
	Question 17: Are the requirements of customers effectively learned when developing new products and services?
	Question 18: Do you think your bank attaches importance to customer loyalty during the development of new products and services?
	Question 19: What is your bank's medium and long-term customer planning in developing new products and services?
	Question 20: Evaluate your bank's feedback mechanism after product and service usage.
Section 5: Personnel and Physical Conditions	Question 21: Evaluate the personnel compliance of your bank in the process of developing new products and services.
	Question 22: Do your bank's staff play an active role in the development of new products and services?
	Question 23: Do you think that the product development team personnel employed by your bank are provided with adequate training?
	Question 24: Do you find the physical conditions of your bank sufficient in the process of developing new products and services?
	Question 25: Are your bank's alternative distribution channels sufficient to develop new products and services?
	Question 26: Evaluate the technological security of your bank in the process of developing new products and services.

Table 3. Summary of responses of public bank employees

Sections	Questions	Personnel 1	Personnel 2
Financial Issues	Question 3	Positive	Negative
	Question 4	Positive	Positive
	Question 5	Positive	Negative
	Question 6	Positive	Positive
	Question 7	Negative	Positive
	Question 8	Positive	Positive
Technology Considerations	Question 9	Positive	Negative
	Question 10	Negative	Negative
	Question 11	Positive	Positive
	Question 12	No Idea	Negative
	Question 13	Positive	Negative
	Question 14	No Idea	No Idea
Customer Considerations	Question 15	Positive	Positive
	Question 16	Negative	Positive
	Question 17	Positive	Positive
	Question 18	Positive	Positive
	Question 19	Negative	Positive
	Question 20	Negative	Positive
Personnel and Physical Conditions	Question 21	Positive	Positive
	Question 22	Negative	Positive
	Question 23	No Idea	No Idea
	Question 24	Positive	Positive
	Question 25	Negative	Negative
	Question 26	Positive	Positive

- Alternative distribution channels are not technologically appropriate for new product and service development processes,
- The Bank does not have competitive technological investment plans,
- The technological infrastructure in the sector is not followed up effectively by the bank,
- Technological infrastructure for customer expectations is not sufficient,
- The Bank does not have medium and long term customer planning in developing new products and services,
- The feedback mechanism after the use of the Bank's products and services does not function effectively,
- The Bank's personnel do not play an active role in the development of new products and services,
- They stated that the Bank's alternative distribution channels were not sufficient for the development of new products and services.

As can be seen from these explanations, it is seen that state banks have deficiencies in all aspects (finance, technology, customer, personnel and physical conditions) for the new product and service development process. In the process, the study also analyzes prepared 26 questions were directed to the staff working in two private banks operating in Turkey. One of these personnel is the head office and branch employees with 13 years and 22 years of experience. A summary of the responses of these personnel is shown in Table 4.

As can be seen from Table 4, the personnel working in private banks did not indicate any negativity regarding the new product and service development process of banks. In addition to the people, has also prepared 26 questions posed to 4 staff working in foreign banks operating in Turkey. These personnel are employees of the headquarters and branches with at least 6 years of experience. A summary of the responses of these personnel is shown in Table 5.

As can be seen from Table 5, the personnel working in foreign banks gave quite positive answers in increasing the efficiency of banks in the new product and service development process. 3 of the 4

Table 4. Summary of answers of private bank employees

Sections	Questions	Personnel 3	Personnel 4
Financial Issues	Question 3	Positive	Positive
	Question 4	Positive	Positive
	Question 5	Positive	Positive
	Question 6	Positive	Positive
	Question 7	Positive	Positive
	Question 8	Positive	Positive
Technology Considerations	Question 9	Positive	Positive
	Question 10	Positive	Positive
	Question 11	Positive	Positive
	Question 12	Positive	Positive
	Question 13	Positive	Positive
	Question 14	Positive	Positive
Customer Considerations	Question 15	Positive	Positive
	Question 16	Positive	Positive
	Question 17	Positive	Positive
	Question 18	Positive	Positive
	Question 19	Positive	Positive
	Question 20	Positive	Positive
Personnel and Physical Conditions	Question 21	Positive	Positive
	Question 22	Positive	Positive
	Question 23	Positive	Positive
	Question 24	Positive	Positive
	Question 25	Positive	Positive
	Question 26	Positive	Positive

Evaluation of Customer Expectations-Based New Product and Service Development Process

Table 5. Summary of answers of foreign bank employees

Sections	Questions	Personnel 5	Personnel 6	Personnel 7	Personnel 8
Financial Issues	Question 3	Positive	Positive	Positive	Positive
	Question 4	Positive	Positive	Positive	Positive
	Question 5	Positive	Positive	Positive	Positive
	Question 6	Positive	Positive	Positive	Positive
	Question 7	Positive	Positive	Positive	Positive
	Question 8	Positive	Positive	Positive	Positive
Technology Considerations	Question 9	Positive	Positive	Positive	Positive
	Question 10	Positive	Positive	Positive	Positive
	Question 11	Positive	Positive	Positive	Positive
	Question 12	Positive	Positive	Positive	Positive
	Question 13	Positive	Positive	**Negative**	Positive
	Question 14	No Idea	Positive	Positive	Positive
Customer Considerations	Question 15	Positive	Positive	Positive	Positive
	Question 16	Positive	Positive	Positive	Positive
	Question 17	Positive	Positive	Positive	Positive
	Question 18	Positive	Positive	Positive	Positive
	Question 19	Positive	Positive	Positive	Positive
	Question 20	Positive	Positive	Positive	Positive
Personnel and Physical Conditions	Question 21	Positive	Positive	Positive	Positive
	Question 22	Positive	Positive	Positive	Positive
	Question 23	Positive	Positive	Positive	Positive
	Question 24	Positive	Positive	Positive	Positive
	Question 25	Positive	Positive	Positive	Positive
	Question 26	Positive	Positive	Positive	Positive

foreign bank personnel answered all the questions positively and 1 of them stated that the technological infrastructure in the sector was not followed up effectively by the bank. On the other hand, it has also prepared 26 questions directed to the staff working in four participation banks operating in Turkey. These personnel are general management and branch employees with at least 7 years of experience. The summary of the responses of these personnel is shown in Table 6.

As can be seen from Table 6, it was determined that the participation bank personnel reported mainly deficiencies in terms of personnel and physical conditions regarding the new product and service development process. However, there have been some shortcomings in technology and customer dimensions. On the other hand, there were no problems with regard to finance. Regarding the process of developing new products and services, personnel told the following topics.

- The technological infrastructure of the Bank in the process of developing new products and services is not sufficient,

Table 6. Summary of responses of participation banks employees

Sections	Questions	Personnel 9	Personnel 10	Personnel 11	Personnel 12
Financial Issues	Question 3	Positive	Positive	Positive	Positive
	Question 4	Positive	Positive	Positive	Positive
	Question 5	Positive	Positive	Positive	Positive
	Question 6	Positive	Positive	Positive	Positive
	Question 7	Positive	Positive	Positive	Positive
	Question 8	Positive	Positive	Positive	No Idea
Technology Considerations	Question 9	**Negative**	**Negative**	Positive	Positive
	Question 10	**Negative**	Positive	Positive	Positive
	Question 11	Positive	Positive	Positive	Positive
	Question 12	Positive	Positive	Positive	Positive
	Question 13	Positive	Positive	Positive	Positive
	Question 14	Positive	Positive	Positive	Positive
Customer Considerations	Question 15	Positive	Positive	Positive	Positive
	Question 16	Positive	Positive	**Negative**	Positive
	Question 17	Positive	No Idea	Positive	Positive
	Question 18	Positive	Positive	Positive	Positive
	Question 19	Positive	No Idea	No Idea	No Idea
	Question 20	**Negative**	Positive	Positive	Positive
Personnel and Physical Conditions	Question 21	Positive	**Negative**	Positive	Positive
	Question 22	Positive	Positive	Positive	Positive
	Question 23	Positive	Positive	Positive	Positive
	Question 24	**Negative**	**Negative**	Positive	Positive
	Question 25	**Negative**	**Negative**	Positive	Positive
	Question 26	Positive	Positive	Positive	Positive

- That alternative distribution channels are not technologically appropriate for new product and service development processes,
- There is no technological infrastructure for customer expectations,
- The feedback mechanism of the Bank after the use of products and services is not working effectively,
- Personnel compliance in the new product and service development process is not successful,
- That the physical conditions of the bank are not sufficient in the process of developing new products and services,
- He stated that the Bank's alternative distribution channels are not sufficient for the development of new products and services.

SOLUTIONS AND RECOMMENDATIONS

When the findings mentioned are taken into consideration, it is understood that public banks have failed to develop new products and services compared to other types of banks. In this context, the details of the proposals developed by us for public banks are given below.

It would be appropriate for state-owned banks to invest technologically. Within this framework, it is important to develop ATMs, mobile banking system and internet banking system by making necessary updates. In this way, state banks will be able to manage this process more effectively with alternative distribution channels with the necessary technological infrastructure while developing new products and services.

Public banks should also pay attention to customer expectations when developing new products and services. In this context, first of all, a wide analysis should be done to determine the expectations of different types of customers. On the other hand, it is important that the bank provides an effective mechanism to receive feedback from customers after the use of products and services. In this way, it will be possible to ensure customer satisfaction while developing new products and services.

Consideration of the opinions of the personnel of public banks in the process of new product and service development will contribute to the success of the bank in this process. In this context, it is important to establish a systematic infrastructure in which the ideas of the personnel can be obtained. In this way, it will be possible to provide suggestions for process improvement while developing new products and services.

FUTURE RESEARCH DIRECTIONS

This study focused on new service development process in the banking industry. This subject is very vital for the banks to increase their competitive power. In the following studies, different methodologies can be taken into consideration for this subject. In this framework, using fuzzy logic makes an important contribution to the literature.

CONCLUSION

With the effect of globalization, financial boundaries between countries have disappeared. This provided many advantages, but also led to an increase in competition in the markets. As a result of increasing competition, many firms could not compete with other big firms and had to go bankrupt. The banking sector was one of the sectors most affected by this process. Therefore, banks have had to take some strategies in order to be able to compete with other competitors.

Developing new products and services is also an application that banks use to survive in a challenging competitive environment. Banks are preferred by customers by developing new products and services and this positively affects the profitability of banks. What is important here is that banks have the effectiveness to develop successful new products and services.

The aim of this study is to analyze the new product and service development process focused on customer expectations in the banking sector. Within this framework, the Turkish banking sector was included in the scope of the review. In the analysis process of the study, in-depth interview technique was used.

In this framework, four different dimensions were determined, namely, finance, technology, customer and personnel and physical conditions for the measurement of new product and service development effectiveness. On the other hand, 12 different criteria have been determined for these dimensions. 26 different questions were prepared by considering these dimensions and criteria. Related questions were asked to 12 different personnel working in Turkish banks.

When the results were taken into consideration, it was determined that public bank personnel reported deficiencies in every dimension regarding the new product and service development process. In this context, the relevant personnel stated that they did not find the budgeting facilities of the bank sufficient, that there was no future output for budgeting and alternative distribution channels were not technologically appropriate for the new product and service development process.

In addition to the aforementioned issues, public bank personnel also stated that their banks do not have competitive technological investment plans, that the technological infrastructure in the sector is not followed up effectively by the bank and that the technological infrastructure for customer expectations is not sufficient. In addition, it is stated that public banks do not have medium and long term customer planning in developing new products and services, that the feedback mechanism of the bank after the use of products and services does not function effectively, that the bank's personnel do not play an active role in the new product and service development process and product and service development.

On the other hand, the personnel working in the private banks did not indicate any negativity regarding the new product and service development process of the banks. In line with this, the personnel working in foreign banks have responded positively in increasing the efficiency of banks in the development of new products and services. 3 of the 4 foreign bank personnel answered all the questions positively and 1 of them stated that the technological infrastructure in the sector was not followed up effectively by the bank.

In addition, it was determined that the participation bank personnel reported mainly deficiencies in terms of personnel and physical conditions regarding the new product and service development process. However, there have been some shortcomings in technology and customer dimensions. On the other hand, there were no problems with regard to finance.

ACKNOWLEDGMENT

This study was derived from Gülcan Ergül's master thesis written in İstanbul Medipol University.

REFERENCES

Abedin, B. (2016). Diffusion of adoption of Facebook for customer relationship management in Australia: An exploratory study. *Journal of Organizational and End User Computing*, *28*(1), 56–72. doi:10.4018/JOEUC.2016010104

Agolla, J. E., Makara, T., & Monametsi, G. (2018). Impact of banking innovations on customer attraction, satisfaction and retention: The case of commercial banks in Botswana. *International Journal of Electronic Banking*, *1*(2), 150–170. doi:10.1504/IJEBANK.2018.095598

Ahrens, T., & Ferry, L. (2015). Newcastle City Council and the grassroots: Accountability and budgeting under austerity. *Accounting, Auditing & Accountability Journal*, *28*(6), 909–933. doi:10.1108/AAAJ-03-2014-1658

Akhisar, İ., Tunay, K. B., & Tunay, N. (2015). The effects of innovations on bank performance: The case of electronic banking services. *Procedia: Social and Behavioral Sciences*, *195*, 369–375. doi:10.1016/j.sbspro.2015.06.336

Ali, F., Dey, B. L., & Filieri, R. (2015). An assessment of service quality and resulting customer satisfaction in Pakistan International Airlines: Findings from foreigners and overseas Pakistani customers. *International Journal of Quality & Reliability Management*, *32*(5), 486–502. doi:10.1108/IJQRM-07-2013-0110

Altinirmak, S., Okoth, B., Ergun, M., & Karamasa, C. (2017). Analyzing mobile banking quality factors under neutrosophic set perspective: A case study of TURKEY. *J. Econ. Finance Accounting*, *4*(4), 354–367.

Amavilah, V., Asongu, S. A., & Andrés, A. R. (2017). Effects of globalization on peace and stability: Implications for governance and the knowledge economy of African countries. *Technological Forecasting and Social Change*, *122*, 91–103. doi:10.1016/j.techfore.2017.04.013

Anshari, M., Alas, Y., Yunus, N., Sabtu, N. I., & Hamid, M. H. (2015). Social customer relationship management and student empowerment in online learning systems. *International Journal of Electronic Customer Relationship Management*, *9*(2-3), 104–121. doi:10.1504/IJECRM.2015.071711

Ascarza, E., Ebbes, P., Netzer, O., & Danielson, M. (2017). Beyond the target customer: Social effects of customer relationship management campaigns. *Journal of Marketing Research*, *54*(3), 347–363. doi:10.1509/jmr.15.0442

Atsalakis, G. S., Atsalaki, I. G., & Zopounidis, C. (2018). Forecasting the success of a new tourism service by a neuro-fuzzy technique. *European Journal of Operational Research*, *268*(2), 716–727. doi:10.1016/j.ejor.2018.01.044

Aysan, A. F., Disli, M., & Ozturk, H. (2018). Bank lending channel in a dual banking system: Why are Islamic banks so responsive? *World Economy*, *41*(3), 674–698. doi:10.1111/twec.12507

Bouzgarrou, H., Jouida, S., & Louhichi, W. (2018). Bank profitability during and before the financial crisis: Domestic versus foreign banks. *Research in International Business and Finance*, *44*, 26–39. doi:10.1016/j.ribaf.2017.05.011

Burton, J., Story, V. M., Raddats, C., & Zolkiewski, J. (2017). Overcoming the challenges that hinder new service development by manufacturers with diverse services strategies. *International Journal of Production Economics*, *192*, 29–39. doi:10.1016/j.ijpe.2017.01.013

Carbonell, P., & Rodriguez Escudero, A. I. (2015). The negative effect of team's prior experience and technological turbulence on new service development projects with customer involvement. *European Journal of Marketing*, *49*(3/4), 278–301. doi:10.1108/EJM-08-2013-0438

Chang, C. J., & Hung, C. Y. (2018). Investigation on income tax system of consolidated income from house and land transactions—in-depth interview method. *International Journal of Research in Business and Social Science (2147-4478), 7*(1), 11-24.

Chang, W., & Taylor, S. A. (2016). The effectiveness of customer participation in new product development: A meta-analysis. *Journal of Marketing, 80*(1), 47–64. doi:10.1509/jm.14.0057

Chopra, V., Veeraraghavan, S., Griffioen, A. T. E., Sun, H., Liberman, D. S., Niergarth, J. D., . . . Friedman, L. (2019). *U.S. Patent Application No. 15/720,319.*

Clay, C. (2016). State borrowing and the Imperial Ottoman Bank in the bankruptcy era (1863–1877). In East Meets West-Banking, Commerce and Investment in the Ottoman Empire (pp. 129-142). Routledge.

Consiglio, J. A., Oliva, J. C. M., Tortella, G., Fraser, M. P., & Fraser, I. L. (2016). Stability against all odds: The Imperial Ottoman Bank, 1875–1914. In Banking and Finance in the Mediterranean (pp. 111-134). Routledge.

Cook, C., Schaafsma, J., & Antheunis, M. (2018). Under the bridge: An in-depth examination of online trolling in the gaming context. *New Media & Society, 20*(9), 3323-3340.

Cornaggia, J., Mao, Y., Tian, X., & Wolfe, B. (2015). Does banking competition affect innovation? *Journal of Financial Economics, 115*(1), 189–209. doi:10.1016/j.jfineco.2014.09.001

Coulibaly, S. K., Erbao, C., & Mekongcho, T. M. (2018). Economic globalization, entrepreneurship, and development. *Technological Forecasting and Social Change, 127*, 271–280. doi:10.1016/j.techfore.2017.09.028

Cridland, E. K., Phillipson, L., Brennan-Horley, C., & Swaffer, K. (2016). Reflections and recommendations for conducting in-depth interviews with people with dementia. *Qualitative Health Research, 26*(13), 1774–1786. doi:10.1177/1049732316637065 PMID:27055496

Crumbly, J., & Carter, L. (2015). Social media and humanitarian logistics: The impact of task-technology fit on new service development. *Procedia Engineering, 107*, 412–416. doi:10.1016/j.proeng.2015.06.099

Cui, A. S., & Wu, F. (2016). Utilizing customer knowledge in innovation: Antecedents and impact of customer involvement on new product performance. *Journal of the Academy of Marketing Science, 44*(4), 516–538. doi:10.100711747-015-0433-x

Dewnarain, S., Ramkissoon, H., & Mavondo, F. (2019). Social customer relationship management: An integrated conceptual framework. *Journal of Hospitality Marketing & Management, 28*(2), 172–188. doi:10.1080/19368623.2018.1516588

Diffley, S., McCole, P., & Carvajal-Trujillo, E. (2018). Examining social customer relationship management among Irish hotels. *International Journal of Contemporary Hospitality Management, 30*(2), 1072–1091. doi:10.1108/IJCHM-08-2016-0415

Dinçer, H., Hacıoğlu, Ü., & Yüksel, S. (2017). Balanced scorecard-based performance measurement of European airlines using a hybrid multicriteria decision making approach under the fuzzy environment. *Journal of Air Transport Management, 63*, 17–33. doi:10.1016/j.jairtraman.2017.05.005

Dinçer, H., & Yüksel, S. (2018a). Comparative evaluation of BSC-based new service development competencies in Turkish banking sector with the integrated fuzzy hybrid MCDM using content analysis. *International Journal of Fuzzy Systems*, *20*(8), 2497–2516. doi:10.100740815-018-0519-y

Dinçer, H., & Yüksel, S. (2018b). Financial sector-based analysis of the G20 economies using the integrated decision-making approach with DEMATEL and TOPSIS. In *Emerging trends in banking and finance* (pp. 210–223). Cham, Switzerland: Springer. doi:10.1007/978-3-030-01784-2_13

Dinçer, H., & Yüksel, S. (2019a). Multidimensional evaluation of global investments on the renewable energy with the integrated fuzzy decision-making model under the hesitancy. *International Journal of Energy Research*, *43*(5), 1775–1784. doi:10.1002/er.4400

Dincer, H., & Yuksel, S. (2019b). IT2-based fuzzy hybrid decision making approach to soft computing. *IEEE Access: Practical innovations, open solutions*, *7*, 15932–15944. doi:10.1109/ACCESS.2019.2895359

Dinçer, H., Yüksel, S., & Adalı, Z. (2019j). Economic effects in Islamic stock development of the European countries: policy recommendations for ethical behaviors. In Handbook of research on managerial thinking in global business economics (pp. 58-78). Hershey, PA: IGI Global.

Dinçer, H., Yüksel, S., Adalı, Z., & Aydın, R. (2019l). Evaluating the role of research and development and technology investments on economic development of E7 countries. In Organizational transformation and managing innovation in the fourth industrial revolution (pp. 245-263). Hershey, PA: IGI Global.

Dinçer, H., Yüksel, S., & Çetiner, İ. T. (2019c). Strategy selection for organizational performance of Turkish banking sector with the integrated multi-dimensional decision-making approach. In Handbook of research on contemporary approaches in management and organizational strategy (pp. 273–291). Hershey, PA: IGI Global. doi:10.4018/978-1-5225-6301-3.ch014

Dinçer, H., Yüksel, S., Eti, S., & Tula, A. (2019i). Effects of demographic characteristics on business success: an evidence from Turkish banking sector. In Handbook of research on business models in modern competitive scenarios (pp. 304–324). Hershey, PA: IGI Global. doi:10.4018/978-1-5225-7265-7.ch016

Dinçer, H., Yüksel, S., Kartal, M. T., & Alpman, G. (2019k). Corporate governance-based evaluation of alternative distribution channels in the Turkish banking sector using quality function deployment with an integrated fuzzy MCDM method. In Intergenerational governance and leadership in the corporate world: emerging research and opportunities (pp. 39-77). Hershey, PA: IGI Global.

Dinçer, H., Yüksel, S., Korsakienė, R., Raišienė, A. G., & Bilan, Y. (2019b). IT2 hybrid decision-making approach to performance measurement of internationalized firms in the Baltic states. *Sustainability*, *11*(1), 296. doi:10.3390u11010296

Dincer, H., Yüksel, S., & Martinez, L. (2019a). Balanced scorecard-based analysis about European energy investment policies: A hybrid hesitant fuzzy decision-making approach with quality function deployment. *Expert Systems with Applications*, *115*, 152–171. doi:10.1016/j.eswa.2018.07.072

Dinçer, H., Yüksel, S., & Martínez, L. (2019f). Analysis of balanced scorecard-based SERVQUAL criteria based on hesitant decision-making approaches. *Computers & Industrial Engineering*, *131*, 1–12. doi:10.1016/j.cie.2019.03.026

Dinçer, H., Yüksel, S., & Martínez, L. (2019h). Interval type 2-based hybrid fuzzy evaluation of financial services in E7 economies with DEMATEL-ANP and MOORA methods. *Applied Soft Computing*, *79*, 186–202. doi:10.1016/j.asoc.2019.03.018

Dinçer, H., Yüksel, S., & Pınarbaşı, F. (2019d). SERVQUAL-based evaluation of service quality of energy companies in Turkey: strategic policies for sustainable economic development. In The circular economy and its implications on sustainability and the green supply chain (pp. 142-167). Hershey, PA: IGI Global.

Dinçer, H., Yüksel, S., & Pınarbaşı, F. (2019m). Technology acceptance model-based website evaluation of service industry: an application on the companies listed in BIST via hybrid MCDM. In Multi-criteria decision-making models for website evaluation (pp. 1-28). Hershey, PA: IGI Global.

Dinçer, H., Yüksel, S., Pınarbaşı, F., & Çetiner, İ. T. (2019g). Measurement of economic and banking stability in emerging markets by considering income inequality and nonperforming loans. In Maintaining financial stability in times of risk and uncertainty (pp. 49–68). Hershey, PA: IGI Global. doi:10.4018/978-1-5225-7208-4.ch003

Dinçer, H., Yüksel, S., Yazici, M., & Pınarbaşı, F. (2019e). Assessing corporate social responsibilities in the banking sector: as a tool of strategic communication during the global financial crisis. In Handbook of research on global issues in financial communication and investment decision making (pp. 1-27). Hershey, PA: IGI Global.

Diviani, N., Van den Putte, B., Meppelink, C. S., & van Weert, J. C. (2016). Exploring the role of health literacy in the evaluation of online health information: Insights from a mixed-methods study. *Patient Education and Counseling*, *99*(6), 1017–1025. doi:10.1016/j.pec.2016.01.007 PMID:26817407

Eisner, E., Drake, R., Lobban, F., Bucci, S., Emsley, R., & Barrowclough, C. (2018). Comparing early signs and basic symptoms as methods for predicting psychotic relapse in clinical practice. *Schizophrenia Research*, *192*, 124–130. doi:10.1016/j.schres.2017.04.050 PMID:28499766

Elmes, M. B., Mendoza-Abarca, K., & Hersh, R. (2016). Food banking, ethical sensemaking, and social innovation in an era of growing hunger in the United States. *Journal of Management Inquiry*, *25*(2), 122–138. doi:10.1177/1056492615589651

Eti, S. (2019). Ulakbim İndeksinde Taranan Sosyal Bilimler Alanındaki Dergilerde Öne Çıkan Konu Ve Yöntemlerin Metin Madenciliği Yaklaşımı İle Belirlenmesi. *Uluslararası Hukuk ve Sosyal Bilim Araştırmaları Dergisi*, *1*(1), 61–66.

Eti, S., Dinçer, H., & Yüksel, S. (2019). G20 Ülkelerinde Bankacılık Sektörünün 5 Yıllık Geleceğinin Arıma Yöntemi İle Tahmin Edilmesi. *Uluslararası Hukuk ve Sosyal Bilim Araştırmaları Dergisi*, *1*(1), 26–38.

Farouk, S., Abu Elanain, H. M., Obeidat, S. M., & Al-Nahyan, M. (2016). HRM practices and organizational performance in the UAE banking sector: The mediating role of organizational innovation. *International Journal of Productivity and Performance Management*, *65*(6), 773–791. doi:10.1108/IJPPM-01-2016-0010

Filip, B. F. (2015). The quality of bank loans within the framework of globalization. *Procedia Economics and Finance*, *20*, 208–217. doi:10.1016/S2212-5671(15)00067-2

Fraser, M. P. (2016). A general survey of the history of the Imperial Ottoman Bank. In East meets West-banking, commerce and investment in the Ottoman Empire (pp. 117-128). Routledge.

Fuertes, A. M., Phylaktis, K., & Yan, C. (2016). Hot money in bank credit flows to emerging markets during the banking globalization era. *Journal of International Money and Finance*, *60*, 29–52. doi:10.1016/j.jimonfin.2014.10.002

Ghosh, A. (2016). Banking sector globalization and bank performance: A comparative analysis of low income countries with emerging markets and advanced economies. *Review of Development Finance*, *6*(1), 58–70. doi:10.1016/j.rdf.2016.05.003

Gozzi, J. C., Levine, R., Peria, M. S. M., & Schmukler, S. L. (2015). How firms use corporate bond markets under financial globalization. *Journal of Banking & Finance*, *58*, 532–551. doi:10.1016/j.jbankfin.2015.03.017

Guha, S., Harrigan, P., & Soutar, G. (2018). Linking social media to customer relationship management (CRM): A qualitative study on SMEs. *Journal of Small Business and Entrepreneurship*, *30*(3), 193–214. doi:10.1080/08276331.2017.1399628

Haberland, N. A., Kelly, C. A., Mulenga, D. M., Mensch, B. S., & Hewett, P. C. (2016). Women's perceptions and misperceptions of male circumcision: A mixed methods study in Zambia. *PLoS One*, *11*(3), e0149517. doi:10.1371/journal.pone.0149517 PMID:26937971

Haeberle, D., Imran, S., van Husen, C., & Droll, C. (2016). A new approach for the development of services for industrial product-service systems. *Procedia CIRP*, *47*, 353–357. doi:10.1016/j.procir.2016.04.079

Hargreaves, I., Roth, D., Karim, M. R., Nayebi, M., & Ruhe, G. (2018). Effective customer relationship management at atb financial: A case study on industry-academia collaboration in data analytics. In *Highlighting the importance of big data management and analysis for various applications* (pp. 45–59). Cham, Switzerland: Springer. doi:10.1007/978-3-319-60255-4_4

Hassan, R. S., Nawaz, A., Lashari, M. N., & Zafar, F. (2015). Effect of customer relationship management on customer satisfaction. *Procedia Economics and Finance*, *23*, 563–567. doi:10.1016/S2212-5671(15)00513-4

Hoffman, K. D., Kelley, S. W., & Rotalsky, H. M. (2016). Retrospective: Tracking service failures and employee recovery efforts. *Journal of Services Marketing*, *30*(1), 7–10. doi:10.1108/JSM-10-2015-0316

Jaakkola, E., Meiren, T., Witell, L., Edvardsson, B., Schäfer, A., Reynoso, J., ... Weitlaner, D. (2017). Does one size fit all? New service development across different types of services. *Journal of Service Management*, *28*(2), 329–347. doi:10.1108/JOSM-11-2015-0370

Kalkavan, H., & Ersin, I. (2019). Determination of factors affecting the South East Asian crisis of 1997 probit-logit panel regression: The South East Asian crisis. In Handbook of research on global issues in financial communication and investment decision making (pp. 148-167). Hershey, PA: IGI Global.

Kaushik, A. K., & Rahman, Z. (2015). Innovation adoption across self-service banking technologies in India. *International Journal of Bank Marketing*, *33*(2), 96–121. doi:10.1108/IJBM-01-2014-0006

Kiliç, M. (2016). Online corporate social responsibility (CSR) disclosure in the banking industry: Evidence from Turkey. *International Journal of Bank Marketing, 34*(4), 550–569. doi:10.1108/IJBM-04-2015-0060

Kleymenova, A., Rose, A. K., & Wieladek, T. (2016). Does government intervention affect banking globalization? *Journal of the Japanese and International Economies, 40*, 43–58. doi:10.1016/j.jjie.2016.03.002

Laukkanen, T. (2015, January). How uncertainty avoidance affects innovation resistance in mobile banking: The moderating role of age and gender. In *2015 48th Hawaii International Conference on System Sciences* (pp. 3601-3610). IEEE.

Lillard, L. L., & Al-Suqri, M. N. (2019). Librarians learning from the retail sector: reaching out to online learners using customer relationship management. *Journal of Arts and Social Sciences, 9*(3), 15–26. doi:10.24200/jass.vol9iss3pp15-26

Liu, C. H., Chang, A. Y. P., Horng, J. S., Chou, S. F., & Huang, Y. C. (2019). Co-competition, learning, and business strategy for new service development. *Service Industries Journal*, 1–25. doi:10.1080/02642069.2019.1571045

Maecker, O., Barrot, C., & Becker, J. U. (2016). The effect of social media interactions on customer relationship management. *Business Research, 9*(1), 133–155. doi:10.100740685-016-0027-6

Mahmoud, M. A., Hinson, R. E., & Anim, P. A. (2018). Service innovation and customer satisfaction: The role of customer value creation. *European Journal of Innovation Management, 21*(3), 402–422. doi:10.1108/EJIM-09-2017-0117

Masood, A., & Java, J. (2015, April). Static analysis for web service security-Tools & techniques for a secure development life cycle. In *2015 IEEE International Symposium on Technologies for Homeland Security (HST)* (pp. 1-6). IEEE 10.1109/THS.2015.7225337

Miller, G. J., Hildreth, W. B., & Rabin, J. (2018). Performance-based budgeting: An ASPA classic. In *Performance based budgeting* (pp. 1–504). Taylor and Francis.

Mittal, S., Pant, A., & Bhadauria, S. S. (2017). An empirical study on customer preference towards payment banks over universal banks in Delhi NCR. *Procedia Computer Science, 122*, 463–470. doi:10.1016/j.procs.2017.11.394

Muda, I., & Putra, A. S. (2018, January). Institutional fishermen economic development models and banking support in the development of the innovation system of fisheries and marine area in North Sumatera. IOP Publishing. *IOP Conference Series. Materials Science and Engineering, 288*(1), 012082. doi:10.1088/1757-899X/288/1/012082

Navimipour, N. J., & Soltani, Z. (2016). The impact of cost, technology acceptance and employees' satisfaction on the effectiveness of the electronic customer relationship management systems. *Computers in Human Behavior, 55*, 1052–1066. doi:10.1016/j.chb.2015.10.036

Nesvetailova, A. (2015). A crisis of the overcrowded future: Shadow banking and the political economy of financial innovation. *New Political Economy, 20*(3), 431–453. doi:10.1080/13563467.2014.951428

Niepmann, F., & Schmidt-Eisenlohr, T. (2017). International trade, risk and the role of banks. *Journal of International Economics, 107*, 111–126. doi:10.1016/j.jinteco.2017.03.007

Noth, F., & Busch, M. O. (2016). Foreign funding shocks and the lending channel: Do foreign banks adjust differently? *Finance Research Letters, 19*, 222–227. doi:10.1016/j.frl.2016.08.003

Nyadzayo, M. W., & Khajehzadeh, S. (2016). The antecedents of customer loyalty: A moderated mediation model of customer relationship management quality and brand image. *Journal of Retailing and Consumer Services, 30*, 262–270. doi:10.1016/j.jretconser.2016.02.002

Ojasalo, K., Koskelo, M., & Nousiainen, A. K. (2015). Foresight and service design boosting dynamic capabilities in service innovation. In *The handbook of service innovation* (pp. 193–212). London, UK: Springer. doi:10.1007/978-1-4471-6590-3_10

Parameswar, N., Dhir, S., & Dhir, S. (2017). Banking on innovation, innovation in banking at ICICI bank. *Global Business and Organizational Excellence, 36*(2), 6–16. doi:10.1002/joe.21765

Parente, R. C., Geleilate, J. M. G., & Rong, K. (2018). The sharing economy globalization phenomenon: A research agenda. *Journal of International Management, 24*(1), 52–64. doi:10.1016/j.intman.2017.10.001

Rahimi, R. (2017). Customer relationship management (people, process and technology) and organisational culture in hotels: Which traits matter? *International Journal of Contemporary Hospitality Management, 29*(5), 1380–1402. doi:10.1108/IJCHM-10-2015-0617

Rahimi, R., & Kozak, M. (2017). Impact of customer relationship management on customer satisfaction: The case of a budget hotel chain. *Journal of Travel & Tourism Marketing, 34*(1), 40–51. doi:10.1080/10548408.2015.1130108

Reim, W., Parida, V., & Örtqvist, D. (2015). Product–Service Systems (PSS) business models and tactics–a systematic literature review. *Journal of Cleaner Production, 97*, 61–75. doi:10.1016/j.jclepro.2014.07.003

Roberts, D. L., & Darler, W. (2017). Consumer co-creation: An opportunity to humanise the new product development process. *International Journal of Market Research, 59*(1), 13–33. doi:10.2501/IJMR-2017-003

Rosenthal, M. (2016). Qualitative research methods: Why, when, and how to conduct interviews and focus groups in pharmacy research. *Currents in pharmacy teaching and learning, 8*(4), 509-516.

Rubin, I. S. (2019). *The politics of public budgeting: Getting and spending, borrowing and balancing.* CQ Press.

Rubleske, J., & Kaarst-Brown, M. L. (2019). Mindful new service conception in not-for-profit organisations: A study of sustainable innovation with scarce resources. *International Journal of Business Innovation and Research, 18*(1), 87–108. doi:10.1504/IJBIR.2019.096897

Rus, S., Mocan, M., Ardelean, B. O., Ivascu, L., & Cioca, L. I. (2016). Conceptualization and examination of success factors in the banking system. *Procedia Economics and Finance, 39*, 679–684. doi:10.1016/S2212-5671(16)30289-1

Samina, Q. S., & Hossain, M. (2019). Current position of banks in the practice of green banking in Bangladesh: An analysis on private sector commercial banks in Bangladesh. *Current Position of Banks in the Practice of Green Banking in Bangladesh: An Analysis on Private Sector Commercial Banks in Bangladesh (Jan. 5, 2019)*.

Santouridis, I., & Veraki, A. (2017). Customer relationship management and customer satisfaction: The mediating role of relationship quality. *Total Quality Management & Business Excellence, 28*(9-10), 1122–1133. doi:10.1080/14783363.2017.1303889

Schnittker, R., Marshall, S., Horberry, T., & Young, K. L. (2018). Human factors enablers and barriers for successful airway management–an in-depth interview study. *Anaesthesia, 73*(8), 980–989. doi:10.1111/anae.14302 PMID:29660772

Şimşek, H., Bayındır, S., & Ustaoğlu, M. (2017). Dual banking systems' dynamics and a brief development history of Islamic finance in select emerging Islamic economies. In *Balancing Islamic and conventional banking for economic growth* (pp. 9–26). Cham, Switzerland: Palgrave Macmillan. doi:10.1007/978-3-319-59554-2_2

Snyder, H., Witell, L., Gustafsson, A., Fombelle, P., & Kristensson, P. (2016). Identifying categories of service innovation: A review and synthesis of the literature. *Journal of Business Research, 69*(7), 2401–2408. doi:10.1016/j.jbusres.2016.01.009

Soltani, Z., & Navimipour, N. J. (2016). Customer relationship management mechanisms: A systematic review of the state of the art literature and recommendations for future research. *Computers in Human Behavior, 61*, 667–688. doi:10.1016/j.chb.2016.03.008

Srinivasan, K., & Saravanan, S. (2015). Principles and practices of customer relationship management in Ethiopian banks. *EXCEL International Journal of Multidisciplinary Management Studies, 5*(8), 8–20.

Su, C. H., & Chen, P. K. (2016). Applying project management for new service development. *International Journal of Innovation Science, 8*(3), 185–198. doi:10.1108/IJIS-09-2016-013

Sun, P. H., Mohamad, S., & Ariff, M. (2017). Determinants driving bank performance: A comparison of two types of banks in the OIC. *Pacific-Basin Finance Journal, 42*, 193–203. doi:10.1016/j.pacfin.2016.02.007

Talón-Ballestero, P., González-Serrano, L., Soguero-Ruiz, C., Muñoz-Romero, S., & Rojo-Álvarez, J. L. (2018). Using big data from customer relationship management information systems to determine the client profile in the hotel sector. *Tourism Management, 68*, 187–197. doi:10.1016/j.tourman.2018.03.017

Tatoğlu, F. Y., Tunalı, H., & Ustaoğlu, M. (2017). The Turkish economy and financing growth by dual banking: empirical evidence. In *Balancing Islamic and conventional banking for economic growth* (pp. 47–68). Cham, Switzerland: Palgrave Macmillan. doi:10.1007/978-3-319-59554-2_4

Ting, X., Yong, B., Yin, L., & Mi, T. (2016). Patient perception and the barriers to practicing patient-centered communication: A survey and in-depth interview of Chinese patients and physicians. *Patient Education and Counseling, 99*(3), 364–369. doi:10.1016/j.pec.2015.07.019 PMID:26776708

Tosun, C., & Bağdadioğlu, N. (2016). Evaluating gender responsive budgeting in Turkey. *International Journal of Monetary Economics and Finance, 9*(2), 187–197. doi:10.1504/IJMEF.2016.076481

Vezzoli, C., Ceschin, F., Diehl, J. C., & Kohtala, C. (2015). New design challenges to widely implement 'Sustainable product–service systems'. *Journal of Cleaner Production, 97*, 1–12. doi:10.1016/j.jclepro.2015.02.061

Visnjic, I., Wiengarten, F., & Neely, A. (2016). Only the brave: Product innovation, service business model innovation, and their impact on performance. *Journal of Product Innovation Management, 33*(1), 36–52. doi:10.1111/jpim.12254

Wang, S., Cavusoglu, H., & Deng, Z. (2016). Early mover advantage in e-commerce platforms with low entry barriers: The role of customer relationship management capabilities. *Information & Management, 53*(2), 197–206. doi:10.1016/j.im.2015.09.011

Wang, Z., & Kim, H. G. (2017). Can social media marketing improve customer relationship capabilities and firm performance? Dynamic capability perspective. *Journal of Interactive Marketing, 39*, 15–26. doi:10.1016/j.intmar.2017.02.004

Witell, L., Anderson, L., Brodie, R. J., Colurcio, M., Edvardsson, B., Kristensson, P., ... Wallin Andreassen, T. (2015). Exploring dualities of service innovation: Implications for service research. *Journal of Services Marketing, 29*(6/7), 436–441. doi:10.1108/JSM-01-2015-0051

Yang, Y., Lee, P. K., & Cheng, T. C. E. (2016). Continuous improvement competence, employee creativity, and new service development performance: A frontline employee perspective. *International Journal of Production Economics, 171*, 275–288. doi:10.1016/j.ijpe.2015.08.006

Ylimäki, J., & Vesalainen, J. (2015). Relational development of a service concept: Dialogue meets efficiency. *Journal of Business and Industrial Marketing, 30*(8), 939–950. doi:10.1108/JBIM-05-2014-0100

Yu, E., & Sangiorgi, D. (2018). Exploring the transformative impacts of service design: The role of designer–client relationships in the service development process. *Design Studies, 55*, 79–111. doi:10.1016/j.destud.2017.09.001

Yüksel, S., Dinçer, H., & Emir, Ş. (2017). Comparing the performance of Turkish deposit banks by using DEMATEL, Grey Relational Analysis (GRA) and MOORA approaches. *World Journal of Applied Economics, 3*(2), 26–47. doi:10.22440/wjae.3.2.2

Yuksel, S., Dinçer, H., & Emir, S. (2018). Analysis of service innovation performance in Turkish banking sector using a combining method of fuzzy MCDM and text mining. *MANAS Sosyal Araştırmalar Dergisi, 7*(3).

Yuksel, S., Dincer, H., & Hacioglu, U. (2015). CAMELS-based determinants for the credit rating of Turkish deposit banks. *International Journal of Finance & Banking Studies (2147-4486), 4*(4), 1-17.

Yüksel, S., Dinçer, H., & Meral, Y. (2019). Financial analysis of international energy trade: A strategic outlook for EU-15. *Energies, 12*(3), 431. doi:10.3390/en12030431

Zaitseva, N. A., Larionova, A. A., Minervin, I. G., Yakimenko, R. V., & Balitskaya, I. V. (2015). Foresight technologies usage in working out long term. Forecasts of service and tourism personnel training system development. *Journal of Environmental Management & Tourism, 6*(2 (12)), 410.

Zaleska, M., & Kondraciuk, P. (2019). Theory and practice of innovation development in the banking sector. *Financial Sciences. Nauki o Finansach, 24*(2), 76-87.

KEY TERMS AND DEFINITIONS

ATM: Automatic Teller Machine
FED: Federal Reserve Bank
IMF: International Monetary Fund
R&D: Research and Development
US: United States
USD: American Dollar

Chapter 15
Role of Agility in the Banking Sector in Competitive Globalization Era:
Evidence From the Turkish Banking Sector

Kagan Cenk Mızrak
Nisantası University, Turkey

Filiz Mızrak
Istanbul Medipol University, Turkey

ABSTRACT

In today's rapidly changing market conditions, organizations need to be agile to gain a competitive market advantage. This chapter details the key points required for agility. Although there has been ongoing discussion whether finance and banking sector can be agile due to rigid structures, processes, and regulators, the chapter aims to prove the vital role of agility in banking sector with the case of Garanti Bank. Thanks to the case, the strategies both on the basis organization structure and marketing level that banks need to apply in agile transformation process, have been exemplified. As a result of the case, the importance of flexibility, speed, monitoring the latest trend, making quick decisions, and being customer-focused in the banking sector is stressed. On the other hand, banks are suggested to engage all their units, shareholders together with their customers in the process to have a more smooth translation.

INTRODUCTION

In this period of rapid technological development and change, the industry is experiencing the first phase of a new revolution, which makes it much more difficult for companies to produce products and services and survive. Competition has moved to a global dimension, product and service life has been shortened and customers' need to satisfy their personal and special needs has increased. In the past, the success of a manufacturer of goods and services was measured with the ability to produce a single product at

DOI: 10.4018/978-1-7998-2559-3.ch015

the lowest cost, but today it is being measured with flexibility, speed, the ability to manage continuous development and change, and the ability to anticipate and react to changes in customer needs and market. In order to survive in this dynamic and uncertain competition environment, companies had to develop new and improved production paradigms. As a result, highly agile companies have emerged in terms of both organizational structure and operation and business processes and have gained great competitive advantage by using technology.

Today, competition has become a factor that seriously affects the sector and the institution in which it operates (Yağcılar, 2011). Again, within the framework of important financial developments and global conditions, the concept of competition has become an indispensable element for both banks and other institutions in the markets. Banks, one of the main actors of the economy, appear as institutions that need to be in constant competition both in terms of sustaining their activities in the market and being ahead of their competitors and need to determine strong strategies for the future (Gök and Özdemir, 2011).

The purpose of the study is to analyze the key points of the agility and stress the importance of it in the banking sector. In this scope, the case of Garanti Bank which has been leading Turkish banking sector with its innovative services and products for a long time, has been analyzed. The requirements for organizations to be agile; flexibility, speed, ability to change, ability to monitor the latest trend, adopting the advanced technology, being customer focused, have been detected in Garanti Bank. Although, it has been doubted whether banks can be transformed into agile model, with the help of the case study, it has been proved that agility has vital role in the success of the banks.

There are 3 main parts in the study. In the first part, the concept of agility, the definitions of agility and lean management are made with the help of the different perspectives in the literature. In the second part competition in the banking sector has been discussed in the framework of literature. In the last part, the case of Garanti Bank has been analyzed.

LITERATURE REVIEW

Agile Approach

The developing competitive environment has forced today's businesses to use technology effectively and created a different competitive environment in order to meet human needs more quickly and effectively. In a globalized competitive environment, it has become very important to see how accurately companies use information and how they reflect this to the market. Accordingly, efforts to create organizational culture that quickly learn and implement information are seen as the primary duties of enterprises.

In a changing and rapidly developing market environment, organizations need flexible and adaptive structures that are open to changes and can respond to new developments (Jayaram et al., 2004). The rapidly changing customer demands and expectations, with the contributions of Marketing 3.0 understanding along with the developments in the industry, exceeded the customer satisfaction. As a result of this situation, the business executives have come to the stage of organizing the administrative process with an understanding that constructs and designs the speed which is more than just keeping pace. Agile production approach that comes into play at this point directly enables companies to keep up with these customer demands and changes in demands as soon as possible (Jayaram et al., 2004).

It is seen that the explanations made while defining the concept of agility may overlap with different facts in the literature. In fact, while trying to explain the concept of agility, many expressions that are intrinsically relevant but are insufficient to directly explain agility are seen in the literature. In this regard, especially in order to better understand the concept of agility to reveal the difference from other similar concepts will provide a better understanding of the subject.

Today, the concept of agile production is seen as equivalent to the concepts such as lean production, flexible production and computerized production. it is possible to define the change as following, covering and easily adapting. For companies, agility refers to the adaptation process to rapidly changing strategic environments, market and industrial developments (Akman & Keskin, 2012). Nagel and Bhargava (1994) described agility as the ability to act quickly, skillfully, and adaptively. For this reason, agility competition in large and small organizations is based on the ability to develop over change and uncertainty.

In a different definition, agility can be considered as a descriptor of both promptness and responsiveness when confronted with internal and external events or stimuli. Although many businesses understand the need to be fast and responsive in a global economy and in an ever-changing market, many are not structured to do so (Ambrose and Morello, 2004).

Gunesakaran (1999) interprets agility as a virtual company with market knowledge and created to use profitable opportunities in a volatile market. It also describes the necessity of flexibility and responsiveness in strategy, technology, system and individuals.

An agile company is a company that embraces change and adapts to it quickly and easily. Agility means efficient restructuring of operations, processes and business relationships, while at the same time enabling development in an environment of continuous change. Companies attempting to implement such production should take care not to implement strategies very quickly. These new production techniques should be well thought out as long-term strategic plans (Hormozi, 2001).

The ability of an organization to create or implement effective strategies, to communicate efficiently within its own hierarchy, to act innovative, to establish partnerships with customers and suppliers, to benefit from market opportunities or to create such opportunities are also explained with corporate agility (Araza and Aslan, 2006).

To be fast and flexible is not to be afraid of change. It means to renew itself regularly, to benefit from the opportunities brought by uncertainty, to be protected from dangers, to provide competitive advantage, to ensure that customers can read correctly. This is what makes corporate agility and being agile company valuable (İleri and Soylu, 2010).

In the literature, it is seen that in the essence of the definitions that try to explain agility, it is imperative that enterprises develop an adaptive structure for all kinds of changes. In order to fulfill this obligation, some of the capabilities of the enterprises must be developed. One of them is to be able to keep up with the speed, which necessitates adaptive structure. In order to adapt, the speed range of changes necessitates, of course, being flexible during periods of unpredictability. At this stage, in order to make unknowns known, in other words, proactive, requires a high prediction. However, it is understood that the concept of agility, which rests on all these basic building blocks, is not independent from the fact that businesses know themselves very well. At one point, when this situation, also called self-awareness, is combined with foresight, it is possible to detect positive and negative changes that may develop in the market, while at the same time, it will be possible for businesses to recognize themselves and understand how they can respond. This will enable the business to see its weaknesses. Nowadays, it is evident that in today's modern business understanding, businesses are a whole with their internal and external environments and their success is to ensure the integration of this whole body effectively. In this respect, it is seen that a total perspective has a direct and non-breaking relationship with the suppliers, employees, proximity to resources, and the ability to use the resources they have. In addition, in many studies, it is understood that outsourcing to improve business capabilities in order to respond to changes, and even shrinking movements to make the activities that businesses can do better, faster and more rapidly, are the main lines that contribute to agility.

Lean Management

As the competition conditions in the market become more difficult, it is necessary to keep up with the changes. In order to develop long-term strategies, companies have to take quick and accurate steps in the short term. For this, they need to have a management approach in flexible structures that can adapt quickly. Although agility corresponds to this, it is necessary to adopt the lean management approach in order to be agile.

The main purpose of the lean management idea is to transfer the value from the raw material to the customer in a continuous manner and to move the product from a holistic point of view which aims to prevent wastes and create value for the customer (Birgün et al., 2006). According to the lean management approach, organizations go through a transformation process and eliminate all activities that do not provide added value to the organization and aim to reduce the time spent for the works that provide added value. At this point, lean management is a management approach that aims to prevent waste by eliminating processes or process steps (Womack et al., 2005).

The fundamentals of today's lean management approach were examined by Japanese engineers Eiji Toyoda and Taiichi Ohno's Ford in the 1950s with the idea, the "mass production" system in America was not suitable for Japan and Toyoto. For this reason, Toyota, a Japanese company, tried a new production and management model for its production practices.

The idea that the "mass production" system, which operates smoothly in America, causes waste, and that this waste is not suitable for Japan and also that Japan's own conditions are not suitable for mass production, allows the foundations of what we call today "lean production" (Kocakoç, 2008).

Lean management is essential to compete in today's conditions. The Toyota Production System, which forms the basis of the separation of value-adding and non-value-added works and lean thinking, has very well explained 14 basic principles of lean management. These principles are (Liker, 2010)

Principle 1 "Base Management Decisions on a Long-Term Philosophy, even at the Cost of Short-Term Financial Targets": It speaks of the benefit of focusing on long-term outcomes rather than short-term results. On the basis of this principle, there is a philosophy that the organization need to adopt to achieve these long-term outcomes, so that employees can be provided with unification around a common goal (Liker, 2010).

Principle 2 "Create an Uninterrupted Process Flow to Reveal Problems": The purpose of this principle is to make the working processes that add high value to the organization more prominent in all areas of the organization by regulating and continuously improving them. Improving the organization and its employees can eliminate waste for both customers, suppliers and every stage of the organization, and if possible, it can reveal the causes of the waste and thus provide added value to the enterprise. The waste may be due to production, inventory handling may be due to errors in the movement and process system and may be due to a lack of system or a lack of information technology. At this point, it is necessary to plan improvements and facilitate transformation in order to meet customer demands (Baysan and Durmuşoğlu, 2015).

Principle 3 "Use "Withdrawal" systems in order to avoid overproduction": The underlying principle of the withdrawal system is the philosophy of delivering the customers what they want at any time and in quantity. At this point, the understanding of replacing the amount consumed refers to the withdrawal system. For this reason, the fact that the organizations have too much stock is an obstacle at this point. With the withdrawal system, it is aimed to reduce the stages without any added value to the organization and the time to meet the demand of the customer decreases and excessive consumption is prevented (Apilioğulları, 2010).

Principle 4 "Straighten Workload": Compression of production to a fixed period of time and work done in order is the activity of smoothing the workload. Sequencing of production with equal load distribution plays an active role in achieving flattening. Balancing the load is one of the factors that facilitate the equal distribution of the workload. Its most important advantage is that it does not reflect to internal processes with balanced production and sequencing techniques in changing customer demands (Apilioğulları, 2016)

Principle 5 "Developing a Stopping Culture to Solve Problems to Ensure Quality from the Beginning": This concept, also called automation, plays an important role in stopping power to use quality effectively. The responsible person at the beginning of the line should have the authority to stop the line in order to ensure quality at the points he deems necessary and to prevent wastage after the work is finished. Jidoka is an application used for this purpose and is actively applied with a visual warning system called "andon". According to some views, quality in the organization can be achieved in a system where everyone is equal, and doing it with machines will be less useful than a system that people observe (Liker, 2010).

Principle 6 "Standardized Tasks are the Basis for Continuous Improvement and Empowerment of Employees": In a lean management system, standardization forms the basis for empowering workers. It is not a structure to routinize normal systems and to frame strict standards. Standardization in management of the year is carried out on the basis of continuous improvement and standardization is realized by measuring the performance of the process at the end of the solutions implemented. At this point, employees are not only the ones who do what they have to do, but also those who perform analyzes and play an active role in solving problems (Liker, 2010).

Principle 7 "Use Visual Control in a way that no problems remain hidden". This principle adopts the principle of "make it clear and visible". The important thing is to use a system in which abnormalities can be detected.

Principle 8 "Serve only Your People and the Process, Use Carefully Tested Technology": It is the process of exploring how a process can be faced before implementing any technology in the organization. What is important here is the use of technologies to support people instead of technologies that replace people. It is not possible to use any program that does not comply with the organizational culture and which the organization cannot adopt or cannot implement. The transition to any new technology is a difficult and costly process. the unpredictable wastes during the acclimatization of the organization and perhaps the inadequacy of the applied technology may have unpredictable results if proper measurements are not performed (Liker, 2010).

Principle 9 "Bring in Leaders Who Understand Business, Live Philosophy and Teach to Others": It is one of the most important principles of lean management that the top management should receive training, develop their leadership and participate in the process together with the employees. The fact that the leaders are raised from within the organization and the leaders dominating the organization are important conditions for the implementation of lean management. The formation of organizational culture in any organization can take a long time and it would be a waste of time for someone who does not know the organizational culture to try to understand the culture. Therefore, a leader who may come from outside contradicts the lean management approach. Leaders who adopt a lean philosophy will be able to guide, teach and coach the employees in the field. It prevents employees from being afraid of making mistakes by motivating them and increases entrepreneurship and opens up opportunities (Liker, 2010).

Principle 10 "Bring in Exceptional People and Teams Following Your Company's Philosophy": Organizations that want to switch to a lean management approach should first understand the lean management philosophy completely and place it in the organization. If management philosophy is implemented from the top without adopting it to employees, the result will be absolute failure. Because the basic purpose of achieving success in lean management is to understand this philosophy and the spirit of philosophy and to live it together with all employees (Liker, 2010).

Principle 11 "Respect Your Partners and Wide Network" Businesses that adopt a lean management approach should continue by creating an integrated network with their suppliers. Strong ties of suppliers with suppliers will also strengthen production and efficiency. The fact that suppliers become a learning organization is one of the important factors that will enable them to solve the problems they encounter immediately and eliminate the waste of time for the enterprises. Within the framework of that trust and respect, the long-term relations of both sides will cause them to overcome the crisis in the easiest way in case of any crisis (Liker, 2010).

Principle 12 "Go and see the situation for yourself to fully undertstand". To understand any problems that will occur within the organization cannot be done only by analyzing the existing data. Leaning to the root of the problem and observing and analyzing it from its formation is one of the important points of lean management. The fact that needs and problems are identified on-site means that they can be understood in depth and should be adopted in the solution of all problems (Liker, 2010).

Principle 13 "Take Your Decisions Without Hurrying, Evaluating All Options Thoroughly, Reconcile and Apply Your Decision Quickly": Decision-making is a process that varies from organization to organization, from person to person, even from country to country. Some of the organizations adopt the idea of quick decision making while others want to make decisions in a systematically standardized manner. It is very important to think well when making decisions in the organization within the philosophy of lean management and it is one of the basic principles of lean management. Decisions taken quickly without much analysis will result in waste both time and money, so the decisions to be taken need to be analyzed from the very beginning of the process and then concluded with a common decision (Liker, 2010).

Principle 14 "Become a Learning Organization through Reflection (Hansei) and Continuously Improve (Kaizen): The improvement of small problems that arise is referred to as "Kaizen". Finding what went wrong and improving the process is the basis for improvement. As a result of this process, existing information is made to benefit the customers while sharing these exchange needs with employees and suppliers becomes part of the process. "Hansei"is refeered to reflection. When something wrong is done, studies should be done to solve the problem and emotionally be willing that this will not be repeated (Liker, 2010).

Agility and Characteristics of Agile Organizations

Agility of any organization plays a very important role in protecting organizations against situations that may develop out of control and provides the fight against unexpected variables. Agility studies reveal that agility has certain characteristics. These are (Candan et al., 2017):

- Starting the production process dynamically
- Focusing on the production of upgradeable products

- Starting production of new or updated products immediately
- Ensuring that the products can be adapted to the demands

The process was not developed within the scope of a plan program before the change became completely necessary; together with the changing thinking and management approach, these thoughts have been abandoned, and especially as it has been realized that change is inevitable, all kinds of change scenarios have been emphasized even more. The necessity of thinking and organization as flexible as possible pushes organizations to agile management understanding (Bititci et al., 1999).

While flexibility is one of the basic steps of agility, it is a necessary feature to adapt to change. If organizations are agile, they are also flexible.

Agility of organizations is defined as a process that occurs with certain situations. These;

- Almost everything in the current market starts to change unexpectedly,
- The market requires high quality and customized products with low budgets,
- Short planning and delivery times of these products demanded by the market,
- Customers wish to receive special treatment.

With this process, the characteristics of agility are as follows (Candan et al., 2017):

- Categorizing customer demands according to their priorities by strengthening communication with the customer,
- Performing function-based authorizations in the organization instead of taking decisions from a single center,
- Reducing the unit costs of the products and personalizing them,
- Flexibility to provide a noticeable change in the volume of production,
- Working with agile suppliers,
- Conducting business analysis meticulously,
- Collaborating with competitors when necessary,
- Strengthening the communication network in the organization,
- Employees being well trained, skilled and experienced.

Agility is seen as one of the basic strategies in today's enterprises where competition is intense and it is possible to list the characteristics of enterprises in agile production, which is frequently applied by enterprises in order to provide competitive advantage (Baki, 2003);

- Concurrency in all activities in the organization should be considered,
- In-service training of employees should be made continuous,
- The organization should be sensitive to its customers,
- Organization employees should be considered as a value of the enterprise,
- The organization should be able to authorize its employees and bring them to the qualification to be authorized,
- Organization should be relevant and sensitive to the environment of the organization,
- The organization must have accessible and available information,
- The organization should be positioned and design correctly from the first moment,

- Organization should pay attention to total quality management,
- Organization should recruit employees that have technology and leadership knowledge,
- The vision of the organization must be clear and consistent.

Organizations have to become agile to survive. This is a necessity in order to remain competitive in fast changing market conditions and customer demands.

In addition, an agile organization should have the following characteristics (Devor et al., 1997):

Adding value to the customer: Agile organization must add value not only to itself but also to its customers.

Cooperation in competition: Strategic cooperation in and around the enterprise should be one of the choices of agile businesses.

Expertise in the process of change or uncertainty: Agile businesses should be built with the flexibility to keep up with all uncertainties right from the start.

Agile organizations are also defined as the company that can best adapt to change. Being intertwined with change, giving importance to communication in the organization, giving importance to a certain speed and continuity in product delivery, keeping testing in the foreground, making simple plans are the characteristics of agile organizations (Hormozi, 2001).

By applying these administrative features, organizations take a step towards agility. Their dynamic employees, their flexible structure and their ability to make quick decisions and to respond quickly lead them to the agile organization class.

The agility of any organization helps to combat variables that cannot be controlled. In this context, agility is defined as an ability to affect the growth and development of organizations in environments where unforeseen and continuous changes begin to spread (Maskell, 2001).

Agility is of vital importance when a strategy has been developed with consideration. Agility of an organization also allows for faster response to customer demands that can often vary, shortening production times, avoiding waste, increasing the efficiency of the use of expensive resources, producing more personalized products and expanding the product range (Candan et al., 2017).

Agility basically has four dimensions, and the ability of an organization to become agile depends on these four basic dimensions. These;

- The organization provides the customer with as much value as possible,
- Cooperating with other enterprises in order to increase competitiveness,
- Ensuring the structure to grow and grow even in situations where change and competition are uncertain,
- Increasing the scope and knowledge of the employees connected to the organization

There are three main factors to achieve agility. These are (Ambrose and Morello, 2004):

Awareness: The organization must understand changing market and competition conditions, changing technology. In order to foresee the uncertainties that may be experienced in the organization and to communicate more effectively, awareness of the organizations should be increased.

Flexibility: Organizations are in a position to respond to a wide range of requests, and to create funds for existing or new models, benefiting from external sources in terms of human resources are the factors that shape and direct the flexibility of the organization.

Table 1. Organizational characteristics of agile organizations

Administrative Basis	Features
Authority	Distributed information and control Less authority levels Less commitment to authority and control Commitment and loyalty to the project group Project based authorization Change of authority through project change
Rules and Procedures	Fewer rules and procedures Edit a low-level image Fluid role definitions Informal organization
Coordination	Informal and personal coordination Duties and authorization in decision making Network communication Targeted
Structure	Flat, horizontal, matrix, network or virtual organization structure Teamwork, cross-functional connections Functional and interdepartmental flexible boundaries
Human Resources	Staff empowerment Personnel participation Business expansion Business enrichment Autonomy in decision making Access to knowledge and experience Team work Multifunctional tools Multidisciplinary skills Labor development and education Differentiation and variety development

Source: Sherehiy, Karwowski, Layer, A Review of Enterprise Agility: Concepts, Frameworks and attributes, International Journal of Industrial Ergonomics, 37, 2007, 445-460

Production: Changes in organizational structure, competitive conditions, technological developments and adaptation times are seen as uncertain market variables that will increase both production and agility of enterprises. Good management of this process will contribute to agile organizations.

What distinguishes agile organizations from other organizations are as follows;

In this study, it is aimed to stress the importance of agility approach in banking sector which is perceived as the most difficult sector to be agile since it is a line of business carried out under heavy laws, regulations and audits, where process management is intense, every business / transaction is documented, traces are created compulsorily and managed with fixed targets, budgets and plans annually.

COMPETITION IN BANKING SECTOR IN GLOBALIZATION ERA

Competition is often considered as a positive factor for most sectors that promotes innovation, improving productivity and supply quality. However, there are different opinions in the literature regarding the impact of competition in the banking sector. The competition-fragility view advocates the idea that high competition in the banking sector can increase the financial instability and fragility of banks. In the highly competitive banking sector, bank managers may be willing to undertake high-risk operations

Table 2. Features that distinguish agile organizations from others

Features	Explanation
Speed	Fast detection, fast analysis, fast decision, fast implementation, fast results, fast production, fast distribution are indispensable priorities.
Flexibility	Flexible organizations build a flexible structure, act flexible, offer flexible products to their customers, see themselves as an option creator.
Customer Focused	Direct, sincere and deep relationship and communication with the customer is the main strategy. Customer focused organizations want to be the first to know what customers want.
Ability to Observe	They perceive market changes, opportunities and threats, changes in customer demands in real time, instantly.
Quick Decisiom Making	This kind of organizations allow immediate decision-making by authorizing the person to implement the decision.
Tendency to Change and Experiment	They do not tolerate fault. They create an innovative identity, periodically renew themselves, show interest in the different.
Use of Technology	They adapt the newest or best technology to their work.
Continuous Measurement of Process and Human Performance	In such organizations, the determining factor is performance, not seniority, and real-time, fresh information is analyzed in order to reach a conclusion. For measurement, not manual documents, but technology is used, objective measurement is very important.
Action Oriented	They perceive that not only knowing something, but also applying that knowledge to work would bring benefits and success.
Result Oriented	They give great importance to finishing work. Nothing replaces success, results. The best job for them is the finished job.

Source: Sekman ve Utku (2009), Kurumsal Ataleti Yenmek, 6. Baskı, Alfa Yayınların, 43-44

to meet their profit objectives. In other words, in the view of competition-fragility, competition erodes the market forces of banks, decreases profit margins and decreases market values. This may encourage banks to pursue more risky policies to protect their old profits (Keeley, 1990).Examples of risky policies include taking more credit risk in the loan portfolio and lowering the capital level. These more risky policies can increase NPL ratios and lead to bankruptcy (Jimenez et al., 2013).

On the other hand, it is argued that the competition in the banking literature enables banks to use their resources more efficiently and the inspection and supervision mechanism becomes more effective. It is also stated that the likelihood of loss from non-performing loans is lower (Petersen and Rajan, 1995). In contrast, in non-competitive markets, bank managers are allowed to avoid problems; thus, costs cannot be controlled which results in banks operating with low efficiency (Pagano, 1993; Berger and Hannan, 1998).

The competition-stability view suggests that in a highly market banking market where the number of banks is low, banks may increase their bank portfolio risks because they want to create more profit margins than credit interest rates. In this case, customers must pay a higher cost for borrowing, which may increase the likelihood of an increase in non-performing loans (Boyd and De Nicoló, 2005). Depending on this point, high competition can have an impact on the cost of capital and companies and individuals can reach lower interest rates, increase the profitability of investment projects, reduce credit risks and ultimately contribute to financial stability.

According to "the competition-efficiency view" adopted by the effective structure hypothesis proposed by Demsetz (1973), the increase in competition forces banks to minimize costs and provide services at lower prices, and consequently an increase in profitability is provided. Padoa-Schioppa (2001) stated that in a competitive environment, the banking system would be stronger and more resistant to shocks.

Although there are different views on the competition in the banking industry about whether or not competition increases the efficiency of organizations, the existence of fierce competition in the sector is a common view. The question is most probably how the players in the sector can have competitive advantage in the race. In this study, the solution is proposed to be gaining agility which requires companies to pay attention to teamwork, collaborative management, customer relationship management, project management, virtual technologies, new product development, product diversification, and so on.

THE CASE OF GARANTI BANK IN TURKEY

General Information about Garanti Bank

Founded in 1946, Garanti Bank, as of December 31, 2017 with its total consolidated assets 356.3 billion Turkish liras (94.4 billion US dollars) has become Turkey's second largest private bank. Garanti, operates in all business lines of the banking sector including corporate, commercial, SME, retail, private and investment banking, and payment systems, it is also an integrated financial services group with its international subsidiaries in the Netherlands and Romania, as well as its financial subsidiaries in the areas of private pension and life insurance, leasing, factoring, investment and portfolio management. (Annual report 2017, Garanti Bank)

As of December 31, 2017, with a widespread distribution network consisting of 937 branches in Turkey, seven branches in Cyprus, one in Malta and eight branches abroad, one representative in London, Düsseldorf and Shanghai, and more than 15 million customers with 19,000 employees meets financial need of its customers. (Annual report 2017, Garanti Bank)

Garanti Bank Provides an uninterrupted experience and ease of integrated channels with its more than 5,000 ATMs with the latest technological infrastructure, award-winning Call Center, internet, mobile and social banking platforms. Aiming to achieve sustainable growth by creating value for all its stakeholders, Garanti strives to provide its customers with products and services that meet their needs with a transparent, understandable and responsible approach. Its competent and dynamic human resources, uninterrupted investments in technology, and innovative products and services offered without compromising quality and customer satisfaction make Garanti a leader in the Turkish banking sector. (Annual report 2017, Garanti Bank)

Garanti's ever-evolving business model is successful thanks to responsible and sustainable development, customer experience, employee happiness, digitalization, optimum use of capital and productivity-oriented strategies. Having world-class integrated management of financial and non-financial risks, Garanti creates sustainable value for all of its stakeholders thanks to effective risk management and "organizational agility" in capturing new opportunities. (Annual report 2017, Garanti Bank)

Strategies of Garanti Bank

Human Resource:

Garanti Bank is conscious of the fact that it is the human resource behind all the advances, it is the fundamental building blocks of the whole system to constantly add young and creative minds to Garanti to train and develop them, to provide the employees with the opportunities to show their talents, to present opportunities, to see their success and to reward them.

Human resources policy of Garanti is to give importance and priority to people, to invest continuously, to allocate the necessary resources for trainings, to give priority to rise within the institution, to implement programs for this purpose, to develop human resources systems, to provide participation by pioneering an open communication environment, to exhibit fair and objective attitude and develop practices in international standards.

The Bank and its employees observe fair behavior in business relations without making any distinctions on language, race, gender, political ideology, philosophical belief, religion, sect and similar, sexual orientation, family responsibilities, disability, age, health status, union membership and the like. Knowing the business objectives of Garanti, Human Resources department uses different measurement and valuation tools and methods, which are built on competencies, are objective, position-specific and developed in line with the needs, in order to place the right person on the right task as well as being close to the business lines and the field.

On the other hand, Garanti's performance system measures the performance of employees based on the objectives and the realization of these objectives. Systematic premiums and performance models are important and effective management tools. In this context, criteria such as customer satisfaction, service quality and effective management are among the main factors that affect performance-based payments as well as the Bank's numerical targets. (Annual report 2017, Garanti Bank)

Innovative Products and Services:

While the global banking sector tries to defend its market share against increasing market types, it requires both strategy-driven and technology-driven development to meet consumer expectations. In order to digitize basic business processes and to better prepare the banking structures for the future, great importance is given to re-evaluation of corporate structures and internal capabilities. This transformation shows that the desire of banks to become "digital bank" has increased. While innovation has become more important, developing new solutions that benefit from data, advanced analysis, digital technologies and new distribution platforms has never been more important.

Garanti Bank was able to achieve the following successes by using the developing technology;

-All-in-house developed information technology solutions,
-Uninterrupted processing capability and infrastructure security,
-Dynamic and advanced technology providing fast customer service time,
-Uninterrupted investment in technology since the 90s,
-Data-based and agile decision-making processes,
-Data consistency, the reliability and efficiency in the production reports.

With its investments in digital platforms, Garanti Bank aims to continue to lead the digital transformation by offering its customers a unique experience, ease of operation and pioneering solutions. While expanding its digital customer base, it aims to increase the share of digital channels in its sales. In its 2018 annual report, Garanti Bank announced some statistics to show its success in digital platforms. Some of them are;

-Mobile Application: According to Forrester's Global Mobile Banking Functionality Benchmark Study, 2017 based on customers experience, Garanti Bank became the most successful in Europe in terms of mobile application. In the same year, statistically, 60 percent of financial transactions excluding cash were made through mobile application.

-Internet: Garanti Bank offers its customers more than 500 different transaction through Internet. Except for cash, 24 percent of financial transactions were made through internet in 2017.

-ATM: In 2017, through Garanti ATMs the rate of deposit to withdrawal rate is 102%. Garanti Bank also provides services to non-bank customers with the transactions which do not require cards.

-Social Media:

In 2017, Garanti Bank became the most followed financial institution in Europe with 5.3 million followers.

It is active on 17 different platforms with 50 accounts.

-Call Center: In 2017, 77.4 million customers were able to be communicated and while call response time was approximately 81 seconds in the sector, Garanti could decrease it to 33 seconds. (Annual report 2018, Garanti Bank)

Customer Experience Management:

Customer experience has always been a cornerstone of Garanti's strategy. Customer experience is even more important in today's world, which is changing at a dizzying pace with the momentum created by technology. Digital business models set new standards in all commercial areas, while the boundaries between sectors disappear. Solutions that make customers happy can become the new norm. Moreover, these norms apply not only to one sector but to all sectors,

Garanti Bank's customer experience strategies are a long-standing and robust strategy that combines technology which has become the most fundamental determinants of our era and human elements. Customers' needs and expectations are constantly changing in line with technological advances; however, the common denominator remains the same. People want to experience time-saving, short and trouble-free journeys, smart solutions that improve their lives and personal touches that they find fun. It is this understanding that shapes all of Garanti's customer experience management efforts.

Garanti's success in implementing its customer experience strategy is based on four core competencies: customer understanding, designed philosophy, empathy culture and measurement systems.

Customer Understanding: Today's rapidly changing world requires customers to understand the needs, expectations, thoughts and emotions that are constantly in motion. Therefore, Garanti Bank uses different methods such as discovery research, social listening, qualitative and quantitative research, instant feedback to develop a deeper understanding of customers. In addition, customers can send all kinds of feedback through the telephone line answered only by the dedicated teams or via e-mail, websites and social media.

In 2017, Garanti Bank received more than 850,000 feedback from its customers and reviewed it extensively. Again last year, the number of employees' suggestions was 1,313. It continuously analyzes the data pool enriched by customers and employees by using the latest technologies and turns them into actionable insights.

-Designed Philosophy: In order to improve the customer experience, not only the individual contact moments, but the whole journey from head to toe needs to be improved. Every step of designing customer journeys is experienced through the eyes of customers and solutions are produced to meet the current needs and expectations at the highest level possible. The journey perspective requires that digital and physical channels be considered in the same context to provide a consistent and uninterrupted experience.

-Empathy Culture: In order for customers to experience products and services as they are designed, it is very important that the customer experience practice is embedded in the corporate culture. For this reason, employees adopt the idea of customers in their daily work and they need to understand their needs and emotions. In line with this principle, Garanti Bank launched a program called "Empati Garanti" at the end of 2016. "Garanti Empati" offers a platform that ensures all Garanti employees are constantly informed about the Bank's customer experience projects, that they have knowledge of good practices both within the organization and around the world, that they have access to tools such as trainings, tips and information to improve themselves, and that they share empathy stories with other employees to create new ones. In this way, the platform aims to inspire its workers to empathy the customers.

-Measurement Systems: Garanti Bank measures the impact of efforts to improve the customer experience in various ways. One of the most important of these is post-service surveys for all employees who are in contact with customers and all critical points in contact. In this way, employees can monitor customer feedback on a daily basis so that they can take quick action to improve their experience.

Optimum Capital Use:

Optimum capital utilization is the capital structure that minimizes the cost of capital and the maximum value of the enterprise. There is no exact formula to determine the optimal capital structure of firms. The fact that an increase in the borrowing level of the firm in the similar business risk category makes a disproportionately large increase in capital cost may be an indication that the borrowing has reached the optimal level. As a result, while borrowing to a certain level is meaningful, borrowing after a certain level can disrupt the optimal capital structure. In this context, while focusing on disciplined and sustainable growth, Garanti Bank aims to maximize the value it creates by using its capital effectively and to maintain its commitment to sound asset quality.

Responsible and Sustainable Development:

In order to achieve responsible and sustainable development, Garanti Bank continues to implement its advanced corporate governance model that reinforces the core values it adopts and aims to act with the principles of trust, accuracy, accountability and transparency towards all its stakeholders.

Furthermore, at the same time, it proves once again the importance it attaches to agility by managing financial and non-financial risks integrated with world standards and providing effective risk management.

Another strategy implemented for this purpose is to create value for the society by focusing on social investment programs and taking into account the principles of impact-oriented investment and creating common value with the loans it provides. At the same time, Garanti Bank aims to be a bank that leads to positive change through strategic partnerships that it has established without being bound to a single plan by adopting the principle of being flexible under changing conditions. (Annual Report 2018, Garanti Bank,9

RECOMMENDATIONS

When competition resulting from globalization and the case of Garanti Bank has been taken into consideration, the necessity for banks to adopt the changing trends has been stressed once again. Within the frame work of agility, banks need to simply its operating process with what is called "lean management" and by doing so, they will have changed their main banking systems in a flexible and easy-to-manage and modular way. Building modern banking practices on state of the latest technology provides banks with a phased, strategic transition that allows them to develop operations, reduce costs and accelerate growth.

Traditional banking is a thing of the past, now banking should be based on agility. If banks do not launch new products and services as quickly as possible, their chances of existence will be greatly reduced. If they fail to adapt to the market; they should seriously consider replacing the existing back office system that is complex and far from flexible, which prevents their business from succeeding.

Banks, in order to adapt to the changes brought by the new market and sector; need to begin to redefine their main activities. What most bank managers want today is; to create more agile organizations according to their competitiveness and to find a place in the market rapidly. This is possible by replacing outdated approaches with real and reliable technology solutions.

Furthermore, corporate culture is also important in terms of corporate transformation. However, the key to this issue is that regulatory or existing units of banks responding to external audit institutions should be able to understand the concept of agility well, learn the basic values, assimilate and be able to adapt these regulations within the scope of their expertise.

The transformation within the organization may require time and process, in order to achieve this, banks should form project teams that can manage and accelerate the agile transformation of the bank. Teams should be formed as cross-functional as possible, with a combination of business lines and technology teams. The units from which the team players will come should be shaped according to the need for the development of the project or product. In the agile transformation process, there should be also coach consultants who help the team and team members to adopt and develop agile methods and thinking. With this method, banks can engage all the members within the organizations as well as customers in the process and it will enable more smooth transition in the end.

FUTURE RESEARCH DIRECTIONS

The purpose of the study was to stress the importance of agility in banking sector. The subject is sensitive and essential when the rigid structure of banking and finance system is taken into consideration. In the following studies, with the help of different methodologies such as fuzzy logic, the importance of agility on the level of each department of banks could be analyzed and discussed.

CONCLUSION

Along with globalization, national competition conditions as well as international competition conditions change rapidly. Organizations operate in a dynamic, constantly changing, competitive environment affected by customers. At the same time, shortening of product life span, increasing product variety and rapidly changing technology have an effect on the enterprises. Especially the change in customer expectations forces companies to develop new management approaches. Companies that can adapt and respond to these changes, in other words, develop and implement agile management strategies, will be able to survive in the future. The most important question for the future is whether firms will abandon their old management understanding and adopt the agile management system and structure. In order to be successful in applying the agile management system, companies should have well-trained workforce and they must follow the technological developments and adapt to themselves very quickly. In addition, talented managers and employees who are prone to teamwork are of great importance in this process.

When it comes to banking sector, the fact that the services and products in banking are more or less the same in every bank, that they can be easily substituted and easily accessible leads to initiatives to create value in the marketing field. For this reason, value creation can only be achieved through the right strategies.

Businesses need to design new processes, activities and studies by focusing on the future in order to gain competitive advantage. Choosing the right strategy starts with setting goals and objectives in particular. The next step is to develop action-specific action plans to achieve these goals.

In this scope, organizations operating in banking sector, need to be agile to be able to survive in this competition. However, agility requires individuals and interactions rather than processes and tools, it requires services and products that work instead of extensive services and documentation, rather than negotiation with customers there needs to be cooperation with them, it also requires stretching to varying needs rather than blindly adhering to a plan.

Although, one of the sectors which is thought to be the most difficult to be agile is the banking and finance sector, Garanti Bank, which has been operating in Turkish Banking sector since 1946, with its annual reports, could prove that the role of agility in banking sector cannot be underestimated. Strategies, Garanti bank has applied to be agile consist of adapting most of financial transactions to the most advanced technology, valuing both the concerns of its customers and employees, managing financial and non-financial risks integrated with world standards and ensuring effective risk management, teamwork model within the organization and innovative and inspiring services and products.

As a result of the case study of Garanti Bank, it was found out that like other sectors, organizations operating in banking need to move to a new model called "agile" in order to adapt to changing business conditions and provide competitive advantage. This model envisages changes in all units of a company for teamwork, collaboration, change compliance and simplification of processes.

ACKNOWLEDGMENT

This study was derived from Kağan Cenk Mızrak's PHD thesis written in Beykent University.

REFERENCES

Akman, G., & Keskin, G. A. (2012). İmalat Firmalarında Çevik Üretimin Algılanma Seviyesinin Değerlendirilmesi. *Dumlupınar Üniversitesi Fen Bilimleri Enstitüsü Dergisi, 28*, 53–66.

Ambrose, C., & Morello, D. (2004). Designing the agile organization: design principles and practices. *Strategic Analysis Report, 21*, 7532.

Apilioğulları, L. (2016). *Yalın Dönüşüm*. Aura Kitapları.

Araza, A., & Aslan, G. (2016). *Yönetimde Yeni Paradigmalar*. Nobel Yayınevi.

Baki, B., 21. Yüzyılın Üretim Paradigması: Çevik Üretim, İktisadi ve İdari Bilimler Dergisi, 17, 1-2, 291-305, 2003.

Baysan, S., & Durmuşoğlu, B. (2015). Systematic literature review for lean product development principles and tools. *Sigma Mühendislik ve Fen Bilimleri Dergisi, 33*(3), 305–323.

Berger, A. N., & Hannan, T. H. (1998). The efficiency cost of market power in the banking industry: A test of the "quiet life" and related hypotheses. *The Review of Economics and Statistics, 80*(3), 454–465. doi:10.1162/003465398557555

Birgün, S., Gülen, K. G., & Özkan, K. (2006). *Yalın Üretime Geçiş Sürecinde Değer Akışı Haritalama Tekniğinin Kullanılması, İstanbul Ticaret Üniversitesi Fen Bilimleri Dergisi, 5*(9), 47–59.

Bititci, U., Turner, T., & Ball, P. (1999). The viable business structure for managing agility. *International Journal of Agile Management Systems, 1*(3), 190–199. doi:10.1108/14654659910296571

Boyd, J. H., & De Nicolo, G. (2005). The theory of bank risk taking and competition revisited. *The Journal of Finance, 60*(3), 1329–1343. doi:10.1111/j.1540-6261.2005.00763.x

Candan, A., Çankır, B., & Seker, S. E. (2017)Organizasyonlarda Çeviklik. *Ansiklopedi, 4*(3), 3–9.

Demsetz, H. (1973). Industry structure, market rivalry, and public policy. *The Journal of Law & Economics, 16*(1), 1–9. doi:10.1086/466752

Devor, R., Graves, R., & Mills, J. J. (1997). Agile manufacturing research: accomplishments and opportunities. *IIE Transactions, 29*(10), 813–823. doi:10.1080/07408179708966404

Garanti Bankası. (n.d.). Retrieved from https://surdurulebilirlik.garantibbva.com.tr/

Göçmen Yağcılar, G. (2011). *Türk bankacılık sektörünün rekabet yapısının analizi*. Ankara, Turkey: BDDK.

Gök, A. C., & Özdemir, A. (2011). Lojistik Regresyon Analizi ile Banka Sektör Paylarinin Tahminlenmesi. *Dokuz Eylül Üniversitesi İşletme Fakültesi Dergisi, 12*(1), 43–51.

Gunasekaran, A. (1999). Agile manufacturing: A framework for research and development. *International Journal of Production Economics, 62*(2), 87–105. doi:10.1016/S0925-5273(98)00222-9

Hormozi, A. M. (2001). Agile manufacturing: The next logical step. Benchmarking. *International Journal (Toronto, Ont.), 8*(2), 132–143.

İleri, Y. Y., Soylu, Y., Bir Rekabet Üstünlüğü Olarak Çeviklik Kavramı ve Örgüt Yapısına Olası Etkileri, Selçuk Üniversitesi Sosyal Bilimler Dergisi, 12, 1-2, 13-28, 2010.

Jayaram, J., Kannan, V. R., & Tan, K. C. (2004). Influence of initiators on supply chain value creation. *International Journal of Production Research, 42*(20), 4377–4399. doi:10.1080/00207540410001716516

Jiménez, G., Lopez, J. A., & Saurina, J. (2013). How does competition affect bank risk-taking? *Journal of Financial Stability*, *9*(2), 185–195. doi:10.1016/j.jfs.2013.02.004

Keeley, M. C. (1990). Deposit insurance, risk, and market power in banking. *The American Economic Review*, 1183–1200.

Kocakoç, M. (2008). *Montaj Süreçlerinde Yalın Üretim Verileri Analizi*. Doktora Tezi, Dokuz Eylül Üniversitesi.

Liker, J. K. (2010). Toyota's lost its quality edge? Not so fast. *Business Week*, 28.

Maskell, B. (2001). The age of agile manufacturing. *Supply Chain Management*, *6*(1), 1, 5–11. doi:10.1108/13598540110380868

Nagel, R., & Bhargava, P. (1994). Agility: The ultimate requirement for world - class manufacturing performance. *National Productivity Review*, *13*(3), 331–340. doi:10.1002/npr.4040130304

Padoa-Schioppa, T. (2001). Bank competition: A changing paradigm. *Review of Finance*, *5*(1-2), 13–20. doi:10.1023/A:1012612610825

Pagano, M. (1993). Financial markets and growth: An overview. *European Economic Review*, *37*(2-3), 613–622. doi:10.1016/0014-2921(93)90051-B

Petersen, M. A., & Rajan, R. G. (1995). The effect of credit market competition on lending relationships. *The Quarterly Journal of Economics*, *110*(2), 407–443. doi:10.2307/2118445

Sekman ve Utku (2009). Kurumsal Ataleti Yenmek, 6. Baskı, Alfa Yayınların, 43-44.

Sherehiy, K., Karwowski, W., & Layer, J. K. (2007). Layer, a review of enterprise agility: concepts, frameworks and attributes. *International Journal of Industrial Ergonomics*, *37*(5), 445–460. doi:10.1016/j.ergon.2007.01.007

Womack, J. P., Byme, A. P., Flume, O. J., Kaplan, S. G., & Toussaint, J. (2005). Going lean in health care. *Institute for Healthcare Improvement, 7,* 1-20. Retrieved from https://www.garantibbvainvestor-relations.com/en/images/annualreport/pdf/GBFR17_eng_FULL.pdf

KEY TERMS AND DEFINITIONS

ATM: Automatic Teller Machine
NPL: Non Performing Loan

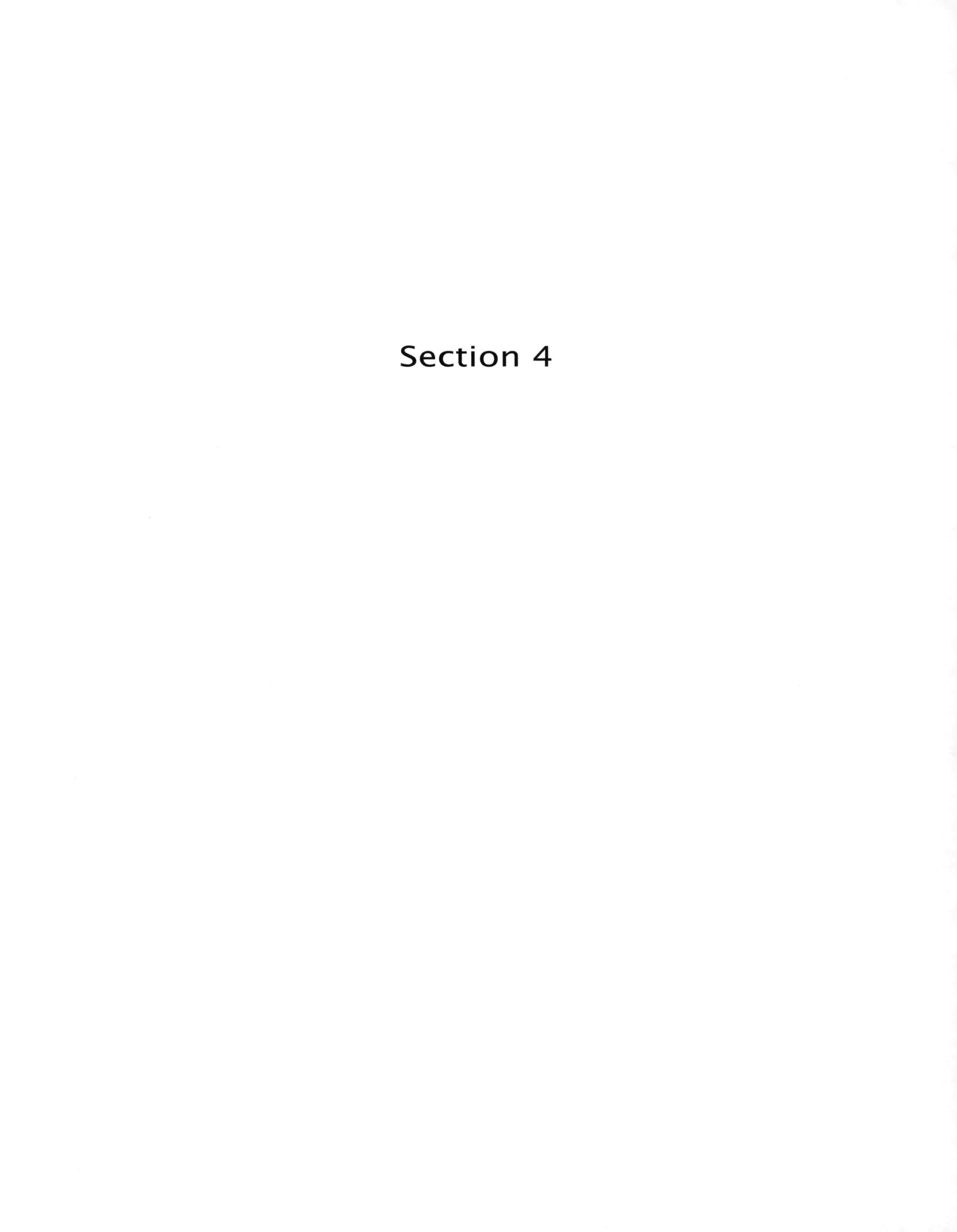

Section 4

Chapter 16
The Importance of PESTEL Analysis for Environmental Scanning Process

Tuğberk Çitilci
Nisantasi University, Turkey

Murat Akbalık
Marmara University, Turkey

ABSTRACT

Strategy and tactic are two inseparable dynamics for organization which can be the same as a chess game. Organizations' theoretical infinite life cycle needs well-established strategic management. To create competitive advantage among competitors, top management of organizations must scan environmental factors very carefully. Without environmental scanning process organization can be viewed as blind and deaf in an ecosystem which definitely ends with shutdown of activity. Environmental scanning has two parts; internal environmental analysis and external analysis which aim to create early signals for organization. Internal analysis deals with micro-based factors which can be controlled by organization whereas external analysis universe is larger and wider when compared to internal analysis. External analysis covers all the factors such as political, economic, social, technological, environmental, and legal, which an organization cannot control and cannot affect. This type of analysis can be named as top-down approach analysis aims to create competitive advantage.

INTRODUCTION

The word origin of strategy comes from ancient Greeks which is the combination of "stratos" and "ago". Evolution of strategy backs to 400 - 200 B.C. and depends on Chinese Sun Tzu's "The art of war". Use of strategy has a very large universe which covers lots of disciplines. One of these discipline is Strategic Management for business organizations. The main assumption of business organizations is having an infinite life cycle. With this assumption firms need the best strategic management process. The process

DOI: 10.4018/978-1-7998-2559-3.ch016

The Importance of PESTEL Analysis for Environmental Scanning Process

can start from delineating environmental analysis and can be classified as external environmental and internal environmental factors. External factors cannot be controlled and replaced by firms so there is a need of well –managed/ designed top down approach in order to adapt these factor for infinite life cycle. External environmental analysis process can be categorized by scanning, monitoring, forecasting and assessing dynamics.

Actors of this ecosystem are competitors, customers, suppliers, regulatory authorities and social/ political etc. As a whole ecosystem external and internal analysis cannot be separated from each other. This can be summarized as from macro analysis to industry analysis.

Development of strategic management starts from military literature and transformed into business organizations in 1950 – 1960 periods.

Starting with brief history of strategy and environmental analysis let it come to main purpose of this book chapter. As planned chapter will cover detailed external analysis on behalf of PESTEL analysis. (Different variations for PESTEL can be mentioned). It is the combination of political, economic, social, technological, environmental and legal factors.

PEST concept was mentioned in "Scanning the business environment" book by Francis J. Aguilar. After his contribution, PEST analysis started non-stop development process.

Authors briefly explain history, evolution and analysis process of PESTEL analysis on behalf of these factors.

Examples of some subtitles of main topics;

- *Political factors* can cover subtitles such as; tax laws, government policies, political risks, elections and stability/instability, trade restrictions etc.
- *Economic factors* can cover subtitles such as; central bank monetary policies, fiscal policies, growth, interest rates, Exchange rates, inflation, wages and taxes etc.
- *Social factors* can cover subtitles such as; Demographics/population, NGO, health/insurance system etc.
- *Technological factors* can cover subtitles such as; innovations, computer systems, copyrights etc.
- *Environmental factors* can cover subtitles such as; climate/weather/nature, raw materials, pollution etc.
- *Legal factors* can cover subtitles such as; labor laws, legislation, consumer rights/law etc.

Subtitles as mentioned above will be detailed during book chapter process.

Topics will go further with details of PESTEL components and searching for main questions about analysis. These questions can be what is the pros and cons of analysis? How to setup template and setup variations of analysis or what is the difference of PESTEL from well-known SWOT analysis (Strengths, Weaknesses, Opportunities and Threats) and other well-known commonly used strategic management tools.

At the end of chapter, further topics and debates about PESTEL model will be discussed in order to support academic literature

The Concept of Strategic Management

Strategy

The strategy word comes from ancient Greeks with military concept. The interesting part is how military approach transforms to corporate environment and changes strategy to business level. The process of transformation is a way of art which combines social and economic factors at the first stage of strategy. As an only word strategy sounds like simple to explicate and characterize but it is not as can be seen due to its complex methodology. In other words strategy has no exact single definite definition in literature. Strategy concept keep in touch with tactics, aims, goals, visions and missions again same question come to mind what is the definition of strategy? Or what is strategy?

Literature scan gives different answers for exact definition of strategy.

- von Neumann & Morgenstern (1947), strategy is a major part of operations by organizations based on particular situation
- Ansoff (1965), the strategy is a bulk of principles of making decisions specified by competitive advantage, product - market range, synergy and growth vector.
- Ackoff (1974), the strategy is interested in long-term goals and style of chasing long term goals which has an impact on the system.
- Mintzberg (1979), the strategy as an influence factor, combines organization and organization's internal environmental and external environmental factors together.

Porter (1996) briefly explained that operational Effectiveness Is Not Strategy which is a breaking point for strategy misunderstood. In general effectiveness equals to strategy, in other word if system has effectiveness strategy is successful but these are totally different concepts. Porter takes effectiveness and strategy as a whole to achieve superior performance which firms want to create.

Strategy word has conflict with other concepts causes from not having exact definition. Simple example of this is relation between strategy and tactic. These two words sound like as same definition but meaning works in different ways. Strategy focuses on long term achievements while tactic helps in short term in order to achieve long term based strategy which is similar to a chess game.

Strategy can be named as the way of art which combines long terms targets with pro-active efficient management taking into consideration of huge internal and external environment as a whole.

Mintzberg (1987) introduced "Five Ps for strategy" with perspective, pattern, ploy, position and plan. He stated that strategy has two critical characteristics which are made in advance of the actions and developed consciously and purposefully. Five Ps gives the definitions of strategy concept.

Hierarchy of strategy is a combination of layers starting with base layer functional strategy then goes up by business strategy and corporate strategy. Hierarchy plays a crucial role on top-down or bottom-up analyze approaches.

The concept of strategic management deals with competitive advantage maximization under strategy methodology. Strategic environmental analysis which named as SEAN, starts with identification of vision, mission, objectives, goals, targets, environmental (internal and external) scanning, strategic thinking, strategic management, strategy formulation / setup, strategic planning, strategy implementation, evolution and ends with control. This process of strategic management is crucial to catch edge of competitive advantage in industry.

The Importance of PESTEL Analysis for Environmental Scanning Process

Under "SEAN", hierarchy of internal needs start with vision which is named as future position of organization in business industry. Vision also viewed as the dream of future, gives the motivation to achieve optimum competitive advantage. In different perspectives vision can be named as the most complex base layer of hierarchy but sometimes complex definition is insufficient to address the situation. The vision is the key starting point of everything because of this importance to set up vision perfectly is sine qua non. Process continues with deleting "v" letter from vision word, adding "m" letter and adding extra "s" to create mission word.

Mission is the purpose of an organization which examines why the organization exits in business industry. Huge universe of goals and objectives of the organization relies on mission.

Vision and mission must be taken into consideration as whole concepts which are very difficult to separate each other. In literature ongoing debates about vision and mission order raises with the question of which one comes first? In general beliefs base layer starts with vision and there will be no mission without vision. This sounds like fact without question mark but is it seems like that or can it be opened to argument. The mixture of vision and mission concepts cannot easily and clearly separate from each other which is a situation like chicken or Egg? Dilemma. Objectives come as outputs of planned activities and goals named as intermediate outputs of planned activities in short term with relation of objectives.

The Identification of Environment

The most important part of this process is the perfectly define what is environment and how to understand it? Environment is a huge universe of internal and external environments that puts the scanning facility at the number one level.

Environment surrounds organization/corporate like a cell membrane, it is not possible to escape from truth for organization.

Environmental analysis plays a crucial role on corporate's life-cycle. It is very difficult to define environment internal and external factors as an only one sentence due to it's complexity and deep universe.

Ecosystem has ongoing and updating process because of this system must be well understood and combined within strategy as a milestone.

Environment and organization must be think as a whole, impossible to separate these two dynamic because of this approach organization must adapt to environment.

Organization and actors behave differently from each other to different environmental factors.

At the environmental analysis part, management experience and success comes to action with top management staff such as strategist, CEO, consultant, board of directors, managers etc. Also these actors crucial for internal environment analysis.

The beginning point of strategic management starts with organization/corporate ecosystem analysis which is can be defined as environment. Large universe of environment covers internal and external environment factors. Internal environment can be viewed as micro –level factors which effect the organization dynamics. External environment universe is larger than internal environment with macro – level factors.

The Essentials of Environmental Analysis

Environmental analysis is a concept of filter all the following information from internal environmental sources and external environmental sources. The complex structure of how to identify which information or data crucial for organization? This raises the need of optimal essentials of environmental analysis.

The essentials of environmental analysis grouped as 4 activities, which are *"scanning"*, *"monitoring"*, *"forecasting" and "assessing"*.

Scanning: The scanning process is the most important part of environmental analysis, organization get lot of information and data from internal and external analysis to understand what is going on around. Inputs catch from scanning activity setup road map of strategy.

Scanning modes are named as; specific (ad-hoc), regular and continuous. Due to complexity of scanning concept it is very difficult to discount scanning into 3 modes but these are the well-known ones to identify.

Scanning activities give facilitation to organization to setup early signal from internal and external environment threats. With potential early signals (not to possible create accurate perfect signal alert!) organization investigate what is the potential threats or what is the weaknesses on vision/mission/objectives/goals. This guard system sounds like perfectly but organization must be act very carefully because environment ecosystem is so complex to setup easily.

Monitoring: The second activity of environmental analysis is monitoring which is related the base layer of scanning. After scanning process with creation of early signal mechanism organization has a protection from environment. But in order to sustainable protection organization carefully make observation about environmental internal and external analysis changes. Monitoring complements scanning activity with performance monitoring and situation monitoring activities.

Monitoring asks questions related to how, who, what, which, where and when to find answers These are;

- How to monitor?
- Who is monitoring?
- What to monitor?
- Which factors to monitor?
- Where are the factors to monitor?

Monitoring activity sometimes confused with evolution activity which is defined as a periodic check list of applied plans/strategies etc. Evaluation simply focuses on outcomes of actions

Forecasting: After scanning and monitoring activities inputs/information and data become more meaningful for organization and management in order to make assumption internally and externally. Forecasting is set of assumption in order to take action about future internal and external environment factors changes. Despite definition of forecasting, it is a very hard and complex methodology to sustain accuracy which makes it as a way of art.

Starting from ancient time's human beings has indispensable aim to know future events. When combine future and strategic management these are the same aims to achieve while having lots of black swans and unknowns.

Forecasting of environmental analysis deals with external analysis factors such as social, economic, political, technological, ethics and legal factors which have direct impact on organization future life cycle.

First of all organization and management staff must identify how to make accurate forecast for industry or business cycle. In this content expectation/guess/forecast definitions difference must be well understood. Forecast is based on more theoretical and numerical approaches but there is no exact one way solution to which forecast method or approach to use.

Forecasting as a crucial part of decision making must be informed about unexpected sudden events which named as black swans. In theoretical way, all inputs (information/data) create huge pool for organization to analyze setup and forecast on what is happening. This process has lack points due to proactive ecosystem.

Assessing: Scanning, monitoring and forecasting activities briefly explain huge information set for organization. Now with this knowledge organization is ready for shocks for this maybe it is too early to say yes without assessing activity. In different perspective activity defined as the importance of environmental factors changes by taking into consideration timing.

The Actors of Environmental Analysis

Strategic management process at the micro level analysis deals with actors at the internal environment. These actors are; competitors, customers, suppliers, industry intermediaries, regulatory authorities, and social/public/political actors.

From now on frequency of environment in chapter will sound more loudly. Organization's main aim to survive from this wild environment with achieving its long-term strategy road map. To achieve this layer of environment must be well-understood and well-analyzed. Without this approach life cycle of organization/corporate will be very short. A layer of environment starts with largest universe, which is the macro-environment, goes with industry/sector and competitors. The core part of this layers is organization/corporate which continuously adapts its self. Some special analysis tools can be used to examine environment with categorization process.

The main problem for environment is how to define it and what is the depth of ecosystem. This process can be start with scanning. The father this area named by Aguilar he mentioned environmental scanning's important for firms. His areas of external information approach based on five factors.

These are;

1. **Market tidings** ; Answer of what is going on market question with taking into consideration of customers, competitors, market dynamics, growth potential, pricing and structural changes
2. **Technical tidings** ; Focuses on product dynamics (problems, new products entrance, costs, licensing/patents
3. **Broad issues** ; Environmental factors/conditions, government policies
4. **Acquisition leads** ; Merger and acquisitions
5. **Other tidings** ; Suppliers, resources, available, miscellaneous

Academic literature of environmental scan started with Aguilar, process developed further by Miles&Snow (1974), Miles (1978) and Hambrick (1979) studies.

Hambrick, dissertation based on environmental scanning process with company management professionals. He examined the factors which affect executives "field of vision"

Under strategy the most important question is to identify which company/organization is unique and most successful in order to answer these complex questions environmental scanning comes to help. The exact answer of this question is company which has adapts the environment easily with efficient strategies.

Miles and Snow's book examined different methods & applications of strategic behaviors. Companies need to create their proactive adaptive strategies according to their own environmental Dynamics. This will create competition with other competitors and increase the chance of company's discrimination in area.

Miles & Snow further detailed solution of adaptive cycle problems by adding four new dimensions in content of competitive advantage

These are;

1. **Defender approach**: Focus on narrow product within environment, aims to achieve success with existing products. Status qua, conservative and focuses on existing products
2. **Prospector approach**: Entering markets with new products and more open on search and maybe defined as aggressive
3. **Analyzer approach**: Combines defender and prospector style. Cost analysis or optimization can be named as crucial part of this approach.
4. **Reactor approach**: Shortage of strategy causes not to catch competitive advantage and environmental adjustment unstable and inconsistent.

The study of Aguilar, examined more than 40 managers in chemistry sector, found that internal sources plays more crucial role in personal when compared to impersonal factors. Also small scale companies take internal sources more than the other companies.

Scanning process environment done by company's managers without a well-managed systematic outcomes from scanning comes from staff and internal interaction more efficient.

According to Aguilar (1967), managers get external information by some methods. These are specified as; undirected viewing, conditioned viewing, unofficial search and official search.

Keegan (1974), found similar results as Aguilar managers did not pay attention on systematic scanning methods

Road map for literature on environmental scan;

- Fahey & King (1977)
- Thomas (1980)
- Fahey & King & Narayanan (1981)
- Stubbart (1982)
- Diffenbach (1983)
- Jain (1984)
- Engledow & Lenz (1986)
- Preble, Rau & Reichel (1988)

As seen from the road map of literature, 1980 period raises as milestone studies which contributes the development of environmental scan

Aguilar's findings suggest that qualified managers depend more on external environmental information while top executives beware of internal environmental information.

The environmental scanning approach can be viewed as a parcel of strategic planning cycle usually allocate the external environmental factors into significant parts of sectors.

Company's survive depends on competitiveness and strategy Dynamics because of this environmental analysis plays a crucial role in other word it takes an x-ray of internal environment. Environmental scanning process simply understands what's going on industry and customers/suppliers needs.

Strategy without environmental scanning cannot be thinkable; it is a must requirement for firm.

Environmental scanning differs from small company to big company approaches. Some studies suggest small companies focus on more internal dynamics, whereas big companies rely more on Professional systems. But there is no exact redline separation between small versus big companies. Maybe this causes from company's different cultural/managerial differences. Strategy and environmental scanning can be defined as a part of puzzle which creates success of failure for firm's life cycle.

Environmental scanning process starts with information filter, comes from internal and external sources. This information is very unique for strategy development. Mangers need to exactly know which Dynamics/sources should be taken into consideration. In this part experience should play a crucial role. With this coming information company/management must adopt to environment because it is an inseparable part of whole environment. To achieve competitiveness this adaptation process is a *"sine qua non"* condition

Basically, strategy road map categories are as;

- Ansoff (1977), Matrix
- Miles & Snow (1978) The typology
- Porter (1980), Competitive Strategy
- Porter (1985), Competitive Advantage
- Porter (1986), Competition in Global Industries
- Porter (1987), From Competitive Advantage to Corporate Strategy
- Mintzberg (1988), Generic Strategies; Toward a Comprehensive Framework

Names and studies can be expended, but these are well known milestones of strategy development roadmap

Miles and Snow, typology systematic opened a new door for strategic management classification.

Also they focused on 3 fundamental problems; firstly the entrepreneurial problem, secondly the engineering problem and thirdly the administrative problem.

The ability of pro-active react to external environment changes/dynamics is a key issue for organization.

The Types of External Analysis Methods

Strategic Management Tools:

1. Porter's Five Forces
2. SWOT Analysis
3. Boston Consulting Group Growth Matrix
4. Value Chain Analysis

5. Balanced Score Card
6. PEST (EL) Analysis

Porter's Five Forces

Michael E. Porter focuses on competition in an industry with 5 basic competitive forces.

These forces are classified as; threat of new entrants, bargaining power of buyers, threat of substitute products or services, bargaining power of suppliers and rivalry among existing firms.

These factors must be well planned & managed because determines the profit potential for company in the industry.

SWOT (Strengths, Weakness, Opportunities and Threats) Analysis

SWOT analysis, which is created by Stanford University professor Alfred Humphrey, a well-known tool for strategy analysis.

SWOT analysis is a synthesis of strengths, weakness, opportunities and threats factors.

SWOT analysis of "O" and "T" letters comes to priority of organization. One of the well-known strategic management tools is SWOT analysis and "S" and "W" letter refers to internal (micro) analysis, letters of "W" and "O" refers to external analysis. Weakness and opportunities give what is the advantages and disadvantages of industry or in other words which sectors to enter or exit.

Internal analysis as a part of SWOT analysis strengths and weakness these are controllable factors by organization but when it comes to external analysis related with SWOT analysis opportunities and threats are not controllable factors.

Boston Consulting Group Growth Matrix

Boston Consulting Group created 2x2 matrix in 1970 by Henderson Bruce Doolan. The aim of matrix is to help firms to increase efficiency with decision process of facilities where to invest in industry, which facilities to shut down in industry. Matrix is also named as growth-share matrix.

Matrix has 4 business product types such as; stars, question marks, cash cows and pets. These categories based on market share and growth factors;

Cash cows : products have high market share and slow growth
Pet : products have low market share and slow growth (undesirable case)
Question marks : low market share and high growth
Star : high share and high growth (desirable case)

Value Chain Analysis

Porter mentioned the importance of analyzing the roots of competitive advantage in competitive with describing the fundamental role of the value chain in his *"competitive advantage creating and sustaining superior performance"* book.

The larger stream activities compose value chain of firm which is defined as value system by Porter (1985)

Competitive scope plays an important role on firms' value chains which causes from industry differences and companies backgrounds

Value chain elements are defined as; Firm infrastructure, human resource management, technology development, procurement, inbound operations, logistics, outbound logistics, service and marketing & sales.

Porter (1985) mentioned value chain as showing total value, value activities and margin. Value activities which are physical and technological activities, create the difference on product which supplies to customers buy opportunity. The spread between total value and cost of value activities gives the margin definition which can be measured in different ways.

Balanced Score Card (BSC)

The roots of balanced scorecard depend on Rober S. Kaplan's (a professor at the Harvard Business School) David P. Norton's (co-founder of Renaissance Worldwide Inc.) research project in 1990. Research, examined 12 large companies and focused on disadvantages of focusing only financial accounting based criteria's. These criteria's not fully reflect the big picture of company and causes in efficiency and ineffectiveness on firms/companies decision making process.

Kaplan and Norton introduced a new approach by combining financial and operational factors in a balanced way in order to measure performance accurately. BSC is not only focus on financial dynamics but only companies/firms other dynamics (for example, operational).

Kaplan and Norton's balanced score card approach published as 3 papers in Harvard Business Review starting with 1992. Also this approach mentioned in "the balanced score card: Translating Strategy into Action" Kaplan and Norton's book (1996)

Balanced Score Card is based on 4 perspectives; firstly financial perspective, secondly innovation and learning perspective, thirdly customer perspective and lastly internal business perspective

Customer Perspective : The top priority of organization is to maximize customer satisfaction. Kaplan and Norton mentioned the importance of customer perspective by focusing on customer concerns with time, quality, cost and performance factors.

Internal Business Perspective : IBP can be defined as a part of customer perspective. Company must take internal dynamics to manage customer's needs.

Innovation and Learning Perspective : The adaption to external environment needs pro-active adaptive management process to catch new development going on industry or the World.

Financial Perspective : Organization's one of the most priority is to maximize the shareholders welfare which can be done by optimum financial management. In order to achieve this aim financial measurement analysis such as financial multiples (price to earnings, price to book value, earnings per share, return on assets, price to sales, EV/EBITDA, EV/Sales, etc.) and valuation approaches plays a crucial role.

PEST (EL) Analysis

One of the vital factors of strategic management is environmental scanning process for these lots of strategic management tools are using. The authors briefly explained tools and from now on focusing on external environment scanning with political, economic, social and technological factors which combines PEST analysis.

PEST analysis, named as a guard of organization's to external macro environment changes in order to protect organization's competitive position in competitive environment. Ecosystem is the hearth of organization which creates success or failure. Because of this concept adaptation and analyze approaches of macro environment scanning determines the faith of life cycle of organization.

Environment scanning process divides into 2 sub-groups as *"internal analysis"* and *"external analysis"*. External analysis universe is larger than internal analysis when compared to factors taking into consideration.

Internal factors analysis comes from SWOT analysis, which focuses on "S" and "W". Strengths and weakness factors of firm are; management, company culture, capabilities and resources (inputs need to produce products). These factors adjust the importance of company's/firm's competitive advantage in industry. Internal analysis with strengths and weakness factors can be named as bottom up analysis approach or from micro to macro analysis. Firstly focusing on company's/firm's heart and adapts this to competitive advantage and to external environment. While doing this top management must setup well designed strategy because it's the first but the most important step for strategic management.

Internal analysis efficiency plays curial role on production line, for example management needs to deal with how to maximize productivity with minimizing cost. If this achieved competitive advantage difference among industry comes to result and differs organization from competitors. Sometimes it is very difficult to setup this ongoing process in other words with only internal factors strategy every organization cannot achieve optimized production or well-designed adaptation to industry.

Internal analysis components are; *"Production"*, *"Financial"*, *"Suppliers"*, *"Resources"* and *"Distribution Channels"* which combines organizational functions.

When taking all of these factors into internal analysis, management faces inefficiency problems due to which factor to take most importantly. The rapidly changing and developing ecosystem creates new black swans for industry in other words unexpected and un thinkable because of these it is not so easy to write down all internal factors and analyze them to create strategy will not setup perfect result of strategic management.

Top management must take environment scanning especially internal analysis factors as infinite learning curve style which combines learning and experience. Every new black swan increases the experience and reaction to event with the content of protecting competitive advantage aim.

Environmental scanning process's micro or internal analysis dynamics focuses on competitive advantage as a whole picture scanning shift from internal to external analysis. External analysis covers the large universe of eco system with analyzing macro environment of industry. When combining macro environment and SWOT analysis "O" and "T" letters comes to priority of organization. One of the well-known strategic management tools is SWOT analysis and "S" and "W" letter refers to internal (micro) analysis, letters of "W" and "O" refers to external analysis. Weakness and opportunities give what is the advantages and disadvantages of industry or in other words which sectors to enter or exit.

Internal analysis as a part of SWOT analysis strengths and weakness these are controllable factors by organization but when it comes to external analysis related with SWOT analysis opportunities and threats are not controllable factors.

External analysis is a part of organization vision, mission and strategic ongoing process. On behalf of this external factors divided into 3 subgroups; 1) competitors environment 2) industry environment and 3) general environment

The Importance of PESTEL Analysis for Environmental Scanning Process

General environment analysis examination done by PEST analysis which is the sum of political, economic, social and technology components. These are the unbreakable parts of macro or external environment (out of control of organization)

The History and Evolution of PESTEL Analysis

History of PEST analysis started with Aguilar study, from this important step PEST analysis continues it's ongoing and inexorably process. The root of PEST factors creates different combinations of analysis and sequence of letters (P, E, S, T) of main dynamic can be different.

In common use PEST acronym refers to political, economic, social and technological factors.

PEST analysis creates matrix with different variations of main dynamics.

The Variations of PEST analysis

- **PEST** : Political + Economic + Social + Technological
- **PESTEL** : Political + Economic + Social + Technological + Environmental + Legal
- **PEEST** : Political + Economic + Environmental + Social + Technological
- **SPENT** : Social + Political + Economic + Nature + Technological
- **SPEENT** : Social + Political + Economic + Environmental + Nature + Technological
- **STEEPLEN** : Social + Technological + Economic + Environmental + Political + Legal Ethical + Nature
- **STEEPLED** : Social + Technological + Economic + Environmental + Political + Legal + Ethical + Demographics
- **PESTLIED** : Political + Economic + Social + Technological + Legal + International + Environmental + Demographics
- **STEEPV** : Social + Technological + Economic + Environmental + Political + Value
- **STEER** : Social + Technological + Economic + Environmental + Regulatory
- **PESTELI** : Political + Economic + Social + Technological + Environmental + International
- **SLEPT** : Social + Legal + Technological + Economic + Political + Technological
- **SLEEPT** : Social + Legal + Technological + Economic + Environmental + Political + Technological
- **LoNGPEST** : Local + National + Global + Political + Economic + Social + Technological

These combinations as mentioned above can be expanded with adding new dynamic come to industry.

Main Factors of PEST Analysis

Political Factors

Political environment and organization integration must be taken into consideration importantly. Sub factors of political factors directly impact competitive advantage and transforms competitive environment.

Political factors can be classified as 2 groups with their impact level; 1) supranational and 2) national

Insane raise of globalization with technological developments makes supranational concept more important for analysis. Big forces, such as U.S.A, can effect whole political system with actions and decisions. Starting from November 2016 Donald Trump who is the president of U.S.A has changed the global view from its roots. He started with trade wars in order to protect U.S.A economy; his targets are mainly China, European Union and Japan. Trade regulations especially for China impact whole trade system around the World. When Trump takes action instantly China takes against action to Trump and this deadlock stops the system working efficiently.

National level political factors effect rely on heavily companies/firms strategic management, for example labor, tax and trade which are components of fiscal policy, related actions can strict competitive advantage for industry.

The political component of PEST analysis tries to answer *"how the political factors impact economy and industry"* question.

Political factors have a large universe sometimes it is very difficult to mention exactly all related factors. What are the major factors of political analysis question becomes more important day by day.

Political factors;

1. Political stability / instability / conflicts
2. Political
3. General / local elections, early elections
4. Government policies
5. Regulation
6. Lobby activities
7. Domestic legislation for country
8. Tax, labor, trade arrangements
9. Foreign trade regulations
10. Specific restrictions for multinational or foreign companies
11. Immigration laws and future of free mobility of labor
12. Global warning regulations
13. Protectionist actions on trade
14. Antitrust and environmental regulations
15. Monopoly and oligopoly restrictions
16. Relation with U.S.A – EU - G20 etc.
17. Terrorist attacks protection regulations
18. Minimum wage view of governments
19. Corruption and bribery cases
20. Political parties changing views on politics
21. Government policies on fiscal policies
22. Health, education and infrastructure systems consumption decisions
23. Government relation between labor and trade unions/organizations
24. International relations

Economic Factors

Starting with political factors defines the big picture when it comes to narrow PEST analysis economic factors have massive effect on competitive advantage and profitability of organization. Global and local economy dynamics surround strategic management and competitive advantage concept of industry which will create domino effect.

When it comes to measure economic impact, gross domestic product data plays a crucial role. GDP examines and outlines the whole economic activity as a snapshot which gives accurate signals economic activity.

The economic component of PEST analysis tries to answer *"how the economic factors impact strategic management"* question.

Under the big umbrella of GDP, the other economic factors such as inflation, disposable income, exchange rate appreciation/depreciation, central bank monetary policy decisions, fiscal policy actions totally effect households and industries. While GDP shows the whole economy it does not mean the other factors are least important. GDP is an output while sub categories factors (such as monetary policies, central bank rate decisions, inflation rates and exchange rates) is input to examine ongoing activity of economies.

Economic factors;

1. Gross Domestic Product (GDP) – Gross National Product (GNP) trends
2. Growth
3. Purchasing power of household
4. Central banks
5. Interest rates
6. Exchange rate appreciation / depreciation
7. Dollar value
8. Fiscal policy impact on households
9. Credit mechanisms
10. Business cycles
11. Money supply
12. Inflation
13. Global and local economy Dynamics
14. Capital / labor / prices
15. Trade / Exchange rate wars
16. Seasonality on economic variables
17. Money markets and stock exchanges
18. Minimum wage standards
19. Income distribution
20. Disposable income
21. Industrial production
22. Opportunity cost / competitive advantage / global – local competition

Social Factors

The political and economic factors have discussed until now, third letter "S" comes to game which is social factors. PEST analysis steps started with politics then continued by economic dynamic these are more industry related but social factors gives more priority to human beings in other word customers for companies/firms

With globalization and technological environmental rapid changes customer's preferences have changed and this causes new adaptation to business models. Strategic management without customer's satisfaction maximization cannot be thinkable which has an impact on business cycles

The social component of PEST analysis tries to answer *"how cultural dynamics shape the industry"* question.

Social factors;

1. Population / demographics
2. Growth rate of population
3. Population pyramid
4. Birth rate / mortality rate / infant mortality rate
5. Lifestyle / changing preferences of households
6. Social media / broadcast
7. Immigration – refugee problems
8. Non-government organizations
9. Natural factors
10. Wages / disposable income
11. Educational levels
12. Attitudes – behaviors

Technological Factors

Technology as a component of PEST analysis may be seen as least important factor when compared to political and economic factors. New innovations under technological development process have power to open and close business cycles. When compact disc (CD) introduced to media and computers sectors satisfaction level of this new innovation went insane among consumer. CD development shifted to DVD then to blue ray products. But how about asking "can anyone remember compact disc nowadays" questions, large distribution of sample probably says no.

Mobile phone sector developments are not different from compact disc developments, Blackberry killed Ericsson brand name and Apple killed all of them on telecom sector. These are the net examples of how technological factors end brand names and business cycles.

Internet and e-commerce have changed technological perspective of business models and well-known brands such as Amazon and eBay are trend setters for customers.

The technological component of PEST analysis tries to answer *"how technological developments dynamics impact the business cycles"* question.

Technological factors;

1. New technology on computers such as quantum computing
2. Technological developments of hardware and software
3. Artificial intelligence
4. Wireless communication
5. Impact of social media (Twitter, Facebook, LinkedIn and Instagram)

The Importance of PESTEL Analysis for Environmental Scanning Process

Environmental Factors

The main root of strategic management tools comes from environmental scan as like PEST (EL) analysis. Environment covers internal and external analysis and taking environmental factors into consideration external analysis impact increases. Environmental factors can be nature related events that will change business model of distribution channel of industry or business cycle.

The environmental component of PEST analysis tries to answer *"how ecological, climate and nature events change the industry"* question.

Environmental factors;

1. Nature
2. Weather conditions
3. Climate changes
4. Global warming
5. Natural disaster
6. Pollution
7. Recycling processes
8. Renewable energy policies
9. Waste optimization
10. Water and air pollution regulations

Ethical Factors

The maximization process of customer needs is the crucial role of top executives under organizations. This priority approach sometimes it is very difficult to care about customer's ethical expectations. Ethical norms as a basic rule of society changes very rapidly in wild capitalist ecosystem. Customers expects to obey ethical rules from business industry, business industry also expects from customers not to focus on ethical norms. This trade off creates mismatch for strategic management and competitive advantage optimization which is a two sided mechanism affects customers and business industry positively or negatively.

The concept of social responsibilities cover ethical and discretionary norms for customers and business industry. There is a slightly differences between ethical and discretionary norms firstly ethical norms reflects the general behaviors accepted by society secondly discretionary norms can be named less strict when compared to ethical norms and based on more voluntary approach.

Some arguments going on whether social responsibilities concept conflicting with economic and legal factors on behalf of priority. The answer of question is must be think as a hole

The ethical component of PEST analysis tries to answer *"how ethical norms affect business models"* question.

Ethical factors;

1. Cultural and religious adaptation
2. Respect for social responsibilities
3. Working safety and conditions
4. Products recycling

5. Prevent gender discrimination

Legal Factors

PEST analysis factors such as political, economic, social and technological factors affect business models and management strategic decisions in order to sustain competitive advantage. These factors are important to obey but cannot be named as must conditions when compared to legal factors. Organization has no chance to pass away obligatory arrangement because there is negative or positive impact on business models. The management must be up to date on law changes and globally/locally adapts to legal factors which affects business models.

Also regulatory factor of PEST analysis can be named under legal factors because of its content similarity

The legal component of PEST analysis tries to answer "how global and local law restrictions, affect business model" question.

Legal factors;

1. Antitrust laws
2. Patent and copyrights
3. Consumer and labor protection laws
4. Trade restrictions (trade wars)
5. Health, education and safety law
6. Data protection
7. Tax law
8. Corporate tax and income tax arrangements
9. Custom law
10. Export and import restrictions

The Pros and Cons of PESTEL Analysis

PESTEL analysis, with major components as Political, Economic, Social and Technological factors, aims to scan external environment of huge ecosystem while taking into consideration of competitive advantage and strategic management. These factors are the starting point of analysis roadmap. First of all, factors are identified in a detailed way for external environment scanning then with the light of PESTEL factors possible impact on organization analyze comes into process. After analyzing possible impact on organization or business model categorize opportunities and threats (which comes from SWOT analysis) management sets importance level of "O" and "W" in order to create well managed / optimized strategic management to sustain competitive advantage. Expected outcome of well managed /optimized strategic management is to eliminate all possible negative effects and transform threats to opportunity for organization.

In a theoretical concept PESTEL analysis may be seen as a perfect solution for organization to create competitive advantage maximization. When it comes to this part some question marks must be taken into consideration. Simply root of PEST and variations from PEST analysis scan only external environment with lots lot detailed and ongoing development process of factors. Because of this, PESTEL analysis

The Importance of PESTEL Analysis for Environmental Scanning Process

seems like a strict guard for organization which protect from all of the external environment factors threats. To sum up PESTEL has lots of pros but cons of it seems like not a perfect rescuer with only itself.

PESTEL analysis efficiency can be maximized if the other strategic management tools are integrated to systematic thinking/analyzing mechanism. These tools are; SWOT Analysis, Porter's Five Forces, Boston Consulting Group Growth Matrix, Value Chain Analysis, Balanced Score Card, Competitive Analysis as mentioned in chapter of book. All of tools have pros and cons when compared with each other, in other words no perfect tool maximizes competitive advantage.

The Comparison of Strategic Management Tools versus PESTEL Analysis

- **PESTEL versus SWOT:** SWOT analysis with combination of Strengths, Weakness, Opportunities and Threats factors focus on "S" and "W" for internal analysis, "O" and "T" for external analysis which comes a part of PESTEL analysis. PEST analysis dynamics focus on detailed external factors which creates the important difference between PEST and SWOT analysis.
- **SWOT versus Porter's Five Forces:** as mentioned above SWOT analysis with combination of Strengths, Weakness, Opportunities and Threats factors focus on "S" and "W" for internal analysis, "O" and "T" for external analysis when compare SWOT to five forces there is differences. Firstly universe of SWOT analysis is larger and has more extensive dynamics covering both internal and external environment. Five-forces focus on the threat of new entrants, the threat of substitutes, existing competitors, bargaining power of buyers and suppliers. Five forces analysis can be more suitable for small to mid-cap organization strategic management decision making processes.
- **Value Chain versus Boston Consulting Group Growth Matrix:** BCG growth matrix consider four dominant product types as, stars, question marks, cash cows and pets in order to beat market growth and achieve revenue growth maximization. This concept is a good solution for different segmentation business industries. Value chain analysis focuses on value creating approach and cost cutting optimization.
- **Balanced Score Card and Competitive Analysis**: BSC has priority on competitors which threats company where as competitive analysis deals with external environment factors. Competitive analysis with external dynamics approaches is similar to PESTEL analysis.

When analyzing the pros and cons of major PESTEL and other strategic management tools differs on environment subgroups as internal and external analysis. Management must consider which strategic management tool to use to get competitive advantage maximization and optimal strategic management.

To sum up, the best solution to support business industry life cycle is combining strategic management tools with management needs and aims.

The chapter of book started with the concept of strategic management and shifted to environmental scanning of internal and external dynamics. With the content of PESTEL analysis external environment factors plays a crucial role in strategic management but again to remind it is not a magical solution tool. What can be done to develop PESTEL furthermore will be new concept for management and technology sector. Due to PESTEL analysis complex and detailed factor artificial intelligence and machine learning system comes to help to reduce the complexity and increase the efficiency. External environment factors ongoing development process sometimes becomes so difficult to follow. AI and machine learning will be solution for managements to maximize competitive advantages with the corporation of technology sector members. Factor input upload to AI and cloud computers scan external environment in a nanoseconds with machine learning approaches optimum analysis comes as output.

CONCLUSION

Strategic management is a complex and ongoing process which cannot be stopped during infinite life cycle of organizations. Top executives must create a guard or early warning signal from eco system threats and changes which affect organization destiny. Environmental scanning is a best solution to survive and fight against competitors. External analysis is a big umbrella which protects organization from heavy rains by giving area to transform threats to opportunities. A well-designed external analysis scans political, economic, social, technological, environmental and legal factors which names as PESTEL analysis. All of the related information of eco-system comes from this analysis and its huge universe is a guard for organization. This sounds everything is fine and top management created best early warning system with PESTEL analysis but when it comes to say yes some question marks arise. PESTEL approach tries to make external scan very deeply but it is not a perfect solution. The other strategic management tools should be blended to catch the maximum efficiency for organization. Top executives setup early warning signal based on PESTEL analysis and develop by adding SWOT, BSC, BCG matrix, value analysis etc. If this setup works fine, organization bounces the top layer of competitive advantage among competitors.

SOLUTIONS AND RECOMMENDATIONS

To sum up, the best solution to support business industry life cycle is combining strategic management tools with management needs and aims. The chapter of book started with the concept of strategic management and shifted to environmental scanning of internal and external dynamics. With the content of PESTEL analysis external environment factors plays a crucial role in strategic management but again to remind it is not a magical solution tool.

FUTURE RESEARCH DIRECTIONS

What can be done to develop PESTEL furthermore will be new concept for management and technology sector. Due to PESTEL analysis complex and detailed factor artificial intelligence and machine learning system comes to help to reduce the complexity and increase the efficiency. External environment factors ongoing development process sometimes becomes so difficult to follow. AI and machine learning will be solution for managements to maximize competitive advantages with the corporation of technology sector members. Factor input upload to AI and cloud computers scan external environment in a nanoseconds with machine learning approaches optimum analysis comes as output.

REFERENCES

Ackoff, R. (1974). *Redesigning the future*. New York: John Wiley & Sons.

Aguilar, F. J. (1967). *Scanning the business environment*. New York: Macmillan.

Ansoff, H. I. (1965). *Corporate strategy an analytic approach to business policy for growth and expansion*. New York: Mcgraw-Hill Book.

David, F. R. (2011). *Strategic management: concepts and cases* (13th ed.). New Jersey: Pearson Education.

Diffenbach, J. (1983). Corporate environmental analysis in large U.S. corporations. *Long Range Planning*, *16*(3), 107–116. doi:10.1016/0024-6301(83)90037-7 PMID:10263400

Drummond, G., Ashford, R., & Ensor, J. (2007). *Strategic marketing: planning and control*. Amsterdam, The Netherlands: Elsevier. doi:10.4324/9780080498270

Fahey, L., & King, W. R. (1977). Environmental scanning for corporate planning. *Business Horizons*, *20*(4), 61–71. doi:10.1016/0007-6813(77)90010-6

Fahey, L., King, W. R., & Narayanan, V. K. (1981). Environmental scanning and forecasting in strategic planning—the state of the art. *Long Range Planning*, *14*(1), 32–39.

Hambrick, D. C. (1979). Environmental scanning, organizational strategy, and executive roles: A study in three industries. (Ph.D. dissertation, Pennsylvania State University).

Hitt, M. A., Ireland, R. D., & Hoskisson, R. E. (2009). *Strategic management: concepts & cases: competitiveness and globalization*. Mason, OH: South-Western Cengage Learning.

Jain, R. K., & Triandis, H. C. (1997). *Management of research and development organizations: managing the unmanageable*. New York: Wiley.

Jain, S. C. (1984). Environmental scanning in U.S. corporations. *Long Range Planning*, *17*(2), 117–128. doi:10.1016/0024-6301(84)90143-2 PMID:10299516

Kaplan, R. S., & Norton, D. P. (n.d.). *The balanced scorecard: translating strategy into action*. Boston, MA: Harvard Business School Press.

Keegan, W. J. (1974). Multinational scanning: a study of the information sources utilized by headquarters executives in multinational companies. *Administrative Science Quarterly*, *19*(3), 411. doi:10.2307/2391981

Lenz, R. T., & Engledow, J. L. (1986). Environmental analysis: The applicability of current theory. *Strategic Management Journal*, *7*(4), 329–346. doi:10.1002mj.4250070404

Macmillan, H., & Tampoe, M. (2000). *Strategic management: process, content and implementation*. Oxford, UK: Oxford University Press.

Mainardes, E. W., Ferreira, J., & Raposo, M. L. (2014). Strategy and strategic management concepts: are they recognised by management students? *E+M. Ekonomie a Management*, *17*(1), 43–61. doi:10.15240/tul/001/2014-1-004

Miles, R. E., Snow, C. C., Meyer, A. D., & Coleman, H. J. Jr. (1978). Organizational strategy, structure, and process. *Academy of Management Review*, *3*(3), 546–562. doi:10.5465/amr.1978.4305755 PMID:10238389

Miles, R. E., Snow, C. C., & Pfeffer, J. (1974). Organization-environment: concepts and issues. *Industrial Relations*, *13*(3), 244–264. doi:10.1111/j.1468-232X.1974.tb00581.x

Mintzberg, H. (1979). *The structuring of organizations: A synthesis of the research*. Englewood Cliffs, NJ: Prentice-Hall.

Mintzberg, H. (1987). The strategy concept I: Five Ps for strategy. *California Management Review*, *30*(1), 11–24. doi:10.2307/41165263

Mintzberg, H. (1988). Generic strategy: Toward a comprehensive framework. *Advances in Strategic Management*, *5*, 1–67.

Neumann, J. V., & Morgenstern, O. (1947). *Theory of games and economic behavior*. Princeton, NJ: Princeton Univ. Pr.

Porter, M. E. (1980). *Competitive strategy: techniques for analyzing industries and competitors*. New York: Free Press.

Porter, M. E. (1985). *Competitive advantage: creating and sustaining superior performance*. New York: Free Press.

Porter, M. E. (1986). *Competition in global industries*. Boston, MA: Harvard Business School Press.

Porter, M. E. (1987). *From competitive advantage to corporate strategy*. Boston, MA: Harvard Business School Pub.

Porter, M. E. (1996). What is strategy? *Harvard Business Review*, *74*(6), 61–78. PMID:10158474

Preble, J. F., Rau, P. A., & Reichel, A. (1988) The environmental scanning practices of US multinationals in the late 1980s. Management International Review 28(4), 4-14.

Smith, K. G., & Hitt, M. A. (2009). *Great minds in management: the process of theory development*. Oxford, UK: Oxford University Press.

Steiss, A. W. (2003). *Strategic management for public and nonprofit organizations*. New York: Marcel Dekker. Strategic planning: The state of the art. *Long Range Planning*, *14*(2), 32–39.

Stubbart, C. (1982). Are environmental scanning units effective? *Long Range Planning*, *15*(3), 139–145. doi:10.1016/0024-6301(82)90035-8 PMID:10298730

Thomas, P. S. (1980). Environmental scanning— The state of the art. *Long Range Planning*, *13*(1), 20–28. doi:10.1016/0024-6301(80)90051-5

Weigl, T. (2008). *Strategy, structure and performance in a transition economy. Gabler*. GWV.

Wheelen, T. L., Hunger, J. D., & Hoffman, A. N. (2012). *Strategic management and business policy toward global sustainability* (13th ed.). New Jersey: Pearson Education.

KEY TERMS AND DEFINITIONS

BCG: Boston Consulting Group
BSC: Balanced Score Card
PESTEL: Political, Economic, Social, Technological, Environmental and Legal
SWOT: Strengths, Weakness, Opportunities and Threats

Chapter 17
The Relationship Between Economic Growth and Innovation:
Panel Data Analysis on Chosen OECD Countries

Samet Akça
https://orcid.org/0000-0003-3460-733X
KTO Karatay University, Turkey

Bilge Afşar
KTO Karatay University, Turkey

ABSTRACT

This chapter studies innovation and economic growth and emphasizes their relationship. In this context; innovation and economic growth outputs of 16 OECD countries between 2005 and 2015 are analyzed. GDP is considered as economic growth variable, R&D investments in GDP (%), and patent applications are considered as innovation variables. In light of these variables, panel data analyze is used. Unit root, Pedroni co-integration and FMOLS tests were applied with the order. As a result, the increase in patent applications and R&D investments was found to have a positive effect on economic growth.

INTRODUCTION

Innovation is an activity that helps the companies gain and earn more. In the globalizing world, innovation is very important for catching the age and competing the markets with other firms. Firms competed only with other firms in the domestic market in the past, but now they compete with all the world's companies in the same sector. On the other hand, when the effects of innovation are considered as macro-based, the economic benefits provided to countries are also very crucial. According to Global Innovation Index 2017 report, 14 of the top 20 countries in Innovation Score List are also in the top

DOI: 10.4018/978-1-7998-2559-3.ch017

The Relationship Between Economic Growth and Innovation

Gross Domestic Product (GDP) list. Accordingly, it is obvious that the favorable relationship between economic growth and innovation investments. In this study, this essential relationship between economic growth and innovation is studied.

The purpose of this study is to present the importance of the innovation in order to achieve sustainable economic growth. In this context, this study consist of three main parts. In the first part of study, the concept of innovation is defined. Innovation sources, innovation types and models are described in this part. Innovation is a dynamic structure which is continuous, developing and constantly changing. Therefore, the measurement of this process is not possible with a simple single technique and different parameters and data are used in this measurement process. For this reason, significant innovations indicators are also explained in this part.

In the second part of study, the concept of economic growth is explained. Different definition of economic growth is given and then, the basic resources of economy which is consisting of human, nature, fund, technological change and innovation are studied. Achieving economic growth and improving the quality of life is desirable by all countries and peoples. Therefore, the policies and measures to be prepared for this purpose are very important. In this context, economic models focusing on innovation are examined.

In the third and last the part of study, literature review, relationship between innovation and economic growth is examined with the help with panel data analysis. The number of patent applications and the share of R&D Investments in GDP are considered as innovation data and national income as economic growth data. The activities of 16 OECD countries which is selected according to GDP between the year of 2005 and 2015 are analyzed by the mentioned innovation and economic growth data. Panel data analysis is chosen as the method and unit root, Pedroni co-integration and FMOLS tests are performed. E-views program is used to perform all these tests. In the conclusion part, all the results obtained are interpreted and the relationship between economic growth and innovation is stated in a concrete way.

CONCEPT AND DEVELOPMENT OF INNOVATION

Definition of Innovation

Innovation word is based on the Latin term "innovatus". The word innovates is derived from the verb "innovare" which has the meaning of change, metamorphosis and renewal. (Akalın, 2007). According to Oslo Guidelines which is co-published by Eurostat (European Statistical Office) and OECD, (Organization for Economic Co-Operation and Development) innovation means a new or significantly improved product, service or process, new marketing or an organizational method. Besides, the minimum requirement for an innovation to occur is that the method to be used is new or significantly improved. (Lowe and Marriot, 2006).

According to Lundvall, innovation is a system in which all the sub-parts of economic system and institutional structure should be evaluated in a single framework. Competitors and subcontractors, suppliers can help to shape the innovation capacity of the company as a source of knowledge, experience and technological solutions.

According to European Union Commission, innovation is the successful discovery and exploitation of renewal in social as well as economic environments (European Commission, 2014).

According to Dosi, innovation is a research activity. This activity may be on a new production system, a new organization installation, a new implementation process, a discovery, experiment or a new product. In addition, innovation have a risk because of the uncertainties as a result of innovation activities in the product or production process. (Dosi, 1988).

Schumpeter is the creator of the first modern innovation definition. Schumpeter uses the innovation in the meaning of creative and beneficial change. It is defined as everything that come in sight the technological developments thanks to a financial return to the entrepreneur. The study of Schumpeter is very important because of its great influence to the innovation theories. Schumpeter says that economic developments are taking action according to a dynamic process created by the replacement of old technologies with the new technologies under the name of "creative destruction". In this view, innovation can be radical or stepwise. Radical innovation refers to innovations that have emerged as a result of the intensive work and completely new to the sector. The application of radical innovation in companies results in significant changes in business areas. On the other hand, stepwise innovation is continuous development of existing products, processes or services with small changes. According to this scope, Schumpeter defines innovation as follows (Schumpeter, 1934):

- Presentation of a new product or a new version of an existing product that is not familiar to consumers,
- Establishing a market that has never been before in the country or region,
- Creation or development of a new supply channels of raw material or other product inputs,
- Establishing a new market structures or organizations in any industry.

It is important to understand why companies are tend to innovation activities. The main purpose of these activities is to increase the profitability of the company by decreasing costs or increasing consumer demand through changes and developments. Developing a new product, service or process in the competitive market can provide significant advantages in terms of market share. The fact that an existing product, service or process which can be defined as stepwise innovation is included in small developments and innovative works enable the company gain cost advantage over its competitors. As a result, it will play an important role in increasing its financial gain and market share over the price in the market (Eurostat and OECD, 2005).

As is seen, there are many different definitions of innovation. But all these definitions of innovation have one thing in common which is helping companies achieve greater financial gain. In a globalized world, innovation is inevitable for both countries and companies. While the competitors of companies in the past were only from domestic market, now they are in the same market and compete with different companies from all over the world. An innovative process that is planned correctly takes companies one step ahead in this competitive global market (Kırım, 2008).

Sources of Innovation

Increasing competitive environment with the globalizing world, the decrease in the profitability rates, changing cultural and social characteristics are pushing the companies to change in the desire to hold on to the market and to increase their market share and profitability. Innovation is the main factor which is driving this change. With the development of technology and changing consumption habits of people, innovation has made its place in economic systems more robust and its effect has become more notice-

The Relationship Between Economic Growth and Innovation

able. Within this framework, innovation has become a necessity for companies to keep up with the times. According to Peter Drucker, there are seven different sources of innovation to implement this requirement. Four of these seven sources are internal resources which consist of situations that occur within enterprises or markets themselves. The other three sources are external. It is due to external independent differentiation of businesses or markets (Drucker, 2017):

- **The Unexpected Situations:** An unexpected success or failure is defined as the first resource that will lead companies to innovate. Unexpected success brings innovation opportunity to companies and this opportunity is very beneficial for company. However, as this opportunity arises after an unexpected success, it is often overlooked because of the languor. Although this opportunity for innovation is very low in risk, it is not implemented because of this risk. In the opposite case which is an unexpected failure, companies make an effort to fix this situation and innovation is an opportunity so as to do achieve the target.
- **The Incongruity:** Drucker defines the contradiction between the expected situation and the current situation is discrepancy. This discrepancy is the result of a mistake and this mistake and if this mistake is detected by the company, it can be used as a source of innovation.
- **Process Need:** When a process that is being used in a company cannot meet the required demand and need, this process needs to be improved. If this improvement is a small change or a new addition at any point in the process, it is defined as stepwise innovation. If the system is redesigned, it is defined as radical innovation (Schumpeter, 1934).
- **Industry and Market Structure Change:** Industry and market structure is not a static but dynamic in a continuous state of change. Companies that try to take their place in this dynamic structure must adapt to dynamism and fulfill their requirements. These requirements are met by innovation. But the important point here is that the acceptance this dynamic structure by the company authorities. Staying behind the times and watching the technological developments from a distance will bring harm to company. For this reason, dynamic structure should be accepted, industry and market structure should be well analyzed and necessary changes should be provided by innovation.
- **Demographic Changes:** Demography is a science that examines the population structure and the dynamic diversity of a population in a small or large scale region (Scheidel, 2006). Both economic and social aspects such as birth, death and migration movements, marriage, age, education and livelihoods of the present population are examined by demography and changes in all these elements are recorded over time. The impact of these demographic changes on the production, sales and marketing processes of any product or service is considerable. Many factors such as the type of production, marketing channel, sales area and sales price of the products and services should be prepared on the basis of demographic changes.
- **Changes in Perception:** In mathematical sense, there is no difference between saying "the glass is half empty" and "the glass is half full". But the meanings and results of these two statements are quite different. If the change from the view of "the glass is half empty" to view of "the glass is half full" is provided, this change will lead to many innovative opportunities. The power of perceptions-based innovations is also accepted by company executives. But at the same time, perceptual innovations are not preferred by the same company executives because these innovations are impractical and have a possibility of dangerous consequences. In order to avoid these problems and risks, it should be understood whether the change in perception is permanent or not. Then the

necessary analysis should be performed and the process should be advanced. To minimize risk, perceptional innovations begin in a very small scale and continue in a special way.
- **New Knowledge:** When the historical journey of human being is examined, it is a miraculous event to have reached the opportunities that currently available. When the battles, natural disasters, epidemics and cruelty of human beings were evaluated from the first human creation to the present day, our species could be expected to have disappeared decades ago. However, human beings have always used their wisdom throughout this historical process, always attached importance to information, and added new things to the knowledge that was possessed with the flowing time and ensured the continuity of the process. They have experienced what has happened in any natural disaster or epidemic and have taken the necessary precautions to prevent the same problems. They were not content with the invention of fire and wheel and provided the necessary infrastructure for the development of all technological developments that human being has today. As time went on, the importance of knowledge increased. Today, companies that are capable of technological innovation are always one step ahead in their markets. Technological innovation requires a certain process of research and development. The main purpose of this process is to reach new information in the first stage and to shape the innovative process through this information. When the new knowledge is examined within this scope, it is considered as the most important of the innovation sources and is considered as external.

Innovation Models and Indicators

Innovation models are the most important indicators which examine the technological improvements, the emergence of new products and the process of their marketing forms and sales. Especially in the 1950s after the World War II, researches gained momentum thanks to the characteristics of the period. The most essential reason for this momentum is the inability of the production speed and techniques to reach the demand of the society.

Rothwell created "Five Generation Innovation Process (5G Innovation Process)" with the adoption of American structure in 1994. This model. This model determines which innovation is based on which method and for what reason. It also examines the relationship between economic factors and innovation. After 1994, the studies accepted this 5G Innovation Process created by Rothwell as the main source and used this model with minor additions or changes in other studies. For example, bot Hobday in 2005 and Tidd in 2006 worked on innovation models with quoting Rothwells's work. In 2003, Marinova and Philimore added the sixth generation to Rothwell's work and defined the first as "black box model" (Marinova and Philimore, 2003). According to Rothwell's model, 5G Innovation Process is as follows:

- **First Generation Innovation Model (From 1950 to mid-1960's):** This model has the characteristics of World War II. The researches have the understanding that the development of technology and the development of technology contribute to the needs of the market. In other words, the perspective of this understanding is that science paves the way for technology and technology paves the way for markets (Edquist, 2005). This model is defined as "technology-push". The more investment in innovation within the scope of research and development activities is the more the amount of new products that will emerge. Since technological developments are accepted and supported by the society, they form the basis of other innovation models.

- **Second Generation Innovation Model (Mid-1960's to early 1970):** The mid-1960's was a period in which companies developed and the competitive environment become more heated. In this competitive environment, marketing has become an important agenda item for companies in order to achieve success and to increase their market share. This period is considered as a period in which customer demands and needs lead the market and the innovation process is seriously driven by customers. Innovations in the first-generation innovation model are accepted as the result of research and development activities based on science and technology. in this model, it is assumed that innovations are directly proportional to customer demands. Accordingly, the second-generation innovation model is also defined as the demand-driven innovation model. The innovation process is carried out in the form of research and development, production, research of market conditions and sales after the determination of customer needs and desires.
- **Third Generation Innovation Model (From the mid-1970's to mid-1980's):** With the oil crisis in 1973, the price of oil increased by 400%. This situation, especially in America, based on the production of cheap oil-based economic structure of countries put serious problems. This change in oil prices which led to an increase in costs caused also inflation to increase rapidly. During this short period from 1973 to 1974, the New York stock exchange lost $ 100 billion. When a similar crisis was experienced again in 1978, the 1970s and 1980s became a period in which economic structures changed throughout the world (Öztürk and Saygın, 2017). This economic turmoil has led to the formation of the third-generation innovation model. Rising oil prices have led countries to move to different sectors and markets. Japan, for example, has changed the direction of its investments due to the oil crisis and has begun to attach more importance to the electronics industry. As a result of this change, Japan produced vehicles that consumed less fuel and used this crisis environment in its favor. They exported vehicles that consumed less fuel to America. The third-generation innovation model is defined as interactive and togetherness because it blends technology push and demand traction (Badulescu et al., 2012).
- **Fourth Generation Innovation Model (From early 1980's to early 1990's):** The globalization of the innovations made in the Japanese automotive industry, which is mentioned in the third-generation innovation model, has made a significant contribution to the formation of the fourth-generation innovation model. This model is defined as an integrated model and requires the integration of different departments such as product development, accounting, quality and marketing. The fact that all company departments work together in a single product or process innovation has enabled the innovation processes to be shortened. With this process shortening, companies have reached the position of being able to take a more rapid position in the market and achieve market share increase in a healthier way. Integration, parallelism and concurrency are very important within the scope of the fourth-generation innovation model. As a result of the studies carried out within this scope, Japan was able to complete the production of a new vehicle in a period of 30 months while competitors completed between 48 and 60 months. The gap between 18 and 30 months has increased the competitiveness of Japanese car companies in the market (Barbieri and Alvares, 2016).
- **Fifth Generation Innovation Model (1990's onwards):** The innovation model adopted and used in the 1990s shifted from integration to a networked system. In the fourth-generation innovation model, it is seen that the association structure for the firm is not sufficient in time. In order to maintain the innovative structure of the companies, it was concluded that in addition to the internal cooperation, it is inevitable to cooperate with institutions and organizations, customers and

other companies in the sector. The fifth-generation innovation model is defined as system integration and network systems (Rothwell, 1994). In this model, all combinations of technology are used to cope with the complex problems encountered in the formation of new products. In this context, Rothwell stated that the fifth-generation innovation model is the new form of fourth-generation model which is changing and improving with technological developments.

According to European Commission, innovation is a dynamic structure that is continuous, constantly changing and developing. Evaluation of a process with this structure is not possible with a single simple technique (EIS, 2019). Therefore, a report has been published under the name of the European Innovation Scoreboard (EIS), which analyzes various data and innovation performances since 2001. Although the report prepared in 2016 was examined under three headings as company activities, suppliers and outputs, the report in 2017 was examined under four headings as framework conditions, investments, innovation activities and impacts. These headings are also used in the report in 2018 and 2019 invariably. This research is based on the most recent report prepared in 2019. In the EIS report, 27 parameters were examined under 4 main headings. In this study, basic and important parameters is examined (EIS, 2019).

- **Research and Development Activities (R&D):** R&D is based on a systematic foundation. This foundation has a structure that increases the knowledge of the society with the support of science and technology and enables this information to be used in new applications. In this context, R&D consists of three main processes which are basic research, applied research and experimental development. Basic research is the studies that are carried out in order to have more detailed information about the planned work. This stage is considered as the starting point of R&D. Secondly, applied research is more specific than basic research. It is carried out for a specific purpose and provides a more detailed understanding of the information obtained through basic research. Thirdly, experimental development is considered as the last process used in R&D activities. The information obtained in the basic and applied research stages is used in the creation of new products or processes through experimental development activities (Erkiletlioğlu, 2013). Expenditures for R&D are very important in the development of new products, services or processes, in the effective use of imported or existing technologies, in the modification and adaptation of these technologies. In this respect, the difference in development of countries in recent years stems from the size of developments in science and technology. Developments in science and technology are possible thanks to R&D studies (Dura ve Atik, 2002).
- **Patent:** In addition to R&D activities and investments, another indicator of technological and scientific development of a company or country is the number of patents received. When we consider spending on R&D as an input for innovation activities, the number of patents obtained as a result of this is an output of these activities and expenditures. At this point, it is worth noting that R&D is not only related to technological innovation but also includes better use of existing or imported products and services. In this respect, the relationship between R&D expenditures and patent numbers is not one-to-one, but thinking in parallel will provide more efficient results (Saygılı, 2003).
- **Education:** One of the most basic and essential indicators of innovation is education. It is necessary to reach a sufficient level of science and technology in order to compete in the developing knowledge economy and to meet the expectations of the changing society structure. This is possible with the continuity of innovation. Quality is one of the most important elements of the age

The Relationship Between Economic Growth and Innovation

of knowledge in education systems that enable individuals to grow in order to make progress and to make innovation continuous. Therefore, education and training and related social innovations are one of the four most important elements of innovation systems implemented in Japan, one of the leading countries in innovation (Freeman, 1982). Manpower equipped with good education is the main source of innovation. It is pointless to expect that R&D costs incurred in a company or country without qualified manpower will reach an innovative result. It is possible to fulfill the requirements of the age by following science and technology. The education system should be maintained with the support of science and technology and focusing on training high-skilled scientists and engineers in order to be successful in innovation.

- **Brain drain:** One of the main problems in the world economy is the huge economic difference between the wealth and poverty of countries. One of the important reasons for this difference is seen as differences in education level. Growing time and cost of qualified personnel which is needed for the development of countries has gradually increased over time. This increase has led to the emergence of the concept of brain drain and globalization has accelerated with the spread of the brain drain. Developed countries meet their labor needs from developing or underdeveloped countries. This situation leads to an increase in economic imbalance. Although developed countries provide financial assistance to the countries where they meet their labor force, these donations do not cover the labor force received (Ersel, 2003). In order to prevent brain drain, it is necessary to determine the causes and take necessary precautions. The main reason for brain drain is the fact that the world economy is composed of countries that are industrialized with high technology on the one hand, and countries with an agriculture-based economy struggling with capital shortage on the other hand.
- **Advanced Technology Export:** According to Tom and Jushi (2011), high-tech products should be considered as radical innovation and should be fed with technology that is significantly different from the rest of the market (Tom and Jushi, 2011). According to Gardner (2000), high-tech products have a unique technology that transforms from laboratory to real practice. These products use technologies that are pioneering or considered to be pioneers in a particular field. According to Eurostat data, the products considered as high technology are the production of basic pharmaceutical and pharmacy-related materials, computers, the production of electronic and optical materials, aircraft, spacecraft and related materials (Eurostat, 2018).
- **Number of Researches:** The researcher is the protagonist of R&D and innovation processes. Researchers are central to the emergence of a new knowledge, product, service, method or technique. Therefore, the number of researchers in a country or company is an important indicator in terms of innovative developments.

CONCEPT OF ECONOMIC GROWTH

Definition of Economic Growth

Economic growth should be defined under two headings as micro and macro scale. On a microeconomic basis, economic growth for a company means increasing production capacity and increasing the market value of the company. Because a company is founded for profit and shapes all its processes in line with this purpose. Macro-scale objectives, such as regulating the balance of payments or reducing unemployment, are not the purpose or objective of a company.

The countries where companies are obliged to comply with the laws and all companies in these countries should be defined within the scope of macroeconomics. In this context, workers in all companies in a country constitute the labor force of the country. At the same time, the imports and exports of all these enterprises within a certain period of time are considered as macroeconomic activities on a country basis (Gürak, 2016). In this research, macroeconomics on the basis of countries will be examined.

According to Parasız (2003), economic growth is the increase in the employment potential in time (Parasız, 2003). According to Lipsey (1990), economic growth is a long-term increase in output per unit factor as a result of productivity (Lipsey et al., 1990).

According to Robinson's most general and accepted definition, economic growth is the increase in per capita or total production of a country. In this context of economic growth, any changes in the structure of the economy or social and cultural elements are ignored (Robinson, 1972).

According to Todaro and Smith (2003), economic growth is a stable process. In this stable process, production capacities have been accepted as the main instrument for increasing the national income.

Kuznets (1949), on the other hand, added advanced technology, institutional and ideological conditions to the concept of economic growth. These three components are very important for the economic growth of a country. Economic growth is the long-term increase in goods and supply capacities shaped by these three factors. These long-term capacity increases symbolize economic growth. Kuznets argued that quantitative factors should be considered when examining economic growth as well as qualitative factors (Kuznets, 1949).

Sources of Economic Growth

The four main sources of economic growth that are mentioned by Samuelson and Nordhaus are (Samuelson and Nordhaus, 2010);

- **Human Resources:** All elements that contribute to the development of individuals can be considered as human resources. Its quality is more important than the size of the total population. A training or motivation seminar to be provided to employees, discipline and labor supply are human resources that will trigger economic growth.
- **Natural Resources:** Natural gas, water, mine, forest resources are defined as natural resources. Countries without fertile soil cannot engage in agriculture and renewable energy sources cannot be used if the climate and weather conditions are not suitable. Mining or forestry cannot be carried out if the underground and above resources are insufficient. Therefore, natural resources are a very basic requirement in order to realize production and achieve economic growth. For example, while the Arab countries have provided their economic growth from oil, which is an underground source, Norway has achieved economic growth with fishing and Canada with natural gas (Samuelson and Nordhaus, 2010). Although natural resources are a fundamental requirement for economic growth, it is not a sufficient condition alone, especially in the age of technology. n this era, if natural resources are not supported by technology and old methods continue to be implemented, only the livelihood of the country is achieved, not economic growth. As a matter of fact, there is a concept under the name of "natural resource curse". According to this concept, it is seen that countries with rich natural resources grow slower than poor ones (Sachs and Warner,

The Relationship Between Economic Growth and Innovation

2001). This concept is described by Jean Bodin as "While people living in fertile lands generally have a shy and sentimental character, people living in infertile lands tend to be more careful, calm, cautious and resourceful character." (Sachs and Warner, 1995)

- **Capital:** Capital can be defined as the means of production or it can be defined as all assets that increase the productivity planned to be used in the production of a product or service. Heavy equipment, manufacturing building and cash money are considered as capital. Inadequate capital in underdeveloped countries leads to very low productivity in production. This has a negative impact on economic growth rates in these countries. Capital accumulation is very important in order to achieve economic growth with capital. According to Somashekar (2003). According to Somashekar (2003), one of the most important conditions of capital accumulation is the increase in saving assets, the existence of financial institutions that will enable these savings to be activated, and finally the use of savings in investments for capital goods. n this context, economic growth in the country will be achieved through the use of capital (Somashekar, 2003). However, as with other sources of economic growth, capital accumulation alone is not enough for economic growth. Capital accumulation should be supported by technology and science in accordance with the conditions of the time.
- **Technological Change and Innovation:** With the contribution of technology that changes and evolves with innovation, production efficiency increases at a positive level. A company using high technology makes its efficiency in the form of time and cost savings. Although the initial capital remains the same with savings, the profitability increases thanks to the increase in the output and the quality of these outputs. For example, in a building built using old technology, more materials and labor need to be used. It is possible to build larger buildings with the same cost by using less materials and labor with high technology (Dwivedi, 2010).

Models of Economic Growth

The first studies on economic growth models and the first thoughts that emerged as a result date back to the 16th century. Increasing prosperity and quality of life thanks to economic growth is desirable by all countries and peoples. Therefore, the policies to be followed and the precautions to be taken to provide economic growth are also very important. In this study, innovation-oriented economic growth models will be examined in order to better understand the relationship between innovation and economic growth.

Shumpeter Model

An Austrian economist Schumpeter published "The Theory of Economic Development" in 1912. In this study, innovation theory is mentioned for the first time and thus Schumpeter is considered the founder of this theory (Lundvall, 2007). According to Schumpeter, capitalism is not static but has a dynamic structure that is constantly changing. Unlike Marx, instead of the view that capitalism must disappear for its recovery; he advocated that capitalism can be repaired through change, R&D and innovation. He also states that long-term economic growth can be achieved with the support of technological innovations as well as innovations in products and processes.

In the economies dominated by capitalism, the demand for innovation by firms and producers starts with the incentive that will arise with the support of technology in terms of production and consumption stages. The market may shrink, grow or disappear completely with these incentives. As a result of these incentives, Schumpeter defines the growth of the market as creative accumulation and defines its destruction as creative destruction. The state of creative destruction should not be considered as an end, but as the end of an old and useless product or process and the beginning of an innovative process.

According to Schumpeter, technological developments and innovations are very important for economic growth. According to this perspective, Schumpeter examined economic growth under two sub-headings as the concept of innovations and initiatives. Firstly, innovation is defined as the availability of new resources or progress in the technical structure. In this context, it is accepted as innovation to create a new production element by using the production elements in a new composition while remaining the same amount. Secondly, entrepreneurship is crucial in Schumpeter's innovation-based economic growth model. Schumpeter states that the factor that constantly changes capitalism is entrepreneurs, not businessmen without taking risk. Entrepreneur is one who is not afraid of taking risks when it is necessary, strives to innovate and shapes his investments for this purpose. Their main purpose in implementing these investments is not only economic returns. Behind the entrepreneurial spirit is the ambition of struggle, the seizure and the desire to be superior. These instincts enable entrepreneurs to take risks more easily than other individuals. An entrepreneur needs two things to achieve his goals. The first of these is the technical knowledge and inventions necessary to implement innovation. According to Schumpeter, since there are many inventions and technical information that are not used and not included in the economic system, there will be no lack of resources in this respect. The second is the financial resources necessary for achieving the innovation goals that can be achieved with technical knowledge or invention. The most important obstacle to the realization of an initiative is the lack of financial capital (Günsoy, 2013).

Romer Model

Romer emphasized the importance of innovation and technological developments for economic growth (Romer, 1986). In 1990, Romer published his original work "Endogenous Technological Change". This study is defined as the first innovation-based economy model and technology is at the center of this model (Jones, 1998). The technology mentioned here symbolizes the technologies and innovations that companies ultimately achieve in order to increase their current profit rates. The technologies that emerged as a result of this process are defined as non-competitive and excluded. In addition, innovation or technology used by one individual does not preclude the use of another individual. In other words, these technologies and innovations can be used by an unlimited number of individuals at the same time. According to Romer's technology-oriented model, there are a total of four inputs in the economy and these are capital, unskilled labor, human capital and technology. These four inputs are used in three sectors as innovation, final goods and intermediate goods. Innovation is the main sector where knowledge is produced and new designs are developed. The final product is the sector in which consumable products are formed and skilled and unskilled labor and capital are used to achieve this formation. Finally, intermediate goods is the intermediate sector that enables new knowledge, technology and designs produced in innovation to be used in final product landing (Valdes, 1999). Romer's model of economic growth based on technology depends on three important elements. These are as follows (Romer, 1990):

- Technological advances enable the use of raw materials to be used together during production process. The products formed as a result of this usage form the basis of economic growth and technology ensures the continuous capital accumulation indirectly. At the same time, thanks to technological support, the amount of output is increasing, although the labor spent remains constant.

The Relationship Between Economic Growth and Innovation

- Although there are technological developments made by academicians in order to reach new information without profit, mostly companies or entrepreneurs who want to increase their profits turn to technological developments. Therefore, technology is an internal change and development.
- The cost of creating new information is paid only once. There is not any new cost for repeated use of this created new information. This is considered a defining feature of technology.

Grossman-Helpman Model

In 1989, 1990 and 1991, Grossman and Helpman focused on the relationship between economic growth and technology in their researches. The most notable of these is the study titled "Innovation and Growth in the Global Economy" published in 1991. According to this study, it will be easier for a country to achieve economic growth through incentives for innovation.

According to Grossman and Helpman, new information and technologies that are generated using economic methods should be considered as an internal element of the economy. Thanks to the investments in technology, efficiency will be increased and economic growth will be accompanied by this increase as a result. Grossman and Helpman focus particularly on the relationship between foreign trade and technology. In this context, there is an important relationship between new and different products created in countries and foreign trade policies of that country. New products created with innovation investments and technological support strengthen the hand of the countries in the competition market. Countries that can compete in the international market thanks to new and different products provide economic growth in this way. Underdeveloped or developing countries provide their needs by transferring products or technologies they cannot produce from other countries with free trade. In this way, although they do not have the necessary power, they can reach new information and technology through free trade. This is beneficial not only for the countries that receive the technology, but also for the countries that provide it because it will increase the employment (Grossman and Helpman, 1991). Quotas and tariffs are the obstacles to this trade. Therefore, both national and international policies are crucial for achieving technology-supported economic growth.

Aghion-Howitt Model

Their work which named is "A Model of Growth Through Creative Destruction" published in 1992 and supports the relationship between innovation and economic growth with Schumpeter's creative destruction model. According to Aghion and Howitt, technology is an inherent phenomenon, but has a goal to improve the quality of the product. Thanks to the increase in quality and innovation support, better and new products will be available and will replace the old ones in time. This process will bring Schumpeter's model of creative destruction.

According to Aghion and Howitt, the scope and size of the innovations to be apply are very important. The more investments mean that the higher the impact of innovations on economic growth. In addition, individual innovation studies with an entrepreneurial spirit have the chance to have a significant potential according to the scope of the research and the selected sectors.

In addition to creative destruction, vertical technologies are another key element of Aghion and Howitt's innovation-driven economic growth model. Vertical technologies are the process of launching new products in line with customer demand rather than making existing products better with innovation studies (Taban, 2013). Thanks to an ongoing innovation with vertical technologies, productivity has the capacity to expand exponentially forever. The main source of competition is shown as vertical technologies (Aghion and Howitt, 1992).

According to Aghion and Howitt, there are two different sectors which are production and research in general. The production process ensures the final product formation. In the research process, the production of intermediate goods which will be used in the production of final goods is provided. In addition, inventions and innovations may emerge as a result of research studies. Thanks to these, it is aimed to produce new products and put the old products on the shelf and end the rent provided by them. This change does not happen at once. In order for creative destruction to occur, new products must first compete with the old ones in the market and take their place (Aghion and Howitt, 1992).

LITERATURE REVIEW

There are many studies in the literature examining the relationship between innovation and economic growth. With the internalization of technological changes and the acceptance of the impact of innovation studies on economic growth, the number of research in this direction has increased. The leading studies on the relationship between innovation and economic growth over the years are as follows.

Lichtenberg (1993) examined 74 countries which is covering the period between 1964 and 1989. The research focused on the relationship between public and private sector funded R&D spending and economic growth associated with productivity. As a result of this study, R & D expenditures financed by the public sector have no effect on economic growth. However, it is stated that there is a positive relationship between R & D expenditures and economic growth and productivity.

Goel and Ram (1994) studied the activities 52 countries which consist of 34 underdeveloped and 18 developed countries between the years 1960 and 1980. As a result of the research, it is concluded that there is a long-term relationship between economic growth and R & D expenditures but the direction of causality in this relationship is not clear.

Coe and Helpman (1995) examined the relationship between total factor productivity and domestic, international R&D activities between 1971 and 1990. As a result, both domestic and international R & D activities have a positive relationship with total factor productivity.

Jones (1995) improved Romer's current model and examined the impact of R&D-based economic growth models on industrialized countries. The result of this model is that a permanent increase in R&D has no effect on economic growth.

Freire-Serén (1999) examined the relationship between economic growth and R&D investments of 21 OECD countries between 1965 and 1990. As a result of the researches, there is a strong positive relationship between R&D and economic growth. It is concluded that 1% increase in R&D expenditures will increase 0.08% in real gross domestic product.

Sylwester (2001) examined the relationship between economic growth and R&D with multivariate regression analysis on 20 OECD countries. As a result of this research, no relationship was found between R&D and economic growth in 20 OECD countries. However, it was also noted that the positive relationship between the economic growth and R&D was clearly seen among the G-7 countries.

Ülkü (2004) examined the relationship between economic growth and innovation between 1981 and 1997 in 20 OECD and 10 non-OECD countries. According to the results of the research, there is a positive relationship between innovation and economic growth in both OECD and non-OECD countries. However, innovation investments do not cause a continuous increase in economic growth.

Zachariadis (2004) examined the relationship between R&D investments and economic growth of 10 OECD countries between 1971 and 1995. In this study, it is concluded that the increase in R&D expenditures will increase economic growth rate and productivity.

Falk (2007) examined the relationship between high technology investments and per capita income of 15 OECD countries between 1970 and 2004. As a result of the study, a positive relationship was found between R&D expenditures and high technology investments and national income per capita.

Wang (2007) examined a total of 30 countries which consists of 7 OECD and 23 non-OECD countries. As a result of this study, it is concluded that effective R&D expenditure will lead to a better economic growth performance.

Saraç (2009) examined the R&D activities of 10 OECD countries between 1983 and 2004. As a result of the study, a positive relationship was found between economic growth and R&D investments.

Korkmaz (2010) investigated the existence of long-term relationship between R&D activities and economic growth in Turkey between 1990 and 2008 by Johansen co-integration test. In the study, it was concluded that each variable affects each other in the long run and there is a co-integration relationship between the variables. As a result of the study, it was stated that both short-term and long-term R&D expenditures had a positive effect on GDP.

Horvath (2011) examined the relationship between long-term economic growth and R&D investments. As a result, it is stated that R & D investments had a positive effect on economic growth.

Eid (2012) examined the relationship between productivity and R&D expenditures of 17 OECD countries for higher education between 1981 and 2006. The study concluded that there was a positive relationship between productivity and R&D expenditures.

Gülmez and Yardımcıoğlu (2012) conducted a research on the R&D expenditures and economic growth of 21 OECD countries between 1990 and 2010. As a result of the research, it was found that 1% increase in R&D expenditures resulted in 0.77% increase in economic growth.

Işık (2014) analyzed the relationship between patent expenditure and economic growth between 1990 and 2010 in Turkey. As a result of the analysis, it was concluded that there is a one-way causality relationship between economic growth and patent expenditures.

Galindo and Mendez (2014) examined the effects of entrepreneurship and innovation on economic growth for 13 developed countries. As a result, it has been found that innovation has a positive effect on economic growth and economic activities.

In the study conducted by Mike and Oransay (2015), the relationship between foreign investment and the number of patents was examined. The study is based on data between 1975 and 2013 in Turkey. As a result, it is stated that there is a positive relationship between GDP, exchange rate, number of patents and foreign capital investments.

In the study conducted by Bozkurt (2015), the relationship between R&D and GDP was researched. In this study, data from Turkey between 1998 and 2013 were examined. As a result of the research, although there was a one-way causality relationship from GDP to R&D, no causality from R&D to GDP was found.

Hanush et al. (2016) examined the impact of public spending on economic growth for the G20 countries. In their studies, it has been shown that innovation-oriented public expenditures have a higher impact on economic growth than other expenditures.

Bujari and Martinez (2016) have studied the relationship between technological innovation and economic growth in Latin American countries. In this study, it was concluded that the investment in patent and high-tech exports increased factor productivity and GDP per capita in most Latin American countries.

Yüksel (2017) analyzed the effect of R&D expenditures on export and economic growth. In this context, annual data of 28 European Union countries between 1996 and 2014 were examined. As a result of this analyze, no significant relationship was found between economic growth and innovation. On the other hand, a causality relationship has been found from exports to R&D expenditures.

THE RELATIONSHIP BETWEEN ECONOMIC GROWTH AND INNOVATION

There are two important ways to increase the output in an economy. The first is to increase the amount of input included in the system for production. The second is to find a new way to achieve more output without changing the amount of input in production. The first study was conducted by Abramovitz (1956) on determining which of these two ways would be more efficient. In this study, Abramovitz examined the amount of input and output of the American economy from 1870 to 1950 and aimed to determine their impact on economic growth. As a result of the researches, it has been stated that the increase in the inputs affects only 15% of the increase in the output and the remaining 85% is an unexplained residue. In the following years, Fabricant (1954), Kendrick (1956), Denison (1962), Jorgenson and Griliches (1967) carried out similar studies for different time intervals and obtained similar results to Abramovitz's work. Apart from these studies, the most remarkable one is Solow's work. Although Solow uses a different method and time frame from Abromovitz, a very similar result has been reached. The amount of unexplained residues between input and output is also referred to in the economic literature as the "Solow residual" (Sungur et al., 2016). The surprising result of Solow's study is that 87% of economic growth is explained by the Solow residual under the name of technical change. But Solow could not find a clear answer to the question of how this technical change was produced and technology has been recognized as an external factor (Gülmez and Yardımcıoğlu, 2012).

In the following studies, R&D, technological change, number of patents and innovation expenditures were included in economic growth models as internal variables, not externally. Aghion and Howitt (1992), Grossman and Helpman (1991) and Romer (1986) are the main people who have included changes in technology into their internal economic growth models (Sungur et al., 2016).

When internal economic growth models are analyzed, it is observed that R&D expenditures are widely used as an indicator of change in order to measure the technological changes easily and reliably. In many studies, it has been found that R&D expenditures are the most important indicators of both changes in output and innovation-oriented studies. For example, Geroski (1989) examined 79 firms between 1976 and 1979 and researched the impact of innovation on total factor productivity. As a result of this research, it is concluded that approximately 50% of the total factor productivity can be explained by innovation. Budd and Hobbis (1989) explored the source of productivity in the UK manufacturing industry between 1968 and 1985. As a result of the research, it has been concluded that the patent activities created by the firms as a result of innovation studies have a positive relationship with efficiency.

In internal economic growth models, innovative activities are seen as the most important factor in achieving sustainable and long-term economic growth. Technological innovations trigger economic growth and create a positive impact both at the firm and national level. According to Romer (1986), there is a strong correlation between innovation and economic growth. Howitt (1999) states that incentives for innovation will increase long-term economic growth.

In this study, the relationship between economic growth and innovation activities is examined. Innovation activities of selected 16 OECD countries between 2005 and 2015 were subjected to panel data analysis.

Panel Data Analysis

Panel data analysis method which has significant advantages for this study compared with other techniques is chosen. The benefits of panel data analysis are as follows (Tarı, 2016):

- Panel data analysis provides the opportunity to work with more complex behavior models.
- In this way, it is in a more advantageous position than the time series and horizontal section data models.
- Panel data is more suitable for investigating the dynamics of change when examining repeated horizontal cross-sectional observations.
- Panel data analysis can better measure and identify effects that are not easily observed in time series data and cross-sectional data.
- Panel data analysis considers differences such as the countries which are specific to cross-sectional units have different trends and behaviors. These differences can be controlled and measured within the model.

Although panel data analysis has advantages, it has some disadvantages. These are as follows (Baltagi, 2005):

- Data collection and design is problematic in panel data analysis.
- The shorter time series makes the prediction weak.
- There may be disturbances caused by measurement errors. Problems such as incorrect recording of data and deliberate inaccuracy of the responses obtained during data collection are the main causes of these errors.

The model to be used in the research within the scope of panel data analysis is as follows:

$$Y_{it} = \alpha_{it} + \beta_{kit} X_{1kit} \quad i = 1,\ldots\ldots N \,;\, t = 1,\ldots\ldots T.$$

- Y : Dependent variable
- X_k : Independent variable
- β : Coefficient
- i : Countries
- t : Time (Year)

Research Method and Findings

The OECD is the forum for countries that account for about three quarters of total world production. It is an international organization that makes continuous evaluations and recommendations about the world economy with its approaches and activities (Akbulut, 2002). Therefore, in order to achieve more efficient results, OECD member countries are included in this study. The selection of the countries included in the study was made from top to bottom according to the world GDP ranking. At this point, the total number of countries including Turkey to be able to research has been identified as 16. In order to obtain more accurate results in the research, it is very important to keep the time interval examined wide. However, access to reliable country data from previous years is a problem at this point. Therefore, the research was limited to year from 2005 to 2015. The GDP data, the share of R&D investments in GDP and the number of patent applications are the variables to be used in the research. GDP and patent application data were obtained from the World Bank and the share of R&D investments in GDP was obtained from OECD. The 16 countries used in the study are shown in Table 1.

The model that will be used in the research is arranged according to the data as follows:

$GDP_{it} = \alpha_{it} + PATENT_{kit}$ i = 1....15 ve t = 1....10.
$GDP_{it} = \alpha_{it} + RD_{kit}$ i = 1....15 ve t = 1....10.

Accordingly, *GDPit* representing economic growth is defined as the dependent variable of the model. The number of patent applications is defined as *PATENTkit* and the share of R&D investments in GDP is defined as independent variables as *RDkit*. The hypotheses regarding the relationship between economic growth and other independent variables are established as follows:

- *H1 = GDP is positively affected by the increase in the number of patent applications.*
- *H2 = GDP is positively affected by the increase in R&D investments.*

Firstly, the presence of unit root was investigated in panel data analysis. In this context, Im, Pesaran and Shin, one of the leading studies that give unit root testing in panel data models, are applied.

As seen in Table 2, t statistics and probabilities are not stationary at I (0) level in unit root test results applied to variables. Therefore, the primary differences of the variants are investigated. When the primary differences are examined for the variables, it is seen that the primary differences of GDP, number of patent application and R&D expenditures are I (1) stable.

After investigating the unit roots, co-integration analysis is applied to determine whether there is a long term relationship between the variables. Pedroni co-integration analysis is used to investigate the long-term relationship between GDP, R&D expenditures and GDP, number patent applications.

As seen in Table 3, four of the seven statistics in the Pedroni co-integration test show that there is co-integration between R&D investments and GDP. Co-integration analysis is used to understand whether

Table 1. 16 selected OECD countries used in the research

U.S.A	France	South Korea	Turkey
China	United Kingdom	Russia	Holland
Japan	Italy	Spain	Sweden
Germany	Canada	Mexico	Belgium

The Relationship Between Economic Growth and Innovation

Table 2. Im, Pesaran and Shin Test

	GDP			
	t statistic I(0)	*Probability I(0)*	*t statistic I(1)*	*Probability I(1)*
Im, Pesaran & Shin	1.21832	0.1116	5.39376	0.0000
	Number of Patent Applications			
	t statistic I(0)	*Probability I(0)*	*t statistic I(1)*	*Probability I(1)*
Im, Pesaran & Shin	0.01978	0.4921	2.96904	0.0015
	R&D Investments			
	t statistic I(0)	*Probability I(0)*	*t statistic I(1)*	*Probability I(1)*
Im, Pesaran & Shin	0.68022	0.2482	3.36392	0.0004

there is a long-term relationship between the variables. In Pedroni panel co-integration analysis, there are 7 different tests which are Panel v-Statistic, Panel rho-Statistic, Panel PP-Statistic, Panel ADF-Statistic, Group rho-Statistic, Group PP-Statistic and Group ADF-Statistic. This methodology is suitable while making evaluation by using panel data (Dinçer and Yüksel, 2019). Within this framework, it can be stated that these two variables are long-term co-integrated.

As seen in Table 4, four of the seven statistics in the Pedroni co-integration test show that there is co-integration between number of patent applications and GDP. Within this framework, it can be stated that the two variables are long-term co-integrated.

After the co-integration tests, FMOLS (Full Modified Ordinary Least Square) method was applied to determine the coefficients of these relationships.

Table 5 shows the FMOLS results. When these results are evaluated, there is a long-term positive interaction between GDP and R&D investments as well as between GDP and number of patent applications.

Table 3. Pedroni co-integration test (GDP and R&D expenditures)

Within Dimension				
	t – statistic	*Probability*	*Weighted t – statistic*	*Probability*
Panel v-Statistic	-3.378382	0.9996	-4.425550	1.0000
Panel rho-Statistic	1.537322	0.9379	1.373496	0.9152
Panel PP-Statistic	-7.002628	0.0000	-9.415250	0.0000
Panel ADF-Statistic	-4.595523	0.0000	-6.869689	0.0000
Between Dimension				
	t – statistic	*Probability*		
Group rho-Statistic	3.202291	0.9993		
Group PP-Statistic	-9.913919	0.0000		
Group ADF-Statistic	-6.899606	0.0000		

Table 4. Pedroni co-integration test (GDP number of patent applications)

	Within Dimension			
	t – statistic	*Probability*	*Weighted t – statistic*	*Probability*
Panel v-Statistic	-4.412455	1.0000	-4.753381	1.0000
Panel rho-Statistic	1.971470	0.9757	1.549849	0.9394
Panel PP-Statistic	-9.080435	0.0000	-11.19756	0.0000
Panel ADF-Statistic	-6.031895	0.0000	-7.703631	0.0000
	Between Dimension			
	t – statistic	*Probability*		
Group rho-Statistic	3.195662	0.9993		
Group PP-Statistic	-12.46051	0.0000		
Group ADF-Statistic	-7.137606	0.0000		

As a result of the analysis, it is accepted that both *H1* (*GDP is positively affected by the increase in the number of patent applications.*) and *H2* (*GDP is positively affected by the increase in R&D investments.*) hypotheses are correct. Moreover, the increase in R&D investments affected positively economic growth more than the increase in the number of patent applications.

SOLUTIONS AND RECOMMENDATIONS

In summary, the results of panel data analyze shows the importance of innovation. In this context, there are studies that a country needs to carry out in order to achieve economic growth through innovation studies. Based on all these points, the following studies should be conducted on innovation (Karagöl and Karahan, 2014):

- It is very important to produce goods that have no or less production, which will reduce imports and the current account deficit in countries. In order to achieve this, it is very important to increase R&D investments efficiently.
- One of the most important building blocks of innovation activities is human resources. In this context, countries should be able to create human resources needed to ensure the needs of technological development. Therefore, national education policies should be revised and reformed ac-

Table 5. FMOLS test results

GDP and R&D Expenditures FMOLS Results				
Variable	*Coefficient*	*Standard Deviation*	*t – statistic*	*Probability*
R&D	0.006807	0.002570	2.649167	0.0090
GDP and Number of Patent Applications FMOLS Results				
Variable	*Coefficient*	*Standard Deviation*	*t – statistic*	*Probability*
Patent	7.19E-06	1.96E-06	3.675737	0.0003

The Relationship Between Economic Growth and Innovation

cordingly. In order to conduct efficient R&D research, people at doctoral level are needed. Hence, especially brain drain should be prevented and valuable human resources should be kept inside the country.
- Research should be conducted in order to realize R&D expenditures efficiently. Then, strategic areas should be focused. Countries should focus on sectoral needs and products.
- R&D investment per capita should be increased efficiently based on the identified sectors and products.

Especially in recent years, companies have started to give more importance to R&D in order to increase their productivity and profitability. In addition, most countries are encouraging companies to lower tax rates and increase subsidies. Therefore, it is clear that the studies which are analyzing the R&D are very important (Yüksel, 2017).

FUTURE RESEARCH DIRECTIONS

In this study, the data of 16 countries between 2005 and 2015 were examined. In the next step of this research, more countries and longer time intervals would be used. In this way, the findings of the research will be more efficient thanks to the benefits of panel data analysis.

EVALUATIONS AND CONCLUSION

Today, as technology is developing rapidly, economic competition between companies and countries becomes equally difficult. For this reason, it is very important to follow technology closely and carry out innovative activities in order to stand out from the competitors. This study is carried out to show how important innovation is in order to ensure the continuous and stable economic growth.

The study examined the GDP, the share of R&D investments in GDP and the number of patent applications of 16 selected OECD countries between 2005 and 2015. Thanks to its advantages, panel data analysis is used in the research. The hypothesis of the research is specified that increase in number of patent applications and R&D investments will increase GDP. In this context, unit root, Pedroni co-integration and FMOLS tests are applied to the data by using E-Views program. As a result of the tests, both hypotheses are positive and increase in the number of patent applications and the increase in R&D investments would have a positive effect on economic growth. This study also coincides with the results of other studies conducted in this direction in previous years. In addition, the validity of the years based on the research, the selected innovation indicators and the tests performed after the selection of panel data analysis differentiate this study from the other studies in the literature. These differences constitute the original side of the study and show its contribution to the literature.

As can be seen, innovation affects economic growth positively. Therefore, realizing the innovation activities through technology integration are very important in order to compete in the global market and increase market share, profitability and quality. South Korea is the most prominent example of this.

South Korea has become one of the poorest countries in the world due to the Korean wars between 1950 and 1953. Between 1962 and 1997, seven "Five-Year Development Plans" were prepared and all of them were successfully implemented. Innovation is at the center of these development plans.

With the importance given to innovation by South Korea, per capita R&D investments increased from 0.38% in 1970 to 0.54% in 1980 and 1.68% in 1990. This ratio continued to increase in 2000s. The R&D investments per capita increased to 2.3% in 2000, to 3.12% in 2008 and to 4.2% in 2015. This ratio is even higher than other developed countries. For example, in 2015, this rate is 2.74% in the United States and 3.2% in Japan. In addition to the increase in R&D investments, the share of total R&D expenditures in South Korea in private sector increased from 26% in 1975 to 75% in 1985. These increases clearly show the importance that South Korea attaches to innovation (Çakmak, 2016).

As it is seen, while South Korea was one of the poorest countries in the world, it ranks ninth in the national income ranking thanks to its innovation policies (Worldbank, 2017). In this context, it is very important for countries to invest in innovation in order to achieve sustainable economic growth. For example, according to TUIK data, Turkey's imports by 90% of the sector is seen as consisting of capital goods and intermediate goods. On the other hand, when examining Turkey's foreign trade in the manufacturing industry according to technology intensity, it is seen that the ratio of low and medium technology products in exports and the ratio of high and medium high technology products in imports are higher. The reason for this is that Turkey cannot perform the production of high-tech products that require R&D investments. This situation shows that there is not enough innovative studies in the country.

Although South Korea's GDP was 65,22 billion dollars in 1980, its GDP in 2015 was 1.382,76 billion dollars. On the other hand, Turkey's GDP was 96,52 billion dolars in 1980, its GDP in 2015 was 859,45 billion dollars. Considering that 35-year period shows that South Korea had a much better economic growth than Turkey. This is because of the innovation activities carried out by South Korea is much more than Turkey.

ACKNOWLEDGMENT

This study was derived from Samet Akça's master thesis written in Karatay University in 2018.

REFERENCES

Aghion, P., & Howitt, P. (1992). A model of growth through creative destruction. *Econometrica*, *60*(2), 323. doi:10.2307/2951599

Akalın, Ş. (2007). Innovation, İnovasyon: Yenileşim. *Türk Dili Dil ve Edebiyat Dergisi*, 483.

Badulescu, N., & Mirela, A. D. (2012). Different types of innovation modeling. *Annals of DAAAM for 2012 & Proceedings of the 23rd International DAAAM Symposium, 23*(1), 1071.

Baltagi, B. H. (2005). *Econometric analysis of panel data*. UK: John Wiley & Sons.

Barbieri, J. C., & Alvares, A. C. T. (2016). *Sixth generation innovation model: description of a success model*. Brazil: Getulio Vargas Foundation Sao Paulo.

Bozkurt, C. (2015). R&D expenditures and economic growth relationship in Turkey. *International Journal Economics and Financial Issues.*, *5*(1), 188.

Bujari, A. A., & Martinez, F. V. (2016). Technological innovation and economic performance in services: a firm-level analysis. *Cambridge Journal of Economics*, *30*(3), 435–458.

Çakmak, U. (2016) Güney Kore'nin Ekonomik Kalkınmasının Temel Dinamikleri. Süleyman Demirel Üniversitesi, *İktisadi ve İdari Bilimler Fakültesi Dergisi*, 21(1), 151,171.

Coe, D., Helpman, E., & Hoffmaister, A. W. (1995). International R&D spillovers and institutions. *IMF Working Paper*.

Dinçer, H., & Yüksel, S. (2019). Identifying the causality relationship between health expenditure and economic growth: an application on E7 countries. *Journal of Health Systems and Policies*, *1*, 14.

Dosi, G. (1988). Sources procedures and microeconimic effects of innovation. *Journal of Economic Literature*, *3*, 1122.

Drucker, F. P. (2017). *İnovasyon ve Girişimcilik – Uygulama ve İlkeler*. İstanbul, Turkey: Optimist Yayım Dağıtım.

Dura, C., & Atik, H. (2002). *Bilgi Tohumu, Bilgi Ekonomisi ve Türkiye. Literatür Yayınları, 1* (p. 209). İstanbul, Turkey: Basım.

Dwivedi, D. N. (2010). Macroeconomics theory and policy. New Delhi, India: Tata McGraw-Hill Education, 388.

Edquist, C. (2005). *Systems of innovation* (p. 64). Routhledge, Oxon: Technologies, Institutions and Organizations.

Eid, A. (2012). Higher education R&D and productivity growth: an empirical study on high-income OECD countries. *Education Economics*, *20*(1), 53–68. doi:10.1080/09645291003726855

Erkiletlioğlu, H. (2013). Dünyada ve Türkiye'de AR-GE Faaliyetleri. İktisadi Araştırmalar Bölümü, Türkiye İş Bankası Yayınları, 2.

Ersel, B. (2003). Bilgi Çağında Çalışma İlkeleri ve Beyin Göçü. *II. Ulusal Bilgi, Ekonomi ve Yönetim Kongresi Bildiriler Kitabı*, Kocaeli Üniversitesi., 717.

Eurostat & OECD. (2005). *Oslo Kılavuzu Yenilik Verilerinin Toplanması ve Yorumlanması İçin İlkeler. 3. Baskı*. TUBİTAK.

Falk, M. (2007). R&D spending in the high-tech sector and economic growth. *Research in Economics*, 61.

Freire-Serén & Jesus M. (1999). Aggregate R&D expenditure and endogenous economic growth. *UFAE and IAE Working Papers* 436, 99.

Galindo, M., & Mendez, M. T. (2014). Entrepreneurship, economic growth and innovation: are feedback effect at work? *Journal of Business Research*, *67*(5), 825–829. doi:10.1016/j.jbusres.2013.11.052

Goel, R. K., & Ram, R. (1994). Research and development expenditures and economic growth: a cross-country study. *Economic development and cultural change*, *42*(2), 403–411. doi:10.1086/452087

Grossman, G. M., & Helpman, E. (1991). *Innovation and growth: in the global economy* (p. 43). Cambridge, MA: MIT Press.

Gülmez, A., & Yardımcıoğlu, F. (2012). OECD Ülkelerinde AR-GE Harcamaları ve Ekonomik Büyüme İlişkisi: Panel Eşbütünleşme ve Panel Nedensellik Analizi (1990-2010). *Maliye Dergisi, 163*, 336.

Güloğlu, B., & Tekin, B. (2012). A panel causality analysis of the relationship among research and development, innovation and economic growth in high-income OECD countries. *Eurasion Economic Review, 2*(1).

Günsoy, B., ... (2013). İktisadi Büyüme. T.C Anadolu Üniversitesi Yayını No:2898 Web-Ofset, Eskişehir.

Gürak, H. (2016). *Ekonomik Büyüme ve Küresel Ekonomi* (pp. 19–62). Bursa, Turkey: Ekin Kitabevi.

Hanusch, H., Chakraborty, L., & Khurana, S. (2016) Public expenditures, innovation and economic growth: empirical evidence from G20 countries. *Beitrag: Institut für Volkswirtschaftslehre.*

Horvath, R. (2011). Research and development and growth: a Bayesion model averaging analysis. *Economic Modelling, 28*(6), 2669–2673. doi:10.1016/j.econmod.2011.08.007

Howitt, P. (1999). Steady endogenous growth with population and R&D inputs growing. *Journal of Political Economy, 107*(4), 715–730. doi:10.1086/250076

Işık, C. (2014). Patent Harcamaları ve İktisadi Büyüe Arasındaki İlişki: Türkiye Örneği. *Sosyoekonomi, 1*, 69.

Jones, C. I. (1995). R&D based models of economic growth. *Journal of Political Economy, 103*(4), 759–784. doi:10.1086/262002

Jones, C. I. (1998). *Introduction to economic growth* (p. 2). New York: W.W. Norton Company.

Kasza, A. (2004). Innovation networks, policy networks and regional development in transition economies: a conceptual review and research perspectives. *Paper for EPSNET Conference*, 5-7.

Kuznets, S. (1949). Suggestions for an inquiry into the economic growth of nations. NBER, In Problems in the Study of Economic Growth, 6.

Lichtenberg, F. R. (1993). R&D investment and international productivity differences. *NBER Working Paper Series Working Paper* No: 4161.

Lipsey, R. G., ... (1990) Economics. Longman Higher Education; 9th edition, 333.

Lowe, R., & Marriot, S. (2006). *Innovation management: enterprise, entrepreneurship and innovation, concepts, contexts and commercialization.* USA: Elsevier.

Lundvall, B. A. (2007). Innovation system research and policy. Where it came from and where it might go. In CAS Seminar, Oslo, 10.

Marinova, D. P. (2003). Models of innovation in the international handbook of innovation. Elsevier Science, 44-53.

Mike, F., & Oransay, G. (2015). Altyapı ve İnovasyon Değişimlerinin Doğrudan Yabancı Yatırımlar Üzerine Etkisi: Türkiye Üzerine Ampirik Bir Uygulama. *The Journal of Academic Social Science, 12*(12), 372. doi:10.16992/ASOS.645

Öztürk, S., & Saygın, S. (2017). 1973 Petrol Krizinin Ekonomiye Etkileri ve Stagflasyon Olgusu. *Balkan Sosyal Bilimler Dergisi, 6*(12), 3.

Parasız, İ. (2003). *Makro Ekonomi Teori ve Politika* (p. 840). Bursa, Turkey: Ezgi Kitabevi Yayınları.

Robinson, S. (1972). Theories of economic growth and development: methodology and content. economic development and culturel change, 52.

Romer, P. M. (1986). Increasing returns and long-run growth. *Journal of Political Economy, 94*(5), 1002–1037. doi:10.1086/261420

Romer, P. M. (1990). Endogenous technological change. *Journal of Political Economy*, 75.

Rothwell, R. (1994). *Towards the fifth-generation innovation process. science policy research unit* (pp. 7–9). UK: University of Sussex.

Sachs, J. D., & Warner, A. M. (1995). Naturel resource abundance and economic growth. *National Bureau of Economic Research Working Paper*, 4.

Sachs, J. D., & Warner, A. M. (2001). The curse of naturel resources. *European Economic Review, 45*(4-6), 827–838. doi:10.1016/S0014-2921(01)00125-8

Samuelson, P. A. & Nordhaus, W. D. (2010). Economics. New Delhi, India: McGraw-Hill Companies, 503.

Saraç, B. T. (2009). Araştırma ve Geliştirme Harcamalarının Ekonomik Buyüme Üzerindeki Etkisi: Panel Veri Analizi. Anadolu International Conference in Economics. Eskişehir, Türkiye.

Scheidel, W. (2006). Population and Demography. Princeton/Stanford Working Class Papers in Classics, Stanford University. 2.

Schumpeter, J. A. (1934). The theory of economic growth. Transaction Publishers (10th Ed.). 2004.

Somashekar, N. T. (2003). *Development and environmental economics* (p. 239). New Delhi, India: New Age International Publishers.

Sylwester, K. (2001). R&D and economic growth. *Knowledge, Technology, & Policy, 13*(4), 71–84. doi:10.1007/BF02693991

Taban, S., Günsoy, B., Günsoy, G., Erdinç, Z., & Aktaş, M. (2013). İktisadi Büyüme. T.C Anadolu Üniversitesi Yayını No: 2898 Web-Ofset, Eskişehir, 147.

Tarı, R. (2016). *Ekonometri. Küv Yayınları 12*. İstanbul, Turkey: Baskı.

Todaro, M., & Smith, S. C. (2003). *Economic development*. New York: Addison Wesley.

Sungur, O., Aydin, H., & Mehmet, E. R. E. N. (2016). Türkiye'de AR-GE, İnovasyon, İhracat ve Ekonomik Büyüme Arasındaki İlişki: Asimetrik Nedensellik Analizi. *Süleyman Demirel Üniversitesi İktisadi ve İdari Bilimler Fakültesi Dergisi, 21*(1), 174.

Ülkü, H. (2004). R&D, innovation and economic growth: an empirical analysis. *IMF Working Paper, 4*(185), 1. doi:10.5089/9781451859447.001

Valdes, B. (1999). *Economic growth: theory, empirics and policy* (p. 137). UK: Edward Elgar.

Wang, E. C. (2007). R&D efficiency and economic performance: a cross-country analysis using the stochastics frontier approach. *Journal of Policy Modeling, 29*(2), 345–360. doi:10.1016/j.jpolmod.2006.12.005

Yüksel, S. (2017). The impacts of research and development expenses on export and economic growth. *International Business and Accounting Research Journal, 1*(1), 1–8. doi:10.15294/ibarj.v1i1.1

Zachariadis, M. (2004). R&D-induced growth in the OECD? *Review of Development Economics, 8*(3), 423–439. doi:10.1111/j.1467-9361.2004.00243.x

KEY TERMS AND DEFINITIONS

EIS: European Innovation Scoreboard
FMOLS: Full Modified Ordinary Least Square
GDP: Gross Domestic Products
OECD: Organization for Economic Co-Operation and Development
R&D: Research and Development
TUIK: Türkiye İstatistik Kurumu (Turkish Statistical Institute)

Chapter 18
The Role of Central Bank in Competitive Environment:
A Study for Interest Rate Corridor Systems

Mustafa Eser Kurum
Yeni Yüzyıl University, Turkey

Suat Oktar
Marmara University, Turkey

ABSTRACT

This chapter evaluates the macroeconomic impact of the interest rate corridor policy implemented by the central bank in Turkey. In this context, firstly the general framework, types and application of interest rate corridor policy are explained. Then, the interest rate corridor policy implemented by the CBRT after the global crisis was examined in detail. In addition, domestic and foreign literature examining the macroeconomic effects of the interest rate corridor policy has been included. This chapter examines the macroeconomic impact of the interest rate corridor policy implemented in Turkey using data from the 2011-2018 period. In the study, Engle-Granger Cointegration Analysis and Toda-Yamamoto Causality Analysis were used as models. As a result of the study, it was concluded that interest rate corridor had an effect on economic growth, foreign direct investment, and exchange rate variables.

INTRODUCTION

Prior to the 2008 Global Crisis, many central banks had implemented conventional monetary policies aimed at price stability, using short-term interest rates as instruments through the transmission mechanism. The transmission mechanism is one of the most important factors in ensuring the macroeconomic stability of monetary policies. Because the transmission mechanism can affect the overall level of demand, GDP, employment and prices through monetary policy (Bain and Howells, 2009). The short-term interest rate, which is called the policy rate, refers to the interest rate that is generally applicable to overnight or weekly term transactions (Özatay, 2011a; Kalkavan and Ersin, 2019).

DOI: 10.4018/978-1-7998-2559-3.ch018

However, in times of crisis, traditional monetary policy instruments focused on price stability are insufficient for central banks to achieve their targets (Smaghi, 2009). In this case, central banks are turning to traditional monetary policy instruments. The interest rate corridor policy is one of these policies. Corridor systems are a system developed to help ensure that interest rates in the money market move in close relation to the policy rate of central banks. Because this close relationship between the policy interest rate and the market interest rates is the basis of the transmission mechanism of the monetary policy. Since interest rates in the interest rate corridor system closely follow the policy interest rate, central banks can also create an effective policy signal (Revised Framework Monetary Operations, 2016).

In this study, the effectiveness of interest rate corridor policy has been examined. The general framework of the interest rate corridor policy, implementation, types, advantages and disadvantages are given. The second section provides information about the application of the interest rate corridor after the global crisis in Turkey.

In the third chapter, literature review related to interest rate corridor is made. In this context, domestic and foreign literature examining the macroeconomic effects of the interest rate corridor has been included.

Finally, theoretical information about Engle-Granger Cointegration Analysis and Toda-Yamamoto Causality Analysis are given. In addition, the data used in the model is explained. The results obtained by cointegration analysis and causality analysis are evaluated.

GENERAL INFORMATION ABOUT INTEREST RATE CORRIDOR SYSTEM

Since the intraday transactions in the interbank market are uncertain, the reserve requirement of each bank at the end of the day is uncertain. For example, a bank with a surplus liquidity surplus may deposit deposits to the central bank in order to assess this surplus, while a bank with temporary liquidity shortage may benefit from the short-term credit facilities of the central bank (Whitesell, 2006).

In the corridor systems, a central bank provides two facilities, namely the possibility of lending to commercial banks provided that they pay a certain interest, and the possibility of deposit income in exchange for a deposit interest. While the central banks implement a corridor policy, the overnight market interest rate in the money market can be determined in close proximity to the targeted interest rate (Berentsen and Monnet, 2008).

In a classical corridor system, the policy rate of the central bank will be below the lending rate and above the deposit rate. Therefore, the lending rate constitutes an upper limit for short-term interest rates. (Revised Framework Monetary Operations, 2016). In corridor systems, there are two types of applications: interest rate corridor system and floor system. Below it will be given information about these systems.

Interest Rate Corridor System

In the interest rate corridor system, the overnight borrowing rate applied by a central bank for short-term credit facilities constitutes a floor, while the lending rate applied in return for the evaluation of the excess liquidity creates a ceiling (Bernhardsen and Kloster, 2010). The interest rate at the middle of this area, which is called the interest rate corridor between the floor interest rate and the ceiling interest rate, constitutes the policy rate (Whitesell, 2006). If the policy rate is determined as the middle point of the interest rate corridor, it is called the symmetric interest corridor. If the policy rate is determined

The Role of Central Bank in Competitive Environment

to be close to the ceiling interest rate or the floor interest rate, the case is called the asymmetric interest rate corridor.

The interest corridor system, where the policy rate moves between the base rate and the ceiling rate, enables the central banks to change the interest rates in the market without requiring any open market transactions (Disyatat, 2008).

The interest rate corridor system prevents the interest rate on the inter-bank market from leaving this corridor determined by the central bank (Clews et al., 2010). Theoretically, central banks can isolate interest policy from balance sheet size by limiting the volatility in policy interest in the corridor system. In the corridor system, the central bank sets a target for overnight policy rate in line with the inflation and economic growth targets as in the traditional structure. In addition, this loan facility, which shows that the central bank is ready to supply the overnight liquidity demand demanded from a fixed interest rate, can be likened to the rediscount window (Kahn, 2010).

In addition, central banks can set narrowing or expanding policies without changing the target interest rate through the interest rate corridor system. For example, the central bank's symmetrical expansion of the interest rate corridor around the set target interest rate makes it difficult for banks to access the central bank's facilites (Berentsen and Monnet, 2008).

With the interest rate corridor system, central banks can freely implement their liquidity policy and interest policy. For example, while official interest rates can be raised against speculative pressures in exchange rates, market interest rates can also be reduced to the lower boundary of the interest rate corridor to provide or even increase the liquidity needed by the domestic financial system (Goodhart, 2010).

Floor System

Basically, the floor system is very similar to the interest corridor system. In the floor system, the target interest rate is defined to be very close or equal to the base interest rate (borrowing interest rate). In the interest rate corridor policy implemented by central banks, the policy rate (i_p) occurs at a point between the borrowing interest rate (i_B) and the lending interest rate (i_L). However, in the floor system, the policy rate (p) of the central bank is close to or equal to the borrowing interest rate (i_B).

Although the floor system is not a widely used policy, it allows commercial banks to gain interest from all their reserves and thus helps the financial system to operate more efficiently. On the other hand, in the corridor system, since the lending interest of central banks will be lower than the market interest, commercial banks obtain income from the reserves by lending money to other commercial banks or by purchasing other assets (Keister, 2012).

The targeted policy interest rate in the floor system is equal to the borrowing interest rate of the central bank. For this, the central bank should provide liquidity to the banking system in order to bring the overnight interest rate closer to the borrowing interest rate of the central bank. In fact, an advantage of the floor system is that the central bank increases the liquidity supply in the banking system without lowering the short-term market interest rates below the policy interest rate. This indicates that central banks have two independent instruments, namely interest rate and liquidity supply. Especially during the global financial crisis in 2008, many central banks have temporarily switched from a corridor system to a floor system (Bernhardsen and Kloster, 2010).

Commercial banks need reserve money to perform interbank payments and many daily banking operations. The amount of interbank payments during the day can easily exceed the end-of-day balances of banks. The central bank may have to increase its reserve supply (daylight credit) during the day to ensure that the payment system operates smoothly. In the floor system, central banks will not have to reduce their reserve supply at the end of the day to achieve the targeted overnight interest rate. This helps to reduce the pressure between the central bank's monetary policy targets and the payment system (Maehle, 2014).

In recent years, due to the large-scale asset purchases of central banks and increasing quantitative easing policies, there has been a significant increase in the reserve amount of commercial banks. For example, the amount of reserves in the USA, which was $ 11 billion in July 2007, increased to $ 2.8 trillion in 2014 and 2015. In case of large increases in reserve supply, it is not possible for central banks to direct market interest rates using the interest rate corridor system. In such a case, the application of a floor system may be more effective than an interest rate corridor system (Keister et al., 2015).

INTEREST RATE CORRIDOR POLICY IN TURKEY

The CBRT used its interest rate corridor policy quite frequently during the global crisis. The interest rate corridor is the width between the CBRT's overnight borrowing interest rate and the lending interest rate. In January 2006, the interest rate corridor, which was 4 points, was reduced to 3 by reducing the lending interest rate by 1 point. In May, CBRT increased the interest rate corridor to 5 points by increasing the lending interest rate by 2 percentage points as the fluctuations in the markets increased (CBRT, 2006).

In May and December 2010, the CBRT cut the overnight borrowing interest rate from 5.75% to 1.50%, and increased the overnight lending rate by 0.25 percentage points to 9% (CBRT, 2010). In addition to the fall in policy rates, overnight borrowing interest rates were lowered in January 2011, allowing the interest rate corridor to widen and market rates to be lower than the policy rate. Thus, the reduction of short-term capital inflows are provided. However, starting from August, the depreciation of TL due to global risk caused inflation to increase in the short term. Therefore, the interest rate corridor was widened in October by increasing interest rates on lending considerably (CBRT,2011).

In 2012, the CBRT narrowed the interest rate corridor by decreasing the lending interest rate by 1 point in February, 1.5 points in September, 0.50 points in October and 0.50 points in November. Despite the increase in global risk seeking in the last quarter of 2012, the CBRT narrowed the interest rate corridor by taking the financial risks into account with the improvement in inflation and macroeconomic stability (CBRT, 2012).

Against strong capital inflows in 2013, the upper and lower limits of the interest rate corridor were reduced by 0.25 points in January and February. In March, the interest rate corridor was narrowed only by lowering the lending interest rate by 1 point. The upper and lower limits were reduced by 0.50 points in April. In order to maintain financial stability as a result of ongoing capital inflows during the year, both interest rates were reduced by 0.50 points in May. In the third quarter of the year, uncertainties in global markets increased, TL depreciated and inflation rates increased. Therefore, the lending interest rate was raised by 0.75 points in July, and by 0.50 points in August, thus extending the interest rate corridor upwards (CBRT, 2013).

The lower limit of the interest rate corridor decreased by 0.50 points in July 2014. In August, the upper limit of the interest rate corridor (marginal funding rate) was reduced from 12% to 11.25%, making the interest rate corridor symmetrical (CBRT, 2014). In February 2015, the CBRT cut the upper limit of the interest rate corridor to 10.75% and the lower limit to 7.25% (CBRT, 2015).

As a result of the fluctuations in global markets in the first quarter of 2016, the need for interest rate corridor decreased. In March and September 2016, the CBRT started to simplify the interest rate cor-

The Role of Central Bank in Competitive Environment

ridor policy due to the slowdown in inflation. In this context, the lending interest rate was reduced by 2.5 points in total in March and September, from 10.75% to 8.25%. Thus, the interest rate corridor was 3.5 points in March and 1.0 points in September. In this period, the borrowing interest rate remained unchanged and remained at 7.25%. However, as uncertainties persisted in the global economy, the CBRT increased the lending interest rate to 8.50% in November and widened the corridor. Thus, as of end-2016, the interest rate corridor was between 7.25-8.50%. The share of marginal funding in CBRT funding was quite high in 2016 (CBRT, 2016).

In order to limit the effects of fluctuations in foreign exchange rates on inflation in the first quarter of 2017, the CBRT implemented a tight monetary policy and raised the upper limit of the interest rate corridor from 8.5% to 9.25% (CBRT, 2017).

High levels of inflation in 2018 posed a risk to pricing behavior. In this context, the CBRT implemented monetary tightening in June and raised the upper limit of the interest rate corridor to 19.25% and the lower limit to 16.25%. At the beginning of August, TL depreciated rapidly due to excessive volatility in financial markets. Thus, the lower limit of the interest rate corridor was raised to 22.50% and the upper limit of the interest rate corridor to 25.50% (CBRT, 2018).

INTEREST RATE CORRIDOR LITERATURE

In this section, domestic and foreign studies related to interest rate corridor will be examined. Özatay (2011) examined the compliance of the new monetary policy instruments implemented by the CBRT after 2010 on an observational basis. In this study, which examined the framework of the new monetary policy implemented by the CBRT, the results and difficulties of these policies were revealed. The CBRT uses two intermediate targets to ensure financial stability; one is to reduce short-term capital inflows, and the other is to narrow credit expansion. For this purpose, short-term policy rate, required reserve ratios and interest rate corridor are used as instruments. The study emphasized that the interest rate corridor should be kept wide and the borrowing interest rate should be reduced to very low levels in order to reduce short-term capital inflows (Özatay, 2011b).

Oktar and Dalyancı (2011) examined the relationship between inflation and interest rates in Turkey using Granger Causality Analysis and Johansen Cointegration Analysis in the period between 2003 and 2011. As a result of the study, it was found that there is a one-way causality relationship from inflation to CBRT policy rate in the short term. It was also found that a two-way cointegration relationship between CBRT policy rate and inflation in the long term (Oktar and Dalyancı, 2011).

Cicioğlu et al. (2013) investigated the instruments of monetary policy implemented between 2003 and 2013 in Turkey and the effect on the current account deficit. In this study which Toda-Yamamoto causality analysis and SVAR analysis were used; current account deficit, open market operations, nominal exchange rate, bank loans, policy interest and rediscount transactions are used as variables. According to the results, there is an inverse relationship between interest rates and current account deficit. A causality relationship between the open market operations and the current account deficit could not be determined. However, it is calculated that there is a causal relationship from the current account deficit to rediscount transactions (Cicioğlu et al., 2013).

Serel and Bayır (2013) have examined the effects of monetary policy in 2008 global crisis on Turkey based on observation. With the global crisis, it was stated that the CBRT started to implement policies that emphasize price and financial stability. It was emphasized that the policies implemented in this process were one-week repo auction interest rate, required reserve ratios, interest rate corridor and supporting policies implemented by the BRSA (Banking Regulation and Supervision Agency). As a result of the study, it was emphasized that the expansionary monetary policies implemented by the CBRT gave positive results. In addition, it was determined that the monetary policies developed against the danger posed by foreign capital used to finance the current account deficit were successful (Serel and Bayır, 2013).

Demirhan (2013) examined the monetary policy instruments implemented by the TMCB to ensure financial stability after the global crisis, the impact channels of these instruments. In this study, by diversifying the monetary policy instruments of the CBRT aimed at ensuring financial stability; It is emphasized that it tries to prevent the contradiction with the aim of price stability. It has been revealed that the required reserve application, which is one of the tools for ensuring financial stability, is used to adjust the credit volume and reduce the volatility in short-term interest rates; but the asymmetric interest rate corridor and ROM application is used to reduce the negative effects of foreign capital inflows on the economy and ensure financial stability (Demirhan, 2013).

Aysan et al. (2014) examined the effectiveness of the asymmetric interest rate corridor and reserve option mechanism within the framework of the CBRT's new monetary policy implementation. It was emphasized that these two policy combinations, which were applied to mitigate the negative effects of short-term capital movements, yielded effective results. According to the study, the interest rate corridor policy limits the fluctuations in foreign exchange supply by changing the returns of foreign capital, while ROM prevents the fluctuations in exchange rates (Aysan et al., 2014).

Serel and Özkurt (2014) examined the unconventional monetary policies implemented by the CBRT to overcome the global crisis since 2010 and the results of these policies based on observation. Interest rate corridor, reserve requirement ratios and ROM were considered as non-traditional monetary policies and these policies were found to be successful. In addition, it has been concluded that ROM application decreases volatility in TL and has a positive effect on financial stability. However, it was emphasized that a longer period should be passed while evaluating the impact of the policies (Serel and Özkurt, 2014).

Yücememiş et al. (2015) using monthly data between 2003 and 2014 examined the relationship between interest rate corridor and inflation in Turkey. In this study, time series analysis with multiple structural breaks was applied. As a result, it was determined that the interest rate corridor policy had an impact on inflation. So; an inverse relationship between borrowing interest, lending interest, interbank interest and inflation was calculated (Yücememiş et al., 2015).

Duramaz and Dilber (2015) examined the monetary policies implemented by the CBRT for price stability and financial stability after the global crisis and especially the effects of the interest rate corridor. In this study, it was found that interest rate corridor policy has a faster impact on markets than traditional policies, thus the effectiveness of this policy was high during the crisis. Ayrıca, bu politikanın krizden önce ve sonra birçok ülke tarafından uygulandığını belirtti. As a result of the study, it was emphasized that the interest rate corridor policy implemented by the CBRT since 2011 is an effective policy against the crisis both on the banking sector and other sectors (Duramaz and Dilber, 2015).

Tetik and Ceylan (2015) examined the effect of the CBRT's interest rate corridor policy on exchange rate and stock prices. The study was divided into two periods before interest rate corridor policy (January 2009-December 2010) and after interest rate corridor policy (December 2010-December 2014) and analyzed by VAR (SVAR) method. As a result of the study, it was determined that the investments made in stocks before the interest rate corridor application were extremely sensitive to the policy shocks in the markets. However, with the implementation of the interest rate corridor policy, the response to these shocks was found to be less. The response of the exchange rate to the policy interest rates was calculated as negative in the period before the interest rate corridor and as positive in the period when the interest rate corridor policy was applied (Tetik and Ceylan, 2015).

Çetin (2016) conducted a study on the monetary policies implemented from the date of the CBRT's inception to the present day, which puts the impact of these policies on the economy after the 2001 crisis. In this study, information about reserve option mechanism and interest rate corridor which has been implemented since 2011 is given. In this observational study, it was stated that the CBRT reduced the volatility in exchange rates by affecting foreign exchange liquidity in the market by means of required reserve ratios, interest rate corridor and ROM after in the 2010. In 2014 and 2015, the increase in geopolitical risks and global uncertainties caused exchange rate volatility and thus the CBRT reserves decreased. It is emphasized that the CBRT will maintain its tight monetary policy stance against these risks in the coming periods (Çetin, 2016).

Gökalp (2016) investigated the impact of the asymmetric interest rate corridor policy implemented by the CBRT on the stocks traded on Borsa Istanbul. In this study, case study and GMM (Generalized Moments Method) methods are used. As a result of this study conducted using data between May 2010 and November 2014, it was found that the changes in the lending interest rate and the borrowing interest rate had a reverse effect on stock prices. Accordingly, if the lending interest rate or the borrowing interest rate increases, stock prices decrease. It has been determined that the most affected sector is the financial sector (Gökalp, 2016).

Atılğan (2016) examines the concept of financial stability after the 2008 crisis in Turkey and the role of unconventional monetary policies as based on observation. As a result of the study, it is emphasized that non-traditional monetary policies implemented in developed and developing countries lower long-term interest rates. In addition, the CBRT's interest rate corridor, required reserves and reserve option mechanism policies were successful and set an example for many countries, but deviated from the price stability target. The importance of the independence of central banks was also mentioned in this study (Atılğan, 2016).

Eroğlu and Kara (2017) examined the relationship between unconventional monetary policies implemented by the CBRT after the 2008 Global Crisis and selected macroeconomic variables by using VAR analysis in their monthly data between 2010 and 2016. As a result of the study, it was found that the changes in reserve requirements had a negative effect on inflation. Moreover, it is concluded that the effect of policy interest on macroeconomic variables remains weak and changes in the lending interest rate partially affect the foreign trade balance. No relationship was found between capacity utilization rates and variables. As a result, they emphasized that it is difficult to talk about the existence of a strong relationship between the unconventional monetary policy instruments implemented by the CBRT after 2010 and macroeconomic variables (Eroğlu and Kara, 2017).

Karaş (2017) examined non-traditional monetary policies developed and implemented by the CBRT, FED and ECB against the global crisis between 2008 and 2017. Firstly theoretical information about non - traditional monetary policies which are open market transactions, rediscount rates and required reserve ratios are given in this study. Subsequently, other non-traditional monetary policies implemented against the crisis were grouped under four main headings: quantitative easing, credit expansion, interest commitment, and interest rate corridor. These policies were examined within the scope of CBRT, FED and ECB practices (Karaş, 2017).

Arabacı (2017) evaluated the CBRT's new monetary policy framework since 2010. It was stated that CBRT policy rates were lowered, VAT (KDV) and SCT (ÖTV) reductions were made and regional incentive packages were announced against the crisis in this study. In addition, CBRT has started to implement required reserve ratios, interest rate corridor and reserve option mechanism in order to prevent short-term capital inflows, current account balance deterioration and limit credit expansion. In order to prevent the crisis from adversely affecting the public budget, debt stock, uncertainties and investments, it was recommended to implement an expansionary fiscal policy (Arabacı, 2017).

İçellioğlu (2017) evaluated the monetary policies implemented by the CBRT in line with price stability and financial stability since 2010 and the effects of these policies. In this study, it was stated that the CBRT has implemented an expansionary monetary policy towards the liquidity need in the market. In this context; with a broad interest rate corridor, the CBRT provided flexibility to interest rate policies, strengthened the balance sheet of financial institutions with required reserve ratios, limited capital flows through the reserve option mechanism and alleviated the pressure on exchange rates (İçellioğlu, 2017).

Kuzu (2017) examined the impact of the CBRT's interest rate corridor policy on the stock market and exchange rate between 2011 and 2017. The variables used in the study are the TCMB weighted average cost of funds, the BIST100 index, the XBANK index and the dollar exchange rate. DKK, DCC GARCH and ML GARCH methods were used as methods. As a result of the study, a direct causal relationship was determined between the weighted average funding cost of the CBRT and the BIST Index. At the same time, direct causality relationship was determined between CBRT weighted average fund cost and XBANK Index. On the other hand, there is an indirect causal relationship between the weighted average fund cost of the CBRT and the dollar rate. According to the study, it was emphasized that the interest rate corridor policy had an impact on the stock market and the dollar rate (Kuzu, 2017).

Arıkan et al. (2018) of the applied interest rate corridor between the years 2010-2016 have studied the impact on Turkey's economy. The variables used were the lower and upper limits of the interest rate corridor, money supply, real exchange rate (RER), domestic credit volume of the banking sector, industrial production index and CPI. As a result of the study, it was determined that interest rate corridor policy yielded an economically effective result (Arıkan et al., 2018).

Kara and Afsal (2018) examined the effectiveness of non-traditional monetary policy instruments implemented by the CBRT in terms of price stability and financial stability in the period between 2010 and 2016. In this study using VAR model, interest rate corridor, reserve requirement ratios and ROM are considered as unconventional monetary policies. As a result of the study, a causality relationship was determined from interest rate corridor, real exchange rate and CPI to credit volume. In addition, the credit volume depends on the changes in the interest rate corridor. A causality relationship was determined from real exchange rate (RER) to CPI. Because the increase in real exchange rates increases the prices of imported goods and causes cost inflation. In addition, a causality relationship was found from the required reserve ratios to the CPI. It was also emphasized that the interest rate corridor may have an impact on financial stability and exchange rate. The interest rate corridor and policy rate did not have a significant effect on CPI (Kara and Afsal, 2018).

Öner (2018) examined the monetary policies implemented by the CBRT since the 2008 global crisis on an observational basis. In this study, in which the policies implemented were handled in a chronological order, it was stated that the global crisis in 2008 made financial stability as well as price stability important and the CBRT started to implement non-traditional monetary policies starting from 2010. The study reveals in this process that the CBRT uses tools such as interest rate corridor, required reserves, ROM and communication policy (Öner, 2018).

Peersman (2011) investigated the effect of unconventional monetary policies on macroeconomic variables by increasing the monetary base between 1999 and 2009 in the Euro Area. SVAR model was used in the study. In this study, the differences between the policy rate application and the monetary base application were also determined. While the effect on consumer prices with interest rate changes was effective after 1 year, it was found to be effective after 6 months with monetary base application. While spreads in banks decreased after the increase in the monetary base, the decrease in policy interest rates increased the spreads significantly. Politika faiz uygulamasının kısa vadede likidite etkisinin bulunmadığı, bilanço genişleme politikasının para çarpanını önemli ölçüde azalttığı tespit edilmiştir. As a result of the study, it is emphasized that unconventional monetary policies can effectively stimulate the economy by affecting macroeconomic variables (Peersman, 2011).

Areosa and Coelho (2013) tried to determine the impact of the reserve requirement policy on macroeconomic variables in Brazil and the main differences between these effects and the policy rate effect. In this study, DSGE Model was used as the model. The quarterly data between 1993: Q3 and 2010: Q2 were used. As a result of the study, it was found that a decrease in reserve requirement ratios had the same qualitatively effect as the decrease in policy interest rates, but had a smaller quantitative effect. For example, if the central bank cuts the policy rate by 1%, GDP will increase by 0.34%, while a permanent 10% reduction in required reserve ratios will increase the GDP by 0.12% (Areosa and Coelho, 2013).

Ellison and Tishbirek (2013) found that long-term borrowings had an impact on GDP, whereas short-term interest rates affected inflation. DSGE model was used in this study. Under the non-traditional monetary policy, the FED sold short-term treasury bills and purchased long-term government bonds with the income it generated, thus extending the average maturity of bonds in the portfolio. In this case, it is emphasized that short and long term interest rates should be managed carefully. As a result of the study, it is revealed that unconventional monetary policies will not lose their importance even when the financial crisis ends (Ellison and Tishbirek, 2013).

Hayashi and Koeda (2014) examined the macroeconomic effects of quantitative expansion policies in Japan on inflation and production by using monthly data between January 1988 and December 2012. SVAR Model was used in this study where inflation, output gap, policy interest and excessive reserve ratio were selected as variables. As a result of the study, they found that a decrease in policy interest rates also reduced inflation, but the increase in excess reserves increased both inflation and output (Hayashi and Koeda, 2014).

Cova et al. (2015) evaluated the internal and external macroeconomic effects of the Asset Purchase Program (APP), which was implemented in the Euro Area, using a calibrated three-country dynamic general equilibrium model (DSGE). They found that increasing liquidity through asset purchases and lowering long-term interest rates increased domestic inflation and economic activity. The international spread of these policies is widening depending on the monetary policy stance of other EU member countries and the response of international relative prices (Cova et al., 2015).

Glocker and Towbin (2015) examined the macroeconomic effects of changes in policy interest and reserve requirements in Brazil using monthly data between July 1999 and June 2014. In this study using VAR model as the method, required reserves, CPI, unemployment rate, interest rate corridor, policy rate, nominal effective exchange rate, total loans, GDP and required reserves of banks are used as variables. It was determined that an increase in the required reserves caused a contraction in loans, increased the unemployment rate, decreased the effective exchange rate, improved the current account balance and raised the general level of prices. These results emphasize that reserve requirements policy are complementary to interest rate policy (Glocker and Towbin, 2015).

Hanisch (2017) examined the effectiveness of traditional and non-traditional monetary policies targeting both policy interest and monetary base in the Japanese economy using a data set of 135 variables between 1985 and 2014. As a result this study using the structural dynamic factor (SDF) model, it has been found that lowering the policy interest rate has a strong positive effect on the output and a moderate positive effect on the general level of prices. An unconventional monetary policy shock focused on balance sheet expansion, which raised the monetary base, was found to have a low, positive, temporary impact on output and a strong impact on prices overall (Hanisch, 2017).

Jawadi et al. (2017) examined the effects of unconventional monetary policies on macroeconomics and wealth in the USA between 2008 and 2013 with the Bayesian SVAR model. The housing price index, CPI, PPI, industrial production index, central bank reserve growth rate, interest rate corridor and stock prices index were used as variables. It was determined that the central bank's widening of its balance sheet through large-scale asset purchases increased housing prices, commodity prices and most importantly stock prices. In this study, it was emphasized that this policy did not create any change in CPI, but it had a very low impact on industrial production (Jawadi et al., 2017).

Nam (2018) evaluated the impact of quantitative easing policies implemented by the USA, Euro Union, UK and Japan between 2009 and 2014 on inflation in South Korea. In the research using the VAR-X model, it is estimated that the quantitative easing policies implemented by these central banks through the purchase of assets put downward pressure on inflation in South Korea. When the responses of macroeconomic variables to quantitative expansion shocks are taken into consideration, it is determined that this spread effect is not through trade channel but through exchange rate channel. In this analysis, where each central bank impact was assessed separately, the impact of FED and ECB was estimated to be higher. The study also proved that long-term interest rates can be effective even when used as an alternative to quantitative expansion (Nam, 2018).

AN ANALYSIS ON TURKEY

In this section, theoretical information about the working methods of this study will be given. First of all, theoretical knowledge about Engle-Granger cointegration analysis which shows the direction of this relationship in case of long term relationship between variables and application of this analysis will be explained. Another analysis to be used in the study is the Toda-Yamamoto causality analysis. After that, theoretical information about Toda-Yamamoto causality analysis will be given and application of this analysis will be explained.

The data of the variables between 2011:09- 2018:12 are used. The data are obtained from the data distribution systems of the CBRT and TURKSTAT. Empirical analyzes are performed with Eviews-9 version. The variables used in this study are given in Table 1.

Engle Granger Cointegration Analysis

Many methods are used to determine the long-term equilibrium relationship between time series. One of these methods is Engle-Granger cointegration analysis proposed by Engle and Granger (1987). The prerequisite for the implementation of Engle-Granger cointegration analysis is that the time series are not stationary in the level values. However, the variables should be stationary at the same level after receiving the difference while performing this test. If the variables do not stationarity to the same degree, this analysis cannot be used. This analysis tests whether there is a long-term cointegration relationship between the non-stationary and the same level of stationary time series (Enders, 2004).

The Role of Central Bank in Competitive Environment

Table 1. Variables

Independent Variable	Dependent Variables
Interest Rate Corridor (IRC)	Inflation Rate (INF)
	Unemployment Rate (UNM)
	Capacity Utilization Rate (CUR)
	Export/Import Coverage Ratio (EICR)
	Dollar Exchange Rate (DER)
	Industrial Production Index (IPI)
	Growth Rate (GRW)
	Foreign Direct Investments/Total Liabilities (FDI)

Stationarity testing is performed by unit root tests. The Advanced Dickey Fuller (ADF) test is usually used for this purpose. In this case, an economic time series can be stationary at the level or stationary when the difference is taken (Gujarati, 2010). In the Engle-Granger Cointegration analysis, after the stationarity test of variables, the level of stationarity of error term series must be tested. If the error term series is stationary at level, the problem of spurious regression will be eliminated and the existence of long-term cointegration relationship will be demonstrated. Below is the OLS estimation equation between non-stationary Y_t and X_t variables;

$$Y_t = \beta_. + \beta_. X_t + \varepsilon_t.$$

The existence of a possible cointegration relationship between the variables Y_t and X_t in the above equation is dependent on the fact that the error term ε_t is stationary. Unit root tests are also used to test whether the time series are stationary or not. The long-term property of a time series is determined by how the value of that variable in the previous period affects this period. The value of the series in each period should be calculated by regression with the value of the previous period. There are various methods and tests for this (Tarı, 2002). The most important of these tests is the Augmented Dickey-Fuller (ADF) analysis performed by Dickey-Fuller (1981). Equations of ADF analysis are given below.

$$\Delta Y_t = \gamma Y_{t-1} + \sum_{i=2}^{k} \beta_i \Delta Y_{t-i+1} + \varepsilon_t.$$

$$\Delta Y_t = a_0 + \gamma Y_{t-1} + \sum_{i=2}^{k} \beta_i \Delta Y_{t-i+1} + \varepsilon_t.$$

$$\Delta Y_t = a_0 + \gamma Y_{t-1} + \beta_t \sum_{i=2}^{k} \beta_i \Delta Y_{t-i+1} + \varepsilon_t.$$

The hypothesis tests of the above equations are also given below;

H_0: $\gamma \geq 0$.(There is unit root problem, ie variables are not stationary)
H_1: $\gamma < 0$.(There is no unit root problem, ie variables are stationary)

In short, when performing the Engle Granger cointegration test, both variables must be of the same degree of stability. In the second step, whether the error terms of the equation are stationary is examined. If the error terms of the equation are stationary, the cointegration relationship is mentioned.

Toda-Yamamoto Causality Analysis

The most commonly used method to determine the causality relationship between two variables is the causality analysis developed by Granger (1969). The variables should be stationarity when performing this analysis. If the variables are not stationary, it should be made stationary. However, the distinction process applied while making the series stationary may cause loss of information in the series. Toda and Yamamoto (1995) developed this causality analysis and found that causality analysis could be also done with non-stationary series.

Toda-Yamamoto causality analysis is carried out in three stages. First, the delay length (k) of the installed VAR model is determined. In the second stage, the maximum stationary degree (d_{max}) of the analyzed variables is determined. After determining these values, a VAR model with delay length (k + d_{max}) is established and Toda-Yamamoto causality analysis is performed. Finally, with the application of the standard Wald test, the hypothesis is decided (Yüksel and Özsarı, 2016). The equation of the Toda-Yamamoto analysis is as follows;

$$Y_t = a_0 + \sum_{i=1}^{k} a_{1i} Y_{t-i} + \sum_{j=k+1}^{k+d_{max}} a_{2j} Y_{t-j} + \sum_{i=1}^{k} \beta_{1i} X_{t-i} + \sum_{j=k+1}^{k+d_{max}} \beta_{2j} X_{t-j} + \varepsilon_t$$

H_0: $\beta_{1i} = 0$ (X is not the cause of Y)
H_1: $\beta_{1i} \neq 0$ (X is the cause of Y)

The rejection of the H_0 hypothesis according to the above equations and hypotheses means that according to the Toda-Yamamoto analysis, X causes the Y variable.

Interest Rate Corridor Unit Root Test

Table 2 shows the ADF unit root test of the interest rate corridor variable. The interest rate corridor variable is indicated by IRC. Unit root test results are as follows.

According to the results of the unit root test in Table 2, the ADF unit root test probability (Prob *) value of the interest rate corridor (IRC) variable was calculated as 0.3920. Since the probability value is greater than 0.05, it is found that the interest rate corridor variable is not stable at the level value. In order to perform the Engle-Granger cointegration test in the next step, first the stationarity process of the variable IRC must be performed. First, the first difference should be taken to ensure the stability of the interest rate corridor variable.

The Role of Central Bank in Competitive Environment

Table 2. Unit root test results of IRC variable

Null Hypothesis: IRC has a unit root				
Exogenous: None				
Lag Length: 0 (Automatic - based on SIC, maxlag=11)				
			t-Statistic	Prob.*
Augmented Dickey-Fuller test statistic			-0.742505	0.3920
Test critical values:	1% level		-2.591813	
	5% level		-1.944574	
	10% level		-1.614315	
*MacKinnon (1996) one-sided p-values.				
Augmented Dickey-Fuller Test Equation				
Dependent Variable: D(IRC)				
Method: Least Squares				
Date: 03/18/19 Time: 17:58				
Sample (adjusted): 2011M10 2018M12				
Included observations: 87 after adjustments				
Variable	Coefficient	Std. Error	t-Statistic	Prob.
IRC(-1)	-0.008568	0.011539	-0.742505	0.4598
R-squared	0.005575	Mean dependent var		-0.011494
Adjusted R-squared	0.005575	S.D. dependent var		0.408678
S.E. of regression	0.407537	Akaike info criterion		1.054058
Sum squared resid	14.28343	Schwarz criterion		1.082402
Log likelihood	-44.85152	Hannan-Quinn criter.		1.065471
Durbin-Watson stat	1.297788			

The ADF unit root test results in Table 3 show the stationarity test by taking the first difference of the IRC variable.

In Table 3, the first difference of the interest rate corridor variable is taken. In this case, the ADF unit root test probability value of IRC variable was calculated as 0.0000. This value is less than 0.05. Therefore, the interest rate corridor variable became stationarity by taking the first difference according to the ADF test.

Unit Root Tests of Dependent Variables

In this section, the stationarity test of the dependent variables of the model will be performed and the stationarity of the non-stationary dependent variables will be performed. The dependent variables of the model are inflation rate (INF), unemployment rate (UNM), capacity utilization rate (CUR), export/import coverage ratio (EICR), dollar exchange rate (DER), industrial production index (IPI), growth rate (GRW) and foreing direct investments / total liabilities ratio (FDI). In this section, as an example, the unit root test of inflation and stationary of inflation are explained. Outputs of unit root tests of other dependent variables were not included. Because these analyzes are made with the same logic. However, the results of these analyzes made with the Eviews program are included.

Inflation Unit Root Test

Table 4 shows the ADF unit root test of the inflation rate variable. The inflation variable is indicated by INF. Unit root test results are as follows.

According to the results of ADF unit root test in Table 4, the probability (Prob *) value of the ADF unit root test of the inflation rate (INF) variable was calculated as 0.1425. Since the probability value of INF variable is greater than 0.05, it is calculated that the inflation variable is not stationary at the level value. In order to perform the Engle-Granger cointegration test in the next step, first the stationarity process of the variable INF must be performed. The first difference will be taken while to stationarity testing the inflation rate variable. Table 5 shows the results of the ADF unit root test performed by taking the first difference of the inflation rate variable.

Table 5 shows the stationarity process of the inflation rate variable by taking the first difference of the inflation rate variable. According to the table, the probability value of ADF unit root test of INF variable was calculated as 0.0000. Since this value is 0.0000 < 0.05, it is understood that the inflation rate variable becomes the first aware stationary according to the ADF unit root test.

Engle-Granger Cointegration Tests

In the previous section, the stationarity test of dependent and independent variables was performed. As a result of the stationarity tests performed with ADF unit root tests, it was calculated that all of the dependent and independent variables were not stationary in their level values and they became stationary by taking the first differences. In this section, the cointegration relationship of each independent variable on macroeconomic variables will be calculated separately by Engle-Granger cointegration analysis.

Engle-Granger cointegration analysis is performed in two stages. First, each independent variable and each dependent variable, which were made stationary in the previous section, are subjected to separate regression analysis. The regression analysis performed so far is a prediction analysis. Therefore, the

Table 3. Receiving the first difference of IRC

Null Hypothesis: D(IRC) has a unit root				
Exogenous: None				
Lag Length: 0 (Automatic - based on SIC, maxlag=11)				
			t-Statistic	Prob.*
Augmented Dickey-Fuller test statistic			-10.82781	0.0000
Test critical values:	1% level		-2.592129	
	5% level		-1.944619	
	10% level		-1.614288	

*MacKinnon (1996) one-sided p-values.

Augmented Dickey-Fuller Test Equation	
Dependent Variable: D(IRC,2)	
Method: Least Squares	
Date: 03/18/19 Time: 18:08	
Sample (adjusted): 2011M11 2018M12	
Included observations: 86 after adjustments	

Variable	Coefficient	Std. Error	t-Statistic	Prob.
D(IRC(-1))	-0.869565	0.080309	-10.82781	0.0000

R-squared	0.578075	Mean dependent var	-0.029070
Adjusted R-squared	0.578075	S.D. dependent var	0.468757
S.E. of regression	0.304485	Akaike info criterion	0.471169
Sum squared resid	7.880435	Schwarz criterion	0.499708
Log likelihood	-19.26025	Hannan-Quinn criter.	0.482654
Durbin-Watson stat	1.823238		

Table 4. Unit root test results of INF variable

			t-Statistic	Prob.*
Null Hypothesis: INF has a unit root				
Exogenous: None				
Lag Length: 4 (Automatic - based on SIC, maxlag=11)				
Augmented Dickey-Fuller test statistic			-1.425590	0.1425
Test critical values:	1% level		-2.593121	
	5% level		-1.944762	
	10% level		-1.614204	

*MacKinnon (1996) one-sided p-values.

Augmented Dickey-Fuller Test Equation
Dependent Variable: D(INF)
Method: Least Squares
Date: 03/18/19 Time: 18:19
Sample (adjusted): 2012M02 2018M12
Included observations: 83 after adjustments

Variable	Coefficient	Std. Error	t-Statistic	Prob.
INF(-1)	-0.152210	0.106770	-1.425590	0.1580
D(INF(-1))	-0.169108	0.134256	-1.259595	0.2116
D(INF(-2))	-0.708220	0.148807	-4.759312	0.0000
D(INF(-3))	-0.108585	0.148274	-0.732326	0.4662
D(INF(-4))	-0.432883	0.131343	-3.295833	0.0015

R-squared	0.454129	Mean dependent var		-0.011566
Adjusted R-squared	0.426135	S.D. dependent var		1.194426
S.E. of regression	0.904823	Akaike info criterion		2.696196
Sum squared resid	63.85902	Schwarz criterion		2.841910
Log likelihood	-106.8921	Hannan-Quinn criter.		2.754736
Durbin-Watson stat	2.024762			

The Role of Central Bank in Competitive Environment

Table 5. Receiving the first difference of INF

Null Hypothesis: D(INF) has a unit root				
Exogenous: None				
Lag Length: 3 (Automatic - based on SIC, maxlag=11)				
			t-Statistic	Prob.*
Augmented Dickey-Fuller test statistic			-7.701162	0.0000
Test critical values:	1% level		-2.593121	
	5% level		-1.944762	
	10% level		-1.614204	

*MacKinnon (1996) one-sided p-values.

Augmented Dickey-Fuller Test Equation				
Dependent Variable: D(INF,2)				
Method: Least Squares				
Date: 03/18/19 Time: 18:21				
Sample (adjusted): 2012M02 2018M12				
Included observations: 83 after adjustments				
Variable	Coefficient	Std. Error	t-Statistic	Prob.
D(INF(-1))	-2.807440	0.364548	-7.701162	0.0000
D(INF(-1),2)	1.520305	0.310529	4.895850	0.0000
D(INF(-2),2)	0.689470	0.216511	3.184460	0.0021
D(INF(-3),2)	0.495108	0.124684	3.970893	0.0002
R-squared	0.764682	Mean dependent var		0.012771
Adjusted R-squared	0.755746	S.D. dependent var		1.842730
S.E. of regression	0.910716	Akaike info criterion		2.697821
Sum squared resid	65.52288	Schwarz criterion		2.814392
Log likelihood	-107.9596	Hannan-Quinn criter.		2.744653
Durbin-Watson stat	2.055641			

results of regression analysis may not reflect the exact truth. Therefore, there is a series of error terms in regression analysis. At this stage, the error term series of the regression analysis are created first.

In the second stage of Engle-Granger cointegation analysis, the stationarity of the error term series generated according to the results of the regression analysis is tested. Stationarity testing is performed by applying ADF unit root test to error term series. As a result of the ADF unit root test, the fact that these error term series are stationary at the level proves the existence of the cointegration relationship between the two variables. If the error terms are not stationary at the level, it is not possible to say that there is a cointegration relationship (Dinçer et al., 2019; Yüksel and Kavak, 2019; Alhan and Yüksel, 2018).

Interest Rate Corridor and Cointegration Analysis of Dependent Variables

The interest rate corridor variable and macroeconomic data are become stationarity at the same degree. At this stage, the cointegration relationship between the interest rate corridor and macroeconomic variables will be examined. However, only the impact of the interest rate corridor on inflation is shown as an example.

IRC and Inflation Engle-Granger Cointegration Analysis

Some findings have been obtained in the analysis performed so far. In this context, when we conducted the ADF unit root tests of the interest rate corridor variable expressed by IRC and the inflation variable expressed by INF;

- Both series are not stationary in their level values.
- The first difference is taken to render the stationary of both series. So the stationary of both series is the same.
- Both variables are suitable for Engle-Granger cointegration analysis.

In the first step, regression analysis will be performed. In the second stage, the ADF unit root test will be performed to test the stationary of the error term series generated according to the results of the regression analysis.

Regression Analysis

Since the effect of interest rate corridor on the inflation variable is examined during the regression analysis, the interest rate corridor is considered as an independent variable. Inflation is treated as a dependent variable. Regression analysis is performed in this direction.

In the regression analysis, first the first aware stationary dependent variable INF1 and second the first aware stationary independent variable IRC1 are selected. Because the analysis examines whether the interest rate corridor has an impact on the inflation rate. In the table above, the coefficient of IRC1 is calculated as 0.435777. If this coefficient is positive, if a possible cointegration relationship between the interest rate corridor and inflation is determined, it will be the right direction.

The Role of Central Bank in Competitive Environment

Table 6. Results of regression analysis of IRC1 and INF1 variables

Dependent Variable: INF1				
Method: Least Squares				
Date: 03/19/19 Time: 14:57				
Sample (adjusted): 2011M10 2018M12				
Included observations: 87 after adjustments				
Variable	Coefficient	Std. Error	t-Statistic	Prob.
IRC1	0.435777	0.319076	1.365748	0.1756
C	-0.008209	0.129699	-0.063296	0.9497
R-squared	0.021473	Mean dependent var		-0.013218
Adjusted R-squared	0.009961	S.D. dependent var		1.215339
S.E. of regression	1.209271	Akaike info criterion		3.240633
Sum squared resid	124.2986	Schwarz criterion		3.297321
Log likelihood	-138.9675	Hannan-Quinn criter.		3.263459
F-statistic	1.865267	Durbin-Watson stat		2.318797
Prob(F-statistic)	0.175621			

Unit Root Test of Error Term Series

The regression analysis performed so far is a prediction analysis. Therefore, the results of regression analysis may not reflect the exact truth. Therefore, there is an series of error term in regression analysis. In the second stage of the Engle-Granger cointegration analysis, the error term series of the regression analysis between INF1 and IRC1 are analyzed. First, the error term series of the regression analysis are generated. These generated error term series are subjected to ADF unit root test. As a result of the ADF unit root test, the fact that these error term series are stationary at the level indicates the presence of cointegration relationship. If the error terms are not stationary at the level, it is not possible to say that there is a cointegration relationship. Table 7 shows the staitonarity test of the error term series with the ADF unit root test.

According to Table 7, the ADF test statistic probability (Probe *) value is calculated as 0.000. Because of 0.000 < 0.05; There is a co-integration relationship between interest rate corridor and inflation. In other words, Turkey's interest rate corridor policy affects the inflation rate in the long term.

Table 7. Unit root test of error term series of IRC1 and INF1 variables

Null Hypothesis: RESID27 has a unit root				
Exogenous: None				
Lag Length: 3 (Automatic - based on SIC, maxlag=11)				
			t-Statistic	Prob.*
Augmented Dickey-Fuller test statistic			-7.589319	0.0000
Test critical values:	1% level		-2.593121	
	5% level		-1.944762	
	10% level		-1.614204	

*MacKinnon (1996) one-sided p-values.

Augmented Dickey-Fuller Test Equation				
Dependent Variable: D(RESID27)				
Method: Least Squares				
Date: 03/19/19 Time: 14:59				
Sample (adjusted): 2012M02 2018M12				
Included observations: 83 after adjustments				
Variable	Coefficient	Std. Error	t-Statistic	Prob.
RESID27(-1)	-2.641654	0.348075	-7.589319	0.0000
D(RESID27(-1))	1.396954	0.296384	4.713316	0.0000
D(RESID27(-2))	0.617264	0.208752	2.956922	0.0041
D(RESID27(-3))	0.472758	0.126231	3.745169	0.0003
R-squared	0.749637	Mean dependent var		0.012771
Adjusted R-squared	0.740130	S.D. dependent var		1.841118
S.E. of regression	0.938555	Akaike info criterion		2.758042
Sum squared resid	69.58992	Schwarz criterion		2.874612
Log likelihood	-110.4587	Hannan-Quinn criter.		2.804873
Durbin-Watson stat	2.015741			

Causality Analysis of Interest Corridor and Dependent Variables

In this section, the macroeconomic impact of the interest rate corridor will be examined with the help of Toda-Yamamoto causality analysis. However, only the impact of the interest rate corridor on inflation is shown as an example.

IRC and Inflation Toda-Yamamoto Causality Analysis

Toda-Yamamoto causality analysis will be carried out for the interest rate corridor and inflation variables which are found to have cointegration relations according to Engle-Granger analysis. Accordingly, firstly, the lag order is determined by VAR analysis and then the model is estimated.

Lag Order Determination

At this stage, when determining the appropriate number of delays, firstly VAR analysis is performed between the interest rate corridor variable and the inflation variable. When doing VAR analysis, firstly the stationary INF1 variable and secondly the stationary IRC1 variable is selected. Since monthly data is used in the series, the maximum number of lag orders is determined as 12.

Table 8 shows the results of 5 different information criteria in which the lag length is determined by VAR analysis. The numbers with asterisks indicate the optimal length. 3 information criteria show 4 for the appropriate delay length. The 2 information criteria show 2. If the one with the most asterisks is preferred, the delay length is 4. Toda-Yamamoto causality analysis is estimated as (d_{max} + k).

k: The appropriate lag length of the estimated VAR model;
d: Maximum degree of integration of variables in the model;
Since d_{max} + k = 1 + 4 = 5, the estimation coefficent is 5.

Estimation of Model

At this stage, VAR analysis will be conducted between interest rate corridor variable and inflation variable. Table 9 presents the results of the Toda-Yamamoto causality analysis between the interest rate corridor and the inflation variable.

Table 9 shows the results of the Toda-Yamamoto causality analysis. According to Toda-Yamamoto causality analysis between IRC1 and INF1, Dependent Variable = INF1 shows the effect of interest rate corridor on inflation rate. Probability Value (Prob.) of IRC1 is calculated as 0.1526. Since this number is greater than 0.05, there is no significant relationship between the interest rate corridor and the inflation rate. In other words, the interest rate corridor in Turkey is not a major cause of inflation.

Evaluation Of Empirical Results

In the model, firstly, the cointegration relationship between independent variable and dependent variables is examined. In order to examine this cointegration relationship, regression analysis is performed between the independent interest rate corridor variable and each dependent variable. Coefficient of independent variables in this regression analysis is shown in Table 10.

Table 8. Determination of lag length by IRC1 and INF1 VAR analysis

VAR Lag Order Selection Criteria						
Endogenous variables: INF1 IRC1						
Exogenous variables: C						
Date: 03/26/19 Time: 23:03						
Sample: 2011M09 2018M12						
Included observations: 75						
Lag	LogL	LR	FPE	AIC	SC	HQ
0	-131.6560	NA	0.121045	3.564161	3.625961	3.588837
1	-126.4703	9.956611	0.117287	3.532541	3.717940	3.606569
2	-109.8976	30.93576	0.083903	3.197269	3.506267*	3.320648*
3	-107.8501	3.712790	0.088449	3.249335	3.681933	3.422067
4	-99.09928	15.40139*	0.078021*	3.122648*	3.678845	3.344731
5	-98.18273	1.564245	0.084871	3.204873	3.884669	3.476308
6	-94.58569	5.947120	0.086030	3.215618	4.019014	3.536405
7	-90.36405	6.754611	0.085853	3.209708	4.136703	3.579847
8	-85.79252	7.070640	0.084987	3.194467	4.245062	3.613958
9	-85.08991	1.049227	0.093406	3.282398	4.456592	3.751240
10	-80.14046	7.127210	0.091818	3.257079	4.554872	3.775274
11	-79.39802	1.029512	0.101163	3.343947	4.765340	3.911494
12	-77.58841	2.412822	0.108562	3.402358	4.947350	4.019256
* indicates lag order selected by the criterion						
LR: sequential modified LR test statistic (each test at 5% level)						
FPE: Final prediction error						
AIC: Akaike information criterion						
SC: Schwarz information criterion						
HQ: Hannan-Quinn information criterion						

Table 10 shows independ variable in the row section and dependent variables in the column section. These coefficients in Table 10 show the direction of the possible cointegration relationship between the two variables. For example; The regression analysis coefficient between the interest rate corridor and capacity utilization rate is -0.145444. The second step of Engle-Granger cointegration analysis is the application of ADF unit root test to error term series obtained as a result of regression analysis. As

Table 9. IRC and INF Toda Yamamoto causality analysis

VAR Granger Causality/Block Exogeneity Wald Tests			
Date: 03/26/19 Time: 23:05			
Sample: 2011M09 2018M12			
Included observations: 82			
Dependent variable: INF1			
Excluded	Chi-sq	df	Prob.
IRC1	8.066365	5	0.1526
All	8.066365	5	0.1526
Dependent variable: IRC1			
Excluded	Chi-sq	df	Prob.
INF1	6.275112	5	0.2804
All	6.275112	5	0.2804

Table 10. Coefficients of independent variables after regression analysis

	INF	UNM	CUR	EICR	DER	IPI	GRW	FDI
IRC	0,435777	0,100666	-0,145444	3,235569	0,032836	-2,790090	-0,538473	-0,001230

a result of ADF unit root test applied to error term series, cointegration relationship between independent variable and all dependent variables was determined. The results of Engle-Granger cointegration relationship are given in Table 11.

According to the table, for example; The relationship between the interest rate corridor and the capacity utilization rate is negative. This indicates an inverse cointegration relationship between the interest rate corridor and capacity utilization rate. This means; if interest rate corridor increases, capacity utilization rate decreases. In other words, narrowing the interest rate corridor increases the capacity utilization rate.

In the second stage of the analysis, the effect of nontraditional monetary policies on macroeconomic stability was examined by Toda-Yamamoto causality analysis. The results of the Toda-Yamamoto causality analysis are summarized in Table 12.

Table 12 shows the probability values between the interest rate corridor and dependent variables. Values less than 0.05 indicate a Toda-Yamamoto causality relationship. For example, the Toda-Yamamoto causality analysis between the interest rate corridor and the growth rate was calculated as 0.0000. This shows that the interest rate corridor has a significant effect on the growth rate. In addition, it is stated that there was a negative Engle-Granger cointegration relationship between the two variables. In this case, it is found that the interest rate corridor had a negative and significant effect on the growth rate.

SOLUTIONS AND RECOMMENDATIONS

The analysis of the study shows that the interest rate corridor, which represents the breadth between the borrowing interest rate and the lending interest rate, affects the dollar exchange rate, foreign direct investments and growth.

However, the effect of the interest rate corridor on inflation, unemployment, capacity utilization rate, export/import coverage ratio and industrial production index could not be determined. The effectiveness of the interest rate corridor policy on price stability needs to be reviewed. Policies complementing the interest rate corridor policy may be effective in price stability and macroeconomic stability.

It is determined that narrowing the interest rate corridor may cause the exchange rate to fall. In addition, if the interest rate corridor is narrowed, it may increase economic growth and foreign direct investment.

Table 11. Engle-Granger cointegration test results

	INF	UNM	CUR	EICR	DER	IPI	GRW	FDI
IRC	Positive	Positive	Negative	Positive	Positive	Negative	Negative	Negative

Table 12. Toda-Yamamoto causality analysis probability values

	INF	UNM	CUR	EICR	DER	IPI	GRW	FDI
IRC	0.1526	0.7601	0.5983	0.3204	0.0435	0.6293	0.0000	0.0068

FUTURE RESEARCH DIRECTIONS

It is clear that interest rates or interest rate corridor are not the only policy on price stability and macroeconomic stability. Therefore, studies examining the results of complementary policies (reserve requirements, reserve option mechanism etc.) in addition to the interest rate corridor policy should be developed.

CONCLUSION

In a corridor system, the policy rate of the central bank will be below the lending rate and above the deposit rate. The lending rate constitutes an upper limit for short-term interest rates. Interest rate corridor in the aftermath of the global crisis in Turkey has been used quite often a policy.

In the studies conducted to examine the effectiveness of the interest rate corridor, it was found that this policy had an impact on inflation and macroeconomic stability. However, no impact of interest rate corridor on inflation was determined in this study.

On the other hand, the interest rate corridor has a negative and strong effect on growth and foreign direct investments. In this respect, it can be said that the expansion of the interest rate corridor decreases growth and foreign direct investments, while narrowing the corridor increases growth and foreign direct investments. The effect of the interest rate corridor on the exchange rate was found to be positive and low.

ACKNOWLEDGMENT

This study was derived from Mustafa Eser Kurum's doctoral thesis written in Marmara University.

REFERENCES

Alhan, O., & Yüksel, S. (2018). Kadın Çalışanların Banka Büyüklüğü Ve Karlılığına Etkisi: Engle-Granger Eş Bütünleşme Analizi İle Türkiye Üzerine Bir Uygulama. *İş'te Davranış Dergisi, 3*(2), 140-147.

Arabacı, H. (2017). Küresel Kriz Sonrası Türkiye'de Uygulanan Ekonomi Politikaları. *Sosyal Bilimler Araştırma Dergisi, 6*(4), 1–10.

Areosa, W. D., & Coelho, C. A. (2013). Using a DSGE model to assess the macroeconomic effects of reserve requirements in Brazil. *Banco Central Do Brasil Working Paper Series*, (303).

Arıkan, C., Görgün, S., & Yalçın, Y. (2018). Parasal Aktarım Sürecinde Faiz Koridorunun Yeri. *Maliye Dergisi, 174*, 1–25.

Atılgan, M. H. (2016). Yeni Para Politikası Anlayışı ve Finansal İstikrar. *Çankırı Karatekin Üniversitesi İİBF Dergisi, 6*(2), 249-268.

Aysan, A. F., Fendoglu, S., & Kilinc, M. (2014). Managing short-term capital flows in new central banking: Unconventional monetary policy framework in Turkey. *Eurasian Economic Review, 4*(1), 45–69. doi:10.100740822-014-0001-6

Bain, M. K., & Howells, P. (2009). *Monetary economics: policy and its theoretical basis*. Macmillan International Higher Education. doi:10.1007/978-1-137-01342-2

Berentsen, A., & Monnet, C. (2008). Monetary policy in a channel system. *Journal of Monetary Economics*, 55(6), 1067–1080. doi:10.1016/j.jmoneco.2008.07.002

Bernhardsen, T., & Kloster, A. (2010). Liquidity management system: Floor or corridor?.

Central Bank of the Republic of Turkey. (2006). *CBRT Annual Report 2006*. CBRT.

Central Bank of the Republic of Turkey. (2010). *CBRT Annual Report 2010*. CBRT.

Central Bank of the Republic of Turkey. (2011). *CBRT Annual Report 2011*. CBRT.

Central Bank of the Republic of Turkey. (2012). *CBRT Annual Report 2012*. CBRT.

Central Bank of the Republic of Turkey. (2013). *CBRT Annual Report 2013*. CBRT.

Central Bank of the Republic of Turkey. (2014). *CBRT Annual Report 2014*. CBRT.

Central Bank of the Republic of Turkey. (2015). *CBRT Annual Report 2015*. CBRT.

Central Bank of the Republic of Turkey. (2016). *CBRT Annual Report 2016*. CBRT.

Central Bank of the Republic of Turkey. (2017). *CBRT Annual Report 2017*. CBRT.

Central Bank of the Republic of Turkey. (2018). *CBRT Annual Report 2018*. CBRT.

Çetin, M. (2016). Türkiye Cumhuriyeti Merkez Bankası (TCMB) Para Politikası Uygulamalarının Gelişimi. *Finansal Araştırmalar ve Çalışmalar Dergisi*, 8(14), 67–101. doi:10.14784/jfrs.87278

Cicioğlu, Ş., Ağuş, A., & Torun, P. (2013). Para Politikası Araçlarının Cari Açık Üzerindeki Etkinliği: Türkiye Ekonomisi Üzerine Bir Uygulama. *Küresel İktisat ve İşletme Çalışmaları Dergisi*, 2(4), 37–48.

Clews, R., Salmon, C., & Weeken, O. (2010). The bank's money market framework. Bank of England Quarterly Bulletin, Q4, 50, 4, 296.

Cova, P., Pagano, P., & Pisani, M. (2019). Domestic and international effects of the eurosystem expanded asset purchase programme: a structural model-based analysis. *IMF Economic Review*, 67(2), 315–348. doi:10.105741308-018-0071-7

Demirhan, B. (2013). Türkiye'de Yeni Yaklaşım Çerçevesinde Para Politikalarinin Finansal İstikrari Sağlama Yönünde Uygulanmasi. *Afyon Kocatepe Üniversitesi İktisadi ve İdari Bilimler Fakültesi Dergisi*, 15(2), 567–589.

Dickey, D. A., & Fuller, W. A. (1981). Likelihood ratio statistics for autoregressive time series with a unit root. *Econometrica*, 49(4), 1057–1072. doi:10.2307/1912517

Dinçer, H., Yüksel, S., Pınarbaşı, F., & Çetiner, İ. T. (2019). Measurement of economic and banking stability in emerging markets by considering income inequality and nonperforming loans. In Maintaining financial stability in times of risk and uncertainty (pp. 49–68). Hershey, PA: IGI Global. doi:10.4018/978-1-5225-7208-4.ch003

Disyatat, P. (2008). *Monetary policy implementation: Misconceptions and their consequences (No. 269)*. Bank for International Settlements.

Duramaz, S., & Dilber, İ. (2015). Küresel Kriz Sürecinde Para Politikasında Yeni Bir Araç Olarak Faiz Koridoruna Genel Bir Bakış. *Maliye Araştırmaları Dergisi, 1*(1), 29–38.

Ellison, M., & Tischbirek, A. (2014). Unconventional government debt purchases as a supplement to conventional monetary policy. *Journal of Economic Dynamics & Control, 43*, 199–217. doi:10.1016/j.jedc.2014.03.012

Enders, W. (2004). *Applied econometric time series*. Hamilton Printing.

Engle, R. F., & Granger, C. W. (1987). Co-integration and error correction: Representation, estimation, and testing. *Econometrica, 55*(2), 251–276. doi:10.2307/1913236

Eroğlu, N., & Kara, F. (2017). Türkiye'de makro ihtiyati para politikası araçlarının makroekonomik değişkenlere etkisinin var analizi ile incelenmesi. *İstanbul İktisat Dergisi, 67*(2), 59-88.

Glocker, C., & Towbin, P. (2015). Reserve requirements as a macroprudential instrument–Empirical evidence from Brazil. *Journal of Macroeconomics, 44*, 158–176. doi:10.1016/j.jmacro.2015.02.007

Gökalp, B. T. (2016). Para Politikası Kararlarının Hisse Senetlerinin Fiyatları Üzerindeki Etkileri. *Suleyman Demirel University Journal of Faculty of Economics & Administrative Sciences, 21*(4).

Goodhart, C. (2010). *The changing role of central banks (No. 326)*. Bank for International Settlements.

Granger, C. W. J. (1969). Investigating causal relations by econometric models and cross-spectral methods. *Econometrica, 37*(3), 424–438. doi:10.2307/1912791

Gujarati, D. N. (2010). *Temel Ekonometri (Çev. Ümit Senesen ve Gülay Günlük Senesen)*. Literatür Yayınları.

Hanisch, M. (2017). The effectiveness of conventional and unconventional monetary policy: Evidence from a structural dynamic factor model for Japan. *Journal of International Money and Finance, 70*, 110–134. doi:10.1016/j.jimonfin.2016.08.002

Hayashi, F., & Koeda, J. (2014). *Exiting from QE (No. w19938)*. National Bureau of Economic Research. doi:10.3386/w19938

Jawadi, F., Sousa, R. M., & Traverso, R. (2017). On the macroeconomic and wealth effects of unconventional monetary policy. *Macroeconomic Dynamics, 21*(5), 1189–1204. doi:10.1017/S1365100515000292

Kahn, G. A. (2010). Monetary policy under a corridor operating framework. *Economic Review-Federal Reserve Bank of Kansas City*, 5.

Kalkavan, H., & Ersin, I. (2019). Determination of factors affecting the South East Asian crisis of 1997 probit-logit panel regression: The South East Asian crisis. In Handbook of research on global issues in financial communication and investment decision making (pp. 148-167). Hershey, PA: IGI Global.

Kara, M., & Afsal, M. Ş. (2018). The effectiveness of monetary policy instruments applied for financial stability in Turkey. *Itobiad: Journal of the Human & Social Science Researches, 7*(3).

Karaş, Z. (2017). 2008 Küresel Krizi Sırasında Merkez Bankaları Tarafından Uygulanan Geleneksel Olmayan Para Politikaları. *Journal of International Social Research*, *10*(48), 630–639. doi:10.17719/jisr.2017.1534

Keister, T. (2012). *Corridors and floors in monetary policy*. Liberty Street Economics.

Keister, T., Martin, A., & McAndrews, J. (2015). *Floor systems and the Friedman rule: the fiscal arithmetic of open market operations (No. 754)*. Federal Reserve Bank of New York.

Kuzu, S. (2017). Türkiye Cumhuriyeti Merkez Bankası (TCMB) Faiz Koridoru Stratejisinin Hisse Senedi Piyasası ve Döviz Kuru Üzerine Etkisinin Analiz Edilmesi. *Uygulamalı Sosyal Bilimler Dergisi*, *1*(2), 46–61.

Maehle, N. (2014). Monetary policy implementation: operational issues for countries with evolving monetary policy regimes. *IMF Working Paper*.

Nam, M. H. (2018). The effect of quantitative easing on inflation in Korea. *East Asian Economic Review*, *22*(4), 507–529. doi:10.11644/KIEP.EAER.2018.22.4.352

Oktar, S., & Dalyancı, L. (2011). Türkiye Ekonomisinde Para Politikası ve Enflasyon Arasındaki İlişkinin Analizi. *Marmara Üniversitesi İktisadi ve İdari Bilimler Dergisi*, *31*(2), 1–20.

Öner, S. (2018). 2008 Küresel Krizi Sonrası Dönem Türkiye Cumhuriyeti Merkez Bankası Para Politikası Uygulamaları. *Avrasya Sosyal ve Ekonomi Araştırmaları Dergisi*, *5*(12), 409–416.

Özatay, F. (2011). *Parasal iktisat: kuram ve politika*. Efil Yayınevi.

Özatay, F. (2011b). Merkez Bankası'nın yeni para politikası: İki hedef-üç ara hedef-üç araç. *Iktisat Isletme ve Finans*, *26*(302), 27–43.

Peersman, G. (2011). *Macroeconomic effects of unconventional monetary policy in the euro area (No. 1397)*. European Central Bank.

Revised framework for monetary operations under the BSP interest rate corridor (IRC) system. (2016). Retrieved from http://www.bsp.gov.ph/downloads/publications/FAQs/IRC.pdf

Şarkaya, C. (2017). Finansal İstikrar ve Türkiye Cumhuriyet Merkez Bankasının Para Politikası Stratejisi. *Mehmet Akif Ersoy Üniversitesi Sosyal Bilimler Enstitüsü Dergisi*, *9*(20), 20–38.

Serel, A., & Bayır, M. (2013). 2008 Finansal Krizinde Para Politikası Uygulamaları: Türkiye Örneği. *Yönetim ve Ekonomi Araştırmaları Dergisi*, *11*(19), 59–80.

Serel, A., & Özkurt, İ. C. (2014). Geleneksel Olmayan Para Politikası Araçları ve Türkiye Cumhuriyet Merkez Bankası. *Yönetim ve Ekonomi Araştırmaları Dergisi*, *12*(22), 56–71.

Smaghi, L. B. (2009). *Conventional and unconventional monetary policy* (p. 28). Geneva, Switzerland: Speech at the Center for Monetary and Banking Studies.

Tarı, R. (2002). *Ekonometri*. Alfa Basım Yayım Dağıtım.

Tetik, M., & Ceylan, R. (2015). Faiz Koridoru Stratejisinin Hisse Senedi Fiyatlari ve Döviz Kuru Üzerine Etkisinin Incelenmesi/Analysis of the effect of interest rate corridor strategy on common stock and exchange rate. *Business and Economics Research Journal*, *6*(4), 55.

Toda, H. Y., & Yamamoto, T. (1995). Statistical inference in vector autoregressions with possibly integrated processes. *Journal of Econometrics*, *66*(1-2), 225–250. doi:10.1016/0304-4076(94)01616-8

Whitesell, W. (2006). Interest rate corridors and reserves. *Journal of Monetary Economics*, *53*(6), 1177–1195. doi:10.1016/j.jmoneco.2005.03.013

Yücememiş, B. T., Alkan, U., & Ağırdır, C. (2015). Yeni Bir Para Politikası Aracı Olarak Faiz Koridoru: Türkiye'de Para Politikası Kurulu Faiz Kararlarının Enflasyon Üzerindeki Etkisi. *Journal of Financial Researches & Studies/Finansal Arastirmalar ve Calismalar Dergisi*, *7*(13), 449-478.

Yüksel, S., & Kavak, P. T. (2019). Do financial investment decisions affect economic development?: An analysis on mortgage loans in Turkey. In Handbook of research on global issues in financial communication and investment decision making (pp. 168-191). Hershey, PA: IGI Global.

Yüksel, S., & Özsarı, M. (2016). Impact of consumer loans on inflation and current account deficit: A Toda Yamamoto causality test for Turkey. *World Journal of Applied Economics*, *2*(2), 3–14. doi:10.22440/wjae.2.2.1

Chapter 19
Analysis of the Effects of Macroeconomic Factors on Entrepreneurship:
An Application on E7 Countries

İrfan Ersin
https://orcid.org/0000-0002-7407-3654
Istanbul Medipol University, Turkey

Ercan Karakeçe
https://orcid.org/0000-0003-0807-4496
Istanbul Medipol University, Turkey

ABSTRACT

Entrepreneurship is an important field in the increase and diversification of investments in a country. Entrepreneurship is gaining importance in today's world where financial marketing has become an important sector. The aim of this study is to determine the macroeconomic factors that determine entrepreneurship in E7 countries. In the study using logit method, the period of 1992-2018 was discussed. In the analysis results, the variables of unemployment, financial loans and current account deficit were found to be macroeconomic factors determining entrepreneurship. Given that entrepreneurship is important in the financial field, E7 countries should take into account the financial credit markets, focus on economic policies to reduce unemployment and address the current account deficit problem.

INTRODUCTION

We live in a world where interdisciplinary studies are becoming increasingly significant. When we talk about a matter, we do not just address it anymore. Everyone accepts that the issue may have different sides. Now the obstacles are solved as different attitudes come together (Chabowski, 2017; Venkataraman, 2019; Huda et al., 2019). For these reasons, it becomes even more essential to have a holistic approach.

DOI: 10.4018/978-1-7998-2559-3.ch019

Although we know that finance is a field and marketing is a separate profession, we can mention both of them into the same structure; financial marketing (Rawhouser et al., 2019; Bolton, 2004; Geçit, 2018). We can even combine with financial marketing and the concept of entrepreneurship which is studied economically, sociologically and psychologically (Adıgüzel et al., 2017; Wiklund et al., 2019; Saebi et al., 2019).

When you converse with someone about the business, it attracts your attention that the other person will surely mention one of the alternatives; to survive, to gain, to be more efficient and effective, to get more shares from the market, to be (or/and remain) the leader, etc. (Drucker, 2012; Akgün et al., 2019; Rehan et al., 2019). Even if you have to talk to people from different departments within the company, you will immediately notice that they are trying to accomplish the same purpose in different ways. This also reveals the influence of multidisciplinary performances. But above all, there is an extra detail to be regarded, that is an entrepreneur (Ryff, 2019; Martin-Rojas et al., 2019; Browder et al., 2019; Bohnsack and Margonlina, 2019).

Some parts of the actions in the macroeconomic environment are on the entrepreneur. S/he both affects the environment and is also affected by the system (Klapper et al., 2007; Kreiser et al., 2019; Shepherd et al., 2019). Understanding the needs of a market, realizing the problems of customers, and creating the solutions and values for them are expected from our hero, sometimes it is done by destructing and setting new economic order (Schumpeter, 2003; Duran & Zehir, 2011; Anderson et al., 2019; Molina and García-Morales, 2019). Whether this responsibility is done by any private sector or a public one, it is at the origin. Unless the entrepreneur locates in the equation, notions, and solutions cannot be real; the needs cannot be satisfied; projects and products cannot come to life even though ventures are tiny or giant, they are the backbones of commercial life (Sadiku-Dushi, 2019; Konon and Kritikos, 2019). Companies compete to produce goods and services. At the same time, they are still demanding products and services while performing this production. In other words, they stimulate the market with both demanding goods and services. In situations where distances between the manufacturer and the consumer are distant, new intermediaries may need to intervene. This gradually creates new entrepreneurs to make a better supply. For these reasons, as the production is supported, the reviving market will need a labor force (Zou et al., 2018; Hechavarria et al., 2019; Schenkel et al., 2019). This will positively affect employment figures. As unemployment decreases, individuals' earnings will increase, which will increase social welfare (Hediger, 2000; Ibeh et al., 2019). Besides, the individual whose earnings increase will turn to savings and consumption again with the income he earns (Meyer and Mok, 2019; Henrekson and Sanandaji, 2019). Also, the tax revenue of the state due to production will be higher and higher. The contributions paid by the entrepreneur will compensate for social security expenditures. All show us the importance of entrepreneurs in our system (Baumol, 1996; Roberts et al., 2019).

Fundamentally, the things that should be brought together to activate a commercial structure are entrepreneur, labor force, raw material, and capital. As it is seen, capital is essential for the entrepreneur to take action as well as natural resources and labor forces. The organizer may not always have the financial capital required at the foundation stage (Fotopoulos and Storey, 2019; Content et al., 2019). In such a case it must be financially assisted. Moreover, the venture's requirement for money should not be limited to the establishment part. Under competitive market conditions, the entrepreneur may sometimes desire to develop his business. So, the current savings may not be sufficient to achieve the growth he envisions. And then, financial support at this step becomes a requirement for the extension of the business (Vaznyte and Andries, 2019; Ersin and Baş, 2019; Mansoori and Lackéus, 2019).

As stated above, the entrepreneur tries to strengthen his position by applying to financial markets. Entrepreneurs try to find funds by issuing valuable papers on financial assets (Cassar, 2004). The counterparty (buyer) hopes to make a profit by buying and selling such securities. Within the framework of administrative and legal rules, the companies those who submit these documents, clientele and regulatory authorities come together to form financial markets. In other words, both those in need of funds and those who want to evaluate the surplus fund are transferring funds through intermediary institutions (Berger and Udell, 1998).

Additionally, there is a meaningful relationship between the level of economic progress in society and the entrepreneurial spirit (Zhang et al, 2010). Evidence for the existence of the mentioned connection has also found in studies related to the entrepreneurial activity (Arıkan, 2004). In the past, while referring the richness, technological developments, and productive forces of countries, today the ones are stated about companies (Durak, 2011). Principally providing technological developments and improving productivity are also matters related to the financial structures of businesses. As explained above, financing is one of the inputs most needed by entrepreneurs. The companies can reach the support of finance from different resources such as family, acquaintances, banks, government, capital markets, and other firms (Cumming and Johan, 2017). Indeed, since the financial composition is very indispensable in entrepreneurship, the venture is affected by monetary developments. The amount of credit in a country, developments in the capital market (foreign capital inflow, etc.), SME funds are expressed as financial factors affecting entrepreneurial finance (Tosunoğlu, 2003; Gün, 2018). Besides, one of the most notable elements affecting entrepreneurship is the conditions of the national economy (Thai and Turkina, 2014). Entrepreneurship is generally more common in countries with high-income inequalities and developing countries. It can be said that necessity-oriented entrepreneurship has a wider existence than opportunity entrepreneurship in this kind of structure (Devece et al., 2016; Gregory, 2019). When economic coefficients affecting entrepreneurship are further elaborated, some veins are encountered such as economic uncertainty, stability, growth, unemployment, debt ratio, FDI, income distribution balance and innovation (Acs et al., 2008; İlhan, 2003; Wennekers et al., 2005; Koellinger and Roy Thurik, 2012).

Literature Review

The literature review on macroeconomic factors determining entrepreneurship has been extensively conducted. Literature section is presented under two sub-titles. In the first of these titles, literature searches related to our study are included, and in the second chapter, the studies about the method are presented.

Studies on Macroeconomic Factors Determining Entrepreneurship

Researchers add new academic studies to their literature and make contributions to entrepreneurship in cross-cutting areas. Entrepreneurial activities can be perceived as the intersection point of macroeconomics and microeconomics fields. For instance, macro-level issues such as rates of growth, unemployment, and entrepreneurship have scoped together. It is possible to relate both the economy and entrepreneurship with the indications revealed in the investigated subjects. In short, with the analysis put forward, the relations of the parties with each other have revealed. However, Naudé (2011) has drawn attention to the "black box" in his research and reminds us of the issues that need to be considered. The studies on macroeconomic factors determining entrepreneurship are presented in Table 1.

Devece and his friends (2016) made research to clarify the relationship between entrepreneurship and different economic context. They focus on two stages in Spain's economy in the analysis: "the 2008 economic crisis and the financial boom before this downturn". They utilized from the data of GEM (he Global Entrepreneurship Monitor) survey and fuzzy-set qualitative comparative analysis (fsQCA) to identify the principal entrepreneurial properties. Their study explicates us that "necessity-driven entrepreneurial activities are weak during recessions and that opportunity perception and innovation are more relevant as success factors during times of recession than as duration of expansion."

Additionally, Simón-Moya et al. (2014) asserted the association within entrepreneurial activity and economic environment. They focus on relationship economic and institutional circumstances on the entrepreneurship. They use the data for the years 2009-2011 about 68 countries in cluster analysis. The results of the study told us that "entrepreneurial activity level is significantly higher in countries with lower levels of development, with greater income inequality and relatively higher levels of unemployment. Necessity-driven entrepreneurship performs a more relevant role in these countries and innovation results are relatively weaker. If the conditions convert to higher levels of financial freedom, relatively elastic job markets opportunity, and comparatively low and stable levels of inflation, open to foreign trade with rare intervention in the financial system, the market become more proper for business."

In addition to this research, Gregory (2019) studied panel data analysis from 1995 to 2013 using data from 62 countries and analyzed the effect of financial openness on changes in entrepreneurship rates in the developing and developed economies. According to their findings, together with capital controls, these factors affect entrepreneurship negatively in developing market countries, but they positively influence entrepreneurship in developed markets. Coulibaly and his colleagues (2018) examined the contribution of economic globalization and entrepreneurship to growth and development in their studies on BRICS countries with the data of 2002-2013. As a result of their studies, they found a positive relationship between these variables.

Sanders and colleagues hypothesized a U-shaped correlation among a country's rate of dynamics of business and financial progress. They utilized from regression GEM 2002 data for nascent entrepreneurial (NE) activities in 36 countries on the level of financial improvement as measured either by per capita income or by an index for innovative capacity. The conclusions submit that a 'natural rate' of NE is to some extent governed by 'laws' related to the level of financial advancement. For the developed countries, promoting incentive structures for business start-ups and improving the economic exploitation of systematic conclusions submit the most encouraging method for public policy. However, developing countries are better pursuing the exploitation of scale economies, encouraging foreign direct investment.

Ashcroft & Love (1996) observed that new establishments in the market and employment rate positively associated. They focused on Britain countries between 1981-1989 years. They also discovered support that company formation is strongly associated with net employment change. Acs et al. (2008) studied in the U.S territory by using the data 1991-1996 by the geographic unit of analysis. They reach that positive correlation between "new firm formation and regional employment growth". Baptista et al. (2005) made a similar analysis with the Portuguese 1982-2002 data utilizing Huber-White-Sandwich regression model. They also reached previous results but they propounded the long-run effect.

Also, Klapper remarked about meaningful relationships between entrepreneurial action and indicators of economic and financial advancement and growth. The scope of their research reaches 84 countries with the data of 2003-2005. By using basic regression, they approached a positive relationship between entrepreneurial activities and growth rate. Similarly, Wong et al. (2005) have made an equivalent study

Table 1. Literature review

Author	Content	Method	Period	Finding(s)
Devece, et al. (2016)	Spain	Fuzzy-set qualitative comparative analysis (fsQCA)	2004- 2010	"Necessity-driven entrepreneurship is ineffective during recessions."
Simón-Moya, et al. (2014)	68 countries	Cluster analysis, analysis of the variables	2009-2011	*Entrepreneurial activity is significantly greater in countries with lower levels of development, greater income inequality and considerable levels of unemployment in more developed countries. *The effects of environment on entrepreneurial activity and innovation results.
Gregory (2019)	62 countries	Panel Data	1995-2013	"The imposition of financial controls in emerging markets is associated with a decline in entrepreneurialism, while ones in developed markets is associated with an increase in entrepreneurial activity."
Coulibaly et al. (2018)	BRICS	Unbalanced panel data	2002-2013	"Entrepreneurial activity makes contribution to growth and development."
Wennekers et al. (2005)	36 countries	Regression	2002	"U-shaped relationship between a country's rate of entrepreneurial dynamics and its level of economic development."
Ashcroft & Love (1996)	Great Britain	Augmented factor-demand model	1981-1989	"Strong positive relationship between entry and employment"
Acs and Armington (2004)	U.S.	The geographic unit of analysis	1991-1996	"Strong relationship between new firm formation and regional employment growth."
Baptista et al. (2005)	Portugal	Huber-White-Sandwich regression	1982-2002	"New firm formation positively related to regional employment. The positive effect appears after eight years."
Klapper et al. (2007)	84 countries	Panel Regression Analysis	2003-2005	"Positive relationship between entrepreneurship and growth."
Wong et al. (2005)	37 countries	Augmented Cobb–Douglas production	2002	"The existence of entrepreneurs defined as high growth potential entrepreneurs is positive for economic growth"
Karagöz (2016)	Turkey	VAR Analysis	1968-2012	"Turkey between entrepreneurship and economic growth in the short term is a positive correlation was detected."
Braunerhjelm et al. (2010)	17 OECD Countries	Panel Regression Analysis	1981-2002	"Entrepreneurship is an important resource for economic growth."
Box et al. (2014)	Sweden	VAR Analysis	1850-2000	"The relationship between entrepreneurship and economic growth was found as positive for the long term."
Audretsch et al. (2015)	127 Europe Countries	Augmented Cobb–Douglas production	1994-2009	it emerged that Entrepreneurship affects economic growth positively in small, medium and large cities.
Mueller (2007)	West Germany Region	Cobb–Douglas Production Function	1990-2002	It was concluded that entrepreneurship positively affected regional economic growth.
Martinez (2005)	Spain	Regression	1998-2002	Entrepreneurship is affected by the level of GDP.
Arin et al. (2015)	GEM Countries	Multiple Regression Model	1999-2005	Growth, unemployment, inflation and taxes were found as macroeconomic factors determining entrepreneurship.
Özkul and Örün (2016)	9 OECD Countries	Panel Regression Analysis	2002-2013	It was concluded that entrepreneurship positively affected economic growth.
Antonie et al. (2017)	33 European Countries	Modeling the Complex Structural Equations (SEM)	2006-2015	Economic efficiency positively affects entrepreneurship.
Khyareh et al. (2019)	97 countries	MIMIC model	2008-2017	Cultural and social norms as an infrastructure play an encouraging role for entrepreneurial behavior of entrepreneurs. High-level entrepreneurial behavior also has positive and / or medium-term impacts on gross domestic product, exports, imports and employment.

covering 37 countries with data from 2002. They claimed that entrepreneurial activity supports to economic improvement.

Apart from these studies, Peris-Ortiz and her friends (2014) executed the effect of the economic crisis on entrepreneurial innovation and performance. Yueh (2009) told that entrepreneurship has a significant role in the progress of the non-state sector. With this fact, Acs and Armington (2004) observed regional circumstances in this relationship.

On the other hand, while there are such supportive studies related to entrepreneurship and increase in employment, some researchers have pointed out some suspicious points about this issue. For example, Fritsch and Mueller (2008) linked that relationship to regional factors. Moreover, Fritsch (1997) denoted the periodical fluctuations in another research. van Stel and Storey (2004) emphasized the value of policies. In their study, Audretsch and Fritsch (2002) observed the aforementioned relationship to be meaningful only in a certain period. Blanchflower (2000), Carree et al. (2007) observed negative relationships and deviations in their studies.

Arin et al. (2014) studied macroeconomic factors that determine entrepreneurship. In the study which analyzed 1999-2005 period, Global Entrepreneurship Monitor (GEM) countries were taken as samples. As a result of the study using Multiple Regression Method, growth, unemployment, inflation and taxes were determined as macroeconomic factors determining entrepreneurship. 32 macroeconomic variables were used in this study. Khyareh et al. (2019) analyzed the factors that determine entrepreneurship and the effect of entrepreneurship on macroeconomic variables. Multiple Indicator Multiple Causes (MIMIC) model was used in the study, which analyzed 97 countries and analyzed for 2008-2017 period. As a result of this study, it has been found that cultural and social policies as infrastructure investments encourage entrepreneurship and high level entrepreneurship positively affects macroeconomic variables such as GDP, employment, exports and imports. Martinez (2005), in his study for 1998-2002 data from Spain, examined the factors that affect the development of entrepreneurship in the literature first and then analyzed the relationship between entrepreneurial development rate and economic development. The author concluded that the relationship between entrepreneurship and economic development initially declined but then increased. It was also stated that entrepreneurship is affected by the GDP level. Antonie et al. (2017) investigated the effect of economic productivity on entrepreneurship. In the research conducted on 33 different European economies, the period of 2006-2015 was taken into consideration and the structural equation model (SEM) was used. As a result of this study, it was found that economic efficiency had a positive effect on entrepreneurs. In addition, it was concluded that senior entrepreneurs positively affected economic growth thanks to productivity in the long run.

Karagoz (2016) analyzed the relationship between entrepreneurship and economic growth in Turkey for the 1968-2012 period. In the study, VAR Analysis and Granger Causality tests were applied. It was found that there is a long-term relationship between entrepreneurship and economic growth. However, no causality was found between entrepreneurship and economic growth. Braunerhjelm et al. (2010) examined the relationship between entrepreneurship and economic growth for 17 OECD countries with the data of 1981-2002 and used the self-employed variable as an indicator of entrepreneurship. As a result of the study using regression method, it is stated that entrepreneurship is an important resource for economic growth. Box et al. (2014) examined the impact of entrepreneurship on economic growth for the Swedish economy and used the VAR analysis method for the period 1850-2000. In this study, self-employed entrepreneurs were used as indicators of entrepreneurship and it was found that there was a positive long-term relationship between self-employed and economic growth in Sweden in the said period.

Audretsch et al. (2015) tried to determine how entrepreneurship affects growth in 127 European cities with the Cobb-Douglas production function. In this study, new firms were used as an indicator of entrepreneurship and entrepreneurship positively affected economic growth in small, medium and large cities. Mueller (2007) tried to determine how the increase in entrepreneurship with the Cobb-Douglas type production function affects the economic output by using the 1990-2002 data for the West Germany regions. In this study, firm institutions were taken into consideration as an indicator of entrepreneurship and it was determined that entrepreneurship positively affected regional economic growth. In the study of Özkul and Örün (2016), the effect of entrepreneurship and innovation on economic growth was examined by using panel data analysis for the 2002-2013 period in 9 OECD countries. Entrepreneurship, which is considered as creating a company, has a positive and significant effect on economic growth only in models where entrepreneurship is designed as immature entrepreneurship rate and obligation-based entrepreneurship activity. As can be seen from Table 1, studies on the macroeconomic factor determining entrepreneurship are not sufficient. Overall, the studies were conducted on the economic effects of entrepreneurship. Therefore, this study is thought to make an important contribution to literature.

Studies Using Logit Method

Logit method, which can be used in quantitative and qualitative research, has been used in many studies. Logit method, which is a powerful method especially in financial crisis forecasts, has been taken into consideration in macroeconomic studies (Eti, 2019; Barışık and Tay, 2010). Yüksel (2017) analyzed the strategic success of developing countries in overcoming the 2008 global economic crisis. He concluded that government debt is an important indicator of economic crisis in developing countries. In the study of Kalkavan and Ersin (2019), the factors determining the Asian crisis were emphasized and logit method was used. In this study, the period of 1975-2006 was examined and money supply, growth and financial loans were determined as factors affecting the crisis.

In the studies of Alifiah and Tahir (2018), the factors that affect financially distressed firms in manufacturing and non-manufacturing sectors in Malaysia were analyzed by logit method. As a result of this study, the financial asset companies in manufacturing sector affected total asset turnover ratio, current ratio, net income / total asset ratio and money supply (M2), while non-manufacturing firms in financial sector were affected by debt ratio, working capital ratio, net income to total assets and money supply (M2) variables. Yüksel and Zengin (2016a) investigated the leading indicators of the global mortgage crisis in the US in 2008. They concluded that nonperforming loans ratio is one of the important causes of the crisis. Additionally, Rise and Rich (2016), Metwally (1997), Yüksel et al. (2015), Yüksel et al. (2016), Dinçer et al. (2016), Mukhtarov et al. (2018) and Yüksel et al. (2016) are other significant studies in the literature which considered logit analysis in their studies.

AN APPLICATION ON E7 ECONOMIES

Data Set and Method

In our study, the E7 countries (China, Russia, Brazil, India, Indonesia, Mexico and Turkey) the impact of macroeconomic factors of entrepreneurship via the logit method are analyzed. In our study using the Logit method, the data of 1992-2018 period were used and macroeconomic variables used in the litera-

Analysis of the Effects of Macroeconomic Factors on Entrepreneurship

ture were considered as data set indicators. In our study, the reason for choosing the sub-period of 1992 is that the macroeconomic data in E7 countries can be presented in all of these periods. The definition and data sources of the variables used in the analysis are given in Table 2.

Logit Model

Regression calculates the effects of independent variables on result variables as probabilities and determines these risk factors as probabilities. Logistic Regression is a method that interrogates the relationship between the result variable and independent variables in binary and multiple stages. When dummy variables with two or more values are included in the regression models as dependent variables, dependent variables indicate preference or decision (Erdoğan, 2002; Gujarati, 2006; Ege & Bayrakdaroğlu, 2009). In preference models with two or more values of the dependent variable, the objective is to determine the probability of selection. Linear Probability Models, which are called the simplest of preference models, may encounter problems in order to realize some assumptions in practice (Cebeci, 2012; Aldric & Nelson, 1984; Atan & Çatalbaş, 2004; Güriş & Çağlayan, 2005; İhal et al., 2006; Ege & Bayrakdaroğlu, 2009; Demirci & Astar, 2011). The model is formulated in the following equation 1 with significant variables.

$$Y = \beta_0 + +\beta_2 X_2 + \beta_4 X_4 + \beta_7 X_7 + \epsilon \tag{1}$$

The dependent variable, Y, represents the entrepreneurial variable. Y = 0 indicates that entrepreneurship decreased compared to the previous year, Y = 1 indicates that entrepreneurship increased compared to the previous year. In addition, the employer data of 1991 period were taken into consideration in order to make Y equal 1 or 0 in 1992 during the period in question. In other words, the increase or decrease of entrepreneurship data from 1991 to 1992 determined that the entrepreneurial dummy variable of 1992

Table 2. Definition of variables used and data sources

Name of Variable	Definition of Variable	Formula Symbol of Variable	Data Source
Inflation	Inflation, consumer prices (annual %)	X1	World Bank
Growth	GDP growth (annual %)	X2	World Bank
Unemployment rate	Unemployment, total (% of total labor force) (modeled ILO estimate)	X3	World Bank
Domestic Credit	Domestic credit provided by financial sector (% of GDP)	X4	World Bank
Exchange Rate	Official exchange rate (LCU per US$, period average)	X5	World Bank
Current Account	Current Account balance (% of GDP)	X6	World Bank
Total Debt Service	Total debt service (% of GNI)	X7	World Bank
Fdi	Foreign direct investment, net inflows (% of GDP)	X8	World Bank
Real Interest Rate	Real interest rate (%)	X9	World Bank, OECD

should be 1 or 0. In this study, domestic financial credit, current account deficit and unemployment rate variables were found to be significant in logit method in periods of increasing entrepreneurship.

Analysis Results

In our study, macroeconomic factors affecting entrepreneurship in E7 countries were analyzed in Eview8 program by logit method in 1992-2018 period. The analysis results are given in Table 3. In this study, 9 independent variables were used and 6 of these variables were meaningless.

Logit analysis test results for macroeconomic factors affecting entrepreneurship are given in Table 3. The first data in the table is the LR statistical value. The LR statistical value provides information about whether the model is generally significant or not. A LR probability of less than 0.05 indicates that the model is generally significant. As a matter of fact, in Table 3, the probe (LR statistic) value was realized as 0.004 and our model was generally significant. The next data is the McFadden R-squared value, which shows how much the arguments explain the model. This value is realized as 0.095. In other words, independent variables, which are macroeconomic indicators, explain entrepreneurship at a level of about 10%. Although this ratio seems weak, it gives us an idea in terms of macroeconomic factors. It also shows that there may be different variables that explain entrepreneurship more strongly.

When the significance of the independent variables is analyzed, the probability value of 6 out of 9 independent variables is higher than 0.10 and they become meaningless. The independent variables Unemployment rate and Domestic Credit's prob values were less than 0.05 and Current Account's probability values were less than 0.10 and gained significance in the model. In addition, it would be appropriate to examine the coefficients of statistically significant variables. The value of the unemployment rate coefficient was -0.16. This shows that entrepreneurship and unemployment rate is inversely proportional. When unemployment rate increases by one unit, entrepreneurship decreases by 0.16 units. The increase in unemployment in E7 countries can be expressed as a macroeconomic factor that negatively affects entrepreneurship. The coefficient of the current account deficit was 0.07. When the current account deficit increases by one unit, entrepreneurship increases by 0.07 units. It is possible to interpret this situation as the current account deficit in E7 countries is a macroeconomic factor affecting entrepreneurship. The last significant variable, domestic credit, was found to be 0.01. Obviously, domestic loans are an important factor in entrepreneurship. Ultimately, credit growth is also an important variable for investments. Increasing and diversifying investments is an event that will develop with entrepreneurship. Our findings are similar to some studies in the literature. Arin et al. (2014), unemployment variable, which is one of the macroeconomic factors determining entrepreneurship in its studies, was also detected in our study. In addition, Khyareh et al. (2019), in their study, employment variable was found to be an influential factor.

SOLUTIONS AND RECOMMENDATIONS

The current account deficit is a major problem of developing countries. The positive effect of the current account deficit on the entrepreneurship in E7 countries reveals a contradictory situation. As a matter of fact, the increase in the current account deficit becomes a structural problem of the national economy and affects entrepreneurship. Therefore, E7 countries should focus on how the current account deficit occurs and on what reasons it affects entrepreneurship. In addition, the finding that domestic loans positively affect entrepreneurship is an important outcome. As a matter of fact, the increase in domestic loans not

Table 3. Logit analysis results

Depent Variable: Employer				
Method: ML - Binary Logit (Quadratic hill climbing)				
Date:: 07/15/19 Time: 13:28				
Sample: 1992 2018				
Included observations: 189				
Convergence achieved after 4 iterations				
Covariance matrix computed using second derivatives				
Variable	Coefficient	Std. Error	z-Statistic	Prob.
Inflation (X1)	0.000423	0.000748	0.565238	0.5719
Growth (X2)	0.060294	0.042813	1.408310	0.1590
Unemployment rate (X3)	-0.157929	0.070137	2.251721	**0.0243****
Domestic Credit (X4)	0.011092	0.005290	2.096984	**0.0360****
Exchange Rate (X5)	-4.79E-05	5.01E-05	-0.956583	0.3388
Current Account (X6)	0.074793	0.044002	1.699780	**0.0892*****
Total Debt Service (X7)	0.104203	0.068603	1.518927	0.1288
Fdi (X8)	0.190979	0.133475	1.430818	0.1525
Real Interest Rate (X9)	0.016790	0.010323	1.626538	0.1038
C	-0.566893	0.633654	0.894641	0.3710
McFadden R-squared	0.095948	Mean dependent var		0.613757
S.D. dependent var	0.488181	S.E. of regression		0.472483
Akaike info criterion	1.311895	Sum squared resid		39.95995
Schwarz criterion	1.483416	Log likelihood		-113.9740
Hannan-Quinn criter.	1.381382	Deviance		227.9481
Restr. deviance	252.1404	Restr. log likelihood		-126.0702
LR statistic	24.19230	Avg. log likelihood		-0.603037
Prob(LR statistic)	0.004007			
Obs with Dep=0	73	Total obs		189
Obs with Dep=1	116			

Note: * symbol represents 1%, ** symbol represents 5% and *** symbol represents 10% significance level.

only affects investments but also increases entrepreneurship in the country. In other words, investments are realized not only by certain firms but also by the addition of new firms.

FUTURE RESEARCH DIRECTIONS

In the future studies, different methodology can be taken into consideration, such as panel regression, GMM, MARS, VAR and probit. Hence, it can be possible to compare the results of this study with others.

CONCLUSION

The most important feature in the formation of entrepreneurship is the existence of concepts of ideas and courage. The first step of entrepreneurship is a market research in which the results can be analyzed correctly in order to bring the idea to life. As a result of the market research, the realization of the idea is possible with the right plan, good budget and financial resources. Funding and successful financial management are important factors that pave the way for entrepreneurship and help them grow. For this reason, the macroeconomic situation of the country should be taken into consideration in the formation of financial resources.

Entrepreneurship is an issue that affects economies as well as other economic indicators. As a matter of fact, the weakness of the economic performance of a country may also prevent the establishment of new companies in that country. Unemployment, which is an important indicator of macroeconomics, has a direct relationship with entrepreneurship. In the event of economic contraction, companies decrease, and this situation emerges as a factor that increases unemployment. In addition, the weakness of the country's financial structure is one of the macroeconomic events that adversely affect entrepreneurship.

Entrepreneurship is an important field in the increase and diversification of investments in a country. Entrepreneurship has gained importance in today's world where financial marketing has become an important sector. There are many factors that determine entrepreneurship. Economic, financial, psychological, sociological and cultural factors should be considered. In this study, macroeconomic factors affecting entrepreneurship were analyzed for E7 countries. In our study using the Logit method, the period 1992-2018 was discussed. As a result of this study, it was determined that unemployment rate, current account deficit and domestic credits are macroeconomic factors affecting entrepreneurship. While the increase in unemployment rate in E7 countries affects entrepreneurship negatively, the current account deficit and the increase in domestic loans positively affect entrepreneurship.

REFERENCES

Acs, Z., & Armington, C. (2004). Employment growth and entrepreneurial activity in cities. *Regional Studies*, *38*(8), 911–927. doi:10.1080/0034340042000280938

Acs, Z. J., Desai, S., & Hessels, J. (2008). Entrepreneurship, economic development and institutions. *Small Business Economics*, *31*(3), 219–234. doi:10.100711187-008-9135-9

Adıgüzel, Z., Artar, M., & Erdil, O. (2017). *A study of psychological contract violation*. Organizational Trust, Intention To Leave Work.

Akgün, A. E., Keskin, H., Çemberci, M., & Karakeçe, E. (2019). *Korku ve Önyargıların Girişimcilik Zihniyetine Etkilerinin Araştırılması: Kavramsal Model Önerisi. II.* Elazığ: Uluslararası Sosyal Bilimler&İnovasyon Kongresi.

Aldric, J. H., & Nelson, F. D. (1984). *Linear Probability, Logit and Probit Models.* Thousand Oaks, CA: Sage. doi:10.4135/9781412984744

Alifiah, M., & Tahir, M. (2018). Predicting financial distress companies in the manufacturing and non-manufacturing sectors in Malaysia using macroeconomic variables. *Management Science Letters, 8*(6), 593–604. doi:10.5267/j.msl.2018.4.031

Anderson, B. S., Wennberg, K., & McMullen, J. S. (2019). Enhancing quantitative theory-testing entrepreneurship research. *Journal of Business Venturing, 34*(5), 105928. doi:10.1016/j.jbusvent.2019.02.001

Arıkan, S. (2004). *Girişimcilik, Temel Kavramlar ve Bazı Güncel Konular, Genişletilmiş 2.* Ankara, Turkey: Baskı, Siyasal Kitabevi.

Arin, K. P., Huang, V. Z., Minniti, M., Nandialath, A. M., & Reich, O. F. (2015). Revisiting the determinants of entrepreneurship: A Bayesian approach. *Journal of Management, 41*(2), 607–631. doi:10.1177/0149206314558488

Ashcroft, B., & Love, J. H. (1996). Firm births and employment change in the British counties: 1981–89. *Papers in Regional Science, 75*(4), 483–500. doi:10.1007/BF02412291

Atan, M., & Çatalbaş, E. (2004). Çok Değişkenli İstatistiksel Analiz Yöntemleri ile Türk Bankacılık Sektöründe Çok Boyutlu Mali Başarısızlık Tahmin Modelleri Oluşturulması. *4. İstatistik Günleri Sempozyumu*, 19-22.

Audretsch, D. B., Belitski, M., & Desai, S. (2015). Entrepreneurship and economic development in cities. *The Annals of Regional Science, 55*(1), 33–60. doi:10.100700168-015-0685-x

Audretsch, D. B., & Fritsch, M. (2002). Growth regimes over time and space. *Regional Studies, 36*(2), 113–124. doi:10.1080/00343400220121909

Barisik, S., & Tay, A. (2010). An analysis of financial crisis by early warning systems approach: the case of transition economies and emerging markets (1994-2006 period panel logit model). *Journal of Economic & Management Perspectives, 4*(2), 403.

Blanchflower, D. G. (2000). Self-employment in OECD countries. *Labour Economics, 7*(5), 471–505. doi:10.1016/S0927-5371(00)00011-7

Bohnsack, R., & Margonlina, A. (2019). Teaching entrepreneurship and business model innovation in a blended-learning curriculum with the Smart Business Modeler. *Journal of Business Models, 7*(3).

Bolton, R. N. (2004). Linking marketing to financial performance and firm value. *Journal of Marketing, 68*(4), 73–75. doi:10.1509/jmkg.68.4.73.42727

Box, M., Lin, X., & Gratzer, K. (2014). Linking entrepreneurship and economic growth in Sweden, 1850-2000. *PESO Working Papers, School of Social Sciences,* Södertörn University.

Braunerhjelm, P., Acs, Z. J., Audretsch, D. B., & Carlsson, B. (2010). The missing link: knowledge diffusion and entrepreneurship in endogenous growth. *Small Business Economics*, *34*(2), 105–125. doi:10.100711187-009-9235-1

Browder, R. E., Aldrich, H. E., & Bradley, S. W. (2019). The emergence of the maker movement: Implications for entrepreneurship research. *Journal of Business Venturing*, *34*(3), 459–476. doi:10.1016/j.jbusvent.2019.01.005

Carree, M., Van Stel, A., Thurik, R., & Wennekers, S. (2007). The relationship between economic development and business ownership revisited. *Entrepreneurship and Regional Development*, *19*(3), 281–291. doi:10.1080/08985620701296318

Cebeci, İ. (2012). *Krizleri İncelemede Kullanılan Nitel Tercih Modelleri: Türkiye İçin Bir Probit Model Uygulaması (1988-2009)*. İstanbul Üniversitesi İktisat Fakültesi Mecmuası.

Content, J., Frenken, K., & Jordaan, J. A. (2019). Does related variety foster regional entrepreneurship? Evidence from European regions. *Regional Studies*, 1–13.

Coulibaly, S. K., Erbao, C., & Mekongcho, T. M. (2018). Economic globalization, entrepreneurship, and development. *Technological Forecasting and Social Change*, *127*, 271–280. doi:10.1016/j.techfore.2017.09.028

Devece, C., Peris-Ortiz, M., & Rueda-Armengot, C. (2016). Entrepreneurship during economic crisis: Success factors and paths to failure. *Journal of Business Research*, *69*(11), 5366–5370. doi:10.1016/j.jbusres.2016.04.139

Dinçer, H., Hacıoğlu, Ü., & Yüksel, S. (2016). The impacts of financial variables on employment planning in Turkish banking sector. [IJSECSR]. *International Journal of Sustainable Entrepreneurship and Corporate Social Responsibility*, *1*(2), 1–20. doi:10.4018/IJSECSR.2016070101

Durak, İ. (2011). Girişimciliği etkileyen çevresel faktörlerle ilgili girişimcilerin tutumları: Bir alan araştırması. *Yönetim Bilimleri Dergisi*, *9*(2), 191–213.

Duran, S., & Zehir, C. (2011). Analyzing the technical efficiency on the effects of foreign portfolio investment in the financing of small and medium-sized enterprises (SMEs) in Turkey. *African Journal of Business Management*, *5*(21), 8567–8575. doi:10.5897/AJBM11.1027

Ege, İ., & Bayrakdaroğlu, A. (2009). İMKB Şirketlerinin Hisse Senedi Getiri Başarılarının Lojistik Regresyon tekniği ile Analizi. ZKÜ Sosyal Bilimler Dergisi, Cilt 5. *Sayı*, *10*, 139–158.

Ersin, İ., & Baş, H. (2019). Güney Avrupa Refah Ülkelerinde Sosyal Harcamalar ve Ekonomik Büyüme Arasındaki İlişkinin İncelenmesi. *SGD-Sosyal Güvenlik Dergisi*, *9*(1), 193–213. doi:10.32331gd.582752

Eti, S. (2019). The use of quantitative methods in investment decisions: a literature review. In Handbook of research on global issues in financial communication and investment decision making (pp. 256–275). Hershey, PA: IGI Global. doi:10.4018/978-1-5225-9265-5.ch013

Fotopoulos, G., & Storey, D. J. (2019). Public policies to enhance regional entrepreneurship: Another programme failing to deliver? *Small Business Economics*, *53*(1), 189–209. doi:10.100711187-018-0021-9

Fritsch, M. (1997). New firms and regional employment change. *Small Business Economics*, *9*(5), 437–448. doi:10.1023/A:1007942918390

Geçit, B. B. (2018). Yöneticilerde Finansal Pazarlama Algısının Ölçümü. *Beykent Üniversitesi Sosyal Bilimler Dergisi*, *11*(1), 24–34.

Gregory, R. P. (2019). Financial openness and entrepreneurship. *Research in International Business and Finance*, *48*, 48–58. doi:10.1016/j.ribaf.2018.12.006

Gujarati, N. D. (2006). *Temel Ekonometri, Çev.* İstanbul, Turkey: Ümit Şenesen ve Gülay Günlük Şenesen, Literatür Yayıncılık.

Gün, M. (2018). The relationship between credit default swap spreads and equity indices in emerging markets. *Current Debates in Social Sciences*, 57.

Güriş, S., & Çağlayan, E. (2005). *Ekonometri ve Temel Kavramlar*. İstanbul, Turkey: Der Yayınları.

Hechavarria, D., Bullough, A., Brush, C., & Edelman, L. (2019). High-growth women's entrepreneurship: fueling social and economic development. *Journal of Small Business Management*, *57*(1), 5–13. doi:10.1111/jsbm.12503

Henrekson, M., & Sanandaji, T. (2019). Measuring entrepreneurship: do established metrics capture Schumpeterian entrepreneurship? *Entrepreneurship Theory and Practice*, 1042258719844500.

Huda, M., Qodriah, S. L., Rismayadi, B., Hananto, A., Kardiyati, E. N., Ruskam, A., & Nasir, B. M. (2019). Towards cooperative with competitive alliance: insights into performance value in social entrepreneurship. In Creating Business Value and Competitive Advantage with Social Entrepreneurship (pp. 294-317). Hershey, PA: IGI Global.

Ibeh, K., Crick, D., & Etemad, H. (2019). International marketing knowledge and international entrepreneurship in the contemporary multi speed global economy. *International Marketing Review*, *36*(1), 2–5. doi:10.1108/IMR-02-2019-377

Ihal, M. E., Topuz, D., & Uçan, O. (2006). Dogrusal Olasilik ve Logit Modelleri ile Parametre Tahmini/ Linear Probability and Parameter Estimation with Logit Models. *Sosyoekonomi*, (1), 47.

İlhan, S. (2003). Sosyo-Ekonomik Bir Fenomen Olarak Girişimciliğin Oluşumunu Etkileyen Başlıca Faktörler. *Muğla Üniversitesi Sosyal Bilimler Enstitüsü Dergisi*, (11), 61-79.

Karagöz, K. (2016). Girişimcilik-Ekonomik Büyüme İlişkisi: Türkiye İçin Ekonometrik Bir Analiz. *Girişmcilik ve Kalkınma Dergisi*, 11(2).

Khyareh, M. M., Khairandish, M., & Torabi, H. (2019). Macroeconomic effects of entrepreneurship: evidences from factor, efficiency and innovation driven countries. *International Journal of Entrepreneurship*, *23*(1), 1–21.

Klapper, L., Laeven, L., & Rajan, R. (2006). Entry regulation as a barrier to entrepreneurship. *Journal of Financial Economics*, *82*(3), 591–629. doi:10.1016/j.jfineco.2005.09.006

Koellinger, P. D., & Thurik, A. R. (2012). Entrepreneurship and the business cycle. *The Review of Economics and Statistics*, *94*(4), 1143–1156. doi:10.1162/REST_a_00224

Konon, A., & Kritikos, A. S. (2019). Prediction based on entrepreneurship-prone personality profiles: Sometimes worse than the toss of a coin. *Small Business Economics, 53*(1), 1–20. doi:10.100711187-018-0111-8

Kreiser, P. M., Kuratko, D. F., Covin, J. G., Ireland, R. D., & Hornsby, J. S. (2019). Corporate entrepreneurship strategy: Extending our knowledge boundaries through configuration theory. *Small Business Economics*, 1–20.

Mansoori, Y., & Lackéus, M. (2019). Comparing effectuation to discovery-driven planning, prescriptive entrepreneurship, business planning, lean startup, and design thinking. *Small Business Economics*, 1–28.

Martin-Rojas, R., Garcia-Morales, V. J., & Gonzalez-Alvarez, N. (2019). Technological antecedents of entrepreneurship and its consequences for organizational performance. *Technological Forecasting and Social Change, 147*, 22–35. doi:10.1016/j.techfore.2019.06.018

Martinez, J. A. B. (2005). Equilibrium entrepreneurship rate, economic development and growth. evidence from Spanish regions. *Entrepreneurship and Regional Development, 17*(2), 145–161. doi:10.1080/08985620500032633

Molina, L. M., & García-Morales, V. J. (2019). Combined influence of absorptive capacity and corporate entrepreneurship on performance. *Sustainability, 11*(11), 1–26.

Mueller, P. (2007). Exploiting entrepreneurial opportunities: The impact of entrepreneurship on growth. *Small Business Economics, 28*(4), 355–362. doi:10.100711187-006-9035-9

Mukhtarov, S., Yüksel, S., & Mammadov, E. (2018). Factors that increase credit risks of Azerbaijani banks. *Journal of International Studies, 11*(2).

Naudé, W. (2011). Entrepreneurship is not a binding constraint on growth and development in the poorest countries. *World Development, 39*(1), 33–44. doi:10.1016/j.worlddev.2010.05.005

Nițu-Antonie, R., Feder, E. S., & Munteanu, V. (2017). Macroeconomic effects of entrepreneurship from an international perspective. *Sustainability, 9*(7), 1159. doi:10.3390u9071159

Nyström, K. (2008). *Is entrepreneurship the salvation for enhanced economic growth?* (No. 143). Royal Institute of Technology, CESIS-Centre of Excellence for Science and Innovation Studies.

Özkul, G., & Örün, E. (2016). Girişimcilik ve İnovasyonun Ekonomik Büyüme Üzerindeki Etkisi: Ampirik Bir Araştırma. *Girişimcilik ve İnovasyon Yönetimi Dergisi, 5*(2), 17–51.

Peris-Ortiz, M., Fuster-Estruch, V., & Devece-Carañana, C. (2014). Entrepreneurship and innovation in a context of crisis. In *Entrepreneurship, innovation and economic crisis* (pp. 1–10). Cham, Switzerland: Springer. doi:10.1007/978-3-319-02384-7_1

Rawhouser, H., Cummings, M., & Newbert, S. L. (2019). Social impact measurement: Current approaches and future directions for social entrepreneurship research. *Entrepreneurship Theory and Practice, 43*(1), 82–115. doi:10.1177/1042258717727718

Rehan, F., Block, J. H., & Fisch, C. (2019). (Forthcoming). Entrepreneurship in Islamic communities: How do Islamic values and Islamic practices influence entrepreneurship intentions? *Journal of Enterprising Communities: People and Places in the Global Economy*, (ahead-of-print). doi:10.1108/JEC-05-2019-0041

Roberts, E. B., Murray, F., & Kim, J. D. (2019). Entrepreneurship and innovation at MIT: Continuing global growth and impact—an updated report. *Foundations and Trends® in Entrepreneurship, 15*(1), 1-55.

Ryff, C. D. (2019). Entrepreneurship and eudaimonic well-being: Five venues for new science. *Journal of Business Venturing, 34*(4), 646–663. doi:10.1016/j.jbusvent.2018.09.003 PMID:31105380

Saebi, T., Foss, N. J., & Linder, S. (2019). Social entrepreneurship research: Past achievements and future promises. *Journal of Management, 45*(1), 70–95. doi:10.1177/0149206318793196

Schenkel, M. T., Farmer, S., & Maslyn, J. M. (2019). Process improvement in SMEs: The impact of harmonious passion for entrepreneurship, employee creative self-efficacy, and time spent innovating. *Journal of Small Business Strategy, 29*(1), 64–77.

Shepherd, D. A., Wennberg, K., Suddaby, R., & Wiklund, J. (2019). What are we explaining? A review and agenda on initiating, engaging, performing, and contextualizing entrepreneurship. *Journal of Management, 45*(1), 159–196. doi:10.1177/0149206318799443

Simón-Moya, V., Revuelto-Taboada, L., & Guerrero, R. F. (2014). Institutional and economic drivers of entrepreneurship: An international perspective. *Journal of Business Research, 67*(5), 715–721. doi:10.1016/j.jbusres.2013.11.033

Tosunoğlu, B. T. (2003). *Girişimcilik ve Türkiye'nin ekonomik gelişme sürecinde girişimciliğin yeri*. Eskişehir Anadolu Üniversitesi Sosyal Bilimler Enstitüsü Yayımlanmamış Doktora Tezi.

Van Stel, A., & Storey, D. (2004). The link between firm births and job creation: Is there a Upas tree effect? *Regional Studies, 38*(8), 893–909. doi:10.1080/0034340042000280929

Venkataraman, S. (2019). The distinctive domain of entrepreneurship research. In *Seminal ideas for the next twenty-five years of advances* (pp. 5–20). Emerald Publishing. doi:10.1108/S1074-754020190000021009

Wennekers, S., Van Wennekers, A., Thurik, R., & Reynolds, P. (2005). Nascent entrepreneurship and the level of economic development. *Small Business Economics, 24*(3), 293–309. doi:10.100711187-005-1994-8

Wiklund, J., Lomberg, C., Alkærsig, L., & Miller, D. (2019, July). When ADHD helps and harms in entrepreneurship: an epidemiological approach. In Academy of Management Proceedings (Vol. 2019, No. 1, p. 17481). Briarcliff Manor, NY 10510: Academy of Management.

Wong, P. K., Ho, Y. P., & Autio, E. (2005). Entrepreneurship, innovation and economic growth: Evidence from GEM data. *Small Business Economics, 24*(3), 335–350. doi:10.100711187-005-2000-1

Yueh, L. (2009). China's entrepreneurs. *World Development, 37*(4), 778–786. doi:10.1016/j.worlddev.2008.07.010

Yüksel, S. (2017). Strategies out of global recession in emerging markets: an application for 2008 global crisis. In *Global business strategies in crisis* (pp. 57–75). Cham, Switzerland: Springer. doi:10.1007/978-3-319-44591-5_5

Yüksel, S., Canöz, İ., & Özsarı, M. (2016). Analyzing foreign exchange (FX) positions of participation banks in Turkey. *Journal*, 6(12). Retrieved from http://www. ijmra. us

Yüksel, S., Dincer, H., & Hacioglu, U. (2015). CAMELS-based determinants for the credit rating of Turkish deposit banks. *International Journal of Finance & Banking Studies*, 4(4), 1–17.

Yüksel, S., Eroğlu, S., & Özsarı, M. (2016). An analysis of the reasons of internal migration in Turkey with logit method. *Business and Management Horizons*, 4(2), 34. doi:10.5296/bmh.v4i2.10350

Yüksel, S., & Zengin, S. (2016). Identifying the determinants of interest rate risk of the banks: a case of Turkish banking sector. *International Journal of Research in Business and Social Science (2147-4478)*, 5(6), 12-28.

Yüksel, S., & Zengin, S. (2016a). Leading indicators of 2008 global crisis: an analysis with logit and mars methods. *Finansal Araştırmalar ve Çalışmalar Dergisi*, 8(15), 495–518.

Chapter 20
PESTEL Analysis–Based Evaluation of Marketing Strategies in the European Banking Sector:
An Application With IT2 Fuzzy DEMATEL

Hasan Dinçer
Istanbul Medipol University, Turkey

Fatih Pınarbaşı
https://orcid.org/0000-0001-9005-0324
Istanbul Medipol University, Turkey

ABSTRACT

This chapter evaluates the marketing strategies in European banking sector. In this context, six dimensions of PESTEL analysis (politic, economic, sociological, technologic, environmental, and legal) are taken into the consideration. On the other side, interval type-2 fuzzy DEMATEL approach is used to weight the importance of these dimensions. The findings show that technological and political factors have the highest importance. Therefore, it is recommended that technological innovations in the banking sector should be followed by European banks. Within this framework, these banks should design a market research department to follow these developments in the market so that new products and services can be identified. Therefore, technological development should be adopted in the strategy development process. In addition, interest rates defined by the central bank should also be considered by these banks. Hence, adopting marketing strategies according to the interest rate policy of the central banks provides a competitive advantage to the European banks.

DOI: 10.4018/978-1-7998-2559-3.ch020

INTRODUCTION

Although there are many advantages of globalization, it also causes same problems for the companies, such as increasing competition. Due to this situation, companies had to compete with more powerful competitors than before. The banking sector was also affected from this competitive environment. The main reason for this is the increase in international trade as a result of globalization. This condition resulted that banks that will mediate to international trade have to perform different operations. Therefore, banks are now in a more difficult environment (Allen et al., 2019; Dinçer et al., 2018a; Bai et al., 2019; Yüksel, 2017). For example, in many countries, the local banks must compete with many big international banks. In this circumstance, many strategies are required to be able to attract the attentions of the customers (Zaleska and Kondraciuk, 2019; Dinçer et al., 2018b; Beyers et al., 2019; Yüksel et al., 2016; Baabdullah et al., 2019).

Banks are trying to take many new actions just to survive in this competitive environment. Within this framework, they employ very different departments for this purpose, such as market research and financial analysis departments. One of the important actions in this context is the marketing strategy. In other words, they need to develop new marketing strategies in order to increase their competitiveness. In this context, new strategies should be developed considering customer expectations. As an example, different alternative distribution channels can be developed, and new advertisements can be made (Cooke et al., 2019; Dinçer and Yüksel, 2018).

One of the most important strategic planning techniques is PESTEL analysis. The main purpose of this approach is to consider environmental issues to develop new strategies. There are mainly six different dimensions of this method. First of all, political factors in the country may affect the strategies of the companies. Also, economical aspects play a key role in this context. Additionally, sociological issues can have an influence on the strategies. Moreover, technological factors may direct companies in this framework. Finally, environmental and legal aspects may affect strategy development process.

PESTEL analysis also plays a crucial role for the banking sector. It is obvious that banks are required to analyze the issues mentioned in PESTEL model in order to survive in a competitive environment. The main reason is that many different factors can have an effect on the performance of the banking sector (Yüksel et al., 2018). For instance, economic conditions directly influence interest rate which represents the cost of the banks. Additionally, if the banks do not consider political factors in the country while generating strategy, they may take high amount of risks. These issues show that an unnecessary marketing strategy could lead to a reduction in the company's profitability.

The level of the competition also increased in European banking industry especially after the globalization. Europe has become a market that attracts the attention of many international banks both as location and economic size. Therefore, many international large-scale banks have entered the European market (Goddard et al., 2007). This situation has increased the competition in this region. Because of this situation, European banks try to develop new strategies to survive in this difficult environment. However, it is not so easy to understand which factors should be mainly focused on (Dinçer, 2018; Carbó et al., 2009).

In this study, it is aimed to assess marketing strategies of the banking industry. Within this scope, European banking sector is taken into the consideration. In addition to them, six different dimensions of PESTEL analysis are used to measure the success of marketing strategies of these banks. In the analysis process, interval type-2 fuzzy DEMATEL approach is considered to weight these six dimensions. As a result of this analysis, it can be understood which factors are more significant in the performance of marketing strategies in European banking industry.

PESTEL Analysis-Based Evaluation of Marketing Strategies in the European Banking Sector

This study has some novelties in many different aspects. Firstly, there are limited studies which consider PESTEL analysis in banking industry. This situation shows that by assessing marketing strategies of European banking industry with PESTEL-based dimensions, this study contributes to the literature. In addition to this aspect, interval type-2 fuzzy DEMATEL is the new approach and was firstly used in this study regarding the evaluation of the marketing strategies. Therefore, this issue increases the originality of this study.

There are four different sections in this study. This introduction section includes general information about the main concepts. After that, the second section reviews the literature by analyzing the studies related to PESTEL analysis. Moreover, the third section identifies the application on European banking industry. For this purpose, firstly, the details of internal type-2 fuzzy DEMATEL approach are explained. Additionally, this section also focuses on the analysis results for European banking industry. In the final section, recommendations are shared based on analysis results.

Literature Review

PESTEL analysis is a significant strategic planning technique in the literature. The main advantage of this method is that it considers many different factors at the same time in this process. Hence, this model is very important in terms of developing company's vision for the future (Ramirez et al., 2019; Türkyılmaz et al., 2019). By focusing on many different factors, this method is helpful for the companies to adopt the changes in the environment in process development process. There are six different dimensions of PESTEL analysis which are political, economic, sociological, technological, legal and environment factors (González Ortega et al., 2019; Tsangas et al., 2019).

With respect to the political dimension, it is aimed to identify the role of the governments on the industries. For example, tax increase may affect some industries negatively. Economic factors include the influences of macroeconomic conditions of the country to the companies' performances (Masih et al., 2019; Calderón Ramírez et al., 2019). In this context, high inflation rates in the country increase the uncertainty which has a decreasing effect on the investment amount. Additionally, sociological factors are also very significant for the companies in strategic decision-making process. In this circumstance, the number of populations in the country is accepted as an important indicator (Song et al., 2017; Strzelczyk and Chłąd, 2019; Padilla, 2019).

In addition to them, technological development also affects the performance of the companies. For instance, innovations can provide an important advantage for some industries (Pan et al., 2018; Graham, 2018; Patil, 2018; Nurmi and Niemelä, 2018). Hence, if the companies do not consider this technological development, they can lose their competitive power in the market. Moreover, environmental factors can have a strong influence especially for some specific industries. Finally, legal factors should be taken into the consideration for the companies in the development of new strategies (Walsh, 2005; Schuetz et al., 2018; Kara, 2018; Nicolae, 2018; Höpel, 2018).

In the literature, PESTEL analysis was assessed by many different researchers. Some of these studies considered this approach in energy industry. For example, Song et al. (2017) used PESTEL analysis in order to evaluate the performance of energy companies in China. They concluded that technological and environmental items play a more significant role in this process. Similarly, Widya Yudha et al. (2018), Zalengera et al. (2014) and Fozer et al. (2017) focused on the renewable energy alternatives with the help of this method. Also, Shilei and Yong (2009) identified that economic and technological dimensions of PESTEL analysis are important in energy industry. Additionally, de Andres et al. (2017) also employed this method for investigating risks and uncertainties about wave and tidal energy technology.

Furthermore, food and construction are other industries in which PESTEL analysis was taken into the consideration. As an example, Zhao and Pan (2015) used this approach to evaluate zero carbon buildings. Similarly, alternative construction models are measured by PESTEL analysis by Kremer and Symmons (2015). On the other side, Damasceno and Abreu (2018) and Oraman (2014) evaluated energy industry in Brazil and organic food industry in Turkey by considering the dimensions of this approach. Parallel to this study, Bees and Williams (2017) focused on food waste collections by PESTEL analysis and concluded that legal issues have the highest importance. In addition, Stoyanova and Harizanova-Bartos (2017), Zhiyong (2017) and Lamas Leite et al. (2017) are other studies which considered PESTEL model in their analysis.

PESTEL analysis was also considered in many different industries. For example, Ziout and Azab (2015), Mitter et al. (2018) and Srdjevic et al. (2012) used PESTEL analysis for agriculture industry. Morover, Leviäkangas (2016), Li et al. (2009), Nataraja and Al-Aali (2011) and Ziolkowska and Ziolkowski (2015) made an analysis for transportation industry by considering this method. In addition to them, tourism industry was also evaluated by Fernández et al. (2011) and Sridhar et al. (2016). Additionally, some other concepts were also assessed with PESTEL analysis, such as air pollution (Gheibi et al., 2018), insurance industry (Kampanje, 2014) and education industry (Versloot, 2016).

On the other side, the subject of marketing strategies in the banking industry was also evaluated in many different aspects. Most of these studies identified the influences of effective marketing strategy on the financial performance of the banks. Rhee and Mehra (2009) examined organizational performance in banking industry. In this context, different aspects are taken into the consideration. They determined that effective marketing strategy is the most important item for the financial performance of the banks. Additionally, Li et al. (2016), Neilson and Chadha (2008), Vegholm (2011), Gilbert and Choi (2003) and Zineldin (2005) stated that successful marketing strategies increase the quality of customer relationship and this situation has an increasing profitability of the banks. Adegbola (2014) also pointed out the importance of corporate social responsibility in the performance of the banks.

Additionally, the importance of marketing in new product or service development was also analyzed by different researchers. For instance, Alalwan et al. (2017) evaluated the adoption of mobile banking in Jordanian banking industry. They concluded that marketing performance of the banks plays a key role in the success of new product. Similar to this study, Chaouali et al. (2017) also underlined the importance of understanding customer expectations in the success of new product development. Durkin et al. (2007), Mitic and Kapoulas (2012) and Chaouali and Souiden (2018) also evaluated this subject and concluded that effective marketing is important in the success of new product or service development of the banks.

According to the results of literature review, it is defined that PESTEL analysis was preferred by many researchers to make analysis in different sectors, such as energy, transportation, food and construction. This situation gives information that the quality of this approach is high. In addition to this condition, marketing strategies of the banking sector were evaluated in various aspects. However, it is determined that there are very limited studies which considered PESTEL analysis in the banking sector. Additionally, it is also seen that there is not such as study in the last years. Thus, it is believed that this kind of study will be beneficial in this context. Also, by making this analysis for European banking sector can provide many opportunities for these banks to increase their profitability.

Methodology

Interval Type-2 Fuzzy Sets

Interval type-1 fuzzy sets are also named as classical fuzzy sets. It is claimed that these fuzzy sets can be insufficient in order to solve uncertainty conditions. Therefore, interval type-2 fuzzy sets were generated for this purpose (Sola et al., 2015). In this context, type-2 fuzzy set is named as $\tilde{A}$. Additionally, type-2 membership function can be represented by $\mu_{\tilde{A}(x,u)}$. Also, this function has a value between 0 and 1. This situation is explained on the equation (1).

$$\tilde{A} = \left\{ \left((x,u), \mu_{\tilde{A}(x,u)}\right) | \forall_x \in X, \forall_u \in J_x \subseteq [0,1] \right\}. \text{ or } \tilde{A} = \int_{x \in X} \int_{u \in J_x} \mu_{\tilde{A}}(x,u)/(x,u) J_x \subseteq [0,1]. \quad (1)$$

When $\mu_{\tilde{A}(x,u)}$ is equal to "1", $\tilde{A}$ can be demonstrated on the equation (2).

$$\tilde{A} = \int_{x \in X} \int_{u \in J_x} 1/(x,u) J_x \subseteq [0,1]. \quad (2)$$

In addition, "lower trapezoidal membership function" is named as $\tilde{A}_i^L$. Moreover, $\tilde{A}_i^U$ represents "the upper trapezoidal membership function". Equation (3) gives information about this situation.

$$\tilde{A}_i = \left(\tilde{A}_i^U, \tilde{A}_i^L\right) = \left(\left(a_{i1}^U, a_{i2}^U, a_{i3}^U, a_{i4}^U; H_1\left(\tilde{A}_i^U\right), H_2\left(\tilde{A}_i^U\right)\right), \left(a_{i1}^L, a_{i2}^L, a_{i3}^L, a_{i4}^L; H_1\left(\tilde{A}_i^L\right), H_2\left(\tilde{A}_i^L\right)\right)\right). \quad (3)$$

On the other side, equations (4)-(8) identify the construction of interval type-2 fuzzy sets.

$$\tilde{A}_1 \oplus \tilde{A}_2 = (\tilde{A}_1^U, \tilde{A}_1^L) \oplus (\tilde{A}_2^U, \tilde{A}_2^L) = ((a_{11}^U + a_{21}^U, a_{12}^U + a_{22}^U, a_{13}^U + a_{23}^U, a_{14}^U +$$
$$a_{24}^U; min(H_1(\tilde{A}_1^U), H_1(\tilde{A}_2^U)), min(H_2(\tilde{A}_1^U), H_2(\tilde{A}_2^U))), (a_{11}^L + a_{21}^L, a_{12}^L + a_{22}^L, a_{13}^L + a_{23}^L, a_{14}^L + \quad (4)$$
$$a_{24}^L; min(H_1(\tilde{A}_1^L), H_1(\tilde{A}_2^L)), min(H_2(\tilde{A}_1^L), H_2(\tilde{A}_2^L))))$$

$$\tilde{A}_1 \ominus \tilde{A}_2 = (\tilde{A}_1^U, \tilde{A}_1^L) \ominus (\tilde{A}_2^U, \tilde{A}_2^L) = ((a_{11}^U - a_{24}^U, a_{12}^U - a_{23}^U, a_{13}^U - a_{22}^U, a_{14}^U -$$
$$a_{21}^U; min(H_1(\tilde{A}_1^U), H_1(\tilde{A}_2^U)), min(H_2(\tilde{A}_1^U), H_2(\tilde{A}_2^U))), (a_{11}^L - a_{24}^L, a_{12}^L - a_{23}^L, a_{13}^L - a_{22}^L, a_{14}^L - \quad (5)$$
$$a_{21}^L; min(H_1(\tilde{A}_1^L), H_1(\tilde{A}_2^L)), min(H_2(\tilde{A}_1^L), H_2(\tilde{A}_2^L))))$$

$$\tilde{A}_1 \otimes \tilde{A}_2 = (\tilde{A}_1^U, \tilde{A}_1^L) \otimes (\tilde{A}_2^U, \tilde{A}_2^L) = ((a_{11}^U \times a_{21}^U, a_{12}^U \times a_{22}^U, a_{13}^U \times a_{23}^U, a_{14}^U \times a_{24}^U$$
$$; min(H_1(\tilde{A}_1^U), H_1(\tilde{A}_2^U)), min(H_2(\tilde{A}_1^U), H_2(\tilde{A}_2^U))), (a_{11}^L \times a_{21}^L, a_{12}^L \times a_{22}^L, a_{13}^L \times a_{23}^L, a_{14}^L \times a_{24}^L \quad (6)$$
$$; min(H_1(\tilde{A}_1^L), H_1(\tilde{A}_2^L)), min(H_2(\tilde{A}_1^L), H_2(\tilde{A}_2^L))))$$

$$k\tilde{A}_1 = \left(k \times a_{11}^U, k \times a_{12}^U, k \times a_{13}^U, k \times a_{14}^U; H_1\left(\tilde{A}_1^U\right), H_2\left(\tilde{A}_1^U\right)\right), \left(k \times a_{11}^L, k \times a_{12}^L, k \times a_{13}^L, k \times a_{14}^L; H_1\left(\tilde{A}_1^L\right), H_2\left(\tilde{A}_1^L\right)\right). \quad (7)$$

$$\frac{\tilde{A}_1}{k} = \left(\frac{1}{k} \times a_{11}^U, \frac{1}{k} \times a_{12}^U, \frac{1}{k} \times a_{13}^U, \frac{1}{k} \times a_{14}^U; H_1\left(\tilde{A}_1^U\right), H_2\left(\tilde{A}_1^U\right)\right), \left(\frac{1}{k} \times a_{11}^L, \frac{1}{k} \times a_{12}^L, \frac{1}{k} \times a_{13}^L, \frac{1}{k} \times a_{14}^L; H_1\left(\tilde{A}_1^L\right), H_2\left(\tilde{A}_1^L\right)\right). \quad (8)$$

Interval Type-2 Fuzzy DEMATEL

"Decision making trial and evaluation laboratory" is represented as DEMATEL. In this approach, it is aimed to measure the interdependence between the dimensions. Additionally, with the help of this methodology, significance levels of these dimensions can be defined. DEMATEL approach can also be considered by considering interval type-2 fuzzy sets (Abdullah and Zulkifli, 2015). This process can be analyzed in five different steps. The first step is related to the collection of the decision makers' evaluations and conversion them to the fuzzy sets. On the other side, "the initial direct-relation fuzzy matrix" is constructed in the second step. In this circumstance, "initial direct-relation fuzzy matrix" $\tilde{Z}$ .is generated by considering the average scores of the evaluations. Equations (9) and (10) summarize this process.

$$\tilde{Z} = \begin{bmatrix} 0 & \tilde{z}_{12} & \cdots & \cdots & \tilde{z}_{1n} \\ \tilde{z}_{21} & 0 & \cdots & \cdots & \tilde{z}_{2n} \\ \vdots & \vdots & \ddots & \cdots & \cdots \\ \vdots & \vdots & \vdots & \ddots & \vdots \\ \tilde{z}_{n1} & \tilde{z}_{n2} & \tilde{z}_{n3} & \cdots & 0 \end{bmatrix} \quad (9)$$

$$\tilde{Z} = \frac{\tilde{Z}^1 + \tilde{Z}^2 + \tilde{Z}^3 + \ldots \tilde{Z}^n}{n}. \quad (10)$$

Moreover, the third step includes the normalization of this matrix. In this scope, the equations (11)-(13) are taken into the consideration.

$$\tilde{X} = \begin{bmatrix} \tilde{x}_{11} & \tilde{x}_{12} & \cdots & \cdots & \tilde{x}_{1n} \\ \tilde{x}_{21} & \tilde{x}_{22} & \cdots & \cdots & \tilde{x}_{2n} \\ \vdots & \vdots & \ddots & \cdots & \cdots \\ \vdots & \vdots & \vdots & \ddots & \vdots \\ \tilde{x}_{n1} & \tilde{x}_{n2} & \cdots & \cdots & \tilde{x}_{nn} \end{bmatrix} \quad (11)$$

$$\tilde{x}_ij = \frac{\tilde{z}_{aij}}{r} = (\frac{Z_{(a_i j)}}{r}, \frac{Z_{(b_i j)}}{r}, \frac{Z_{(c_i j)}}{r}, \frac{Z_{(d_i j)}}{r}; H_1(z_{ij}^U), H_2(z_{ij}^U)), (\frac{Z_{(e_i j)}}{r}, \frac{Z_{(f_i j)}}{r}, \frac{Z_{(g_i j)}}{r}, \frac{Z_{(h_i j)}}{r}; H_1(z_{ij}^L), H_2(z_{ij}^L))$$
(12)

$$r = \max\left(\max_{1 \le i \le n} \sum_{j=1}^{n} Z_{d_{ij}}, \max_{1 \le i \le n} \sum_{j=1}^{n} Z_{d_{ij}}\right).$$
(13)

Furthermore, "the total influence fuzzy matrix" is constructed in the fourth step by using the equations (14)-(18).

$$X_a \cdot \begin{bmatrix} 0 & a'_{12} & \cdots & \cdots & a'_{1n} \\ a'_{21} & 0 & \cdots & \cdots & a'_{2n} \\ \vdots & \vdots & \ddots & \cdots & \cdots \\ \vdots & \vdots & \vdots & \ddots & \vdots \\ a'_{n1} & a'_{n2} & \cdots & \cdots & 0 \end{bmatrix}, \ldots, X_h \cdot \begin{bmatrix} 0 & h'_{12} & \cdots & \cdots & h'_{1n} \\ h'_{21} & 0 & \cdots & \cdots & h'_{2n} \\ \vdots & \vdots & \ddots & \cdots & \cdots \\ \vdots & \vdots & \vdots & \ddots & \vdots \\ h'_{n1} & h'_{n2} & \cdots & \cdots & 0 \end{bmatrix}$$
(14)

$$\tilde{T} = \lim_{k \to \infty} \tilde{X} + \tilde{X}^2 + \ldots + \tilde{X}^k.$$
(15)

$$\tilde{T} \cdot \begin{bmatrix} \tilde{t}_{11} & \tilde{t}_{12} & \cdots & \cdots & \tilde{t}_{1n} \\ \tilde{t}_{21} & \tilde{t}_{22} & \cdots & \cdots & \tilde{t}_{2n} \\ \vdots & \vdots & \ddots & \cdots & \cdots \\ \vdots & \vdots & \vdots & \ddots & \vdots \\ \tilde{t}_{n1} & \tilde{t}_{n2} & \cdots & \cdots & \tilde{t}_{np} \end{bmatrix}$$
(16)

$$\tilde{t}_{ij} = \left(a''_{ij}, b''_{ij}, c''_{ij}, d''_{ij}; H_1\left(\tilde{t}_{ij}^U\right), H_2\left(\tilde{t}_{ij}^U\right)\right), \left(e''_{ij}, f''_{ij}, g''_{ij}, h''_{ij}; H_1\left(\tilde{t}_{ij}^L\right), H_2\left(\tilde{t}_{ij}^L\right)\right).$$
(17)

$$\left[a''_{ij}\right] = X_a \times \left(I - X_a\right)^{-1} \ldots, \left[h''_{ij}\right] = X_h \times \left(I - X_h\right)^{-1}.$$
(18)

Finally, the last step includes the calculation of "the defuzzified total influence matrix" by using the equations (19)-(22).

$$Def_T = \frac{\frac{(u_U - l_U) + (^2_U \times m_{1U} - l_U) + (\pm_U \times m_{2U} - l_U)}{4} + l_U + \left[\frac{(u_L - l_L) + (^2_L \times m_{1L} - l_L) + (\pm_L \times m_{2L} - l_L)}{4} + l_L\right]}{2}.$$
(19)

$$Def_T = T = \left[t_{ij}\right]_{n \times n}., \; i,j = 1,2,\ldots,n. \tag{20}$$

$$\tilde{D}_i^{def} = r = \left[\sum_{j=1}^{n} t_{ij}\right]_{n \times 1} . = (r_i)_{n \times 1} = (r_1,\ldots,r_i,\ldots,r_n). \tag{21}$$

$$\tilde{R}_i^{def} = y = \left[\sum_{i=1}^{n} t_{ij}\right]_{1 \times n}' . = (y_j)'_{1 \times n} = (y_1,\ldots,y_i,\ldots,y_n). \tag{22}$$

Next, the values of $\left(\tilde{D}_i + \tilde{R}_i\right)^{def}$ .and $\left(\tilde{D}_i - \tilde{R}_i\right)^{def}$ .re used in the defuzzification process. In this context, $\tilde{D}_i^{def}$ .ives information about the sum of all vector rows. On the other hand, the sum of all vector columns is represented by $\tilde{R}_i^{def}$. Thus, high $\left(\tilde{D}_i + \tilde{R}_i\right)^{def}$ .alue means being closer to the central point. Additionally, $\left(\tilde{D}_i - \tilde{R}_i\right)^{def}$ .represents degree of causality. Many different studies considered fuzzy DEMATEL method in their studies (Lo et al., 2019; Dinçer et al., 2019a,b,c,d; Addae et al., 2019; Dinçer and Yüksel, 2019a; Hatefi and Tamošaitienė, 2019; Uzunkaya et al., 2019; Wang et al., 2019). Additionally, interval type-2 DEMATEL approach was preferred in many different studies in the literature especially in the last years (Pandey et al., 2019; Dinçer et al., 2019e,f,g; Zhang et al., 2019; Dinçer and Yüksel, 2019b,c; Liu et al., 2019; Tang and Dinçer, 2019; Yüksel et al., 2019).

An Application on European Banking Industry

6 dimensions based on PESTEL have been defined to measure the marketing strategies in the European Banking Industry. For this purpose, 3 decision makers that are experts in the field of international finance and marketing have been appointed to provide their linguistic scales for the criteria. Table 1 defines the linguistic scales and interval type 2 fuzzy numbers to evaluate the criteria of marketing strategies in the European banking sector.

Impact-relationship matrix for the dimensions have been constructed based on the linguistic evaluations of the decision makers and Table 2 illustrates the dependency degrees among the dimensions.

Initial direct relation matrix has been defined by the formulas (9)-(10) as seen in Table 3.

Initial direct relation matrix has been normalized by the equations (11)-(13) and the results are represented in Table 4.

Normalized values have been used for computing the total relation matrix by the formulas (14)-(18). The values are seen in Table 5.

The defuzzified values have been calculated to weight the criteria and rank the factors. By the formulas (19)-(22), defuzzified total relation matrix and the results of weighting have been computed as seen in Table 6.

Table 6 demonstrates that technologic dimension (D4) is the most influencing factor among the dimensions of marketing strategies as the environmental factor (D5) is the most influenced. Accordingly,

Table 1. Linguistic scales and interval type-2 trapezoidal fuzzy numbers for the dimensions

Criteria	IT2TrFNs
Absolutely Low (AL)	((0.0,0.0,0.0,0.0;1.0), (0.0,0.0,0.0,0.0;1.0))
Very Low (VL)	((0.0075, 0.0075, 0.015, 0.0525;0.8), (0.0,0.0,0.02,0.07;1.0))
Low (L)	((0.0875, 0.12, 0.16, 0.1825;0.8), (0.04,0.10,0.18,0.23;1.0))
Medium Low (ML)	((0.2325, 0.255, 0.325, 0.3575;0.8), (0.17,0.22,0.36,0.42;1.0))
Medium (M)	((0.4025, 0.4525, 0.5375, 0.5675;0.8), (0.32,0.41,0.58,0.65;1.0))
Medium High (MH)	((0.65, 0.6725, 0.7575, 0.79;0.8), (0.58,0.63,0.80,0.86;1.0))
High (H)	((0.7825, 0.815, 0.885, 0.9075;0.8), (0.72,0.78,0.92,0.97;1.0))
Very High (VH)	((0.9475, 0.985, 0.9925, 0.9925;0.8), (0.93,0.98,1.0,1.0;1.0))
Absolutely High (AH)	((1.0, 1.0, 1.0, 1.0; 1.0), (1.0, 1.0, 1.0, 1.0; 1.0))

Source: Chen et al. 2013.

D4 has the most importance between the dimensions whereas D5 is the weakest factor with 15.7 percentage. This situation shows that technological factors play the highest significant role in the performance of the marketing strategies for the banks. Jaworski (2018), Lorenzo-Romero et al. (2014) and Maduku et al. (2016) stated that technological improvement is the most important item that should be taken into the consideration in generating marketing strategies. For this purpose, it is thought that a department which evaluated technological development in the market may be very beneficial. Marketing strategy development team of the banks can adjust their strategies according to the information obtained from this department.

On the other side, political factors have the second degree regarding this aspect. This conclusion was also emphasized in many different researchers in the literature, such as Schlegelmilch (2016) and Jimenez and Boehe (2018). Within this framework, macroeconomic indicators of the countries, such as economic growth, unemployment level and interest rates, should be taken into the consideration by the banks in marketing strategy development process. The main reason is that this situation gives information to the banks while adopting their strategies. For example, aggressive strategy cannot be appropriate when macroeconomic factors in the country go worse.

Table 2. Dependency degrees among the dimensions

	D1			D2			D3			D4			D5			D6		
	DM1	DM2	DM3	DM1	DM2	DM3	DM1	DM2	DM3	DM1	DM2	DM3	DM1	DM2	DM3	DM1	DM2	DM3
Politic (D1)	-	-	-	H	VH	VH	MH	H	H	ML	M	M	H	H	VH	M	M	MH
Economic (D2)	L	ML	ML	-	-	-	MH	MH	H	ML	M	M	MH	MH	M	M	M	MH
Sociological (D3)	ML	ML	ML	ML	ML	M	-	-	-	ML	ML	L	M	M	MH	L	ML	ML
Technologic (D4)	MH	H	H	MH	H	VH	H	VH	VH	-	-	-	VH	VH	VH	MH	H	VH
Environmental (D5)	L	ML	ML	ML	ML	ML	ML	ML	ML	L	L	L	-	-	-	ML	ML	ML
Legal (D6)	ML	M	M	ML	M	MH	M	MH	MH	ML	ML	M	MH	MH	MH	-	-	-

Table 3. Initial direct relation matrix

	D1	D2	D3
D1	((0.0,0.0,0.0,0.0;0.8), (0.0,0.0,0.0,0.0;1.0))	((0.89,0.93,0.96,0.96;0.80), (0.86,0.91,0.97,0.99;1.00))	((0.74,0.77,0.84,0.87;0.80), (0.67,0.73,0.88,0.93;1.00))
D2	((0.18,0.21,0.27,0.30;0.80), (0.13,0.18,0.30,0.36;1.00))	((0.0,0.0,0.0,0.0;0.8), (0.0,0.0,0.0,0.0;1.0))	((0.69,0.72,0.80,0.83;0.80), (0.63,0.68,0.84,0.90;1.00))
D3	((0.23,0.26,0.33,0.36;0.80), (0.17,0.22,0.36,0.42;1.00))	((0.29,0.32,0.40,0.43;0.80), (0.22,0.28,0.43,0.50;1.00))	((0.0,0.0,0.0,0.0;0.8), (0.0,0.0,0.0,0.0;1.0))
D4	((0.74,0.77,0.84,0.87;0.80), (0.67,0.73,0.88,0.93;1.00))	((0.79,0.82,0.88,0.90;0.80), (0.74,0.80,0.91,0.94;1.00))	((0.89,0.93,0.96,0.96; 0.80), (0.86,0.91,0.97,0.99;1.00))
D5	((0.18,0.21,0.27,0.30; 0.80), (0.13,0.18,0.30,0.36;1.00))	((0.23,0.26,0.33,0.36;0.80), (0.17,0.22,0.36,0.42;1.00))	((0.23,0.26,0.33,0.36;0.80), (0.17,0.22,0.36,0.42;1.00))
D6	((0.35,0.39,0.47,0.50; 0.80), (0.27,0.35,0.51,0.57;1.00))	((0.43,0.46,0.54,0.57;0.80), (0.36,0.42,0.58,0.64;1.00))	((0.57,0.60,0.68,0.72;0.80), (0.49,0.56,0.73,0.79;1.00))
	D4	**D5**	**D6**
D1	((0.35,0.39,0.47,0.50;0.80), (0.27,0.35,0.51,0.57;1.00))	((0.84,0.87,0.92,0.94;0.80), (0.79,0.85,0.95,0.98;1.00))	((0.49,0.53,0.61,0.64;0.80), (0.41,0.48,0.65,0.72;1.00))
D2	((0.35,0.39,0.47,0.50;0.80), (0.27,0.35,0.51,0.57;1.00))	((0.57,0.60,0.68,0.72;0.80), (0.49,0.56,0.73,0.79;1.00))	((0.49,0.53,0.61,0.64;0.80), (0.41,0.48,0.65,0.72;1.00))
D3	((0.18,0.21,0.27,0.30; 0.80), (0.13,0.18,0.30,0.36;1.00))	((0.49,0.53,0.61,0.64;0.80), (0.41,0.48,0.65,0.72;1.00))	((0.18,0.21,0.27,0.30; 0.80), (0.13,0.18,0.30,0.36;1.00))
D4	((0.0,0.0,0.0,0.0;0.8), (0.0,0.0,0.0,0.0;1.0))	((0.95,0.99,0.99,0.99;0.80), (0.93,0.98,1.00,1.00;1.00))	((0.79,0.82,0.88,0.90;0.80), (0.74,0.80,0.91,0.94;1.00))
D5	((0.09,0.12,0.16,0.18; 0.80), (0.04,0.10,0.18,0.23;1.00))	((0.0,0.0,0.0,0.0;0.8), (0.0,0.0,0.0,0.0;1.0))	((0.23,0.26,0.33,0.36;0.80), (0.17,0.22,0.36,0.42;1.00))
D6	((0.29,0.32,0.40,0.43;0.80), (0.22,0.28,0.43,0.50;1.00))	((0.65,0.67,0.76,0.79;0.80), (0.58,0.63,0.80,0.86;1.00))	((0.0,0.0,0.0,0.0;0.8), (0.0,0.0,0.0,0.0;1.0))

SOLUTIONS AND RECOMMENDATIONS

It is recommended that European banks should design a department which follows the technological development in the banking sector. Within this context, new products and services should be identified so that banks should adopt their marketing strategies according to these developments. In addition, with respect to the political factors, interest rates defined by the central bank also influence marketing strategies of these banks. Therefore, these interest rates determined by the central bank should be monitored effectively by banks. If the marketing strategies are not developed based on these interest rates, it has a negative effect on the performance of these banks.

FUTURE RESEARCH DIRECTIONS

This study focuses on the success of marketing strategies in European banking sector. With this analysis, some recommendations can be presented for the improvement of the European banking industry. Additionally, in the future studies, the marketing strategies of developing economies can also be evaluated.

Table 4. Normalized initial direct relation matrix

	D1	D2	D3
D1	((0.0,0.0,0.0,0.0;0.8), (0.0,0.0,0.0,0.0;1.0))	((0.19,0.20,0.21,0.21;0.80), (0.19,0.20,0.21,0.21;1.00))	((0.16,0.17,0.18,0.19;0.80), (0.15,0.16,0.19,0.20;1.00))
D2	((0.04,0.05,0.06,0.06;0.80), (0.03,0.04,0.06,0.08;1.00))	((0.0,0.0,0.0,0.0;0.8), (0.0,0.0,0.0,0.0;1.0))	((0.15,0.16,0.17,0.18;0.80), (0.14,0.15,0.18,0.19;1.00))
D3	((0.05,0.06,0.07,0.08;0.80), (0.04,0.05,0.08,0.09;1.00))	((0.06,0.07,0.09,0.09;0.80), (0.05,0.06,0.09,0.11;1.00))	((0.0,0.0,0.0,0.0;0.8), (0.0,0.0,0.0,0.0;1.0))
D4	((0.16,0.17,0.18,0.19;0.80), (0.15,0.16,0.19,0.20;1.00))	((0.17,0.18,0.19,0.19;0.80), (0.16,0.17,0.20,0.20;1.00))	((0.19,0.20,0.21,0.21;0.80), (0.19,0.20,0.21,0.21;1.00))
D5	((0.04,0.05,0.06,0.06; 0.80), (0.03,0.04,0.06,0.08;1.00))	((0.05,0.06,0.07,0.08;0.80), (0.04,0.05,0.08,0.09;1.00))	((0.05,0.06,0.07,0.08;0.80), (0.04,0.05,0.08,0.09;1.00))
D6	((0.07,0.08,0.10,0.11; 0.80), (0.06,0.08,0.11,0.12;1.00))	((0.09,0.10,0.12,0.12;0.80), (0.08,0.09,0.13,0.14;1.00))	((0.12,0.13,0.15,0.15;0.80), (0.11,0.12,0.16,0.17;1.00))
	D4	**D5**	**D6**
D1	((0.07,0.08,0.10,0.11; 0.80), (0.06,0.08,0.11,0.12;1.00))	((0.18,0.19,0.20,0.20;0.80), (0.17,0.18,0.20,0.21;1.00))	((0.11,0.11,0.13,0.14;0.80), (0.09,0.10,0.14,0.16;1.00))
D2	((0.07,0.08,0.10,0.11; 0.80), (0.06,0.08,0.11,0.12;1.00))	((0.12,0.13,0.15,0.15;0.80), (0.11,0.12,0.16,0.17;1.00))	((0.11,0.11,0.13,0.14;0.80), (0.09,0.10,0.14,0.16;1.00))
D3	((0.04,0.05,0.06,0.06; 0.80), (0.03,0.04,0.06,0.08;1.00))	((0.11,0.11,0.13,0.14;0.80), (0.09,0.10,0.14,0.16;1.00))	((0.04,0.05,0.06,0.06; 0.80), (0.03,0.04,0.06,0.08;1.00))
D4	((0.0,0.0,0.0,0.0;0.8), (0.0,0.0,0.0,0.0;1.0))	((0.21,0.21,0.21,0.21;0.80), (0.20,0.21,0.22, 0.22;1.00))	((0.17,0.18,0.19,0.19;0.80), (0.16,0.17,0.20,0.20;1.00))
D5	((0.02,0.03,0.03,0.04; 0.80), (0.01,0.02,0.04,0.05;1.00))	((0.0,0.0,0.0,0.0;0.8), (0.0,0.0,0.0,0.0;1.0))	((0.05,0.06,0.07,0.08;0.80), (0.04,0.05,0.08,0.09;1.00))
D6	((0.06,0.07,0.09,0.09;0.80), (0.05,0.06,0.09,0.11;1.00))	((0.14,0.15,0.16,0.17;0.80), (0.13,0.14,0.17,0.19;1.00))	((0.0,0.0,0.0,0.0;0.8), (0.0,0.0,0.0,0.0;1.0))

On the other hand, another methodology can be considered in the analysis process, such interval type-2 fuzzy QUALIFLEX and internal type-2 fuzzy VIKOR.

CONCLUSION

The level of competition increases in the banking industry especially after the globalization. Due to this aspect, many banks now have to compete with large scale international banks. Therefore, these banks should take many different actions in order to be successful in this competitive market. Otherwise, the globalization can decrease the profitability of them. Within this context, the performance of the marketing strategies of the banks plays a key role. With the help of effective marketing, banks can increase their profitability.

In this study, it is aimed to measure the marketing performance of European banking industry. In this framework, six different dimensions of PESTEL analysis (politic, economic, sociological, technologic, environmental and legal) are taken into the consideration. With the help of this method, many different aspects can be considered at the same time to reach this objective. On the other side, interval type-2 fuzzy DEMATEL approach is used so as to identify the weights of these dimensions.

Table 5. Total relation matrix

	D1	D2	D3
D1	((0.07,0.09,0.14,0.17;0.80), (0.04,0.07,0.18,0.26;1.00))	((0.28,0.31,0.38,0.41;0.80), (0.24,0.28,0.42,0.52;1.00))	((0.28,0.31,0.39,0.43;0.80), (0.23,0.27,0.45,0.56;1.00))
D2	((0.09,0.11,0.17,0.20;0.80), (0.06,0.09,0.21,0.29;1.00))	((0.08,0.10,0.15,0.18;0.80), (0.05,0.08,0.19,0.27;1.00))	((0.23,0.25,0.33,0.37;0.80), (0.18,0.22,0.38,0.48;1.00))
D3	((0.08,0.10,0.14,0.17;0.80), (0.05,0.08,0.17,0.24;1.00))	((0.11,0.13,0.18,0.21;0.80), (0.07,0.11,0.22,0.30;1.00))	((0.06,0.07,0.12,0.15;0.80), (0.03,0.06,0.16,0.23;1.00))
D4	((0.24,0.26,0.33,0.37;0.80), (0.19,0.23,0.38,0.47;1.00))	((0.30,0.33,0.41,0.45;0.80), (0.25,0.30,0.46,0.56;1.00))	((0.34,0.38,0.46,0.50;0.80), (0.29,0.34,0.52,0.63;1.00))
D5	((0.06,0.08,0.11,0.14; 0.80), (0.04,0.06,0.14,0.20;1.00))	((0.08,0.10,0.15,0.18;0.80), (0.05,0.08,0.18,0.25;1.00))	((0.09,0.11,0.16,0.19;0.80), (0.06,0.09,0.20,0.27;1.00))
D6	((0.12,0.14,0.20,0.23; 0.80), (0.08,0.12,0.24,0.33;1.00))	((0.16,0.19,0.26,0.29;0.80), (0.12,0.16,0.30,0.40;1.00))	((0.21,0.23,0.31,0.35;0.80), (0.16,0.20,0.36,0.46;1.00))
	D4	**D5**	**D6**
D1	((0.13,0.16,0.22,0.25; 0.80), (0.09,0.13,0.26,0.34;1.00))	((0.31,0.35,0.43,0.47;0.80), (0.26,0.31,0.49,0.60;1.00))	((0.19,0.22,0.30,0.33;0.80), (0.14,0.19,0.34,0.44;1.00))
D2	((0.11,0.13,0.19,0.21; 0.80), (0.08,0.11,0.22,0.30;1.00))	((0.22,0.25,0.33,0.37;0.80), (0.17,0.22,0.38,0.49;1.00))	((0.16,0.19,0.25,0.29;0.80), (0.12,0.16,0.29,0.38;1.00))
D3	((0.06,0.08,0.12,0.14; 0.80), (0.04,0.06,0.15,0.21;1.00))	((0.16,0.19,0.25,0.29;0.80), (0.12,0.16,0.30,0.39;1.00))	((0.08,0.10,0.15,0.18; 0.80), (0.05,0.08,0.18,0.26;1.00))
D4	((0.08,0.10,0.15,0.18; 0.80), (0.05,0.08,0.19,0.27;1.00))	((0.38,0.41,0.50,0.54;0.80), (0.32,0.38,0.55, 0.67;1.00))	((0.27,0.30,0.38,0.42;0.80), (0.23,0.27,0.43,0.53;1.00))
D5	((0.04,0.05,0.099,0.11; 0.80), (0.02,0.04,0.11,0.16;1.00))	((0.05,0.07,0.11,0.13;0.80), (0.03,0.05,0.14,0.21;1.00))	((0.08,0.09,0.14,0.16;0.80), (0.05,0.08,0.17,0.23;1.00))
D6	((0.10,0.12,0.17,0.20;0.80), (0.07,0.10,0.21,0.29;1.00))	((0.24,0.26,0.34,0.38;0.80), (0.19,0.23,0.40,0.50;1.00))	((0.07,0.08,0.14,0.17;0.80), (0.04,0.07,0.17,0.25;1.00))

As a result, it is defined that technological factors play the most significant role in the marketing strategies of European banking industry. In addition to this issue, politic factors are on the second rank regarding this condition. However, it is also determined that environmental issues have the lowest importance. This situation gives information that innovation in the banking sector has an important impact on the performance of European banks. In other words, these innovations should be followed by the

Table 6. Defuzzified total relation matrix and the weights for the dimensions

	D1	D2	D3	D4	D5	D6			$\left(\tilde{D}_i - \tilde{R}_i\right)^{def}$	Weights	Ranking
D1	0.12	0.34	0.35	0.19	0.38	0.26	1.637	0.961	2.598	0.677	0.171	2
D2	0.15	0.13	0.29	0.16	0.29	0.22	1.234	1.341	2.576	-0.107	0.170	3
D3	0.12	0.16	0.11	0.10	0.22	0.13	0.839	1.569	2.408	-0.730	0.159	5
D4	0.30	0.36	0.41	0.13	0.45	0.34	1.983	0.804	2.786	1.179	0.184	1
D5	0.10	0.13	0.14	0.07	0.09	0.12	0.651	1.734	2.386	-1.083	0.157	6
D6	0.18	0.23	0.27	0.15	0.30	0.12	1.244	1.179	2.424	0.065	0.160	4

banks in the development process of the marketing strategy. Otherwise, banks cannot develop effective marketing strategy if they do not consider these innovations.

REFERENCES

Abdullah, L., & Zulkifli, N. (2015). Integration of fuzzy AHP and interval type-2 fuzzy DEMATEL: An application to human resource management. *Expert Systems with Applications*, *42*(9), 4397–4409. doi:10.1016/j.eswa.2015.01.021

Addae, B. A., Zhang, L., Zhou, P., & Wang, F. (2019). Analyzing barriers of smart energy city in Accra with two-step fuzzy DEMATEL. *Cities (London, England)*, *89*, 218–227. doi:10.1016/j.cities.2019.01.043

Adegbola, E. A. (2014). Corporate social responsibility as a marketing strategy for enhanced performance in the Nigerian banking industry: A granger causality approach. *Procedia: Social and Behavioral Sciences*, *164*, 141–149. doi:10.1016/j.sbspro.2014.11.062

Alalwan, A. A., Dwivedi, Y. K., & Rana, N. P. (2017). Factors influencing adoption of mobile banking by Jordanian bank customers: Extending UTAUT2 with trust. *International Journal of Information Management*, *37*(3), 99–110. doi:10.1016/j.ijinfomgt.2017.01.002

Allen, F., Qian, Y., Tu, G., & Yu, F. (2019). Entrusted loans: A close look at China's shadow banking system. *Journal of Financial Economics*, *133*(1), 18–41. doi:10.1016/j.jfineco.2019.01.006

Baabdullah, A. M., Alalwan, A. A., Rana, N. P., Kizgin, H., & Patil, P. (2019). Consumer use of mobile banking (M-Banking) in Saudi Arabia: Towards an integrated model. *International Journal of Information Management*, *44*, 38–52. doi:10.1016/j.ijinfomgt.2018.09.002

Bai, C., Shi, B., Liu, F., & Sarkis, J. (2019). Banking credit worthiness: Evaluating the complex relationships. *Omega*, *83*, 26–38. doi:10.1016/j.omega.2018.02.001

Bees, A. D., & Williams, I. D. (2017). Explaining the differences in household food waste collection and treatment provisions between local authorities in England and Wales. *Waste Management (New York, N.Y.)*, *70*, 222–235. doi:10.1016/j.wasman.2017.09.004 PMID:28918870

Beyers, C., De Freitas, A., Essel-Mensah, K. A., Seymore, R., & Tsomocos, D. P. (2019). A Computable general equilibrium model for banking sector risk assessment in South Africa. *Saïd Business School WP*, *11*.

Calderón Ramírez, M. A., de Jesús Arrias Añez, J. C., Ronquillo Riera, O. I., Herráez Quezada, R. G., Ríos Vera, Á. A., Torres Cegarra, J. C., & Ojeda Sotomayor, P. M. (2019). Pestel based on neutrosophic cognitive maps to characterize the factors that influence the consolidation of the neo constitutionalism in Ecuador. *Neutrosophic Sets & Systems, 26*.

Carbó, S., Humphrey, D., Maudos, J., & Molyneux, P. (2009). Cross-country comparisons of competition and pricing power in European banking. *Journal of International Money and Finance*, *28*(1), 115–134. doi:10.1016/j.jimonfin.2008.06.005

Chaouali, W., & Souiden, N. (2018). The role of cognitive age in explaining mobile banking resistance among elderly people. *Journal of Retailing and Consumer Services.*

Chaouali, W., Souiden, N., & Ladhari, R. (2017). Explaining adoption of mobile banking with the theory of trying, general self-confidence, and cynicism. *Journal of Retailing and Consumer Services, 35*, 57–67. doi:10.1016/j.jretconser.2016.11.009

Chen, T. Y., Chang, C. H., & Lu, J. F. R. (2013). The extended QUALIFLEX method for multiple criteria decision analysis based on interval type-2 fuzzy sets and applications to medical decision making. *European Journal of Operational Research, 226*(3), 615–625. doi:10.1016/j.ejor.2012.11.038

Cooke, F. L., Cooper, B., Bartram, T., Wang, J., & Mei, H. (2019). Mapping the relationships between high-performance work systems, employee resilience and engagement: A study of the banking industry in China. *International Journal of Human Resource Management, 30*(8), 1239–1260. doi:10.1080/09585192.2015.1137618

Damasceno, V. S., & Abreu, Y. V. D. (2018). Avaliação da energia eólica no Brasil utilizando a análise SWOT e PESTEL. *Interações (Campo Grande), 19*(3), 503–514. doi:10.20435/inter.v19i3.1649

de Andres, A., MacGillivray, A., Roberts, O., Guanche, R., & Jeffrey, H. (2017). Beyond LCOE: A study of ocean energy technology development and deployment attractiveness. *Sustainable Energy Technologies and Assessments, 19*, 1–16. doi:10.1016/j.seta.2016.11.001

Dincer, H. (2018). HHI-based evaluation of the European banking sector using an integrated fuzzy approach. *Kybernetes.*

Dincer, H., Uzunkaya, S. S., & Yüksel, S. (2019g). An IT2-based hybrid decision-making model using hesitant fuzzy linguistic term sets for selecting the development plan of financial economics. *International Journal of Computational Intelligence Systems, 12*(2), 460–473. doi:10.2991/ijcis.d.190312.001

Dinçer, H., & Yüksel, S. (2018). Comparative evaluation of BSC-based new service development competencies in Turkish banking sector with the integrated fuzzy hybrid MCDM using content analysis. *International Journal of Fuzzy Systems*, 1–20.

Dinçer, H., & Yüksel, S. (2019a). Analyzing the possibility of violent conflict in the Middle East economies using determinants of global conflict risk index with an integrated fuzzy multicriteria decision making model. In The impact of global terrorism on economic and political development: Afro-Asian perspectives (pp. 155-166). Emerald Publishing.

Dincer, H., & Yuksel, S. (2019b). Balanced scorecard-based analysis of investment decisions for the renewable energy alternatives: A comparative analysis based on the hybrid fuzzy decision-making approach. *Energy, 175*, 1259–1270. doi:10.1016/j.energy.2019.03.143

Dincer, H., & Yuksel, S. (2019c). IT2-based fuzzy hybrid decision making approach to soft computing. *IEEE Access: Practical Innovations, Open Solutions, 7*, 15932–15944. doi:10.1109/ACCESS.2019.2895359

Dinçer, H., Yuksel, S., & Adalı, Z. (2018b). Relationship between non-performing loans, industry, and economic growth of the african economies and policy recommendations for global growth. In Globalization and Trade Integration in Developing Countries (pp. 203–228). Hershey, PA: IGI Global. doi:10.4018/978-1-5225-4032-8.ch009

Dinçer, H., Yüksel, S., & Çetiner, İ. T. (2019b). Strategy selection for organizational performance of Turkish banking sector with the integrated multi-dimensional decision-making approach. In Handbook of research on contemporary approaches in management and organizational strategy (pp. 273–291). Hershey, PA: IGI Global. doi:10.4018/978-1-5225-6301-3.ch014

Dinçer, H., Yüksel, S., Kartal, M. T., & Alpman, G. (2019c). Corporate governance-based evaluation of alternative distribution channels in the Turkish banking sector using quality function deployment with an integrated fuzzy MCDM method. In Intergenerational governance and leadership in the corporate world: emerging research and opportunities (pp. 39-77). Hershey, PA: IGI Global.

Dinçer, H., Yüksel, S., Korsakienė, R., Raišienė, A. G., & Bilan, Y. (2019f). IT2 hybrid decision-making approach to performance measurement of internationalized firms in the Baltic states. *Sustainability*, *11*(1), 296. doi:10.3390u11010296

Dinçer, H., Yüksel, S., & Martínez, L. (2019e). Interval type 2-based hybrid fuzzy evaluation of financial services in E7 economies with DEMATEL-ANP and MOORA methods. *Applied Soft Computing*, *79*, 186–202. doi:10.1016/j.asoc.2019.03.018

Dinçer, H., Yüksel, S., & Pınarbaşı, F. (2019a). SERVQUAL-based evaluation of service quality of energy companies in Turkey: strategic policies for sustainable economic development. In The circular economy and its implications on sustainability and the green supply chain (pp. 142-167). Hershey, PA: IGI Global.

Dinçer, H., Yüksel, S., & Şenel, S. (2018a). Analyzing the global risks for the financial crisis after the great depression using comparative hybrid hesitant fuzzy decision-making models: policy recommendations for sustainable economic growth. *Sustainability*, *10*(9), 3126. doi:10.3390u10093126

Dinçer, H., Yüksel, S., Yazici, M., & Pınarbaşı, F. (2019d). Assessing corporate social responsibilities in the banking sector: as a tool of strategic communication during the global financial crisis. in Handbook of research on global issues in financial communication and investment decision making (pp. 1-27). Hershey, PA: IGI Global.

Durkin, M., O'Donnell, A., Mullholland, G., & Crowe, J. (2007). On e-banking adoption: From banker perception to customer reality. *Journal of Strategic Marketing*, *15*(2-3), 237–252. doi:10.1080/09652540701318815

Fernández, J. I. P., Cala, A. S., & Domecq, C. F. (2011). Critical external factors behind hotels' investments in innovation and technology in emerging urban destinations. *Tourism Economics*, *17*(2), 339–357. doi:10.5367/te.2011.0033

Fozer, D., Sziraky, F. Z., Racz, L., Nagy, T., Tarjani, A. J., Toth, A. J., ... Mizsey, P. (2017). Life cycle, PESTLE and multi-criteria decision analysis of CCS process alternatives. *Journal of Cleaner Production*, *147*, 75–85. doi:10.1016/j.jclepro.2017.01.056

Gheibi, M., Karrabi, M., Mohammadi, A., & Dadvar, A. (2018). Controlling air pollution in a city: A perspective from SOAR-PESTLE analysis. *Integrated Environmental Assessment and Management*, *14*(4), 480–488. doi:10.1002/ieam.4051 PMID:29663693

Gilbert, D. C., & Choi, K. C. (2003). Relationship marketing practice in relation to different bank ownerships: A study of banks in Hong Kong. *International Journal of Bank Marketing*, *21*(3), 137–146. doi:10.1108/02652320310469511

Goddard, J., Molyneux, P., Wilson, J. O., & Tavakoli, M. (2007). European banking: An overview. *Journal of Banking & Finance*, *31*(7), 1911–1935. doi:10.1016/j.jbankfin.2007.01.002

González Ortega, R., Oviedo Rodríguez, M. D., Leyva Vázquez, M., Estupiñán Ricardo, J., Sganderla Figueiredo, J. A., & Smarandache, F. (2019). Pestel analysis based on neutrosophic cognitive maps and neutrosophic numbers for the Sinos River Basin management. *Neutrosophic Sets & Systems, 26*.

Graham, D. (2018). PESTEL factors for e-learning revisited: The 4Es of tutoring for value added learning. *E-Learning and Digital Media*, *15*(1), 17–35. doi:10.1177/2042753017753626

Hatefi, S. M., & Tamošaitienė, J. (2019). An integrated fuzzy DEMATEL-fuzzy ANP model for evaluating construction projects by considering interrelationships among risk factors. *Journal of Civil Engineering and Management*, *25*(2), 114–131. doi:10.3846/jcem.2019.8280

Höpel, T. (2018). Friedemann Pestel, Kosmopoliten wider Willen. Die „monarchiens "als Revolutionsemigranten.(Pariser Historische Studien, Bd. 104.) Berlin/Boston, De Gruyter Oldenbourg 2015. *Historische Zeitschrift*, *306*(1), 225–227. doi:10.1515/hzhz-2018-1048

Jaworski, B. J. (2018). Commentary: Advancing marketing strategy in the marketing discipline and beyond. *Journal of Marketing Management*, *34*(1-2), 63–70. doi:10.1080/0267257X.2017.1398770

Jimenez, A., & Boehe, D. (2018). How do political and market exposure nurture ambidexterity? *Journal of Business Research*, *89*, 67–76. doi:10.1016/j.jbusres.2018.03.016

Kampanje, B. (2014). PESTEL analysis of Malawi's non-life insurance industry. *African Journal of Economic and Management Studies*, *5*(1). doi:10.1108/AJEMS-01-2013-0002

Kara, E. (2018). A contemporary approach for strategic management in tourism sector: pestel analysis on the city Muğla, Turkey. *İşletme Araştırmaları Dergisi, 10*(2), 598-608.

Kremer, P. D., & Symmons, M. A. (2015). Mass timber construction as an alternative to concrete and steel in the Australia building industry: A PESTEL evaluation of the potential. *International Wood Products Journal*, *6*(3), 138–147. doi:10.1179/2042645315Y.0000000010

Lamas Leite, J. G., de Brito Mello, L. C. B., Longo, O. C., & Cruz, E. P. (2017). Using analytic hierarchy process to optimize PESTEL scenario analysis tool in huge construction projects. [Trans Tech Publications Ltd.]. *Applied Mechanics and Materials*, *865*, 707–712. doi:10.4028/www.scientific.net/AMM.865.707

Leviäkangas, P. (2016). Digitalisation of Finland's transport sector. *Technology in Society*, *47*, 1–15. doi:10.1016/j.techsoc.2016.07.001

Li, H. H., Hsieh, M. Y., & Chang, W. L. (2016). Lucky names: Superstitious beliefs in Chinese corporate branding strategy for bank marketing. *The North American Journal of Economics and Finance, 35*, 226–233. doi:10.1016/j.najef.2015.10.011

Li, X., Mao, Z., & Qi, E. (2009, September). Study on global logistics integrative system and key technologies of Chinese automobile industry. In *International Conference on Management and Service Science, 2009. MASS'09.* (pp. 1-4). IEEE. 10.1109/ICMSS.2009.5301609

Liu, Z., Ming, X., & Song, W. (2019). A framework integrating interval-valued hesitant fuzzy DEMATEL method to capture and evaluate co-creative value propositions for smart PSS. *Journal of Cleaner Production, 215*, 611–625. doi:10.1016/j.jclepro.2019.01.089

Lo, H. W., Liou, J. J., & Tzeng, G. H. (2019). Comments on "Sustainable recycling partner selection using fuzzy DEMATEL-AEW-FVIKOR: A case study in small-and-medium enterprises". *Journal of Cleaner Production, 228*, 1011–1012. doi:10.1016/j.jclepro.2019.04.376

Lorenzo-Romero, C., Constantinides, E., & Alarcón-del-Amo, M. D. C. (2014). Social media as marketing strategy: an explorative study on adoption and use by retailers. This study is framed within research project with reference number ECO2009-08708 (Ministerio de Ciencia e Innovación, Gobierno de España, 2009–2013). In Social media in strategic management (pp. 197-215). Emerald Group.

Maduku, D. K., Mpinganjira, M., & Duh, H. (2016). Understanding mobile marketing adoption intention by South African SMEs: A multi-perspective framework. *International Journal of Information Management, 36*(5), 711–723. doi:10.1016/j.ijinfomgt.2016.04.018

Masih, J., Rajkumar, R., Matharu, P. S., & Sharma, A. (2019). Market capturing and business expansion strategy for gluten-free foods in India and USA using PESTEL model. *The Sciences, 10*, 202–213.

Mitic, M., & Kapoulas, A. (2012). Understanding the role of social media in bank marketing. *Marketing Intelligence & Planning, 30*(7), 668–686. doi:10.1108/02634501211273797

Mitter, H., Schönhart, M., Larcher, M., & Schmid, E. (2018). The stimuli-actions-effects-responses (SAER)-framework for exploring perceived relationships between private and public climate change adaptation in agriculture. *Journal of Environmental Management, 209*, 286–300. doi:10.1016/j.jenvman.2017.12.063 PMID:29306145

Nataraja, S., & Al-Aali, A. (2011). The exceptional performance strategies of Emirate Airlines. *Competitiveness Review, 21*(5), 471–486. doi:10.1108/10595421111171966

Neilson, L. C., & Chadha, M. (2008). International marketing strategy in the retail banking industry: The case of ICICI Bank in Canada. *Journal of Financial Services Marketing, 13*(3), 204–220. doi:10.1057/fsm.2008.21

Nicolae, P. (2018). Use of the PESTEL model in the management of the tourism branch of the Republic of Moldova. *Ovidius University Annals. Economic Sciences Series, 18*(1), 370–375.

Nurmi, J., & Niemelä, M. S. (2018, November). PESTEL analysis of hacktivism campaign motivations. In *Nordic Conference on Secure IT Systems* (pp. 323-335). Cham, Switzerland: Springer. 10.1007/978-3-030-03638-6_20

Oraman, Y. (2014). An analytic study of organic food industry as part of healthy eating habit in Turkey: market growth, challenges and prospects. *Procedia: Social and Behavioral Sciences, 150*, 1030–1039. doi:10.1016/j.sbspro.2014.09.115

Padilla, G. A. (2019). PESTEL analysis with neutrosophic cognitive maps to determine the factors that affect rural sustainability. Case study of the South-Eastern plain of the province of Pinar del Río.

Pan, W., Chen, L., & Zhan, W. (2018). PESTEL analysis of construction productivity enhancement strategies: A case study of three economies. *Journal of Management Engineering, 35*(1), 05018013. doi:10.1061/(ASCE)ME.1943-5479.0000662

Pandey, M., Litoriya, R., & Pandey, P. (2019). Identifying causal relationships in mobile app issues: An interval type-2 fuzzy DEMATEL approach. *Wireless Personal Communications*, 1–28.

Patil, D. A. (2018). Sustainable bio-energy through bagasse co-generation technology: a PESTEL analysis of sugar hub of India, Solapur. *Journal of Emerging Technologies and Innovative Research, 5*(12).

Ramírez, M. A. C., Añez, J. C. D. J. A., Ronquillo, O. I., Riera, R. G. H. Q., Vera, Á. A. R., Cegarra, J. C. T., & Sotomayor, P. M. O. (2019). Pestel based on neutrosophic cognitive maps to characterize the factors that influence the consolidation of the neo constitutionalism in Ecuador. *Neutrosophic Sets and Systems*, 60.

Rhee, M., & Mehra, S. (2006). Aligning operations, marketing, and competitive strategies to enhance performance: An empirical test in the retail banking industry. *Omega, 34*(5), 505–515. doi:10.1016/j.omega.2005.01.017

Schlegelmilch, B. B. (2016). Assessing global marketing opportunities. In *Global marketing strategy* (pp. 21–41). Cham, Switzerland: Springer. doi:10.1007/978-3-319-26279-6_2

Schuetz, C. G., Mair, E., & Schrefl, M. (2018, October). PESTEL Modeler: Strategy analysis using MetaEdit+, iStar 2.0, and semantic technologies. In *2018 IEEE 22nd International Enterprise Distributed Object Computing Workshop (EDOCW)*(pp. 216-219). IEEE.

Şenel Uzunkaya, S., Dinçer, H., & Yüksel, S. (2019). Evaluating the financial and nonfinancial functions of the waqfs in Ottoman economy.

Shilei, L., & Yong, W. (2009). Target-oriented obstacle analysis by PESTEL modeling of energy efficiency retrofit for existing residential buildings in China's northern heating region. *Energy Policy, 37*(6), 2098–2101. doi:10.1016/j.enpol.2008.11.039

Sola, H. B., Fernandez, J., Hagras, H., Herrera, F., Pagola, M., & Barrenechea, E. (2015). Interval type-2 fuzzy sets are generalization of interval-valued fuzzy sets: Toward a wider view on their relationship. *IEEE Transactions on Fuzzy Systems, 23*(5), 1876–1882. doi:10.1109/TFUZZ.2014.2362149

Song, J., Sun, Y., & Jin, L. (2017). PESTEL analysis of the development of the waste-to-energy incineration industry in China. *Renewable & Sustainable Energy Reviews, 80*, 276–289. doi:10.1016/j.rser.2017.05.066

Srdjevic, Z., Bajcetic, R., & Srdjevic, B. (2012). Identifying the criteria set for multicriteria decision making based on SWOT/PESTLE analysis: A case study of reconstructing a water intake structure. *Water Resources Management*, *26*(12), 3379–3393. doi:10.100711269-012-0077-2

Sridhar, R., Sachithanandam, V., Mageswaran, T., Purvaja, R., Ramesh, R., Senthil Vel, A., & Thirunavukkarasu, E. (2016). A political, economic, social, technological, legal, and environmental (PESTLE) approach for assessment of coastal zone management practice in India. *International Review of Public Administration*, *21*(3), 216–232. doi:10.1080/12294659.2016.1237091

Stoyanova, Z., & Harizanova-Bartos, H. (2017). PESTEL analysis of project management in water sector in Bulgaria. In *Conference Proceedings/International scientific conference ITEMA 2017 Recent Advances in Information Technology, Tourism, Economics, Management and Agriculture*. Association of Economists and Managers of the Balkans, Belgrade, Serbia.

Strzelczyk, M., & Chłąd, M. (2019). Use of Pestel analysis for assessing the situation of Polish transport enterprises (Part II). *Organizacja i Zarządzanie: kwartalnik naukowy*, (1 (45)), 61-75.

Tang, Z., & Dinçer, H. (2019). Selecting the house-of-quality-based energy investment policies for the sustainable emerging economies. *Sustainability*, *11*(13), 3514. doi:10.3390u11133514

Tsangas, M., Jeguirim, M., Limousy, L., & Zorpas, A. (2019). The application of analytical hierarchy process in combination with PESTEL-SWOT analysis to assess the hydrocarbons sector in Cyprus. *Energies*, *12*(5), 791. doi:10.3390/en12050791

Turkyilmaz, A., Guney, M., Karaca, F., Bagdatkyzy, Z., Sandybayeva, A., & Sirenova, G. (2019). A comprehensive construction and demolition waste management model using PESTEL and 3R for construction companies operating in Central Asia. *Sustainability*, *11*(6), 1593. doi:10.3390u11061593

Vegholm, F. (2011). Relationship marketing and the management of corporate image in the bank-SME relationship. *Management Research Review*, *34*(3), 325–336. doi:10.1108/01409171111116330

Versloot, M. (2016). *Turbulence in the higher education publishing industry due to open access: a PESTEL analysis* (Bachelor's thesis, University of Twente).

Walsh, P. R. (2005). Dealing with the uncertainties of environmental change by adding scenario planning to the strategy reformulation equation. *Management Decision*, *43*(1), 113–122. doi:10.1108/00251740510572524

Wang, Y., Tian, L., & Chen, Z. (2019). A reputation bootstrapping model for E-commerce based on fuzzy DEMATEL method and neural network. *IEEE Access: Practical Innovations, Open Solutions*, *7*, 52266–52276. doi:10.1109/ACCESS.2019.2912191

Widya Yudha, S., Tjahjono, B., & Kolios, A. (2018). A PESTLE policy mapping and stakeholder analysis of Indonesia's fossil fuel energy industry. *Energies*, *11*(5), 1272. doi:10.3390/en11051272

Yüksel, S. (2017). Determinants of the credit risk in developing countries after economic crisis: A case of Turkish banking sector. In *Global financial crisis and its ramifications on capital markets* (pp. 401–415). Cham, Switzerland: Springer. doi:10.1007/978-3-319-47021-4_28

Yüksel, S., Dinçer, H., & Meral, Y. (2019). Financial analysis of international energy trade: A strategic outlook for EU-15. *Energies*, *12*(3), 431. doi:10.3390/en12030431

Yüksel, S., Mukhtarov, S., & Mammadov, E. (2016). Comparing the efficiency of Turkish and Azerbaijani banks: An application with data envelopment analysis. *International Journal of Economics and Financial Issues*, *6*(3), 1059–1067.

Yüksel, S., Mukhtarov, S., Mammadov, E., & Özsarı, M. (2018). Determinants of profitability in the banking sector: an analysis of post-Soviet countries. *Economies*, *6*(3), 41. doi:10.3390/economies6030041

Zalengera, C., Blanchard, R. E., Eames, P. C., Juma, A. M., Chitawo, M. L., & Gondwe, K. T. (2014). Overview of the Malawi energy situation and a PESTLE analysis for sustainable development of renewable energy. *Renewable & Sustainable Energy Reviews*, *38*, 335–347. doi:10.1016/j.rser.2014.05.050

Zaleska, M., & Kondraciuk, P. (2019). Theory and practice of innovation development in the banking sector. *Financial Sciences. Nauki o Finansach, 24*(2), 76-87.

Zhang, H., Gao, H., & Liu, P. (2019). Interval type-2 fuzzy multiattribute group decision-making for logistics services providers selection by combining QFD with partitioned heronian mean operator. *Complexity*.

Zhang, N., Williams, I. D., Kemp, S., & Smith, N. F. (2011). Greening academia: Developing sustainable waste management at Higher Education Institutions. *Waste Management, 31*(7), 1606-1616.

Zhao, X., & Pan, W. (2015). Delivering zero carbon buildings: The role of innovative business models. *Procedia Engineering*, *118*, 404–411. doi:10.1016/j.proeng.2015.08.440

Zhiyong, X. (2017, August). PESTEL model analysis and legal guarantee of tourism environmental protection in China. In *IOP Conference Series: Earth and Environmental Science*, 81, 1, 012092). IOP Publishing. 10.1088/1755-1315/81/1/012092

Zineldin, M. (2005). Quality and customer relationship management (CRM) as competitive strategy in the Swedish banking industry. *The TQM Magazine*, *17*(4), 329–344. doi:10.1108/09544780310487749

Ziolkowska, J. R., & Ziolkowski, B. (2015). Energy efficiency in the transport sector in the EU-27: A dynamic dematerialization analysis. *Energy Economics*, *51*, 21–30. doi:10.1016/j.eneco.2015.06.012

Ziout, A., & Azab, A. (2015). Industrial product service system: a case study from the agriculture sector. *Procedia CIRP*, *33*, 64–69. doi:10.1016/j.procir.2015.06.013

KEY TERMS AND DEFINITIONS

DEMATEL: Decision-Making Trial and Evaluation Laboratory
EU: European Union
R&D: Research and Development
VIKOR: vlsekriterijumska optimizacija i kompromisno resenje, which means Multiple Criteria Optimization and Compromise Solution

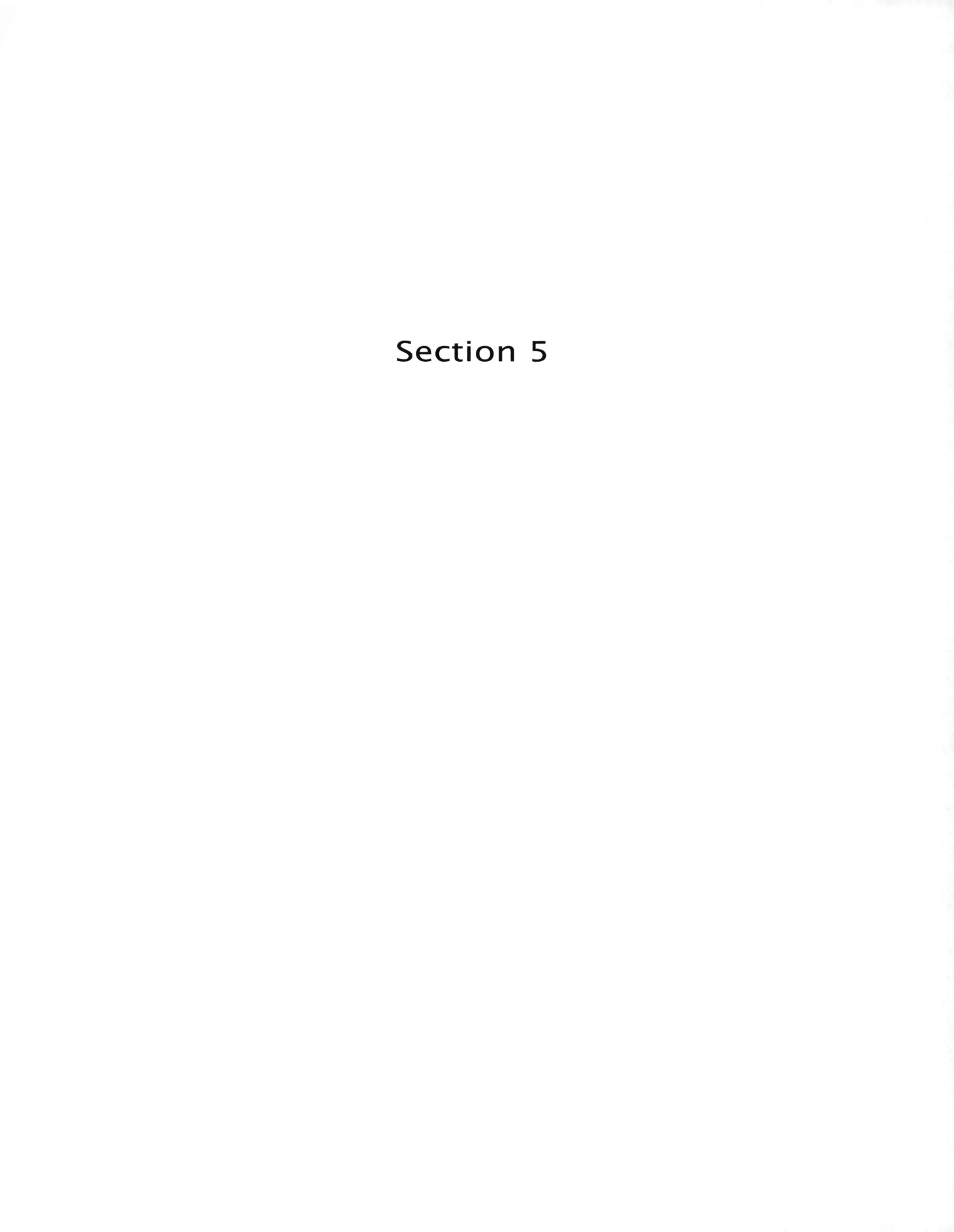

Section 5

Chapter 21
Testing the Validity of Taylor's Rule on Developing Countries for Effective Financial Marketing

Ali Doğdu
Konya Food and Agriculture University, Turkey

Gökçe Kurucu
https://orcid.org/0000-0003-3121-8953
Konya Food and Agriculture University, Turkey

İhsan Erdem Kayral
https://orcid.org/0000-0002-8335-8619
Konya Food and Agriculture University, Turkey

ABSTRACT

This chapter examines whether the central bank policy behaviors of E-7 countries are valid by using a Taylor type monetary policy response function. In this context, the policy response function of banks is analyzed by using monthly data for the 2008-2018 period. Then, unit root tests of ADF (Augmented Dickey Fuller), PP (Philips Perron), IPS (Im Peseran Shin) and LLC (Levin Lin Chu) were performed and analyzed by using Dumitrescu-Hurlin methodology. As a result of the analyses conducted using inflationary data, it was observed that short-term interest rates of the central bank affect price stability by causing inflation, but inflation rates did not cause an increase or decrease in short-term interest rates. According to the findings, although inflation does not cause interest rates to change in E7 countries, a causality relationship has emerged from interest rates to inflation rates. These results indicate that the monetary policies implemented in these countries are not carried out in accordance with the Taylor rule.

DOI: 10.4018/978-1-7998-2559-3.ch021

INTRODUCTION

Today, the central banks have tried to fulfill the most important function of monetary policy by focusing on the objective of achieving price stability as a result of many studies showing that the uncertainties experienced in increasing inflation due to new developments in financial markets and high inflation rates negatively affect sustainable economic growth. In line with a target of inflation rates with monetary policy instruments, it tries to achieve the inflation target by aiming at reaching a numerically proportional rate determined in a certain period in order to achieve price stability, which is the central bank's target (Aguiar-Conraria et al., 2018; Dinçer et al., 2019a,b). Although the objectives of monetary policy and economic / economic policy are the same in many aspects, there are differences. Benjamin Friedman (2000) described monetary policy as one of two methods used to regularly influence the direction and speed of economic activities, including financial factors such as the rate of change in prices in the free market economy, as well as non-financial factors such as output and employment. Full employment, price stability, financial stability, economic development, fair income distribution and closing the balance of payments deficits are the objectives of monetary policy (Ince et al., 2016; Yüksel and Özsarı, 2017).

Full Employment means that all production factors in the economy can be fully and effectively exploited. In the narrow definition of monetary policy, full employment means the full and effective use of labor among production factors (Dinçer et al., 2016). The aim of full employment for monetary policy is defined as the elimination or prevention of unemployment. However, because of the fact that seasonal and incidental unemployment constitutes the natural unemployment rate in economies, an unemployment rate of 3-5% is accepted as natural unemployment rate in all current economies (Morley et al., 2018).

Price stability is the most important one of the objectives of monetary policy and the absence of phenomena such as deflation, inflation, slumpflation and stagflation in an economy, and maintaining the balance of the general level of prices. If the general level of prices goes below or exceeds a certain level, this results in the occurrence of one of the aforementioned phenomena by disturbing price stability. It is not possible to talk about price stability in these economies. Inflation refers to the continuous increase in prices at the general level. Every price increase is not inflation. Deflation is a continuous and rapid decrease in prices at the general level. Slump inflation is the situation of inflation in an economy while shrinking / shrinking in that economy (Caporale et al., 2018).

Stagflation is the simultaneous stagnation of the economy while inflation continues (stagnation in inflation). In cases where price stability cannot be achieved, individual decision-makers cannot make a rational decision by looking at economic activities such as savings, spending and investment with risk, prices cannot easily distinguish the changes and do not have the necessary / sufficient information. In cases where price stability cannot be achieved, political power cannot implement a more comprehensive economic policy since confidence in the policies implemented is diminished. For such reasons, providing price stability is the most important objective of monetary policy. Price stability is shown as the indispensable objective of monetary policies (Beckmann et al., 2017).

Financial stability, directing capital mobility in open economies is directly related to stability in financial markets. In a financial market where there is no stability, capital outflows are experienced even though there is no capital inflow, and on the contrary, stability and confidence in the market attract capital mobility (Wang et al., 2019; Dinçer and Yüksel, 2018). In today's conditions where globalization is gradually increasing, the increase in international trade and capital mobility creates significant changes in money and financial markets (Dinçer et al., 2018a,b; Kim et al., 2015). Savers can transfer their resources to international markets, which will provide higher returns than domestic markets. When governments find it difficult to finance public expenditures, they may borrow from international financial markets. When considered in the size of firms, they can find new international partners with stocks and borrow them at lower costs by issuing bonds and bills in foreign currency. For such reasons, stability in financial markets is an important factor (Bauer and Neuenkirch, 2017).

Economic development, the importance of economic integration in a globalized world cannot be ignored. The difference between underdeveloped and developed countries in economic terms continues to increase day by day. The main problems in underdeveloped countries can prevent the economy from responding positively to monetary policies. The changes in the free market economy and foreign trade reveal that monetary policies are also the factors that shape the economy. It is possible for the Central Banks to give direction to many national and international factors by providing monetary resources to be injected into the economy or to be the forefront with monetary policies (Hurn et al., 2018).

From the financing of public expenditures to the provision of resources by rational individuals, from public borrowing to private sector borrowing, many necessary instruments are directly related to the monetary policies of the Central Banks. The economic position of underdeveloped countries is not capable of carrying out many transactions such as industrial production, financial markets, foreign trade transactions, lending or borrowing to international institutions and organizations. On the other hand, in developed countries, it is seen that it is capable of directing these transactions by applying monetary policies economically in terms of accelerations in foreign trade, the situation in financial and capital markets, technological industrial production, outsourcing and outsourcing. Economic development, growth and development as a whole can only be realized through a dynamic economic policy. At this point, monetary policy has serious duties and constitutes one of the main objectives of monetary policies (Lansing and Ma, 2017).

The debates on whether the policies to be implemented for this purpose in economic theory should be carried out according to a rule or should be realized with discretionary policies occupied the agenda. At this stage, John B. Taylor (1993) proposed a policy in his study and stated that the use of short-term nominal interest rates as a monetary policy tool should change the nominal interest rate if inflation deviates from the specified target and output potential (Gallmeyer et al., 2017).

In this study, a Taylor-type interest rate reaction function is tried to be estimated under the hypothesis that the interest rate and inflation series have unit roots in order to better understand the monetary policies applied by the central banks and to determine whether they comply with a rule while determining the interest rate. In the second part; The concept of money, the systems used in monetary terms and the monetary institutions that are still present are discussed. Monetary policy regimes have been mentioned, the aims and instruments of monetary policies have been discussed and voluntary and rule-based policies have been discussed. Inflation measurement indices and inflation types are mentioned.

In the third chapter, the theoretical approach of Taylor Rule is discussed, its historical development is explained, classical and extended Taylor rule are mentioned, and criticisms, advantages and disadvantages are mentioned. The general information about the central banks of the E-7 countries selected as a sample was given. Finally, the data and method are mentioned, and the model used after theoretical explanations is presented and the empirically obtained results are evaluated and the conclusions reached are summarized.

GENERAL INFORMATION ABOUT INFLATION

Definition and Calculation of Inflation

We can briefly describe inflation as the continuous upward trend seen in general prices. According to classical economists, one of the proponents of quantity theory, it is considered to be synonymous with the increase in the amount of money in circulation. According to the Keynesian economic approach, while the economy is at full employment level, it is a surplus that results from the fact that total demand is higher than total supply (Parasız, 2007).

One of the most important problems experienced in all economies today is the phenomenon of inflation. We defined inflation as the continuous increase in prices. The inflation rate is the change in the general level of prices in a certain period. The fact that the total demand that occurs at the current prices level is more than the total supply causes additional inflation, socially and economically, leading to inflation. On the other hand, long-term and high rates of inflation, on the other hand, have a significant role in decreasing social welfare (Ozturk, 2011; Dinçer et al., 2018).

Inflation rates can be calculated using five different price indices. We can measure how selected goods and services change within a certain period with the help of price indices. In order to observe the change occurring at the general level of prices, a basket is formed from certain goods and services and the changes that occur in the prices of goods and services in this basket are determined (Barnett and Duzhak, 2017; Yüksel, 2016). With the help of the basket formed by the prices of goods and services such as food, beverages, tobacco, clothing, housing, rent, household goods, health, transportation, communication, entertainment, culture, education, restaurants, and hotels, the consumer price index can transfer the average consumption trends of the households in Turkey. shows the change in prices. In short, CPI is the index that measures the change in the prices of goods and services purchased by consumers (Wang et al., 2019).

It is called the index which can measure the changes in the prices of raw materials and semi-products used as inputs in the production process in the economy at the supplier stage. It measures the change in the prices of raw materials and semi-finished products used by some sectors (agriculture and animal husbandry, forestry, fisheries, mining, manufacturing industry, electricity, gas, water, etc.). in Turkey until 2005, WPI (Wholesale Price Index) has taken place while you are using the PPI began to be calculated in the same year. The difference in content is seen in the units where prices are measured. The WPI measures the change in producer prices of goods produced domestically but is also determined at wholesale points other than producers. In PPI, price changes are collected from producers and they consist of cash sales prices excluding some spending taxes (VAT, SCT etc.). With the PPI, which was started to be calculated in 2005, the calculation of WPI was abandoned (Heimonen et al., 2017; Öztürk, 2011; Dinçer et al., 2017).

Core inflation is used to evaluate and calculate the change in prices in general. It is an index that is calculated by subtracting certain items that cause changes in some groups of goods and prices by assuming that inflation calculations, which consist of the basket of goods and services which are generally open to use such as consumer, producer and wholesale price index, do not fully reflect those that cause an inflationist tendency (Ozturk, 2011; Kim et al., 2015).

The main objective here is to determine the factors that make the increase in the general level of prices continuous and to decide to implement more realistic policies towards these factors. In countries with policies targeting inflation, such indices are created and used in different forms. outside the scope of core inflation in Turkey, leaving some items from the CPI, Consumer Price Index was created Specified Coverage.

Types of the Inflation

In order to sustain economic activities in the formation of inflation, if the necessary resources are scarce, a higher price is requested or formed for the same types of goods and services. It often occurs when more fees are charged for the same amount of goods and services, or if the total demand exceeds the total supply in the whole economy. Increases in the price of input costs used during production and increases in the price of imported products cause different types of inflation. The structurally separated inflation in their occurrences are described below.

When the total demand for goods and services exceeds the total supply in current prices, prices are defined as the increase in the general level (Madeira and Palma, 2018; Parasız, 2007). In economies where an expansionary economic policy is implemented, total demand is rapidly increasing, creating surplus demand, and as a result, the general level of prices is increasing. Demand inflation; consumption expenditures of households, investment expenditures of firms, public expenditures made by public authority or factor income generated by the net external world.

According to Parasız (2016), the inflation brought about by the increase in demand caused by the increase in the costs of production as a result of the reflection of this on prices is called cost inflation. Cost increases, wages, raw material prices and some public goods and services may be caused by decreases in the marginal output of labor as a result of the release of prices that have been limited for a long time or the policy of overemployment (Carvalho et al., 2018).

In the real economy, prices do not always occur in full competition. In case of imperfect competition, prices can be raised as desired in the expansionary phase of the economy, and a behavior that may affect prices may be formed by decreasing production amounts in contractionary phases. The prices of some goods may have a political character in terms of the characteristics of the sectors producing these goods and in terms of the income distribution policy that the state is trying to realize (Zhu and Chen, 2017; Öztürk, 2011).

The government buys these products at a fair price where the prices of agricultural products are very low in the market. From this point of view, the state provides more income to producers of various agricultural products than the market value. Under the conditions of imperfect competition, the companies that make agreements between them find the opportunity to sell their products at the price they want by taking advantage of the unity that does not occur in the consumers. As a result of this imperfect competition, some firms may cause unjust profits through the products they sell higher than the market price and cause inflation (Hafner and Lauwers, 2017; Sawhney et al., 2017).

General Information about Taylor Rule

In the past, monetary policy was used as the most basic instruments by adopting fixed exchange rate and fixed monetary expansion instruments. In recent years, in the globalizing world, economic integration has been included as a result of the interaction of countries in many ways by coming closer to each other. As a result of increasing capital movements and emerging market failures, these monetary policy instruments, which have been implemented in the past, have lost their effectiveness. Instead of these policies, policies that show how central banks can participate and integrate in developing economic processes have started to dominate. Central banks have focused on these developments and focusing on monetary policy response functions as modeling in monetary policy changes during the integration process. The Taylor Rule first appeared by the American economist, John Taylor, in 1993 as an argument for the functioning and implementation of monetary policies by central banks. In accordance with this rule, it demonstrates how central banks should establish response functions when implementing monetary policy instruments (Lee et al., 2015; Caputo and Díaz, 2018).

The origin of the Taylor rule dates back to the 1970s. The monetary policies implemented as a result of the high levels of growth in oil crisis inflation rates in the 70s and low figures have been in line with the theoretical simple monetary policies implemented in the previous periods. In this period, the policies implemented did not go beyond rational expectations and the theories of stickiness of prices called new macroeconomic models, leading to a complex monetary policy. However, the suggestion and use of these models led to the emergence of the Taylor Rule. The Lucas critique and the time-inconsistency approach to rational expectations and stickiness theories have been enlightening. Initially, simple monetary policies were proposed with new models, and then, with optimal control theory and micro foundations, these simple policies took their place in the literature (Efthymios and David, 2018; Beckworth and Hendrickson, 2015; Özcan, 2016).

In the Taylor rule, short-term interest rates are determined according to the difference between the targeted value of inflation and the potential level of production. Demand pressures can be observed as the targeted value of inflation exceeds the potential level of production. In order to prevent this pressure, nominal interest rates are used as policy instruments. The most important feature of the Taylor Rule is that central banks act as if they were bound by a rule in determining interest rates, although they did not set targets based on a specific policy (Nguyen et al., 2018; Siami-Namini et al., 2018).

Taylor (1993) showed that in this model, the coefficients and the Fed should react against the decreases and increases in real GDP in price levels, and as a result of this study, they reached a common conclusion in the signs of model coefficients and in the functional formula of the model. In the model applied by Taylor, the interest rate is taken as 1 quarter average and the real GDP is taken into consideration for the output level. Between 1984 and 1992, the potential output level was determined by considering the average of 2.2. The inflation rate is delayed as the average of the previous four quarters. Taylor adopted inflation targeting at 2% (De Truchis et al., 2017).

When the inflation rate and real output level are equalized to the target values, the monetary policy nominal interest rate is 4% and the real interest rate is 2%. In the model discussed in the study, the balance interest rate is established as 2%, which is close to the potential growth rate of 2.2%, which is determined as the long-term fixed growth rate. Coefficients of inflation and real output deviations were equal to 0.5 in the model. In order to enable policy decision makers to make easy decisions, it has been deemed appropriate to treat them as round digits in multiple numbers (Alcidi et al., 2016).

The Taylor Rule states that central banks, which are monetary policy decision makers, act within a rule and respond to changes in indicators taking into account certain economic indicators. The error term found in the rule, on the other hand, as an example of Taylor's own study in 1993, prevents the deviations causing supply shocks such as the liquidity crisis resulting from the Iraq-Kuwait war. While working on this rule, John Taylor first examined a simple Taylor Rule model. Then, there was no consensus among economists in determining the details of the rule. In terms of measurement, timing, weighting and correction, many contributions have been made to the Taylor Rule over time by economists, and new inferences have been created by trying various Taylor type models that differ within the framework of the basic rules. Today, in terms of policy objectives, no central bank is responsible for inflation, production, employment and so on. as such. Depending on the economic conjuncture, exchange rates and central bank interest rates of other countries (such as the US-Fed interest rate) also contributed to the formation of an expanded Taylor Rule (Chen et al., 2017).

Although the Taylor Rule is accepted in terms of monetary policy in developed countries such as the USA, as Taylor has stated in his own statement, it refers to the differentiation of this rule among developing countries. It is stated in different studies that the target strategies of the central banks of the developing countries in the current global economies should be formed by a tri-structure consisting of inflation targeting, flexible exchange rate policy and monetary policy rules (Kim and Park, 2016; Chen and Kashiwagi, 2017).

John Taylor included the exchange rate variable in his 2001 study by looking at the results of the new studies. In this study, Taylor realized that the effect of the exchange rate variable on the model was quite low and stated that this effect was implicitly present in the classical Taylor Rule approach found in his previous study. He argued that there will be a decrease in the interest rate due to exchange rate pass-through in a change / valuation that occurs in the exchange rate. In his study on New Zealand using this data between 1989 and 1999, he analyzed the classical Taylor Rule during the period in which flexible exchange rate and inflation targeting were adopted. policy explained clearly through the Taylor Rule (Huber, 2017; Wang et al., 2016).

Since the temporary fluctuations in the exchange rate will have little effect on inflation expectations, applying the exchange rate variable in the model by assuming that interest rates will be indirectly affected by the changes in the exchange rate will have more meaningful results. In some cases, including the exchange rate among the variables in the model will have a distorting effect on the consistency in the implementation of monetary policies (Baerg and Lowe, 2018).

General criticisms of rule-based monetary policies, how to reach the information required in the implementation of policies, when necessary and how and in some way to make calculations of some values are brought in some criticisms. Leading economists such as Milton Friedman, Karl Brunner and Altan Meltzer argue that simple rules such as fixed monetary growth would be more useful than the rules presented by activist policies because of the difficulties in obtaining the information and data required to implement discretionary monetary policies. Taylor failed to produce a fall in inflation due to the fact that the policies implemented between 1960 and 1970 were at a looser level than they should have been, failing and the interest rate was lower than it should have been. It is defined that the interest rates used by the Fed between the 1960s and 1970s in the United States were largely deviated from what they were supposed to be (the value calculated in terms of the Taylor Rule) and that such policies failed in real terms (Kim and Park, 2019; Lafuente et al., 2018).

When Taylor created and uncovered the rule mentioned in his name in his 1993 study, he benefited from the data obtained as a result of the policies implemented between 1988 and 1992 in support of this rule. The point to note here is that these data used by Taylor consist of revised data. However, it is impossible for the monetary authority to obtain and use these data during the policies to be implemented. Another criticism of Taylor-type policies was previously made by Fed president Greenspan (Bhattarai and Carter, 2018). He argues that even if some data such as output gap is obtained in the implementation of such policies, it is based on a basic assumption that past economic relations will exist in the future. Based on the experience gained in the past, no one and no institution can guarantee that something that has occurred in the past will also occur in the future. The rules of simple monetary policy give more consistent results compared to a complex and complex model formed by the optimization approach. When the literature is examined and an evaluation is made, it is understood that simple monetary policy rules have higher performance in terms of macroeconomics than optimization rules (Hudson and Vespignani, 2018).

In contrast to complex sets of variables based on more sets of variables, advanced statistical applications, econometric and mathematical approaches, the Taylor Rule is mainly concerned with three economic variables (inflation, interest rates, and output amount). At the same time, the Taylor Rule is quite simple, allowing it to be easily understood and controlled by other economic agents. In addition, in his study conducted in 2007, John Taylor argued that the abandonment of simple monetary policies could lead to the formation of housing bubbles and financial crises. The Taylor model stated that simple monetary policy approaches can eliminate the causes of financial crises in the long run (McCulloch, 2015; Dräger and Lamla, 2017).

Rudebusch (1998, 2002), which uses the lagged interest rate variable in its studies, has been published by Söderlind et al. (2003) concluded that the Taylor Rule was not valid in their analysis of data sets between 1988 and 2000 for the US economy. The Taylor rule has been criticized by some economic circles because it is retroactive and does not take into account future prospects. The reason for this is that the monetary policies used by the central banks and the delays in the effects of these implementations on inflation rates and the inability to take measures in the future. This shows that monetary policy decision makers may be too late in practice (López and Neira, 2017; Liu, 2018; Yüksel et al., 2018).

AN ANALYSIS ON DEVELOPING ECONOMIES

General Information about the Analysis

The analysis was performed using Eviews-10 package program. Before the Dumitrecu-Hurlin panel causality test which will be used as the basic analysis in the study, it is necessary to check the stationarity of the data in horizontal section, to determine the stationary ones and to make them stationary in horizontal section. Stability of variables; it can be expressed as having a constant mean, a constant variance and a covariance depending on the level of delay by approaching a certain value over time. Time series, which do not contain unit root or show a stationary characteristic, appear as series with a constant average, variance and covariance for each delay period. Different methods have been developed and applied in the literature for testing stability. One of the most commonly used tests is the Augmented Dickey Fuller (ADF) test. However, in his 1989 study, the Perron data set failed the ADF test in cases of structural breaks and proposed the Philips-Perron (PP) test. In this study, unit root test analyzes of ADF (Augmented Dickey Fuller), PP (Philips Perron), IPS (Im Peseran Shin) and LLC (Levin Lin Chu) will be calculated. In order to analyze non-stationary original data, unit root stationarity test analysis will be performed by taking the first differences. Then, for Dumitrescu-Hurlin analysis, three lag lengths are determined, and three separate lag tests are applied.

Dumitrescu Hurlin Panel Causality Analysis

It is the causality analysis method that was first introduced into the literature by Granger (1969). It allows us to investigate whether variables that affect the analysis other than that data contribute to the estimation of the value of a data at a future time (Yüksel & Oktar, 2017). This causality is described by Holtz-Eakin et al. (1988), the panel has been added to the literature in recent years with new techniques in terms of causality relationship. The main purpose of the Granger causality test in the framework of panel data is to take advantage of the structural advantages of these models. Panel data analyzes can reflect the modeling of the behavior of data sets in a more flexible way than classical time series analyzes. In addition, since it has more observations than single time series, it allows to produce more useful results especially in short-term periods than classical Granger tests.

According to Dumitrescu and Hurlin (2012), the causality relationship which is valid for one country in terms of economic conditions is likely to be valid for other countries as well. Thus, the causal relationship with more observable data in the panel data light can be analyzed more effectively. The existence of a horizontal cross-sectional information requires that the heterogeneity between the units is taken into consideration in the Granger panel causality analysis. In 1988, Hoaltz-Eakin et al. and hypothesized that there was no causal relationship between the variables of all units and the hypothesis in the alternative hypothesis was that there was a causal relationship between the variables of all units. In summary, the basic hypothesis showing that there is no homogeneous Granger causality relationship is tested with the alternative hypothesis that there is homogeneous Granger causality relationship. As a result of these homogeneous hypotheses, in fact only one subgroup of the sample had a causality relationship, while the hypothesis that Granger-causality was not valid for all horizontal sections obtained was rejected and the hypothesis that this relationship was accepted in all horizontal sections was accepted. This methodology was considered in many different studies in the literature (Doğan and Arslan, 2017; Yüksel, 2017; Ülgen and Özalp, 2017; Dinçer et al., 2019c,d,e,f; Amin et al., 2019; Dinçer et al., 2017b; Furuoka, 2017; Adalı and Yüksel, 2017; Doğan et al., 2016; Dinçer and Yüksel, 2019; Zaman et al., 2017).

Analysis Results

The results of the statistical analysis performed will be explained below. Both the trends and intercepts were determined during stasis analysis. As the result of the calculations was above the statistical stagnation requirement of 0.05, it was observed that the original form of the series was not stable. Therefore, the first differences of the data will be taken and again subjected to stasis analysis. When the first difference is taken for the interest rate variable, the data set is stable. Therefore, the first difference of the data set will be used in the analysis. On the other hand, the inflation rate variable is not stable in its original state. In the last table, the first difference is tried to be stabilized and the values of statistical stasis is reached below 0.05. In the analysis, the first difference of the inflation variable will be taken into consideration. The details of the stationary analysis are given on the Appendix Part.

This analysis is a Granger causality analysis based on the lag length of whether there is a causality relationship between the two variables. In order for this test to yield positive results, three delay lengths were determined; lag1, lag2, lag3 3 different analyzes were made. If the test is validated for all 3 lags, it means that there is a causal relationship. If it is not confirmed in any of them, it is concluded that there is no causality. The Dumitrescu-Hurlin test gives us the value of whether the analysis is statistically significant. If these values are below 0.05, the test statistic is significant and there will be a causality between them. To summarize, for all 3 lags, the probe value should be less than 0.05 for causality.

In Table 1 above, the first line tests the hypothesis "Interest is not the cause of inflation." Probe. value (0.0000) is less than 0.05, this hypothesis is rejected. So interest for lag1 is the cause of inflation. In the second line, the hypothesis that inflation is not the cause of interest was tested. This hypothesis must be accepted since the probe value (0.3699) is above 0.05. In other words, inflation is not the cause

Table 1. Lag1 analysis results

Pairwise Dumitrescu Hurlin Panel Causality Tests			
Date: 05/18/19 Time: 13:04			
Sample: 2008M01 2018M12			
Lags: 1			
Null Hypothesis:	W-Stat.	Zbar-Stat.	Prob.
CBIR1 does not homogeneously cause INF1	16.0918	27.4276	0.0000
INF1 does not homogeneously cause CBIR1	1.50890	0.89675	0.3699

of interest. According to the results of our first test, inflation is not the cause of interest. But interest for lag1 is the cause of inflation. For all this to be clear, lag2 and lag3 should give the same results.

The Probe value in the first row of Table 2 is 0.000. that is less than 0.05. Thus, interest is not the cause of inflation, the hypothesis is rejected. Hence, interest for lag2 is the cause of inflation. So far, interest rates have been the cause of inflation in both lag1 and lag2 tests. In order to reach a clear result, we will look at the results of our last lag, lag3.

When we look at the results in Table 3 Probe value 0.0000. as we can see. So for lag 3, the hypothesis that interest is not the cause of inflation is rejected, and interest has resulted in the cause of inflation for lag1, lag2 and lag3.

SOLUTIONS AND RECOMMENDATIONS

Analysis of the study showed that central bank interest rates were not used as instruments in E-7 countries in order to ensure price stability during inflationary periods. High inflation rates in many devel-

Table 2. Lag2 analysis results

Pairwise Dumitrescu Hurlin Panel Causality Tests			
Date: 05/18/19 Time: 13:10			
Sample: 2008M01 2018M12			
Lags: 2			
Null Hypothesis:	W-Stat.	Zbar-Stat.	Prob.
CBIR1 does not homogeneously cause INF1	20.0660	23.0893	0.0000
INF1 does not homogeneously cause CBIR1	3.04923	1.30142	0.1931

Table 3. Lag3 analysis results

Pairwise Dumitrescu Hurlin Panel Causality Tests			
Date: 05/18/19 Time: 13:11			
Sample: 2008M01 2018M12			
Lags: 3			
Null Hypothesis:	W-Stat.	Zbar-Stat.	Prob.
CBIR1 does not homogeneously cause INF1	22.1861	19.9064	0.0000
INF1 does not homogeneously cause CBIR1	5.65723	2.71180	0.0067

oping countries, which emerge periodically, can be seen in E-7 countries, and monetary policies to be implemented by monetary authorities during these inflationary periods should not be evaluated within the framework of the Classical Taylor Rule. As a result of the analysis made for E7 countries, it was concluded that the Taylor Rule is not valid in these countries.

FUTURE RESEARCH DIRECTIONS

In addition to the inflation and CBRT interest rates, future studies may include other variables such as GDS, Bonds, Bills, Exchange rate, Deposit interest rates, and more consistent results in real terms.

CONCLUSION

As a result of the analyzes conducted using inflationary data, it was observed that short-term interest rates of the central bank caused inflation to affect price stability, but inflation rates did not cause an increase or decrease in short-term interest rates. According to the findings, although there is no reason for inflation interest rates in E7 countries, a causality relationship has emerged from interest rates to inflation rates. These results indicate that the monetary policies implemented in these countries are not carried out in accordance with the Taylor rule.

According to the Classic Taylor Rule, the increase in inflation rates should increase interest rates. When the Taylor Rule equation is examined, the short-term central bank interest rate (policy rate) is increased by 1.5% every time there is a 1% increase in inflation rate. The increase in the short-term real interest rate, which will have a decreasing effect on aggregate demand, will result in a decrease in the inflation rate, thus enabling inflation to move towards the targeted rate. The most important point in this model is that although it depends on a rule, it has a flexible structure considering the changes in both variables in the equation. Accordingly, it is expected that the amount of money circulating in the market will be reduced by the interest rates and the recovery of deposits from the market by applying narrowing monetary policies will have an impact on the inflationary tendency. In short, while inflation should have been a cause of interest, such a causality could not be reached as a result of our analysis.

ACKNOWLEDGMENT

This study was derived from Ali Doğdu's master thesis written in Konya Food and Agriculture University.

REFERENCES

Adalı, Z., & Yüksel, S. (2017). Causality relationship between foreign direct investments and economic improvement for developing economies. *Marmara İktisat Dergisi, 12*, 109–118.

Aguiar-Conraria, L., Martins, M. M., & Soares, M. J. (2018). Estimating the Taylor rule in the time-frequency domain. *Journal of Macroeconomics, 57*, 122–137. doi:10.1016/j.jmacro.2018.05.008

Alcidi, C., Busse, M., & Gros, D. (2016). Is there a need for additional monetary stimulus? Insights from the original Taylor rule. *Insights from the Original Taylor Rule (April 15, 2016). CEPS Policy Brief*, (342).

Amin, S. B., Kabir, F. A., & Khan, F. (2019). Tourism and energy nexus in selected South Asian countries: A panel study. *Current Issues in Tourism*, 1–5. doi:10.1080/13683500.2019.1638354

Baerg, N., & Lowe, W. (2018). A textual Taylor rule: estimating central bank preferences combining topic and scaling methods. *Political Science Research and Methods*, 1-17.

Barnett, W. A., & Duzhak, E. A. (2017). Structural stability of the generalized Taylor rule. *Macroeconomic Dynamics*, 1–15.

Bauer, C., & Neuenkirch, M. (2017). Forecast uncertainty and the Taylor rule. *Journal of International Money and Finance, 77*, 99–116. doi:10.1016/j.jimonfin.2017.07.017

Beckmann, J., Belke, A., & Dreger, C. (2017). The relevance of international spillovers and asymmetric effects in the Taylor rule. *The Quarterly Review of Economics and Finance, 64*, 162–170. doi:10.1016/j.qref.2016.11.004

Beckworth, D., & Hendrickson, J. R. (2015). Nominal GDP targeting and the Taylor rule on an even playing field. *Journal of Money, Credit, and Banking*.

Bhattarai, K., & Carter, M. (2018). An empirical analysis of the Taylor rule and its application to monetary policy: a case for the United Kingdom and Euro area. *Asian Journal of Economics and Empirical Research, 5*(2), 173–182. doi:10.20448/journal.501.2018.52.173.182

Caporale, G. M., Helmi, M. H., Çatık, A. N., Ali, F. M., & Akdeniz, C. (2018). Monetary policy rules in emerging countries: Is there an augmented nonlinear Taylor rule? *Economic Modelling, 72*, 306–319. doi:10.1016/j.econmod.2018.02.006

Caputo, R., & Díaz, A. (2018). Now and always, the relevance of the Taylor rule in Europe. *International Journal of Finance & Economics, 23*(1), 41–46. doi:10.1002/ijfe.1601

Carvalho, C., Nechio, F., & Tristao, T. (2018). Taylor rule estimation by OLS. Available at *SSRN 3265449*.

Chen, C., Yao, S., & Ou, J. (2017). Exchange rate dynamics in a Taylor rule framework. *Journal of International Financial Markets, Institutions and Money, 46*, 158–173. doi:10.1016/j.intfin.2016.07.008

Chen, J. E., & Kashiwagi, M. (2017). The Japanese Taylor rule estimated using censored quantile regressions. *Empirical Economics*, 52(1), 357–371. doi:10.100700181-016-1074-8

De Truchis, G., Dell'Eva, C., & Keddad, B. (2017). On exchange rate comovements: New evidence from a Taylor rule fundamentals model with adaptive learning. *Journal of International Financial Markets, Institutions and Money*, 48, 82–98. doi:10.1016/j.intfin.2016.12.006

Dinçer, H., Hacıoğlu, Ü., & Yüksel, S. (2016). The impacts of financial variables on employment planning in Turkish banking sector. [IJSECSR]. *International Journal of Sustainable Entrepreneurship and Corporate Social Responsibility*, 1(2), 1–20. doi:10.4018/IJSECSR.2016070101

Dinçer, H., Hacıoğlu, Ü., & Yüksel, S. (2017). A strategic approach to global financial crisis in banking sector: a critical appraisal of banking strategies using fuzzy ANP and fuzzy topsis methods. [IJSEM]. *International Journal of Sustainable Economies Management*, 6(1), 1–21. doi:10.4018/ijsem.2017010101

Dinçer, H., Hacıoğlu, Ü., & Yüksel, S. (2018a). Determining influencing factors of currency exchange rate for decision making in global economy using MARS method. In Geopolitics and strategic management in the global economy (pp. 261–273). Hershey, PA: IGI Global. doi:10.4018/978-1-5225-2673-5.ch013

Dinçer, H., Hacıoğlu, Ü., & Yüksel, S. (2018b). Evaluating the effects of economic imbalances on gold price in Turkey with MARS method and discussions on microfinance. In Microfinance and its impact on entrepreneurial development, sustainability, and inclusive growth (pp. 115-137). Hershey, PA: IGI Global.

Dinçer, H., & Yüksel, S. (2018). Financial sector-based analysis of the G20 economies using the integrated decision-making approach with DEMATEL and TOPSIS. In *Emerging trends in banking and finance* (pp. 210–223). Cham, Switzerland: Springer. doi:10.1007/978-3-030-01784-2_13

Dinçer, H., & Yüksel, S. (2019). Identifying the causality relationship between health expenditure and economic growth: An application on E7 countries. *Journal of Health Systems and Policies*, 1, 5.

Dinçer, H., Yüksel, S., & Adalı, Z. (2017b). Identifying causality relationship between energy consumption and economic growth in developed countries. *International Business and Accounting Research Journal*, 1(2), 71–81. doi:10.15294/ibarj.v1i2.9

Dinçer, H., Yüksel, S., & Adalı, Z. (2019e). Economic effects in Islamic stock development of the european countries: policy recommendations for ethical behaviors. In Handbook of research on managerial thinking in global business economics (pp. 58-78). Hershey, PA: IGI Global.

Dinçer, H., Yüksel, S., Adalı, Z., & Aydın, R. (2019c). Evaluating the role of research and development and technology investments on economic development of E7 countries. In Organizational transformation and managing innovation in the fourth industrial revolution (pp. 245-263). Hershey, PA: IGI Global.

Dinçer, H., Yüksel, S., & Canbolat, Z. N. (2019f). A strategic approach to reduce energy imports of E7 countries: use of renewable energy. In Handbook of research on economic and political implications of green trading and energy use (pp. 18-38). Hershey, PA: IGI Global.

Dinçer, H., Yüksel, S., Eti, S., & Tula, A. (2019d). Effects of demographic characteristics on business success: an evidence from Turkish banking sector. In Handbook of research on business models in modern competitive scenarios (pp. 304–324). Hershey, PA: IGI Global. doi:10.4018/978-1-5225-7265-7.ch016

Dinçer, H., Yüksel, S., & Kartal, M. T. (2019b). The role of bank interest rate in the competitive emerging markets to provide financial and economic stability. *Ekonomi, İşletme ve Maliye Araştırmaları Dergisi, 1*(2).

Dinçer, H., Yüksel, S., Pınarbaşı, F., & Çetiner, İ. T. (2019a). Measurement of economic and banking stability in emerging markets by considering income inequality and nonperforming loans. In Maintaining financial stability in times of risk and uncertainty (pp. 49–68). Hershey, PA: IGI Global. doi:10.4018/978-1-5225-7208-4.ch003

Dinçer, H., Yüksel, S., & Şenel, S. (2018). Analyzing the global risks for the financial crisis after the great depression using comparative hybrid hesitant fuzzy decision-making models: Policy recommendations for sustainable economic growth. *Sustainability, 10*(9), 3126. doi:10.3390u10093126

Dogan, E., & Aslan, A. (2017). Exploring the relationship among CO2 emissions, real GDP, energy consumption and tourism in the EU and candidate countries: Evidence from panel models robust to heterogeneity and cross-sectional dependence. *Renewable & Sustainable Energy Reviews, 77*, 239–245. doi:10.1016/j.rser.2017.03.111

Dogan, E., Sebri, M., & Turkekul, B. (2016). Exploring the relationship between agricultural electricity consumption and output: New evidence from Turkish regional data. *Energy Policy, 95*, 370–377. doi:10.1016/j.enpol.2016.05.018

Dräger, L., & Lamla, M. J. (2017). Explaining disagreement on interest rates in a Taylor-rule setting. *The Scandinavian Journal of Economics, 119*(4), 987–1009. doi:10.1111joe.12217

Dumitrescu, E. I., & Hurlin, C. (2012). Testing for Granger non-causality in heterogeneous panels. *Economic Modelling, 29*(4), 1450–1460. doi:10.1016/j.econmod.2012.02.014

Efthymios, G. P., & David, A. P. (2018). Modeling changes in US monetary policy with a time-varying nonlinear Taylor rule. *Studies in Nonlinear Dynamics and Econometrics, 22*(5).

Friedman, B. M. (2000). Decoupling at the margin: The threat to monetary policy from the electronic revolution in banking. *International Finance, 3*(2), 261–272. doi:10.1111/1468-2362.00051

Furuoka, F. (2017). Renewable electricity consumption and economic development: New findings from the Baltic countries. *Renewable & Sustainable Energy Reviews, 71*, 450–463. doi:10.1016/j.rser.2016.12.074

Gallmeyer, M., Hollifield, B., Palomino, F., & Zin, S. (2017). Term premium dynamics and the Taylor rule. *The Quarterly Journal of Finance, 7*(04), 1750011. doi:10.1142/S2010139217500112

Granger, C. W. (1969). Investigating causal relations by econometric models and cross-spectral methods. *Econometrica, 37*(3), 424–438. doi:10.2307/1912791

Hafner, C. M., & Lauwers, A. R. (2017). An augmented Taylor rule for the federal reserve's response to asset prices. *International Journal of Computational Economics and Econometrics, 7*(1/2), 115-151.

Heimonen, K., Junttila, J., & Kärkkäinen, S. (2017). Stock market and exchange rate information in the Taylor rule: Evidence from OECD countries. *International Review of Economics & Finance, 51*, 1–18. doi:10.1016/j.iref.2017.05.001

Holtz-Eakin, D., Newey, W., & Rosen, H. S. (1988). Estimating vector autoregressions with panel data. *Econometrica, 56*(6), 1371–1395. doi:10.2307/1913103

Huber, F. (2017). Structural breaks in Taylor rule based exchange rate models—Evidence from threshold time varying parameter models. *Economics Letters, 150*, 48–52. doi:10.1016/j.econlet.2016.11.008

Hudson, K. B., & Vespignani, J. (2018). Understanding the deviation of Australian policy rate from the Taylor rule. *Applied Economics, 50*(9), 973–989. doi:10.1080/00036846.2017.1346367

Hurn, S., Johnson, N., Silvennoinen, A., & Teräsvirta, T. (2018). *Transition from the Taylor rule to the zero lower bound (No. 2018-31)*. Department of Economics and Business Economics, Aarhus University.

In Carnegie-Rochester Conference Series on Public Policy (Vol. 39, pp. 195-214). North-Holland.

Ince, O., Molodtsova, T., & Papell, D. H. (2016). Taylor rule deviations and out-of-sample exchange rate predictability. *Journal of International Money and Finance, 69*, 22–44. doi:10.1016/j.jimonfin.2016.06.002

Kim, C. J., & Park, C. (2016). *Real exchange rate dynamics and the Taylor rule: importance of Taylor-rule fundamentals*. Monetary Policy Shocks, and Risk-premium Shocks.

Kim, C. J., & Park, C. (2019). Real exchange rate dynamics: Relative importance of Taylor-rule fundamentals, monetary policy shocks, and risk-premium shocks. *Review of International Economics, 27*(1), 201–219. doi:10.1111/roie.12372

Kim, H., Fujiwara, I., Hansen, B. E., & Ogaki, M. (2015). Purchasing power parity and the Taylor rule. *Journal of Applied Econometrics, 30*(6), 874–903. doi:10.1002/jae.2391

Lafuente, J. A., Pérez, R., & Ruiz, J. (2018). *Disentangling permanent and transitory monetary shocks with a non-linear Taylor rule (No. 2018-19)*. Universidad Complutense de Madrid, Facultad de Ciencias Económicas y Empresariales, Instituto Complutense de Análisis Económico.

Lansing, K. J., & Ma, J. (2017). Explaining exchange rate anomalies in a model with Taylor-rule fundamentals and consistent expectations. *Journal of International Money and Finance, 70*, 62–87. doi:10.1016/j.jimonfin.2016.08.004

Lee, K., Morley, J., & Shields, K. (2015). The meta Taylor rule. *Journal of Money, Credit and Banking, 47*(1), 73–98. doi:10.1111/jmcb.12169

Liu, X. (2018). How is the Taylor rule distributed under endogenous monetary regimes? *International Review of Finance, 18*(2), 305–316. doi:10.1111/irfi.12131

López, J. L. V., & Neira, M. A. A. (2017). The Taylor rule and the sandpile: the Taylor contribution and other matters. *Open Journal of Modelling and Simulation, 5*(04), 183–188. doi:10.4236/ojmsi.2017.54014

Madeira, J., & Palma, N. (2018). Measuring monetary policy deviations from the Taylor rule. *Economics Letters, 168*, 25–27. doi:10.1016/j.econlet.2018.03.034

McCulloch, J. H. (2015). The Taylor rule, the zero lower bound, and the term structure of interest rates. In Monetary policy in the context of the financial crisis: New challenges and lessons (pp. 405-417). Emerald Group. doi:10.1108/S1571-038620150000024023

Morley, B., Wang, R., & Stamatogiannis, M. (2018). Forecasting the exchange rate using non-linear Taylor rule based models. *International Journal of Forecasting*.

Nguyen, A. D., Pavlidis, E. G., & Peel, D. A. (2018). Modeling changes in US monetary policy with a time-varying nonlinear Taylor rule. *Studies in Nonlinear Dynamics and Econometrics*, *22*(5).

Özcan, M. (2016). Asymmetric Taylor monetary rule: The case of Turkey. *Eurasian Academy of Sciences Social Sciences Journal*, *10*, 68–92.

Öztürk, N. (2011). *Para banka kredi*. Ekin Yayınevi.

Parasız, M. İ. (2007). *Para teorisi ve politikası*. Ezgi Kitabevi.

Sawhney, B., Kulkarni, K. G., & Cachanosky, N. (2017). Monetary policy in India and the US: Is the Taylor rule irrelevant? *International Review of Business and Economics*, *1*(1), 75.

Siami-Namini, S., Hudson, D., Trindade, A. A., & Lyford, C. (2018). *Commodity prices, monetary policy and the Taylor rule* (No. 2015-2018-283).

Taylor, J. B. (1993, December). Discretion versus policy rules in practice.

Ülgen, G., & Özalp, L. F. A. (2017). Bir Refah Devleti Analizi: Ekonomik ve Sosyal Sonuçlar. *Siyasal Bilimler Dergisi*, *5*(2), 219–243.

Wang, R., Morley, B., & Ordóñez, J. (2016). The Taylor rule, wealth effects and the exchange rate. *Review of International Economics*, *24*(2), 282–301. doi:10.1111/roie.12213

Wang, R., Morley, B., & Stamatogiannis, M. P. (2019). Forecasting the exchange rate using nonlinear Taylor rule based models. *International Journal of Forecasting*, *35*(2), 429–442. doi:10.1016/j.ijforecast.2018.07.017

Yüksel, S. (2016). Rusya Ekonomisinde Büyüme, Issizlik ve Enflasyon Arasindaki Nedensellik Iliskileri/ The causality relationship between growth, unemployment and inflation in Russian economy. *Finans Politik & Ekonomik Yorumlar*, *53*(614), 43.

Yüksel, S. (2017). The impacts of research and development expenses on export and economic growth. *International Business and Accounting Research Journal*, *1*(1), 1–8. doi:10.15294/ibarj.v1i1.1

Yüksel, S., Mukhtarov, S., Mammadov, E., & Özsarı, M. (2018). Determinants of profitability in the banking sector: An analysis of post-Soviet countries. *Economies*, *6*(3), 41. doi:10.3390/economies6030041

Yüksel, S., & Oktar, S. (2017). Okun Yasasının Farklı Gelişme Düzeyindeki Ülkelere İlişkin Ekonometrik Analizi. *Marmara Üniversitesi İktisadi ve İdari Bilimler Dergisi*, *39*(1), 323–332. doi:10.14780/muiibd.329945

Yüksel, S., & Özsari, M. (2017). Türkiye Cumhuriyet Merkez Bankası'nın Döviz Rezervlerine Etki Eden Makroekonomik Faktörlerin Belirlenmesi. *Finans Politik & Ekonomik Yorumlar*, *54*(631), 41–53.

Zaman, K., Moemen, M. A. E., & Islam, T. (2017). Dynamic linkages between tourism transportation expenditures, carbon dioxide emission, energy consumption and growth factors: Evidence from the transition economies. *Current Issues in Tourism*, *20*(16), 1720–1735. doi:10.1080/13683500.2015.1135107

Zhu, Y., & Chen, H. (2017). The asymmetry of US monetary policy: Evidence from a threshold Taylor rule with time-varying threshold values. *Physica A*, *473*, 522–535. doi:10.1016/j.physa.2017.01.023

KEY TERMS AND DEFINITIONS

ADF: Augmented Dickey Fuller
IPS: Im Peseran Shin
LLC: Levin Lin Chu
PP: Philips Perron
Stationary Analysis: It aims to identify whether there is a unit root in the series or not.

APPENDIX

Table 4. Interest rates unit root test (original form)

Panel unit root test: Summary				
Series: CENTRAL BANK INTEREST RATE (CBIR)				
Date: 05/18/19 Time: 12:50				
Sample: 2008M01 2018M12				
Exogenous variables: Individual effects, individual linear trends				
User-specified lags: 4				
Newey-West automatic bandwidth selection and Bartlett kernel				
Balanced observations for each test				
Method	Statistic	Prob.**	Cross-sections	Obs
Null: Unit root (assumes common unit root process)				
Levin, Lin & Chu t*	-0.47190	0.3185	7	889
Breitung t-stat	0.76338	0.7774	7	882
Null: Unit root (assumes individual unit root process)				
Im, Pesaran and Shin W-stat	0.14768	0.5587	7	889
ADF - Fisher Chi-square	11.5692	0.6409	7	889
PP - Fisher Chi-square	4.56479	0.9910	7	917
** Probabilities for Fisher tests are computed using an asymptotic Chi-square distribution. All other tests assume asymptotic normality.				

Table 5. Interest rates unit root test (first difference)

Panel unit root test: Summary				
Series: D(CBIR)				
Date: 05/18/19 Time: 12:51				
Sample: 2008M01 2018M12				
Exogenous variables: Individual effects, individual linear trends				
User-specified lags: 4				
Newey-West automatic bandwidth selection and Bartlett kernel				
Balanced observations for each test				
Method	Statistic	Prob.**	Cross-sections	Obs
Null: Unit root (assumes common unit root process)				
Levin, Lin & Chu t*	-1.62352	0.0522	7	882
Breitung t-stat	-5.11175	0.0000	7	875
Null: Unit root (assumes individual unit root process)				
Im, Pesaran and Shin W-stat	-6.08829	0.0000	7	882
ADF - Fisher Chi-square	62.8184	0.0000	7	882
PP - Fisher Chi-square	332.368	0.0000	7	910
** Probabilities for Fisher tests are computed using an asymptotic Chi-square distribution. All other tests assume asymptotic normality.				

Table 6. Inflation rates unit root test (original form)

Panel unit root test: Summary				
Series: INF				
Date: 05/18/19 Time: 12:57				
Sample: 2008M01 2018M12				
Exogenous variables: Individual effects, individual linear trends				
User-specified lags: 4				
Newey-West automatic bandwidth selection and Bartlett kernel				
Balanced observations for each test				
Method	Statistic	Prob.**	Cross-sections	Obs
Null: Unit root (assumes common unit root process)				
Levin, Lin & Chu t*	2.70178	0.9966	7	889
Breitung t-stat	1.14912	0.8747	7	882
Null: Unit root (assumes individual unit root process)				
Im, Pesaran and Shin W-stat	1.84332	0.9674	7	889
ADF - Fisher Chi-square	17.0191	0.2552	7	889
PP - Fisher Chi-square	11.7598	0.6256	7	917
** Probabilities for Fisher tests are computed using an asymptotic Chi-square distribution. All other tests assume asymptotic normality.				

Table 7. Inflation rates unit root test (first difference)

Panel unit root test: Summary				
Series: D(INF)				
Date: 05/18/19 Time: 12:58				
Sample: 2008M01 2018M12				
Exogenous variables: Individual effects, individual linear trends				
User-specified lags: 4				
Newey-West automatic bandwidth selection and Bartlett kernel				
Balanced observations for each test				
Method	Statistic	Prob.**	Cross-sections	Obs
Null: Unit root (assumes common unit root process)				
Levin, Lin & Chu t*	-4.54234	0.0000	7	882
Breitung t-stat	-2.69930	0.0035	7	875
Null: Unit root (assumes individual unit root process)				
Im, Pesaran and Shin W-stat	-8.19827	0.0000	7	882
ADF - Fisher Chi-square	93.5310	0.0000	7	882
PP - Fisher Chi-square	418.191	0.0000	7	910
** Probabilities for Fisher tests are computed using an asymptotic Chi-square distribution. All other tests assume asymptotic normality.				

Chapter 22
The Concentration From the Competition Perspective in the Turkish Banking Sector:
An Examination for the Period of 1999-2018

Mustafa Tevfik Kartal
https://orcid.org/0000-0001-8038-8241
Borsa İstanbul, Turkey

ABSTRACT

With the globalization, the world has been becoming a much smaller place. New types of business have been emerging. Depending on this situation, new corporations are founded in current and emerging sectors. This causes an increase in competition. On the other hand, a variety of sectors are regulated intensively which result in a high concentration. Banking sectors is one of these sectors at where regulations are much and entry barriers are high. It is aimed at examining concentration from competition perspectives Turkish Banking Sector (TBS). It is concluded that TBS generally has a non-concentrated industry structure in terms of total assets, total credits, total deposits, total equities, and total net profits. Exceptions are seen in total net profits and in total deposits. Concentration level generally has decreased from 1999 (1,172 on average) to 2018 (899 on average calculated by Herfindahl-Hirschman Index (HHI). It is recommended that necessary precautions should be taken by regulatory bodies in order to decrease concentration and increase competition in TBS.

INTRODUCTION

Depending on the increasing globalization and digitalization, the business environment has been in rapid change and it has been much more complex. Sectors' structures have also been changing. This cause exits from/new entries to the sectors. So, giving a quick response to changes is crucially important.

DOI: 10.4018/978-1-7998-2559-3.ch022

With the changes in the business environment, countries should provide respond quickly in order to maintain economic growth, financial stability, and competitive power. With increasing globalization, everything has been becoming much more global than it has ever been. This means that there are international issues, which should be considered, besides national issues to be taken into consideration. This structure causes increases in competition for almost every sector including financial sectors.

When examining the structure of financial sectors in different countries, it can be seen that banks are generally the most important financial player in the sector (Çam & Özer, 2018). That is why banks have a bridge role between investors and deposit holders (Demirhan, 2013; Djalilove & Piesse, 2016). Similar to most of the countries, Turkey has also a financial system in which banks have the highest share and important financial intermediary role providing monetary and credit services (Coşkun et al., 2012; Çetin & Kartal, 2019). Development in financial systems and efficient working of the sector has importance in terms of economy as a whole (Kar et al., 2008).

Similar to most of the countries, TBS is also highly regulated sector because of its high importance for the economy and country. Besides Banking Law (BL), Banking Regulation and Supervision Agency (BRSA) also made lots of secondary regulations about a variety of issues which are accepted as important for the TBS. With the intensive regulations, specifically made after the banking crisis in 2000 and 2001, some banks have gotten out of the business while new banks have entered the sector. Depending on this condition, concentration in TBS has also changed over years.

Concentration means how much players operate in the sector and each player has how much industry shares. Concentration is important because of the fact that firms could get high revenues and profits if there is high concentration and they have an opportunity using monopoly power (Hazar et al., 2017). Also, the concentration may cause some problems such as adverse selection, moral hazard, and high-interest rates which could result in negative effects on the economies. It is important that banking sector, specifically TBS in this study, should have a market structure to be efficient and effective in order to be able to make a positive contribution to the economy (Coşkun et al., 2012). Banks can make a positive contribution to the economy by providing sources to economic parties. The most possible way for providing a contribution to economies is to be a competitive sector. That is the main reason why concentration and competition have been gaining importance (Ural, 2014).

This paper is prepared to make an evaluation upon concentration from the perspectives of competition in Turkey. Development trend of concentration is examined upon TBS, because Turkey has a bank-based financial system (Depren et al., 2018). Also, HHI is preferred for simplicity in the study.

The study consists of four parts. Literature related to the topic is reviewed in the second part. The concentration situation in TBS for the period of 1999-2018 is examined in the third part. Finally, an evaluation is made in the fourth part with determining solutions, proposing some recommendations and stating future research directions.

LITERATURE REVIEW

There are various studies about concentration and competition in both Turkey and other countries. Some of the selected studies in Turkey are included in Table 1.

Besides studies in Turkey, there are also a variety of studies about concentration and competition in other countries. Same of the selected studies are included in Table 2.

Table 1. Some selected studies in Turkey

Author	Year	Period	Results
Kasman	2001	1988 1996	Concentration is positively related with profitability and concentration in TBS.
Emek	2005	1990 2003	There is no meaningful relationship between stability and efficiency in TBS:
Abbasoğlu et al.	2007	1995 2005	There is not a statistically significant relationship between competition and concentration.
Yayla	2007	1995 2005	Concentration decreased between 1995 and 1999 and it increased between 2000 and 2005 according to HHI.
Çelik & Ürünveren	2009	2002 2007	The entrance of foreign banks to Turkey has not any contribution to the increase in the level of competition except for the year 2006. TBS has a competitive structure in 2006 while it has a monopolistic structure in all other years.
Tunay	2009	1988 2007	Competition is negatively related with fragility of banks in terms of national banks in TBS. The more concentration and growth in banks' scale, the more fragility. Competition in TBS should be increased.
Çelik & Kaplan	2010	2002 2007	Competition is linearly related with the efficiency in TBS. Competition increases while efficiency increases in 2005 and 2006.
Yaldız & Bazzana	2010	2001 2009	Intensive regulations made in 2000 causes a decrease in the number of banks and hence competition decreased.
Yağcılar	2011	1992 2008	There is a significant and negative relationship between competitive power and market share.
Özcan	2012	2002 2009	It is defined that there is monopolistic competition in TBS.
İskenderoğlu & Tomak	2013	2002 2012	There is not a relationship between competition and concentration.
Ayaydın & Karakaya	2014	2003 2011	Concentration has a positive effect on the banks' profits. It means that the decrease in competition increases the possibility of profit.
Çelik et al.	2015	1990 2011	There is no causality between concentration and competition in TBS. Also, efficiency in TBS increases when competition increases.
Dilvin Taşkın	2015	2003 2013	Competition decreases in short-run and long-run in case of increasing financial stability.
Özcan & Çiftçi	2015	2006 2013	Market share (concentration) is positively related with the profitability.
Korkmaz et al.	2016	2007 2014	Concentration has a two-way interaction with the financial fragility in TBS.
Hazar	2017	1998 2015	There is an increasing trend in concentration after the 2001 banking crisis.
Çam & Özer	2018	2003 2012	It is concluded that there is TBS has a monopolistic competition market structure. Also, scale size is a crucial variable affecting market structure.
Ustaoğlu et al.	2018	2017	It is concluded that there is not enough competition in the press sector in Turkey and so, it has a monopoly sector structure according to HHI.
Aydın	2019	2005 2015	There is a statistically important relationship between return on equity and concentration in TBS.

Source: Authors

Table 2. Some selected studies in other countries

Author	Year	Period	Scope	Results
Short	1979	1972 1974	12 Developed Countries	The profitability of banks increases when concentration in the banking sector increases.
Smirlock	1985	1973 1978	USA	Market share (concentration) is positively related with the profitability when concentration is kept under control in the banking sector.
Keeley	1990	1971 1986	USA	Increasing competition causes a decrease in profit margin, so banks would take excessive risk in order to increase returns. Therefore, there was an increase in bankruptcies.
Shaffer	1993	1968 1989	Canada	Concentration would not affect competition in the banking sector.
Bofondi & Gobbi	2004	1986 1996	Italy	Increase in the competition (i.e. the number of operating banks) causes an increase in credit default rates.
Maudos & De Guevara	2004	1993 2000	5 Selected Countries	Deregulation of competition regulations causes decrease in interest margin.
Beck et al.	2006	1980 1997	69 Selected Countries	Economies having more concentrated banking systems have less likely crises.
Boyd et al.	2006	1993 2004	USA & 134 Non-industrialized Countries	Competition increases financial stability.
Schaeck et al.	2006	1980 2003	38 Countries	More competitive banking sectors tend to have a low crisis possibility.
Yeyati & Micco	2007	1993 2002	8 Selected Latin America Countries	Increasing concentration does not weaken competition of banking. Besides, foreign participation in the banking sectors causes less competitiveness in the banking sector.
Fischer & Hempell	2008	1993 2001	Germany	Concentration in the local market is associated with the market power of banks.
Schaeck & Cihak	2008	1995 2005	Europe & USA	Increase in market power (concentration) increases costs efficiency.
Berger et al.	2009	1999 2005	23 Developed Countries	Much more competition decreases the profit margin of banks.
Carbo-Valverde et al.	2009	1994 2002	Spain	Small and medium-sized enterprises (SMEs) could reach credits easily when competition in banking sectors increases.
Davydenko	2011	2005 2009	Ukraine	Concentration in the sector is one of the most influential factors affecting the level of profitability.
Liu & Mirzaei	2013	1993 2007	48 Developed & Emerging Countries	More competitive and concentrated banking sectors increase industrial growth.
Fu et al.	2014	2003 2010	14 Selected Asia Pacific Countries	Much more concentration increases financial fragility.
Arrawatia et al.	2015	1996 2011	India	Competition affects productivity positively.
Fernandez & Garza-Garcia	2015	2001 2008	Mexico	Bank competition is negatively related to financial stability.
Apriadi et al.	2016	2005 2013	Indonesia	Competition decreases productivity and stability of banking.
Yaldız Hanedar	2016	2002 2010	79 Countries	Competition in the banking sector is positively related with the financial difficulties which firms face.
Cuestas et al.	2017	2000 2014	3 Selected Baltic Countries	Low competition is associated with risk-taking and bank failures.
Ekinci & Kök	2017	2006 2014	26 European Countries	Competition power of European banking system increased. Also, there is positive causality from competition to efficiency.
Leroy & Lucotte	2017	2004 2013	Europe	High competitiveness increases banking risks and banking fragility.
Eyüboğlu & Eyüboğlu	2018	1996 2015	16 Emerging Countries	Competition moves together with the financial soundness in short-run and long-run.

Source: Authors

The Concentration From the Competition Perspective in the Turkish Banking Sector

When appraising studies in the literature regarding competition and concentration in the literature, it can be said that concentration has an important role for banks for many ways especially profitability. For this reason, concentration is examined from a variety of perspectives in current studies taking place in the literature. It is possible to say that concentration has a substantial role for the banking sector. In this study, concentration in TBS is examined from competition perspectives for the period of 2000 and 2018 by using HHI.

AN EXAMINATION REGARDING CONCENTRATION UPON TURKISH BANKING SECTOR FOR THE PERIOD OF 1999-2018

After reviewing the conceptual background in the previous parts of the study, an examination regarding concentration upon TBS based on HHI calculation is made in this part. Hence, it is possible to determine the trend and current situation in TBS about concentration.

In this part of the study, firstly current structure of TBS is examined shortly. Secondly, HHI method is examined conceptually. Thirdly, the results of some selected studies applied with HHI are examined. Fourthly, concentration in TBS is calculated by using HHI. Fifthly, results of concentration calculation are discussed from competition perspectives as last.

Current Structure of TBS

Although there are over 90 banks before the year 2000 in Turkey, the number of banks operating has decreased substantially due to banking crisis seen in 2000 and 2001, removal of operating licenses of some banks, voluntary liquidation of some banks, and merger of some banks (Çetin, 2018). With the economic and financial stability achieved after the 2001 crisis in Turkey, some banks are permitted to be established such Ziraat Participation, Vakıf Participation, and Emlak Participation banks. As a recent case, Golden Global Investment Banks has taken establishment permission from BRSA in 2019. However, it is still in progress to be operating.

By excluding Golden Global Investment Banks because of the fact that it is in the establishment process, there are 53 banks operating in Turkey which are listed in the Appendix. Most of the banks are deposit banks which counts for 32. Besides, there are 13 investment and development banks. Also, there are 6 participation banks. Moreover, 2 banks operate under the Saving and Deposit Insurance Fund (SDIF) (BRSA, 2019).

The Requirements of Banks Establishment in Turkey

As mentioned in the introduction part of the study, the banking sector in Turkey is highly regulated by BL and BRSA regulations. Main regulations take place in BL. According to BL, the following establishment requirements should be provided in order to take establishment permission from BRSA (BL, 2005):

- *"Establishment as a joint-stock company,*
- *Issuance of the shares against cash and all of them are registered shares,*
- *Founders should have conditions specified in BL,*

- *Members of the board of directors should have qualifications specified in the provisions of the corporate governance of BL and the professional experience to carry out the planned activities,*
- *Compliance of the foreseen activities with the planned financial, management and organizational structure,*
- *Paid-in-capital should be at least TL 30 million Turkish Liras,*
- *Articles of association should comply with provisions of BL,*
- *Having a transparent and open partnership structure and organizational chart that will not prevent effective supervision of BRSA,*
- *Absence of any issues preventing a consolidated audit,*
- *Submitting an activity program showing the budget plan and structural organization for the first three years including the internal control, risk management, and internal audit system, including the business plans, projections related to the financial structure of the organization and capital adequacy for the activities foreseen."*

Besides, establishment requirements, the following operating requirements should be provided in order to take operating permission from BRSA (BL, 2005):

- *"Its capital should be paid in cash and it is capable of carrying out the planned activities,*
- *Submission of a document by founders of the bank that TL 750.000 system entrance fee is paid to the account of SDIF,*
- *Ensuring the compliance of its activities with the provisions of corporate governance and having sufficient personnel and technical equipment,*
- *Executives should have qualifications specified in the corporate governance provisions,*
- *BRSA Board should consider that the bank has the competence to carry out its activities."*

Besides regulation taking place in BL, BRSA made a secondary regulation regarding the establishment and operating licenses of banks named as Charter about the Permitted Transactions of Banks and Indirect Shareholders (Charter). Some additional obligations take place in this Charter (BRSA, 2006).

All these regulations summarized above show that the establishment of a bank in Turkey is not so easy. This causes not to increase the number of operating banks in Turkey after the banking crisis seen in 2000 and 2001.

About HHI

HHI index is a method used frequently to determine concentrate ratios in a sector (Evren et al., 2018). HHI takes all players into consideration in the sector. HHI can be calculated as (Hazar et al., 2017):

$$HHI = \sum_{i=1}^{k} s_i^2 \quad (1)$$

s_i symbolizes the market share of the company i. When s_i is used as a percentage, then HHI would be maximum 10,000; when s_i is used as share, then HHI would be the maximum 100%.

According to HHI calculation, concentration level in an industry can be described as (Coşkun et al., 2012):

- *"There is a highly competitive industry if HHI is below 0.01 (or 100),*
- *There is a non-concentrated industry if HHI is below 0.15 (or 1,500),*
- *There is a moderate concentration industry if HHI is between 0.15 to 0.25 (or 1,500 to 2,500),*
- *There is a high/strong concentration industry if HHI is above 0.25 (above 2,500)."*

Some Studies Published with HHI

There are a variety of studies prepared by using HHI. Some of them are included in Table 3.

Concentration in TBS Calculated Based on HHI

Concentration situation in TBS is calculated in terms of total assets, total credits, total deposits, total equities, and total net profits by using HHI.

Due to the fact that participation banking in TBS has 5.3% in terms of total assets as of 2018 end and their data before 2008 are not available, participation banks are excluded from the analysis. There are totally 47 deposit and investment and development banks as of 2018 end. So, the total number of banks is 47 for the year 2018 end and it changes for previous years.

Table 3. Some selected studies prepared with HHI

Author	Year	Scope	Results
Boyd et al.	2006	USA & 134 Countries	Increasing competition makes a positive effect on financial stability.
Abbasoğlu et.al.	2007	Turkey	There is no meaningful relationship between competition and concentration.
Jimenez et al.	2007	Spain	Concentration in banking does not take effect on repayment of commercial credits which is an indicator of risk.
Yayla	2007	Turkey	Concentration decreased between 1995 and 1999 and it has been in increasing trend between 2000 and 2005 according to HHI.
Berger et al.	2009	23 Developed Countries	Banks with high market share, i.e. high concentration, have lover risk.
Tushaj	2010	Albania	When concentration increases, the lending capacity of banks decreases.
Khan	2014	5 Selected Countries	There is an increase in concentration in S. Korea, Malaysia, and Thailand due to consolidations.
Kumar et al.	2015	India	Financial liberalizations policies decrease concentration significantly over time.
Memic	2015	Bosnia & Herzegovina	There is a high concentration between 2008 and 2012.
Korkmaz et al.	2016	Turkey	Concentration has two-way interaction with the financial fragility.

Source: Authors

Concentration in Terms of Total Assets

Concentration in terms of total assets is calculated and summarized in Table 4.

As Table 4 indicates, concentration in TBS in terms of total assets is nearly at the level of 1,200 in 1999 and decreased steadily to 2008. After 2010, it decreased less than 1,000 which are at the level of 938 for the year 2011. Concentration in TBS is 866 as of 2018 end which means that it is a non-concentrated industry in terms of total assets.

In addition to the general concentration level in TBS, when we examine concentration for first 5 banks, we can see that the concentration for them is under the level of TBS. On the other hand, when we examine concentration for first 10 banks, we can see that the concentration for them is nearly equal to the concentration in TBS. This shows that concentration level in TBS in terms of total assets results from the concentration of first 10 banks.

Concentration in Terms of Total Credits

Concentration in terms of total credits is calculated and summarized in Table 5.

Table 4. Concentration in terms of total assets

Year	Number of Banks	HHI	HHI for First 5 Banks	HHI for First 10 Banks
1999	42	1,199	1,050	1,191
2000	42	1,141	975	1,132
2001	42	1,042	841	1,027
2002	42	1,038	805	1,022
2003	42	1,083	837	1,070
2004	41	1,057	808	1,042
2005	42	1,085	780	1,069
2006	42	998	751	978
2007	42	976	719	955
2008	42	984	731	964
2009	42	1,019	767	1,004
2010	42	1,003	759	987
2011	42	938	696	914
2012	43	915	652	892
2013	44	883	630	857
2014	46	873	627	848
2015	46	867	633	843
2016	46	864	629	843
2017	46	872	634	854
2018	47	866	640	850

Source: The Bank Association of Turkey (BAT) 2019, Participation Bank Association of Turkey (PBAT) 2019, Author's calculation.

Table 5. Concentration in terms of total credits

Year	Number of Banks	HHI	HHI for First 5 Banks	HHI for First 10 Banks
1999	42	1,072	707	1,060
2000	42	1,053	699	1,039
2001	42	1,001	553	983
2002	42	982	506	954
2003	42	882	444	846
2004	41	850	469	810
2005	42	920	534	882
2006	42	895	530	859
2007	42	887	519	852
2008	42	906	570	877
2009	42	886	605	860
2010	42	909	626	888
2011	42	894	615	864
2012	43	875	578	845
2013	44	855	579	825
2014	46	851	574	822
2015	46	845	581	817
2016	46	857	605	834
2017	46	860	623	840
2018	47	875	657	858

Source: BAT (2019), PBAT (2019), Author's calculation.

As Table 5 indicates, concentration in TBS in terms of total credits is nearly at the level of 1,100 in 1999 and decreased steadily to 2004. After 2010, it has shown a variable trend which increases and decreases over the years. Concentration in TBS has reached the lowest level in 2015 which is 845. Concentration in TBS is 875 as of 2018 end which means that it is a non-concentrated industry in terms of total credits.

In addition to the general concentration level in TBS, when we examine concentration for first 5 banks, we can see that the concentration for them is under nearly 50% of TBS level. On the other hand, when we examine concentration for first 10 banks, we can see that the concentration for them is nearly equal to the concentration in TBS. This shows that concentration level in TBS in terms of total credits results from the concentration of first 10 banks.

Concentration in Terms of Total Deposits

Concentration in terms of total deposits is calculated and summarized in Table 6.

As Table 6 indicates, concentration in TBS in terms of total deposits is above 1,500 for the year 1999 and 2000. This means that TBS has a moderate concentration for these years. After these years,

Table 6. Concentration in terms of total deposits

Year	Number of Banks	HHI	HHI for First 5 Banks	HHI for First 10 Banks
1999	42	1,603	1,471	1,599
2000	42	1,502	1,348	1,497
2001	42	1,139	919	1,123
2002	42	1,177	930	1,165
2003	42	1,226	962	1,215
2004	41	1,250	1,020	1,237
2005	42	1,222	933	1,210
2006	42	1,110	883	1,095
2007	42	1,102	858	1,088
2008	42	1,103	862	1,090
2009	42	1,136	897	1,126
2010	42	1,157	938	1,149
2011	42	1,023	780	1,014
2012	43	998	742	988
2013	44	972	716	960
2014	46	945	694	931
2015	46	955	699	941
2016	46	962	718	951
2017	46	973	720	964
2018	47	989	772	981

Source: BAT (2019), PBAT (2019), Author's calculation.

concentration began to decrease and it has been 1,023 in 2011. After 2011, it has continuing to decrease and 989 as of 2018 end which means that it is a non-concentrated industry in terms of total deposits.

In addition to the general concentration level in TBS, when we examine concentration for first 5 banks, we can see that the concentration for them is very close to the level of TBS. In addition, when we examine concentration for first 10 banks, we can see that the concentration for them is so much close and nearly equal to the concentration in TBS. This shows that concentration level in TBS in terms of total deposits results from the concentration of first 10 banks.

Concentration in Terms of Total Equities

Concentration in terms of total equities is calculated and summarized in Table 7.

As Table 7 indicates, concentration in TBS in terms of total equities is at the level of 949 in 1999 and increased over the level of 1,100 because of effects of 2000 and 2001 crisis in the following two years. After, it has decreased to the level of 799 until the 2009 global crisis. Due to the global crisis, it has increased in 2009 and 2010. Concentration in TBS is 860 as of 2018 end which means that it is a non-concentrated industry in terms of total equities.

The Concentration From the Competition Perspective in the Turkish Banking Sector

Table 7. Concentration in terms of total equities

Year	Number of Banks	HHI	HHI for First 5 Banks	HHI for First 10 Banks
1999	42	949	817	883
2000	42	1,132	1,029	1,087
2001	42	1,105	1,004	1,049
2002	42	989	866	949
2003	42	985	861	945
2004	41	937	799	901
2005	42	947	750	907
2006	42	866	670	833
2007	42	857	681	825
2008	42	799	625	765
2009	42	846	681	816
2010	42	881	722	859
2011	42	832	657	804
2012	43	845	671	823
2013	44	819	635	795
2014	46	848	680	828
2015	46	844	671	824
2016	46	849	681	830
2017	46	864	698	846
2018	47	860	693	842

Source: BAT (2019), PBAT (2019), Author's calculation.

In addition to the general concentration level in TBS, when we examine concentration for first 5 banks, we can see that the concentration for them is under the level of TBS. On the other hand, when we examine concentration for first 10 banks, we can see that the concentration for them is nearly equal to the concentration in TBS. This shows that concentration level in TBS in terms of total credits results from the concentration of first 10 banks.

Concentration in Terms of Total Net Profits

Concentration in terms of total net profits is calculated and summarized in Table 8.

As Table 8 indicates, concentration in TBS in terms of total assets is at the level of 1,036 in 1999 and increased to 1,241 with the crisis in 2000 for the next year. With the 2001 crisis, it has reached to 3,640 which show that TBS has a high/strong concentration in terms of total profits in 2001 because of the effects of the crisis. With the effect of the stabilization program applied in Turkey, concentration began to decrease and it is 906 as of 2018 end which means that it is a non-concentrated industry in terms of total assets.

Table 8. Concentration in terms of total net profits

Year	Number of Banks	HHI	HHI for First 5 Banks	HHI for First 10 Banks
1999	42	1,036	906	984
2000	42	1,241	1,158	1,207
2001	42	3,640	-	-
2002	42	1,187	832	1,111
2003	42	1,193	1,028	1,139
2004	41	1,195	965	1,138
2005	42	1,295	1,208	1,265
2006	42	979	784	947
2007	42	1,065	908	1,044
2008	42	1,011	872	992
2009	42	1,107	962	1,097
2010	42	1,137	987	1,130
2011	42	1,040	833	1,033
2012	43	993	778	981
2013	44	1,056	855	1,045
2014	46	1,017	848	1,002
2015	46	1,026	856	1,006
2016	46	1,013	868	998
2017	46	984	814	970
2018	47	906	758	890

Source: BAT (2019), PBAT (2019), Author's calculation.

In addition to the general concentration level in TBS, when we examine concentration for first 5 banks, we can see that the concentration for them is under the level of TBS. On the other hand, when we examine concentration for first 10 banks, we can see that the concentration for them is nearly equal to the concentration in TBS. This shows that concentration level in TBS in terms of total net profits results from the concentration of first 10 banks.

Discussion about Concentration and Competition

Before this part of the study, concentration has been examined from the perspectives of total assets, total credits, total deposits, total equities, and total net profits by using HHI method. It is time to summarize all of the analysis made according to these criteria. The summary of calculated HHI based on these criteria is shown in Figure 1.

As it can be seen from Figure 1, concentration in TBS, calculated by using HHI, is under the level of 1,500 which is the boundary of indicator of non-concentrated industry. In other words, TBS generally has a non-concentrated industry structure in terms of total assets, total credits, total deposits, total equities, and total net profits. However, there are also some exceptions that deviate from this situation.

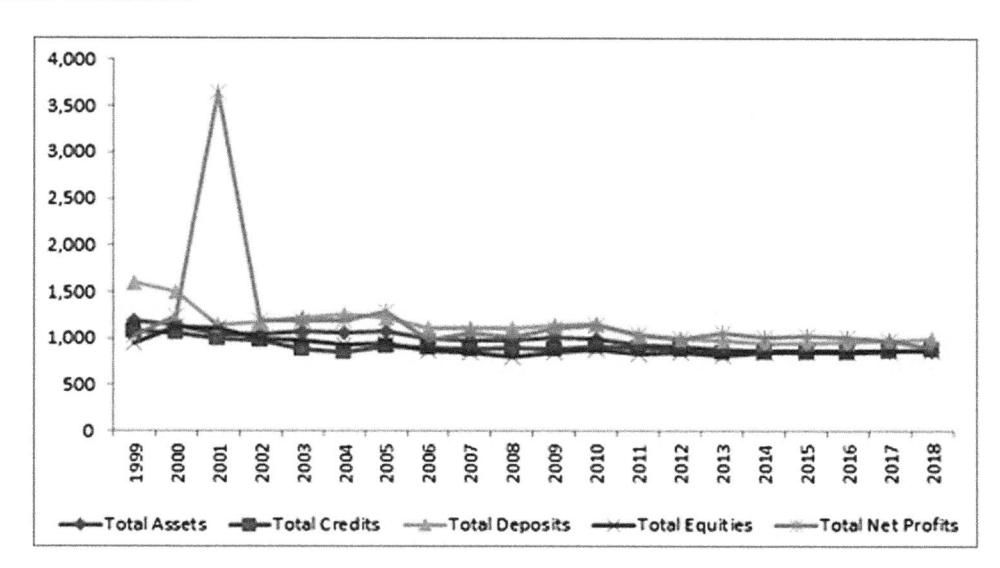

The Concentration From the Competition Perspective in the Turkish Banking Sector

Figure 1. Summary of concentration in terms of different indicators
Source: *Author's calculation.*

As Figure 1 indicates, the first (major) exception is seen in total profits. Due to the fact that Turkey experienced two heavy banking crises in 2000 and 2001, concentration in TBS has reached to 3,640 in the year 2001 which means that TBS has moderate concentration. Concentration has also continued to increase till 2004 and began to decrease in 2005. Similarly, concentration has increased after the 2009 global crisis in 2010 and after that, it has begun to decrease.

As Figure 1 indicates, the second exception is seen in the total deposit. TBS has moderate concentration. Then with the banking crises in 2000 and 2001, concentration in TBS has decreased to 1,139 as of 2011 end. It has increased again in 2002 and 2013. Similarly, concentration has increased after the 2009 global crisis in 2010 and after that, it has begun to decrease.

TBS is a non-concentrated industry in terms of concentration which has values between 100 and 1,500 except for two exceptions detailed in above. Although concentration has been increased in terms of total assets, total deposits, and total net profits after 2000 and 2001 crises, a similar situation has not been seen in terms of total credits and total equities. Moreover, concentration has been increased in terms of total credits, total deposits, total equities, and total net profits; but not increased in total assets after 2008 and 2009 global crises. At the end of the year of 2018, TBS has a level average 899 concentration in terms of total assets, total credits, total deposits, total equities, and total net profit which means that TBS has non-concentrated industry structure. The highest concentration is calculated in total deposits whereas the smallest concentration is calculated in total equities. However, it shows that there is a long way to reach a highly competitive industry structure for TBS at the same time.

The situation is not so bod for TBS. TBS has in stage two in terms of concentration and competition. As it is known, the increase in HHI shows that there a decrease in competition balance (Owen et al., 2007). Taking into consideration this information, Turkey should take necessary precautions to decrease the current level of concentration in order to be a highly competitive industry.

As an important point, it should be underlined that the concentration of the first 10 banks is nearly equal to the concentration in TBS. ın other words, it can be said that behaviors and status of first 10 banks in TBS affect the general position and indicators of TBS. Names and orders of first 5 banks and first 10 banks in terms of total assets, total credits, total deposits, total equities, and total net profits in Turkey based on 2018 financial figures are listed in the Appendix for readers who may want to know which banks they are.

SOLUTIONS AND RECOMMENDATIONS

In this study, the concentration level of TBS is examined by using HHI method for the period of 1999 and 2018. In the study, it is identified that TBS has a non-concentrated industry structure as general except for some years in terms of different indicators. TBS had a high/strong concentration in 2001 in terms of total net profits. On the other hand, TBS had a moderate concentration in 1999 and 2000 in terms of total deposits. Taking into consideration that Turkey experienced two important banking crises in 2000 and 2001, these abnormal exceptions may be evaluated as normal in the context of crisis periods. Besides the national crisis, there were also increasing trend after 2008 and 2009 global crises in terms of concentration. The latest concentration level of TBS as of the 2018 year-end is still far from being a highly competitive industry, unfortunately.

Taking into consideration that concentration prevents competition and lower competition would result in a variety of negative effects on the economies, Turkey should decrease concentration level in TBS in order to make TBS a highly competitive industry. In order for this, establishing a bank in Turkey should be eased. With the new establishment of banks in Turkey, it is anticipated that concentration would decrease and competition would increase. Hence, TBS would be a highly competitive industry.

FUTURE RESEARCH DIRECTIONS

In this study, it is aimed at examining concentration in TBS and its development. In the study, it is intended to make examination covering two important cornerstones in Turkey, which are national banking crisis in 2000 and 2001 and global crisis in 2008 and 2009, as well as using HHI method. In order for aim, data examination is carried out covering the period between 1999 and 2018.

By measuring the latest condition regarding concentration in TBS, it is thought that this study contributes to the literature. On the other hand, at the beginning of the study, it was thought that all banks would be included study. However, the examination is made upon deposit banks and investment and development banks only due to the fact that gathering data of participation banks before 2008 is not easy. For this reason, it is thought that new studies focusing on concentration in the sector including all players would be beneficial.

CONCLUSION

Due to the fact that the world has been much more global and smaller. For this reason, every countries and activity have been interdependent each other. This phenomenon in the world causes an increase in competition in every area. In addition to a variety of sectors, the banking sector is one of the most important sectors to be affected by this development and trends in many ways specifically competition.

Countries try to attract investment to their countries, specifically foreign direct investments. However, this is not easy, the competition also occurs in this area. For this reason, using national resources effectively is so important if a country fails in attracting new investments. As it is known, the main national resources in providing financing are banks. So, being competitive in the banking sectors has crucial importance for countries which have bank-based financial systems like Turkey. If the banking sector has a competitive structure, it means that it would provide a maximum positive contribution to the economy. However, competition largely depends on concentration. For this reason, having un-concentrated banking sector is important in terms of competitiveness.

In this study, taking into consideration the importance of concentration mentioned above, concentration in TBS is examined. As a result, it is defined that TBS generally has a non-concentrated industry structure in terms of total assets, total credits, total deposits, total equities, and total net profits. There are also some exceptions. The first one is seen in total net profit in 2001 which results in that TBS has high/strong concentration. The second one is seen in total deposits in 1999 and 2000 which results in that TBS has moderate concentration. However, the concentration level generally has decreased from 1999 to 2018. In other words, concentration has been calculated as 899 on average in terms of mentioned indicators by Herfindahl-Hirschman Index (HHI) as of the 2018 year-end while it was 1,172 as of the 1999 year-end. The highest concentration is determined in total deposits whereas the smallest concentration is defined in total equities. Moreover, concentration has increasing due to deterioration in TBS after critical times such as 2000 and 2001 banking crises in Turkey and 2008 and 2009 global crises. Lastly, total share of the first 10 banks has important effects on the indicators of TBS including concentration.

Taken into consideration findings determined in the study, it is recommended that some precautions should be taken by regulatory bodies in order to decrease concentration and increase competition in TBS. When thinking about possible precautions, it should not be forgotten that the most possible way to decrease concentration and increase competition is those which protect small and medium-sized banks in the sector, develop these banks, and ease new entries to the sector. It should also not be forgotten that every precaution, including wrong precautions, would have the influence in shaping concentration and competition structure of TBS. For this reason, regulatory bodies should be careful when taking precautions. However, by taking the necessary and right steps, it is possible to make TBS less concentrated and much more competitive.

REFERENCES

Abbasoğlu, O. F., Aysan, A. F., & Güneş, A. (2007). Concentration, competition, efficiency, and profitability of the Turkish banking sector in the post-crisis period. *MPRA Working Paper*, No. 5494.

Altunöz, U. (2013). Empirical analysis of competition dynamics in Turkish banking via competition determination approaches. *International Conference on Eurasian Economies 2013*.

Apriadi, I., Sembel, R., Santosa, P. W., & Firdaus, M. (2016). Banking fragility in Indonesia: A panel vector autoregression approach. *IJABER*, *14*(14), 1193–1224.

Arrawatia, R., Misra, A., & Dawar, V. (2015). Bank competition and efficiency: Empirical evidence from Indian market. *International Journal of Law and Management*, *57*(3), 217–231. doi:10.1108/IJLMA-03-2014-0029

Ayaydın, H., & Karakaya, A. (2014). The effect of bank capital on profitability and risk in Turkish banking. *International Journal of Business and Social Science*, 5, 252–271.

Aydın, Y. (2019). Türk bankacılık sektöründe karlılığı etkileyen faktörlerin panel veri analizi ile incelenmesi. *Gümüşhane Üniversitesi Sosyal Bilimler Enstitüsü Elektronik Dergisi*, 10(1), 181–189.

BAT. (2019). Retrieved from https://verisistemi.tbb.org.tr

Beck, T., Demirgüç-Kunt, A., & Levine, R. (2006). Bank concentration, competition, and crises: First results. *Journal of Banking & Finance*, 30(5), 1581–1603. doi:10.1016/j.jbankfin.2005.05.010

Berger, A. N., Klapper, L. F., & Turk-Ariss, R. (2009). Bank competition and financial stability. *Journal of Financial Services Research*, 35(2), 99–118. doi:10.100710693-008-0050-7

BL. (2005). Banking Law. Published in Turkish Official Gazette dated 11.01.2005 and numbered 25983.

Bofondi, M., & Gobbi, G. (2004). Bad loans and entry into local credit markets. *Bank of Italy Temi di Discussione del Servizio Studi*. No. 509, 1-49.

Boyd, J. H., Nicolo, G. D., & Jalal, A. M. (2006). Bank risk-taking and competition revisited: New theory and new evidence. *IMF Working Paper*, No: 06/297.

BRSA. (2006). C charter about the permitted transactions of banks and indirect shareholders. Published in Turkish Official Gazette dated 11.01.2006 and numbered 26333.

BRSA. (2019). Banks. Retrieved from https://www.bddk.org.tr/Institutions-Category/Banks/22

Çam, Ü., & Özer, H. (2018). Türk bankacılık sektörünün piyasa yapısının rekabet ve yarışılabilirlik açısından analizi: Panzar-rosse modeli. *Cumhuriyet Üniversitesi İktisadi ve İdari Bilimler Dergisi*, 18(1), 336–360.

Carbo-Valverde, S., Rodriguez-Fernandez, F., & Udell, G. F. (2009). Bank market power and SME financing constraints. *Review of Finance*, 13(2), 309–340. doi:10.1093/rof/rfp003

Çelik, T., & Kaplan, M. (2010). Türk Bankacılık Sektöründe Etkinlik ve Rekabet: 2002-2007. *Sosyoekonomi*, 6(13), 7–28.

Çelik, T., Kaplan, M., & Şahin, F. (2015). Efficiency, concentration and competition in the Turkish banking sector. *İktisat İşletme ve Finans*, 30(346), 81-104.

Çelik, T., & Ürünveren, Ç. (2009). Yabancı banka girişlerinin Türk bankacılık sektörüne rekabet etkisi: 2002-2007. *Niğde Üniversitesi İİBF Dergisi*, 2(2), 42–59.

Çetin, A. (2018). Katılım ve mevduat bankalarının piyasa etkinliğinin karşılaştırmali analizi ve bir uygulama. *TBB Yayınları*, Yayın No: 329.

Çetin, A., & Kartal, M. T. (2019). Deposit insurance in participation banking: A comprehensive examination upon interest-free participation fund insurance in Turkey and model proposal. *Journal of Islamic Economics and Finance*, 5(1), 1–38.

Coşkun, N., Ardor, H. N., Çermikli, A. H., Eruygur, H. O., Öztürk, F., Tokatlıoğlu, İ., . . . Dağlaroğlu, T. (2012), Türkiye'de bankacılık sektörü, piyasa yapısı, firma davranışları ve rekabet analizi. *Türkiye Bankalar Birliği Yayınları*, Yayın No: 280. Retrieved from http://www.tbb.org.tr/Dosyalar/userfiles/file/ecg/rekabetKitap.pdf

Cuestas, J. C., Yannick, L., & Reigl, N. (2017). Banking sector concentration, competition and financial stability: The case of the Baltic countries. *Bank of Estonia Working Paper*, No. wp2017-7.

Davydenko, A. (2011). Determinants of bank profitability in Ukraine. *Undergraduate Economic Review*, 7(1), 1–30.

Demirhan, D. (2013). Effects of the recent financial crisis on the determinants of bank profitability: Case of Turkish banking industry. *Journal of Yasar University*, 8(31), 5203–5228.

Depren, Ö., Kartal, M. T., & Kılıç Depren, S. (2018). Bibliometric analysis of the academic studies published about volatility in exchanges. *Banking and Capital Market Research Journal*, 2(6), 1–15.

Dilvin Taşkın, F. (2015). Türk bankacılık sektöründe finansal istikrar-rekabet ilişkisi. *Maliye Finans Yazıları*, 103(103), 175–204. doi:10.33203/mfy.307961

Djalilov, K., & Piesse, J. (2016). Determinants of bank profitability in transition countries: What matters most? *Research in International Business and Finance*, 38, 69–82. doi:10.1016/j.ribaf.2016.03.015

Ekinci, R., & Kök, R. (2017). Rekabet ve etkinlik: Avrupa Birliği bankacılık endüstrisi üzerine bir uygulama. *Çankırı Karatekin Üniversitesi İİBF Dergisi*, 7(2), 171-200.

Emek, U. (2005). Bankacılık sisteminde rekabet ve istikrar ikileminin analizi: Türkiye örneği. (Unpublished Doctorate Thesis, Ankara University Social Sciences Institute).

Evren, A. A., Ustaoğlu, E., & Bayer, Z. A. (2018). Piyasaların yoğunlaşma derecelerinin belirlenmesinde entropi kavramından türetilen Herfindahl-Hirschmann ve benzeri egemenlik ölçüleri. *Uygulamalı Sosyal Bilimler Dergisi*, 2(1), 1–13.

Eyüboğlu, K., & Eyüboğlu, S. (2018). Testing the relationship between competition and soundness in banking sector: Panel ARDL model in emerging countries. *Eskişehir Osmangazi Üniversitesi İktisadi ve İdari Bilimler Dergisi*, 13(3), 219-234. Retrieved from https://dergipark.org.tr/oguiibf/article/450138

Fernandez, R. O., & Garza-Garcia, J. G. (2015). The relationship between bank competition and financial stability: A case study of the Mexican banking industry. [Ensayos Journal of Economics]. *Ensayos Revista de Economía*, 34(1), 103–120.

Fischer, K. H., & Hempell, H. S. (2005). Oligopoly and conduct in banking-An empirical analysis. *Deutsche Bundesbank Research Centre, Discussion paper*.

Fu, X. M., Yongjia, R. L., & Molyneux, P. (2014). Bank competition and financial stability in Asia Pacific. *Journal of Banking & Finance*, 38, 64–77. doi:10.1016/j.jbankfin.2013.09.012

Hazar, A., Sunal, O., Babuşçu, Ş., & Alp, Ö. S. (2017). Türk bankacılık sektöründe piyasa yoğunlaşması: 2001 krizi öncesi ve sonrasının karşılaştırılması. *Maliye ve Finans Yazıları*, 1(107), 41–68.

İskenderoğlu, Ö., & Tomak, S. (2013). Competition and stability: An analysis of the Turkish banking system. *International Journal of Economics and Financial, 3*(3), 752–762.

Jimenez, G., Lopez, J., & Saurina, J. (2007). How does competition impact bank risk taking? *Banco de Espana Working Papers*, No: 1005.

Kar, M., Taş, S., & Ağır, H. (2008). *Finansal sistem ve kalkınma. Editörler: Sami Taban, Muhsin Kar. Kalkınma Ekonomisi*. Bursa, Turkey: Ekin Yayınları.

Kasman, A. (2001). The profit-structure relationship in the Turkish banking industry using direct measures of efficiency. *Ege Akademik Bakış, 1*(1), 141–164.

Keeley, M. (1990). Deposit insurance, risk and market power in banking. *The American Economic Review, 80,* 1183–1200.

Khan, S. J. M. (2014). Concentration in Southeast Asia banking. *American Journal of Economics, 4*(3), 150–158.

Korkmaz, Ö., Erer, D., & Erer, E. (2016). The relationship between concentration and financial fragility in banking sector: The case of Turkey (2007-2014). *The Journal of Accounting and Finance,* (69), 127-146.

Kumar, P., Bishnoi, N. K., & Chauhan, P. (2015). Bank market structure and concentration in Indian banking sector. *The Journal of Institute of Public Enterprise, 38*(1-2), 103–127.

Leroy, A., & Lucotte, Y. (2017). Is there a competition-stability trade-off in European banking? *Journal of International Financial Markets, Institutions and Money, 46,* 199–215. doi:10.1016/j.intfin.2016.08.009

Liu, G., & Mirzaei, A. (2013). Industrial growth: Does bank competition, concentration and stability constraint matter? Evidence from developed and emerging economics. *Brunel University Economics and Finance Working Paper Series*, No: 13-23.

Maudos, J., & De Guevara, J. F. (2004). Factors explaining the interest margin in the banking sectors of the European Union. *Journal of Banking & Finance, 28*(9), 2259–2281. doi:10.1016/j.jbankfin.2003.09.004

Memic, D. (2015). Banking competition and efficiency: Empirical analysis on Bosnia and Herzegovinia using Panzar-Rosse model. *Business Systems Research, 6*(1), 72–92. doi:10.1515/bsrj-2015-0005

Owen, P. D., Ryan, M., & Weatherston, C. R. (2007). Measuring competitive balance in professional team sports using the Herfindahl-Hirschman index. *Review of Industrial Organization, 31*(4), 289–302. doi:10.100711151-008-9157-0

Özcan, A. (2012). Türkiye'de ticari bankacılık sektöründe rekabet düzeyinin belirlenmesi (2002-2009). *Cumhuriyet Üniversitesi İktisadi ve İdari Bilimler Dergisi, 13*(1), 195–211.

Özcan, A., & Çiftçi, C. (2015). Türkiye'de mevduat bankacılığında yoğunlaşma ve karlılık ilişkisi (2006-2013 Dönemi). *Niğde Üniversitesi İktisadi ve İdari Bilimler Fakültesi Dergisi, 8*(3), 1–12.

PBAT. (2019). Retrieved from http://www.tkbb.org.tr/sector-comparison

Schaeck, K., & Cihak, M. (2008). How does competition affect efficiency and soundness in banking? New empirical evidence. *ECB Working Papers Series*, No. 932.

Schaeck, K., Martin, C., & Wolfe, S. (2006). Are more competitive banking systems more stable? *IMF Working Paper*, No. WP/06/143.

Shaffer, S. (1993). A test of competition in Canadian banking. *Journal of Money, Credit, and Banking*, *25*(1), 49–61. doi:10.2307/2077819

Short, B. K. (1979). The relation between commercial bank profit rates and banking concentration in Canada, Western Europe and Japan. *Journal of Banking & Finance*, *3*(3), 209–219. doi:10.1016/0378-4266(79)90016-5

Smirlock, M. (1985). Evidence on the (non) relationship between concentration and profitability in banking. *Journal of Money, Credit and Banking*, *17*(1), 69–83. doi:10.2307/1992507

Tunay, K. B. (2009). Competition and fragility in Turkish banking sector. *Bankacılar Dergisi*, 68, 30-55. Retrieved from https://www.tbb.org.tr/Dosyalar/Arastirma_ve_Raporlar/kirilganlik.pdf

Tushaj, A. (2010). Market concentration in the banking sector: Evidence from Albania. BERG Working Paper Series No. 73.

Ural, M. (2014). *Bankacılıkta yoğunlaşma, rekabet ve füzyon. Editorlör: O. Altay, C. Küçüközmen, M. Ural, E. Demireli. Banka İktisadı ve İşletmeciliği*. Ankara, Turkey: Detay Yayıncılık.

Ustaoğlu, E., Evren, A. A., & Bayer, Z. A. (2018). Piyasaların yoğunlaşma derecelerinin belirlenmesinde entropi kavramından türetilen Herfindahl-Hirschmann ve benzeri egemenlik ölçüleri. *Uygulamalı Sosyal Bilimler Dergisi*, *2*(1), 1–13.

Yağcılar, G. G. (2011). *Türk bankacılık sektörünün rekabet yapısının analizi*. Ankara, Turkey: BRSA Books.

Yaldız, E., & Bazzana, F. (2010). The effect of market power on bank risk taking in Turkey. *Financial Theory and Practice*, *34*(3), 297–314.

Yaldız Hanedar, E. (2016). Rekabetçi bankacilik sektörü firmalarin krediye erişimlerini kolaylaştirir mi? *BDDK Bankacılık ve Finansal Piyasalar Dergisi*, *10*(2), 9–27.

Yayla, M. (2007). Türk bankacılık sektöründe yoğunlaşma ve rekabet. *BDDK Bankacılık ve Finansal Piyasalar Dergisi*, *1*(1), 35–59.

Yeyati, E. L., & Micco, A. (2007). Concentration and foreign penetration in Latin American banking sectors: Impact on competition and risk. *Journal of Banking & Finance*, *31*(6), 1633–1647. doi:10.1016/j.jbankfin.2006.11.003

APPENDIX

Table 9. Banks List in Turkey

Bank Name	Bank Type	Bank Detail
Adabank A.Ş.	Deposit	in Saving and Deposit Insurance Fund
Akbank T.A.Ş.	Deposit	Private
Aktif Yatırım Bankası A.Ş.	Development and Investment	Private
Alternatifbank A.Ş.	Deposit	Foreign
Anadolubank A.Ş.	Deposit	Private
Arap Türk Bankası A.Ş.	Deposit	Foreign
Bank Mellat	Deposit	Foreign (Branch)
Bank of Tokyo-Mitsubishi UFJ Turkey A.Ş.	Deposit	Foreign
BankPozitif Kredi ve Kalkınma Bankası A.Ş.	Development and Investment	Foreign
Birleşik Fon Bankası A.Ş.	Deposit	in Saving and Deposit Insurance Fund
Burgan Bank A.Ş.	Deposit	Foreign
Citibank A.Ş.	Deposit	Foreign
Denizbank A.Ş.	Deposit	Foreign
Deutsche Bank A.Ş.	Deposit	Foreign
Diler Yatırım Bankası A.Ş.	Development and Investment	Private
Fibabanka A.Ş.	Deposit	Private
Finans Bank A.Ş.	Deposit	Foreign
GSD Yatırım Bankası A.Ş.	Development and Investment	Private
Habib Bank Limited	Deposit	Foreign (Branch)
HSBC Bank A.Ş.	Deposit	Foreign
ICBC Turkey Bank A.Ş.	Deposit	Foreign
ING Bank A.Ş.	Deposit	Foreign
Intesa Sanpaolo S.p.A.	Deposit	Foreign (Branch)
İller Bankası A.Ş.	Development and Investment	Public
İstanbul Takas ve Saklama Bankası A.Ş.	Development and Investment	Public
JPMorgan Chase Bank N.A.	Deposit	Foreign (Branch)
Merrill Lynch Yatırım Bank A.Ş.	Development and Investment	Foreign
Nurol Yatırım Bankası A.Ş.	Development and Investment	Private
Odea Bank A.Ş.	Deposit	Foreign
Pasha Yatırım Bankası A.Ş.	Development and Investment	Foreign
Rabobank A.Ş.	Deposit	Foreign
Société Générale (SA)	Deposit	Foreign (Branch)
Standard Chartered Yatırım Bankası Türk A.Ş.	Development and Investment	Foreign
Şekerbank T.A.Ş.	Deposit	Private

continued on following page

Table 9. Continued

Bank Name	Bank Type	Bank Detail
Turkish Bank A.Ş.	Deposit	Private
Turkland Bank A.Ş.	Deposit	Foreign
Türk Ekonomi Bankası A.Ş.	Deposit	Private
Türkiye Cumhuriyeti Ziraat Bankası A.Ş.	Deposit	Public
Türkiye Garanti Bankası A.Ş.	Deposit	Foreign
Türkiye Halk Bankası A.Ş.	Deposit	Public
Türkiye İhracat Kredi Bankası A.Ş.	Development and Investment	Public
Türkiye İş Bankası A.Ş.	Deposit	Private
Türkiye Kalkınma Bankası A.Ş.	Development and Investment	Public
Türkiye Sınai Kalkınma Bankası A.Ş.	Development and Investment	Private
Türkiye Vakıflar Bankası T.A.O.	Deposit	Public
Yapı ve Kredi Bankası A.Ş.	Deposit	Private
Albaraka Türk Katılım Bankası A.Ş.	Participation	Private
Kuveyt Türk Katılım Bankası A.Ş.	Participation	Private
Türkiye Finans Katılım Bankası A.Ş.	Participation	Private
Vakıf Katılım Bankası A.Ş.	Participation	Public
Ziraat Katılım Bankası A.Ş.	Participation	Public

Source: BRSA

Table 10. Orders of First 5 and 10 Banks Based on Total Assets, Total Credits, Total Deposits, Total Equities, and Total Net Profits in Turkey According to 2018 Financial Figures

Order	Total Assets	Total Credits	Total Depotis	Total Equities	Total Net Profits
1	Türkiye Cumhuriyeti Ziraat Bankası A.Ş.	Türkiye Cumhuriyeti Ziraat Bankası A.Ş.	Türkiye Cumhuriyeti Ziraat Bankası A.Ş.	Türkiye Cumhuriyeti Ziraat Bankası A.Ş.	Türkiye Cumhuriyeti Ziraat Bankası A.Ş.
2	Türkiye İş Bankası A.Ş.	Türkiye İş Bankası A.Ş.	Türkiye Halk Bankası A.Ş.	Türkiye İş Bankası A.Ş.	Türkiye İş Bankası A.Ş.
3	Türkiye Halk Bankası A.Ş.	Türkiye Halk Bankası A.Ş.	Türkiye İş Bankası A.Ş.	Türkiye Garanti Bankası A.Ş.	Türkiye Garanti Bankası A.Ş.
4	Türkiye Garanti Bankası A.Ş.	Türkiye Garanti Bankası A.Ş.	Türkiye Garanti Bankası A.Ş.	Akbank T.A.Ş.	Akbank T.A.Ş.
5	Yapı ve Kredi Bankası A.Ş.	Türkiye Vakıflar Bankası T.A.O.	Yapı ve Kredi Bankası A.Ş.	Yapı ve Kredi Bankası A.Ş.	Yapı ve Kredi Bankası A.Ş.
6	Türkiye Vakıflar Bankası T.A.O.	Yapı ve Kredi Bankası A.Ş.	Akbank T.A.Ş.	Türkiye Halk Bankası A.Ş.	Türkiye Vakıflar Bankası T.A.O.
7	Akbank T.A.Ş.	Akbank T.A.Ş.	Türkiye Vakıflar Bankası T.A.O.	Türkiye Vakıflar Bankası T.A.O.	Türkiye Halk Bankası A.Ş.
8	QNB Finansbank A.Ş.	Türkiye İhracat Kredi Bankası A.Ş.	QNB Finansbank A.Ş.	İller Bankası A.Ş.	QNB Finansbank A.Ş.
9	Türkiye İhracat Kredi Bankası A.Ş.	QNB Finansbank A.Ş.	Denizbank A.Ş.	Denizbank A.Ş.	Denizbank A.Ş.
10	Denizbank A.Ş.	Denizbank A.Ş.	Türk Ekonomi Bankası A.Ş.	QNB Finansbank A.Ş.	İller Bankası A.Ş.

Source: BAT (2019), Author's calculation.

Chapter 23
The Impact of US Monetary Growth on Bitcoin Trading Volume in the Current Economic Uncertainty

İsmail Canöz
https://orcid.org/0000-0002-3351-6754
İstanbul Arel University, Turkey

ABSTRACT

This study examines the effect of US monetary growth on Bitcoin trading volume. To achieve this purpose, firstly, the symmetric causality test is used. Following this test, another symmetric causality test is used to reveal a time-varying causal effect between variables. The data set covers the period from July 2010 to July 2019. The results of the first symmetric causality test, which considers the time interval of the study data as a whole, show that there is no causal relationship between variables. According to the results of the second causality test, these support the previous results substantially. However, an interesting detail is the causal relationship between variables for the period between April 2019 and July 2019. The reason for this relationship could be that investors who are indecisive during the current economic uncertainty add Bitcoin to their portfolios in response to the Federal Reserve's decisions.

INTRODUCTION

Recent political events and macroeconomic developments in the world have pushed the global economy into a recession. Thus, the uncertainty in the global economy has gradually increased. The trade war between the US and China has led to a slowdown in the world economy. These two countries constantly impose tariffs on each other. In the struggle of the two largest economies of the world, more tariffs mean less trade. Less trade means less economic growth. A decrease in trade affects the global companies most and they start to shrink. Therefore, they have lower turnover and profit. For this reason, stock markets have been falling all over the world for almost a year. This situation causes investors to adopt a wealth-

DOI: 10.4018/978-1-7998-2559-3.ch023

protecting attitude. Investors sell their shares and seek safe havens. Other leading political and economic situations influencing the global uncertainty are stated below:

- The recession in the European economy,
- Disputes in the process of the United Kingdom's exit from the European Union (EU),
- The resignation of the Prime Minister of Italy,
- Yellow vests protests in France,
- Terrorist actions in Syria and the Middle East,
- Protests in Hong Kong since June 2019,
- The economic crisis in Argentina,
- The economic crisis in Venezuela,
- An increase in the number of central banks with interest rates at negative levels,
- Due to a seeking safe havens, an increase in demand for government bonds with negative returns.

Considering all of these above, the world is struggling with many problems at the same time. Under these circumstances, investors are considering the idea of adding a new financial instrument to their portfolios to preserve the value of their wealth. If there is uncertainty in the global economy, returns on financial assets are on the agenda more than usual. When the current economic period is observed, it is understood that the fluctuations in the prices of financial assets are higher than during stable periods. Similar incidents have led to a decline in the confidence of some investors in certain financial assets and a new pursuit for a safe haven. Especially in recent times, many currencies in the world have lost their value, whereas gold has gained value. This is due to the increase in investors' demand for gold to protect their wealth. In addition to gold, silver returns, which are a cheap alternative to gold, have also risen significantly. Among other currencies, the Japanese yen stands out with its solid stance against the American dollar. Today, the number of people who think that Bitcoin is among these financial assets is considerable. This is probably since some countries are unable to purchase gold. These countries can, however, take advantage of the decentralization of Bitcoin.

Bitcoin, which emerged at a time when the effects of the economic crisis in 2008 were continuing, has not encountered what could be called a crisis in its ten-year life yet. Nevertheless, it has had a first on something lately. At the end of July 2019, Bitcoin faced a Federal Reserve's interest rate cut for the first time in its history. This has never happened before. It seems that Bitcoin's trading volume has positively reacted to this interest rate cut. From this point of view, the question of which parameters affect Bitcoin is also considered in terms of monetary growth.

In order to link Bitcoin trading volume with US monetary growth, the background to money supply and monetary policy will be briefly outlined in section 2. Section 3 is divided into two parts. The first part discusses primary studies related to the relationship between monetary growth and financial assets. The second part submits a literature of Bitcoin as a financial asset. Section 4 consists of the data set and model of the study. Section 5 describes the methodology of the study. Section 6 is devoted to methodological findings and presents the results of the analysis with the aid of tables and figures. In the 7th and last section, the conclusion of the study is discussed.

A BRIEF OF THEORETICAL BACKGROUND OF MONETARY GROWTH

Money Supply and Definitions of Money Supply

Emission means issuing banknotes to the market. The amount of money issued by the Central Bank or the total amount of banknotes circulating in the market refers to the volume of emissions. On the other hand, money supply refers to a concept that has a broader meaning than the volume of emission. The money supply includes banknotes and coins in circulation as well as other means of purchasing. From this point of view, money supply means the stock of money that is available in the market in an economy at a specific period and is briefly indicated by the letter "M". It is generally measured in two ways: a narrow definition of money supply and a broad definition of money supply (Eğilmez, 2018). The narrow money definition is divided into Money 0 (M0) and Money 1 (M1). On the other hand, the broad definition of the money supply is divided into Money 2 (M2) and Money 3 (M3). M0 is the narrowest definition of money supply. This concept represents all money that is readily available or in a liquid state.

The definitions of the money supply may vary between countries. According to the Federal Reserve, there are several standard measures of money supply, including monetary base, M1 and M2, calculated by the sum of some of the central bank's balance sheet accounts. The monetary base is the sum of money in circulation and deposits held by banks and other custody institutions in accounts in the Federal Reserve. M1 is the sum of the money held by the public and the transaction deposits at the depository institutions. The sum of M1, savings deposits, small-denomination time deposits and the retail money market mutual fund shares equals M2 (FED, August 2019).

Instruments of Monetary Policy

Milton Friedman argues that money supply provides important information about the near-term direction for an economy and determines the level of price and inflation in the long-term. Central banks, including the Federal Reserve, have occasionally used money supply measures as an important guide in the implementation of monetary policy (FED, August 2019). The main task of the Federal Reserve is to be responsible for money supply management and economic stability. The Federal Reserve has some main instruments of that it uses to implement monetary policy (FED, August 2019):

- Reserve requirements,
- Discount rate,
- Open market operation,
- Expired policy tools,
- Overnight reserve repurchase agreement facilities,
- Interest on required reserve balance and excess balances.

Monetary Expansion (Quantitative Easing) and Monetary Tightening (Quantitative Tightening)

In an economy, an increase in the amount of money in circulation causes a depreciation of the currency, while a decrease in the amount of money causes an appreciation of the currency. Since the value of money is measured by interest, a change for money causes interest rates to rise or fall. Due to this effect, the money supply is very important for economic management. Central banks aim to control the general level of prices by intervening in money supply through tools of monetary policy.

Monetary expansion is the state of open market operation that has reached enormous amounts. When the central banks want to increase the liquidity in the market, they buy bonds and bills from the market and give money to the market in return. The Federal Reserve is the first central bank to initiate monetary expansion. On the one hand, the Federal Reserve provides liquidity to banks by buying bonds and bills. On the other hand, it tries to ensure that banks can provide loans by lowering interest rates. The purpose of this is to stimulate demand and the economy (Eğilmez, 2015). Monetary tightening is the opposite of monetary expansion. The Central Bank sells bonds and bills to the market and withdraws money from the market. The main purpose of the monetary tightening is to stop the increase in total demand, which is seen as the main reason for inflation.

LITERATURE REVIEW

Literature Related to the Effects of Monetary Growth on Financial Assets

As stated by Renaud (2003: 152), three main assets support growth in any economy. The most important of these is human capital. The other two are real estate assets and financial assets. It should be noted that many studies are investigating the effects of monetary policies on investments in financial assets and real estate assets in the literature. Some of them are summarized below.

When the studies related to the relationship between monetary policy and stock are investigated, Thorbecke (1997) aims to examine how stock returns react to monetary policy shocks. The findings of the study show that the expansionary monetary policy increases ex-post stock returns. Patelis (1997) investigates whether monetary policy variables, as well as various financial variables, predict stock returns. The results show that monetary policy variables are important determinants of future stock returns, but they do not fully explain the predictability of stock returns. Ioannidis and Kontonikas (2008) investigate the impact of monetary policy on stock returns in 13 OECD countries in the period between 1972 and 2002. The results show that changes in monetary policy have a significant effect on stock returns. Bjørnland and Leitemo (2009) investigate the mutual statistical relationship between US monetary policy and the S&P 500 using the vector autoregressive (VAR) model. According to the results of the analysis, a significant interaction has been found between interest rate setting and real stock prices.

Much research has been done on the relationship between monetary policy and commodity. Frankel (2006) seeks to argue that monetary policy is an important determinant of the real price of oil and other mineral and agricultural products. According to Frankel's findings, the decline in real interest rates has a negative effect on commodity prices. Anzuini et. al. (2010) aim to examine the empirical relationship between US monetary policy and commodity prices. For this purpose, they used a standard VAR model, which is widely used to analyze the effects of monetary policy shocks. As a result of the study, it is understood that the expansionary monetary policy shocks increase the commodity price index and its components, but the degree of this effect is low. Belke et. al. (2014) examine the interactions between money, interest rates, goods and commodities prices in a study covering the period 1970-2008 for OECD countries. This interaction is tested with the VAR model. The results of the analysis show that a global liquidity aggregate determines the long-term homogeneity of goods and commodity price movements while controlling different monetary policy stances through interest rates. Hammoudeh et.

al. (2015) have aimed to examine the effects of US monetary policy on sectoral commodity prices and macroeconomic activity using a Structural VAR (SVAR) model. According to empirical evidence, the commodity price index suddenly rises when the US monetary tightening occurs. This rise then erodes as the positive interest shock disappears at the end of the six quarters.

Several publications have appeared on the subject of the relationship between monetary policy and real estate. Gupta et. al. (2010) assess the impact of monetary policy on real house price growth in South Africa. To achieve this objective, a factor-augmented vector autoregression (FAVAR) model is used and the study includes the period from January 1980 to April 2006. The results show that the house price reacts negatively to the monetary policy shock and this reaction changes in the middle, luxury and affordable options of the housing market. Xu and Chen (2012) investigate the effects of key monetary policy variables on the dynamics of growth on property prices in China. To achieve this aim, the authors have used both the data from the 1st quarter of 1998 to the 4th quarter of 2009 and the data from July 2005 to February 2010. According to the empirical results, while expansionary monetary policy tends to accelerate the increase in housing prices, restrictive monetary policy tends to slow the increase in housing prices.

In conclusion, the majority of studies reviewed in the relevant literature support a significant relationship between monetary policy and financial assets (stocks, commodities, and real estate).

Literature Related to Bitcoin as a Financial Asset

Academic studies on Bitcoin include many different disciplines. For example, when a payment transaction with Bitcoin is made, an accountant is interested in how to record this transaction, while a tax officer may be interested in how to tax it. Alternatively, a computer engineer can research Bitcoin software. On the other hand, studies in economics and finance generally focus on Bitcoin as an investment instrument. The reason why Bitcoin is seen as an investment instrument is obvious because Bitcoin has failed to prove its adequacy as a means of payment yet. Although the number of companies accepting payments with Bitcoin in the world is increasing day by day, it is difficult to say that it fully fulfills the requirements of being an instrument of payment due to its price volatility in the cryptocurrency markets. This is because not many people in the world have adopted it as one of the means of payment available to them. Based on this statement, the studies that evaluate Bitcoin as a financial instrument are summarized below.

Studies on cryptocurrencies are relatively recent and previous research has documented whether they are mediums of exchange or financial assets. Luther and White (2014) evaluate whether Bitcoin is used as a means of payment or as a speculative investment instrument. The authors argue that it is difficult to use it as a means of payment because of its volatility and that there may be entrepreneurial efforts to prevent it. Glaser et. al. (2014) aim to provide empirical evidence of whether cryptocurrencies are considered as a financial asset or a currency by their users. The results show that new Bitcoin users describe it as a financial asset, not a currency. Dyhrberg (2015) examines whether Bitcoin has the characteristics of a financial asset using the GARCH model. Initial findings suggest that there are some similarities between the dollar, gold, and Bitcoin. The results show that Bitcoin can be useful in risk management for risk-averse investors. Bianchi (2017) explores the relationship between cryptocurrencies and standard assets and the main factors behind their market activity. Analysis results indicate that there is a significant relationship between cryptocurrencies and commodities such as gold and energy in terms of returns. Moreover, it is understood that macroeconomic factors do not significantly affect trading activities in cryptocurrency markets. Baur et. al. (2018) aim to analyze whether Bitcoin is a medium of exchange or a financial asset. The results show that Bitcoin is not associated with traditional assets (such as stocks, bonds, and commodities) in both normal and financial uncertainty periods. Besides, Bitcoin is not used as an alternative currency and medium of exchange, but it is used as a speculative investment instrument. Ji et. al. (2018) investigate the relationship between Bitcoin and other financial assets using the acyclic graph method. The results show that the Bitcoin market has its characteristics and there is no specific asset affecting this market. In addition to this, if Bitcoin is operating in the bear market, lagged relationships between Bitcoin and some assets have been identified.

Recently, some researchers have suggested a new perspective evaluating Bitcoin's role in risk management, portfolio diversification, and hedge funds. Yermack (2015) examines whether bitcoin should be considered as currency. According to the author, the fact that its high volatility is much higher than the volatility of other major currencies creates short-term risks for users. Based on the findings, it is said that Bitcoin has almost no correlation with major currencies and gold. This explains why Bitcoin is useless for risk management. In opposition to this study, Dyhrberg (2016) aims to test Bitcoin's ability to hedge. It is concluded that Bitcoin can be appropriate as a hedge against stocks in the Financial Times Stock Exchange Index. Furthermore, it can be a hedging instrument against the dollar. Thus, Bitcoin can show similarities to gold when hedging. Bouri et. al. (2017) examine Bitcoin's suitability for hedge and its preferability as a safe haven compared to important financial assets such as stocks, bonds, gold, oil, dollar, and commodity. The empirical results demonstrate that Bitcoin is weak to hedge and is only appropriate for portfolio diversification. Moreover, Bitcoin can serve as a safe haven in case of a weekly downward movement in Asian stocks. Similar to this study, Corbet et. al. (2018) aim to test the relationship between the three most important cryptocurrencies and various other financial assets. The findings indicate that cryptocurrencies can be effective in portfolio diversification and offer safe havens for investors. Guesmi et. al. (2019) focus on the nature of the interaction between Bitcoin and financial assets and their transmission mechanisms in portfolio diversification and hedge. To achieve this objective, they use the DCC-GARCH model. According to the model's findings, the portfolio including gold, oil, emerging stocks, and Bitcoin has a lower variance than the portfolio including gold, oil, and stocks.

Consequently, some studies reveal the differences between Bitcoin's being a medium of exchange and a financial asset. On the other hand, some studies already accept it as a financial asset and examine how it performs in portfolio diversification and hedge.

DATA AND MODEL

This study covers the period from July 2010 to July 2019. It corresponds to a total of 109 months of observation obtained from the Federal Reserve and one of the biggest cryptocurrency data providers. M2, which is one of the definitions of money supply, is used as the variable to represent monetary growth (M2 is a seasonally adjusted time series). When the literature is reviewed, it is seen that M2 variable is generally used in the analysis of most studies related to monetary policy (Kesbiç et al., 2004; Grauwe and Polan, 2005; Owoye and Onafowora, 2007; Altıntaş et al., 2008; Korap, 2009; Xu and Chen, 2012). For this reason, M2 has been preferred for analysis. The growth rate of M2 has been calculated and included in the model.

Another variable used in the analysis for the study is Bitcoin trading volume. Trading volume is the most significant criteria and measurement for Bitcoin with increasing supply and market capitalization. Briefly, it means how many Bitcoins have changed hands over a period of time. These periods are usu-

The Impact of US Monetary Growth on Bitcoin Trading Volume in the Current Economic Uncertainty

ally the last 24 hours, last week or last 30 days. Trading volume can also be expressed in currencies such as dollars or euros. However, in the analysis of the study, it has been tested as BTC, not currency. The following table summarizes the information about the variables.

In this study, the data set of the variables has been evaluated with raw conditions without any conversion to prevent information loss. The graphs of the variables are shown in Figure 1.

According to Figure 1, when the data of BTCVOL and M2_G is examined, it is seen that it is a fractured series. These fractures have been taken into consideration in the analysis. Therefore, the unit root test that considers the breakpoint has been preferred in the analysis.

The main model predicted in the study is presented in equation (1):

$$BTCVOL_t = \beta_0 + \beta_1 M2\_G_t + u_t \quad (1)$$

The dependent variable in the model is the Bitcoin trade volume (BTCVOL). Besides, M2_G is an independent variable and represents monetary growth. The term error is expressed by u_t. The letter "t", which is the subscript of the variables, defines that the related variables are time series. Beta (β) is the long-term parameter coefficient.

METHODOLOGY

If there is a time-lagged relationship between the two variables, the method that determines the causality direction of this relationship in terms of statistical analysis is called the causality test. This method

Table 1. Summary of the variables

Variables	Abbreviation	Economic size unit	Source
Monetary growth	M2_G	$	https://www.federalreserve.gov/datadownload/
Bitcoin trading volume	BTCVOL	BTC	https://bitcoinity.org/

Figure 1. Graphical display of the variables (2010:07-2019:07)

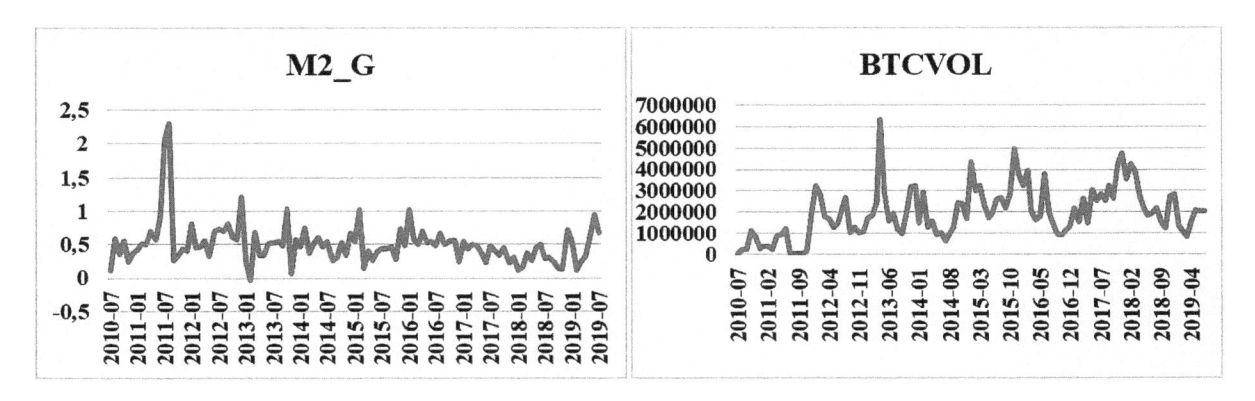

tests whether another variable provides useful information in the future estimation of one variable. Sims (1972), Hsiao (1981), Toda and Yamamoto (1995), and Hacker and Hatemi-J (2006) followed the traditional causality test, which began with Granger (1969). These tests accept the effect of positive shocks and negative shocks experienced by the variables. In other words, these are symmetric causality tests (Yılancı and Bozoklu, 2014: 213-214).

On the other hand, looking at the time dimension of the causality relationship is important in terms of examining whether causality changes over time. The time-varying causality analysis serves to illustrate the period in which causality occurs between variables. Therefore, the methodologies of both the Hacker and Hatemi-J (2006) Symmetric Causality Test and the Time-Varying Symmetric Causality Test will be examined in this study.

The Hacker and Hatemi-J (2006) Symmetric Causality Test

Hacker and Hatemi-J (2006) developed an analysis, which is a continuation of the causality test of Toda and Yamamoto (1995). They outline the causality test of Toda and Yamamoto as follows (Hacker and Hatemi-J, 2006: 1489):

- The test has an absence of pre-testing distortions.
- The test does not require variables to be stationary.
- The test is based on a standard asymptotic distribution regardless of the cointegration characteristics of the variables.
- The application of the test is simple.

Hacker and Hatemi-J (2006) examined the dimensional characteristics of the Wald statistics in the Toda-Yamamoto (1995) Causality Test and found that the test statistic was insufficient in small samples. To prevent deterioration of dimensions in small samples, the authors proposed a new test statistic (Modified-Wald). The MWALD statistics obtained by the authors based on bootstrap distributions show a much weaker deterioration of dimension compared to the results of Monte Carlo simulations performed by the authors. When the test statistic calculated in this analysis is greater than the bootstrap critical values obtained by Monte Carlo simulation, the null hypothesis claiming the absence of Granger causality is rejected (Topal, 2018: 189). The equation of the Hacker and Hatemi-J (2006) test adapted for this study can be expressed as follows:

$$\begin{bmatrix} BTCVOL_t \\ M2\_G_t \end{bmatrix} = \partial_0 + \partial_1 \begin{bmatrix} BTCVOL_{t-1} \\ M2\_G_{t-1} \end{bmatrix} + \ldots + \partial_{k+d_{max}} \begin{bmatrix} BTCVOL_{t-k+d_{max}} \\ M2\_G_{t-k+d_{max}} \end{bmatrix} + w_t \quad (2)$$

In Equation 2, the letter "k" represents the optimal lag length determined by the VAR model. Also, the maximum degree of integration between the two series is expressed by the abbreviation "d_{max}".

The optimal lag length is determined using various information criteria. Generally, if the Hannan-Quinn and Schwarz information criteria point to the same lag length, this is the optimal lag length. Furthermore, when determining optimal lag length, certain conditions must be carried out in the $VAR_{(k)}$ model. These are a normal distribution, heteroscedasticity and autocorrelation.

Occasionally, the Hannan-Quinn and Schwarz information criteria do not signal the same lag length. Hatemi-J (2003) has wanted to avoid confusion in such a situation. The author, therefore, proposed a procedure. This procedure has been referred to as the Hatemi-J Information Criterion (HJC) in the literature. If such a situation is encountered, the optimal lag length is determined by the following formula:

$$HJC = ln(|\Omega| + j\left(\frac{n^2 lnT + 2n^2 ln(lnT)}{2T}\right), j = 0......, k \quad (3)$$

The symbol (Ω) denotes the variance-covariance matrix of the error terms of the VAR model estimated by the lag length up to j. The letter "n" is the number of equations in the model and the letter "T" is the number of observations (Değer and Pata, 2017: 38).

The Time-Varying Symmetric Causality Test

The rolling window method is applied in the Time-Varying Symmetric Causality Test and the sub-sample dimension to be applied should be decided. Firstly, the sub-sample dimension up to "n" is selected in the application of the test. Then, the Hacker and Hatemi-J (2006) Causality Test is applied to the data from the first observation to the nth observation (Kamışlı et. al., 2017: 577).

The Hacker and Hatemi-J (2006) Causality Test's approaches is to examine the period as a whole. However, as stated by Tang (2008), causality relationships may change over time with the effect of economic and political events (Ertekin and Kırca, 2017: 56). A political or an economic shock in the global economy affects many indicators related to financial markets and the duration of this impact may vary with time. From this point of view, the use of a time-varying causality test focuses on the intertemporal change of causality relationships between variables. Besides, this test provides information about the stability level of a continuous causality relationship between them (Bölükbaş, 2019: 10). For this reason, it is important to use methods that take into account time-varying relationships in the studies to be carried out. To obtain different results from the traditional methods and to show that the relationships can change in different periods, the Time-Varying Symmetric Causality Test has been included in the study.

Before the Time-Varying Symmetric Causality Test is used, some criteria must be selected. Firstly, the sub-sample dimension should be selected. In this test, the sub-sample dimension is expressed as the number of windows. There is no clear technique for determining it. However, not being able to determine it correctly may cause erroneous results. In addition to this, selecting it too large or too small a sub-sample makes it difficult to obtain healthy results. Therefore, it is necessary to choose the most appropriate window number that will balance the accuracy and representativeness (Açık, et al. 2019: 7).

ANALYSIS AND FINDINGS

The analysis of the relationship between monetary growth and Bitcoin trading volume consists of three stages. In the first stage, the stationarity of the variables will be examined. In the second stage, the Hacker and Hatemi-J (2006) Causality Test will be conducted. In the third stage, the Time-Varying Causality Test will be performed to determine the causality periods between the variables. The results of the analysis have been obtained with Gauss 10 Package Program. Moreover, the necessary steps for performing the tests mentioned above have been achieved with the EViews 9.5 Package Program.

The Result of the Unit Root Test

Before starting the symmetric causality analysis, it is necessary to determine the maximum degree of integration of two variables. First of all, the stationary of the variables included in the analysis has been controlled with the Two-Break LM Unit Root Test developed by Lee and Strazicich (2003). According to Perron (1989), the regression line estimated using the sample data is different from the actual regression line in case of a structural break. This situation leads to a weakening of the estimation that is intended to be made by the stationary test. As Charemza and Deadman (1997) also remark, tests that do not include structural breaks despite structural breaks give deviant results.

The characteristic of The LM Unit Root Test is that it allows two structural breaks when performing unit root testing in the series. In The Two-Break LM Unit Root Test, the null hypothesis is accepted when the test statistic is greater than the critical value without considering their absolute values. In the case of structural breaks, it is decided that the series has a unit root. This test is one of the most advanced unit root tests. The use of this test provides an opportunity for more accurate results.

As is clear from Table 2, the M2_G series does not contain a unit root in both Model A and Model C at a 1% significance level because the test statistic value of it is less than its critical value. Looking at the structural breaks for M2_G, as Eğilmez (2017) remark, the Federal Reserve launched a new monetary expansion program called Quantitative Easing 2 (QE2), which lasted until July 2011. In September 2011, the Federal Reserve also staged an application called Operation Twist (QT). This application resembled QE and served banks by providing funds. In other words, long-term bonds and mortgage-based derivative products were taken from banks. In general, these two applications gave successful results. The breakpoints of M2_G coincide with QE2 and QT.

On the other hand, since the test statistic value of BTCVOL is less than its critical value, the null hypothesis is rejected. Therefore, when the results of Model A and Model C are examined together, it is understood that BTCVOL does not have a unit root at the level. Also, structural breaks for Bitcoin's trading volume have been observed in May 2011 and April 2018. These results show that the maximum degree of integration of the two variables is zero ($d_{max}=0$). The two-break LM Unit root test results are presented in the table below.

The Result of the Hacker and Hatemi-J (2006) Causality Test

Before applying the symmetric causality test, the optimal lag length must be selected in the VAR model. To achieve this goal, the procedure proposed by Hatemi-J (2003) has been used. This procedure suggests that the Hatemi-J information criterion should be consulted to select the optimal lag length. The optimal lag length has been calculated as one (k=1). After the necessary steps are completed, the test is started. It should also be noted that normal distribution, autocorrelation and heteroscedasticity conditions are provided. The causality test results based on leveraged bootstrap technique are presented in Table 3.

From Table 3 it is concluded that there is no evidence of any causal relationship between the variables. In other words, there is no symmetric causality relationship between M2_G and BTCVOL. This can be understood from the fact that the Wald statistics obtained with the bootstrap are smaller than the critical value.

Table 2. The results of the two-break LM unit root test

Variables	Model A			Model C		
	Test statistic	Critical value*	Breakpoint	Test statistic	Critical value*	Breakpoint
M2_G	-7,070295	-4,101000	2011-05, 2011-07	-7,940711	-5,667000	2011-05, 2011-12
BTCVOL	-5,869866	-4,101000	2011-05, 2011-12	-5,91853	-5,783000	2011-05, 2018-04

Note: The Two-Break LM Unit Root Test uses intercept (Model A) and trend and intercept (Model C) models. The models allow two structural breaks. *: It represents critical values at a 1% significance level.

The Result of the Time-Varying Symmetric Causality Test

Initially, the sub-sample dimension must be selected in this method. The number of window has been determined as 40 in this study. After selecting the sub-sample dimension, the type of information criterion, and the maximum degree of integration, the maximum number of lags and the bootstrap must be determined. The selected information criterion is the Hatemi-J information criterion (HJC). Because of using a monthly data set, 12 has been determined the maximum number of lags. 10000 bootstrap simulation has been performed. Finally, the maximum degree of integration was calculated as one above. After the completion of all steps, the results of the test are shown in Figure 2.

Figure 2 shows the causality periods from M2_G to BTCVOL. The null hypothesis of this test represents the absence of a causal relationship. The red line shows the critical value at a 10% significance level. If the probability value indicated by the green color is above the red line, there is a causal relationship between the variables in the relevant period. Accordingly, no causal relationship has been observed in the vast majority of the period covered. When both the Hacker and Hatemi-J (2006) and the Time-Varying Causality tests are evaluated together, it is seen that the two results support each other. But, there is a causal relation in a minimal period. The related table is given below.

Nevertheless, even if the duration is minimal, the Time-Varying Causality Test indicates the existence of a causal relationship between April 2019 and July 2019.

SOLUTIONS AND RECOMMENDATIONS

In general, there is no causality between M2_G and BTCVOL. But recently, there is a significant causal relationship from M2_G to BTCVOL when looking at Figure 2 and Table 4. If the results are evaluated, it is normal for investors to search for new financial assets, while uncertainty prevails in the economy. In parallel to this, the following points are recommended for investors. In response to economic uncertainty,

Table 3. The results of the Hacker and Hatemi-J (2006) causality test*

Hypothesis	Wald statistic	Critical value (1%)**	Lag***
M2_G is not the Granger cause of BTCVOL.	0,212	7,109	1
BTCVOL is not the Granger cause of M2_G.	0,461	7,243	1

Note: *: 10000 bootstrap simulation has been performed to obtain critical values. **: It represents critical values at a 1% significance level. ***: The optimal lag length has been determined with HJC.

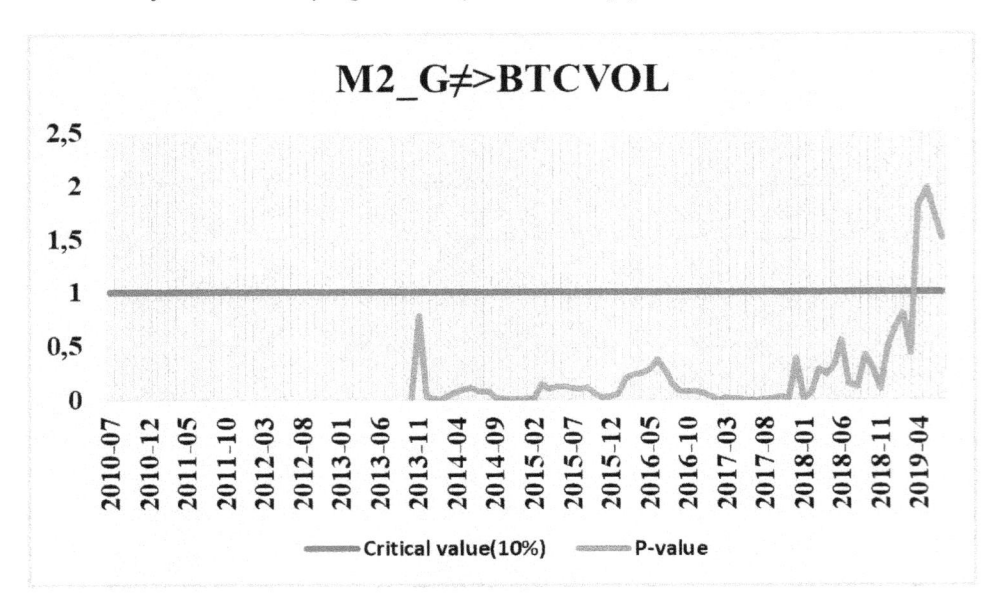

Figure 2. The result of the time-varying causality relationship from M2_G to BTCVOL

M2_G≠>BTCVOL

the Federal Reserve reacts by taking prudential measures using monetary policy instruments. At its July 2019 meeting, it decided to reduce interest rates by 25 basis points and pursued a monetary easing policy. Bitcoin investors reacted positively to this decision and the price of Bitcoin increased immediately after this decision. Bitcoin traders should consider this experience when making a decision. For example, they should take positions in advance according to possible decisions to be taken at the next the Federal Reserve meeting. They should closely monitor the market and evaluate the views of professional analysts to estimate the Federal Reserve's decision. In addition to this advice, investors should diversify their portfolio. While there is uncertainty in the economy, it is important to add other financial assets, which are seen as the safe havens by many investors, in their portfolio. It also reduces this risk.

Apart from these, Bitcoin investors should not forget that even though they rely on its technology, cryptocurrencies are traded in extremely speculative markets. Compared to any financial asset, Bitcoin is a more speculative investment tool. Investors should closely monitor not only global economic developments but also the developments in the universe of cryptocurrencies.

Bitcoin has been on the radar of many financial institutions due to both being the first cryptocurrency and dominance in the cryptocurrency market. Recently, there have been financial institutions in the United States applying for the futures transactions of Bitcoin and its trading as the Exchange Traded Fund (ETF). These developments undoubtedly affect both the institutional investors' interest in Bitcoin and its prices.

Table 4. Causality date and durations

Period	Start Date	Ending Date	Duration
1	April 2019	July 2019	4

FUTURE RESEARCH DIRECTION

After the 2008 Global Crisis, the global economy, which expanded with measures taken all over the world, began to contract in the second half of 2018 with the effect of the trade war between the USA and China. This global economic contraction continues day by day and shows its effects by increasing. As this study was written while economic uncertainty continued, the duration of the expected causal relationship seems limited. In the following periods, re-performing this analysis with different methods may provide more results that are meaningful. Also, while many parameters are affecting Bitcoin's trading volume, only monetary growth is considered here.

Compared to other financial assets, the cryptocurrency market has a very small market capacity. Besides, Bitcoin has a history of only 10 years. In this case, it is a very new financial instrument. In other words, more time is needed to ensure the confidence of other financial assets on the investor. With its development, the study subjects and sample size in this field will increase.

This research has concentrated on investors' positions towards Bitcoin if the economy is uncertain. Due to the intense contribution of current global developments to this issue, this research differs from other researches related to Bitcoin by revealing its originality. To our knowledge, this is the first study to explore a statistic relationship between US monetary growth and Bitcoin trading volume. Most important, though, it has offered a framework about this issue. This study supports other studies that treat Bitcoin as a financial instrument. It also argues that Bitcoin is a safe haven during times of economic uncertainty. Moreover, it is a modest contribution to the ongoing debates about the effects of monetary policies on Bitcoin.

CONCLUSION

While economic uncertainty in the world continues to increase day by day, there are positive developments concerning Bitcoin. Even the developed countries of the world are now aware of its existence. For example, employees in New Zealand will be able to choose to receive a part of their salary in cryptocurrency. The Bank of Japan announced that it approves of Bitcoin technology and supported it in a controlled manner. Also, recent developments will attract more institutional investors in Bitcoin. In September 2019, it is planned to establish a platform that allows a Bitcoin futures contract. Considering such developments, confidence in Bitcoin may increase if there are no extreme speculative attacks and hacking incidents. On the other hand, during this time of economic uncertainty, investors may be in search of new investment instruments to protect their wealth. Some investors are eager to add this instrument to their portfolio at a time when technology continues to develop and investors' awareness of Bitcoin is increasing. They may have started to see it as a safe haven.

The cryptocurrency economy and its technology continue to grow progressively. It is now debated whether or not a few of the existing cryptocurrencies can be adapted to the real world. For now, it can be said that Bitcoin and other cryptocurrencies exist in their universes, but they have no significant impact on the national economies. However, the opposite can also be said in this conjuncture. While there are many negative situations in the global economy, Bitcoin still exists and is capable of making its investors happy.

There are external and internal dynamics affecting Bitcoin's trading volume. However, recent developments signal that there may be a significant relationship between US monetary growth and Bitcoin trading volume due to investors' search for safe havens. When considered from this point of view, this study aims to investigate the relationship between US monetary growth and Bitcoin trading volume.

If the results obtained from Table 3 are evaluated in general terms, it is seen that US monetary growth is not the Granger cause of Bitcoin's trading volume. However, in recent months, which is characterized as a period of increasing economic uncertainty in the world, there is a causal relationship from US monetary growth to Bitcoin trading volume. This period consists of four months between April 2019 and July 2019. Recent Federal Reserve's decisions have been affecting Bitcoin investments. Investors are adding Bitcoin to their portfolios to preserve their wealth while there is economic uncertainty. Because Bitcoin has recently experienced lower volatility than before some investors are eager to buy it.

REFERENCES

Açık, A., Sağlam, B. B., & Tepe, R. (2019). Time-varying causality between exchange rate and container handling volume in Turkish ports. *Transport & Logistics: the International Journal*, *19*(46), 1–11.

Altıntaş, H., Çetintaş, H., & Taban, S. (2008). Türkiye'de bütçe açığı, parasal büyüme ve enflasyon arasındaki ilişkinin ekonometrik analizi: 1992–2006. *Anadolu University Journal of Social Science*, *8*(2), 185–208.

Anzuini, A., Lombardi, M. J., & Pagano, P. (2012). The impact of monetary policy shocks on commodity prices. *Bank of Italy Temi di Discussione Working Paper*, (851).

Baur, D. G., Hong, K., & Lee, A. D. (2018). Bitcoin: Medium of exchange or speculative assets? *Journal of International Financial Markets, Institutions, and Money*, *54*, 177–189. doi:10.1016/j.intfin.2017.12.004

Belke, A. H., Bordon, I. G., & Hendricks, T. W. (2014). Monetary policy, global liquidity and commodity price dynamics. *The North American Journal of Economics and Finance*, *28*, 1–16. doi:10.1016/j.najef.2013.12.003

Bianchi, D. (2018). Cryptocurrencies as an asset class? An empirical assessment. *An Empirical Assessment (June 6, 2018). WBS Finance Group Research Paper*.

Bjørnland, H. C., & Leitemo, K. (2009). Identifying the interdependence between US monetary policy and the stock market. *Journal of Monetary Economics*, *56*(2), 275–282. doi:10.1016/j.jmoneco.2008.12.001

Bölükbaş, M. (2019). Kamu büyüklüğü işsizliğin ve genç işsizliğin nedeni midir? Türkiye örneği. *Aydın İktisat Fakültesi Dergisi*, *3*(2), 1–17.

Bouri, E., Molnár, P., Azzi, G., Roubaud, D., & Hagfors, L. I. (2017). On the hedge and safe haven properties of Bitcoin: Is it really more than a diversifier? *Finance Research Letters*, *20*, 192–198. doi:10.1016/j.frl.2016.09.025

Charemza, W., & Deadman, D. F. (1997). *New directions in econometric practice*. Edward Elgar.

Corbet, S., Meegan, A., Larkin, C., Lucey, B., & Yarovaya, L. (2018). Exploring the dynamic relationships between cryptocurrencies and other financial assets. *Economics Letters*, *165*, 28–34. doi:10.1016/j.econlet.2018.01.004

Değer, M. K., & Pata, U. K. (2017). Türkiye'de dış ticaret ve karbondioksit salınımı arasındaki ilişkilerin simetrik ve asimetrik nedensellik testleriyle analizi. *Doğuş Üniversitesi Dergisi, 18*(1), 31–44. doi:10.31671/dogus.2018.20

Dyhrberg, A. H. (2016). Bitcoin, gold and the dollar–A GARCH volatility analysis. *Finance Research Letters, 16*, 85–92. doi:10.1016/j.frl.2015.10.008

Dyhrberg, A. H. (2016). Hedging capabilities of bitcoin. Is it the virtual gold? *Finance Research Letters, 16*, 139–144. doi:10.1016/j.frl.2015.10.025

Eğilmez, M. (2018, July 10). Para arzı nedir ve nasıl ölçülür? [Blog post]. Retrieved from http://www.mahfiegilmez.com/2018/07/para-arz-nedir-ve-nasl-olculur.html

Eğilmez, M. (2015, Sept. 5). Parasal genişleme uygulamaları. [Blog post]. Retrieved from http://www.mahfiegilmez.com/2015/09/parasal-genisleme-uygulamalar.html

Eğilmez, M. (2017, Sept. 22). Niceliksel genişlemeden niceliksel sıkılaştırmaya. [Blog post]. Retrieved from http://www.mahfiegilmez.com/2017/09/niceliksel-gevsemeden-niceliksel.html

Ertekin, M., & Kırca, M. (2017). Türkiye'de kentleşme ve iktisadi büyüme ilişkisinin zamanla değişen nedensellik analizi yöntemiyle incelenmesi. *Journal of Emerging Economies and Policy, 2*(2), 44–63.

FED. (n.d.). Policy tools. Retrieved from https://www.federalreserve.gov/monetarypolicy/policytools.htm

FED. (n.d.). What is the money supply? Is it important? Retrieved from https://www.federalreserve.gov/faqs/money_12845.htm

Frankel, J. A. (2006). *The effect of monetary policy on real commodity prices (No. w12713)*. National Bureau of Economic Research. doi:10.3386/w12713

Glaser, F., Zimmermann, K., Haferkorn, M., Weber, M. C., & Siering, M. (2014). *Bitcoin-asset or currency? Revealing users' hidden intentions. Revealing Users' Hidden Intentions (April 15, 2014)*. ECIS.

Granger, C. W. (1969). Investigating causal relations by econometric models and cross-spectral methods. *Econometrica, 37*(3), 424–438. doi:10.2307/1912791

Grauwe, P. D., & Polan, M. (2005). Is inflation always and everywhere a monetary phenomenon? *The Scandinavian Journal of Economics, 107*(2), 239–259. doi:10.1111/j.1467-9442.2005.00406.x

Guesmi, K., Saadi, S., Abid, I., & Ftiti, Z. (2019). Portfolio diversification with virtual currency: Evidence from bitcoin. *International Review of Financial Analysis, 63*, 431–437. doi:10.1016/j.irfa.2018.03.004

Gupta, R., Jurgilas, M., & Kabundi, A. (2010). The effect of monetary policy on real house price growth in South Africa: A factor-augmented vector autoregression (FAVAR) approach. *Economic Modelling, 27*(1), 315–323. doi:10.1016/j.econmod.2009.09.011

Hacker, R. S., & Hatemi-J, A. (2006). Tests for causality between integrated variables using asymptotic and bootstrap distributions: Theory and application. *Applied Economics, 38*(13), 1489–1500. doi:10.1080/00036840500405763

Hammoudeh, S., Nguyen, D. K., & Sousa, R. M. (2015). US monetary policy and sectoral commodity prices. *Journal of International Money and Finance*, *57*, 61–85. doi:10.1016/j.jimonfin.2015.06.003

Hatemi-J, A. (2003). A new method to choose optimal lag order in stable and unstable VAR models. *Applied Economics Letters*, *10*(3), 135–137. doi:10.1080/1350485022000041050

Hsiao, C. (1981). Autoregressive modelling and money-income causality detection. *Journal of Monetary Economics*, *7*(1), 85–106. doi:10.1016/0304-3932(81)90053-2

https://data.bitcoinity.org/markets/volume/30d?c=e&t=b

https://www.federalreserve.gov/datadownload/Choose.aspx?rel=H6

Ioannidis, C., & Kontonikas, A. (2008). The impact of monetary policy on stock prices. *Journal of Policy Modeling*, *30*(1), 33–53. doi:10.1016/j.jpolmod.2007.06.015

Ji, Q., Bouri, E., Gupta, R., & Roubaud, D. (2018). Network causality structures among Bitcoin and other financial assets: A directed acyclic graph approach. *The Quarterly Review of Economics and Finance*, *70*, 203–213. doi:10.1016/j.qref.2018.05.016

Kamışlı, M., Kamışlı, S., & Temizel, F. (2017). Bölgesel İslami hisse senedi endeksleri arasındaki ilişkilerin analizi. *Uluslararası Yönetim İktisat ve İşletme Dergisi*, *13*(5), 574–587.

Kesbiç, C. Y., Baldemir, E., & Bakımlı, E. (2004). Bütçe açıkları ile parasal büyüme ve enflasyon arasındaki ilişki: Türkiye için bir model denemesi. *Atatürk Üniversitesi İktisadi ve İdari Bilimler Dergisi*, *19*(1), 81–98.

Korap, L. (2011). Parasal büyüme ve tüketici enflasyonu değişim oranı arasındaki nedensellik ilişkisi üzerine bir deneme: Türkiye örneği. *Ekonometri ve İstatistik e-Dergisi*, (9), 56-74.

Lee, J., & Strazicich, M. C. (2003). Minimum Lagrange multiplier unit root test with two structural breaks. *The Review of Economics and Statistics*, *85*(4), 1082–1089. doi:10.1162/003465303772815961

Luther, W. J., & White, L. H. (2014). Can bitcoin become a major currency? *George Mason University Department of Economics Working Paper No. 14-17*

Owoye, O., & Onafowora, O. A. (2007). M2 targeting, money demand, and real GDP growth in Nigeria: Do rules apply. *Journal of Business and Public Affairs*, *1*(2), 1–20.

Patelis, A. D. (1997). Stock return predictability and the role of monetary policy. *The Journal of Finance*, *52*(5), 1951–1972. doi:10.1111/j.1540-6261.1997.tb02747.x

Perron, P. (1989). The great crash, the oil price shock, and the unit root hypothesis. *Econometrica*, *57*(6), 1361–1401. doi:10.2307/1913712

Renaud, B. (2003). Speculative behaviour in immature real estate markets, lessons of the 1997 Asia financial crisis. *Urban Policy and Research*, *21*(2), 151–173. doi:10.1080/08111140309950

Sims, C. A. (1972). Money, income, and causality. *The American Economic Review*, *62*(4), 540–552.

Tang, C. F. (2008). Wagner's law versus Keynesian hypothesis: New evidence from recursive regression-based causality approaches. *The IUP Journal of Public Finance*, *6*(4), 29–38.

Thorbecke, W. (1997). On stock market returns and monetary policy. *The Journal of Finance*, *52*(2), 635–654. doi:10.1111/j.1540-6261.1997.tb04816.x

Toda, H. Y., & Yamamoto, T. (1995). Statistical inference in vector autoregressions with possibly integrated processes. *Journal of Econometrics*, *66*(1-2), 225–250. doi:10.1016/0304-4076(94)01616-8

Topal, M. H. (2018). Türkiye'de askeri harcamalar ile ekonomik büyüme arasındaki ilişkinin bir analizi (1960-2016). *Maliye Dergisi*, *174*, 175–202.

Wikipedia. Transaction deposit. Retrieved from https://en.wikipedia.org/wiki/Transaction_deposit

Xu, X. E., & Chen, T. (2012). The effect of monetary policy on real estate price growth in China. *Pacific-Basin Finance Journal*, *20*(1), 62–77. doi:10.1016/j.pacfin.2011.08.001

Yermack, D. (2015). Is Bitcoin a real currency? An economic appraisal. In *Handbook of digital currency* (pp. 31–43). Academic Press. doi:10.1016/B978-0-12-802117-0.00002-3

Yılancı, V., & Bozoklu, Ş. (2014). Türk sermaye piyasasında fiyat ve işlem hacmi ilişkisi: Zamanla Değişen Asimetrik Nedensellik Analizi. *Ege Academic Review*, *14*(2), 211–220.

KEY TERMS AND DEFINITIONS

FED: It means the central banking system of the US.

Safe Haven: It identifies financial assets with the lowest risk of loss by investors.

Transaction Deposit: A type of deposit in a bank that can be withdrawn, transferred or otherwise used immediately by the holder without restriction or limits.

US: It is a federal constitutional republic on the continent of North America, whose citizens are called "American" and consist of fifty states and a federal territory.

Chapter 24
The Relationship Between Commodity Prices and Selected Macroeconomic Variables in Turkey:
Evidence From Fourier Cointegration Test

Mustafa Uysal
Artvin Çoruh University, Turkey

Zafer Adalı
Artvin Çoruh University, Turkey

ABSTRACT

This chapter determines whether there is a long-run relationship among oil, copper, natural gas, export figures and import figures, and BIST 100. Within this context, the study employs monthly periods from January 2006 to June 2019. ADF, Fourier ADF, and Banerjee Cointegration Test were applied. Banerjee Cointegration Test revealed that copper, oil, and natural gas and import figures move together in the long run but the existence of the long-run relationship between the selected inputs and export figures and BIST 100 has not been found. This evidence can be interpreted as the change in oil, copper, and natural gas may influence the amount of Turkish import figures.

INTRODUCTION

The notable of oil, copper and natural gas in the all developed and developing countries has received immense attention among researchers, politicians and business environments. Three of them are accepted as important inputs which can influence on the cost of production, household's welfare and even change economic structure. The sight of economics and politicians for commodity prices depends on countries' sectoral compositions, their economic development, and commodity importing or exporting

DOI: 10.4018/978-1-7998-2559-3.ch024

that's why the effects of the change in commodity prices on the economics activities is associated with the country's specifics situations. Researchers have interested in the relationship between commodity prices and the fundamentals consisting of inflation, the economic growth, industrial production indexes, trade balance, and government expenditures, etc. As we will understand, the literature is not able to achieve a consensus pertaining to the relationship between commodities and the economic activities; owing to this condition, it can be stated that studies, which investigate the effects of change in oil, copper, natural gas prices on export, imports and stock prices are very significant. In this context, the main purpose of this study is to give a policy recommendation to policymakers and investors. For this purpose, monthly data for the period between January 2006- June 2019 was evaluated by Banerjee Cointegration Test analysis. According to the results of the analysis, it will be possible to give some recommendation to these countries regarding this concept.

This study is composed of four sections. After introduction part, the second section reviews the literature. In this part, different studies related to this issue will be examined. Furthermore, third part contains research and methodology and the fourth part emphasized data. Moreover, in the fifth part, analysis results will be highlighted and eventually the final part summarizes results and emphasizes recommendation.

LITERATURE REVIEW

The studies which analyzing the effects of the change in oil, natural gas and copper prices on export, import and stock prices has been taken huge interest by researchers and there are a great number of studies in the literature. Some of these studies are presented on table 1.

For oil-exporting countries, many studies concluded that an increasing oil price is one of the important determinants affecting the current account. For example, Huntington (2015) conducted a study to inspect the effects of change in oil prices on the current account and the results achieved from regression analysis showed that an increase in oil prices is the main cause of current account surplus. As for oil-importing countries, the change in oil prices has been carefully observed by policymakers and businessman because many researchers and economics confirm that oil is an irreplaceable input, especially for oil-importing country. An increase in oil prices unequivocally leads to the depression of the economy since the increase in oil prices causes the higher cost of productions which leads to higher inflation and hence the deterioration of trade balance experiences because of lower net exports. Many studies reached the detrimental impacts of oil prices on the economics activities of oil-importing countries (Hamilton, 1983, Brown and Yücel, 1999; Burbidge and Harrison, 1984; Finn, 2000). Briefly, majority of studies emphasized that oil price shocks have a detrimental impact on economic activities. On the one hand, the current account in oil-importing countries became very sensitive to change in oil prices and many studies found results parallel to this event. For example, Bitzis et. al. (2008) conducted a study to test the relationship between oil prices and the current account in Greece. As a result of cointegration analysis, it was affirmed that oil price appears to be strong factors impacting the current account deficit. Also, Turkey is important in oil-importing countries and its economic structures are very associated with oil prices. The response of the current account to change oil prices has been very interesting topics and generally many studies by using different econometric methodology highlighted that higher oil prices raises the current account deficit for oil-importing countries (Demirbaş et. al, 2006; Karabulut and Danışoglu, 2006; Kayhan 2018; Beşel, 2017). In addition to these,, Altınbas (2013) underlined that oil price does

Table 1. Featured studies in the literature

Author	Scope	Method	Result
Faria et. al. (2009)	China	ARDL Model	It was emphasized that there is a positive correlation between Chinese exports and oil prices.
Du et. al. (2010)	China	VAR Model	Higher oil price leads to a decline in Chinese export performances.
Qianqian (2011)	China	VECM Model	The long-run negative relationship between oil price and Chinese exports is found.
Farzanegan and Markwardt (2009)	Iran	VAR Model	The relationship between industrial production indexes and oil prices is found as positive and strong.
Bitzis et. al. (2008)	Greece	Cointegration Analysis	It was found that oil prices seem to be an important factor impacting the current account deficit.
Huntington (2015)	91 countries	Regression	Oil is found as an important determinant affecting the current account.
Aristovnik (2007)	MENA Countries	Regression	Oil prices stimulate foreign trade balance.
Bayraktar	Fragile Five Countries	Regression	Oil prices are important determinants of current account deficit.
Altınbaş (2013)	Turkey	ARDL Model	It was showed that the increase in oil prices does not impair export
Başarır and Erçakar (2016)	Turkey	VAR Model	It was identified that there is a mutual relationship between crude oil prices and the current account.
Çulha et. al. (2016)	Turkey	Dynamic Panel	It was affirmed that the effects of oil prices on the exports appear to be very limited.
Aydın (2017)	Turkey	Regression	It was reported that change in oil prices has direct effect on the current account deficit.
Kayhan (2018)	Turkey	Johansen Cointegration Analysis	It was determined that a sharp increase in oil prices has a detrimental impact on the current account.
Arouri et. al. (2014)	India	Frequency Domain Causality Analysis	Oil prices are one of the main determinants for Indian trade balance
Bayat et. al. (2013)	Turkey	Frequency Domain Causality Analysis	In the long run, oil price changes do not influence on the foreign trade balance of Turkey.
Beşel (2017)	Turkey	Toda-Yamamoto Causality Analysis	It was reported that oil prices influence current account deficit.
Güngör et. al. (2016)	Turkey	GARCH	The current account deficit reduces the oil prices.
Karabulut and Danışoglu (2006)	Turkey	ECM Model	It was underlined that an increase in oil prices spurs the current account deficit.
Demirbaş et. al. (2009)	Turkey	ECM Model	Higher oil prices deteriorate the current account.
Wang et. al. (2013)	Oil Importing and Exporting Countries	SVAR Model	Higher oil price stimulates stock market prices.
Park and Ratti (2008)	The US and 13 European Countries	VAR Model	It was underlined that oil prices play an active role in the stock markets.
Basher et. al. (2012)	Emerging Economies	SVAR Model	Change in oil prices is important factors affecting stock market prices.
Killian and Park (2009)	US	VAR Model	Oil demand shocks have a greater effect on the stock market than oil supply shocks.
Apergis and Miller (2009)	8 Developed	SVAR Model	It was stated that oil market shocks have unimportant impact on the stock prices.
Basher and Sadorsky (2006)	Emerging Countries	Regression	It was emphasized that oil price risks impair the stock market returns.
Hammoudeh and Li (2005)	US, Norway, and Mexico	VECM and APT Model	It was understood that oil-related stocks are linked with oil price growth.
El-Sharif et. al. (2005)	The UK	Regression	Oil prices have a positive impact on stock market prices.
Huang et. al. (1996)	US	VAR Model	The relationship between daily oil futures returns and daily stock returns is positive for individual oil company stock returns.

continued on following page

The Relationship Between Commodity Prices and Selected Macroeconomic Variables in Turkey

Table 1. Continued

Author	Scope	Method	Result
Sadorsky (1999)	US	VAR Model	Oil prices movements are an important determinant of the stock markets.
Broadstock and Filis (2014)	US and China	Scalar-BEKK Model	It was identified that the US is more vulnerable to oil price shock than China
Papapetrou (2001)	Greece	VAR Model	It is posed that oil price is a substantial determinant of stock price movement.
Boyer and Filion (2007)	Canada	Regression	It was determined that the Canadian oil and gas companies' stock returns are positively affected by a rise in oil price
Fayyad and Daly (2011)	GCC countries the UK and USA	VAR Model	Qatar, the UAE, and the UK are seemingly more sensitive to oil price shocks than other markets' stock prices.
Zarour (2006)	5 Gulf Countries	VAR Model	An increase in oil prices leads to raising at studied countries' stock prices.
Miller and Ratti (2009)	6 OECD Countries	VECM Model	It was determined that Positive oil price shocks impair the stock market returns in the long run
Dagher and Hariri (2013)	Lebanon	VAR Model	Higher oil price is a determinant that increases stock prices.
Basher et. al. (2017)	Major Oil-Exporting Countries	Markov Switching Approach	Various oil shocks matter of stock price movement.
Narayan and Gupta (2015)	US	Regression	Stock prices are highly influenced by oil price shocks.
Degiannakis et. al. (2014)	European Countries	SVAR Model	It was identified that oil demand shocks increase stock market volatility in Europe.
Ghosh and Kanjilal (2016)	India	Threshold cointegration Test	Change in oil prices has indirectly effect on stock prices through the channel of government, inflation and exchange rates.
Salisu and Isah (2017)	Oil Exporting and Importing Countries	Non-linear Panel ARDL	Oil price shocks have asymmetrically effect on both oil-importing and exporting countries' stock prices.
Zhu et. al. (2014)	OECD and Non-OECD Countries	A Panel Threshold Cointegration	It is found that stock markets are associated with crude oil shocks.
Reboredo and Rivera-Castro (2014)	US and European Countries	Wavelets Method	It was defined that oil price shocks have no impact on stock prices in the pre-crisis period.
Lee and Zeng (2011)	G7 Countries	Quantile Regression	It was underlined that asymmetric oil price shock has largely impact on real stock returns.
Jouini and Harrathi (2014)	GCC Countries	BEKK-GARCH	Asymmetric effects of stock prices matter for GCC countries.
Asteriou and Bashmakova (2013)	Central and Eastern European Countries	Rolling Regression Method	Oil price is found as an important role in determining stock prices.
Şener et. al. (2013)	Turkey	Hidden Cointegration Test	It was found that the change in oil price affects stock prices.
İşcan (2010)	Turkey	Cointegration and Causality Analysis	Oil prices are seemingly not determinant of stock prices
Güler and Nalın (2013)	Turkey	Granger Causality Analysis	Oil prices seem to be unimportant factors influencing stock prices.
Zortuk and Bayrak (2016)	Turkey	ADL Threshold Cointegration Test	It was understood that there is a long-run the relationship between crude oil prices and stock prices.
Özmerdivanlı (2014)	Turkey	Granger Causality Analysis	There are unidirectional causalities from oil prices to stock prices.
Ünlü and Topcu (2012)	Turkey	Cointegration and Causality Analysis	It was emphasized that oil prices have a positive impact on stock prices.
Kaya and Binici (2014)	Turkey	Cointegration and Causality Analysis	It was found that oil prices are important determinants of oil related companies' stock prices.
Sandal et. al. (2017)	Turkey	Cointegration and Causality Analysis	It was defined that the relationship between stock prices and oil prices do not exist.

continued on following page

Table 1. Continued

Author	Scope	Method	Result
Akgun and Sahin (2016)	Turkey	Johansen-Juselius Cointegration Analysis	The long run relationship between Brent petrol barrel prices and BIST Industry index returns has been not found.
Acaravci et. al. (2012)	EU-15 Countries	Cointegration and Causality Analysis	There is a long-run linkage between natural gas prices and stock prices in Austria, Denmark, Finland, Germany, and Luxembourg but for other EU-15 countries.
Arshad and Bashir (2015)	Pakistan	Regression	It was found that gas price impairs stock prices.
Oberndorfer (2009)	European Countries	Regression	It was identified that stock prices are not associated with natural gas.
Ahmed (2018)	Qatar	GARCH	Natural gas has an impact on stock price and a change in natural gas prices leads to higher volatility.
Lin et. al. (2019)	China	GARCH	It was underlined that the directional causality form natural gas to the Chinese stock markets exists in crisis regime.
Gatfaoui (2016)	US	Copula Model	The linkage between natural gas and stock prices appear to unstable over time.
Makridis (2014)	East Mediterranean Countries	VAR Model	It was found that no relationship between natural gas and stock price exists.

not seem to be an important factor reducing Turkish export performance and a study made by Güngör (2016) using GARCH model posed that the current account deficit reduces the oil prices.

Naturally, as for an oil-importing country, the increase in oil prices has usually a detrimental impact on the economics activities but the Chinese economy is a unique example about the effects of oil prices on net oil importer country. Chinese phenomenon can be explained through its large labor surplus. When an increase in oil price occurs, the Chinese economy can replace oil with labor in its production function so China is less vulnerable to the oil prices than its competitors. This phenomenon is found by many studies. Another possible explanation for the positive relationship between the oil price and the economic activities, Chinese exports are not based on energy-intensive so energy inputs do not play active role in the Chinese economy on the contrary to labor; therefore, the change in oil prices or other energy commodities have little impact on the production costs. For example, Faria et. al. (2009) conducted a study for Chinese economy to explain the relationship between oil price and Chinese export by using ARDL model and they concluded that there is a positive correlation between oil prices and Chinese export. With the differences of this study, Du et. al. (2010) made a study to achieve the results of the impacts of oil prices on Chinese economy based on a monthly data from 1995:1to 2008:12 with the help of VAR model. As a result, it is concluded that oil prices dramatically impact on Chinese activities composed of economic growth and inflation but the relation is found as nonlinear. However, it is also underlined that China has not yet an influential on the world oil prices it means that the oil prices are exogenous regarding Chinese economy. Parallel to this study, Qianqian (2011) also achieved the similar findings for China by using VECM and according to the results, there is a long-run negative relationship between the oil prices and Chinese output, CPI and the total amount of net exports.

There is a great deal number of studies analyzing the relationship between changes in oil prices and stock market returns. As for oil prices and stock market activities, there are numerous studies in the literature and this interesting topic has been always on the researchers' agenda and its importance seem to continue because durations, results, magnitudes, and even causality directions differ widely depending on whether the shocks result from demand or supply, whether the econometric methodology is based on linear or nonlinear and whether the country is an oil-exporting or oil-importing.

Basher et. al. (2012) made a study to research the dynamic relationship between oil prices and stock market prices in emerging countries by using SVAR Model. According to their results, it was concluded that higher oil prices tend to reduce the stock market returns and it is also proven that an increase in emerging stock market prices is prone to increase oil prices.

The change in oil prices can be driven by oil a demand shocks, a supply shocks and a global demand shock. Each shock has different impacts on the real economic activities so Killian (2009) identified a structure framework by using VAR model to resolve the effects of each shock on real economic activities. An approach modeled by Killian (2009) has been used to examine the effect of oil price shocks on stock prices. Killian and Park (2009) use the same framework modeled by Killian (2009) to analyze the relationship between oil price shocks and US stock prices. They reported that the effects of an oil demand shock on US stock prices became more effective in case that oil shocks are driven by oil demand shocks. There is also evidence that oil demand shocks tend to depress US stock prices. Moreover, Apergis and Miller (2009) tried to achieve the results of the impacts of structural oil price shocks on the stock prices in eight advanced economies by using SVAR approach. They affirmed that oil market shocks have an unimportant impact on the stock prices. Killian approach is also applied for key selected industries stock. For example, Broadstock and Filis (2014) analyzed the reaction of US and Chinese key selected industries stock prices by using Scalar-BEKK Model and they highlighted that US stock markets are apparently more vulnerable to oil price shock than China and each sector differently response to oil price shocks.

Hammoudeh and Li (2005) tried to investigate the effects of oil price shocks on firms operating in the different sectors as well as the world capital represented by MSCI in Norway, Mexico, and US. Their econometric models are based on VECM and APT Model. According to study findings, an increase in oil price contribute to oil-related firms' stocks but higher oil prices lead to lower world capital. There is also evidence that the APT model reached an adverse relationship between the US transportation industry and the oil price in contrast with the results of VECM Model.

Park and Ratti (2008) made a study in order to understand the dynamic relationship between oil price shocks and real stock market returns in the US and 13 European countries by using VAR model. Their findings are associated with countries' specific situations. For instances, higher oil prices lead to higher stock returns in Norway and an increase in volatility of oil prices tend to depress real stock returns for many European countries, except the US. With the help of VAR and VECM Model, Fayyad and Daly (2011), Zarour (2006), Miller and Ratti (2009), Dagher and Hariri (2013), Degiannakis et. al. (2014) determined that oil price is important determinant in the prediction of stock prices parallel to Park and Ratti (2008)' findings. On the other hand, Reboredo and Rivera-Castro (2014) reached a different conclusion than oil price shocks have no effect on stock prices in the pre-crisis period by using Wavelets Method.

El-Sharih (2005) tried to define the relationship between oil prices and oil-gas sectors' equity value in the UK with the bits of help of regression. It was confirmed that there is a positive and important relationship oil prices and oil-gas sectors' equity value in the UK. Parallel to El-Sharih (2005)' findings, Boyer and Filion (2007) investigated the reaction of Canadian oil companies' stock returns to oil prices by using regression and it was identified that an increase in oil price improves oil companies' stock returns.

Huang et. al. (1996) tested the linkage between daily oil future returns and daily stock return in the US used VAR Model and they posed that oil futures returns have a positive effect on individual company stock but its effects on the S&P 500 represented as the broad-based market indices is insignificant. On the contrary to Huang et. al. (1999), Sadorksy (1999) found that the S&P 500 movement is mainly driven by the oil price movement.

Jones and Kaul (1996) using quarterly data analyzed the response of US, UK, Japanese and Canadian stock prices to oil price shocks by utilizing a standard cash-flow dividend valuation model and it was reported that the movement of US and Canada stock market prices is influenced by the oil price shocks but oil price shocks do not have impact on the UK and Japanese stock market prices.

Papapetrou (2001) conducted a study to analyze the effects of oil price on real economic activity using by VAR Model and it was found that the real economic activity, employment, stock price movement are accounted for oil price shocks.

Narayan and Gupta (2015) tried to conduct a study in order to investigate the role of oil price movement in predicting stock price in US by using monthly data spanning over 150 years (1859:10-2013:12) with the help of regression model. According to the results, it was suggested that both an increase and a decrease in oil prices are used to predict US stock returns and it is also proven that negative oil price change has a more powerful impact on US stock returns.

In addition to the linear approach, there are many studies using nonlinear test techniques to investigate the linkage between oil prices and stock prices. Basher et. al. (2017) used Markow Switching Approach in order to analyze the effects of various oil price shocks on major oil-exporting countries and many important findings are unraveled that Stock returns in Canada, Norway, Russia, Kuwait, Saudi Arabia, and the UAE is very sensitive to oil-demand shocks and oil-supply shock have largely effect on the UK, Kuwait and UAE. On the other hands, Oil price shocks do not play an active role in Mexico. Ghosh and Kanjilal (2016) conducted a study for India by using threshold cointegration test. It was identified that change in oil prices has indirectly effect on stock prices via the channel of inflation, government and exchange rates. Besides, Slisu and Isah (2017) used nonlinear panel ARDL approach to investigate the relationship between oil prices and stock prices in oil-exporting and importing countries. As a result of the test, it was posed that the effects of change in oil prices are asymmetric for both oil-exporting and importing countries. Also, Zhu et. al. (2014) made a study for OECD and Non-OECD countries by using Panel Threshold Cointegration test to analyze the relationship between oil prices and stock prices. It was highlighted that oil price seem to be important factors impacting stock markets.

In addition to them, some studies focus on the relationship between oil prices and stock prices in Turkey by using different econometric approach. For example, Kaya and Binici (2014) conducted a study by using Cointegration and Causality Analysis and they detailed that oil prices do have an impact on stock prices. Besides, Özmerdivanlı (2014), Şener et. al. (2013), Zortuk and Bayrak (2016), Akgun and Sahin (2016) reached a similar conclusion that the relationship between oil prices and stock prices exists for Turkey. However, some studies in the literature reached the different conclusion and they are reported that oil prices are not used to predict stock prices in Turkey. Besides, Ünlü and Topcu (2012) determined that oil prices spur stock prices.

Though the relationship between oil prices and stock prices have been well examined and prevailing topics in the literature, there are few studies investigated the impacts of natural gas on stock prices. On the other hand, natural gas seems to be an important energy source in the world energy market since its importance is driven by it utilized in a variety of field and areas involving industrial, power generation, residential and eventually natural gas is used as vehicle fuel also. With gaining importance for many areas, few researchers have tried to analyze the potential role of natural gas in the stock market. For instances, A study conducted by Acaravci et. al. (2012) can be accepted as a prominent study in this topic. They employed quarterly data covering the period from 1990:1 to 2008:1 by using Granger Causality and JJ cointegration analyze for the EU-15 countries. Their results indicated that there is long-run relationship between the natural gas and stock prices in Austria, Denmark, Finland, Germany, and Luxembourg though they detect any long-run relationship in the other ten EU-countries. Similiarly, Ahmed (2018) and Lin et. al. (2019) used the same methodology for different scope and they reported that natural gas price does not impact on stock prices. However, Oberndorfer (2009) conducted a study to investigate the reaction of European energy company equity prices to change in natural gas prices by using regression and it was identified that natural gas prices seem to be an unimportant factor for energy stocks. Makridis (2014) also reached a similar conclusion for East Mediterranean Countries using VAR model. Also, Arshad and Bashir (2015) suggested that an increase in natural gas prices impair stock prices in Pakistan.

As for the linkage between copper prices and stock prices as well as export-import, there are no direct studies but copper is one of the important commodities used various areas consisting of telecommunication, industry, construction, automobile, etc. ; that's why, taking into the importance of the copper in the economy, a study testing the linking between copper and stock prices as well as import-export will improve the literature. Also, natural gas is generally used to test the Dutch Disease but natural gas is irreplaceable energy and highly imported from MENA and Russia. Change in natural gas prices has a direct impact on the industries, heating cost and transportation cost so when the effects of change in natural gas prices on export, import, and stock prices will be directly examined, politicians, households, and investors can mitigate their risks.

METHODOLOGY

At this study, the long-run relationship commodities involving copper, natural gas and oil and BIST100, and export figure, and import figures, respectively. Before starting analyzing, all variables used in this study are detected whether they are stationary or not by applying standard Augment Dickey-Fuller (ADF) AND Fourier Augmented Dickey-Fuller (FADF) developed by Christopoulos & León-Ledesma (2010). First of all, all variables are used in logarithmic form then unit roots were employed in order to determine their stationary level. After obtaining the results of both ADF and FADF, the cointegration between all variables were analyzed with the help of applying the novel approach of Fourier ADL (Autoregressive Distributive Lag) cointegration test developed by Banerjje et. al. (2017).

Period, type or number of structural breaks appears to be one of the problems affecting the results of econometric analysis so Fourier unit root test enhanced by by Christopoulos and León-Ledesma (2010) (CL) is considered as powerful kinds of unit roots to eliminate these problems. FADF seems to be superior against similar tests because the numbers of unknowns as well as kinds of structural breaks can be identified by using FADF. Besides, CL Fourier unit roots involving trigonometric expression is one of other advantages since the large change is the deterministic components of variables can be revealed by using trigonometric expression. Cl Fourier unit root test equations are presented as follows: (Christopoulos ve León-Ledesma, 2010):

$$y_t = \omega_0 + \omega_1 \sin\left(\frac{2\pi k t}{T}\right) + \omega_2 \cos\left(\frac{2\pi k t}{T}\right) + \nu_t \qquad (1)$$

where t refers trend term, T is population size, π is taken as 3.1416, k represents proper frequency. In order to detect proper frequency, k is given value between 1 and 5.Subsequently, k is then selected as the optimal frequency (k^A) in the model that results in minimum the sum of the residual squares (SSR) minimum. The null hypothesis of the unit root test is detailed as follows:

$H_0: v_t = \mu_t, \mu_t = \mu_{t-1} + h_t$

Here, h_t is supposed to be a stationary process where the mean is zero, and when the optimal frequency is selected, the least squares OLS residuals are achieved using equation number (2)

$$vE = y_t + \left[\omega E_0 + \omega E_1 \sin\left(\frac{2\pi kF}{T}\right) \right] + \omega E_2 \cos\left(\frac{2\pi kF}{T}\right) \tag{2}$$

The OLS residuals obtained from the 2nd equation is employed for unit root test using equation number (3) below.

$$\Delta v_t = \alpha_1 v_{t-1} + \sum_{j=1}^{p} \beta_j \Delta v_{t-j} + u_t \tag{3}$$

Equation 3 is associated with Fourier ADF and the null hypothesis states that the series have unit. The critical values of Christopoulos and León-Ledesma (2010) are used in order test hypothesis. The acceptation of the null hypothesis means that the variables is not stationary around the deterministic trend of the break. In this approach, Becker et. al. (2006) underlined some precautions for more stable analysis that one or two frequencies appears to be sufficient to determine significant breaks in the data since more than two frequencies used in test would impair the detection power. (Yılancı ve Eriş, 2013: 24).

Banerjee et al. (2017) Fourier ADL Cointegration Test was employed to determine the possible long-term relationship between series. Banerjee et. al. (1998) added ADL approach to the cointegration approach and in accordance with this new approach, later a cointegration test based on the fourier function in the deterministic term regarding the unknown forms of nonlinear fractures linking to ADL was developed by Banerjee et. al. (2017). The model is known as FADL and is detailed as the following equation (Banerjee et. al. 2017):

$$\Delta y_{1t} = d(t) + \delta_1 y_{1,t-1} + \gamma' y_{2,t-1} + \varphi' \Delta y_{2t} + \epsilon_t \tag{4}$$

According to equation 4, γ', φ' ve y_{2t}, nx1 state vectors of parameter and explanatory variables, d(t) refers the deterministic term d(t) and the y_{1t} means the dependent variable. In order to reduce the serial correlation, it would be added the error term (ϵ_t) lagged values of the variables difference on the right side of the equation and hence the d(t) in the equation can be presented as follows:

$$d(t) = \gamma_0 + \sum_{k=1}^{q} \gamma_{1,k} \sin\left(\frac{2\pi kt}{T}\right) + \sum_{k=1}^{q} \gamma_{2,k} \cos\left(\frac{2\pi kt}{T}\right) \quad q \leq T/2 \tag{5}$$

The equation 5 showed that the usual deterministic trend consisting of constant and linear trend in γ_0 express the number of T observations, the single frequency component and the frequency of q. Furthermore, the null (H_0: $\delta_1 = 0$) states that the series are not cointegrated but alternative hypothesis (H_1:

$\delta_1 < 0$) express that the series are cointegrated. Therefore, the critical values obtained from Banerjee et al. (2017) compare with the result of the test in order to test the null hypothesis against the alternative hypothesis.

DATA

In this study, we investigate the long-run relationship between commodities involving copper, oil and natural gas and selected fundamentals comprising of export figures, import figures and BIST 100.monthly data for copper, natural gas, oil prices, BIST 100, Export and Import figures covering period from January 2006- June 2019 are taken consideration and this data was obtained from data provider ''Finnet''. Beginning period in this study is selected as January 2006 because of limited data. Moreover, all prices associated with variables used in this study are monthly data and in terms of dollar.

EMPIRICIAL RESULTS

First of all, logarithm of all variables was used and then the descriptive statistics of all variables was examined. Table 2 poses descriptive statistics of all variables analyzed in the study. According to the results, though the highest volatility belongs to natural gas and it is also observed that the export and import variables have very close volatility.

Before starting the analysis, initially, ADF test was employed to detect whether the variables used in this study are stationary or not and then Fourier ADF (FADF) unit root test was used in accordance with same purpose. The results of the ADF Unit Root Test are showed in Table 2. Considering the ADF tests, the null hypothesis is not rejected so the series have unit roots in their level forms.

Not a, b and c refer significance at the 1,5 and 10% level, respectively. The null hypothesis is that the series has a unit root. The optimal lags for ADF Test were determined by The Schwartz Information Criterion.

After obtaining the results of the standard ADF unit root test, FADF unit root test was employed to variables regarding the structural breaks. Table 4 details the FADF unit root test results for all variables and it was emphasized that all variables have unit roots at the levels but they become stationary by after taking their first differences. Then, the F test was examined to determine the significance of stationary series in order to analyze the significance of trigonometric terms. The results of the F test showed that all variables were meaningless since F statistical values of the variables less than critical values. That is to say, the series become stationary at their first differences as a consequence of FADF test are. Therefore, the standard ADF unit root test results will be considered in subsequent analyzes.

a,b and c refer significance at the 1,5 and 10% level, respectively. Values in the parenthesis present optimal lags. Critical values for the FKPSS (k =1) test were4.43, -3.85 and -3.52, respectively, at %1, %5 and 10% levels. The F-test critical values used to evaluate the significance of trigonometric terms are 64.133, 4.929 and 6.730, respectively, at %1, %5 and 10%.

After the stationary analyze, Banerjee Cointegration test was applied to test the long-run relationship between commodities consisting of copper, natural gas and oil and BIST 100 index, export and import. Table 5 presents the long-run relationship between commodities and BIST 100 index, Table 6 and commodities and export, and Table 7 shows the long-run relationship between commodities and export. Table 5, Table 6 and Table 7 detail the results obtaining from the Banerjee cointegration test below.

Not: Critical values for the Banerjee cointegration test at levels of 1%, 5% and 10% were -4.79, -4.03 and -3.65

According to the results of Banerjee Cointegration test acquired from Table 5 and Table 6, it was understood that test statistics is less than critical values in other words the null hypothesis is accepted. Therefore, there is no long-run relationship between copper, natural gas and oil prices and BIST 100 as well as export figure.

Besides, it was seen in Table 7 that the test statistics resulting from Banerjee cointegration test applied to analyze the long-run relationship between commodities and import figures is more than critical values at the levels of %10. Accordingly, it was revealed that the long-run relationship between commodities and import figures exists.

According to the results of the test statistics achieved from Banerjee cointegration tests, it was understood that a sudden change in commodities price do not play active role in the BIST 100 index and export figures in the long run but change in commodities prices has strong impact on import figures in Turkey.

SOLUTIONS AND RECOMMENDATIONS

With respect to the results, following policy recommendations will be presented in this section to build more strong Turkish economy. Firstly, the study revealed that import figures is related to commodities so Turkish economy should create alternative energy sources such as solar and wind. Also, like Chinese firms, Turkish firms should invest in energy sectors in order to reduce the burden of import. Therefore, in order to have a low volatile, sustainable GDP growth and low unemployment rate, Turkey should look for different alternatives in terms of obtaining such commodities. Otherwise there will always be negative fluctuations and in fact financial turmoil in times of inflationary periods in commodity prices.

FUTURE RESEARCH DIRECTION

Taking into this study consideration, more effective policy recommendation can be achieved by adding some extension in order to design more healthy and strong Turkish economy policy. Firstly, the study which can be composed of other commodities and energy sources such as coal, iron, electricity, solar and aluminum will result in more realistic results. Turkish firms' performance is based on change in many commodities prices so each commodity should be monitored in order to mitigate their effects. Also, change in commodity prices have a different impact on each sector since production function in each sector appear to be complicated and unique. Besides, if the study is done with a longer data set, the relationship between change in commodity prices and economic activities can be more properly investigated. Also, the study can be extended via adding other economic fundamentals such as inflation, government debt, expenditure which are important factors affecting the economy. Another significant limitation is that Banerjee co-integration test was used to detect whether there is long-run relationship between commodities and economic activities, or not. In addition to the long-run relationship, the study which can be done to investigate the short run relationship or the dynamic relationship between commodities and economic activities by using causality analyses, VAR model, VECM model and SVAR model.

Table 2. Descriptive statistics

	Lcopper	Lnaturalgas	Loil	Lexport	Limport	LBİST 100
Mean	1.095565	1.388699	4.326137	23.12643	23.53957	11.05927
Median	1.129626	1.341686	4.307166	23.19279	23.58516	11.11066
Maximum	1.499177	2.591741	4.940427	23.49312	23.86937	11.69131
Minimum	0.332894	0.537078	3.579344	22.35897	22.82074	10.08692
St. Deviation	0.220496	0.412754	0.319593	0.221199	0.221582	0.362404
Skewness	-0.862170	0.656303	-0.133139	-0.891086	-0.843531	-0.549512
Kurtosis	4.035394	2.786391	2.016652	3.240433	3.137670	2.680433
Observations	162	162	162	162	162	162

Table 3. The results of ADF unit root test

	I (0)		I (1)	
Variables	Constant	Constant and Trend	Constant	Constant and Trend
Lcopper	-2.85 (11)	-3.03 (11)	-3.90[a] (11)	-3.89[a] (11)
Lnaturalgas	-1.73 (9)	-3.49[b] (0)	-5.03[a] (8)	-5.02[a] (8)
Loil	-2.44 (1)	-2.66 (1)	-6.04[a] (4)	-6.02[a] (4)
Lexport	-2.21 (11)	-3.10 (13)	-4.23[a] (11)	-5.78[a] (10)
Limport	-3.12 (13)	-3.20 (13)	-3.01[b] (11)	-3.16[c] (11)
LBIST 100	-1.45 (10)	-3.74 (12)	-4.46[a] (13)	-4.44[a] (13)

Table 4. FADF unit root test results

Variables	Frequency (k)	Min SSR	FADF	F-statistic F(k)
Lcopper	2	5.872	-3.220[c] (11)	26.474
Lnaturalgas	1	14.700	-2.820 (0)	68.842
Loil	1	9.746	-3.137 (1)	54.643
Lexport	1	4.956	-2.949 (13)	46.866
Limport	1	4.840	-4.550 (13)	50.332
LBIST 100	1	8.871	-2.400 (10)	109.100
ΔLcopper	4	1.034	-4.607[a] (11)	3.182
ΔLnaturalgas	5	2.693	-5.292[a] (8)	1.565
ΔLoil	4	1.249	-6.398[a] (4)	2.638
ΔLexport	4	2.090	-6.400[a] (10)	0.365
ΔLimport	4	1.795	-3.877[a] (11)	1.347
ΔLBIST 100	5	0.864	-4.245[a] (13)	3.466

Table 5. Banerjee cointegration test results

Frequency	Min SSR	Banerjee Cointegration test Statistics	Independent Variables	Lag of Independent Variables
4	-2.382	-3.009	Lcopper	3
			Lnaturalgas	1
			Loil	1

Table 6. Banerjee cointegration test results

Frequency	Min SSR	Banerjee Cointegration test Statistics	Independent Variables	Lag of Independent Variables
1	-1.947	-3.850	Lcopper	1
			Lnaturalgas	1
			Loil	1

Note: Critical values for the Banerjee cointegration test at levels of 1%, 5% and 10% were 5.17, -4.51 and. -4.17

Table 7. Banerjee cointegration test results

Frequency	Min SSR	Banerjee Cointegration test Statistics	Independent Variables	Lag of Independent Variables
1	-1.987	-4.418	Lcopper	1
			Lnaturalgas	1
			Loil	1

Note: Critical values for the Banerjee cointegration test at levels of 1%, 5% and 10% were -5.17, -4.51 and -4.17.

Some of the limitations that designed this study are presented above. Therefore, when further studies can regard these constraints and expand their studies in terms of this direction, more appropriate results can be obtained and policy makers, households and business environment are able to minimize risks.

CONCLUSION

Copper, oil and natural gas are substantial inputs for production and economic growth in a country and the level of industrialization of countries is a significant determinant of the demand for these products. Insufficiency of all these inputs in the economy results in the import of the products. Eventually, the stock prices, the export and the import figures of the countries are expected to be linked to the change in the prices of these products.

In this study, it has been tried to test the long-run relationship between commodities involving copper, oil and natural gas and selected fundamentals comprising of export figures, import figures and BIST 100.Monthly data for copper, natural gas, oil prices, BIST 100, Export and Import figures covering the period from January 2006- June 2019 were taken consideration. Then, standard ADF unit root test and Fourier ADF unit root test were employed and it was emphasized that all variables used in this study have unit roots at their level and after taking first differences, they become stationary. After the stationary process, the existence of long-run relationship was analyzed by using Banerjee cointegration test. The results of the test showed that the existence of a the long-run relationship between selected inputs and BIST 100 and export figures has been not detected but there is long-run relationship copper, natural gas and oil prices and import figures; in other words, selected inputs comprising of copper, natural gas and oil prices and import figures move together in the long run. As a result, it can be said that the amount of copper, natural gas and oil are significant factors affecting the amount of Turkish imports figures. In other words, existence of a long run relationship can be considered as a proof for the general consensus which says to have a healthy and sustainable GDP growth Turkey, as a commodity poor country, need raw materials. Absence of such commodities will result a strong negative hit for Turkey in terms of production, unemployment and inflationary pressures. Therefore, in order to have a low volatile, sustainable GDP growth and low unemployment rate, Turkey should look for different alternatives in terms of obtaining such commodities. Otherwise there will always be negative fluctuations and in fact financial turmoil in times of inflationary periods in commodity prices.

All in all, when interpreting export figures or investing in BIST 100, it is assumed to consider other commodities prices or economic fundamentals associated with BIST 100 and export rather than copper, oil and natural gas. As for import figures, the prices of copper, natural gas and oil should be monitored.

REFERENCES

Acaravci, A., Ozturk, I., & Kandir, S. Y. (2012). Natural gas prices and stock prices: Evidence from EU-15 countries. *Economic Modelling, 29*(5), 1646–1654. doi:10.1016/j.econmod.2012.05.006

Ahmed, W. M. (2018). On the interdependence of natural gas and stock markets under structural breaks. *The Quarterly Review of Economics and Finance, 67,* 149–161. doi:10.1016/j.qref.2017.06.003

Akgun, A., & Sahin, I. E. (2016). Effects of oil prices fluctuation on stock returns of the industry Sector Firms: Borsa Istanbul Industry Index Application. *On Designs of Rotating Savings and Credit Associations,* 121.

Altıntaş, H. (2013). Türkiye'de petrol fiyatları, ihracat ve reel döviz kuru ilişkisi: ARDL sınır testi yaklaşımı ve dinamik nedensellik analizi. *Uluslararası Yönetim İktisat ve İşletme Dergisi, 9*(19), 1–30.

Apergis, N., & Miller, S. M. (2009). Do structural oil-market shocks affect stock prices. *Energy Economics, 31*(4), 569–575. doi:10.1016/j.eneco.2009.03.001

Aristovnik, A. (2007). Short-and medium-term determinants of current account balances in Middle East and North Africa countries.

Arouri, M., Tiwari, A., & Teulon, F. (2014). Oil prices and trade balance: A frequency domain analysis for India. *Economic Bulletin, 34*(2), 663–680.

Arshad, R., & Bashir, A. (2015). Impact of oil and gas prices on stock returns: Evidence from Pakistan's energy intensive industries. *International Review of Social Sciences*, *3*(4), 156–168.

Asteriou, D., & Bashmakova, Y. (2013). Assessing the impact of oil returns on emerging stock markets: A panel data approach for ten Central and Eastern European Countries. *Energy Economics*, *38*, 204–211. doi:10.1016/j.eneco.2013.02.011

Aydın, G. K. (2017). Ödemler dengesi ve cari açık: Türkiye'de 2014-2016 yılları arsında cari açık ve petrol fiyatları etkilişimi. *Fırat Üniversitesi Uluslararası İktisadi ve İdari Bilimler Dergisi*, *1*(2), 27–66.

Banerjee, A., Dolado, J., & Mestre, R. (1998). Error correction mechanism tests for cointegration in a single equation framework. *Journal of Time Series Analysis*, *19*(3), 267–283. doi:10.1111/1467-9892.00091

Banerjee, P., Arcabic, V., & Lee, H. (2017). Fourier ADL cointegration test to approximate smooth breaks with new evidence from crude oil market. *Economic Modelling*, *67*, 114–124. doi:10.1016/j.econmod.2016.11.004

Başarır, Ç., & Erçakar, M. E. (2016). An analysis of the relationship between crude oil prices, current account deficit and exchange rates: Turkish experiment. *International Journal of Economics and Finance*, *8*(11), 48. doi:10.5539/ijef.v8n11p48

Basher, S. A., Haug, A. A., & Sadorsky, P. (2012). Oil prices, exchange rates and emerging stock markets. *Energy Economics*, *34*(1), 227–240. doi:10.1016/j.eneco.2011.10.005

Basher, S. A., Haug, A. A., & Sadorsky, P. (2017). The impact of oil-market shocks on stock returns in major oil-exporting countries: a Markov switching approach. Available at *SSRN 3046052*.

Basher, S. A., & Sadorsky, P. (2006). Oil price risk and emerging stock markets. *Global Finance Journal*, *17*(2), 224–251. doi:10.1016/j.gfj.2006.04.001

Bayat, T., Şahbaz, A., & Akçacı, T. (2013). Petrol fiyatlarının dış ticaret açığı üzerindeki etkisi: Türkiye örneği. *Erciyes Üniversitesi İktisadi ve İdari Bilimler Fakültesi Dergisi*, (42), 67-90.

Bayraktar, Y., Taha, E., & Yildiz, F. (2016). A causal relationship between oil prices current account deficit, and economic growth: an empirical analysis from fragile five countries. *Ecoforum Journal*, *5*(3).

Becker, R., Enders, W., & Lee, J. (2006). A stationarity test in the presence of an unknown number of smooth Breaks. *Journal of Time Series Analysis*, *27*(3), 381–409. doi:10.1111/j.1467-9892.2006.00478.x

Beşel, F. (2017). Oil prices affect current account deficit: Empirical evidence from Turkey. *Journal of Applied Research in Finance and Economics*, *3*(2), 13–21.

Bitzis, G., Paleologos, J. M., & Papazoglou, C. (2008). The determinants of the Greek current account deficit: The EMU experience. *Journal of International and Global Economic Studies*, *1*(1), 105–122.

Boyer, M. M., & Filion, D. (2007). Common and fundamental factors in stock returns of Canadian oil and gas companies. *Energy Economics*, *29*(3), 428–453. doi:10.1016/j.eneco.2005.12.003

Broadstock, D. C., & Filis, G. (2014). Oil price shocks and stock market returns: New evidence from the United States and China. *Journal of International Financial Markets, Institutions and Money, 33,* 417–433. doi:10.1016/j.intfin.2014.09.007

Brown, S. P., & Yücel, M. (2000). Oil prices and the economy. *Southwest Economy,* (Jul), 1-6.

Burbidge, J., & Harrison, A. (1984). Testing for the effects of oil-price rises using vector autoregressions. *International Economic Review, 25*(2), 459–484. doi:10.2307/2526209

Christopoulos, D. K., & Leon-Ledesma, M. A. (2010). Smooth breaks and non-linear mean reversion: Post-bretton woods real exchange rates. *Journal of International Money and Finance, 29*(6), 1076–1093. doi:10.1016/j.jimonfin.2010.02.003

Çulha, O. Y., Özmen, M. U., & Yılmaz, E. (2016). Impact of oil price changes on Turkey's exports. *Applied Economics Letters, 23*(9), 637–641. doi:10.1080/13504851.2015.1095993

Dagher, L., & El Hariri, S. (2013). The impact of global oil price shocks on the Lebanese stock market. *Energy, 63,* 366–374. doi:10.1016/j.energy.2013.10.012

Degiannakis, S., Filis, G., & Kizys, R. (2014). The effects of oil price shocks on stock market volatility: Evidence from European data. *Energy Journal,* 35–56.

Demirbaş, M., Türkay, H., & Türkoğlu, M. (2009). Petrol fiyatlarındaki gelişmelerin Türkiye'nin cari açığı üzerine etkisinin analizi. *Süleyman Demirel Üniversitesi İktisadi ve İdari Bilimler Fakültesi Dergisi, 14*(3), 289–299.

Du, L., Yanan, H., & Wei, C. (2010). The relationship between oil price shocks and China's macroeconomy: An empirical analysis. *Energy Policy, 38*(8), 4142–4151. doi:10.1016/j.enpol.2010.03.042

El-Sharif, I., Brown, D., Burton, B., Nixon, B., & Russell, A. (2005). Evidence on the nature and extent of the relationship between oil prices and equity values in the UK. *Energy Economics, 27*(6), 819–830. doi:10.1016/j.eneco.2005.09.002

Faria, J. R., Mollick, A. V., Albuquerque, P. H., & León-Ledesma, M. A. (2009). The effect of oil price on China's exports. *China Economic Review, 20*(4), 793–805. doi:10.1016/j.chieco.2009.04.003

Farzanegan, M. R., & Markwardt, G. (2009). The effects of oil price shocks on the Iranian economy. *Energy Economics, 31*(1), 134–151. doi:10.1016/j.eneco.2008.09.003

Fayyad, A., & Daly, K. (2011). The impact of oil price shocks on stock market returns: Comparing GCC countries with the UK and USA. *Emerging Markets Review, 12*(1), 61–78. doi:10.1016/j.ememar.2010.12.001

Finn, M. G. (2000). Perfect competition and the effects of energy price increases on economic activity. *Journal of Money, Credit, and Banking, 32*(3), 400–416. doi:10.2307/2601172

Gatfaoui, H. (2016). Linking the gas and oil markets with the stock market: Investigating the US relationship. *Energy Economics, 53,* 5–16. doi:10.1016/j.eneco.2015.05.021

Ghosh, S., & Kanjilal, K. (2016). Co-movement of international crude oil price and Indian stock market: Evidences from nonlinear cointegration tests. *Energy Economics, 53*, 111–117. doi:10.1016/j.eneco.2014.11.002

Güler, S., & Nalın, H. T. (2013). *Petrol fiyatlarının IMKB endeksleri üzerindeki etkisi.* Ekonomik ve Sosyal Araştırmalar Dergisi.

Güngör, S., Sönmez, L., Korkmaz, Ö., & Karaca, S. S. (2016). Petrol fiyatlarındaki değişimlerin Türkiye'nin cari işlemler açığına etkileri. *Maliye ve Finans Yazıları*, (106), 29-48.

Hamilton, J. D. (1983). Oil and the macroeconomy since World War II. *Journal of Political Economy, 91*(2), 228–248. doi:10.1086/261140

Hammoudeh, S., & Li, H. (2005). Oil sensitivity and systematic risk in oil-sensitive stock indices. *Journal of Economics and Business, 57*(1), 1–21. doi:10.1016/j.jeconbus.2004.08.002

Huang, R. D., Masulis, R. W., & Stoll, H. R. (1996). Energy shocks and financial markets. *Journal of Futures Markets: Futures, Options, and Other Derivative Products, 16*(1), 1–27. doi:10.1002/(SICI)1096-9934(199602)16:1<1::AID-FUT1>3.0.CO;2-Q

Huntington, H. G. (2015). Crude oil trade and current account deficits. *Energy Economics, 50*, 70–79. doi:10.1016/j.eneco.2015.03.030

İşcan, E. (2010). Petrol fiyatının hisse senedi piyasası üzerindeki etkisi. *Maliye Dergisi, 158*, 607–617.

Jones, C. M., & Kaul, G. (1996). Oil and the stock markets. *The Journal of Finance, 51*(2), 463–491. doi:10.1111/j.1540-6261.1996.tb02691.x

Jouini, J., & Harrathi, N. (2014). Revisiting the shock and volatility transmissions among GCC stock and oil markets: A further investigation. *Economic Modelling, 38*, 486–494. doi:10.1016/j.econmod.2014.02.001

Karabulut, G., & Danışoğlu, A. Ç. (2006). Türkiye'de cari işlemler açığının büyümesini etkileyen faktörler. *Gazi Üniversitesi İktisadi ve İdari Bilimler Fakültesi Dergisi, 8*(1), 47–63.

Kaya, A., & Binici, Ö. (2014). BIST kimya, petrol, plastik endeksi hisse senedi fiyatları ile petrol fiyatları arasındaki ilişkinin incelenmesi. *Cumhuriyet Üniversitesi İktisadi ve İdari Bilimler Dergisi, 15*(1), 383–395.

Kayhan Unutur, P. (2018). *The effect of crude oil prices on the foreign trade deficit-case of Turkey (2000-2015)* (Master's thesis, Dogus University Institute of Social Science).

Kilian, L. (2009). Not all oil price shocks are alike: Disentangling demand and supply shocks in the crude oil market. *The American Economic Review, 99*(3), 1053–1069. doi:10.1257/aer.99.3.1053

Kilian, L., & Park, C. (2009). The impact of oil price shocks on the US stock market. *International Economic Review, 50*(4), 1267–1287. doi:10.1111/j.1468-2354.2009.00568.x

Lee, C. C., & Zeng, J. H. (2011). The impact of oil price shocks on stock market activities: Asymmetric effect with quantile regression. *Mathematics and Computers in Simulation, 81*(9), 1910–1920. doi:10.1016/j.matcom.2011.03.004

Lin, L., Zhou, Z., Liu, Q., & Jiang, Y. (2019). Risk transmission between natural gas market and stock markets: Portfolio and hedging strategy analysis. *Finance Research Letters*, *29*, 245–254. doi:10.1016/j.frl.2018.08.011

Makridis, C. A. (2014). *Measuring the impact of oil and gas price volatility on East Mediterranean stock markets*. Theses, Dissertations, and Projects.

Miller, J. I., & Ratti, R. A. (2009). Crude oil and stock markets: Stability, instability, and bubbles. *Energy Economics*, *31*(4), 559–568. doi:10.1016/j.eneco.2009.01.009

Narayan, P. K., & Gupta, R. (2015). Has oil price predicted stock returns for over a century? *Energy Economics*, *48*, 18–23. doi:10.1016/j.eneco.2014.11.018

Oberndorfer, U. (2009). Energy prices, volatility, and the stock market: Evidence from the Eurozone. *Energy Policy*, *37*(12), 5787–5795. doi:10.1016/j.enpol.2009.08.043

Özmerdivanlı, A. (2014). Petrol fiyatlari ile Bist 100 endeksi kapaniş fiyatlari arasindaki ilişki. *Akademik Bakış Uluslararası Hakemli Sosyal Bilimler Dergisi*, (43).

Papapetrou, E. (2001). Oil price shocks, stock market, economic activity and employment in Greece. *Energy Economics*, *23*(5), 511–532. doi:10.1016/S0140-9883(01)00078-0

Qianqian, Z. (2011). The impact of international oil price fluctuation on China's economy. *Energy Procedia*, *5*, 1360–1364. doi:10.1016/j.egypro.2011.03.235

Reboredo, J. C., & Rivera-Castro, M. A. (2014). Wavelet-based evidence of the impact of oil prices on stock returns. *International Review of Economics & Finance*, *29*, 145–176. doi:10.1016/j.iref.2013.05.014

Sadorsky, P. (1999). Oil price shocks and stock market activity. *Energy Economics*, *21*(5), 449–469. doi:10.1016/S0140-9883(99)00020-1

Salisu, A. A., & Isah, K. O. (2017). Revisiting the oil price and stock market nexus: A nonlinear Panel ARDL approach. *Economic Modelling*, *66*, 258–271. doi:10.1016/j.econmod.2017.07.010

Sandal, M., Çemrek, F., & Yıldız, Z. (2017). Bist 100 endeksi ile altın ve petrol fiyatları arasındaki fiyatları arasındaki nedensellik ilişkisinin incelenmesi *Çukurova Üniversitesi Sosyal Bilimler Enstitüsü Dergisi*, *26*(3), 155-170.

Şener, S., Yılancı, V., & Tıraşoğlu, M. (2013). Petrol fiyatları ile Borsa İstanbul kapanış fiyatları arasındaki saklı ilişkinin analizi. *Sosyal Ekonomik Araştırmalar Dergisi*, *13*(26), 231–248.

Ünlü, U., & Topcu, M. (2012). Petrol fiyatları hisse senedi piyasalarını doğrudan etkiler mi: İMKB örneği. *İktisat İşletme ve Finans*, *27*(319), 75-88.

Wang, Y., Wu, C., & Yang, L. (2013). Oil price shocks and stock market activities: Evidence from oil-importing and oil-exporting countries. *Journal of Comparative Economics*, *41*(4), 1220–1239. doi:10.1016/j.jce.2012.12.004

Yılancı, V., & Eris, Z. A. (2013). Purchasing power parity in African countries: further evidence from fourier unit root tests based on linear and nonlinear models. *The South African Journal of Economics*, *81*(1), 20–34. doi:10.1111/j.1813-6982.2012.01326.x

Zarour, B. A. (2006). Wild oil prices, but brave stock markets! The case of GCC stock markets. *Operations Research*, *6*(2), 145–162. doi:10.1007/BF02941229

Zhu, H. M., Li, R., & Li, S. (2014). Modelling dynamic dependence between crude oil prices and Asia-Pacific stock market returns. *International Review of Economics & Finance*, *29*, 208–223. doi:10.1016/j.iref.2013.05.015

Zortuk, M., & Bayrak, S. (2016). Ham petrol fiyat şokları-hisse senedi piyasası ilişkisi: ADL eşik değerli koentegrasyon testi. *Eskişehir Osmangazi Üniversitesi İİBF Dergisi*, *11*(1), 7–22.

KEY TERMS AND DEFINITIONS

Cointegration Analysis: It aims to determine whether the series are cointegrated in the long run or not.

Chapter 25
From the Working Order of Akhi–Tradesmen Organization to Economic Geography:
Regional Production, Competition, and Tanner Tradesmen

Çiğdem Gürsoy
Istinye University, Turkey

ABSTRACT

It is possible to take the concepts of economic geography, regional production, and competition, often mentioned nowadays, back to the transition to the established order in the historical process, in other words, to the agricultural revolution. However, systematically developing and implementing methods was started by Ahi Evran about 800 years ago. The working order of the Akhi-Tradesmen Organization created by Evran, based on the understanding of the economy will serve the human, not human to economy, bears a resemblance to today's agglomeration system. The fact that production factors, which are agglomerated in a specified geographical area, work with optimum efficiency spurs competitiveness. Within this framework, this chapter reveals the implementation of regional agglomeration model in Ottoman territories in historical process, which is discussed in the economic geography studies. In addition, within the scope of institutionalization, the period spent by organization of Akhi-Tradesmen in the Ottoman Empire will be mentioned.

INTRODUCTION

Regional agglomeration, which is one of the main areas of economic geography studies that has started to increase since the middle of 20th century, has focused on getting optimum efficiency with the least possible use of natural resources from the start of production date until the time it reaches the customer. Regional production, in other words, regional agglomeration traces were investigated in the past, and the

DOI: 10.4018/978-1-7998-2559-3.ch025

Akhi-Tradesmen Organization as an economic organization model in the Seljuk Dynasty was encountered 800 years ago. After the Seljuks, the organization continued its existence in the Ottoman Empire and over time, it became a center of the production of goods and services by becoming tradesmen associations with laws after some arrangements. Considering the fact that the courtiers, senior staff and almost everyone except the catechism class were registered in a branch of tradesmen, the limits of extensiveness will be better understood.

Due to the assemblage of the tradesmen in the same region, it is easier to follow up the stages of production from raw material procurement to finished goods, and on the other hand, a timely intervention on possible disruptions in the process is provided. It is understood that the sustainability of the system is supported by the positive economic exogeneities it produces in addition to its internal advantages. Within this framework, the tradesmen's/producer's backward linkages with raw material and intermediate goods suppliers, forward linkages with merchants and retail end sellers contribute to expand the boundaries of regional agglomeration. Furthermore, the desire for a qualified workforce, bring with it the training of expert staff in the work of producers with knowledge. This is for the benefit of both individual producers and the professional association established in the same region. As it is seen, agglomeration is interrelated and supportive, in other words, it is a collaborative economic formation. In addition, regional agglomeration in economic geography studies is seen as a remarkable element of competition.

It was determined that the regional agglomeration model, where business partnerships and competition nourish each other, is valid within the Ottoman trades system. Considering the points where the tanner tradesmen, which are taken as an example in the study, are examined, it is seen that there are slaughterhouses and butcher's trades in the immediate vicinity. Warehouses were built to store the tanned leather according to the density of tradesmen gathered in five different regions in İstanbul. The distribution of raw materials from butchers and tanner tradesmen required a more complicated grouping. The leather tanned by tanner tradesmen is distributed to tradesmen such as shoemakers, binders, saddlers, whippers, who process the leather different. In addition to this, the meat of the animal was distributed to sheep, lamb, goat butchers, the animal fat to candlemakers, and the offal part of the animal to the different tradesmen such as soup sellers and sellers of liver. (Kala, 1992) Such horizontal and vertical organizations have helped the tradesmen to exist and make each other sustainable, and have developed a control mechanism. This mechanism has the characteristic preventing unfair competition between the organized tradesmen in themselves and the associations of the same tradesmen established in different regions.

In this context, the aim of this study is to examine the regional agglomeration model, which is discussed in economic geography studies, on Ottoman tradesmen in order to ensure optimum production efficiency. As an example, tanner tradesmen and their sub-associations will be discussed, micro, meso and macro regularisations will be mentioned, and information about where the regional professional agglomerations are located in İstanbul will be presented. It will focus on the creation of sub-professional associations in micro-scale, the division of labor between the associations in the agglomeration regions located in the meso-scale cities, and how the cross-sectoral cooperation is provided in these regions in macro-scale, raw material procurement and product distribution. The study, which is carried out on the documents obtained from the records of Ottoman archives, will point out that the historical trade axes, in other words, the regional trade organization areas, have not lost their old positions.

In the research done upon the related topic up to now, economic geography, regional production and competition issues and forms of Akhi-Tradesmen organization are generally handled alone. The study aims to draw attention to the gap in interdisciplinary fields by bringing all three issues together under the same roof. In this way, the Ottoman system of provisionalism arranged on the regional basis will be compared to today's location/region-based production system known also as economic geography.

Within this framework, before the 2000s, it is seen that Akhi-Tradesmen organization is generally examined from the historical perspective under the titles of Akhi philosophy, work and professional ethics, and the organization of tradesmen etc. In the following years, it has been determined that these titles are discussed in terms of today's concepts as marketing, quality management, competition, aggregation, poverty and unemployment. Muhittin Şimşek's examination of Total Quality Management study through Akhism is one of the first examples of interdisciplinary work. (Şimşek, 2002)

In a study conducted on the same issue in 2018, it was mentioned that the concept of Total Quality Management was first appeared in 1957 and its effective date was 1962 in Japan, much earlier than that in 13th century, it was used very broadly with emphasis on professional ethics. In the system, a human and value-oriented approach was exhibited, and it was pointed out that quality should be adopted not only in business life, but also as a philosophy of life. As a result, based on the philosophy of Akhism, 12 item Turkish Quality Management System principles were proposed. (Karatop & Kubat, 2018) It was seen that the structures of this study were laid out in the 2011 declaration of Karatop and Kubat. (Karatop, Karahan, & Kubat, 2011)

In another study in 2011, the concepts of economy-marketing and business, and the 21st century markets of the Akhi-Tradesmen Organizations were associated. It is explained how the marketing concepts come from 4P to 4C, and its historical background can be found in the philosophy of Akhism in the 13th century. (Erbaşı & Ersöz, 2011) In other words, one of the marketing strategies (4P) focused on the similarities of customer oriented 4C's "customer is always right" oriented Akhi-Tradesmen organizations. It is stated that when Akhism philosophy is examined closely, it will be useful in finding solutions to the problems of enterprises.

In the same year in another study, the importance of Akhism principles' tacit knowledge between craftsman and tradesman in creating a sustainable advantage in today's competitive conditions is emphasized. Doğan described the tacit knowledge in the present day, where competition often brings imitation to the forefront, as *"do not know more than you can tell, write and explain"*. In the study, it was stated that the tacit knowledge, which cannot be symbolized because it is not based on formulas, stems from long-term experience and accumulation, and covers 90% of our knowledge. This 90% was claimed to be the basis of innovation and creativity, in other words, social capital. (Doğan, 2011)

In a study in 2013, aims to determine the place of Akhism principles and implementations in the success of enterprises. It is stated that today's competitive market implementations increase bribery, unemployment and poverty in society. In order to prevent this, it is pointed out that global enterprises should be based on ethical values day by day, and they should take care of the interests of the entire society as well as their own interests. By this means, it was determined that production and distribution would be more egalitarian, in other words, resource productivity would be achieved. (Soysal, 2013)

Eraslan and Güngören's studies in 2013 are about the journey of the aggregation in economic history. It is stated that the first aggregation examples were seen in Akhi associations. They pointed out that the associations had many elements such as cultural norms, competing companies while cooperatig with each other, interrelated institutions, specialised producers, the people who make the standards and audits, institutions producing information, educational institution. In this context, Jingdezhen's ceramic and porcelain production, which is the first given example of aggregation in history, and the sericulture in Jiangsu are not aggregation, but consists of only small unit transaction. (Eraslan & Güngören, 2013)

In this study, the concept of economic geography, which brings together the concepts of regional agglomeration and competition under the same roof, will be examined in the example of tanner tradesmen in the historical process of İstanbul.

Regional Agglomeration, Competition and Economic Geography

The concept of regional agglomeration in the economic sense was laid by Marshall's article, entitled "Industrial Regions and External Economies (1890-1920)", published in the early 20th century. The area Marshall calls industrial regions is a geographic location created by the regional agglomeration of small firms with similar characteristics. In addition, the agglomerations in these regions bring local and specialized labor pool, division of labor, low-priced and simple logistics services, and easy access to commercial and technical information etc. (Paul, 2012)

Economic activity concentrations have expedited the information flow, face-to-face interactions, the creation of talented workforce, in brief, they have facilitated the development of social capital.

After 1970s, the political, social, economic, environmental and institutional disadvantages of the industrial system based on mass production began to emerge. Unemployment growth is one of them, perhaps the most important one. The increase in unemployment triggered new models of organization, which included small and medium-sized enterprises as well as big business. At this stage, there has been a strong shift to regional agglomerations, from mass production based on vertical integration to flexible production, and from independent firm-based systems to regional network based systems. (Öcal & Uçar, 2011) The concept of regional network is used for sectors that share a certain geographical area. These agglomerations play a role in increasing the productivity of the sectors with low added value, while bringing the competiveness of the sectors with high added value into the forefront in the region.

In the 1990s, Michael Porter added the concepts of cluster and competition to regional agglomeration. According to Porter, the cluster is the geographic agglomeration of firms that are both competitive and cooperating in the same business segment, suppliers specialized in a particular field, service providers, firms in the relevant sectors and the related institutions. The main three topics on the road from agglomeration to cluster are; regional economic competition, specialization and cooperation. It has been determined that productivity increases with the participation of competition in specialization and cooperation that often take place in the regional agglomeration. With the contribution of competition, cluster programs are becoming more visible day by day due to income growth.

Competition;

- It increases the productivity of the enterprises established by clustering method.
- It leads innovation that will increase productivity and generate new products in the future.
- It encourages the emergence of new business areas that expand and strengthen the cluster itself. (Eraslan Hakkı, 2008)

It is also possible to see the competition-cluster interaction under three topics in the competition analysis. In the analysis known as the diamond model, all factors are assumed to be related with each other and among others. The firm's strategy and competitiveness, factor conditions, relevant-supportive industries and the state, in short, all major variables of the sector are handled together. (Eraslan & Dönmez, 2017)

İstanbul tanner tradesmen the sample area of the research, has agglomerated in five different regions considering various factors such as raw material procurement, lojistics conditions, the presence of the

From the Working Order of Akhi-Tradesmen Organization to Economic Geography

army (a significant part of the leather demand is used for military supplies), overpopulation of the city, access to financial needs and trained personnel. Moreover, due to agglomeration, low-priced and immediate access to production factors has played a role in cost reduction. The presence of butchers from which tanner tradesmen procure raw materials and tradesmen groups such as shoemakers, binders, leather bottle makers, saddler, who use processed leather as raw materials, retail traders and merchants in the same region, can be seen as supportive institutions. The efforts of all these sectors on quality, service and product differentiation in order to be sustainable bring about competition, in other words, innovativeness.

Within the scope of regional agglomeration, firms are the producers of external demands while they are also customers of each other. These demands are spread through mutual trade relations in all firms, and affect many firms and industries in the region. Mutual interactions affect both the existing market and intraregional demand. (Öcal & Uçar, 2011)Butchers are customers of drovers, tanner tradesmen are butchers', saddlers are tanner tradesmen's and leather bottle makers are saddlers'. The saddlers, who are the customers of tanner tradesmen, are the producers of coachman tradesmen. Especially in times of war, the demand for processed leather is highter than usual and this affects all tradesmen producing munitions of war associated with leather, particularly drovers. Intermediaries, which are one of the important elements of rise in price in the system, were eliminated and it was ensured that the products were sent directly to the market or to new tradesmen organizations within the region for processing.

In the 2000s, the necessity of explaining economic relations of regional agglomerations, focusing on the causalities, evaluating the results and establishing connections with different production units outside the region started economic geography studies. Local economic balances and geographical structures that emerge at different stages of economic development or in different institutional settings vary. Economic geography, which tries to explain and predict local economic relations by establishing various theoretical models on these main problems, is defined as a special professional field of general economics on the need. The question to be answered at this stage is why regions and cities specialize in different economic efficiencies? (Küçüker, 2000) Krugman, one of the pioneers of the issue, defined three main reasons for regional agglomeration by calling it localization. It is seen that in this ranking, Krugman follows Marshall externalities one by one. Marshall lists the externalities that cause an industry to agglomerate in a region. 1- The fact that firms are agglomerated in a single position provides a cumulative market for laborers with industry specific abilities. This leads to decrease of possible unemployment and lack of labor power. 2- Firms producing intermediate goods want to be close to raw material providers and final goods producers, and final goods producers want to be close to both intermediate goods producers and consumers. Due to the agglomeration in the same geography, forward-backward linkages between firms are strengthened. 3- Information dissemination provides clustered firms with a better production function than isolated producers. (Paul, 2012)

As can be seen from the studies; it is possible to mention non-sectoral economies that are conceptualized as external economies of skilled labor, technology development, value added products and expanding market as external economies with the agglomeration of firms in the same sector in a specific geographical region. Regardless of its line, every type of exogeneity, leads to spatial agglomeration and growth of economic efficiency. (Eraslan & Güngören, 2013) The important point that has not yet been resolved and to be emphasized here is whether external economies expand regional agglomeration, or regional agglomeration triggers external economies as a centre of attention. It seems that as the world economy becomes complicated, knowledge-based and dynamic, the need for agglomerations-clusters increases.

Economic Model Of Akhi-Tradesmen Organizations

As can be seen from the explanations, economic geography and regional agglomeration are fed from the same sources and focus on the same concepts. Akhism and tradesmen organizations were examined in terms of economic geography and regional competition by briefly mentioning the basic concepts rather than historical information based on the emergence of Futuwwa teaching. Akhism developed within the framework of the rules and laws known as rules and regulations of Turkish-Islamic guild, Futuwwa. These rules and laws include not only tradesmen, but notably sultans, and then political-governmental administrators, ulemas, students, merchants, in other words, teachings for all segments of society. Based on this comprehensiveness, it is seen that in the historical process, the state and Akhism Organization act in unison to maintain the socio-economic order. The most important philosophy in this order is to have a people oriented economic mentality. The economy will serve the people, not people to economy.

In people-oriented production, a person's work, idea or artifact has been considered as an indicator for his/her individuality. Based on the "a good job is wasted in the wrong hands" philosophy, in Akhism, the importance and priority has been given to the fact that individuals being knowledgeable, honest and having a strong personality. In a sense, the production of quality goods has been tried to be guaranteed by the presence of quality personalities. Moreover, in Akhism, the division of labor idea is not "me", but "us", and this bring about Akhi-Tradesmen togetherness. It must have been understood that the optimum efficiency of regional agglomeration in economic terms, because these kind of expressions are often used; "If people who produce their own needs, work in harmony and collaborate with others, then they would see both their needs and the needs of the society all together." The term knowledgeable is used herein to mean the tacit knowledge of tradesmen agglomerated in the same region. (Howells, 2002)

Akhi-Tradesmen Organization model was introduced by Ahi Evran in Kayseri, in Anatolian territories, dominated by Seljuq Dynasty at the beginning of 13th century. Then it was adopted and developed as a model of economic organization in the Ottoman Empire. (Kala, 2012) In this model, it is possible to find traces of regional agglomeration and economic geography studies with it. For the first time in an economy, Evran has shown that production that will meet the need can be made by establishing a professional-industrial production organizations by free enterprise. In the meantime, he argued that by regulating the relations between different sectors, production and productivity can be increased, economic progress-development can be achieved by creating subprofessional organizations and production region, and providing a competitive advantage. The competitivenes here, lies in local elements such as knowledge, connections and motivation that the competitors who are far from there, cannot replicate. He pointed out that at this stage, the state should prepare the legal basis for the new production system, and take an indirect and regulatory role in economic life. It is seen that the organization of the tradesmen organizations and the cooperation with the state make tradesmen the main responsible of economic life. They aimed to fulfill the duty assigned to them with statutes, hierarchical order and a firm hand. In addition, with the self-regulation system based on the bail they developed, they have alleviated the work of the state by keeping the tradesmen, thus the system under control. (Kazıcı, 2014) In a clustered tradesmen organization, the implementation of the self-regulation mechanism was ensured by bail of all tradesmen within the organization. Nowadays, in the agglomerated tradesmen organizations where the first examples of the implementation known as the quality control circle are seen, all members are responsible for the working, production and audit of each other.

Akhi-Tradesmen organization model was used by the Ottomans, especially in the organization of industrial and trade sectors, and in regulating the relations between industrial-trade-agricultural sectors

From the Working Order of Akhi-Tradesmen Organization to Economic Geography

based on the industry. According to Ahi Evran, meeting the needs of the society with adequate production will increase the welfare level of the society. Sustainability of this level is possible by regulating the production-consumption relations. Thus, a relationship has been established between scare resources and meeting the unlimited wants. The scare resources are an important problem, and primarily, making production with the efficient use of resources in the region is once again brings cooperation into the forefront. In this context, the coexistence of the producers using the same raw material will increase the efficiency obtained from the raw material and bring about progress. It is predicted that production will increase in quality and quantity by virtue of the method that encourages the agglomeration of tradesmen in certain regions. The aim of the model is determined to meet not only the needs of the people in the region but also the needs of people in the country and even in the nearby countries. Thus, each region would meet its own needs and provide regional development while contributing to different regions with the external economies it created. This model, which is based on export of inconsumable raw mateials and production to other regions, has been the primary resource of the classical regional surplus product export policies of the Seljuks and Ottomans.

In addition, according to regional production factors, the professional organizations agglomerating in certain regions would naturally be able to produce regional needs at a cheaper price and with higher quality by providing a competitive advantage to other regions. Outside products would always be more expensive than replacement products produced in the region, so they would not find buyers. In this way, regional competitive advantage would emerge automatically. As it is in this day and age, taking into account the advantages of the model, production efficiency was increased by means of horizontal expansion due to different cross-sectoral interoperability established between professional-industrial organizations. Moreover, the efficiency and sustainability of the organization was ensured by creating sub-professional groups through vertical cluster. With the network system established through vertical and horizontal organizations, the management of production regions within itself is controlled while on the other hand, competitive advantage is achieved in different regions. It should be emphasized once again that the state does not play any role other than to ensure the healthy functioning of the production and being the protector of it carried out by the professional organizations, by making legal arrangements. Micro-meso-macro scale policies have been developed as more comprehensive policies are needed in terms of increasing, interrelating and harmonizing regional agglomeration locations. In micro scale; tradesmen to establish their own sub-professional organizations, meso scale cities in the agglomeration of the division of labor between the organizations in the region, the macro scale in these regions, by providing cooperation between sectors of raw material procurement and product distribution was regulated. (Kala, 2012) The regional agglomeration model, which was developed in the 13th century, has reorganized production and apportionment, while changing sectoral and regional economic relations. For instance; the leather industry had made good use of the regional agglomeration advantage and has created an important trade item in the horse equipment made of leather and adorned with silver. Examples of the 17th century saddlery can be found in the Russian Tsar Palace. In addition, the French bought the leather they used in book binding from the Ottomans. (Faroqhi, 2018)

It was possible to sustain the established economic organization through professional development in the 13th century as it is today. The optimum use of scarce resources and the ability to sell quality products to consumers were related to the production being made by those mastered in the profession. The profession should have been learned by the master who knows it. Since qualified labor force was needed, experienced tradesmen were encouraged to train experts of their work. Qualified staff who are very important in terms of professional sustainability were beneficial to both individual producers and the professional organization operating in the same region. The profession taught starting from the apprenticeship, went into the stage of benefiting from the tacit knowledge of the master after becoming an assistant master and then further developed. (Doğan, 2011) The organizational behavior, which means the formation and development of professional organizations, has diversified production even more. Porter's commitment to merit of staff quality in the diamond model draws attention in the apprencite-master relationship in the teachings of Akhism. It is known that the profession did not pass from father to son, and if the son did not train from apprenticeship and assistant master, then he could not continue the profession.

The employment policy of the Ottoman classical period was exactly in this direction, not based on finding employment, but on learning a profession. Learning a profession, between the ages of 12-15, began with being an apprentice next to the master. However, being an apprentice did not mean being employed. At the end of the period of learning the profession, if the apprentice became an assistant master, then he was employed. The assistant master had the status of being a wageworker. The assitant master was getting a share or earning full time from the sale of the product he helped to produce. Becoming an assistant master started at the age of 15-16, and the time to become a master varied according to his profession. In the profession of tanner tradesmen, the average time to become a master from an assistant master was ten years, this period could extend to 20 years in jewellery. After becoming a master, the assistant master could continue to work as his master's business partner or take over a vacant store, if there were any. This process, which changed from apprenticeship to workmanship and then to entreprenuership, was a process of professional development. Apprentices who could not become a assistant master were changing the profession with the advice of his master. (Kala, 2012) The solidarity of the tradesmen clusters, a young person's sense of belonging to a group of tradesmen, who entered as an apprentice, and a profession that he could continue until the end of his life, in short, a job security brought about quality production. (Mantran, C.I. 1990)

As it can be seen, in the teaching of Akhism, it was possible to regulate economic and social life when the interoperability envisaged by the system and the value given to the people combined with professional education. The development of social capital naturally affected the development of the region. The main factor that enables differentiation in the profession should be sought in the cooperation of the region in changing the social capital in the historical process. (Öcal & Uçar, 2011)

Ottoman Tradesmen and Regional Agglomeration

Within the framework of Akhi-Tradesmen Organization model in the Ottoman Empire, it is seen that production is made in cooperation and in designated regions. In addition, it has been determined that the subdivisions of the line of business operating in the region are organized into separate groups accoording to quality of each product and services. The difference in quality between them arises from the differentiation of a particular product and service in the production phase. It is known that in the production of a prartricular product, separate tradesmen organizations operate at every phase from raw material procurement to final goods. For instance, in the leather business; many different organizations were clustered such as drovers who provided the livestock needed for the leather raw material, buthcers who cut the livestock in slaughterhouses and gave their skin to tanners, tanners in the processing of the leather raw materials, shoemakers and saddlers in the manufacturing the leather. In Scheme 1, horizontal and vertical organization of drover tradesmen are given.

If the difference in quality of products and services was not only in different production stages but also in the same production stage, different organizations would formed again. For instance, butchers were organized into sheep butchers and cattle butchers. According to the differences in the quality of the products and services produced, the tradesmen were going to form independent organizations within certain location limits. The same tradesmen could go to different regions to be organized in such a way that the numbers would change according to the needs of the regions. In the districts of İstanbul in 1682, there were four sheep butchers in Tahtakale, 10 in Yedikule, nine in Langa and 13 in Aksaray, while there was no sheep butcher in Cibali. (Kazıcı, 2014)

The fact that tradesmen formed independent organizations had important implications for the competition between the organizations. The organizations also played a role in the close-out of tradesmen. The organized tradesmen, limited the production of products and services to the number of tradesmen involved in the organization and in a sense, closed out. Thus, it was possible for people outside the organization to prevent them from producing products and services based on the monopoly rights provided to them by the state.

Some mechanisms have been developed to prevent the monopoly rights provided to tradesmen, in other words, the loff of quality of the products and services produced due to non-competition and the fact that the tradesmen who do not develop new techniques become completely closed. When the existing tradesmen organizations started to produce new substitute goods that the economy needed, unliked the products they were producing, the legal system came into play. The tradesmen who produced the substitute goods was sending firman to Muslim judges in order to prevent the intervene from the tradesmen organization who had the right to production. As can be seen, there was always the possibility that tradesmen organization would encounter the competition of new substitute goods to be produced outside their own organization. Tradesmen organizations must had to keep the quality of the products and services that they produced high, and the efforts to develop new production techniques within the organization. This had a vital importance for the future of the tradesmen organizations.

Moreover, since the raw material inputs of the tradesmen who produce substitute goods and services were generally based on the joint products used by the other tradesmen, the competition between the organizations was quite high in the procurement phase of such joint raw materials. Competition ceased to be only within a certain region and turned into the competition of tradesmen organizations using the same joint product within the empire. The competition between the tradesmen producing inter-regional substitute goods was primarily in the production of necessary foodstuff. This raw material competition, which started with grain products, emerged in the procurement of bovine and ovine animals and then raw materials such as wool, silk, cotton and leather, which were the inputs of industrial production. (Kala, 2012)

The substitute goods could be produced in the existing tradesmen organization and also by those outside the organized tradesmen organizations. In order for a new product or service production to be valid, primarily it had to be for the benefit of the economy, the use of a new technique, a reasonable price and high quality. When such products and services started to be produced, a new tradesmen organization were established. (Kala, 2012)

İstanbul and Tradesmen Organizations

In the Middle Ages, where transportation in general and particularly the land transport was costly, it was seen that metropolitans were built on the seashores and riversides. İstanbul is one of these cities and it has used the advantage of its being built by the seashore in every period. For the convenience of logistics services, it is seen that tradesmen and craftsmen prefer İstanbul's waterfront settlements as their agglomeration places. The entrance and exit of the products to the city were made mostly by the piers established on the shore of Halic. There is an obligation to bring down the products to certain piers. As is evident from their names; Honey Trap Pier, Vegetable and Fruit Pier, Wood Pier, Flour Trap Pier, Lemon Pier, Wicker Pier, Fish Market Pier, etc... (Kazıcı, 2014) The shipments of items, especially foodstuffs, leather and wood from the Halic Coast are frequent, continuous and bulky. The fact that the large storehouses, fruit and vegetable cases are close to the piers also minimized the transportation and storage costs of products. Within this framework, locationally, the piers and the areas where the tradesmen organizations are located are the center of production and trade. In the maps 1 and 2, the settlements of the producer, merchant and wholesaler are marked on the coast of Halic in the second half of the 17th century.

In the same years on the maps, other agglomeration places of tradesmen and trade outside Halic, too much tradesmen organizations such as seamen in Galata and Kasımpaşa, spice sellers in Spice Bazaar, iron smiths in Galata-Azap Gate, oilers and candlemakers in Oil Trap, flour makers in Flour Trap, saddlers in Saddlery, carpenters and wood mills in Wood Gate, tailors in Hagia Sophia, goldsmiths and jewerllers in covered Turkish are enumerated. (Mantran, C. II. 1990)

Moreover, when the placement of tradesmen was examined on a micro scale, it was determined that the place was agglomerated from time to time according to the living spaces around it. Such as the agglomeration of the stationer, binders, bibliopoles and ink sellers around the educational institutions/madrassas around the Beyazıt Mosque, or the butchers near the settlements. In addition, between Beyazıt and Eminönü, Long Bazaar and Mahmut Pasha Street were two main roads and around them, tradesmen of various professions were operating. It is known that wholesalers store and sell their products in the inns on these two roads. The largest covered place in İstanbul was the Grand Bazaar, which accomodated all tradesmen groups. In the 18 gates, 61 streets and 4,000 stores different groups of tradesmen were operating together. There were 61 different tradesmen who gave their name to the streets such as carpet stores, quilt makers, tailors, goldsmiths, sandal sellers and mirror stores. (Mantran, C. II. 1990)

When all these settlements are examined, it is clear that the tradesmen are in the rectangle of Eminönü-Beyazıt-Saddlery-Flour Trap. There are also commercial lines from Hagia Sophia to Beyazıt, Beyazıt to Aksaray, Vefa to Saddlery, Saddlery to Suleymaniye and Flour Trap. When the agglomeration places are examined visually, Map 1 shows the locations of the producer tradesmen, Map 2 shows the merchant and wholesaler tradesmen. When the both maps are overlapped, it is seen that wholesaler and producers are agglomerated in almost the same place. This co-operation has facilitated production, price determination, audit, catering and taxation policies. Co-operations giving certain rights to tradesmen have brought certain obligations. In this way, tradesmen have monopolies to buy, produce and sell which give them great advantages. And the state has determined which products and services, which quality, in which region, at which price, who will buy and produce and have rights to sell. (Kala, 2012) These production and franchise are implemented in two policy titles with social and economic content. Production and price/price fixing policies. The first one of these was to meet the needs of the people, in other words, to assure the production of the quality determined to satisfy the demand and to make it sustainable. The second one was to fix a reasonable price for each produced product and service, both for the producer and the consumer, and to assure its implementation.

The control of prices and production were monitored through the officials called constabulary. The consutabularies had many control issues such as quality, bribery in measures and weight, tax and especially price. (Kazıcı, 2014) The name of the system used to control price fixation was officially fixed price. While the officially fixed price was determining, the constabulary could not act on his own. Guild chairs such as tradesmen elders, chamberlain are invited after receiving information about the product, and price was determined by looking at the seasonal conditions, money value of the day, abudance and failure of crops, military and social events. The frequency of price changes can be expressed in weeks, months, a year or years. Thus, it was tried to soften the effect of supply not increasing in proportion to demand or the decrease in supply even though the demand reimained the same. (Kazıcı, 2014) After the officially fixed price determined for various kinds of shoes with raw material Morocco leather in 1814, the second price determination was made in 1827, after 13 years. (Kala, 2012)

The laws imposed by the state had also negative effects on prices. The tradesmen wanted to monopolize by closing out from time to time and regulate prices as they wanted. In this case, the rising prices also raise the officially fixed price than they should have. Tanner tradesmen in İstanbul had the monopoly of purchase privilege of acorns with raw materials from the acorn tradesmen. But they did not buy to lower purchase price. Due to the monopoly, acorn tradesmen could not sell acorns to anyone other than the tanner tradesmen, and because they could not hold the products for a long time, they had to sell at a cheaper price. Tanners started to buy not only the acorns they needed but they did not need too, and then sold them to the merchant at a higher price. As can be seen, tanners began to do the acorn tradesmen's acorn trade, and in some way, they tended to turn into tradesmen-merchant. This behavior allowed tanners to lower and raise the prices as they wanted, based on their monopoly rights. Towards the end of the 18th century Selim III, argued that the reason for the monopolization of the tradesmen in a damaging way to peoplewas the order given by the state, and he demanded abolition of monopolies other than essential foodstuff. (Kala, 2012)

In order to avoid problems in the provisionalism of İstanbul, which is the consumption center, the city population should be kept under control so that controling supply and demand along with the prices would be possible. For this reason, utmost importance was given to assure that the population remained stable, regardless of the settlement centers. Since the production and distribution, in other words, impeded supply and demand, it was forbidden for farmers to leave their plantation and engage in other jobs and go to cities, which was called quitting being a farmer. Those who came to the city without a guarantor for such reasons would be sent to their hometowns with the fear that it would cause social disorganization. Thus, the transition from production to consumerism was prevented and raw material provisionalism was made regular and sustainable. It is understood that all the remedies have been resorted, in order to not deteriorate the system and not to go out of the determined clusters. For instance, cattles brought to İstanbul after slaughtering had to be sold in Edirnekapı to make pastrami. Some people were found to secretly sell meat elsewhere in order to avoid taxes and the necessary penalties were imposed. (Kazıcı, 2014)

As can be seen, the basis of economic development and sustainable competitiveness was connected with the spatial proximity and cooperation of related sectors and related institutions/organizations as it is today. The fact that people operate in cetain places/regions and work in collaboration to produce products and services has emerged in parallel with the development of the urbanization culture, resulting in today's competitive industrial clusters. (Eraslan & Güngören, 2013) In this context, the tanner tradesmen will be examined as an example.

Tanner Tradesmen

Leather, shoes, horse harness and other military ammunition, water bottles, bags, sandals are used in various fields needed by the people and the army is an important substance. Leather finishing is called tanning, dressing and tannery, and the tradesmen doing this work is called tanner. The animal slaughtering places/stores, which are frequently mentioned in the text, are called slaughterhouse. Since leather tanning process requires abundant water, the tanner tradesmen in İstanbul, where they agglomerate on the waterfront far away from the settlements, are also found to operate in seaside locations such as Kasımpaşa, Eyüp, Yedikule and Tophane. Map 1 and 2.

The procurement of raw materials for the tanner tradesmen in İstanbul starts with the animals brought from the villages to be slaughtered. Wholesalers who had a certain amount of money, called drover, were assigned to bring bovine and ovine animals to the city centers. Being a drover as a profession was not desired because of its difficulties and risks. For this reason, as there were not enough butchers, duties were done by instructions, and if not followed, they would serve with fine and receive imprisonment, and in some cases be sentenced with capital punishment. (Kazıcı, 2014) (Özkul, 2018)The animals that were brought to İstanbul by the drover evaluated by two different methods, delivery to İstanbul Muslim judge and his constabulary-officials, or slaughtering in designated stores and selling them to certain butchers.

With both methods, an average of 4,000,000 sheep, 3,000,000 lambs and 200,000 cattle were slaughtered annually. It was recorded in the butcher's book that how many butchers would buy and sell meat to İstanbul every year. In the butcher's book about İstanbul, butcher would consider the financial situation of the person who was written, and recorded clearly how many sheep could buy and how much meat would be sell to people from the butcher store in the designated place. It should be emphasized that most of the slaughtered meat is taken by the court kitchen and the guild of janissaries. In the İstanbul account book dated 1682, a total of 183 sheep butcher stores were determined in 15 tax regions within the city wall. 105 of these belong to Muslims and 78 to dhimmis. (Kazıcı, 2014) The animals were sold alive to the butchers of İstanbul, and were slaughtered in the slaughterhouse to which the butcher was affiliated, and sold to the costumer by the butcher to provide meat need for a wide range of people including palaces, military and charitable institutions. In addition, the distribution of slaughtered animals according to predetermined shares was preventing overpayment of the tradesmen or rich tradesmen to volume buying of products and other tradesmen, who were doing the same job, to not being able to find products. And it is understood that the situations which get tradesmen in the soup and distort competitiveness, in short, make the stability of the market difficult, are prevented. Furthermore, it has a great importance that the slaughtering is controled in slaughterhouses in order to assure the full use of meat, skin, fat and other by-products of the slaughtered animal without wasting. It is seen that the importance of regional agglomeration in regulating supply-demand conditions, in other words, market conditions has been understood by the 13th century. The distribution of slaughtered animals to horizontal and vertical tradesmen groups from one place ensures the optimum efficient use of the raw material while minimizing the waste and environmental pollution. (Kala, 1992)

It was an advantage for food security that it was inspected in terms of health and cleanliness while complying with hygiene requirements during slaughtering. Sheep and goat meats were not intermixed. Even the butchers' were asked to be separate. In addition, detailed code of laws were prepared, including the cleanliness of eating houses in close relationship with buthcers, how they cook the food and wash dishes. (Kazıcı, 2014) Slaughtering in designated stores also provided price control. With this control, not only the meat but the fat that was given to the candlemakers, the leather to tanners, the giblets to eating house owners' price control was also ensured. Moreover, since it is determined how much distribution will be made to which tradesmen, it has been tried to minimize the fact that some tradesmen take more than others and make a lot of profit, or the effects of destabilizing market stability such as stockpiling. As a result, the government encouraged tradesmen to agglomerate in certain regions in order to maintain the hygiene control and price control, and prevent monopoly tendencies, in short, to make provisionalism system sustainable.

In addition to market regulations, in terms of İstanbul being the capital, the life satisfaction of the army, tradesmen and the people had to be provided at the highest level possible. Considering that it would be difficult to recover from a disturbance in a possible famine, the largest wheat storehouses, army accommodation centers and abattoirs were established in İstanbul. In other words, İstanbul served as a warehouse for products arriving by land and sea. Along the southern coast of the Halic, there were piers specialized in certain products. The logistics chain, which was stored in warehouses and went into retail sales, also reflected the way tradesmen were organized. It is seen that grouping and agglomeration came into the forefront here. (Mantran, C. I. 1990)

The drovers gathered the sheep mostly from Thrace, Bulgaris, Macedonia, Wallachia and Bogdan. Also sheep were brought from Central Anatolia, Karaman and Turkmen. (Mantran, C.I. 1990) How many sheep would be brought decided by looking at the previous year, the demands were conveyed by the Muslim judges to various local units and given to the butchers under the supervision of the constabulary-officials. The orders for frequent and continuous supervisions are recorded in the 16th and 17th century documents. (Kala, 2012) In order to avoid shortage of raw materials in the market, tanned raw leather was also brought from Rumelia and Anatolia in addition to livestocks, and distributed to tanneries, painters and other leather and material producers. (Mantran, C. II. 1990)

When animal gathering areas are examined, it is understood that most of the raw materials come to the consumption center İstanbul, from the outside. Since the priority of Ottoman provisionalism policies was to meet the needs of the domestic market, export prohibitions were imposed on some strategic goods. Ox, goat and sheep leather and their by-products Morocco leather, gon, buff, beewax and tallow export was prohibited. It was prohibited to export goods such as weapons, gunpowder, leaded copper, sulphur, bitumen, horse, fleece, cotton, sailcloth, cotton yarn, timber and grain, where the prohibitions were not limited with leather products. Exports were made with dispensation after meeting the needs of the domestic market. Otherwise, deterrent penalties were imposed. In a control made by the constabulary-official, the necessary procedures were carried out on the indication that the foreign ships were loaded with gon/processed leather and left without permission in 1584. (Kazıcı, 2014) (Mantran, C.I. 1990)

There were also code of laws issued by padishahs on the same subject. Mehmet IV's code of laws, penalties and sanctions for tradesmen and constabulary-officials, which were prepared in 1680 is one of them. In the code of laws, there are provisions stating that separate the sheep and goats from males to females, not slaughter the weak animal, preserve the fat, butchers that do not have meat in their stores will be penalized, shoemakers will make quality products, candlemakers won't use corrupt or bad tallow, eating house owners will meet the cleaning requirements, tanners won't close the sell to anyone other than the places given to them and they will be penalized if their prices are above the officially fixed price. (Mantran, C.I. 1990)

In order to maintain the balance of supply and demand, raw leather was brought from Anatolia and Rumelia when necessary. After the customs and taxes were paid at the place called "Guild Place", these leathers were distributed to the tanner tradesmen according to share proportion as one for a store owner, two for two stores owner. (Tekin, 1997) According to the type of leather (waterbuffalo skin, goat skin, lamb skin) to be processed, they were divided into sections. Their workers were also separated. When another tradesmen produced a leather processing type, that production would be flimsy and of poor quality. For this purpose, the tanner tradesmen had decided on the type of process to be made among themselves and provided the necessary tools and sales booth. After determining which type of leather each tanner was going to process, another type of leather was prohibited. All of the slaughtered sheep, goat and lamb skins were given to tanner tradesmen in the summer and winter without wasting even a single skin. It was regulated by law, not to produce Morocco leather in a cowhide leather (bovine animal leather) processing tannery. Morocco leather tradesmen and vellum tradesmen were also separated from each other. A tanner processing vellum would only did that. As can be seen, the vertical and horizontal organization of tradesmen was quite complicated.

Tanner tradesmen in İstanbul were agglomerated in five different regions; Eyup, Kasımpaşa, Tophane, Üsküdar and Castle of Seven Towers. (Tekin, 1997) The first tannery was established in the middle of the 15th century by Mehmed the Conqueror in Castle of Seven Towers and its income was given to the Hagia Sophia Foundation. It is understood that the regional agglomeration started in these years with 27 tanneries and 33 abattoirs/salughterhouses clustered around Castle of Seven Towers. About 200 years later, in the middle of the 17th century, the number of tanneries in Castle of Seven Towers region had increased from 360 to 700 throughout İstanbul. The number of workers was approximately 3000 master-assistant master-apprentice. In the early 20th century, due to the regional agglomeration that Marshall put forward to, it has been determined that 300 years ago, the tanner tradesmen in İstanbul implemented the theory about the gains to be obtained.

Although the organization and working principles of the tanner tradesmen, which are agglomerated in five different regions, were the same, it is useful to briefly mention the regional characteristics such as raw material procurement, distributive points, processed leather variety and interregional competition. Castle of Seven Towers tanners procured the leather/raw material to be processed from slaughterhouses at the seaside in İstanbul, slaughterhouses outside Edirnekapı and black cattle skins slaughtered in Eyup. Since the abovementioned vellum production was prohibited within the boundaries of İstanbul, the vellum production belonged only to Castle of Seven Towers tanners located outside of İstanbul. Butchers had to give their lambskin to Castle of Seven Towers tanners for vellum production. The Castle of Seven Towers tanner tradesmen, who were producing multiple different products, often conflicted with tanner tradesmen in other districts about leather. Since the conquest of İstanbul, the Castle of Seven Towers tanners used to buy black cattle skins and used them to produce cowhide leather. Tanners of Eyup could not process these leathers. On July 22, 1662, when tanners of Eyup sold these leathers to foreigners, the Castle of Seven Towers tanners raised an objection. When the situation is understood and asked from the butchers in Eyup, the Castle of Seven Towers tanners were justified and met the case. (Tekin, 1997) Furthermore, the Castle of Seven Towers objected to the establishment of tanneries in Yenibahçe and Cibali, and issued a decision not to establish tannery there. Organizations seem to be strong enough to influence the authority.

After custom duties were paid, the Castle of Seven Towers tanners distributed the intermediate goods such as Morocco leather, cowhide leather that they produced and the leather brought from Thrace and Anatolia for shoemaking, to merchants and other tradesmen at the Coral Bazaar. Some of the tanners sold the Morocco leather, buff and cowhide leather they produced at high prices around the corners and solitary places outside of the designated areas, therewith Morocco leather merchants sued them on May 12, 1793, and stated that tanners could come to Coral Bazaar like they used to and merchants would give them three stores so that they could sell their products at market value. (Tekin, 1997)

From the Working Order of Akhi-Tradesmen Organization to Economic Geography

In the middle of the 15th century, Kasımpaşa region was ranked as number two among the tanneries in İstanbul with a total of 36 stores affiliated to Kasımpaşa Foundation and Sinanpaşa Foundation. These tanneries bought their raw materials from the slaughterhouses in Galata Kazası and from three other slaughterhouses located in Balat Gate, Hasır Pier and Samatya Gate, and bought the skins of 600 kilos sheep slaughtered for the Old Palace. In addition, in the middle of the 15th century, when the tanneries were first established, the total of slaughtered sheep and goat skins in the inner and outer regions in Kasımpaşa and Galata, divided into three parts and then distributed two shares to the Castle of Seven Towers tanners and one share to Kasımpaşa tanners. As soon as the inconveniences of the method were observed, everyone was allowed to buy the skins in their own area. (Tekin, 1997)

There was a competition between Kasımpaşa and Castle of Seven Towers tanners in terms of production quality besides leather procurement. On March 30, 1610, the Castle of Seven Towers tanners took action on Kasımpaşa tanners that they were making fake manufacturing, and in a research upon this, it is understood that Kasımpaşa tanners processed gon and cowhide leather better than Castle of Seven Towers tanners.

Kasımpaşa tanners processed the skin of the local and foreign cows and oxen they bought, and produced intermediate products and then sold them to slaughterhouses, merchants, leather bottle makers and tailor tradesmen. Also they provided cowhide leather, chamois leather and Morocco leather used in the navy, guild of janissaries and pumps, and buff for powder bag, straps and Morocco leather for car palanquin. (Tekin, 1997)

In the 15th century, the third cluster place of İstanbul tanneries is Eyup District with 39 stores. 36 of the stores were affiliated to Eyyüb Ensari Foundation, and 3 of them were affiliated to Pirî Mehmed Pasha Foundation in Hasköy. Tanneries in Eyup usually bought leather they needed from the slaughterhouses of Eyup district. However they Pirî Mehmed Pasha tanners also had the rights of 24 sheep skins outside Castle of Seven Towers for each day. The 47 butcher shops, which were subjected to slaughterhouses that Eyup tanneries procured leather to, were distributed to different regions of İstanbul. (Tekin,1997) Conflicts between Eyup tanners and Castle of Seven Towers tanners had occured as in other slaughterhouse cluster centers. When the three tanneries established by Pirî Mehmet Pasha in Hasköy took the skins belonging to Castle of Seven Towers, the Castle of Seven Towers tanners got in a bind. Because they broke the order, their wells and guilds were demolished and removed, and those who resisted were penalized. Castle of Seven Towers tanners said "we will give stores and shares", as long as Pirî Mehmet Pasha tanners work with them and give their rents to their foundations/Hagia Sophia Foundation, so that three tanneries transferred to Castle of Seven Towers. In the following years, Eyup tanners wanted the tanners in Hasköy to relocate to their old place, and take their rents from Hagia Sophia Foundation and affiliate to Eyup Foundation again. From a firman dated April 2, 1843, it is understood that Pirî Mehmet Pasha tanners in Hasköy returned to their old places. This example demonstrates that producers can be mobile between regions when it is necessary. (Kala, 2012)

Üsküdar tanneries, which ranked fourth in terms of capacity among cluster locations of İstanbul tanners, were three groups. In total, 8 of the 31 tanneries were from Mihrimah Sultan's Foundations, 12 of them were from Atik Valide Sultan's Foundations and 11 of them were from the foundation tanneries established by Safiye Sultan. They processed the leather procured from slaughterhouses within the borders of Üsküdar and from the places where shares were assigned to them. Also the Jewish community in İstanbul used to give the skins of the sheep that they slaughtered to Üsküdar tanneries. In 1572, Jews were prohibited to slaughter sheep in İstanbul, and it was adjudicated that they could slaughter sheep outside the Edirne Gate. The Castle of Seven Towers tanners wanted to own these leathers because the authority to buy leathers outside İstanbul borders belonged to them. The provision sent on the subject, ordered the animal skins slaughtered by Jews, will continue to be given to Üsküdar tanneries as usual. It is understood that competition is at its highest level because in a possible change, other cluster regions are immediately involved in order to benefit them. (Tekin, 1997)

In addition to these, from the Great Pier in Üsküdar to Zincirlikuyu and At Bazaar, the slaughtered sheep skins were assigned to 11 tanneries which were affiliated to Üsküdar Safiye Sultan Foundation. Also, the skins in Gunner Mehmet Pasha's butcher shop in Kumkapi, the skins of butchers who gave meat to the Old Palace, the animal skins of butchers who slaughter sheep from Eminönü to Hagia Sophia belonged to the tanners of Safiye Sultan Foundation.

The tanners operating the eight tanneries affiliated to Mihrimah Sultan Foundation, could also buy sheep skins slaughtered in Gülfem Hatun Foundation stores in Balat Gate, Galatasaray, Beşiktaş, Jewish Neighbourhood and from Great Pier in Üsküdar to Zincirlikuyu, in adition to two shares of Castle of Seven Towers slaughterhouses. (Kala, 2012)

Since all of the animal skins slaughtered in existing butcher shops and slaughterhouses were allocated, the secretly established tanneries were threatining the existing structure. As a matter of fact, in 1692, it was determined that Castle of Seven Towers worker Mehmet and his partner secretly established a tannery in a mansion in Istavros Village, and they bought the leather around them at a highter price and then processed them. Upon the complaints of tanners who were affected by this, Atik Valide Sultan had removed the tanneries established without permission. It is understood that state immediately intervened in this situation, which disrupts supply-demand balance and is contrary to the interregional competition, and implemented the necessary legal sanctions. (Kala, 2012)

People, wishing to establish a tannery within the limits of the law would inform the official authorities and if deemed reasonable, they would rent to the foundation which the settled tanners affliated to, in the region and they would receive a share from the production share in return. In the same way, in 1655, a person named Mehmet rented a land belonged to Mihrimah Sultan Foundtaion to establish a tannery. The order was sent to the Üsküdar Muslim judge, and this person was included in the share and it was reported that he was allowed to tanning.

In terms of production, Tophane tanneries brought up the rear among İstanbul tanneries. Within the boundaries of Galata, besides the eight tanneries which were affiliated to Kılıç Ali Pasha Foundation, in Tophane, it was also mentioned that those affiliated to Hagia Sophia Foundation, however their exact number is unknown. Kılıç Ali Pasha tanneries were sharing the slaughtered animal skins in Galata with Kasım Pasha and Sinan Pasha. Disagreements have occured from time to time between two groups receiving raw materials from the same region. According to a document dated 1740; all animal skins slaughtered in Galata and its vicinity belonged to Tophane tanners. Tanner tradesmen in Tophane, shared the skins they received, with the tradesmen groups in their region, and used to produce wares from buff, cowhide leather and yellow buff leather which were necessary in shipyards, ammunitions, saddleries, powder mills and paper mills, and then they would sold the wares to designated places. Because of the abundant of leather is needed for production, the slaughtered ox, cow, buffalo, sheep, lamb and goat skins in slaughterhouses were not sold to foreigners without being processed, and sold to Tophane tanners for summer and winter market price, and the fair share of leathers between them was required by the law. It is understood that tanner tradesmen benefited from the advantages of regional agglomeration. (Kala, 2012)

In another case record dated 1764, it is possible to determine that Kılıç Ali Pasha tanners and the tanners affliated to Hagia Sophia Foundation bought and processed the animal skins slaughtered in all slaughterhouses and butcher shops inside and outside of Galata and from Tophane to Beşiktaş and from there to Sarıyer. In 1801, the court was held on the claim of Tophane tanners, that some butchers and sailor tradesmen sold the best skins to foreigners by choosing, so they guaranteed to sell the animal skins of the butcher tradesmen to Tophane tanners in accordance with Castle of Seven Towers order without any process.

In another record, Castle of Seven Towers tanners say that they are less favored then Kasımpaşa tanners. Because the animal skins slaughtered in Castle of Seven Towers' abattoir are given to Kasımpaşa tanners. However, according to an old provision, these should be given to Castle of Seven Towers tanners. Similarly, tanners in Kasımpaşa wanted to take the skins slaughtered in Galata with the allowance given by Mehmet the Conqueror. (Mantran, C.I. 1990) The objections are examined, and firstly an agreement is reached between the parties, otherwise the penalties and sanctions are applied.

As can be seen, the tanner tradesmen clustered in five different regions of İstanbul, had many horizontal and vertical elements of competition within themselves and between regions. It is understood that competition is at its highest level, besides the internal control of the tradesmen, the efforts to control different organizations producing the same product. How this complex organization is structured over each other is illustrated in Scheme 1 through tanner tradesmen. As it is understood, in the Ottoman tradesmen cluster, the necessity to change and the articulation of different tradesmen organizations due to production innovations is an indication that the organization is open to development. Thus, it is possible for any tradesmen who has developed a different style or technique, to take part in this.

SOLUTIONS AND RECOMMENDATIONS

The importance of economic geography and regional agglomeration examined in the historical process has become more evident today. In other words, the transition from agglomeration to cluster has started. Within this framework, increasing the opportunities of working, contributes to the region determined from different fields such as research institutions, educational and medical institutions, financial institutions, non-governmental institutions. In order to make the contribution sustainable, it is inevitable for the firms to go to sectoral cooperation. Cooperating firms may have some advantages that they cannot reach on their own in many fields, especially in the reduction of input costs. Increasing the export efficiency of firms, increasing the level of innovation, networking among enterprises and attracting new enterprises to the region are among the main benefits provided to firms by the cluster structure.

It should not be forgotten that clustering is not a legal obligation, but trust and cooperation between the firms. Furthermore, the cluster does not preclude the profitability of firms. On the contrary, intracluster competition continues. This competition makes it easier for keep up with the global competitive environment. Media and communication firms have a big role in the development of the cluster, giving a demonstration, inclusion of missing or needed new actors in the cluster.

As a solution, support should be provided to the cluster coopeation that SMEs will establish among themselves, with big enterprises and other actors in the field of entrepreneurship. Support programs should be implemented considering sectoral needs. The sectors, which Turkey will compete in foreign markets should be chosen and they should be supported. Vocational education should be ensured to act in harmony with these clusters. Also, about the withdrawal of International direct investmets in Turkey, the advantageous sectors should be determined.

FUTURE RESEARCH DIRECTIONS

The study is limited to the Ottoman period and İstanbul. In addition, tanner tradesmen were selected as tradesmen. It would be useful to examine economic geography, regional production and competition within the scope of other tradesmen organizations. Another limitation of the study is that it does not cover enclosed spaces. In the 16th century, the functioning of the bazaars in themselves, where the tanner tradesmen and their sub-units were clustered such as Grand Bazaar, Saddlery Market, is also worth examining. Considering the diversity of tradesmen that are covered by Grand Bazaar, it presents a research subject in its own dynamics.

While the Ottoman tradesmen organization was conceptualized as an agglomeration, at this point reached today, clusters are mentioned. Then it should be another research subject to examine the process from agglomeration to cluster. The current situation of economic geography, regional production and competition, and the position of leather business line in this context can be considered as another subject of study. Within this framework, it can be investigated how the tanner tradesmen's agglomeration places are used today. Thus, it may be possible to compare the vertical and horizontal organization of the leather business line in both time periods.

Another subject of study may be to examine the status of the tradesmen, tanner tradesmen especially, in Europe and around the World in the 16th century. For comparison, China, one of the leaders in the leather industry today, and the following countries such as Italy, Spain, Pakistan, Indonesia can be examined in terms of regional production and competition. Between the mentioned countries, the status of Turkey and what measures should be taken for Turkey to be at the top can be pointed out.

CONCLUSION

At the end of the research, it is determined that the agglomeration of Akhi-Tradesmen organizations developed by Ahi Evran in certain regions, covers the subjects of economic thought, organization for production and distribution, development through regional and sectoral economic relations. Furthermore, it is understood that many current business concepts such as employee empowerment, quality management, institutionalization, human capital, branding, mission, vision and strategy exist in the Seljuk-Ottoman tradition. It is seen that transportation was expensive and risky, production was made for the domestic market at the local scale, and in those centuries, regional agglomeration has ben given priority. In addition to the increase in the number of existing tradesmen groups with the development, the emergence of new occupational groups has led to an increase in forward and backward movements in production. Regional agglomeration has been seen as an important advantage in order to make this mobility sustainable and to use the resources with optimum efficiency.

In addition to the forward and backward movement freedom of tradesmen in the production region, it was determined that the model was developed with vertical and horizontal extensions in order to adapt to the new conditions. One of the main reasons behind the encouragement of specialized tradesmen to agglomerate in certain geographical areas was that they would not be able to engage in large investments requiring fixed capital. Within this framework, it was not possible for tradesmen who were vulnerable to the effects of economic-politics and social events to produce by making use of economy of scale. Also, another well-known characteristic of Ottoman economic mentality is the policies that prevent people from accumulating too much money. For these and similar reasons, the way out of tradesmen who could not take cost-cutting measures by making batch production, was to take an advantage of regional agglomeration.

Also, due to the agglomerations, the combination of cultural affinity and social relations brought about increasing knowledge and experience sharing, and this created regional superiority. Moreover, easy access to raw materials, the combination of tradesmen using the same raw materials and the convenience of logistics falities were used as competitive advantages. Another advantage that creates competition superiority in regional agglomerations is the existence of tacit knowledge expressed as internal knowledge in the Ottoman tradesmen system. In the Ottoman economic system, where economic life is strengthened by social associations, the sustainability of tacit knowledge draws attention as an important competitive advantage. In this sense, it is undoubtedly that using the common knowledge pool triggers innovation.

As a result, it was understood that the sustainability of the Ottoman tradesmen system for many years, was provided by specialized labor power, back-and-forth connections between the tradesmen and the agglomeration of knowledge. This sustainability has been supported by state policies which have an indirect role in economic life with the necessary regulations and controls by preparing the legal basis for the production system. Moreover, the cooperation between the state and the tradesmen has made tradesmen the main responsible for socio-economic life. It is possible to benefit from the experiences of the past by investigating all aspects of Akhi-Tradesmen organization system and comparing it with the concepts of today's economic geography, regional agglomeration and competition.

REFERENCES

Doğan, H. (2011). Development and spread examples of tacit knowledge from. *Gümüşhane University Journal of Social Sciences Electronic*, 77-100.

Eraslan, İ. H., & Dönmez, C. Ç. (2017). The analysis of industrial cluster implications in wordwide: an evaluation for agriculture, manufacturing and service industries. *Electronic Journal of Social Sciences*, 719-755.

Eraslan, İ. H., & Güngören, M. (2013). The economic history and evolution progress of industrial. *Electronic Journal of Social Sciences*, 171-197.

Eraslan Hakkı, M. B. (2008). Clusters and their effects on innovations: implementations in the Turkish tourism sector. *Magazine for Travel and Hotel Management*, 15-29.

Erbaşı, A., & Ersöz, S. (2011). The relationship between Akhism and 4C Marketing Mix: A view from historical perspective. *Turkish Culture and Hacı Bektas Veli Research Quarterly*, 135-146.

Faroqhi, S. (2018). *Osmanlı dünyasında üretmek, pazarlamak, yaşamak*. İstanbul, Turkey: Yapı Kredi Yayınları.

Howells, J. R. (2002). Tacit knowledge, innovation and economic geography. Policy Research in Engineering, Science & Technology (PREST) (871-844). içinde Manchester: University of Manchester.

Kala, A. (1992). Organization of İstanbul Butcher Shopman Until The 19th Century. *Journal of Social Politics Conferences*, 111-117.

Kala, A. (2012). *DebbağlıktanEriciliğe İstanbul Merkezli Deri Sektörünün Doğuşu ve Gelişimi*. İstanbul, Turkey: Zeytinburnu Municipality.

Karatop, B., Karahan, A. G., & Kubat, C. (2011). First application of total quality management in Ottoman Empire: Ahi organization. *7th Research/Expert Conference with International Participations*, (1109-1114).

Karatop, B., & Kubat, C. (2018). Akhi order's effect on Turkish quality management system. *Journal of Academic Studies*, 351-368.

Kazıcı, Z. (2014). *Osmanlı Medeniyeti Tarihi: Osmanlı'da Yerel Yönetim: (ihtisab müessesesi)*.

Küçüker, C. (2000). New Economic Geography. *Ekonomik Yaklaşım*, 1-45.

Mantran, R. (C. II. 1990). Istanbul in The Second Half of The 17th Century. Ankara, Turkey: Turkish Historical Society.

Mantran, R. (C.I. 1990). Istanbul in The Second Half of The 17th Century. Ankara, Turkey: Turkish Historical Society.

Öcal, T., & Uçar, H. (2011). Structural change and competitiveness in clusters. *Journal of Social Policy Conferences*, 285-321.

Özkul, A. E. (2018). Butchers and activities in Cyprus in the Ottoman Rule. *Gazi Academic View*, 165-198.

Paul, K. (2012). Increasing returns and economic geography. *Maliye Dergisi*, 396-410.

Şimşek, M. (2002). *Total quality management and an application in history: Akhism*. İstanbul, Turkey: Hayat Yayınları.

Soysal, A. (2013). The importance of Akhism principles and applications in business success: an evaluation. *Çimento Endüstri İşverenleri Sendikası*, 6-19.

Tekin, Z. (1997). İstanbul Debbağhaneleri. *Ankara Üniversitesi Osmanlı Tarihi Araştırma ve Uygulamaları Merkezi Dergisi*, 348-397.

KEY TERMS AND DEFINITIONS

Abattoir: A store where animals are slaughtered.

Agglomeration: Refers to the number and size distribution of units that control or own a certain economic integration.

Cluster: The gathering of producers and their supporting firms and institutions that are operating in the same or similar line of business, geographically close to each other, cooperating and competing with each other.

Drover: A person who trades animals.

SME: Refers to small, medium and big sized enterprises.

Tanner Tradesmen: Tradesmen who buy and process raw leather.

From the Working Order of Akhi-Tradesmen Organization to Economic Geography

APPENDIX

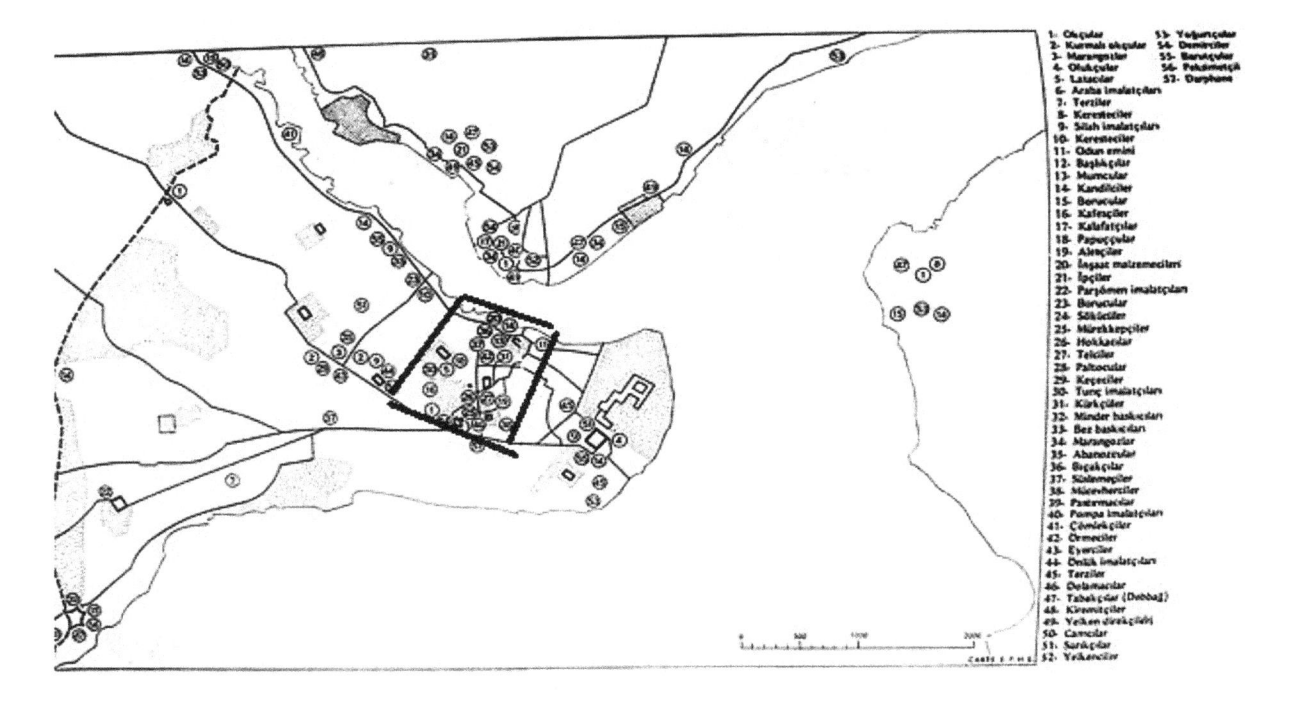

Figure 1. Locations of manufacturers and tradesmen (17th century)
Source: (Mantran, Istanbul in The Second Half of The 17 th Century, C. II. 1990)

Figure 2. Trade and wholesaler's place (17th century)
Source: (Mantran, Istanbul in The Second Half of The 17 th Century, C. II. 1990)

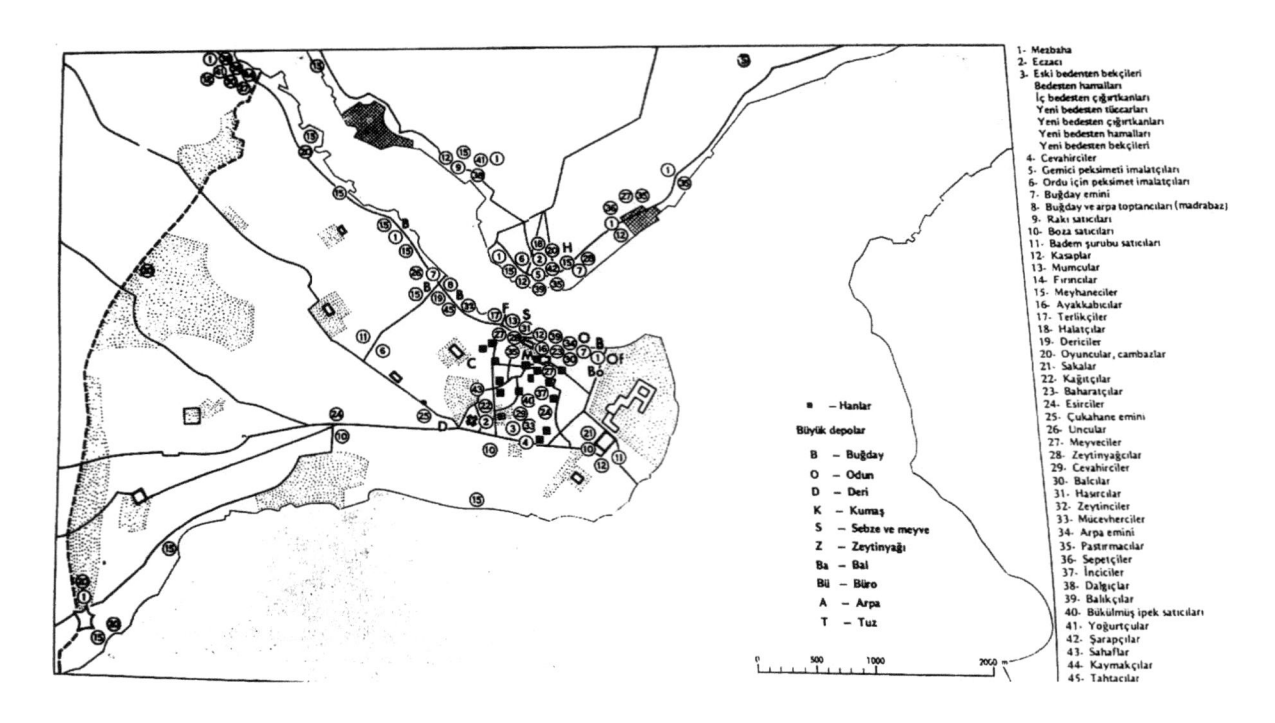

Figure 3. Vertical and horizontal aggloremation of drover tradesmen
Source: Çiğdem Gürsoy

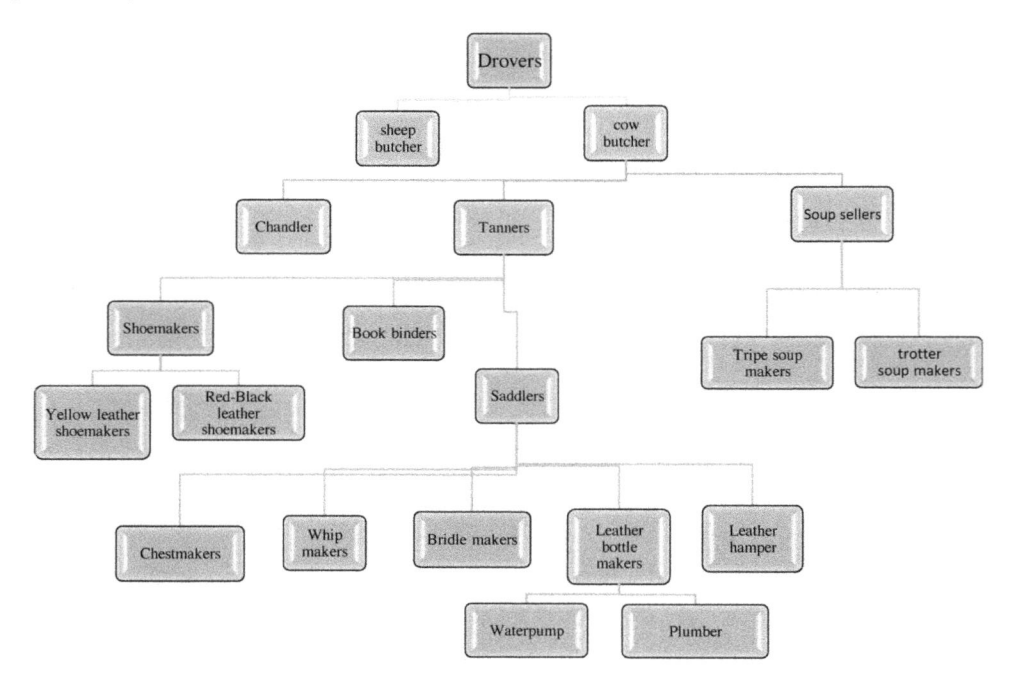

Compilation of References

Aaby, N. E., & Slater, S. F. (1989). Management influences on export performance: A review of the empirical literature 1978-1988. *International Marketing Review*, *6*(4). doi:10.1108/EUM0000000001516

Abbasoğlu, O. F., Aysan, A. F., & Güneş, A. (2007). Concentration, competition, efficiency, and profitability of the Turkish banking sector in the post-crisis period. *MPRA Working Paper*, No. 5494.

Abbey, B. S., & Doukas, J. A. (2015). Do individual currency traders make money? *Journal of International Money and Finance*, *56*, 158–177. doi:10.1016/j.jimonfin.2014.10.003

Abdul-Jabbar, A., Yilmaz, E., Fisahn, C., Drazin, D., Blecher, R., Uppal, M., ... Chapman, J. R. (2019). Disaster scenarios in spine surgery: A survey analysis. *Spine*, *44*(14), 1018–1024. doi:10.1097/BRS.0000000000003040 PMID:30921295

Abdullah, L., & Zulkifli, N. (2015). Integration of fuzzy AHP and interval type-2 fuzzy DEMATEL: An application to human resource management. *Expert Systems with Applications*, *42*(9), 4397–4409. doi:10.1016/j.eswa.2015.01.021

Abedin, B. (2016). Diffusion of adoption of Facebook for customer relationship management in Australia: An exploratory study. *Journal of Organizational and End User Computing*, *28*(1), 56–72. doi:10.4018/JOEUC.2016010104

Abubakar, H. A. (2015). Entrepreneurship development and financial literacy in Africa. *World Journal of Entrepreneurship, Management and Sustainable Development*, *11*(4), 281–294. doi:10.1108/WJEMSD-04-2015-0020

Acaravci, S. K. (2016). Finansal Oranlar ve Hisse Senedi Getirisi İlişkisi: Borsa İstanbul Üzerine Bir Uygulama / Financial Ratios - Stock Return Nexus: An Applicaton on BIST. *Mustafa Kemal Üniversitesi Sosyal Bilimler Enstitüsü Dergisi*, *13*(35), 0–0.

Acaravcı, A., ve Öztürk, İ. (2003). Döviz kurundaki değişkenliğin türkiye ihracatı üzerine etkisi: Ampirik bir çalışma. Review of Social. *Economic ve Business Studies*, *2*, 197–206.

Acaravci, A., Ozturk, I., & Kandir, S. Y. (2012). Natural gas prices and stock prices: Evidence from EU-15 countries. *Economic Modelling*, *29*(5), 1646–1654. doi:10.1016/j.econmod.2012.05.006

Açık, A., Sağlam, B. B., & Tepe, R. (2019). Time-varying causality between exchange rate and container handling volume in Turkish ports. *Transport & Logistics: the International Journal*, *19*(46), 1–11.

Ackoff, R. (1974). *Redesigning the future*. New York: John Wiley & Sons.

Acs, Z. J., Desai, S., & Hessels, J. (2008). Entrepreneurship, economic development and institutions. *Small Business Economics*, *31*(3), 219–234. doi:10.100711187-008-9135-9

Acs, Z., & Armington, C. (2004). Employment growth and entrepreneurial activity in cities. *Regional Studies*, *38*(8), 911–927. doi:10.1080/0034340042000280938

Adalı, Z., & Yüksel, S. (2017). *Causality relationship between foreign direct investments and economic improvement for developing economies*. Retrieved from http://dspace.marmara.edu.tr/xmlui/handle/11424/6146

Adalı, Z., & Yüksel, S. (2017). Causality relationship between foreign direct investments and economic improvement for developing economies. *Marmara İktisat Dergisi, 12*, 109–118.

Addae, B. A., Zhang, L., Zhou, P., & Wang, F. (2019). Analyzing barriers of smart energy city in Accra with two-step fuzzy DEMATEL. *Cities (London, England), 89*, 218–227. doi:10.1016/j.cities.2019.01.043

Adegbola, E. A. (2014). Corporate social responsibility as a marketing strategy for enhanced performance in the Nigerian banking industry: A granger causality approach. *Procedia: Social and Behavioral Sciences, 164*, 141–149. doi:10.1016/j.sbspro.2014.11.062

Adeniyi, O., Omisakin, O., Egwaikhide, F. O., & Oyinlola, A. (2012). Foreign direct investment economic growth and financial sector development in small open developing economies. *Economic Analysis and Policy, 42*(1), 105–127. doi:10.1016/S0313-5926(12)50008-1

Adıgüzel, Z., Artar, M., & Erdil, O. (2017). *A study of psychological contract violation*. Organızatıonal Trust, Intentıon To Leave Work.

Adler, N. J., & Jelinek, M. (1986). Is "organization culture" culture bound? *Human Resource Management, 25*(1), 73–90. doi:10.1002/hrm.3930250106

Agarwal, S., Amromin, G., Ben-David, I., Chomsisengphet, S., & Evanoff, D. D. (2015). Financial literacy and financial planning: Evidence from India. *Journal of Housing Economics, 27*, 4–21. doi:10.1016/j.jhe.2015.02.003

Aghion, P., & Howitt, P. (1992). A model of growth through creative destruction. *Econometrica, 60*(2), 323. doi:10.2307/2951599

Ağırman, E., & Akyol, Ş. (2019). *Finanasal Okuryazarlık İİBF Öğrencileri Üzerine Bir Araştırma*. Bursa, Turkey: Ekin Yayınları.

Agolla, J. E., Makara, T., & Monametsi, G. (2018). Impact of banking innovations on customer attraction, satisfaction and retention: The case of commercial banks in Botswana. *International Journal of Electronic Banking, 1*(2), 150–170. doi:10.1504/IJEBANK.2018.095598

Aguiar-Conraria, L., Martins, M. M., & Soares, M. J. (2018). Estimating the Taylor rule in the time-frequency domain. *Journal of Macroeconomics, 57*, 122–137. doi:10.1016/j.jmacro.2018.05.008

Aguilar, F. J. (1967). *Scanning the business environment*. New York: Macmillan.

Ahmad, F., Draz, M. U., & Yang, S.-C. (2016). *The nexus between exchange rate, exports and economic growth: Further evidence from Asia*. Retrieved from https://ssrn.com/abstract=2758505

Ahmed, N., Ahmad, Z., & Khan, S. K. (2011). Behavioral finance: shaping the decisions of small investors of Lahore stock exchange. *Interdisciplinary Journal of Research in Business, 1*(2), 38–43.

Ahmed, W. M. (2018). On the interdependence of natural gas and stock markets under structural breaks. *The Quarterly Review of Economics and Finance, 67*, 149–161. doi:10.1016/j.qref.2017.06.003

Ahrens, T., & Ferry, L. (2015). Newcastle City Council and the grassroots: Accountability and budgeting under austerity. *Accounting, Auditing & Accountability Journal, 28*(6), 909–933. doi:10.1108/AAAJ-03-2014-1658

Aiginger, K. (1998). A framework for evaluating the dynamic competitiveness of countries. *Structural Change and Economic Dynamics, 9*(2), 159–188. doi:10.1016/S0954-349X(97)00026-X

Aiginger, K. (2006). Competitiveness: From a dangerous obsession to a welfare creating ability with positive externalities. *Journal of Industry, Competition and Trade*, *6*(2), 161–177. doi:10.100710842-006-9475-6

Akalın, Ş. (2007). Innovation, İnovasyon: Yenileşim. *Türk Dili Dil ve Edebiyat Dergisi*, 483.

Akal, M., & Gökmenoğlu, S. M. (2012). OECD Ülkelerinde Rekabet Gücünün Nedensellik İlişkisi: Ampirik Bir Analiz. *TISK Akademi*, *7*(13), 102–129.

Akal, M., Kabasakal, A., & Gökmenoğlu, S. M. (2012). OECD Ülkelerinin Rekabet Gücünü Açıklayıcı Kurumsal ve Karma Modeller. *Business and Economics Research Journal*, *3*(1), 109–130.

Akgun, A., & Sahin, I. E. (2016). Effects of oil prices fluctuation on stock returns of the industry Sector Firms: Borsa Istanbul Industry Index Application. *On Designs of Rotating Savings and Credit Associations*, 121.

Akgün, A. E., Keskin, H., Çemberci, M., & Karakeçe, E. (2019). *Korku ve Önyargıların Girişimcilik Zihniyetine Etkilerinin Araştırılması: Kavramsal Model Önerisi*. II. Elazığ: Uluslararası Sosyal Bilimler&İnovasyon Kongresi.

Akhisar, İ., Tunay, K. B., & Tunay, N. (2015). The effects of innovations on bank performance: The case of electronic banking services. *Procedia: Social and Behavioral Sciences*, *195*, 369–375. doi:10.1016/j.sbspro.2015.06.336

Akhtar, M. A., & Hilton, R. S. (1984). *Exchange rate uncertainty and international trade: Some conceptual issues and new estimates for Germany and the United States*. Federal Reserve Bank.

Akman, G., & Keskin, G. A. (2012). İmalat Firmalarında Çevik Üretimin Algılanma Seviyesinin Değerlendirilmesi. *Dumlupınar Üniversitesi Fen Bilimleri Enstitüsü Dergisi*, *28*, 53–66.

Akpınar, H., & Edin, İ. (2007). Rekabet İstihbaratı, Öneri, *7*(28), 1–8.

Aksin, Z., Armony, M., & Mehrotra, V. (2007). The modern call center: A multi-disciplinary perspective on operations management research. *Production and Operations Management*, *16*(6), 665–688. doi:10.1111/j.1937-5956.2007.tb00288.x

Aktan, C. C. (1999). Global Ekonomik Entegrasyon ve Türkiye. *Dış Ticaret Dergisi*, (12), 1-29.

Aktan, C., & Vural, İ. Y. (2004a). Rekabet Dizisi: 2 Rekabet Gücü ve Rekabet Stratejileri. *Ankara: Türkiye İşveren Sendikaları Konfederasyonları Yayını, Yayın*, (254), 9-23.

Aktan, C. C., & Vural, İ. Y. (2004b). *Yeni ekonomi ve rekabet*. Türkiye İşveren Sendikaları Konfederasyonu Rekabet Dizisi, Ajans Türk Basım.

Aktan, C. C., & Vural, İ. Y. (2006). *Çokuluslu şirketler: Global sermaye ve global yatırımlar*. Konya, Turkey: Çizgi Kitabevi Yayınları.

Aktaş, C. (2010). Türkiye'de reel döviz kuru ile ihracat ve ithalat arasındaki ilişkinin VAR tekniğiyle analizi. *ZKÜ Sosyal Bilimler Dergisi*, *6*(11), 123–140.

Aktaş, K. (2015). Uluslararası İşletmelerde Stratejik Yönetim. *Uluslararası Yönetim ve Sosyal Araştırmalar Dergisi*, *3*(1), 16.

Alalwan, A. A., Dwivedi, Y. K., & Rana, N. P. (2017). Factors influencing adoption of mobile banking by Jordanian bank customers: Extending UTAUT2 with trust. *International Journal of Information Management*, *37*(3), 99–110. doi:10.1016/j.ijinfomgt.2017.01.002

Al-Bahrani, A., Weathers, J., & Patel, D. (2019). Racial differences in the returns to financial literacy education. *The Journal of Consumer Affairs*, *53*(2), 572–599. doi:10.1111/joca.12205

Albaity, M., & Rahman, M. (2012). Behavioural finance and Malaysian culture. *International Business Research*, *5*(11), 65. doi:10.5539/ibr.v5n11p65

Albeni, M., & Demir, Y. (2005). Makro Ekonomik Göstergelerin Mali Sektör Hisse Senedi Fiyatlarına Etkisi (IMKB Uygulamalı). *Muğla Üniversitesi Sosyal Bilimler Enstitüsü Dergisi*, (14), 1–18.

Alcidi, C., Busse, M., & Gros, D. (2016). Is there a need for additional monetary stimulus? Insights from the original Taylor rule. *Insights from the Original Taylor Rule (April 15, 2016). CEPS Policy Brief*, (342).

Aldric, J. H., & Nelson, F. D. (1984). *Linear Probability, Logit and Probit Models*. Thousand Oaks, CA: Sage. doi:10.4135/9781412984744

Alexander, C. (Ed.). (2003). *Operational risk: regulation, analysis and management*. Pearson Education.

Alfaro, L., Chanda, A., Özcan, S. K., & Sayek, S. (2003). FDI and economic growth: the role of local financial markets. *Journal of International Economics*, *64*(1), 89–112. doi:10.1016/S0022-1996(03)00081-3

Alhan, O., & Yüksel, S. (2018). Kadın Çalışanların Banka Büyüklüğü Ve Karlılığına Etkisi: Engle-Granger Eş Bütünleşme Analizi İle Türkiye Üzerine Bir Uygulama. *İş'te Davranış Dergisi*, *3*(2), 140-147.

Ali, A., Rahman, M. S. A., & Bakar, A. (2015). Financial satisfaction and the influence of financial literacy in Malaysia. *Social Indicators Research*, *120*(1), 137–156. doi:10.100711205-014-0583-0

Ali, F., Dey, B. L., & Filieri, R. (2015). An assessment of service quality and resulting customer satisfaction in Pakistan International Airlines: Findings from foreigners and overseas Pakistani customers. *International Journal of Quality & Reliability Management*, *32*(5), 486–502. doi:10.1108/IJQRM-07-2013-0110

Alifiah, M., & Tahir, M. (2018). Predicting financial distress companies in the manufacturing and non-manufacturing sectors in Malaysia using macroeconomic variables. *Management Science Letters*, *8*(6), 593–604. doi:10.5267/j.msl.2018.4.031

Aliyu, S., Hassan, M. K., Mohd Yusof, R., & Naiimi, N. (2017). Islamic banking sustainability: a review of literature and directions for future research. *Emerging Markets Finance & Trade*, *53*(2), 440–470. doi:10.1080/1540496X.2016.1262761

Allen, F., Qian, Y., Tu, G., & Yu, F. (2019). Entrusted loans: A close look at China's shadow banking system. *Journal of Financial Economics*, *133*(1), 18–41. doi:10.1016/j.jfineco.2019.01.006

Allen, T. T., Xiong, H., & Afful-Dadzie, A. (2016). A directed topic model applied to call center improvement. *Applied Stochastic Models in Business and Industry*, *32*(1), 57–73. doi:10.1002/asmb.2123

Allexandre, D., Bernstein, A. M., Walker, E., Hunter, J., Roizen, M. F., & Morledge, T. J. (2016). A web-based mindfulness stress management program in a corporate call center: A randomized clinical trial to evaluate the added benefit of onsite group support. *Journal of Occupational and Environmental Medicine*, *58*(3), 254–264. doi:10.1097/JOM.0000000000000680 PMID:26949875

Allgood, S., & Walstad, W. B. (2016). The effects of perceived and actual financial literacy on financial behaviors. *Economic Inquiry*, *54*(1), 675–697. doi:10.1111/ecin.12255

Allport, G. W. (1961). *Pattern and growth in personality*. London, UK: Holt, Reinhart, and Winston.

Almeida, J. H., Sapienza, H. J., & Michael, J. (2000). Growth through internationalization: Patterns among British firms. *Frontier of Entrepreneurship Research*, *4*, 402.

Almenberg, J., & Dreber, A. (2015). Gender, stock market participation and financial literacy. *Economics Letters*, *137*, 140–142. doi:10.1016/j.econlet.2015.10.009

Compilation of References

Alpar, R. (2010). *Spor, sağlık ve eğitim bilimlerinden örneklerle uygulamalı istatistik ve geçerlik-güvenirlik*. Detay Yayıncılık.

Alpar, R. (2013). *Uygulamalı çok değişkenli istatistiksel yöntemler*. Detay Yayıncılık.

Altay, B., & Gürpınar, K. (2008). Açıklanmış Karşılaştırmalı Üstünlükler Ve Bazı Rekabet Gücü Endeksleri: Türk Mobilya Sektörü Üzerine Bir Uygulama. *Afyon Kocatepe Üniversitesi İktisadi ve İdari Bilimler Fakültesi Dergisi*, *10*(1), 257–274.

Alti, A., & Titman, S. (2019). *A dynamic model of characteristic-based return predictability (No. w25777)*. National Bureau of Economic Research. doi:10.3386/w25777

Altınbaşak, İ., Akyol, A., Alkibay, S., & Arslan, F. M. (2008). *Küresel pazarlama yönetimi*. İstanbul, Turkey: Beta Basım Yayım Dağıtım AŞ.

Altinirmak, S., Okoth, B., Ergun, M., & Karamasa, C. (2017). Analyzing mobile banking quality factors under neutrosophic set perspective: A case study of TURKEY. *J. Econ. Finance Accounting*, *4*(4), 354–367.

Altıntaş, H. (2013). Türkiye'de petrol fiyatları, ihracat ve reel döviz kuru ilişkisi: ARDL sınır testi yaklaşımı ve dinamik nedensellik analizi. *Uluslararası Yönetim İktisat ve İşletme Dergisi*, *9*(19), 1–30.

Altıntaş, H., Çetintaş, H., & Taban, S. (2008). Türkiye'de bütçe açığı, parasal büyüme ve enflasyon arasındaki ilişkinin ekonometrik analizi: 1992–2006. *Anadolu University Journal of Social Science*, *8*(2), 185–208.

Altunöz, U. (2013). Empirical analysis of competition dynamics in Turkish banking via competition determination approaches. *International Conference on Eurasian Economies 2013*.

Alvarez, I., & Marin, R. (2013). FDI and technology as levering factors of competitiveness in developing countries. *Journal of International Management*, *19*(3), 232–246. doi:10.1016/j.intman.2013.02.005

Alvesson, M. (2012). Understanding organizational culture. Atlanta, GA: Sage.

Amavilah, V., Asongu, S. A., & Andrés, A. R. (2017). Effects of globalization on peace and stability: Implications for governance and the knowledge economy of African countries. *Technological Forecasting and Social Change*, *122*, 91–103. doi:10.1016/j.techfore.2017.04.013

Amaya, A., Lau, C., Owusu-Amoah, Y., & Light, J. (2018). Evaluation of gaining cooperation methods for IVR surveys in low-and middle-income countries. *Survey Methods: Insights from the Field*, 8.

Ambrose, C., & Morello, D. (2004). Designing the agile organization: design principles and practices. *Strategic Analysis Report*, *21*, 7532.

AMF. (2014, Oct. 13). *The AMF warns of the dangers of forex market trading for individual investors*. Retrieved from https://www.amf-france.org/en_US/Actualites/Communiques-depresse/AMF/annee_2014.html?docId=workspace%3A%2F%2FSpacesStore%2F96c52a14-3900-464f-8fff-7d4700ff37e3

Amin, S. B., Kabir, F. A., & Khan, F. (2019). Tourism and energy nexus in selected South Asian countries: A panel study. *Current Issues in Tourism*, 1–5. doi:10.1080/13683500.2019.1638354

Andersen, T. J. (Ed.). (2006). *Perspectives on strategic risk management*. Copenhagen Business School Press DK.

Anderson, B. S., Wennberg, K., & McMullen, J. S. (2019). Enhancing quantitative theory-testing entrepreneurship research. *Journal of Business Venturing*, *34*(5), 105928. doi:10.1016/j.jbusvent.2019.02.001

Anderson, C. R., & Zeithaml, C. P. (1984). Stage of the product life cycle, business strategy, and business performance. *Academy of Management Journal*, *27*(1), 5–24.

Anderson-Levitt, K. M. (2012). Complicating the concept of culture. *Comparative Education*, *48*(4), 441–454. doi:10.1080/03050068.2011.634285

Andersson, C. (2015). Comparison of WEB and interactive voice response (IVR) methods for delivering brief alcohol interventions to hazardous-drinking university students: A randomized controlled trial. *European Addiction Research*, *21*(5), 240–252. doi:10.1159/000381017 PMID:25967070

Ang, J. B. (2009). Foreign direct investment and its impact on the Thai economy: The role of financial development. *Journal of Economics and Finance*, *33*(3), 316–323. doi:10.100712197-008-9042-6

Anshari, M., Alas, Y., Yunus, N., Sabtu, N. I., & Hamid, M. H. (2015). Social customer relationship management and student empowerment in online learning systems. *International Journal of Electronic Customer Relationship Management*, *9*(2-3), 104–121. doi:10.1504/IJECRM.2015.071711

Ansoff, H. I. (1965). *Corporate strategy an analytic approach to business policy for growth and expansion*. New York: Mcgraw-Hill Book.

Anzuini, A., Lombardi, M. J., & Pagano, P. (2012). The impact of monetary policy shocks on commodity prices. *Bank of Italy Temi di Discussione Working Paper*, (851).

Apergis, N., & Miller, S. M. (2009). Do structural oil-market shocks affect stock prices. *Energy Economics*, *31*(4), 569–575. doi:10.1016/j.eneco.2009.03.001

Apergis, N., & Ozturk, I. (2015). Testing environmental Kuznets curve hypothesis in Asian countries. *Ecological Indicators*, *52*, 16–22. doi:10.1016/j.ecolind.2014.11.026

Apilioğulları, L. (2016). *Yalın Dönüşüm*. Aura Kitapları.

Apriadi, I., Sembel, R., Santosa, P. W., & Firdaus, M. (2016). Banking fragility in Indonesia: A panel vector autoregression approach. *IJABER*, *14*(14), 1193–1224.

Arabacı, H. (2017). Küresel Kriz Sonrası Türkiye'de Uygulanan Ekonomi Politikaları. *Sosyal Bilimler Araştırma Dergisi*, *6*(4), 1–10.

Araza, A., & Aslan, G. (2016). *Yönetimde Yeni Paradigmalar*. Nobel Yayınevi.

Aren, S., Aydemir, S. D., & Şehitoğlu, Y. (2016). Behavioral biases on institutional investors: A literature review. *Kybernetes*, *45*(10), 1668–1684. doi:10.1108/K-08-2015-0203

Aren, S., & Zengin, A. N. (2016). Influence of financial literacy and risk perception on choice of investment. *Procedia: Social and Behavioral Sciences*, *235*, 656–663. doi:10.1016/j.sbspro.2016.11.047

Areosa, W. D., & Coelho, C. A. (2013). Using a DSGE model to assess the macroeconomic effects of reserve requirements in Brazil. *Banco Central Do Brasil Working Paper Series*, (303).

Arıkan, C., Görgün, S., & Yalçın, Y. (2018). Parasal Aktarım Sürecinde Faiz Koridorunun Yeri. *Maliye Dergisi*, *174*, 1–25.

Arıkan, S. (2004). *Girişimcilik, Temel Kavramlar ve Bazı Güncel Konular, Genişletilmiş 2*. Ankara, Turkey: Baskı, Siyasal Kitabevi.

Arin, K. P., Huang, V. Z., Minniti, M., Nandialath, A. M., & Reich, O. F. (2015). Revisiting the determinants of entrepreneurship: A Bayesian approach. *Journal of Management*, *41*(2), 607–631. doi:10.1177/0149206314558488

Aristotelous, K. (2001). Exchange-rate volatility, exchange-rate regime, and trade volume: Evidence from the UK–US export function (1889–1999). *Economics letters*, *72*(1), 87–94. doi:10.1016/S0165-1765(01)00414-1

Aristovnik, A. (2007). Short-and medium-term determinants of current account balances in Middle East and North Africa countries.

Arize, A. C., Malindretos, J., & Kasibhatla, K. M. (2003). Does exchange-rate volatility depress export flows: The case of LDCs. *International Advances in Economic Research*, *9*(1), 7–19. doi:10.1007/BF02295297

Arize, A. C., & Osang, T., ve Slottje, D. J. (2000). Exchange-rate volatility and foreign trade: Evidence from thirteen LCD's. *Journal of Business & Economic Statistics*, *18*(1), 10–17.

Arkan, T. (2016). The importance of financial ratios in predicting stock price trends: A case study in emerging markets. *Finanse, Rynki Finansowe. Ubezpieczenia*, *79*(1), 13–26.

Armutlu, C., & Ari, G. S. (2010). Yönetim modalarinin yüksek lisans ve doktora tezlerine yansimalari: Bibliyometrik bir analiz. *ODTÜ Gelisme Dergisi*, *37*(1), 1.

Arouri, M., Tiwari, A., & Teulon, F. (2014). Oil prices and trade balance: A frequency domain analysis for India. *Economic Bulletin*, *34*(2), 663–680.

Arrawatia, R., Misra, A., & Dawar, V. (2015). Bank competition and efficiency: Empirical evidence from Indian market. *International Journal of Law and Management*, *57*(3), 217–231. doi:10.1108/IJLMA-03-2014-0029

Arshad, R., & Bashir, A. (2015). Impact of oil and gas prices on stock returns: Evidence from Pakistan's energy intensive industries. *International Review of Social Sciences*, *3*(4), 156–168.

Artan, S., & Hayaloğlu, P. (2015). Doğrudan Yabancı Sermaye Yatırımlarının Kurumsal Belirleyicileri: OECD Ülkeleri Örneği. *Ege Akademik Bakış*, *15*(4), 551–564. doi:10.21121/eab.2015416654

Ascarza, E., Ebbes, P., Netzer, O., & Danielson, M. (2017). Beyond the target customer: Social effects of customer relationship management campaigns. *Journal of Marketing Research*, *54*(3), 347–363. doi:10.1509/jmr.15.0442

Ashby, S., Palermo, T., & Power, M. (2012). Risk culture in financial organisations: An interim report.

Ashcroft, B., & Love, J. H. (1996). Firm births and employment change in the British counties: 1981–89. *Papers in Regional Science*, *75*(4), 483–500. doi:10.1007/BF02412291

Ashraf, N., Camerer, C. F., & Loewenstein, G. (2005). Adam Smith, behavioral economist. *The Journal of Economic Perspectives*, *19*(3), 131–145. doi:10.1257/089533005774357897

Aslan, N. (2005). *Dünya Ekonomisinde Gelişmeler: Küreselleşme ve Ekonomik Entegrasyon Küresel ve Bölgesel Yaklaşım* (O. Küçükahmetoğlu, Ed.). Ankara, Turkey: Ekin Yayınevi.

Asseery, A., & Peel, D. A. (1991). The effects of exchange rate volatility on exports: Some new estimates. *Economics letters*, *37*(2), 173–177. doi:10.1016/0165-1765(91)90127-7

Asteriou, D., & Bashmakova, Y. (2013). Assessing the impact of oil returns on emerging stock markets: A panel data approach for ten Central and Eastern European Countries. *Energy Economics*, *38*, 204–211. doi:10.1016/j.eneco.2013.02.011

Asteriou, D., Masatci, K., & Pılbeam, K. (2016). Exchange rate volatility and international trade: International evidence from the MINT countries. *Economic Modelling*, *58*, 133–140. doi:10.1016/j.econmod.2016.05.006

Asutay, M. (2008). *Islamic banking and finance: social failure*. New Horizon, No. 169 (pp. 1–3). October-December; doi:10.2139srn.1735674

Ataman, G., & Gegez, E. (1991). Dış Çevrenin Pazarlama Üzerindeki Etkisi ve Pazarlama Yönetimi Açısından Önemi. *Pazarlama Dünyası*, *5*(26), 28–35.

Atan, M., & Çatalbaş, E. (2004). Çok Değişkenli İstatistiksel Analiz Yöntemleri ile Türk Bankacılık Sektöründe Çok Boyutlu Mali Başarısızlık Tahmin Modelleri Oluşturulması. *4. İstatistik Günleri Sempozyumu*, 19-22.

Atasoy, F. (2005). *Küreselleşme ve Milliyetçilik*. İstanbul, Turkey: Ötüken Yayınları.

Atılğan, M. H. (2016). Yeni Para Politikası Anlayışı ve Finansal İstikrar. *Çankırı Karatekin Üniversitesi İİBF Dergisi, 6*(2), 249-268.

Atsalakis, G. S., Atsalaki, I. G., & Zopounidis, C. (2018). Forecasting the success of a new tourism service by a neuro-fuzzy technique. *European Journal of Operational Research, 268*(2), 716–727. doi:10.1016/j.ejor.2018.01.044

Audretsch, D. B., Belitski, M., & Desai, S. (2015). Entrepreneurship and economic development in cities. *The Annals of Regional Science, 55*(1), 33–60. doi:10.100700168-015-0685-x

Audretsch, D. B., & Fritsch, M. (2002). Growth regimes over time and space. *Regional Studies, 36*(2), 113–124. doi:10.1080/00343400220121909

Australia, D. (2012). *Cultivating an intelligent risk culture: a fresh perspective*. Sydney, Australia: Deloitte Touche Tohmatsu Ltd.

Aven, T. (2011). *Quantitative risk assessment: the scientific platform*. Cambridge, UK: Cambridge University Press. doi:10.1017/CBO9780511974120

Ayaydın, H., & Karakaya, A. (2014). The effect of bank capital on profitability and risk in Turkish banking. *International Journal of Business and Social Science, 5*, 252–271.

Aydemir, M., & Demirci, M. K. (2006). *İşletmelerin Küreselleşme stratejileri ve kobi örnekleminde bir uygulama*. Ankara, Turkey: Gazi Kitabevi.

Aydemir, O. (2008). Hisse Senedi Getirileri Ve Reel Sektör Arasındaki İlişki: Ampirik Bir Çalışma. *Afyon Kocatepe Üniversitesi İktisadi ve İdari Bilimler Fakültesi Dergisi, 10*(2), 37–55.

Aydın, A. (2008). Endüstri içi ticaret ve Türkiye: Ülkeye özgü belirleyicilerin tespitine yönelik bir araştırma. *Marmara Üniversitesi İİBF Dergisi, 25*(2), 881–921.

Aydin, E., Brounen, D., & Kok, N. (2018). Information provision and energy consumption: Evidence from a field experiment. *Energy Economics, 71*, 403–410. doi:10.1016/j.eneco.2018.03.008

Aydın, G. K. (2017). Ödemler dengesi ve cari açık: Türkiye'de 2014-2016 yılları arsında cari açık ve petrol fiyatları etkilişimi. *Fırat Üniversitesi Uluslararası İktisadi ve İdari Bilimler Dergisi, 1*(2), 27–66.

Aydın, M. (2004). Uluslararası İlişkilerin Gerçekçi Teorisi: Kökeni, Kapsamı,Kritiği. *Uluslararası İlişkiler, 1*(1), 33–60.

Aydin, M., & Malcioglu, G. (2016). Financial development and economic growth relationship: The case of OECD countries. *Journal of Applied Research in Finance and Economics, 2*(1), 1–7.

Aydın, Y. (2019). Türk bankacılık sektöründe karlılığı etkileyen faktörlerin panel veri analizi ile incelenmesi. *Gümüşhane Üniversitesi Sosyal Bilimler Enstitüsü Elektronik Dergisi, 10*(1), 181–189.

Aysan, A. F., Disli, M., & Ozturk, H. (2018). Bank lending channel in a dual banking system: Why are Islamic banks so responsive? *World Economy, 41*(3), 674–698. doi:10.1111/twec.12507

Aysan, A. F., Fendoglu, S., & Kilinc, M. (2014). Managing short-term capital flows in new central banking: Unconventional monetary policy framework in Turkey. *Eurasian Economic Review, 4*(1), 45–69. doi:10.100740822-014-0001-6

Compilation of References

Baabdullah, A. M., Alalwan, A. A., Rana, N. P., Kizgin, H., & Patil, P. (2019). Consumer use of mobile banking (M-Banking) in Saudi Arabia: Towards an integrated model. *International Journal of Information Management*, *44*, 38–52. doi:10.1016/j.ijinfomgt.2018.09.002

Bachmann, K., De Giorgi, E. G., & Hens, T. (2019). Behavioral finance for private banking: from the art of advice to the science of advice. *Structure*, *8*(2).

Badia, M. M., Slootmaekers, V., Beveren, I., & Van Beveren, I. (2008). *Globalization drives strategic product switching (No. 2008-2246)*. International Monetary Fund.

Badie, B. (2001). Realism under praise, or a requiem? The praradigmatic debate in international relations. *International Political Science Review*, *22*(3), 45–46. doi:10.1177/0192512101223003

Badulescu, N., & Mirela, A. D. (2012). Different types of innovation modeling. *Annals of DAAAM for 2012 & Proceedings of the 23rd International DAAAM Symposium*, *23*(1), 1071.

Baerg, N., & Lowe, W. (2018). A textual Taylor rule: estimating central bank preferences combining topic and scaling methods. *Political Science Research and Methods*, 1-17.

Bagirov, M., & Mateus, C. (2019). Oil prices, stock markets and firm performance: Evidence from Europe. *International Review of Economics & Finance*, *61*, 270–288. doi:10.1016/j.iref.2019.02.007

Bağış, B. (2016). *Döviz kuru sistemleri, uluslararası ticaret ve parite ilişkileri. (Editör: N. Eroğlu, H. Dinçer, ve Ü. Hacıoğlu), Uluslararası Finans Teori ve Politika* (pp. 361–408). Ankara, Turkey: Orion Kitabevi.

Bahmani-Oskooee, M., & Gelan, A. (2018). Exchange-Rate volatility and international trade performance: Evidence from 12 African countries. *Economic Analysis and Policy*, *58*, 14–21. doi:10.1016/j.eap.2017.12.005

Bahmani-Oskooee, M., & Harvey, H. (2012). US–Malaysia trade at commodity level and the role of the real exchange rate. *Global Economic Review*, *41*(1), 55–75. doi:10.1080/1226508X.2012.655028

Bahmani-Oskooee, M., & Hegerty, S. W. (2007). Exchange rate volatility and trade flows: A review article. *Journal of Economic Studies (Glasgow, Scotland)*, *34*(3), 211–255. doi:10.1108/01443580710772777

Bahmani-Oskooee, M., Iqbal, J., & Salam, M. (2016). Short run and long run effects of exchange rate volatility on commodity trade between Pakistan and Japan. *Economic Analysis and Policy*, *52*, 131–142. doi:10.1016/j.eap.2016.09.002

Bai, C., Shi, B., Liu, F., & Sarkis, J. (2019). Banking credit worthiness: Evaluating the complex relationships. *Omega*, *83*, 26–38. doi:10.1016/j.omega.2018.02.001

Bain, M. K., & Howells, P. (2009). *Monetary economics: policy and its theoretical basis*. Macmillan International Higher Education. doi:10.1007/978-1-137-01342-2

Baker, H. K., Kumar, S., Goyal, N., & Gaur, V. (2019). How financial literacy and demographic variables relate to behavioral biases. *Managerial Finance*, *45*(1), 124–146. doi:10.1108/MF-01-2018-0003

Baki, B., 21. Yüzyılın Üretim Paradigması: Çevik Üretim, İktisadi ve İdari Bilimler Dergisi, 17, 1-2, 291-305, 2003.

Balanda, K. P., & MacGillivray, H. (1988). Kurtosis: A critical review. *The American statistician*, *42*(2), 111–119.

Ball, D. A., McCulloch, W. H., Frantz, P., Geringer, M., & Minor, M. (1999). International business: The challenge of global competition.

Baltagi, B. H. (2005). *Econometric analysis of panel data*. UK: John Wiley & Sons.

Banerjee, A., Dolado, J., & Mestre, R. (1998). Error correction mechanism tests for cointegration in a single equation framework. *Journal of Time Series Analysis*, *19*(3), 267–283. doi:10.1111/1467-9892.00091

Banerjee, P., Arcabic, V., & Lee, H. (2017). Fourier ADL cointegration test to approximate smooth breaks with new evidence from crude oil market. *Economic Modelling*, *67*, 114–124. doi:10.1016/j.econmod.2016.11.004

Banks, E. (2012). *Risk culture: A practical guide to building and strengthening the fabric of risk management*. Palgrave Macmillan. doi:10.1057/9781137263728

Bannock, G., & Manser, W. (2003). *International dictionary of finance (the economist series)*. Profile Books.

Baranoff, E. Z., & Baranoff, E. Z. (2004). *Risk management and insurance* (pp. 48–52). Danvers, MA: Wiley.

Barber, B. M., & Odean, T. (2013). The behavior of individual investors. In *Handbook of the Economics of Finance* (Vol. 2, pp. 1533–1570). Elsevier.

Barbieri, J. C., & Alvares, A. C. T. (2016). *Sixth generation innovation model: description of a success model*. Brazil: Getulio Vargas Foundation Sao Paulo.

Barışık, S. (2001). Para kurulu sistemi, üstünlükleri ve zayıf yönleri. *Gazi Üniversitesi İktisadi ve İdari Bilimler Fakültesi Dergisi*, *3*(2), 51–68.

Barisik, S., & Tay, A. (2010). An analysis of financial crisis by early warning systems approach: the case of transition economies and emerging markets (1994-2006 period panel logit model). *Journal of Economic & Management Perspectives*, *4*(2), 403.

Barker, W. (2007). The global foreign exchange market: Growth and transformation. *Bank of Canada Review*, *2007*(Autumn), 4–13.

Barnett, W. A., & Duzhak, E. A. (2017). Structural stability of the generalized Taylor rule. *Macroeconomic Dynamics*, 1–15.

Barney, J. (1991). Firm resources and sustained competitive advantage. *Journal of Management*, *17*(1), 99–120. doi:10.1177/014920639101700108

Barney, J. B., & Hesterly, W. S. (2009). *Concepts-strategic management and competitive advantage*. Pearson India.

Baron, D. P. (1976). Fluctuating exchange rates and the pricing of exports. *Economic Inquiry*, *14*(3), 425–438. doi:10.1111/j.1465-7295.1976.tb00430.x

Barrick, M. R., & Mount, M. K. (1991). The big five personality dimensions and job performance: A meta-analysis. *Personnel Psychology*, *44*(1), 1–26. doi:10.1111/j.1744-6570.1991.tb00688.x

Başarır, Ç., & Erçakar, M. E. (2016). An analysis of the relationship between crude oil prices, current account deficit and exchange rates: Turkish experiment. *International Journal of Economics and Finance*, *8*(11), 48. doi:10.5539/ijef.v8n11p48

Basher, S. A., Haug, A. A., & Sadorsky, P. (2017). The impact of oil-market shocks on stock returns in major oil-exporting countries: a Markov switching approach. Available at *SSRN 3046052*.

Basher, S. A., Haug, A. A., & Sadorsky, P. (2012). Oil prices, exchange rates and emerging stock markets. *Energy Economics*, *34*(1), 227–240. doi:10.1016/j.eneco.2011.10.005

Basher, S. A., & Sadorsky, P. (2006). Oil price risk and emerging stock markets. *Global Finance Journal*, *17*(2), 224–251. doi:10.1016/j.gfj.2006.04.001

Basher, S. A., & Sadorsky, P. (2016). Hedging emerging market stock prices with oil, gold, VIX, and bonds: A comparison between DCC, ADCC and GO-GARCH. *Energy Economics*, *54*, 235–247. doi:10.1016/j.eneco.2015.11.022

Baştürk, Ş. (2001). Bir Olgu Olarak Küreselleşme. *ISGUC The Journal of Industrial Relations and Human Resources*, *3*(2).

BAT. (2019). Retrieved from https://verisistemi.tbb.org.tr

Bateh, J., & Farah, J. (2017). Reducing call center wait times through six sigma. *Journal of Business Inquiry*, *17*(2), 131–148.

Bauer, C., & Neuenkirch, M. (2017). Forecast uncertainty and the Taylor rule. *Journal of International Money and Finance*, *77*, 99–116. doi:10.1016/j.jimonfin.2017.07.017

Bauman, Z. (1999). *Küreselleşme*. İstanbul, Turkey: Ayrıntı Yayınları.

Bauman, Z. (2010). *Küreselleşme Topumsal Sonuçları* (A. Yılmaz, Trans.). İstanbul, Turkey: Ayrıntı Yayınları.

Baum, C. F., Caglayan, M., & Ozkan, N. (2004). Nonlinear effects of exchange rate volatility on the volume of bilateral exports. *Journal of Applied Econometrics*, *19*(1), 1–23. doi:10.1002/jae.725

Baum, C., Schäfer, D., & Talavera, O. (2011). The impact of the financial system's structure on firms' financial constraints. *Journal of International Money and Finance*, *30*(4), 678–691. doi:10.1016/j.jimonfin.2011.02.004

Baur, D. G., Hong, K., & Lee, A. D. (2018). Bitcoin: Medium of exchange or speculative assets? *Journal of International Financial Markets, Institutions, and Money*, *54*, 177–189. doi:10.1016/j.intfin.2017.12.004

Bayar, F. (2008). Küreselleşme Kavramı ve Küreselleşme Sürecinde Türkiye. *Uluslararası Ekonomik Sorunlar Dergisi*, *32*, 25–34.

Bayat, T., Şahbaz, A., & Akçacı, T. (2013). Petrol fiyatlarının dış ticaret açığı üzerindeki etkisi: Türkiye örneği. *Erciyes Üniversitesi İktisadi ve İdari Bilimler Fakültesi Dergisi*, (42), 67-90.

Bayraç, N. (2006). *Yeni Ekonomi'nin Toplumsal*. Ekonomik Ve Teknolojik Boyutları.

Bayraktar, Y., Taha, E., & Yildiz, F. (2016). A causal relationship between oil prices current account deficit, and economic growth: an empirical analysis from fragile five countries. *Ecoforum Journal*, *5*(3).

Baysan, S., & Durmuşoğlu, B. (2015). Systematic literature review for lean product development principles and tools. *Sigma Mühendislik ve Fen Bilimleri Dergisi*, *33*(3), 305–323.

Becker, R., Enders, W., & Lee, J. (2006). A stationarity test in the presence of an unknown number of smooth Breaks. *Journal of Time Series Analysis*, *27*(3), 381–409. doi:10.1111/j.1467-9892.2006.00478.x

Beckmann, J., Belke, A., & Dreger, C. (2017). The relevance of international spillovers and asymmetric effects in the Taylor rule. *The Quarterly Review of Economics and Finance*, *64*, 162–170. doi:10.1016/j.qref.2016.11.004

Beck, T., Demirgüç-Kunt, A., & Levine, R. (2006). Bank concentration, competition, and crises: First results. *Journal of Banking & Finance*, *30*(5), 1581–1603. doi:10.1016/j.jbankfin.2005.05.010

Beckworth, D., & Hendrickson, J. R. (2015). Nominal GDP targeting and the Taylor rule on an even playing field. *Journal of Money, Credit, and Banking*.

Bees, A. D., & Williams, I. D. (2017). Explaining the differences in household food waste collection and treatment provisions between local authorities in England and Wales. *Waste Management (New York, N.Y.)*, *70*, 222–235. doi:10.1016/j.wasman.2017.09.004 PMID:28918870

Beilis, A., Dash, J. W., & Wise, J. V. (2014). Psychology, stock/FX trading and option prices. *Journal of Behavioral Finance*, *15*(3), 251–268. doi:10.1080/15427560.2014.943227

Bekiros, S., Gupta, R., & Kyei, C. (2016). On economic uncertainty, stock market predictability and nonlinear spillover effects. *The North American Journal of Economics and Finance*, *36*, 184–191. doi:10.1016/j.najef.2016.01.003

Belke, A. H., Bordon, I. G., & Hendricks, T. W. (2014). Monetary policy, global liquidity and commodity price dynamics. *The North American Journal of Economics and Finance*, *28*, 1–16. doi:10.1016/j.najef.2013.12.003

Bell, J., Crick, D., & Young, S. (2004). Small firm internationalization and business strategy: An exploratory study of 'knowledge-intensive' and 'traditional' manufacturing firms in the UK. *International Small Business Journal*, *22*(1), 23–56. doi:10.1177/0266242604039479

Bell, J., & Young, S. (1998). Towards an integrative framework of the internationalization of the firm. In *Internationalization* (pp. 5–28). London, UK: Palgrave Macmillan. doi:10.1007/978-1-349-26556-5_1

Ben-David, B. M., & Icht, M. (2016). Voice changes in real speaking situations during a day, with and without vocal loading: Assessing call center operators. *Journal of Voice*, *30*(2), 247–e1. doi:10.1016/j.jvoice.2015.04.002 PMID:26320758

Bengil, D. (2003). Uluslararası Pazarlamada Reklam Mesajı Yaratılmasında Kültür ve Önemi. Marmara Üniversitesi Sosyal Bilimler Enstitüsü (Yayınlanmamış Yüksek Lisan Tezi), 97 s., İstanbul.

Benk, S., & Akdemir, T. (2004). Globalleşme ve Ekonomik Değişim. *Çimento İşveren Dergisi*, *18*(1), 12-27.

Berentsen, A., & Monnet, C. (2008). Monetary policy in a channel system. *Journal of Monetary Economics*, *55*(6), 1067–1080. doi:10.1016/j.jmoneco.2008.07.002

Berger, A. N., & Hannan, T. H. (1998). The efficiency cost of market power in the banking industry: A test of the "quiet life" and related hypotheses. *The Review of Economics and Statistics*, *80*(3), 454–465. doi:10.1162/003465398557555

Berger, A. N., Klapper, L. F., & Turk-Ariss, R. (2009). Bank competition and financial stability. *Journal of Financial Services Research*, *35*(2), 99–118. doi:10.100710693-008-0050-7

Bergeron, P., & Hiller, C. A. (2002). Competitive intelligence. *Annual Review of Information Science and Technology (Arist)*, *36*(1), 353–390. doi:10.1002/aris.1440360109

Bernhardsen, T., & Kloster, A. (2010). Liquidity management system: Floor or corridor?.

Beşel, F. (2017). Oil prices affect current account deficit: Empirical evidence from Turkey. *Journal of Applied Research in Finance and Economics*, *3*(2), 13–21.

Beşel, F., & Yardımcıoğlu, F. (2017). Maliye Dergisi'nin bibliyometrik analizi: 2007-2016 Dönemi. *Maliye Dergisi*, *172*, 133–151.

Best, R., Langston, C. A., & De Valence, G. (Eds.). (2003). *Workplace strategies and facilities management*. Routledge.

Beyers, C., De Freitas, A., Essel-Mensah, K. A., Seymore, R., & Tsomocos, D. P. (2019). A Computable general equilibrium model for banking sector risk assessment in South Africa. *Saïd Business School WP*, *11*.

Beyer, S., Jensen, G., Johnson, R., & Hughen, J. C. (2015). Stock returns and the US dollar: The importance of monetary policy. *Managerial Finance*.

Bhardwaj, P., Chatterjee, P., Demir, K. D., & Turut, O. (2018). When and how is corporate social responsibility profitable? *Journal of Business Research*, *84*, 206–219. doi:10.1016/j.jbusres.2017.11.026

Compilation of References

Bharucha, J. P. (2019). Determinants of financial literacy among Indian youth. In *Dynamic Perspectives on Globalization and Sustainable Business in Asia* (pp. 154–167). Hershey, PA: IGI Global. doi:10.4018/978-1-5225-7095-0.ch010

Bhattarai, K., & Carter, M. (2018). An empirical analysis of the Taylor rule and its application to monetary policy: a case for the United Kingdom and Euro area. *Asian Journal of Economics and Empirical Research*, *5*(2), 173–182. doi:10.20448/journal.501.2018.52.173.182

Bianchi, D. (2018). Cryptocurrencies as an asset class? An empirical assessment. *An Empirical Assessment (June 6, 2018). WBS Finance Group Research Paper*.

Bilici, İ. (2017). *Medya Okuryazarlığı ve Eğitimi*. Ankara, Turkey: Nobel Akademik Yayınları.

Birchall, J. (2004). Cooperatives and the millennium development goals.

Birgün, S., Gülen, K. G., & Özkan, K. (2006). *Yalın Üretime Geçiş Sürecinde Değer Akışı Haritalama Tekniğinin Kullanılması, İstanbul Ticaret Üniversitesi Fen Bilimleri Dergisi*, *5*(9), 47–59.

Birindelli, G., Ferretti, P., Intonti, M., & Iannuzzi, A. P. (2015). On the drivers of corporate social responsibility in banks: Evidence from an ethical rating model. *The Journal of Management and Governance*, *19*(2), 303–340. doi:10.100710997-013-9262-9

BIS. (2016, Dec. 11). *Triennial Central Bank Survey of foreign exchange and OTC derivatives markets in 2016*. Retrieved from www.bis.org/publ/rpfx16.htm

Bititci, U., Turner, T., & Ball, P. (1999). The viable business structure for managing agility. *International Journal of Agile Management Systems*, *1*(3), 190–199. doi:10.1108/14654659910296571

Bitzis, G., Paleologos, J. M., & Papazoglou, C. (2008). The determinants of the Greek current account deficit: The EMU experience. *Journal of International and Global Economic Studies*, *1*(1), 105–122.

Bjørnland, H. C., & Leitemo, K. (2009). Identifying the interdependence between US monetary policy and the stock market. *Journal of Monetary Economics*, *56*(2), 275–282. doi:10.1016/j.jmoneco.2008.12.001

BL. (2005). Banking Law. Published in Turkish Official Gazette dated 11.01.2005 and numbered 25983.

Blackburn, R. A., Hart, M., & Wainwright, T. (2013). Small business performance: Business, strategy and owner-manager characteristics. *Journal of Small Business and Enterprise Development*, *20*(1), 8–27. doi:10.1108/14626001311298394

Blajer-Gołębiewska, A., Wach, D., & Kos, M. (2018). Financial risk information avoidance. *Economic research- Ekonomska Istrazivanja*, *31*(1), 521–536. doi:10.1080/1331677X.2018.1439396

Blanchflower, D. G. (2000). Self-employment in OECD countries. *Labour Economics*, *7*(5), 471–505. doi:10.1016/S0927-5371(00)00011-7

Blenkhorn, D. L., & Fleisher, C. S. (Eds.). (2005). *Competitive intelligence and global business*. Greenwood Publishing Group.

Bofondi, M., & Gobbi, G. (2004). Bad loans and entry into local credit markets. *Bank of Italy Temi di Discussione del Servizio Studi*. No. 509, 1-49.

Bohnsack, R., & Margonlina, A. (2019). Teaching entrepreneurship and business model innovation in a blended-learning curriculum with the Smart Business Modeler. *Journal of Business Models*, *7*(3).

Boisclair, D., Lusardi, A., & Michaud, P. C. (2017). Financial literacy and retirement planning in Canada. *Journal of Pension Economics and Finance*, *16*(3), 277–296. doi:10.1017/S1474747215000311

Bolívar, L. M., Casanueva, G., & Castro, I. (2019). Global foreign direct investment: a network perspective. *International Business Review*, 1–17.

Boltho, A. (1996). The assessment: International competitiveness. *Oxford Review of Economic Policy*, *12*(3), 1–16. doi:10.1093/oxrep/12.3.1

Bolton, R. N. (2004). Linking marketing to financial performance and firm value. *Journal of Marketing*, *68*(4), 73–75. doi:10.1509/jmkg.68.4.73.42727

Bölükbaş, M. (2019). Kamu büyüklüğü işsizliğin ve genç işsizliğin nedeni midir? Türkiye örneği. *Aydın İktisat Fakültesi Dergisi*, *3*(2), 1–17.

Bonelli, R. (1999). A note on foreign direct investment and industrial competitiveness in Brazil. *Oxford Development Studies*, *27*(3), 305–327. doi:10.1080/13600819908424180

Borders, M. A., Irfaeya, W., & Liu, L. (1991). International management.

Borensztein, E., & Gregorio, J. D. (1998). How does foreign direct investment affect economic growth? *Journal of International Economics*, *45*(1), 115–135. doi:10.1016/S0022-1996(97)00033-0

Bornmann, L., & Mutz, R. (2015). Growth rates of modern science: A bibliometric analysis based on the number of publications and cited references. *Journal of the Association for Information Science and Technology*, *66*(11), 2215–2222. doi:10.1002/asi.23329

Bose, R. (2008). Competitive intelligence process and tools for intelligence analysis. *Industrial Management & Data Systems*, *108*(4), 510–528. doi:10.1108/02635570810868362

Boter, H., & Lundström, A. (2005). SME perspectives on business support services: The role of company size, industry and location. *Journal of Small Business and Enterprise Development*, *12*(2), 244–258. doi:10.1108/14626000510594638

Bouri, E., Jain, A., Biswal, P. C., & Roubaud, D. (2017). Cointegration and nonlinear causality amongst gold, oil, and the Indian stock market: Evidence from implied volatility indices. *Resources Policy*, *52*, 201–206. doi:10.1016/j.resourpol.2017.03.003

Bouri, E., Molnár, P., Azzi, G., Roubaud, D., & Hagfors, L. I. (2017). On the hedge and safe haven properties of Bitcoin: Is it really more than a diversifier? *Finance Research Letters*, *20*, 192–198. doi:10.1016/j.frl.2016.09.025

Bouzgarrou, H., Jouida, S., & Louhichi, W. (2018). Bank profitability during and before the financial crisis: Domestic versus foreign banks. *Research in International Business and Finance*, *44*, 26–39. doi:10.1016/j.ribaf.2017.05.011

Bowden, A. R., Lane, M. R., & Martin, J. H. (2002). *Triple bottom line risk management: enhancing profit, environmental performance, and community benefits*. John Wiley & Sons.

Box, M., Lin, X., & Gratzer, K. (2014). Linking entrepreneurship and economic growth in Sweden, 1850-2000. *PESO Working Papers, School of Social Sciences,* Södertörn University.

Boyacıoğlu, M. A., & Çürük, D. (2016). Döviz Kuru Değişimlerinin Hisse Senedi Getirisine Etkisi: Borsa İstanbul 100 Endeksi Üzerine Bir Uygulama. *Muhasebe ve Finansman Dergisi*, (70), 143–156. doi:10.25095/mufad.396686

Boyd, J. H., Nicolo, G. D., & Jalal, A. M. (2006). Bank risk-taking and competition revisited: New theory and new evidence. *IMF Working Paper*, No: 06/297.

Boyd, J. H., & De Nicolo, G. (2005). The theory of bank risk taking and competition revisited. *The Journal of Finance*, *60*(3), 1329–1343. doi:10.1111/j.1540-6261.2005.00763.x

Boyer, M. M., & Filion, D. (2007). Common and fundamental factors in stock returns of Canadian oil and gas companies. *Energy Economics*, *29*(3), 428–453. doi:10.1016/j.eneco.2005.12.003

Bozeman, B., & Kingsley, G. (1998). Risk culture in public and private organizations. *Public Administration Review*, *58*(2), 109–118. doi:10.2307/976358

Bozkurt, V. (2001). Küreselleşme Kavram, Gelişim Yaklaşımlar. *3*(2).

Bozkurt, C. (2015). R&D expenditures and economic growth relationship in Turkey. *International Journal Economics and Financial Issues.*, *5*(1), 188.

Brada, J. C., & Méndez, J. A. (1988). Exchange rate risk, exchange rate regime and the volume of international trade. *Kyklos*, *41*(2), 263–280. doi:10.1111/j.1467-6435.1988.tb02309.x

Bradley, F. (2002). Uluslararası Pazarlama Stratejisi.(Çev.: Ġçlem Er). *Financial Times Prentice Hall, Ankara: Bilim Teknik Yayın Evi*.

Braunerhjelm, P., Acs, Z. J., Audretsch, D. B., & Carlsson, B. (2010). The missing link: knowledge diffusion and entrepreneurship in endogenous growth. *Small Business Economics*, *34*(2), 105–125. doi:10.100711187-009-9235-1

Briers, S. (2000). The development of an integrated model of risk. (Doctoral thesis, The University of South Africa).

Broadstock, D. C., & Filis, G. (2014). Oil price shocks and stock market returns: New evidence from the United States and China. *Journal of International Financial Markets, Institutions and Money*, *33*, 417–433. doi:10.1016/j.intfin.2014.09.007

Brocklesby, J., & Campbell-Hunt, C. (2004). The evolution of competitive capability: A cognition and complex systems perspective. *Journal of Organisational Transformation & Social Change*, 1.

Brooks, C. (2014). *Introductory econometrics for finance*. Cambridge University Press. doi:10.1017/CBO9781139540872

Brout, D., Scolnic, D., Kessler, R., D'Andrea, C. B., Davis, T. M., Gupta, R. R., . . . Macaulay, E. (2019). First cosmology results using SNe Ia from the dark energy survey: Analysis, systematic uncertainties, and validation [First cosmology results using type IA supernovae from the dark energy survey: Analysis, systematic uncertainties, and validation]. *The Astrophysical Journal (Online)*, *874*(arXiv: 1811.02377; FERMILAB-PUB-18-541-AE).

Browder, R. E., Aldrich, H. E., & Bradley, S. W. (2019). The emergence of the maker movement: Implications for entrepreneurship research. *Journal of Business Venturing*, *34*(3), 459–476. doi:10.1016/j.jbusvent.2019.01.005

Brown, S. P., & Yücel, M. (2000). Oil prices and the economy. *Southwest Economy*, (Jul), 1-6.

Brown, L., Gans, N., Mandelbaum, A., Sakov, A., Shen, H., Zeltyn, S., & Zhao, L. (2005). Statistical analysis of a telephone call center: A queueing-science perspective. *Journal of the American Statistical Association*, *100*(469), 36–50. doi:10.1198/016214504000001808

Brown, M., Henchoz, C., & Spycher, T. (2018). Culture and financial literacy: Evidence from a within-country language border. *Journal of Economic Behavior & Organization*, *150*, 62–85. doi:10.1016/j.jebo.2018.03.011

BRSA. (2006). C charter about the permitted transactions of banks and indirect shareholders. Published in Turkish Official Gazette dated 11.01.2006 and numbered 26333.

BRSA. (2019). Banks. Retrieved from https://www.bddk.org.tr/Institutions-Category/Banks/22

Buckley, P. J., Pass, C. L., & Prescott, K. (1988). Measures of international competitiveness: A critical survey. *Journal of Marketing Management*, *4*(2), 175–200. doi:10.1080/0267257X.1988.9964068

Bujari, A. A., & Martinez, F. V. (2016). Technological innovation and economic performance in services: a firm-level analysis. *Cambridge Journal of Economics*, *30*(3), 435–458.

Bulut, N. (2003). Küreselleşme: Sosyal Devletin Sonu Mu? *Ankara Üniversitesi Hukuk Fakültesi Dergisi*, *52*(2), 185.

Burbidge, J., & Harrison, A. (1984). Testing for the effects of oil-price rises using vector autoregressions. *International Economic Review*, *25*(2), 459–484. doi:10.2307/2526209

Burdon, S., Chelliah, J., & Bhalla, A. (2009). Structuring enduring strategic alliances: The case of Shell Australia and Transfield Services. *The Journal of Business Strategy*, *30*(4), 42–51. doi:10.1108/02756660910972640

Burton, J., Story, V. M., Raddats, C., & Zolkiewski, J. (2017). Overcoming the challenges that hinder new service development by manufacturers with diverse services strategies. *International Journal of Production Economics*, *192*, 29–39. doi:10.1016/j.ijpe.2017.01.013

Byrne, S., & Popoff, L. (2008). *International joint ventures handbook*. Baker & McKenzie.

Çabuk, U. C., Şenocak, T., Demir, E., & Çavdar, A. (2017). A Proposal on initial remote user enrollment for IVR-based voice authentication systems. *Int. J. of Advanced Research in Computer and Communication Engineering*, *6*, 118–123.

Çakırer, M. (2019). *Finanasal Okuryazarlık*. Bursa, Turkey: Ekin Basım Yayın Dağıtım.

Çakmak, H. K. (2004). Stratejik dış ticaret politikaları. Akdeniz İ. İ. B. F. Dergisi, 7, 48–66.

Çakmak, U. (2016) Güney Kore'nin Ekonomik Kalkınmasının Temel Dinamikleri. Süleyman Demirel Üniversitesi, *İktisadi ve İdari Bilimler Fakültesi Dergisi*, *21*(1), 151,171.

Calderón Ramírez, M. A., de Jesús Arrias Añez, J. C., Ronquillo Riera, O. I., Herráez Quezada, R. G., Ríos Vera, Á. A., Torres Cegarra, J. C., & Ojeda Sotomayor, P. M. (2019). Pestel based on neutrosophic cognitive maps to characterize the factors that influence the consolidation of the neo constitutionalism in Ecuador. *Neutrosophic Sets & Systems*, *26*.

Calof, J., & Skinner, B. (1999). Government's role in competitive intelligence: What's happening in Canada. *Competitive Intelligence Magazine*, *2*(2), 20–23.

Calvo, G. A., & Mishkin, F. S. (2003). The mirage of exchange rate regimes for emerging market countries. *Journal of Economic Perspectives*, *17*(4), 99–118. doi:10.1257/089533003772034916

Campa, D., & Zijlmans, E. W. A. (2019). Corporate social responsibility recognition and support for the arts: Evidence from European financial institutions. *European Management Journal*. doi:10.1016/j.emj.2019.01.003

Campbell, J. L. (2004). *Institutional change and globalization*. Princeton University Press.

Çam, Ü., & Özer, H. (2018). Türk bankacılık sektörünün piyasa yapısının rekabet ve yarışılabilirlik açısından analizi: Panzar-rosse modeli. *Cumhuriyet Üniversitesi İktisadi ve İdari Bilimler Dergisi*, *18*(1), 336–360.

Canbaş, S., Doğukanlı, H., Düzakın, H., & İskenderoğlu, Ö. (2005). Performans Ölçümünde Tobin Q Oranının Kullanılması: Hisse Senetleri İMKB''de İşlem Gören Sanayi İşletmeleri Üzerinde Bir Deneme. *Muhasebe ve Finansman Dergisi*, (28), 24–36.

Candan, A., Çankır, B., & Seker, S. E. (2017)Organizasyonlarda Çeviklik. *Ansiklopedi*, *4*(3), 3–9.

Caporale, G. M., Helmi, M. H., Çatık, A. N., Ali, F. M., & Akdeniz, C. (2018). Monetary policy rules in emerging countries: Is there an augmented nonlinear Taylor rule? *Economic Modelling*, *72*, 306–319. doi:10.1016/j.econmod.2018.02.006

Caputo, R., & Díaz, A. (2018). Now and always, the relevance of the Taylor rule in Europe. *International Journal of Finance & Economics*, *23*(1), 41–46. doi:10.1002/ijfe.1601

Compilation of References

Carbaugh, R. J. (2005). *International economics* (10th ed.). Canada: South-Western.

Carbonell, P., & Rodriguez Escudero, A. I. (2015). The negative effect of team's prior experience and technological turbulence on new service development projects with customer involvement. *European Journal of Marketing*, *49*(3/4), 278–301. doi:10.1108/EJM-08-2013-0438

Carbó, S., Humphrey, D., Maudos, J., & Molyneux, P. (2009). Cross-country comparisons of competition and pricing power in European banking. *Journal of International Money and Finance*, *28*(1), 115–134. doi:10.1016/j.jimonfin.2008.06.005

Carbo-Valverde, S., Rodriguez-Fernandez, F., & Udell, G. F. (2009). Bank market power and SME financing constraints. *Review of Finance*, *13*(2), 309–340. doi:10.1093/rof/rfp003

Carmeli, A., & Tishler, A. (2004). The relationships between intangible organizational elements and organizational performance. *Strategic Management Journal*, *25*(13), 1257–1278. doi:10.1002mj.428

Carree, M., Van Stel, A., Thurik, R., & Wennekers, S. (2007). The relationship between economic development and business ownership revisited. *Entrepreneurship and Regional Development*, *19*(3), 281–291. doi:10.1080/08985620701296318

Carvalho, C., Nechio, F., & Tristao, T. (2018). Taylor rule estimation by OLS. Available at *SSRN 3265449*.

Castillo, O. N., Santibáñez, A. L. V., & Bolívar, H. R. (2011). Technological determinants of market shares of Mexican manufacturing exports. *Asian Journal of Latin American Studies*, *24*(1).

Cebeci, İ. (2012). *Krizleri İncelemede Kullanılan Nitel Tercih Modelleri: Türkiye İçin Bir Probit Model Uygulaması (1988-2009)*. İstanbul Üniversitesi İktisat Fakültesi Mecmuası.

Çekmecelioğlu, H. G., Günsel, A., & Ulutaş, T. (2012). Effects of emotional intelligence on job satisfaction: An empirical study on call center employees. *Procedia: Social and Behavioral Sciences*, *58*, 363–369. doi:10.1016/j.sbspro.2012.09.1012

Çelik, T., Kaplan, M., & Şahin, F. (2015). Efficiency, concentration and competition in the Turkish banking sector. *İktisat İşletme ve Finans*, *30*(346), 81-104.

Çelik, S., & Kaya, H. (2010). Real exchange rates and bilateral trade dynamics of Turkey: Panel cointegration approach. *Applied Economics Letters*, *17*(8), 791–795. doi:10.1080/13504850802388993

Çelik, T., & Kaplan, M. (2010). Türk Bankacılık Sektöründe Etkinlik ve Rekabet: 2002-2007. *Sosyoekonomi*, *6*(13), 7–28.

Çelik, T., & Ürünveren, Ç. (2009). Yabancı banka girişlerinin Türk bankacılık sektörüne rekabet etkisi: 2002-2007. *Niğde Üniversitesi İİBF Dergisi*, *2*(2), 42–59.

Central Bank of the Republic of Turkey. (2006). *CBRT Annual Report 2006*. CBRT.

Central Bank of the Republic of Turkey. (2010). *CBRT Annual Report 2010*. CBRT.

Central Bank of the Republic of Turkey. (2011). *CBRT Annual Report 2011*. CBRT.

Central Bank of the Republic of Turkey. (2012). *CBRT Annual Report 2012*. CBRT.

Central Bank of the Republic of Turkey. (2013). *CBRT Annual Report 2013*. CBRT.

Central Bank of the Republic of Turkey. (2014). *CBRT Annual Report 2014*. CBRT.

Central Bank of the Republic of Turkey. (2015). *CBRT Annual Report 2015*. CBRT.

Central Bank of the Republic of Turkey. (2016). *CBRT Annual Report 2016*. CBRT.

Central Bank of the Republic of Turkey. (2017). *CBRT Annual Report 2017*. CBRT.

Central Bank of the Republic of Turkey. (2018). *CBRT Annual Report 2018*. CBRT.

Çetin, A. (2018). Katılım ve mevduat bankalarının piyasa etkinliğinin karşılaştırmali analizi ve bir uygulama. *TBB Yayınları*, Yayın No: 329.

Çetin, A., & Kartal, M. T. (2019). Deposit insurance in participation banking: A comprehensive examination upon interest-free participation fund insurance in Turkey and model proposal. *Journal of Islamic Economics and Finance*, 5(1), 1–38.

Çetin, M. (2016). Türkiye Cumhuriyeti Merkez Bankası (TCMB) Para Politikası Uygulamalarının Gelişimi. *Finansal Araştırmalar ve Çalışmalar Dergisi*, 8(14), 67–101. doi:10.14784/jfrs.87278

Çetin, M., & Şeker, F. (2014). Ticari Açıklık ve Finansal Gelişmenin Doğrudan Yabancı Yatırımlar Üzerindeki Etkisi: Oecd Ülkeleri Üzerine Dinamik Panel Veri Analizi. *Atatürk Üniversitesi İktisadi ve İdari Bilimler Dergisi*, 28(1), 125–147.

Cetorelli, N., & Peristiani, S. (2015). Firm value and cross listings: The impact of stock market prestige. *Journal of Risk and Financial Management*, 8(1), 150–180. doi:10.3390/jrfm8010150

Chang, C. J., & Hung, C. Y. (2018). Investigation on income tax system of consolidated income from house and land transactions—in-depth interview method. *International Journal of Research in Business and Social Science (2147-4478)*, 7(1), 11-24.

Chang, C. H., & Lin, S. J. (2015). The effects of national culture and behavioral pitfalls on investors' decision-making: Herding behavior in international stock markets. *International Review of Economics & Finance*, 37, 380–392. doi:10.1016/j.iref.2014.12.010

Chang, T. Y., Graff Zivin, J., Gross, T., & Neidell, M. (2019). The effect of pollution on worker productivity: Evidence from call center workers in China. *American Economic Journal. Applied Economics*, 11(1), 151–172. doi:10.1257/app.20160436

Chang, W., & Taylor, S. A. (2016). The effectiveness of customer participation in new product development: A meta-analysis. *Journal of Marketing*, 80(1), 47–64. doi:10.1509/jm.14.0057

Chaouali, W., & Souiden, N. (2018). The role of cognitive age in explaining mobile banking resistance among elderly people. *Journal of Retailing and Consumer Services*.

Chaouali, W., Souiden, N., & Ladhari, R. (2017). Explaining adoption of mobile banking with the theory of trying, general self-confidence, and cynicism. *Journal of Retailing and Consumer Services*, 35, 57–67. doi:10.1016/j.jretconser.2016.11.009

Charemza, W. W., & Deadman, D. F. (1992). *New directions in econometric practice*. Cambridge, UK: Edward Elgar.

Chau, J. Y., Sukala, W., Fedel, K., Do, A., Engelen, L., Kingham, M., ... Bauman, A. E. (2016). More standing and just as productive: Effects of a sit-stand desk intervention on call center workers' sitting, standing, and productivity at work in the Opt to Stand pilot study. *Preventive Medicine Reports*, 3, 68–74. doi:10.1016/j.pmedr.2015.12.003 PMID:26844191

Cheema, M. A., & Nartea, G. V. (2017). Momentum returns, market states, and market dynamics: Is China different? *International Review of Economics & Finance*, 50, 85–97. doi:10.1016/j.iref.2017.04.003

Chen, C., Yao, S., & Ou, J. (2017). Exchange rate dynamics in a Taylor rule framework. *Journal of International Financial Markets, Institutions and Money*, 46, 158–173. doi:10.1016/j.intfin.2016.07.008

Chen, G., Kim, K. A., Nofsinger, J. R., & Rui, O. M. (2007). Trading performance, disposition effect, overconfidence, representativeness bias, and experience of emerging market investors. *Journal of Behavioral Decision Making*, 20(4), 425–451. doi:10.1002/bdm.561

Chen, J. E., & Kashiwagi, M. (2017). The Japanese Taylor rule estimated using censored quantile regressions. *Empirical Economics*, *52*(1), 357–371. doi:10.100700181-016-1074-8

Chen, J., Tang, T. L. P., & Tang, N. (2014). Temptation, monetary intelligence (love of money), and environmental context on unethical intentions and cheating. *Journal of Business Ethics*, *123*(2), 197–219. doi:10.100710551-013-1783-2

Chen, T. Y., Chang, C. H., & Lu, J. F. R. (2013). The extended QUALIFLEX method for multiple criteria decision analysis based on interval type-2 fuzzy sets and applications to medical decision making. *European Journal of Operational Research*, *226*(3), 615–625. doi:10.1016/j.ejor.2012.11.038

Cheung, Y. W., & Sengupta, R. (2013). Impact of exchange rate movements on exports: An analysis of Indian non-financial sector firms. *Journal of International Money and Finance*, *39*, 231–245. doi:10.1016/j.jimonfin.2013.06.026

Chew, B., Tan, L., & Hamid, S. (2016). Ethical banking in practice: A closer look at the Co-operative Bank UK PLC. *Qualitative Research in Financial Markets*, *8*(1), 70–91. doi:10.1108/QRFM-02-2015-0008

Chiang, T. C., & Chen, X. (2016). Stock returns and economic fundamentals in an emerging market: An empirical investigation of domestic and global market forces. *International Review of Economics & Finance*, *43*, 107–120. doi:10.1016/j.iref.2015.10.034

Chien, M. S., Lee, C. C., Hu, T. C., & Hu, H. T. (2015). Dynamic Asian stock market convergence: Evidence from dynamic cointegration analysis among China and ASEAN-5. *Economic Modelling*, *51*, 84–98. doi:10.1016/j.econmod.2015.06.024

Choi, I. (2001). Unit root tests for panel data. *Journal of International Money and Finance*, *20*(2), 249–272. doi:10.1016/S0261-5606(00)00048-6

Choong, C.-K., & Lim, K.-P. (2009). Foreign direct investment, financial development and economic growth: the case of Malaysia. *Macroeconomics and Finance in Emerging Market Economies*, *2*(1), 13–30. doi:10.1080/17520840902726227

Chopra, V., Veeraraghavan, S., Griffioen, A. T. E., Sun, H., Liberman, D. S., Niergarth, J. D., . . . Friedman, L. (2019). *U.S. Patent Application No. 15/720,319*.

Choudhry, T., & Hassan, S. S. (2015). Exchange rate volatility and UK imports from developing countries: The effect of the global financial crisis. *Journal of International Financial Markets, Institutions and Money*, *39*, 89–101. doi:10.1016/j.intfin.2015.07.004

Choudhry, T., Papadimitriou, F. I., & Shabi, S. (2016). Stock market volatility and business cycle: Evidence from linear and nonlinear causality tests. *Journal of Banking & Finance*, *66*, 89–101. doi:10.1016/j.jbankfin.2016.02.005

Chowdhury, A. R. (1993). Does exchange rate volatility depress trade flows? Evidence from error-correction models. *The Review of Economics and Statistics*, *75*(4), 700–706. doi:10.2307/2110025

Christopoulos, D. K., & Leon-Ledesma, M. A. (2010). Smooth breaks and non-linear mean reversion: Post-bretton woods real exchange rates. *Journal of International Money and Finance*, *29*(6), 1076–1093. doi:10.1016/j.jimonfin.2010.02.003

Chuang, Y. T., Church, R., & Zikic, J. (2004). Organizational culture, group diversity and intra-group conflict. *Team Performance Management: An International Journal*, *10*(1/2), 26–34. doi:10.1108/13527590410527568

Chu, Z., Wang, Z., Xiao, J. J., & Zhang, W. (2017). Financial literacy, portfolio choice and financial well-being. *Social Indicators Research*, *132*(2), 799–820. doi:10.100711205-016-1309-2

Cicioğlu, Ş., Ağuş, A., & Torun, P. (2013). Para Politikası Araçlarının Cari Açık Üzerindeki Etkinliği: Türkiye Ekonomisi Üzerine Bir Uygulama. *Küresel İktisat ve İşletme Çalışmaları Dergisi*, *2*(4), 37–48.

Čihák, M., Demirguc-Kunt, A., Feyen, E., & Levine, R. (2012). Benchmarking financial development around the world. *World Bank Policy Research Working Paper*, 6175. World Bank, Washington, DC.

Çivi, E., Erol, İ., İnanlı, T., & Erol, E. D. (2008). *Uluslararası rekabet gücüne farklı bakışlar*. Ekonomik ve Sosyal Araştırmalar Dergisi.

Clark, P. B. (1973). Uncertainty, exchange risk, and the level of international trade. *Economic Inquiry*, *11*(3), 302–313. doi:10.1111/j.1465-7295.1973.tb01063.x

Clark, R., Lusardi, A., & Mitchell, O. S. (2017). Employee financial literacy and retirement plan behavior: A case study. *Economic Inquiry*, *55*(1), 248–259. doi:10.1111/ecin.12389

Clay, C. (2016). State borrowing and the Imperial Ottoman Bank in the bankruptcy era (1863–1877). In East Meets West-Banking, Commerce and Investment in the Ottoman Empire (pp. 129-142). Routledge.

Clews, R., Salmon, C., & Weeken, O. (2010). The bank's money market framework. Bank of England Quarterly Bulletin, Q4, 50, 4, 296.

Coe, D., Helpman, E., & Hoffmaister, A. W. (1995). International R&D spillovers and institutions. *IMF Working Paper*.

Çömlekçi, İ., & Özer, A. (2018). Behavioral finance models, anomalies, and factors affecting investor psychology. In *Global Approaches in Financial Economics, Banking, and Finance* (pp. 309–330). Cham, Switzerland: Springer. doi:10.1007/978-3-319-78494-6_15

Consiglio, J. A., Oliva, J. C. M., Tortella, G., Fraser, M. P., & Fraser, I. L. (2016). Stability against all odds: The Imperial Ottoman Bank, 1875–1914. In Banking and Finance in the Mediterranean (pp. 111-134). Routledge.

Content, J., Frenken, K., & Jordaan, J. A. (2019). Does related variety foster regional entrepreneurship? Evidence from European regions. *Regional Studies*, 1–13.

Cook, C., Schaafsma, J., & Antheunis, M. (2018). Under the bridge: An in-depth examination of online trolling in the gaming context. *New Media & Society, 20*(9), 3323-3340.

Cooke, F. L., Cooper, B., Bartram, T., Wang, J., & Mei, H. (2019). Mapping the relationships between high-performance work systems, employee resilience and engagement: A study of the banking industry in China. *International Journal of Human Resource Management*, *30*(8), 1239–1260. doi:10.1080/09585192.2015.1137618

Cooper, C. A., Cartwright, S., & Earley, P. C. (2001). *The international handbook of organizational culture and climate*.

Cooper, D. F. (2005). *Project risk management guidelines: managing risk in large projects and complex procurements*. Hoboken, NJ: John Wiley & Sons

Corbet, S., Meegan, A., Larkin, C., Lucey, B., & Yarovaya, L. (2018). Exploring the dynamic relationships between cryptocurrencies and other financial assets. *Economics Letters*, *165*, 28–34. doi:10.1016/j.econlet.2018.01.004

Cornaggia, J., Mao, Y., Tian, X., & Wolfe, B. (2015). Does banking competition affect innovation? *Journal of Financial Economics*, *115*(1), 189–209. doi:10.1016/j.jfineco.2014.09.001

Cornalba, C., & Giudici, P. (2004). Statistical models for operational risk management. *Physica A*, *338*(1-2), 166–172. doi:10.1016/j.physa.2004.02.039

Cornett, M. M., & Saunders, A. (2003). *Financial institutions management: A risk management approach*. McGraw-Hill/Irwin.

Cortez, A. (2011). *Winning at risk: strategies to go beyond Basel* (Vol. 638). Hoboken, NJ: John Wiley & Sons.

Compilation of References

Coşkun, N., Ardor, H. N., Çermikli, A. H., Eruygur, H. O., Öztürk, F., Tokatlıoğlu, İ., . . . Dağlaroğlu, T. (2012), Türkiye'de bankacılık sektörü, piyasa yapısı, firma davranışları ve rekabet analizi. *Türkiye Bankalar Birliği Yayınları*, Yayın No: 280. Retrieved from http://www.tbb.org.tr/Dosyalar/userfiles/file/ecg/rekabetKitap.pdf

Costa, D. F., Carvalho, F. D. M., & Moreira, B. C. D. M. (2019). Behavioral economics and behavioral finance: A bibliometric analysis of the scientific fields. *Journal of Economic Surveys*, *33*(1), 3–24. doi:10.1111/joes.12262

Costa, D. F., de Melo Carvalho, F., de Melo Moreira, B. C., & do Prado, J. W. (2017). Bibliometric analysis on the association between behavioral finance and decision making with cognitive biases such as overconfidence, anchoring effect and confirmation bias. *Scientometrics*, *111*(3), 1775–1799. doi:10.100711192-017-2371-5

Costa, P. T., & McCrae, R. R. (2003). *NEO-FFI: NEO Five Factor Inventory*. Lutz, FL: Psychological Assessment Resources.

Côté, A. (1994). *Exchange rate volatility and trade*. Bank of Canada.

Coulibaly, S. K., Erbao, C., & Mekongcho, T. M. (2018). Economic globalization, entrepreneurship, and development. *Technological Forecasting and Social Change*, *127*, 271–280. doi:10.1016/j.techfore.2017.09.028

Cova, P., Pagano, P., & Pisani, M. (2019). Domestic and international effects of the eurosystem expanded asset purchase programme: a structural model-based analysis. *IMF Economic Review*, *67*(2), 315–348. doi:10.105741308-018-0071-7

Cox-Fuenzalida, L. E., Swickert, R., & Hittner, J. B. (2004). Effects of neuroticism and workload history on performance. *Personality and Individual Differences*, *36*(2), 447–456. doi:10.1016/S0191-8869(03)00108-9

Cridland, E. K., Phillipson, L., Brennan-Horley, C., & Swaffer, K. (2016). Reflections and recommendations for conducting in-depth interviews with people with dementia. *Qualitative Health Research*, *26*(13), 1774–1786. doi:10.1177/1049732316637065 PMID:27055496

Crumbly, J., & Carter, L. (2015). Social media and humanitarian logistics: The impact of task-technology fit on new service development. *Procedia Engineering*, *107*, 412–416. doi:10.1016/j.proeng.2015.06.099

Cuestas, J. C., Yannick, L., & Reigl, N. (2017). Banking sector concentration, competition and financial stability: The case of the Baltic countries. *Bank of Estonia Working Paper*, No. wp2017-7.

Cui, A. S., & Wu, F. (2016). Utilizing customer knowledge in innovation: Antecedents and impact of customer involvement on new product performance. *Journal of the Academy of Marketing Science*, *44*(4), 516–538. doi:10.100711747-015-0433-x

Çulha, O. Y., Özmen, M. U., & Yılmaz, E. (2016). Impact of oil price changes on Turkey's exports. *Applied Economics Letters*, *23*(9), 637–641. doi:10.1080/13504851.2015.1095993

Cummins, J. D., Phillips, R. D., & Smith, S. D. (1998). The rise of risk management. *Economic Review (Atlanta, Ga.)*, *83*(1), 30–41.

Ćumurović, A., & Hyll, W. (2019). Financial literacy and self-employment. *The Journal of Consumer Affairs*, *53*(2), 455–487. doi:10.1111/joca.12198

Cushman, D. O. (1986). Has exchange risk depressed international trade? The impact of third country exchange risk. *Journal of International Money and Finance*, *5*(3), 361–379. doi:10.1016/0261-5606(86)90035-5

Custódio, C., Mendes, D., & Metzger, D. (2019). The impact of financial literacy on medium and large enterprises–Evidence from a randomized controlled trial in Mozambique.

Czinkota, M. R. (1999). *Marketing: best practices*. Holt Rinehart & Winston.

Daft, R. L. (2015). *Organization theory and design*. Cengage Learning.

Dagher, L., & El Hariri, S. (2013). The impact of global oil price shocks on the Lebanese stock market. *Energy*, *63*, 366–374. doi:10.1016/j.energy.2013.10.012

Damasceno, V. S., & Abreu, Y. V. D. (2018). Avaliação da energia eólica no Brasil utilizando a análise SWOT e PESTEL. *Interações (Campo Grande)*, *19*(3), 503–514. doi:10.20435/inter.v19i3.1649

Daniel, K., & Hirshleifer, D. (2015). Overconfident investors, predictable returns, and excessive trading. *The Journal of Economic Perspectives*, *29*(4), 61–88. doi:10.1257/jep.29.4.61

Daniel, K., Hirshleifer, D., & Teoh, S. H. (2002). Investor psychology in capital markets: Evidence and policy implications. *Journal of Monetary Economics*, *49*(1), 139–209. doi:10.1016/S0304-3932(01)00091-5

Daniels, J. D., Radebaugh, L. H., & Sullivan, D. P. (1998). *International business: Environments and operations*. Addison-Wesley.

Danışoğlu, A. Ç. (2004). Küreselleşmenin Gelir Eşitsizliği ve Yoksulluk Üzerindeki Etkisi. *İstanbul Ticaret Üniversitesi Dergisi, 3*(5), 215-216.

Das, S. S., Hackbarth, K. R., Jensen, K. B., Kohler, J. E., Matula, V. C., & Windhausen, R. A. (2005). *U.S. Patent No. 6,847,714*. Washington, DC: U.S. Patent and Trademark Office.

David, F. R. (2011). *Strategic management: concepts and cases* (13th ed.). New Jersey: Pearson Education.

David, F. R., & David, F. R. (2013). *Strategic management concepts and cases: A competitive advantage approach*. Pearson.

David, F. R., & David, F. R. (2013). *Strategic management: Concepts and cases: A competitive advantage approach*. Pearson.

Davydenko, A. (2011). Determinants of bank profitability in Ukraine. *Undergraduate Economic Review*, *7*(1), 1–30.

de Andres, A., MacGillivray, A., Roberts, O., Guanche, R., & Jeffrey, H. (2017). Beyond LCOE: A study of ocean energy technology development and deployment attractiveness. *Sustainable Energy Technologies and Assessments*, *19*, 1–16. doi:10.1016/j.seta.2016.11.001

De Bock, D., Leuven, K. U., De Win, I., & Van Campenhout, G. (2019). Inclusion of financial literacy goals in secondary school curricula: role of financial mathematics. *MEDITERRANEAN JOURNAL*, 33.

De Bondt, W. F. (1998). A portrait of the individual investor. *European Economic Review*, *42*(3-5), 831–844. doi:10.1016/S0014-2921(98)00009-9

De Bortoli, D., da Costa, N. Jr, Goulart, M., & Campara, J. (2019). Personality traits and investor profile analysis: A behavioral finance study. *PLoS One*, *14*(3), e0214062. doi:10.1371/journal.pone.0214062 PMID:30917175

De Truchis, G., Dell'Eva, C., & Keddad, B. (2017). On exchange rate comovements: New evidence from a Taylor rule fundamentals model with adaptive learning. *Journal of International Financial Markets, Institutions and Money*, *48*, 82–98. doi:10.1016/j.intfin.2016.12.006

Deardoff, A. V. (2008). Dünya Ekonomisi ve Dünya Ticaret Sistemi Nereye Gidiyor. *Uluslararası Ekonomi ve Dış Ticaret Politikaları, 3*(1-2), 7–24.

Deenanath, V., Danes, S. M., & Jang, J. (2019). Purposive and unintentional family financial socialization, subjective financial knowledge, and financial behavior of high school students. *Journal of Financial Counseling and Planning*, *30*(1), 83–96. doi:10.1891/1052-3073.30.1.83

Değer, M. K., & Pata, U. K. (2017). Türkiye'de dış ticaret ve karbondioksit salınımı arasındaki ilişkilerin simetrik ve asimetrik nedensellik testleriyle analizi. *Doğuş Üniversitesi Dergisi, 18*(1), 31–44. doi:10.31671/dogus.2018.20

Degiannakis, S., Filis, G., & Kizys, R. (2014). The effects of oil price shocks on stock market volatility: Evidence from European data. *Energy Journal*, 35–56.

Delgado, M., Ketels, C., Porter, M. E., & Stern, S. (2012). The determinants of national competitiveness. *Nber Working Paper Series*, National Bureau of Economic Research, Cambridge, 1-47.

Delmar, F. (1996). *Entrepreneurial behavior and business performance*. EFI.

Demir, G. (2001). Küreselleşme üzerine. *Ankara Üniversitesi SBF Dergisi, 56*(01).

Demirbaş, M., Türkay, H., & Türkoğlu, M. (2009). Petrol fiyatlarındaki gelişmelerin Türkiye'nin cari açığı üzerine etkisinin analizi. *Süleyman Demirel Üniversitesi İktisadi ve İdari Bilimler Fakültesi Dergisi, 14*(3), 289–299.

Demirhan, B. (2013). Türkiye'de Yeni Yaklaşım Çerçevesinde Para Politikalarinin Finansal İstikrari Sağlama Yönünde Uygulanmasi. *Afyon Kocatepe Üniversitesi İktisadi ve İdari Bilimler Fakültesi Dergisi, 15*(2), 567–589.

Demirhan, D. (2013). Effects of the recent financial crisis on the determinants of bank profitability: Case of Turkish banking industry. *Journal of Yasar University, 8*(31), 5203–5228.

Demir, İ. (2001). *Türkiye beyaz eşya sanayiinin rekabet gücü ve geleceği*. Devlet Planlama Teşkilatı.

Demsetz, H. (1973). Industry structure, market rivalry, and public policy. *The Journal of Law & Economics, 16*(1), 1–9. doi:10.1086/466752

Depren, Ö., Kartal, M. T., & Kılıç Depren, S. (2018). Bibliometric analysis of the academic studies published about volatility in exchanges. *Banking and Capital Market Research Journal, 2*(6), 1–15.

Dereli, B. (2005). Çok Uluslu İşletmelerde İnsan Kaynakları Yönetimi. *İstanbul Ticaret Üniversitesi Sosyal Bilimler Dergisi, 7*, 59-81.

Deresky, H. (2017). *International management: Managing across borders and cultures*. Pearson Education India.

Derici, O., Tüysüz, Z., & Sarı, A. (2007). Kurumsal Risk Yönetimi ve Sayıştay Uygulaması. *Sayıştay Dergisi, 65*, 151–172.

Desbordes, R., & Wei, S.-J. (2017). The effects of financial development on foreign direct investment. *Journal of Development Economics, 127*, 153–168. doi:10.1016/j.jdeveco.2017.02.008

Deshmukh, G. K., & Joseph, S. (2016). Behavioural finance: An introspection of investors psychology. *Indian Journal of Commerce and Management Studies, 7*(1), 97.

Deshpandé, R., & Farley, J. U. (2004). Organizational culture, market orientation, innovativeness, and firm performance: An international research odyssey. *International Journal of Research in Marketing, 21*(1), 3–22. doi:10.1016/j.ijresmar.2003.04.002

Dessaint, O., Foucault, T., Frésard, L., & Matray, A. (2018). Noisy stock prices and corporate investment. *Review of Financial Studies, 32*(7), 2625–2672. doi:10.1093/rfs/hhy115

Dess, G. G., Lumpkin, G. T., & Covin, J. G. (1997). Entrepreneurial strategy making and firm performance: Tests of contingency and configurational models. *Strategic Management Journal, 18*(9), 677–695. doi:10.1002/(SICI)1097-0266(199710)18:9<677::AID-SMJ905>3.0.CO;2-Q

Devece, C., Peris-Ortiz, M., & Rueda-Armengot, C. (2016). Entrepreneurship during economic crisis: Success factors and paths to failure. *Journal of Business Research, 69*(11), 5366–5370. doi:10.1016/j.jbusres.2016.04.139

Devor, R., Graves, R., & Mills, J. J. (1997). Agile manufacturing research: accomplishments and opportunities. *IIE Transactions*, *29*(10), 813–823. doi:10.1080/07408179708966404

Dewnarain, S., Ramkissoon, H., & Mavondo, F. (2019). Social customer relationship management: An integrated conceptual framework. *Journal of Hospitality Marketing & Management*, *28*(2), 172–188. doi:10.1080/19368623.2018.1516588

Dhar, R., & Zhu, N. (2006). Up close and personal: Investor sophistication and the disposition effect. *Management Science*, *52*(5), 726–740. doi:10.1287/mnsc.1040.0473

Dicken, P. (2006). Yeni Jeo Ekonomi (A. Ağca, Trans. B. K. Ed.). Ankara, Turkey: Kadim Yayınları.

Dickey, D. A., & Fuller, W. A. (1981). Likelihood ratio statistics for autoregressive time series with a unit root. *Econometrica*, *49*(4), 1057–1072. doi:10.2307/1912517

Diener, E., & Seligman, M. E. (2004). Beyond money: Toward an economy of well-being. *Psychological Science in the Public Interest*, *5*(1), 1–31. doi:10.1111/j.0963-7214.2004.00501001.x PMID:26158992

Diffenbach, J. (1983). Corporate environmental analysis in large U.S. corporations. *Long Range Planning*, *16*(3), 107–116. doi:10.1016/0024-6301(83)90037-7 PMID:10263400

Diffley, S., McCole, P., & Carvajal-Trujillo, E. (2018). Examining social customer relationship management among Irish hotels. *International Journal of Contemporary Hospitality Management*, *30*(2), 1072–1091. doi:10.1108/IJCHM-08-2016-0415

Digman, J. M. (1997). Higher-order factors of the Big Five. *Journal of Personality and Social Psychology*, *73*(6), 1246–1256. doi:10.1037/0022-3514.73.6.1246 PMID:9418278

Dilber, İ., ve Kılıç, J. (2018). Türkiye'de turizm gelirleri ile ekonomik büyüme ilişkisi: Engle granger eşbütünleşme testi ve VAR model. TESAM Akademi Dergisi, 5(2), 95–118.

Dilek, M. Ş. (2019, 5 15). *Ekonomiye Giriş Ders Tanıtımı Formu*. Retrieved from İletişim Fakültesi - Halkla İlişkiler ve Reklamcılık Programı EKONOMİYE GİRİŞ: http://www.medipol.edu.tr/ders-detayi?DersBolumID=202966#DersTanimi

Dilvin Taşkın, F. (2015). Türk bankacılık sektöründe finansal istikrar-rekabet ilişkisi. *Maliye Finans Yazıları*, *103*(103), 175–204. doi:10.33203/mfy.307961

Dinçer, H., & Yüksel, S. (2019a). Analyzing the possibility of violent conflict in the Middle East economies using determinants of global conflict risk index with an integrated fuzzy multicriteria decision making model. In The impact of global terrorism on economic and political development: Afro-Asian perspectives (pp. 155-166). Emerald Publishing.

Dinçer, H., Hacıoğlu, Ü., & Yüksel, S. (2018). Conflict risk and defense expenses and their impact on the economic growth. In Handbook of research on military expenditure on economic and political resources (pp. 1–23). Hershey, PA: IGI Global. doi:10.4018/978-1-5225-4778-5.ch001

Dinçer, H., Hacıoğlu, Ü., & Yüksel, S. (2018b). Determining influencing factors of currency exchange rate for decision making in global economy using MARS method. In Geopolitics and strategic management in the global economy (pp. 261–273). Hershey, PA: IGI Global. doi:10.4018/978-1-5225-2673-5.ch013

Dinçer, H., Hacıoğlu, Ü., & Yüksel, S. (2018b). Evaluating the effects of economic imbalances on gold price in Turkey with MARS method and discussions on microfinance. In Microfinance and its impact on entrepreneurial development, sustainability, and inclusive growth (pp. 115-137). Hershey, PA: IGI Global.

Compilation of References

Dinçer, H., Hacıoğlu, Ü., & Yüksel, S. (2018c). Evaluating the effects of economic imbalances on gold price in Turkey with MARS method and discussions on microfinance. In Microfinance and its impact on entrepreneurial development, sustainability, and inclusive growth (pp. 115-137). Hershey, PA: IGI Global.

Dinçer, H., Yuksel, S., & Adalı, Z. (2018b). Relationship between non-performing loans, industry, and economic growth of the African economies and policy recommendations for global growth. In Globalization and trade integration in developing countries (pp. 203–228). Hershey, PA: IGI Global. doi:10.4018/978-1-5225-4032-8.ch009

Dinçer, H., Yüksel, S., & Adalı, Z. (2019). Economic effects in Islamic stock development of the European countries: Policy recommendations for ethical behaviors. In Handbook of research on managerial thinking in global business economics (pp. 58-78). Hershey, PA: IGI Global.

Dinçer, H., Yüksel, S., & Adalı, Z. (2019a). Economic effects in Islamic stock development of the European countries: Policy recommendations for ethical behaviors. In Handbook of research on managerial thinking in global business economics (pp. 58-78). Hershey, PA: IGI Global.

Dinçer, H., Yüksel, S., & Adalı, Z. (2019c). Determining the effects of monetary policies on capital markets of the emerging economies: An evidence from E7 countries. The impacts of monetary policy in the 21st century: Perspectives from emerging economies. Emerald Publishing Limited, 3-16.

Dinçer, H., Yüksel, S., & Adalı, Z. (2019e). Economic effects in Islamic stock development of the european countries: policy recommendations for ethical behaviors. In Handbook of research on managerial thinking in global business economics (pp. 58-78). Hershey, PA: IGI Global.

Dinçer, H., Yüksel, S., & Adalı, Z. (2019j). Economic effects in Islamic stock development of the European countries: policy recommendations for ethical behaviors. In Handbook of research on managerial thinking in global business economics (pp. 58-78). Hershey, PA: IGI Global.

Dinçer, H., Yuksel, S., & Bozaykut-Buk, T. (2018b). Evaluation of financial and economic effects on green supply chain management with multi-criteria decision-making approach: Evidence from companies listed in BIST. In Handbook of research on supply chain management for sustainable development (pp. 144–175). Hershey, PA: IGI Global. doi:10.4018/978-1-5225-5757-9.ch009

Dinçer, H., Yüksel, S., & Canbolat, Z. N. (2019d). A strategic approach to reduce energy imports of E7 countries: Use of renewable energy. In Handbook of research on economic and political implications of green trading and energy use (pp. 18-38). Hershey, PA: IGI Global.

Dinçer, H., Yüksel, S., & Canbolat, Z. N. (2019f). A strategic approach to reduce energy imports of E7 countries: use of renewable energy. In Handbook of research on economic and political implications of green trading and energy use (pp. 18-38). Hershey, PA: IGI Global.

Dinçer, H., Yüksel, S., & Çetiner, İ. T. (2019c). Strategy selection for organizational performance of Turkish banking sector with the integrated multi-dimensional decision-making approach. In Handbook of research on contemporary approaches in management and organizational strategy (pp. 273–291). Hershey, PA: IGI Global. doi:10.4018/978-1-5225-6301-3.ch014

Dinçer, H., Yüksel, S., & Kartal, M. T. (2019b). The role of bank interest rate in the competitive emerging markets to provide financial and economic stability. *Ekonomi, İşletme ve Maliye Araştırmaları Dergisi, 1*(2).

Dinçer, H., Yüksel, S., & Kartal, M. T. (2019d). The role of bank interest rate in the competitive emerging markets to provide financial and economic stability. *Ekonomi, İşletme ve Maliye Araştırmaları Dergisi, 1*(2).

Dinçer, H., Yüksel, S., & Pınarbaşı, F. (2019a). SERVQUAL-based evaluation of service quality of energy companies in Turkey: strategic policies for sustainable economic development. In The circular economy and its implications on sustainability and the green supply chain (pp. 142-167). Hershey, PA: IGI Global.

Dinçer, H., Yüksel, S., & Pınarbaşı, F. (2019b). Technology acceptance model-based website evaluation of service industry: an application on the companies listed in BIST via hybrid MCDM. In Multi-Criteria Decision-Making Models for Website Evaluation (pp. 1-28). Hershey, PA: IGI Global.

Dinçer, H., Yüksel, S., & Pınarbaşı, F. (2019d). SERVQUAL-based evaluation of service quality of energy companies in Turkey: strategic policies for sustainable economic development. In The circular economy and its implications on sustainability and the green supply chain (pp. 142-167). Hershey, PA: IGI Global.

Dinçer, H., Yüksel, S., & Pınarbaşı, F. (2019m). Technology acceptance model-based website evaluation of service industry: an application on the companies listed in BIST via hybrid MCDM. In Multi-criteria decision-making models for website evaluation (pp. 1-28). Hershey, PA: IGI Global.

Dinçer, H., Yüksel, S., Adalı, Z., & Aydın, R. (2019a). Evaluating the role of research and development and technology investments on economic development of E7 countries. In Organizational transformation and managing innovation in the fourth industrial revolution (pp. 245-263). Hershey, PA: IGI Global.

Dinçer, H., Yüksel, S., Adalı, Z., & Aydın, R. (2019a). Evaluating the role of research and development and technology investments on economic development of E7 countries. In Organizational Transformation and Managing Innovation in the Fourth Industrial Revolution (pp. 245-263). Hershey, PA: IGI Global.

Dinçer, H., Yüksel, S., Adalı, Z., & Aydın, R. (2019c). Evaluating the role of research and development and technology investments on economic development of E7 countries. In Organizational transformation and managing innovation in the fourth industrial revolution (pp. 245-263). Hershey, PA: IGI Global.

Dinçer, H., Yüksel, S., Adalı, Z., & Aydın, R. (2019l). Evaluating the role of research and development and technology investments on economic development of E7 countries. In Organizational transformation and managing innovation in the fourth industrial revolution (pp. 245-263). Hershey, PA: IGI Global.

Dinçer, H., Yüksel, S., Eti, S., & Tula, A. (2019d). Effects of demographic characteristics on business success: an evidence from Turkish banking sector. In Handbook of research on business models in modern competitive scenarios (pp. 304–324). Hershey, PA: IGI Global. doi:10.4018/978-1-5225-7265-7.ch016

Dinçer, H., Yüksel, S., Kartal, M. T., & Alpman, G. (2019c). Corporate governance-based evaluation of alternative distribution channels in the Turkish banking sector using quality function deployment with an integrated fuzzy MCDM method. In Intergenerational governance and leadership in the corporate world: emerging research and opportunities (pp. 39-77). Hershey, PA: IGI Global.

Dinçer, H., Yüksel, S., Kartal, M. T., & Alpman, G. (2019e). Corporate governance-based evaluation of alternative distribution channels in the turkish banking sector using quality function deployment with an integrated fuzzy MCDM method. In Intergenerational governance and leadership in the corporate world: Emerging research and opportunities (pp. 39-77). Hershey, PA: IGI Global.

Dinçer, H., Yüksel, S., Kartal, M. T., & Alpman, G. (2019k). Corporate governance-based evaluation of alternative distribution channels in the Turkish banking sector using quality function deployment with an integrated fuzzy MCDM method. In Intergenerational governance and leadership in the corporate world: emerging research and opportunities (pp. 39-77). Hershey, PA: IGI Global.

Dinçer, H., Yüksel, S., Pınarbaşı, F., & Çetiner, İ. T. (2019b). Measurement of economic and banking stability in emerging markets by considering income inequality and nonperforming loans. In Maintaining financial stability in times of risk and uncertainty (pp. 49–68). Hershey, PA: IGI Global. doi:10.4018/978-1-5225-7208-4.ch003

Dinçer, H., Yüksel, S., Yazici, M., & Pınarbaşı, F. (2019). Assessing corporate social responsibilities in the banking sector: as a tool of strategic communication during the global financial crisis. In Handbook of research on global issues in financial communication and investment decision making (pp. 1–27). Hershey, PA: IGI Global. doi:10.4018/978-1-5225-9265-5.ch001

Dinçer, H., Yüksel, S., Yazici, M., & Pınarbaşı, F. (2019b). Assessing corporate social responsibilities in the banking sector: as a tool of strategic communication during the global financial crisis. In Handbook of research on global issues in financial communication and investment decision making (pp. 1-27). Hershey, PA: IGI Global.

Dinçer, H., Yüksel, S., Yazici, M., & Pınarbaşı, F. (2019d). Assessing corporate social responsibilities in the banking sector: as a tool of strategic communication during the global financial crisis. in Handbook of research on global issues in financial communication and investment decision making (pp. 1-27). Hershey, PA: IGI Global.

Dinçer, H., Yüksel, S., Yazici, M., & Pınarbaşı, F. (2019e). Assessing corporate social responsibilities in the banking sector: as a tool of strategic communication during the global financial crisis. In Handbook of research on global issues in financial communication and investment decision making (pp. 1-27). Hershey, PA: IGI Global.

Dincer, H. (2015). Profit-based stock selection approach in banking sector using Fuzzy AHP and MOORA method. *Global Business and Economics Research Journal*, *4*(2), 1–26.

Dincer, H. (2018). HHI-based evaluation of the European banking sector using an integrated fuzzy approach. *Kybernetes*.

Dincer, H., Hacioglu, U., Tatoglu, E., & Delen, D. (2016). A fuzzy-hybrid analytic model to assess investors' perceptions for industry selection. *Decision Support Systems*, *86*, 24–34. doi:10.1016/j.dss.2016.03.005

Dincer, H., Hacioglu, U., Tatoglu, E., & Delen, D. (2019d). Developing a hybrid analytics approach to measure the efficiency of deposit banks. *Journal of Business Research*, *104*, 131–145. doi:10.1016/j.jbusres.2019.06.035

Dinçer, H., Hacıoğlu, Ü., & Yüksel, S. (2016). The impacts of financial variables on employment planning in Turkish banking sector. *International Journal of Sustainable Entrepreneurship and Corporate Social Responsibility*, *1*(2), 1–20. doi:10.4018/IJSECSR.2016070101

Dinçer, H., Hacıoğlu, Ü., & Yüksel, S. (2017). A strategic approach to global financial crisis in banking sector: a critical appraisal of banking strategies using fuzzy ANP and fuzzy topsis methods. *International Journal of Sustainable Economies Management*, *6*(1), 1–21. doi:10.4018/ijsem.2017010101

Dinçer, H., Hacıoğlu, Ü., & Yüksel, S. (2017). Balanced scorecard-based performance measurement of European airlines using a hybrid multicriteria decision making approach under the fuzzy environment. *Journal of Air Transport Management*, *63*, 17–33. doi:10.1016/j.jairtraman.2017.05.005

Dincer, H., Uzunkaya, S. S., & Yüksel, S. (2019c). An IT2-based hybrid decision-making model using hesitant fuzzy linguistic term sets for selecting the development plan of financial economics. *International Journal of Computational Intelligence Systems*, *12*(2), 460–473. doi:10.2991/ijcis.d.190312.001

Dinçer, H., & Yüksel, S. (2018a). Financial sector-based analysis of the G20 economies using the integrated decision-making approach with DEMATEL and TOPSIS. In *Emerging trends in banking and finance* (pp. 210–223). Cham, Switzerland: Springer. doi:10.1007/978-3-030-01784-2_13

Dinçer, H., & Yüksel, S. (2018b). Comparative evaluation of BSC-based new service development competencies in Turkish banking sector with the integrated fuzzy hybrid MCDM using content analysis. *International Journal of Fuzzy Systems*, *20*(8), 2497–2516. doi:10.100740815-018-0519-y

Dinçer, H., & Yüksel, S. (2019). An integrated stochastic fuzzy MCDM approach to the balanced scorecard-based service evaluation. *Mathematics and Computers in Simulation*.

Dinçer, H., & Yüksel, S. (2019). Identifying the causality relationship between health expenditure and economic growth: an application on E7 countries. *Journal of Health Systems and Policies*, *1*, 14.

Dinçer, H., & Yüksel, S. (2019). Identifying the causality relationship between health expenditure and economic growth: An application on E7 countries. *Journal of Health Systems and Policies*, *1*, 5.

Dinçer, H., & Yüksel, S. (2019a). Multidimensional evaluation of global investments on the renewable energy with the integrated fuzzy decision-making model under the hesitancy. *International Journal of Energy Research*, *43*(5), 1775–1784. doi:10.1002/er.4400

Dincer, H., & Yuksel, S. (2019b). Balanced scorecard-based analysis of investment decisions for the renewable energy alternatives: A comparative analysis based on the hybrid fuzzy decision-making approach. *Energy*, *175*, 1259–1270. doi:10.1016/j.energy.2019.03.143

Dincer, H., & Yuksel, S. (2019b). IT2-based fuzzy hybrid decision making approach to soft computing. *IEEE Access: Practical innovations, open solutions*, *7*, 15932–15944. doi:10.1109/ACCESS.2019.2895359

Dinçer, H., Yüksel, S., & Adalı, Z. (2017). Identifying causality relationship between energy consumption and economic growth in developed countries. *International Business and Accounting Research Journal*, *1*(2), 71–81. doi:10.15294/ibarj.v1i2.9

Dinçer, H., Yüksel, S., Korsakienė, R., Raišienė, A. G., & Bilan, Y. (2019e). IT2 hybrid decision-making approach to performance measurement of internationalized firms in the Baltic states. *Sustainability*, *11*(1), 296. doi:10.3390u11010296

Dincer, H., Yüksel, S., & Martinez, L. (2019a). Balanced scorecard-based analysis about European energy investment policies: A hybrid hesitant fuzzy decision-making approach with quality function deployment. *Expert Systems with Applications*, *115*, 152–171. doi:10.1016/j.eswa.2018.07.072

Dinçer, H., Yüksel, S., & Martínez, L. (2019b). Interval type 2-based hybrid fuzzy evaluation of financial services in E7 economies with DEMATEL-ANP and MOORA methods. *Applied Soft Computing*, *79*, 186–202. doi:10.1016/j.asoc.2019.03.018

Dinçer, H., Yüksel, S., & Martínez, L. (2019f). Analysis of balanced scorecard-based SERVQUAL criteria based on hesitant decision-making approaches. *Computers & Industrial Engineering*, *131*, 1–12. doi:10.1016/j.cie.2019.03.026

Dinçer, H., Yüksel, S., & Şenel, S. (2018a). Analyzing the global risks for the financial crisis after the great depression using comparative hybrid hesitant fuzzy decision-making models: Policy recommendations for sustainable economic growth. *Sustainability*, *10*(9), 3126. doi:10.3390u10093126

Dinçer, Ö. (1998). *Stratejik Yönetim ve Politikası, Genişletilmiş ve Yenilenmiş 5*. İstanbul, Turkey: Baskı, Beta Yay.

Disyatat, P. (2008). *Monetary policy implementation: Misconceptions and their consequences (No. 269)*. Bank for International Settlements.

Diviani, N., Van den Putte, B., Meppelink, C. S., & van Weert, J. C. (2016). Exploring the role of health literacy in the evaluation of online health information: Insights from a mixed-methods study. *Patient Education and Counseling*, *99*(6), 1017–1025. doi:10.1016/j.pec.2016.01.007 PMID:26817407

Compilation of References

Dizdarlar, H. I., & Derindere, S. (2008). *Hisse Senedi Endeksini Etkileyen Faktörler: İMKB 100 Endeksini Etkileyen Makroekonomik Göstergeler Üzerine Bir Araştırma. 19*(61), 113–124.

Djalilov, K., & Piesse, J. (2016). Determinants of bank profitability in transition countries: What matters most? *Research in International Business and Finance, 38*, 69–82. doi:10.1016/j.ribaf.2016.03.015

Doğan, H. (2011). Development and spread examples of tacit knowledge from. *Gümüşhane University Journal of Social Sciences Electronic*, 77-100.

Dogan, E., & Aslan, A. (2017). Exploring the relationship among CO2 emissions, real GDP, energy consumption and tourism in the EU and candidate countries: Evidence from panel models robust to heterogeneity and cross-sectional dependence. *Renewable & Sustainable Energy Reviews, 77*, 239–245. doi:10.1016/j.rser.2017.03.111

Dogan, E., Sebri, M., & Turkekul, B. (2016). Exploring the relationship between agricultural electricity consumption and output: New evidence from Turkish regional data. *Energy Policy, 95*, 370–377. doi:10.1016/j.enpol.2016.05.018

Dosi, G. (1988). Sources procedures and microeconimic effects of innovation. *Journal of Economic Literature, 3*, 1122.

Dräger, L., & Lamla, M. J. (2017). Explaining disagreement on interest rates in a Taylor-rule setting. *The Scandinavian Journal of Economics, 119*(4), 987–1009. doi:10.1111joe.12217

Drucker, F. P. (2017). *İnovasyon ve Girişimcilik – Uygulama ve İlkeler*. İstanbul, Turkey: Optimist Yayım Dağıtım.

Drucker, P. (2012). *Management*. Routledge. doi:10.4324/9780080939063

Drummond, G., Ashford, R., & Ensor, J. (2007). *Strategic marketing: planning and control*. Amsterdam, The Netherlands: Elsevier. doi:10.4324/9780080498270

Duasa, J. (2009). Exchange rate shock on Malaysian prices of imports and exports: An empirical analysis. *Journal of Economic Cooperation and Development, 30*(3), 99–114.

Du, L., Yanan, H., & Wei, C. (2010). The relationship between oil price shocks and China's macro-economy: An empirical analysis. *Energy Policy, 38*(8), 4142–4151. doi:10.1016/j.enpol.2010.03.042

Dulupçu, M. A. (2001). *Küresel rekabet gücü: Türkiye üzerine bir değerlendirme*. Nobel.

Dumitrescu, E. I., & Hurlin, C. (2012). Testing for Granger non-causality in heterogeneous panels. *Economic Modelling, 29*(4), 1450–1460. doi:10.1016/j.econmod.2012.02.014

Dunning, J. H. (1998). Location and the multinational enterprise: A neglected factor? *Journal of International Business Studies, 29*(1), 45–66. doi:10.1057/palgrave.jibs.8490024

Dunning, J. H., & Zhang, F. (2008). *Foreign direct investment and the locational competitiveness of countries. Transnational Corporations, 17(3)* (pp. 1–30). New York: United Nations.

Dura, C., & Atik, H. (2002). *Bilgi Tohumu, Bilgi Ekonomisi ve Türkiye. Literatür Yayınları, 1* (p. 209). İstanbul, Turkey: Basım.

Durak, İ. (2011). Girişimciliği etkileyen çevresel faktörlerle ilgili girişimcilerin tutumları: Bir alan araştırması. *Yönetim Bilimleri Dergisi, 9*(2), 191–213.

Duramaz, S., & Dilber, İ. (2015). Küresel Kriz Sürecinde Para Politikasında Yeni Bir Araç Olarak Faiz Koridoruna Genel Bir Bakış. *Maliye Araştırmaları Dergisi, 1*(1), 29–38.

Durand, R. B., Newby, R., & Sanghani, J. (2008). An intimate portrait of the individual investor. *Journal of Behavioral Finance, 9*(4), 193–208. doi:10.1080/15427560802341020

Duran, S., & Zehir, C. (2011). Analyzing the technical efficiency on the effects of foreign portfolio investment in the financing of small and medium-sized enterprises (SMEs) in Turkey. *African Journal of Business Management*, *5*(21), 8567–8575. doi:10.5897/AJBM11.1027

Durkin, M., O'Donnell, A., Mullholland, G., & Crowe, J. (2007). On e-banking adoption: From banker perception to customer reality. *Journal of Strategic Marketing*, *15*(2-3), 237–252. doi:10.1080/09652540701318815

Dursun, A., & Özcan, M. (2019). Enerji Fiyat Değişimleri İle Borsa Endeksleri Arasındaki İlişki: OECD Ülkeleri Üzerine Bir Uygulama. *Energy price changes and stock exchange relationship: an application on OECD countries*, (82), 177–198. doi:10.25095/mufad.536069

Dursun, İ. T. (2013). Örgüt Kültürü ve Strateji İlişkisi: Hofstede'nin Boyutları Açısından Bir Değerlendirme. *Siyaset, Ekonomi ve Yönetim Araştırmaları Dergisi, 1*(4).

Dwivedi, D. N. (2010). Macroeconomics theory and policy. New Delhi, India: Tata McGraw-Hill Education, 388.

Dyhrberg, A. H. (2016). Bitcoin, gold and the dollar–A GARCH volatility analysis. *Finance Research Letters*, *16*, 85–92. doi:10.1016/j.frl.2015.10.008

Dyhrberg, A. H. (2016). Hedging capabilities of bitcoin. Is it the virtual gold? *Finance Research Letters*, *16*, 139–144. doi:10.1016/j.frl.2015.10.025

Easterby-Smith, M., Thorpe, R., & Jackson, P. R. (2012). Management research. *Atlanta, GA: Sage*.

Edin, İ. (2008). Rekabet İstihbaratı Sürecinde Anahtar İstihbarat Konularının Belirlenmesi, *Marmara Üniversitesi İ. İ. B. F. Dergisi*, C.XXV, 2, 589-600.

Edirisuriya, P., Gunasekarage, A., & Dempsey, M. (2015). Bank diversification, performance and stock market response: Evidence from listed public banks in South Asian countries. *Journal of Asian Economics*, *41*, 69–85. doi:10.1016/j.asieco.2015.09.003

Edquist, C. (2005). *Systems of innovation* (p. 64). Routhledge, Oxon: Technologies, Institutions and Organizations.

Efremidze, L., Rutledge, J., & Willett, T. D. (2016). Capital flow surges as bubbles: Behavioral finance and McKinnon's over-borrowing syndrome extended. *The Singapore Economic Review*, *61*(02), 1640023. doi:10.1142/S0217590816400233

Efthymios, G. P., & David, A. P. (2018). Modeling changes in US monetary policy with a time-varying nonlinear Taylor rule. *Studies in Nonlinear Dynamics and Econometrics*, *22*(5).

Ege, İ., & Bayrakdaroğlu, A. (2012). İMKB Şirketlerinin Hisse Senedi Getiri Başarılarının Lojistik Regresyon Tekniği İle Analizi. *Uluslararası Yönetim İktisat ve İşletme Dergisi*, *5*(10), 139-158. doi:10.11122/ijmeb.2014.5.10.203

Ege, İ., & Bayrakdaroğlu, A. (2009). İMKB Şirketlerinin Hisse Senedi Getiri Başarılarının Lojistik Regresyon tekniği ile Analizi. ZKÜ Sosyal Bilimler Dergisi, Cilt 5. *Sayı, 10*, 139–158.

Eğilmez, M. (2012). Tarife dışı engeller. Retrieved from http://www.mahfiegilmez.com/2012/11/tarife-ds-engeller.html. Erişim Tarihi: 26.11.2012.

Eğilmez, M. (2015, Sept. 5). Parasal genişleme uygulamaları. [Blog post]. Retrieved from http://www.mahfiegilmez.com/2015/09/parasal-genisleme-uygulamalar.html

Eğilmez, M. (2017, Sept. 22). Niceliksel genişlemeden niceliksel sıkılaştırmaya. [Blog post]. Retrieved from http://www.mahfiegilmez.com/2017/09/niceliksel-gevsemeden-niceliksel.html

Eğilmez, M. (2018, July 10). Para arzı nedir ve nasıl ölçülür? [Blog post]. Retrieved from http://www.mahfiegilmez.com/2018/07/para-arz-nedir-ve-nasl-olculur.html

Eğinli, A. T. (2011). Kültürlerarası Yeterliliğin Kazanılmasında Kültürel Farklılık Eğitimlerinin Önemi. *Öneri Dergisi, 9*(35), 215-227.

Ehtiyar, R. (2003). Kültürel Sinerji: Uluslararası İşletmelere Yönelik Kavramsal Bir İrdeleme. *Akdeniz University Faculty of Economics & Administrative Sciences Faculty Journal/Akdeniz Universitesi Iktisadi ve Idari Bilimler Fakultesi Dergisi, 3*(5).

Eid, A. (2012). Higher education R&D and productivity growth: an empirical study on high-income OECD countries. *Education Economics, 20*(1), 53–68. doi:10.1080/09645291003726855

Eisen, M. L., Winograd, E., & Qin, J. (2002). Individual differences in adults' suggestibility and memory performance. *Memory and Suggestibility in the Forensic Interview*, 205-234.

Eisner, E., Drake, R., Lobban, F., Bucci, S., Emsley, R., & Barrowclough, C. (2018). Comparing early signs and basic symptoms as methods for predicting psychotic relapse in clinical practice. *Schizophrenia Research, 192*, 124–130. doi:10.1016/j.schres.2017.04.050 PMID:28499766

Ekin, N. (1999). Küreselleşme ve Gümrük Birliği. *İstanbul Ticaret Odası Yayın*, (1999-47), 432.

Ekinci, R., & Kök, R. (2017). Rekabet ve etkinlik: Avrupa Birliği bankacılık endüstrisi üzerine bir uygulama. *Çankırı Karatekin Üniversitesi İİBF Dergisi, 7*(2), 171-200.

Ellison, M., & Tischbirek, A. (2014). Unconventional government debt purchases as a supplement to conventional monetary policy. *Journal of Economic Dynamics & Control, 43*, 199–217. doi:10.1016/j.jedc.2014.03.012

Ellwood, W. (2002). *Küreselleşmeyi Anlama Kılavuzu*. İstanbul, Turkey: Metis Yayınları.

Elmes, M. B., Mendoza-Abarca, K., & Hersh, R. (2016). Food banking, ethical sensemaking, and social innovation in an era of growing hunger in the United States. *Journal of Management Inquiry, 25*(2), 122–138. doi:10.1177/1056492615589651

El-Sharif, I., Brown, D., Burton, B., Nixon, B., & Russell, A. (2005). Evidence on the nature and extent of the relationship between oil prices and equity values in the UK. *Energy Economics, 27*(6), 819–830. doi:10.1016/j.eneco.2005.09.002

Emek, U. (2005). Bankacılık sisteminde rekabet ve istikrar ikileminin analizi: Türkiye örneği. (Unpublished Doctorate Thesis, Ankara University Social Sciences Institute).

Emin, Ç., & Çavuşgil, S. T. (2001). Yeni Dünya Düzeninde Güç Kazanan Ülkeler: Yükselen Ekonomiler. *Yönetim ve Ekonomi: Celal Bayar Üniversitesi İktisadi ve İdari Bilimler Fakültesi Dergisi, 8*(1), 113–128.

Emin, Ç., & Erol, E. D. (2008). Ulusal Rekabet Gücünü Arttırma Yolları: Literatür Araştırması. *Yönetim ve Ekonomi: Celal Bayar Üniversitesi İktisadi ve İdari Bilimler Fakültesi Dergisi, 15*(1), 99–114.

Emir, S., Dincer, H., Hacioglu, U., & Yuksel, S. (2016). Random regression forest model using technical analysis variables. *International Journal of Finance & Banking Studies (2147-4486), 5*(3), 85-102.

Enders, W. (2004). *Applied econometric time series*. Hamilton Printing.

Engelberg, J., & Parsons, C. A. (2016). Worrying about the stock market: Evidence from hospital admissions. *The Journal of Finance, 71*(3), 1227–1250. doi:10.1111/jofi.12386

Engle, R. F., & Granger, C. W. J. (1987). Co-integration and error correction : Representation, estimation, and testing. *Econometrica, 55*(2), 251–276. doi:10.2307/1913236

Eraslan Hakkı, M. B. (2008). Clusters and their effects on innovations: implementations in the Turkish tourism sector. *Magazine for Travel and Hotel Management*, 15-29.

Eraslan, İ. H., & Dönmez, C. Ç. (2017). The analysis of industrial cluster implications in wordwide: an evaluation for agriculture, manufacturing and service industries. *Electronic Journal of Social Sciences*, 719-755.

Eraslan, İ. H., & Güngören, M. (2013). The economic history and evolution progress of industrial. *Electronic Journal of Social Sciences*, 171-197.

Erbaşı, A., & Ersöz, S. (2011). The relationship between Akhism and 4C Marketing Mix: A view from historical perspective. *Turkish Culture and Hacı Bektas Veli Research Quarterly*, 135-146.

Erdogan, A. I. (2018). Factors affecting SME access to bank financing: An interview study with Turkish bankers. *Small Enterprise Research*, 25(1), 23–35. doi:10.1080/13215906.2018.1428911

Ergün, K. (2018). Financial literacy among university students: A study in eight European countries. *International Journal of Consumer Studies*, 42(1), 2–15. doi:10.1111/ijcs.12408

Erinç, S. M. (2014). Kültürde kültür, kültür de kültür. *Cogito Düşünce Dergisi*, 2, 107–112.

Erkiletlioğlu, H. (2013). Dünyada ve Türkiye'de AR-GE Faaliyetleri. İktisadi Araştırmalar Bölümü, Türkiye İş Bankası Yayınları, 2.

Erkılıç, S. (2006). *Türkiye'de Cari Açığın Belirleyicileri*. Ankara, Turkey: Uzmanlık Yeterlilik Tezi.

Eroğlu, N., & Kara, F. (2017). Türkiye'de makro ihtiyati para politikası araçlarının makroekonomik değişkenlere etkisinin var analizi ile incelenmesi. *İstanbul İktisat Dergisi*, 67(2), 59-88.

Ersel, B. (2003). Bilgi Çağında Çalışma İlkeleri ve Beyin Göçü. *II. Ulusal Bilgi, Ekonomi ve Yönetim Kongresi Bildiriler Kitabı,* Kocaeli Üniversitesi., 717.

Ersin, İ. (2018). İhracata Dayalı Büyüme Hipotezinin Test Edilmesi: MINT Ülkeleri Örneği. *Ekonomi İşletme ve Maliye Araştırmaları Dergisi*, 1(1), 26–38.

Ersin, İ., & Baş, H. (2019). Güney Avrupa Refah Ülkelerinde Sosyal Harcamalar ve Ekonomik Büyüme Arasındaki İlişkinin İncelenmesi. *SGD-Sosyal Güvenlik Dergisi*, 9(1), 193–213. doi:10.32331gd.582752

Ersin, İ., & Eti, S. (2017). Measuring the waste-conscious and saving habits of the youth in Turkey: The sample of Istanbul Medipol University. *Uluslararası İslam Ekonomisi ve Finansı Araştırmaları Dergisi*, 3(3), 41–49.

Ertekin, M., & Kırca, M. (2017). Türkiye'de kentleşme ve iktisadi büyüme ilişkisinin zamanla değişen nedensellik analizi yöntemiyle incelenmesi. *Journal of Emerging Economies and Policy*, 2(2), 44–63.

Esen, Ö. (2012). Türkiye'de döviz kuru belirsizliğinin ihracat üzerine etkisi. *Finans Politik ve Ekonomik Yorumlar*, 49(568), 89.

Etemad, H. (Ed.). (2004). *International entrepreneurship in small and medium size enterprises: orientation, environment and strategy*. Edward Elgar. doi:10.4337/9781845421557

Ethier, W. (1973). International trade and the forward exchange market. *The American Economic Review*, 63(3), 494–503.

Eti, S. (2016). Üniversitelerdeki akademik üretkenliğe etki eden faktörlerin incelenmesi. *İş'te Davranış Dergisi*, 1(1), 67-73.

Eti, S. (2019). The use of quantitative methods in investment decisions: a literature review. In Handbook of research on global issues in financial communication and investment decision making (pp. 256–275). Hershey, PA: IGI Global. doi:10.4018/978-1-5225-9265-5.ch013

Compilation of References

Eti, S. (2019). Ulakbim İndeksinde Taranan Sosyal Bilimler Alanındaki Dergilerde Öne Çıkan Konu Ve Yöntemlerin Metin Madenciliği Yaklaşımı İle Belirlenmesi. *Uluslararası Hukuk ve Sosyal Bilim Araştırmaları Dergisi, 1*(1), 61–66.

Eti, S. (2019a). ULAKBİM İndeksinde Taranan Sosyal Bilimler Alanındaki Dergilerde Öne Çıkan Konu Ve Yöntemlerin Metin Madenciliği Yaklaşımı İle Belirlenmesi. *Uluslararası Hukuk ve Sosyal Bilim Araştırmaları Dergisi, 1*(1), 61–66.

Eti, S., Dinçer, H., & Yüksel, S. (2019). G20 Ülkelerinde Bankacılık Sektörünün 5 Yıllık Geleceğinin Arıma Yöntemi İle Tahmin Edilmesi. *Uluslararası Hukuk ve Sosyal Bilim Araştırmaları Dergisi, 1*(1), 26–38.

Eugster, N., & Isakov, D. (2019). Founding family ownership, stock market returns, and agency problems. *Journal of Banking & Finance, 107*, 105600. doi:10.1016/j.jbankfin.2019.07.020

Eurostat & OECD. (2005). *Oslo Kılavuzu Yenilik Verilerinin Toplanması ve Yorumlanması İçin İlkeler. 3. Baskı.* TUBİTAK.

EViews downloads. (n.d.). Retrieved from https://www.eviews.com/download/download.shtml#eviews9

Evren, A. A., Ustaoğlu, E., & Bayer, Z. A. (2018). Piyasaların yoğunlaşma derecelerinin belirlenmesinde entropi kavramından türetilen Herfindahl-Hirschmann ve benzeri egemenlik ölçüleri. *Uygulamalı Sosyal Bilimler Dergisi, 2*(1), 1–13.

Ewing, B. T., & Malik, F. (2016). Volatility spillovers between oil prices and the stock market under structural breaks. *Global Finance Journal, 29*, 12–23. doi:10.1016/j.gfj.2015.04.008

Eyüboğlu, K., & Eyüboğlu, S. (2018). Testing the relationship between competition and soundness in banking sector: Panel ARDL model in emerging countries. *Eskişehir Osmangazi Üniversitesi İktisadi ve İdari Bilimler Dergisi, 13*(3), 219-234. Retrieved from https://dergipark.org.tr/oguiibf/article/450138

Fagerberg, J. (1988). International competitiveness. *Economic Journal (London), 98*(391), 355–374. doi:10.2307/2233372

Fagerberg, J. (1996). Technology and competitiveness. *Oxford Review of Economic Policy, 12*(3), 39–51. doi:10.1093/oxrep/12.3.39

Fagerberg, J., Srholec, M., & Knell, M. (2007). The competitiveness of nations: Why some countries prosper while others fall behind. *World Development, 35*(10), 1595–1620. doi:10.1016/j.worlddev.2007.01.004

Fahey, L. (2007). Connecting strategy and competitive intelligence: Refocusing intelligence to produce critical strategy inputs. *Strategy and Leadership, 35*(1), 4–12. doi:10.1108/10878570710717236

Fahey, L., & King, W. R. (1977). Environmental scanning for corporate planning. *Business Horizons, 20*(4), 61–71. doi:10.1016/0007-6813(77)90010-6

Fahey, L., King, W. R., & Narayanan, V. K. (1981). Environmental scanning and forecasting in strategic planning—the state of the art. *Long Range Planning, 14*(1), 32–39.

Fahimnia, B., Sarkis, J., & Davarzani, H. (2015). Green supply chain management: A review and bibliometric analysis. *International Journal of Production Economics, 162*, 101–114. doi:10.1016/j.ijpe.2015.01.003

Falk, M. (2007). R&D spending in the high-tech sector and economic growth. *Research in Economics, 61*.

Faria, J. R., Mollick, A. V., Albuquerque, P. H., & León-Ledesma, M. A. (2009). The effect of oil price on China's exports. *China Economic Review, 20*(4), 793–805. doi:10.1016/j.chieco.2009.04.003

Faroqhi, S. (2018). *Osmanlı dünyasında üretmek, pazarlamak, yaşamak.* İstanbul, Turkey: Yapı Kredi Yayınları.

Farouk, S., Abu Elanain, H. M., Obeidat, S. M., & Al-Nahyan, M. (2016). HRM practices and organizational performance in the UAE banking sector: The mediating role of organizational innovation. *International Journal of Productivity and Performance Management, 65*(6), 773–791. doi:10.1108/IJPPM-01-2016-0010

Farrel, J. M., & Hoon, A. (2009). What's your company risk culture. National Association of Corporate Directors Directorship, 50-62.

Farzanegan, M. R., & Markwardt, G. (2009). The effects of oil price shocks on the Iranian economy. *Energy Economics, 31*(1), 134–151. doi:10.1016/j.eneco.2008.09.003

Fayad, A. A., Ayoub, R., & Ayoub, M. (2017). Causal relationship between CSR and FB in banks. *Arab Economic and Business Journal, 12*(2), 93–98. doi:10.1016/j.aebj.2017.11.001

Fayyad, A., & Daly, K. (2011). The impact of oil price shocks on stock market returns: Comparing GCC countries with the UK and USA. *Emerging Markets Review, 12*(1), 61–78. doi:10.1016/j.ememar.2010.12.001

FED. (n.d.). Policy tools. Retrieved from https://www.federalreserve.gov/monetarypolicy/policytools.htm

FED. (n.d.). What is the money supply? Is it important? Retrieved from https://www.federalreserve.gov/faqs/money_12845.htm

Feigin, P. (2006). *Analysis of customer patience in a bank call center. Working paper.* Haifa, Israel: The Technion.

Feinberg, R. A., Hokama, L., Kadam, R., & Kim, I. (2002). Operational determinants of caller satisfaction in the banking/financial services call center. *International Journal of Bank Marketing, 20*(4), 174–180. doi:10.1108/02652320210432954

Feng, S. P., Hung, M. W., & Wang, Y. H. (2016). The importance of stock liquidity on option pricing. *International Review of Economics & Finance, 43*, 457–467. doi:10.1016/j.iref.2016.01.008

Fernández, J. I. P., Cala, A. S., & Domecq, C. F. (2011). Critical external factors behind hotels' investments in innovation and technology in emerging urban destinations. *Tourism Economics, 17*(2), 339–357. doi:10.5367/te.2011.0033

Fernandez, R. O., & Garza-Garcia, J. G. (2015). The relationship between bank competition and financial stability: A case study of the Mexican banking industry. [Ensayos Journal of Economics]. *Ensayos Revista de Economía, 34*(1), 103–120.

Ferreira, F. A. F., Jalali, M. S., & Ferreira, J. J. M. (2016). Experience-focused thinking and cognitive mapping in ethical banking practices: From practical intuition to theory. *Journal of Business Research, 69*(11), 4953–4958. doi:10.1016/j.jbusres.2016.04.058

Ferris, S. P., Haugen, R. A., & Makhija, A. K. (1988). Predicting contemporary volume with historic volume at differential price levels: Evidence supporting the disposition effect. *The Journal of Finance, 43*(3), 677–697. doi:10.1111/j.1540-6261.1988.tb04599.x

Field, A. (2013). *Discovering statistics using IBM SPSS statistics*. Thousand Oaks, CA: Sage.

Field, A. (2000). *Discovering Statistics Using SPSS for Windows*. New Delhi, India: Sage Publications.

Fikirkoca, M. (2003). *Bütünsel risk yönetimi*. Ankara, Turkey: Pozitif Matbaacılık.

Filbeck, G., Hatfield, P., & Horvath, P. (2005). Risk aversion and personality type. *Journal of Behavioral Finance, 6*(4), 170–180. doi:10.120715427579jpfm0604_1

Filip, B. F. (2015). The quality of bank loans within the framework of globalization. *Procedia Economics and Finance, 20*, 208–217. doi:10.1016/S2212-5671(15)00067-2

Filiztekin, A., & Karata, S. (2010). Türkiye'nin Dış Ticarette Rekabet Gücü: Seçilmiş Ülkeler, Sektörler-Mal Grupları ve Endeksler Bazında Karşılaştırmalı Bir Analiz. *TÜSİAD-Sabancı Üniversitesi Rekabet Forumu (REF) ve Sektörel Dernekler Federasyonu'nun, 1*, 1-47.

Financial Times. (2011, April 1). *Forex investing: no place for amateurs*. Retrieved from https://www.ft.com/content/62cb6258-5c4c-11e0-8f48-00144feab49a

Findler, L., Wind, L. H., & Barak, M. E. M. (2007). The challenge of workforce management in a global society: Modeling the relationship between diversity, inclusion, organizational culture, and employee well-being, job satisfaction and organizational commitment. *Administration in Social Work*, *31*(3), 63–94. doi:10.1300/J147v31n03_05

Finn, M. G. (2000). Perfect competition and the effects of energy price increases on economic activity. *Journal of Money, Credit, and Banking*, *32*(3), 400–416. doi:10.2307/2601172

Fischer, K. H., & Hempell, H. S. (2005). Oligopoly and conduct in banking-An empirical analysis. *Deutsche Bundesbank Research Centre, Discussion paper*.

Fischer, S. (2003). Globalization and its challenges. *The American Economic Review*, *93*(2), 2. doi:10.1257/000282803321946750

Flory, J. A., Leibbrandt, A., & List, J. A. (2016). *The effects of wage contracts on workplace misbehaviors: Evidence from a call center natural field experiment (No. w22342)*. National Bureau of Economic Research.

Fogel, S. O. C., & Berry, T. (2006). The disposition effect and individual investor decisions: The roles of regret and counterfactual alternatives. *Journal of Behavioral Finance*, *7*(2), 107–116. doi:10.120715427579jpfm0702_5

Fornero, E., & Prete, A. L. (2019). Voting in the aftermath of a pension reform: The role of financial literacy. *Journal of Pension Economics and Finance*, *18*(1), 1–30. doi:10.1017/S1474747218000185

Forseth, U., Røyrvik, E. A., & Clegg, S. (2015). Brave new world? The global financial crisis' impact on Scandinavian banking's sales rhetoric and practices. *Scandinavian Journal of Management*, *31*(4), 471–479. doi:10.1016/j.scaman.2015.06.003

Fotopoulos, G., & Storey, D. J. (2019). Public policies to enhance regional entrepreneurship: Another programme failing to deliver? *Small Business Economics*, *53*(1), 189–209. doi:10.100711187-018-0021-9

Fozer, D., Sziraky, F. Z., Racz, L., Nagy, T., Tarjani, A. J., Toth, A. J., ... Mizsey, P. (2017). Life cycle, PESTLE and multi-criteria decision analysis of CCS process alternatives. *Journal of Cleaner Production*, *147*, 75–85. doi:10.1016/j.jclepro.2017.01.056

Frankel, J. A. (2006). *The effect of monetary policy on real commodity prices (No. w12713)*. National Bureau of Economic Research. doi:10.3386/w12713

Fraser, M. P. (2016). A general survey of the history of the Imperial Ottoman Bank. In East meets West-banking, commerce and investment in the Ottoman Empire (pp. 117-128). Routledge.

Fraser, J. R., & Simkins, B. J. (2016). The challenges of and solutions for implementing enterprise risk management. *Business Horizons*, *59*(6), 689–698. doi:10.1016/j.bushor.2016.06.007

Freeman, R. E. (2010). *Strategic management: A stakeholder approach*. Cambridge, UK: Cambridge University Press. doi:10.1017/CBO9781139192675

Freire-Serén & Jesus M. (1999). Aggregate R&D expenditure and endogenous economic growth. *UFAE and IAE Working Papers* 436, 99.

Friedman, B. M. (2000). Decoupling at the margin: The threat to monetary policy from the electronic revolution in banking. *International Finance*, *3*(2), 261–272. doi:10.1111/1468-2362.00051

Frimpong, E., Oduro-Mensah, E., Vanotoo, L., & Agyepong, I. A. (2018). An exploratory case study of the organizational functioning of a decision-making and referral support call center for frontline providers of maternal and new born care in the Greater Accra Region of Ghana. *The International Journal of Health Planning and Management*, *33*(4), e1112–e1123. doi:10.1002/hpm.2595 PMID:30095184

Fritsch, M. (1997). New firms and regional employment change. *Small Business Economics*, *9*(5), 437–448. doi:10.1023/A:1007942918390

Frolick, M. N., & Ariyachandra, T. R. (2006). Business performance management: One truth. *IS Management*, *23*(1), 41–48.

Froot, K. A., Scharfstein, D. S., & Stein, J. C. (1993). Risk management: Coordinating corporate investment and financing policies. *Journal of Finance*, *48*(5), 1629-1658.

Fuertes, A. M., Phylaktis, K., & Yan, C. (2016). Hot money in bank credit flows to emerging markets during the banking globalization era. *Journal of International Money and Finance*, *60*, 29–52. doi:10.1016/j.jimonfin.2014.10.002

Funston, R. (2003). Creating a risk-intelligent organization: Using enterprise risk management, organizations can systematically identify potential exposures, take corrective action early, and learn from those actions to better achieve objectives. *Internal Auditor*, *60*(2), 59–64.

Furnham, A., & Argyle, M. (1998). *The psychology of money*. Psychology Press.

Furuoka, F. (2017). Renewable electricity consumption and economic development: New findings from the Baltic countries. *Renewable & Sustainable Energy Reviews*, *71*, 450–463. doi:10.1016/j.rser.2016.12.074

Fu, X. M., Yongjia, R. L., & Molyneux, P. (2014). Bank competition and financial stability in Asia Pacific. *Journal of Banking & Finance*, *38*, 64–77. doi:10.1016/j.jbankfin.2013.09.012

Galindo, M., & Mendez, M. T. (2014). Entrepreneurship, economic growth and innovation: are feedback effect at work? *Journal of Business Research*, *67*(5), 825–829. doi:10.1016/j.jbusres.2013.11.052

Gallmeyer, M., Hollifield, B., Palomino, F., & Zin, S. (2017). Term premium dynamics and the Taylor rule. *The Quarterly Journal of Finance*, *7*(04), 1750011. doi:10.1142/S2010139217500112

Gamble, J. E., Peteraf, M. A., & Thompson, A. A. (2014). *Essentials of strategic management: The quest for competitive advantage*. McGraw-Hill Education.

Gans, N., Shen, H., Zhou, Y. P., Korolev, N., McCord, A., & Ristock, H. (2015). Parametric forecasting and stochastic programming models for call-center workforce scheduling. *Manufacturing & Service Operations Management: M & SOM*, *17*(4), 571–588. doi:10.1287/msom.2015.0546

Gao, Y. C., Zeng, Y., & Cai, S. M. (2015). Influence network in the Chinese stock market. *Journal of Statistical Mechanics*, *2015*(3), P03017. doi:10.1088/1742-5468/2015/03/P03017

Garanti Bankası. (n.d.). Retrieved from https://surdurulebilirlik.garantibbva.com.tr/

Garcia, M. J. R. (2013). Financial education and behavioral finance: New insights into the role of information in financial decisions. *Journal of Economic Surveys*, *27*(2), 297–315. doi:10.1111/j.1467-6419.2011.00705.x

Garcia-Zamor, J. C. (2003). Workplace spirituality and organizational performance. *Public Administration Review*, *63*(3), 355–363. doi:10.1111/1540-6210.00295

Garg, N., & Singh, S. (2018). Financial literacy among youth. *International Journal of Social Economics*, *45*(1), 173–186. doi:10.1108/IJSE-11-2016-0303

Garrett, G., Benden, M., Mehta, R., Pickens, A., Peres, S. C., & Zhao, H. (2016). Call center productivity over 6 months following a standing desk intervention. *IIE Transactions on Occupational Ergonomics and Human Factors*, *4*(2-3), 188–195. doi:10.1080/21577323.2016.1183534

Gatfaoui, H. (2016). Linking the gas and oil markets with the stock market: Investigating the US relationship. *Energy Economics*, *53*, 5–16. doi:10.1016/j.eneco.2015.05.021

Gebler, D. (2006). Is your culture a risk factor? *Business And Society Review-Boston And New York*, *111*(3), 337.

Geçit, B. B. (2018). Yöneticilerde Finansal Pazarlama Algısının Ölçümü. *Beykent Üniversitesi Sosyal Bilimler Dergisi*, *11*(1), 24–34.

Gegez, E., Arslan, M., Cengiz, E., & Uydacı, M. (2003). *Uluslararası Pazarlama Çevresi*. İstanbul, Turkey: Der Yayınları.

Geiersbach, N. (2010). The impact of international business on the global economy. *Business Intelligence Journal*, *3*(2), 119–129.

Genc, E. G., & Artar, O. K. (2014). The effect of exchange rates on exports and imports of emerging countries. *European Scientific Journal*, *10*(13), 128–141.

Gerrans, P., & Heaney, R. (2019). The impact of undergraduate personal finance education on individual financial literacy, attitudes and intentions. *Accounting and Finance*, *59*(1), 177–217. doi:10.1111/acfi.12247

Gheibi, M., Karrabi, M., Mohammadi, A., & Dadvar, A. (2018). Controlling air pollution in a city: A perspective from SOAR-PESTLE analysis. *Integrated Environmental Assessment and Management*, *14*(4), 480–488. doi:10.1002/ieam.4051 PMID:29663693

Gheitani, A., Imani, S., Seyyedamiri, N., & Foroudi, P. (2019). Mediating effect of intrinsic motivation on the relationship between Islamic work ethic, job satisfaction, and organizational commitment in banking sector. *International Journal of Islamic and Middle Eastern Finance and Management*, *12*(1), 76–95. doi:10.1108/IMEFM-01-2018-0029

Ghosh, A. (2016). Banking sector globalization and bank performance: A comparative analysis of low income countries with emerging markets and advanced economies. *Review of Development Finance*, *6*(1), 58–70. doi:10.1016/j.rdf.2016.05.003

Ghoshal, S., & Bartlett, C. A. (1988). Creation, adoption and diffusion of innovations by subsidiaries of multinational corporations. *Journal of International Business Studies*, *19*(3), 365–388. doi:10.1057/palgrave.jibs.8490388

Ghosh, S., & Kanjilal, K. (2016). Co-movement of international crude oil price and Indian stock market: Evidences from nonlinear cointegration tests. *Energy Economics*, *53*, 111–117. doi:10.1016/j.eneco.2014.11.002

Giacalone, R. A., & Jurkiewicz, C. L. (Eds.). (2003). *Handbook of workplace spirituality and organizational performance*. Me Sharpe.

Giddens, A. (2006). *Modernitenin Küreselleşmesi* (K. Bülbül, Trans.). Ankara, Turkey: Kadim Yayınları.

Giddings, B., Hopwood, B., & O'Brien, G. (2002). Environment, economy and society: Fitting them together into sustainable development. *Sustainable Development*, *10*(4), 187–196. doi:10.1002d.199

Gilani, H. (2015). Exploring the ethical aspects of Islamic banking. *International Journal of Islamic and Middle Eastern Finance and Management*, *8*(1), 85–98. doi:10.1108/IMEFM-09-2012-0087

Gilbert, D. C., & Choi, K. C. (2003). Relationship marketing practice in relation to different bank ownerships: A study of banks in Hong Kong. *International Journal of Bank Marketing*, *21*(3), 137–146. doi:10.1108/02652320310469511

Gilpin, R. (2016). *The political economy of international relations*. Princeton University Press.

Glaser, F., Zimmermann, K., Haferkorn, M., Weber, M. C., & Siering, M. (2014). *Bitcoin-asset or currency? Revealing users' hidden intentions. Revealing Users' Hidden Intentions (April 15, 2014)*. ECIS.

Glocker, C., & Towbin, P. (2015). Reserve requirements as a macroprudential instrument–Empirical evidence from Brazil. *Journal of Macroeconomics, 44*, 158–176. doi:10.1016/j.jmacro.2015.02.007

Göçer, İ. (2013). *Yabancı Doğrudan Yatırımların Makroekonomik ve Verimlilik Etkileri: Türkiye Çin ve Hindistan Örneği*. Adnan Menderes Üniversitesi Sosyal Bilimler Enstitüsü Doktora Tezi.

Göçmen Yağcılar, G. (2011). *Türk bankacılık sektörünün rekabet yapısının analizi*. Ankara, Turkey: BDDK.

Goddard, J., Molyneux, P., Wilson, J. O., & Tavakoli, M. (2007). European banking: An overview. *Journal of Banking & Finance, 31*(7), 1911–1935. doi:10.1016/j.jbankfin.2007.01.002

Go, E. M., Ong, K. B., San Juan, J. L., Sia, W. G., Tiu, R. H., & Li, R. (2018, August). Development of fuzzy data envelopment risk analysis applied on auditory ergonomics for call center agents in the Philippines. In *Congress of the International Ergonomics Association* (pp. 13–22). Cham, Switzerland: Springer.

Goel, R. K., & Ram, R. (1994). Research and development expenditures and economic growth: a cross-country study. *Economic development and cultural change, 42*(2), 403–411. doi:10.1086/452087

Gök, A. (2006). Alternatif döviz kuru sistemleri. *Marmara Üniversitesi İİBF Dergisi, 21*(1), 131–145.

Gök, A. C., & Özdemir, A. (2011). Lojistik Regresyon Analizi ile Banka Sektör Paylarinin Tahminlenmesi. *Dokuz Eylül Üniversitesi İşletme Fakültesi Dergisi, 12*(1), 43–51.

Gökalp, B. T. (2016). Para Politikası Kararlarının Hisse Senetlerinin Fiyatları Üzerindeki Etkileri. *Suleyman Demirel University Journal of Faculty of Economics & Administrative Sciences, 21*(4).

Gökmen, H. (2012). *Finansal Okuryazarlık*. İstanbul, Turkey: Hiperlik Yayınları.

Goldberg, L. R. (1993). The structure of phenotypic personality traits. *The American Psychologist, 48*(1), 26–34. doi:10.1037/0003-066X.48.1.26 PMID:8427480

González Ortega, R., Oviedo Rodríguez, M. D., Leyva Vázquez, M., Estupiñán Ricardo, J., Sganderla Figueiredo, J. A., & Smarandache, F. (2019). Pestel analysis based on neutrosophic cognitive maps and neutrosophic numbers for the Sinos River Basin management. *Neutrosophic Sets & Systems, 26*.

Goodhart, C. (2010). *The changing role of central banks (No. 326)*. Bank for International Settlements.

Gorbachev, O., & Luengo-Prado, M. J. (2019). The credit card debt puzzle: The role of preferences, credit access risk, and financial literacy. *The Review of Economics and Statistics, 101*(2), 294–309. doi:10.1162/rest_a_00752

Gordon, C. (2008). Cashing in on corporate culture: An organization with a well-defined culture can achieve higher profitability. *CA Magazine (Toronto), 141*(1), 49.

Gorzeń-Mitka, I. (2015). Management challenges in the context of risk culture. *Problems of Management in the 21st Century, 10*(2), 60-61.

Gozzi, J. C., Levine, R., Peria, M. S. M., & Schmukler, S. L. (2015). How firms use corporate bond markets under financial globalization. *Journal of Banking & Finance, 58*, 532–551. doi:10.1016/j.jbankfin.2015.03.017

Graham, D. (2018). PESTEL factors for e-learning revisited: The 4Es of tutoring for value added learning. *E-Learning and Digital Media, 15*(1), 17–35. doi:10.1177/2042753017753626

Granger, C. W. (1988). Some recent development in a concept of causality. *Journal of Econometrics*, *39*(1-2), 199–211. doi:10.1016/0304-4076(88)90045-0

Granger, C. W. J. (1969). Investigating causal relations by econometric models and cross-spectral methods. *Econometrica*, *37*(3), 424–438. doi:10.2307/1912791

Grant, R. M. (1991). The resource-based theory of competitive advantage: Implications for strategy formulation. *California Management Review*, *33*(3), 114–135. doi:10.2307/41166664

Grant, R. M. (2002). *Contemporary strategy analysis: concept, techniques, applications. Massachusetts*: Blackwell.

Grauwe, P. D., & Polan, M. (2005). Is inflation always and everywhere a monetary phenomenon? *The Scandinavian Journal of Economics*, *107*(2), 239–259. doi:10.1111/j.1467-9442.2005.00406.x

Gregory, R. P. (2019). Financial openness and entrepreneurship. *Research in International Business and Finance*, *48*, 48–58. doi:10.1016/j.ribaf.2018.12.006

Griffts, J. H. M. M. (1965). *Politics among nations: the struggle for power and peace* (pp. 24–38). New York: Routledge.

Grimwade, N. (2003). *International trade: new patterns of trade, production and investment*. Routledge. doi:10.4324/9780203401668

Grohmann, A. (2018). Financial literacy and financial behavior: Evidence from the emerging Asian middle class. *Pacific-Basin Finance Journal*, *48*, 129–143. doi:10.1016/j.pacfin.2018.01.007

Grohmann, A., Kouwenberg, R., & Menkhoff, L. (2015). Childhood roots of financial literacy. *Journal of Economic Psychology*, *51*, 114–133. doi:10.1016/j.joep.2015.09.002

Grosse, R. (1996). International technology transfer in service journal of technology business studies, *27*, 781–800.

Grosse, R. (2012). Bank regulation, governance and the crisis: A behavioral finance view. *Journal of Financial Regulation and Compliance*, *20*(1), 4–25. doi:10.1108/13581981211199399

Grossman, G. M., & Helpman, E. (1991). *Innovation and growth: in the global economy* (p. 43). Cambridge, MA: MIT Press.

Grover, P. (2015). Study on behavioural factors influencing investment decision in real estate: a case study of Udham Singh Nagar (Uttrakhand). *International Journal of Engineering Technology, Management and Applied*, 150-158.

Guesmi, K., Saadi, S., Abid, I., & Ftiti, Z. (2019). Portfolio diversification with virtual currency: Evidence from bitcoin. *International Review of Financial Analysis*, *63*, 431–437. doi:10.1016/j.irfa.2018.03.004

Guha, S., Harrigan, P., & Soutar, G. (2018). Linking social media to customer relationship management (CRM): A qualitative study on SMEs. *Journal of Small Business and Entrepreneurship*, *30*(3), 193–214. doi:10.1080/08276331.2017.1399628

Gujarati, D. N. (2010). *Temel Ekonometri (Çev. Ümit Senesen ve Gülay Günlük Senesen)*. Literatür Yayınları.

Gujarati, D. N., & Porter, D. C. (2008). *Basic econometrics* (5th ed.). The McGraw-Hill Series Economics.

Gujarati, N. D. (2006). *Temel Ekonometri, Çev*. İstanbul, Turkey: Ümit Şenesen ve Gülay Günlük Şenesen, Literatür Yayıncılık.

Gül, E., ve Ekinci, A. (2006). Türkiye'de reel döviz kuru ile ihracat ve ithalat arasındaki nedensellik ilişkisi: 1990 – 2006. Dumlupınar Üniversitesi Sosyal Bilimler Dergisi, (16), 165–190.

Güler, S., & Nalın, H. T. (2013). *Petrol fiyatlarının IMKB endeksleri üzerindeki etkisi*. Ekonomik ve Sosyal Araştırmalar Dergisi.

Gülmez, A., & Yardımcıoğlu, F. (2012). OECD Ülkelerinde AR-GE Harcamaları ve Ekonomik Büyüme İlişkisi: Panel Eşbütünleşme ve Panel Nedensellik Analizi (1990-2010). *Maliye Dergisi, 163*, 336.

Güloğlu, B., & Tekin, B. (2012). A panel causality analysis of the relationship among research and development, innovation and economic growth in high-income OECD countries. *Eurasion Economic Review, 2*(1).

Gün, M. (2018). The relationship between credit default swap spreads and equity indices in emerging markets. *Current Debates in Social Sciences, 57*.

Gün, M. (2019). Cointegration between carbon emission, economic growth, and energy consumption in two neighbor countries: a study on Georgia and Turkey. *Uluslararası İktisadi ve İdari İncelemeler Dergisi*, (22), 39–50. doi:10.18092/ulikidince.397486

Gunasekaran, A. (1999). Agile manufacturing: A framework for research and development. *International Journal of Production Economics, 62*(2), 87–105. doi:10.1016/S0925-5273(98)00222-9

Güngör, S., Sönmez, L., Korkmaz, Ö., & Karaca, S. S. (2016). Petrol fiyatlarındaki değişimlerin Türkiye'nin cari işlemler açığına etkileri. *Maliye ve Finans Yazıları*, (106), 29-48.

Günsoy, B., ... (2013). İktisadi Büyüme. T.C Anadolu Üniversitesi Yayını No:2898 Web-Ofset, Eskişehir.

Gupta, K., & Banerjee, R. (2019). Does OPEC news sentiment influence stock returns of energy firms in the United States? *Energy Economics, 77*, 34–45. doi:10.1016/j.eneco.2018.03.017

Gupta, R., Jurgilas, M., & Kabundi, A. (2010). The effect of monetary policy on real house price growth in South Africa: A factor-augmented vector autoregression (FAVAR) approach. *Economic Modelling, 27*(1), 315–323. doi:10.1016/j.econmod.2009.09.011

Gürak, H. (2016). *Ekonomik Büyüme ve Küresel Ekonomi* (pp. 19–62). Bursa, Turkey: Ekin Kitabevi.

Gürbüz, S., & Şahin, F. (2016). *Sosyal Bilimlerde Araştırma Yöntemleri*. Ankara, Turkey: Seçkin Yayıncılık.

Güriş, S., & Çağlayan, E. (2005). *Ekonometri ve Temel Kavramlar*. İstanbul, Turkey: Der Yayınları.

Gustavsson, K., L'Ecuyer, P., & Olsson, L. (2018). Modeling bursts in the arrival process to an emergency call center. In *Winter Simulation Conference 2018*.

Güven, A. B., & Öniş, Z. (2010). The global economic crisis and the future of neoliberal globalization: Rupture versus continuity. *Available at SSRN 1676730*.

Güven, S., & Mert, M. (2016). Uluslararası Turizm Talebinin Eşbütünleşme Analizi: Antalya İçin Panel Ardl Yaklaşımı. *Cumhuriyet Üniversitesi İktisadi ve İdari Bilimler Dergisi, 17*(1), 133–152.

Haberland, N. A., Kelly, C. A., Mulenga, D. M., Mensch, B. S., & Hewett, P. C. (2016). Women's perceptions and misperceptions of male circumcision: A mixed methods study in Zambia. *PLoS One, 11*(3), e0149517. doi:10.1371/journal.pone.0149517 PMID:26937971

Hacıoğlu, Ü., Dinçer, H., & Parlak, B. (2015). An assessment on inflation risk and its effects on business operations. In Handbook of research on strategic developments and regulatory practice in global finance (pp. 197–216). Hershey, PA: IGI Global. doi:10.4018/978-1-4666-7288-8.ch013

Compilation of References

Hacıoğlu, Ü., & Dinçer, H. (2013). Evaluation of conflict hazard and financial risk in the E7 economies' capital markets. *Zbornik radova Ekonomskog fakulteta u Rijeci, časopis za ekonomsku teoriju i praksu-Proceedings of Rijeka Faculty of Economics. Journal of Economics and Business*, *31*(1), 79–102.

Hacker, R. S., & Hatemi-J, A. (2006). Tests for causality between integrated variables using asymptotic and bootstrap distributions: Theory and application. *Applied Economics*, *38*(13), 1489–1500. doi:10.1080/00036840500405763

Haeberle, D., Imran, S., van Husen, C., & Droll, C. (2016). A new approach for the development of services for industrial product-service systems. *Procedia CIRP*, *47*, 353–357. doi:10.1016/j.procir.2016.04.079

Hafner, C. M., & Lauwers, A. R. (2017). An augmented Taylor rule for the federal reserve's response to asset prices. *International Journal of Computational Economics and Econometrics*, *7*(1/2), 115-151.

Haider, M. A., Khan, M. A., Saddique, S., & Hashmi, S. H. (2017). *The impact of stock market performance on foreign portfolio investment in China*, *7*(2), 9.

Hair, J. F., Black, W. C., Babin, B. J., Anderson, R. E., & Tatham, R. L. (2006). Multivariate data analysis (Vol. 6).

Halaba, A., & Coşkun, A. (2016). Behavioral finance perspective on managerial decision making under risk in commercial banks. *Regional Economic Development: Entrepreneurship and Innovation*, 161.

Hambrick, D. C. (1979). Environmental scanning, organizational strategy, and executive roles: A study in three industries. (Ph.D. dissertation, Pennsylvania State University).

Hamilton, J. D. (1983). Oil and the macroeconomy since World War II. *Journal of Political Economy*, *91*(2), 228–248. doi:10.1086/261140

Hammoudeh, S., & Li, H. (2005). Oil sensitivity and systematic risk in oil-sensitive stock indices. *Journal of Economics and Business*, *57*(1), 1–21. doi:10.1016/j.jeconbus.2004.08.002

Hammoudeh, S., Nguyen, D. K., & Sousa, R. M. (2015). US monetary policy and sectoral commodity prices. *Journal of International Money and Finance*, *57*, 61–85. doi:10.1016/j.jimonfin.2015.06.003

Hanak, E. (1982). *The Tanzanian balance of payments crisis: causes, consequences, and lessons for a survival strategy*: Economic Research Bureau, University of Dar es Salaam.

Hanisch, M. (2017). The effectiveness of conventional and unconventional monetary policy: Evidence from a structural dynamic factor model for Japan. *Journal of International Money and Finance*, *70*, 110–134. doi:10.1016/j.jimonfin.2016.08.002

Hanke, S. H. (2002). Currency boards. *The annals of the American academy of political and social science*, *579*(1), 87–105. doi:10.1177/000271620257900107

Hanusch, H., Chakraborty, L., & Khurana, S. (2016) Public expenditures, innovation and economic growth: empirical evidence from G20 countries. *Beitrag: Institut für Volkswirtschaftslehre*.

Han, W., Zhuangxiong, Y., & Jie, L. (2018). Corporate social responsibility, product market competition, and product market performance. *International Review of Economics & Finance*, *56*, 75–91. doi:10.1016/j.iref.2018.03.019

Hargreaves, I., Roth, D., Karim, M. R., Nayebi, M., & Ruhe, G. (2018). Effective customer relationship management at atb financial: A case study on industry-academia collaboration in data analytics. In *Highlighting the importance of big data management and analysis for various applications* (pp. 45–59). Cham, Switzerland: Springer. doi:10.1007/978-3-319-60255-4_4

Harris, P. R., Moran, R. T., & Andrews, J. (1991). *Managing cultural differences* (Vol. 3). Houston, TX: Gulf Publishing.

Harvey, B. (1995). Ethical banking: The case of the Co-operative bank. *Journal of Business Ethics*, *14*(12), 1005–1013. doi:10.1007/BF00872116

Hassan, R. S., Nawaz, A., Lashari, M. N., & Zafar, F. (2015). Effect of customer relationship management on customer satisfaction. *Procedia Economics and Finance*, *23*, 563–567. doi:10.1016/S2212-5671(15)00513-4

Hassler, U., & Hosseinkouchack, M. (2016). Panel cointegration testing in the presence of linear time trends. *Econometrics*, *4*(4), 45. doi:10.3390/econometrics4040045

Hatch, M. J. (2018). *Organization theory: Modern, symbolic, and postmodern perspectives*. Oxford, UK: Oxford University Press.

Hatch, M. J., & Schultz, M. (1997). Relations between organizational culture, identity and image. *European Journal of Marketing*, *31*(5/6), 356–365. doi:10.1108/eb060636

Hatefi, S. M., & Tamošaitienė, J. (2019). An integrated fuzzy DEMATEL-fuzzy ANP model for evaluating construction projects by considering interrelationships among risk factors. *Journal of Civil Engineering and Management*, *25*(2), 114–131. doi:10.3846/jcem.2019.8280

Hatemi-J, A. (2003). A new method to choose optimal lag order in stable and unstable VAR models. *Applied Economics Letters*, *10*(3), 135–137. doi:10.1080/1350485022000041050

Hatzichronoglou, T. (1996). *Globalisation and competitiveness: relevant indicators (No. 1996/5)*. OECD Publishing.

Hausmann, R., Hwang, J., & Rodrik, D. (2007). What you export matters. *Journal of Economic Growth*, *12*(1), 1–25. doi:10.100710887-006-9009-4

Hayashi, F., & Koeda, J. (2014). *Exiting from QE (No. w19938)*. National Bureau of Economic Research. doi:10.3386/w19938

Hazar, A., Sunal, O., Babuşçu, Ş., & Alp, Ö. S. (2017). Türk bankacılık sektöründe piyasa yoğunlaşması: 2001 krizi öncesi ve sonrasının karşılaştırılması. *Maliye ve Finans Yazıları*, *1*(107), 41–68.

Hechavarria, D., Bullough, A., Brush, C., & Edelman, L. (2019). High-growth women's entrepreneurship: fueling social and economic development. *Journal of Small Business Management*, *57*(1), 5–13. doi:10.1111/jsbm.12503

Heenan, D. A., & Perlmutter, H. V. (1979). *Multinational organization development*. Addison-Wesley.

Heimonen, K., Junttila, J., & Kärkkäinen, S. (2017). Stock market and exchange rate information in the Taylor rule: Evidence from OECD countries. *International Review of Economics & Finance*, *51*, 1–18. doi:10.1016/j.iref.2017.05.001

Heldman, K. (2010). *Project manager's spotlight on risk management*. Hoboken, NJ: John Wiley & Sons.

Henager, R., & Cude, B. J. (2019). Financial literacy of high school graduates: Long-and short-term financial behavior by age group. *Journal of Family and Economic Issues*, 1–12.

Henrekson, M., & Sanandaji, T. (2019). Measuring entrepreneurship: do established metrics capture Schumpeterian entrepreneurship? *Entrepreneurship Theory and Practice*, 1042258719844500.

Hens, T., & Vlcek, M. (2011). Does prospect theory explain the disposition effect? *Journal of Behavioral Finance*, *12*(3), 141–157. doi:10.1080/15427560.2011.601976

Hersey, P., Blanchard, K. H., & Johnson, D. E. (2007). *Management of organizational behavior* (Vol. 9). Upper Saddle River, NJ: Prentice Hall.

Hertz, D. B., & Thomas, H. (1983). *Risk analysis and its applications*. Singapore: John Wiley & Sons.

Hidayah Ibrahim, S. N., Suan, C. L., & Karatepe, O. M. (2019). The effects of supervisor support and self-efficacy on call center employees' work engagement and quitting intentions. *International Journal of Manpower*, *40*(4), 688–703. doi:10.1108/IJM-12-2017-0320

Hill, C. (2008). International business: Competing in the global marketplace. *Strategic Direction*, *24*(9).

Hill, C. W., Jones, G. R., & Schilling, M. A. (2014). *Strategic management theory: an integrated approach*. Cengage Learning.

Hillson, D., Linsley, P., Smith, K., Hindson, A., & Murray-Webster, R. (2012). Models of risk culture. *Risk culture: Resources for practitioners*, 22-27.

Hillson, D. (2012). *How much risk is too much risk: understanding risk appetite*. Project Management Institute.

Hindson, A. (2012). A practical approach to risk culture. *Risk culture: Resources for Practitioners*, 16-19.

Hirshleifer, D. (2015). Behavioral finance. *Annual Review of Financial Economics*, *7*(1), 133–159. doi:10.1146/annurev-financial-092214-043752

Hitt, M. A., Ireland, R. D., & Hoskisson, R. E. (2009). *Strategic management: concepts & cases: competitiveness and globalization*. Mason, OH: South-Western Cengage Learning.

Hitt, M. A., Ireland, R. D., & Hoskisson, R. E. (2012). *Strategic management cases: competitiveness and globalization*. Cengage Learning.

Hoerl, R., & Snee, R. D. (2012). *Statistical thinking: Improving business performance* (Vol. 48). Hoboken, NJ: John Wiley & Sons. doi:10.1002/9781119202721

Hoffman, K. D., Kelley, S. W., & Rotalsky, H. M. (2016). Retrospective: Tracking service failures and employee recovery efforts. *Journal of Services Marketing*, *30*(1), 7–10. doi:10.1108/JSM-10-2015-0316

Hofstede, G. (1998). Attitudes, values and organizational culture: Disentangling the concepts. *Organization Studies*, *19*(3), 477–493. doi:10.1177/017084069801900305

Hofstede, G., Hofstede, G. J., & Minkov, M. (2005). *Cultures and organizations: Software of the mind* (Vol. 2). New York: McGraw-Hill.

Holt, D. H., & Wigginton, K. W. (2002). *International management*. South-Western Pub.

Holtz-Eakin, D., Newey, W., & Rosen, H. S. (1988). Estimating vector autoregressions with panel data. *Econometrica*, *56*(6), 1371–1395. doi:10.2307/1913103

Hooper, P., & Kohlhagen, S. W. (1978). The effect of exchange rate uncertainty on the prices and volume of international trade. *Journal of International Economics*, *8*(4), 483–511. doi:10.1016/0022-1996(87)90001-8

Höpel, T. (2018). Friedemann Pestel, Kosmopoliten wider Willen. Die „monarchiens" als Revolutionsemigranten.(Pariser Historische Studien, Bd. 104.) Berlin/Boston, De Gruyter Oldenbourg 2015. *Historische Zeitschrift*, *306*(1), 225–227. doi:10.1515/hzhz-2018-1048

Horioka, C. Y., & Niimi, Y. (2019). *Financial literacy*. Incentives, and Innovation to Deal with Population Aging.

Hormozi, A. M. (2001). Agile manufacturing: The next logical step. Benchmarking. *International Journal (Toronto, Ont.)*, *8*(2), 132–143.

Horvath, R. (2011). Research and development and growth: a Bayesion model averaging analysis. *Economic Modelling*, *28*(6), 2669–2673. doi:10.1016/j.econmod.2011.08.007

Hotamışlı, M., & Erem, I. (2014). Muhasebe ve Finansman Dergisi'nde yayınlanan makalelerin bibliyometrik analizi. *Muhasebe ve Finansman Dergisi*, (63), 1-20.

Howells, J. R. (2002). Tacit knowledge, innovation and economic geography. Policy Research in Engineering, Science & Technology (PREST) (871-844). içinde Manchester: University of Manchester.

Howitt, P. (1999). Steady endogenous growth with population and R&D inputs growing. *Journal of Political Economy*, *107*(4), 715–730. doi:10.1086/250076

Hsiao, C. (1981). Autoregressive modelling and money-income causality detection. *Journal of Monetary Economics*, *7*(1), 85–106. doi:10.1016/0304-3932(81)90053-2

Hsiao, H. F., Zhong, T., & Dincer, H. (2019). Analysing managers' financial motivation for sustainable investment strategies. *Sustainability*, *11*(14), 3849. doi:10.3390u11143849

Hsiao, Y. J., & Tsai, W. C. (2018). Financial literacy and participation in the derivatives markets. *Journal of Banking & Finance*, *88*, 15–29. doi:10.1016/j.jbankfin.2017.11.006

https://data.bitcoinity.org/markets/volume/30d?c=e&t=b

https://www.federalreserve.gov/datadownload/Choose.aspx?rel=H6

Huang, R. D., Masulis, R. W., & Stoll, H. R. (1996). Energy shocks and financial markets. *Journal of Futures Markets: Futures, Options, and Other Derivative Products*, *16*(1), 1–27. doi:10.1002/(SICI)1096-9934(199602)16:1<1::AID-FUT1>3.0.CO;2-Q

Huang, S., An, H., Gao, X., & Sun, X. (2017). Do oil price asymmetric effects on the stock market persist in multiple time horizons? *Applied Energy*, *185*, 1799–1808. doi:10.1016/j.apenergy.2015.11.094

Huber, F. (2017). Structural breaks in Taylor rule based exchange rate models—Evidence from threshold time varying parameter models. *Economics Letters*, *150*, 48–52. doi:10.1016/j.econlet.2016.11.008

Huda, M., Qodriah, S. L., Rismayadi, B., Hananto, A., Kardiyati, E. N., Ruskam, A., & Nasir, B. M. (2019). Towards cooperative with competitive alliance: insights into performance value in social entrepreneurship. In Creating Business Value and Competitive Advantage with Social Entrepreneurship (pp. 294-317). Hershey, PA: IGI Global.

Hudson, K. B., & Vespignani, J. (2018). Understanding the deviation of Australian policy rate from the Taylor rule. *Applied Economics*, *50*(9), 973–989. doi:10.1080/00036846.2017.1346367

Huntington, H. G. (2015). Crude oil trade and current account deficits. *Energy Economics*, *50*, 70–79. doi:10.1016/j.eneco.2015.03.030

Huntington, S. (2004). *Biz Kimiz: Amerika'nın Ulusal Kimlik Arayışı* (A. Özer, Trans.). İstanbul, Turkey: CSA Yayınları.

Hurn, S., Johnson, N., Silvennoinen, A., & Teräsvirta, T. (2018). *Transition from the Taylor rule to the zero lower bound (No. 2018-31)*. Department of Economics and Business Economics, Aarhus University.

Ibeh, K., Crick, D., & Etemad, H. (2019). International marketing knowledge and international entrepreneurship in the contemporary multi speed global economy. *International Marketing Review*, *36*(1), 2–5. doi:10.1108/IMR-02-2019-377

Ibrahim, R., Ye, H., L'Ecuyer, P., & Shen, H. (2016). Modeling and forecasting call center arrivals: A literature survey and a case study. *International Journal of Forecasting*, *32*(3), 865–874. doi:10.1016/j.ijforecast.2015.11.012

İçke, B. T. (2017). *Finansal Okur Yazarlık*. İstanbul, Turkey: Beta Basım Yayın.

Compilation of References

Idris, I., & Bala, H. (2015). Firms' specific characteristics and stock market returns (Evidence from listed food and beverages firms in Nigeria). *Research Journal of Finance and Accounting, 6*(16), 188-200–200.

Ihal, M. E., Topuz, D., & Uçan, O. (2006). Dogrusal Olasilik ve Logit Modelleri ile Parametre Tahmini/Linear Probability and Parameter Estimation with Logit Models. *Sosyoekonomi*, (1), 47.

İleri, Y. Y., Soylu, Y., Bir Rekabet Üstünlüğü Olarak Çeviklik Kavramı ve Örgüt Yapısına Olası Etkileri, Selçuk Üniversitesi Sosyal Bilimler Dergisi, 12, 1-2, 13-28, 2010.

İlhan, S. (2003). Sosyo-Ekonomik Bir Fenomen Olarak Girişimciliğin Oluşumunu Etkileyen Başlıca Faktörler. *Muğla Üniversitesi Sosyal Bilimler Enstitüsü Dergisi*, (11), 61-79.

IMF. (1984). *Exchange rate volatility and world trade.* International Monetary Fund, Occasional Paper No: 28. Retrieved from https://www.imf.org/en/Publications/Occasional-Papers/

IMF. (2006). Glossary of selected financial terms. Retrieved from http://www.imf.org/external/np/exr/glossary/showTerm.asp#91

IMF. (2014). Annual report on exchange rate arrangements and exchange restrictions. Retrieved from https://www.imf.org/en/Publications

IMF. (n.d.). Financial development index database. Retrieved from https://data.imf.org/?sk=F8032E80-B36C-43B1-AC26-493C5B1CD33B&sId=1480712464593

Im, K. S., Pesaran, M. H., & Shin, Y. (2003). Testing for unit roots in heterogeneous panels. *Journal of Econometrics, 115*(1), 53–74. doi:10.1016/S0304-4076(03)00092-7

In Carnegie-Rochester Conference Series on Public Policy (Vol. 39, pp. 195-214). North-Holland.

İnal, K. (2009). *Medya Okuryazarlığı El Kitabı*. Ankara, Turkey: Ütopya Yayınevi.

İnan, E. A. (2002). Kur rejimi tercihi ve Türkiye. Bankacılık Dergisi, 1–10.

İnançli, S., Altintaş, N., & İnal, V. (2016). Finansal Gelişme ve Ekonomik Büyüme İlişkisi: D-8 Örneği. *Kastamonu Üniversitesi İktisadi ve İdari Bilimler Fakültesi Dergisi, 14*(4), 36–49.

İnançlı, S., & Aydın, F. (2015). Doğrudan Yabancı Sermaye Yatırımı ve Dış Rekabet Gücü İlişkisi: Türkiye İçin Nedensellik Analizi. *Sakarya İktisat Dergisi, 4*(1), 52–69.

Ince, O., Molodtsova, T., & Papell, D. H. (2016). Taylor rule deviations and out-of-sample exchange rate predictability. *Journal of International Money and Finance, 69*, 22–44. doi:10.1016/j.jimonfin.2016.06.002

İnceoğlu, Y. (2007). Medyayı Doğru Okumak. In *N. Türkoğlu, & M. Cinman Şimşek, Medya Okuryazarlığı* (pp. 21–26). İstanbul, Turkey: Kalemus Yayınları.

Invernizzi, A. C. (2018). Managerial overconfidence. In *Overconfidence in SMEs* (pp. 1–20). Cham, Switzerland: Palgrave Macmillan. doi:10.1007/978-3-319-66920-5_1

Ioannidis, C., & Kontonikas, A. (2008). The impact of monetary policy on stock prices. *Journal of Policy Modeling, 30*(1), 33–53. doi:10.1016/j.jpolmod.2007.06.015

Iqbal, Z., & Mirakhor, A. (1999). Progress and challenges of Islamic banking. *Thunderbird International Business Review, 41*(4-5), 381–405. doi:10.1002/tie.4270410406

İşcan, E. (2010). Petrol fiyatının hisse senedi piyasası üzerindeki etkisi. *Maliye Dergisi, 158*, 607–617.

Işık, C. (2014). Patent Harcamaları ve İktisadi Büyüe Arasındaki İlişki: Türkiye Örneği. *Sosyoekonomi*, *1*, 69.

İskenderoğlu, Ö., & Tomak, S. (2013). Competition and stability: An analysis of the Turkish banking system. *International Journal of Economics and Financial*, *3*(3), 752–762.

İslamoğlu, A. H. (1999). *Pazarlama yönetimi: stratejik ve global yaklaşım*. Beta Basım Yayım Dağıtım AŞ.

Ison, S., & Wall, S. (2007). Economics (4th Ed.). London, UK: Pearson Education.

Jaakkola, E., Meiren, T., Witell, L., Edvardsson, B., Schäfer, A., Reynoso, J., ... Weitlaner, D. (2017). Does one size fit all? New service development across different types of services. *Journal of Service Management*, *28*(2), 329–347. doi:10.1108/JOSM-11-2015-0370

Jain, R. K., & Triandis, H. C. (1997). *Management of research and development organizations: managing the unmanageable*. New York: Wiley.

Jain, S. C. (1984). Environmental scanning in U.S. corporations. *Long Range Planning*, *17*(2), 117–128. doi:10.1016/0024-6301(84)90143-2 PMID:10299516

Jarblad, A. (2003). The global political economy of transnational corporations: a theory of asymmetric interdependence.

Jariwala, H. V. (2015). Analysis of financial literacy level of retail individual investors of Gujarat State and its effect on investment decision. *Journal of Business & Finance Librarianship*, *20*(1-2), 133–158. doi:10.1080/08963568.2015.977727

Jarque, C. M., & Bera, A. K. (1980). Efficient tests for normality, homoscedasticity and serial independence of regression residuals. *Economics letters*, *6*(3), 255–259. doi:10.1016/0165-1765(80)90024-5

Jasson, E. M. V. (2009). *A study of Argentine competitiveness: an extension of Porter's Diamond Model*, (Doctoral Dissertation, York University).

Jawadi, F., Sousa, R. M., & Traverso, R. (2017). On the macroeconomic and wealth effects of unconventional monetary policy. *Macroeconomic Dynamics*, *21*(5), 1189–1204. doi:10.1017/S1365100515000292

Jaworski, B. J. (2018). Commentary: Advancing marketing strategy in the marketing discipline and beyond. *Journal of Marketing Management*, *34*(1-2), 63–70. doi:10.1080/0267257X.2017.1398770

Jayaram, J., Kannan, V. R., & Tan, K. C. (2004). Influence of initiators on supply chain value creation. *International Journal of Production Research*, *42*(20), 4377–4399. doi:10.1080/00207540410001716516

Jennings, J. D., Quinn, C., Ly, J. A., & Rehman, S. (2019). Orthopaedic surgery resident financial literacy: An assessment of knowledge in debt, investment, and retirement savings. *The American Surgeon*, *85*(4), 353–358. PMID:31043194

Jimenez, G., Lopez, J., & Saurina, J. (2007). How does competition impact bank risk taking? *Banco de Espana Working Papers*, No: 1005.

Jimenez, A., & Boehe, D. (2018). How do political and market exposure nurture ambidexterity? *Journal of Business Research*, *89*, 67–76. doi:10.1016/j.jbusres.2018.03.016

Jiménez, G., Lopez, J. A., & Saurina, J. (2013). How does competition affect bank risk-taking? *Journal of Financial Stability*, *9*(2), 185–195. doi:10.1016/j.jfs.2013.02.004

Ji, Q., Bouri, E., Gupta, R., & Roubaud, D. (2018). Network causality structures among Bitcoin and other financial assets: A directed acyclic graph approach. *The Quarterly Review of Economics and Finance*, *70*, 203–213. doi:10.1016/j.qref.2018.05.016

Ji, Y., Park, T., & Lee, Y. S. (2017). The impact of severe weather announcement on the Korea meteorological administration call center counseling demand. *Atmosphere*, *27*(4), 377–384.

Johansen, S. (1991). Estimation and hypothesis testing of cointegration vectors in Gaussian vector autoregressive models. *Econometrica*, *59*(6), 1551–1580. doi:10.2307/2938278

Johansen, S. (1995). *Likelihood-based inference in cointegrated vector autoregressive models*. Oxford University Press on Demand. doi:10.1093/0198774508.001.0001

Johansen, S., & Juselius, K. (1990). Maximum likelihood estimation and inference on cointegration—With applications to the demand for money. *Oxford Bulletin of Economics and Statistics*, *52*(2), 169–210. doi:10.1111/j.1468-0084.1990.mp52002003.x

Johanson, J. M., & Mattsson, L. G. (1988). Internationalization in industrial systems–a network approach. Strategies in Global Competition. London, UK: Croom Helm. 287-314.

Johanson, J., & Mattsson, L. G. (1994). The markets-as-networks tradition in Sweden. In *Research traditions in marketing* (pp. 321–346). Dordrecht, The Netherlands: Springer. doi:10.1007/978-94-011-1402-8_10

Johanson, J., & Mattsson, L. G. (2015). Internationalisation in industrial systems—a network approach. In *Knowledge, networks and power* (pp. 111–132). London, UK: Palgrave Macmillan. doi:10.1057/9781137508829_5

Johanson, J., & Wiedersheim-Paul, F. (1975). The internationalization of the firm—Four Swedish cases 1. *Journal of Management Studies*, *12*(3), 305–323. doi:10.1111/j.1467-6486.1975.tb00514.x

John, O. P., Donahue, E. M., & Kentle, R. L. (1991). The big five inventory—versions 4a and 54.

Jones, C. I. (1995). R&D based models of economic growth. *Journal of Political Economy*, *103*(4), 759–784. doi:10.1086/262002

Jones, C. I. (1998). *Introduction to economic growth* (p. 2). New York: W.W. Norton Company.

Jones, C. M., & Kaul, G. (1996). Oil and the stock markets. *The Journal of Finance*, *51*(2), 463–491. doi:10.1111/j.1540-6261.1996.tb02691.x

Jones, C., Fouty, J. R., Lucas, R. B., & Frye, M. A. (2019). Integrating individual student advising into financial education to optimize financial literacy in veterinary students. *Journal of Veterinary Medical Education*, 1–11. doi:10.3138/jvme.1117-156r1 PMID:31194629

Jones, G. R. (2013). *Organizational theory, design, and change*. Upper Saddle River, NJ: Pearson.

Jones, M. V., & Coviello, N. E. (2005). Internationalisation: Conceptualising an entrepreneurial process of behaviour in time. *Journal of International Business Studies*, *36*(3), 284–303. doi:10.1057/palgrave.jibs.8400138

Jordan, D., & Diltz, J. D. (2004). Day traders and the disposition effect. *Journal of Behavioral Finance*, *5*(4), 192–200. doi:10.120715427579jpfm0504_2

Jouini, J., & Harrathi, N. (2014). Revisiting the shock and volatility transmissions among GCC stock and oil markets: A further investigation. *Economic Modelling*, *38*, 486–494. doi:10.1016/j.econmod.2014.02.001

Jouini, O., Akşin, O. Z., Karaesmen, F., Aguir, M. S., & Dallery, Y. (2015). Call center delay announcement using a newsvendor-like performance criterion. *Production and Operations Management*, *24*(4), 587–604. doi:10.1111/poms.12259

Judge, T. A., Higgins, C. A., Thoresen, C. J., & Barrick, M. R. (1999). The big five personality traits, general mental ability, and career success across the life span. *Personnel Psychology*, *52*(3), 621–652. doi:10.1111/j.1744-6570.1999.tb00174.x

Kadoya, Y., & Khan, M. S. R. (2018). Can financial literacy reduce anxiety about life in old age? *Journal of Risk Research*, *21*(12), 1533–1550. doi:10.1080/13669877.2017.1313760

Kahaner, L. (1997). *Competitive intelligence: How to gather analyze and use information to move your business to the top*. Simon and Schuster.

Kahn, G. A. (2010). Monetary policy under a corridor operating framework. *Economic Review-Federal Reserve Bank of Kansas City*, 5.

Kahneman, D., & Tversky, A. (1979). On the interpretation of intuitive probability: A reply to Jonathan Cohen. *Cognition*, *7*(4), 409–411. doi:10.1016/0010-0277(79)90024-6

Kahneman, D., & Tversky, A. (1979). Prospect theory: An analysis of decision under risk. *Econometrica*, *47*(2), 263–291. doi:10.2307/1914185

Kaiser, H. F. (1974). An index of factorial simplicity. *Psychometrika*, *39*(1), 31–36. doi:10.1007/BF02291575

Kala, A. (1992). Organization of İstanbul Butcher Shopman Until The 19th Century. *Journal of Social Politics Conferences*, 111-117.

Kala, A. (2012). *Debbağlıktan Dericiliğe İstanbul Merkezli Deri Sektörünün Doğuşu ve Gelişimi*. İstanbul, Turkey: Zeytinburnu Municipality.

Kalaycı, Ş. (2006). *SPSS Uygulamalı Çok Değişkenli İstatistik Teknikleri*. Asil Yayınevi.

Kalkavan, H., & Ersin, I. (2019). Determination of factors affecting the South East Asian crisis of 1997 probit-logit panel regression: The South East Asian crisis. In Handbook of research on global issues in financial communication and investment decision making (pp. 148-167). Hershey, PA: IGI Global.

Kalkavan, H., & Ersin, I. (2019). Determination of factors affecting the South East Asian crisis of 1997 Probit-Logit panel regression: The South East Asian crisis. In Handbook of research on global issues in financial communication and investment decision making (pp. 148-167). Hershey, PA: IGI Global.

Kamışlı, M., Kamışlı, S., & Temizel, F. (2017). Bölgesel İslami hisse senedi endeksleri arasındaki ilişkilerin analizi. *Uluslararası Yönetim İktisat ve İşletme Dergisi*, *13*(5), 574–587.

Kampanje, B. (2014). PESTEL analysis of Malawi's non-life insurance industry. *African Journal of Economic and Management Studies*, *5*(1). doi:10.1108/AJEMS-01-2013-0002

Kanaan, O. (2000). Tanzania's experience with trade liberalization. *Finance & Development*, *37*(2). Retrieved from https://www.imf.org/external/pubs/ft/fandd/2000/06/kanaan.htm

Kang, W., Ratti, R. A., & Vespignani, J. (2016). The impact of oil price shocks on the US stock market: A note on the roles of US and non-US oil production. *Economics Letters*, *145*, 176–181. doi:10.1016/j.econlet.2016.06.008

Kao, C. (1999). Spurious regression and residual-based tests for cointegration in panel data. *Journal of Econometrics*, *90*(1), 1–44. doi:10.1016/S0304-4076(98)00023-2

Kaplan, R. S., & Norton, D. P. (n.d.). *The balanced scorecard: translating strategy into action*. Boston, MA: Harvard Business School Press.

Kaplan, R. S., & Norton, D. P. (2005). *Creating the office of strategy management*. Boston, MA: Division of Research, Harvard Business School.

Compilation of References

Kara, E. (2018). A contemporary approach for strategic management in tourism sector: pestel analysis on the city Muğla, Turkey. *İşletme Araştırmaları Dergisi, 10*(2), 598-608.

Karaaslan, A., & Tuncer, G. (1994). Uluslararası Rekabet Gücünün Artırılmasında Temel Devlet Politikaları. *Management Decision, 32*(2), 49.

Karabıçak, M. (2002). Küreselleşme Sürecinde Gelişmekte Olan Ülke Ekonomilerinde Ortaya Çıkan Yönelim ve Tepkiler. *Süleyman Demirel Üniversitesi İktisadi ve İdari Bilimler Fakültesi, 7*(1), 113–116.

Karabulut, G., & Danışoğlu, A. Ç. (2006). Türkiye'de cari işlemler açığının büyümesini etkileyen faktörler. *Gazi Üniversitesi İktisadi ve İdari Bilimler Fakültesi Dergisi, 8*(1), 47–63.

Karaçor, Z., & Gerçeker, M. (2012). Reel döviz kuru ve dış ticaret ilişkisi: Türkiye örneği (2003 - 2010). SÜ İİBF Sosyal ve Ekonomik Araştırmalar Dergisi, (23), 289–312.

Karagöz, K. (2016). Girişimcilik-Ekonomik Büyüme İlişkisi: Türkiye İçin Ekonometrik Bir Analiz. *Girişmcilik ve Kalkınma Dergisi*, 11(2).

Karagöz, M., & Doğan, Ç. (2005). Döviz kuru dış ticaret ilişkisi: Türkiye örneği. *Fırat Üniversitesi Sosyal Bilimler Dergisi, 15*(2), 219–228.

Karakurum-Ozdemir, K., Kokkizil, M., & Uysal, G. (2019). Financial literacy in developing countries. *Social Indicators Research, 143*(1), 325–353. doi:10.100711205-018-1952-x

Kara, M., & Afsal, M. Ş. (2018). The effectiveness of monetary policy instruments applied for financial stability in Turkey. *Itobiad*: *Journal of the Human & Social Science Researches, 7*(3).

Karan, M. B. (2011). *Yatırım Analizi ve Portföy Yönetimi* (3rd ed.). Ankara, Turkey: Gazi Kitabevi.

Karaş, Z. (2017). 2008 Küresel Krizi Sırasında Merkez Bankaları Tarafından Uygulanan Geleneksel Olmayan Para Politikaları. *Journal of International Social Research, 10*(48), 630–639. doi:10.17719/jisr.2017.1534

Karatop, B., & Kubat, C. (2018). Akhi order's effect on Turkish quality management system. *Journal of Academic Studies*, 351-368.

Karatop, B., Karahan, A. G., & Kubat, C. (2011). First application of total quality management in Ottoman Empire: Ahi organization. *7th Research/Expert Conference with International Participations*, (1109-1114).

Kara, U. (2004). *Sosyal Devletin Yükselişi ve Düşüşü*. Ankara, Turkey: Özgür Üniversite Kitaplığı.

Karluk, R. (2009). *Uluslararası Ekonomi Teori Politika*. İstanbul, Turkey: Beta Yayınevi.

Kar, M., Taş, S., & Ağır, H. (2008). *Finansal sistem ve kalkınma. Editörler: Sami Taban, Muhsin Kar. Kalkınma Ekonomisi*. Bursa, Turkey: Ekin Yayınları.

Kasman, A. (2001). The profit-structure relationship in the Turkish banking industry using direct measures of efficiency. *Ege Akademik Bakış, 1*(1), 141–164.

Kasman, A., ve Kasman, S. (2005). Exchange rate uncertainty in turkey and its impact on export volume. *ODTÜ Gelisme Dergisi, 32*(1), 41–58.

Kasman, A., & Kasman, S. (2005). Exchange rate uncertainty in Turkey and its impact on export volume. *ODTÜ Gelisme Dergisi, 32*(1), 41–58.

Kassavou, A., & Sutton, S. (2016). Supporting medication adherence using Interactive Voice response (IVR): development and delivery of a theory and evidence-based intervention. *Eur Heal Psychol, 18*.

Kassavou, A., & Sutton, S. (2016). *Developing and pre-testing a tailored interactive voice response (IVR) intervention to support adherence to anti-hypertensive medications: a research protocol*. Cambridge, UK: Cambridge University.

Kasza, A. (2004). Innovation networks, policy networks and regional development in transition economies: a conceptual review and research perspectives. *Paper for EPSNET Conference*, 5-7.

Katırcıoğlu, E. (2008). *Küreselleşme Çağında Sol Ekonomik Politikalar"Yeni Toplum Yeni Siyaset Küreselleşme Çağında Sosyal Demokrat Yaklaşımlar*. İstanbul, Turkey: Kalkedon Yayınları.

Kaushik, A. K., & Rahman, Z. (2015). Innovation adoption across self-service banking technologies in India. *International Journal of Bank Marketing*, *33*(2), 96–121. doi:10.1108/IJBM-01-2014-0006

Kavitha, V. (2017). *The relationship and effect of role overload, role ambiguity, work-life balance and career development on work stress among call center executives of business process outsourcing (BPO) in Selangor* (Doctoral dissertation, Universiti Utara Malaysia).

Kaya, A., & Öztürk, M. (2015). Muhasebe Kârları ile Hisse Senedi Fiyatları Arasındaki İlişki: BİST Firmaları Üzerine Bir Uygulama. *The relationship between accounting profits and stock prices: an application on BIST firms*, 37–54.

Kaya, F. (2011). *Dış Ticaret İşlemleri Yönetimi*. İstanbul, Turkey: Beta Yayınevi.

Kaya, A. A., ve Güçlü, M. (. (2005). Döviz kuru rejimleri, krizler ve arayışlar. *Ekonomik Yaklaşım Dergisi*, *16*(55), 1–15. doi:10.5455/ey.10517

Kaya, A., & Binici, Ö. (2014). BIST kimya, petrol, plastik endeksi hisse senedi fiyatları ile petrol fiyatları arasındaki ilişkinin incelenmesi. *Cumhuriyet Üniversitesi İktisadi ve İdari Bilimler Dergisi*, *15*(1), 383–395.

Kaygın, Y. C. (2013). Hisse Senetleri Fiyatını Etkileyen Faktörlerin Panel Veri Analizi İle İncelenmesi: İmalat Sektörü Üzerine Bir Uygulama. Atatürk Üniversitesi SBE, Yayımlanmamış Doktora Tezi, Erzurum.

Kayhan Unutur, P. (2018). *The effect of crude oil prices on the foreign trade deficit-case of Turkey (2000-2015)* (Master's thesis, Dogus University Institute of Social Science).

Kaymakcı, O., Avcı, N., & Şen, R. (2007). *Uluslararası Ticarete Giriş*. Ankara, Turkey: Nobel Yayıncılık.

Kazakos, K., Asthana, S., Balaam, M., Duggal, M., Holden, A., Jamir, L., ... Murthy, G. V. S. (2016, May). A real-time IVR platform for community radio. In *Proceedings of the 2016 CHI Conference on Human Factors in Computing Systems* (pp. 343-354). ACM. 10.1145/2858036.2858585

Kazıcı, Z. (2014). *Osmanlı Medeniyeti Tarihi: Osmanlı'da Yerel Yönetim: (ihtisab müessesesi)*.

Keegan, W. J. (1974). Multinational scanning: a study of the information sources utilized by headquarters executives in multinational companies. *Administrative Science Quarterly*, *19*(3), 411. doi:10.2307/2391981

Keeley, M. (1990). Deposit insurance, risk and market power in banking. *The American Economic Review*, *80*, 1183–1200.

Keeley, M. C. (1990). Deposit insurance, risk, and market power in banking. *The American Economic Review*, 1183–1200.

Keister, T. (2012). *Corridors and floors in monetary policy*. Liberty Street Economics.

Keister, T., Martin, A., & McAndrews, J. (2015). *Floor systems and the Friedman rule: the fiscal arithmetic of open market operations (No. 754)*. Federal Reserve Bank of New York.

Kemeç, A., & Kösekahyaoğlu, L. (2015). J eğrisi analizi ve türkiye üzerine bir uygulama. Uluslararası İktisadi ve İdari Bilimler Dergisi, (December), 5–29.

Kenen, P. (2001). *The international financial architecture: What's new? What's missing?* Washington, DC: Institute for International Economics.

Kenen, P. B., & Rodrik, D. (1986). Measuring and analyzing the effects of short-term volatility in real exchange rates. *The Review of Economics and Statistics*, *68*(2), 311–315. doi:10.2307/1925511

Kesbiç, C. Y., Baldemir, E., & Bakımlı, E. (2004). Bütçe açıkları ile parasal büyüme ve enflasyon arasındaki ilişki: Türkiye için bir model denemesi. *Atatürk Üniversitesi İktisadi ve İdari Bilimler Dergisi*, *19*(1), 81–98.

Kester, W. C., & Luehrman, T. A. (1989). Are we feeling more competitive yet? The exchange rate gambit. *MIT Sloan Management Review*, *30*(2), 19.

Khan, S. J. M. (2014). Concentration in Southeast Asia banking. *American Journal of Economics*, *4*(3), 150–158.

Khosa, J., Botha, I., & Pretorius, M. (2015). The impact of exchange rate volatility on emerging market exports: Original research. *Acta Commercii*, *15*(1), 1–11. doi:10.4102/ac.v15i1.257

Khyareh, M. M., Khairandish, M., & Torabi, H. (2019). Macroeconomic effects of entrepreneurship: evidences from factor, efficiency and innovation driven countries. *International Journal of Entrepreneurship*, *23*(1), 1–21.

Kibritçioğlu, A. (1996). Uluslararası rekabet gücüne kavramsal bir yaklaşım. *MPM Verimlilik Dergisi*, *96*(3), 109–122.

Kılavuz, E., & Altay Topcu, B., & Tülüce, N. S. (2011). Yükselen ekonomilerde döviz kuru rejimi seçimi: Ampirik bir analiz. *Erciyes Üniversitesi Sosyal Bilimler Enstitüsü Dergisi*, *1*(30), 83–109.

Kilian, L. (2009). Not all oil price shocks are alike: Disentangling demand and supply shocks in the crude oil market. *The American Economic Review*, *99*(3), 1053–1069. doi:10.1257/aer.99.3.1053

Kilian, L., & Park, C. (2009). The impact of oil price shocks on the US stock market. *International Economic Review*, *50*(4), 1267–1287. doi:10.1111/j.1468-2354.2009.00568.x

Kılıç, E. (2009). Türk imalat sektöründe ihracat, ithalat ve döviz kuru arasındaki ilişkilerin zaman serisi analizi. In Econ Anadolu 2009: Anadolu International Conference in Economics. Eskişehir, Turkey.

Kiliç, M. (2016). Online corporate social responsibility (CSR) disclosure in the banking industry: Evidence from Turkey. *International Journal of Bank Marketing*, *34*(4), 550–569. doi:10.1108/IJBM-04-2015-0060

Kiliyanni, A. L., & Sivaraman, S. (2016). The perception-reality gap in financial literacy: Evidence from the most literate state in India. *International Review of Economics Education*, *23*, 47–64. doi:10.1016/j.iree.2016.07.001

Kim Jean Lee, S., & Yu, K. (2004). Corporate culture and organizational performance. *Journal of Managerial Psychology*, *19*(4), 340–359. doi:10.1108/02683940410537927

Kimball, R. C. (2000). Failures in risk management. *New England Economic Review*, 3–12.

Kim, C. B. (2017). Does exchange rate volatility affect Korea's seaborne import volume? *Asian Journal of Shipping and Logistics*, *33*(1), 43–50. doi:10.1016/j.ajsl.2017.03.006

Kim, C. J., & Park, C. (2016). *Real exchange rate dynamics and the Taylor rule: importance of Taylor-rule fundamentals*. Monetary Policy Shocks, and Risk-premium Shocks.

Kim, C. J., & Park, C. (2019). Real exchange rate dynamics: Relative importance of Taylor-rule fundamentals, monetary policy shocks, and risk-premium shocks. *Review of International Economics*, *27*(1), 201–219. doi:10.1111/roie.12372

Kim, C., Klimenok, V. I., & Dudin, A. N. (2016). Priority tandem queueing system with retrials and reservation of channels as a model of call center. *Computers & Industrial Engineering*, *96*, 61–71. doi:10.1016/j.cie.2016.03.012

Kim, H., Fujiwara, I., Hansen, B. E., & Ogaki, M. (2015). Purchasing power parity and the Taylor rule. *Journal of Applied Econometrics*, *30*(6), 874–903. doi:10.1002/jae.2391

Kim, J. I., & Choi, B. R. (2015). Convergence study on emotional labor, stress response and turnover intention of call-center worker. *Journal of the Korea Convergence Society*, *6*(6), 139–146. doi:10.15207/JKCS.2015.6.6.139

Kim, J., & Kang, P. (2016). Late payment prediction models for fair allocation of customer contact lists to call center agents. *Decision Support Systems*, *85*, 84–101. doi:10.1016/j.dss.2016.03.002

Kisman, Z., & Restiyanita, S. (2015). M. The validity of capital asset pricing model (CAPM) and arbitrage pricing theory (APT) in predicting the return of stocks in Indonesia stock exchange. *American Journal of Economics. Financial Management*, *1*, 184–189.

Kızıldemir, C. (2013). Klasik Yaklaşım. Retrieved from https://www.paranomist.com/klasik-yaklasim.html, Erişim Tarihi: 17.09.2013.

Klaas Jagersma, P. (2005). Cross-border alliances: Advice from the executive suite. *The Journal of Business Strategy*, *26*(1), 41–50. doi:10.1108/02756660510575041

Klapper, L., Laeven, L., & Rajan, R. (2006). Entry regulation as a barrier to entrepreneurship. *Journal of Financial Economics*, *82*(3), 591–629. doi:10.1016/j.jfineco.2005.09.006

Kleine, J., Wagner, N., & Weller, T. (2016). Openness endangers your wealth: Noise trading and the big five. *Finance Research Letters*, *16*, 239–247. doi:10.1016/j.frl.2015.12.002

Kleymenova, A., Rose, A. K., & Wieladek, T. (2016). Does government intervention affect banking globalization? *Journal of the Japanese and International Economies*, *40*, 43–58. doi:10.1016/j.jjie.2016.03.002

Knight, G. A., & Cavusgil, S. T. (2004). Innovation, organizational capabilities, and the born-global firm. *Journal of International Business Studies*, *35*(2), 124–141. doi:10.1057/palgrave.jibs.8400071

Koçak, O., Arslan, H., & Eti, S. (2017). Belediyelerde sosyal politika uygulamaları ve Pendik belediyesi örneği. *Uluslararası Toplum Araştırmaları Dergisi*, *7*(12), 119–144. doi:10.26466/opus.311278

Koçak, O., Beki, A., & Eti, S. (2018). The effects of the different activities on the depression level of older people. *OPUS Uluslararası Toplum Araştırmaları Dergisi*, *8*(15), 1241–1266.

Kocakoç, M. (2008). *Montaj Süreçlerinde Yalın Üretim Verileri Analizi*. Doktora Tezi, Dokuz Eylül Üniversitesi.

Kodongo, O., & Ojah, K. (2013). Real exchange rates, trade balance and capital flows in Africa. *Journal of Economics and Business*, *66*, 22–46. doi:10.1016/j.jeconbus.2012.12.002

Koellinger, P. D., & Thurik, A. R. (2012). Entrepreneurship and the business cycle. *The Review of Economics and Statistics*, *94*(4), 1143–1156. doi:10.1162/REST_a_00224

Kohler, A., & Ferjani, A. (2018). Exchange rate effects: A case study of the export performance of the swiss agriculture and food Sector. *World Economy*, *41*(2), 494–518. doi:10.1111/twec.12611

Konon, A., & Kritikos, A. S. (2019). Prediction based on entrepreneurship-prone personality profiles: Sometimes worse than the toss of a coin. *Small Business Economics*, *53*(1), 1–20. doi:10.100711187-018-0111-8

Korap, L. (2011). Parasal büyüme ve tüketici enflasyonu değişim oranı arasındaki nedensellik ilişkisi üzerine bir deneme: Türkiye örneği. *Ekonometri ve İstatistik e-Dergisi*, (9), 56-74.

Compilation of References

Koray, F., & Lastrapes, W. D. (1989). Real exchange rate volatility and US bilateral trade: A VAR approach. *The review of economics and statistics, 71*(4), 708–712. doi:10.2307/1928117

Korgaonkar, C. (2012). Analysis of the impact of financial development on foreign direct investment: a data mining approach. *Journal of Economics and Sustainable Development, 3*(6), 70–78.

Korkmaz, Ö., Erer, D., & Erer, E. (2016). The relationship between concentration and financial fragility in banking sector: The case of Turkey (2007-2014). *The Journal of Accounting and Finance,* (69), 127-146.

Köse, Ö. (2003). Küreselleşme Sürecinde Devletin Yapısal ve İşlevsel Dönüşümü. *Sayıştay Dergisi, 49*(Nisan-Haziran), 3-4.

Köse, N., & Ay, A., & Topallı, N. (2008). Döviz kuru oynaklığının ihracata etkisi: Türkiye örneği (1995 - 2008). *Gazi Üniversitesi İktisadi ve İdari Bilimler Fakültesi Dergisi, 10*(2), 25–45.

Köseoğlu, M. A., & Akdeve, E. (2013). *Rekabet İstihbaratı (Competitive Intelligence).* Ankara, Turkey: Nobel Yayın.

Kotabe, M., Helsen, K., & Kotabe, M. (1998). *Global marketing management.* New York, NY: Wiley.

Kotabe, M., & Kothari, T. (2016). Emerging market multinational companies' evolutionary paths to building a competitive advantage from emerging markets to developed countries. *Journal of World Business, 51*(5), 729–743. doi:10.1016/j.jwb.2016.07.010

Kozak, S., Nagel, S., & Santosh, S. (2018). Interpreting factor models. *The Journal of Finance, 73*(3), 1183–1223. doi:10.1111/jofi.12612

Kreiser, P. M., Kuratko, D. F., Covin, J. G., Ireland, R. D., & Hornsby, J. S. (2019). Corporate entrepreneurship strategy: Extending our knowledge boundaries through configuration theory. *Small Business Economics,* 1–20.

Kremer, P. D., & Symmons, M. A. (2015). Mass timber construction as an alternative to concrete and steel in the Australia building industry: A PESTEL evaluation of the potential. *International Wood Products Journal, 6*(3), 138–147. doi:10.1179/2042645315Y.0000000010

Krugman, P. (1989). Difference in income elasticities and trends in real exchange rates. *European Economic Review, 33*(5), 1301–1046. doi:10.1016/0014-2921(89)90013-5

Krugman, P. (1994). Competitiveness: A dangerous obsession. *Foreign Affairs, 73*(2), 28. doi:10.2307/20045917

Küçüker, C. (2000). New Economic Geography. *Ekonomik Yaklaşım,* 1-45.

Kumar, S., & Goyal, N. (2015). Behavioural biases in investment decision making–a systematic literature review. *Qualitative Research in Financial Markets, 7*(1), 88-108.

Kumar, P., Bishnoi, N. K., & Chauhan, P. (2015). Bank market structure and concentration in Indian banking sector. *The Journal of Institute of Public Enterprise, 38*(1-2), 103–127.

Kuntze, R., Wu, C., Wooldridge, B. R., & Whang, Y. O. (2019). Improving financial literacy in college of business students: Modernizing delivery tools. *International Journal of Bank Marketing, 37*(4), 976–990. doi:10.1108/IJBM-03-2018-0080

Kurt, G., & Köse, A. (2017). Türkiye'de Bankaların Finansal Oranları ile Hisse Senedi Getirisi Arasındaki Panel Nedensellik İlişkisi. *Çukurova Üniversitesi Sosyal Bilimler Enstitüsü Dergisi, 26*(3), 302–312.

Kusi, N. K. (2002). *Trade liberalization and South Africa's export performance.* Paper presented at the 2002 Annual Forum at Glenburn Lodge, Muldersdrift: Trade and Industrial Policy Strategies.

Kuznets, S. (1949). Suggestions for an inquiry into the economic growth of nations. NBER, In Problems in the Study of Economic Growth, 6.

Kuzu, S. (2017). Türkiye Cumhuriyeti Merkez Bankası (TCMB) Faiz Koridoru Stratejisinin Hisse Senedi Piyasası ve Döviz Kuru Üzerine Etkisinin Analiz Edilmesi. *Uygulamalı Sosyal Bilimler Dergisi, 1*(2), 46–61.

Lafuente, J. A., Pérez, R., & Ruiz, J. (2018). *Disentangling permanent and transitory monetary shocks with a non-linear Taylor rule (No. 2018-19).* Universidad Complutense de Madrid, Facultad de Ciencias Económicas y Empresariales, Instituto Complutense de Análisis Económico.

Lall, S. (2000). *Turkish performance in exporting manufactures: a comparative structural analysis.* Queen Elizabeth House.

Lamas Leite, J. G., de Brito Mello, L. C. B., Longo, O. C., & Cruz, E. P. (2017). Using analytic hierarchy process to optimize PESTEL scenario analysis tool in huge construction projects. [Trans Tech Publications Ltd.]. *Applied Mechanics and Materials, 865*, 707–712. doi:10.4028/www.scientific.net/AMM.865.707

Landesmann, M., & Stehrer, R. (2000). Potential switchovers in comparative advantage: patterns of industrial convergence. *WIIW Working Papers,* No. 14.

Lansing, K. J., & Ma, J. (2017). Explaining exchange rate anomalies in a model with Taylor-rule fundamentals and consistent expectations. *Journal of International Money and Finance, 70*, 62–87. doi:10.1016/j.jimonfin.2016.08.004

Lash, S. (2000). Risk culture. *The risk society and beyond: Critical issues for social theory*, 47-62.

Laukkanen, T. (2015, January). How uncertainty avoidance affects innovation resistance in mobile banking: The moderating role of age and gender. In *2015 48th Hawaii International Conference on System Sciences* (pp. 3601-3610). IEEE.

Lawler, E. E. III, & Worley, C. G. (2011). *Management reset: Organizing for sustainable effectiveness.* Hoboken, NJ: John Wiley & Sons.

Lee, C. C., & Chang, C. P. (2006). Social security expenditure and GDP in OECD countries: A cointegrated panel analysis. *International Economic Journal, 20*(3), 303–320. doi:10.1080/10168730600879372

Lee, C. C., & Zeng, J. H. (2011). The impact of oil price shocks on stock market activities: Asymmetric effect with quantile regression. *Mathematics and Computers in Simulation, 81*(9), 1910–1920. doi:10.1016/j.matcom.2011.03.004

Lee, J. (1999). The effect of exchange rate volatility on trade in durables. *Review of International Economics, 7*(2), 189–201. doi:10.1111/1467-9396.00156

Lee, J., & Strazicich, M. C. (2003). Minimum Lagrange multiplier unit root test with two structural breaks. *The Review of Economics and Statistics, 85*(4), 1082–1089. doi:10.1162/003465303772815961

Lee, K., Morley, J., & Shields, K. (2015). The meta Taylor rule. *Journal of Money, Credit and Banking, 47*(1), 73–98. doi:10.1111/jmcb.12169

Legros, B., Jouini, O., & Koole, G. (2018). Blended call center with idling times during the call service. *IISE Transactions, 50*(4), 279–297. doi:10.1080/24725854.2017.1387318

Lenz, S., & Neckel, S. (2019). Ethical banks between moral self-commitment and economic expansion. In S. Schiller-Merkens, & P. Balsiger (Eds.), The Contested Moralities of Markets (Research in the Sociology of Organizations, Vol. 63). Emerald. pp. 127-148. doi:10.1108/S0733-558X20190000063015

Lenz, R. T., & Engledow, J. L. (1986). Environmental analysis: The applicability of current theory. *Strategic Management Journal, 7*(4), 329–346. doi:10.1002mj.4250070404

Leroy, A., & Lucotte, Y. (2017). Is there a competition-stability trade-off in European banking? *Journal of International Financial Markets, Institutions and Money, 46*, 199–215. doi:10.1016/j.intfin.2016.08.009

Compilation of References

Leung, K., Bhagat, R. S., Buchan, N. R., Erez, M., & Gibson, C. B. (2005). Culture and international business: Recent advances and their implications for future research. *Journal of International Business Studies*, *36*(4), 357–378. doi:10.1057/palgrave.jibs.8400150

Leviäkangas, P. (2016). Digitalisation of Finland's transport sector. *Technology in Society*, *47*, 1–15. doi:10.1016/j.techsoc.2016.07.001

Levi, M. D. (2009). *International finance* (5th ed.). London, UK: Routledge.

Levin, A., Lin, C. F., & Chu, C. S. J. (2002). Unit root tests in panel data: Asymptotic and finite-sample properties. *Journal of Econometrics*, *108*(1), 1–24. doi:10.1016/S0304-4076(01)00098-7

Levy-Yeyati, E., & Sturzenegger, F. (2003). A de facto classification of exchange rate regimes: A methodological note. *The American Economic Review*, *93*(4), 1173–1193. doi:10.1257/000282803769206250

Lewis, M. K., & Algaoud, L. M. (2001). *Islamic banking*. Edward Elgar.

Li, S., Wang, Q., & Koole, G. (2018, November). Predicting call center performance with machine learning. In *INFORMS International Conference on Service Science* (pp. 193-199). Cham, Switzerland: Springer.

Li, X., Mao, Z., & Qi, E. (2009, September). Study on global logistics integrative system and key technologies of Chinese automobile industry. In *International Conference on Management and Service Science, 2009. MASS'09.* (pp. 1-4). IEEE. 10.1109/ICMSS.2009.5301609

Lichtenberg, F. R. (1993). R&D investment and international productivity differences. *NBER Working Paper Series Working Paper* No: 4161.

Li, H. H., Hsieh, M. Y., & Chang, W. L. (2016). Lucky names: Superstitious beliefs in Chinese corporate branding strategy for bank marketing. *The North American Journal of Economics and Finance*, *35*, 226–233. doi:10.1016/j.najef.2015.10.011

Liker, J. K. (2010). Toyota's lost its quality edge? Not so fast. *Business Week*, 28.

Lilienthal, D. E. (1960). *The multinational corporation: A review of some problems and opportunities for business management in a period of world-wide economic change*. Development and Resources Corporation.

Lillard, L. L., & Al-Suqri, M. N. (2019). Librarians learning from the retail sector: reaching out to online learners using customer relationship management. *Journal of Arts and Social Sciences*, *9*(3), 15–26. doi:10.24200/jass.vol9iss3pp15-26

Li, M., Liu, C., & Scott, T. (2019). Share pledges and firm value. *Pacific-Basin Finance Journal*, *55*, 192–205. doi:10.1016/j.pacfin.2019.04.001

Lin, L., Zhou, Z., Liu, Q., & Jiang, Y. (2019). Risk transmission between natural gas market and stock markets: Portfolio and hedging strategy analysis. *Finance Research Letters*, *29*, 245–254. doi:10.1016/j.frl.2018.08.011

Lin, W. L., Law, S. H., Ho, J. A., & Sambasivan, M. (2019). The causality direction of the corporate social responsibility – Corporate financial performance Nexus: Application of Panel Vector Autoregression approach. *The North American Journal of Economics and Finance*, *48*, 401–418. doi:10.1016/j.najef.2019.03.004

Lin, X., Bruhn, A., & William, J. (2019). Extending financial literacy to insurance literacy: A survey approach. *Accounting and Finance*, *59*(S1), 685–713. doi:10.1111/acfi.12353

Lin, Y. H., Chen, C. Y., Hong, W. H., & Lin, Y. C. (2010). Perceived job stress and health complaints at a bank call center: Comparison between inbound and outbound services. *Industrial Health*, *48*(3), 349–356. doi:10.2486/indhealth.48.349 PMID:20562511

Li-Ping Tang, T., Shin-Hsiung Tang, D., & Luna-Arocas, R. (2005). Money profiles: The love of money, attitudes, and needs. *Personnel Review*, *34*(5), 603–618. doi:10.1108/00483480510612549

Lipsey, R. G., ... (1990) Economics. Longman Higher Education; 9th edition, 333.

LiPuma, E. (1993). Culture and the concept of culture in a theory of practice. *Bourdieu: critical perspectives,* 14-34.

Lipumba, N., Ndulu, B., Horton, S., & Plourde, A. (1988). A supply constrained macroeconometric model of Tanzania. *Economic Modelling*, *5*(4), 354–376. doi:10.1016/0264-9993(88)90009-0

Liu, G., & Mirzaei, A. (2013). Industrial growth: Does bank competition, concentration and stability constraint matter? Evidence from developed and emerging economics. *Brunel University Economics and Finance Working Paper Series*, No: 13-23.

Liu, C. H., Chang, A. Y. P., Horng, J. S., Chou, S. F., & Huang, Y. C. (2019). Co-competition, learning, and business strategy for new service development. *Service Industries Journal*, 1–25. doi:10.1080/02642069.2019.1571045

Liu, X. (2018). How is the Taylor rule distributed under endogenous monetary regimes? *International Review of Finance*, *18*(2), 305–316. doi:10.1111/irfi.12131

Liu, Z., Ming, X., & Song, W. (2019). A framework integrating interval-valued hesitant fuzzy DEMATEL method to capture and evaluate co-creative value propositions for smart PSS. *Journal of Cleaner Production*, *215*, 611–625. doi:10.1016/j.jclepro.2019.01.089

Ljungwall, C., & Li, J. (2007). Financial sector development, FDI and economic growth in China. *Center for Economic Research (CCER)* Peking University. Working Paper Series, No: E2007005.3.

Lloyd-Reason, L., & Mughan, T. (2002). Strategies for internationalisation within SMEs: The key role of the owner-manager. *Journal of Small Business and Enterprise Development*, *9*(2), 120–129. doi:10.1108/14626000210427375

Lo, A. W., Repin, D. V., & Steenbarger, B. N. (2005). Fear and greed in financial markets: A clinical study of day-traders. *The American Economic Review*, *95*(2), 352–359. doi:10.1257/000282805774670095

Locke, P. R., & Mann, S. C. (2005). Professional trader discipline and trade disposition. *Journal of Financial Economics*, *76*(2), 401–444. doi:10.1016/j.jfineco.2004.01.004

Loerwald, D., & Stemmann, A. (2016). Behavioral finance and financial literacy: Educational implications of biases in financial decision making. In *International handbook of financial literacy* (pp. 25–38). Singapore: Springer. doi:10.1007/978-981-10-0360-8_3

Loh, A. M., Peong, K. K., & Peong, K. P. (2019). Determinants of personal financial literacy among young adults in Malaysian accounting firms. *Global J. Bus. Soc. Sci. Review, 7*(1), 08-19.

Lo, H. W., Liou, J. J., & Tzeng, G. H. (2019). Comments on "Sustainable recycling partner selection using fuzzy DEMATEL-AEW-FVIKOR: A case study in small-and-medium enterprises". *Journal of Cleaner Production*, *228*, 1011–1012. doi:10.1016/j.jclepro.2019.04.376

Longo, J. M. (2014). Trading and investment strategies in behavioral finance. *Investor behavior: The psychology of financial planning and investing*, 495-512.

López, J. L. V., & Neira, M. A. A. (2017). The Taylor rule and the sandpile: the Taylor contribution and other matters. *Open Journal of Modelling and Simulation*, *5*(04), 183–188. doi:10.4236/ojmsi.2017.54014

Lorenzo-Romero, C., Constantinides, E., & Alarcón-del-Amo, M. D. C. (2014). Social media as marketing strategy: an explorative study on adoption and use by retailers. This study is framed within research project with reference number ECO2009-08708 (Ministerio de Ciencia e Innovación, Gobierno de España, 2009–2013). In Social media in strategic management (pp. 197-215). Emerald Group.

Love, I. (2003). Financial development and financing constraints: international evidence from the structural investment model. *Review of Financial Studies, 16*(3), 765–791. doi:10.1093/rfs/hhg013

Lowe, R., & Marriot, S. (2006). *Innovation management: enterprise, entrepreneurship and innovation, concepts, contexts and commercialization*. USA: Elsevier.

Lu, B., Song, X. Y., & Li, X. D. (2012). Bayesian analysis of multi-group nonlinear structural equation models with application to behavioral finance. *Quantitative Finance, 12*(3), 477–488. doi:10.1080/14697680903369500

Lu, F., Suggs, A., Ezaldein, H. H., Ya, J., Fu, P., Jamora, J., ... Baron, E. D. (2019). The effect of shift work and poor sleep on self-reported skin conditions: a survey of call center agents in the Philippines. *Clocks & Sleep, 1*(2), 273–279. doi:10.3390/clockssleep1020023

Lundvall, B. A. (2007). Innovation system research and policy. Where it came from and where it might go. In CAS Seminar, Oslo, 10.

Lusardi, A. (2019). Financial literacy and the need for financial education: Evidence and implications. *Schweizerische Zeitschrift für Volkswirtschaft und Statistik, 155*(1), 1.

Luthans, F., & Doh, J. P. (2012). *International management: Culture, strategy, and behavior*. New York: McGraw-Hill.

Luther, W. J., & White, L. H. (2014). Can bitcoin become a major currency? *George Mason University Department of Economics Working Paper No. 14-17*

Lyons, A. C., Grable, J., & Zeng, T. (2019). Impacts of financial literacy on the loan decisions of financially excluded households in the People's Republic of China.

Macmillan, H., & Tampoe, M. (2000). *Strategic management: process, content and implementation*. Oxford, UK: Oxford University Press.

Maddala, G. S., & Shaowen, W. (1999). Comparative study of unit root tests with panel data and a new simple test. *Oxford Bulletin of Economics and Statistics, 61*(Special Issue), 631–652. doi:10.1111/1468-0084.61.s1.13

Madeira, J., & Palma, N. (2018). Measuring monetary policy deviations from the Taylor rule. *Economics Letters, 168*, 25–27. doi:10.1016/j.econlet.2018.03.034

Madsen, T. L., & Walker, G. (2015). *Modern competitive strategy*. McGraw Hill.

Maduku, D. K., Mpinganjira, M., & Duh, H. (2016). Understanding mobile marketing adoption intention by South African SMEs: A multi-perspective framework. *International Journal of Information Management, 36*(5), 711–723. doi:10.1016/j.ijinfomgt.2016.04.018

Madura, J. (2011). *International financial management*. Cengage Learning.

Maecker, O., Barrot, C., & Becker, J. U. (2016). The effect of social media interactions on customer relationship management. *Business Research, 9*(1), 133–155. doi:10.100740685-016-0027-6

Maehle, N. (2014). Monetary policy implementation: operational issues for countries with evolving monetary policy regimes. *IMF Working Paper*.

Mahmoud, M. A., Hinson, R. E., & Anim, P. A. (2018). Service innovation and customer satisfaction: The role of customer value creation. *European Journal of Innovation Management*, *21*(3), 402–422. doi:10.1108/EJIM-09-2017-0117

Mainardes, E. W., Ferreira, J., & Raposo, M. L. (2014). Strategy and strategic management concepts: are they recognised by management students? *E+M. Ekonomie a Management*, *17*(1), 43–61. doi:10.15240/tul/001/2014-1-004

Makridis, C. A. (2014). *Measuring the impact of oil and gas price volatility on East Mediterranean stock markets.* Theses, Dissertations, and Projects.

Malandri, L., Xing, F. Z., Orsenigo, C., Vercellis, C., & Cambria, E. (2018). Public mood–driven asset allocation: The importance of financial sentiment in portfolio management. *Cognitive Computation*, *10*(6), 1167–1176. doi:10.100712559-018-9609-2

Mancebón, M. J., Ximénez-de-Embún, D. P., Mediavilla, M., & Gómez-Sancho, J. M. (2019). Factors that influence the financial literacy of young Spanish consumers. *International Journal of Consumer Studies*, *43*(2), 227–235. doi:10.1111/ijcs.12502

Mannan, M. A. (1986). *Islamic economics: Theory and practice*. Cambridge, UK: Hodder & Stoughton.

Mansoori, Y., & Lackéus, M. (2019). Comparing effectuation to discovery-driven planning, prescriptive entrepreneurship, business planning, lean startup, and design thinking. *Small Business Economics*, 1–28.

Mantran, R. (C. II. 1990). Istanbul in The Second Half of The 17th Century. Ankara, Turkey: Turkish Historical Society.

Mantran, R. (C.I. 1990). Istanbul in The Second Half of The 17th Century. Ankara, Turkey: Turkish Historical Society.

Maqbool, S., & Zameer, M. N. (2018). Corporate social responsibility and financial performance: An empirical analysis of Indian banks. *Future Business Journal*, *4*(1), 84–93. doi:10.1016/j.fbj.2017.12.002

Ma, R., Anderson, H. D., & Marshall, B. R. (2019). Risk perceptions and international stock market liquidity. *Journal of International Financial Markets, Institutions and Money*, *62*, 94–116. doi:10.1016/j.intfin.2019.06.001

Marhavilas, P. K., & Koulouriotis, D. E. (2012). Developing a new alternative risk assessment framework in the work sites by including a stochastic and a deterministic process: A case study for the Greek public electric power provider. *Safety Science*, *50*(3), 448–462. doi:10.1016/j.ssci.2011.10.006

Marinova, D. P. (2003). Models of innovation in the international handbook of innovation. Elsevier Science, 44-53.

Marr, B., & Schiuma, G. (2003). Business performance measurement–past, present and future. *Management Decision*, *41*(8), 680–687. doi:10.1108/00251740310496198

Martin, J. (2001). Organizational culture: Mapping the terrain. Thousand Oaks, CA: Sage.

Martinez, J. A. B. (2005). Equilibrium entrepreneurship rate, economic development and growth. evidence from Spanish regions. *Entrepreneurship and Regional Development*, *17*(2), 145–161. doi:10.1080/08985620500032633

Martinez, R. J., & Eden, E. L. L. (1996). The production transfer and spillover of technology: comparing large and small multinationals as technology producer. *Small Business Economics*, *9*, 53–66.

Martin-Rojas, R., Garcia-Morales, V. J., & Gonzalez-Alvarez, N. (2019). Technological antecedents of entrepreneurship and its consequences for organizational performance. *Technological Forecasting and Social Change*, *147*, 22–35. doi:10.1016/j.techfore.2019.06.018

Masih, J., Rajkumar, R., Matharu, P. S., & Sharma, A. (2019). Market capturing and business expansion strategy for gluten-free foods in India and USA using PESTEL model. *The Sciences*, *10*, 202–213.

Maskell, B. (2001). The age of agile manufacturing. *Supply Chain Management*, 6(1), 1, 5–11. doi:10.1108/13598540110380868

Masood, A., & Java, J. (2015, April). Static analysis for web service security-Tools & techniques for a secure development life cycle. In *2015 IEEE International Symposium on Technologies for Homeland Security (HST)* (pp. 1-6). IEEE 10.1109/THS.2015.7225337

Masum, M., & Fernandez, A. (2008). Internationalization process of SMEs: Strategies and methods.

Maudos, J., & De Guevara, J. F. (2004). Factors explaining the interest margin in the banking sectors of the European Union. *Journal of Banking & Finance*, 28(9), 2259–2281. doi:10.1016/j.jbankfin.2003.09.004

Mayfield, C., Perdue, G., & Wooten, K. (2008). Investment management and personality type. *Financial Services Review*, 17(3), 219–236.

Maysami, R. C., Howe, L. C., & Rahmat, M. A. (2005). Relationship between macroeconomic variables and stock market indices: cointegration evidence from stock exchange of Singapore's all-S sector indices. *Jurnal Pengurusan (UKM Journal of Management)*, 24. Retrieved from http://ejournal.ukm.my/pengurusan/article/view/1454

McCulloch, J. H. (2015). The Taylor rule, the zero lower bound, and the term structure of interest rates. In Monetary policy in the context of the financial crisis: New challenges and lessons (pp. 405-417). Emerald Group. doi:10.1108/S1571-038620150000024023

McKenzie, M. D. (1999). The impact of exchange rate volatility on international trade flows. *Journal of Economic Surveys*, 13(1), 71–106. doi:10.1111/1467-6419.00075

McKenzie, M. D., & Brooks, R. D. (1997). The impact of exchange rate volatility on German-US trade flows. *Journal of International Financial Markets, Institutions and Money*, 7(1), 73–87. doi:10.1016/S1042-4431(97)00012-7

McNeil, A. J., Frey, R., & Embrechts, P. (2005). *Quantitative risk management: Concepts, techniques, and tools* (Vol. 3). Princeton, NJ: Princeton University Press.

McShane, M. (2018). Enterprise risk management: History and a design science proposal. *The Journal of Risk Finance*, 19(2), 137–153. doi:10.1108/JRF-03-2017-0048

Memic, D. (2015). Banking competition and efficiency: Empirical analysis on Bosnia and Herzegovinia using Panzar-Rosse model. *Business Systems Research*, 6(1), 72–92. doi:10.1515/bsrj-2015-0005

Meshal, H. (1997). *Comparative and competitive advantage as determinants of 'foreign policy formulation in Australia*, (Doctoral Thesis, The Fletcher School).

Metin Camgoz, S., Karan, B., & Ergeneli, A. (2011). Relationship between the Big-Five personality and the financial performance of fund managers. *Current Topics in Management*, 15, 137–152.

Mike, F., & Oransay, G. (2015). Altyapı ve İnovasyon Değişimlerinin Doğrudan Yabancı Yatırımlar Üzerine Etkisi: Türkiye Üzerine Ampirik Bir Uygulama. *The Journal of Academic Social Science*, 12(12), 372. doi:10.16992/ASOS.645

Miles, M. P., Arnold, D. R., & Thompson, D. L. (1993). The interrelationship between environmental hostility and entrepreneurial orientation. *Journal of Applied Business Research*, 9(4), 12–23. doi:10.19030/jabr.v9i4.5984

Miles, R. E., Snow, C. C., Meyer, A. D., & Coleman, H. J. Jr. (1978). Organizational strategy, structure, and process. *Academy of Management Review*, 3(3), 546–562. doi:10.5465/amr.1978.4305755 PMID:10238389

Miles, R. E., Snow, C. C., & Pfeffer, J. (1974). Organization-environment: concepts and issues. *Industrial Relations*, 13(3), 244–264. doi:10.1111/j.1468-232X.1974.tb00581.x

Miller, G. J., Hildreth, W. B., & Rabin, J. (2018). Performance-based budgeting: An ASPA classic. In *Performance based budgeting* (pp. 1–504). Taylor and Francis.

Miller, J. I., & Ratti, R. A. (2009). Crude oil and stock markets: Stability, instability, and bubbles. *Energy Economics*, *31*(4), 559–568. doi:10.1016/j.eneco.2009.01.009

Miller, M. H. (1977). Debt and Taxes. *The Journal of Finance*, 261–275.

Mintzberg, H. (1979). *The structuring of organizations: A synthesis of the research.* Englewood Cliffs, NJ: Prentice-Hall.

Mintzberg, H. (1987). The strategy concept I: Five Ps for strategy. *California Management Review*, *30*(1), 11–24. doi:10.2307/41165263

Mintzberg, H. (1988). Generic strategy: Toward a comprehensive framework. *Advances in Strategic Management*, *5*, 1–67.

Mishkin, F. S. (2018). *Makroekonomi Politika ve Uygulama. (Edsitör: S. Sezgin ve M. Şentürk)* (2nd ed.). Ankara, Turkey: Nobel Yayıncılık.

Mitic, M., & Kapoulas, A. (2012). Understanding the role of social media in bank marketing. *Marketing Intelligence & Planning*, *30*(7), 668–686. doi:10.1108/02634501211273797

Mittal, S., Pant, A., & Bhadauria, S. S. (2017). An empirical study on customer preference towards payment banks over universal banks in Delhi NCR. *Procedia Computer Science*, *122*, 463–470. doi:10.1016/j.procs.2017.11.394

Mitter, H., Schönhart, M., Larcher, M., & Schmid, E. (2018). The stimuli-actions-effects-responses (SAER)-framework for exploring perceived relationships between private and public climate change adaptation in agriculture. *Journal of Environmental Management*, *209*, 286–300. doi:10.1016/j.jenvman.2017.12.063 PMID:29306145

Mocan, M., Rus, S., Draghici, A., Ivascu, L., & Turi, A. (2015). Impact of corporate social responsibility practices on the banking industry in Romania. *Procedia Economics and Finance*, *23*, 712–716. doi:10.1016/S2212-5671(15)00473-6

Molina, L. M., & García-Morales, V. J. (2019). Combined influence of absorptive capacity and corporate entrepreneurship on performance. *Sustainability*, *11*(11), 1–26.

Moosa, I. A. (2006). *Exchange rate regimes: fixed, flexible or something in between?* New York: Palgrave Macmillan.

Moran, R. T., Harris, P. R., & Moran, S. V. (2011). *Managing cultural differences: global leadership strategies for cross-cultural business success.* Routledge.

Morgan, P. J., Huang, B., & Trinh, L. Q. (2019). *The need to promote digital financial literacy for the digital age.* IN THE DIGITAL AGE.

Morgan, R. E., & Strong, C. A. (2003). Business performance and dimensions of strategic orientation. *Journal of Business Research*, *56*(3), 163–176. doi:10.1016/S0148-2963(01)00218-1

Morley, B., Wang, R., & Stamatogiannis, M. (2018). Forecasting the exchange rate using non-linear Taylor rule based models. *International Journal of Forecasting*.

Mouna, A., & Jarboui, A. (2015). Financial literacy and portfolio diversification: An observation from the Tunisian stock market. *International Journal of Bank Marketing*, *33*(6), 808–822. doi:10.1108/IJBM-03-2015-0032

Mousavi, D., & Leelavathi, D. (2013). Agricultural export and exchange rates in India: The Granger causality approach. *International Journal of Scientific and Research Publications*, *3*(2), 1–8.

Mtigwe, B. (2005). The entrepreneurial firm internationalization process in the Southern African context: A comparative approach. *International Journal of Entrepreneurial Behaviour & Research*, *11*(5), 358–377. doi:10.1108/13552550510615006

Muda, I., & Putra, A. S. (2018, January). Institutional fishermen economic development models and banking support in the development of the innovation system of fisheries and marine area in North Sumatera. IOP Publishing. *IOP Conference Series. Materials Science and Engineering*, *288*(1), 012082. doi:10.1088/1757-899X/288/1/012082

Mudliar, P., & Donner, J. (2015). Experiencing interactive voice response (IVR) as a participatory medium: The case of CGNet Swara in India. *Mobile Media & Communication*, *3*(3), 366–382. doi:10.1177/2050157915571591

Mueller, P. (2007). Exploiting entrepreneurial opportunities: The impact of entrepreneurship on growth. *Small Business Economics*, *28*(4), 355–362. doi:10.100711187-006-9035-9

Muermann, A., & Volkman Wise, J. (2006). Regret, pride, and the disposition effect. *Available at SSRN 930675*.

Mukhtarov, S., Yüksel, S., & Mammadov, E. (2018). Factors that increase credit risks of Azerbaijani banks. *Journal of International Studies*, *11*(2).

Murendo, C., & Mutsonziwa, K. (2017). Financial literacy and savings decisions by adult financial consumers in Zimbabwe. *International Journal of Consumer Studies*, *41*(1), 95–103. doi:10.1111/ijcs.12318

Murphy, C. (2016). *Competitive intelligence: gathering, analysing and putting it to work*. Routledge. doi:10.4324/9781315573151

Mutlu, E. C. (1999). *Uluslararası İşletmecilik*. İstanbul, Turkey: Beta Yayınları.

Nadolny, L., Nation, J., & Fox, J. (2019). Supporting motivation and effort persistence in an online financial literacy course through game-based learning. *International Journal of Game-Based Learning*, *9*(3), 38–52. doi:10.4018/IJGBL.2019070103

Nagel, R., & Bhargava, P. (1994). Agility: The ultimate requirement for world - class manufacturing performance. *National Productivity Review*, *13*(3), 331–340. doi:10.1002/npr.4040130304

Nam, M. H. (2018). The effect of quantitative easing on inflation in Korea. *East Asian Economic Review*, *22*(4), 507–529. doi:10.11644/KIEP.EAER.2018.22.4.352

Naoum, S. (2001). *People and organizational management in construction*. Thomas Telford. doi:10.1680/paomic.28746

Narayan, P. K., & Gupta, R. (2015). Has oil price predicted stock returns for over a century? *Energy Economics*, *48*, 18–23. doi:10.1016/j.eneco.2014.11.018

Nataraja, S., & Al-Aali, A. (2011). The exceptional performance strategies of Emirate Airlines. *Competitiveness Review*, *21*(5), 471–486. doi:10.1108/10595421111171966

Naudé, W. (2011). Entrepreneurship is not a binding constraint on growth and development in the poorest countries. *World Development*, *39*(1), 33–44. doi:10.1016/j.worlddev.2010.05.005

Navimipour, N. J., & Soltani, Z. (2016). The impact of cost, technology acceptance and employees' satisfaction on the effectiveness of the electronic customer relationship management systems. *Computers in Human Behavior*, *55*, 1052–1066. doi:10.1016/j.chb.2015.10.036

NBC News. (2012, Nov. 19). *Dozens of forex traders arrested*. Retrieved from http://www.nbcnews.com/id/3540930/ns/business-corporate_scandals/t/dozens-FOREX-traders-arrested/#.XSGISegzbDc

NBS. (2016). National bureau of statistics: Foreign trade statistics 2013.

Neaime, S. (2016). Financial crises and contagion vulnerability of MENA stock markets. *Emerging Markets Review*, *27*, 14–35. doi:10.1016/j.ememar.2016.03.002

Neely, A. (Ed.). (2007). *Business performance measurement: Unifying theory and integrating practice*. Cambridge University Press. doi:10.1017/CBO9780511488481

Negruş, M. (1986). *Mijloace şi modalităţi de plată internaţionale*. Editura Academiei Republicii Socialiste România.

Neilson, L. C., & Chadha, M. (2008). International marketing strategy in the retail banking industry: The case of ICICI Bank in Canada. *Journal of Financial Services Marketing*, *13*(3), 204–220. doi:10.1057/fsm.2008.21

Nelson, R. R., & Winter, S. G. (1982). The Schumpeterian tradeoff revisited. *The American Economic Review*, *72*(1), 114–132.

Nesvetailova, A. (2015). A crisis of the overcrowded future: Shadow banking and the political economy of financial innovation. *New Political Economy*, *20*(3), 431–453. doi:10.1080/13563467.2014.951428

Neumann, J. V., & Morgenstern, O. (1947). *Theory of games and economic behavior*. Princeton, NJ: Princeton Univ. Pr.

Nicholson, N., Soane, E., Fenton-O'Creevy, M., & Willman, P. (2005). Personality and domain-specific risk taking. *Journal of Risk Research*, *8*(2), 157–176. doi:10.1080/1366987032000123856

Nicolae, P. (2018). Use of the PESTEL model in the management of the tourism branch of the Republic of Moldova. *Ovidius University Annals. Economic Sciences Series*, *18*(1), 370–375.

Niepmann, F., & Schmidt-Eisenlohr, T. (2017). International trade, risk and the role of banks. *Journal of International Economics*, *107*, 111–126. doi:10.1016/j.jinteco.2017.03.007

Niţu-Antonie, R., Feder, E. S., & Munteanu, V. (2017). Macroeconomic effects of entrepreneurship from an international perspective. *Sustainability*, *9*(7), 1159. doi:10.3390u9071159

Nkurunziza, F. (2016). Exchange rate volatility and Rwanda's balance of trade. *International Journal of Learning and Development*, *6*(1), 104–135.

Noori, M. (2016). Cognitive reflection as a predictor of susceptibility to behavioral anomalies. *Judgment and Decision Making*, *11*(1), 114.

Noth, F., & Busch, M. O. (2016). Foreign funding shocks and the lending channel: Do foreign banks adjust differently? *Finance Research Letters*, *19*, 222–227. doi:10.1016/j.frl.2016.08.003

Nurettin, A. Y. A. Z., & Türkmen, B. M. (2018). Yöresel yiyecekleri konu alan lisansüstü tezlerin bibliyometrik analizi. *Gastroia: Journal of Gastronomy and Travel Research*, *2*(1), 22–38.

Nur, H. B., & Dilber, İ. (2017). Gelişmekte Olan Ülkelerde Doğrudan Yabancı Yatırımları Belirleyen Temel Unsurlar. *Dokuz Eylül Üniversitesi İktisadi ve İdari Bilimler Fakültesi Dergisi*, *32*(2), 15–45. doi:10.24988/deuiibf.2017322551

Nurmi, J., & Niemelä, M. S. (2018, November). PESTEL analysis of hacktivism campaign motivations. In *Nordic Conference on Secure IT Systems* (pp. 323-335). Cham, Switzerland: Springer. 10.1007/978-3-030-03638-6_20

Nyadzayo, M. W., & Khajehzadeh, S. (2016). The antecedents of customer loyalty: A moderated mediation model of customer relationship management quality and brand image. *Journal of Retailing and Consumer Services*, *30*, 262–270. doi:10.1016/j.jretconser.2016.02.002

Nyström, K. (2008). *Is entrepreneurship the salvation for enhanced economic growth?* (No. 143). Royal Institute of Technology, CESIS-Centre of Excellence for Science and Innovation Studies.

Oates, G., & Dias, R. (2016). Including ethics in banking and finance programs: Teaching "we shouldn't win at any cost". *Education + Training*, *58*(1), 94–111. doi:10.1108/ET-12-2014-0148

Oberndorfer, U. (2009). Energy prices, volatility, and the stock market: Evidence from the Eurozone. *Energy Policy, 37*(12), 5787–5795. doi:10.1016/j.enpol.2009.08.043

Obrecht, J. J. (2004). Entrepreneurial capabilities: A resource-based systemic approach to international entrepreneurship. Handbook of research on international entrepreneurship, 248-266.

Öcal, T., & Uçar, H. (2011). Structural change and competitiveness in clusters. *Journal of Social Policy Conferences*, 285-321.

Odean, T. (1998). Are investors reluctant to realize their losses? *The Journal of Finance, 53*(5), 1775–1798. doi:10.1111/0022-1082.00072

Odebiyi, D. O., Akanle, O. T., Akinbo, S. R. A., & Balogun, S. A. (2016). Prevalence and impact of work-related musculoskeletal disorders on job performance of call center operators in Nigeria. *Int J Occup Environ Med (The IJOEM), 7*(2 April), 622-98.

OECD. (2011). *Measuring Financial Literacy: Questionnaire and Guidance Notes for Conducting an Internationally Comparable Survey of Financial Literacy*. Paris, France: OECD.

OECD. (2013). *Advancing National Strategies for Financial Education A Joint Publication by Russia's G20 Presidency and the OECD*. Russia: OECD.

OECD. (n.d.). FDI regulatory restrictiveness index. Retrieved from https://www.oecd.org/investment/fdi index.htm

OECD. (n.d.). Retrieved from https://stats.oecd.org/Index.aspx?datasetcode=FDIINDEX#

OECD. (n.d.). Retrieved from https://www.oecd-ilibrary.org/finance-and-investment/oecd-s-fdi-restrictiveness-index5k-m91p02zj7g-en

Oehler, A., Wendt, S., Wedlich, F., & Horn, M. (2018). Investors' personality influences investment decisions: Experimental evidence on extraversion and neuroticism. *Journal of Behavioral Finance, 19*(1), 30–48. doi:10.1080/15427560.2017.1366495

Oğuztürk, A. G. D. B. S. (2003). Yenilik kavramı ve teorik temelleri. *Süleyman Demirel Üniversitesi İktisadi ve İdari Bilimler Fakültesi Dergisi, 8*(2).

Oh, H., Park, H., & Boo, S. (2017). Mental health status and its predictors among call center employees: A cross-sectional study. *Nursing & Health Sciences, 19*(2), 228–236. doi:10.1111/nhs.12334 PMID:28295980

Ojasalo, K., Koskelo, M., & Nousiainen, A. K. (2015). Foresight and service design boosting dynamic capabilities in service innovation. In *The handbook of service innovation* (pp. 193–212). London, UK: Springer. doi:10.1007/978-1-4471-6590-3_10

Oktar, S., & Dalyancı, L. (2011). Türkiye Ekonomisinde Para Politikası ve Enflasyon Arasındaki İlişkinin Analizi. *Marmara Üniversitesi İktisadi ve İdari Bilimler Dergisi, 31*(2), 1–20.

Oktar, S., & Yüksel, S. (2016). Bankalarin Türev Ürün Kullanimini Etkileyen Faktörler: Mars Yöntemi ile Bir Inceleme/Determinants of the use derivatives in banking: An analysis with MARS Model. *Finans Politik & Ekonomik Yorumlar, 53*(620), 31.

Olivares-Mesa, A., & Cabrera-Suarez, K. (2006). Factors affecting the timing of the export development process: Does the family influence on the business make a difference? *International Journal of Globalisation and Small Business, 1*(4), 326–339. doi:10.1504/IJGSB.2006.012183

Olivares-Mesa, A., & Suarez-Ortega, S. (2006). Factors affecting the timing of the export development process in Spanish manufacturing firms. In *International Marketing Research* (pp. 89–105). Emerald Group. doi:10.1016/S1474-7979(06)17003-9

Omran, M., & Bolbol, A. (2003). Foreign direct investment financial development and economic growth: evidence from the Arab countries. *Review of Middle East Economics and Finance*, *1*(3), 231–249. doi:10.1080/1475368032000158232

Onafowora, O. A., & Owoye, O. (2008). Exchange rate volatility and export growth in Nigeria. *Applied Economics*, *40*(12), 1547–1556. doi:10.1080/00036840600827676

Öner, S. (2018). 2008 Küresel Krizi Sonrası Dönem Türkiye Cumhuriyeti Merkez Bankası Para Politikası Uygulamaları. *Avrasya Sosyal ve Ekonomi Araştırmaları Dergisi*, *5*(12), 409–416.

Oral, M. (2004). *Rekabet Gücü Ölçümü Ve Strateji Saptanması*. Laval Üniversitesi, Yönetim Bilimleri Fakültesi, Ste-Foy Québec, RQ. GİK 7P4. Canada.

Oral, M., Singer, A. E., & Kettani, O. (1989). The level of international competitiveness and its strategic implications. *International Journal of Research in Marketing*, *6*(4), 267–282. doi:10.1016/0167-8116(89)90054-2

Oraman, Y. (2014). An analytic study of organic food industry as part of healthy eating habit in Turkey: market growth, challenges and prospects. *Procedia: Social and Behavioral Sciences*, *150*, 1030–1039. doi:10.1016/j.sbspro.2014.09.115

Oran, B. (2001). *Küreselleşme ve Azınlıklar* (4th ed.). Ankara, Turkey: İmaj Yayınevi.

Oruç, K. E., Armaneri, Ö., & Yalçınkaya, Ö. (2008). 360 Derece Performans Değerleme ve Web Tabanlı Bir Model İle Kurumsal Verimliliğin Arttırılması, İzmir Büyükşehir Belediyesi, Ulaşım Dairesi, Dokuz Eylül Üniversitesi, Mühendislik Fakültesi, Endüstri Mühendisliği Bölümü, *Endüstri Mühendisliği Dergisi*. Makina Mühendisleri Odası, *19*(1), 4–18.

Ostroff, C., Kinicki, A. J., & Muhammad, R. S. (2012). Organizational culture and climate. Handbook of psychology, Second Edition, 12.

Ott, J. S. (1989). *The organizational culture perspective* (pp. 221–243). Chicago, IL: Dorsey Press.

Oviatt, B. M., & McDougall, P. P. (2005). Defining international entrepreneurship and modeling the speed of internationalization. *Entrepreneurship Theory and Practice*, *29*(5), 537–553. doi:10.1111/j.1540-6520.2005.00097.x

Owen, P. D., Ryan, M., & Weatherston, C. R. (2007). Measuring competitive balance in professional team sports using the Herfindahl-Hirschman index. *Review of Industrial Organization*, *31*(4), 289–302. doi:10.100711151-008-9157-0

Owoye, O., & Onafowora, O. A. (2007). M2 targeting, money demand, and real GDP growth in Nigeria: Do rules apply. *Journal of Business and Public Affairs*, *1*(2), 1–20.

Oyewumi, O. R., Ogunmeru, O. A., & Oboh, C. S. (2018). Investment in corporate social responsibility, disclosure practices, and financial performance of banks in Nigeria. *Future Business Journal*, *4*(2), 195–205. doi:10.1016/j.fbj.2018.06.004

Özalp, İ. (1998). *Çokuluslu İşletmeler: Uluslararası Yaklaşım*. Anadolu Üniversitesi Yayınları.

Özalp, İ. (Ed.). (2004). *Uluslararasi İşletmecilik*. Anadolu Universitesi.

Özatay, F. (2011). *Parasal iktisat: kuram ve politika*. Efil Yayınevi.

Özatay, F. (2011b). Merkez Bankası'nın yeni para politikası: İki hedef-üç ara hedef-üç araç. *Iktisat Isletme ve Finans*, *26*(302), 27–43.

Ozbay, P. (1999). *The effect of exchange rate uncertainty on exports: A case study for Turkey*. Citeseer. Retrieved from www.citeseerx.ist.psu.edu

Compilation of References

Özbek, D. (1998). Doviz kuru sisteminde seçenekler. *Ekonomik Yaklaşım Dergisi*, *9*(29), 17–36. doi:10.5455/ey.10285

Özcan, A. (2012). Türkiye'de ticari bankacılık sektöründe rekabet düzeyinin belirlenmesi (2002-2009). *Cumhuriyet Üniversitesi İktisadi ve İdari Bilimler Dergisi*, *13*(1), 195–211.

Özcan, A., & Çiftçi, C. (2015). Türkiye'de mevduat bankacılığında yoğunlaşma ve karlılık ilişkisi (2006-2013 Dönemi). *Niğde Üniversitesi İktisadi ve İdari Bilimler Fakültesi Dergisi*, *8*(3), 1–12.

Özcan, M. (2016). Asymmetric Taylor monetary rule: The case of Turkey. *Eurasian Academy of Sciences Social Sciences Journal*, *10*, 68–92.

Özdemir, E. (2010). Rekabet istihbarati toplama ve etik: Bir alan arastirmasi. *İstanbul Üniversitesi Siyasal Bilgiler Fakültesi Dergisi*, (43), 67-95.

Özdemir, K. A., & Şahinbeyoğlu, G. (2000). Alternatif döviz kuru sistemleri. Türkiye Cumhuriyet Merkez Bankası Araştırma Genel Müdürlüğü Tartışma Tebliği.

Özel, Ç. H., & Kozak, N. (2012). Turizm pazarlaması alanının bibliyometrik profili (2000-2010) ve bir atıf analizi çalışması. *Türk Kütüphaneciliği*, *26*(4), 715–733.

Özerol, H., Selin, M. C., Karan, M. B., & Ergeneli, A. (2011). Determining the performance of individual investors: The predictive roles of demographic variables and trading strategies. *International Journal of Business and Social Science*, *2*(18).

Özgür, M. I., & Demirtaş, C. (2015). Finansal Gelişme ve Doğrudan Yabancı Yatırımların Ekonomik Büyüme Üzerindeki Etkileri: Türkiye Örneği. *E-Journal of New World Sciences Academy*, *10*(3), 76–91.

Özkul, A. E. (2018). Butchers and activities in Cyprus in the Ottoman Rule. *Gazi Academic View*, 165-198.

Özkul, G., & Örün, E. (2016). Girişimcilik ve İnovasyonun Ekonomik Büyüme Üzerindeki Etkisi: Ampirik Bir Araştırma. *Girişimcilik ve İnovasyon Yönetimi Dergisi*, *5*(2), 17–51.

Özmerdivanlı, A. (2014). Petrol fiyatlari ile Bist 100 endeksi kapaniş fiyatlari arasindaki ilişki. *Akademik Bakış Uluslararası Hakemli Sosyal Bilimler Dergisi*, (43).

Oztaysi, B., Onar, S. C., & Kahraman, C. (2017). Integrated call center performance measurement using hierarchical intuitionistic fuzzy axiomatic design. In *Advances in fuzzy logic and technology 2017* (pp. 94–105). Cham, Switzerland: Springer.

Öztürk, N. (2011). *Para banka kredi*. Ekin Yayınevi.

Öztürk, S., & Gövdere, B. (2004). Para kurulu yaklaşımı ve bulgaristan deneyimi. *Journal of Political Science*, *31*, 95–112.

Öztürk, S., & Saygın, S. (2017). 1973 Petrol Krizinin Ekonomiye Etkileri ve Stagflasyon Olgusu. *Balkan Sosyal Bilimler Dergisi*, *6*(12), 3.

Padilla, G. A. (2019). PESTEL analysis with neutrosophic cognitive maps to determine the factors that affect rural sustainability. Case study of the South-Eastern plain of the province of Pinar del Río.

Padoa-Schioppa, T. (2001). Bank competition: A changing paradigm. *Review of Finance*, *5*(1-2), 13–20. doi:10.1023/A:1012612610825

Pagano, M. (1993). Financial markets and growth: An overview. *European Economic Review*, *37*(2-3), 613–622. doi:10.1016/0014-2921(93)90051-B

Pandey, M., Litoriya, R., & Pandey, P. (2019). Identifying causal relationships in mobile app issues: An interval type-2 fuzzy DEMATEL approach. *Wireless Personal Communications*, 1–28.

Pang, M. F. (2019). Enhancing the generative learning of young people in the domain of financial literacy through learning study. *International Journal for Lesson and Learning Studies*.

Pan, W., Chen, L., & Zhan, W. (2018). PESTEL analysis of construction productivity enhancement strategies: A case study of three economies. *Journal of Management Engineering*, *35*(1), 05018013. doi:10.1061/(ASCE)ME.1943-5479.0000662

Papapetrou, E. (2001). Oil price shocks, stock market, economic activity and employment in Greece. *Energy Economics*, *23*(5), 511–532. doi:10.1016/S0140-9883(01)00078-0

Pappas, D., Androutsopoulos, I., & Papageorgiou, H. (2015, October). Anger detection in call center dialogues. In *2015 6th IEEE International Conference on Cognitive Infocommunications (CogInfoCom)* (pp. 139-144). IEEE. 10.1109/CogInfoCom.2015.7390579

Parameswar, N., Dhir, S., & Dhir, S. (2017). Banking on innovation, innovation in banking at ICICI bank. *Global Business and Organizational Excellence*, *36*(2), 6–16. doi:10.1002/joe.21765

Parasız, İ. (2003). *Makro Ekonomi Teori ve Politika* (p. 840). Bursa, Turkey: Ezgi Kitabevi Yayınları.

Parasız, M. İ. (2007). *Para teorisi ve politikası*. Ezgi Kitabevi.

Parente, R. C., Geleilate, J. M. G., & Rong, K. (2018). The sharing economy globalization phenomenon: A research agenda. *Journal of International Management*, *24*(1), 52–64. doi:10.1016/j.intman.2017.10.001

Patelis, A. D. (1997). Stock return predictability and the role of monetary policy. *The Journal of Finance*, *52*(5), 1951–1972. doi:10.1111/j.1540-6261.1997.tb02747.x

Patil, D. A. (2018). Sustainable bio-energy through bagasse co-generation technology: a PESTEL analysis of sugar hub of India, Solapur. *Journal of Emerging Technologies and Innovative Research*, *5*(12).

Paul, K. (2012). Increasing returns and economic geography. *Maliye Dergisi*, 396-410.

Paulet, E., Parnaudeau, M., & Relano, F. (2015). Banking with ethics: strategic moves and structural changes of the banking industry in the aftermath of the subprime mortgage crisis. *Journal of Business Ethics*, *131*(1), 199–207. doi:10.100710551-014-2274-9

PBAT. (2019). Retrieved from http://www.tkbb.org.tr/sector-comparison

Pearce, J. A., & Robinson, R. B. (2005). Formulation, implementation, and control of competitive strategy. McGraw-Hill.

Pedroni, P. (2001). Fully modified OLS for heterogeneous cointegrated panels. In Nonstationary panels, panel cointegration, and dynamic panels. Emerald Group, 15, 93-130.

Pedroni, P. (1999). Critical values for cointegration tests in heterogeneous panels with multiple regressors. *Oxford Bulletin of Economics and Statistics*, *61*(1), 653–670. doi:10.1111/1468-0084.61.s1.14

Peersman, G. (2011). *Macroeconomic effects of unconventional monetary policy in the euro area (No. 1397)*. European Central Bank.

Peiró, A. (2016). Stock prices and macroeconomic factors: Some European evidence. *International Review of Economics & Finance*, *41*, 287–294. doi:10.1016/j.iref.2015.08.004

Perée, E., & Steinherr, A. (1989). Exchange rate uncertainty and foreign trade. *European Economic Review*, *33*(6), 1241–1264. doi:10.1016/0014-2921(89)90095-0

Peris-Ortiz, M., Fuster-Estruch, V., & Devece-Carañana, C. (2014). Entrepreneurship and innovation in a context of crisis. In *Entrepreneurship, innovation and economic crisis* (pp. 1–10). Cham, Switzerland: Springer. doi:10.1007/978-3-319-02384-7_1

Perron, P. (1989). The great crash, the oil price shock, and the unit root hypothesis. *Econometrica*, *57*(6), 1361–1401. doi:10.2307/1913712

Pervin, L. A., & John, O. P. (Eds.). (1999). *Handbook of personality: theory and research*. Elsevier.

Petersen, M. A., & Rajan, R. G. (1995). The effect of credit market competition on lending relationships. *The Quarterly Journal of Economics*, *110*(2), 407–443. doi:10.2307/2118445

Phatak, A. V. (1989). *Uluslararası Yönetim, (Çev. Atilla Baransel, Tomris Somay)*. İstanbul, Turkey: İÜ İşletme Fakültesi Yayını.

Phatak, A. V., Bhagat, R. S., & Kashlak, R. J. (2005). *International management: Managing in a diverse and dynamic global environment*. New York, NY: McGraw-Hill Irwin.

Phua, C. Y., Ang, W. H., Chua, H. E., Hong, Y. W., & Peng, S. C. (2017). *Does domestic stock market returns depend on the stock market of its major trading partners? Evidence from Malaysia* (Doctoral dissertation, UTAR).

Picanso, J. M., Swinkels, C. M., Hill, M., Hess, T. H., Straits-Tröster, K. A., Glynn, S., & Sayers, S. L. (2017, March). The development and initial evaluation of a call center for concerned family members of military veterans. In Annals of Behavioral Medicine (Vol. 51, pp. S229-S229). 233 Spring St., New York, NY 10013: Springer.

Pikoulakis, E. (1995). *The exchange rate and the current account when prices evolve sluggishly: A simplification of the dynamics and a reconciliation with the absorption approach*. International Macroeconomics (pp. 126–143). Macmillan Education UK.

Polychronidou, P., Ioannidou, E., Kipouros, A., Tsourgiannis, L., & Simet, G. F. (2014). Corporate social responsibility in Greek banking sector – an empirical research. *Procedia Economics and Finance*, *9*, 193–199. doi:10.1016/S2212-5671(14)00020-3

Pompian, M. (2016). *Risk profiling through a behavioral finance lens*. CFA Institute Research Foundation.

Porter, M. E. (1998). Clusters and competition. *On competition*, *7*, 91.

Porter, M. E. (2008a). Competitive advantage: Creating and sustaining superior performance, New York City.

Porter, M. E., & Kramer, M. R. (2002). The competitive advantage of corporate.

Porter, M. (1990). e. (1990). The competitive advantage of nations. *Harvard Business Review*, *68*(2), 73–93.

Porter, M. (2010). *Rekabet üzerine*. İstanbul, Turkey: Optimist Yayınları.

Porter, M. E. (1980). *Competitive strategy: techniques for analyzing industries and competitors*. New York: Free Press.

Porter, M. E. (1980). *Techniques for analyzing industries and competitors. Competitive Strategy*. New York: Free.

Porter, M. E. (1985). *Competitive advantage: creating and sustaining superior performance*. New York: Free Press.

Porter, M. E. (1986). *Competition in global industries*. Boston, MA: Harvard Business School Press.

Porter, M. E. (1987). *From competitive advantage to corporate strategy*. Boston, MA: Harvard Business School Pub.

Porter, M. E. (1990). *The competitive advantage of nations*. New York: The Free Press. doi:10.1007/978-1-349-11336-1

Porter, M. E. (1996). What is strategy? *Harvard Business Review*, *74*(6), 61–78. PMID:10158474

Porter, M. E. (2000). *Rekabet Stratejisi, Sektör ve Rakip Analizi Teknikleri (Çeviri: Gülen Ulubilgen) Sistem Yayıncılık*, *1* (p. 16). İstanbul, Turkey: Basım.

Porter, M. E. (2008b). *Competitive strategy: Techniques for analyzing industries and competitors*. Simon and Schuster.

Pothukuchi, V., Damanpour, F., Choi, J., Chen, C. C., & Park, S. H. (2002). National and organizational culture differences and international joint venture performance. *Journal of International Business Studies*, *33*(2), 243–265. doi:10.1057/palgrave.jibs.8491015

Potrich, A. C. G., Vieira, K. M., Coronel, D. A., & Bender Filho, R. (2015). Financial literacy in Southern Brazil: Modeling and invariance between genders. *Journal of Behavioral and Experimental Finance*, *6*, 1–12. doi:10.1016/j.jbef.2015.03.002

Potrich, A. C. G., Vieira, K. M., & Mendes-Da-Silva, W. (2016). Development of a financial literacy model for university students. *Management Research Review*, *39*(3), 356–376. doi:10.1108/MRR-06-2014-0143

Power, M., Ashby, S., & Palermo, T. (2013). *Risk culture in financial organisations: A research report*. CARR-Analysis of Risk and Regulation.

Pradhan, R. P. (2010). Financial deepening foreign direct investment and economic growth: are they cointegrated. *International Journal of Financial Research*, *1*(1), 37–43. doi:10.5430/ijfr.v1n1p37

Prahalad, C. K., & Hamel, G. (1990). The core competence of the corporation. *Harvard Business Review*, 3.

Preble, J. F., Rau, P. A., & Reichel, A. (1988) The environmental scanning practices of US multinationals in the late 1980s. Management International Review 28(4), 4-14.

Presbitero, A. (2017). It's not all about language ability: Motivational cultural intelligence matters in call center performance. *International Journal of Human Resource Management*, *28*(11), 1547–1562. doi:10.1080/09585192.2015.1128464

Preston, A. C., & Wright, R. E. (2019). Understanding the gender gap in financial literacy: Evidence from Australia. *The Economic Record*, *95*(S1), 1–29. doi:10.1111/1475-4932.12472

Pritchard, A. (1969). Statistical bibliography or bibliometrics. *The Journal of Documentation*, *25*(4), 348–349.

Pruna, R. T., Polukarov, M., & Jennings, N. R. (2018). Avoiding regret in an agent-based asset pricing model. *Finance Research Letters*, *24*, 273–277. doi:10.1016/j.frl.2017.09.014

Pugh, W. (2017). *Call center experience optimization: a case for a virtual predictive queue* (Doctoral dissertation, University of the Incarnate Word).

Qianqian, Z. (2011). The impact of international oil price fluctuation on China's economy. *Energy Procedia*, *5*, 1360–1364. doi:10.1016/j.egypro.2011.03.235

Rafaeli, A., Ziklik, L., & Doucet, L. (2008). The impact of call center employees' customer orientation behaviors on service quality. *Journal of Service Research*, *10*(3), 239–255. doi:10.1177/1094670507306685

Raheem, I. D., & Oyınlola, M. A. (2013). Foreign direct investment-economic nexus: the role of the level of financial sector development in Africa. *Journal of Economics and International Finance*, *5*(9), 327–337. doi:10.5897/JEIF2013.0542

Rahimi, R. (2017). Customer relationship management (people, process and technology) and organisational culture in hotels: Which traits matter? *International Journal of Contemporary Hospitality Management*, *29*(5), 1380–1402. doi:10.1108/IJCHM-10-2015-0617

Rahimi, R., & Kozak, M. (2017). Impact of customer relationship management on customer satisfaction: The case of a budget hotel chain. *Journal of Travel & Tourism Marketing*, *34*(1), 40–51. doi:10.1080/10548408.2015.1130108

Rakow, K. C. (2019). Incorporating financial literacy into the accounting curriculum. *Accounting Education*, 1–17.

Ramiah, V., Xu, X., & Moosa, I. A. (2015). Neoclassical finance, behavioral finance and noise traders: A review and assessment of the literature. *International Review of Financial Analysis*, *41*, 89–100. doi:10.1016/j.irfa.2015.05.021

Ramírez, M. A. C., Añez, J. C. D. J. A., Ronquillo, O. I., Riera, R. G. H. Q., Vera, Á. A. R., Cegarra, J. C. T., & Sotomayor, P. M. O. (2019). Pestel based on neutrosophic cognitive maps to characterize the factors that influence the consolidation of the neo constitutionalism in Ecuador. *Neutrosophic Sets and Systems*, 60.

Rawhouser, H., Cummings, M., & Newbert, S. L. (2019). Social impact measurement: Current approaches and future directions for social entrepreneurship research. *Entrepreneurship Theory and Practice*, *43*(1), 82–115. doi:10.1177/1042258717727718

Raza, N., Shahzad, S. J. H., Tiwari, A. K., & Shahbaz, M. (2016). Asymmetric impact of gold, oil prices and their volatilities on stock prices of emerging markets. *Resources Policy*, *49*, 290–301. doi:10.1016/j.resourpol.2016.06.011

Reboredo, J. C., & Rivera-Castro, M. A. (2014). Wavelet-based evidence of the impact of oil prices on stock returns. *International Review of Economics & Finance*, *29*, 145–176. doi:10.1016/j.iref.2013.05.014

Reboredo, J. C., Rivera-Castro, M. A., & Ugolini, A. (2016). Downside and upside risk spillovers between exchange rates and stock prices. *Journal of Banking & Finance*, *62*, 76–96. doi:10.1016/j.jbankfin.2015.10.011

Rehan, F., Block, J. H., & Fisch, C. (2019). (Forthcoming). Entrepreneurship in Islamic communities: How do Islamic values and Islamic practices influence entrepreneurship intentions? *Journal of Enterprising Communities: People and Places in the Global Economy*, (ahead-of-print). doi:10.1108/JEC-05-2019-0041

Reich, C. M., & Berman, J. S. (2015). Do financial literacy classes help? An experimental assessment in a low-income population. *Journal of Social Service Research*, *41*(2), 193–203. doi:10.1080/01488376.2014.977986

Reim, W., Parida, V., & Örtqvist, D. (2015). Product–Service Systems (PSS) business models and tactics–a systematic literature review. *Journal of Cleaner Production*, *97*, 61–75. doi:10.1016/j.jclepro.2014.07.003

Reís, Ş. G., & Aydin, N. (2014). Causality relationship between stock liquidity and financial performance: an example of Borsa İstanbul. *Gaziantep University Journal of Social Sciences*, *13*(3), 607–617.

Rejda, G. E. (2011). *Principles of risk management and insurance*. Pearson Education India.

Remund, D. L. (2010). Financial Literacy Explicated: The Case for a Clearer Definition in an Increasingly Complex Economy. *The Journal of Consumer Affairs*, *44*(2), 276–295. doi:10.1111/j.1745-6606.2010.01169.x

Renaud, B. (2003). Speculative behaviour in immature real estate markets, lessons of the 1997 Asia financial crisis. *Urban Policy and Research*, *21*(2), 151–173. doi:10.1080/08111140309950

Republic of Turkey Official Gazette. (2017, Feb. 10). *Notice Number 29975*. Retrieved from http://www.resmigazete.gov.tr/eskiler/2017/02/20170210-5.htm

Revised framework for monetary operations under the BSP interest rate corridor (IRC) system. (2016). Retrieved from http://www.bsp.gov.ph/downloads/publications/FAQs/IRC.pdf

Rezaee, Z., Dou, H., & Zhang, H. (2019). Corporate social responsibility and earnings quality: Evidence from China. *Global Finance Journal*, *100473*. doi:10.1016/j.gfj.2019.05.002

Rhee, M., & Mehra, S. (2006). Aligning operations, marketing, and competitive strategies to enhance performance: An empirical test in the retail banking industry. *Omega*, *34*(5), 505–515. doi:10.1016/j.omega.2005.01.017

Rhinesmith, S. H. (2000). *Yöneticinin Küreselleşme Rehberi*. İstanbul, Turkey: Sabah Kitapçılık.

Richard, P. J., Devinney, T. M., Yip, G. S., & Johnson, G. (2009). Measuring organizational performance: Towards methodological best practice. *Journal of Management*, *35*(3), 718–804. doi:10.1177/0149206308330560

Riff, S., & Yagil, Y. (2016). Behavioral factors affecting the home bias phenomenon: Experimental tests. *Journal of Behavioral Finance*, *17*(3), 267–279. doi:10.1080/15427560.2016.1203324

Rime, D., & Schrimpf, A. (2013). The anatomy of the global FX market through the lens of the 2013 Triennial Survey. *BIS Quarterly Review,* December.

Ritchie, B., & Brindley, C. (2007). Supply chain risk management and performance: A guiding framework for future development. *International Journal of Operations & Production Management*, *27*(3), 303–322. doi:10.1108/01443570710725563

Ritter, J. R. (2003). Behavioral finance. *Pacific-Basin Finance Journal*, *11*(4), 429–437. doi:10.1016/S0927-538X(03)00048-9

Robbins, T. R. (2017). Complexity and flexibility in call center scheduling models. *International Journal of Business and Social Science*, *8*(12).

Roberts, E. B., Murray, F., & Kim, J. D. (2019). Entrepreneurship and innovation at MIT: Continuing global growth and impact—an updated report. *Foundations and Trends® in Entrepreneurship*, *15*(1), 1-55.

Roberts, D. L., & Darler, W. (2017). Consumer co-creation: An opportunity to humanise the new product development process. *International Journal of Market Research*, *59*(1), 13–33. doi:10.2501/IJMR-2017-003

Robinson, S. (1972). Theories of economic growth and development: methodology and content. economic development and culturel change, 52.

Robinson, J., Glean, A., & Moore, W. (2018). How does news impact on the stock prices of green firms in emerging markets? *Research in International Business and Finance*, *45*, 446–453. doi:10.1016/j.ribaf.2017.07.176

Rocha, L. E., Glina, D. M. R., Marinho, M. F., & Nakasato, D. (2005). Risk factors for musculoskeletal symptoms among call center operators of a bank in Sao Paulo, Brazil. *Industrial Health*, *43*(4), 637–646. doi:10.2486/indhealth.43.637 PMID:16294918

Rodrigues, L. F., Oliveira, A., Rodrigues, H., & Costa, C. J. (2019). Assessing consumer literacy on financial complex products. *Journal of Behavioral and Experimental Finance*, *22*, 93–104. doi:10.1016/j.jbef.2019.02.005

Rodriguez-Fernandez, M. (2016). Social responsibility and financial performance: The role of good corporate governance. *BRQ Business Research Quarterly*, *19*(2), 137–151. doi:10.1016/j.brq.2015.08.001

Roeschmann, A. Z. (2014). Risk culture: What it is and how it affects an insurer's risk management. *Risk Management & Insurance Review*, *17*(2), 277–296. doi:10.1111/rmir.12025

Rogers, P., Rogers, D., & Securato, J. R. (2015). About psychological variables in application scoring models. *Revista de Administração de Empresas*, *55*(1), 38–49. doi:10.1590/S0034-759020150105

Rohde, E. (2018). Olympic Games and values in disruption: The fundamental renewal of Coubertinian renewal seems necessary. *Diagoras: International Academic Journal on Olympic Studies*, *2*, 193–214.

Romer, P. M. (1986). Increasing returns and long-run growth. *Journal of Political Economy*, *94*(5), 1002–1037. doi:10.1086/261420

Romer, P. M. (1990). Endogenous technological change. *Journal of Political Economy*, 75.

Rooij, M. V., Lusardi, A., & Alessie, R. (2007, September). Financial Literacy and Stock Market Participation. *Tjalling C. Koopmans Research Institute Discussion Paper Series nr: 07-23*, pp. 1-50.

Root, F. R. (1994). *Entry strategies for international markets* (pp. 22–44). New York: Lexington Books.

Rosen, R. C., Stephens-Shields, A. J., Cunningham, G. R., Cifelli, D., Cella, D., Farrar, J. T., ... Snyder, P. J. (2016). Comparison of interactive voice response (IVR) with paper administration of instruments to assess functional status, sexual function, and quality of life in elderly men. *Quality of Life Research: An International Journal of Quality of Life Aspects of Treatment, Care and Rehabilitation*, *25*(4), 811–821. doi:10.100711136-015-1133-1 PMID:26358063

Rosenthal, M. (2016). Qualitative research methods: Why, when, and how to conduct interviews and focus groups in pharmacy research. *Currents in pharmacy teaching and learning, 8*(4), 509-516.

Rothaermel, F. T. (2013). *Strategic management: concepts*. New York, NY: McGraw-Hill Irwin.

Rothwell, R. (1994). *Towards the fifth-generation innovation process. science policy research unit* (pp. 7–9). UK: University of Sussex.

Rubin, I. S. (2019). *The politics of public budgeting: Getting and spending, borrowing and balancing*. CQ Press.

Rubleske, J., & Kaarst-Brown, M. L. (2019). Mindful new service conception in not-for-profit organisations: A study of sustainable innovation with scarce resources. *International Journal of Business Innovation and Research*, *18*(1), 87–108. doi:10.1504/IJBIR.2019.096897

Ruhanen, L., Weiler, B., Moyle, B. D., & McLennan, C. L. J. (2015). Trends and patterns in sustainable tourism research: A 25-year bibliometric analysis. *Journal of Sustainable Tourism*, *23*(4), 517–535. doi:10.1080/09669582.2014.978790

Rus, S., Mocan, M., Ardelean, B. O., Ivascu, L., & Cioca, L. I. (2016). Conceptualization and examination of success factors in the banking system. *Procedia Economics and Finance*, *39*, 679–684. doi:10.1016/S2212-5671(16)30289-1

Rutasitara, L. (2004). *Exchange rate regimes and inflation in Tanzania*. The African Economic Research Consortium.

Rweyemamu, J. (1973). *Underdevelopment and industrialization in Tanzania: A study of perverse capitalist industrial development*. Oxford University Press.

Ryff, C. D. (2019). Entrepreneurship and eudaimonic well-being: Five venues for new science. *Journal of Business Venturing*, *34*(4), 646–663. doi:10.1016/j.jbusvent.2018.09.003 PMID:31105380

Saatçioğlu, C., & Karaca, O. (2004). Döviz kuru belirsizliğinin ihracata etkisi: Türkiye örneği. *Doğuş Üniversitesi Dergisi*, *5*(2), 183–195. doi:10.31671/dogus.2019.296

Sabir, S. A., Mohammad, H. B., & Shahar, H. B. K. (2019). The role of overconfidence and past investment experience in herding behaviour with a moderating effect of financial literacy: Evidence from Pakistan stock exchange. *Asian Economic and Financial Review*, *9*(4), 480–490. doi:10.18488/journal.aefr.2019.94.480.490

Sachs, J. D., & Warner, A. M. (1995). Naturel resource abundance and economic growth. *National Bureau of Economic Research Working Paper,* 4.

Sachs, J. D., & Warner, A. M. (2001). The curse of naturel resources. *European Economic Review*, *45*(4-6), 827–838. doi:10.1016/S0014-2921(01)00125-8

Sadorsky, P. (1999). Oil price shocks and stock market activity. *Energy Economics*, *21*(5), 449–469. doi:10.1016/S0140-9883(99)00020-1

Saebi, T., Foss, N. J., & Linder, S. (2019). Social entrepreneurship research: Past achievements and future promises. *Journal of Management*, *45*(1), 70–95. doi:10.1177/0149206318793196

Saeidi, S. P., Sofian, S., Saeidi, P., Saeidi, S. P., & Saaeidi, S. A. (2015). How does corporate social responsibility contribute to firm financial performance? The mediating role of competitive advantage, reputation, and customer satisfaction. *Journal of Business Research*, *68*(2), 341–350. doi:10.1016/j.jbusres.2014.06.024

Sağlam, S. (2007a). Küreselleşmeye Yaklaşımlar. *Genç Sosyal Bilim Forumu*, *13*, 7.

Sahay, R., Čihák, M., N'Diaye, P., Barajas, A., Bi, R., Ayala, D., ... Yousefi, S. R. (2015). Rethinking financial deepening: stability and growth in emerging markets. *IMF Staff Discussion Note, SDN*, *15*(08), 1–41. doi:10.5089/9781498312615.006

Şahin, D. (2018). Apec Ülkelerinde Doğrudan Yabancı Sermaye Yatırımlarının Belirleyicileri. *Kırıkkale Üniversitesi Sosyal Bilimler Dergisi*, *8*(2), 415–430.

Saidi, K., & Mbarek, M. B. (2016). Nuclear energy, renewable energy, CO2 emissions, and economic growth for nine developed countries: Evidence from panel Granger causality tests. *Progress in Nuclear Energy*, *88*, 364–374. doi:10.1016/j.pnucene.2016.01.018

Salgado, J. F. (1997). The five factor model of personality and job performance in the European Community. *The Journal of Applied Psychology*, *82*(1), 30–43. doi:10.1037/0021-9010.82.1.30 PMID:9119797

Salisu, A. A., & Isah, K. O. (2017). Revisiting the oil price and stock market nexus: A nonlinear Panel ARDL approach. *Economic Modelling*, *66*, 258–271. doi:10.1016/j.econmod.2017.07.010

Salmanov, O., Babina, N., Bashirova, S., Samoshkina, M., & Bashirov, R. (2016). The Importance of the country's GDP in the evaluation of companies using multiples on the European stock market. *Regional and Sectoral Economic Studies*, *16*, 1.

Samina, Q. S., & Hossain, M. (2019). Current position of banks in the practice of green banking in Bangladesh: An analysis on private sector commercial banks in Bangladesh. *Current Position of Banks in the Practice of Green Banking in Bangladesh: An Analysis on Private Sector Commercial Banks in Bangladesh (Jan. 5, 2019)*.

Samuelson, P. A. & Nordhaus, W. D. (2010). Economics. New Delhi, India: McGraw-Hill Companies, 503.

Sancak, E. (2012). *Bireysel Tasarruf ve Yatırımları Koruma Rehberi*. Ankara, Turkey: Gazi Kitabevi.

Sancak, E. (2014). *Sermaye Piyasası Sözlüğü - Temel Düzey*. İstanbul, Turkey: Scala Yayıncılık.

Sandal, M., Çemrek, F., & Yıldız, Z. (2017). Bist 100 endeksi ile altın ve petrol fiyatları arasındaki fiyatları arasındaki nedensellik ilişkisinin incelenmesi *Çukurova Üniversitesi Sosyal Bilimler Enstitüsü Dergisi*, *26*(3), 155-170.

Sandu, C., & Ghiba, N. (2011). The relationship between exchange rate and exports in Romania using a vector autoregressive model. *Annales Universitatis Apulensis: Series Oeconomica*, *13*(2), 476–482.

San-Jose, L., & Cuesta, J. (2019). Are Islamic banks different? The application of the Radical Affinity Index. *International Journal of Islamic and Middle Eastern Finance and Management*, *12*(1), 2–29. doi:10.1108/IMEFM-07-2017-0192

San-Jose, L., Retolaza, J. L., & Gutierrez-Goiria, J. (2011). Are ethical banks different? A comparative analysis using the radical affinity index. *Journal of Business Ethics*, *100*(1), 151–173. doi:10.100710551-011-0774-4

Compilation of References

Santouridis, I., & Veraki, A. (2017). Customer relationship management and customer satisfaction: The mediating role of relationship quality. *Total Quality Management & Business Excellence, 28*(9-10), 1122–1133. doi:10.1080/14783363.2017.1303889

Saraç, B. T. (2009). Araştırma ve Geliştirme Harcamalarının Ekonomik Buyüme Üzerindeki Etkisi: Panel Veri Analizi. Anadolu International Conference in Economics. Eskişehir, Türkiye.

Saray, M. O., & Hark, R. (2015). OECD Ülkelerinin İleri-Teknoloji Ürünlerindeki Rekabet Güçlerinin Değerlendirilmesi. *Çankırı Karatekin Üniversitesi İktisadi ve İdari Bilimler Fakültesi Dergisi, 5*(1), 347-372.

Sardžoska, E. G., & Tang, T. L. P. (2009). Testing a model of behavioral intentions in the Republic of Macedonia: Differences between the private and the public sectors. *Journal of Business Ethics, 87*(4), 495–517. doi:10.100710551-008-9955-1

Sarıbay, A. Y. (2000). Global ve Yerel Eksende Türkiye. In A. Sarıbay (Ed.), Yirmibirinci Yüzyıla Doğru Global Kapitalizm, Oryantalizm, Yerlicilik", Global ve Yerel Eksende Türkiye. İstanbul, Turkey: Alfa Yayınları.

Sarıçoban, B. S. O. K. (2013). Küresel Rekabette Kümelenme ve İnovasyonun Rolü. *Sosyal ve Beşeri Bilimler Dergisi, 5*(1), 94–104.

Sarıdoğan, E. (2010). *Mikroekonomi ve makroekonomi düzeyinde küresel rekabet gücünü etkileyen faktörler ve stratejiler*. İTO.

Sarıgül, H. (2015). Finansal Okuryazarlık Tutum Ve Davranış Ölçeği: Geliştirme, Geçerlik Ve Güvenirlik. *Yönetim ve Ekonomi Araştırmaları Dergisi, 13*(1), 200–218.

Şarkaya, C. (2017). Finansal İstikrar ve Türkiye Cumhuriyet Merkez Bankasının Para Politikası Stratejisi. *Mehmet Akif Ersoy Üniversitesi Sosyal Bilimler Enstitüsü Dergisi, 9*(20), 20–38.

Sawhney, B., Kulkarni, K. G., & Cachanosky, N. (2017). Monetary policy in India and the US: Is the Taylor rule irrelevant? *International Review of Business and Economics, 1*(1), 75.

Schaeck, K., & Cihak, M. (2008). How does competition affect efficiency and soundness in banking? New empirical evidence. *ECB Working Papers Series*, No. 932.

Schaeck, K., Martin, C., & Wolfe, S. (2006). Are more competitive banking systems more stable? *IMF Working Paper*, No. WP/06/143.

Scheidel, W. (2006). Population and Demography. Princeton/Stanford Working Class Papers in Classics, Stanford University. 2.

Schein, E. H. (2010). *Organizational culture and leadership* (Vol. 2). Hoboken, NJ: John Wiley & Sons.

Schenkel, M. T., Farmer, S., & Maslyn, J. M. (2019). Process improvement in SMEs: The impact of harmonious passion for entrepreneurship, employee creative self-efficacy, and time spent innovating. *Journal of Small Business Strategy, 29*(1), 64–77.

Schlegelmilch, B. B. (2016). Assessing global marketing opportunities. In *Global marketing strategy* (pp. 21–41). Cham, Switzerland: Springer. doi:10.1007/978-3-319-26279-6_2

Schnittker, R., Marshall, S., Horberry, T., & Young, K. L. (2018). Human factors enablers and barriers for successful airway management–an in-depth interview study. *Anaesthesia, 73*(8), 980–989. doi:10.1111/anae.14302 PMID:29660772

Schuetz, C. G., Mair, E., & Schrefl, M. (2018, October). PESTEL Modeler: Strategy analysis using MetaEdit+, iStar 2.0, and semantic technologies. In *2018 IEEE 22nd International Enterprise Distributed Object Computing Workshop (EDOCW)* (pp. 216-219). IEEE.

Schumpeter, J. A. (1934). *The theory of economic growth*. Transaction Publishers (10th Ed.). 2004.

Schwab, K., & Sala-i-Martín, X. (2016, April). The global competitiveness report 2013–2014: Full data edition. World Economic Forum.

Schwartz, S. P., Adair, K. C., Bae, J., Rehder, K. J., Shanafelt, T. D., Profit, J., & Sexton, J. B. (2019). Work-life balance behaviours cluster in work settings and relate to burnout and safety culture: A cross-sectional survey analysis. *BMJ Quality & Safety*, *28*(2), 142–150. doi:10.1136/bmjqs-2018-007933 PMID:30309912

Sefil, S., & Çilingiroğlu, H. K. (2011). Davranışsal finansın temelleri: karar vermenin bilişsel ve duygusal eğilimleri.

Sekman ve Utku (2009). Kurumsal Ataleti Yenmek, 6. Baskı, Alfa Yayınların, 43-44.

Şen, C. C. A. H. (1999). Globalleşme Ekonomik Kriz ve Türkiye. *Tosyöv Yayınları*, 10-12.

Senadza, B., & Diaba, D. D. (2017). Effect of exchange rate volatility on trade in Sub-Saharan Africa. *Journal of African Trade*, *4*(1-2), 20–36. doi:10.1016/j.joat.2017.12.002

Şenel Uzunkaya, S., Dinçer, H., & Yüksel, S. (2019). Evaluating the financial and nonfinancial functions of the waqfs in Ottoman economy.

Şener, S., Yılancı, V., & Tıraşoğlu, M. (2013). Petrol fiyatları ile Borsa İstanbul kapanış fiyatları arasındaki saklı ilişkinin analizi. *Sosyal Ekonomik Araştırmalar Dergisi*, *13*(26), 231–248.

Serel, A., & Bayır, M. (2013). 2008 Finansal Krizinde Para Politikası Uygulamaları: Türkiye Örneği. *Yönetim ve Ekonomi Araştırmaları Dergisi*, *11*(19), 59–80.

Serel, A., & Özkurt, İ. C. (2014). Geleneksel Olmayan Para Politikası Araçları ve Türkiye Cumhuriyet Merkez Bankası. *Yönetim ve Ekonomi Araştırmaları Dergisi*, *12*(22), 56–71.

Serenis, D., & Tsounis, N. (2013). Exchange rate volatility and foreign trade: The case for Cyprus and Croatia. *Procedia Economics and Finance*, *5*, 677–685. doi:10.1016/S2212-5671(13)00079-8

Sewell, W. H. (2004). The concept(s) of culture. In *Practicing history* (pp. 90–110). Routledge.

Seyidoğlu, H. (2003a). *Uluslararası Finans (4.Baskı)*. İstanbul, Turkey: Güzem Can Yayınları.

Seyidoğlu, H. (2003a). *Uluslararası İktisat Teori Politika Ve Uygulama*. İstanbul, Turkey: Güzem Can Yayınları.

Seymen, T. B. O. A. (2005). Çok uluslu İşletmelerin Kavramsal Açıdan İncelenmesi. In T. Seymen (Ed.), Küreselleşme ve Çok Uluslu İşletmecilik (pp. 53-67). Ankara, Turkey: Nobel Yayın Dağıtım.

Sghaier, I. M., & Abida, Z. (2013). Foreign direct investment, financial development and economic growth: empirical evidence from North African countries. *Journal of International and Global Economic Studies*, *6*(1), 1–13.

Shaffer, S. (1993). A test of competition in Canadian banking. *Journal of Money, Credit, and Banking*, *25*(1), 49–61. doi:10.2307/2077819

Shefrin, H. M., & Statman, M. (1984). Explaining investor preference for cash dividends. *Journal of Financial Economics*, *13*(2), 253–282. doi:10.1016/0304-405X(84)90025-4

Shefrin, H., & Statman, M. (1985). The disposition to sell winners too early and ride losers too long: Theory and evidence. *The Journal of Finance*, *40*(3), 777–790. doi:10.1111/j.1540-6261.1985.tb05002.x

Sheikh, S. (2019). Corporate social responsibility and firm leverage: The impact of market competition. *Research in International Business and Finance*, *48*, 496–510. doi:10.1016/j.ribaf.2018.11.002

Compilation of References

Shenkar, O., Luo, Y., & Chi, T. (2014). *International business*. Routledge. doi:10.4324/9780203584866

Shepherd, D. A., Wennberg, K., Suddaby, R., & Wiklund, J. (2019). What are we explaining? A review and agenda on initiating, engaging, performing, and contextualizing entrepreneurship. *Journal of Management*, *45*(1), 159–196. doi:10.1177/0149206318799443

Shepherd, D. A., & Wiklund, J. (2005). *Entrepreneurial small businesses: a resource-based perspective*. Edward Elgar. doi:10.4337/9781845425692

Sherehiy, K., Karwowski, W., & Layer, J. K. (2007). Layer, a review of enterprise agility: concepts, frameworks and attributes. *International Journal of Industrial Ergonomics*, *37*(5), 445–460. doi:10.1016/j.ergon.2007.01.007

Sherman, A. W. Jr, & Bohlander, G. W. (1992). Managing human resources. Cincinnati: South. *Western Publishing Co., Wright, BE, Davis, BS (2003). Job Satisfaction in the Public Sector: The Role of the Work Environment. American Review of Public Administration*, *33*(1), 70–90.

Shilei, L., & Yong, W. (2009). Target-oriented obstacle analysis by PESTEL modeling of energy efficiency retrofit for existing residential buildings in China's northern heating region. *Energy Policy*, *37*(6), 2098–2101. doi:10.1016/j.enpol.2008.11.039

Shiller, R. J. (2003). From efficient markets theory to behavioral finance. *The Journal of Economic Perspectives*, *17*(1), 83–104. doi:10.1257/089533003321164967

Shi, X., Prevett, P., Farnsworth, V., Kwong, K. C., Wan, W., He, F., ... Zhen, L. (2019). Modeling changes to survey response items over time in a Britain financial literacy education study. *Journal of Financial Counseling and Planning*, *30*(1), 56–66. doi:10.1891/1052-3073.30.1.56

Short, B. K. (1979). The relation between commercial bank profit rates and banking concentration in Canada, Western Europe and Japan. *Journal of Banking & Finance*, *3*(3), 209–219. doi:10.1016/0378-4266(79)90016-5

Siami-Namini, S., Hudson, D., Trindade, A. A., & Lyford, C. (2018). *Commodity prices, monetary policy and the Taylor rule* (No. 2015-2018-283).

Siddiqi, M. N. (2006). Islamic banking and finance in theory and practice: A survey of state of the art. *Islamic Economic Studies*, *13*(2).

Siganos, A., Vagenas-Nanos, E., & Verwijmeren, P. (2017). Divergence of sentiment and stock market trading. *Journal of Banking & Finance*, *78*, 130–141. doi:10.1016/j.jbankfin.2017.02.005

Sığrı, Ü., & Tığlı, M. (2014). Hofstede'nin" belirsizlikten kaçınma" kültürel boyutunun yönetsel-örgütsel süreçlerde ve pazarlama açısından tüketici davranışlarına etkisi. *İktisadi ve İdari Bilimler Dergisi; Cilt 21, Sayı 1 (2006); 327-342*.

Simón-Moya, V., Revuelto-Taboada, L., & Guerrero, R. F. (2014). Institutional and economic drivers of entrepreneurship: An international perspective. *Journal of Business Research*, *67*(5), 715–721. doi:10.1016/j.jbusres.2013.11.033

Sims, C. A. (1972). Money, income, and causality. *The American Economic Review*, *62*(4), 540–552.

Şimşek, G. G., & Noyan, F. (2009). Türkiye'de cep telefonu cihazı pazarında marka sadakati için bir model denemesi. *Middle East Technical University Studies in Development*, *36*(1).

Şimşek, H., Bayındır, S., & Ustaoğlu, M. (2017). Dual banking systems' dynamics and a brief development history of Islamic finance in select emerging Islamic economies. In *Balancing Islamic and conventional banking for economic growth* (pp. 9–26). Cham, Switzerland: Palgrave Macmillan. doi:10.1007/978-3-319-59554-2_2

Şimşek, M. (2002). *Total quality management and an application in history: Akhism*. İstanbul, Turkey: Hayat Yayınları.

Sivaramakrishnan, S., Srivastava, M., & Rastogi, A. (2017). Attitudinal factors, financial literacy, and stock market participation. *International Journal of Bank Marketing*, *35*(5), 818–841. doi:10.1108/IJBM-01-2016-0012

Sivrikaya, D. (2012a). *Küreselleşme Sürecinde Çokuluslu Şirketler ile Sivil Toplum Kuruluşlarının İktisadi Etkileşimi. (Yüksek Lisans)*. Ordu, Turkey: Ordu Üniversitesi.

Sivrikaya, D. (2012c). *Küreselleşme Sürecinde Çokuluslu Şirketler ile Sivil Toplum Kuruluşlarının İktisadi Etkileşimleri. (Yüksek Lisans)* (p. 134). Ordu, Turkey: Ordu Üniversitesi.

Skalicky, S., Friginal, E., & Subtirelu, N. (2016). A corpus-assisted investigation of nonunderstanding in outsourced call center discourse. In *Talking at Work* (pp. 127–153). London, UK: Palgrave Macmillan. doi:10.1057/978-1-137-49616-4_6

Skipper, H. D. (2008). *Risk management and insurance: perspectives in a global economy*. Hoboken, NJ: John Wiley & Sons.

Slywotzky, A., & Hoban, C. (2007). Stop competing yourself to death: Strategic collaboration among rivals. *The Journal of Business Strategy*, *28*(3), 45–55. doi:10.1108/02756660710746274

Smaghi, L. B. (2009). *Conventional and unconventional monetary policy* (p. 28). Geneva, Switzerland: Speech at the Center for Monetary and Banking Studies.

Smales, L. A. (2017). The importance of fear: Investor sentiment and stock market returns. *Applied Economics*, *49*(34), 3395–3421. doi:10.1080/00036846.2016.1259754

Smallman, C. (1996). Risk and organizational behaviour: A research model. *Disaster Prevention and Management: An International Journal*, *5*(2), 12–26. doi:10.1108/09653569610112880

Smart, D. T., & Conant, J. S. (1994). Entrepreneurial orientation, distinctive marketing competencies and organizational performance. *Journal of Applied Business Research*, *10*(3), 28–38. doi:10.19030/jabr.v10i3.5921

Smirlock, M. (1985). Evidence on the (non) relationship between concentration and profitability in banking. *Journal of Money, Credit and Banking*, *17*(1), 69–83. doi:10.2307/1992507

Smith, A. (1950). An inquiry into the nature and causes of the wealth of nations, (1776).

Smith, K. G., & Hitt, M. A. (2009). *Great minds in management: the process of theory development*. Oxford, UK: Oxford University Press.

Snowdon, B., & Stonehouse, G. (2006). Competitiveness in a globalised world: Michael Porter on the microeconomic foundations of the competitiveness of nations, regions, and firms. *Journal of International Business Studies*, *37*(2), 163–175. doi:10.1057/palgrave.jibs.8400190

Snyder, H., Witell, L., Gustafsson, A., Fombelle, P., & Kristensson, P. (2016). Identifying categories of service innovation: A review and synthesis of the literature. *Journal of Business Research*, *69*(7), 2401–2408. doi:10.1016/j.jbusres.2016.01.009

Sofyalıoğlu, Ç., & Aktaş, R. (2001). Kültürel farklılıkların uluslararası işletmelere etkisi. *Yönetim ve Ekonomi: Celal Bayar Üniversitesi İktisadi ve İdari Bilimler Fakültesi Dergisi*, *8*(1), 75–92.

Soh, S. B., & Gurvich, I. (2016). Call center staffing: Service-level constraints and index priorities. *Operations Research*, *65*(2), 537–555. doi:10.1287/opre.2016.1532

Sola, H. B., Fernandez, J., Hagras, H., Herrera, F., Pagola, M., & Barrenechea, E. (2015). Interval type-2 fuzzy sets are generalization of interval-valued fuzzy sets: Toward a wider view on their relationship. *IEEE Transactions on Fuzzy Systems*, *23*(5), 1876–1882. doi:10.1109/TFUZZ.2014.2362149

Solan, E., & Yenice, S. (2017). Finansal Gelişmişliğin Finansal Kısıtlara Etkisi: Borsa İstanbul Uygulaması. *Kara Harp Okulu Bilim Dergisi, 27*(1), 25–52.

Soltani, Z., & Navimipour, N. J. (2016). Customer relationship management mechanisms: A systematic review of the state of the art literature and recommendations for future research. *Computers in Human Behavior, 61*, 667–688. doi:10.1016/j.chb.2016.03.008

Somashekar, N. T. (2003). *Development and environmental economics* (p. 239). New Delhi, India: New Age International Publishers.

Song, J., Sun, Y., & Jin, L. (2017). PESTEL analysis of the development of the waste-to-energy incineration industry in China. *Renewable & Sustainable Energy Reviews, 80*, 276–289. doi:10.1016/j.rser.2017.05.066

Sönmez, M. (2011). *Analysis of knowledge and technology transfer by multinational companies to local suppliers in the Turkish automotive industry.* In M. B. Steger (Ed.), *Küreselleşme* (A. Ersoy, Trans.), Ankara, Turkey: Dost Kitabevi.

Soysal, A. (2013). The importance of Akhism principles and applications in business success: an evaluation. *Çimento Endüstri İşverenleri Sendikası*, 6-19.

Srdjevic, Z., Bajcetic, R., & Srdjevic, B. (2012). Identifying the criteria set for multicriteria decision making based on SWOT/PESTLE analysis: A case study of reconstructing a water intake structure. *Water Resources Management, 26*(12), 3379–3393. doi:10.100711269-012-0077-2

Sridhar, R., Sachithanandam, V., Mageswaran, T., Purvaja, R., Ramesh, R., Senthil Vel, A., & Thirunavukkarasu, E. (2016). A political, economic, social, technological, legal, and environmental (PESTLE) approach for assessment of coastal zone management practice in India. *International Review of Public Administration, 21*(3), 216–232. doi:10.1080/12294659.2016.1237091

Srinivasan, K., & Saravanan, S. (2015). Principles and practices of customer relationship management in Ethiopian banks. *EXCEL International Journal of Multidisciplinary Management Studies, 5*(8), 8–20.

Statman, M. (2017). Financial advertising in the second generation of behavioral finance. *Journal of Behavioral Finance, 18*(4), 470–477. doi:10.1080/15427560.2017.1365236

Steiss, A. W. (2003). *Strategic management for public and nonprofit organizations.* New York: Marcel Dekker. Strategic planning: The state of the art. *Long Range Planning, 14*(2), 32–39.

Stepanov, E., Favre, B., Alam, F., Chowdhury, S., Singla, K., Trione, J., ... Riccardi, G. (2015, December). Automatic summarization of call-center conversations. In *Proc. of the IEEE Automatic Speech Recognition and Understanding Workshop (ASRU 2015).* IEEE.

Stoyanova, Z., & Harizanova-Bartos, H. (2017). PESTEL analysis of project management in water sector in Bulgaria. In *Conference Proceedings/International scientific conference ITEMA 2017 Recent Advances in Information Technology, Tourism, Economics, Management and Agriculture.* Association of Economists and Managers of the Balkans, Belgrade, Serbia.

Strzelczyk, M., & Chłąd, M. (2019). Use of Pestel analysis for assessing the situation of Polish transport enterprises (Part II). *Organizacja i Zarządzanie: kwartalnik naukowy*, (1 (45)), 61-75.

Stubbart, C. (1982). Are environmental scanning units effective? *Long Range Planning, 15*(3), 139–145. doi:10.1016/0024-6301(82)90035-8 PMID:10298730

Stulz, R. M. (1996). Rethinking risk management. *Journal of Applied Corporate Finance, 9*(3), 8–25. doi:10.1111/j.1745-6622.1996.tb00295.x

Subba, D., & Kumar, S. (2018). Employees' responses to corporate social responsibility: A study among the employees of banking industry in India. *Decision (Washington, D.C.), 45*(4), 301–312. doi:10.100740622-018-0194-8

Su, C. H., & Chen, P. K. (2016). Applying project management for new service development. *International Journal of Innovation Science, 8*(3), 185–198. doi:10.1108/IJIS-09-2016-013

Sui, L., & Sun, L. (2016). Spillover effects between exchange rates and stock prices: Evidence from BRICS around the recent global financial crisis. *Research in International Business and Finance, 36,* 459–471. doi:10.1016/j.ribaf.2015.10.011

Sümer, N., Lajunen, T., & Özkan, T. (2005). Big five personality traits as the distal predictors of road accident. *Traffic and Transport Psychology: Theory and Application, 215,* 215–227.

Sungur, O., Aydin, H., & Mehmet, E. R. E. N. (2016). Türkiye'de AR-GE, İnovasyon, İhracat ve Ekonomik Büyüme Arasındaki İlişki: Asimetrik Nedensellik Analizi. *Süleyman Demirel Üniversitesi İktisadi ve İdari Bilimler Fakültesi Dergisi, 21*(1), 174.

Sung, Y., Lee, J.-A., & Choi, S. M. (2016). Why we post selfies: Understanding motivations for posting pictures of oneself. *Personality and Individual Differences, 97,* 260–265. doi:10.1016/j.paid.2016.03.032

Sun, P. H., Mohamad, S., & Ariff, M. (2017). Determinants driving bank performance: A comparison of two types of banks in the OIC. *Pacific-Basin Finance Journal, 42,* 193–203. doi:10.1016/j.pacfin.2016.02.007

Sürgevil, O., & Budak, G. (2008). İşletmelerin farklılıkların yönetimi anlayışına yaklaşım tarzlarının saptanmasına yönelik bir araştırma. *Dokuz Eylül Üniversitesi Sosyal Bilimler Enstitüsü Dergisi, 10*(4), 65–96.

Svirydzenka, K. (2016). Introducing a new broad-based index of financial development. IMF Working Paper WP/16/5. Retrieved from https://www.imf.org/external/pubs/ft/wp/ 2016/wp1605.pdf

Swendeman, D., Jana, S., Ray, P., Mindry, D., Das, M., & Bhakta, B. (2015). Development and pilot testing of daily interactive voice response (IVR) calls to support antiretroviral adherence in India: A mixed-methods pilot study. *AIDS and Behavior, 19*(2), 142–155. doi:10.100710461-014-0983-9 PMID:25638037

Sylwester, K. (2001). R&D and economic growth. *Knowledge, Technology, & Policy, 13*(4), 71–84. doi:10.1007/BF02693991

Taban, S., Günsoy, B., Günsoy, G., Erdinç, Z., & Aktaş, M. (2013). İktisadi Büyüme. T.C Anadolu Üniversitesi Yayını No: 2898 Web-Ofset, Eskişehir, 147.

Taggart, J. H., & McDermott, M. C. (1993). *The essence of international business.* London, UK.

Talón-Ballestero, P., González-Serrano, L., Soguero-Ruiz, C., Muñoz-Romero, S., & Rojo-Álvarez, J. L. (2018). Using big data from customer relationship management information systems to determine the client profile in the hotel sector. *Tourism Management, 68,* 187–197. doi:10.1016/j.tourman.2018.03.017

Tanaka, S., Murakami, K., & Takebayashi, Y. (2019). Survey analysis on the installation utilization pattern and renovation details of the cogeneration systems in the district heat supply system of the Tokyo metropolitan area. *Journal of Environmental Engineering (Japan), 84*(757), 303–312. doi:10.3130/aije.84.303

Tang, C. F. (2008). Wagner's law versus Keynesian hypothesis: New evidence from recursive regression-based causality approaches. *The IUP Journal of Public Finance, 6*(4), 29–38.

Tang, T. L. P., & Chen, Y. J. (2008). Intelligence vs. wisdom: The love of money, Machiavellianism, and unethical behavior across college major and gender. *Journal of Business Ethics, 82*(1), 1–26. doi:10.100710551-007-9559-1

Tang, T. L. P., & Chiu, R. K. (2003). Income, money ethic, pay satisfaction, commitment, and unethical behavior: Is the love of money the root of evil for Hong Kong employees? *Journal of Business Ethics, 46*(1), 13–30. doi:10.1023/A:1024731611490

Tang, T. L. P., & Liu, H. (2012). Love of money and unethical behavior intention: Does an authentic supervisor's personal integrity and character (ASPIRE) make a difference? *Journal of Business Ethics*, *107*(3), 295–312. doi:10.100710551-011-1040-5

Tang, Z., & Dinçer, H. (2019). Selecting the house-of-quality-based energy investment policies for the sustainable emerging economies. *Sustainability*, *11*(13), 3514. doi:10.3390u11133514

Tan, L., Chew, B., & Hamid, S. (2017). A holistic perspective on sustainable banking operating system drivers. *Qualitative Research in Financial Markets*, *9*(3), 240–262. doi:10.1108/QRFM-12-2016-0052

Tarı, R., & Yıldırım, D. Ç. (2009). Döviz Kuru Belirsizliğinin İhracata Etkisi: Türkiye İçin Bir Uygulama. Celal Bayar Üniversiteis İİBF Yönetim ve Ekonomi, 16(2), 95–105.

Tarı, R. (2002). *Ekonometri*. Alfa Basım Yayım Dağıtım.

Tarı, R. (2016). *Ekonometri. Küv Yayınları 12*. İstanbul, Turkey: Baskı.

Taşkıran Öncel, N. (2007). *Medya Okuryazarlığına Giriş*. İstanbul, Turkey: Beta Yayınları.

Taşlıca, A. O. (1999). *Çok Uluslu İşletmeler ve Türkiye*. Paper presented at the Anadolu Üniversitesi, İİBF Yayınları Eskişehir.

Taştan, S. (2005). Küreselleşme ve Küresel Strateji.

Tatoğlu, F. Y., Tunalı, H., & Ustaoğlu, M. (2017). The Turkish economy and financing growth by dual banking: empirical evidence. In *Balancing Islamic and conventional banking for economic growth* (pp. 47–68). Cham, Switzerland: Palgrave Macmillan. doi:10.1007/978-3-319-59554-2_4

Tauni, M. Z., Fang, H. X., & Yousaf, S. (2015). The influence of Investor personality traits on information acquisition and trading behavior: Evidence from Chinese futures exchange. *Personality and Individual Differences*, *87*, 248–255. doi:10.1016/j.paid.2015.08.026

Taylor, J. B. (1993, December). Discretion versus policy rules in practice.

Taylor, J. W. (2008). A comparison of univariate time series methods for forecasting intraday arrivals at a call center. *Management Science*, *54*(2), 253–265. doi:10.1287/mnsc.1070.0786

Tchankova, L. (2002). Risk identification–basic stage in risk management. *Environmental Management and Health*, *13*(3), 290–297. doi:10.1108/09566160210431088

Tease, W. (1993). The stock market and investment. *Behaviour*, *1*, 11.

Tekin, Z. (1997). İstanbul Debbağhaneleri. *Ankara Üniversitesi Osmanlı Tarihi Araştırma ve Uygulamaları Merkezi Dergisi*, 348-397.

Terdudomtham, K. T. T. (2004). *Evolution of inter-firm techonology transfer and technological capability formation of local parts firms in the Thai automobile industry journal of technology innovation*, *12*, 2–20.

Terpstra, V., Foley, J., & Sarathy, R. (2012). *International marketing*. Naper Press.

Tetik, M., & Ceylan, R. (2015). Faiz Koridoru Stratejisinin Hisse Senedi Fiyatlari ve Döviz Kuru Üzerine Etkisinin Incelenmesi/Analysis of the effect of interest rate corridor strategy on common stock and exchange rate. *Business and Economics Research Journal*, *6*(4), 55.

Thaler, R. H., & Ganser, L. J. (2015). *Misbehaving: The making of behavioral economics*. New York: WW Norton.

Thomas, P. (2009). *Strategic management*. Course at Chalmers University of Technology.

Thomas, P. S. (1980). Environmental scanning—The state of the art. *Long Range Planning, 13*(1), 20–28. doi:10.1016/0024-6301(80)90051-5

Thompson, P. H. G. (2007). *Küreselleşme Sorgulanıyor* (Ç. E. v. E. Yücel, Trans.). Ankara, Turkey: Dost Kitabevi

Thorbecke, W. (1997). On stock market returns and monetary policy. *The Journal of Finance, 52*(2), 635–654. doi:10.1111/j.1540-6261.1997.tb04816.x

Ting, X., Yong, B., Yin, L., & Mi, T. (2016). Patient perception and the barriers to practicing patient-centered communication: A survey and in-depth interview of Chinese patients and physicians. *Patient Education and Counseling, 99*(3), 364–369. doi:10.1016/j.pec.2015.07.019 PMID:26776708

Toda, H. Y., & Yamamoto, T. (1995). Statistical inference in vector autoregressions with possibly integrated processes. *Journal of Econometrics, 66*(1–2), 225–250. doi:10.1016/0304-4076(94)01616-8

Todaro, M., & Smith, S. C. (2003). *Economic development*. New York: Addison Wesley.

Tolga, O. R. A. L., Polat, E., & Ahmet, Ş. İ. T. (2017). *Borsa İstanbul Kurumsal Yönetim Endeksinde Yer Alan Şirketlerin Sermaye Yapıları İle Hisse Senedi Getirileri Arasındaki İlişkinin İncelenmesi, 8*(1), 16.

Tomanbay, M. (2014). *Uluslararası Ticaret ve Finansmanı*. Ankara, Turkey: Gazi Kitabevi.

Topal, M. H. (2018). Türkiye'de askeri harcamalar ile ekonomik büyüme arasındaki ilişkinin bir analizi (1960-2016). *Maliye Dergisi, 174*, 175–202.

Tosun, C., & Bağdadioğlu, N. (2016). Evaluating gender responsive budgeting in Turkey. *International Journal of Monetary Economics and Finance, 9*(2), 187–197. doi:10.1504/IJMEF.2016.076481

Tosunoğlu, B. T. (2003). *Girişimcilik ve Türkiye'nin ekonomik gelişme sürecinde girişimciliğin yeri*. Eskişehir Anadolu Üniversitesi Sosyal Bilimler Enstitüsü Yayımlanmamış Doktora Tezi.

Truslow, D. K. (2003). Operational risk management? It's everyone's job. *The R Journal, 85*(5), 34–37.

Tsangas, M., Jeguirim, M., Limousy, L., & Zorpas, A. (2019). The application of analytical hierarchy process in combination with PESTEL-SWOT analysis to assess the hydrocarbons sector in Cyprus. *Energies, 12*(5), 791. doi:10.3390/en12050791

Tunay, K. B. (2009). Competition and fragility in Turkish banking sector. *Bankacılar Dergisi*, 68, 30-55. Retrieved from https://www.tbb.org.tr/Dosyalar/Arastirma_ve_Raporlar/kirilganlik.pdf

Tunay, N., Yüksel, S., & Tunay, K. B. (2019). The Effects of Technology on Bank Performance in Advanced and Emerging Economies: An Empirical Analysis. In Handbook of research on managerial thinking in global business economics (pp. 263–280). Hershey, PA: IGI Global. doi:10.4018/978-1-5225-7180-3.ch015

Tuncel, G., & Alpan, G. (2010). Risk assessment and management for supply chain networks: A case study. *Computers in Industry, 61*(3), 250–259. doi:10.1016/j.compind.2009.09.008

Turan, Z., & Öztürk, Y. K. (2016). Keynes sistemi ve bekleyişlerin sisteme katkısı. *Niğde Üniversitesi İktisadi ve İdari Bilimler Fakültesi Dergisi*, 9(2).

Turkyilmaz, A., Guney, M., Karaca, F., Bagdatkyzy, Z., Sandybayeva, A., & Sirenova, G. (2019). A comprehensive construction and demolition waste management model using PESTEL and 3R for construction companies operating in Central Asia. *Sustainability, 11*(6), 1593. doi:10.3390u11061593

Tushaj, A. (2010). Market concentration in the banking sector: Evidence from Albania. BERG Working Paper Series No. 73.

Ulengin, F., Önsel, Ş., & Kaaata, S. (2011). Türkiye'nin Küresel Rekabet Düzeyi: Dünya Ekonomik Forumu Küresel Rekabetçilik Raporu'na Göre Bir Değerlendirme. *TÜSİAD-Sabancı Üniversitesi Rekabet Forumu, Sektörel Dernekler Federasyonu Yayını, 1*.

Ülgen, G., & Özalp, L. F. A. (2017). Bir Refah Devleti Analizi: Ekonomik ve Sosyal Sonuçlar. *Siyasal Bilimler Dergisi, 5*(2), 219–243.

Ülkü, H. (2004). R&D, innovation and economic growth: an empirical analysis. *IMF Working Paper, 4*(185), 1. doi:10.5089/9781451859447.001

UNCTAD. (1997). Transnational corporations, market structure and competition policy. UN.

UNCTAD. (2003). *FDI policies for development: National and international perspectives. World Investment Report*. New York: UNCTAD.

UNCTAD. (2019). World Investment Report 2019. Special economic zones key messages and overview. United Nations, Geneva. Retrieved from https://unctad.org/en/Publications Library/wir2019_overview_en.pdf

Ünlü, U., & Topcu, M. (2012). Petrol fiyatları hisse senedi piyasalarını doğrudan etkiler mi: İMKB örneği. *İktisat İşletme ve Finans, 27*(319), 75-88.

Ural, M. (2014). *Bankacılıkta yoğunlaşma, rekabet ve füzyon. Editorlör: O. Altay, C. Küçüközmen, M. Ural, E. Demireli. Banka İktisadı ve İşletmeciliği*. Ankara, Turkey: Detay Yayıncılık.

Usmani, M. M. T. (2001). An introduction to Islamic finance. In *An introduction to Islamic finance*. Brill Publishing.

Valdes, B. (1999). *Economic growth: theory, empirics and policy* (p. 137). UK: Edward Elgar.

Valentine, S., & Godkin, L. (2017). Banking employees' perceptions of corporate social responsibility, value-fit commitment, and turnover intentions: ethics as social glue and attachment. *Employee Responsibilities and Rights Journal, 29*(2), 51–71. doi:10.100710672-017-9290-8

Van Stel, A., & Storey, D. (2004). The link between firm births and job creation: Is there a Upas tree effect? *Regional Studies, 38*(8), 893–909. doi:10.1080/0034340042000280929

Vegholm, F. (2011). Relationship marketing and the management of corporate image in the bank-SME relationship. *Management Research Review, 34*(3), 325–336. doi:10.1108/01409171111116330

Venkataraman, S. (2019). The distinctive domain of entrepreneurship research. In *Seminal ideas for the next twenty-five years of advances* (pp. 5–20). Emerald Publishing. doi:10.1108/S1074-754020190000021009

Venkatraman, N., & Ramanujam, V. (1986). Measurement of business performance in strategy research: A comparison of approaches. *Academy of Management Review, 11*(4), 801–814. doi:10.5465/amr.1986.4283976

Vergil, H. (2002). Exchange rate volatility in Turkey and its effect on trade flows. *Journal of Economic and Social Research, 4*(1), 83–99.

Versloot, M. (2016). *Turbulence in the higher education publishing industry due to open access: a PESTEL analysis* (Bachelor's thesis, University of Twente).

Vezzoli, C., Ceschin, F., Diehl, J. C., & Kohtala, C. (2015). New design challenges to widely implement 'Sustainable product–service systems'. *Journal of Cleaner Production, 97*, 1–12. doi:10.1016/j.jclepro.2015.02.061

Visnjic, I., Wiengarten, F., & Neely, A. (2016). Only the brave: Product innovation, service business model innovation, and their impact on performance. *Journal of Product Innovation Management*, *33*(1), 36–52. doi:10.1111/jpim.12254

Vissing-Jorgensen, A. (2003). Perspectives on behavioral finance: Does" irrationality" disappear with wealth? Evidence from expectations and actions. *NBER Macroeconomics Annual*, *18*, 139–194. doi:10.1086/ma.18.3585252

Vitor Jordão da Gama Silva, P., Brandalise Santos, J., & Portes Pereira, G. (2019). Behavioral finance in Brazil: A bibliometric study from 2007 to 2017. *Latin American Business Review*, 1–22.

Vohs, K. D., Mead, N. L., & Goode, M. R. (2006). The psychological consequences of money. *Science*, *314*(5802), 1154–1156. doi:10.1126cience.1132491 PMID:17110581

Wallace, C. M., Eagleson, G., & Waldersee, R. (2000). The sacrificial HR strategy in call centers. *International Journal of Service Industry Management*, *11*(2), 174–184. doi:10.1108/09564230010323741

Walsh, P. R. (2005). Dealing with the uncertainties of environmental change by adding scenario planning to the strategy reformulation equation. *Management Decision*, *43*(1), 113–122. doi:10.1108/00251740510572524

Wang, E. C. (2007). R&D efficiency and economic performance: a cross-country analysis using the stochastics frontier approach. *Journal of Policy Modeling*, *29*(2), 345–360. doi:10.1016/j.jpolmod.2006.12.005

Wang, R., Morley, B., & Ordóñez, J. (2016). The Taylor rule, wealth effects and the exchange rate. *Review of International Economics*, *24*(2), 282–301. doi:10.1111/roie.12213

Wang, R., Morley, B., & Stamatogiannis, M. P. (2019). Forecasting the exchange rate using nonlinear Taylor rule based models. *International Journal of Forecasting*, *35*(2), 429–442. doi:10.1016/j.ijforecast.2018.07.017

Wang, S., Cavusoglu, H., & Deng, Z. (2016). Early mover advantage in e-commerce platforms with low entry barriers: The role of customer relationship management capabilities. *Information & Management*, *53*(2), 197–206. doi:10.1016/j.im.2015.09.011

Wang, Y. Y., Chih, H. H., & Chou, R. K. (2016). Review of behavioral finance studies in Taiwan. *Jing Ji Lun Wen Cong Kan*, *44*(1), 1–55.

Wang, Y., Tian, L., & Chen, Z. (2019). A reputation bootstrapping model for E-commerce based on fuzzy DEMATEL method and neural network. *IEEE Access: Practical Innovations, Open Solutions*, *7*, 52266–52276. doi:10.1109/ACCESS.2019.2912191

Wang, Y., Wu, C., & Yang, L. (2013). Oil price shocks and stock market activities: Evidence from oil-importing and oil-exporting countries. *Journal of Comparative Economics*, *41*(4), 1220–1239. doi:10.1016/j.jce.2012.12.004

Wang, Z., & Kim, H. G. (2017). Can social media marketing improve customer relationship capabilities and firm performance? Dynamic capability perspective. *Journal of Interactive Marketing*, *39*, 15–26. doi:10.1016/j.intmar.2017.02.004

Wang, Z., & Sarkis, J. (2017). Corporate social responsibility governance, outcomes, and financial performance. *Journal of Cleaner Production*, *162*, 1607–1616. doi:10.1016/j.jclepro.2017.06.142

Weber, M., & Camerer, C. F. (1998). The disposition effect in securities trading: An experimental analysis. *Journal of Economic Behavior & Organization*, *33*(2), 167–184. doi:10.1016/S0167-2681(97)00089-9

Weigl, T. (2008). *Strategy, structure and performance in a transition economy*. Gabler. GWV.

Weinberg, J., Brown, L. D., & Stroud, J. R. (2007). Bayesian forecasting of an inhomogeneous Poisson process with applications to call center data. *Journal of the American Statistical Association*, *102*(480), 1185–1198. doi:10.1198/016214506000001455

Welch, L. S., & Luostarinen, R. (1988). Internationalization: Evolution of a concept. *Journal of General Management*, *14*(2), 34–55. doi:10.1177/030630708801400203

Wennekers, S., Van Wennekers, A., Thurik, R., & Reynolds, P. (2005). Nascent entrepreneurship and the level of economic development. *Small Business Economics*, *24*(3), 293–309. doi:10.100711187-005-1994-8

Westfall, P. H. (2014). Kurtosis as peakedness, 1905–2014. RIP. *The American statistician*, *68*(3), 191–195. doi:10.1080/00031305.2014.917055 PMID:25678714

Wheelen, T. L., & Hunger, J. D. (2011). *Concepts in strategic management and business policy*. Pearson Education India.

Wheelen, T. L., Hunger, J. D., & Hoffman, A. N. (2012). *Strategic management and business policy toward global sustainability* (13th ed.). New Jersey: Pearson Education.

Wheelen, T. L., Hunger, J. D., Hoffman, A. N., & Bamford, C. E. (2010). *Strategic management and business policy*. Upper Saddle River, NJ: Prentice Hall.

Whitesell, W. (2006). Interest rate corridors and reserves. *Journal of Monetary Economics*, *53*(6), 1177–1195. doi:10.1016/j.jmoneco.2005.03.013

Widana, G. O., Wiryono, S. K., Purwanegara, M. S., & Toha, M. (2015). Exploring the impact of Islamic business ethics and relationship marketing orientation on business performance: the Islamic banking experience. Asian Academy of Management Journal, 20(1).

Widya Yudha, S., Tjahjono, B., & Kolios, A. (2018). A PESTLE policy mapping and stakeholder analysis of Indonesia's fossil fuel energy industry. *Energies*, *11*(5), 1272. doi:10.3390/en11051272

Wikipedia. Transaction deposit. Retrieved from https://en.wikipedia.org/wiki/Transaction_deposit

Wiklund, J., Lomberg, C., Alkærsig, L., & Miller, D. (2019, July). When ADHD helps and harms in entrepreneurship: an epidemiological approach. In Academy of Management Proceedings (Vol. 2019, No. 1, p. 17481). Briarcliff Manor, NY 10510: Academy of Management.

Wiklund, J., & Shepherd, D. (2005). Entrepreneurial orientation and small business performance: A configurational approach. *Journal of Business Venturing*, *20*(1), 71–91. doi:10.1016/j.jbusvent.2004.01.001

Williams, C. A., Smith, M. L., & Young, P. C. (1998). *Risk management and insurance* (Doctoral dissertation, Univerza v Mariboru, Ekonomsko-poslovna fakulteta).

Williams, L. J., & Anderson, S. E. (1991). Job satisfaction and organizational commitment as predictors of organizational citizenship and in-role behaviors. *Journal of Management*, *17*(3), 601–617. doi:10.1177/014920639101700305

Williams, M. J., Bélanger, J. J., Horgan, J., & Evans, W. P. (2018). Experimental effects of a call-center disclaimer regarding confidentiality on callers' willingness to make disclosures related to terrorism. *Terrorism and Political Violence*, 1–15. doi:10.1080/09546553.2018.1476347

Williamson, S. D. (2014). *Macroeconomics* (5th ed.). London, UK: Pearson Education.

Wilson, R. S., Yu, L., James, B. D., Bennett, D. A., & Boyle, P. A. (2017). Association of financial and health literacy with cognitive health in old age. *Neuropsychology, Development, and Cognition. Section B, Aging, Neuropsychology and Cognition*, *24*(2), 186–197. doi:10.1080/13825585.2016.1178210 PMID:27263546

Witell, L., Anderson, L., Brodie, R. J., Colurcio, M., Edvardsson, B., Kristensson, P., ... Wallin Andreassen, T. (2015). Exploring dualities of service innovation: Implications for service research. *Journal of Services Marketing*, *29*(6/7), 436–441. doi:10.1108/JSM-01-2015-0051

Womack, J. P., Byrne, A. P., Flume, O. J., Kaplan, S. G., & Toussaint, J. (2005). Going lean in health care. *Institute for Healthcare Improvement, 7,* 1-20. Retrieved from https://www.garantibbvainvestorrelations.com/en/images/annualreport/pdf/GBFR17_eng_FULL.pdf

Wong, P. K., Ho, Y. P., & Autio, E. (2005). Entrepreneurship, innovation and economic growth: Evidence from GEM data. *Small Business Economics, 24*(3), 335–350. doi:10.100711187-005-2000-1

Woods, M. (2012). *Risk management in organizations: An integrated case study approach.* Routledge. doi:10.4324/9780203815922

Wu, F., Mahajan, V., & Balasubramanian, S. (2003). An analysis of e-business adoption and its impact on business performance. *Journal of the Academy of Marketing Science, 31*(4), 425–447. doi:10.1177/0092070303255379

Wu, M.-W., & Shen, C.-H. (2013). Corporate social responsibility in the banking industry: Motives and financial performance. *Journal of Banking & Finance, 37*(9), 3529–3547. doi:10.1016/j.jbankfin.2013.04.023

Xiaoming, C., & Junchen, H. (2012). A literature review on organization culture and corporate performance. *International Journal of Business Administration, 3*(2), 28–37.

Xue, R., Gepp, A., O'Neill, T., Stern, S., & Vanstone, B. J. (2019, April). Financial literacy and financial decision-making: The mediating role of financial concerns. In The 10th Financial Markets & Corporate Governance Conference: Capital Markets, Sustainability and Disruptive Technologies.

Xue, R., Gepp, A., O'Neill, T. J., Stern, S., & Vanstone, B. J. (2019). Financial literacy amongst elderly Australians. *Accounting and Finance, 59*(S1), 887–918. doi:10.1111/acfi.12362

Xu, X. E., & Chen, T. (2012). The effect of monetary policy on real estate price growth in China. *Pacific-Basin Finance Journal, 20*(1), 62–77. doi:10.1016/j.pacfin.2011.08.001

Xu, Y., He, K., Kenneth, L. K. K., & Lai, K. K. (2014, July). A behavioral finance analysis on ETF investment behavior. In *2014 Seventh International Joint Conference on Computational Sciences and Optimization* (pp. 386-389). IEEE. 10.1109/CSO.2014.81

Yalçıner, K., Atan, M., & Boztosun, D. (2005). Finansal Oranlarla Hisse Senedi Getirileri Arasındaki İlişki. *Muhasebe ve Finansman Dergisi,* (27), 176–187.

Yaldız Hanedar, E. (2016). Rekabetçi bankacilik sektörü firmalarin krediye erişimlerini kolaylaştirir mi? *BDDK Bankacılık ve Finansal Piyasalar Dergisi, 10*(2), 9–27.

Yaldız, E., & Bazzana, F. (2010). The effect of market power on bank risk taking in Turkey. *Financial Theory and Practice, 34*(3), 297–314.

Yamak, R., & Korkmaz, A. (2005). Reel döviz kuru ve dış ticaret dengesi ilişkisi. *İstanbul Üniversitesi İktisat Fakültesi Ekonometri ve İstatistik Dergisi,* (2), 16–38.

Yamak, R., & Akyazı, H. (2010). Fiyat istikrarının sağlanmasında para kurulu sistemi ve Türkiye. *Atatürk Üniversitesi İktisadi ve İdari Bilimler Dergisi, 12*(1), 1–26.

Yanar, R. (2008). Gelişmekte olan ülkelerde döviz kuru rejim tercihinin makro ekonomik performans üzerine etkileri. *Gaziantep Üniversitesi Sosyal Bilimler Dergisi, 7*(2), 255–270.

Yang, Y., Lee, P. K., & Cheng, T. C. E. (2016). Continuous improvement competence, employee creativity, and new service development performance: A frontline employee perspective. *International Journal of Production Economics, 171,* 275–288. doi:10.1016/j.ijpe.2015.08.006

Compilation of References

Yapraklı, S. (2009). Türkiye'de esnek döviz kuru rejimi altında dış açıkların belirleyicileri: Sınır testi yaklaşımı giriş. *Ankara Üniversitesi Sbf Dergisi*, 141–164.

Yayla, M. (2007). Türk bankacılık sektöründe yoğunlaşma ve rekabet. *BDDK Bankacılık ve Finansal Piyasalar Dergisi*, *1*(1), 35–59.

Yazidi, J. (2013). *Impact of exchange rate on trade balance*. The Open University of Tanzania.

Yee, L. S., Mun, H. W., Zhengyi, T., Ying, L. J., & Xin, K. K. (2016). Determinants of export: Empirical study in Malaysia. *Journal of International Business and Economics*, *4*(1), 61–75. doi:10.15640/jibe.v4n1a6

Ye, J., & Kulathunga, K. M. M. C. B. (2019). How does financial literacy promote sustainability in SMEs? A developing country perspective. *Sustainability*, *11*(10), 2990. doi:10.3390u11102990

Yermack, D. (2015). Is Bitcoin a real currency? An economic appraisal. In *Handbook of digital currency* (pp. 31–43). Academic Press. doi:10.1016/B978-0-12-802117-0.00002-3

Yeyati, E. L., & Micco, A. (2007). Concentration and foreign penetration in Latin American banking sectors: Impact on competition and risk. *Journal of Banking & Finance*, *31*(6), 1633–1647. doi:10.1016/j.jbankfin.2006.11.003

Yiğit, F., & Muzır, E. (2019). Efficiency of the Major Borsa Istanbul indexes: An empirical investigation about the interaction between corporate governance and equity prices through a market model approach. *Ekonomi İşletme ve Maliye Araştırmaları Dergisi*, *1*(3), 237–245.

Yılancı, V., & Bozoklu, Ş. (2014). Türk sermaye piyasasında fiyat ve işlem hacmi ilişkisi: Zamanla Değişen Asimetrik Nedensellik Analizi. *Ege Academic Review*, *14*(2), 211–220.

Yılancı, V., & Eris, Z. A. (2013). Purchasing power parity in African countries: further evidence from fourier unit root tests based on linear and nonlinear models. *The South African Journal of Economics*, *81*(1), 20–34. doi:10.1111/j.1813-6982.2012.01326.x

Yılmaz, A. (2007). *Romantizmden Gerçeğe Küreselleşme*. Ankara, Turkey: Minima Yayıncılık.

Yılmaz, G. (2017). Restoranlarda bahşiş ile ilgili yayınlanan makalelerin bibliyometrik analizi. *Seyahat ve Otel İşletmeciliği Dergisi*, *14*(2), 65–79. doi:10.24010oid.335082

Ylimäki, J., & Vesalainen, J. (2015). Relational development of a service concept: Dialogue meets efficiency. *Journal of Business and Industrial Marketing*, *30*(8), 939–950. doi:10.1108/JBIM-05-2014-0100

Young, J. (2006). *Operational risk management-the practical application of a qualitative approach*. Pretoria, South Africa: Van Schaik Publishers.

Yücel, F. (2006). Dış ticaretin belirleyicileri üzerine teorik bir yaklaşım. *Sosyo Ekonomi*, *2*, 46–68.

Yücel, R. (1999). İnsan kaynakları yönetiminde başarı değerlendirme. *Dokuz Eylül Üniversitesi Sosyal Bilimler Enstitüsü Dergisi*, *1*(3), 110–128.

Yücememiş, B. T., Alkan, U., & Ağırdır, C. (2015). Yeni Bir Para Politikası Aracı Olarak Faiz Koridoru: Türkiye'de Para Politikası Kurulu Faiz Kararlarının Enflasyon Üzerindeki Etkisi. *Journal of Financial Researches & Studies/Finansal Arastirmalar ve Calismalar Dergisi*, *7*(13), 449-478.

Yu, E., & Sangiorgi, D. (2018). Exploring the transformative impacts of service design: The role of designer–client relationships in the service development process. *Design Studies*, *55*, 79–111. doi:10.1016/j.destud.2017.09.001

Yueh, L. (2009). China's entrepreneurs. *World Development*, *37*(4), 778–786. doi:10.1016/j.worlddev.2008.07.010

Yüksel, S., & Kavak, P. T. (2019). Do financial investment decisions affect economic development?: An analysis on mortgage loans in Turkey. In Handbook of research on global issues in financial communication and investment decision making (pp. 168-191). Hershey, PA: IGI Global.

Yüksel, S., & Zengin, S. (2016). Identifying the determinants of interest rate risk of the banks: a case of Turkish banking sector. *International Journal of Research in Business and Social Science (2147-4478), 5*(6), 12-28.

Yuksel, S., Dinçer, H., & Emir, S. (2018). Analysis of service innovation performance in turkish banking sector using a combining method of fuzzy MCDM and text mining. *MANAS Sosyal Araştırmalar Dergisi, 7*(3).

Yuksel, S., Dinçer, H., & Emir, S. (2018). Analysis of service innovation performance in Turkish banking sector using a combining method of fuzzy MCDM and text mining. *MANAS Sosyal Araştırmalar Dergisi, 7*(3).

Yuksel, S., Dincer, H., & Hacioglu, U. (2015). CAMELS-based determinants for the credit rating of Turkish deposit banks. *International Journal of Finance & Banking Studies (2147-4486), 4*(4), 1-17.

Yuksel, H., Kuzey, C., & Sevinc, E. (2012). The impact of exchange rate volatility on exports in Turkey. *European Journal of Economic and Political Studies, 5*(2), 5–19.

Yüksel, Ö. (1999a). *Uluslararası İşletme Yönetimi ve Türkiye Uygulamaları*. Ankara, Turkey: Gazi Kitabevi.

Yüksel, S. (2016). Rusya ekonomisinde büyüme, işsizlik ve enflasyon arasındaki nedensellik ilişkileri. *Finans Politik ve Ekonomik Yorumlar, 53*(614), 43–56.

Yüksel, S. (2016). Rusya Ekonomisinde Büyüme, Issizlik ve Enflasyon Arasindaki Nedensellik Iliskileri/The causality relationship between growth, unemployment and inflation in Russian economy. *Finans Politik & Ekonomik Yorumlar, 53*(614), 43.

Yüksel, S. (2017). Determinants of the credit risk in developing countries after economic crisis: A case of Turkish banking sector. In *Global financial crisis and its ramifications on capital markets* (pp. 401–415). Cham, Switzerland: Springer. doi:10.1007/978-3-319-47021-4_28

Yüksel, S. (2017). Strategies out of global recession in emerging markets: an application for 2008 global crisis. In *Global business strategies in crisis* (pp. 57–75). Cham, Switzerland: Springer. doi:10.1007/978-3-319-44591-5_5

Yüksel, S. (2017). The impacts of research and development expenses on export and economic growth. *International Business and Accounting Research Journal, 1*(1), 1–8. doi:10.15294/ibarj.v1i1.1

Yüksel, S., & Canöz, İ. (2017). Does Islamic banking contribute to economic growth and industrial development in Turkey? *IKONOMIKA, 2*(1), 93–102. doi:10.24042/febi.v2i1.945

Yüksel, S., Canöz, İ., & Özsarı, M. (2016). Analyzing foreign exchange (FX) positions of participation banks in Turkey. *Journal, 6*(12). Retrieved from http://www. ijmra. us

Yüksel, S., Dinçer, H., & Emir, Ş. (2017). Comparing the performance of Turkish deposit banks by using DEMATEL, Grey Relational Analysis (GRA) and MOORA approaches. *World Journal of Applied Economics, 3*(2), 26–47. doi:10.22440/wjae.3.2.2

Yüksel, S., Dincer, H., & Hacioglu, U. (2015). CAMELS-based determinants for the credit rating of Turkish deposit banks. *International Journal of Finance & Banking Studies, 4*(4), 1–17.

Yüksel, S., Dinçer, H., & Meral, Y. (2019). Financial analysis of international energy trade: A strategic outlook for EU-15. *Energies, 12*(3), 431. doi:10.3390/en12030431

Yüksel, S., Eroğlu, S., & Özsarı, M. (2016). An analysis of the reasons of internal migration in Turkey with logit method. *Business and Management Horizons, 4*(2), 34. doi:10.5296/bmh.v4i2.10350

Yüksel, S., Mukhtarov, S., & Mammadov, E. (2016). Comparing the efficiency of Turkish and Azerbaijani banks: An application with data envelopment analysis. *International Journal of Economics and Financial Issues, 6*(3), 1059–1067.

Yüksel, S., Mukhtarov, S., Mammadov, E., & Özsarı, M. (2018). Determinants of profitability in the banking sector: an analysis of post-Soviet countries. *Economies, 6*(3), 41. doi:10.3390/economies6030041

Yüksel, S., & Oktar, S. (2017). Okun Yasasının Farklı Gelişme Düzeyindeki Ülkelere İlişkin Ekonometrik Analizi. *Marmara Üniversitesi İktisadi ve İdari Bilimler Dergisi, 39*(1), 323–332. doi:10.14780/muiibd.329945

Yüksel, S., & Özsarı, M. (2016). Impact of consumer loans on inflation and current account deficit: A Toda Yamamoto causality test for Turkey. *World Journal of Applied Economics, 2*(2), 3–14. doi:10.22440/wjae.2.2.1

Yüksel, S., & Özsari, M. (2017). Identifying the factors influence Turkish deposit banks to join corporate social responsibility activities by using panel probit method. *International Journal of Finance & Banking Studies, 6*(1), 39.

Yüksel, S., & Özsari, M. (2017). Türkiye Cumhuriyet Merkez Bankası'nın Döviz Rezervlerine Etki Eden Makroekonomik Faktörlerin Belirlenmesi. *Finans Politik & Ekonomik Yorumlar, 54*(631), 41–53.

Yüksel, S., & Zengin, S. (2016a). Leading indicators of 2008 global crisis: an analysis with logit and mars methods. *Finansal Araştırmalar ve Çalışmalar Dergisi, 8*(15), 495–518.

Zachariadis, M. (2004). R&D-induced growth in the OECD? *Review of Development Economics, 8*(3), 423–439. doi:10.1111/j.1467-9361.2004.00243.x

Zadeh, H. A., & Madani, Y. (2012). Financial market development FDI and economic growth in Iran. *Journal of Basic and Applied Scientific Research, 2*(1), 228–230.

Zainuldin, M., Lui, T., & Yii, K. (2018). Principal-agent relationship issues in Islamic banks: A view of Islamic ethical system. *International Journal of Islamic and Middle Eastern Finance and Management, 11*(2), 297–311. doi:10.1108/IMEFM-08-2017-0212

Zaitseva, N. A., Larionova, A. A., Minervin, I. G., Yakimenko, R. V., & Balitskaya, I. V. (2015). Foresight technologies usage in working out long term. Forecasts of service and tourism personnel training system development. *Journal of Environmental Management & Tourism, 6*(2 (12)), 410.

Zalengera, C., Blanchard, R. E., Eames, P. C., Juma, A. M., Chitawo, M. L., & Gondwe, K. T. (2014). Overview of the Malawi energy situation and a PESTLE analysis for sustainable development of renewable energy. *Renewable & Sustainable Energy Reviews, 38*, 335–347. doi:10.1016/j.rser.2014.05.050

Zaleska, M., & Kondraciuk, P. (2019). Theory and practice of innovation development in the banking sector. *Financial Sciences. Nauki o Finansach, 24*(2), 76-87.

Zaman, K., Moemen, M. A. E., & Islam, T. (2017). Dynamic linkages between tourism transportation expenditures, carbon dioxide emission, energy consumption and growth factors: Evidence from the transition economies. *Current Issues in Tourism, 20*(16), 1720–1735. doi:10.1080/13683500.2015.1135107

Zarour, B. A. (2006). Wild oil prices, but brave stock markets! The case of GCC stock markets. *Operations Research, 6*(2), 145–162. doi:10.1007/BF02941229

Zengingönül, O. (2004). *Yoksulluk Gelişmişlik Ve İşgücü Piyasaları Ekseninde Küreselleşme*. Ankara, Turkey: Adres Yayınları.

Zengin, S., & Yüksel, S. (2016). A comparison of the views of internal controllers/auditors and branch/call center personnel of the banks for operational risk: A case for Turkish banking sector. *International Journal of Finance & Banking Studies*, *5*(4), 10.

Zengin, S., Yüksel, S., & Kartal, M. T. (2018). Understanding the factors that affect foreign direct investment in Turkey by using mars method. *Finansal Araştırmalar ve Çalışmalar Dergisi*, *10*(18), 1309–1123.

Zhang, N., Williams, I. D., Kemp, S., & Smith, N. F. (2011). Greening academia: Developing sustainable waste management at Higher Education Institutions. *Waste Management, 31*(7), 1606-1616.

Zhang, Y., & Jin, Y. (2015). Thematic and episodic framing of depression: How Chinese and American newspapers framed a major public health threat. *Athens Journal of Mass Media and Communications*, 91.

Zhang, H., Gao, H., & Liu, P. (2019). Interval type-2 fuzzy multiattribute group decision-making for logistics services providers selection by combining QFD with partitioned heronian mean operator. *Complexity*.

Zhang, K. H. (2014). How does foreign direct investment affect industrial competitiveness? Evidence from China. *China Economic Review*, *30*, 530–539. doi:10.1016/j.chieco.2013.08.003

Zhao, X., & Pan, W. (2015). Delivering zero carbon buildings: The role of innovative business models. *Procedia Engineering*, *118*, 404–411. doi:10.1016/j.proeng.2015.08.440

Zheng, Y., & Osmer, E. (2019). Housing price dynamics: The impact of stock market sentiment and the spillover effect. *The Quarterly Review of Economics and Finance*. doi:10.1016/j.qref.2019.02.006

Zhiyong, X. (2017, August). PESTEL model analysis and legal guarantee of tourism environmental protection in China. In *IOP Conference Series: Earth and Environmental Science*, 81, 1, 012092). IOP Publishing. 10.1088/1755-1315/81/1/012092

Zhu, A. Y. F., Yu, C. W. M., & Chou, K. L. (2019). Improving financial literacy in secondary school students: A randomized experiment. *Youth & Society*, 0044118X19851311.

Zhu, H. M., Li, R., & Li, S. (2014). Modelling dynamic dependence between crude oil prices and Asia-Pacific stock market returns. *International Review of Economics & Finance*, *29*, 208–223. doi:10.1016/j.iref.2013.05.015

Zhu, Y., & Chen, H. (2017). The asymmetry of US monetary policy: Evidence from a threshold Taylor rule with time-varying threshold values. *Physica A*, *473*, 522–535. doi:10.1016/j.physa.2017.01.023

Zineldin, M. (2005). Quality and customer relationship management (CRM) as competitive strategy in the Swedish banking industry. *The TQM Magazine*, *17*(4), 329–344. doi:10.1108/09544780310487749

Ziolkowska, J. R., & Ziolkowski, B. (2015). Energy efficiency in the transport sector in the EU-27: A dynamic dematerialization analysis. *Energy Economics*, *51*, 21–30. doi:10.1016/j.eneco.2015.06.012

Ziout, A., & Azab, A. (2015). Industrial product service system: a case study from the agriculture sector. *Procedia CIRP*, *33*, 64–69. doi:10.1016/j.procir.2015.06.013

Zito, M., Emanuel, F., Molino, M., Cortese, C. G., Ghislieri, C., & Colombo, L. (2018). Turnover intentions in a call center: The role of emotional dissonance, job resources, and job satisfaction. *PLoS One*, *13*(2), e0192126. doi:10.1371/journal.pone.0192126 PMID:29401507

Zortuk, M., & Bayrak, S. (2016). Ham petrol fiyat şokları-hisse senedi piyasası ilişkisi: ADL eşik değerli koentegrasyon testi. *Eskişehir Osmangazi Üniversitesi İİBF Dergisi*, *11*(1), 7–22.

Zou, J., & Deng, X. (2019). Financial literacy, housing value and household financial market participation: Evidence from urban China. *China Economic Review*, *55*, 52–66. doi:10.1016/j.chieco.2019.03.008

Compilation of References

Zoundi, Z. (2017). CO2 emissions, renewable energy and the Environmental Kuznets Curve, a panel cointegration approach. *Renewable & Sustainable Energy Reviews*, *72*, 1067–1075. doi:10.1016/j.rser.2016.10.018

Zuckerman, M. (1994). *Behavioral expressions and biosocial bases of sensation seeking*. Cambridge, UK: Cambridge University Press.

Zur Muehlen, M. (2004). Organizational management in workflow applications–issues and perspectives. *Information Technology Management*, *5*(3-4), 271–291. doi:10.1023/B:ITEM.0000031582.55219.2b

About the Contributors

Hasan Dinçer is an Associate Professor of finance at Istanbul Medipol University, Faculty of Economics and Administrative Sciences, Istanbul-Turkey. Dr. Dinçer has BAs in Financial Markets and Investment Management at Marmara University. He received PhD in Finance and Banking with his thesis entitled "The Effect of Changes on the Competitive Strategies of New Service Development in the Banking Sector". He has work experience in finance sector as portfolio specialist and his major academic studies focusing on financial instruments, performance evaluation, and economics. He is the executive editor of the International Journal of Finance and Banking Studies (IJFBS) and the founder member of the Society for the Study of Business and Finance (SSBF).

Serhat Yüksel is Associate Professor of finance in İstanbul Medipol University. Before this position, he worked as a senior internal auditor for seven years in Finansbank, Istanbul-Turkey and 1 year in Konya Food and Agriculture University as an assistant professor. Dr. Yüksel has a BS in Business Administration (in English) from Yeditepe University (2006) with full scholarship. He got his master degree from the economics in Boğaziçi University (2008). He also has a PhD in Banking from Marmara University (2015). His research interests lie in banking, finance and financial crisis. He has more than 150 publications (books, book chapters, scientific articles, etc.).

* * *

Zafer Adıgüzel graduated from Kocaeli University, Business Administration in Faculty of Economics and Administrative Sciences in 2006. Received his MBA degree from Cardiff Metropolitan University, And Master of Science degree from Istanbul University. He earned her Business PhD from Gebze Technical University. His main areas of interest cover Management and Organization, Strategy and Leadership. Currently, Dr. Adiguzel is an academic member at Istanbul Medipol University, Medipol Business School.

Selin Metin Camgoz works as a full-time Professor at the Department of Business Administration, Hacettepe University, Turkey. Her recent research interests include organizational behavior, heuristics and biases in decision making processes, behavioral finance, gender issues and leadership & motivation. She has published several papers in journals including Journal of Business Research, Sex Roles, Entrepreneurship & Regional Development: An International Journal, Emerging Markets Finance and Trade, Leadership & Organization Development Journal and Social Behavior and Personality.

About the Contributors

İsmail Canöz is a research assistant at İstanbul Arel University. His department is in Banking and Finance. His studying areas are cryptocurrencies, banking, financial crises and so on.

Nildag Basak Ceylan is a Professor of Finance at Ankara Yildirim Beyazit University, Business School, Department of Banking and Finance, Ankara, Turkey. She was born and grew up in Ankara, Turkey. Dr. Ceylan has a BS in Mathematics from METU (1996), MSc in Management from Baskent University (1999) and a PhD in Management (Finance) from Gazi University (2004). Prior to joining the Ankara Yildirim Beyazit University, Dr. Ceylan was a lecturer in Business Administration, Atilim University from 2002 to 2011. Her research interests include international finance, behavioral finance, and financial markets and institutions. She has taught International Finance, Financial Markets and Institutions and Real Estate Finance courses at both graduate and undergraduate levels. Dr. Ceylan has published numerous articles in finance and economics journals.

Ihsan Eken was born in 1986 in Istanbul. He studied Visual Communication Design at Istanbul Commerce University. Later on, he received his master's degree in Advertising and Brand Management at Bahcesehir University. He received his doctorate degree with his thesis on "Accessible Communication for Everyone, Mobile Accessibility of Visually Impaired Users: Analysis of Mobile Applications With Usability Approach" in Istanbul Commerce University Media and Communication Program. He is currently working as an assistant professor at Istanbul Medipol University Communication Faculty. He is Media and Visual Arts Program Vice Head of Department. He has won awards in national and international festivals. His work has been published in national and international scientific publications.

Serkan Eti is a mathematics graduate at Yildiz Technical University. I am a graduate of Quantitive Methods at Marmara University. I am a doctorate in Quantitive Methods. At the same time, I am a lecturer at Medipol University since 2017.

Başak Gezmen was born in 1978 in Izmir. She received her master's degree in Journalism at Marmara University. She received her doctorate degree with her thesis on "Technological developments in Journalism in Turkey" in Marmara University Journalism Program. She is working as an assistant professor at Istanbul Medipol University Communication Faculty. She has published in national and international scientific publications.

Çiğdem Gürsoy completed her undergraduate studies in Faculty of Engineering of Istanbul University in 1986. Then she completed her master's degreeat İstanbul Reseraches Department in Istanbul University in 2011. Çiğdem Gürsoy completed her doctorate at the Department of Economics in Istanbul University in 2015, she also gave lectures as a lecturer in the Faculty of Economics and Administrative Sciences of Maltepe University and Marmara University, Institute of Middle East and Islamic Countries Research Institute, Middle East Economy Policy Department. Since April 2017, she is at the Department of Economics of the Faculty of Economics and Administrative Sciences in Istinye University as Lecturer. She is a member of the academic staff.

Ayhan Kapusuzoglu is a Professor of Finance at Ankara Yildirim Beyazit University, Business School, Department of Banking and Finance, Ankara, Turkey. He was born and grew up in Ankara, Turkey. He holds a BA and MSc in Business Administration from Abant Izzet Baysal University as well as a PhD in

Business Administration (Finance) from Hacettepe University. Prior to joining Ankara Yildirim Beyazit University, Dr. Kapusuzoglu was a research assistant in Business Administration, Hacettepe University from 2008 to 2011. He has been as a visiting scholar at many institutions in United Kingdom, including Bangor University, The University of Hull, University of Dundee and The University of Edinburgh from 2011 to 2018. His research interests include energy finance and markets, risk management, behavioral finance, financial markets and institutions, and financial development. He has taught Theory of Finance and Investment, Corporate Finance, Financial Management, Behavioral Finance and Financial Derivatives courses at both graduate and undergraduate levels. Dr. Kapusuzoglu has published numerous articles in finance and economics journals.

Ercan Karakeçe is a lecturer at Medipol University, Vocational School of Social Sciences. He graduated from International Trade Department at Boğaziçi University in 2006. He has worked for 10 years as a founder and administrator in the business life. He started his master's degree in Entrepreneurship Innovation and Management Department at Yıldız Technical University in 2017.

Mehmet Baha Karan works as a Professor at the Department of Business Administration, Hacettepe University, Turkey. Her recent research interests include investments, financial and energy markets, behavioral finance, risk management and market efficiency. He has published several papers in journals including European Journal of Finance, Energy Markets Finance and Trade, Corporate Governance: An International Review, Journal of Business Economics and Management and Applied Economics.

Mustafa Tevfik Kartal is a capital markets professional. He received an MBA degree in business administration from Sakarya University, Turkey, in 2009, and a Ph.D. degree in banking from Marmara University, Turkey, in 2017. His research interests focus on accounting, audits, banking, capital markets, economics, finance, Islamic finance, laws, and legislation. He has authored 1 book, 15 book chapters, 38 articles, and 8 proceedings in Turkish and English. In addition, his 3 proceedings, 5 book chapters, and 15 articles have been in the reviewing process. As well, he has taken a role as referee in 21 national and international journals.

İhsan Erdem Kayral was born in Ankara in 1987, Assist. Prof. Dr. İhsan Erdem Kayral graduated from the Department of Economics at Hacettepe University as the top student of faculty and department. He received his MSc and PhD degrees in the field of Finance in the Department of Business Administration at the same university. Completing his studies, Assist. Prof. Dr. İhsan Erdem Kayral started to work in Tubitak (The Scientific and Technological Research Council of Turkey) as a Chief Expert in 2010 and he served there over 8 years. Currently, he works in the Department of Economics in Konya Food and Agriculture University. Assist. Prof. Dr. İhsan Erdem Kayral has lots of awards in various fields. He also gets National Tubitak Master's Degree Scholarship and Turkish Economics Association Achievement Grant in Bachelor's Degree Level.

Haroub Omar was born and raised in Zanzibar islands, Tanzania. He graduated from the Zanzibar University in 2013 with BBA in Accounting & Finance. He worked for Zanzibar Telecom Limited (Zantel); one of the four biggest telecom companies in Tanzania before joining Madrasa Early Childhood Program-Zanzibar (MECP-Z: Aga Khan Foundation) as Finance and Administration Officer. He later on enrolled on MA program in Banking & Finance in the Ankara Yildirim Beyazit University and graduated

About the Contributors

in July 2017. He is now working as Finance & Administration Officer with D-Tree International, Zanzibar with strong desire and drive to continue further his education and contribute into the world of science.

Yilmaz Yildiz is a senior lecturer in Accountancy, Finance, and Economics in Huddersfield Business School. He has research interests on empirical corporate finance, including topics such as ownership structure, accounting conservatism, and in environmental economics. He has papers published in several journals such as The European Journal of Finance, Applied Economics, and Emerging Markets Finance and Trade.

Index

A

Abattoir 17, 20
actors of globalization 1
ADF 1, 7-19, 22, 24
agglomeration 1-2, 4-8, 10, 12-14, 16-20
agility 1-4, 6-9, 11, 14-16
ARDL 5, 7, 10, 18
ATM 3-4, 6-12, 18, 27, 30

B

banking 1-17, 19
banking sector 1-17, 19
BCG 19, 22
behavioral finance 1-5, 7, 9-15, 17, 19
bibliometric analysis 1, 10, 13, 15, 17
Big-Five Personality Traits 4, 8, 10, 19
Bitcoin trading volume 1-2, 6, 9, 13-14
BOT 5, 9-10, 21
BRICS 2, 4-5, 12, 18
BSC 10, 19, 22
budget 2, 4, 6, 8, 11, 16-18, 22

C

CAPM 3, 22
cluster 4, 7-8, 12, 15-18, 20
cointegration 1-3, 5-22, 24
cointegration analysis 1-3, 5, 7-8, 10-11, 13-16, 18-20, 22
commodity price 4-5
competition 1-21
competitiveness 1-19
concentration 1-2, 5, 7-16
corporate social responsibility 1-4, 6-7, 10-12
CRM 27
CTI 27
culture 1-2, 4-5, 7-21

D

DEMATEL 1-3, 6, 8, 10-11, 20
disposition effect 1, 3, 7-14, 19
drover 8, 12, 20, 22

E

economic geography 1-6, 9, 17-19
economic growth 1-3, 5-17, 19-21, 24
economics 1-5, 8-10, 12, 15-20
economic uncertainty 1, 3, 11, 13-14
economy 1-20, 22
EIS 7, 25
Engle-Granger cointegration 1-2, 10-12, 14-16, 18-20, 22, 24
entrepreneurship 1-4, 6-11, 14, 17
environmental factors 1-5, 8, 10, 16, 18
ethical banking 1-4, 11-12
EU 9, 11, 20, 27
European banking sector 1-2, 4, 8, 10
exchange rate 1-21, 24-25
export 1-18, 20-21, 24
export-import 8

F

FED 3, 6-7, 9-10, 17-18, 30
finance 1-20, 22
financial assets 2-6, 11-13, 17
Financial Competition 1
financial development 1-3, 5-11, 18
financial literacy 1-11, 13-14, 18-19, 22
financial marketing 1-3, 10-11, 20
FMOLS 1-2, 18, 20, 25
foreign demand 1-2, 9-11, 14-17
foreign direct investment 1-4, 6-8, 10-11, 13, 18, 24
foreign trade 1-4, 6-15, 17-21
FOREX 1-5, 7-10, 12-14, 19

Index

FOREX markets 1-2, 5, 7
Fourier Cointegration Test 1
Fourier unit root test 8

G

GDP 1-2, 4, 6, 9, 11, 14, 17-21, 25
Globalization Phenomenon 1
GNP 5, 9-10, 19
Granger Causality 1, 3, 5-11, 13, 16-18

H

HHI 1-2, 5-7, 12-15

I

IMF 1-4, 6, 8, 10, 15, 21, 30
in-depth interview 1-2, 12-13, 19
individual investors 1-3, 5, 7-8
industrial production index 8, 10-11, 13-17, 21, 24
inflation 1-11, 14-21, 24-25
innovation 1-21, 25
innovation management 2, 6-8
interest rate 1-16, 18-22, 24-25
interest rate corridor 1-10, 12, 14, 18-19, 21-22, 24-25
interval type-2 fuzzy DEMATEL 1-3, 6, 11
investment 1-15, 17-18, 20, 22, 24
IPS 1, 7-8, 17-18
Islamic banking 1-4, 10-12
İstanbul 1-5, 7-22
IVR 2, 10, 14, 17-19, 21, 27
IVR Tree 2, 14, 17

K

KMO 8-9, 20

L

literacy 1-11, 13-14, 18-19, 22
LLC 1, 7-8, 17-18
logit method 1, 7, 9, 11
love of money 1, 3, 6-10, 12, 14, 19

M

macroeconomic factors 1, 3, 5-7, 9, 11
management 1-21, 27
marketing strategy 2, 4, 9, 13
MINT 2, 10, 26

monetary growth 1-4, 6-7, 9, 13-14
multinational companies 1, 4, 7-8, 12

N

NGO 7, 14, 19
NPL 10, 18

O

OECD 1-11, 13-18, 20, 25
Ottoman 1-4, 6, 8, 13, 17-19

P

panel data analysis 1-4, 6-7, 11, 16-17, 20
patent 1-2, 5-6, 14-15, 17-20
Pedroni cointegration 3, 6, 8
Pedroni panel cointegration analysis 7-8
performance 1-14, 16-20
personality 1, 3-6, 8-14, 17, 19
PESTEL 1-4, 8, 11-12, 17-19, 22
PESTEL analysis 1-4, 11-12, 17-19
PP 1, 8, 17-18

Q

questionnaire 2-6, 8-9, 12-17, 22

R

R&D 1-2, 6, 10, 13-15, 17-21, 25-27, 30
regional production 1-2, 7, 18
risk 1-14, 16-17, 19-20

S

safe haven 2, 6, 13, 17
saving 2, 4-6, 9, 11, 18, 22
savings 1-16, 18-20
SME 3, 5, 11, 13, 20
social environment 1, 8, 17
SSCI 2, 20
Stationary Analysis 7, 9, 13, 17, 26
stock market 1-3, 5-11
strategy 1-4, 6-11, 13-18, 20
Survey analysis 7
sustainable financial system 11
SWOT 2, 9, 11, 17-19, 22
Symmetric Causality 1, 8-11

T

tanner tradesmen 1-2, 4-5, 8, 11-14, 16-18, 20
Tanzania 1-5, 8-11, 16-18, 21
Taylor Rule 1, 3, 5-8, 11
TBS 1-2, 5, 7-15
technology 1-21
TL 4-8, 10-16, 19-20
Toda-Yamamoto causality 1-2, 5, 10, 12, 17-21, 24
Transaction Deposit 17
TUIK 21, 25
Turkey 1-8, 10-21, 25-26

Turkish Academic Studies 1

U

UNCTAD 7, 13-14, 19
US 1-15, 17, 19-20, 26-27, 30
USA 3-7, 10, 12-13, 18, 20
USD 5-6, 10-11, 22, 26-27, 30

V

VAR 1, 4-13, 15-19, 21
VIKOR 11, 20

Purchase Print, E-Book, or Print + E-Book

IGI Global's reference books are available in three unique pricing formats:
Print Only, E-Book Only, or Print + E-Book.
Shipping fees may apply.

www.igi-global.com

Recommended Reference Books

Digital Currency
ISBN: 978-1-5225-6201-6
© 2019; 341 pp.
List Price: $345

Business Transformations in the Era of Digitalization
ISBN: 978-1-5225-7262-6
© 2019; 360 pp.
List Price: $215

Intergenerational Governance and Leadership in the Corporate World
ISBN: 978-1-5225-8003-4
© 2019; 216 pp.
List Price: $205

Smart Marketing With the Internet of Things
ISBN: 978-1-5225-5763-0
© 2019; 304 pp.
List Price: $205

Breaking Down Language and Cultural Barriers Through Contemporary Global Marketing Strategies
ISBN: 978-1-5225-6980-0
© 2019; 325 pp.
List Price: $235

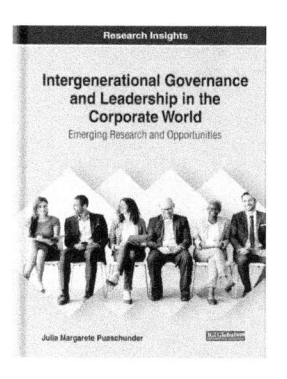

Green Finance for Sustainable Global Growth
ISBN: 978-1-5225-7808-6
© 2019; 397 pp.
List Price: $215

Do you want to stay current on the latest research trends, product announcements, news and special offers?
Join IGI Global's mailing list today and start enjoying exclusive perks sent only to IGI Global members.
Add your name to the list at **www.igi-global.com/newsletters**.

Publisher of Peer-Reviewed, Timely, and Innovative Academic Research

IGI Global
DISSEMINATOR OF KNOWLEDGE

www.igi-global.com | Sign up at www.igi-global.com/newsletters | facebook.com/igiglobal | twitter.com/igiglobal | linkedin.com/igiglobal

Ensure Quality Research is Introduced to the Academic Community

Become an IGI Global Reviewer for Authored Book Projects

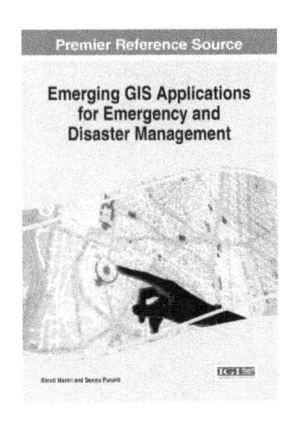

The overall success of an authored book project is dependent on quality and timely reviews.

In this competitive age of scholarly publishing, constructive and timely feedback significantly expedites the turnaround time of manuscripts from submission to acceptance, allowing the publication and discovery of forward-thinking research at a much more expeditious rate. Several IGI Global authored book projects are currently seeking highly-qualified experts in the field to fill vacancies on their respective editorial review boards:

Applications and Inquiries may be sent to:
development@igi-global.com

Applicants must have a doctorate (or an equivalent degree) as well as publishing and reviewing experience. Reviewers are asked to complete the open-ended evaluation questions with as much detail as possible in a timely, collegial, and constructive manner. All reviewers' tenures run for one-year terms on the editorial review boards and are expected to complete at least three reviews per term. Upon successful completion of this term, reviewers can be considered for an additional term.

If you have a colleague that may be interested in this opportunity,
we encourage you to share this information with them.

IGI Global Proudly Partners With eContent Pro International

Receive a 25% Discount on all Editorial Services

Editorial Services

IGI Global expects all final manuscripts submitted for publication to be in their final form. This means they must be reviewed, revised, and professionally copy edited prior to their final submission. Not only does this support with accelerating the publication process, but it also ensures that the highest quality scholarly work can be disseminated.

English Language Copy Editing

Let eContent Pro International's expert copy editors perform edits on your manuscript to resolve spelling, punctuaion, grammar, syntax, flow, formatting issues and more.

Scientific and Scholarly Editing

Allow colleagues in your research area to examine the content of your manuscript and provide you with valuable feedback and suggestions before submission.

Figure, Table, Chart & Equation Conversions

Do you have poor quality figures? Do you need visual elements in your manuscript created or converted? A design expert can help!

Translation

Need your documjent translated into English? eContent Pro International's expert translators are fluent in English and more than 40 different languages.

Hear What Your Colleagues are Saying About Editorial Services Supported by IGI Global

"The service was very fast, very thorough, and very helpful in ensuring our chapter meets the criteria and requirements of the book's editors. I was quite impressed and happy with your service."

– Prof. Tom Brinthaupt,
Middle Tennessee State University, USA

"I found the work actually spectacular. The editing, formatting, and other checks were very thorough. The turnaround time was great as well. I will definitely use eContent Pro in the future."

– Nickanor Amwata, Lecturer,
University of Kurdistan Hawler, Iraq

"I was impressed that it was done timely, and wherever the content was not clear for the reader, the paper was improved with better readability for the audience."

– Prof. James Chilembwe,
Mzuzu University, Malawi

Email: customerservice@econtentpro.com   www.igi-global.com/editorial-service-partners

IGI Global
DISSEMINATOR OF KNOWLEDGE

www.igi-global.com

Celebrating Over 30 Years of Scholarly Knowledge Creation & Dissemination

InfoSci®-Books

A Database of Over 5,300+ Reference Books Containing Over 100,000+ Chapters Focusing on Emerging Research

GAIN ACCESS TO THOUSANDS OF REFERENCE BOOKS AT A FRACTION OF THEIR INDIVIDUAL LIST PRICE.

InfoSci®-Books Database

The **InfoSci®-Books** database is a collection of over 5,300+ IGI Global single and multi-volume reference books, handbooks of research, and encyclopedias, encompassing groundbreaking research from prominent experts worldwide that span over 350+ topics in 11 core subject areas including business, computer science, education, science and engineering, social sciences and more.

Open Access Fee Waiver (Offset Model) Initiative

For any library that invests in IGI Global's InfoSci-Journals and/or InfoSci-Books databases, IGI Global will match the library's investment with a fund of equal value to go toward **subsidizing the OA article processing charges (APCs) for their students, faculty, and staff** at that institution when their work is submitted and accepted under OA into an IGI Global journal.*

INFOSCI® PLATFORM FEATURES

- No DRM
- No Set-Up or Maintenance Fees
- A Guarantee of No More Than a 5% Annual Increase
- Full-Text HTML and PDF Viewing Options
- Downloadable MARC Records
- Unlimited Simultaneous Access
- COUNTER 5 Compliant Reports
- Formatted Citations With Ability to Export to RefWorks and EasyBib
- No Embargo of Content (Research is Available Months in Advance of the Print Release)

*The fund will be offered on an annual basis and expire at the end of the subscription period. The fund would renew as the subscription is renewed for each year thereafter. The open access fees will be waived after the student, faculty, or staff's paper has been vetted and accepted into an IGI Global journal and the fund can only be used toward publishing OA in an IGI Global journal. Libraries in developing countries will have the match on their investment doubled.

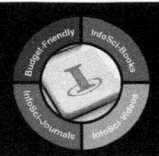

To Learn More or To Purchase This Database:
www.igi-global.com/infosci-books

eresources@igi-global.com • Toll Free: 1-866-342-6657 ext. 100 • Phone: 717-533-8845 x100

IGI Global
DISSEMINATOR OF KNOWLEDGE
www.igi-global.com

IGI Global
DISSEMINATOR OF KNOWLEDGE
www.igi-global.com

Publisher of Peer-Reviewed, Timely, and Innovative Academic Research Since 1988

IGI Global's Transformative Open Access (OA) Model:
How to Turn Your University Library's Database Acquisitions Into a Source of OA Funding

In response to the OA movement and well in advance of Plan S, IGI Global, early last year, unveiled their OA Fee Waiver (Offset Model) Initiative.

Under this initiative, librarians who invest in IGI Global's InfoSci-Books (5,300+ reference books) and/or InfoSci-Journals (185+ scholarly journals) databases will be able to subsidize their patron's OA article processing charges (APC) when their work is submitted and accepted (after the peer review process) into an IGI Global journal.*

How Does it Work?

1. When a library subscribes or perpetually purchases IGI Global's InfoSci-Databases including InfoSci-Books (5,300+ e-books), InfoSci-Journals (185+ e-journals), and/or their discipline/subject-focused subsets, IGI Global will match the library's investment with a fund of equal value to go toward subsidizing the OA article processing charges (APCs) for their patrons.

   Researchers: Be sure to recommend the InfoSci-Books and InfoSci-Journals to take advantage of this initiative.

2. When a student, faculty, or staff member submits a paper and it is accepted (following the peer review) into one of IGI Global's 185+ scholarly journals, the author will have the option to have their paper published under a traditional publishing model or as OA.

3. When the author chooses to have their paper published under OA, IGI Global will notify them of the OA Fee Waiver (Offset Model) Initiative. If the author decides they would like to take advantage of this initiative, IGI Global will deduct the US$ 1,500 APC from the created fund.

4. This fund will be offered on an annual basis and will renew as the subscription is renewed for each year thereafter. IGI Global will manage the fund and award the APC waivers unless the librarian has a preference as to how the funds should be managed.

Hear From the Experts on This Initiative:

"I'm very happy to have been able to make one of my recent research contributions, 'Visualizing the Social Media Conversations of a National Information Technology Professional Association' featured in the *International Journal of Human Capital and Information Technology Professionals*, freely available along with having access to the valuable resources found within IGI Global's InfoSci-Journals database."

– **Prof. Stuart Palmer**, Deakin University, Australia

For More Information, Visit: www.igi-global.com/publish/contributor-resources/open-access or contact IGI Global's Database Team at eresources@igi-global.com.

Are You Ready to Publish Your Research?

IGI Global
DISSEMINATOR OF KNOWLEDGE

IGI Global offers book authorship and editorship opportunities across 11 subject areas, including business, computer science, education, science and engineering, social sciences, and more!

Benefits of Publishing with IGI Global:

- Free one-on-one editorial and promotional support.
- Expedited publishing timelines that can take your book from start to finish in less than one (1) year.
- Choose from a variety of formats including: Edited and Authored References, Handbooks of Research, Encyclopedias, and Research Insights.
- Utilize IGI Global's eEditorial Discovery® submission system in support of conducting the submission and blind review process.
- IGI Global maintains a strict adherence to ethical practices due in part to our full membership with the Committee on Publication Ethics (COPE).
- Indexing potential in prestigious indices such as Scopus®, Web of Science™, PsycINFO®, and ERIC – Education Resources Information Center.
- Ability to connect your ORCID iD to your IGI Global publications.
- Earn royalties on your publication as well as receive complimentary copies and exclusive discounts.

Get Started Today by Contacting the Acquisitions Department at:
acquisition@igi-global.com

www.igi-global.com/infosci-ondemand

InfoSci®-OnDemand

Continuously updated with new material on a weekly basis, InfoSci®-OnDemand offers the ability to search through thousands of quality full-text research papers. Users can narrow each search by identifying key topic areas of interest, then display a complete listing of relevant papers, and purchase materials specific to their research needs.

Comprehensive Service
- Over 125,000+ journal articles, book chapters, and case studies.
- All content is downloadable in PDF and HTML format and can be stored locally for future use.

No Subscription Fees
- One time fee of $37.50 per PDF download.

Instant Access
- Receive a download link immediately after order completion!

"It really provides an excellent entry into the research literature of the field. It presents a manageable number of highly relevant sources on topics of interest to a wide range of researchers. The sources are scholarly, but also accessible to 'practitioners'."

– Lisa Stimatz, MLS, University of North Carolina at Chapel Hill, USA

"It is an excellent and well designed database which will facilitate research, publication, and teaching. It is a very useful tool to have."

– George Ditsa, PhD, University of Wollongong, Australia

"I have accessed the database and find it to be a valuable tool to the IT/IS community. I found valuable articles meeting my search criteria 95% of the time."

– Prof. Lynda Louis, Xavier University of Louisiana, USA

Recommended for use by researchers who wish to immediately download PDFs of individual chapters or articles.

www.igi-global.com/e-resources/infosci-ondemand

IGI Global
DISSEMINATOR OF KNOWLEDGE
www.igi-global.com

Ingram Content Group UK Ltd.
Milton Keynes UK
UKHW030049160323
418650UK00008B/171